WEBSTER'S DICTIONARY

Edited by
Liz Kauffman

Proofread by
Marsha Tischner

Watermill Press

Published by Watermill Press,
an imprint of Troll Associates, Inc.

Printed in the United States of America

10   9

Rules of Spelling

1. The most common way to form the plural of a noun is to add an s (Example: girl, girls; town, towns; hall, halls).

2. The plural of nouns which end in y following a consonant are formed by dropping the y and adding ies.
(Example: country, countries; baby, babies; family, families).

3. The plural of nouns which end in y following a vowel are formed by adding an s.
(Example: toy, toys; boy, boys; attorney, attorneys).

In this quick reference dictionary, a double dash (--) indicates a hyphenated word, and a single dash (-) indicates syllablization.

Each entry is in bold type followed by the part of speech in italic. Sub-entries are indicated in bold type after the main definition.

Abbreviations Used In This Dictionary

abbr.	abbreviation
adj.	adjective
adv.	adverb
aeron.	aeronautics
aeros.	aerospace
archit.	architecture
astron.	astronomy
biol.	biology
bot.	botany
Brit.	British
Can.	Canada
chem.	chemistry
elect.	electricity
econ.	economist
geol.	geology
govt.	government
gram.	grammar
theol.	theology
interj.	interjection
L.	Latin
mech.	mechanics
med.	medicine
meteor.	meteorology
milit.	military
mus.	music
myth.	mythology
naut.	nautical
n.	noun
pathol.	pathology
physiol.	physiology
pl.	plural
poet.	poetry
pref.	prefix
pron.	pronoun
psychol.	psychologist
suff.	suffix
surg.	surgery
v.	verb

A, a The first letter of the English alphabet; the highest grade, meaning excellent or best.

AA *abbr.* Alcoholics Anonymous.

AAA *abbr.* American Automobile Association.

AAAL *abbr.* American Academy of Arts and Letters.

AAAS *abbr.* American Association for the Advancement of Science.

AACS *abbr.* Airways and Air Communications Service.

aah *v.* To exclaim in joy.

AAR *abbr.* Against all risks.

aardvark *n.*

A burrowing African animal, which resembles the anteater and feeds on ants and termites.

aard-wolf *n.* A hyena-like mammal, feeding chiefly on carrion and insects.

AAU *abbr.* Amateur Athletic Union.

AAUN *abbr.* American association for the United Nations.

AB *abbr.* One of the major blood types. One who possesses it may donate blood to type AB and receive blood from types A, B, AB, and O.

AB *abbr.* Bachelor of Arts; academic degree.

aba *n.* A type of fabric which is woven for the camel's hair.

ABA *abbr.* American Booksellers Association; American Bar Association.

ab-a-ca *n.* A plant from the Philippines whose leafstalks are the source of Manila hemp.

a-back *adv.* Unexpectedly; by surprise; startled.

abac-te-ri-al *adj.* Not being caused by bacteria.

ab-a-cus *n.*

A frame holding parallel rods with beads, used for manual computation, especially by the Chinese.

a-baft *adv.* On or toward the stern, aft, or hind part of a ship.

ab-a-lo-ne *n.* A member of the genus of gastropod mollusks that will cling to rocks and have a shell which is flat and lined with mother of pearl.

a-ban-don *v.* To yield utterly; to desert; to forsake; to withdraw protection, support, or help. **abandonment** *n.*, **abandonedly** *adv.*

a-ban-doned *adj.* To be deserted; to be forsaken.

a-ban-don-ee *n.* The person to whom a thing is abandoned.

a-base *v.* To lower in rank, prestige,

position, or estimation; to cast down, to humble.

a-base-ment *n.* A state of depression, degradation, or humiliation.

a-bash *v.* To embarrass; to disconcert; to make ashamed or uneasy.

a-bash-ment *n.* The state of something being abashed.

a-bate *v.* To deduct; to make less; to reduce in quantity, value, force, or intensity. **abater** *n.*, **-able**, **abated** *adj.*

abate-ment *n.* The process of abating something; the amount which is abated.

ab-a-tis *n.* The collection of felled trees of which the smaller branches have already been cut off.

A battery *n.* A type of battery which is used used for the purpose of heating the filaments electron tubes.

ab-at-toir *n.* The public slaughterhouse.

ab-ax-i-al *adj.* To be positioned or situated out of the axis of something.

abb *n.* A type of low grade wool that is from the inferior parts of a fleece.

Ab-ba *n.* The ecclesiastical title that is used in some Eastern churches.

ab-ba-cy *n.* A jurisdiction or an office of an abbot.

ab-ba-tial *adj.* To be pertaining or related to an abbey or abbot.

ab-be *n.* A French title given to a priest.

ab-bess *n.* The female superior of an abbey of nuns and possessing the same authority as an abbot.

ab-bey *n.* An abbey church, a monastery, or convent.

ab-bot *n.* The superior of the monastery.

ab-bre-vi-ate *v.* To make briefer; to abridge; to shorten; to reduce to a briefer form, as a word or phrase.

ab-bre-vi-a-tion *n.* A shortened form of a word or phrase, used to represent the full form. **-tor** *n.*, **abbreviatory** *adj.*

ABC *n.* A rudiments of writing, reading, and spelling.

ABC soil *n.* A type of soil where there are three well-defined layers.

abd *abbr.* Abdomen.

ab-di-ca-ble *adj.* To be pertaining to the one that may renounce.

ab-di-cate *v.* To relinquish power or responsibility formally; to renounce. **abdication** *n.*

ab-do-men *n.* That part of the human body that lies between the thorax and the pelvis and contains the stomach, spleen, liver, kidneys, bladder, pancreas, and intestines. **abdominal** *adj.*, **abdominally** *adv.*

ab-du-cens nerve *n.* The 6th cranial nerves that are motor nerves and supply the eye muscles.

ab-duct *v.* To carry away wrongfully, as by force or fraud; to kidnap; to draw aside or away. **abductor** *n.*

ab-duc-tion *n.* An action of abducting.

a-beam *adv.* At right angles to the keel of a ship.

a-bed *adv.* In bed; on a bed; to bed; restricted to bed.

a-bel-mosk *n.* A type of herb which is

found in Asia and the East Indies and the musky seeds are used to flavor coffee and for perfumes.

Ab-er-deen An-gus *n.* A type of black hornless cattle and whose origin is in Scotland.

ab-er-rant *adj.* Straying from the right way or usual course; not being proper or truthful; abnormal or exceptional. **aberrantly** *adv.*

ab-er-ra-tion *n.* The disorder of the mind; deviation from a type or standard. **aberrational** *adj.*

a-bet *v.* To incite, encourage, or assist by countenance, aid, or approval. **abetter, abetment** *n.*

ab-hor *v.* To dislike intensely; to loathe.

ab-hor-rence *n.* The state of abhorring.

ab-hor-rent *adj.* To be feeling abhorrence; hating; detesting.

a-bid-ance *n.* The state of abiding; compliance.

a-bide *v.* To tolerate; to bear; to remain; to last; to conform to; to comply with.

a-bid-ing *adj.* To be enduring.

ab-i-gail *n.* A personal maid of a lady.

a-bil-i-ty *n.* State of being able; possession of qualities necessary; competence; skill.

-abil-i-ty *n., suffix* Tendency to act in a specified manner or way.

ab-i-o-gen-e-sis *n.* An origination of something living from something that is not living. **abiogenetically** *adv.*

abi-o-log-i-cal *adj.* Not being made or produced by organisms.

abi-ot-ic *adj.* Not being biotic.

ab-ject *adj.* Sunk to a low condition; groveling; mean; despicable; worthless. *n.* A person who is an outcast. **abjectness** *n.*

ab-jec-tion *n.* A state which is downcast.

ab-ju-ra-tion *n.* The process of abjuring.

ab-jure *v.* To renounce solemnly or on oath; to repudiate; to forswear. **-er** *n.*

abl *abbr.* Ablative.

ab-late *v.* To remove something by cutting or erosion.

ab-la-tion *n.* A removal of a part; a process of ablating.

a-blaze *adv.* On fire; brilliantly lighted up; very excited; angry.

a-ble *adj.* Having sufficient ability; capable or talented. **-ness** *n.*, **-y** *adv.*

-able *adj., suffix* To be worthy of.

a-ble--bodied *adj.* Having a sound, strong body; competent for physical service.

a-ble sea-man *n.* A seaman who is experienced to perform routine tasks at sea.

a-bloom *adj.* To be abounding with blooms such as a plant.

ab-lut-ed *adj.* To be washed and clean.

ab-lu-tion *n.* The act of washing, cleansing, or purification by a liquid, usually water; specifically, a washing of the body as a part of religious rites. **ablutionary** *adj.*

ably *adv.* To do something in an able manner.

abn *abbr.* Airborne.

Ab-na-ki *n.* A person who is a member of the Amerindian people of southern Quebec and Maine.

ab-ne-gate *v.* To deny; to refuse or renounce; to relinquish or surrender.

ab-nor-mal *adj.* Not normal; irregular unnatural. **-ity** *n.*, **abnormally** *adv.*

abnormal psychology *n.* A type of psychology that deals with the behaviors of people.

a-board *adv.* On board a ship or other vehicle.

a-bode *n.* A dwelling place; home; place of residence; habitation.

a-boil *adj.* To be at the point of which something, such as a fluid, will boil.

a-bol-ish *v.* To put an end to; to annul. **abolisher, abolishment** *n.*, **-able** *adj.*

ab-o-li-tion *n.* The state of being abolished. **abolitionary** *adj.*

ab-o-li-tion-ism *n.* The measures that will foster abolition.

ab-oma-sum *n.* A fourth digestive stomach of the ruminant, lying next to third stomach or omasum.

A--Bomb *n.* An atomic bomb; a very destructive bomb where energy is released in an explosion with enormous force and heat.

a-bom-i-na-ble *adj.* Detestable; loathsome. **abominably** *adv.*, **-ness** *n.*

a-bom-i-na-ble snow-man *n.* A type of animal which has been reported to exist in the Himalayas; having features similar to those of man.

a-bom-i-nate *v.* To loathe intensely; to detest; to hate extremely; to abhor.

abom-i-na-tion *n.* An extreme hatred; the act of abominating; detestation; hateful vice.

ab-oral *adj.* To be situated away from the mouth.

ab-orig-i-nal *adj.* To be the first in a region and may be primitive when compared with a more advanced type.

a-born-ing *adv.* While being produced or made.

a-bort *v.* To terminate or cause to terminate an operation or procedure before completion; to miscarry in giving birth.

a-bor-ti-fa-cient *adj.* To be able to induce an abortion, especially by inducing drugs.

a-bor-tion *n.* Induced termination of pregnancy before the fetus can survive; something malformed.

a-bor-tion-ist *n.* Something which will produce or cause an abortion; a person who induces abortions especially illegal ones.

a-bor-tive *adj.* To be developed imperfectly. **abortiveness** *n.*

a-bound *v.* To have plenty; to exist in large numbers.

a-bout *adv.* Approximately; on every side, here and there.

a-bout--face *n.* The reversal of one's point of view or attitude.

a-bove *adv.* Higher or greater than; in or at a higher place.

a-bove all *adv.* To be before all other

considerations.

a-bove-board *adv.* To do something in a manner that is straightforward.

a-bove-ground *adj.* To be located or positioned above the level or surface of the ground.

abp *abbr.* Archbishop.

abr. *abbr.* Abridgment.

ab-ra-ca-dab-ra *n.* A word believed by some to have magical powers, used in casting spells; nonsense, foolish talk.

a-brade *v.* To wear or rub off; to grate off; abrasive, scouring.

abra-sion *n.* The grinding of something, such as a surface, with the used of friction.

abra-sive *adj.* To tend to abrade.

ab-re-act *v.* To release an emotion that is forgotten in psychoanalysis.

ab-re-ac-tion *n.* To eliminate a bad experience by reliving it.

a-breast *adv.* or *adj.* Side by side.

a-bridge *v.* To make smaller, fewer, or shorter while maintaining essential contents. **-er** *n.*, **-able, -eable** *adj.*

abridg-ment *n.* The state of being abridged.

abroach *adv.* In agitation or action.

a-broad *adv.* Widely; in many places; outside one's country; at large.

ab-ro-gate *v.* To cancel; to put an end to; to repeal. **abrogation** *n.*, **abrogable, abrogative** *adj.*

ab-rupt *adj.* Happening or coming suddenly with no warning. **abruptness** *n.*, **abruptly** *adv.*

abrup-tion *n.* The sudden breaking away of something.

abs *abbr.* Abstract.

ab-scess *n.* An infected place in the body which becomes sore and swollen and contains pus. **abscessed** *adj.*

ab-scind *v.* To cut off; to sever; to pare away; to separate.

ab-scise *v.* To part or separate with abscission.

ab-scis-ic acid *n.* A type of plant hormone that will promote leaf abscission and dormancy.

ab-scis-sion *n.* A natural separation of fruit, flowers, or the leaves of a plant.

ab-scond *v.* To remove oneself, as to flee from justice. **absconder** *n.*

ab-sence *n.* Being absent, not present; inattention.

ab-sent *adj.* Not present; away; lacking; nonexistent. **absently** *adv.*

ab-sen-tee *n.* A person who is absent.

ab-sen-tee bal-lot *n.* A type of ballot which is submitted to an election by a voter who is not able to be at the polls.

ab-sen-tee-ism *n.* The chronic absence from something, such as school.

ab-sen-tee vot-er *n.* A person who is allowed to vote in an election with an absentee ballot.

ab-sent--mind-ed *adj.* Always forgetting things; dreaming or thinking of something else; not paying attention.

ab-sent with-out leave *adj.* To be absent without permission from the place of duty in the armed forces.

ab-sinthe *n.* A type of green liqueur which has been flavored by wormwood.

ab-so-lute *adj.* Unconditional; without restraint; perfect. **absoluteness** *n.*, **absolutely** *adv.*

ab-so-lute ceil-ing *n.* The height above the sea level which is the highest point a plane is able to fly in a horizontal position.

ab-so-lute hu-mid-i-ty *n.* An amount of water vapor that is present in a unit of volume of air.

ab-so-lu-tion *n.* An act of absolving.

ab-so-lut-ize *v.* To make something absolute.

ab-solve *v.* To set free or release from duties, guilt, or penalty. **absolver** *n.*, **absolvable** *adj.*

ab-sorb *v.* To take in; to take up the full attention; to engage one's whole attention. **absorbability** *n.*, **-able** *adj.*

ab-sor-ben-cy *n.* The state of being absorbent.

ab-for-bent *adj.* To be able to absorb something.

ab-sorp-tion *n.* The act of giving full attention or having great interest.

ab-stain *v.* To refrain from doing something. **abstainer** *n.*

ab-ste-mi-ous *adj.* Showing moderation in the use of drink and food. **abstemiousness** *n.*, **abstemiously** *adv.*

ab-sten-tion *n.* The act of holding off from using or doing something.

ab-stract *v.* To remove from, reduce, or summarize. **abstractness** *n.*

ab-strac-tion *n.* The process of abstracting. **abstractive** *adj.*

ab-strac-tion-ism *n.* The practice of making abstract art.

ab-strict *v.* To cause an abstraction.

ab-stric-tion *n.* A forming of spores with the cutting off of parts of the sporophore.

ab-struse *adj.* Hard or difficult to understand. **-ness** *n.*, **abstrusely** *adv.*

ab-surd *adj.* Contrary to reason; clearly untrue or unreasonable. **absurdity, absurdness** *n.*

ab-surd-ism *n.* The philosophy which is based on the idea and belief that man lives in a meaningless universe and the search for order will bring him and the universe into conflict. **absurdist** *n.*

a-bub-ble *adj.* To be in the process of bubbling.

a-build-ing *adj.* To be in the process of constructing or building.

a-bun-dance *n.* Ample supply; plenty; amount more than enough.

a-bun-dant *adj.* To be amply supplied. **abundantly** *adv.*

a-buse *v.* To use in an improper or wrong way. *n.* Improper treatment.

a-bu-sive *adj.* To be injurious to another. **abusiveness** *n.*

a-but *v.* To border; to touch at one end.

a-bu-ti-lon *n.* A member of the genus of mallow family that has lobed leaves and bell-shaped flowers.

a-but-ment *n.* Support at the end of an arch or bridge.

a-but-ting *adj.* To abut or to serve as an abutment of something.

a-buzz *adj.* To be filled with a buzzing.

a-bys-mal *adj.* Immeasurably deep or low.

a-byss *n.* A deep crack or gap in the earth. **abyssal** *adj.*

Ab-ys-sin-i-an cat *n.* A type of breed of cat of African origin that has short brownish hair.

ac *abbr.* Account.

AC *abbr.* Alternating current.

a-ca-cia *n.* Thorny tree or shrub of warm climates.

acad *abbr.* Academy.

ac-a-deme *n.* The place where instruction is given to pupils.

ac-a-dem-ic *adj.* To be pertaining to or related to an academy.

ac-a-dem-ic free-dom *n.* The freedom for one to teach or learn without an interference from the government.

ac-a-de-mi-cian *n.* A person who follows a philosophical tradition.

ac-a-dem-ic year *n.* A period of sessions of school which will usually start in September and ends in May or June.

a-cad-e-my *n.* A private school for special training, as in music, art, or military.

Aca-di-an *n.* A person who is a native of Acadia.

AC and U *abbr.* Association of Colleges and Universities.

acan-tho-ceph-a-lan *n.* A member of the group of intestinal worms that have a hooked proboscis and will absorb food out of the digestive tract.

a-can-thus *n.* A prickly plant, native to the Mediterranean region.

a-cap-pel-la *adj.* Singing without instrumental accompaniment.

ac-a-ri-a-sis *n.* An infestation that is caused by mites.

ac-a-rid *n.* A member of the order of arachnids that includes the ticks and mites.

ac-a-roid res-in *n.* A type of resin that is alcohol-soluble and is obtained from the Australian grass trees.

acar-pel-ous *adj.* To be without carpels.

a-cat-a-lec-tic *adj.* Not stopping short; having the complete number or syllables, in a line of verse.

a-cau-les-cent *adj.* To have no stem.

ACC *abbr.* Air Coordinating Committee.

ac-cede *v.* To consent; to agree; to arrive at a certain condition or state.

ac-cel-er--ate *v.* To make run or work faster; to increase the speed.

ac-cel-er-a-tion *n.* The process of accelerating something.

ac-cel-er-a-tive *adj.* To be pertaining to acceleration.

ac-cel-er-a-tor *n.* Something that accelerates something else.

ac-cel-er-om-e-ter *n.* A type of device that is used to measure acceleration.

ac-cent *n.* An effort to make one syllable more prominent than the others.

accentless *adj.*

ac-cen-tu-al *adj.* To be pertaining to or having an accent. **accentually** *adv.*

ac-cept *v.* To take what is given; to believe to be true; to agree. **accepter, acceptor** *n.*

ac-cept-able *adj.* Satisfactory; proper; good enough. **acceptableness, acceptability** *n.*, **acceptably** *adv.*

ac-cep-tance *n.* Approval or belief; an accepting or being accepted.

ac-cep-tant *adj.* To be willing to accept something.

ac-cess *n.* Admission, entrance; attack. **accessibility** *n.*, **accessible** *adj.*

ac-ces-sion *n.* In Computer Science, the act of obtaining data from storage.

ac-ces-so-ri-al *adj.* To be pertaining to an accessory.

ac-ces-so-rize *v.* To wear with accessories.

ac-ces-sory *n.*, *pl.* **-ies** Something which is aiding or contributing.

ac-ces-sory nerve *n.* The pair of 11th cranial nerves which supply to the muscles of the upper chest, shoulders, back, and pharynx.

ac-cess road *n.* A type of road which will provide access to an area.

ac-ci-dent *n.* A happening that is not planned or expected. **accidental** *adj.*, **accidentally** *adv.*

ac-ci-dent in-sur-ance *n.* A type of insurance protecting the person against loss due to the injury which may be caused by an accident.

ac-ci-dent--prone *adj.* To have a greater than average amount of accidents.

ac-cip-i-ter *n.* A type of short-winged hawk that has a flight pattern that is darting and low. **accipitrine** *adj.*

ac-claim *v.* To greet with strong approval or loud applause; to hail or cheer.

ac-cla-ma-tion *n.* An expression of approval that can be quite loud.

ac-cli-mate *v.* To get used to a different climate or new surroundings.

ac-cli-ma-ti-za-tion *n.* The result of acclimatizing.

ac-cli-ma-tize *v.* To change to or to adapt to a change in altitude, climate, or temperature.

ac-cliv-i-ty *n.* A slope which is ascending.

ac-co-lade *n.* Award; praise; ceremony used in conferring knighthood.

ac-com-mo-date *v.* To give room or lodging; to make fit; to adjust.

ac-com-mo-dat-ing *adj.* Ready to help; willing to please; obliging.

ac-com-mo-da-tion *n.* Adjustment; change to fit new conditions; help or convenience.

ac-com-mo-da-tion lad-der *n.* A type of ladder which will hang over the ship for the purpose of getting into smaller boats easier.

ac-com-mo-da-tor *n.* Someone or something that will accommodate.

ac-com-pa-ni-ment *n.* Something that goes well with another.

ac-com-pa-nist *n.* A person who plays a musical accompaniment.

ac-com-pa-ny *v.* To be together with; to go along with.

ac-com-plice *n.* Companion who helps another break the law.

ac-com-plish *v.* To perform; to carry out; to complete; to do. **accomplisher** *n.,* **accomplishable** *adj.*

ac-com-plish-ment *n.* Finish; completion.

ac-cord *n.* Harmony; agreement. *v.* To grant or award. **accordance** *n.*

ac-cord-ing-ly *adv.* In a way that is proper and fitting.

ac-cord-ing to *prep.* Attested by.

ac-cor-di-on *n.*

A musical instrument fitted with bellows and button keyboard, played by pulling out and pressing together the bellows to force air through the reeds.

ac-cor-di-on-ist *n.* A player of the accordion.

ac-cost *v.* To come close to and to speak first in an unfriendly manner.

ac-count *n.* A description; a statement of debts and credits in money transactions; a record; a report. **account** *v.*

ac-count-able *adj.* Liable to be held responsible; able to be explained. **accountableness** *n.,* **accountably** *adv.*

ac-coun-tan-cy *n.* The profession of an accountant.

ac-count-ing *n.* A report on how accounts have been balanced; the system of keeping business records or accounts.

ac-count-ing mach-ine *n.* A type of device that will subtract, add, and totals data that is placed into it.

ac-cou-tre *v.* To give or to provide with furnishings.

ac-cred-it *v.* To authorize someone; to give official power. **accreditation** *n.*

ac-crete *v.* To grow together or join. **accretive** *adj.*

ac-cre-tion *n.* The process of enlargement of something. **accretionary** *adj.*

ac-crue *v.* To result naturally; to increase at certain times.

acct *abbr.* Account.

ac-cul-tur-a-tion *n.* The modification of one's culture with a prolonged interaction involving another culture.

ac-cu-mu-late *v.* To collect or gather over a period of time; to pile up.

ac-cu-mu-la-tion *n.* A process of accumulating.

ac-cu-ra-cy *n.* *-cies* Exactness; precision; the fact of being accurate or without mistakes.

ac-cu-rate *adj.* Without mistakes or errors; careful and exact; correct.

ac-curs-ed *adj.* Sure to end badly; under a curse; unpleasant or annoying; very bad. **accursedness** *n.,* **accursely** *adv.*

ac-cu-sa-tion *n.* A charge that a person is guilty of breaking the law.

ac-cu-sa-tive *adj.* Relating to the direct object of a preposition or of a verb.

ac-cu-sa-to-ry *n.* To be expressing accusation.

ac-cuse *v.* To find fault with; to blame; to charge someone with doing wrong or breaking the law. **accuser** *n.*

ac-custom *v.* To familiarize by habit.

ac-custom-ed *adj.* Customary; usual.

ace *n.* The face of a die or a playing card marked with one spot; in tennis and some other sports, a score made by a serve that is not returned.

ACE *abbr.* American Council on Education.

acen-tric *adj.* To be missing a centromere.

aceph-a-lous *adj.* To be without a head.

ace-quia *n.* A type of ditch which can be used for irrigation.

acerb *adj.* To be acid in one's mood.

ac-er-o-la *n.* A type of West Indian shrub that yields cherrylike fruits.

acer-vate *adj.* To be living or growing in heaps. **acervately** *adv.*

ac-e-tab-u-lar-ia *n.* A type of single-celled alga found in the warm seas which look like mushrooms in shape.

ac-e-tab-u-lum *n.* The socket of the hipbone. **acetabular** *adj.*

ac-et-amin-o-phen *n.* A compound which is used for the purpose of relieving pain and fever.

ac-e-tate *n.* Salt formed by union of acetic acid with a base, used in making rayon and plastics.

ace-tic *adj.* To be pertaining to or related to vinegar or acetic acid.

a-ce-tic acid *n.* The main ingredient of vinegar; a sour, colorless liquid that has a sharp smell.

ace-ti-fy *v.* To change or to turn into acetic acid. **acetification** *n.*

ace-to-phe-net-i-din *n.* A type of compound which is used for relief of pain and fever.

ace-tous *adj.* To be pertaining to vinegar.

a-cet-y-lene *n.* A highly inflammable, poisonous, colorless gas that burns brightly with a hot flame, used in blowtorches for cutting metal.

ache *v.* To give or have a dull, steady pain; to want very much; to long for.

ache *n.* A dull, continuous pain.

achene *n.* A type of indehiscent one-seeded fruit that has developed from an ovary. **achneial** *adj.*

a-chieve *v.* To set or reach by trying hard; to do; to succeed in doing; to accomplish. **achiever** *n.,* **-able** *adj.*

a-chieve-ment *n.* Something achieved by work, courage, or skill.

A-chil-les ten-don *n.*

The tendon that connects the heelbone and calf muscles.

achon-drite *n.* A type of stony meteorite that does not have rounded grains.

achon-dro-pla-sia *n.* The failure of the development in a normal manner of the cartilage which results in dwarfism. **achondroplastic** *adj.*

achro-ma-tism *n.* A quality of giving of images practically free from extraneous colors.

achy *adj.* To have aches. **achiness** *n.*

ac-id *n.* A chemical compound containing hydrogen that forms a salt when combined with a base; dissolves in water, has a very sour taste, makes litmus paper turn red.

ac-id head *n.* A user of the drug LSD.

a-cid-i-fy *v.* To make some substance acid.

a-cid-i-ty *n.* Condition or quality of being acid.

acid rain *n.* Acid precipitation that falls as rain.

a-cid-u-late *v.* To become or make somewhat acid.

a-cid-u-lous *adj.* To be slightly acid in taste.

ac-i-nar *adj.* To be pertaining to an acinus.

ac-i-nus *n.* A sac of a racemose gland which is lined with secreting cells.

ack *abbr.* Acknowledge; acknowledgment.

ack-ack *n.* Anti-aircraft fire.

ac-know-ledge *v.* To admit the truth, existence or reality. **acknowledgment** *n.,* **acknowledgeable** *adj.*

ACLS *abbr.* American Council of Learned Societies.

ac-me *n.* The highest point of attainment; peak.

ac-ne *n.* A common inflammatory disease of young people in which pimples continue to appear on the body.

a-cock *adj.* To be in a cocked position.

ac-o-lyte *n.* An altar boy or someone who assists a priest at Mass.

ac-o-nite *n.* A poisonous plant with flowers resembling hoods.

a-corn *n.* A fern or moss-type plant that has no seed leaves.

a-corn squash *n.* An acorn-shaped squash with yellow flesh and a ridged rind.

a-corn tube *n.* A small vacuum tube which is like an acorn in shape.

a-corn worm *n.* A member of the group of burrowing wormlike marine animals having an acorn-shaped proboscis.

a-cot-y-ledon *n.* A plant as a fern or moss, which does not have seed leaves.

a-cous-tic *adj.* Having to do with sound or the sense of hearing; the sense of sound; absorbing sound. **acoustical** *n.,* **acoustically** *adv.*

a-cous-tics *n.* The scientific study of sound; total effect of sound, especially in an enclosed space. **acoustician** *n.*

ACP *abbr.* American College of Physicians.

acpt *abbr.* Acceptance.

ac-quaint *v.* To make familiar; to let know; to make aware; to inform.

ac-quain-tance *n.* A person whom one knows but not as a close friend. **acquaintanceship** *n.*

ac-qui-esce *v.* To agree without arguing; to comply without protest. **-cent** *adj.*

ac-quire *v.* To secure control or possession; to become the owner. **-er** *n.*

ac-quire-ment *n.* The act of acquiring something, as a skill gained by learning.

ac-quir-ed im-mun-ity *n.* Immunity against diseases that one develops during a lifetime.

ac-qui-si-tion *n.* Something that is acquired; the act of acquiring.

ac-quis-i-tive *adj.* Eager to gain and possess things; greedy.

ac-quit *v.* To rule that a person accused of something is not guilty; to conduct oneself; to behave. **acquittal** *n.*

a-cre *n.* A measurement of land that equals 43,560 square feet.

a-cre-age *n.* The total number of acres in a section of land.

ac-rid *adj.* Having a sharp, bitter, or irritating taste or smell. **acridity,** **acridness** *n.,* **acridly** *adv.*

ac-ri-mo-ni-ous *adj.* Sharp or bitter in speech or manner. **-ness** *n.,* **acrimoniously** *adv.*

ac-ro-bat *n.* One who is skilled in gymnastic feats. **acrobatic** *adj.*

ac-ro-bat-ics *n.* The performance of an acrobat.

ac-ro-cen-tric *adj.* To have a centromere that is located so one chromosomal arm is longer that the other arm.

ac-ro-pho-bi-a *n.* Unusual fear of heights.

a-cross *prep.* From side to side; to one side from the other.

across the board *adj.* Designates win, place, and show in one bet on the same contestant.

a-cros-tic *n.* A series of lines or a poem in which certain letters in each line form a name or motto. **acrostically** *adv.*

a-cryl-ic *n.* Relating to or of acrylic acid or its derivatives.

acrylic fiber *n.* A fiber which is made of chemicals, used in making fabrics.

ac-ry-lo-ni-trile *n.* A liquid organic compound used to make acrylic fibers and rubber.

act *n.* Doing something; a thing done; deed; an action; a showing of emotion which is not real or true; a law; decree; one of the main parts of a play, opera, etc. **actability** *n.,* **actable** *adj.*

ACT *abbr.* American College Test.

actg *abbr.* Acting.

ac-tin *n.* A type of protein that is in the muscle and becomes active in muscle contractions.

act-ing *adj.* Temporarily performing the duties, services, or functions of another person.

ac-tin-o-gen *n.* An element which is radioactive.

ac-tion *n.* The process of doing or acting;

an effect produced by something; a lawsuit.

ac-tion-able *adj.* To be affording ground for a suit at law.

ac-tion-less *adj.* To be characterized with inaction and lack of movement.

ac-tion paint-ing *n.* A style of painting where paint is often smeared or dribbled to give a thickly texture surface.

ac-ti-vate *v.* To put into action. **activation** *n.*

ac-tive *adj.* Working; full of action; busy; lively; quick. **activeness** *n.*, **-ly** *adv.*

ac-tive im-mu-ni-ty *n.* A type of immunity where the effects are long lasting and acquired through a response to antigens.

ac-tive trans-port *n.* A type of movement across a membrane of a cell with the used of energy.

ac-tiv-ism *n.* A practice based on direct action to affect changes in government and social conditions.

ac-tiv-i-ty *n.* Being active, in motion; normal power of body or mind.

act of God *n.* An unforseeable, uncontrollable happening caused by nature.

ac-tor *n.* A person who acts in movies, plays, television shows, etc.

ac-tress *n.* A female actor.

ac-tu-al *adj.* Acting or existing in fact or reality; as it really is, true, real. **actualness** *n.*

ac-tu-al-ly *adv.* In truth.

ac-tu-ary *n.* A person who will figure or calculate insurance.

ac-tu-ate *v.* To put into motion or action. **actuation** *n.*

ac-tu-a-tor *n.* Something that will control something else indirectly.

act up *v.* To behave in a manner that is capricious or unruly.

acu-i-ty *n.* A sharp perception of something.

acu-le-ate *adj.* To have a sting.

acu-mi-nate *adj.* To taper to a point which is slender in shape.

ac-u-punc-ture *n.* A traditional Chinese means of treating some illnesses or of lessening pain by putting thin needles into certain parts of the body.

a-cute *adj.* Extremely sensitive; sharp and quick, as pain; shrewd. **acuteness** *n.*, **acutely** *adv.*

acute accent *n.* A mark to indicate heavy stress on a syllable.

ACV *abbr.* Actual cash value.

ad *n.* An advertisement.

AD *abbr. Anno Domini*, Latin for "in the year of the Lord".

ad-age *n.* A proverb; a wise or true saying.

a-da-gi-o *adj.* Term used in music to tell how fast a phrase should be played.

Ad-am *n.* The first man named in the Bible, the husband of Eve.

ad-a-mant *adj.* Standing firm; not giving in easily; unyielding. **adamantly** *adv.*

Ad-am's ap-ple *n.* A projection in the throat, especially noticeable in men, formed by the trachea or a cartilage

the upper end of the windpipe.

a-dapt *v.* To fit or suit; to change oneself as to adjust to new conditions. **adaptedness** *n.*

adapt-able *adj.* Being capable of being adapted. **adaptability** *n.*

ad-ap-ta-tion *n.* An act of changing so as to fit or become suitable.

ad-ax-i-al *adj.* To be positioned on one side of the axis.

ADC *abbr.* Air Defense Command.

add *v.* To join or put something with another so that there will be more; to cause an increase. **add up** *v.* To make sense; to be reasonable. **add up to** *v.* To indicate; to mean. **addable, addible** *adj.*

ad-dax *n.* An African antelope with spiral twisted horns.

ad-dend *n.* The number that is added to another number.

ad-der *n.*

A common poisonous snake found in America and Europe.

ad-der's--tongue *n.* A type of fern who has a fruiting spike that is just like the tongue of a serpent.

ad-dict *n.* A person with a habit so strong that he cannot easily give it up. **addiction** *n.*, **addicted** *v.*

ad-di-tion *n.* An adding of numbers to find their total; the act of joining one thing to another. **additional** *adj.*, **additionally** *adv.*

ad-di-tive *n.* A substance added to another in small amounts to alter it.

ad-dle *v.* To become or make confused; to spoil.

addn *abbr.* Addition.

ad-dress *v.* To direct or aim; to speak to; to give attention to. *n.* The location to which mail or goods can be sent to a person.

ad-dress-ee *n.* The person to whom a letter or a package is addressed to.

ad-duce *v.* To offer as proof or give as a reason. **adducer** *n.*, **adducible** *adj.*

ad-duct *v.* To move or draw, such as a limb, toward the median axis of the body.

ad-duc-tion *n.* The state of being adducted.

ad-duc-tor *n.* The type of muscle which will draw a part of the body toward the median line of the body.

add up *v.* To arrive or to come to the expected total of a group of numbers.

ad-e-ni-tis *n.* The swelling or inflammation of lymph nodes.

ad-e-no-car-ci-no-ma *n.* A type of malignant tumor which originates in the glandular epithelium. **-tous** *adj.*

ad-e-noids *n.* Lymphoid tissue growths in the upper part of the throat behind the nose, that may need to be removed surgically.

ad-e-noi-dal *adj.* To be pertaining to or related to the adenoids.

ad-e-no-ma *n.* A type of benign tumor that will effect a glandular structure.

a-dept *adj.* Highly skilled; expert. **adeptly** *adv.*, **adeptness** *n.*

ad-e-qua-cy *n.* The state of being good enough to fill a requirement.

ad-e-quate *adj.* Sufficient; good enough for what is needed. **adequateness** *n.*, **adequately** *adv.*

ad-here *v.* To stay attached; to stick and not come loose; to stay firm in support.

ad-her-ence *n.* The quality of adhering.

ad-her-end *n.* A surface to which an adhesive is able to adhere to.

ad-her-ent *n.* A person who follows a leader, party, or belief; a believer or supporter.

ad-he-sion *n.* The act or state of sticking to something or of being stuck together.

ad-he-sive *adj.* Tending to stick and not come loose; cling; having a sticky surface. **adhesiveness** *n.*, **adhesively** *adv.*

ad-he-sive tape *n.* A type of tape that has an adhesive on one side.

a-dieu *n.* A word for good-by.

a-di-os *interj.* Spanish for good-by.

ad in-ter-im *adj.* In the meantime.

ad-i-pose tis-sue *n.* A type of connective tissue where fat is stored in the body.

adj *abbr.* Adjective; adjacent; adjourned.

ad-ja-cen-cy *n.* The state of being adjacent.

ad-ja-cent *adj.* Close to or nearby.

ad-ja-cent an-gles *n.* Two angles with a side in common, having the same vertex.

ad-jec-tive *n.* A word used to describe a noun or pronoun.

ad-join *v.* To be next to; to be in or nearly in contact with.

ad-join-ing *adj.* To be touching at a point.

ad-journ *v.* To close a meeting or session for a time. **adjournment** *n.*

ad-judge *v.* To decide by judicial procedure.

ad-ju-di-cate *v.* To settle a dispute judicially. **adjudicator** *n.*, **-ive** *adj.*

ad-ju-di-ca-tion *n.* Judicial decision. **adjudicatory** *adj.*

ad-junct *n.* Something less important added to something with more importance. **adjunctly** *adv.*, **adjunctive** *adj.*

ad-jure *v.* To ask urgently; to command solemnly. **adjuration** *n.*

adjust *v.* To arrange or change; to make work correctly; to regulate. **adjustability** *n.*

ad-just-a-ble *adj.* Anything that can be adjusted.

ad-just-ed *adj.* To have attained or achieved a relationship with the environment that is harmonious.

ad-just-ment *n.* The act or process of changing; a settlement of a suit or claim.

ad-ju-tan-cy *n.* The rank of an adjutant.

ad-ju-tant *n.* An administrative staff officer who serves as a secretary to the commanding officer.

ad-lib *v.* To improvise; to compose or make up spontaneously.

ad-man *n.* A person who works in the business of advertising.

ad-min-is-ter *v.* To direct or manage; to give or carry out instructions. **administrable** *adj.*

ad-min-is-tra-tion *n.* The people who manage a school, company, or organization.

ad-min-is-tra-tor *n.* A person who administers or directs, an executive; a manager.

ad-mi-ra-ble *adj.* Worthy of being admired or praised; excellent.

ad-mi-ral *n.* The highest rank for a naval officer; the commanding officer of a navy.

ad-mi-ral-ty *n.* The department of the British navy; the court and law dealing with ships and shipping.

ad-mire *v.* To hold a high opinion; to regard with wonder, delight, and pleased approval. **admiringly** *adv.*, **admirer** *n.*

ad-mis-si-ble *adj.* Capable of being admitted, accepted or allowed.

ad-mis-sion *n.* The right or act of being admitted; an admitting of the truth of something; a confession.

ad-mit *v.* To take or accept as being the truth; to permit or give the right to enter. **admittedly** *adv.*

ad-mit-tance *n.* Permission to enter.

ad-mit-ted-ly *adv.* One's own admission or confession.

ad-mix-ture *n.* Blend; mingling.

ad-mon-ish *v.* To warn a person to correct a fault; to criticize in a gentle way.

ad-mo-ni-tion *n.* A mild criticism or warning.

a-do-be *n.* A brick or building material made from clay and straw and then dried in the sun.

ad-o-les-cence *n.* The period of physical and psychological development between childhood and adulthood; also known as youth.

ad-o-les-cent *n.* A person in the transitional period between childhood and adulthood.

a-dopt *v.* To legally take into one's family and raise as their own. **adoption** *n.*

a-dor-a-ble *adj.* Very likable; charming. **adorably** *adv.*, **adorableness** *n.*

a-dore *v.* To love greatly; to worship or honor highly; to like very much.

a-dorn *v.* To add splendor or beauty.

a-dorn-ment *n.* Something that adorns; decoration; ornament; the act of adorning.

ad rem *adj.* Relevant to a point at issue.

a-dre-nal gland *n.* A small endocrine gland that consist of a medulla and cortex, located near the kidney.

a-drift *adv.* Drifting; floating freely without being steered; having no clear purpose or aim.

a-droit *adj.* Skillful and clever in difficult circumstances. **adroitly** *adv.*

ad-sorb *v.* To collect and hold as molecules of gases, liquids; to become adsorbed. **adsorbable** *adj.*

ad-ulate *v.* To give greater praise or flattery than is proper or deserved. **adulation** *n.*

a-dult *n.* A man or woman who is fully grown; a mature person. *adj.* Having reached full size and strength. **adulthood** *n.*

a-dul-ter-ate *v.* To make impure or of less quality by adding improper ingredients.

a-dul-tery *n.* The act of sexual intercourse between a married person and someone other than the husband or wife.

adv *abbr.* Adverb; advertisement.

ad-vance *v.* To move ahead; to make or become higher; to increase in value or price.

ad-vanced *adj.* Ahead in time; beyond beginning status.

ad-vance-ment *n.* A promotion in position; progression; money ahead of time.

ad-van-tage *n.* A better chance or more forcible position; a condition, thing or event that can help or benefit; the first point, after deuce scored in the game of tennis.

ad-van-ta-geous *adj.* Giving advantage; favorable.

ad-vent *n.* A coming or arrival; the four Sundays before Christmas.

ad-ven-ture *n.* An exciting and dangerous experience that is remembered; an unusual experience. **adventure** *v.*

ad-ven-tur-er *n.* A person who looks for adventure; one who seeks wealth and social position. **adventurous** *adj.*

ad-verb *n.* A word used with a verb, adjective, or another adverb to tell when, where, how, what kind, or how much. **adverbial** *adj.*, **adverbially** *adv.*

ad-verse *adj.* Opposed; not helpful; against someone or something. **adverseness** *n.*, **adversely** *adv.*

ad-ver-si-ty *n.* Bad luck or misfortune.

ad-ver-tise *v.* To draw public attention to a product you wish to sell. **-er** *n.*

ad-ver-tise-ment *n.* A public notice designed to advertise something.

ad-ver-tis-ing *n.* The job of preparing advertisements for publication or broadcast.

ad-vice *n.* Suggestion or recommendation regarding a course of action or decision.

ad-vis-a-ble *adj.* Fit to be done or advised. **advisability, advisableness** *n.*

ad-vis-ed-ly *adv.* Deliberately; with consideration.

ad-vise-ment *n.* Careful thought and consideration.

ad-viser *n.* A person who gives an opinion or advises.

ad-vis-so-ry *adj.* Exercising or having the power to advise; giving or containing advice.

ad-vo-cate *v.* To write or speak in favor of or support. **advocate** *n.*

AEC *abbr.* Atomic Energy Commission.

a-e-des *n.* A mosquito that transmits yellow fever.

ae-gis *n.* Protection; support or sponsorship.

aer-ate *v.* To purify by exposing to the open air.

aer-i-al *adj.* Of or in the air; pertaining to aircraft. *n.* An antenna for television or radio. **aerially** *adv.*

aer-i-al-ist *n.* An acrobat who does stunts high above the ground on a wire or trapeze.

aer-ie *n.* The nest of a predatory bird, built on a cliff or other high places.

aer-o-bics *n.* Strenuous exercise that increases oxygen to the heart and lungs, therefore strengthening them.

aer-o-nau-tics *pl.*, *n.* The science of designing and constructing aircraft. **aeronautic** *adj.*

aer-o-pause *n.* The region in the upper atmosphere where aircraft cannot fly.

aer-o-plane *n.* British word for airplane.

aer-o-sol *n.* A liquid substance under pressure within a metal container.

Ae-sop *n.* Greek writer of fables from the sixth century B.C.

aes-thet-ic *adj.* Having a love for beauty.

aes-thet-ics *n.* The study of the nature of beauty. **aesthetically** *adv.*

a-far *adv.* Far off; far away.

af-fa-ble *adj.* Good natured, easy to talk to; friendly. **affably** *adv.*

af-fair *n.* An event or happening; matters of business or public concern.

af-fect *v.* To move emotionally; to feel sympathetic or sad; to bring about a change in. **affecting, affected** *adj.*

af-fec-ta-tion *n.* Artificial behavior that is meant to impress others.

af-fec-tion *n.* A tender or fond feeling towards another.

af-fec-tion-ate *adj.* Loving and gentle. **affectionately** *adv.*

af-fi-da-vit *n.* A written statement by a person swearing that something is the truth.

af-fil-i-ate *v.* To join in, connect, or associate with. **affiliation** *n.*

af-fin-i-ty *n.* A special attraction with kinship; a natural attraction or liking.

af-firm *v.* To declare positively and be willing to stand by the truth. **affirmation** *n.*

af-firm-a-tive *adj.* Asserting the fact is true. **affirmative** *n.*

af-fix *n.* To attach; to fasten; to add at the end. *n.* A prefix or suffix added to a word.

af-flict *v.* To cause suffering or pain; to cause mental suffering. **affliction** *n.*

af-flu-ence *n.* Wealth; riches; abundance.

af-flu-ent *adj.* Prosperous; rich; having all the wealth or money needed. **affluently** *adv.*

af-ford *v.* To be able to provide; to have enough money to spare.

af-for-est *v.* To turn open land into

forest. **afforestation** n.

af-fray n. Brawl or noisy fight.

af-front v. To insult one to his face; to confront.

af-ghan n. A crocheted or knitted cover in colorful designs.

Af-ghan-i-stan n. A country in south-western Asia, between Pakistan and Iran.

a-field adv. Away from home or the usual path.

a-fire adv. Burning.

AFL-CIO abbr. American Federation of Labor and Congress of Industrial Organizations.

a-flame adj. Burning; in flames; glowing.

a-float adj. Floating on the surface of water; circulating.

a-flut-ter adj. Nervously excited.

a-foot adj. In the progress of happening; walking; on foot.

a-fore-men-tioned adj. Mentioned before.

a-fore-said adj. Having spoken of something before.

a-fore-thought adj. Premeditated; planned beforehand.

a-foul adv. Tangled; entangled in a collision.

Afr abbr. Africa; African.

a-fraid adj. Hesitant; filled with fear; reluctant.

A-frame n. A structure for a house; a style or model.

a-fresh adv. Once more; again.

Af-ri-ca n.

A continent located in the Eastern Hemisphere, south of Europe and between the Atlantic and Indian Oceans.

Af-ri-kaans n. The spoken language of the Republic of South Africa.

Af-ro n. A bushy hair style; African in style.

aft adv. At, close to, near, or toward the rear of an aircraft or stern of a ship.

af-ter adv. In the rear. prep. Following.

af-ter-birth n. The placenta and fetal matter released by the uterus after childbirth.

af-ter-ef-fect n. An effect coming after.

af-ter-math n. Consequence; result.

af-ter-thought n. An idea occurring later.

a-gain adv. Moreover; another time; once more.

a-gainst prep. In exchange for; in preparation for.

a-gape adv. With expectation; in wonder; open-mouthed.

ag-ate n. The type of quartz that has bands of colors.

a-ga-ve n. Fleshy-leaved tropical American plant.

age n. The length of time from beginning to a certain date; the time of life when a person has full legal rights; the age of 21. v. To grow or become old; to mature.

aged adj. Grown or become old. **agedness** n., **agedly** adv.

age-ism n. Discrimination based on a person's age.

age-less adj. Existing forever; never seems to grow old.

a-gen-cy n. A business or service that acts for others; action; active influence; power.

a-gen-da n. Program or list of things to be done.

a-gent n. One who acts as the representative of another; one who acts or exerts power.

ag-gior-na-men-to n. Bringing up to date.

ag-glom-er-ate v. To collect; to form into a mass. **agglomerate** n.

ag-glu-ti-nate v. To join by adhesion; to cause red blood cells to clump together.

ag-glu-ti-nin n. A substance that causes agglutination; a group or mass formed by the union of separate elements.

ag-gran-dize n. To enlarge, to extend; to increase. **aggrandizement** n.

ag-gra-vate v. To annoy; to make worse.

ag-gre-gate adj. To gather together into a mass or whole. **aggregate** adj.

ag-gres-sion n. Hostile action or behavior; an unprovoked assault.

ag-gres-sive adj. Offensive; distressing; pushy; afflicting. **aggressiveness** n.

a-ghast adj. Appalled; struck with amazement.

ag-ile adj. Marked by the ability to move quickly and easily; nimble. **agility** n.

ag-itate v. To disturb; to upset; to stir or move with violence; to try to arouse the public interest.
agitation, agitator n.

a-gleam adj. Gleaming.

a-glim-mer adv. Glimmering.

a-glitter adj. Glittering.

a-glow adj. Glowing.

ag-nos-tic n. One who doubts that there is a God or life hereafter. **-ism** n.

a-go adj. & adv. In the past; gone by.

a-gog adj. Excited; eagerly expectant.

ag-o-nize v. To afflict with great anguish or to suffer. **agonized, agonizing** adj.

ag-o-ny n., pl. **-nies** Intense mental distress or physical pain; anguish.

ag-o-ra-pho-bi-a n. Fear of open spaces.

agr or **agric** abbr. Agricultural; agriculture.

a-grar-i-an adj. Pertaining to or of land and its ownership; pertaining to farming; agricultural.

a-gree v. To give assent; to consent; to share an understanding or opinion; to be beneficial or suitable; to correspond.

a-gree-a-ble adj. Pleasant; pleasing; willing; ready to consent.
agreeableness n., **agreeably** adv.

a-gree-ment n. Harmony; concord; state or act of agreeing.

ag-ri-busi-ness n. Big business farming, embracing the product, distribution, and processing of farm products and the manufacture of farm equipment.

ag-ri-cul-ture *n.* Raising of livestock; farming and cultivating the crops. **agriculturalist, agriculturist** *n.*

a-ground *adv. & adj.* Stranded; on the ground; to run ashore; beached.

a-gue *n.* Fever accompanied by chills or shivering and sweating. **aguish** *adj.*

a-head *adv.* Before; in advance; to or at the front of something.

a-hoy *interj.* A nautical call or greeting.

aid *v.* To give help or assistance. **aider** *n.*

AIDS *n.* Disease that destroys the body's immunological system; Acquired Immune Deficiency Syndrome.

ail *v.* To feel sick; to make ill or uneasy.

ai-lan-thus *n.* A tree with numerous pointed leaves.

ai-ler-on *v.* Movable control flap on the trailing edge of an airplane wing.

ail-ment *n.* A mild illness.

aim *v.* To direct a weapon; to direct purpose. *n.* Intention.

aim-less *adj.* Lacking of purpose.

ain't *contr.* Am not, are not, is not, has not, or have not.

ai-o-li *n.* Rich garlic-flavored mayonnaise.

air *n.* An odorless, tasteless, colorless, gaseous mixture; primarily composed of nitrogen (78%) and oxygen (21%); the sky; a breeze. **on the air** Broadcast.

air-borne *adj.* Carried through or by the air.

air brake *n.* Brake operated by the power of c mpressed air.

air-brush Machine using compressed · to spray paint and other liquids on , surface.

air con-di-tion-er *n.* Equipment used to lower the temperature and humidity of an enclosure.

air-craft *n.* A machine that flies, such as a helicopter, airplane, or glider.

air-craft car-rier *n.* A large ship which carries airplanes on which they can be landed and launched.

air-crew *n.* A crew that mans an airplane and are responsible for flying the aircraft.

air-drop *n.* Delivery of supplies made by parachute from an airplane while in flight.

air-dry *v.* To dry by exposing to the air.

air-field *n.* Paved runways at an airport; landing strip.

air-flow *n.*

The motion of air around a body as relative to the surface of a body immersed in it.

air-foil *n.* Part of an airplane which controls stability, lift, thrust, etc.

Air Force *n.* Aviation branch of armed forces.

air-frame *n.* The structure of a rocket or airplane without an engine.

air-freight *n.* Freight that is transported from one location to another by air.

air gun *n.* Gun which is operated by compressed air.

air-hole *n.* A hole that is used to discharge or admit air into an area.

air-ing *n.* Exposing something in the open air.

air lane *n.* The regular route of travel for airplanes.

air letter *n.* A letter that is transmitted by means of an aircraft.

air-lift *n.* System of transporting supplies or troops by air when ground routes are blocked.

air-line *n.* An air transportation company or system.

air-lin-er *n.* A large passenger airline.

air lock *n.* Airtight compartment between regions of unequal pressure.

air-mail & air mail *n.* Mail sent by means of air.

air-man *n.* A person enlisted in the air force.

air-man-ship *n.* The skill in navigating or piloting an airplane.

air-plane *n.* A vehicle capable of flight, heavier than air, and propelled by jet engines or propellers.

air pocket *n.* A condition in the atmosphere that can cause an airplane to loose altitude quickly.

air-port *n.* A terminal station for passengers where aircraft take off and land.

air raid *n.* Bombing attack by military aircraft.

air-ship *n.* Dirigible; a self-propelled lighter-than-air aircraft.

air-sick-ness *n.* Nausea resulting from flight in an aircraft. **airsick** *adj.*

air--speed *n.* Speed of an aircraft while airborne.

air-strip *n.* Concrete runway on an airfield; minimally equipped airfield.

air-tight *adj.* Impermeable by air or gas. **airtightness** *n.*

air-wave *n.* The medium of television and radio transmission and communication.

air-way *n.* An air lane; the designated route along which an airplane must travel.

air-wor-thy *adj.* Fit to fly. **-iness** *n.*

air-y *adj.* Open to the air; breezy; light as air; graceful or delicate. **airiness** *n.*, **airily** *adv.*

aisle *n.* Passageway between rows of seats, as in a church, auditorium, or airplane. **aisled** *adj.*

a-jar *adv. & adj.* Partially opened.

AK *abbr.* Alaska.

AKA *abbr.* Also known as.

a-kim-bo *adj. & adv.* Bent; with a crook.

a-kin *adj.* Related, as in family; similar in quality or character.

AL *abbr.* American Legion; Alabama.

Alabama *n.* A state located in the southeastern part of the United States.

al-a-bas-ter *n.* A dense, translucent, tinted or white, fine-grained gypsum. **alabastrine** *adj.*

a la carte *n.* Separate price for each item

on the menu.

a-lack *interj.* An exclamation expressive of sorrow.

a-lac-ri-ty *n.* Readiness; cheerfulness; eagerness; briskness.

a la mode *n.* Served with ice cream, as pie; fashionable.

a-larm *n.* A warning of danger; sudden feeling of fear; the bell or buzzer of a clock. *v.* To frighten or warn by an alarm. **alarming** *adv.*, **alarmingly** *adj.*

a-larm-ist *n.* Someone who needlessly alarms others. **alarmism** *n.*

a-las *interj.* Expressive of anxiety or regret.

Alaska *n.* A state located in the northwestern part of the United States.

a-late *or* **alated** *adj.* Winged; having wings. **alation** *n.*

alb *n.* White linen robe worn by clergy during Mass.

al-ba-core *n.* Large marine fish; major source of canned tuna.

Al-ba-ni-a *n.* A country located in SE Europe.

Al-ba-ni-an *n.* An inhabitant or native of Albania.

al-ba-tross *n.*

Large, web-footed, long-winged sea bird.

al-be-it *conj.* Although; even though.

al-bi-no *n.* An animal or person with an abnormal whiteness of the skin and hair and pink colored eyes.

al-bum *n.* A book for photographs, autographs, stamps; a book of collections.

al-bu-men *n.* White of an egg.

al-bu-min *n.* Several proteins found in the white of eggs, blood serum, milk, and plant and animal tissue.

al-bu-min-ous *adj.* Relating to, having the properties of or containing albumen.

al-caz-ar *n.* A Spanish fortress or palace.

al-che-my *n.* Traditional chemical philosophy concerned primarily with changing base metals into gold.

al-co-hol *n.* Intoxicating liquor containing alcohol; ethanol; a series of related organic compounds.

al-co-hol-ic *adj.* Resulting from alcohol; containing or preserved in alcohol; suffering from alcoholism. **alcoholic** *n.*

al-co-hol-ism *n.* Excessive alcohol consumption; a habit or addiction.

al-co-hol-ize *v.* Saturate or treat something with alcohol.

al-cove *n.* Recess or partly enclosed extension of a room.

al-de-hyde *n.* Any of a class of highly reactive compounds obtained by oxidation of alcohols.

al-der *n.* Tree of the birch family, grows in marshy soil.

al-der-man *n.* Member of a municipal legislative body.

ale *n.* Beverage similar to, but more bitter than beer, made from malt by fermentation.

a-lem-bic *n.* A glass or metal vessel formerly used in distillation.

a-lert *adj.* Vigilant; brisk; watchful; active. *n.* A signal by siren of air attack. **alertly** *adv.*, **alertness** *n.*

al-ex-an-drine *n.* Line of English verse in iambic hexameter; probably from poems dealing with Alexander the Great.

al-fal-fa *n.* Plant with purple flowers, widely resembling the clover widely grown for forage.

al-fres-co *adv.* & *adj.* In the fresh air; outside.

al-gae *pl.*, *n.* Various primitive, chiefly aquatic, one-celled or multicellular plants, as the seaweed.

al-ge-bra *n.* Generalization of math in which symbols represent members of a specified set of numbers and are related by operations that hold for all numbers in the set. **algebraic, -ally** *adv.*, **algebraist** *n.*

a-li-as *n.*, *pl.* **aliases** Assumed name. *adv.* Otherwise known as.

al-i-bi *n.* A form of defense, an attempt by a defendant to prove he was elsewhere when a crime was committed; an excuse.

a-li-en *adj.* Owing allegiance to a government or country, not one's own; unfamiliar; repugnant; a member of another region, or country. *n.* A stranger; a foreigner.

al-ien-a-ble *adj.* Able to be transferred to the ownership of another. **alienability** *n.*

al-ien-ate *v.* To cause to become indifferent or unfriendly. **alienation** *n.*

al-ien-ist *n.* A psychiatrist accepted by a court as an expert on mental stability.

a-light *v.* To settle; to come down; to dismount. *adj.* *or* *adv.* Burning, lighted.

a-lign *v.* To arrange in a line; to take one side of an argument or cause. **aline** *v.*

a-lign-ment *or* **alinement** *n.* Arrange or position in a straight line.

a-like *adj.* Similar, having close resemblance. *adv.* In the same manner, way, or degree.

al-i-ment *n.* Nourishment; food. **alimentation** *n.*, **alimental** *adj.*

al-i-men-ta-ry *adj.* Pertaining to nutrition or food.

al-i-men-ta-ry canal *n.* The tube of the digestive system from the mouth to the anus, including the pharynx, esophagus, stomach, and intestines.

al-i-men-ta-tion *n.* The process or act of affording nutriment. **-ive** *adj.*

al-i-mo-ny *n.*, *pl.* **-nies** Court ordered allowance for support, usually given by a man to his former wife following a divorce or legal separation.

A-line *adj.* Having a close-fitting top and a flared bottom.

al-i-phat-ic *adj.* Having to do with organic chemical compounds where the carbon atoms are linked in open chains.

a-live *adj.* Living; having life; in existence or effect; full of life. **-ness** *n.*

a-li-yah *n.* Immigration of Jewish people to Israel.

a-liz-a-rin *n.* A red-orange compound used in dyes.

al-ka-li *n., pl.* **-lies** or **-lis** A hydroxide or carbonate of an alkali metal, whose aqueous solution is slippery, bitter, caustic, and basic in reactions.

al-ka-li metal *n.* Any of the mostly basic metals comprising lithium, sodium, potassium, francium, etc.

al-ka-line *adj.* Of, relating to, or containing an alkali. **alkalinity** *n.*

al-ka-lin-ize *adj.* To make alkaline.

al-ka-loid *n.* Any of various nitrogen containing organic bases obtained from plants. **alkaloidal** *adj.*

al-ka-lo-sis *n.* Unusually high alkali content in the blood and tissues.

all *adj.* Total extent or total entity; being a whole number, amount, or quantity; every.

Al-lah *n.* The Moslem supreme being.

all-a-round *n.* Variance of all-round.

al-lay *v.* To relieve; to lessen; to calm; to pacify. **allayer** *n.*

al-le-ga-tion *n.* The act or result of alleging.

al-lege *v.* To affirm; to assert to be true; to declare without proof.

Al-le-ghe-ny Mountains *n.* Section of the Appalachians extending from Pennsylvania to Virginia.

al-le-giance *n.* Loyalty to one's nation, cause, or sovereign; obligations of a vassal to an overlord. **allegiant** *adj.*

al-le-go-ry *n., pl.* **-ries** A dramatic, literary, or pictorial device in which each object, character, and event symbolically illustrates a moral or religious principle. **allegoric, -ical** *adj.,* **allegorically** *adv.,* **-ist** *n.*

al-le-gret-to *adv., Mus.* Slower than allegro but faster than andante. **allegretto** *adj.*

al-le-gro *adv., Mus.* Faster than allegretto but slower than presto. **allegro** *adj. & n.*

al-lele *n.* Any of a group of possible mutational forms of a gene. **allelic** *adj.,* **allelism** *n.*

al-le-lu-ia *interj.* Expressing praise to God or of thanksgiving.

al-ler-gen *n.* Substance which causes an allergy. **allergenic** *adj.*

al-ler-gist *n.* A doctor specializing in allergies.

al-ler-gy *n.* **-gies** Pathological or abnormal reaction to environmental substances, as foods, dust, pollens, or microorganisms. **allergic** *adj.*

al-le-vi-ate *v.* To make more bearable. **alleviation, alleviator** *n.*

al-ley *n., pl.* **-leys** Narrow passageway between or behind buildings.

al-li-ance *n.* A union, relationship, or connection by kinship, marriage, or

common interest; a confederation of nations by a formal treaty; an affinity.

al-li-ga-tor *n.*

Large amphibious reptile with very sharp teeth, powerful jaws, and a shorter snout than the related crocodile.

al-li-ga-tor pear *n.* An avocado.

al-lit-er-ate *v.* To arrange or form words beginning with the same sound. **alliterator** *n.*

al-lit-er-a-tion *n.* Occurrence of two or more words having the same initial sound. **alliterative** *adj.*

al-lo-cate *v.* To assign; to allot. **allocation** *n.*

al-lot *v.* To distribute or set aside as a share of something. **allotment, allotter** *n.*

all out *adv.* With every possible effort or resource.

al-low *v.* To make a provision for, to permit; to permit to have; to admit; to concede. **-able** *adj.,* **allowably** *adv.*

al-low-ance *n.* The act of allowing something, a regular amount of money, food, etc.; a price discount.

al-loy *v.* Something that has been added to; item reduced purity or value.

all right *adj.* Meets satisfaction, certainly. *adv.* Satisfactory; correct; unhurt. *adj., Slang* Good; of sound character; dependable.

all-round *adj.* Versatile, including all aspects.

all-spice *n.* Tropical American tree bearing aromatic berries, used as a spice.

all-star *adj.* Composed entirely of star performers.

all-time *adj.* Of all time.

all told *adv.* Everything taken into account.

al-lude *n.* To refer to something indirectly. **allusion** *n.,* **allusive** *adj.,* **allusively** *adv.*

al-lure *v.* To entice; to tempt. *n.* Attraction; charm; enticement; the prospect of attracting. **allurement, allurer** *n.,* **alluringly** *adv.*

al-lu-sion *n.* The act of referring to something indirectly; a hint.

al-lu-vi-um *n.* Sediment deposited by flowing water as in a river bed. **alluvial** *adj.*

al-ly *v.* To connect or unite in a formal or close relationship or bond. *n.* One united with another in a formal or personal relationship.

al-ma ma-ter *n.* College, school, or university one has attended; the anthem of that college, school, or university.

al-ma-nac *n.* Annual publication having calendars with weather forecasts, astronomical information, and other useful facts.

al-might-y *adj.* Having absolute power. **Almighty** *n.* The Almighty God.

al-mond *n.* An oval, edible nut with a

soft, light-brown shell; tree bearing such nuts.

al-most *adv*. Not quite; slightly short of.

alms *pl., n*. Goods or money given to the poor in charity.

alms-house *n*. A poorhouse.

al-oe *n*.

Any of various mostly African plants having fleshy, spiny-toothed leaves; a cathartic drug made from the juice of the leaves of this plant.

a-loft *adv*. Toward the upper rigging of a ship; in or into a high place; in the air.

a-lo-ha *interj*. Hawaiian expression of greeting or farewell.

a-lone *adj*. Away from other people; single; solitary; excluding anyone or anything else; with nothing further; sole; only. **alone** *adv*.

a-long *adv*. In a line with; following the length or path; in association; together; as a companion.

a-long-shore *adv*. Near, along, or by the shore, either on land or in the water.

a-long-side *adv*. Along, at, near, or to the side of; side by side with.

a-loof *adj*. Indifferent; distant. **aloofness** *n*., **aloofly** *adv*.

a-loud *adv*. Orally; audibly.

alp *n*. High mountain.

al-pac-a *n*. South American mammal related to the llama; the wool of the alpaca.

al-pen-horn *n*. Long curved horn used to call cows to pasture.

al-pen-stock *n*. Long staff with an iron point used by mountain climbers.

al-pha *n*. First letter of the Greek alphabet.

al-pha-bet *n*. The letters of a language, arranged in an order fixed by custom.

al-pha-bet-i-cal *adj*. Arranged in the traditional order of the letters of a language. **alphabetically** *adv*.

al-pha-bet-ize *v*. To arrange in alphabetical order.

al-pha de-cay *n*. Decay of an atomic nucleus as it emits an alpha particle.

Al-pha ray *n*. A stream of alpha particles.

Alps *n*. The major mountain system of south-central Europe, forming an arc from Southern France to Albania.

al-read-y *adv*. By this or a specified time.

al-so *adv*. Likewise; besides; in addition.

al-so--ran *n*. One defeated in a competition.

alt *abbr*. Alteration; alternate; altitude.

Al-ta-ic *adj*. A language family of Europe and Asia. **Altaian** *n*.

al-tar *n*. An elevated structure before which religious ceremonies may be held or sacrifices offered.

al-tar-piece *n*. A carving or painting placed above and behind an altar.

al-ter *v*. To make change or become different; to modify; to castrate or spay,

as an animal. **alterability**, **-ation** *n*.

al-ter-a-tive *adj*. Tending to alter or produce alterations.

al-ter-ca-tion *n*. Noisy and heated quarrel.

al-ter e-go *v*. An intimate friend; another aspect of oneself.

al-ter-nate *v*. To happen or follow in turn; to occur in successive turns. *n*. Substitute. **-ly** *adv*., **alternation** *n*.

al-ter-nat-ing cur-rent *n*. Electric current that reverses direction at regular intervals.

al-ter-na-tive *n*. A choice between two or more possibilities; one of the possibilities to be chosen. **-ly** *adv*.

al-ter-na-tive *adj*. Allowing a choice.

al-ter-na-tor *n*. Electric generator producing alternating current.

al-though *conj*. Even though.

al-tim-e-ter *n*. Instrument for measuring and indicating altitude.

al-ti-tude *n*. The height of a thing above a reference level; above the earth's surface; above sea level.

al-to *n*. Low female singing voice; the range between soprano and tenor.

al-to-geth-er *adv*. Entirely; with all included or counted.

al-tru-ism *n*. Selfless concern for the welfare of others. **altruist** *n*., **altruistic** *adj*., **altruistically** *adv*.

al-um *n*. Any one of several similar double sulfates.

a-lu-mi-na *n*. Any of several forms of aluminum oxide.

a-lu-mi-num *n*. A silvery-white, ductile metallic element used to form many hard, light, corrosion-resistant alloys.

a-lum-na *n., pl.* **-nae** Female graduate or former student of a school, college, or university.

a-lum-nus *n., pl.* **-ni** A male graduate or former student of a school, college, or university.

al-ways *adv*. Continuously; forever; on every occasion; at all times.

am *n*. First person, singular, present tense of be.

AM *abbr*. Ante meridian, Latin for "before noon".

AMA *abbr*. American Medical Association.

a-mal-gam *n*. An alloy of mercury with other metals, as with tin or silver; a blend of diverse elements. **-able** *adj*.

a-mal-ga-mate *v*. To mix so as to make a unified whole; to blend. **amalgamation**, **amalgamator** *n*.

a-man-dine *adj*. Made or garnished with almonds.

am-a-ranth *n*. Various weedy plants with greenish or purplish flowers; an imaginary flower that never fades. **amaranthine** *adj*.

am-a-ryl-lis *n*.

A bulbous plant with large, lily-like, reddish or white flowers.

am-a-teur *n*. One who

engages in an activity as a pastime rather than as a profession; one who lacks expertise. **amateurish** *adj.*, **amateurism** *n.*

am-a-to-ry *adj.* Of or expressive of sexual love.

a-maze *v.* To astound; to affect with surprise or wonder. **amazingly** *adv.*, **amazedness**, **-ment** *n.*, **amazing** *adj.*

Am-a-zon *n.* A river of South America, beginning in the Andes and flowing through North Brazil to the Atlantic.

amb *abbr.* Ambassador.

am-bas-sa-dor *n.* Official representative of the highest rank, accredited by one government to another. **ambassadorial** *adj.*, **-ship.** *n.*

am-ber *n.* A hard, translucent, yellow, brownish-yellow, or orange fossil resin, used for jewelry and ornaments; medium to dark orange yellow.

am-ber-gris *n.* A waxy, grayish substance produced by sperm whales, and used in making perfumes.

am-bi-ance *n.* Environment; atmosphere.

am-bi-dex-trous *adj.* Able to use both hands with equal facility.

am-bi-ent *adj.* Surrounding.

am-big-u-ous *adj.* Doubtful; uncertain. **ambiguousness** *n.*, **ambiguously** *adv.*

am-bi-tion *n.* Strong desire to achieve; will to succeed; the goal or object desired.

am-bi-tious *adj.* Challenging. **ambitiousness** *n.*, **ambitiously** *adv.*

am-biv-a-lence *n.* Existence of mutually different feelings about a person or thing.

am-ble *v.* To move at a leisurely pace.

am-bro-sia *n.* Food of the Greek Gods and immortals; food having exquisite flavor or fragrance. **ambrosial** *adj.*

am-bu-lance *n.*

Vehicle equipped to transport the injured or sick.

am-bu-la-to-ry *adj.* Moving about; movable; of or to do with walking.

am-bus-cade *n.* Ambush.

am-bush *n.* Surprise attack made from a hidden position. **ambush** *v.*, **ambusher**, **ambushment** *n.*

A-me-ba also Amoeba *n.*

A single-celled semi-fluid living animal.

a-me-lio-rate *v.* To become or make better. **ameliorator**, **amelioration** *n.*, **ameliorative** *adj.*

a-men *interj.* Used at the end of a prayer to express solemn approval.

a-me-na-ble *adj.* Responsive; tractable; accountable. **-ness**, **amenability** *n.*

a-mend *v.* To correct; to improve; to rectify. **amendable** *adj.*, **amender** *n.*

a-mend-ment *n.* Correction, reformation or improvement; the parliamentary

procedure where such alteration is made.

a-mends *pl.*, *n.* Compensation for insult or injury.

a-men-i-ty *n.*, *pl.* **-ties** Agreeableness; means of comfort or convenience.

Amer *abbr.* America; American.

a-merce *v.* To punish. **amercement** *n.*

America *n.* United States of America; North America; South America.

A-mer-i-ca-n *n.* A native of one of the Americas or a U.S. citizen.

American eagle *n.* The bald eagle.

A-mer-i-can-ism *n.* Language usage, trait, or tradition of the U.S.

American plan *n.* A hotel plan where a guest is charged a fixed daily rate for service, room, and meals.

Am-er-ind *n.* American Indian or an Eskimo.

am-e-thyst *n.* Violet or purple form of transparent corundum or quartz, used as a gemstone. **amethystine** *adj.*

a-mi-a-ble *adj.* Friendly and pleasant. **-ness**, **amiability** *n.*, **amiably** *adv.*

am-i-ca-ble *adj.* Harmonious; friendly. **amicability**, **-ness** *n.*, **amicably** *adv.*

a-mid *prep.* In the middle of; surrounded by.

a-mid-ships *adv.* Halfway between the bow and the stern.

a-midst *prep.* In the middle of; surrounded by; during.

a-mi-go *n.* A friend.

A-mish *pl.*, *n.* Mennonites that settled mostly in southeastern Pennsylvania in the late 1600's. **Amish** *adj.*

a-miss *adj.* Out of order or place; in an improper or wrong way.

am-i-ty *n.* Relationships that are friendly, as between two states.

am-me-ter *n.* A tool measuring electric current.

am-mo *n.* Ammunition.

am-mo-nia *n.* Colorless, pungent gas.

am-mo-nium hy-drox-ide *n.* A colorless, basic aqueous solution of ammonia.

am-mu-ni-tion *n.* Projectiles that can be propelled or discharged from guns; any means of defense.

am-ne-sia *n.* The loss of memory.

am-nes-ty *n.*, *pl.* **-ties** Pardon for political offenders.

a-moe-ba *n.*, *pl.* **-bas** *or* **-bae** Various minute one-celled organisms having an indefinite, changeable form.

a-mong *prep.* In or through the midst of; between one another.

a-mon-til-la-do *n.*, *pl.* **-dos** A pale, dry sherry.

a-mor-al *adj.* Neither moral nor immoral. **amorality** *n.*, **amorally** *adv.*

am-o-rous *adj.* Inclined to or indicative of sexual love. **amorousness** *n.*

a-mor-phous *adj.* Lacking definite form; shapeless; general; vague.

am-or-tize *v.* To liquidate a loan by installment payments; a loan. **-ation** *n.*

a-mount *n.* Aggregate, sum or total quantity. *v.* To be equivalent.

a-mour *n.* A forbidden love affair.

a-mour--pro-pre *n.* Self-respect.

am·per·age *n.* Strength of an electric current, expressed in amperes.

am·pere *n.* Unit of electric current equal to a flow of one amp per second.

am·per·sand *n.* The character or sign that represents and (&).

am·phet·a·mine *n.* Colorless volatile liquid; a drug.

amphi *prefix.* Around, on both sides, all around on all sides.

am·phib·i·an *n.* An organism, as a frog or toad, developing from an aquatic state into an air-breathing state; aircraft that can take off and land on land or water; a vehicle that can take off or land on land or water.

am·phi·the·a·ter *n.* A round or oval building having tiers of seats rising around an arena.

am·pho·ra *n., pl.* -rae *or* -ras Ancient Greek jar with two handles and a narrow neck, used to carry oil or wine.

am·ple *adj.* Sufficient; abundant; large. **ampleness** *n.,* **amply** *adv.*

am·pli·tude *n.* Maximum value of a periodically varying quantity; greatness of size; fullness.

am·pli·tude mod·u·la·tion *n.* The encoding of a carrier wave by variation of its amplitude in accordance with a signal.

am·pul *or* **am·pule** *n.* A small, sealed vial containing a hypodermic injection solution.

am·pu·tate *v.* To cut off; to remove, as a limb from one's body. **amputation** *n.*

am·pu·tee *n.* A person who has had one or more limbs amputated.

amt *abbr.* Amount.

amu *n., Phys.* Atomic mass unit.

a·muck *adv.* In an uncontrolled manner; a murderous frenzy; out of control.

am·u·let *n.* A charm worn as protection against evil or injury.

A·mur *n.* A river of East Asia.

a·muse *v.* To entertain in an agreeable, pleasing way. **-ment** *n.,* **amusable** *adj.*

an *adj.* One; one sort of; each; form of "a" used before words beginning with a vowel or with an unpronounced "h" as an elephant or an honor.

a·nach·ro·nism *n.* Connecting of a thing, of a person or happening with another that came after in history; anything that seems to be out of place in history.

an·a·con·da *n.*

A large tropical American snake which kills its prey by crushing it to death in its coils.

an·a·dem *n.* A wreath for the head.

a·nad·ro·mous *adj.* Migrating up river from the sea to breed in fresh water, as a salmon.

a·nae·mi·a *n.* Variant of anemia.

an·aes·the·sia *n.* Variant of anesthesia.

an·a·gram *n.* Word formed by transposing the letters of another word.

anagrammatical, anagrammatic *adj.*

a·nal *adj.* Of or relating to the anus.

anal *abbr.* Analogous; analogy; analysis; analytic.

an·al·ge·sia *n.* Inability to feel pain while awake. **analgesic** *adj. & n.*

an·a·log com·put·er *n.* A computer where numerical data are represented by measurable quantities as lengths, electrical signals, or voltage.

a·nal·o·gous *adj.* Similar; corresponding in certain ways. **analogously** *adv.*

an·a·logue *n.* Something that bears resemblance to something else.

a·nal·o·gy *n., pl.* -gies Connection between things that are otherwise dissimilar; a conclusion or opinion that if two things are alike in some respects they must be alike in others.

a·nal·y·sis *n.* Breaking up or separation of something into its parts so as to examine them and see how they fit together; result.

an·a·lyst *n.* A person who analyzes or who is skilled in analysis.

an·a·lyze *v.* To make an analysis of.

an·a·pest *n.* Metrical foot make up of two short syllables followed by one long one. **anapestic** *adj.*

an·ar·chic *adj.* Of, like, or promoting confusion or disorder.

an·ar·chism *n.* Belief that all forms of government act in an unfair way against the liberty of a person and should be done away with.

an·ar·chy *n.* Lack of political authority, disorder and confusion; the absence of any purpose or standard.

a·nas·to·mo·sis *n.* Connection or union of branches, as of rivers, leaf veins, or blood vessels. **anastomotic** *adj.*

a·nas·tro·phe *n.* Changing the normal syntactic order of words.

a·nath·e·ma *n.* Curse; ban; or excommunication. **anathematize** *v.*

a·nat·o·mize *v.* To examine in great detail; to analyze; in biology, to dissect. **anatomization** *n.*

a·nat·o·my *n., pl.* -mies Structure of an organ or organism; a detailed analysis. **anatomical, anatomic** *adj.*

an·ces·try *n., pl.* -tries Line of descent; lineage ancestors collectively.

an·ces·tor *n.* A person who comes before one in a family line; someone earlier than a grandparent; forefather. **ancestral** *adj.*

an·chor *n.*

Heavy metal device lowered into the water by a chain to keep a ship from drifting. *v.* To attach or fix firmly.

an·chor·age *n.* A place for anchoring a ship; a strong support that keeps something steady.

an·cho·rite *n.* A religious hermit.

anchor man *n.* The main member of a

team of newscasters.

an-cho-vy *n.*

A very small fish of the herring family; usually salted, canned in oil, and used for making sauces and relishes.

an-cient *adj.* Anything belonging to the early history of people; very old. **ancientness** *n.,* **anciently** *adv.*

and *conj.* Together with; along with; as well as; added to; as a result; plus; also.

an-dan-te *adv., Mus.* Rather slow in tempo. **andante** *adj.*

an-dan-ti-no *adj., Mus.* Slightly faster in tempo than andante.

An-des *n.* A mountain system stretching the length of west South American, from Venezuela to Tierra del Fuego.

and-i-ron *n.* Heavy metal support for logs or wood in a fireplace.

andr *n.* The male sex; masculine.

an-dro-gen *n.* Hormone that develops and maintains masculine characteristics. **androgenic** *adj.*

an-drog-y-nous *adj.* Having the characteristics or nature of both male and female; having both staminate and pistillate flowers in the same cluster with the male flowers uppermost. **androgynal, androgyny** *n.*

an-droid *n.* In science fiction; a synthetic man made to look like a human being.

an-ec-dote *n.* Short account of a story of some happening or about some person. **anecdotal, -ic** *adj.,* **anecdotist** *n.*

an-echo-ic *adj.* Neither having or producing echoes.

a-ne-mi-a *n.* The condition in which a person's blood does not have enough red corpuscles or hemoglobin and, therefore, does not carry a normal amount of oxygen.

a-ne-mic *adj.* Of or having anemia.

an-e-mom-e-ter *n.* Instrument for measuring wind force and speed.

a-nem-o-ne *n.* A plant with purple, white, or red cup-shaped flowers.

a-nent *prep.* Regarding; concerning.

an-es-the-sia *n.* Condition in which one has no feeling of heat, touch, or pain in all or part of the body.

an-es-the-si-ol-o-gy *n.* The medical study and use of anesthetics. **anesthesiologist** *n.*

an-es-thet-ic *adj.* Taking away the feeling of pain. *n.* Drug, gas, etc. used to bring on anesthesia before surgery. **anesthetically** *adv.*

an-es-the-tize *v.* To bring on unconsciousness by giving anesthetics; to remove the capacity to feel pain in a localized area.

a-new *adv.* Again; once more; in a new way.

an-gel *n.* An immortal being attendant upon God; a very kind and lovable person; a helping or guiding spirit. **angelic** *adj.*

an-gel-fish *n.* Several tropical fishes with a flattened body.

an-gel-i-ca *n.* A plant with aromatic seed, used as flavoring.

an-ger *n.* Feeling of extreme hostility; rage; wanting to fight back.

an-gi-na *n.* A disease marked by painful choking spasms and attacks of suffocation pain. **anginous, anginose** *adj.,* **anginal** *adj.*

angina pec-to-ris *n.* Severe pain in the chest, associated with feelings of apprehension and suffocation.

an-gle *v.*

A shape made by two straight lines meeting in a point or two surfaces meeting along a line.

an-gle-worm *n.* Earthworm, used as fishing bait.

An-gli-can *n.* Member of the church of England or any of its related churches.

an-gli-cize *v.* To make English in form, idiom, or character. **anglicization** *n.*

an-gling *n.* The act of fishing with a hook and line.

An-glo *n.* A root word meaning "English."

An-glo--Sax-on *n.* A member of one of the Germanic peoples who settled in Britain in the 5th and 6th centuries A.D.

An-go-la *n.* A country located on the southwestern coast of Africa.

an-go-ra *n.* The long silky hair of the Angora rabbit or Angora goat; yarn or fabric made from the hair of an Angora goat or rabbit.

an-gry *adj.* Feeling or showing anger; having a menacing aspect; inflamed.

an-guish *n.* Great suffering, from worry, grief, or pain; agony.

an-gu-lar *adj.* Having angles or sharp corners; measured by an angle or degrees of an arc; gaunt, bony, lean. **angularity** *n.,* **angularly** *adv.*

an-hy-dride *n.* Chemical compound formed from another by removing the water.

an-hy-drous *adj.* Does not contain any water.

an-i-line *n.* Colorless, oily, poisonous liquid, used to make rubber, dyes, resins, pharmaceuticals, and varnishes.

an-i-mad-vert *v.* To comment with disapproval. **animadversion** *n.*

an-i-mal *n.* Any being other than a human being; any four-footed creature; beast. **animalize** *v.*

an-i-mal-cule *n.* Microscopic or minute animal.

an-i-mate *v.* To give liveliness, life or spirit to; to cause to act; to inspire. **animatedly** *adv.,* **animation** *n.*

a-ni-ma-to *adv., Mus.* In a lively or animated manner; used as a direction.

an-i-ma-tor *n.* One who animates, such as an artist or technician who produces an animation, as a cartoon.

an·i·mism n. A belief in primitive tribes that natural objects and forces have souls. **animist** n., **animistic** adj.

an·i·mos·i·ty n., pl. **-ties** Hostility; bitterness; hatred.

an·i·mus n. Feeling of animosity.

an·i·on n. An ion with a negative charge that is attracted to an anode; electrolysis.

an·ise n. A plant with yellowish-white flower clusters and licorice-flavored seeds; aniseed.

an·i·seed n. Seed used for flavoring and in medicine.

an·i·sette n. Anise-flavored liqueur.

an·kle n. Joint that connects the foot with the leg; slender section of the leg immediately above this joint.

an·klet n. A short sock, an ornament worn around the ankle.

ann abbr. Annals; annual; annuity.

an·nals pl., n. Descriptive record; history. **annalist** n.

an·neal v. To heat and then cool glass slowly to make it less brittle.

an·nex v. To add or join a smaller thing to a larger one. **annexation** n.

an·ni·hi·late v. To destroy completely; totally. **annihilator, annihilation** n.

an·ni·ver·sa·ry n., pl. **-ries** The date on which something happened at an earlier time; this event celebrated on this date each year.

an·no·tate v. To use notes to give one's opinions. **-ion, -or** n., **annotative** adj.

an·nounce v. To proclaim; to give notice. **announcement** n.

an·nounc·er n. A performer on radio or television who provides program continuity and gives commercial and other points of interest.

an·noy v. To bother; to irritate; to make slightly angry. **-ing** adj., **-ingly** adv.

an·noy·ance n. A nuisance; irritation; act of annoying.

an·nu·al adj. Recurring or done at the same time each year; a yearly publication, as a yearbook. **annually** adv.

an·nu·i·tant n. Person who receives an annuity.

an·nu·i·ty n., pl. **-ties** Annual payment of an income or allowance.

an·nul v. To cancel a marriage or a law; to do away with; to put an end to. **annullable** adj., **annulment** n.

an·nu·lar adj. Shaped like or forming a ring. **annularity** n., **annularly** adv.

an·nun·ci·ate v. To proclaim; to announce.

an·nun·ci·a·tion n. An announcement; the act of announcing.

an·ode n. Positively charged electrode. **anodic** adj., **anodically** adv.

an·o·dize v. To coat a metallic surface by electrolysis with a protective oxide.

a·noint v. To apply oil in a religious ceremony. **anointer, anointment** n.

a·nom·a·ly n., pl. **-lies** Anything irregular or abnormal. **anomalistic, -ous** adj.

a·non adv. Soon; in a short period of time.

a·non·y·mous adj. An unknown or withheld name, agency. **anonymity, anonymousness** n., **anonymously** adv.

an·oth·er adj. Additional; one more different, but of the same character.

ans abbr. Answer.

an·swer n. A written or spoken reply, as to a question; a result or solution, as to a problem. v. To respond correctly; to be responsible for.

ant n.

A small insect, usually without wings; which lives in or on the ground, or in wood in large colonies.

ant abbr. Antenna; antonym.

ant·ac·id n. A substance which neutralizes or weakens acids.

an·tag·o·nism n. Hostility; condition of being against; the feeling of unfriendliness toward.

an·tag·o·nize v. To arouse hostility; to make an enemy of someone.

Ant·arc·tic n. Large area of land completely covered with ice; the South Pole.

ant·eat·er n. Animal with a long snout and a long, sticky tongue, feeding mainly on ants.

an·te·ce·dent adj. One event that precedes another; previous.

an·te·date v. To precede in time; to give an earlier date than the actual date.

an·te·lope n. A slender, long-horned, swift-running, hoofed mammal.

an·te me·rid·i·em n. Time before noon, abbreviated as "A.M.".

an·ten·na n., pl. **-nae** Slender feelers on the head of an insect, lobster, crab, etc.; wire or set of wires used in radio and television to send and receive signals.

an·te·pe·nult n. The third syllable from the end of a word. **-imate** adj. & n.

an·te·ri·or adj. Toward or at the front; coming before; earlier.

an·te·room n. Waiting room; a room leading to a larger, more important room.

an·them n. Hymn of praise or loyalty; an official song of a country, school, etc.

an·ther n. The part of the flower where the pollen is located at the end of a stamen.

an·thol·o·gy n. A collection of stories, poems, or other writings.

an·thra·cite n. Coal with a high carbon content and low volatile matter; hard coal. **anthracitic** adj.

an·thrax n. The infectious, usually fatal disease found in animals such as cattle and sheep; disease that can be transmitted to man.

an·thro·po·cen·tric adj. To interpret reality in terms of human experience and values.

an·thro·poid n. Gorillas or chimpanzees resembling man.

an·thro·pol·o·gy n. The science that studies the origin, culture, and development of man. **anthropologic,** **-ical** *adj.*, **-ically** *adv.*, **-ist** *n.*

an-thro-po-mor-phism *n.* The ascribing of human motivation and human characteristics to something that is not human. **anthropomorphic** *adj.*

an-ti *n.* One who opposes a group, policy, practice, or proposal.

an-ti-anx-i-ety *adj.* Preventing or relieving anxiety.

an-ti-bal-lis-tic missile *n.* A missile designed to destroy a ballistic missile.

an-ti-bi-ot-ic *n.* A substance, as streptomycin or penicillin, that is produced by organisms, as fungi and bacteria, effective in the destruction of microorganisms and used widely to prevent or treat diseases.

an-ti-bod-y *n.* Proteins generated in the blood that react to foreign proteins or carbohydrates of certain types, neutralizing them and producing immunity against certain microorganisms or their toxins.

an-tic *n.* Mischievous caper or act.

An-ti-christ *n.* A great enemy of Christ. **Antichristian** *adj.*

an-tic-i-pate *v.* To look forward; to act in advance of; to foresee. **anticipation,** **anticipator** *n.*, **anticipatory** *adj.*

an-ti-cli-max *n.* A letdown or decline; a commonplace conclusion; a series of sign-ificant events or happenings. **anticlimactic** *adj.*, **-ctically** *adv.*

an-ti-dote *n.* A substance that counteracts an injury or poison. **-al** *adj.*

an-ti-freeze *n.* Substance, as ethylene glycol, that is mixed with water or liquid to lower the freezing point.

an-ti-gen *n.* Substance, when introduced into the body, stimulates the production of antibodies. **antigenic** *adj.*, **antigenically** *adv.*, **antigenicity** *n.*

an-ti-his-ta-mine *n.* A drug used to relieve the symptoms of allergies and colds by interfering with the production of histamines. **antihistaminic** *adj.*

an-ti-knock *n.* Substance added to gasoline to reduce engine knock, making the vehicle run smoother.

An-til-les *n.* The main group of islands in the West Indies, forming a chain that separates the Caribbean from the Atlantic.

an-ti-log-a-rithm *n.* The number corresponding to a given logarithm.

antilog *abbr.* Antilogarithm.

an-ti-ma-cas-sar *n.* A protective covering for the backs and arms of chairs and sofas, used to prevent soiling.

an-ti-mat-ter *n.* A form of matter that is composed of antiparticles.

an-ti-mo-ni-al *adj.* Containing or of antimony.

an-ti-mo-ny *n.* Silver-white metallic element used in chemistry, medicine, and alloys, etc.

an-tin-o-my *n.* An opposition or contradiction.

an-ti-par-ti-cle *n.* Identically matched atomic particles, but with exactly opposite electrically charged magnetic properties and spin.

an-ti-pasto *n.* Appetizer including cheese, fish, vegetables, and smoked meat served with oil and vinegar.

an-tip-a-thy *n.*, *pl.* **-thies** Feeling of repugnance or opposition. **antipathetic, antipathetical** *adj.*, **antipathetically** *adv.*

an-ti-per-spi-rant *n.* Substance applied to the underarm to reduce excessive perspiration.

an-tiph-o-ny *n.* One that echoes or answers another; responsive chanting or singing.

an-ti-pode *n.* A direct opposite.

an-ti-pro-ton *n.* The antiparticle of a proton.

an-tique *adj.* Belonging to or of ancient times. *n.* An object that is over 100 years old. **antique** *v.*

an-tiquity *n.*, *pl.* **-ties** Quality of being ancient or old.

an-ti—Sem-ite *n.* A person hostile toward Jews. **anti-Semitic** *adj.*, **-Semitism** *n.*

an-ti-sep-sis *n.* Condition of being free from pathogenic bacteria and the method of obtaining this condition.

an-ti-sep-tic *adj.* Pertaining or capable of producing antisepsis; thoroughly clean. **antiseptically** *adv.*

an-ti-so-cial *adj.* Unsociable; opposed to society.

an-tith-e-sis *n.*, *pl.* **-e -ses** Direct opposition or contrast. **antithetical, antithetic** *adj.*

an-ti-trust *adj.* Having to do with the regulation of trusts, monopolies, and cartels.

ant-ler *n.*

One of a pair of bony growths on the head of a member of the deer family. **-ed** *adj.*

an-to-nym *n.* A word opposite in meaning to another word.

an-uria *n.* The inability to urinate.

a-nus *n.* The lower opening of the alimentary canal.

an-vil *n.* A heavy block of steel or iron on which metal is formed.

anx-i-e-ty *n.* A state of uncertainty; disturbance of the mind regarding uncertain events.

anx-ious *adj.* Troubled in mind or worried about some uncertain matter or event. **-ness** *n.*, **anxiously** *adv.*

any *adj.* One; no matter which; some; every; and quantity or part.

any-body *pron.*, *pl.* **-bodies** Anyone; any person.

any-how *adv.* By any means; in any why; whatever.

any-more *adv.* At present and from now on.

any-one *pron.* Any person; anybody.

any-place *adv.* Anywhere.

any-thing *pron.* Any occurrence, object or matter.

any-time *adv.* At any time whatever.

any-way *adv.* Nevertheless; anyhow; in any manner; carelessly.

any-where *adv.* In, at, or to any place; to any degree or extent.

a-or-ta *n., pl.* **-tas** *or* **-tae** The main artery that carries blood away from the heart; distributes blood to all of the body except the lungs. **aortal, aortic** *adj.*

a-ou-dad *n.* Wild sheep of North Africa having long curved horns and a growth of hair on the neck and chest similar to a beard.

Ap *abbr.* Apostle; April.

AP *abbr.* Associated Press.

APA *abbr.* American Psychiatric Association.

a-pace *adv.* Rapid in pace; quickly.

A-pache *n., pl.* **-es** A member of the Athapaskan-speaking tribe of Indians in North America, settled in the Southwest U.S. and North Mexico.

a-part *adv.* Separate or at a distance; in pieces; to pieces; to set aside. **-ness** *n.*

a-part-heid *n.* In the Republic of South Africa, an official policy of political, social, and economic discrimination and segregation against nonwhites.

a-part-ment *n.* A suite or room in a building equipped for individual living.

ap-a-thy *n.* The lack of emotions or feelings. **apathetic** *adj.,* **apathetically** *adv.*

ap-a-tite *n.* Mineral used as a source of phosphorus compounds.

ape *n.* A large mammal such as a gorilla, chimpanzee, or monkey; a very clumsy, coarse person. **aped** *v.*

Ap-en-nines *n.* A mountain range in Italy extending the length of the peninsula.

a-pe-ri-tif *n.* A drink of alcoholic liquor consumed before a meal.

ap-er-ture *n.* An opening.

a-pex *n., pl.* **apexes** *or* **apices** The highest point; tip; top.

a-pha-sia *n.* Any partial or total loss of the ability to express ideas, resulting from brain damage.

aphasiac *n.,* **aphasic** *adj. & n.*

aphe-lion *n.* The point in an orbit farthest from the sun.

aphid *n.* Small insects that suck sap from plants.

aph-o-rism *n.* Brief statement of truth or principal. **aphorist** *n.,* **aphoristically** *adv.,* **aphoristic** *adj.*

apho-tic *adj.* Without light.

aph-ro-dis-i-ac *adj.* Increasing or arousing the sexual desire or potency.

Aph-ro-di-te *n.* Greek goddess of love and beauty.

a-pi-ary *n.* Place where bees are kept and raised for their honey.

a-piece *adv.* For or to each one.

a-plomb *n.* Assurance; poise; self-confidence.

apmt *abbr.* Appointment.

apo- *pref.* Lack of; separation of; being away from.

APO *abbr.* Army Post Office.

Apoc *abbr.* Apocalypse; Apocrypha; Apocryphal.

A-poc-a-lypse *n.* The last book of the New Testament; Revelation.

apocalyptical, apocalyptic *adj.*

a-poc-ry-pha *n.* Fourteen books not included in the Old Testament by Protestants, considered uncanonical because they are not part of the Hebrew scriptures; eleven of the books are accepted in the Roman Catholic Church.

a-poc-ry-phal *adj.* False; of questionable authenticity. **apocryphally** *adv.*

ap-o-gee *n.* The point most distant from earth in the moon's orbit.

A-pol-lo *n.* Greek sun god; very handsome young man.

a-pol-o-get-ic *adj.* Making an expression of apology. **-al, apologetically** *adv.*

a-pol-o-gize *v.* To make an apology.

a-pol-o-gy *n., pl.* **-gies** A statement expressing regret for an action or fault; a formal justification or defense.

ap-o-plex-y *n.* Sudden loss of muscular control, consciousness, and sensation resulting from a rupture or blockage of the blood vessel in the brain.

a-port *adv., Naut.* To the left side of a ship.

a-pos-ta-sy *n., pl.* **-sies** Desertion of one's political party, religious faith, or cause.

a-pos-tate *n.* One who forsakes his faith or principles.

apos-te-ri-o-ri *adj., L.* Inductive; reasoning from facts to principles or from effect to cause.

a-pos-tle *n.* A person sent on a mission; the first Christian missionary to go into a new area or group; the person who first initiates a moral reform or introduces an important system or belief; a member of a Mormon council of twelve men. **apostleship** *n.*

Apostles' Creed *n.* A Christian statement of belief in God, used in public worship.

a-pos-to-late *n.* A group of people dedicated to spreading a religion or a doctrine.

ap-os-tol-ic *adj.* Relating to an apostle; living by the teachings of the New Testament and the apostles. **-ity** *n.*

Apostolic Father *n.* The church father of the first or second century A.D.

a-pos-tro-phe *n.* The mark (') used to indicate the removal of letters or figures, the plural of letters or figures, and the possessive case; the act of turning away; addressing the usually absent person or a usually personified thing rhetorically.

a-pos-tro-phize *v.* To make use of apostrophe.

a-poth-e-car-ies' mea-sure *pl., n.* A measurement used mainly by pharmacists; a measurement of capacity.

a-poth-e-car-y *n., pl.* **-caries** A person who prepares drugs for medical uses.

apo-the-ci-um *n.* A single-celled structure in many lichens and fungi that consists of a cupped body bearing asci on the exposed flat or concave surface.

ap-o-thegm *n.* A short, essential, and instructive formulation or saying.

apothegmatical, apothegmatic *adj.*

apo-the-o-sis *n.* The perfect way to explain or define something or someone.

app *abbr.* Apparatus; appendix.

ap-pall *v.* To overcome by shock or dismay; to weaken; to fail; to become pale.

ap-pall-ing *adj.* Dismay or disgust caused by an event or a circumstance.

Ap-pa-loo-sa *n.* A horse from the northwestern American region; which has a mottled skin, vertically striped hooves, and a dotted or blotched patch of white hair over the rump.

ap-pa-nage *n.* A rightful adjunct; provision for a younger offspring or child; a section of property or privilege appropriated by or to a person as his share.

ap-pa-ra-tchik *n.* A member of the Communist party.

ap-pa-ra-tus *n., pl.* **-tuses** Appliance or an instrument designed and used for a specific operation.

ap-par-el *v.* To dress or put on clothing; to adorn or embellish. *n.* Clothing. *Naut.* The sails and rigging of a ship.

ap-par-ent *adj.* Clear and opened to the eye and mind; open to view, visible. **apparently** *adv.*, **apparentness** *n.*

ap-par-ent time *n.* Time of day so indicated by a sundial or the sun.

ap-pa-ri-tion *n.* An unusual or unexpected appearance; the act of being visible; a ghostly figure. **-al** *adj.*

ap-par-i-tor *n.* An official person sent to carry out the order of a judge, court, or magistrate.

ap-peal *n.* Power to arouse a sympathetic response; an earnest plea; a legal preceding where a case is brought from a lower court to a higher court for a rehearing. *v.* To make a request; to ask another person for corroboration, vindication, or decision on a matter of importance.
appealable *adj.*, **appealingly** *adv.*

ap-pear *v.* To come into existence; to come into public view; to come formally before an authorized person.

ap-pear-ance *n.* The action or process of appearing; an outward indication or showing.

ap-pease *v.* To give peace; to cause to stop or subside; to calm; to pacify. **appeasable** *adj.*, **appeasement** *n.*

ap-pel-late *adj.* Having the power to hear and review the decisions of the lower courts.

ap-pel-la-tion *n.* Identifying by a name or title.

ap-pel-la-tive *adj.* Having to do with the giving of names; relating to or of a common noun. **appellatively** *adv.*

ap-pend *v.* To add an appendix or supplement, as to a book; to attach.

ap-pend-age *n.* Something added to something more important or larger; a subordinate or a dependent person.

ap-pen-dec-to-my *n.* The surgical removal of the appendix.

ap-pen-dix *n., pl.* **-dixes** *Med.*

Ascending colon

Cecum

Appendix

A medical term that refers to a small, hollow blind process or the vermiform appendix. Supplementary material usually found at the end of something that has been written; the vermiform appendix.

ap-per-cep-tion *n.* The mental understanding of something perceived in terms of previous experience.
apperceptively *adv.*, **apperceptive** *adj.*

ap-per-tain *v.* To belong to or connect with, as a rightful part.

ap-petite *n.* The craving or desire for food. **appetitive** *adj.*

ap-pe-tiz-er *n.* Food or drink served before a meal to stimulate the appetite.

ap-plaud *v.* To express or show approval by clapping the hands. **-able** *adj.*

ap-plause *n.* The expression of public approval. **applausive** *adj.*

ap-ple *n.* The round, red, yellow, or green edible fruit of a tree.

ap-ple-jack *n.* Brandy distilled from hard cider.

ap-ple mag-got *n.* A two-winged fly whose larva burrows into and feeds on apples.

ap-pli-ance *n.* A piece of equipment or device designed for a particular use.

ap-pli-ca-ble *adj.* Appropriate; suitable; capable of being applied. **-ility** *n.*

ap-pli-cant *n.* A person who applies for a job or position.

ap-pli-ca-tion *n.* The act of putting something to use; the act of superposing or administering; request or petition; a form used to make a request.

ap-pli-ca-tor *n.* A device used to apply a substance; one who applies.

ap-plies *adj.* Putting something to practical use to solve definite problems.

ap-ply *v.* To make a request in the form of a written application; to put into use for a practical purpose or reason; to put into operation or to bring into action; to employ with close attention.

ap-pog-gia-tu-ra *n.* A music note or tone that precedes an essential melodic note or tone and usually is written as a note of smaller size.

ap-point *v.* To arrange something; to fix or set officially.
appointable *adj.*, **appointer** *n.*

ap-poin-tee *n.* Someone that is appointed.

ap-point-ive *adj.* Something related to or

filled by appointment.

ap·point·ment *n.* The act of appointing or designating; arrangement for a meeting; a nonelective position or office; engagement or meeting.

ap·por·tion *v.* To divide and share according to a plan. **apportionment** *n.*

ap·pose *v.* To apply one thing to another; to put before. **apposable** *adj.*

ap·po·site *adj.* Highly appropriate or pertinent. **-ness** *n.,* **appositely** *adv.*

ap·po·si·tion *n.* A grammatical construction where a noun or noun phrase is followed by another; the explanatory equivalent. **appositional** *adj.*

ap·pos·i·tive *adj.* Relating to or standing in apposition.

ap·prais·al *n.* The evaluation of property by an authorized person.

ap·praise *v.* To estimate the value, worth, or status of a particular item. **-ment, appraiser** *n.,* **appraising** *adj.*

ap·pre·cia·ble *adj.* Capable of being measured or perceived, noticed, or estimated. **appreciably** *adv.*

ap·pre·ci·ate *v.* To recognize the worth, quality, or significance; to value very highly; to be aware of; to realize; to increase in price or value. **appreciatory** *adj.*

ap·pre·ci·a·tion *n.* The expression of admiration, gratitude, or approval; increase in value.

ap·pre·cia·tive *adj.* Having or showing appreciation.

ap·pre·hend *v.* To anticipate with anxiety, dread or fear; to recognize the meaning of; to grasp; to understand.

ap·pre·hen·si·ble *adj.* Capable of being apprehended.

ap·pre·hen·sion *n.* The act of or comprehending power to comprehend; suspicion or fear of future events.

ap·pre·hen·sive *adj.* Viewing the future with anxiety or fear. **-ly** *adv.*

ap·pren·tice *n.* A person who is learning a trade, art, or occupation under a skilled worker for a prescribed period of time. *v.* To work as an apprentice under the supervision of a skilled worker. **apprenticeship** *n.*

ap·pressed *adj.* Pressed close to or lying flat against.

ap·prise *v.* To inform; to give notice.

ap·proach *v.* To come near to or draw closer; to be close in appearance. *n.* Access to or reaching something. **approachable** *adj.*

ap·pro·ba·tion *n.* A formal approval.

ap·pro·pri·ate *v.* To take possession of; to take without permission. *adj.* Suitable for a use or occasion; fitting. **-ly** *adv.,* **appropriator, -ness** *n.*

ap·pro·pri·a·tion *n.* Money set apart for a particular use; the act or instance of appropriating.

ap·prov·able *adj.* Something or someone that is capable of being approved. **approvably** *adv.*

ap·prov·al *n.* The act of approving; subject to acceptance or refusal.

ap·prove *v.* To regard or express a

favorable opinion; to give formal or official approval. **approvingly** *adv.*

approx *abbr.* Approximate; approximately.

ap·prox·i·mate *adj.* Located close together; almost accurate or exact. *v.* To bring close or near to; to approach; to estimate; to be near the same. **approximately** *adv.*

appt *abbr.* Appoint; appointment; appointed.

ap·pur·te·nance *n.* Something that belongs with another more important thing; an accessory that is passed along with.

ap·pur·te·nant *adj.* Constitutes a legal attachment.

Apr *abbr.* April.

aprax·ia *n.* Inability to execute complex coordinate movement. **apractic, -c** *adj.*

apri·cot *n.* An oval, orange-colored fruit resembling the peach and plum in flavor, varying in color, normally a medium orange.

April *n.* The fourth month of the calendar year.

April fool *n.* A trick or joke played on another person on April Fools' Day.

April Fools' Day *n.* The first day of April, marked by practical joke playing.

apri·o·ri *adj.* Based on theory rather than personal experience; deductive.

apron *n.* A garment used to protect clothing; paved area around an airport terminal building or airport hangar; waterfront edge of a wharf or pier.

apron string *n.* Dominance or complete control over someone.

ap·ro·pos *adv.* At a good time; by the way.

apse *n.* A semicircular or polygonal projection of a building or church.

ap·si·dal *adj.* Relating to an apse.

apt *adj.* Unusually qualified or fitting; appropriate; having a tendency; suitable; quick to understand. **aptly** *adv.,* **aptness** *n.*

ap·ti·tude *n.* A natural talent or ability; quickness in learning or understanding.

aq *abbr.* Aqua; aqueous.

aqua *n.,* *pl.* **aquae, aquas** Water; aquamarine.

aqua·cade *n.* Water entertainment, consisting of swimming and diving exhibitions, with musical accompaniment.

aqua·lunger *n.* A scuba diver.

aqua·marine *n.* A color of pale blue to light green; a mineral that is blue blue-green, or green in color.

aqua·naut *n.* A scuba diver who lives inside and outside of an underwater shelter for an extended period of time.

aqua·plane *n.* A board towed by a speeding boat, ridden by a person while standing.

aqua pura *n.* Very pure water.

aqua regia *n.* Mixture of hydrochloric and nitric acids that dissolves platinum or gold.

aqua·relle *n.* A transparent water-color

drawing.

aquar-ist *n.* A person who takes care of an aquarium.

aquar-i-um *n.* An artificial pond where living plants and aquatic animals are maintained and exhibited.

Aquar-i-us *n.* The eleventh sign of the zodiac; a person born under this sign; (Jan. 20 - Feb. 18).

a-quat-ic *adj.* Anything occurring on or in the water.

aqua-vitae *n.* A very strong liquor; alcohol.

aq-ue-duct *n.* A conduit for carrying a large quantity of flowing water; a bridge-like structure supporting a canal over a river.

aq-ue-ous *adj.* Like or resembling water; dissolved in water; watery.

aqueous humor *n.* The clear fluid in the chamber of the eye between the cornea and lens.

aq-ui-cul-ture or aqua-cul-ture *n.* The cultivation of produce in natural water; hydroponics. **aquicultural** *adj.*

aq-ui-fer *n.* The layer of underground gravel, sand, or rocks where water collects.

aq-ui-line *adj.* Resembling or related to an eagle; hooked or curved like the beak on an eagle.

a-quiv-er *adj.*, *Slang* Trembling or quivering.

ar *abbr.* Arrival; arrive.

AR *abbr.* Arkansas; acknowledgment of receipt; army regulation; accounts receivable.

Ar-ab *n.* A resident or native of Arabia; a member of the Semitic people of North Africa and the Middle East.

ar-a-besque *n.* An intricate style or design of interwoven leaves, flowers, and geometric forms.

A-ra-bi-a *n.* Peninsula of southwest Asia between the Persian Gulf and the Red Sea. **Arbian** *adj. & n.*

Ar-a-bic *adj.* Relating to Arabs, their culture, or their language.

Arabic numeral *n.* One of the number symbols: 0,1,2,3,4,5,6,7,8,9.

Ar-ab-ist *n.* Specialist in the Arabic culture or in the Arabic language.

ar-a-ble *adj.* Land that is suitable for cultivation by plowing.

a-rach-nid *n.* Arthropods that are mostly air-breathing, having four pairs of legs but no antennae; an insect as a spider. **arachnidan** *n.*, **arachnid** *adj.*

Ar-a-ma-ic *n.* A Semitic language used in Southwestern Asia, known since the ninth century B.C. This commercial language was adopted by non-Aramaean people.

Aramaic alphabet *n.* The commercial alphabet for many countries of southwest Asia, dating from the ninth century B.C.

ara-ne-id *n.* A breed of spider.

Arau-ca-ni-an *n.* A member from a group of Indian people of south central Chile.

Ar-a-wak *n.* American Indian people from the Arawakan group, living mainly along the coast of Guyana.

ar-ba-lest *n.* Military weapon from medieval times with a steel bow, used to throw balls and stones. **-er** *n.*

ar-bi-ter *n.* A person chosen to decide a dispute, having absolute power of determining and judging.

ar-bi-tra-ble *adj.* Subject to arbitration.

ar-bi-tra-ment *adj.* The settling of a dispute; settlement; determination; the power or right of deciding.

ar-bi-trar-y *adj.* Something based on a whim or impulse. **-ily** *adv.*, **-iness** *n.*

ar-bi-tra-tor *n.* A person chosen to settle a dispute or controversy between parties.

ar-bor *n.* A garden shelter that is shady and covered with or made of climbing plants. **arborous** *adj.*

Arbor Day *n.* A day assigned as a day for planting trees.

ar-bo-re-al *adj.* Resembling or related to a tree; living in trees. **arboreally** *adv.*

ar-bo-re-tum *n.* A place for studying and exhibiting trees, shrubs, and plants cultivated for educational and for scientific purposes.

ar-bo-ri-cul-ture *n.* The ornamental cultivation of shrubs and trees. **-ist** *n.*

ar-bor-ist *n.* A specialist in the maintenance and care of trees.

ar-bo-ri-za-tion *n.* The formation of an arrangement or figure of a bush or shrub.

ar-bo-rize *v.* To branch repeatedly and freely.

ar-bor-vi-tae *n.* An evergreen tree of the pine family that has closely overlapping or compressed scale leaves, often grown for hedges and for ornamental decorations.

ar-bo-vi-rus *n.* Various viruses transmitted by arthropods, including the causative agents for yellow fever and encephalitis.

ar-bu-tus *n.* A fragrant pinkish flower that blossoms early in the spring.

arc *n.* Something that is curved or arched; the luminous discharge of electric current across a gap of two electrodes.

ARC *abbr.* American Red Cross.

ar-cade *n.* An arched covered passageway supported by columns; a long arched gallery or building, sometimes having shops and stores.

ar-cad-ed *adj.* Furnished with arcades or arches.

ar-ca-di-a *n.* The ancient Greek area usually chosen as background for poetry; region of simple quiet and pleasure.

Ar-ca-di-an *n.* A person living a very quiet and simple life. **Arcadian** *adj.*

arch *n.*

A structure that spans over an open area and gives support.

archly adv., archness n.

ar-chae-ol-o-gy n. Scientific study of ancient times and ancient peoples.

archaeological adj., archaeologist n.

ar-cha-ic adj. Something that belongs to an earlier time; characteristic of an earlier language, now used only in special cases.

ar-cha-ism n. Something that is outdated or old fashioned, as an expression or word. archaistic adj., archaist n.

arch-an-gel n. The highest in order of angels in the celestial. -ic adj.

arch-bishop n. A bishop of the highest rank who has the supervision over the other bishops.

arch-dea-con n. A clergyman who has the duty of assisting a bishop.

archdeaconate n.

arch-di-o-cese n. The territory or district of an archbishop. archdiocesan adj.

arch-du-cal adj. Pertains to an archduke or archduchy.

arch-duch-ess n. A woman who has a rank and right equal to that of an archduke; the wife or widow of an archduke.

arch-duchy n. The territory of an archduchess or of an archduke.

arch-duke n. A royal prince of the imperial family of Austria. -dom n.

arch-en-e-my n. One who is a chief enemy.

arch-er n. A person who is trained in the uses or skill of the bow and arrow.

ar-cher-y n. The practice or art of shooting with a bow and arrow; the equipment used by an archer. archer n.

ar-che-spore n. A single cell or group of cells from which a mother spore is formed.

ar-che-type n. An original from which other things are patterned.

arch-fiend n. A chief or principal friend; a person of great wickedness, especially Satan.

ar-chi-tect n. A person who may design and or supervise the construction of large structures.

ar-chi-tec-ton-ic adj. To resemble architecture in organization or structure. architectonically adv.

ar-chi-tec-ture n. The art or science of designing and building structures; a method or style of construction or building. architectural adj.

ar-chi-trave n. In classical architecture, a horizontal piece supported by the columns of a building.

ar-chives pl., n. Public documents or records; the place where archives are kept. archival adj., archivist n.

arch-way n. A passage or way under an arch; an arch over a passage.

arc lamp n. Electric lamp which produces light as when a current passes between two incandescent electrodes.

arc-tic adj. Extremely cold or frigid; relating to the territory north of the Arctic Circle. n. A waterproof boot that covers of comes just above the ankle.

Arc-tic Cir-cle n. Parallel of the latitude that is approximately 66.5 degrees north of the equator.

-ard or -art suff. A person who is characterized by performing something excessively.

ar-dor n. Extreme warmth or passion; emotion; intense heat.

ar-du-ous adj. Taking much effort to bring forth; difficult; hard, as a task. arduously adv.

are v. First, second, and third person plural and second person singular of the verb "to be".

ar-e-a n. A flat or level piece of ground; field of study; the scope of a concept, activity or operation. areal adj.

area code n. The three-digit number assigned to each telephone area in the United States, used to call another area in the U.S.

ar-e-a-way n. A sunken area in a basement that offers access, light and air.

a-re-ca n. Tall palm of southeast Asia that has white flowers and red or orange egg-shaped nuts.

a-re-na n. Enclosed area for public entertainment, such as football games, concerts, etc.

ar-e-na-ceous adj. Having the properties of sand.

a-re-na the-a-ter n. A theater with the stage located in the center and the audience seated around the stage.

aren't contr. Are not.

Ar-gen-ti-na n. Country of south-eastern South America. Argentinean adj. & n.

ar-gen-tite n. A lustrous ore.

ar-gil-la-ceous adj. Resembling or containing clay.

ar-go-sy n., pl. -sies A fleet of ships; a large merchant ship.

ar-got n. A secret, specialized vocabulary.

ar-gu-able adj. Open to argument; questionable. arguably adv.

ar-gue v. To debate, to offer reason for or against a subject; to dispute, argue, or quarrel; to persuade or influence. argument, arguer n.

ar-gu-men-ta-tion n. The process or act of arguing; debating.

ar-gu-men-ta-tive adj. Given to argument; debating or disputing.

ar-gus pheasant n. A large South Asian bird with long tail feathers brilliantly colored with eye-like spots.

ar-gyle or argyll n. A pattern knitted with varicolored, diamond-shaped designs.

a-ri-a n. A vocal piece with accompaniment sung in solo; part of an opera.

a-ri-bo-fla-vin-o-sis n, Med. A vitamin deficiency, in which the mucous membrane of the mouth becomes irritated and some discoloration of the tongue may occur.

ar-id adj. Insufficient rain; dry; lacking in interest or feeling; dull. aridity n.

Aries n. The first sign of the zodiac; a person born under this sign:

(March 21 - April 19).

-right *adv.* Correctly; rightly; in a right way or form.

r-il *n.* The extra covering of the seed of some plants, such as the nutmeg.

-rise *v.* To come from a source; to come to attention; to come into view; to mount; to move to a higher place; to get out of bed.

ris-ta *n., pl.* **-tae** *or* **-tas** Bristle-like appendage or structure.

r-is-toc-ra-cy *n.* A government by the best individuals or by a small privileged class; class or group viewed as superior; the hereditary privileged ruling nobility or class. **aristocratic** *adj.*

-rith-me-tic *adj.* Branch of math that deals with addition, subtraction, multiplication, division. **arithmetical** *adj.*, **arithmetically** *adv.*

-rith-met-ic mean *n.* The number received by dividing the sum of a set of quantities by the number of quantities in the set.

-rith-met-ic pro-gres-sion *n.* A progression in which the difference between any term and the one before or after is constant, as 2,4,6,8, etc.

ar-i-um *suff.* The place or thing connected to or relating with.

rizona *n.* A state located in the southwestern part of the United States.

rk *n.* The ship Noah built for survival during the Great Flood; the chest which contained the Ten Commandments on stone tables, carried by the Jews; something that gives protection.

rkansas *n.* A state located in the south-central part of the United States.

rm *n.* The part between the shoulder and the wrist; upper limb of the human body. *v.* To furnish with protection against danger. **armer** *n.*

rm *abbr.* Armenian.

r-ma-da *n.* A fleet of warships; a large force of moving things.

r-ma-dil-lo *n.*

A burrowing nocturnal animal with an armor-like covering of jointed, bony plates.

r-ma-ged-don *n.* A final battle between the forces of good and evil.

r-ma-ment *n.* Military supplies and weapons; the process of preparing for battle.

r-ma-ture *n.* The main moving part of an electric device or machine; a piece of soft iron that connects the poles of a magnet.

rm-chair *n.* A chair with armrests or supports. *adj.* Remote from the direct dealing with problems.

rm-ed for-ces *n.* The combined air, military, and naval forces of a nation.

rm-ful *n., pl.* **armfuls** *or* **armsful** As much as the arm can hold.

arm-hole *n.* The opening in a garment for the arm.

ar-mi-stice *n.* The temporary suspension of combat by mutual agreement; truce.

Armistice Day *n.* The armistice ending of World War I; title used before the official adoption of Veterans Day in 1954.

arm-let *n.* A band worn on the upper arm.

ar-moire *n.* A large wardrobe or cupboard.

ar-mor *n.* Covering used in combat to protect the body, made from a heavy metal. **armor** *v.*, **armored** *adj.*

ar-mor-er *n.* A person who makes armor; one who assembles, repairs, and tests firearms.

ar-mory *n., pl.* **-mories** The supply of arms for attack or defense; the place where military equipment is stored.

arm-pit *n.* The hollow area under the arm where it joins the shoulder.

arm-rest *n.* The support for the arm, as on a chair.

arm-twist-ing *n.* The use of direct personal pressure to achieve a desired effect.

arm wrestling *n.* A game in which two opponents sit face to face gripping right hands, with elbows securely on a table, making an attempt to bring the opponent's arm down flat onto the table.

ar-my *n., pl.* **-mies** A group of persons organized for a country's protection; the land forces of a country.

ar-my-worm *n.* Moth whose larvae travels in multitudes from one area to another destroying grain and grass.

ar-ni-ca *n.* Plant of the genus Arnica with yellow flowers from which a form of a tincture, as a liniment, is made.

a-ro-ma *n.* A distinctive fragrance or pleasant odor. **-tical, aromatic** *adj.*

a-round *adv.* To or on all sides; in succession or rotation; from one place to another; in a circle or circular movement.

around-the-clock *adj.* Lasting continuously for a period of 24 hours.

arouse *v.* To wake up from a sleep; to stir; to excite. **arousal** *n.*

ar-peg-gi-o *n.* Tones of a chord produced in succession and not simultaneously.

arr *abbr.* Arranged; arrival; arrive.

ar-rack *n.* An alcoholic beverage distilled from the juices of the coconut palm, from the Far or Near East.

ar-raign *v.* To called before a court to answer a charge or indictment; to accuse of imperfection, inadequacy, or of wrong doing. **arraignment** *n.*

ar-range *v.* To put in correct order or proper sequence; to prepare for something; to take steps to organize something; to bring about an understanding or an agreement; to prepare or change a musical composition for instruments or voices other than those

ar-range-ment *n.* The state or being arranged; something made by arranging things or parts together.

ar-rant *adj.* Extreme; being notoriously without moderation. **arrantly** *adv.*

ar-ras *n.* A screen or wall hanging of tapestry.

ar-ray *v.* To place or set in order; to draw up; to decorate or dress in an impressive attire. **arrayer** *n.*

ar-rears *n., pl.* The state of being behind something, as an obligation, payment, etc.; an unfinished duty.

ar-rear-age *n.* The condition of having something unpaid or overdue.

ar-rest *n.* To stop or to bring an end to; to capture; to seize; to hold in custody by the authority of law. **arrester, arrestor, arrestment** *n.*

arrest-ee *n.* A person under arrest.

ar-rest-ing *adj.* Very impressive or striking; catching the attention. **-ly** *adv.*

ar-rhyth-mia *n.* The alteration in rhythm of the heartbeat, either in force or time.

ar-rhyth-mic *adj.* Lacking regularity or rhythm.

ar-riv-al *n.* The act of arriving.

ar-rive *v.* To reach or get to a destination.

ar-ro-gance *n.* An overbearing manner, intolerable presumption; an insolent pride. **arrogant, arrogantly** *adv.*

ar-row *n.* A weapon shot from a bow; a sign or mark to show direction.

ar-row-head *n.* The striking end of an arrow, usually shaped like a wedge.

ar-row-root *n.* A starch-yielding plant of tropical America.

ar-row-wood *n.* Shrubs with tough pliant shoots that were formerly used in making arrowheads.

ar-se-nal *n.* A collection of weapons; a place where arms and military equipment are manufactured or stored.

ar-se-nic *n.* A solid, poisonous element, steel-gray in color, used to make insecticide or weed killer. **arsenic, arsenical** *adj.*

ar-son *n.* The fraudulent burning of property. **arsonist** *n.,* **arsonous** *adj.*

art *n.* A human skill of expression of other objects by painting, drawing, sculpture, etc.; a branch of learning.

ar-te-ri-ole *n.* One of the small terminal twigs of an artery that ends in capillaries.

ar-ter-y *n., pl.* **-teries** A blood vessel that carries blood from the heart to the other parts of the body; a major means for transportation. **arterial** *adj.*

ar-te-sian well *n.*

A well that produces water without a pump.

art form *n.* The recognized form of an artistic expression.

art-ful *adj.* Showing or performed with skill or art. **artfully** *adv.,* **-ness** *n.*

art glass *n.* Glass designed for decorative purposes; novelty glassware.

ar-thral-gia *n.* Pain that occurs in one or more joints. **arthralgic** *adj.*

ar-thrit-ic *n.* A person who has arthritis. *adj.* Affected with arthritis; showing effects associated with aging.

ar-thri-tis *n.* Inflammation of joints due to infectious or metabolic causes.

ar-thro-pod *n.* An animal with jointed limbs and segmented body, as a spider. **arthropodal, arthropodan, arthropodous** *adj.*

ar-ti-choke *n.* A plant with a thistle-like head, which can be cooked and eaten as a vegetable.

ar-ti-cle *n.* A term or clause in a contract; a paragraph or section; a condition or rule; an object, item or commodity.

ar-tic-u-lar *adj.* Related to or of a joint.

ar-tic-u-late *adj.* Able to express oneself clearly, effectively, or readily; speaking in distinct words, or syllables. **-ness, articulator** *n.,* **articulately** *adv.*

ar-ti-fact *n.* Something made by man showing human modification or workmanship.

ar-ti-fice *n.* An artful or clever skill; ingenuity.

ar-ti-fi-cial *adj.* Not genuine; made by man; not found in nature. **-ly** *adv.*

ar-til-lery *n.* Weapons, especially cannons; troops that are trained in the use of guns and other means of defense.

ar-ti-san *n.* A mechanic or a craftsman.

art-ist *n.* A person who practices the fine arts of painting, sculpture, etc.

ar-tiste *n.* One who is an expert in the theatrical profession.

ar-tis-tic *adj.* Relating to the characteristic of an artist or art. **artistically** *adv.*

art-ist-ry *n.* The artistic ability, or quality of workmanship or effect.

art-less *adj.* Lacking knowledge, art, or skill; crude; natural; simple. **artlessly** *adv.,* **artlessness** *n.*

art-mobile *n.* A trailer that carries an art collection for exhibition on road tours.

art-work *n.* The artistic work of an artist.

ARV *abbr.* American Revised Version.

Ar-y-an *adj.* Relating to or of the Indo-European family of languages.

as *adv.* In the manner like; of the same degree or amount; similar to.

AS *abbr.* After sight, airspeed, Anglo-Saxon.

ASA *abbr.* American Society of Appraisers; American Statistical Association.

asb *abbr.* Asbestos.

as-bes-tos *n.* A noncombustible, fibrous mineral form of magnesium silicate that is used especially in fireproofing. **asbestine** *adj.*

ASCAP *abbr.* American Society of Composers, Authors, and Publishers.

ASCE *abbr.* American Society of Civil Engineers.

as-cend *v.* To rise up from a lower level; to climb; to mount; to walk up. **ascendible, ascendable** *adj.*

as-cen-dant *or* **ascsendent** *adj.* Rising; moving up.

as-cent *n.* A way up; a slope; the act of rising.

as-cer-tain *v.* To find out for certain; to make sure. **ascertainment** *n.*, **ascertainable** *adj.*

as-cet-icism *n.* The practice of strict self-denial through personal and spiritual discipline.

as-cot *n.* A scarf or broad tie that is placed under the chin.

as-cribe *v.* To assign or attribute to something. **ascribable, ascription** *v.*

ASCU *abbr.* Association of State Colleges and Universities.

ASE *abbr.* American Stock Exchange.

a-sex-u-al *adj.* Lacking sexual reproductive organs; without sex. **asexuality** *n.*

asg *abbr.* Assigned, assignment.

ash *n.* A type of tree with a hard, tough elastic wood; the grayish dust remaining after something has burned.

a-shamed *adj.* Feeling guilt, disgrace, or shame; feeling unworthy or inferior.

a-shore *adv.* On or to the shore.

ash-tray *n.* A container or receptacle for discarding tobacco ashes and cigarette and cigar butts.

Ash Wednesday *n.* The first day of Lent.

ASI *abbr.* Airspeed indicator.

aside *adv.* Out of the way; to a side; to one side; something that is said in an undertone and not meant to be heard by someone.

ask *v.* To request; to require or seek information. **asker** *n.*

askance *adv.* With a side glance; with suspicion or distrust.

askew *adv. or adj.* Out of line, not straight.

a-slant *adv.* In a slanting direction.

a-sleep *adv.* In a state of sleep; lacking sensation; numb; not alert.

a-slope *adv.* In a slanting or sloping position or direction.

ASME *abbr.* American Society of Mechanical Engineers.

a-so-cial *adj.* Selfish, not social.

as-par-a-gus *n.*

A vegetable with tender shoots, very succulent when cooked.

as-pect *n.* The situation, position, view, or appearance of something.

as-pen *n.* A tree known as the trembling poplar, having leaves that flutter even in a very light breeze.

as-peri-ty *n., pl.* **-ties** Roughness in manner.

as-persion *v.* False charges or slander; defamation; maligning.

as-phalt *n.* A sticky, thick, blackish-brown mixture of petroleum tar used in paving roads and roofing buildings. **asphaltic** *adj.*

as-phyx-i-ate *v.* To suffocate, to prevent from breathing. **asphyxiation** *n.*

as-pic *n.* A savory jelly made from fish, meat, or vegetable juices.

as-pi-rate *v.* To give pronunciation with a full breathing sound; to draw out using suction. **aspiration** *n.*

as-pire *v.* To desire with ambition; to strive towards something that is higher. **aspiringly** *adv.*, **aspirer** *n.*

as-pi-rin *n.* Medication used for the relief of pain and fever.

ASR *abbr.* Airport surveillance radar; air-sea rescue.

ass *n.* A hoofed animal; a donkey; a stupid or foolish person.

as-sail *v.* To attack violently with words or blows. **assailant** *n.*

as-sas-sin *n.* Murderer especially one that murders a politically important person either for fanatical motives or for hire.

as-sas-si-nate *v.* To murder a prominent person by secret or sudden attack. **assassination, assassinator** *n.*

as-sault *n.* A very violent physical or verbal attack on a person. **assaulter** *n.*

as-say *n.* To evaluate or to assess; to try; to attempt. **assayer** *n.*

as-sem-blage *n.* A collection of things or people; artistic composition made from junk, scraps, and miscellaneous materials.

as-sem-ble *v.* To put together the parts of something; to come together as a group. **assembly** *n.*

as-sem-bly line *n.* The arrangement of workers, machines, and equipment which allows work to pass from operation to operation in the correct order until the product is assembled.

as-sem-bly-man *n.* A member of an assembly line.

as-sent *v.* To agree on something. **-er** *n.*

as-sert *v.* To declare or state positively, to maintain; to defend. **asserter, assertor** *n.*

as-sess *v.* To fix or assign a value to something. **assessor** *n.*

as-sess-ment *n.* The official determination of value for tax purposes.

as-set *n.* A valuable quality or possession; all of the property of a business or a person that can be used to cover liabilities.

as-sev-er-ate *v.* To state positively, firmly, and seriously. **asseveration** *n.*

as-sign *v.* To designate as to duty; to give or allot; to attribute. **assignable** *adj.*

as-sign-ed risk *n.* A poor risk for insuring; one that insurance companies would normally refuse but are forced to insure by state law.

as-sign-ee *n.* The person appointed to act for another; the person to whom property or the right to something is legally transferred.

as-sign-ment *n.* A given amount of work or task to undertake; a post, position, or office to which one is assigned.

as-sim-i-late v. To take in, to understand; to make similar; to digest or to absorb into the system. **assimilator, assimilation** n.

as-sist v. To give support, to aid, to give help. **assistance, assistant** n.

as-size n. A fixed or customary standard.

assoc abbr. Associate.

assn abbr. Association.

as-so-ci-ate v. To connect or join together. n. A partner, colleague, or companion.

as-so-ci-a-tion n. An organized body of people having a common interest; a society. **associational** adj.

as-so-nance n. The repetition of sound in words or syllables.

as-sort v. To distribute into groups of a classification or kind. **assorter** n., **assortative** adj.

as-sort-ed adj. Made up of different or various kinds.

as-sort-ment n. The act or state of being assorted; a collection of different things.

asst abbr. Assistant.

as-suage v. To quiet, pacify; to put an end to by satisfying. **assuagement** n.

as-sua-sive adj. Having a smooth, pleasant effect or quality.

as-sume v. To take upon oneself to complete a job or duty; to take responsibility for; to take for granted. **assumable** adj., **assumably** adv.

as-sump-tion n. An idea or statement believed to be true without proof.

as-sur-ance n. A statement made to inspire confidence of mind or manner; freedom from uncertainty or self-doubt.

as-sure v. To give the feeling of confidence; to make sure or certain.

as-sured adj. Satisfied as to the truth or certainty. **assuredly** adv.

as-sur-er n. A person who gives assurance.

assy abbr. Assembly.

as-ter n.

A plant having white, bluish, purple, or pink daisy-like flowers.

as-ter-isk n. The character (*) used to indicate letters omitted or as a reference to a footnote.

a-stern adv. & adj. Toward the rear or back of an aircraft or ship.

as-ter-oid n. One of thousands of small planets between Jupiter and Mars.

asth-ma n. A respiratory disease marked by labored breathing, accompanied by wheezing, and often coughing and gasping. **asthmatic** adj., **-tically** adv.

as though conj. As if.

astig-ma-tism n. A defect of the lens of an eye resulting in blurred or imperfect images.

a-stir adj. To be out of bed, awake; in motion.

ASTM abbr. American Society for Testing and Materials.

as to prep. With reference to or regard to; concerning; according to.

as-ton-ish v. To strike with sudden fear, wonder, or surprise.

as-ton-ish-ing adj. Causing surprise or astonishment. **astonishingly** adv.

as-ton-ish-ment n. The state of being amazed or astonished.

as-tound v. To fill with wonder and bewilderment. **-ing** adj. **-ingly** adv.

ASTP abbr. Army Specialized Training Program.

as-tra-khan n. The curly fur from a young lamb of the southeast U.S.S.R.

as-tral adj. Resembling, or related to the stars.

a-stray adv. Away from a desirable or proper path or development.

a-stride prep. One leg on either side of something; placed or lying on both sides of; extending across or over.

as-trin-gent adj. Able to draw together or to constricting tissue. **-cy** n.

as-tro-dome n. A large stadium covered by a dome.

as-tro-labe n. Instrument formerly used to determine the altitude of a celestial body.

as-trol-o-gy n. The study of the supposed influences of the planets and stars and their movements and positions on human affairs. **-ical** adj., **astrologer** n.

astron abbr. Astronomer; Astronomy.

as-tro-naut n. A person who travels in a spacecraft beyond the earth's atmosphere.

as-tro-nau-tics n. The technology and science of the construction and operation of a spacecraft. **astronautical** adj. **astronautically** adv.

as-tro-nom-i-cal adj. Relating to astronomy; something inconceivable or enormously large. **-ly** adv.

as-tron-o-my n. The science of the celestial bodies and their motion, magnitudes, and constitution. **-er** n.

as-tro-phys-ics n. Branch of astronomy dealing with the chemical and physical constitution of the celestial bodies. **astrophysical** adj., **astrophysicist** n.

as-tute adj. Sharp in discernment; very shrewd. **astutely** adv., **astuteness** n.

a-sun-der adv. Separate into parts or positions apart from each other.

ASV abbr. American Standard Version.

asy-lum n. A refuge or institution for the care of the needy or sick; a place of security and retreat; an institution providing help and care for the destitute or insane.

a-sym-metric adj. Something that is not symmetrical. **asymmetry** n.

at prep. To indicate presence, occurrence, or condition; used as a function word to indicate a certain time.

AT abbr. Ampere-turn; air temperature.

at-a-vism n. The reappearance a hereditary characteristic that skipped several generations. **atavistic** adj.

a**tax-ia** *n.* Any nervous disorder with an inability to coordinate voluntary muscular movements. **ataxic** *adj.*

a**t-el-ier** *n.* An artist's workshop.

a**-the-ism** *n.* The disbelief that God exists.

a**the-ist** *n.* A person who does not believe in God. **-ic, atheistical** *adj.*

A**th-ens** *n.* The capital city of Greece.

a**-thirst** *adj.* Having a strong, eager desire for something.

a**th-lete** *n.* A person who participates in sports, as football, basketball, soccer, etc.

a**th-lete's foot** *n.* A contagious skin infection of the feet.

a**th-let-ic** *adj.* Relating to athletes; physically strong and active.

a**-thwart** *adv.* Opposition to the expected or right; from one side to another.

a**-tilt** *adj. & adv.* Inclined upward or tilted in some way.

A**t-lan-ta** *n.* The capital city of Georgia.

A**t-lan-tic Ocean** *n.* The second largest ocean.

a**t-las** *n.* A collection or book of maps.

A**TM** *abbr.* Automatic Teller Machine; a banking terminal that allows a customer to deposit or withdraw money by inserting a card and entering a private number code.

a**t-mos-phere** *n.* A gaseous mass that surrounds a celestial body, as the earth; a predominant mood or feeling.

a**t-oll** *n.*

An island of coral that encircles a lagoon either partially or completely.

a**t-om** *n.*

A tiny particle, the smallest unit of an element.

a**tom bomb** *or* **atomic bomb** *n.* A bomb that explodes violently due to the sudden release of atomic energy, occurring from the splitting of nuclei of a heavy chemical element.

a**t-om-ic en-er-gy** *n.* Energy that is released by changes in the nucleus of an atom.

a**-ton-al** *adj.* Marked by the deliberate avoidance of a traditional key or tonal center. **atonality** *n.*, **atonally** *adv.*

a**-tone** *v.* To give satisfaction; to make amends.

a**-tone-ment** *n.* Amends for an injury or a wrongdoing; the reconciliation between God and man.

a**top** *adj.* On the top of something.

a**tri-um** *n.* One of the heart chambers; the main hall of a Roman house.

atrial *adj.*

a**-tro-cious** *adj.* Exceedingly cruel or evil.

a**-troc-i-ty** *n., pl.* **-ties** The condition of being atrocious; an atrocious act.

a**-tro-phy** *v.* To decrease in size or a wasting away.

att *abbr.* Attached; attention; attorney.

a**t-tach** *v.* To bring together; to fasten or become fastened; to bind by personal attachments. **attachable** *adj.*

a**t-ta-che** *n.* An expert on the diplomatic staff of an embassy.

attache case *n.* A briefcase or a small suitcase.

a**t-tach-ment** *n.* The state of being attached; a tie of affection or loyalty; the supplementary part of something.

a**t-tack** *v.* To threaten with force, to assault; to start to work on with vigor.

a**t-tain** *v.* To arrive at or reach a goal. **-ability** *n.*, **-able** *adj.* **attainableness** *n.*

a**t-tain-der** *n.* The loss of civil rights that occurs following a criminal conviction.

a**t-tain-ment** *n.* Accomplishment; an achievement.

a**t-taint** *v.* To disgrace or stain; to achieve or obtain by effort.

a**t-tar** *n.* The fragrant oil from flowers.

a**t-tempt** *v.* To make an effort to do something. **attempt** *n.*

a**t-tend** *v.* To be present; to take charge of or to look after.

a**t-ten-dance** *n.* The fact or act of attending; the number of times a person attends.

a**t-ten-dant** *n.* One who provides a service for another.

a**t-ten-tion** *n.* Observation, notice, or mental concentration. **attentive** *adj.*, **attentively** *adv.*, **attentiveness** *n.*

a**t-ten-u-ate** *v.* To lessen the force, amount or value; to become thin; to weaken. **attenuation** *n.*

a**t-test** *v.* To give testimony or to sign one's name as a witness. **attestation** *n.*

a**t-tic** *n.* The space directly below the roof of a building.

a**t-tire** *n.* A person's dress or clothing. *v.* To clothe; to dress.

a**t-ti-tude** *n.* A mental position; the feeling one has for oneself.

attn *abbr.* Attention.

a**t-tor-ney** *n., pl.* **-neys** A person with legal training who is appointed by another to transact business for him.

a**t-tor-ney gen-er-al** *n.* The chief law officer of a state or nation.

a**t-tract** *v.* To draw by appeal; to cause to draw near by appealing qualities.

a**t-trac-tion** *n.* The capability of attracting; something that attracts or is meant to attract.

a**t-trac-tive** *adj.* Having the power of charming, or quality of attracting. **attractively** *adv.*, **attractiveness** *n.*

a**t-trib-ute** *v.* To explain by showing a cause. *n.* A characteristic of a thing or person. **attributable** *adj.*

a**t-tune** *v.* To bring something into harmony; to put in tune; to adjust.

a**-typ-i-cal** *adj.* Not confirming to the typical type. **atypically** *adv.*

atty *abbr.* Attorney.

atty gen *abbr.* Attorney general.

atwit-ter *adj.* Very excited; or nervously concerned about something.

at wt *abbr.* Atomic Weight.

au-bade *n.* A poem or song for lovers who part at dawn; a love song in the morning.

au-burn *adj.* A reddish brown color; moderately brown; used in describing the color of a person's hair.

au cou-rant *adj.* Fully familiar or informed.

auc-tion *n.* A public sale of merchandise to the highest bidder. **auctioneer** *n.*

auction bridge *n.* A variation in the game of bridge in which tricks made in excess of the contract are scored toward game.

auc-to-ri-al *adj.* Having to do with an author.

au-da-cious *adj.* Bold, daring, or fearless; insolent. **-ly** *adv.,* **audacity** *n.*

au-di-ble *adj.* Capable of being heard.

au-di-ence *n.* A group of spectators or listeners; the opportunity to express views; a formal hearing or conference.

au-di-o *adj.* Of or relating to sound or its high-fidelity reproduction.

au-dit *n.* Verification or examination of financial accounts or records.

au-di-tion *n.* A trial performance given by an entertainer as to demonstrate ability.

au-di-tor *n.* A person who listens or hears; one who audits accounts.

au-di-to-ri-um *n.* A large room in a public building or a school that holds many people.

au-di-to-ry *adj.* Related to the organs or sense of hearing.

Aug *abbr.* August, the 8th month of the calendar year.

au-ger *n.* The tool which is used for the purpose of putting holes in the ground or wood.

aught *n.* Zero (0).

aug-ment *v.* To add to or increase; to enlarge. **augmentation, augmenter** *n.,* **augmentative, augmentable** *adj.*

au jus *adj.* Served in the juices obtained from roasting.

auk *n.* Sea bird with a stocky body and short wings, living in the arctic regions.

au na-tu-rel *adj.* Of a natural state.

aunt *n.* A sister of a person's father or mother; the wife of one's uncle.

au-ra *n., pl.* **-ras, -rae** An emanation said to come from a person's or an animal's body.

au-ral *adj.* Relating to the ear or the sense of hearing. **aurally** *adv.*

au-re-ate *adj.* Of a brilliant golden color.

au-re-ole *n.* A halo.

au re-voir *interj.* Used in expressing farewell to someone.

au-ri-cle *n.* The two upper chambers of the heart.

au-ric-u-lar *adj.* Dealing with the sense of hearing or of being in the shape of the ear.

au-rif-er-ous *adj.* Producing or yielding gold; containing gold

au-ro-ra *n.* The brilliant display of moving and flashing lights in the night sky, believed to be caused by electrically charged particles. **-al** *adj.*

aus-tere *adj.* Stern in manner and appearance. **austerity** *n.*

aus-tral *adj.* Southern.

Aus-tri-a *n.* Country of central Europe.

au-then-tic *adj.* Real; genuine; worthy of acceptance.

au-then-ti-cate *v.* To prove something is true or genuine. **authentication, authenticity, authenticator** *n.*

author *n.* A person who writes an original literary work; the creator of anything. **author** *v.*

au-thor-i-tar-i-an *adj.* Blind submission and absolute, unquestioned obedience to authority. **authoritarianism, authoritarian** *n.* **authoritative** *adj.*

au-thor-i-ty *n., pl.* **-ties** A group or person with power; a government; an expert.

au-thor-i-za-tion *n.* The act of authorizing something.

au-thor-ize *v.* To give authority, to approve, to justify.

au-thor-ship *n.* The character of being an author.

au-tism *n.* Absorption in a self-centered mental state, such as fantasies, daydreams or hallucinations in order to escape from reality. **autistic** *adj.*

auto *abbr.* Automatic; automobile.

au-to-bahn *n.* Highway in Germany.

au-to-bi-og-ra-pher *n.* A person who writes an autobiography.

au-to-bi-og-ra-phy *n., pl.* **-phies** The life story of a person, written by that person. **autobiographer** *n.*

au-toch-tho-nous *adj.* Native to an area.

au-toc-ra-cy *n.* Government by one person who has unlimited power. **autocrat** *n.,* **autocratic** *adj.*

au-to-di-dact *n.* A person who has taught himself. **autodidactic** *adj.*

au-to-graph *n.* A handwritten signature.

au-to-in-tox-i-ca-tion *n.* Self-poisoning caused by metabolic wastes of other toxins in the body.

au-to-mate *v.* To operate by automation, to convert something to automation.

au-to-mat-ic *adj.* Operating with very little control; self-regulating. **automatically** *adv.*

au-to-ma-tion *n.* The equipment and techniques used to acquire automation.

au-to-mo-bile *n.* A four-wheeled passenger vehicle commonly propelled by an internal-combustion engine.

au-to-mo-tive *adj.* Relating to self-propelled vehicles.

au-to-nom-ic *adj.* Pertaining to the autonomic system of the nervous system.

au-to-nom-ic ner-vous sys-tem *n.* The part of the body's nervous system which is regulated involuntarily.

au-ton-o-my *n.* Independence; self-government.

au-to-pilot *n.* The device for automatically steering aircraft and ships.

au-top-sy *n., pl.* **-sies** Postmortem examination; the examination of a body after death to find the cause of death. autopsic, autopsical *adj.*

au-to-stra-da *n.* An expressway in Italy.

au-tumn *n.* The season between summer and winter. autumnal *adj.*

aux-il-ia-ry *adj.* Providing help or assistance to someone; giving support.

aux-il-ia-ry verb *n.* Verbs that accompany a main verb and express the mood, voice, or tense.

auxin *n.* The hormone in a plant that stimulates growth.

av *or* **ave** *abbr.* Avenue.

a-vail *v.* To be of advantage or use; to use. *n.* The advantage toward attaining a purpose or goal.

a-vail-abil-i-ty *n.* The state of being available.

a-vail-able *adj.* Ready or present for immediate use. **-ness** *adj.*, **-y** *adv.*

av-a-lanche *n.* A large amount of rock or snow that slides down a mountainside.

a-vant-garde *n.* The people who apply and invent new ideas and styles in a certain field.

av-a-rice *n.* One's desire to have wealth and riches.

a-vast *interj., Naut.* A command to stop or cease.

a-venge *v.* To take revenge for something. avenger *n.*

av-e-nue *n.* A street lined with trees; a way of achieving something; sometimes called an "avenue of attack".

a-ver *v.* To be firm and to state positively. averment *n.*

av-er-age *n.* Something that is typical or usual, not being exceptional; common.

a-verse *adj.* Having a feeling of distaste or repugnance. **-ness** *n.*, aversely *adv.*

a-ver-sion *n.* A feeling of strong dislike, or distaste for something.

a-vert *v.* To prevent or keep from happening; to turn aside or away from.

av *abbr.* Average.

a-vi-ary *n.* A place where birds are kept.

a-vi-a-tion *n.* The operation of planes and other aircraft.

a-vi-a-tor *n.* Pilot of an aircraft.

av-id *adj.* Greedy; eager; enthusiastic.

av-o-ca-do *n.*

The pear-shaped edible fruit from the avocado tree, having a large seed and yellowish-green pulp.

av-o-ca-tion *n.* A pleasurable activity that is in addition to the regular work a person must do; a hobby.

a-void *v.* To stay away from; to shun; to prevent or keep from happening. avoidable *adj.*, avoidably *adv.*

a-void-ance *n.* The act of making something void

a-vouch *v.* To assert; to guarantee. avouchment *n.*

a-vow *v.* To state openly on a subject. avower, avowal *n.*, avowedly *adv.*

a-wait *v.* To wait for something.

a-wake *v.* To wake up; to be alert or watchful.

a-ward *v.* To give or confer as being deserved needed, or merited. *n.* A judgment or decision; a prize. awardable *adj.*, awarder *n.*

a-ware *adj.* Being conscious or mindful of something. awareness *n.*

a-wash *adj.* Flooded; afloat; to be washed by water.

a-way *adv.* At a distance; apart from.

awe *n.* A feeling of wonder mixed with reverence. awe *v.*

a-wea-ry *adj.* Tired.

a-weigh *adj.* To hang just clear of a ship's anchor.

awe-some *adj.* Expressive of awe. awesomely *adv.*, awsomeness *n.*

aw-ful *adj.* Very unpleasant or dreadful.

a-while *adv.* For a short time.

a-whirl *adj.* To spin around.

awk-ward *adj.* Not graceful; clumsy. awkwardly *adv.*, awkwardness *n.*

awl *n.* Tool used to make holes in leather.

awn *n.* The part of a piece a grass which resembles a bristle. awned, -less *adj.*

awn-ing *n.* Structure that serves as a shelter over a window; roof-like.

AWOL *abbr.* Absent without leave.

a-wry *adv.* In a twisted or turned position.

ax *or* **axe** *n.* Tool used to split wood.

ax-i-om *n.* Statement recognized as being true; something assumed to be true without proof. axiomatic *adj.*, axiomatically *adv.*

ax-is *n., pl.* **axes**

The line around an object or body that rotates or may be thought to rotate.

ax-le *n.* A spindle or shaft around which a wheel or pair of wheels revolve.

ax-le-tree *n.* A bar which a wheel turns upon.

a-yah *n.* A native nursemaid or maid in India.

AZ *abbr.* Arizona.

a-zal-ea *n.* A shrub of the genus Rhododendron group grown for their many colored flowers.

a-zo-ic *adj.* Time period which occurred before life first appeared on the earth.

AZT *abbr.* Azidothymidine; a drug that improves the symptoms of AIDS; (Acquired Immune Deficiency Syndrome), allowing a longer and better life. Approved early 1987 by the Federal Government for prescription use.

Az-tec *n.* The Indian people of Mexico.

az-ure *n.* The blue color of the sky.

azur-ite *n.* A mineral that consists of a blue basic carbonate of copper.

B, b The second letter of the English alphabet; a student's grade rating of good, but not excellent.

BA *abbr.* Bachelor of Arts.

BAAE *abbr.* Bachelor of Aeronautical and Astronautical Engineering.

ba-ba *n.* A rich cake soaked in rum.

babble *v.* To reveal secrets; to chatter senselessly; to talk foolishly.

babe *n.* A very young child or infant.

ba-bel *n.* Babbling noise of many people talking at the same time.

ba-boon *n.* A species of the monkey family with a large body and big canine teeth.

ba-bu *n.* A Hindu gentleman.

ba-bul *n.* A acacia tree in northern Africa and Asia which yields gum arabic as well as fodder and timber.

ba-bush-ka *n.* A kerchief folded into a triangle and worn as a covering on the head.

ba-by *n., pl.* **babies** A young child; infant. **babyish** *adj.*

ba-by car-riage *n.* A push carriage with four wheels and folding capabilities.

ba-by grand *n.* A type of piano, five to six feet long.

bac-ca-lau-re-ate *n* A degree given by universities and colleges.

bac-cha-na-lia *n.* A Roman festival celebrated with dancing and song.

Bac-chus *n.* The Greek god of wine.

bach-e-lor *n.* An unmarried male; the first degree one can receive from a four year university.

bach-e-lor's but-ton *n.* European flower with blue, pink, or white heads.

ba-cil-lus *n., pl.* **bacilli** A rod-like microscopic organism which can cause certain diseases.

bac-i-tra-cin *n.* An antibiotic used topically against cocci.

back *n.* The rear part of the human body from the neck to the end of the spine, also the rear part of an animal; a position in the game of football, in which the player lines up behind the front line of players; the final nine holes of an 18-hole golf course.

back-ache *n.* A pain in the back.

back-bite *v.* To gossip or speak in a nasty way about a person who is not present.

back-board *n.* A board that gives support when placed under or behind something.

back-bone *n.* The spinal column or spine of the vertebrates; the strongest support, or strength; the back of a book with the title and the author's names.

back-drop *n.* A curtain or scene behind the back of a stage set.

back-er *n.* One who gives support to a cause.

back-field *n.* Football players who are positioned behind the line of scrimmage.

back-fire *n.* Premature explosion of unburned exhaust gases or ignited fuel of an internal-combustion engine; a fire deliberately set to check an advancing forest or prairie fire.

back-gam-mon *n.* A game played by two people wherein each player tries to move his counters on the board, at the same time trying to block his opponent.

back-ground *n.* The area or surface behind which objects are represented; conditions leading up to a happening; the collection of a person's complete experience.

background music *n.* Music played to accompany the action of a motion picture, or television drama.

back-hand *n.* A stroke in the game of tennis, made with the back of the hand facing outward. **backhanded** *adj.*

back-hoe *n.* An excavating machine used to dig foundations for homes, etc.

back-ing *n.* Support or aid; a supply in reserve.

back judge *n.* A football official who keeps the official time and identifies eligible pass receivers.

back-lash *n* A violent backward movement or reaction; a snarl in a fishing line. **backlasher** *n.*

back-log *n.* An accumulation of unfinished work; a reserve supply.

back-pack *n.* A piece of equipment used to carry items on the back, mounted on a lightweight frame, and constructed of nylon or canvas. **-packer** *n.*

back-pedal *v.* To move backward or retreat.

back-rest *n.* A support given to the back.

back room *n.* A room in the rear of a building for inconspicuous group meetings.

back-saw *n.* Saw with metal ribs on its back side.

back-seat *n.* The seat in the back of an auto-mobile, etc.; an inferior position.

back-side *n.* The buttocks.

back-slide *v.* To lapse back into a less desirable condition, as in a religious practice. **backsliding** *v.*, **backslider** *n.*

back-spin *n.* A spin which rotates in the reverse direction.

back-stage *n.* The area behind the performing area in a theatre.

back-stitch *n.* A hand stitch made by inserting the needle a stitch to the right and bringing it up an equal stitch to the left.

back-stop *n.* Something that prevents a ball from being hit out of play.

back-stretch *n.* The opposite of the homestretch on a racecourse.

back-stroke *n.* A swimming stroke performed while on the back.

back-swept *adj.* Slanting or swept backward.

back-talk *n.* A smart or insolent reply.

back-track *v.* To reverse a policy; to retrace previous steps. **-ing** *n.*

back-up *n.* One that serves as an alternative or substitute.

back-ward *adv.* Toward the back; to or at the back. **-ness** *n.*, **backwards** *adv.*

back-wash *n.* A backward flow of water.

back-wa-ter *n.* A body of water turned back by an obstruction.

back-woods *n., pl.* A sparsely populated, heavily wooded area. **-man** *n.*

back-yard *n.* An area to the rear of a house.

ba-con *n.* Side and back of a pig, salted and smoked.

bac-ter-emia *n.* The presence of bacteria or microorganisms in the blood.

bac-ter-ia *pl., n.* The plural of bacterium.

bac-te-ri-cide *n.* A substance that kills bacteria.

bac-te-ri-ol-o-gy *n.* Scientific study of bacteria and its relationship to medicine, etc.

bac-te-ri-um *n., pl.* **-ria** Any of various forms of numerous unicellular microorganisms that cause disease. **bacterial** *adj.*

bad *adj.* Naughty or disobedient; unfavorable; inferior; poor; spoiled; invalid. **badly** *adv.*, **badness** *n.*

bad-der-locks *n.* A blackish seaweed sometimes eaten as a vegetable in Europe.

badge *n.* An emblem worn for identification.

bad-ger *n.*

A sturdy burrowing mammal. *v.* To harass or trouble persistently.

bad-lands *pl., n.* Area with sparse life, peaks, and eroded ridges.

Bad-lands *n.* The nickname of very barren regions of southwestern South Dakota and northwestern Nebraska.

bad-min-ton *n.* A court game played with long-handled rackets and a shuttlecock.

bad-mouth *v.* To criticize someone.

baf-fle *v.* To puzzle; to perplex. *n.* A device that checks or regulates the flow of gas, sound, or liquids, etc. **baffled, baffling** *v.* **bafflingly** *adv.*

bag *n.* A flexible container used for holding, storing, or carrying something; a square white canvas container used to mark bases in baseball. **bag** *v.*, **bagful** *n.*, **baggy** *adj.*

ba-gasse *n.* Plant residue.

bag-a-telle *n.* A game played with a cue and balls on an oblong table.

ba-gel *n.* A hard, glazed, round roll with a chewy texture and a hole in the middle.

bag-gage *n.* The personal belongings of a traveler.

bag-gy *adj.* Loose. **baggily** *adv.*

Bagh-dad *n.* The capital of Iraq.

bag-man *n.* A person who collects illicit payments for another.

bag-pipe *n.* A wind instrument with a leather bag and melody pipes. **-er** *n.*

ba-guette *n.* A gem in the shape of a long, narrow rectangle.

bag-wig *n.* An 18th century wig with the hair in the back contained in a small silk bag.

bag-worm *n.* A type of moth larva that lives in a silk case covered with plant debris, very destructive to evergreens.

Ba-ha-ma Islands *n.* Islands in the Atlantic Ocean, southeast of Florida.

bail *n.* The security or money given to guarantee the appearance of a person for trial. *v.* To remove water from a boat by dipping and emptying the water overboard. **bailor, bailer** *n.*

bail-iff *n.* The officer who guards prisoners and keeps order in a courtroom.

bail-i-wick *n.* The office or district of a bailiff.

bails-man *n.* The person who puts up the bail for another.

bait *v.* To lure; to entice. *n.* Food that is used to catch or trap an animal.

baize *n.* A coarse woolen or cotton cloth.

bake *v.* To cook in an oven; to harden or dry. **baking, baked** *v.*, **baker** *n.*

baker's dozen *n.* Thirteen.

bak-ery *n.* A store where baked goods are made and sold.

bak-ing pow-der *n.* A leavening agent used in baking consisting of carbonate, an acid substance, and flour or starch.

bak-ing soda *n.* Sodium bicarbonate.

bak-sheesh *n.* A tip or gratuity.

bal-a-lai-ka *n.* A three-stringed musical instrument.

bal-ance *n.* Device for determining the weight of something; the agreement of totals in the debit and credit of an account.

balance beam *n.* A narrow wooden beam approximately four feet off the ground used for balancing feats in gymnastics.

bal-co-ny *n., pl.* **-nies** Gallery or platform projecting from the wall of a building.

bald *adj.*

Lacking hair on the head. **baldish** *adj.*, **baldness** *n.*

bal-da-chin *n.* An embroidered fabric of silk and gold used to carry over an important person or sacred object.

bald eagle *n.* The eagle of North America that is dark when young but has a white head and neck feathers when mature.

bal-der-dash *n.* Nonsense.

bale *n.* A large, bound package or bundle.

ba-leen *n.* A whalebone.

balk *v.* To refuse to go on; to stop short of something. *n.* A rafter or crossbeam extending from wall to wall. **balking** *v.*, **balky** *adj.*

ball *n.* A round body or mass; a pitched baseball that is delivered outside of the strike zone.

bal-lad *n.* A narrative story or poem of folk origin; a romantic song.

bal-lade *n.* A verse form, consisting of three stanzas with recurrent rhymes and a refrain for each part.

bal-lad-eer *n.* A person who sings ballads.

bal-last *n.* Heavy material placed in a vehicle to give stability and weight.

ball bear-ing *n* A bearing that reduces friction by separating the stationary parts from the moving ones.

bal-le-ri-na *n.* A female ballet dancer in a company.

bal-let *n.* An artistic expression of dance by choreographic design.

bal-lis-tic missile *n.* A projectile that is self-powered, is guided during ascent, and has a free fall trajectory at descent.

bal-lis-tics *n.* The science of motion in flight; the firing characteristics of a firearm.

bal-lo-net *n.* A compartment within the interior of a balloon or airship to control ascent and descent.

bal-loon *n.* A bag inflated with gas lighter than air which allows it to float in the atmosphere, used as a child's toy.

bal-lot *n.* A slip of paper used in secret voting. *v.* To vote by ballot.

ball-park *n.* A stadium where ball games are played.

ball-point *n.* A pen that has a small self-inking writing point.

bal-ly-hoo *n.* Exaggerated advertising.

balm *n.* A fragrant ointment that soothes, comforts, and heals.

bal-ma-caan *n.* A loose overcoat made of woolens and having raglan sleeves, short collar and a closing which may be buttoned up to the throat.

ba-lo-ney *n., Slang* Nonsense.

bal-sa *n.* American tree whose wood is very light in weight.

bal-sam *n.* A fragrant ointment from different trees; a plant cultivated for its colorful flowers.

bal-us-ter *n.* The upright post that supports a handrail.

bam-boo *n.* Tropical, tall grass with hollow, pointed stems.

bam-boo-zle *v.* To trick or deceive. bamboozled, bamboozling *v.*

ban *v.* To prohibit; to forbid. banning, banned *v.*

ba-nal *adj.* Trite; lacking freshness.

ba-nan-a *n.* The crescent-shaped usually yellow, edible fruit of a tropical plant.

band *n.* A strip used to trim, finish, encircle, or bind; the range of a radio wave length; a group of musicians who join together to play their instruments.

band-age *n.* A strip of cloth used to protect an injury. bandage *v.*

ban-dan-na *n.* A brightly colored cotton or silk handkerchief.

ban-deau *n.* A narrow band worn in the hair; a narrow brassiere.

ban-de-ri-lla *n.* A decorated dart that the banderillero thrusts into the neck of the bull in a bullfight.

ban-di-coot *n.* A very large rat of India which is destructive to the rice fields and gardens.

ban-dit *n., pl.* bandits, banditti A gangster or robber. banditry *n.*

ban-do-lier *n.* A belt worn over the shoulder with pockets for cartridges.

ban-dore *n.* A 3-stringed instrument resembling a guitar.

band-stand *n.* A raised platform on which an orchestra or band perform.

ban-dy *adv.* Bent; crooked; curved outward. bandying *v.*

bane *n.* A cause of destruction. baneful *adj.,* banefully *adv.*

bang *n.* A sudden loud noise; short hair cut across the forehead. *v.* To move or hit with a loud noise.

Bang-kok *n.* The capital of Thailand.

ban-gle *n.* A bracelet worn around the wrist or ankle.

ban-ish *v.* To leave; to drive away. banished, banishing *v.,* banisher, banishment *n.*

ban-is-ter *n.* The upright supports of a handrail on a staircase.

ban-jo *n.* A stringed instrument similar to a guitar. banjoist *n.*

bank *n.* A slope of land adjoining water; an establishment that performs financial transactions. bankable *adj.*

bank-rupt *n., pl.* -cies One who is legally insolvent and whose remaining property is divided among creditors. bankrupt *v.,* bankruptcy *n.*

ban-ner *n.* A piece of cloth, such as a flag, that is used as a standard by a commander or monarch.

ban-nock *n.* Unleavened or flat cake made from barley or oatmeal.

banns *pl., n.* The announcement of a forthcoming marriage.

ban-quet *n.* An elaborate dinner or feast.

ban-shee *n.* A spirit in folklore whose appearance warns a family of approaching death of a member.

ban-yan *n.* A tree from the tropics whose aerial roots grow downward to form additional roots.

bap-tism *n.* A Christian sacrament of spiritual rebirth through the application of water. baptismal *adj.*

bar *n.* A rigid piece of material used as a support; a counter where a person can receive drinks. *v.* To prohibit or exclude; to keep out.

barb *n.* A sharp projection that extends backward making it difficult to remove; a breed of horses from Africa noted for their speed and endurance.

bar-bar-i-an *n.* A person or culture thought to be primitive and therefore inferior. barbarous, barbaric *adj.*

bar-be-cue *n.* An outdoor fireplace or pit for roasting meat. barbecue *v.*

barbed wire *n.* Wire that is twisted with sharp points.

bar-bell *n.* A bar with weights at both ends, used for exercise.

bar-ber *n.* A person whose business is

cutting and dressing hair and shaving and trimming beards.

bar-ber-ry n. A shrub having yellow flowers and oblong red berries.

bar-ber-shop n. The place of business where hair is cut; impromptu unaccompanied vocal harmonizing of popular songs, usually consisting of 4 or more men.

bar-bette n. A cylinder protecting a gun turret on a warship.

bar-bi-tal n. A white addictive administered in the form of sodium salt.

bar-ca-role n. A Venetian boat song with a strong and weak beat which suggests a rowing rhythm.

bard n. A poet; a piece of armor for a horse's neck. **bardic** adj.

bare adj. Exposed to view; without coloring. **bare** v., **bareness** n.

bare-back adv. & adj. Riding a horse without a saddle.

ba-rege n. A sheer fabric for women's clothing.

bare-ly adv. Sparsely; by a very little amount.

barf v. Slang To vomit.

bar-gain n. A contract or agreement on the purchase or sale of an item; a purchase made at a favorable or good price. **bargainer** n.

bargain basement n. A section in a store where goods are sold at lower prices.

barge n. A flat-bottomed boat. v. To intrude abruptly.

barge-board n. A board which conceals roof timbers that project over gables.

barge-man n. A deckhand of a barge.

bar-iat-rics n. The branch of medicine which treats obesity.

bari-tone n. The male voice in the range between tenor and bass.

bark n. The outer covering of a tree; the abrupt, harsh sound made by a dog. **barker** n., **barkless** adj.

bark beetle n. A beetle that bores under the bark of trees.

bar-ken-tine n. A 3-masted ship with fore-and-aft rigging.

bark-er n. A person in the circus who stands at the entrance and advertises the show.

bar-ley n. A type of grain used for food and for making whiskey and beer.

bar-low n. A sturdy jackknife.

barm n. A yeast which forms on fermenting malt liquors.

bar mitz-vah n. A Jewish boy who, having reached the age of 13, assumes the moral and religious duties of an adult.

barn n. A farm building used to shelter animals and to store farm equipment and products.

bar-na-cle n. A fish with a hard shell that remains attached to an underwater surface; a European goose which breeds in the Arctic.

barn dance n. A social gathering in a barn featuring square dancing.

barn-storm n. A tour through rural areas to obtain votes during a political campaign.

ba-rom-et-er n. An instrument that records the weight and pressure of the atmosphere. **barometrical** adj.

bar-on n. The lowest rank of nobility in Great Britain. **baroness** n., **-ial** adj.

ba-rong n. A thin-edged knife or sword.

ba-roque adj. An artistic style characterized by elaborate and ornate forms.

ba-rouche n. A four-wheeled carriage.

bar-rack n. A building for housing soldiers.

bar-ra-cu-da n., pl. **-da**, **-das** A fish with a large, narrow body, found in the Atlantic Ocean.

bar-rage n. A concentrated outpouring or discharge of missiles from small arms; an artificial dam to increase the depth of water for use in irrigation or navigation.

bar-ra-try n. The unlawful breach of duty by a ship's crew that results in injury to the ship's owner.

bar-rel n. Wooden container with round, flat ends of equal size and sides that bulge.

bar-ren adj. Lacking vegetation; sterile.

bar-rette n. A clasp or small bar used to hold hair in place.

bar-ri-cade n. Barrier.

bar-ri-er n. A structure that restricts or bars entrance.

barrier reef n. A coral reef parallel to shore separated by a lagoon.

bar-room n. A building or room where a person can purchase alcoholic beverages sold at a counter.

bar-row n. A rectangular, flat frame with handles; a wheelbarrow.

bar-tend-er n. A person who serves alcoholic drinks and other refreshments at a bar.

bar-ter v. To trade something for something else without the exchange of money. **-ing**, **bartered** v., **barterer** n.

bar-ti-zan n. A small structure serving as a lookout.

Barton, Clara n. The founder of the American Red Cross.

ba-salt n. A greenish-black volcanic rock.

base n. The fundamental part; the lowest part; the bottom. **base** v., **baseless** adj., **basely** adv., **baseness** n.

base-ball n. A game played with a ball and bat; the ball used in a baseball game.

base-board n. A molding that covers the area where the wall meets the floor.

base hit n. In baseball, a batted ball which enables the batter to reach base safely.

base-ment n. The foundation of a building or home.

bash v. To smash with a heavy blow. Slang A party. **bashed**, **bashing** v.

bash-ful adj. Socially shy. **bashfully** adv.

ba-sic adj. Forming the basis; fundamental. **basically** adv.

BASIC n. A common computer programming language.

bas-il n. An herb used as seasoning in

cooking.

ba-sil-i-ca *n.* An early Christian church building.

bas-o-lisk *n.* A tropical American lizard related to the iguana.

ba-sin *n.* A sink; a washbowl; a round open container used for washing; an area that has been drained by a river system.

ba-sis *n., pl.* **bases** The main part; foundation.

bask *v.* To relax in the warmth of the sun. **basking, basked** *v.*

bas-ket *n.* An object made of woven material, as straw, cane, or other flexible items. **basketry** *n.*

bas-ket-ball *n.* A game played on a court with two teams, each team trying to throw the ball through the basketball hoop at the opponents' end of the court.

bas mitz-vah *n.* A Jewish girl who having reached the age of thirteen, assumes the moral and religious duties of an adult.

bass *n., pl.* **basses**

A fresh water fish, one of the perch family.

bass drum *n.* A large drum with a low booming sound.

bas-set hound *n.* A breed of short-legged hunting dogs with very long ears.

bas-si-net *n.* A basket on legs used as an infant's crib.

bas-soon *n.* A woodwind instrument with a low-pitched sound.

bas-tard *n.* An illegitimate child. *Slang* A disagreeable, nasty, or mean person. **bastardize** *v.*

baste *v.* To run a loose stitch to hold a piece of material in place for a short time. **basted, basting** *v.*

bas-tille *n.* A tower in France used as a jail.

bat *n.*

A wooden stick made from strong wood; a nocturnal flying mammal. **batter** *n.*

bat boy *n.* A boy who takes care of the equipment of a baseball team.

batch *n.* A group of work entered on a computer at one time; a quantity (as of cookies, etc.) baked at one time.

bath *n., pl.* **-baths** The act of washing the body.

bathe *v.* To take a bath. **bathing** *v.*

ba-thom-e-ter *n.* An instrument which is used to measure the depth of water.

bathy-scaphe *n.* A submersible ship for deep sea exploration.

ba-tik *n.* A method of dying fabric, in which the parts not to be dyed are coated with wax.

ba-tiste *n.* A soft sheer fabric.

bat-tal-ion *n.* A military unit consisting

of a headquarters and three or more companies.

bat-ten *v.* To secure; to fasten together.

bat-ter *v.* To beat or strike continuously; to assault. *n.* A cricket or baseball player at bat. **battering, battered** *v.*

bat-tery *n.* A group of heavy guns.

bat-tle *n.* A struggle; combat between opposing forces. *v.* To engage in a war or battle. **battled, battling** *v.*

battle cruiser *n.* A large armed warship.

bawd *n.* A prostitute. **bawdy** *adj.*

bawl *v.* To cry very loudly.

bay *n.* The inlet of a body of water; a main division or compartment.

bay-berry *n.* Evergreen shrub used for decorations and making candles.

bay-o-net *n.* A spear-like weapon.

bay rum *n.* A fragrant liquid from the leaves of the bayberry used in cosmetics and medicine.

ba-zaar *n.* A fair where a variety of items are sold as a money-making project for charity, clubs, churches, or other such organizations.

ba-zooka *n.* Weapon for firing rockets.

BBA *abbr.* Bachelor of Business Administration.

BC *abbr.* Before Christ.

BD *abbr.* Bank draft.

be *v.* To occupy a position; to exist; used with the present participle of a verb to show action; used as a prefix to construct compound words, as behind, before, because, etc.

beach *n.* Pebbly or sandy shore of a lake, ocean, sea, or river.

bea-con *n.* A coastal guiding or signaling device.

bead *n.* A small round piece of material with a hole for threading. **beading** *n.*

bea-gle *n.* A small breed of hunting dog with short legs.

beak *n.* The bill of a bird. **beaked** *adj.*

beak-er *n.* Large, widemouthed cup for drinking; a cylindrical, glass laboratory vessel with a lip for pouring.

beam *n.* Large, oblong piece of wood or metal used in construction. *v.* To shine.

bean *n.* An edible seed or seed pod.

bean curd *n.* A soft vegetable cheese usually found in the Orient.

bear *n., pl.* **bears**

A carnivorous mammal. *v.* To endure; to carry; to support. **bearable** *adj.*, **bearability** *n.*

beard *n.* Hair growing on the chin and cheeks. **bearded, beardless** *adj.*

beast *n.* A four-legged animal. **-ly** *adj.*

beast of burden *n.* An animal used to perform heavy work and transport heavy materials.

beat *v.* To strike repeatedly; to defeat. *adj.* Exhausted, very tired. **beaten** *adj.*, **beat, beater** *n.*

be-a-tif-ic *adj.* Giving or showing extreme bliss or joy.

be-at-i-tude n. The highest form of happiness; heavenly bliss.

beau n. Sweetheart; dandy.

beau-ty n. Quality that is pleasing to the eye. **beautiful** adj., **beautifully**, adv.

bea-ver n. A large semiaquatic rodent with webbed feet and flat tail which yields valuable fur for coats, hats, etc.

be-bop n. Slang Jazz music.

be-calm v. To make quiet. **becalming** v.

be-cause conj. For a reason; since.

beck n. A summons; a call.

beck-et n. A loop for holding something in place.

beck-on v. To summon someone with a nod or wave.

be-come v. To come, to be, or to grow.

bed n. Furniture for sleeping; a piece of planted or cultivated ground. **bed** v., **bedding** n.

be-dazzle v. To confuse with bright lights. **bedazzling, bedazzled** v.

bed-bug n. A wingless insect that sucks blood and infests human homes, especially beds.

bed-fast adj. Confined to a bed; bedridden.

bed-lam n. A state or situation of confusion.

be-drag-gled adj. Limp and wet; soiled as though pulled through mud.

bee n. A hairy-bodied insect characterized by structures for gathering pollen and nectar from flowers.

beech n. A tree of light-colored bark, with edible nuts.

beef n., pl. **beefs, beeves** A cow, steer, or bull that has been fattened for consumption. **beefy** adj.

bee-keep-er n. A person who raises bee for their honey.

beep n. A warning sound from a horn.

beer n. An alcoholic beverage.

bees-wax n. The wax from bees that is used for their honeycombs.

beet n. The root from a cultivated plant that can be used as a vegetable or a source of sugar.

bee-tle n. An insect with modified, horny front wings, which cover the membranous back wings when it is not in flight.

be-fit v. To be suitable. **befitting** adj.

be-fore adv. Earlier; previously. prep. In front of.

be-friend v. To be a friend to someone.

beg v. To make a living by asking for charity. **beggar** n., **beggarly** adj.

be-gan v. The past tense of begin.

be-get v. To cause or produce.

be-gin v. To start; to come into being; to commence. **beginner, beginning** n.

be-gone v., interj. Go away; depart.

be-go-nia n. A tropical plant with waxy flowers and showy leaves.

be-grime v. To soil with grime.

be-grudge v. To envy someone's possessions or enjoyment.

be-guile v. To deceive; to delight; to charm. **beguiled** v.

be-guine n. A popular dance of the islands which resembles the rumba.

be-gum n. A Muslim woman.

be-gun v. The past participle of begin.

be-half n. The support or interest of another person.

be-have v. To function in a certain manner; to conduct oneself in a proper manner. **-ing** v., **-ior, behaviorism** n.

be-head v. To remove the head from the body; to decapitate.

be-held v. Past participle of behold.

be-hind adv. To or at the back; late or slow in arriving.

be-hold v. To look at; to see.

be-hoove v. To benefit or give advantage.

beige n. or adj. A light brownish, grey color.

being n. One's existence.

be-la-bor v. To work on or to discuss beyond the point where it is necessary; to carry to absurd lengths.

be-lat-ed adj. Tardy; late. **belatedly** adv.

bel can-to n. Operatic singing with rich lyricism and brilliant vocal means.

belch v. To expel stomach gas through the mouth.

bel-fry n., pl. **belfries** The tower that contains the bell of a church.

Bel-grade n. Capital of Yugoslavia.

be-lief n. Something that is trusted or believed.

be-lieve v. To accept as true or real; to hold onto religious beliefs. **believable** adj., **believer** n.

be-lit-tle v. To think or speak in a slighting manner of someone or something. **belittled, belittling** v.

bell n.

A metal instrument that gives a metallic sound when struck.

Bell, Alexander Graham n. Inventor of the telephone.

bel-la-don-na n. A poisonous plant with black berries; a medicine extracted from the belladonna plant.

bell--bot-toms pl., n. Pants with legs that flare at the bottom.

belles--let-tres pl., n. Literature that is regarded not for its value, but for its artistic quality.

bel-lig-er-ent adj. Hostile and inclined to be aggressive. **belligerence, belligerent** n., **belligerently** adv.

bell-ly-ra n. A glockenspiel mounted in a frame and used in marching bands.

bel-low v. To make a deep, powerful roar like a bull. **-ed**, **bellowing** v.

bel-lows n. An instrument that produces air in a chamber and expels it through a short tube.

bell-wort n. An herb of the lilly family with yellow bell-shaped flowers.

bel-ly n., pl. **bellies** The abdomen or the stomach.

be-long v., pl. **belongings** n. To be a part of. **belonging** n.

be-loved adj. To be dearly loved.

be-low *adv.* At a lower level or place. *prep.* To be inferior to.

belt *n.* A band worn around the waist; a zone or region that is distinctive in a special way.

belt-way *n.* A highway that encircles an urban area.

be-lu-ga *n.* A large white whale whose roe is used to make caviar.

be-muse *v.* To bewilder or confuse; to be lost in thought. **-ing** *v.*, **-ed** *adj.*

bench *n.* A long seat for more than two people; the seat of the judge in a court of law.

bench warrant *n.* A warrant issued by a judge against a person guilty of contempt.

bend *v.* To arch; to change the direct course; to deflect. **-ing** *v.*, **bender** *n.*

beneath *adv.* To or in a lower position; below; underneath.

ben-e-dict *n.* A previously confirmed bachelor who was recently married.

ben-e-dic-tion *n.* A blessing given at the end of a religious service.

ben-e-fac-tion *n.* A charitable donation; a gift. **benefactor** *n.*

ben-e-fice *n.* Fixed capital assets of a church that provide a living.

be-nef-i-cence *n.* The quality of being kind or charitable.

ben-e-fi-cia-ry *n.* The person named to receive the estate of another in case of death.

ben-e-fit *n.* Aid; help; an act of kindness; a social event or entertainment to raise money for a person or cause.

be-nev-o-lence *n.* The inclination to be charitable. **benevolent** *adj*

be-night-ed *adj.* Overtaken by night.

be-nign *adj.*, *pl.* **-ities**. Having a gentle and kind disposition; gracious; not malignant. **benignly** *adv.*

ben-i-son *n.* A blessing; benediction

ben-ny *n.* An amphetamine.

bent *adj.* Curved, not straight. *n.* A fixed determination; purpose.

be-numb *v.* To dull; to make numb.

benz-al-de-hyde *n.* An aromatic liquid used in flavoring and perfumery.

ben-zene *n.* A flammable toxic liquid used as a motor fuel.

be-queath *v.* To give or leave to someone by will; to hand down.

be-quest *n.* Something that is bequeathed.

be-rate *v.* To scold severely.

be-reave *v.* To deprive; to suffer the loss of a loved one. **bereft** *adj.*, **bereavement** *n.*

be-ret *n.* A round, woolen cap that has no brim.

berg *n.* A large mass of ice; iceberg.

ber-i-ber-i *n.* Nervous disorder from the deficiency of vitamin B producing partial paralysis of the extremities.

berry *n.*, *pl.* **berries** An edible fruit, such as a strawberry or blackberry.

ber-serk *adj.* Destructively violent.

berth *n.* Space at a wharf for a ship or boat to dock; a built-in bunk or bed on a train or ship.

ber-yl *n.* A mineral composed of silicon, oxygen, and beryllium that is the major source of beryllium.

be-ryl-li-um *n.* A corrosion-resistant, rigid, light-weight metallic element.

be-seech *v.* To ask or request earnestly. **beseechingly** *adv.*

be-side *prep.* At the side of; next to.

be-siege *v.* To surround with troops; to harass with requests.

be-sit *v.* To surround on all sides.

be-smear *v.* To soil; to smear.

be-som *n.* A broom made of twigs that are attached to a handle, used to sweep floors.

be-spat-ter *v.* To splash; to soil.

be-speak *v.* To indicate; to speak.

best *adj.* Exceeding all others in quality or excellence; most suitable, desirable, or useful.

bes-tial *adj.*, *pl.* **-ities** Of or relating to an animal; brutish. **-ly** *adv.*, **bestiality** *n.*

bes-ti-ar-y *n.* A medieval collection of fables about imaginary and real animals, each with a moral.

be-stir *v.* To rouse into action.

best man *n.* The attendant of a bridegroom at a wedding.

be-stow *v.* To present or to give honor.

be-stride *v.* To step over or to straddle.

best-sell-er *n.* A book or an article which has a high rate of sale.

bet *n.* An amount risked on a stake or wager.

bet *abbr.* Between.

be-take *v.* To cause oneself to make one's way; move or to go.

beta particle *n.* High-speed positron or electron coming from an atomic nucleus that is undergoing radioactive decay.

be-ta-tron *n.* Accelerator in which electrons are propelled by the inductive action of a rapidly varying magnetic field.

be-think *v.* To remember or to remind oneself.

Beth-le-hem *n.* The birthplace of Jesus.

be-tide *v.* To happen to; to take place.

be-to-ken *v.* To show by a visible sign.

be-tray *v.* To be disloyal or unfaithful; to indicate; to deceive. **betrayal** *n.*

be-troth *v.* To promise to take or give in marriage. **betrothal** *n.*

be-trothed *n.* A person to whom one is engaged to marry.

bet-ta *n.* A brightly colored freshwater fish of southeastern Asia.

bet-ter *adj.* More suitable, useful, desirable, or higher in quality. *v.* To improve oneself. **betterment** *n.*

be-tween *prep.* The position or time that separates; in the middle or shared by two.

be-twixt *prep.* Not knowing which way one should go; between.

bev-el *n.* The angle at which one surface meets another when they are not at right angles.

bev-er-age *n.* A refreshing liquid for drinking other than water.

bev-y *n.*, *pl.* **-bevies** A collection or

group; a flock of birds.

be-wail v. To express regret or sorrow.

be-ware v. To be cautious; to be on guard.

be-wil-der v. To confuse; to perplex or puzzle. **bewilderment** n.

be-witch v. To fascinate or captivate completely. **-ery** n., **bewitchment** v.

bey n. The Turkish title of respect and honor.

be-yond prep. Outside the reach or scope of; something past or to the far side.

bez-el n. A flange or groove that holds the beveled edge of an object such as a gem in a ring mounting.

be-zique n. A card game that uses a deck of 64 cards, similar to pinochle.

bhang n. An intoxicant obtained from the leaves and flowering tops of hemp.

bi pref. Two; occurring two times; used when constructing nouns.

bi-a-ly n. A baked roll with onions on the top.

bi-an-nu-al adj. Taking place twice a year; semiannual. **biannually** adv.

bi-as n. A line cut diagonally across the grain of fabric; prejudice. v. To be or to show prejudice toward others. **biasness** n., **biased** v., **biased** adj.

bib n. A cloth that is tied under the chin of small children to protect their clothing.

bibb n. A piece of timber bolted to the ship's mast for support.

Bi-ble n. The holy book of Christianity, containing the Old and New Testaments. **Biblical** adj., **Biblically** adv.

Bible Belt n. Section of the United States where the Protestant Fundamentalists prevail.

bib-li-og-ra-phy n., pl. **-phies** A list of work by a publisher or writer; a list of sources of information. **-grapher** n.

bib-lio-phile n. A person who collects books.

bib-li-ot-ics n. The study of handwriting to determine authorship.

bib-u-lous adj. Inclined to drink, of or related to drinking.

bi-cen-ten-ni-al adj. Happening once every 200 years. n. Anniversary or celebration of 200 years.

bi-ceps n.

Large muscle in the front of the upper arm and at the back of the thigh. **bicipital** adj.

bick-er v. To quarrel or argue. **bicker** n.

bi-con-cave adj. Bowing in on two sides.

bi-cul-tur-al adj. Having or containing two distinct cultures.

bi-cus-pid n. A tooth with two roots.

bi-cy-cle n. A two-wheeled vehicle propelled by pedals. **bicyclist** n.

bid v. To request something; to offer to pay a certain price. n. One's intention in a card game. **bidder** n.

bid-dy n. A young chicken; hen. Slang A fussy woman.

bide v. To remain; to wait.

bi-det n. A basin for bathing the genital and anal areas.

bi-en-ni-al adj. Occurring every two years; lasting for only two years. **biennially** adv., **biennial** n.

bier n. A stand on which a coffin is placed before burial.

bi-fo-cal adj. Having two different focal lengths.

bifocals pl., n. Lenses used to correct both close and distant vision.

bi-fur-cate v. To divide into two parts. **bifurcation** n., **bifurcately** adj.

big adj. Very large in dimensions, intensity, and extent; grown-up; bountiful.

big-a-my n., pl. **bigamies** The act of marrying one person while still married to another. **bigamist** n.

big brother n. A person who befriends a boy who usually doesn't have a father.

Big Dipper n. Cluster of seven stars that form a bowl and handle.

big head adj. A conceited person.

big--hearted adj. Being generous and kind.

bighorn n. A sheep from the mountainous western part of North America.

bight n. The slack in a rope; a bend in the shoreline.

big-ot n., pl. **-ries** A person who is fanatically devoted to one group, religion, politics, or race. **bigoted** adj., **bigotry** n.

big-wig n. A person of authority.

bike n. A bicycle. **bike** v., **biker** n.

bi-ki-ni n. A scanty, two-piece bathing suit. **bikinied** adj.

bi-lat-er-al adj. Having or relating to two sides. **bilaterally** adv.

bilbo n. A iron bar with sliding shackles to confine prisoners on shipboard.

bile n. A brownish-yellow alkaline liquid that is secreted by the liver. **-iary** adj.

bi-lev-el adj. Divided into 2 floor levels.

bilge n. Lowest inside part of the hull of a ship.

bilge keel n. A projection like a fin along a ship on either side to check rolling.

bi-lin-gual adj. Able to speak two languages with equal ability.

bil-ious adj. Undergoing gastric distress from a sluggish gallbladder or liver.

bilk v. To cheat or swindle.

bill v. Itemized list of fees for services rendered; a document presented containing a formal statement of a case complaint or petition; the beak of a bird. **bill** v., **biller** n.

bil-la-bong n. A blind channel coming from a river; a dry stream bed which fills up after seasonal rains.

bill-board n. A place for displaying advertisements.

bil-let n. An official document which provides a member of the military with board and lodging.

bill-fold n. Pocket-sized wallet for holding money and personal information.

bil-liards n. Game played on a table with

cushioned edges.

bil-lion *n.* A thousand million.

bil-lion-aire *n.* A person whose wealth equals at least one billion dollars.

bill of lading *n.* A form issued by the carrier for promise of delivery of merchandise listed.

Bill of Rights *n.* The first ten amendments to the United States Constitution.

bil-low *n.* Large swell of water or smoke; wave. **billowy** *adj.*

bil-ly club *n.* A short wooden club used for protection or defense.

billy goat *n.* A male goat.

bi-met-al-lism *n.* The use of two metals, gold and silver, as legal tenders. **bimetallist** *n.,* **bimetallistic** *adj.*

bi-month-ly *adj., pl.* **-lies** Occurring every two months.

bin *n.* An enclosed place for storage.

bi-na-ry *adj.* Made of two different components or parts.

bind *v.* To hold with a belt or rope; to bandage; to fasten and enclose pages of a book between covers. **binding** *n.*

bind-er *n.* A notebook for holding paper; payment or written statement legally binding an agreement.

bind-er-y *n., pl.* **-eries** The place where books are taken to be bound.

binge *n.* Uncontrollable self-indulgence; a spree.

bin-go *n.* A game of chance in which a person places markers on numbered cards in accordance with numbers drawn by a caller.

bin-na-cle *n.* A place where a ship's compass is contained.

bin-oc-u-lar *n.*

A device designed for both eyes to bring objects far away into focus. **-ity** *n.,* **binocularly** *adv.*

bi-o-chem-is-try *n.* Chemistry of substances and biological processes.

bi-o-de-grad-a-ble *adj.* Decomposable by natural processes. **biodegradability, biodegradation** *n.*

bi-o-feed-back *n.* The technique of controlling involuntary bodily functions.

bio-geo-chem-is-try *n.* The science which deals with the relation of earth chemicals to plant and animal life.

bi-og-ra-pher *n.* The person who writes a biography.

bi-o-haz-ard *n.* Biological material that threatens humans and or their environment if infective.

biological warfare *n.* Warfare that uses organic biocides or disease-producing microorganisms to destroy crops, livestock, or human life.

bi-ol-o-gy *n.* Science of living organisms and the study of their structure, reproduction, and growth. **biological** *adj.,* **biologist** *n.*

bi-o-med-i-cine *n.* Medicine that has to do with human response to environmental stress.

bi-on-ics *n.* Application of biological principles to the study and design of engineering systems, as electronic systems.

bi-o-phys-ics *n.* The physics of living organisms. **biophysical** *adj.*

bi-op-sy *n., pl.* **biopsies** The examination for the detection of a disease in tissues removed from a living organism.

bi-ot-ic *adj.* Related to specific life conditions or to life itself.

bi-o-tin *n.* Part of the vitamin B complex found in liver, milk, yeast, and egg yolk.

bi-par-ti-san *adj.* Support by two political parties. **bipartisanship** *n.*

bi-ped *n.* An animal have two feet.

bi-plane *n.* A glider or airplane with wings on two levels.

bi-polar *adj.* Having or related to two poles; concerning the earth's North and South Poles.

bi-racial *adj.* Composed of or for members of two races.

birch *n.* A tree providing hard, close-grained wood.

bird *n.* A warm-blooded, egg-laying animal whose body is covered by feathers.

bird bath *n.* A shallow basin for birds to bathe in.

bird-brain *n., Slang* A person who acts in a silly fashion.

bird-ie *n.* A stroke under par in the game of golf; a shuttlecock.

bi-ret-ta *n.* Cap worn by Roman Catholic clergy, square in shape.

birl-ing *n.* A game of skill in which two lumberjacks try to balance on a floating log while spinning the log with their feet.

birth *n.* The beginning of existence. *v.* To bring forth a baby from the womb.

birth certificate *n.* An official record of a person's birth date and place of birth.

birth con-trol *n.* A technique used to control or prevent the number of children born by lessening the chances of conception.

birth-day *n.* The day a person is born and the anniversary of that day.

birth-mark *n.* A blemish or mark on the skin present at birth.

birth-place *n.* The place of birth.

birth-rate *n.* The ratio of the number of births to a given population over a specified period of time.

birth-right *n.* Privilege granted by virtue of birth, especially to the first-born.

birth-stone *n.* A gemstone that represents the month a person was born in.

birth-wort *n.* A herb with aromatic roots used in medicine to aid in childbirth.

bis *adv.* Again; encore.

bis-cuit *n.* Small piece of bread made with baking soda or baking powder; a cookie.

bi-sect *v.* To divide or cut into two equal parts. **bisection** *n.*

bi-sex-u-al *adj.* Sexually relating to both sexes. **bisexuality** *n.,* **-ly** *adv.*

bish-op *n.* A Christian clergyman with high rank. **bishopric** *n.*

Bis-mark *n.* The capital of North Dakota.

bis-muth *n.* A white, crystalline metallic element.

bi-son *n.*

A large buffalo of northwestern America, with a dark-brown coat and short, curved horns.

bisque *n.* A creamy soup made from fish or vegetables; unglazed clay.

bis-sex-file *adj.* Related to the extra day occurring in a leap year.

bis-tort *n.* An American herb with twisted roots used as astringents.

bis-tro *n.*, *pl.* **bistros** A bar or small nightclub. **bistroic** *adj.*

bit *n.* A tiny piece or amount of something; a tool designed for boring or drilling especially, drilling for oil; in computer science, either of two characters, as the binary digits zero and one, of a language that has only two characters; a unit of information; storage capacity, as of a computer memory.

bitch *n.* A female dog; a spiteful woman. *v.* To complain.

bite *v.* To cut, tear, or crush with the teeth. **bite** *n.*, **bitingly** *adv.*

bit-stock *n.* A brace that secures a drilling bit.

bit-ter *adj.* Having a sharp, unpleasant taste. **bitterly** *adv.*, **bitterness** *n.*

bit-tern *n.* A small to medium-sized heron with a booming cry.

bit-ter-root *n.* A Rocky mountain herb with fleshy roots and pink flowers.

bit-ter-sweet *n.* A woody vine whose root, when chewed, has first a bitter, then a sweet taste.

bi-tu-mi-nous coal *n.* Coal that contains a high ratio of bituminous material and burns with a smoky flame.

bi-valve *n.* A mollusk that has a hinged two-part shell, a clam or oyster.

biv-ou-ac *n.* A temporary military camp in the open air. *v.* To camp overnight in the open air.

bi-week-ly *n.* Occurring every two weeks.

bi-year-ly *n.* Occurring every two years.

bi-zarre *adj.* Extremely strange or odd. **bizarrely** *adv.*, **bizarreness** *n.*

bkpg *abbr.* Bookkeeping.

bkpt *abbr.* Bankrupt.

blab *v.* To reveal a secret by indiscreetly talking; to gossip.

blab-ber *v.* To chatter; to blab. **blabbering** *v.*, **blabber** *n.*

blab-ber-mouth *n.*, *Slang* A person who gossips.

black *adj.* Very dark in color; depressing; cheerless; darkness, the absence of light. **blackness** *n*, **blackly** *adv.*

black--and--blue *adj.* Discolored skin caused by bruising.

black-ball *n.* A vote that prevents a person's admission to an organization or club.

black belt *n.* The rank of expert in karate.

black-berry *n.*, *pl.* **berries** A thorny plant with black edible berries that have small seeds.

black-bird *n.* A small bird, the males of the species having mostly all black feathers.

black-board *n.* Hard, slate-like board written on with chalk.

black box *n.* The container that protects the tape recordings of airline pilots from water and fire, normally recoverable in the event of an accident.

black eye *n.* A bruise or discoloration around the eye.

black--eyed Susan *n.* A North American plant with orange-yellow petals and dark brown centers; the official state flower of Maryland.

black-flag *v.* To signal a race car drive to return to the pits; a pirate's flag with scull and crossbones.

black-head *n.* A small mass of dirt that clogs the pore of the skin.

black-jack *n.* A card game in which each player tries to accumulate cards with points higher than that of the dealer, but not more than 21 points.

black-light *n.* Ultraviolet or invisible infrared light.

black-list *n.* A list which contains the names of people who are to be boycotted.

black lung *n.* A disease of the lungs usually contracted by coal miners from prolonged working in the mines.

black magic *n.* Witchcraft.

black-mail *n.* The threat of exposing a past discreditable act or crime; money paid to avoid exposure. **-er** *n.*

black market *n.* The illegal buying or selling of merchandise or items.

Black Muslim *n.* A member of a Black religious organization that supports the establishment of a Black nation.

black-out *n.* The temporary loss of electrical power. *v.* To conceal lights that might be seen by enemy aircraft.

black pepper *n.* A pungent condiment used for seasoning when cooking.

Black Sea *n.* The inland sea between Asia Minor and Europe.

black sheep *n.* A person who is considered a loser by a respectable family.

black-smith *n.* A person who shapes iron with heat and a hammer.

black-snake *n.* A harmless snake very black in color of the United States.

black--tie *adj.* The wearing of semiformal evening wear by men.

black-top *n.* Asphalt, used to pave or surface roads.

black walnut *n.* A walnut of eastern North America.

black widow *n.* A spider that is extremely poisonous.

blad-der *n.* The expandable sac in the pelvis that holds urine.

blade *n.* The cutting part of a knife; the leaf of a plant or a piece of grass; the runner of an ice skate.

blah *n.* A feeling of general dissatisfaction.

blame *v.* To hold someone guilty for something; to find fault. **-less** *adj.*, **blamelessly** *adv.*, **blamelessness** *n.*

blanch *v.* To remove the color from something, as to bleach; to pour scalding hot water over fresh vegetables.

bland *adj.* Lacking taste or style. **blandly** *adv.*, **blandness** *n.*

blan-dish *v.* To coax by flattery.

blank *adj.* Having no markings or writing; empty; confused. **blankly** *adv.*, **blankness** *n.*

blank check *n.* Carte blanche; freedom of action.

blan-ket *n.* A woven covering used on a bed.

blank verse *n.* A poem of lines that have rhythm but do not rhyme.

blare *v.* To make or cause a loud sound.

blar-ney *n.* Talk that is deceptive or nonsense. **blarney** *v.*

blas-pheme *v.* To speak with irrevence. **blasphemously** *adv.*, **-ousness** *n.*

blast *n.* A strong gust of air; the sound produced when a horn is blown. **blasted** *adj.*, **blaster** *n.*

blast-off *n.* The launching of a space ship.

bla-tant *adj.* Unpleasant; offensively loud; shameless. **blatancy** *n.*

blath-er *v.* To talk, but not making sense. **blatherer** *n.*

blaze *n.* A bright burst of fire; a sudden outburst of anger; a trail marker; a white mark on an animal's face.

blaz-er *n.* A jacket with notched collar and patch pockets.

bla-zon *v.* To make known. **blazoner** *n.*

bldg *abbr.* Building.

bleach *v.* To remove the color from a fabric; to become white.

bleach-ers *pl.*, *n.* Seating for spectators in a stadium.

bleak *adj.* Discouraging and depressing; barren; cold; harsh. **bleakness** *n.*, **bleakly** *adv.*, **bleakish** *adj.*

bleary *adj.* Dull from lack of sleep.

bleat *n.* The cry of a sheep or goat.

bleed *v.* To lose blood, as from an injury; to extort money; to mix or allow dyes to run together.

bleed-ing heart *n.* A plant with pink flowers; a person who feels very sympathetic toward the underprivileged.

bleep *n.* A signal with a quick, loud sound.

blem-ish *n.* A flaw or defect.

blench *v.* To turn aside from lack of courage.

blend *v.* To mix together smoothly, to obtain a new substance. **blender** *n.*

bless *v.* To honor or praise; to confer prosperity or well-being.

bless-ed *adj.* Holy; enjoying happiness. **blessedly** *adv.*

bless-ing *n.* A short prayer before a meal.

blight *n.* A disease of plants that can cause complete destruction.

blimp *n.* A large aircraft with a nonrigid gas-filled hull.

blind *adj.* Not having eyesight; something that is not based on facts. *n.* A shelter that conceals hunters.

blind alley *n.* A mistaken direction.

blind date *n.* A date between two strangers that has been arranged by a third party.

blind-ers *pl.*, *n.* Flaps that are attached to the bridle of a horse, restricting side vision.

blind-fold *v.* To cover the eyes with a cloth; to block the vision. **-ed** *adj.*

blind-man's buff *n.* A game in which a person is blindfolded and then tries to catch another player.

blink *v.* To squint; to open and close the eyes quickly; to take a quick glance.

blink-er *n.* A signaling light that displays a message; a light on a car used to indicate turns.

blintz *n.* A very thin pancake rolled and stuffed with cottage cheese or other fillings.

blip *v.* To remove; erase sounds from a recording. *n.* The brief interruption as the result of blipping.

bliss *n.* To have great happiness or joy. **blissful** *adj.*, **blissfully** *adv.*

blis-ter *n.* The swelling of a thin layer of skin that contains a watery liquid. **blister** *v.*, **blisteringly** *adj.*

blithe *adj.* Carefree or casual. **blithery** *adv.*, **blitheness** *n.*

blitz *n.* A sudden attack; an intensive and forceful campaign.

bliz-zard *n.* A severe winter storm characterized by wind and snow.

blk *abbr.* Black, block.

bloat *v.* To swell or puff out. **bloat**, *n.*, **bloated** *adj.*

blob *n.* A small shapeless mass.

bloc *n.* A united group formed for a common action or purpose.

block *n.* A solid piece of matter; a piece of wood where a person condemned to be executed lays his neck; a platform used at an auction to display goods to be auctioned; the act of obstructing or hindering something. **blockage** *n.*, **blocker** *n.*

block-ade *n.* The closure of an area. **blockader** *n.*, **blockade** *v.*

block and tackle *n.* An apparatus with ropes and pulleys used for hoisting and lifting heavy objects.

block head *n.* A strong-willed person.

blond *adj.* A golden or flaxen color.

blonde *adj.* A woman or girl with blond hair.

blood *n.* The red fluid circulated by the heart throughout the body that carries oxygen and nutrients to all parts of the body.

blood bank *n.* A place where blood is processed, typed, and stored for future needs.

blood count n. The determination of the number of white and red corpuscles in a specific amount of blood.

blood-cur-dling adj. Terrifying; horrifying.

blood-hound n. A breed of dogs with a very keen sense of smell.

blood-let-ting n. The act of bleeding a vein as part of medical therapy.

blood-mobile n. A portable blood bank that visits different locations, drawing and collecting blood from donors.

blood poisoning n. The invasion of the blood by toxin produced by bacteria; septicemia.

blood pressure n. A pressure exerted by the blood against the walls of the blood vessels.

blood-shot adj. Redness; irritation especially of the eyes.

blood-stream n. The circulation of blood in the vascular system.

blood-sucker n. An animal that sucks blood.

blood sugar n. The presence of glucose in the blood.

blood vessel n. Any canal in which blood circulates, such as a vein, artery, or capillary.

blood-wort n. A herb with a red coloring matter in the roots.

blood-y adj. Stained with blood; having the characteristics of containing blood. **bloodiness** n., **bloodied** adj.

bloom v. To bear flowers; to flourish; to have a healthy look. **blooming** adj.

bloom-ers n., pl. Loose trousers that are gathered at the knee or just below.

bloop-er n. An embarrassing blunder made in public; in baseball, a high pitch lobbed to the batter.

blos-som n. A flower or a group of flowers of a plant that bears fruit. v. To flourish; to grow. **blossomy** adj.

blot n. A spot or stain. v. To dry with an absorbent material.

blotch n. An area of a person's skin that is discolored. **blotch** v., **blotchily** adj.

blot-ter n. A piece of paper used to blot ink; a book for temporary entries.

blouse n. A loosely fitting shirt or top.

blow v. To move or be in motion because of a current of air. n. A sudden hit with a hand or fist. **blow one's stack** To become angry. **blow hot and cold** To be friendly at one moment and be unfriendly the next. **blower** n.

blow--by--blow adj. Minutely detailed in description.

blow dry v. To dry one's hair with a hand-held hair dryer.

blow-hole n. A hole in the ice that enables aquatic mammals to come up and breathe; the nostril of a whale and other cetaceans.

blow-out n. The sudden deflation of a tire that occurs while driving.

blow-pipe n. A long metal tube used by a glass blower in order to form shapes made from glass.

blow-torch n. A hand-held tool that generates a flame hot enough to melt soft metals.

blow-up n. An enlargement; a photograph; an explosion of a violent temper.

BLT abbr. Bacon, lettuce, and tomato sandwich.

blubber n. The fat removed from whales and other marine mammals. **-y** adj.

blud-geon n. A stick with a loaded end used as a weapon.

blue n. A color the same as the color of a clear sky; the hue that is between violet and green; the color worn by the Union Army during the Civil War.

blue baby n. An infant with a bluish colored skin, caused by inadequate oxygen in the blood.

blue-berry n., pl.-ries A small, edible, seedless berry.

blue-bird n. A small North American songbird related to the robin.

blue blood n. A member of a socially prominent family.

blue cheese n. A cheese ripened by veins of greenish blue mold

blue chip n. A stock selling at a high price because of its past history of steady earnings.

blue-collar adj. Relating to wage earners who wear work clothes to perform their tasks.

blue-crab n. A large edible blue crab found in the Atlantic and Gulf coasts.

blue-fish n. A game fish of the tropical waters of the Atlantic and Indian Oceans.

blue-gill n. A sunfish found in the eastern and central sections of the United States, sought for both eating and sport fishing.

blue-grass n. Folk music of the southern United States, played on guitars and banjos.

blue jay n. A bird having mostly blue colored feathers.

blue-law n. A law regulating work, commerce, etc. on Sundays.

blue-nose n. A person who advocates a rigorous moral code.

blue--pen-cil v. To correct or edit something before it is printed.

blue-print n. A reproduction of technical drawings or plans, using white lines on a blue background.

blue ribbon n. The award given for placing first in a contest.

blues pl., n. A style of jazz from American Negro songs; a state of depression.

blue spruce n. An evergreen tree from the Rocky Mountains.

bluff v. To deceive or mislead; to intimidate by showing more confidence than the facts can support. n. A steep and ridged cliff. **bluffly** adv., **bluffness** n.

blun-der n. An error or mistake caused by ignorance. v. To move clumsily. **blunderer** n., **blundering** v.

blun-der-buss n. A short gun with a flared muzzle.

blunt adj. Frank and abrupt; a dull end

blur *v.* To smudge or smear; to become hazy. **blurringly** *adv.*

blurt *v.* To speak impulsively.

blush *v.* To be embarrassed from modesty or humiliation and to turn red in the face; to feel ashamed. *n.* Make-up used to give color to the cheekbones. **blushful** *adj.*, **blushingly** *adv.*, **blusher** *n.*

blus-ter *n.* A violent and noisy wind in a storm. **bluster** *v.*, **blusterer** *n.*

blvd *abbr.* Boulevard.

B O *abbr.* Box office; back order.

bo-a *n.*

A large nonvenomous snake of the Boidea family which coils around prey and crushes it.

boar *n.*

A male pig; wild pig.

board *n.* A flat piece of sawed lumber; a flat area on which games are played. *v.* To receive lodging, meals or both, usually for pay; to enter a ship, train, or plane. **boarder** *n.*, **boardlike** *adj.*

board-er *n.* A person who lives in someone's house and is provided food as well as lodging.

board game *n.* A game played by moving pieces or objects on a board.

board-ing-house *n.* A house in which meals and lodging are provided.

board-walk *n.* A wooden walkway along a beach.

boast *v.* To brag about one's own accomplishments. **boastfully** *adv.*, **boastful** *adj.*, **boastfulness** *n.*

boat *n.* A small open craft or ship.

boa-tel *n.* A hotel having docks to accommodate people traveling by boat.

boat-er *n.* A straw hat.

boat-swain *n.* Warrant or petty officer in charge of the rigging, anchors, and crew of a ship.

bob *v.* To cause to move up and down in a quick, jerky movement.

bob-bin *n.* A spool that holds thread in a sewing machine.

bob-by *n.* An English police officer.

bob-by socks *pl.*, *n.* An ankle sock, usually worn by teenaged girls.

bob-cat *n.* A wildcat of North America, with reddish-brown fur, small ears, and a short tail.

bo-beche *n.* A glass collar on a candlestick to catch the wax drippings from the candle.

bob-o-link *n.* An American song bird, the male has black, yellowish and white feathers.

bob-sled *n.* Racing sled which has steering controls on the front runners. **bobsled** *v.*, **bobsledder** *n.*

bob-white *n.* A game bird of the eastern United States.

bo-cac-cio *n.* A large rockfish found principally off the Pacific coast.

bock *n.* A dark rich beer of Germany.

bo-de-ga *n.* A wineshop and grocery store.

bode *v.* To foretell by omen or sign.

bod-ice *n.* The piece of a dress that extends from the shoulder to the waist.

bod-kin *n.* A small instrument with a sharp point for making holes in fabric.

bod-y *n.* The main part of something; the physical part of a person.

bod-y build-ing *n.* The development and toning of the body through diet and exercise.

body-guard *n.* A person hired to protect another person.

body stocking *n.* A sheer one-piece garment for the torso.

body-surf *v.* To ride on a wave without a surfboard. **bodysurfer** *n.*

bog *n.* A poorly drained spongy area.

bo-gey *n.* In golf, one stroke over par for a hole. **bogeyed** *v.*

bo-gey-man *n.* An imaginary figure used in threatening children.

bog-gle *v.* To pull away from with astonishment. **boggle** *n.*

Bo-go-ta *n.* The capital of Colombia.

bo-gus *adj.* Something that is counterfeit; worthless in value.

bo-hea *n.* A black tea from China.

Bo-he-mi-an *n.* An inhabitant or native of Bohemia.

bo-he-mi-an *n.* A person whose life-style is unconventional.

boil *v.* To raise the temperature of water or other liquid until it bubbles; to evaporate; reduce in size by boiling. A very painful, pus-filled swollen area of the skin caused by bacteria in the skin.

boil-er *n.* A vessel that contains water and is heated for power.

Boi-se *n.* The capital of Idaho.

bois-ter-ous *adj.* Violent, rough and stormy; undisciplined. **boisterously** *adv.*, **boisterousness** *n.*

bo-la *n.* A weapon with two or more stones or balls at the end of a cord, which is hurled in the air to entangle an animal.

bold *adj.* Courageous; showing courage; distinct and clear. **-ly** *adv.*, **-ness** *n.*

bold-face *n.* A style of printing type with heavy thick lines.

bole *n.* A tree trunk.

bo-le-ro *n.* A short jacket without sleeves, worn open in the front.

boll *n.* A rounded capsule that contains seeds, as from the cotton plant.

bol-lard *n.* A post of wood on a wharf to fasten mooring lines.

boll wee-vil *n.* A small beetle whose larvae damage cotton bolls.

bo-lo-gna *n.* A seasoned, smoked sausage.

bo-lo tie *n.* A tie made of cord and fastened with an ornamental clasp.

bol-ster *n.* A long, round pillow. *v.* To provide support.

bolt *n.* A threaded metal pin designed with a head at one end and a removable nut at the other; a thunderbolt; a large roll of material. *v.* To run or move suddenly.

bomb *n.* A weapon that is detonated upon impact releasing destructive material as gas or smoke. *Slang* A complete and total failure.

bom-bard *v.* To attack repeatedly with missiles or bombs.
bombarder *n.*, bombardment *n.*

bom-bar-dier *n.* A crew member who releases the bombs from a military aircraft.

bom-bast *n.* Very ornate speech.
bombastic *adj.*, bombastically *adv.*

bom-ba-zine *n.* Silk or cotton fabric woven with diagonal ribbing.

bombe *n.* A frozen dessert with one mixture molded and filled with another.

bombed *adj.*, *Slang* Drunk.

bomber *n.* A military aircraft that carries and drops bombs.

bo-na fide *adj.* Performed in good faith; genuine; authentic.

bo-nan-za *n.* A profitable pocket or vein of ore; great prosperity.

bon-bon *n.* Chocolate or fondant candy with a creamy, fruity, or nutty center.

bond *n.* Something that fastens or binds together; a duty or binding agreement; an insurance agreement in which the agency guarantees to pay the employer in the event an employee is accused of causing financial loss. bonded *adj.*

bond-age *n.* Slavery; servitude.

bond-er-ize *v.* To coat with a solution for protection against corrosion.

bond ser-vant *n.* One who agrees to work without pay.

bonds-man *n.* One who agrees to provide bond for someone else.

bone *n.*

The calcified connecting tissue of the skeleton. bone *v.*

bone--dry *adj.* Completely without water.

bone-head *n.*, *Slang* A stupid person. boneheaded *adj.*

bon-er *n.*, *Slang* A mistake or blunder.

bon-fire *n.* An open outdoor fire.

bon-go *n.* A pair of small drums played with the hands.

bon-i-face *n.* The proprietor a hotel, inn, etc.

bo-ni-to *n.* A game fish related to the tuna.

bon-kers *adj.*, *Slang* Acting in a crazy fashion.

Bonn *n.* Capital of West Germany.

bon-net *n.* A woman's hat that ties under the chin.

bon-ny *adj.* Attractive or pleasing; pretty.

bon-sai *n.* A small ornamental shrub grown in a shallow pot.

bo-nus *n.*, *pl.* -nuses Something that is given over and above what is expected.

bon voyage *n.* A farewell wish for a traveler to have a pleasant and safe journey.

boo *n.* Verbal expression showing disapproval or contempt.

boo--boo *n.*, *Slang* A mistake, blunder, or minor injury.

boo-by *n.* A small fish-eating seabird found in the tropical seas.

booby prize *n.* A prize given for the worst performance.

boog-ie *v.*, *Slang* To dance especially to rock and roll music.

book *n.* A group of pages fastened along the left side and bound between a protective cover; literary work that is written or printed.

book-case *n.* A piece of furniture with shelving for storing books.

book-end *n.* A support for holding a row of books upright.

book-ie *n.*, *Slang* A bookmaker.

book-ing *n.* A scheduled engagement.

book-keep-ing *n.* The business of recording the accounts and transactions of a business. bookkeeper *n.*

book-mak-er *n.* A person that publishes, prints, and binds books; a person who accepts and pays off bets.

book-mark *n.* Something inserted in a book to mark where to begin.

book-mo-bile *n.* A vehicle equipped for use as a mobile book-lending service.

book-plate *n.* A plate attached inside a book, giving the owner's name.

book-report *n.* A written or oral review of a book, given after reading the book. Various insect larvae that feed on the paste and binding of books.

book-mo-bile *n.* A portable library, usually contained in a truck, that travels from one area to another.

book review *n.* A critical review of a book that is usually written.

book-sell-er *n.* A person who specializes in selling books.

book shelf *n.* An open shelf area used to display and store books.

book-store *n.* A place of business that sells reading material especially books.

book value *n.* The value of something as shown in books of the same business.

book-worm *n.* One who spends a lot of time reading or studying.

boom *n.* A deep, resonant sound; a long pole extending to the top of a derrick giving support to guide lifted objects. *v.* To cause to flourish or grow swiftly.

boo-mer-ang *n.* A curved, flat missile that can be thrown so that it returns to the thrower. boomerang *v.*

boom town *n.* *Slang* A town with sudden prosperity or growth.

boon *n.* Something that is pleasant or beneficial; a blessing; favor.

boon-docks *pl.*, *n. Slang* Back country.

boon-dog-gle *n.* A useless activity; a waste of time.

Boone, Daniel *n.* The American pioneer who explored and settled in Kentucky.

boor *n.* A person with clumsy manners and little refinement; rude person. **boorishly** *adv.*, **boorishness** *n.*

boost *v.* To increase; to raise or lift by pushing up from below. *n.* An increase in something.

boost-er *n.* A promoter; a supplementary or additional dose of vaccine.

boost-er cable *n.* Electric cables used to jump start a battery from another power source.

boot *n.*

A protective covering for the foot; any protective sheath or covering. In computer science, to load a computer with an operating system or other software.

boot-black *n.* A person who polishes shoes for a living.

boot camp *n.* A military training camp for new recruits.

boo-tee *n.* A soft, knitted sock for a baby.

booth *n.* A small enclosed compartment or area; display area at trade shows for displaying merchandise for sale; an area in a restaurant with a table and benches.

boot-jack *n.* A device shaped like a V, used to pull boots off.

boot-leg *v.*, *Slang.* To sell, make, or transport liquor illegally.

booze *n.*, *Slang.* An alcoholic drink.

bor *abbr.* Borough.

bo-ra *n.* A cold wind of the Adriatic.

bo-rax *n.* A crystalline compound used in manufacturing detergents and pharmaceuticals.

bor-der *n.* A surrounding margin or edge; a political or geographic boundary.

bor-der-land *n.* Land near or on a border; an indeterminate situation.

bor-der-line *n.* A line or mark indicating a border.

bore *v.* To make a hole through or in something using a drill; to become tired, repetitious, or dull. **boredom** *n.*

bo-re-al *adj.* Located in or of the north.

bor-er *n.* A tool used to bore holes.

bo-ric acid *n.* A colorless or white mixture that is used as a preservative and as a weak antiseptic.

born *adj.* Brought into life or being; having an innate talent.

born-again *adj.* Having accepted Jesus Christ as a person's personal savior.

Bor-ne-o *n.* An island in the western Pacific Ocean divided by Indonesia, Brunei, and Malaysia.

bo-ron *n.* A soft, brown nonmetallic element used in nuclear reactor control elements, abrasives, and flares.

bor-ough *n.* A self-governing incorporated town, found in some United States cities; an incorporated British town that sends one or more representatives to Parliament.

bor-row *v.* To receive money with the intentions of returning it; to use another idea as one's own.

borscht *n.* Hot or cold beet soup.

borscht circuit *n.* The nightclubs associated with the summer resorts in the Catskills.

bor-stal *n.* An institution for delinquent boys and girls.

bort *n.* Imperfect diamond fragments used as an abrasive.

bor-zoi *n.* A breed of longhaired dogs of the greyhound family.

BOS *abbr.* Basic Operating System; the program that handles the routine functions of computer operations, such as accessing the disk drive, displaying information on the screen, handling input and output, etc.

bosh *n.* Foolish talk.

bos-ky *adj.* Thickly covered with trees or shrubs; related to a wooded area.

bos-om *n.* The female's breasts; the human chest; the heart or center of something. **bosomy** *adj.*

Bos-po-rus *n.* The strait which link the Marmara and Black Seas.

boss *n.* An employer or supervisor for whom one works; a projecting block used in architecture. *v.* To command; to supervise. **bossiness** *n.*, **bossy** *adj.*

bos-sa no-va *n.* A Brazilian dance resembling the samba.

bossy *adj.* Tending to be domineering.

Bos-ton *n.* Capital of Massachusetts.

Boston terrier *n.* A breed of small smooth-coated terriers.

bot *abbr.* Botany; botanical; botanist.

bo-tan-i-cal *adj.* Relating to plants.

bot-a-nize *v.* To collect and study plants while on a field trip.

bot-a-ny *n.* The science of plants. **botanical** *adj.*, **botanist** *n.*

botch *v.* To ruin something by clumsiness; to repair clumsily. **botcher** *n.*

both *adj.* Two in conjunction with one another.

both-er *v.* To pester, harass, or irritate; to be concerned about something. **bothersome** *adj.*, **bothering** *v.*

bot-tle *n.* A receptacle, usually made of glass, with a narrow neck and a top that can be capped or corked; formula or milk that is fed to a baby.

bottle gourd *n.* A type of gourd.

bot-tle-neck *n.* A narrow, obstructed passage, highway, road, etc.; a hindrance to progress or production.

bot-tle-nosed dolphin *n.* A stout-bodied whale having a prominent beak and dorsal fin.

bot-tom *n.* The lowest or deepest part of anything; the base; underside; the last; the land below a body of water. *Informal* The buttocks. **bottomless** *adj.*, **bottomed** *adj.*, **bottomer** *n.*

bottom less *adj.* Extremely deep; seemingly without a bottom. **bottomlessness** *n.*, **bottomlessly** *adv.*

bottom line *n.* The end result; lowest line of a financial statement, showing net loss or gain.

bot-tom-most *adj.* Being at the very bottom.

bot-u-lism *n.* Food poisoning, often fatal, caused by bacteria that grows in improperly prepared food.

bou-cle *n.* An uneven yarn which forms loops at different intervals.

bouf-fant *adj.* Full; puffed out.

bou-gain-vil-lea *n.* A flower of the 4 o'clock family with purple or red floral flowers.

bough *n.* The large branch of a tree.

bou-gie *n.* A candle.

bouil-la-baisse *n.* A fish stew using at least 2 kinds of fish which is highly seasoned.

bouil-lon *n.* A clear broth made from meat.

bouillon cube *n.* A compressed cube of seasoned meat extract.

boul-der *n.* A large round rock. **bouldered, bouldery** *adj.*

boul-e-vard *n.* A broad city street lined with trees.

bou-le-ver-se-ment *n.* Violent disorder.

bounce *v.* To rebound or cause to rebound; to leap or spring suddenly; to be returned by a bank as being worthless or having no value. **-ed** *v.*

bounc-er *n.* A person who removes disorderly people from a public place.

bounc-ing *adj.* Healthy; vigorous; robust; lively and spirited.

bound *n.* A leap or bounce. *v.* To limit; to be tied.

bound-a-ry *n., pl.* **-ries** A limit or border.

bound-en *adj.* Under an obligation or agreement.

bound-er *n.* A vulgar person.

bound-less *adj.* Without limits. **boundlessly** *adv.*, **boundlessness** *n.*

boun-te-ous *adj.* Plentiful or generous; giving freely. **-ly** *adv.*, **-ness** *n.*

boun-ti-ful *adj.* Abundant; plentiful. **bountifully** *adv.*

bounty *n.* Generosity; an inducement or reward given for the return of something; a good harvest.

bounty hunter *n.* A person who hunts and captures outlaws when a reward is offered.

bou-quet *n.* A group of cut flowers; the aroma of wine.

bour-bon *n.* Whiskey distilled from fermented corn mash.

bour-geois *pl., n.* A member of the middle class. **bourgeois** *adj.*

bout *n.* A contest or match; the length of time spent in a certain way.

bou-tique *n.* A small retail shop that sells specialized gifts, accessories, and fashionable clothes.

bou-ton-niere *n.* A flower worn in the buttonhole of a man's jacket.

bou-zou-ki *n.* A long-necked stringed instrument resembling a mandolin.

bo-vine *adj.* Of or relating to an ox or cow. **bovinely** *adv.*

bow *n.* The front section of a boat or ship; bending of the head or waist to express a greeting or courtesy; a weapon made from a curved stave and strung taut to launch arrows; a rod strung with horsehair, used for playing stringed instruments.

bowd-ler-ize *v.* To expurgate. **-ation** *n.*

bow-el *n.* The digestive tract located below the stomach; the intestines.

bow-er *n.* A shelter constructed from tree boughs; an anchor.

bow-er-bird *n.* A bird of the Australian region of which, the male builds a passage with twigs and branches to attract the female.

bow-ery *n.* A district in New York City.

bow-ie knife *n.*

A single-edged thick-bladed hunting knife.

bowl *n.* A hemispherical container for food or liquids; a bowl-shaped part, as of a spoon or ladle; a bowl-shaped stadium. *v.* To participate in the game of bowling. **bowled** *adj.*, **bowlful** *n.*

bow-leg *n.* An outward curvature of the leg at the knee.

bowl-er *n.* A person that bowls.

bow-line *n.* A rope to keep the edge of a square sail taut.

bowl-ing *n.* A game in which a person rolls a ball down a wooden alley in order to knock down a triangular group of ten wooden bowling pins.

bowling alley *n.* A building containing alleys for the game of bowling.

bow-man *n.* An oarsman in the front of a boat.

bowl over *v.* To astound; to be astounded.

bow saw *n.* A saw with a narrow blade in a bow-shaped frame.

bow-sprit *n.* A spar that projects forward from the stem of a ship.

box *n.* A small container or chest, usually with a lid; a special area in a theater that holds a small group of people; a shrub or evergreen with leaves and hard wood that is yellow in color. *v.* To fight with the fists.

box-car *n.* An enclosed railway car used for the transportation of freight.

box elder *n.* A North American maple.

box-er *n.* A person who boxes professionally; a German breed of dog with short hair, brownish coat, and a square nose or muzzle.

box-ing *n.* A sport in which two opponents hit each other using padded gloves on their hands, forming fists.

boxing glove *n.* A pair of leather gloves heavily padded on the back used in the sport of boxing.

box kite *n.* A tailless kite with open-ended boxes at each end.

box office *n.* An office where theatre tickets are purchased.

box social *n.* An affair at which box lunches are auctioned off to raise money.

box spring *n.* A cloth-covered frame which supports the mattress.

box turtle *n.* A North American land tortoise.

box-wood *n.* A plant with very heavy tough hard wood.

boy *n.* A male youth or child. -hood *n.*, **boyish** *adj.*, **boyishly** *adv.*

boy-cott *v.* To abstain from dealing with, buying, or using as a means of protest.

boy-friend *n.* A male companion.

Boy Scout *n.* A boy who belongs to a worldwide organization that emphasizes citizenship training and character development.

boy-sen-ber-ry *n.* A trailing hybrid which bears fruit developed by crossing blackberries and raspberries.

B P *abbr.* Bills payable.

B P O E *abbr.* Benevolent and Protective Order of Elks.

Br *abbr.* Britain.

B R *abbr.* Bills receivable.

bra *n.* Brassiere.

brace *n.* A device that supports or steadies something. **brace** *v.*

brace-let *n.* An ornamental band for the wrist.

bra-ce-ro *n.* A Mexican laborer.

brack-en *n.* A large species of fern with tough stems and finely divided fronds.

brack-et *n.* A support attached to a vertical surface that projects in order to hold a shelf or other weight. *v.* To enclose a word in brackets ( ).

brack-ish *adj.* Containing salt; distasteful. **brackishness** *n.*

bract *n.* A leaf-like plant below a flower cluster or flower. **bracteate**, **bracteal**, **bracted**, **bracteolate** *adj.*

brad *n.* A nail that tapers to a small head. **bradding** *v.*

brad-awl *n.* A tool used to make holes for brads or screws.

brag *v.* To assert or talk boastfully. **bragger** *n.*, **braggy** *adj.*

brag-ga-do-ci-o *n.*, *pl.* A cockiness or arrogant manner; empty bragging.

brag-gart *n.* A person who brags.

Brah-ma *n.* A member of the Hindu group that created the universe.

Brah-man-ism *n.* The religious beliefs and practices of ancient India; strict Hinduism.

braid *v.* To interweave three or more strands of something; to plait. **braider**, **braiding** *n.*, **braided** *adj.*

braille *n.* A system of printing for the blind, consisting of six dots, two across and four directly under the first two. Numbers and letters are represented by raising certain dots in each group of six.

brain *n.* The large mass of nerve tissue enclosed in the cranium, responsible for the interpretation of sensory impulses, control of the body, and coordination; the center of thought and emotion in the body. **braininess** *n.*, **brainless** *adj.*, **brainlessness** *n.*, **brainy** *adj.*

brain-child *n.* A product of one's imagination.

brain-storm *n.* A sudden idea or inspiration.

brain-wash-ing *n.* Intensive indoctrination to radically change a person's convictions. **brainwash** *v.*, **brainwasher**, **brainwash** *n.*

brain wave *n.* The rhythmic fluctuation of voltage between parts of the brain.

braise *v.* To cook by first browning in a small amount of fat, adding a liquid such as water, and then simmering in a covered container. **braising** *v.*

brake *n.* A device designed to stop or slow the motion of a vehicle or machine. **brake** *v.*, **brakeless** *n.*

brake fluid *n.* The liquid contained in hydraulic brake cylinders.

brake-man *n.* A train crew member who assists the conductor; the man who operates the brake on a bobsled.

bram-ble *n.* A prickly shrub or plant such as the raspberry or blackberry bush.

bran *n.* The husk of cereal grains that is separated from the flour.

branch *n.* An extension from the main trunk of a tree. *v.* To divide into different subdivisions. **branched** *adj.*, **branchless** *n.*

brand *n.* A trademark or label that names a product; a mark of disgrace or shame; a piece of charred or burning wood; a mark made by a hot iron to show ownership. **brander** *n.*

bran-dish *v.* To wave or flourish a weapon.

brand-ling *n.* A small earthworm.

brand name *n.* A company's trademark.

brand-new *adj.* Unused and new.

bran-dy *n.*, *pl.* -dies An alcoholic liquor distilled from fermented fruit juices or wine. **brandied** *adj.*, **brandy** *v.*

brant *n.* A wild goose which breeds in the Arctic but migrates southward.

brash *adj.* Hasty, rash, and unthinking; insolent; impudent.

brass *n.* An alloy of zinc, copper and other metals in lesser amounts. *Slang.* A high-ranking officer in the military.

bras-sard *n.* A piece of armor to protect the arm.

brass band *n.* A band with brass and percussion instruments only.

bras-siere *n.* A woman's undergarment with cups to support the breasts.

brass tacks *pl.*, *n.* The details of immediate, practical importance.

brat *n.* An ill-mannered child. **brattiness** *n.*, **brattish** *adj.*

brat-wurst *n.* A fresh pork sausage.

braun-schweig-er *n.* Smoked liverwurst.

bra-va-do *n.* A false showing of bravery.

brave *adj.* Having or displaying courage. *n.* An American Indian warrior.

brav-er-y *n.* The quality of or state of being brave.

bra-vo *Interj.* Expressing approval.

bra-vu-ra *n.* A musical passage which takes technical skill.

brawl *n.* A noisy argument or fight. **brawl** *v.*, **brawler** *n.*

brawn *n.* Well-developed and solid muscles. **brawniness** *n.*, **brawny** *adj.*

bray v. To make a loud cry like a donkey.

braze v. To solder using a nonferrous alloy that melts at a lower temperature than that of the metals being joined together.

bra-zen adj. Made of brass; shameless or impudent.

bra-zier n. A person who works with brass; a metal pan that holds burning charcoal or coals.

Bra-zil n. A large South American country.

breach n. Ruptured, broken, or torn condition or area; a break in friendly relations. v. To break the law or obligation.

breach of promise n. The violation of a promise.

bread n. A leavened food made from a flour or meal mixture and baked. Slang Money. v. To cover with bread crumbs before cooking.

bread--and--butter adj. Being the basis of one's livelihood.

bread-basket adj. A major grain producing region of the United States. Slang The stomach.

bread-board n. A board used for cutting bread; a board on which electric or electronic circuit diagrams may be laid out.

bread-fruit n. A tropical tree with lobed leaves and edible fruit.

bread-stuff n. Bread; a cereal product; meal, grain, or flour.

breadth n. The distance or measurement from side to side; width.

bread-win-ner n. The one whose pay supports a household.

break v. To separate into parts with violence or suddenness; to collapse or give way; to change suddenly. break a leg To be a success in the theatre. break even To make neither a profit or loss in business. break the ice To begin a conversation first. break ground To start excavating. Informal A stroke of good luck.

break-age n. Things that are broken.

break-down n. Failure to function; a mental or nervous collapse.

break-er n. A wave that breaks into foam.

break-fast n. The first meal of the day.

break-through n. A sudden advance in knowledge or technique; a thrust that goes farther than anticipated or expected.

break-water n. A barrier that protects a beach from the full force of waves.

breast n. The milk-producing glandular organs on a woman's chest; the area of the body from the neck to the abdomen.

breast-bone n. The sternum.

breast-plate n. A metal plate worn on the chest for protection.

breast-stroke n. A stroke in swimming in which a person lies face down and extends the arms in front of the head, drawing the knees forward and outward and then sweeping the arms back while kicking outward and backward.

breath n. The air inhaled and exhaled in breathing; a very slight whisper, fragrance, or breeze.

breathe v. To draw air into and expel from the lungs; to take a short rest.

breather n. A small opening in an otherwise air-tight enclosure; one that breathes.

breath-less adj. Gasping for breath. **breathlessly** adv., **breathlessness** n.

breath-tak-ing adj. Astonishing; awesome. **breathtakingly** adv.

breech n., pl. -es The buttocks; the hind end of the body; the part of a gun or firearm located at the rear of the bore. plural Trousers that fit tightly around the knees.

breech-es buoy n. A canvas seat used to haul persons from one ship to another or in rescue operations from ship to shore.

breed v. The genetic strain of domestic animals, developed and maintained by mankind. **breeding** n.

breeze n. A slight gentle wind; something that is accomplished with very little effort. **breezy** adj.

breeze-way n. A roofed connection between two buildings or walls.

Bre-men n. A city in West Germany.

Bret-on n. A native of Brittany.

breve n. The curved mark over a vowel to indicate a short or unstressed syllable.

bre-vet n. A commission given a military officer with a higher rank than which he is being paid for.

bre-vi-ar-y n. A book that contains prayers and psalms for the canonical hours.

brev-i-ty n., pl. -ties A brief duration; conciseness.

brew v. To make beer from malt and hops by boiling, infusion, and fermentation. **brewer** n.

brew-er-y n. A building or plant where beer or ale is brewed.

bri-ard n. A breed of large strong black dogs of France.

bribe v. To influence or induce by giving a token or anything of value for a service. **bribe** n., **bribable** adj.

brib-ery n. The practice of giving or receiving a bribe.

bric--a--brac n. A collection of small objects.

brick n. A molded block of baked clay, usually rectangular in shape.

brick-bat n. A piece of a brick used as a weapon when thrown as a missile.

brick-lay-er n. A person who lays bricks as a profession.

bri-dal adj. Relating to a bride or a nuptial ceremony.

bridal wreath n. A flower grown for its small white flowers used in bouquets.

bride n. A women just married or about to be married.

bride-groom n. A man just married or about to be married.

brides-maid *n.* A woman who attends a bride at her wedding.

bridge *n.* A structure that provides passage over a depression or obstacle; a card game for four players.

bridge-head *n.* A military position secured by advance troops in enemy territory, giving protection for the main attack force.

bridge-work *n.* The construction of dental work.

bri-dle *n.* A harness used to restrain or guide a horse. *v.* To restrain or control. **bridling** *v.,* **bridler** *n.*

brief *n.* A concise, formal statement of a client's case. *adj.* Short in duration. *v.* To summarize or inform in a short statement. **briefly** *adv.,* **briefness** *n.*

brief-case *n.* A small, flat, flexible case for holding and carrying papers or books.

brief-ing *n.* The act of giving essential information.

brief-ly *adv.* For a very short span of time.

bri-er *n.* A woody, thorny, or prickly plant. **briery** *adj.*

bri-er-root *n.* A root which is used to make tobacco pipes.

brig *n.* A prison on a ship; a twin-masted, square-rigged sailing ship.

bri-gade *n.* A military unit organized for a specific purpose.

brig-a-dier *n.* An officer in the British army.

brigadier general *n.* A commissioned officer in the armed forces who ranks above a colonel.

brig-and *n.* A person who lives as a robber; a bandit.

brig-an-dine *n.* A medieval body armor.

brig-an-tine *n.* A square-rigged two-masted ship.

bright *adj.* Brilliant in color; vivid; shining and emitting or reflecting light; happy; cheerful; lovely. **brightness** *n.*

bright-en *v.* To make things brighter. **brightener** *n.,* **brightened** *v.*

bril-liant *adj.* Very bright and shiny; sparkling; radiant; extraordinarily intelligent. **brilliantly** *adv.,* **-ness** *n.*

bril-lian-tine *n.* A light woven fabric similar to alpaca.

brim *n.* The edge or rim of a cup. **brimmed** *v.,* **brimless** *adj.*

brim-ful *adj.* Completely full.

brim-stone *n.* Sulfur.

brin-dle *adj.* Having dark streaks or flecks on a gray or tawny background.

brine *n.* Water saturated with salt; the water contained in the oceans and seas.

bring *v.* To carry with oneself to a certain place; to cause, act, or move in a special direction.

brink *n.* The upper edge or margin of a very steep slope.

bri-oche *n.* A roll made from flour, eggs, butter, and yeast.

bri-o-lette *n.* A pear-shaped diamond cut into facets.

bri-quette *n.* A small brick-shaped piece of charcoal.

brisk *adj.* Moving or acting quickly; being sharp in tone or manner; energetic, invigorating or fresh. **briskly** *adv.,* **briskness** *n.*

bris-ket *n.* The meat from the lower chest or breast of an animal.

bris-ling *n.* A small fish that is processed like a sardine.

bris-tle *n.* Short, stiff, coarse hair. *v.* To react in angry defiance. **bristly** *adj.*

britch-es *pl., n.* Trousers; breeches.

Brit-ish *n.* The people and the language spoken in Great Britain.

brit-tle *adj.* Very easy to break; fragile.

bro *abbr.* Brother.

broach *n.* A tapered and serrated tool used for enlarging and shaping a hole. **broach** *v.*

broad *adj.* Covering a wide area; from side to side; clear; bright. **broadly** *adv.,* **broadness** *n.*

broad-cast *v.* To transmit a program by television; to make widely known; to scatter or sow seeds. **broadcaster** *n.*

broad-cloth *n.* A textured woolen cloth with a lustrous finish.

broad-en *v.* To become or make broad or broader.

broad-loom *adj.* Woven on a wide loom. *n.* Carpet woven in this manner.

broad-mind-ed *adj.* Tolerant of varied views; liberal. **broadmindedness** *n.*

broad-side *n.* The side of a ship that is above the water line; a sheet of paper printed on both sides and then folded.

Broad-way *n.* The New York theatre district; a famous street in New York.

bro-cade *n.* A silk fabric with raised patterns in silver and gold.

broc-co-li *n.*

A green vegetable from the cauliflower family, eaten before the small buds open.

bro-chure *n.* A booklet or pamphlet.

brock-et *n.* A small deer of South America.

bro-gan *n.* A sturdy oxford shoe.

brogue *n.* A strong regional accent; a heavy shoe with a hobnail sole.

broil *v.* To cook by exposure to direct radiant heat.

broil-er *n.* A device, usually a part of a stove, that is used for broiling meat; a young chicken.

broke *adj.* Penniless; completely without money.

bro-ken *adj.* Separated violently into parts. **brokenly** *adj.,* **brokenness** *n.*

bro-ken-hearted *adj.* Overcome by despair or grief.

bro-ken home *n.* A family situation in which the parents are not living together.

bro-ker *n.* A person who acts as a negotiating agent for contracts, sales, or purchases in return for payment.

bro-ker-age *n.* The establishment of a broker.

brome-grass *n.* A type of tall grasses having sagging spikelets.

bro-me-li-ad *n.* The family of tropical American plants which includes the pineapple.

bro-mide *n.* A compound of bromine with other elements; a sedative; a commonplace idea or notion.

bro-mine *n.* A nonmetallic element of a deep red, toxic liquid that gives off a disagreeable odor.

bro-mo *n.* A effervescent mixture used as a sedative or a headache remedy.

bron-chi-al *adj.* Pertaining to the bronchi or their extensions.

bron-chi-tis *n.* An acute inflammation of the bronchial tubes.

bron-cho-scope *n.* A tubular instrument which is illuminated for inspecting the bronchi.

bron-chus *n.* Either of two main branches of the trachea that lead directly to the lungs.

bron-co *n.* A wild horse of western North America.

bron-co-bust-er *n.* The man who breaks wild horses.

bron-to-saur *n.* A very large dinosaur.

bronze *n.* An alloy of tin, copper, and zinc; moderate olive brown to yellow in color. **bronze** *v.*, **bronze** *adj.*

Bronze Age *n.* Human culture between the Iron Age and the Stone Age.

brooch *n.* A large decorative pin.

brood *n.* The young of an animal; a family of young. *v.* To produce by incubation; to hatch; to think about at length.

brood-er *n.* An enclosed heated area for raising young chickens.

brook *n.* A small fresh-water stream that contains many rocks.

brook trout *n.* A cold-water fish of eastern North America.

broom *n.* A long-handled implement used for sweeping; a shrub with small leaves and yellow flowers.

bros *abbr.* Brothers.

broth *n.* The liquid in which fish, meat, or vegetables have been cooked; also called stock.

broth-el *n.* A house of prostitution; whorehouse.

broth-er *n.* A male who shares the same parents as another person.

brotherly *adj.*, **brotherliness** *n.*

brother-hood *n.* The state of being brothers; one that is related to another for a particular purpose.

brother--in--law *n.* The brother of one's spouse; the husband of one's sister; the husband of one's spouse's sister.

broug-ham *n.* A vehicle without a cover over the driver's seat.

brought *v.* The past tense of bring.

brow *n.* The ridge above the eye where the eyebrow grows.

brow-beat *v.* To bully; dominate; intimidate. **browbeating** *v.*

brown *n.* A color between yellow and red; a dark or tanned complexion.

brown bag-ging *n.* The practice of bringing one's lunch to work.

Brown Betty *n.* A pudding baked with apples, spices, and bread crumbs.

brown bread *n.* Bread made from whole wheat flour.

brown-ie *n.* A good-natured elf believed to perform helpful services; a square, chewy piece of chocolate cake.

Brownie A member of the Girl Scouts from 7 to 9 years of age.

brown-out *n.* An interruption of electrical power.

brown-stone *n.* A reddish-brown sandstone used for construction; a building faced with brownstone.

brown study *n.* A state of being total absorbed.

brown sugar *n.* Sugar with crystals covered by a film or refined dark syrup.

browse *v.* To look over something in a leisurely and casual way.

bruise *n.* An injury that ruptures small blood vessels and discolors the skin without breaking it.

brum-by *n.* An unbroken horse.

brum-ma-gem *n.* Something inferior.

brunch *n.* A combination of a late breakfast and an early lunch.

bru-net *or* **bru-nette** A person with dark brown hair.

Bruns-wick stew *n.* A stew with vegetables and meats.

brunt *n.* The principal shock, or force.

brush *n.* A device consisting of bristles used for applying paint, scrubbing or grooming the hair; a very dense growth of bushes. *v.* To touch lightly in passing.

brush-off *Slang* To dismiss abruptly.

brush up *v.* To refresh one's memory or skills.

brusque *adj.* Being blunt or short in manner or speech; harsh.

brusquely *adv.*, **brusqueness** *n.*

Brussels lace *n.* A fine bobbin or needlepoint lace with a floral design.

brussels sprout *n.*

The small head of a green vegetable, resembling the cabbage.

bru-tal *adj.* Very harsh or cruel treatment. **brutality** *n.*, **-ly** *adv.*, **-ize** *v.*

bru-tal-i-ty *n.* A brutal course of action.

brute *n.* A person characterized by physical power rather than intelligence; a person who behaves like an animal. **brutish** *adj.*

brux-ism *n.* The unconscious grinding of the teeth during sleep.

bry-o-ny *n.* A vine of the gourd family having large leaves and fruit.

bryo-phyte *n.* A species of nonflowering plant which includes the liverworts.

BS *abbr.* Bachelor of Science

BSA *abbr.* Boy Scouts of America.

bsh *abbr.* bushel.

bsk *abbr.* basket.

bu *abbr.* bureau.

bub-ble *n.* A small round object, usually hollow; a small body of gas contained in a liquid. *v.* To produce bubbles.

bubble gum *n.* A chewing gum that can be blown into bubbles.

bub-bler *n.* A drinking fountain where water bubbles upward.

bub-bly *adj.* Something full of bubbles. *Slang* Champagne.

bu-bo *n.* Inflammatory swelling of the lymphatic glands, especially in the area of the groin or armpits.

bu-bon-ic plague *n.* The contagious and normally fatal disease that is transmitted by fleas from infected rats, characterized by fever, diarrhea, chills, and vomiting.

buc-ca-neer *n.* A pirate preying on Spanish ships in the West Indies in the 17th century; an unscrupulous adventurer.

buck *n.* The adult male deer; the lowest grade in the military category. *v.* To throw a rider; to oppose the system. *Slang* A dollar.

buck-board *n.* An open carriage with four wheels and a seat attached to a flexible board.

buck-et *n.* A vessel used to carry liquids or solids; a pail.

bucket brigade *n.* A line of people who pass buckets of water from hand to hand in order to extinguish a fire.

buck-et seat *n.* A separate seat with a rounded or molded back.

buck-eye *n.* A tree with flower clusters and glossy brown nuts.

buck-le *v.* To warp, crumple, or bend under pressure. *n.* Metal clasp for fastening one end to another. buckle, buckler *n.*, buckling, buckled *v.*

bucko *n.* A person who is domineering.

buck-ram *n.* A coarse, stiff fabric that is sized with glue and used for interlinings in garments and in bookbindings.

buck-shot *n.* A coarse lead shot for shotgun shells.

buck-skin *n.* A soft leather; a light colored horse; riding breeches made from buckskin. buckskin *adj.*

buck-tail *n.* A lure used by a fisherman.

buck-tooth *n.* A large, prominently projecting front tooth. -ed *adj.*

buck-wheat *n.* A plant with small edible seeds that are often ground into flour and used as a cereal grain.

bucolic *n.* A poem.

bud *n.* Something that has not developed completely; a small structure that contains flowers or leaves that have not developed; the early stage of development. budding *v.*

Bu-da-pest *n.* Capital of Hungary.

Bud-dhism *n.* A religion that teaches that suffering is inherited and that one can be released from it by moral and mental self-purification. Buddhist *n. or adj.*

bud-dy *n.* A good companion, partner, or friend.

buddy system *n.* A mutual agreement in which two people are paired for safety in hazardous situations.

budge *v.* To give way to; to cause to move slightly.

bud-ger-i-gar *n.* A small Australian parrot.

bud-get *n.* The total amount of money allocated for a certain purpose.

bud-ge-teer *n.* A person who prepares a budget for someone.

buff *n.* A leather made mostly from skins of buffalo, elk, or oxen, having the color of light to moderate yellow.

buf-fa-lo *n.* A wild ox with heavy forequarters, short horns, and a large muscular hump. *v.* To bewilder, to intimidate.

buff-er *n.* A tool used to polish or shine; in computer science, a part of the memory used to hold information temporarily while data transfers from one place to another. *v.* To lessen, absorb, or protect against the shock of an impact.

buffer zone *n.* A neutral separation between conflicting forces.

buf-fet *n.* A meal placed on a side table so that people may serve themselves; a side table for serving food. *v.* To strike sharply with the hand.

buffing wheel *n.* The round surface of a wheel covered with cloth used to polish or shine something.

buf-foon *n.* A clown; a stupid person; an uneducated person.

bug *n.* Any small insect; a concealed listening device. *v.* To bother or annoy. bugged, bugging *v.*

bug-a-boo *n.* A source of concern or fear.

bug-bane *n.* An herb of the buttercup family but with white flowers.

bug-eye *n.* A small boat with a flat bottom.

bug-gy *n.* A small carriage pulled behind a horse.

bu-gle *n.*

A brass instrument without keys or valves. *v.* To sound a bugle call. bugle *v.*, bugler *n.*

bu-gle-weed *n.* A genus of the mint family which is a mild narcotic.

bug-seed *n.* An annual herb of the goosefoot family.

buhr-stone *n.* A rock used to make a grinding stone.

build *v.* To erect by uniting materials into a composite whole; to fashion or create; to develop or add to. *n.* The form or structure of a person.

build-er *n.* A person who supervises the construction of a building project.

build-ing *n.* A roofed and walled structure for permanent use.

built--in *adj.* Containing something within a structure.

bulb *n.* A rounded underground plant such as a tulip that lies dormant in the winter and blooms in the spring; an incandescent light for electric lamps. **bulbed, -aceous** adj.

bulbous adj Resembling a bulb in shape.

bul-bul n. A songbird often mentioned in poetry.

Bulg abbr. Bulgaria

bulge n. A swelling of the surface caused by pressure from within. **bulging, bulge** v., **bulgy** adj.

bul-gur n. Wheat prepared for human consumption.

bu-lim-ia n. An eating disorder in which a person overeats and then throws up in order to remain thin.

bulk n. A large mass; anything that has great size, volume, or units. **bulky** adj.

bulk-age n. A substance that increases the bulk of material in the intestine, therefore stimulating peristalsis.

bulk-head n. The partition that divides a ship into compartments; a retaining wall along a waterfront.

bulky adj. Having great bulk; out of proportion. **bulkiness** n.

bull n. The adult male in cattle and other large mammals. Slang Nonsense talk.

bull abbr. Bulletin.

bul-la n. A blister or vesicle.

bull-dog n. A short-haired dog with a stocky build and an undershot lower jaw.

bull-doze v. To move or dig up with a bulldozer. Slang To bully.

bull-dozer n. A tractor-like machine with a large metal blade in front for moving earth and rocks.

bul-let n. A cylindrical projectile that is fired from a gun.

bul-le-tin n. A broadcasted statement of public interest; a public notice.

bulletin board n. A board on which messages and notices are posted.

bull-fight n. A Spanish or Mexican spectacle in which men known as matadors engage in fighting bulls.

bull-frog n. A deep-voiced frog.

bull-head-ed adj. Headstrong and stubborn.

bull-horn n. A hand-held loudspeaker.

bul-lion n. Refined gold or silver in the uncoined state.

bull-ish adj. Tending to cause or hopeful of rising prices, as in the stock market.

bull-ock n. A castrated bull.

bull-pen n. The area where pitchers warm up during a baseball game.

bull session n. An informal group discussion.

bull's eye n. The center of a target.

bull snake n. A harmless snake native to North America.

bull-ter-ri-er n. A breed of dog crossed between a terrier and a bulldog.

bul-ly n., pl. -ies A person who is mean or cruel to weaker people.

bul-rush n. Tall grass as found in a marsh.

bul-wark n. A strong protection or support.

bum n. One who begs from others; one who spends time unemployed. v. To loaf.

bum-ble-bee n.

A large hairy bee.

bum-boat n. A boat that has commodities for sale to ships in port.

bum-mer Slang Depressing.

bump v. To collide with, knock, or strike something. n. A swelling or lump on a person's body.

bump-er n. A device on the front of vehicles that absorbs shock and prevents damage.

bumper--to--bumper adj. A long line of cars or other vehicles moving very slowly.

bump-kin n. An awkward, stupid, or unsophisticated country person. -ish adj.

bump-tious adj. Crudely self-assertive and forward; pushy. **bumptiously** adv., **bumptiousness** n.

bumpy adj. Being uneven; having ups and downs.

bun n. Any of a variety of plain or sweet small breads; tightly rolled hair that resembles a bun.

bunch n. A cluster or group of items that are the same.

bunch-flow-er n. A summer-blooming herb of the lily family usually found in the eastern and southern part of the United States.

bun-co n. A game of confidence; a swindling scheme.

bun-dle n. Anything wrapped or held together. Slang A large amount of money. **bundler** n., **bundling** n

bundle up v. To dress warmly, usually using many layers of clothing.

bung n. The cork used to plug the bunghole in a large cask.

bun-ga-low n. A small one-story cottage.

bun-gle v. To work or act awkwardly or clumsily. **bungler** n.

bun-ion n. An inflamed, painful swelling of the first joint of the big toe.

bunk n. A narrow bed that is built in; one of a tier of berths on a ship.

bunk bed n. A bed having two sections, one on top of the other.

bun-ker n. A tank for storing fuel on a ship; an embankment or a sand trap creating a hazard on a golf course.

bunk-house n. A building used as sleeping quarters usually on a ranch.

bun-ny n., pl. -nies A small rabbit.

Bun-sen burner n. An adjustable gas-burning laboratory burner.

bunt v. To tap a pitched ball with a half swing. n. The center of a square sail.

bunt-ing n. A hooded blanket for a baby; a variety of stout-billed birds.

buoy n. A floating object to mark a channel or danger. v. To stay afloat.

buoy-an-cy n. The tendency of an object or body to remain afloat in liquid or to rise in gas or air.

bur-bot *n.* A freshwater fish of the cod family.

bur-den *n.* Something that is hard to bear; a duty or responsibility; a ship's capacity for carrying cargo. **burdening** *v.*, **burdensome** *adj.*

bur-dock *n.* A coarse plant with purplish flowers.

bu-reau *n.*, *pl.* **bureaus, bureaux.** A low chest for storing clothes; a branch of the government or a subdivision of a department.

bu-reauc-ra-cy *n.*, *pl.* **-cies.** A body of nonelected officials in a government; the administration of a government through bureaus.

bu-reau-crat *n.* A government official who has great authority in his own department.

bu-reau-crat-ic *adj.* Having the characteristics of a bureaucrat.

bu-rette *n.* A glass tube for measuring quantities of liquid or gas that are discharged or taken in.

burg *n.* A town or city.

bur-gage *n.* A tenure held under the king for a yearly rent.

bur-gee *n.* A flag used by ships for signals or identification.

bur-geon *v.* To put forth new life as in leaves, buds, etc.

burg-er *n.*, *Slang* A hamburger.

bur-gess *n.* A representative of the legislature of colonial Maryland and Virginia.

bur-glar *n.* A person who steals personal items from another person's home.

bur-glar-ize *v.* To commit burglary.

bur-glar-proof *adj.* Protected and secure against burglary.

bur-gla-ry *n.* The breaking into and entering of a private home with the intent to steal.

bur-go-mas-ter *n.* The chief magistrate in certain countries of Europe.

Bur-gun-dy *n.* A white or red wine produced in Burgundy, an area in southeast France.

bu-rin *n.* An engraver's cutting tool; a flint tool with a beveled point.

burl *n.* A woody, often flat and hard, hemispherical growth on a tree.

bur-la-dero *n.* A wooden barrier to protect the bullfighter from the charge of the bull.

bur-lap *n.* A coarse cloth woven from hemp or jute.

bur-lesque *n.* Theatrical entertainment with comedy and mocking imitations. **burlesque** *adj.*, **burlesquely** *adv.*

bur-ley *n.* A tobacco grown in Kentucky.

bur-ly *adj.* Very heavy and strong. **burlily** *adv.*, **burliness** *n.*

burn *v.* To be destroyed by fire; to consume fuel and give off heat. *n.* An injury produced by fire, heat, or steam; the firing of a rocket engine in space. **burnable** *adj.*, **-ingly** *adv.*, **burned** *v.*

burn-er *n.* The part of a fuel-burning device where the fire is contained.

bur-net *n.* An herb of the rose family

with pinnate leaves and spikes ⊙ flowers.

bur-nish *v.* To make shiny by rubbin to polish. **burnishing** *adj.*

bur-noose *n.* A one-piece hooded cloak

burnt *adj.* Affected by burning.

burp *n.* A belch. *v.* To expel gas fro the stomach.

bur-ro *n.* A small donkey.

bur-row *n.* A tunnel dug in the groun by an animal. *v.* To construct by tur neling through the earth.

bur-sa *n.* A sac between the bone an the tendon.

bur-sar *n.* The person or official i charge of monies at a college.

bur-sa-ry *n.* The treasury of a college; grant to a needy student.

burse *n.* A square cloth used in a Com munion service.

bur-si-tis *n.* An inflammation of th small sac between a tendon of th knee, elbow, or shoulder joints.

burst *adj.* To explode or experienc a sudden outbreak; to very suddenl become visible or audible. *n.* A sud den explosion or outburst.

bur-ton *n.* A single or double blockin tackle used for hoisting.

bury *v.* To hide by covering with earth to inter a body at a funeral service.

bus *n.*, *pl.* **busses** A large passenge vehicle; a small hand truck; a conduc tor for collecting electric currents.

bus *abbr.* Business.

bus boy *n.* A waiter's assistant; one whe removes dirty dishes from a table an the resets it.

bus-by *n.* A fur hat that is worn in cer tain regiments of the British Army.

bush *n.* A low plant with branches nea the ground; a dense tuft or growth land that is covered intensely with un dergrowth.

bush basil *n.* A small annual herb.

bush bean *n.* A variety of green beans grown on bushes.

bush-buck *n.* A small African antelope with spirally twisted horns.

bushed *adj.*, *Slang* Extremely ex hausted; tired.

bush-el *n.* A unit of dry measurement which equals four pecks or 2,150.42 cubic inches; a container that holds a bushel.

bush-fire *n.* A fire burning out of contro in the bush.

bush-ing *n.* A cylindrical lining in ar opening to limit the size of the open ing or serve as a guide.

bush-league *n.* An inferior class or team.

bush lima *n.* A lima bean grown or small bushes instead of poles.

Bush-man *n.* A member of the nomadic hunters of southwestern Africa.

bush-mas-ter *n.* The largest New World venomous snake.

bush-whack *v.* To travel through thick woods by cutting bushes and small trees; to ambush. **bushwhacker** *n.*

bushy *adj.* Overgrown with a dense growth of bushes.

busi-ness *n.* A person's professional dealings or occupation; an industrial or commercial establishment.

business card *n.* A card which informs business associates which company you represent.

busi-ness-man *n.* A representative of a company; a business executive.

busi-ness-wom-an *n.* A female representative of a company.

bus-ing *n.* The practice of busing children to a school outside their area to establish racial balance.

busk-er *n.* A person who entertains on the street corner.

bus-kin *n.* A boot that reaches halfway to the knee; tragedy as that of an ancient Greek drama.

bus-man's holiday *n.* Vacation or holiday where a person follows the same practice of his usual occupation.

buss *n.* A kiss.

bust *n.* A sculpture that resembles the upper part of a human body; the breasts of a women. *v.* To break or burst; to become short of money; to exceed the limit in the game of blackjack.

bust-er *n.* A sturdy child; a person who breaks horses; sudden violent wind coming from the south.

bus-tle *n.* A padding that gives extra bulk to the back of a woman's skirt. **bustlingly** *adv.*, **bustling** *adj.*

bus-y *adj.* Full of activity; engaged in some form of work. *v.* To occupy one's self. **busily** *adv.*, **busyness** *n.*

busy-body *n.* An inquisitive person who interferes with someone else's business.

but *conj.* On the contrary to; other than; if not; except for the fact.

bu-tane *n.* A gas produced from petroleum, used as a fuel refrigerant and aerosol propellant.

butch-er *n.* One who slaughters animals and dresses them for food; a person who kills brutally.

butcher knife *n.* A heavy kitchen knife with a broad blade.

butch-er's-broom *n.* A leafless plant of the lily family with twigs used in brooms.

bu-teo *n.* Hawks with broad wings and soaring flight.

but-ler *n.* A male servant of a household who is in charge of other household employees.

butt *n.* The object of ridicule; the thick large or blunt end of something; a backstop for stopping missiles. *v.* To hit with horns or the head; to be joined at the end.

butte *n.* A small mountain with steep precipitous sides with a smaller summit area than a mesa.

but-ter *n.* A yellow substance churned from milk.

but-ter--and--eggs *n.* A perennial herb of the snapdragon family with yellow and orange flowers.

butter bean *n.* A dried lima bean.

butter clam *n.* A delicately flavored clam of the Pacific coast.

but-ter-cup *n.* A colorful plant with glossy yellow flowers.

but-ter-fat *n.* The natural fat from milk that floats to the top of unpasteurized milk.

but-ter-fin-gers *n.* An awkward or clumsy person.

but-ter-fly *n., pl.* **-flies**

A narrow-bodied insect with four broad, colorful wings; a person occupied with the pursuit of pleasure; a swimming stroke.

butterfly chair *n.* A chair constructed from cloth supported by a frame of metal tubing.

but-ter-milk *n.* The liquid that remains after butter has been churned from milk.

but-ter-nut *n.* The edible nut of the walnut family.

but-ter-scotch *n.* A candy made from brown sugar and melted butter.

butter up *v.* To charm with flattery.

but-ter-wort *n.* An herb of the bladderworth family whose leaves produce a secretion which captures insects.

but-tery *n.* A liquor storeroom.

butt in *v.* To meddle in someone's affairs.

but-tocks *pl., n.* The two round fleshy parts of the rump.

but-ton *n.* A small disk that interlocks with a buttonhole to close a piece of garment; a badge bearing a a stamped design or slogan; an immature mushroom. **buttoned** *v.*, **buttonless** *n.*

but-ton-hole *n.* The slit through which a button is inserted to close a piece of garment.

but-ton-hole stitch *n.* A tightly worked loop stitch used to make a firm edge on a button hole.

but-ton-hole snake-root *n.* A plant having a rose-purple flower head; coarse herb.

but-ton-hook *n.* An offensive play in football; a hook used to draw buttons thru buttonholes.

but-ton-wood *n.* A massive tree that provides useful timber.

but-ton-y *adj.* Having a number of buttons.

but-tress *n.* A support made of either brick or stone and built against or projecting from a building or wall used for the purpose of giving stability; a support or prop.

butt shaft *n.* A barbless arrow.

butt-stock *n.* The stock of a firearm that is situated behind the breech mechanism.

butt weld *n.* A weld that is formed by joining the flat ends of two pieces of metal at a white heat.

bu-tyl al-co-hol *n.* Chemically related form of alcohol that contains the butyl radical, used in manufacturing perfumes, lacquers and other organic compounds.

bu-tyr-a-ceous *adj.* Having the qualities of butter.

bu-ty-rin *n.* A yellowish liquid fat that is present in butter, and is formed from butyric acid.

bux-om *adj.* Lively; happy; amply proportioned. **buxomness** *n.*

bux-om-ly *adv.* Vigorously; briskly.

buy *v.* To purchase in exchange for money; to acquire possession of something. *n.* Anything that is bought.

buy-er *v.* A person who buys from a store or an individual; a person employed to make purchases for a company.

buy out *v.* To obtain release form a responsibility, by making a payment.

buzz *v.* To make a low vibrating humming sound, as a bee.

buz-zard *n.* A broad-winged vulture from the same family as the hawk. *Slang* A mean, old cantankerous man.

buzz-er *n.* An electrical signaling device that makes a buzzing sound.

buzz saw *n.* A circular power saw.

by *prep.* Up to and beyond; to go past; not later than; next to; according to; beside or near; according to; in relation to.

bye *n.* A position in which a contestant has no opponent after pairs are drawn for a tournament, and, therefore, advances to the next round; something that is aside from the main consideration or course.

bye-bye *Slang* Farewell.

by and by *adv.* Before much longer.

by and large *adv.* In general.

by-gone *adj.* Gone by; past; former; departed; out of date.

by-law *n.* A rule or law governing internal affairs of a group or organization.

by--line *n.* A line at the beginning of a newspaper article, news story, or magazine that contains the author's name.

by--name *n.* A nickname or secondary name.

by--pass *n.* A road that goes around an obstructed area; a detour; a secondary route.

by--path *n.* A path that is very seldom used; a private or obscure way.

by--prod-uct *n.* Material that is left over when something is manufactured or produced but also has a market value of its own; an inadvertent consequence.

by-stander *n.* A person who is present at an event but does not participate in it.

byte *n.* In computer science, a sequence of adjacent binary digits operated on as a unit.

by-way *n.* A secondary field of study; a side road; an unfrequented path.

by-word *n.* A well-known proverb; an object of contempt.

By-zan-ti-um *n.* An ancient Greek city on the site of Constantinople; pertaining to the Eastern Roman Empire.

C, c The third letter of the English alphabet; the Roman numeral for 100.

CA *abbr.* California.

cab *n.* A taxicab; the compartment where a person sits to drive a large truck or machinery.

ca-bal *n.* A group that conspires against a government or other public institution.

ca-ban-a *n.* A small building or shelter on the beach or at the side of a pool.

cab-a-ret *n.* A restaurant that provides dancing and live entertainment.

cab-bage *n.*

A plant with large, edible green leaves, eaten as a vegetable.

cab-in *n.* A small, roughly-built house, especially one made from logs; the living quarters on a ship; the area of an airplane for the passengers and crew members.

cab-i-net *n.* A unit for displaying and storing dishes and other objects; a selected group of people appointed by the head of state to officially advise and to take charge of the different government departments.

cab-i-net-maker *n.* A person who specializes in the construction of furniture.

ca-ble *n.* A heavy rope made from fiber or steel; a bound group of insulated conductors.

cable stitch *n.* A knitting stitch that produces the look of a cable.

cable television *n.* A private television system which picks up signals from television stations and transmits them by cable.

ca-boo-dle *n., Slang* The entire unit, amount, or collection.

ca-boose *n.* The last car of a train, that contains the eating and sleeping quarters for the crew.

ca-ca-o *n.* Any tree of the chocolate family; the dried seed of the cacao tree from which chocolate and cocoa are made.

cach-a-lot *n.* A sperm whale.

cache *n.* A safe place to hide and conceal goods.

ca-chet *n.* A mark of distinction or authenticity.

cack-le *v.* To laugh with the characteristic shrill noise a hen makes after laying an egg; to talk or laugh with a similar sound. **cackler** *n.*

ca-coph-o-ny *n.* A harsh and disagreeable sound. **cacophonous** *adj.*, **cacophonously** *adv.*

cac-tus *n., pl.* **-es, -ti** A leafless plant with a thick, prickly surface, which grows primarily in hot and dry regions.

cad *n.* An ungentlemanly man. **-dish** *adj.*

ca-dav-er *n.* The body of a person who has died; pale and gaunt. **-ic** *adj.*

ca-dav-er-ous *adj.* Pale and gaunt.

cad-die *n., pl.* **caddies** A person

employed by a golfer to assist him by carrying his clubs during the game of golf.

ca-dence *n.* A rhythmic movement or flow.

ca-den-za *n.* An elaborate ornamental section for a soloist near the end of a concerto.

ca-det *n.* A student in training at a naval or military academy. **cadetship** *n.*

cadge *v.* To beg or to receive by begging; to mooch. **cadger** *n.*

cad-re *n.* The group of trained personnel that forms the heart of an organization.

ca-du-ce-us *n.* The symbol of the medical profession, a winged staff entwined with two serpents entwined around it.

cae-su-ra *n.* A pause or break in a line of verse or poetry.

caf-e-te-ri-a *n.* A restaurant where a person chooses his own food and then carries it on a tray to his table.

caf-feine *n.* A stimulant found in coffee, tea, and dark colas.

caf-tan *n.* A loose-fitting, full-length garment worn in the Near East.

cage *n.* A box-like structure enclosed with bars or grating for the confinement of animals.

ca-gey *adj.* Shrewd, wary, or cautious.

ca-hoot *n.* A questionable relationship with an associate.

cais-son *n.* A waterproof structure that is used for construction work underwater.

ca-jole *v.* To wheedle or coax someone into doing something.

Ca-jun *n.* A native of Louisiana descended from French-speaking immigrants.

cake *n.* A sweet food made from flour, eggs, and shortening. **cake** *v.*

cal-a-bash *n.* A large hard-shelled gourd that can be used as a utensil.

cal-a-boose *n., Slang* A jail.

cal-a-mine *n.* A pink powder of zinc oxide and ferric oxide mixed with mineral oils to form a lotion for skin irritations such as poison ivy.

ca-lam-i-ty *n., pl.* **-ies** Misfortune or great distress. **calamitous** *adj.*, **calamitously** *adv.*

cal-ci-fy *v.* To become or make chalky or stony. **calcification** *n.*

cal-cine *v.* To heat to a high temperature without melting, but causing loss of moisture and reduction. **-ation** *n.*

cal-ci-um *n.* The alkaline element that is found in teeth and bones; the element symbolized by Ca.

cal-cu-late *v.* To figure by a mathematical process, to evaluate; to estimate. **calculable** *adj.*, **-ably** *adv.*, **-ive** *adj.*

cal-cu-lat-ed *adj.* Worked out beforehand with careful estimation. **calculatedly** *adv.*

cal-cu-lat-ing *adj.* Shrewd consideration of self-interest.

cal-cu-la-tor *n.* A machine with a keyboard for automatic mathematical operation.

cal-cu-lus *n., pl.* **-es** A stone in the gallbladder or kidneys; the mathematics of integral and differential calculus.

cal-dron *n.* A large boiler or kettle.

cal-en-dar *n.* A system for showing time divisions by years, months, weeks, and days; the twelve months in a year.

cal-en-der *n.* A machine that makes paper and cloth smooth and glossy.

cal-ends *n.* The first day of the new moon.

calf *n., pl.* **calves** The young offspring of the domestic cow; the young of large animals as the whale and elephant.

cal-i-ber *n.* The inner diameter of a tube or gun; the quality or worth of something.

cal-i-co *n.* Cotton fabric with figured patterns.

Cal-i-for-nia *n.* A state located on the western coast of the United States.

cal-i-per *n.* An instrument with two curved, hinged legs, used to measure inner and outer dimensions.

ca-liph *n.* A religious and secular head in Islam. **caliphate** *n.*

cal-is-then-ics *n.* Exercises that develop muscular tone and promote good physical condition.

call *v.* To call out to someone; to name or designate; to telephone; to pay a short visit; to demand payment; in card games, to demand the opponent show his cards. **call** *n.*

cal-la *or* **cal-la lily** *n.* A family of white and yellow flowers enclosing a club-like flower stalk.

cal-lig-ra-phy *n.* The art of writing with a pen using different slants and positions.

call-ing *n.* The occupation or profession of a person.

cal-liope *n.* A keyboard musical instrument that is fitted with steam whistles.

Cal-lis-to *n.* The largest of Jupiter's moons.

cal-lous *adj.* Having calluses; to be without emotional feelings. **callously** *adv.*, **callousness** *n.*

cal-lus *n., pl.* **-luses** A thickening of the horny layer of the skin.

calm *adj.* Absence of motion; having little or no wind, storms, or rough water.

cal-o-mel *n.* A white, tasteless compound used as a purgative.

cal-o-rie *n., pl.* **-ries** A measurement of the amount of heat or energy produced by food. **caloric, calorific** *adj.*

cal-u-met *n.* A pipe used by the North American Indians during ceremonies; also known as a peace pipe.

ca-lum-ni-ate *v., pl.* **-nies** To slander; to malign.

cal-um-ny *n., pl.* **-ies** A statement that is malicious, false, and damaging to someone's reputation.

Cal-va-ry *n.* The location where Jesus Christ was crucified.

calve *v.* To give birth to a calf.

Cal-vin-ism n. The doctrine of John Calvin, marked by a strong emphasis on the sovereignty of God.

ca-lyp-so n., pl. calypsos Improvised ballad of the West Indies with lyrics on topical or humorous subjects.

ca-lyx n., pl. calyxes, calyces The outer cover of a flower.

cam n. A curved wheel used to produce a reciprocating motion.

ca-ma-ra-de-rie n Good will among friends.

cam-ber n. A slight curve upward in the middle.

cam-bric n. A cotton fabric or white linen.

came n. A grooved lead bar that is used to hold together the panes of glass in latticework or stained-glass windows. v. Past tense of to come.

cam-el n.

An animal used in desert regions, having either one or two humps on its back.

ca-mel-lia n. A shrub with shiny green leaves and various colored flowers.

ca-mel-o-pard n. A giraffe.

cam-e-o n. A gem usually cut with one layer contrasting another, serving as a background; a brief appearance by a famous performer in a single scene on a television show or in a movie.

cam-er-a n. An apparatus for taking photographs in a lightproof enclosure with an aperture and shuttered lens through which the image is focused and recorded on photosensitive film.

cam-i-sole n. A woman's short, sleeveless undergarment.

cam-ou-flage v. To disguise by creating the effect of being part of the natural surroundings.

camp n. A temporary lodging or makeshift shelter.

cam-paign n. An organized operation designed to bring about a particular political, commercial, or social goal. campaigner n.

cam-pa-ni-le n., pl. -iles A free-standing bell tower that is associated with a church.

camp-er n. A person who camps in makeshift shelters for recreation; a vehicle specially equipped for casual travel and camping.

camp-fire n. An outdoor fire used for cooking and for heat while camping.

camp-ground n. A specially prepared area for camping.

cam-phor n. A crystalline compound used as an insect repellent. -ic adj.

camp-site n. The area used for camping.

cam-pus n. The buildings and grounds of a college, school, or university.

cam-shaft n. The shaft of an engine that is fitted with cams.

can v. To know how to do something; to be physically or mentally able; to have the ability to do something; to preserve fruit or vegetables by sealing in an airtight container. n. An airtight container.

Ca-naan n. In biblical times, known as the Promised Land. Canaanite n.

Can-a-da n. The Commonwealth nation located in the northern half of North America. Canadian adj. & n.

ca-nal n. A man-made water channel for irrigating land.

ca-nal-ize v. To convert into canals; to make new canals.

ca-nar-y n., pl. -ies A green or yellow songbird which is popular as a caged bird.

ca-nas-ta n. A card game using two decks of cards which each player or partnership tries to meld in groups of three or more cards of the same rank; a meld of seven cards that are of the same rank in canasta.

can-can n. A dance performed by women, characterized by high kicking while holding up the front of a full skirt.

can-cel v. To invalidate or annul; to cross out; to neutralize; in mathematics, to remove a common factor from the numerator and the denominator of a fraction; in computer science, to abort or stop a procedure or program. cancellation n.

can-cer n. A malignant tumor that invades healthy tissue and spreads to other areas; the disease marked by such tumors. cancerous adj.

Cancer n. The fourth sign of the zodiac; a person born between June 21 - July 22.

can-de-la-bra n., pl. candelabrum A decorative candlestick with several branching arms for candles.

can-did adj. Free from bias, malice, or prejudice; honest and sincere.

can-di-date n., pl. A person who aspires to or is nominated or qualified for a membership, or office. candidacy, candidature n.

can-dle n. A slender, cylindrical mass of wax or tallow containing a linen or cotton wick which is burned to produce light. v. To hold something between the eye and a light, as to test eggs for blood clots, growths, or fertility. candler n.

candle-holder n. A candlestick.

can-dle-light n. The light emitted from a candle.

can-dor n. Straightforwardness; frankness of expression.

can-dy n., pl. -ies A confection made from sugar and flavored in a variety of ways. v. To preserve, cook, coat, or saturate with syrup or sugar.

can-dy-tuft n. A variety of plants with white, purple, or reddish flower clusters.

cane n. A pithy or hollow, flexible, jointed stem of bamboo or rattan that is split for basketry or wickerwork; a walking stick. **cane** v.

ca-nine adj. Relating to or resembling a dog; of the dog family.

Ca-nis Ma-jor n. A constellation in the Southern Hemisphere that contains the Dog Star.

can-is-ter n. A container made of thin metal, used to store dry foods, such as flour, sugar, coffee, and tea; the cylinder that explodes and scatters shot when fired from a gun.

can-ker n. An ulcerated sore in the mouth.

canned adj. Preserved and sealed under pressure.

can-ner-y n., pl. -ies A company that processes canned meat, vegetables, and other foods.

can-ni-bal n. Any animal who survives by eating one of its own kind; a person who survives by eating the flesh of human beings. **cannibalism** n., **cannibalistic** adj.

can-ni-bal-ize v. To remove parts from a plane for use as replacements in another plane.

can-non n., pl. **cannons** A heavy war weapon made of metal and mounted on wheels or a base for discharging projectiles.

can-non-ball n. An iron projectile fired from a cannon.

can-ny adj. Thrifty; careful; cautious; shrewd. **cannily** adv., **canniness** n.

ca-noe n.

A lightweight, slender boat with pointed ends which moves by paddling. **canoe** v., **canoeist** n.

can-on n. The laws established by a church council; a priest serving in a collegiate church or cathedral. **canonical** adj.

can-on-ize v. To officially declare a deceased person a saint. **-ation** n.

can-o-py n., pl. -ies A cloth covering used as an ornamental structure over a bed; the supporting surface of a parachute; the transparent cover over the cockpit of an airplane.

cant n. The external angle of a building. v. To throw off by tilting.

can't contr. Cannot.

can-ta-bi-le n. A lyrical, flowing style of music.

can-ta-loupe n. A sweet-tasting, orange-colored muskmelon.

can-tan-ker-ous adj. Bad-tempered and argumentative. **cantankerously** adv.

can-ta-ta n. A drama that is sung but not acted.

can-teen n. A small metal container for carrying water or other liquids to drink; a place where a person can buy refreshments.

can-ter n. An easy lope just a little slower than a gallop, but faster than a trot.

can-ti-cle n. A hymn or chant sung in church.

can-ti-lev-er n. A long structure, such as a beam, supported only at one end.

can-ton n. A small area of a country divided into parts. **cantonal** adj.

can-ton-ment n. One or more temporary billets for troops.

can-tor n. The chief singer in a synagogue.

can-vas n. A heavy fabric used in making tents and sails for boats; a piece of canvas that is used for oil paintings.

can-vass v. To travel through a region to solicit opinions or votes; to take a poll or survey. **canvasser** n.

can-yon n. A deep and narrow gorge with steep sides.

cap n. A covering for the head, usually brimless and made of a soft material; the final or finishing touch to something; a small explosive charge that is used in cap guns. **cap** v.

ca-pa-ble adj. Having the ability to perform in an efficient way; qualified. **capability**, n., **capably** adv.

ca-pa-cious adj. Having a lot of room or space.

ca-pac-i-tance n. The property of a body or circuit which allows it to store an electrical charge. **capacitive** adj.

ca-pac-i-tor n. The circuit element composed of metallic plates that are separated by a dielectric and are used to store a charge temporarily.

ca-pac-i-ty n., pl. -ies The ability to contain, receive, or absorb; having the aptitude or ability to do something; the maximum production or output; in computer science, the total amount of data or information that can be processed, stored, or generated.

ca-par-i-son n. An ornamental covering for a horse, saddle, or harness.

cape n. A sleeveless covering for the shoulders that fastens at the neck; a piece or point of land that extends into a lake or sea.

ca-per n. A prank; antic.

cap-il-lary n., pl. -ies Any of the small vessels that connect the veins and arteries. adj. Having a hair-like bore; very fine or small in size.

cap-i-tal n. The town or city that is designated as the seat of government for a nation or state; material wealth in the form of money or property that is used to produce more wealth; funds that are contributed to a business by the stockholders or owners; net worth of a company or business.

cap-i-tal-ism n. The economic system in which the means of distribution and production are privately owned and operated for private profit.

capitalist n. A person who invests in a business. **capitalistic** adj.

cap-i-ta-tion n. A census or tax of equal amount for each person.

Cap-i-tol n. The building used by the United States Congress for meetings.

ca-pit-u-late v. To surrender under terms of an agreement. **capitulator** n., **capitulatory** adj.

ca-pon *n.* A young rooster that has been castrated to improve the meat for eating.

ca-price *n.* A sudden change of action or mind without adequate reason; a whim. **capricious** *adj.*, **-iousness** *n.*

Capricon *n.* The tenth sign of the zodiac; a person born between (December 22 - January 19.)

cap-size *v.* To overturn in a boat.

cap-stan *n., Naut.* A drum-like apparatus rotated to hoist weights by winding in a cable on a ship or boat.

cap-su-lated *adj.* Formed or in a capsule-like state. **capsulation** *n.*

cap-sule *n.* A small gelatinous case for a dose of oral medicine; a fatty sac that surrounds an organ of the body, as the kidney, and protects it; a summary in a brief form. **capsular** *adj.*

cap-tion *n.* The chief leader of a group; the commander or master of a ship. *Naval* The commissioned naval officer who ranks below a commodore or rear admiral; the designated spokesperson of a team. **captaincy** *n.*

cap-tion *n.* A subtitle; a description of an illustration or picture.

cap-tious *adj.* Deceptive; critical.

cap-ti-vate *v.* To hold the attention, fascinate, or charm a person or group of people. **captivation** *n.*, **captivator** *n.*

cap-tive *n.* A person being held as a prisoner.

cap-ture *v.* To take something or someone by force. **capturer** *n.*

car *n.* An automobile; an enclosed vehicle, as a railroad car.

ca-rafe *n.* A glass bottle for serving wine or water.

car-a-mel *n.* A chewy substance primarily composed of sugar, butter, and milk.

car-a-mel-ize *v.* To make into caramel.

car-at *n.* The unit of weight for gems that equals 200 milligrams.

car-a-van *n.* A group of people traveling together.

car-a-way *n.* An aromatic seed used in cooking.

car-bide *n.* A carbon compound with a more electropositive element.

car-bine *n.* A short-barreled rifle, light in weight.

car-bo-hy-drate *n.* A group of compounds, including starches, celluloses, and sugars that contain carbon, hydrogen, and oxygen.

car-bon *n.* A nonmetallic element that occurs as a powdery noncrystalline solid; the element symbolized by C. **carbonization** *n.*, **carbonize** *v.*

car-bon-ate *v.* To add or charge with carbon dioxide gas, as in a beverage. **carbonation** *n.*

car-bon copy *n.* The copy of an original made with carbon paper. *Slang* An exact copy.

car-bon di-ox-ide *n.* An odorless, colorless, nonflammable gas, removed from the atmosphere by the photosynthesis of plants and returned by the respiration of animals.

car-bon mon-ox-ide *n.* An odorless, colorless gas that is formed by the incomplete oxidation of carbon, burns with a blue flame, an is highly poisonous when inhaled.

car-bon pa-per *n.* A thin sheet of paper with dark pigments on one side, which transfers whatever is written or typed on a sheet of paper on top of it onto paper placed beneath it.

car-bon tet-ra-chlo-ride *n.* A nonflammable, colorless, poisonous liquid used as a cleaning fluid and in fire extinguishers.

car-bun-cle *n.* An infection of the skin and deeper tissue which is red, inflamed, full of pus, and painful.

car-bu-re-tor *n.* The device in gasoline engines that mixes vapor, fuel, and air for efficient combustion.

car-cass *n.* The dead body of an animal; something that no longer has life.

car-ci-no-ma *n.* A malignant tumor; cancer. **carcinomatous** *adj.*

card *n.* A small piece of pasteboard or very stiff paper, used in a wide variety of ways, as a greeting card, a business card, a postcard, etc.

card cat-a-log *n.* An alphabetical catalog of books, composed of individual cards for each book, found in libraries.

car-di-ac *adj.* Relating to the heart.

car-di-ac mas-sage *n.* A procedure performed by a physician to restore proper circulation and respiration for someone in distress.

car-di-gan *n.* A sweater with an opening down the front.

car-di-nal *adj.* Of prime importance; principal. *n.* An official of the Catholic Church who ranks just below the Pope and who is appointed by him.

car-di-o-gram *n.* The curve recorded by a cardiograph and is used in the diagnosis of heart defects.

car-di-ol-o-gy *n.* The study of the heart, its diseases, and treatments. **cardiologist** *n.*

car-di-o-pul-mo-nary *adj.* Relating to the heart and lungs.

car-di-o-pul-mo-nary re-sus-ci-ta-tion *n.* A procedure used to restore breathing after cardiac arrest by using mouth-to-mouth resuscitation.

car-di-o-vas-cu-lar *adj.* Involving and relating to the heart and the blood vessels.

card-shark *n.* A person who cheats when playing cards.

care *n.* A feeling of concern, anxiety, or worry; guardianship or custody. *v.* To show interest or regard.

ca-reen *v.* To lurch or twist from one side to another while moving rapidly.

ca-reer *n.* The profession or occupation a person takes in life. **career** *n.*

care-free *adj.* Free from all cares, worries, and concerns.

care-ful *adj.* Exercising care; cautious; watchful.

ca-ress v. To gently show affection by touching or stroking. **caress** n.

car-go n. Freight; the goods and merchandise carried on a ship, plane, or other vehicle.

car-hop n. A person who waits on customers at a drive-in restaurant.

Carib-bean Sea n. An arm of the Atlantic Ocean bounded by the coasts of South and Central America and the West Indies.

car-i-bou n.

A large antlered deer of northern North America.

car-ies n. The decay of a bone or tooth.

car-il-lon n. A set of tuned bells in a tower, that are usually played by a keyboard.

car-mine n. A vivid red color; crimson; deep purplish red.

car-nage n. A bloody slaughter; war; massacre.

car-nal adj. Relating to sensual desires. **carnality** n., **carnally** adv.

car-na-tion n. A fragrant perennial flower in a variety of colors.

car-nel-ian n. A clear red chalcedony that is used as a gem.

car-ni-val n. A traveling amusement show with side shows, a Ferris wheel, and merry-go-rounds; any kind of a happy celebration.

car-ni-vore n. A flesh-eating animal. **carnivorous** adj., **-ously** adv.,

car-ol n. A song to celebrate joy or praise. **caroler** n., **carol** v.

ca-rouse v. To be rowdy and to be in a drunken state. **carouser** n.

carp v. To find unreasonable fault with something or someone; to complain unduly. n. A freshwater fish that contains many small bones but can be eaten with caution.

car-pal adj. Pertaining to the wrist and the bones in the wrist.

car-pel n., Bot. A seed vessel or pistil.

car-pen-ter n. A person who builds and repairs wooden structures. **-ry** n.

car-pet n. A thick, woven or felt floor covering that helps to insulate the floors. **carpeting** n.

car-pet bag n. An old-fashioned traveling bag made from carpet.

car-pet bag-ger n. A person from the North who traveled to the South after the Civil War to seek political or financial gain.

car-port n. A roof attached to the side of a building to give shelter for a vehicle.

car-riage n. A horse-drawn coach.

car-rot n. An orange vegetable that is a root.

car-rou-sel n. A merry-go-round.

car-ry v. To transport from one place to another; to bear the burden, weight, or responsibility of; to keep or have available for sale; to maintain on business books for future settlement.

cart n. A two-wheeled vehicle for moving heavy goods; a small lightweight vehicle that can be moved around by hand. **carter** n.

car-tel n. A group of independent companies that have organized to control prices, production, etc.

Carter, James Earl Jr. (Jimmy) n. The 39th president of the United States 1977-1981.

car-ti-lage n. A tough, elastic substance of connective tissue attached to the surface of bones near the joints. **cartilaginous** adj.

car-tog-ra-phy n. The art of developing charts and maps. **cartographer** n., **cartographic** adj.

carton n. A container made from cardboard.

car-toon n. A caricature depicting a humorous situation; animated cartoons produced by photographing a series of action drawings. **cartoonist** n.

car-tridge n. A case made of metal, pasteboard, etc., that contains a charge of powder; the primer and shot or projectile for a firearm.

cart-wheel n. A sideways handspring with the arms over the head and the legs spread like the spokes of a wheel.

carve v. To slice meat or poultry; to cut into something; to create, as sculpture.

cary-at-id n. A supporting column sculptured in the form of a female figure.

cas-cade n. A waterfall that flows over steep rocks.

case n. A particular occurrence or instance; an injury or disease; an argument, supporting facts, or reasons that justify a situation; a box or housing to carry things in, as a briefcase; in the law, a suit of action brought against a person.

cas-ing n. A protective covering or container; the framework of a window or door.

ca-sein n. A dairy protein that is used in foods and in manufacturing adhesives and plastics.

case-work n. The study of a patient, his family, and his problems in order to help him deal with his problems.

cash-ew n. A tropical American tree that produces an edible nut that can be eaten raw or roasted.

cash-ier n. An employee who handles cash as part of his job description; an officer in a bank in charge of receiving or distributing money.

cash-mere n. The wool from the Kashmir goat; the yarn made from this wool.

ca-si-no n., pl. **-nos** A public establishment open especially for gambling.

cask n. A large wooden vessel or barrel; the quantity that a cask will hold.

cas-ket n. A coffin; a small chest or box.

cas-que n. A helmet. **casqued** adj.

cas-se-role n. A dish in which the food is baked and also served; food cooked and served in this manner.

cas-sette n. A cartridge of magnetic tape

used in tape recorders to play and record.

cas-sock *n.* A close-fitting garment worn by members of the clergy.

cast *v.* To hurl or throw with force; to direct or turn; to shed; to give a certain part or role; to deposit or give a vote on something; to make or throw, as with a fishing line. *Naut.* To fall off, to veer; to be shipwrecked or marooned at sea. *n.* A dressing made from plaster of paris used on a broken bone.

cas-ta-net *n., pl.* **-nets** An instrument made from a pair of ivory or hardwood shells, held in the palm of the hand and clapped together with the fingers.

cast-a-way *adj.* Throw away. *n.* One who is shipwrecked or discarded.

caste *n.* A social separation based on a profession, hereditary, or financial hierarchy.

cas-tel-lat-ed *adj.* Adorned by battlements and turrets.

cast-er *n.* A small set of swiveling rollers that are fastened under pieces of furniture and the like.

cas-ti-gate *v.* To punish or criticize severely. **castigation, castigator** *n.*

cast-ing *n.* The act of one that casts.

cas-tle *n.* A fort or fortified dwelling for nobility; any large house or place of refuge; a stronghold.

cast-off *adj.* Discarded; thrown away.

castor oil *n.* An oil from the seeds of a tropical plant used as a cathartic and lubricant.

cas-trate *v.* To remove the testicles; to remove the ovaries; to spay. **-ion** *n.*

ca-su-al *adj.* Informal; occurring by chance. **casually** *adv.*, **casualness** *n.*

ca-su-al-ty *n., pl* **-ies** One who is injured or killed in an accident. *Milit.* A soldier who is killed, wounded, taken prisoner by the enemy, or missing in action.

cat *n.* A small domesticated animal, a pet; any of the animals in the cat family, such as the lion, lynx, tiger, etc.

cat-a-clysm *n.* A sudden and violent disaster. **cataclysmic, cataclysmal** *adj.*

cat-a-combs *n.* An underground passage with small rooms for coffins.

cat-a-falque *n.* The structure that supports a coffin during a state funeral.

cat-a-lep-sy *n.* A condition in which there is a rigidity of the muscles, causing the patient to remain in a fixed position or posture. **cataleptic** *adj.*

cat-a-log *or* **cat-a-logue** *n.* A publication containing a list of names, objects, etc.

cat-a-lyst *n., Chem.* Any substance that alters and decreases the time it takes a chemical reaction to occur.

cat-a-ma-ran *n.* A boat with twin hulls.

cat-a-pult *n.* An ancient military device for throwing arrows or stones; a device for launching aircraft from the deck of a ship.

cat-a-ract *n.* A large waterfall or downpour. *Pathol.* A disease of the lens of the eye, causing total or partial blindness.

ca-tarrh *n., Pathol.* Inflammation of the nose and throat. **catarrhal** *adj.*

ca-tas-tro-phe *n.* A terrible and sudden disaster. **catastophic** *adj.*, **-ically** *adv.*

cat-bird *n.* A song bird of North America with slate-gray feathers.

cat-call *n.* A shrill whistle to express derision or disapproval.

catch *v.* To take; to seize or capture; to reach in time; to intercept; to become entangled or fastened. **catch** *n.*

catch-all *n.* A container or bag for odds and ends.

catch-er *n.* A person who catches a ball.

Catch-22 *n.* A situation where alternatives can cancel each other out, leaving no means of settling a dilemma.

cat-e-gor-i-cal *adj.* Absolute; certain; related to or included in a category without qualification. **-ly** *adv.*

cat-e-go-rize *v.* To place in categories.

cat-e-go-ry *n., pl.* **-ries** A general group to which something belongs.

ca-ter *v.* To provide a food service; to bring directly to a location. **caterer** *n.*

cat-er-pil-lar *n.*

The very fuzzy, worm-like, brightly-colored spiny larva of a moth or butterfly.

cat-er-waul *n.* The harsh cry made by cats at mating time. **caterwaul** *v.*

cat-fish *n.* A scaleless, freshwater fish that has long barbels or whiskers around the mouth.

cat-gut *n.* A thin, tough cord made from the fried intestines of sheep.

ca-the-dral *n.* A large and important church, containing the seat of a bishop.

cath-e-ter *n., Med.* A thin, flexible tube that is inserted into body cavities for drainage and to draw urine from the bladder. **catheterize** *v.*

cath-ode *n.* The negatively charged electrode which receives positively charged ions during electrolysis.

cath-ode ray tube *n.* The vacuum tube on which images are found, used in a computer screen.

Catholic *n.* A member of the Roman Catholic Church.

Ca-thol-i-cism *n.* The doctrine, practice, and faith of the Roman Catholic Church.

cat-i-on *n.* A positively charged ion that is attracted in electrolytes to a negative electrode. **cationic** *adj.*

cat-nap *n.* A short nap. **catnap** *v.*

cat--o'--nine--tails *n.* A handmade whip with nine knotted cords fastened to a handle.

CAT scan *n.* A cross-sectional picture produced by a scanner, used to x-ray the body by using computerized axial tomography.

CAT scan-ner *n.* The machine used to produce a cross-sectional picture of the body.

cat-sup n., Variation of ketchup

cat-tail n. A long marsh plant that has minute brown flowers and long leaves, used in making chair seats and in dried flower arrangements.

cat-tle n., pl. Farm animals raised for meat and dairy products.

cat-ty adj. Malicious or spiteful. **cattily** adv., **cattiness** n.

cat-ty--cor-nered adj. Not straight; sitting at an angle.

Cau-ca-sian n. An inhabitant of Caucasus. adj. Relating to a major ethnic division of the human race; of or relating to the white race.

cau-cus n. A meeting of a political party to make policy decisions and to select candidates.

caught v. Past tense of catch.

cau-li-flow-er n. A vegetable related to broccoli and cabbage.

caulk v. To seal seams and edges against leakage of water and air. **caulker** n.

cause v. To produce a result, consequence, or effect. n. A goal, principle; a reason; motive. **causer** n.

cau-se-rie n. A short informal conversation or chat.

cause-way n. A paved highway through a marsh tract; raised road over water.

cau-ter-ize v. To sear or burn with a hot instrument. **cauterization** n.

cau-ter-y n. A very hot instrument used to destroy tissue that does not seem normal.

cau-tion n. A warning careful planning.

cau-tious adj. Very careful.

cav-al-cade n. A group of horse-drawn carriages or riders, forming a procession.

cav-a-lier n. A very gallant gentleman; a knight.

cav-al-ry n., pl. -ies Army troops trained to fight on horseback or in armored vehicles. **cavalryman** n.

cave n. An underground tomb or chamber with an opening at the ground surface.

ca-ve-at n. A formal legal notice to stop the proceedings until both sides have a hearing; a warning or caution.

ca-vern n. A very large underground cave. **cavernous** adj.

cav-i-ar or **cav-i-are** n. The eggs of large fish, eaten as an appetizer.

cav-i-ty n., pl. -ies A decayed place in a tooth; a hollow or hole.

CD abbr. Compact disk; civil defense; certificate of deposit.

cease v. To come to an end or put an end to; to stop.

cease-fire v. To stop fighting, usually as a result of a truce.

cease-less adj. Endless. **ceaselessly** adv.

ce-cum or **cae-cum** n., Anat. The pouch where the large intestine begins.

ce-dar n. An evergreen tree with fragrant, reddish wood.

ce-dil-la n. A diacritical mark placed under the letter c in the French vocabulary to indicate a modification

or alteration of the usual phonetic sound.

ceil-ing n. The overhead covering of a room; the maximum limit to something; the maximum height for visibility under specified conditions for aircraft.

cel-e-brate v. To observe with ceremonies, rejoicing, or festivity.

cel-eb-ri-ty n., pl. -ies A famous person.

cel-er-y n.

A green vegetable with an edible stalk.

ce-les-ta n. A musical instrument which produces bell-like tones when the keyboard and metal plates are struck by hammers.

ce-les-tial adj. Heavenly; spiritual.

cel-i-bate n. A person who remains unmarried because of religious vows; one who is sexually abstinent. **celibacy** n., **celibate** adj.

cell n.

A typical cell

A prison; a small room; the smallest unit of any organism that is capable of independent function, is composed of a small mass of cytoplasm, usually encloses a central nucleus and is surrounded by a membrane or a rigid cell wall; a cavity of an ovary or pericarp that is seed-bearing. Electr. The part of a battery that generates the electricity; in computer science, the location in memory that holds a single unit of information; a byte.

cel-lar n. An underground area, beneath a building, used for storage.

cel-lo n. A base instrument of the violin family. **cellist** n.

cel-lo-phane n. A transparent paper-like material made from treated cellulose that has been processed in thin, clear strips.

cel-lu-lar adj. Consisting of cells.

cel-lu-lite n. A fatty deposit or area under the skin.

cel-lu-lose n. A carbohydrate that is insoluble in ordinary solvents and forms the fundamental material for the structure of plants.

ce-ment n. A construction material made up of powdered, calcined rock and clay materials which when added with water, set up as a hard, solid mass.

cem-e-ter-y n., pl. -ies The place for burying the dead.

cen-ser n. A vessel or container for burning incense.

cen-sor n. A person who examines films

and printed materials to determine what might be objectionable. -ship *n.*

cen-sure *n.* An expression of criticism and/or disapproval.

cen-sus *n.* An official count of the population.

cent *n.* One; one hundredth of a dollar.

cen-te-nar-i-an *n.* A person who has reached the age of 100 or more.

cen-ter *n.* The place of equal distance from all sides; the heart; in sports, a person who holds the middle position, as in the forward line.

cen-ti-pede *n.* A flat arthropod with numerous body segments and legs.

cen-tral *adj.* In, near, or at the center; of primary importance. -ly *adv.*, -ize *v.*

cen-tral ner-vous sys-tem *n.* The nervous system that consists of the spinal cord and the brain.

cen-trif-u-gal *adj.* Moving or directing away from a center location.

cen-tu-ry *n., pl.* -ies A period consisting of 100 years.

ce-ram-ic *adj.* Of or relating to a brittle material made by firing a nonmetallic mineral, such as clay.

ce-ram-ics *n.* The art of making a ceramic piece.

ce-re-al *n.* An edible grain eaten as a breakfast food.

cer-e-bel-lum *n., pl.* -bellums The part of the brain responsible for the coordination of voluntary muscular movements.

cer-e-bral hem-or-rhage *n.* The rupture of an artery in the brain, which allows blood to escape.

cer-e-bral pal-sy *n.* A variety of chronic conditions in which brain damage, usually occurring at birth, impairs motor function and control.

cer-e-brum *n., pl.* -brums *or* -bra The brain structure that is divided into two cerebral hemisphere's and occupies most of the cranial cavity.

cer-e-mo-ni-al *adj.* Mark by or relating to a ceremony. ceremonially *adv.*

cer-e-mo-ny *n., pl.* -ies A ritual or formal act performed in a certain manner. ceremonious *adj.*

ce-rise *n.* The color of deep purplish red.

cer-tain *adj., pl.* -ties Being very sure of something; without any doubt; inevitable; not mentioned but assumed. certainly *adv.*

cer-tif-i-cate *n.* A document stating the truth or accuracy of something; a document that certifies fulfillment of duties or requirements, as of a course of study.

cer-tif-i-ca-tion *n.* A certified statement.

cer-ti-fy *v.* To testify in writing that something is true or a fact.

cer-vi-cal *adj.* Relating to the neck of the cervix.

Ce-sar-ean / Ce-sar-i-an *n.* A surgical operation which involves cutting through the abdomen and the uterus to remove or deliver a baby when normal delivery cannot or should not be accomplished.

ce-si-um *n.* An electrometal, white in color, from the alkali group, used in photoelectric cells.

ces-sa-tion *n.* The act of stopping or ceasing.

ces-sion *n.* The act of giving up territory or rights to another.

cess-pool *n.* A pit or hole for the collection of drainage from toilets, and sinks and other waste water.

chafe *v.* To become sore by rubbing; to irritate.

chaf-fer *v.* To bargain; to haggle.

chaf-ing dish *n.* A dish for cooking food and keeping it warm at the table.

cha-grin *n.* A feeling of distress caused by disappointment, failure, or humiliation.

chain *n.* A connection of several links; anything that confines or restrains. chain gang Prisoners that are chained together. chain reaction Series of events that directly affect one another.

chain-smoke *v.* To smoke cigarettes one right after another.

chair *n.* A seat with four legs and a back, intended for one person; a seat of office; the chairman. *Slang* Electric chair. chair lift A chair suspended from cables that is used to carry people and snow equipment up or down the ski slopes.

chair-man *n., pl.* -men The person presiding over a committee, board, or other meeting. -ship, -person *n.*

chaise *n.* A one-horse vehicle for two people.

cha-let *n.* A cottage that has a gently sloping and overhanging roof.

chal-ice *n.* A drinking goblet or cup.

chalk *n.* A soft mineral made from fossil seashells, used for marking on a surface, such as a slate board. chalky *adj.*

chalk-board *n.* A blackboard made from slate.

chal-lah *or* cha-lah A loaf of braided bread made with extra eggs, traditionally eaten by Jews on holidays and the Sabbath.

chal-lenge *n.* A demand for a contest; a protest. *v.* To call into question. challenger *n.*

chal-lis *n.* A lightweight printed cloth in rayon, cotton, or wool.

cham-ber *n.* A bedroom in a large home; a judge's office; a meeting place or hall for a legislative body; the compartment of a gun that holds the charge.

cham-ber-lain *n.* The high-ranking person or official of a royal court.

cham-ber-maid *n.* A maid who takes care of bedrooms at a hotel.

cham-pagne *n.* A white sparkling wine.

cham-pi-on *n.* The holder of first place in a contest; one who defends another person.

cham-pi-on-ship *n.* The competition that determines a winner.

chance *n.* The random existence of something happening; a gamble or a risk. chance *v.*

chan-cel *n.* The area of a church that contains the altar and choir.

chan-cel-lor *n.* The chief director or minister of state in certain countries in Europe. **chancellorship** *n.*

chan-cer-y *n.* The office for the safekeeping of official records.

chan-cre *n.* A lesion that is the first indication of syphilis.

chan-croid *n.* A sore or lesion in the genital area that is similar to a chancre, but does not involve syphilis.

chanc-y *adj.* Risky; dangerous.

chan-de-lier *n.* A light fixture with many branches for lights that is suspended from the ceiling.

chan-dler *n.* A person who makes and sells candles. **chandlery** *n.*

change *v.* To become or make different; to alter; to put with another; to use to take the place of another; to freshen a bed by putting clean coverings on. *n.* Coins; money given back when the payment exceeds the bill.

changeable *adj.,* **changeably** *adv.,* **changeability, changer** *v.*

chan-nel *n.* The deepest part of a stream, river, or harbor; the course that anything moves through or past; a groove.

chant *n.* A melody in which all words are sung on the same note. *v.* To celebrate with a song. **chanter** *n.*

Cha-nu-kah *n., Variation of* Hanukkah

cha-os *n.* Total disorder.

chaotic *adj.,* **chaotically** *adv.*

chap *n., Slang* A fellow; a man. *v.* To dry and split open from the cold and wind.

chap-el *n.* A place to worship, usually contained in a church.

chap-er-on *or* **chap-er-one** *n.* An older woman who supervises younger people. **chaperone** *v.*

chap-lain *n.* A clergyman who conducts religious services for a group.

chap-let *n.* A garland for the head; a string of beads.

chaps *pl., n.* Leather overpants, without a seat, worn over trousers by cowboys to provide protection for their legs.

chap-ter *n.* One division of a book; a branch of a fraternity, religious order, or society.

char-ac-ter *n.* A quality or trait that distinguishes an individual or group; a person that is portrayed in a play; a distinctive quality or trait. *adj.* Distinctive; peculiar.

cha-rades *pl., n.* A game in which the syllables of words are acted out by each player.

char-coal *n.* A carbonaceous material resulting from the imperfect combustion of organic matter, such as wood; material used to draw pictures.

chard *n.* On edible white beet with large, succulent leaves.

charge *v.* To give responsibility; to ask a price; to accuse; to impute something to; to command; to record a debt. *n.* Management; custody; supervision; an expense or price. *Slang* A thrill.

charg-er *n.* An apparatus for recharging a battery.

char-i-ot *n.* An ancient horse-drawn vehicle used to fight battles. **-eer** *n.*

char-i-ty *n.* Money or help given to aid the needy; an organization, fund, or institution whose purpose is to aid those in need.

cha-ri-va-ri *n.* A mock serenade to newlyweds, performed with horns, tin pans, etc.

char-la-tan *n.* One who falsely claims to possess knowledge or a skill he does not have. **charlatanism** *n.*

char-ley horse *n.* A severe muscle cramp in an arm or a leg.

charm *n.* The ability to delight or please; a small ornament that has a special meaning, usually worn on a bracelet.

char-nel *n.* A special room or building that contains the bones or bodies of the dead.

chart *n.* A map, graph, or table that gives information in a form that is easy to read.

char-ter *n.* An official document that grants certain privileges and rights. *v.* To lease or hire a vehicle or aircraft.

char-treuse *n.* A light yellowish green.

char-y *adj.* Wary; cautious; not wasting time, resources, or money.

charily *adv.,* **chariness** *n.*

chase *v.* To follow quickly; to pursue; to run after. **chase, chaser** *n.*

chasm *n.* A very deep crack in the earth's surface.

chas-sis *n.* The rectangular framework that supports the body and engine of a motor vehicle.

chaste *adj.* Morally pure; modest; not guilty of participating in sexual intercourse.

chas-tise *v.* To severely reprimand; to punish by beating. **chastisement** *n.*

chas-u-ble *n.* The vestment without sleeves worn over the alb by a priest when celebrating Mass.

chat *v.* To converse in a friendly manner.

chat-tel *n.* An item of movable personal property.

chauf-feur *n.* A person who is hired to drive an automobile for another person.

chau-vin-ism *n.* The unreasonable belief in the superiority of one's own group. **chauvinist** *n.,* **chauvinistic** *adj.*

cheap *adj.* Inexpensive; low in cost; of poor quality. **-ly** *adv.,* **cheapness** *n.*

cheap-en *v.* To lessen the value; to make cheap.

cheap-skate *n.* A person who is very cheap and refuses to spend money.

cheat *v.* To deprive of by deceit; to break the rules. **cheater** *n.*

check *v.* To control or restrain; to examine for correctness or condition. *n.* The act of verifying, comparing, or testing; a bill one receives at a restaurant; a written order on one's bank to pay money from funds on deposit; the act of comparing item to item; a move in chess which threatens a king and which forces the opponent to move the king to safety.

check-book *n.* A book containing blank checks for a checking account.

check-ers *n.* A game played by two people on a red-and-black checkered board.

check-er-board *n.* A game board used to play various games; a pattern that is arranged like a checkerboard.

check-mate *n.* The move in chess which places the opponent's king in a check from which escape is impossible.

check-up *n.* A complete physical examination.

ched-dar *n.* A firm, smooth cheese which ranges in flavor from mild to sharp.

cheek *n.* The fleshy part of the face just below the eye and above and to the side of the mouth.

cheek-bone *n.* The facial bone below the eyes.

cheep *n.* To utter high-pitched sounds.

cheer *v.* To give courage to; to instill with courage or hope; to make glad or happy; to shout with encouragement or applause. *n.* Good spirits; happiness.

cheer-ful *adj.* Having good spirits.

cheer-leader *n.* Someone who leads cheers at a sporting event.

cheese *n.* A food made from the curd of milk that is seasoned and aged.

cheese-cake *n.* A dessert cake made from cream cheese, cottage cheese, eggs, and sugar, which and may be topped with a variety of fruit.

cheese-cloth *n.* A loosely-woven cotton gauze.

chee-tah *n.* A swift-running, long-legged African wildcat.

chef *n.* A male cook who manages a kitchen; the head cook.

che-la *n.* The pincer-like claw of an arachnid.

chem-i-cal *adj.* Of or related to chemistry. **chemically** *adv.*

che-mise *n.* A woman's loose undergarment which resembles a slip; a loose-fitting dress that hangs straight down from the shoulders.

chem-ist *n.* A person who is versed in chemistry.

chem-is-try *n.* The scientific study of the composition, structure, and properties of substances and their reactions.

che-mo-ther-a-py *n.* The treatment of a disease, such as cancer, with chemicals. **chemotherapeutic** *adj.*

che-nille *n.* A fuzzy, soft cord used to make rugs, bedspreads, and other fabrics.

cher-ish *v.* To treat with love; to hold dear.

Cher-o-kee *n.* A tribe of Iroquoian Indians who formerly lived in northern Georgia and North Carolina, now living in the state of Oklahoma.

che-root *n.* A cigar that is cut off square at both ends.

cher-ry *n., pl.* **-ies** A fruit tree bearing a small, round, deep, or purplish red fruit with a small, hard stone.

cher-ub *n., pl.* **-cherubs** A beautiful young child; a representation of an angel resembling a child with a rosy face and wings.

chess *n.* A game played on a chessboard by two people, each of whom has sixteen pieces and tries to checkmate his opponent's king in order to win the game.

chess-board *n.* A board with sixty-four squares, which can be used to play chess or checkers.

chess-man *n., pl.* **chessmen** Any of the pieces necessary to play chess.

chest *n.* The part of the upper body that is enclosed by the thorax; the ribs; a box usually having a hinged lid, used for storage.

ches-ter-field *n.* An overcoat with concealed buttons and a velvet collar.

chest-nut *n.* A tree bearing edible reddish-brown nuts; a nut from a chestnut tree.

chev-ron *n.* An insignia or emblem consisting of stripes that meet at an angle, indicating rank, length of service, or merit.

chew *v.* To crush or grind with the teeth; to masticate. *n.* The act of chewing. **chewer** *n.*, **chewy** *adj.*

Chi-an-ti *n.* A dry red or white wine from Italy.

chi-a-ro-scu-ro *n.* The distribution of shade and light in a picture.

Chi-ca-na *n.* An American woman with Mexican ancestry.

chick *n.*

A young chicken or bird. *Slang* A young woman.

chick-a-dee *n.* A North American bird with dark feathers on the throat and the top of the head.

chick-en *n.* A domestic fowl; the edible meat of a chicken. *Slang* Cowardly; afraid; losing one's nerve.

chick-en feed *n.* Food for chickens. *Slang* Very little money.

chick-en--heart-ed *adj.* Timid or cowardly.

chick-en pox *n.* A contagious childhood disease, characterized by fever and skin eruptions.

chick-pea *n.* A bushy plant from Mediterranean regions and central Asia bearing edible pea-like seeds.

chick-weed *n.* A small, weedy plant with small white flowers.

chic-le *n.* The milky juice of a tropical tree; the principal ingredient of chewing gum.

chic-o-ry *n., pl.* **-ies** An herb with blue flowers used in salads, the dried, roasted roots of which are used as a coffee substitute.

chide *v.* To scold or find fault. **chider** *n.*

chief *n.* The person of highest rank. **chiefly** *adv., or adj.*

chief-tain *n.* The head of a group, clan

or tribe.

chif-fon *n.* A sheer fabric made from rayon or silk. *adj.* In cooking, having a fluffy texture.

chif-fo-nier *n.* A tall chest of drawers with a mirror at the top.

chig-ger *n.* A mite that attaches itself to the skin and causes intense itching.

chi-gnon *n.* A roll of hair worn at the back of the neck.

chil-blain *n.* An inflammation of the hands and feet caused by exposure to cold.

child *n., pl.* **children** A young person of either sex; adolescent; a person between infancy and youth. **childish** *adj.*

child abuse *n.* Sexual or physical maltreatment of a child by a guardian, parent, or other adult.

child-birth *n.* The act of giving birth.

child-hood *n.* The time or period of being a child.

child-like *adj.* Characteristic of a child.

chil-i *or* **chile** *or* **chil-li** *n.* A hot pepper; a sauce made of meet and chili or chili powder.

chil-i con car-ne *n.* A spicy dish made of chili powder, beans, ground meat, and tomato sauce.

chill *v.* To be cold, often with shivering; to reduce to a lower temperature. *n.* A feeling of cold.

chill-y *adj.* Very cold; without warmth of temperature or feeling.

chime *n.* A group or set of bells tuned to a scale. *v.* To announce on the hour, by sounding a chime.

chi-me-ra *n.* An absurd fantasy; an imaginary monster with a goat's body, a lion's head, and a serpent's tail.

chim-ney *n.* A flue for smoke to escape, as from a fireplace.

chim-pan-zee *n.* An anthropoid ape with large ears and dark brown hair, smaller and more intelligent than the gorilla.

chin *n.* The lower part of the face. *v.* To lift oneself up while grasping an overhead bar until the chin is level with the bar.

chin-chil-la *n.* A rodent from South America raised for its soft fur.

chine *n.* The spine or backbone of animals.

chink *n.* A narrow crack.

chintz *n.* A printed cotton fabric which is glazed.

chintz-y *adj.* Cheap.

chip *n.* A small piece that has been broken or cut from another source; a disk used in the game of poker; in Computer Science, an integrated circuit engraved on a silicone substrate.

chip-munk *n.*

A striped rodent of the squirrel family.

chi-ro-prac-tic *n.* A method of therapy in which the body is manipulated to adjust the spine. **chiropractor** *n.*

chirp *n.* The high-pitched sound made by a cricket or a small bird. **chirp** *v.*

chis-el *n.* A tool with a sharp edge which is used to shape and cut metal, wood, or stone.

chit *n.* A voucher indicating the amount owed for food or drink; a lively girl.

chit-chat *n.* Casual conversation or small talk.

chi-tin *n.* The substance that forms the hard outer cover of insects.

chit-ter-lings *pl., n.* The small intestines of a pig, used as food.

chiv-al-ry *n., pl.* **-ies** The brave and courteous qualities of an ideal knight.

chive *n.* An herb used as flavoring in cooking.

chlo-ride *n.* A compound of chlorine with a double positive element.

chlo-rine *n.* A greenish-yellow compound used to purify water, bleach, and disinfectant.

chlo-ro-phyll *n.* The green pigment that is found in photosynthetic organisms.

chock *n.* A wedge or block placed under a wheel to prevent motion. **chock** *v.*

choc-o-late *n.* A preparation of ground and roasted cacao nuts that is usually sweetened; a candy or beverage made from chocolate. **chocolaty** *adj.*

Choc-taw *n.* A member of the tribe of North American Indians from the Muskhogean group, now residing in Oklahoma.

choice *n.* To select or choose; the opportunity, right, or power to choose.

choir *n.* An organized group of singers that usually perform in a church.

chok-er *n.* A necklace that fits tightly around the neck.

cho-les-ter-ol *n.* A fatty crystalline substance that is derived from bile and is present in most gallstones, the brain, and blood cells.

choose *v.* To select or pick out; to prefer; to make a choice. **chosen** *adj.*, **choosy** *or* **choosey** *adj.*

chop *v.* To cut by making a sharp downward stroke; to cut into bits or small pieces.

chop-per *n., Slang* A helicopter.

chop-pers *pl., n., Slang* False teeth.

chop-py *adj.* Rough; irregular; jerky.

chop-sticks *pl., n.* Slender sticks of ivory or wood, Chinese in origin, used in pairs of two as eating utensils.

cho-ral *adj.* Pertaining to, written for, or sung by a choir or chorus. **-ly** *adv.*

cho-rale *n.* A Protestant hymn with a simple melody, sung in unison.

chore *n.* A daily task; a task that becomes unpleasant or burdensome.

cho-re-a *n.* An acute nervous disease especially of children, marked by irregular and uncontrollable movement of muscles.

cho-re-og-ra-phy *n.* The creation of a dance routine. **choreograph** *v.*, **choreographer** *n.*, **-ic** *adj.*, **-ically** *adv.*

chor-is-ter *n.* A choirboy or a member of

a choir.

chor-tle v. To chuckle with glee, especially in triumph or joy.
chortle, chortler n.

cho-rus n., pl. -ses A group of people who sing together; the repeated verses of a song.

chose v. The past tense of choose.

cho-sen adj. Selected or preferred above all.

chow-der n. A soup dish made with fish or clams, often having a milk base.

Christ n. Jesus; The Messiah; God's son who died to save Christians from sin.

chris-ten v. To baptize; to give a Christian name at baptism; to use for the first time. christening n.

Chris-tian n. A believer and follower of the teachings of Jesus.
Christianly adv., Christianity n.

Christ-mas n. December 25th, the anniversary of the birth of Jesus Christ, observed as a holiday or holy day.

chro-mat-ic adj. Relating to color.

chro-mo-some n. One of several small bodies in the nucleus of a cell, containing genes responsible for the determination and transmission of hereditary characteristics.

chron-ic adj. Frequently recurring; continuing for long periods of time; affected by a disease for a long time. chronically adv.

chron-i-cle n. A record of events written in the order in which they occurred.
chronicle v., chronicler n.

chrys-a-lis n., pl.-ses The enclosed pupa from which a moth or butterfly develops.

chry-san-the-mum n. A cultivated plant having large, showy flowers.

chub n. A freshwater fish related to the carp.

chub-by adj. Plumb; rounded. -iness n.

chuck v. To tap or pat affectionately under the chin. Slang To throw out or to throw away; to quit; to give up. n. A cut of beef extending from the neck to the ribs.

chuck-hole n. A hole in the street or the pavement.

chuck-le v. To laugh quietly with satisfaction. chuckler n.

chum n. A close friend or pal.

chunk n. A thick piece of anything; a large quantity of something; a lump.

church n. A building for Christian worship; a congregation of public Christian worship.

churl n. A rude or rustic person.
churlish adj., churlishness n.

churn n. The container in which cream or milk is beaten vigorously to make butter. v. To agitate in a churn in order to make butter; to agitate violently.

chute n. An incline passage through which water, coal, etc., may travel to a destination. Slang A parachute.

chut-ney n. An agreeable condiment of fruit, spices, and herbs.

ci-der n. The juice from apples.

ci-gar n. Rolled tobacco leaves used for smoking.

cig-a-rette n. or **cig-a-ret** A small amount of tobacco rolled in thin paper for smoking.

cinch n. The strap for holding a saddle. v. To assure. Slang Something easy to do.

cin-cho-na n. A tree in South America whose bark yields quinine.

cinc-ture n. A belt or cord to put around the waist. v. To encircle or surround with a cincture.

cin-der n. A piece of something that is partially burned. cindery adj.

cin-e-ma n., pl. -mas A motion picture; a motion picture theatre; the business of making a motion picture.

cin-e-mat-o-graph n. A movie projector or camera.

cin-e-ma-tog-ra-phy n. The art of photographing a motion picture.
cinematographer n.

cin-na-bar n. A mineral which is the principal source of mercury.

cin-na-mon n. The aromatic inner bark of a tropical Asian tree, used as a spice, reddish brown in color.

ci-pher n. The symbol for the absence of quantity; O; secret writing that has a prearranged key or scheme.

cir-cle n. A process that ends at its starting point; a group of people having a common interest or activity.

cir-cuit n. The closed path through which an electric current flows.

cir-cuit break-er n. A relay switch that automatically stops the flow of an electric current in an overloaded circuit.

cir-cuit court n. The lowest court of record, located in various counties or districts over which its jurisdiction extends.

cir-cu-lar adj. Moving in a circle or round-like fashion; relating to something in a circle; having free motion, as the air. circularity n.

cir-cu-late v. To pass from place to place or person to person; to distribute in a wide area. -ion, -or n., -ory adj.

cir-cum-cise v. To remove the foreskin on the male penis. circumcision n.

cir-cum-fer-ence n. The perimeter or boundary of a circle. -ential adj.

cir-cum-flex n. A mark indicating the quality or sound of vowels as they appear in words.

cir-cum-scribe v. To confine something within drawn boundaries; to surround.

cir-cum-stance n. A fact or condition that must be considered when making a decision.

cir-cum-stan-tial adj. Incidental; not essential; dependent on circumstances.

cir-cum-stan-ti-ate adj. Providing support or circumstantial evidence.

cir-cum-vent v. To outwit or gain advantage; to avoid or go around.
circumvention n., circumventive adj.

cir-cus n., pl. -cuses Entertainment featuring clowns, acrobats, and trained animals.

cir-rho-sis n. A liver disease that is ultimately fatal. **cirrhotic** adj.

cir-rus n., pl. **-cirri** A high altitude, white, wispy cloud.

cis-tern n. A man-made tank or artificial reservoir for holding rain water.

cit-a-del n. A fortress commanding a city; a stronghold.

ci-ta-tion n. An official summons from a court; a quotation used in literary or legal material; an honor.

cite v. To bring forward as proof; to summon to action; to rouse; to summon to appear in court. **-able** adj., n.

cit-i-zen n. A resident of a town or city; a native or naturalized person entitled to protection from a government. **citizenship** n.

citizen's band n. A two-way radio frequency band for private use.

citric acid n. A colorless acid found in lime, lemon, and other juices.

cit-ron n. A fruit resembling a lemon, but less acidic and larger in size.

cit-rus n., pl. **citrus, citruses** Any of a variety of trees bearing fruit with thick skins, as limes, oranges, lemons, and grapefruits.

city n. A place larger than a town.

civ-et n. A cat-like mammal that secretes a musky fluid from the genital glands, which is used in perfumery.

civ-ic adj. Relating to or of a citizen, city, or citizenship.

civ-il adj. Relating to citizens; relating to the legal proceedings concerned with the rights of private individuals.

civ-il de-fense n. A civilian program of volunteers ready to take action in case of a natural disaster, invasion, or enemy attack.

ci-vil-ian n. A person not serving in the military, as a firefighter, or as a policeman.

civ-i-li-za-tion n. A high level of social, cultural, and political development.

civ-i-lize v. To bring out of a state of savagery into one of education and refinement.

civ-il rights pl., n. Rights guaranteed to citizens; the rights provided by the 13th and 14th amendments of the United States Constitution.

civ-il ser-vice n. The administrative or executive service of a government.

civ-il war n. A war between two regions of the same country; English Civil War (1642-1646); United States Civil War (1861-1865); Spanish Civil War (1936-1939).

claim v. To ask for one's due; to hold something to be true; to make a statement that something is true. **claim, claimant** n.

clair-voy-ance n. The ability to visualize in the mind distant objects or objects hidden from the senses. **clairvoyant** n.

clam n. Any of various marine and freshwater bivalve mollusks. Slang To become silent; to clam up.

clam-bake n. An outside gathering in which clams are cooked over hot coals.

clam-ber v. To climb by using both the hands and feet. **clamberer** n.

clam-my adj. Damp, cold, and sticky. **clammily** adv., **clamminess** n.

clam-or n. A loud noise or outcry; a vehement protest or demand. **clamorous** adj., **clamorously** adv.

clamp n. A device for holding or fastening things together.

clan n. A large group of people who are related to one another by a common ancestor. **-nish** adj., **-sman** n.

clan-des-tine adj. Kept or done in secrecy for a purpose.

clang v. To cause or make a loud, ringing, metallic sound.

clan-gor n. A loud series of clangs.

clank n. A sharp, quick, metallic sound.

clap v. To applaud; to strike the hands together with an explosive sound.

clap-board n. A narrow board with one end thicker than the other, used to cover the outside of buildings so as to weatherproof the inside.

clap-per n. The part of a bell that hits against the side.

clar-i-fy v. To become or make clearer. **clarification** n.

clar-i-net n.

A woodwind instrument with a single reed. **clarinetist** n.

clar-i-ty n. The state or quality of being clear.

clash v. To bring or strike together; to collide; to conflict.

clasp n. A hook to hold parts of objects together; a grasp or grip of the hands.

class n. A group or set that has certain social or other interests in common; a group of students who graduate at the same time.

clas-sic adj. Belonging in a certain category of excellence; having a lasting artistic worth.

clas-si-cal adj. Relating to the style of the ancient Roman or Greek classics; standard and authoritative, not experimental or new.

clas-si-cism n. A belief in the esthetic principles of ancient Rome and Greece. **classicist** n.

clas-si-fy v. To arrange or assign items, people, etc., into the same class or category. **classification** n.

clat-ter v. To make or to cause a rattling sound. **clatter** n.

clause n. A group of words which are part of a simple compound, or complex sentence, containing a subject and predicate.

claus-tro-pho-bia n. A fear of small or enclosed places.

clav-i-chord n. A keyboard instrument which is one step down from the piano.

clav-i-cle n. The bone that connects the breastbone and the shoulder blade.

cla-vier *n.* An instrument with a keyboard, such as the harpsichord.

claw *n.*

A sharp, curved nail on the foot of an animal; the pincer of certain crustaceans, such as the crab, lobster, etc.

clay *n.* A fine-grained, pliable earth that hardens when fired, used to make pottery, bricks, and tiles.

clay pig-eon *n.* A clay disk that is hurled into the air as a target for trapshooting and skeet.

clean *adj.* Free from impurities, dirt, or contamination; neat in habits.

cleanse *v.* To make pure or clean.

clear *adj.* Free from precipitation and clouds; able to hear, see, or think easily; free from doubt or confusion; free from a burden, obligation, or guilt. **clearly** *adv.*, **clearness** *n.*

clearance *n.* The distance that one object clears another by; a permission to proceed.

cleat *n.* A metal projection that provides support, grips, or prevents slipping.

cleav-age *n.* The process, act, or result of splitting; the cleft a woman displays in low-cut clothes.

cleav-er *n.* A knife used by butchers.

clef *n.* A symbol indicating which pitch each line and space represents on a musical staff.

clem-ent *adj.* Merciful; mild.

cler-gy *n.* The group of men and women who are ordained as religious leaders and servants of God.

cler-gy-man *n.* A member of the clergy.

cler-i-cal *adj.* Trained to handle office duties.

clerk *n.* A worker in an office who keeps accounts, records, and correspondence up to date; a person who works in the sales department of a store.

Cleveland, Stephen Grover *n.* The 22nd and 24th president of the United States from, 1885-1889 and 1893-1897.

clev-er *adj.* Mentally quick; showing dexterity and skill. **cleverly** *adv.*, **-ness** *n.*

cli-ent *n.* A person who secures the professional services of another.

cli-en-tele *n.* A collection of patients, customers, or clients.

cliff *n.* A high, steep edge or face of a rock.

cliff-hanger *n.* Anything which causes suspense and anticipation until the final outcome is known.

cli-mac-ter-ic *n.* A time in life when physiological changes.

cli-mate *n.* The weather conditions of a certain region generalized or averaged over a period of years; the prevailing atmosphere. **-ic** *adj.*, **-ically** *adv.*

cli-max *n.* The point of greatest intensity and fullest suspense; the culmination.

climb *v.* To move to a higher or lower location; to advance in rank or status. **climbable** *adj.*, **climber** *n.*

clinch *v.* To secure; to fasten; to settle definitively. **clinch** *n.*

cling *v.* To hold fast to; to grasp or stick; to hold on and resist emotional separation. **clinger** *n.*

clin-ic *n.* A medical establishment connected with a hospital; a center that offers instruction or counseling.

clink *v.* To cause a light ringing sound.

clip *v.* To cut off; to curtail; to cut short. *n.* Something that grips, holds, or clasps articles together.

clip-per *n.* A sailing vessel that travels at a high rate of speed.

clique *n.* A small and exclusive group of people.

cloak *n.* A loose outer garment that conceals or covers.

clob-ber *v.*, *Slang* To hit repeatedly and violently.

cloche *n.* A bell-shaped, close-fitting hat.

clock *n.*

An instrument that measures time. *v.* To time with a watch, clock, stop-watch, etc.

clod *n.* A large piece or lump of earth; a stupid, ignorant person.

clog *v.* To choke up. *n.* A shoe with a wooden sole.

clone *n.* An identical reproduction grown from a single cell of the original. **clone** *v.*

close *adj.* Near, as in time, space, or relationship; nearly even, as in competition; fitting tightly. *v.* To shut.

clos-et *n.* A small cabinet, compartment, or room for storage. **closet** *v.*

close-up *n.* A picture that is taken at close range; a close view or examination of something.

clot *n.* A thick or solid mass, as of blood.

cloth *n.*, *pl.* **cloths** A knitted, woven, or matted piece of fabric, used to cover a table; the professional clothing of the clergy.

clothe *v.* To provide clothes; to cover with clothes; to wrap.

clo-ture *n.* A parliamentary action that calls for an immediate vote.

cloud *n.* A visible body of water or ice particles floating in the atmosphere; something that obscures. **cloudy** *adj.*, **cloudiness** *n.*

clout *n.* A heavy blow with the hand. *Slang* The amount of influence or pull a person may have. **clout** *v.*

clove *n.* A spice from an evergreen tree; a small bud that is part of a larger group, as a clove of garlic.

clo-ver *n.* A plant that has a dense flower and trifoliolate leaves.

clover-leaf *n.* A junction of highways that cross each other at different levels and are connected by curving ramps.

clown *n.* A professional comedian who entertains by jokes, tricks, and funny jest; a circus comedian who dresses in outlandish costumes and wears heavy makeup on his face. **clownish** *adj.*

cloy *v.* To make one sick or disgusted with too much sweetness. **-ingly** *adv.*

club *n.* A heavy wooden stick, used as a weapon; a group of people who have organized themselves with or for a common purpose.

clump *n.* A very thick cluster or group; a dull, heavy sound. *v.* To plant or place in a clump.

clum-sy *adj.* Lacking coordination, grace, or dexterity; not tactful or skillful. **clumsily** *adv.*, **clumsiness** *n.*

clus-ter *n.* A bunch; a group.

clutch *v.* To seize or attempt to seize and hold tightly. *n.* A tight grasp; a device for connecting and disconnecting the engine and the drive shaft in an automobile or other mechanism.

clut-ter *n.* A confused mass of disorder.

coach *n.* An automobile that is closed and usually has four doors and four wheels; a trainer and/or director of athletics, drama, etc.

co-ad-ju-tor *n.* An assistant.

co-ag-u-lant *n.* A substance that causes coagulation.

co-ag-u-late *v.* To clot. **coagulation** *n.*

coal *n.* A mineral widely used as a natural fuel; an ember.

co-a-lesce *v.* To come together or to grow as one.

co-ali-tion *n.* A temporary alliance.

coarse *adj.* Lacks refinement; of inferior or low quality; having large particles; harsh. **coarseness** *n.*

coast *v.* To move without propelling oneself; to use the force of gravity alone; to slide or glide along. *n.* The land bordering the sea. **coaster** *n.*

coat *n.* An outer garment with sleeves, worn over other clothing; a layer that covers a surface. **coat** *v.*, **coating** *n.*

coax *v.* To persuade by tact, gentleness, or flattery. **coaxingly** *adv.*

co-ax-i-al *adj.* Having common coincident axes.

co-ax-i-al cable *n.* A cable that has two or more insulated conductors that are capable of transmitting television or radio signals or multiple telephone or telegraph messages.

cob *n.* A male swan; a corncob; a thickset horse that has short legs.

co-balt *n.* A hard, lustrous metallic element that resembles iron and nickel.

cob-ble *v.* To make or repair shoes; to make or put together roughly.

CO-BOL *n.* In Computer Science, computer programming that is simple and based on English.

co-bra *n.* A venomous snake from Asia or Africa. When excited, the neck dilates into a broad hood.

cob-web *n.* The fine thread from a spider which is spun into a web and used to catch prey.

co-caine *n.* An alkaloid used as an anesthetic and narcotic.

coc-cyx *n.* The small bone at the bottom of the spinal column.

coch-i-neal *n.* A brilliant scarlet dye prepared from the dried, pulverized bodies of certain female insects of tropical America.

coch-le-a *n.* The spiral tube of the inner ear, forming an essential part for hearing.

cock *n.* The adult male in the domestic fowl family; the rooster; the hammer of a firearm and the readiness for firing. *v.* To raise in preparation for hitting; to ready a firearm for firing.

cock-ade *n.* A knot of ribbon or something similar worn on a hat as a badge.

cock-a-too *n.* A crested parrot of the East Indies.

cock-a-trice *n.* A mythical serpent said to be hatched from a cock's egg, deadly to those who meet its glance or feel its breath.

cock-le *n.* European bivalve mollusk of the edible species, having ridged, somewhat heart-shaped shells.

cock-pit *n.* The compartment of an airplane where the pilot and the crew sit.

cock-roach *n.* A flat-bodied, fast running, chiefly nocturnal insect, many of which are household pests.

co-co *n.* The fruit obtained from the coconut palm.

co-coa *n.* The powder from the roasted husked seed kernels of the cacoa.

co-coon *n.* The protective fiber or silk pupal case that is spun by insect larvae.

cod *n.* A large fish of the North Atlantic that is important as food.

cod-dle *v.* To cook just below the boiling point; to simmer.

code *n.* A system of set rules; a set of secret words, numbers, or letters used as a means of communication; in Computer Science, the method of representing information or data by using a set sequence of characters, symbols, or words. **code** *v.*

co-dex *n.* An ancient manuscript of the classics or Scriptures.

codg-er *n.* An odd or eccentric old man.

co-ed-u-ca-tion *n.* An educational system for both men and women at the same institution. **coeducational** *adj.*

co-erce *v.* To restrain or dominate with force; to compel by law, authority, fear, or force.

co-e-val *adj.* Of the same time period.

co-ex-ist *v.* To exist at the same time or together; the ability to live peaceably with others in spite of differences.

cof-fee *n.* A beverage prepared from ground beans of the coffee tree.

cof-fee cake *n.* A sweet dough containing raisins or nuts and shaped into a ring or braid.

cof-fer *n.* A strongbox or chest made for valuables.

cof-fin *n.* A box in which a corpse is buried.

cog *n.* A tooth or one of series of a teeth on the rim of wheel in a machine or a mechanical device.

co-gent *adj.* Compelling; forceful; convincing.

cog-i-tate *v.* To think carefully about or to ponder. **cogitation** *n.*, **-ive** *adj.*

co-gnac *n.* A fine brandy made in France.

cog-nate *adj.* From a common ancestor; identical or similar in nature; related.

cog-ni-zance *n.* Perception of fact; awareness; recognition; observation.

cog-no-men *n.*, *pl.* **cognomens** A person's surname; nickname.

co-hab-it *v.* To live together as husband and wife.

co-here *v.* To stick or hold together.

co-hort *n.* A group of people who are united in one effort; an accomplice.

coif *n.* A close-fitting hat that is worn under a nun's veil.

coil *n.* A series of connecting rings. *v.* To wind in spirals.

coin *n.* A flat, rounded piece of metal used as money. *v.* To invent or make a new phrase or word.

co-in-cide *v.* To happen at the same time; to agree exactly.

co-in-ci-dence *n.* Two events happening at the same time by accident but appearing to have some connection.

co-i-tus *n.* Physical union of male and female sexual organs; sexual intercourse.

coke *n.* A solid, carbonaceous fuel made by heating soft coal until some of its gases have been removed. *Slang* Cocaine.

cold *adj.* Having a low temperature; feeling uncomfortable; without sufficient warmth; lacking in affection or sexual desire; frigid. *n.* An infection of the upper respiratory tract resulting in coughing, sneezing, etc. **coldness** *n.*

cold--blooded *adj.* Done without feeling; having a body temperature that varies according to the temperature of the surroundings. **cold-bloodedly** *adv.*

cold boot *n.* In Computer Science, the boot performed when power is turned on for the first time each day.

cold cuts *pl.*, *n.* A selection of freshly sliced cold meats.

cole *n.* A plant such as the cabbage or a vegetable of the same family.

col-ic *n.* A sharp pain in the abdomen caused by muscular cramps or spasms, occurring most often in very young babies.

col-i-se-um *n.* A large amphitheater used for sporting games.

col-lab-o-rate *v.* To cooperate or work with another person. **collaboration**, **collaborator** *n.*

col-lapse *v.* To fall; to give way; to fold and assume a smaller size; to lose all or part of the air in a lung.

col-lar *n.* The upper part of a garment that encircles the neck and is often folded over.

col-lar-bone *n.*, *Anat.* The clavicle, located near the neck.

col-late *v.* To compare in a critical fashion; to assemble in correct sequence or order.

col-lat-er-al *adj.* Serving to support; guaranteed by stocks, property, bonds, etc.

col-league *n.* Someone who works in the same profession or official body.

col-lect *v.* To gather or assemble; to gather donations or payments. **collectible**, **collection** *n.*

col-lege *n.* An institution of higher education which grants a bachelor's degree; a school of special instruction or special fields.

col-lide *v.* To come together with a direct impact; to clash; to come into conflict.

col-lo-cate *v.* To compare facts and arrange in correct order.

col-lo-di-on *n.* A highly flammable spray solution used to protect wounds and used for photographic plates.

col-loid *n.* A glue-like substance, such as gelatin, that cannot pass through animal membranes.

col-lo-quy *n.*, *pl.* **-quies** A formal conversation or conference.

col-lusion *n.* A secret agreement between two or more people for an illegal purpose.

co-lon *n.* A punctuation mark (:) used to introduce an example or series; the section of the large intestine that extends from the cecum to the rectum.

colo-nel *n.* An officer in the armed forces that ranks above a lieutenant colonel and below a brigadier general.

col-o-ny *n.*, *pl* **-ies** A group of emigrants living in a new land away from, but under the control of, the parent country; a group of insects, as ants.

col-o-phon *n.* The inscription at the end of a book that gives the publication facts.

col-or *n.* The aspect of things apart from the shape, size, and solidity; a hue or tint that is caused by the different degrees of light that are reflected or emitted by them. **colored**, **colorful** *adj.*, **coloring** *n.*, **color** *v.*

Col-o-ra-do *n.* A state located in the western central part of the United States.

col-or-a-tion *n.* The arrangement of different colors or shades.

col-or--blind *adj.* Unable to distinguish colors, either totally or partially.

col-or-fast *adj.* Color that will not run or fade with washing or wearing. **colorfastness** *n.*

co-los-sal *adj.* Very large or gigantic in degree or size.

co-los-sus *n.* Something that is very large, as a huge state, thing, or person.

colt *n.* A very young male horse. **-ish** *adj.*

Columbus, Christopher *n.* The person credited with finding the New World.

col-umn *n.* A decorative and/or supporting pillar used in construction; a vertical division of typed or printed lines on paper. **columnar** *adj.*

col-um-nist *n.* A person who writes a

newspaper or magazine column.

co-ma *n.* A deep sleep or unconsciousness caused by an illness or injury.

co-ma-tose *adj.* Unconscious.

comb *n.* A toothed instrument made from a material such as plastic used for smoothing and arranging the hair; the fleshy crest on the head of a fowl.

com-bat *v.* To fight against; to oppose; to contend. *n.* A struggle; a fight or contest especially with armed conflict, as a battle. **combatant** *n.*

com-bi-na-tion *n.* The process of combining or the state of being combined; a series of numbers or letters needed to open certain locks.

com-bine *v.* To unite; to merge. *n.* A farm machine that harvest by cutting, threshing, and cleaning the grain.

com-bus-ti-ble *adj.* Having the capability of burning. *n.* A combustible material as paper or wood.

com-bus-tion *n.* The chemical change that occurs rapidly and produces heat and light; a burning. **combustive** *adj.*

come *v.* To arrive; to approach; to reach a certain position, state, or result; to appear; to come into view.

com-e-dy *n., pl.* -ies A humorous, entertaining performance with a happy ending; a real-life comical situation.

co-mes-ti-ble *n.* Something that is fit to eat. *adj.* Fit to eat.

com-et *n.* A celestial body that moves in an orbit around the sun, consisting of a solid head that is surrounded by a bright cloud with a long, vaporous tail.

com-fort *v.* To console in time of grief or fear; to make someone feel better; to help; to assist. **comfortingly** *adv.*

com-fort-a-ble *adj.* In a state of comfort; financially secure. **comfortably** *adv.*

com-fort-er *n.* A heavy blanket or quilt; someone who comforts.

com-ic *adj.* Characteristic of comedy. *n.* A comedian. **Comics** Comic strips.

com-i-cal *adj.* Amusing; humorous.

com-ma *n.* The punctuation mark (,) used to indicate separation of ideas or a series in a sentence.

com-mand *v.* To rule; to give orders; to dominate. *n.* In computer science, the instruction given that specifies an operation to be performed.

com-mand-ing *adj.* Dominating by size or position.

com-mem-o-rate *v.* To honor the memory of; to create a memorial to. **commemoration** *n.,* -ive *adj.& n.,* -or *n.*

com-mence *v.* To begin; to start.

com-mence-ment *n.* A graduation ceremony.

com-mend *v.* To give praise; to applaud. -able *adj.,* -ably *adv.,* -ion *n.*

com-men-su-rate *adj.* Equal in duration, extent, or size. **commensuration** *n.*

com-ment *n.* A statement of criticism, analysis, or observation.

com-merce *n.* The exchanging of products or materials; buying and selling.

com-mer-cial *adj.* Of or relating to a product; supported by advertising. *n.* An advertisement on radio or television.

com-mis-er-ate *v.* To display or feel sympathy for someone. **commiserative** *adj.,* **commiseration** *n.*

com-mis-sar *n.* An official of the Communist Party whose duties include enforcement of party loyalty and political indoctrination.

com-mis-sar-y *n., pl.* -ies A store that sells food and supplies on a military base.

com-mis-sion *n.* The moneys paid to a person for his service in the area of sales; the act of entrusting to another; the command or authorization to act as specified.

com-mit-tee *n.* A group of persons appointed or elected to perform a particular task or function. **committeeman, committeewoman** *n.*

com-mode *n.* A movable washstand with storage underneath; a toilet; a low chest of drawers or bureau.

com-mo-di-ous *adj.* Roomy; spacious. **commodiously** *adv.*

com-mo-dore *n.* A naval officer ranking above a captain and below a rear admiral; the senior captain of a naval squadron or of a merchant fleet.

com-mon *adj.* Having to do with, belonging to, or used by an entire community or public; vulgar; unrefined.

com-mon de-nom-i-na-tor *n.* A number that can be evenly divided by all the denominators of a set of fractions.

com-mon frac-tion *n.* A fraction with both the denominator and numerator being whole numbers.

com-mon law *n.* The unwritten system of law that is based on judicial decisions, customs, and usages.

com-mon-weal-th *n.* The common good of the whole group of people.

com-mu-ni-ca-ble *adj.* Capable of being transmitted, as with a disease. **communicability** *n.,* -y *adv.*

com-mu-ni-cate *v.* To make known; to cause others to partake or share something.

com-mu-ni-ca-tion *n.* The act of transmitting ideas through writing or speech; the means to transmit messages between person or places.

com-mun-ion *n.* The mutual sharing of feelings and thoughts; a religious fellowship between members of a church.

com-mun-ion *n.* A sacrament in which bread and wine are consumed to commemorate the death of Christ.

com-mu-nism *n.* A system of government in which goods and production are commonly owned; the theory of social change and struggle toward communism through revolution.

com-mu-ni-ty *n., pl.* -ies A group of people living in the same area and under the same government; a class or group having common interests and likes.

com-mu-ni-ty pro-per-ty *n.* Property not belonging to only a husband or wife but owned jointly.

com-mute *v.* To travel a long distance to one's job each day; to exchange or to substitute.

com-muter *n.* One who travels a long distance on a regular basis.

com-pact *adj.* Packed together or solidly united; firmly and closely united.

com-pac-tor *n.* A device for compressing trash into a small mass for disposal.

com-pan-ion *n.* An associate; a person employed to accompany or assist another; one hired to travel or live with another. companionship *n.*

com-pan-ion-a-ble *adj.* Friendly; sociable. companionably *adv.*

com-pan-ion-way *n.*, *Naut.* A stairway leading from a ship's deck to the cabin below.

com-pa-ny *n., pl.* -ies The gathering of persons for a social purpose; a number of persons who are associated for a common purpose, as in business; a business.

com-pa-ra-ble *adj.* Capable of comparison; worthy of comparison; similar. comparability *n.*, comparably *adv.*, comparative *adj.*

com-pare *v.* To speak of or represent as similar or equal to; to note the similarities or likenesses of.

com-par-i-son *n.* Likeness; similarity. *Gram.* Modification of an verb or adjective that indicates the positive, comparative, or superlative degree.

comparison--shop *v.* To shop and look for bargains by comparing the prices of different brands found available in different stores.

com-part-ment *n.* One of the sections into which an enclosed area is divided.

com-pass *n.*

An instrument used to determine geographic direction; an enclosed area or space; the extent of reach of something; range or area; scope. a pair of compasses A device shaped like a V that is used for drawing circles.

com-pas-sion *n.* Sympathy for someone who is suffering or distressed in some way. compassionate *adj.*

com-pat-i-ble *adj.* Able to function, exist, or live together harmoniously. compatibility *n.*, compatibly *adv.*

com-pa-tri-ot *n.* A person of the same country.

com-peer *n.* A person that is a peer or equal.

com-pel *v.* To urge or force action.

com-pen-di-um *n., pl.* -diums A short summary.

com-pen-sate *v.* To make up for; to make amends; to pay; to neutralize or counterbalance. compensation *n.*, compensatory *adj.*

com-pete *v.* To contend with others; to engage in a contest or competition.

com-pe-tent *adj.* Having sufficient ability; being capable. competence, competency *n.*

com-pe-ti-tion *n.* The act of rivalry or competing; a trial of skill or ability; a contest between teams or individuals. competitive *adj.*

com-pet-i-tor *n.* One who competes against another.

com-pile *v.* To put together material gathered from a number of sources; in Computer Science, to convert our language into machine language. compilation *n.*, compiler *n.*

com-plain-ant *n.* A person filing a formal charge.

com-plaint *n.* An expression of pain, dissatisfaction, or resentment; a cause or reason for complaining; a grievances.

com-plai-sance *n.* The willingness to please, to oblige. complaisant *adj.*

com-ple-ment *n.* Something that perfects, completes, or adds to. -ary *adj.*

com-plete *adj.* Having all the necessary parts; whole; concluded. completion *n.*

com-plex *adj.* Consisting of various intricate parts. -ity *n.*, complexly *adv.*

com-plex-ion *n.* The natural color and texture of the skin. complexioned *adj.*

com-pli-ance *n.* The act of agreeing passively to a request, rule, or demand; the tendency to yield to others. compliant *adj.*, compliancy *n.*

com-pli-cate *v.* To make or become involved or complex.

com-plic-i-ty *n.* An involvement or association with a crime.

com-pli-ment *n.* An expression of praise or admiration.

com-pli-men-ta-ry *adj.* Conveying a compliment.

com-ply *v.* To agree, to consent to, or obey a command or wish. complier *n.*

com-po-nent *n.* A constituent part.

com-port *v.* To behave or conduct oneself in a certain way.

com-pose *v.* To make up from elements or parts; to produce or create a song; to arrange, as to typeset. composer *n.*

com-posed *adj.* Calm.

com-pos-ite *adj.* Made up from separate elements or parts; combined or compounded. **Bot.** Characteristic of a plant with densely clustered flowers.

com-po-si-tion *n.* The act of putting together artistic or literary work; a short essay written for an assignment in school. compositional *adj.*

com-post *n.* A fertilizing mixture that consists of decomposed vegetable matter.

com-po-sure *n.* Tranquillity; calm self-possession.

com-pote *n.* Fruit that is preserved or stewed in syrup; a dish used for holding fruit, candy, etc.

com-pound *n.* The combination of two or more parts, elements, or ingredients. In grammar, a new word that is composed of two or more words joined with a hyphen or written as a solid word. *Chem.* A definite substance that results form combining specific radicals or elements in certain or fixed proportions. *v.* To combine; to increase. **compoundable** *adj.*

com-pound frac-ture *n.* A fracture (broken bone) that breaks and protrudes through the skin.

com-pre-hend *v.* To perceive, to grasp mentally, or to understand fully; to comprise; to include. **-sion** *n.*

com-pre-hen-si-ble *adj.* Capable of being understood. **comprehensibility** *n.*, **comprehensibly** *adv.*

com-pre-hen-sive *adj.* Large in content or scope.

com-press *v.* To press together into a smaller space; to condense. *n.* A soft pad sometimes medicated, for applying cold, heat, moisture, or pressure to a part of the body. **compressibility**, **compression** *n.*, **compressible** *adj.*

com-pres-sed air *n.* Air that is under greater pressure than the atmosphere.

com-pres-sor *n.* Something that compresses; a machine that is used for compressing air to utilize its expansion.

com-prise *v.* To consist of; to be made up of. **comprisable** *adj.*

com-pro-mise *n.* The process of settling or the settlement of differences between opposing sides, with each side making concessions. **compromiser** *n.*, **compromise** *v.*

comp-trol-ler *n.* A person appointed to examine and verify accounts.

com-pul-sion *n.* The act or state of being compelled; an irresistible urge or impulse to act irrationally.

com-pul-sive *n.* An act or state of being compelled

com-pul-so-ry *adj.* Enforced, mandatory.

com-punc-tion *n.* Anxiety arising from guilt or awareness.

com-pur-ga-tion *n.* The clearing of an accused person by the oaths of persons who swear his innocence.

com-pu-ta-tion *n.* The action or act of computing. The operation of a computer.

com-pute *v.* To ascertain or determine by the use of mathematics; to determine something by the use of a computer. **computability**, **computation** *n.*, **computable** *adj.*

com-puter *n.* A person who computes; a high speed, electronic machine which performs logical calculations, processes, stores, and retrieves programmed information.

com-put-er-ese *n.* The language or jargon used by computer technologists.

com-puter-ize *v.* To process or store information on a computer; to switch from manual operations to computer.

com-puter lan-guage *n.* The various codes and information that are used to give data and instructions to computers.

com-rade *n.* An associate, friend, or companion who shares one's interest or occupation. **comradeship** *n.*

con *v.* To study carefully. *Slang* To swindle or trick.

co-na-tus *n.* A natural impulse, tendency or striving.

con brio *adv.* In a brisk or vigorous manner.

conc *abbr.* Concentrated; concentration or concentrate.

con-cat-e-r ate *v.* To join, connect, or link tog..ther. **concatenation** *n.*

con-cave *adj.*

Hollowed and curved inward. **concavely** *adv.*, **concave** *n.*

con-ceal *v.* To keep from disclosure, sight, or knowledge; to hide. **concealable** *adj.*, **-er**, **concealment** *n.*

con-cede *v.* To grant or yield to a right or privilege; to acknowledge as true. **conceder** *n.*, **conceded** *adj.*

con-ceive *v.* To become pregnant; to create a mental image. **-ability** *n.*, **conceivable** *adj.*, **conceivably** *adv.*

con-cen-trate *v.* To give intense thought to; to draw to a common point; to intensify by removing certain elements; to become compact. **-ive** *adj.*, **-or** *n.*

con-cen-tra-tion *n.* The state of being concentrated or the act of concentrating; the process or act of giving complete attention to a certain problem or task.

con-cen-tra-tion camp *n.* An enclosed camp for the confinement of political dissidents, aliens, or prisoners of war.

con-cept *n.* A generalized idea formed from particular occurrences or instances; an opinion. **conceptual** *adj.*

con-cep-tion *n.* The union of sperm and egg; a mental thought or plan.

con-cern *n.* Something to consider; sincere interest; something that affects one's business or affairs. *v.* To be interested in; to be involved with. **concerned** *adj.*

con-cert *n.* A musical performance for a group of people; agreement in purpose, action, or feeling. *v.* To act or plan together. **concerted** *adj.*

con-cer-to *n.*, *pl.* **-tos**, **-ti** A composition that features one or more solo instruments.

con-ces-sion *n.* The act of conceding; something that has been conceded; a tract of land that is granted by a government for a particular use.

con-ces-sion-aire *n.* The operator or holder of a concession.

conch *n.* A tropical marine mollusk having a large spiral shell and flesh that is edible.

con-chol-o-gy *n.* The study of mollusks and shells. **-ical** *adj.*, **conchologist** *n.*

con-cil-i-ate *v.* To win over or to gain a friendship. **-ion**, **-or** *n.*, **-ory** *adj.*

con-cise *adj.* Short and to the point.

con-clave *n.* A private or secret meeting; the private meeting of the Roman Catholic cardinals to elect a new pope.

con-clude *v.* To close or bring to an end; to bring about an agreement; to arrive at a decision; to resolve. **conclusion** *n.*

con-clu-sive *adj.* Putting an end to any questions or doubt.

con-coct *v.* To make by combining ingredients; to devise or to plan. **-tion** *n.*

con-com-i-tant *adj.* Accompanying. **concomitance** *n.*, **concomitantly** *adv.*

con-cord *n.* Accord; harmony; friendly and peaceful relationships.

con-cor-dance *n.* A condition of concord or agreement; the alphabetical index of major words used by an author, listed in the order of use in a book.

con-cor-dant *adj.* Exist in agreement; harmonious. **concordantly** *adv.*

con-course *n.* A large, open space for the assembling or passage of crowds.

con-cres-cence *n.* Increase by the addition of particles; growing together.

con-crete *adj.* Pertaining to a specific instance or thing; naming a specific class of things. *n.* A construction material made from sand, gravel, and cement. *v.* To bring together in one body or mass. **-ly** *adv.*, **concreteness** *n.*

con-cu-bine *n.* A woman living with a man and not being legally married to him. **concubinage** *n.*

con-cu-pis-cence *n.* A strong sexual desire; lust. **concupiscent** *adj.*

con-cur *v.* To agree or express approval; to cooperate; to happen at the same time; to coincide. **concurrence** *n.*

con-cur-rent *adj.* Referring to an event that happens at the same time as another; acting together.

con-cus-sion *n.* A sudden and violent jolt; a violent injury to an organ, especially the brain. **concussive** *adj.*

con-demn *v.* To find to be wrong; to show the guilt; to announce judgment upon; to officially declare unfit for use. **condemnable**, **-atory** *adj.*, **condemnation**, **condemner** *n.*

con-dense *v.* To make more concentrated or compact; to change something from a liquid state to a solid state or from a gaseous to a liquid state. **condensability**, **-ation**, **condenser** *n.*, **-able**, **condensible** *adj.*

con-di-ment *n.* A relish, spice, or sauce used to season food.

con-di-tion *n.* The mode or state of existence of a thing or person; a circumstance that is found to be necessary to the occurrence of another; a provision in a contract or will that leaves room for modification or changes at a future date. *Slang* A sickness or ailment. **condition** *v.*

con-di-tion-al *adj.* Tentative; depending on a condition; implying or expressing

a condition. *Gram.* A mood, clause, tense, or condition. **conditionality** *n.*, **conditionally** *adv.*

con-di-tioned *adj.* Prepared for a certain process or action by past experience.

con-di-tion-er *n.* An application that improves the usability of a substance.

con-do *n.*, *Slang* Condominium.

con-dom *n.* A thin rubber sheath used to cover the penis, serving as an antivenereal or contraceptive purpose during sexual intercourse.

con-do-min-i-um *n.* A joint ownership; an apartment in which all units are owned separately; a building in which the units are owned by each tenant.

con-done *n.* To overlook; to forgive; to disregard. **condoner** *n.*

con-dor *v.* One of the largest flying birds, with a bare head and a white downy neck.

con-du-cive *adj.* Contributing towards or promotion; helpful. **conduce** *v.*

con-duct *v.* To lead and direct a performance of a band or orchestra; to guide or show the way; to lead; to direct or control the course of; to transmit heat, electricity, or sound. *n.* Behavior. **conductibility**, **conduction** *n.*, **conductible** *adj.*

con-duc-tor *n.* A person who conducts a musical ensemble; one who is in charge of a railroad or streetcar. *Phys.* Any substance that conducts light, electricity, heat, or sound.

con-duit *n.* A pipe used to pass electric wires or cable through; a channel or pipe that water passes through.

cone *n.* A solid body that is tapered evenly to a point from a base that is circular; a wafer that is cone-shaped and used for holding ice cream.

con-fab-u-late *v.* To chat or speak informally. **confabulation**, **-or** *n.*, **-ory** *adj.*

con-fec-tion-er-y *n.* Candy and sweets as a whole; a store that sells candy and sweets. **confection** *n.*

con-fed-er-a-cy *n.*, *pl.* **-ies** The union of eleven southern states that seceded from the United States during the Civil War of 1861-1865 and established the Confederate Sate of America.

con-fed-er-ate *n.* An ally or friend; a person who supports the Confederacy.

con-fer *v.* To consult with another; to hold a conference; to give or grant. **-ment**, **conferral**, **conferrer** *n.*

con-fer-ence *n.* A formal meeting for discussion; a league of churches, schools, or athletic teams.

con-fess *v.* To disclose or admit to a crime, fault, sin, or guilt; to tell a priest or God of one's sins. **confessedly** *adv.*

con-fes-sion *n.* The act of confessing.

con-fes-sion-al *n.* The small enclosure where a priest hears confessions.

con-fet-ti *pl.*, *n.* Small pieces of paper thrown during a happy occasion.

con-fide *v.* To entrust a secret to another. **-er** *n.*, **-ing** *adj.*, **-ingly** *adv.*

con-fi-dence *n.* A feeling of self-assurance; a feeling of trust in a person; reliance; good faith.

con-fi-den-tial *adj.* Hold as a secret; having another's entrusted confidence. **confidentiality** *n.*, **confidentially** *adv.*

con-fig-u-ra-tion *n.* An arrangement of parts or things; the arrangement of elements. **configurationally** *adv.*

con-fine *v.* To keep within a certain boundary or limit. **confines, confinement, confiner** *n.*

con-firm *v.* To establish or support the truth of something; to make stronger; to ratify and bind by a formal approval. **-able, confirmatory** *adj.*

con-fir-ma-tion *n.* The act of confirming to show proof; a religious rite that admits a person to full membership in a church.

con-fis-cate *v.* To seize for public use; to officially seize. **confiscation, -or** *n.*

con-flate *v.* To combine two different ideas into a whole. **conflation** *n.*

con-flict *n.* A battle; clash; a disagreement of ideas, or interests. **conflict** *v.*, **conflictive** *adj.*

con-flu-ence *n.* The flowing together of two streams or rivers; the point where the two join. **confluent** *adj. & n.*, **confluently** *adv.*

con-form *v.* To be similar in form or character; to adhere to prevailing customs or modes. **-able** *adj.*, **-ably** *adv.*

con-for-ma-tion *n.* The manner in which something is shaped, structured, or arranged.

con-found *v.* To amaze, confuse, or perplex; to confuse one thing for another.

con-front *v.* To put or stand face to face with defiance. **confrontation** *n.*, **confrontational** *adj.*

con-fuse *v.* To mislead or bewilder; to jumble or mix up. **confusedness** *n.*, **confusingly** *adv.*

con-fu-sion *n.* The state of being confused.

con-fute *v.* To prove to be invalid or false. **-able** *adj.*, **-ion** *n.*, **-ive** *adj.*

con-geal *v.* To jell; to solidify; to change from a liquid to a solid form.

con-gen-ial *adj.* Having similar character habits, or tastes; sociable; friendly. **congeniality** *n.*, **congenially** *adv.*

con-gen-i-tal *adj.* Existing from the time of birth, but not from heredity.

con-gest *v.* To enlarge with an excessive accumulation of blood; to clog. **congestion** *n.*, **congestive** *adj.*

con-glom-er-ate *n.* A business consisting of many different companies; gravel that is embedded in cement material.

con-grat-u-late *v.* To acknowledge an achievement with praise. **congratulator** *n.*, **congratulatory** *adj.*

con-grat-u-la-tions *pl., n.* The expression of or the act of congratulating.

con-gre-gate *v.* To assemble together in a crowd. **congregator** *n.*

con-gre-ga-tion *n.* A group of people meeting together for worship.

Con-gress *n.* The United States legislative body, consisting of the Senate and the House of Representatives. **Congressional** *adj.*, **-ally** *adv.*

con-gress-man *n.* An elected member of the United States House of Representatives.

con-gress-wom-an *n.* A woman elected as a member of the United States House of Representatives.

con-gru-ent *adj.* Agreeing to conform; in mathematics, having exactly the same size and shape.

con-ic *or* **con-i-cal** *adj.* Related to and shaped like a cone.

conj *abbr.* Conjunction.

con-jec-ture *n.* A guess or conclusion based on incomplete evidence. **-able, conjectural** *adj.*, **conjecture** *v.*

con-join *v.* To unite; join to together.

con-ju-gal *adj.* Pertaining to the relationship or marriage of husband and wife.

con-ju-gate *adj.* To change the form of a verb; to join in pairs. **conjugately** *adv.* **conjugative** *adj.*, **conjugator** *n.*

con-junct *adj.* Combined; joined together.

con-junc-tion *n.* The act of joining; the state of being joined. *Gram.* A word used to join or connect other words, phrases, sentences, or clauses.

con-junc-ti-va *n., pl.* **-vas, -vae** The membrane lining of the eyelids. **-l** *adj.*

con-junc-tive *adj.* Connective; joining. *Gram.* Serving as a conjunction.

con-junc-ti-vi-tis *n., Pathol.* Inflammation of the membrane that lines the eyelids.

con-jure *v.* To bring into the mind; to appeal or call on solemnly; to practice magic.

con-nect *v.* To join; to unite; to associate, as to relate. **connectedly** *adv.*, **connector, connecter** *n.*

Con-nect-i-cut *n.* A state located in the northeastern part of the United States.

con-nec-tion *n.* An association of one person or thing to another; a union, link, or bond; an influential group of friends or associates.

con-nec-tive *adj.* Capable of connecting; tending to connect. *n.* something that connects as a word. **connectivity** *n.*

con-nive *v.* To ignore a known wrong, therefore implying sanction; to conspire; to cooperate in secret.

con-nois-seur *n.* A person whose expertise in an area of art or taste allows him to be a judge; an expert. **-ship** *n.*

con-no-ta-tion *n.* The associative meaning of a word in addition to the literal meaning. **connotative** *adj.*

con-note *v.* To imply along with the literal meaning.

con-nu-bi-al *adj.* Having to do with marriage or the state of marriage. **connubiality** *n.*, **connubially** *adv.*

con-quer *v.* To subdue; to win; to overcome by physical force.

con-quis-ta-dor *n., pl.* **-dors** A Spanish conqueror of the sixteenth century.

con-san-guin-e-ous *adj.* Having the same

blood; descended from the same ancestor. **consanguineously** *adv.*

con-science *n.* The ability to recognize right and wrong regarding one's own behavior.

con-sci-en-tious *adj.* Honest; scrupulous; careful.

con-scious *adj.* Aware on one's own existence and environment; aware of facts or objects.

con-script *n.* One who is drafted or forced to enroll for a service or a job.

con-se-crate *v.* To declare something to be holy; to dedicate to sacred uses. **consecration, consecrator** *n.*

con-sec-u-tive *adj.* Following in uninterrupted succession. **consecutively** *adv.*, **consecutiveness** *n.*

con-sen-sus *n.* A general agreement; a collective opinion.

con-sent *v.* To agree; an acceptance.

con-se-quence *n.* The natural result from a preceding condition or action; the effect.

con-se-quent *adj.* Following as a natural result or effect. **consequently** *adv.*

con-se-quen-tial *adj.* Having or showing self-importance. **consequentially** *adv.*

con-ser-va-tive *adj.* Opposed to change; desiring the preservation of the existing order of things; moderate; cautious; wanting to conserve. **conservatively** *adv.*, **-ness** *n.*

con-ser-va-to-ry *n.*, *pl.* **-ries** A school of dramatic art or music; a greenhouse.

con-serve *v.* To save something from decay, loss, or depletion; to maintain; to preserve fruits with sugar. *n.* A mixture of several fruits cooked together with sugar and sometimes raisins or nuts. **conservable** *adj.*, **conserver** *n.*

con-sid-er *v.* To seriously think about; to examine mentally; to believe or hold as an opinion; to deliberate.

con-sid-er-a-ble *adj.* Large in amount or extent; important; worthy of consideration. **considerably** *adv.*

con-sid-er-a-tion *n.* The taking into account of circumstance before forming an opinion; care and thought; a kind or thoughtful treatment or feeling. **considering** *prep.*

con-sign *v.* To commit to the care of another; to deliver or forward, as merchandise; to put aside, as for specific use. **consignee** *n.*, **consignable** *adj.*, **consignor, consignment** *n.*

con-sist *v.* To be made up of.

con-sis-ten-cy *n.*, *pl.* **-cies** Agreement or compatibility among ideas, events, or successive acts; the degree of texture, viscosity, or density. **consistent** *adj.*

con-sis-to-ry *n.*, *pl.* **-ries** In the Roman Catholic Church, the assembly of all cardinals with the pope presiding over them.

con-sole *v.* To give comfort to someone. **consolable** *adj.*, **-ation** *n.*, **-ingly** *adv.*

con-sol-i-date *v.* To combine in one or to form a union of; to form a compact mass. **consolidation, consolidator** *n.*

con-so-nant *n.* A sound produced by complete or partial blockage of the air from the mouth, as the sound of b, f, k, s, t; the letter of the alphabet that represents such a sound. *adj.* In agreement. **consonantal** *adj.*, **-ly** *adv.*

con-sort *n.* A spouse; companion or partner. *v.* To unite or keep in company.

con-sor-ti-um *n.*, *pl.* **-tia** *n.* An association with banks or corporations that require vast resources.

con-spic-u-ous *adj.* Noticeable. **conspicuously** *adv.*, **conspicuousness** *n.*

con-spir-a-cy *n.*, *pl.* **-ies** A plan or act of two or more persons to do an evil act.

con-spire *v.* To plan a wrongful act in secret; to work or act together.

con-sta-ble *n.* A peace officer.

con-stant *adj.* Faithful; unchanging; steady in action, purpose, and affection. *Math* A quantity that remains the same throughout a given problem. **constancy** *n.*, **constantly** *adv.*

con-ster-na-tion *n.* Sudden confusion or amazement.

con-sti-pa-tion *n.* A condition of the bowels characterized by difficult or infrequent evacuation. **constipate** *v.*

con-stit-u-en-cy *n.*, *pl.* **-cies** A group of voters that is represented by an elected legislator.

con-stit-u-ent *adj.* Having the power to elect a representative. *n.* A necessary element or part.

con-sti-tu-tion *n.* The fundamental laws that govern a nation; structure or composition. **constitutional** *adj.*, **constitutionality** *n.*, **-ally** *adv.*

con-strain *v.* To restrain by physical or moral means. **constrained** *adj.*

con-straint *n.* The threat or use of force; confinement; restriction.

con-strict *v.* To squeeze, compress, or contract. **constriction** *n.*, **constrictive** *adj.*, **constrictively** *adv.*

con-struct *v.* To create, make, or build. **constructor, constructer** *n.*

con-struc-tion *n.* The act of constructing or building something. *Gram.* The arrangement of words in a meaningful clause or sentence. **constructional** *adj.*

con-struc-tive *adj.* Useful; helpful; building, advancing, or improving; resulting in a positive conclusion. **-ly** *adv.*, **constructiveness** *n.*

con-strue *v.* To interpret; to translate; to analyze grammatical structure.

con-sul *n.* An official that resides in a foreign country and represents his or her government's commercial interests and citizens. **consular** *adj.*, **-ship** *n.*

con-sul-ate *n.* The official premises occupied by a consul.

con-sult *v.* To seek advice or information from; to compare views. **consultant, consultation** *n.*

con-sume *v.* To ingest; to eat or drink; to destroy completely; to absorb; to engross. **consumable** *adj.* & *n.*

con-sum-er *n.* A person who buys services or goods.

con-sum-mate *v.* To conclude; to make a

marriage complete by the initial act of sexual intercourse.

con·sump·tion n. Fulfillment; the act of consuming; the quantity consumed; tuberculosis.

con·sump·tive adj. Tending to destroy or waste away; affected with or pertaining to pulmonary tuberculosis. **consumptively** adv., **consumptiveness** n.

con·tact n. The place, spot, or junction where two or more surfaces or objects touch; the connection between two electric conductors. **contacts** Slang Contact lens; thin lens of plastic or glass with an optical prescription, worn directly on the cornea of the eye.

con·ta·gion n. The transmitting of a disease by contact. **contagious** adj., **contagiously** adv., **contagiousness** n.

con·tain v. To include or enclose; to restrain or hold back. **containable** adj., **containment** n.

con·tain·er v. Something that holds or carries, as a box or can.

con·tain·er ship n. A ship that is designed to carry containerized cargo.

con·tam·i·nate v. To pollute or make inferior by adding undesirable elements; to taint; to infect; to make dirty or to soil. **contaminant**, **contamination** n.

con·temn v. To scorn or despise.

con·tem·plate v. To look over; to ponder; to consider thoughtfully. **contemplation** n., **-ive** adj. & n.

con·tem·po·ra·ne·ous adj. Occurring or living at the same time; contemporary. **contemporaneously** adv., **-ness** n.

con·tempt n. The act of viewing something as mean, vile, or worthless scorn; legally, the willful disrespect or disregard of authority. **-ible** adj., **contemptibleness** n., **contemptibly** adv.

con·temp·tu·ous adj. Feeling or showing contempt. **contemptuously** adv.

con·tend v. To dispute; to fight; to debate; to argue. **contender** n.

con·tent n. Something contained within; the subject matter of a book or document; the proportion of a specified part. adj. Satisfied. **contentment** n., **contentedly** adv., **contented** adj.

con·ten·tion n. Competition; rivalry; controversy; argument. **contentious** adj., **contentiously** adv.

con·test n. A competition; strife; conflict. v. To challenge. **contestable** adj., **contestant**, **contester** n.

con·text n. A sentence, phrase, or passage so closely connected to a word or words that it affects their meaning; the environment in which an event occurs.

con·ti·nent n. One of the seven large masses of the earth: Asia, Africa, Australia, Europe, North America, South America and Antarctica.

con·ti·nen·tal adj. Of or characteristic of a continent.

con·ti·nen·tal di·vide n. A divide separating rivers or streams that flow to opposite sides of a continent.

con·tin·ue v. To maintain without interruption a course or condition; to resume; to postpone or adjourn a judicial proceeding. **continuance**, **continuer** n.

con·ti·nu·i·ty n., pl. **-ties** The quality of being continuous.

con·tin·u·ous adj. Uninterrupted. **continuously** adv., **continuousness** n.

con·tort v. To severely twist out of shape.

con·tor·tion·ist n. An acrobat who exhibits unnatural body positions.

con·tour n. The outline of a body, figure, or mass.

con·tra·band n. Illegal or prohibited traffic; smuggled goods.

con·tra·bass n. A double bass, also called a contrabassoon.

con·tra·cep·tion n. The voluntary prevention of impregnation. **-ive** adj.

con·tract n. A formal agreement between two or more parties to perform the duties as stated.

con·trac·tion n. The act of contracting; a shortening of a word by omitting a letter or letters and replacing them with an apostrophe (').

con·trac·tile adj. Having the power to contract.

con·tra·dict v. To express the opposite side or idea; to be inconsistent. **contradictable**, **contradictory** adj., **contradicter**, **contradictor**, **-ion** n.

con·tral·to n., pl. **-tos** The lowest female singing voice.

con·trap·tion n. A gadget.

con·tra·pun·tal adj. Relating to counterpoint. **contrapuntally** adv.

con·trar·y adj. Unfavorable; incompatible with another. **contrarily** adv., **contrariness** n.

con·trast v. To note the differences between two or more people, things, etc.

con·tra·vene v. To be contrary; to violate; to oppose; to go against.

con·trib·ute v. To give something to someone; to submit for publication. **contribution**, **contributor** n., **-ive**, **contributory** adj., **contributively** adv.

con·trite adj. Grieving for sin or shortcoming. **contritely** adv., **contrition** n.

con·trol v. To have the authority or ability to regulate, direct, or dominate a situation. **controllable** adj.

con·trol·ler n. The chief accounting officer of a business, also called the comptroller.

con·tro·ver·sy n. A dispute; a debate; a quarrel **controversial** adj.

con·tro·vert v. To contradict; to deny.

con·tu·me·ly n., pl **-lies** Rude treatment.

co·nun·drum n. A riddle with an answer that involves a pun; a question or problem with only a surmise for an answer.

con·va·lesce v. To grow strong after a long illness. **convalescence** n., **convalescent** adj.

con·vec·tion n. The transfer of heat by the movement of air, gas, or heated liquid between areas of unequal density. **convectional** adj.

con·vene v. To meet or assemble formally. **convenable** adj., **convener** n.

con-ven-ience *n.* The quality of being convenient or suitable.

con-vent *n.* A local house or community of a religious order, especially for nuns.

con-ven-ti-cle *n.* A secret meeting for religious study or worship.

con-ven-tion *n.* A formal meeting; a regulatory meeting between people, states, or nations on matters that affect all of them.

con-ven-tion-al *adj.* Commonplace, ordinary.

con-verge *v.* To come to a common point. convergence *n.*, covergent *adj.*

con-ver-sa-tion *n.* An informal talk. conversational *adj.*, -ally *adv.*

converse *v.* To involve oneself in conversation with another.

con-ver-sion *n.* The act or state of changing to adopt new opinions or beliefs; a formal acceptance of a different religion. conversional *adj.*

con-vert-i-ble *adj.* A car with a top that folds back or can be removed completely.

con-vex *adj.* Curved outward like the outer surface of a ball. convexity *n.*

con-vey *v.* To transport; to pass information on to someone else; to conduct.

con-vey-ance *n.* The action of conveying; the legal transfer of property or the document effecting it.

con-vict *v.* To prove someone guilty. *n.* A prisoner.

con-vic-tion *n.* The act of being convicted.

con-vince *v.* To cause to believe without doubt. convincingly *adv.*

con-vo-ca-tion *n.* A formal or ceremonial assembly or meeting.

con-voke *v.* To call together for a formal meeting.

con-voy *n.* A group of cars, trucks, etc., traveling together. *v.* To escort or guide.

con-vulse *v.* To move or shake violently. convulsive *adj.*, convulsively *adv.*

con-vul-sion *n.* A violent involuntary muscular contraction.

cook *v.* To apply heat to food before eating; to prepare food for a meal. *n.* A person who prepares food.

cook-book *n.* A book containing directions for preparing and cooking food.

cook-ie *n.*, *pl.* -ies A sweet, flat cake.

cool *adj.* Without warmth; indifferent or unenthusiastic. *Slang* First-rate; composure.

cool-ant *n.* The cooling agent that circulates through a machine.

Coolidge, John Calvin *n.* The 30th president of the United States, from 1923-1929.

coon *n.*, *Informal* A raccoon.

coop *n.* A cage or enclosed area to contain animals, as chickens.

co--op *n.* A cooperative.

co-op-er-ate *v.* To work together toward a common cause. -ion, -or *n.*

co-op-er-a-tive *adj.* Willing to cooperate with others. cooperatively *adv.*,

cooperativeness *n.*

co--opt *v.* To elect or choose as a new member.

co-or-di-nate *v.* To be equal in rank, importance, or degree; to plan a wardrobe or outfit so that it goes well together. *n.* Any of a set of numbers which establishes position on a graph, map, etc. coordinately *adv.*, -or *n.*

co-or-di-na-tion *n.* The state of being coordinated.

coot *n.* A short-winged bird. *Slang* A silly old man.

coot-ie *n.*, *Slang* A body louse.

cop *n.*, *Informal* A police officer.

cope *v.* To strive; to struggle or contend with something. *n.* The long cape worn by a priest on special ceremonial occasions.

cop-ier *n.* A machine that makes copies of original material.

co-pi-lot *n.* The assistant pilot on an aircraft.

co-pi-ous *adj.* Large in quantity; abundant.

cop--out *n.*, *Slang* A way to avoid responsibility.

cop-per *n.* A metallic element that is a good conductor of electricity and heat, reddish-brown in color.

cop-per-head *n.* A venomous snake found in the eastern United States, having brownish-red markings.

cop-ra *n.* Dried coconut meat that yields coconut oil.

copse *n.* A thicket made up of trees or small bushes.

cop-ter *n.*, *Slang* A helicopter.

cop-u-la *n.*, *Gram.* A word or words which connect a subject and predicate.

cop-u-late *v.* To have sexual intercourse.

copy *v.*, *pl.* -ies To reproduce an original. *n.* A single printed text. copyist *n.*

copy edit *v.* To edit and correct a written copy for publication. copy editor *n.*

copy-right *n.* The statutory right to sell, publish, or distribute a literary or artistic work.

copy writer *n.* A person who writes copy for advertisements.

coq au vin *n.* Chicken cooked in wine.

co-quette *n.* A woman who flirts.-ish *adj.*

cor-al *n.* The stony skeleton of a small sea creature, often used for jewelry.

Cor-al Sea *n.* An arm of the southwest Pacific, located southeast of New Guinea and northeast of Australia.

cor-al reef *n.* A marine mound formed chiefly of broken pieces and grains of coral that have become a hard mass.

cor-al snake *n.* A venomous snake of tropical America and the southern United States, brightly colored with red, black, and yellow rings.

cord *n.* A string or twine; an insulated wire used to supply electricity to another source; a measurement for firewood that equals 128 cubic feet; a raised rib of fabric, as corduroy. cord *v.*, corder *n.*

cor-dial *adj.* Warm-hearted and sincere. *n.* A liqueur. cordiality *n.*, -ly *adv.*

cord-ite *n.* A smokeless gunpowder.

cor-don *n.* A circle of men or ships positioned to guard or enclose an area; an ornamental ribbon or braid worn as an insignia of honor.

con-dor *n.*

A very large American vulture with a bare neck and head with dull black plumage and white patches on the wings and neck.

cor-du-roy *n.* A durable cotton fabric which has a ribbed pile.

core *n.* The innermost or central part of something; the inedible center of a fruit that contains the seeds. *v.* To remove the core from a piece of fruit.

co-re-spon-dent *n.* A person charged with having committed adultery with the defendant in a divorce case.

cork *n.* The elastic bark of the oak tree used for bottle stoppers and craft projects.

cork-age *n.* The fee that must be paid when one consumes a bottle of liquor not purchased on the premises.

cork-screw *n.* A pointed metal spiral attached to a handle used for removing corks from bottles.

corn *n.* An American cultivated cereal plant bearing seeds on a large ear or cob; the seed of this plant; a horny thickening of the skin, usually on the toe.

Corn Belt *n.* The major corn growing states of the United States; Illinois, Indiana, Iowa, Kansas, Missouri, Nebraska, and Ohio.

corn bread *n.* A bread made from crushed cornmeal, eggs, flour, and milk.

corn cob *n.* The woody core around which the corn kernels grow.

corn-crib *n.* The building used for storing and drying corn.

cor-ne-a *n.* The transparent membrane of the eyeball. **corneal** *adj.*

cor-ner *n.* The point formed when two surfaces or lines meet and form an angle; the location where two streets meet.

corner-back *or* **corner back** *n.* In football, the defensive halfback who defends the flank and covers the pass receiver.

corner-stone *n.* A stone that forms part of the corner of a building, usually laid in place with a special ceremony.

cor-net *n.* A three valved, brass musical instrument. **cornetist** *n.*

corn-meal *n.* Meal made from corn.

corn-row *v.* To braid the hair in rows very close to the head.

corn-stalk *n.* A stalk of corn.

corn-starch *n.* A starch made from corn and used to thicken food while cooking.

corn syrup *n.* A sweet syrup made from cornstarch, containing maltose, dextrins, and dextrose.

cor-nu-co-pi-a *n.* A curved goat's horn overflowing with flowers, fruit, and corn to signify prosperity.

corn-y *adj.*, *Slang* Trite or mawkishly old-fashioned.

co-rol-la *n.* The petals of a flower.

cor-ol-lary *n.*, *pl.* **-ies** Something that naturally or incidentally follows or accompanies.

cor-o-nar-y *adj.* Of or relating to the two arteries that supply blood to the heart muscles. **coronary** *n.*

cor-o-nary throm-bo-sis *n.* A blockage of the coronary artery of the heart.

cor-po-ral *n.* A noncommissioned officer who ranks above a private first class but below a sergeant. *adj.* Relating to the body.

cor-po-rate *adj.* Combined into one joint body; relating to a corporation.

cor-po-ra-tion *n.* A group of merchants united in a trade guild; any group or persons that act as one.

cor-po-re-al *adj.* Of a physical nature.

corps *n.*, *pl.* **corps** A branch of the armed forces; the body of persons under common direction.

corpse *n.* A dead body.

cor-pu-lence *n.* The excessive accumulation of body fat; obesity.

cor-pus-cle *n.* A minute particle or living cell, especially as one in the blood. **corpuscular** *adj.*

cor-pus de-lic-ti *n.* The essential evidence pertaining to a crime.

cor-ral *n.* An enclosure for containing animals. *v.*, *Slang* To take possession of.

cor-rect *v.* To make free from fault or mistakes. **correctable**, **-ible** *adj.*, **correctional**, **correction**, **-ness** *n.*, **corrective** *adj. & n.*, **correctly** *adv.*

cor-rel-a-tive *adj.* Having a mutual relation.

cor-re-spond *v.* To communicate by letter or written words; to be harmonious, equal or similar. **correspondingly** *adv.*

cor-ri-dor *n.* A long hall with rooms on either side; a piece of land that forms a passage through a foreign land.

cor-ri-gen-dum *n.*, *pl.* **-da** An error in print that is accompanied by its correction.

cor-ri-gi-ble *adj.* Able to correct; capable of being corrected.

cor-rob-o-rate *v.* To support a position or statement with evidence. **corroboration** *n.*, **corroborative** *adj.*

cor-rode *v.* To eat away through chemical action. **corrodible** *adj.*, **corrosion** *n.*, **corrosive** *adj. & n.*

cor-rupt *adj.* Dishonest; evil. *v.* To become or make corrupt. **corrupter** *n.*

cor-sage *n.* A small bouquet of flowers worn on a woman's shoulder or wrist.

cor-sair *n.* A pirate; a fast moving vessel.

cor-set *n.* An undergarment that is tightened with laces and reinforced with stays, worn to give shape and support to a woman's body.

cor-tege *n.* A ceremonial procession; a funeral procession.

cor-tex *n., pl.* -tices The external layer of an organ, especially the gray matter that covers the brain; the bark of trees and the rinds of fruits.

cor-ti-sone *n.* A hormone produced by the adrenal cortex, used in the treatment of rheumatoid arthritis.

co-run-dum *n.* An aluminum oxide used as an abrasive.

cor-us-cate *v.* To sparkle. **coruscation** *n.*

cor-vette *n.* An armed warship smaller than a destroyer, used as an escort vessel.

co-ry-za *n.* An acute inflammation of the upper respiratory system.

co-sign *v.* To sign a document jointly.

co-sig-na-to-ry *n., pl.* -ies One who jointly cosigns a document.

cos-met-ic *n.* A preparation designed to beautify the face. **cosmetically** *adv.*

cos-me-tol-o-gy *n.* The study of cosmetics and their use. **cosmetologist** *n.*

cos-mog-o-ny *n.* The creation of the universe.

cos-mo-naut *n.* A Soviet astronaut.

cos-mo-pol-i-tan *adj.* Being at home anywhere in the world.

cos-mop-o-lite *n.* A cosmopolitan person.

cos-mos *n.* An orderly and harmoniously systematic universe.

Cos-sack *n.* A member of a group of people of southern Russia, famous as horsemen.

cos-set *v.* To pamper; pet.

cost *n.* The amount paid or charged for a purchase. **cost** *v.,* **costly** *adj.*

cos-tive *adj.* Affected with or causing constipation.

cos-tume *n.* A suit, dress, or set of clothes characteristic of a particular season or occasion; clothes worn by a person playing a part or dressing up in a disguise.

cot *n.* A small, often collapsible bed.

cot-tage *n.* A small house, usually for vacation use.

cot-ter pin *n.* A metal pin whose ends can be flared after being inserted through a slot or hole.

cot-ton *n.* A plant or shrub cultivated the fiber surrounding its seeds; a fabric created by the weaving of cotton fibers; yarn spun from cotton fibers.

cot-ton can-dy *n.* Spun sugar.

cot-ton-mouth *n.* The water moccasin. *Slang* Having a dry mouth.

couch *n.* A piece of furniture, such as a sofa or bed on which one may sit or recline for rest or sleep. *v.* To phrase in a certain manner; to lie in ambush.

cou-gar *n.* A large brown cat, also called a mountain lion, panther, and puma.

cough *v.* To suddenly expel air from the lungs with an explosive noise.

could *v.* Past tense of can.

could-n't *contr.* Could not.

cou-lomb *n.* The unit of quantity used to measure electricity; the amount conveyed by one amphere in one second.

coun-cil *n.* A group of people assembled for consultation or discussion; an official legislative or advisory body. **councilman, councilor** *n.*

coun-sel *n.* Advice given through consultation; a lawyer engaged in the management or trial of a court case.

coun-sel-or *n.* One who gives advice; a lawyer.

count *v.* To name or number so as to find the total number of units involved; to name numbers in order; to take account of in a tally or reckoning; to rely or depend on something or someone; to have significance. *n.* A nobleman found in various countries throughout Europe, having rank corresponding to that of a British earl; a tally.

count-down *n.* An audible counting in descending order to mark the time remaining before an event.

coun-te-nance *n.* The face as an indication of mood or character; bearing or expression that would suggest approval or sanction.

coun-ter *n.* A level surface over which transactions are conducted, on which food is served, or on which articles are displayed; a person or device that counts to determine a number or amount. *v.* To move or act in a contrary, or opposing direction or wrong way.

coun-ter-act *v.* To oppose and, by contrary action, make ineffective.

coun-ter-attack *n.* An attack made in response to an enemy attack.

coun-ter-bal-ance *n.* A force or influence that balances another; a weight that balances another. **counterbalance** *v.*

coun-ter-claim *n.* A contrary claim made to offset another.

coun-ter-clock-wise *adj. & adv.* In a direction contrary to that in which the hands of a clock move.

coun-ter-cul-ture *n.* A culture with values opposite those of traditional society.

coun-ter-es-pi-o-nage *n.* Espionage aimed at discovering and thwarting enemy espionage.

coun-ter-feit *v.* To closely imitate or copy with the intent to deceive; to forge. *adj.* Marked by false pretense. *n.* Something counterfeit.

coun-ter-foil *n.* A stub, as on a check or ticket, usually serving as a record of the transaction.

coun-ter-in-tel-li-gence *n.* An intelligence agency function designed to block information, deceive the enemy, prevent sabotage, and gather military and political material and information.

coun-ter-ir-ri-tant *n.* An irritation that diverts attention from another.

coun-ter-man *n.* One who works at a counter.

coun-ter-mand *v.* To reverse or revoke a command by issuing a contrary order *n.* An order which reverses or contradicts a previous order.

coun-ter-of-fen-sive *n.* A military offensive designed to thwart an enemy attack.

coun-terpane *n.* A covering.

coun-terpart *n.* One that matches or complements another.

coun-ter-plea *n.* A plea made in answer to a previous plea.

coun-ter-point *n., Mus.* The combining of melodies into a harmonic relationship while retaining the linear character.

coun-ter-pro-duc-tive *adj.* Tending to hinder rather than aid in the attainment of a goal.

coun-ter-re-vo-lu-tion *n.* A revolution designed to overthrow a government previously seated by a revolution.

coun-ter-sign *n.* A signature confirming the authenticity of a document already signed by another; a sign or signal given in response to another.

coun-ter-sink *n.* A funnel-shaped enlargement on the outer end of a drilled hole designed to allow the head of a nail or screw to lie flush with or below the surface; a tool for making a countersink. *v.* To set the head, as of a nail or screw at or below the surface.

coun-ter-ten-or *n.* An adult tenor with a very high range, higher than that of the average tenor.

coun-ter-vail *v.* To counteract.

coun-ter-weight *n.* An equivalent weight, used as a counterbalance.

count-ess *n.* The wife or widow of an earl or count; a woman who, in her own right, holds the rank of earl or count.

count-ing house *n.* A building or room used for keeping books and doing business.

count-less *adj.* Too many or too numerous to be counted.

coun-tri-fied *adj.* Of or relating to country life; rural; unsophisticated.

coun-try *n., pl.* **-ies** A given area or region; the land of one's birth, residence, or citizenship; a state, nation, or its territory.

coun-try club *n.* A suburban club for social and recreational activities.

coun-try-man *n.* A compatriot; one living in the country or having country ways.

coun-try music *n.* Music derived from the folk style of the southern United States and from the cowboy.

coun-try-side *n.* A rural area or its inhabitants.

coun-ty *n., pl.* **-ies** A territorial division for local government within a state.

coup *n.* A brilliant, sudden move that is usually highly successful.

cou-ple *n.* A pair; something that joins two things together; a few. *v.* To join in marriage or sexual union.

cou-plet *n.* Two rhyming lines of poetry in succession.

cou-pon *n.* A statement of interest due, to be removed from a bearer bond and presented for payment when it is payable; a form surrendered to obtain a product, service, or discount on same; a form to be clipped from a magazine or paper and mailed for discounts or gifts.

cour-age *n.* Mental or moral strength to face danger without fear. **courageous** *adj.*, **courageously** *adv.*

cou-ri-er *n.* A messenger; a person who carries contraband for another.

course *n.* The act of moving in a path from one point to another; the path over which something moves; a period of time; a series or sequence; a series of studies.

court *n.* The residence of a sovereign or similar dignitary; a sovereign's family and advisors; an assembly for the transaction of judicial business; a place where trials are conducted; an area marked off for game playing. *v.* To try to win favor or dispel hostility.

cour-te-ous *adj.* Marked by respect for and consideration of others.

cour-te-san *n.* A prostitute, one who associates with or caters to high-ranking or wealthy men.

cour-te-sy *n., pl.* **-ies** Courteous behavior; general allowance despite facts.

court-house *n.* A building for holding courts of law.

court-i-er *n.* One in attendance at a royal court.

court-yard *n.* An open space enclosed by walls.

cous-in *n.* A child of one's uncle or aunt; a member of a culturally similar race or nationality.

cove *n.* A small inlet or bay, generally sheltered; a deep recess or small valley in the side of a mountain.

cov-e-nant *n.* A formal, binding agreement; a promise or pledge.

cov-er *v.* To place something on or over; to lie over; to spread over; to guard from attack; to hide or conceal. *Slang* To be all-encompassing; to act as a stand-in during another's absence; to have within one's gun sights. **cover** *n.*

cov-et *v.* To wish for enviously; to crave possession of that which belongs to someone else.

cov-ey *n.* A small group of birds, especially quail or partridges.

cow *n., pl.* **cows**

The mature female of cattle or of any species when the adult male is referred to as a bull.

cow-ard *n.* One who shows great fear or timidity. **cowardice** *n.*

cowl *n.* A hood or long hooded cloak such as that of a monk; a covering for a chimney that is designed to improve the air draft; the top portion at the front of an automobile where the windshield and dashboard are attached.

cow-slip n. A common British primrose with yellow or purple flowers.

cox-comb n. A conceited foolish person.

cox-swain n. One who steers a boat or racing shell.

coy adj. Quieting or shy, or to pretending to be so. **coyness** n.

coy-o-te n. A small wolf-like animal that is native to North America.

coz-en v. To swindle, cheat, deceive, win over, or induce to do something by coaxing or trickery. **cozener** n.

co-zy adj. Comfortable and warm; snug. n. A cover placed over a teapot to retain the warmth. **-ily** adv., **-iness** n.

crab n., pl. **crabs**

Any one of numerous chiefly marine crustaceans with a short, broad shell, four pairs of legs, and one pair of pincers; sideways motion of an airplane headed into a crosswind. **crabs** Infestation with crab lice. **-ber** n.

crab-bed adj. Morose or peevish; difficult to read or understand. **crabbedly** adv., **crabbedness** n.

crab-by adj. Being ill-tempered and cross.

crack v. To make a loud explosive sound; to break, snap, or split apart; to break without completely separating; to lose control under pressure (often used with up); to go at a good speed; to break with a sudden, sharp sound; to solve; to reduce petroleum compounds to simpler forms by heating. n. A sharp, witty remark; a weakness caused by decay or age; an attempt or try. *Slang* A highly dangerous and addictive form of cocaine.

crack-le v. To make sharp, sudden, repeated noises; to develop a network of fine cracks.

cra-dle n. A small bed for infants, usually on rockers or rollers; a framework of support, such as that for a telephone receiver; a small platform on casters used by mechanics when working under a vehicle; a device used for rocking in panning for gold.

craft n. A special skill or ability; a trade that requires dexterity or artistic skill; the ability to use cunning and skill in deceiving; an aircraft, boat, or ship.

crag n. A steep, jagged rock or cliff. **cragged, craggy** adj.

cram v. To pack tightly or stuff; to thrust in a forceful manner; to eat in a greedy fashion; to prepare hastily for an exam.

cramp n. A painful involuntary contraction of a muscle; sharp abdominal pain.

cran-ber-ry n., pl. **-berries** A North American shrub which grows in damp soil and bears edible, tart red berries.

crane n. A large bird with long legs and a long neck; a machine used for lifting or moving heavy objects. v. To strain or stretch the neck.

cra-ni-um n., pl. **crania** The skull, especially the part in which the brain is enclosed. **cranial** adj.

crank n. An arm bent at right angles to a shaft and turned to transmit motion; an eccentric person; a bad-tempered person; a grouch. v. To operate or start by crank.

crank-case n. The housing of a crankshaft.

crank-shaft n. A shaft propelled by a crank.

crank-y adj. Grouchy, irritable. **-iness** n.

cran-ny n., pl. **-ies** A small break or crevice; an obscure nook or corner.

craps v. A gambling game played with two dice.

crap-shoot-er n. A person who plays craps.

crash v. To break violently or noisily; to damage in landing, usually an airplane; to collapse suddenly, usually a business; to cause to make a loud noise; to enter into without an invitation. *Slang* To spend the night in a particular place; to return to normalcy from a drug-induced state. n. In computer science, the unplanned termination of a computer operation or program.

crass adj. Insensitive and unrefined.

crate n. A container, usually made of wooden slats, for protection during shipping or storage. **crate** v.

cra-ter n. A bowl-shaped depression at the mouth of a volcano; a depression formed by a meteorite; a hole made by an explosion. **cratered** adj.

cra-vat n. A necktie.

crave v. To desire intensely.

cra-ven adj. Completely lacking courage.

crav-ing n. An intense longing or desire.

craw n. The crop of a bird; the stomach of a lower animal.

craw-fish n. A crayfish.

crawl v. To move slowly by dragging the body along the ground in a prone position; to move on hands and knees; to progress slowly.

cray-on n. A stick of white or colored chalk or wax used for writing or drawing.

craze v. To make insane or as if insane; to become insane; to develop a fine mesh of narrow cracks. n. Something that lasts for a short period of time; a fad.

cra-zy adj. Insane; impractical; unusually fond. **crazily** adv., **craziness** n.

creak v. A squeaking or grating noise. **creaky** adj., **creakily** adv.

cream n. The yellowish, fatty part of milk, containing a great amount of butterfat; something having the consistency of cream; the best part; a pale yellow-white color. **creaminess** n., **creamy** adj.

crease n. A line or mark made by folding and pressing a pliable substance.

cre-ate v. To bring something into existence; to give rise to.

re-a-tion *n*. The act of creating; something that is created; the universe.

re-a-tive *adj*. Marked by the ability to create; inventive; imaginative. creatively *adv*., creativeness *n*.

rea-tor *n*. One that creates. **The Creator.** God.

rea-ture *n*. Something created; a living being.

re-dence *n*. Belief.

re-den-za *n*. A buffet or sideboard, usually without legs.

red-i-ble *adj*. Offering reasonable grounds for belief. credibility *n*., credibly *adv*.

red-it *n*. An amount at a person's disposal in a bank; recognition by name for a contribution; acknowledgment; recognition by a learning institution that a student has completed a requirement leading to a degree.

red-u-lous *adj*. Gullible; ready to believe on slight or uncertain evidence. -ly *adv*., credulousness *n*.

reed *n*. A brief authoritative statement of religious belief.

reek *n*. A narrow stream. **up the creek** In a difficult or perplexing situation.

reel *n*. A wicker basket for holding fish.

reep *v*. To advance at a slow pace; to go timidly or cautiously; to grow along a surface, clinging by means of tendrils or aerial roots.

re-mate *v*. To reduce to ashes by burning.

re-ole *n*. A person of European descent born in Spanish America or the West Indies; a person of mixed African and European ancestry.

re-o-sote *n*. An oily liquid mixture obtained by distilling coal tar, used especially as a wood preservative.

rept *v*. The past tense of creep.

re-pus-cu-lar *adj*. Of, resembling, or relating to twilight.

re-scen-do *adv*. In music, gradually increasing in loudness.

res-cent *n*.

The shape of the moon in its first and fourth quarters, defined with a convex and a concave edge.

ress *n*. Any of numerous plants with sharp-tasting edible leaves.

rest *n*. A tuft or comb on the head of a bird or animal; the top line of a mountain or hill.

re-tin *n*. One afflicted with cretinism; a person with marked mental deficiency.

re-tin-ism *n*. A condition marked by physical stunting and mental deficiency.

re-tonne *n*. A strong cotton or linen cloth, used especially for curtains and upholstery.

re-vasse *n*. A deep crack or crevice.

rev-ice *n*. A narrow crack.

rew *n*. A group of people that work together; the whole company belonging to an aircraft or ship.

crew-el *n*. Slackly twisted worsted yarn, used in embroidery.

crib *n*. A small bed with high sides for an infant; a feeding bin for animals.

crick-et *n*. A leaping orthopteran insect, the male of the species producing a high pitched chirping sound by rubbing the front wings together; a game played with a bat and ball by two teams of eleven players each.

cri-er *n*. One who calls out public notices.

crime *n*. An act or the commission of an act that is forbidden by law.

crimp *v*. To cause to become bent or crinkled; to pinch in or together.

crim-son *n*. A deep purplish color. *v*. To make or become crimson.

cringe *v*. To shrink or recoil in fear.

crin-kle *v*. To wrinkle. crinkly *adj*.

crin-o-line *n*. An open-weave fabric used for lining and stiffening garments.

crip-ple *n*. One who is lame or partially disabled; something flawed or imperfect. *adj*. Being a cripple. *v*. To deprive one of the use of a limb or limbs.

cri-sis *n*., *pl*. **crises** An unstable or uncertain time or state of affairs, the outcome of which will have a major impact; the turning point for better or worse in a disease or fever.

crisp *adj*. Easily broken; brittle; brisk or cold; sharp; clear. *v*. To make or become crisp. crisply *adv*., crispness *n*., crispy *adj*.

crisp-er *n*. A compartment within a refrigerator used to keep fruits and vegetables fresh.

criss-cross *v*. To mark with crossed lines; to mark with intersecting lines. crisscross *adj. & adv*.

cri-te-ri-on *n*., *pl*. **criteria** A standard by which something can be judged.

crit-ic *n*. A person who is critical; a person who examines a subject and expresses an opinion as to its value; a person who judges or evaluates art or artistic creations, as a theatre critic.

crit-i-cal *adj*. Very important, as a critical decision; tending to criticize harshly. critically *adv*.

crit-i-cism *n*. The act of criticizing, usually in a severe or negative fashion.

crit-i-cize *v*. To be a critic; to find fault with; to judge critically; to blame.

croak *n*. A hoarse, raspy cry such as that made by a frog. *v*. To utter a croak. *Slang* To die.

cro-chet *n*. The needlework achieved by looping thread with a hooked needle.

crock *n*. An earthenware pot or jar most often used for cooking or storing food.

croc-o-dile *n*.

Any of various large, thick-skinned, long-bodied reptiles of tropical and subtropical regions.

croc-o-dile tears *n., pl.* Insincere grief.

cro-cus *n., pl.* **crocuses** A plant having solitary, long-tubed flowers and slender, linear leaves.

crone *n.* A witch-like, withered old woman.

cro-ny *n., pl.* **-ies** A close friend.

crook *n.* A bent or hooked implement; a bend or curve; a person given to dishonest acts. *v.* To bend or curve.

croon *v.* To sing in a gentle, low voice; to make a continued moaning sound. **croon** *n.*

crop *n.* A plant which is grown and then harvested for use or for sale; a riding whip. *v.* To cut off short; to appear unexpectedly.

cro-quet *n.* An outdoor game played by driving wooden balls through hoops with long-handled mallets.

cro-quette *n.* A small patty or roll of minced food that is breaded and deep fried.

cross *n.*

A structure consisting of an upright post and a crossbar, used especially by the Romans for execution, such as the cross on which Jesus was crucified; something that tries one's virtue or patience; a medal with the shape of the cross, such as the one used as a Christian emblem; a mark formed by the intersection of two lines. *v.* In biology, to interbreed a plant or an animal with one of a different kind; to go over; to intersect; to turn against; to go against. *adj.* Ill-tempered.

cross-bar *n.* A horizontal bar or line.

cross-bones *n.* Two leg or arm bones placed crosswise, as in a skull and crossbones.

cross-bow *n.* A weapon consisting chiefly of a bow mounted crosswise near the end of a wooden stock.

cross-breed *v.* To produce a hybrid plant or animal by interbreeding different breeds and varieties.

cross-cur-rent *n.* A current flowing against another; a conflicting tendency.

crotch *n.* The angle formed by the junction of two parts, such as legs or branches. **crotched** *adj.*

crotch-et *n.* A peculiar opinion or preference.

crouch *v.* To bend at the knees and lower the body close to the ground.

croup *n.* A spasmodic laryngitis, especially of children, marked by a loud, harsh cough and difficulty in breathing. **croupy** *adj.*

crou-pi-er *n.* One who collects and pays bets at a gambling table.

crou-ton *n.* A small piece of toasted or fried bread.

crow *n.* A large, black bird.

crowd *n.* A large group of people gathered together. *v.* To assemble in large numbers; to press close.

crown *n.* A circular ornament or he covering made of precious metal a jewels, worn as the headdress of sovereign; the highest point; the to most part of the skull; the tile rep senting the championship of a sport; reward or honor for achievement; t part of a tooth that rises above t gum line. *v.* To place a checker another checker to make a king; adorn something with a crown; to on the head.

CRT *abbr.* Cathode Ray Tube.

cru-cial *adj.* Extremely important; cr cal.

cru-ci-ble *n.* A vessel used for melti and calcining materials at high te peratures; a hard test of someone.

cru-ci-fy *v.* To put to death by nailing a cross; to treat cruelly; to torment.

crude *adj.* Unrefined; lacking refineme or tact; haphazardly made. *n.* U refined petroleum. **-ly** *adv.*, **-ness** *n.*

cruel *adj.* Inflicting suffering; causi pain. **cruelly** *adv.*, **cruelty** *n.*

cru-et *n.* A small glass bottle norma used as a container for oil or vinegar

cruise *v.* To drive or sail about f pleasure; to move about the streets leisure; to travel at a speed th provides maximum efficiency.

crumb *n.* A small fragment of materi particularly bread.

crum-ble *v.* To break into small pieces.

crum-ple *v.* To bend or crush out shape; to cause to collapse; to crumpled.

crunch *v.* To chew with a crackli noise; to run, walk, etc., with a crus ing noise. **crunch** *n.*

cru-sade *n.* Any of the military expe tions undertaken by Christian leade during the 11th, 12th, and 13th ce turies to recover the Holy Land fro the Moslems. **crusade** *v.*

crush *v.* To squeeze or force by pressu so as to damage or injure; to reduce particles by pounding or grinding; put down or suppress. **crushable** *adj.*, **crusher** *n.*

crust *n.* The hardened exterior or surfa of bread; a hard or brittle surfa layer; the outer layer of the earth; t shell of a pie, normally made pastry. *v.* To cover or become cover with crust.

crus-ta-cean *n.* Any one of a large cla of aquatic arthropods, includi lobsters and crabs, with a segmente body and paired, jointed limbs.

crutch *n.* A support usually designed fit in the armpit and to be used as aid in walking; any support or prop.

crux *n.* An essential or vital moment; main or central feature.

cry *v.* To shed tears; to call out loudly; utter a characteristic call or sound; proclaim publicly. **cry** *n.*

crypt *n.* An underground chamber vault primarily used to bury the dead

cryp-tic *adj.* Intended to be obscur serving to conceal.

cryp-tog-ra-phy *n.* The writing and deciphering of messages in secret code. **cryptographer** *n.*

crys-tal *n.* Quartz that is transparent or nearly transparent; a body that is formed by the solidification of a chemical element; a clear, high-quality glass. **crystalline** *adj.*

crys-tal ball *n.* A glass globe for fore-telling the future.

crys-tal-lize *v.* To cause to form crystals or assume crystalline form; to cause to take a definite form; to coat with crystals, especially sugar crystals.

CT *abbr.* Connecticut.

cub *n.* The young of the lion, wolf, or bear; an awkward child or youth.

cub-by-hole *n.* A small enclosed area.

cube *n.*

A regular solid with six equal squares, having all its angles right angles. **cube** *v.*

cube root *n.* A number whose cube is a given number.

cubic *adj.* Having the shape of a cube; having three dimensions; having the volume of a cube with the edges of a specified unit.

cu-bi-cle *n.* A small partitioned area.

cub-ism *n.* An art style that portrays the subject matter with geometric forms.

cu-bit *n.* An ancient unit of measurement that equals approximately eighteen to twenty inches.

Cub Scout *n.* A member of the Boy Scout organization from the ages of eight to ten.

cuck-oo *n., pl.* **cuckoos** A European bird, gray in color, which lays its eggs in the nests of other birds. *Slang* Silly.

cu-cum-ber *n.* A fruit with a green rind and white, seedy flesh.

cud *n.* Food forced up into the mouth of a ruminating animal from the first stomach and chewed again.

cud-dle *v.* To caress fondly and hold close; to snuggle. **cuddly** *adj.*

cue *n.* A signal given to an actor or someone making a speech, letting him know it is his turn; a long rod for playing pool and billiards.

cue ball *n.* The white ball that is struck with the cue in billiards and pool.

cuff *n.* The lower part of a sleeve; the part of the pant legs which is turned up. *v.* To strike someone.

cuffs *n.* Handcuffs.

cui-rass *n.* A piece of armor for the breast and back, used for protection.

cui-sine *n.* A style of cooking and preparing food; the food prepared.

cu-li-nar-y *adj.* Relating to cooking.

cull *v.* To select the best from a group.

cul-mi-nate *v.* To reach or rise to the highest point. **culmination** *n.*

cu-lotte *n.* A woman's full pants made to look like a skirt.

cul-pa-ble *adj.* Meriting blame.

cul-prit *n.* A person guilty of a crime.

cult *n.* A group or system of religious worship. **cultic** *adj.*, **cultist** *n.*

cul-ti-vate *v.* To improve land for planting by fertilizing and plowing; to improve by study; to encourage. **-able** *adj.*, **cultivation**, **cultivator** *n.*

cul-ture *n.* The act of developing intellectual ability with education; a form of civilization, particularly the beliefs, arts, and customs. *Biol.* The growth of living material in a prepared nutrient media. **culture** *v.*

cul-vert *n.* A drain that runs under a road or railroad.

cum-ber *v.* To burden someone.

cum-ber-some *adj.* Clumsy; unwieldy.

cum-mer-bund *n.* A wide sash worn by men in formal attire.

cu-mu-lus *n., pl.* **cumuli** A white, fluffy cloud with a rounded top and a flat base.

cu-ne-i-form *n.* Wedge-shaped characters used in ancient Babylonian, Assyrian, and Sumerian writing.

cun-ning *adj.* Crafty; sly. **cunningly** *adv.*

cup *n.* A small, open container with a handle, used for drinking; a measure of capacity that equals 1/2 pint, 8 ounces, or 16 tablespoons.

Cu-pid *n.* The god of love in Roman mythology.

cu-pid-ity *n.* An excessive desire for material gain.

cu-po-la *n.* A rounded roof; a small vaulted structure that usually rises above a roof.

cur *n.* A mongrel; a dog of mixed breeds.

cu-rate *n.* A member of the clergy that assists the priest.

cu-ra-tor *n.* A person in charge of a museum.

curb *n.* Something that restrains or controls; the raised border along the edge of a street. **curb** *v.*

curd *n.* The coagulated portion of milk used for making cheese.

cure *n.* Recovery from a sickness; a medical treatment; the process of preserving food with the use of salt, smoke, or aging.

cu-ret-tage *n.* Surgical cleaning and scraping.

cur-few *n.* An order for people to clear the streets at a certain hour; the hour at which an adolescent has been told to be home by his or her parents.

cu-ri-o *n.* An unusual or rare object.

cu-ri-ous *adj.* Questioning; inquisitive; eager for information. **curiousity** *n.*, **curiously** *adv.*

curl *v.* To twist into curves; shape like a coil. *n.* A ringlet of hair. **curler**, **curliness** *n.*, **curly** *adj.*

cur-lew *n.* A migratory bird with long legs and a long slender curved bill.

cur-mudg-eon *n.* An ill-tempered person.

cur-rant *n.* A small seedless raisin.

cur-ren-cy *n., pl.* **-cies** Money in circulation.

cur-rent *adj.* Belonging or occurring in the present time. *n.* Water or air that has a steady flow in a definite direction. **currently** *adv.*

cur-ric-u-lum *n., pl.* **-la, -lums** The courses offered in a school.

cur-ry *v.* To groom a horse with a brush. *n.* A pungent spice used in cooking.

cur-ry-comb *n.* A special comb used to curry a horse.

curse *n.* A prayer or wish for harm to come to someone or something. **cursed** *adj.,* **curse** *v.*

cursor *n.* In computer science, the flashing square, underline, or other indicator on the CRT screen of a computer that shows where the next character will be deleted or inserted.

cur-sive *n.* A flowing writing in which the letters are joined together. **-ly** *adv.*

curt *adj.* Abrupt; rude. **curtly** *adv.,* **curtness** *n.*

cur-tail *v.* To shorten. **curtailment** *n.*

cur-tain *n.* A piece of material that covers a window and can be either drawn to the sides or raised.

curt-sy *n., pl.* **-sies** A respectful gesture made by bending the knees and lowering the body.

cush-ion *n.* A pillow with a soft filling. *v.* To absorb the shock or effect.

cus-pid *n.* A pointed canine tooth.

cus-pi-dor *n.* A spittoon.

cuss *v.* To use profanity.

cus-tard *n.* A mixture of milk, eggs, sugar, and flavoring that is baked.

cus-to-di-an *n.* One who has the custody or care of something or someone.

cus-to-dy *n., pl.* **-dies** The act of guarding; the care and protection of a minor.

cus-tom *n.* An accepted practice of a community or people; the usual manner of doing something. **customs** The tax one must pay on imported goods.

custom--built *adj.* Built to one's special order.

cus-tomer *n.* A person with whom a merchant or business person must deal, usually on a regular basis.

cus-tom house *n.* An office of business where customs are paid and ships are cleared for entering or leaving a country.

cut *v.* To penetrate with a sharp edge, as with a knife; to omit or leave something out; to reap or harvest crops in the fields. *Slang* To cut class; to share in the profits. **cut** *n.*

cut back *v.* To reduce; to prune.

cute *adj.* Attractive in a delightful way.

cut glass *n.* Glass shaped and decorated by using a cutting instrument.

cut-lass *or* **cut-las** *n.* A thick, short, curved sword.

cut-lery *n.* Cutting instruments used at the dinner table and used to prepare food for cooking.

cut-let *n.* A thin piece of meat for broiling or frying, usually lamb or veal.

cut-off *n.* A short cut; the act of cutting something off.

cut-out *n.* Something intended to be cut or already cut out. *v.* To shape by cutting; to eliminate. *Slang* **cut it out**

Stop it.

cut--rate *adj.* Offering merchandise at a lower than normal price.

cut-ter *n., Naut.* A fast-sailing vessel with a single mast.

cut-throat *n.* A murderer; a thug.

cut up *v.* To act foolishly; to behave like a clown; to cut into pieces.

cut-work *n.* A type of ornamental embroidery in which a design is stitched and the material inside the design is cut away.

cu-vette *n.* A small vessel or tube used in a laboratory.

cy-a-nide *n., Chem.* A compound of cyanogen with a metallic element; a poison.

cyc-la-men *n.* A plant with red, white, or pink flowers.

cy-cle *n.* A recurring time in which an event occurs repeatedly; a bicycle or motorcycle. **cyclical** *adj.*

cy-clist *n.* A person who rides a cycle.

cy-clone *n.* A storm with wind rotating about a low pressure center, accompanied by destructive weather.

cy-clo-tron *n.* Machine that obtains high-energy electrified particles by whirling at a high speed in a strong magnetic field.

cyl-in-der *n.*

A long, round body that is either hollow or solid. **cylindrical** *adj.*

cym-bal *n.* A pair of brass plates which produce a clashing tone when struck together.

cyn-ic *n.* One who believes that all people have selfish motives. **cynical** *adj.,* **cynicism** *n.*

cy-no-sure *n.* A person or object that attracts admiration and interest.

cy-press *n.* An evergreen tree that grows in a warm climate and bears small scale-like needles.

cyst *n.* An abnormal sac or vesicle which may collect and retain fluid. **cystic** *adj.*

cyst-ic fi-bro-sis *n.* A congenital disease usually developing in childhood and resulting in disorders of the lungs and pancreas.

cys-ti-tis *n.* An inflammation of the bladder.

cy-tol-ogy *n.* The scientific study of cell formation, function, and structure. **cytological, cytologic** *adj.,* **cytologist** *n.*

cy-to-tech-nol-o-gist *n.* A trained medical technician in the identification of cell abnormalities.

czar *n.* An emperor or king or one of the former emperors or kings of Russia. *Slang* One who has authority.

czar-das *n.* Hungarian dance to music that starts out slow and ends with fast whirl.

cza-ri-na *n.* The woman married to the czar of Russia.

czar-ism *n.* The former Russian system of government. **czarist** *n.*

, d The fourth letter of the English alphabet; the Roman numeral for 500.

A *abbr.* District Attorney.

ab *v.* To touch quickly with light, short strokes.

ab-ble *v.* To play in a liquid, as water, with the hands; to work in or play with in a minor way. **dabbler** *n.*

achs-hund *n.* A small dog with very short legs, drooping ears, and a long body.

ad *n., Informal* Father.

ad-dy *n., pl.* **-dies** *Informal* Father.

ad-dy--long-legs *n.* An insect with very long legs and a rounded body that resembles a spider.

af-fo-dil *n.* A bulbous plant with solitary yellow flowers.

aft *adj.* Insane; crazy; foolish. **daftly** *adv.*, **daftness** *n.*

ag-ger *n.*

A pointed, short-edged weapon which is used for stabbing.

a-querre-o-type *n.* A very early photographic process which used silver-coated metallic plates that were sensitive to light.

ahl-ia *n.* A perennial plant having tuberous roots and showy purple, red, yellow, or white flowers.

ai-ly *adj., pl.* **-lies** To occur, appear, or happen every day of the week. *n.* A newspaper which is published daily.

ai-ly dou-ble *n.* A bet that is won by picking the winners of two specified races occurring on the same day.

ain-ty *adj., pl.* **-ties** Having or showing refined taste; delicately beautiful. **daintily** *adv.*, **daintiness** *n.*

ai-qui-ri *n.* A cocktail made with rum and lime juice.

air-y *n., pl.* **-ies** A commercial establishment which processes milk for resale. **dairymaid, dairyman** *n.*

ai-sy *n., pl.* **-ies** A plant having flowers with yellow disks and white rays.

ale *n.* A small valley.

al-ly *v.* To waste time; to dawdle; to flirt. **dallier, dalliance** *n.*

al-ma-tian *n.* A breed of dog with short, smooth white hair with black spots. *adj.* Pertaining to Dalmatia or its people.

am *n.* A barrier constructed for controlling or raising the level of water; female animal who has had offspring.

am-age *n.* An injury to person or property; in law, the compensation given for loss or injury. **damageable** *adj.*, **damagingly** *adv.*

am-ask *n.* An elaborately patterned, reversible fabric, originally made of silk.

ame *n.* A mature woman or matron. *Slang* A woman. **Dame** *Brit.* A title given to a woman, the female equivalent of a British Lord.

amn *v.* To swear or curse at; to pronounce as bad, worthless, or a failure. **damnation, damnableness** *n.*

damp *adj.* Between dry and wet; of or relating to poisonous gas or foul air found in a mine. **-ish** *adj.*, **-ly** *adv.*

dam-sel *n.* A maiden; a young unmarried woman.

dam-son *n.* The tree that produces an oval purple plum of the same name.

dance *v.* To move rhythmically to music using improvised or planned steps and gestures. **dance, dancer** *n.*

dan-de-lion *n.* A plant considered a weed in North America, having yellow flowers and green notched leaves, sometimes used in salads and in making wines.

dan-dle *v.* To move a child or infant up and down on the knees or in the arms with a gentle movement. **dandler** *n.*

dan-druff *n.* A scaly material which forms on the scalp and is shed from time to time.

dan-dy *n., pl.* **-dies** A man who is very interested in an elegant appearance and fine clothes. *Informal adj.* Excellent, very fine. **dandify** *v.*, **dandy, dandyish** *adj.*, **dandyism** *n.*

dan-ger *n.* An exposure to injury, evil, or loss.

dan-ger-ous *adj.* Unsafe. **dangerously** *adv.*, **dangerousness** *n.*

dan-gle *v.* To hang loosely and swing to and fro; to have an unclear grammatical relation in a sentence.

dank *adj.* Uncomfortably damp; wet and cold. **dankly** *adv.*, **dankness** *n.*

dan-seuse *n., pl.* **-seuses** A female ballet dancer.

dap-per *adj.* Stylishly dressed.

dap-ple *v.* To make variegated or spotted in color.

dare *v.* To have the boldness or courage to undertake an adventure; to challenge a person as to show proof of courage. **daring** *adj.*, **daringly** *adv.*

dare-devil *n.* A person who is bold or reckless. **daredevilry, daredeviltry** *n.*

dark *adj.* Dim; to have little or no light; to be difficult to comprehend; of a deep shade of color, as black or almost black. **in the dark** To do in secret; to be in a state of ignorance.

Dark Ages *n.* The early part of the Middle Ages.

dark-en *v.* To become or make dark or darker. **darkish** *adj.*, **darkly** *adv.*

dar-ling *n.* A favorite person; someone who is very dear; a person tenderly loved. **darlingly** *adv.*, **darlingness** *n.*

darn *v.* To mend a hole by filling the gap with interlacing stitches. **darner** *n.*

dart *n.* A pointed missile either shot or thrown. **darts** *pl.* The game of throwing darts at a usually round target.

dash *v.* To break or shatter with a striking violent blow; to move quickly; to rush; to finish or perform a duty in haste. **dash, dasher** *n.*

das-tard *n.* A coward; a sneak. **dastardliness** *n.*, **dastardly** *adj.*

da-ta *pl., n.* The figures or facts from

which conclusions may be drawn.

da-ta bank *n.* In computer science, the location in a computer where information is stored.

da-ta pro-cess-ing *n.* In computer science, the business of handling and storing information using computers and other available machines.

date *n.* A particular point in time; a day, month, or year; the exact time at which something happens; a social engagement; a person's partner on such an occasion. **date** *v.*

date-line *n.* The line or phrase at the beginning of a periodical giving the date and place of publication; the 180th meridian on a map or globe which is where a day begins.

da-tum *n., pl.* **-ta** A single piece of information.

daub *v.* To coat or smear with grease, plaster, or an adhesive substance.

daugh-ter *n.* The female offspring of a man or woman; a female descendant.

daughter--in--law *n.* One's son's wife.

daunt *v.* To intimidate or discourage.

Davis, Jefferson *n.* President of the Confederate States of America, from 1861-1865.

dav-it *n.* A small crane on the side of a ship, for lifting its boats.

daw-dle *v.* To waste; to take more time than is needed. **dawdler** *n.*

dawn *n.* The beginning of a new day; to begin to understand, expand, or develop. **dawning** *n.*

day *n.* The period of time that falls between dawn and nightfall; the time that is represented by one rotation of the earth upon its axis, twenty-four hours; the large portion of a day spent in a particular way.

day-care *n.* A service provided for working mothers and fathers, offering daytime supervision, training, and safe keeping for their children while they work.

day-light sav-ings time *n.* The period of the year, beginning in the spring, when clocks are moved ahead by one hour.

Day of A-tone-ment *n.* Yom Kippur.

daze *v.* To bewilder or stun with a heavy blow or shock. **dazedly** *adv.*

DBA *abbr.* Doing business as.

DC *abbr.* District of Columbia.

D--Day *n., Milit.* June 6, 1944, the day on which the Allies invaded France in World War II.

dea-con *n.* The clergyman who ranks immediately below a priest.
deaconess, deaconry, deaconship *n.*

dead *adj.* Without life; no longer in existence or use; dormant; quiet; in law, no longer in force.

dead-beat *n., Slang* A person who avoids paying his debts.

dead-end *n.* A point from which one cannot progress; a street having no outlet.

dead-eye *n.* A sharpshooter.

dead heat *n.* A contest where two or more entrants finish at the same time.

dead-line *n.* A time limit when something must be finished.

dead-fy *adj.* Very dangerous; likely to cause death.

dead pan *adj., Slang* Having no expression on one's face.

dead reck-on-ing *n., Naut.* A method of computing a vessel's position by compass and log without the use of astronomical observation.

Dead Sea *n.* The salt lake between Jordan and Israel.

deaf *adj.* Totally or partially unable to hear; refusing or unwilling to listen.
deaf *n.*

deal *v.* To distribute or pass out playing cards; to be occupied or concerned with a certain matter; to discuss, consider, or take affirmative action. *n.* An indefinite amount; a business transaction. **dealer** *n.*

deal-er-ship *n.* A franchise to sell a certain item in a specified area, as a car dealer.

deal-ing *n., Slang* Involved in the buying and selling of illegal drugs.

dean *n.* The head administrator of a college, high school, or university.

dear *adj.* Greatly cherished; loved.
dearly *adv.,* **dearness** *n.*

death *n.* Termination; the permanent cessation of all vital functions.

death-bed *n.* The bed on which a person dies; the last hours.

death-blow *n.* An event or blow that is fatal.

death-cup *n.* A poisonous mushroom.

death-less *adj.* Immortal; not subject to death.

death-ly *adj.* Fatal; causing death.

death rate *n.* Ratio of deaths to the population of a certain area.

death-trap *n.* An unsafe structure.

death-watch *n.* A vigil kept on a person who is dying.

de-ba-cle *n.* A sudden downfall, failure, or collapse.

de-bark *v.* To disembark.

de-base *v.* To lower in character or value; demean. **-ment,** **debaser** *n.*

de-bate *v.* To discuss or argue opposing points; to consider; to deliberate.
debate *n.,* **debatable** *adj.,*
debatably *adv.,* **debater** *n.*

de-bauch *v.* To lead away from morals; to corrupt. **debauchery, -ment** *n.*

de-ben-ture *n.* A voucher given as an acknowledgment of debt.

de-bil-i-tate *v.* To make feeble or weak.
debilitation *n.,* **debilitative** *adj.*

deb-it *n.* A debt or item recorded in an account. *v.* To enter a debt in a ledger.

de-brief *v.* To interrogate or question in order to obtain information.

de-bris *n.* Scattered or discarded remains or waste.

debt *n.* That which someone owes, as money, services, or goods; an obligation to pay or render something to another.

debt-or *n.* A person owing a debt to another.

e-bug v. To find and remove a concealed electronic listening device; in computer science, to remove errors in a computer program.

e-bunk v., *Informal* To expose false pretensions.

e-but n. A first public appearance; the formal introduction to society; the beginning of a new career. **debut** v.

eb-u-tante n. A young woman making her debut in society.

ec-ade n. A period of ten years; a set or group of ten.

e-ca-dence n. A process of decay or deterioration; a period or condition of decline, as in morals. **decadent** adj., **decadently** adv.

e-caf-fein-at-ed adj. Having the caffeine removed.

ec-a-gon n., *Geom.*

A polygon with ten sides and ten angles. **decagonal** adj., **decagonally** adv.

ec-a-gram or **del-a-gram** n. In the metric system, a measure of weight equal to 10 grams.

e-cal n. A design or picture transferred by decalcomania.

e-cal-co-ma-ni-a n. The process of transferring pictures or designs printed on special paper to glass, wood, and other materials.

ec-a-li-ter or **dek-a-li-ter** n. In the metric system, a measure of capacity equal to 10 liters.

ec-a-logue or **dec-a-log** n. The Ten Commandments.

ec-a-me-ter or **dek-a-me-ter** n. In the metric system, a measure of length equal to 10 meters.

e-camp v. To break camp; to leave or depart suddenly.

e-cant v. To pour off liquid without disturbing the sediments; to pour from one container to another. **-ation** n.

e-cant-er n. A decorative stoppered bottle for serving wine or other liquids.

e-cap-i-tate v. To cut off the head; to behead. **decapitation, decapitator** n.

e-cath-lon n. An athletic event with ten different track and field events in all of which each contestant participates.

e-cay v. To decline in quantity or quality; to rot. *Phys.* To diminish or disintegrate by radioactive decomposition.

e-cease v. To die. **decedent** n., **-ed** adj.

e-ceit n. Deception; the quality of being deceptive; falseness. **deceitful** adj., **deceitfully** adv.

e-ceive v. To mislead by falsehood; to lead into error; to delude. **deceivable** adj., **deceiver** n.

e-cel-er-ate v. To decrease in velocity. **deceleration, decelerator** n.

De-cem-ber n. The 12th month of the year, having 31 days.

e-cen-ni-al adj. Happening once every 10 years; continuing for ten years.

de-cent adj. Adequate; satisfactory; kind; generous; characterized by propriety of conduct, speech, or dress; respectable. *Informal* Properly or adequately clothed. **decently** adv., **decentness** n.

de-cen-tral-ize v. To divide the administrative functions of a central authority among several local authorities; to reorganize into smaller and more dispersed parts. **-ation** n.

de-cep-tion n. The act of deceiving; the fact or state of being deceived; anything which deceives or deludes.

de-cep-tive adj. Having the tendency or power to deceive. **deceptively** adv., **deceptiveness** n.

dec-i-are n. In the metric system, one tenth of an are.

de-ci-bel n. A measurement of sound; one tenth of a bel.

de-cide v. To settle; to determine, as a controversy or contest; to determine the conclusion or issue of; to make up one's mind. **decider** n.

de-cid-ed adj. Definite or unquestionable; exhibiting determination. **decidedly** adv., **decidedness** n.

de-cid-u-ous adj., *Biol.* Shedding or falling off at maturity or at a certain season, such as fruit, leaves, petals, antlers, or snake skins.

dec-i-gram n. In the metric system, the tenth part of a gram.

dec-i-li-ter n. In the metric system, the tenth part of a liter.

de-cil-lion n. The cardinal number written as one followed by thirty-three zeros; a thousand nonillions. **decillionth** adj. & n.

dec-i-mal n. A proper fraction based on the number 10 and indicated by the use of a decimal point; every decimal place indicating a multiple of a power of 10; a number with a decimal point; a decimal fraction or one of its digits.

de-c-i-mal point n. A period placed to the left of a decimal fraction.

dec-i-mate v. To destroy or kill a large proportion of something; to select by lot and kill one out of every ten.

dec-i-meter n. In the metric system, the tenth part of a meter.

de-ci-pher v. To determine the meaning of something obscure, as a poor handwriting; to translate from code or cipher into plain text; to decode.

de-ci-sion n. The act of deciding; a judgment or conclusion reached by deciding; in boxing, a victory decided when there has not been a knockout.

de-ci-sive adj. Ending uncertainty or dispute; conclusive; characterized by firmness; un-questionable; unmistakable. **decisively** adv.

dec-i-stere n. In the metric system, a cubic decimeter, or the tenth part of a stere.

deck n. A set of playing cards. *Naut.* A horizontal platform that covers or extends across a vessel, and serves as both a floor and a roof. **hit the deck**

To rise from bed; to get up early; to be ready for action. **on deck** Present and ready for action. **all decked out** To decorate or dress elegantly. *v.* To knock someone or something down with a punch.

deck hand *or* **deck-hand** *n.* A member of a ship's crew assigned to work on deck.

de-claim *v.* To speak or deliver loudly and rhetorically; to give a formal speech; to attack verbally. **declamation** *n.*, **declamatory** *adj.*

de-clare *v.* To make known or clear; to state formally or officially; to say emphatically; to avow; to assert; to make full claim to, as goods liable to duty; to proclaim an opinion or choice for or against something. **declarer**, **declaration** *n.*, **declarative** *adj.*

de-clas-si-fy *v.* To remove the security classification of a document. **declassification** *n.*

de-clen-sion *n.* A descent; a sloping downward; a decline; a deviation, as from a belief. *Gram.* The inflection of nouns, pronouns, and adjectives according to case, number, and gender.

dec-li-na-tion *n.* The act of bending downward or inclining; deviation, as in conduct or direction; the angle formed between the direction of a compass needle and the true north; a polite refusal.

de-cline *v.* To reject or refuse something; to grow frail gradually, as in health; to bend or incline to the side or downward; to refuse politely. *Gram.* To give the inflected form of a noun, pronoun, or adjective. *n.* The act or result of deterioration. **declinable**, **declinational** *adj.*, **declination**, **decliner**, **decline** *n.*

de-cliv-i-ty *n.*, *pl.* **-ties** A steep downward slope or surface. **declivous** *adj.*

de-coct *v.* To extract by boiling; to condense. **decoction** *n.*

de-code *v.* To convert from a coded message into plain language. **decoder** *n.*

de-com-pose *v.* To decay; to separate into constituent parts. **-able** *adj.*, **decomposer, decomposition** *n.*

de-com-press *v.* To relieve of pressure; to bring a person back to normal air pressure, as divers or caisson workers. **decompression** *n.*

de-con-ges-tant *n.* An agent that relieves congestion.

de-con-tam-i-nate *v.* To make free of contamination by destroying or neutralizing poisonous chemicals, radioactivity, or other harmful elements. **-ion**, **decontaminator** *n.*

de-con-trol *v.* To free from the control of, especially from governmental control.

de-cor *n.* The style of decorating a room, office, or home.

dec-o-rate *v.* To adorn or furnish with fashionable or beautiful things; to confer a decoration or medal upon.

dec-o-ra-tion *n.* The process, art, or act of decorating; a thing or group o things which decorate; an emblem badge, medal, or award.

Dec-o-ra-tion Day *n.* Memorial Day, th day set aside to honor all fallen sol diers with special services and flower placed on their graves.

dec-o-ra-tive *adj.* Suitable for decora tion; ornamental. **decoratively** *adv.*, **decorativeness** *n.*

dec-o-rous *adj.* Marked by decorum seemly; proper. **-ly** *adv.*, **-ness** *n.*

de-co-rum *n.* Proper behavior; good o fitting conduct.

de-coy *n.* An artificial animal used t lure game, especially ducks; a mean to mislead, trap, or lure into danger.

de-crease *v.* To grow or cause to grow gradually less or smaller; to diminish *n.* The process or act of decreasing o the resulting state; a decline.

de-cree *n.* An authoritative and forma order or decision; a judicial judgment.

dec-re-ment *n.* The process or act o decreasing; the amount lost by gradua waste or diminution. **decremental** *adj*

de-crep-it *adj.* Broken down or worn ou by old age or excessive use. **decrepitly** *adv.*, **decrepitude** *n.*

de-cre-scen-do *n.*, *pl.* **-dos** *Mus.* A gradual decrease in force or loudness. **decrescendo** *adj.* & *adv.*

de-crim-i-nal-ize *v.* To remove th criminal classification of; to no longe prohibit.

de-cry *v.* To disparage or condem openly; to denounce. **decrier** *n.*

ded-i-cate *v.* To set apart, as for sacre uses; to set apart for special use, duty or purpose; to address or inscribe work of literature, art or music to someone; to commit oneself to a cer tain cause, course of action, o thought; to unveil or open to th public. **dedication** *n.*, **dedicatory** *adj.*

de-duce *v.* To derive a conclusion b reasoning. **deducible** *adj.*

de-duc-tion *n.* The act of deducing o subtracting; an amount that is or ma be deducted; the process or act o deducting. **deductive** *adj.*, **-ively** *adv.*

deed *n.* Anything performed or done; notable achievement or feat; in law, legal document, especially one relatin to the transference of property.

deem *v.* To judge or consider.

deep *adj.* Extending far below a surface extending far backward from front t rear or far inward from an outer su face; penetrating to or coming from depth; hard to understand; extreme intense; vivid and rich in shade; low i pitch; resonant. *n.*, *Naut.* The interva between two fathoms marked in suc cession. **to go off the deep end** To be come excited or hysterical. **the dee** *Poet.* The ocean or sea. **deeply** *adv.*, **deepness** *n.*

deep-en *v.* To become or make deep o deeper.

deep-freeze *v.* To quick-freeze. *Slang* A appliance for storing frozen foods.

deep--root-ed *adj.* Firmly implanted, said of beliefs; of or relating to a plant with very long roots.

deep-six *v.*, *Slang* To throw overboard; to get rid of; to toss out.

deer *n.*, *pl.* **deer**

A hoofed ruminant mammal having deciduous antlers, usually in the male only, as the elk, moose, and reindeer.

deer fly *n.* Any of the various bloodsucking flies.

deer-skin *n.* A deer's hide or the leather made from it.

de-es-ca-late *v.* To decrease or be decreased gradually, as in intensity, scope, or effect.

de-face *v.* To spoil or mar the appearance or surface of something.

de fac-to *adj.* Really or actually exercising authority.

de-fal-cate *v.* To embezzle; to misuse funds. **defalcation** *n.*

de-fame *v.* To slander or libel. **-ion**, defamatory *adj.*, **defamer** *n.*

de-fault *v.* To neglect to fulfill an obligation or requirement, as to pay money due or to appear in court; to forfeit by default. *n.* The failure to participate or compete in a competition. **defaulter** *n.*

de-feat *v.* To win a victory; to beat; to prevent the successful outcome of; to frustrate; to baffle; in law, to make void; to annul.

de-feat-ism *n.* The practice of those accepting defeat as inevitable. **defeatist** *n.* & *adj.*

def-e-cate *v.* To discharge feces from the bowels. **defecation**, **defecator** *n.*

de-fect *n.* The lack of something desirable or necessary for completeness or perfection; a fault or imperfection. **defection**, **defector** *n.*

de-fec-tive *adj.* Having a defect; imperfect. *Gram.* Lacking one or more of the infected forms normal for its class. *Psychol.* Having less than normal intelligence. **defectively** *adv.*, **-ness** *n.*

de-fend *v.* Protect.

de-fend-ant *n.* The person charged in a criminal or civil lawsuit.

de-fense *n.* The action of defending.

de-fer *v.* To delay or postpone. **-ment** *n.*

de-fi-ance *n.* The instance or act of defying; a challenge. **defiant** *adj.*, **-ly** *adv.*

de-fi-cient *adj.* Lacking in a necessary element.

def-i-cit *n.* Deficiency in amount.

de-flate *v.* To cause to collapse by removing gas or air; to remove self-esteem or conceit. *Econ.* To reduce or restrict money or spending so that prices decline.

deflation *n.*, **deflationary** *adj.*

de-flect *v.* To turn aside; to swerve from a course. **deflectable**, **deflective** *adj.*, **deflection**, **deflector** *n.*

de-flower *v.* To rob one's virginity; to violate; to rob of charm or beauty.

de-fog *v.* To remove fog from, as from the inside of an automobile. **-ger** *n.*

de-fo-li-ant *n.* A chemical sprayed or dusted on plants or trees to cause the leaves to drop off. **defoliate** *v.*

de-for-est *v.* To clear of forests or trees. **deforestation** *n.*

de-form *v.* To distort the form of; to be distorted; to mar the beauty or excellence of; to spoil the natural form of. **deformable** *adj.*, **deformation** *n.*

de-fraud *v.* To cheat; to swindle.

de-fray *v.* To provide for or to make payment on something. **-able** *adj.*, **-al** *n.*

de-frost *v.* To cause to thaw out; to remove the ice or frost from. **-er** *n.*

deft *adj.* Skillful and neat in one's actions. **deftly** *adv.*, **deftness** *n.*

de-funct *adj.* Dead; deceased. **defunctive** *adj.*, **defunctness** *n.*

de-fuse *v.* To remove the detonator or fuse from; to remove or make less dangerous, tense, or hostile.

de-fy *v.*, *pl.* **-fies** To confront or resist boldly and openly; to challenge someone to do some-thing or not do something; to dare. **defier** *n.*

deg *abbr.* Degree.

De Gaulle, Charles *n.* (1890-1970) French general and statesman.

de-gauss *v.* To neutralize the magnetic field of something.

de-gen-er-ate *v.* To decline in quality, value, or desirability; to deteriorate; to become worse. *adj.* Morally depraved or sexually deviant. **degenerate**, **degeneracy** *n.*, **-ly** *adv.*, **-ive** *adj.*

de-grade *v.* To reduce in rank, status, or grade; to demote; to reduce in quality or intensity. **degraded** *adj.*, **degradingly** *adv.*, **degradedness** *n.*

de-gree *n.* One of a succession of stages and/or steps; relative manner, condition or respect; the academic title given by an institution of learning upon completion of a course of study or as an honorary distinction; a unit on a temperature or thermometer scale; in law, a measure of severity, as murder in the first degree. *Gram.* A form used in the comparison of adjectives and adverbs. **by degrees** Little by little. **to a degree** Somewhat.

de-horn *v.* To remove the horns from an animal.

de-hu-man-ize *v.* To deprive of human qualities, especially to make mechanical and routine.

de-hu-mid-i-fy *v.* To remove the moisture from. **dehumidifier** *n.*

de-hy-drate *v.* To cause to lose moisture or water. **dehydration** *n.*

de-ice *v.* To rid of or keep free of ice.

de-i-fy *v.* To glorify or idealize; to raise in high regard; to worship as a god. **deification** *n.*

deign *v.* To think it barely worthy of one's dignity; to condescend.

De·i gra·ti·a *adv.*, L. By the grace of God.

de·in·sti·tu·tion·al·ize *v.* To remove a person who is developmentally handicapped or mentally ill from an institution; to remove the institutional nature of.

de·ism *n.* A belief in the existence of God but a denial of the validity of revelation. deist *n.*

de·ject *v.* To lower the spirits; to dishearten. dejection, -edness *n.*, -edly *adv.*

de·jec·tion *n.* The state or condition of being dejected; depression.

de ju·re *adv.*, L. By right; legally or rightfully.

deka- *or* deca- *combining form* In the metric system, ten times a specified unit.

dek·a·gram *n.* See decagram.

dek·a·liter *n.* See decaliter.

dek·a·meter *n.* See decameter.

dek·are *or* dec·are *n.* In the metric system, a thousand square meters or 10 ares.

dek·a·stere *or* dec·a·stere *n.* In the metric system, a measure of volume equal to 10 steres.

deke *v.*, *Slang* In hockey, to outmaneuver an opponent by faking a shot or movement.

del *abbr.* Delete.

Del·a·ware *n.* A state located on the eastern coast of the United States.

de·lay *v.* To put off until a later time; to defer; to cause to be late or detained; to linger; to waste time; to procrastinate. *n.* The time period that someone is delayed. delayer *n.*

de·le *n.*, *Print.* A mark in typesetting which indicates something is to be deleted or taken out of the manuscript.

de·lec·ta·ble *adj.* Giving great pleasure; delightful; savory; delicious. delectability *n.*

de·lec·ta·tion *n.* Enjoyment or pleasure.

del·e·gate *n.* A person with the power to act as a representative for another; a deputy or agent; a person appointed or elected to represent a territory in the House of Representatives, where he may speak but not vote; a member of the lower legislature in Maryland, Virginia, and West Virginia. *v.* To entrust and commit to another.

del·e·ga·tion *n.* The act of delegating or the state of being delegated; a person or group of people appointed to represent others.

de·lete *v.* To cancel; to take out. -ion *n.*

del·e·te·ri·ous *adj.* Causing moral or physical injury; harmful. deleteriously *adv.*, deleteriousness *n.*

delft *n.* A glazed earthenware, usually blue and white in color, originating in Delft, Holland, in 1310.

Del·hi *n.* A city in north central India.

del·i *n.*, *Slang* A delicatessen.

de·lib·er·ate *v.* To say or do something intentionally; to plan in advance. *adj.* Premeditated; to be leisurely or slow in manner or motion. deliberateness, deliberation *n.*, -ly *adv.*, -ive *adj.*

del·i·ca·cy *n.*, *pl.* -cies A select or choice food; the quality or state of being delicate.

del·i·cate *adj.* Pleasing to the senses; exquisite and fine in workmanship, texture, or construction; pleasing, as in color, taste, or aroma; sensitive and subtle in perception, feeling, or expression; frail in constitution; easily broken or damaged; considerate of the feelings of others. delicately *adv.*, delicateness *n.*

del·i·ca·tes·sen *n.* A store which sells cooked meats, preserved cheeses, pickles, and other delicacies.

de·li·cious *adj.* Extremely enjoyable and pleasant to the taste. deliciously *adv.*, deliciousness *n.*

de·li·cious *n.* A variety of red, sweet apples.

de·light *n.* A great joy or pleasure. *v.* To give or take great pleasure; to rejoice to gratify or please highly. delighted *adj.*, delightedly *adv.*

de·light·ful *adj.* Extremely pleasing. delightfully *adv.*, delightfulness *n.*

Delilah *n.* The Philistine woman who betrayed Samson by cutting off his hair, thus depriving him of his strength; a pleasant but treacherous woman.

de·lim·it *v.* To give or prescribe the limits of.

de·lin·e·ate *v.* To represent by a drawing; to draw or trace the outline of something; to sketch; to represent in gestures or words. delineation *n.*

de·lin·quent *adj.* Neglecting to do what is required by obligation or law; falling behind in a payment. *n.* A juvenile who is out of control, as violating the law. delinquency, delinquent *n.*, delinquently *adv.*

del·i·quesce *v.*, *Chem.* To become liquid by absorbing atmospheric moisture; to melt. deliquescent *adj.*

de·lir·i·um *n.* A temporary or sporadic mental disturbance associated with fever, shock, or intoxication and marked by excitement, incoherence, and hallucination; uncontrolled excitement and emotion. delirious *adj.*, deliriously *adv.*, deliriousness *n.*

de·lir·i·um tre·mens *n.* Acute delirium resulting from chronic and excessive use of alcohol.

de·liv·er *v.* To surrender; to hand over; to set free; to liberate; to give or send forth; to assist in the birth of an offspring; to do what is expected or desired; to take to the intended recipient. to be delivered of To give birth. deliverable *adj.*, deliverance, deliverer *n.*

de·liv·er·y *n.*, *pl.* -ies The act of conveying or delivering; a transferring or handing over; the process or act of giving birth, as parturition; the act or manner of throwing.

dell *n.* A small, secluded, usually wooded

valley.

Del-phia *n.* An ancient town of central Greece near Mount Parnassus.

del-phin-ium *n.* Any of a genus of perennial plants of the crowfoot with spurred flowers which are usually blue.

del-ta *n.* The fourth letter in the Greek alphabet; a typically triangular-shaped silt deposit at or in the mouth of a river; anything triangular in shape.

del-ta ray *n.* An electron ejected from matter ionizing radiation.

del-ta wing *n.* An aircraft with wings that sweep back.

de-lude *v.* To mislead the mind or judgment; to deceive; to cause to be deceived.

del-uge *v.* To flood with water; to overwhelm; to destroy. *n.* A great flood.

de-lu-sion *n.* A false, fixed belief held in spite of contrary evidence. delusional, delusive *adj.*

de luxe *or* **de-luxe** *adj.* High elegance or luxury.

delve *v.* To search for information with careful investigation.

Dem *abbr.* Democratic; Democrat.

de-mag-net-ize *v.* To remove the magnetic properties of. -ation *n.*

dem-a-gogue *n.* A person who leads the populace by appealing to emotions and prejudices. -ry, demagogy *n.*

de-mand *v.* To ask for in a firm tone; to claim as due; to have the need or requirement for; in law, to summon to court; to make a formal claim to property. *Econ.* The ability and desire to purchase something; the quantity of merchandise wanted at a certain price. **in demand** Sought after; desired. **on demand** On request or presentation; a note payable whenever the lender demands it. -able *adj.*, demander *n.*

de-mar-cate *v.* To set boundaries or limits; to separate or limit. -ion *n.*

de-mean *v.* To behave or conduct oneself in a particular manner; to degrade; to humble oneself or another.

de-mean-or *n.* A person's conduct toward others; a person's general behavior.

de-ment-ed *adj.* Insane.

de-men-tia *n.* An irreversible deterioration of intellectual faculties.

de-mer-it *n.* A fault; a defect; a mark against one's record, especially for bad conduct in school.

de-mesne *n.* A manor house with the adjoining lands; a domain; a region; in law, lands held in one's own power.

dem-i-god *n.* A mythological, semidivine being, especially the offspring of a mortal and a god.

dem-i-john *n.* A large, narrow-necked bottle usually enclosed in wicker.

de-mil-i-ta-rize *v.* To remove the military characteristics from. -ation *n.*

dem-i-mon-daine *n.* A woman who belongs to the demimonde.

dem-i-monde *n.* A class of women who are supported by wealthy protectors or

lovers.

de-mise *n.* Death; in law, a transfer of an estate by lease or will.

dem-i-tasse *n.* A small cup of very strong coffee; the name of the cup used to hold this beverage.

dem-o *n., pl.* -os *Slang* A demonstration to show product use and purpose.

de-mo-bi-lize *v.* To disband; to release from the military service.

de-moc-ra-cy *n., pl.* -cies A form of government exercised either directly by the people or through their elected representatives; rule by the majority; the practice of legal, political, or social equality.

dem-o-crat *n.* One who prefers a democracy; one who believes in social and political equality. *adj.* Marked by or advocating democracy. democratically *adv.*, democratize *v.*

Dem-o-crat-ic Par-ty *n.* One of the two major political parties in the United States, the other being the Republican Party.

de-mog-ra-phy *n.* Study of the characteristics of human population, such as growth, size, and vital statistics. demographic *adj.*, -ically *adv.*

de-mol-ish *v.* To tear down; to raze; to completely do away with; to end. demolisher, demolishment *n.*

dem-o-li-tion *n.* The process of demolishing, especially destruction with explosives.

de-mon *n.* An evil spirit; a devil. *Informal* A person of great skill or zeal.

de-mon-e-tize *v.* To deprive the currency of its standard value; to withdraw currency from use. demonetization *n.*

de-mo-ni-ac *adj.* Like or befitting a demon; to be influenced or possessed by or as by demons; of, resembling, or suggestive of a demon.

de-mon-ol-o-gy *n.* The belief or study in demons.

de-mon-stra-ble *adj.* Obvious or apparent. demonstrability *n.*, -ly *adv.*

dem-on-strate *v.* To show or prove by reasoning or evidence; to make a public protest. demonstration, demonstrator *n.*

de-mon-stra-tive *adj.* Serving to point out or demonstrate; able to prove beyond any doubt; conclusive and convincing. *Gram.* Indicating the object or person referred to; a demonstrative pronoun. demonstratively *adv.*, -ness *n.*

de-mor-al-ize *v.* To undermine the morale or confidence of someone; to degrade; to corrupt. demoralization, demoralizer *n.*

de-mote *v.* To reduce in rank, grade, or position. demotion *n.*

de-mul-cent *n.* A soothing substance.

de-mur *v.* To take issue; to object.

de-mure *adj.* Reserved and modest; coy.

de-mur-rer *n.* In law, a plea to dismiss a lawsuit on the grounds that the plaintiff's statements are insufficient to prove claim.

den *n.* The shelter for a wild animal; a small room in a home used for private study or relaxation.

de-na-ture *v.* To change the nature or natural qualities of, especially to make unfit for consumption.
denaturant, denaturation *n.*

den-drite *n., Physiol.* The branching process of a nerve cell which conducts impulses toward the cell body.
dendritic *adj.*, **dendritically** *adv.*

den-drol-ogy *n.* The botanical study of trees.

den-gue *n., Pathol.* An infectious tropical disease transmitted by mosquitoes, characterized by severe joint pains and fever.

de-ni-al *n.* A refusal to comply with a request; refusal to acknowledge the truth of a statement; abstinence; self-denial.

den-i-grate *v.* To slander; to defame.

den-im *n.* A strong, twilled cotton used for jeans, overalls, and work clothes.

Den-mark *n.* A country of northern Europe consisting of an archipelago and a peninsula between the Baltic and North seas.

de-nom-i-nate *v.* To give a name to; to designate.

de-nom-i-na-tion *n.* The name of a group or classification; the act of calling by name or naming; an organization of similar religious congregations.

de-nom-i-na-tor *n.* In mathematics, the term for the bottom half of a fraction, which indicates the number of equal parts into which the unit is divided; a common characteristic or trait.

de-no-ta-tion *n.* The meaning of, or the object or objects designated by a word; an indication, as a sign.

de-note *v.* To make known; to point out; to indicate; to signify; to designate; to mean, said of symbols or words.
denotable, denotative *adj.*

de-noue-ment *n.* The final solution of a novel, play, or plot.

de-nounce *v.* To attack or condemn openly and vehemently; to accuse formally; to announce the ending of something in a formal way. **-er** *n.*

dense *adj.* Compact; thick; close; slow to understand; stupid. **-ly** *adv.*, **-ness** *n.*

den-si-ty *n., pl.* **-ties** The state or quality of being dense or close in parts; the quantity or amount of something per unit measure, area, volume, or length.

dent *n.* A small surface depression made by striking or pressing. *v.* To put a dent in something; to make meaningful progress or headway.

den-tal *adj.* Pertaining to the teeth; of or pertaining to dentistry.

den-tal floss *n.* A strong thread, either waxed or unwaxed, used to clean between the teeth.

den-tal hy-gien-ist *n.* A licensed dental professional who provides preventive dental care, as cleaning and instruction on how to care for teeth at home.

den-ti-frice *n.* A preparation in powder or paste form for cleaning the teeth.

den-tine *or* **den-tin** *n.* The hard, calcified part of the tooth beneath the enamel containing the pulp chamber and root canals.

den-tist *n.* A licensed person whose profession is the diagnosis, treatment, and prevention of diseases of the gums and teeth. **dentistry** *n.*

den-ti-tion *n.* The kind, number, and arrangement of teeth, as in humans and other animals; the process of cutting teeth.

den-ture *n.* A set of artificial teeth either partial or full; also called a dental plate.

de-nude *v.* To remove all covering; to be or cause to be naked. *Geol.* To come into view by erosion. **denudation** *n.*

de-nun-ci-a-tion *n.* Open disapproval of a person or action; an accusation; warning or threat.

Den-ver *n.* The capital of the state of Colorado.

de-ny *v.* To declare untrue; to refuse to acknowledge or recognize; to withhold; to refuse to grant. **to deny oneself** To refuse oneself something desired; self-denial.

de-o-dor-ant *n.* A product designed to prevent, mask, or destroy unpleasant odors.

de-o-dor-ize *v.* To destroy, modify, or disguise the odor of. **-ation, -er** *n.*

de-ox-i-dize *v.* To remove the oxygen from; to reduce from the state of an oxide. **deoxidization, deoxidizer** *n.*

de-ox-y-ri-bo-nu-cle-ic acid *n.* A nucleic acid which forms a principal constituent of the genes and is known to play a role of importance in the genetic action of the chromosomes, also known as DNA.

dep *abbr.* Depart; deposit; deputy.

de-part *v.* To leave; to go away; to deviate.

de-part-ment *n.* The distinct division or part of something, as in a business, college, or store. *Informal* An area of special activity or knowledge.

de-part-men-tal-ize *v.* To divide into organized departments. **-ation** *n.*

de-part-ment store *n.* A large retail store selling various types of merchandise and services.

de-par-ture *n.* The act of taking leave or going away; a divergence; a deviation; the act of starting out on a new course of action or going on a trip.

de-pend *v.* To rely on; to trust with responsibilities; to be determined or conditioned.

de-pend-a-ble *adj.* Capable of being depended upon; trustworthy. **-ability**, **dependableness** *n.*, **dependably** *adv.*

de-pend-ence *or* **de-pend-ance** *n.* The quality or state of being dependent; trust or reliance; the state of being contingent on or determined by something else.

de-pend-en-cy *or* **de-pend-an-cy** *n., pl.* **-cies** The state of being dependent; a territory separate from but still subject to another state, territory, or country.

de-pend-ent *adj.* Depending or needing the help of another for support; determined by or contingent on something or someone else. *n., also* **de-pend-ant** A person who depends on another person for financial support. -ly *adv.*

de-pict *v.* To represent in a sculpture or a picture; to describe or represent in words. **depiction** *n.*

dep-i-late *v.* To remove the hair from. **depilation, depilator** *n.*

de-pil-a-to-ry *n., pl.* -ries A chemical which removes hair, usually in cream or liquid form.

de-plane *v.* To disembark or leave an aircraft.

de-plete *v.* To exhaust, empty, or use up a supply of something. **depletion** *n.*

de-plor-a-ble *adj.* Grievous; lamentable; very bad; wretched. **deplorably** *adv.*

de-plore *v.* To have, show, or feel great disapproval of something.

de-ploy *v.* To spread out; to place or position according to plans. -ment *n.*

de-po-lit-i-cize *v.* To remove the political status or aspect from.

de-po-nent *n.* A person who testifies under oath giving sworn testimony, especially in writing.

de-pop-u-late *v.* To quickly remove or lower the population greatly, as by massacre or disease. **depopulation** *n.*

de-port *v.* To banish or expel someone from a country; to behave in a specified manner. -ation, **deportee** *n.*

de-port-ment *n.* One's conduct; behavior.

de-pose *v.* To remove from a powerful position or office; in law, to declare or give testimony under oath. **deposable** *adj.,* **deposal** *n.*

de-pos-it *v.* To put, place, or set something down; to entrust money to a bank; to put down in the form of a layer, as silt; to give as security or partial payment. **deposit, depositor** *n.*

dep-o-si-tion *n.* The act of deposing, as from an office; that which is deposited; in law, written testimony given under oath.

de-pos-i-to-ry *n., pl.* -ries A place where anything is deposited for safekeeping.

de-pot *n.* A railroad station. *Milit.* The place where military materials are manufactured, stored, and repaired; an installation for processing personnel; a warehouse or storehouse.

de-prave *v.* To render bad or worse; in morals, to corrupt or pervert. **depraved** *adj.,* **depravity** *n.*

dep-re-cate *v.* To express regret for or disapproval of; to belittle. **deprecatingly** *adv.,* -ion, **deprecator** *n.*

de-pre-ci-ate *v.* To lessen in value or price. **depreciator** *n.,* -ive, -ory *adj.*

de-pre-ci-a-tion *n.* A loss in efficiency or value resulting from age or usage; the decline in the purchasing value of money.

de-press *v.* To make gloomy; to lower the spirits of; to lessen in energy or vigor; to press down; to lower; to diminish in value or price. -or *n.*

de-pres-sant *adj.* Acting to lower the nervous or functional activities. *n.* A sedative; a depressant agent.

de-pres-sed *adj.* Dejected; sad; low in spirits; lower than, even with, or below the surface; reduced in amount, value, or power.

de-pres-sed area *n.* An area or region characterized by severe unemployment.

de-pres-sion *n.* The state of being or the act of depressing; a severe decline in business, accompanied by increasing unemployment and falling prices. *Psych.* A condition of deep dejection characterized by lack of response to stimulation and withdrawal.

de-pres-sive *adj.* Tending to depress; related to psychological depression.

de-prive *v.* To take something away from; to keep from using, acquiring, or enjoying. **deprivable** *adj.*

depth *n.* The degree or state of being deep; the distance or extent backward, downward, or inward; the most intense part of something; intensity or richness of sound or color; the range of one's comprehension. **depths** *pl.* A deep part or place; an intense state of feeling or being.

depth charge *n.* A drum-shaped bomb which is designed to detonate underwater at a desired depth.

dep-u-ta-tion *n.* A person or persons who are acting for another or others; the act of deputing or the state of being deputed.

de-pute *v.* To appoint as a deputy, an agent, or other figure of authority; to delegate; to transfer.

dep-u-tize *v.* To act as a deputy; to appoint as a deputy.

dep-u-ty *n., pl.* -ties The person designated or authorized to act for in the absence of, or to assist another, generally a sheriff; a member of a legislative body in certain countries.

de-rail *v.* To run off the rails; to cause a train to run off the rails. **derailment** *n.*

de-range *v.* To disturb the arrangement or normal order of; to unbalance the reason; to make insane. -ment *n.*

der-by *n., pl.* -bies An annual horse race especially for 3-year-olds; a race open to all contestants; a stiff hat made from felt with a round crown and a narrow, curved brim.

de-reg-u-late *v.* To decontrol or remove from regulation or control. -ion *n.*

der-e-lict *adj.* Neglectful of obligations; remiss. *n.* Abandoned or deserted, as a ship at sea; a vagrant; a social outcast.

der-e-lic-tion *n.* Voluntary neglect, as of responsibility; the fact or state of being abandoned.

de-ride *v.* To ridicule; to treat with scornful mirth. **derider, derision** *n.,* **deridingly** *adv.,* **derisive** *adj.*

de ri-gueur *adj.* Prescribed or required by manners, custom, or fashion.

der-i-va-tion *n.* The act of or process of deriving; the process used to form new words by the addition of affixes to roots, stems, or words.

de-riv-a-tive *adj.* Of or relating to something derived.

de-rive *v.* To receive or obtain from a source. *Chem.* To produce a compound from other substances by chemical reaction.

der-mal *or* **der-mic** *adj.* Relating to or of the skin.

der-ma-ti-tis *n., Pathol.* An inflammation of the skin.

der-ma-tol-o-gy *n.* The medical study of the skin and the diseases related it. **dermatologist** *n.*

der-o-gate *v.* To take or cause to take away from; to distract; to cause to become inferior. **derogation** *n.*

de-rog-a-tory *adj.* Having the effect of belittling; lessening. **derogatorily** *adv.*

der-rick *n.* A machine which uses a tackle to lift heavy loads; the framework over the open hole of an oil well, used to support the heavy objects necessary to drill the well.

der-ri-ere *n.* The buttocks.

der-ring--do *n.* A courageous or daring action or spirit.

der-rin-ger *n.* A short-barreled, large-bored, pocket-sized pistol.

der-vish *n.* A member of a Moslem religious order, some of whom express their devotion in whirling dances.

de-salt *v.* To remove the salt from sea or saline water.

des-cant *v.* To play or sing a varied melody.

de-scend *v.* To move from a higher to a lower level; to pass through inheritance; to come from a particular family. *Astron.* Moving toward the horizon.

de-scen-dent *n.* One who descends from another individual; an offspring.

de-scen-dant *or* **de-scen-dent** *adj.* Proceeding downward; descending from an ancestor.

de-scent *n.* A slope; lowering or decline, as in level or status.

de-scribe *v.* To explain in written or spoken words; to draw or trace the figure of. **-able** *adj.*, **describer** *n.*

de-scrip-tion *n.* The technique or act of describing; an account or statement that describes. **descriptive** *adj.*

de-scry *v.* To catch sight of; to discover by observation. **descrier** *n.*

des-e-crate *v.* To violate something sacred, turning it into something common or profane. **desecration** *n.*

de-seg-re-gate *v.* To remove or eliminate racial segregation in. **desegregation** *n.*

de-sen-si-tize *v.* To make less sensitive; to eliminate the sensitivity of an individual, tissue, or organ, as to an allergen. **-er**, **desensitization** *n.*

des-ert *v.* To abandon or forsake. *Milit.* To be absent without leave with the plan of not returning. AWOL. *n.* A dry, barren region incapable of supporting any considerable population or vegetation without an artificial water supply.

de-ser-tion *n.* The act of deserting or leaving; in law, the willful abandonment of one's spouse, children, or both.

de-serve *v.* To be worthy of or entitled to.

de-served *adj.* Merited; earned. **deserving** *adj.*, **deservingly** *adv.*

des-ic-cant *n.* A silica gel used to absorb moisture; any material used to absorb moisture.

des-ic-cate *v.* To preserve by drying, such as food; dehydrate. **desiccation** *n.*, **desiccative** *adj.*

de-sid-er-a-tum *n., pl.* **-ta** A desired and necessary thing.

de-sign *v.* To draw and sketch preliminary outlines; to invent or create in the mind; to have as an intention or goal. *n.* An artistic or decorative piece of work; a project; a plan; a well thought-out intention. **designedly** *adv.*, **designer** *n.*

des-ig-nate *v.* To assign a name or title to; to point out; to specify; to appoint or select, as to an office. **designate** *adj.*, **designation** *n.*

de-sign-ing *adj.* Of or relating to the art or act of making designs; scheming or plotting; crafty. **designingly** *adv.*

de-sir-a-ble *adj.* Pleasing, attractive, or valuable; worthy of desire. **desirability**, **desirableness** *n.*

de-sire *v.* To long for; to wish; to crave; to request or ask for; to have sexual appetite.

de-sir-ous *adj.* Having a craving or strong desire.

de-sist *v.* To stop doing something; to cease from an action.

desk *n.*

A table or piece of furniture usually with drawers or compartments and a top for writing; a stand or table to hold reading materials; a department in a newspaper office, as the copy desk.

Des Moines *n.* The capital of the state of Iowa.

des-o-late *adj.* Made unfit for habitation; useless; forlorn; forsaken. **-ly** *adv.*

des-o-la-tion *n.* A wasteland; the condition of being ruined or deserted; loneliness.

de-spair *v.* To lose or give up hope; to abandon all purpose. **despair** *n.*, **despairing** *adj.*, **despairingly** *adv.*

des-per-a-do *n., pl.* **-does** *or* **-dos** A dangerous, desperate, or violent criminal.

des-per-ate *adj.* Rash, violent, reckless and without care, as from despair; intense; overpowering.

des-per-a-tion *n.* The state of being desperate.

des-pi-ca-ble *adj.* Deserving scorn or contempt. **despicably** *adv.*

de-spise *v.* To regard with contempt; to regard as worthless. **despiser** *n.*

de-spite *prep.* Notwithstanding; in spite of.

de-spoil *v.* To rob; to strip of property or possessions by force. **despoiler, despoilment, despoliation** *n.*

de-spond *v.* To lose hope, courage, or spirit. **despondently** *adv.*

de-spon-den-cy *n.* A dejection of spirits from loss of courage or hope. **-ent** *adj.*

des-pot *n.* An absolute ruler; a tyrant. **despotic** *adj.*, **-ically** *adv.*, **-ism** *n.*

des-sert *n.* A serving of sweet food, as pastry, ice cream, or fruit, as the last course of a meal.

des-ti-na-tion *n.* The point or place to which something or someone is directed; the purpose or end for which something is created or intended.

des-tine *v.* To be determined in advance; to design or appoint a distinct purpose. **destined** *adj.*

des-ti-ny *n., pl.* -nies The inevitable loss or fate to which a person or thing is destined; fate; a predetermined course of events.

des-ti-tute *adj.* Utterly impoverished; not having; extremely poor. **destitution** *n.*

de-stroy *v.* To ruin; to tear down; to demolish; to kill; to make useless or ineffective.

de-stroy-er *n.* One that destroys. *Milit.* A small maneuverable warship.

de-struct *n., Aeros.* The deliberate destruction of a defective or dangerous missile or rocket after launch.

de-struc-ti-ble *adj.* Capable of being destroyed. **destructibility** *n.*

de-struc-tion *n.* The state of or the act of being destroyed. **destructive** *adj.*, **destructively** *adv.*, **destructiveness** *n.*

des-ue-tude *n.* A condition or state of disuse.

de-sul-fur-ize *v.* To remove sulfur from. **desulfurizer, desulfurizationer** *n.*

des-ul-to-ry *adj.* Something that occurs by chance; lacking continuity; aimless.

de-tach *v.* To unfasten, disconnect, or separate; to extricate oneself; to withdraw.

de-tached *adj.* Separate; apart.

de-tach-ment *n.* The process of separating. *Milit.* A shipment of military equipment or personnel from a larger unit for special duty.

de-tail *n.* A part or item considered separately. *Milit.* Military personnel selected for a particular duty.

de-tain *v.* To stop; to keep from proceeding; to delay.

de-tect *v.* To find out or perceive; to expose or uncover, as a crime. **-able, detectible** *adj.*, **detection, detector** *n.*

de-tec-tive *n.* A person whose work is to investigate crimes, discover evidence, and capture criminals.

de-tent *n.* A pawl.

de-ten-tion *n.* The act of or state of being detained; in law, a time or period of

temporary custody which precedes disposition by a court.

de-ter *v.* To prevent or discourage someone from acting by arousing fear, uncertainty, intimidation, or other strong emotion. **determent** *n.*

de-ter-gent *n.* A cleansing agent which is chemically different from soap. **detergency, detergence** *n.*

de-te-ri-o-rate *v.* To worsen; to depreciate. **-ion** *n.*, **deteriorative** *adj.*

de-ter-mi-nate *adj.* Definitely fixed or limited; conclusive. *Bot.* The terminating in a bud or flower, as each axis of an inflorescence. **determinately** *adv.*, **determinateness** *n.*

de-ter-mine *v.* To settle or decide conclusively or authoritatively; to limit to extent or scope; to fix or ascertain; to give direction or purpose to; in law, to come to an end. **determinable** *adj.*, **determinably** *adv.*, **determination** *n.*

de-ter-mined *adj.* Showing or having a fixed purpose; resolute; firm. **-ly** *adv.*

de-ter-rent *n.* Something which deters. *adj.* Serving to deter. **deterrently** *adv.*

de-test *v.* To dislike strongly. **-able** *adj.*, **detestably** *adv.*, **detestation** *n.*

de-throne *v.* To remove from the throne, to depose, as a king.

det-o-nate *v.* To explode suddenly and violently. **detonation** *n.*

det-o-na-tor *n.* The device, such as a fuse or percussion cap, used to detonate an explosive.

de-tour *n.* A road used temporarily instead of a main road; a deviation from a direct route or course of action.

de-tox-i-fy *v.* To free oneself from dependence on drugs or alcohol.

de-tract *v.* To take away from; to diminish; to divert. **detraction, detractor** *n.*, **detractive** *adj.*

de-train *v.* To leave or cause to leave a railroad train. **detrainment** *n.*

det-ri-ment *n.* Damage; injury; loss; something which causes damage, injury, or loss. **-al** *adj.*, **-ally** *adv.*

de-tri-tus *n.* Loose fragments or particles formed by erosion, glacial action, and other forces; debris.

deuce *n.* Two; a playing card or the side of a die with two spots or figures; in tennis, a tie in which each side has 40 points. *Informal* The devil, bad luck, or a mild oath.

De-us *n., L.* God.

deu-te-ri-um *n.* The isotope of hydrogen which contains one more neutron in its nucleus than hydrogen does.

Deu-ter-on-o-my *n.* The fifth book of the Old Testament.

deut-sche mark *n.* The standard monetary unit of East and West Germany, equivalent to 100 pfennigs.

de-val-u-ate *v.* To reduce or lessen the value of. **devaluation** *n.*

dev-as-tate *v.* To destroy; to ruin; to overwhelm; to overpower. **-ion** *n.*

de-vel-op *v.* To bring out or expand the potentialities; to make more elaborate; to enlarge; to advance from a lower to a higher stage or from an earlier to a later stage of maturation. *Photog.* To process an image upon a sensitized plate that has been exposed to the action of light. **developer, development** *n.*, **developmental** *adj.*

de-vi-ant *adj.* Anything which deviates from a norm, especially from an accepted standard. **deviance, deviant** *n.*

de-vi-ate *v.* To turn away from a specified prescribed behavior or course. **deviation** *n.*

de-vice *n.* Something constructed and used for a specific purpose, as a machine; a crafty or evil scheme or plan; an ornamental design; a motto or an emblem.

dev-il *or* **Devil** *n.* The spirit of evil, the ruler of Hell; Satan; a wicked or malevolent person; a daring, clever, and energetic person; a printer's apprentice, also called a printer's devil. **the devil to pay** Trouble to be expected as a consequence of something.

dev-il-fish *n.*, *pl.* **-fishes** Any of the large cephalopods, as the octopus.

dev-il-ish *adj.* To resemble or have the characteristics of a devil. *Informal* Extreme.

dev-il--may--care *adj.* Reckless; careless.

dev-il-ment *n.* Mischief.

dev-il's ad-vo-cate *n.* One who argues about something with which he or she may not disagree, as for the sake of argument.

devil's food cake *n.* A chocolate cake made from dark chocolate, flour, and eggs.

dev-il-try *n.*, *pl.* **-tries** Malicious mischief; cruelty or wickedness.

de-vi-ous *adj.* Leading away from the straight, regular, or direct course; rambling; straying from the proper way. *Slang* Underhanded. **deviously** *adv.*, **deviousness** *n.*

de-vise *v.* To form in the mind; to contrive; to plan; to invent; in law, to transmit or give by will. *n.* The act of bequeathing lands; a clause in a will conveying real estate.

de-vi-see *n.* In law, the person to whom a devise is made.

de-vi-sor *n.* In law, the person who devises property.

de-vi-tal-ize *v.* To make weak; to destroy the vitality. **devitalization** *n.*

de-void *adj.* Empty; utterly lacking; without.

de-voir *n.* The act or expression of courtesy or respect; duty or responsibility.

de-volve *v.* To pass duty or authority on to a successor.

de-vote *v.* To apply time or oneself completely to some activity, purpose, or cause. **devotement** *n.*

de-vot-ed *adj.* Feeling or showing devotion; set apart, as by a vow; consecrated. **-ly** *adv.*, **devotedness** *n.*

dev-o-tee *n.* An enthusiastic supporter; one who is deeply devoted to anything; one marked by religious ardor.

de-vo-tion *n.* A strong attachment or affection, as to a person or cause; zeal or ardor in the performance of religious duties or acts; the state or act of being devoted.

devotional *adj.*, **devotionally** *adv.*

de-vour *v.* To destroy or waste; to eat up greedily; to engulf. **devourer** *n.*

de-vout *adj.* Extremely and earnestly religious; showing sincerity; displaying piety or reverence. **-ly** *adv.*, **-ness** *n.*

dew *n.* Moisture condensed from the atmosphere in minute drops onto cool surfaces; something which is refreshing or pure.

dew-ber-ry *n.* The fruit of many species of trailing blackberries; the plant which bears such fruit.

dew-claw *n.* A rudimentary toe in some dogs and other mammals.

dew-lap *n.* The loose skin under the throat and neck of cattle and certain dogs.

dew point *n.* The temperature at which condensation of vapor occurs.

dex-ter-i-ty *n.* Proficiency or skill in using the hands or body; cleverness.

dex-ter-ous *or* **dex-trous** *adj.* Skillful or adroit in the use of the hands, body, or mind. **dexterously** *adv.*, **-ness** *n.*

dex-trose *n.* Sugar found in animal and plant tissue and derived synthetically from starches.

dia *abbr.* Diameter.

di-a-be-tes *n.*, *Pathol.* A metabolic disorder characterized by deficient insulin secretion, leading to excess sugar in the urine and blood, extreme hunger, and thirst.

di-a-bet-ic *adj.*, *Med.* Pertaining to, or affected with diabetes. **diabetic** *n.*

di-a-bol-ic *or* **di-a-bol-i-cal** *adj.* Wicked; proceeding from the devil; satanic or infernal. **diabolically** *adv.*, **-ness** *n.*

di-a-crit-ic *n.* A mark near or through a phonetic character or combination of characters, to indicate a special phonetic value or to distinguish words otherwise graphically identical. **diacritical, diacritic** *adj.*

di-a-dem *n.* A crown or headband worn to symbolize or indicate royalty or honor.

di-aer-e-sis *n.* Variation of dieresis.

di-ag-no-sis *n.*, *pl.* **-ses** An analysis and examination to identify a disease; the result of diagnosis. **diagnose** *v.*, **diagnostic** *adj.*, **diagnostician** *n.*

di-ag-o-nal *adj.* In mathematics, joining two opposite corners of a polygon which are not adjacent. *n.* A diagonal or slanting plane or line. **-ly** *adv.*

di-a-gram *n.* A sketch, plan, drawing, or outline designed to demonstrate or clarify the similarity among parts of a whole or to illustrate how something works. **diagram** *v.*, **diagrammatic, diagrammatical** *adj.*, **-matically** *adv.*

di-al *n.* Any graduated circular plate or face upon which a measurement, as pressure or temperature, is indicated by means of a needle or pointer; the face of a clock, watch, or sundial; a control for selecting a radio or television station. *v.* To make a call by means of a dial telephone.

di-a-lec-tic *n.* The act or practice of argument or exposition in which the conflict between contradictory facts or ideas is resolved. **dialectical, dialectic** *adj.*

di-a-logue *or* **dialog** *n.* A conversation involving two or more persons; a conversational passage in a literary work.

di-al-y-sis *n., pl.* **-ses** The separation of substances in solution, which is accomplished by passing them through membranes or filters. **kidney dialysis** A form of *dialysis* used to cleanse the blood of impurities and wastes when the kidneys are unable to perform this function.

di-am-e-ter *n.* In mathematics, a straight line which passes through the center of a circle or sphere and stops at the circumference or surface; a measurement of that distance.

di-a-met-ri-cal *or* **diametric** *adj.* Along or relating to a diameter; exactly opposite; contrary. **diametrically** *adv.*

di-a-mond *n., pl.* **-s**

A very hard, highly refractive, colorless, or white crystalline of carbon used as a gem; a playing card with a red, lozenge-shaped figure; a precious gem; in baseball, the shape of a baseball field.

di-a-mond an-ni-ver-sa-ry *n.* The 60th or 75th anniversary.

di-a-mond-back *n.*

A large, venomous rattle-snake of the south and western United States and Mexico; an edible turtle of the southern United States.

Di-a-mond State *n.* The nickname of the state of Delaware.

di-a-pa-son *n.* The full range of a voice or an instrument; in a pipe organ, either of two principal stops which form the tonal basis for the entire scale.

di-a-per *n.* A folded piece of soft, absorbent material placed between a baby's legs and fastened at the waist. *v.* To put a diaper on.

di-aph-a-nous *adj.* Of such fine texture as to be transparent or translucent; delicate. **diaphanously** *adv.*

di-a-phragm *n., Anat.* The muscular wall which separates the abdominal and thoracic cavities. *Photog.* The disk with an adjustable aperture that can control the amount of light which passes through the lens of a telescope, camera, etc.; a contraceptive device usually made of a rubber or rubber-like material and shaped like a cap to cover the uterine cervix.

di-ar-rhe-a *or* **di-ar-rhoe-a** *n., Pathol.* A disorder of the intestines causing excessively frequent, loose bowel movements.

di-a-ry *n., pl.* **-ries** A daily record, especially a personal record of one's activities, experiences, or observations; a journal; a book for keeping such records. **diarist** *n.*

di-as-to-le *n., Physiol.* The normal rhythmic dilatation and relaxation of the heart cavities during which they fill with blood. **diastolic** *adj.*

di-as-tro-phism *n., Geol.* Any of the processes through which the earth's crust, as mountains and continents, are formed.

di-a-ther-my *n., pl.* **-mies** *Med.* The generation of heat in the body tissues by high-frequency electromagnetic waves.

di-a-tom *n.* Any of various tiny planktonic algae whose walls contain silica.

di-a-tom-ic *adj.* Having two atoms in a molecule.

di-a-ton-ic *adj., Mus.* Relating to a standard major or minor scale of eight tones without the chromatic intervals.

di-a-tribe *n.* A bitter, often malicious criticism or denunciation.

dib-ble *n.* A gardener's pointed tool used to make holes in soil, especially for planting bulbs or seedlings. **dibble** *v.*

dice *pl., n.*

Two or more small cubes of wood, bone, or ivory having the sides marked with dots from one to six; a game of chance. *v.* To gamble with dice; to cut food into small cubes.

di-chot-o-my *n., pl.* **-mies** A division into two mutually exclusive subclasses. *Bot.* The branching of something in which each successive axis forks into two equally developed branches. **-ous** *adj.*

di-chro-mate *n., Chem.* A chemical compound with two chromium atoms per anion.

di-chro-mat-ic *adj., Zool.* Having two color phases within the species apart from the changes due to age or sex. *Pathol.* Having the ability to see only two of the three primary colors.

Dickens, Charles John Huffam *n.* (1812-1870). English novelist.

dick-er *v.* To haggle or work towards a deal or bargain.

dick-ey *or* **dick-ie** *or* **dick-y** *n., pl.* **-eys** *or* **-ies** A woman's blouse front worn under a jacket or low-necked dress; the detachable shirtfront for a man; a small bird.

di-cot-y-le-don *n.* A plant which has two seed leaves. **dicotyledonous** *adj.*

dic-tate *v.* To read or speak aloud for another to record or transcribe; to give commands, terms, rules, or other orders with authority. *n.* A directive or guiding principle. **dictation** *n.*

dic-ta-ting ma-chine *n.* A phonographic machine which records and reproduces speech, as for dictation.

dic-ta-tor *n.* A person having absolute authority and supreme governmental powers; one who dictates. -ship *n.*

dic-ta-to-ri-al *adj.* Tending to dictate; relating to or characteristic of a dictator. **dictatorially** *adv.*

dic-tion *n.* The selection and arrangement of words in speaking and writing; the manner of uttering speech sounds.

dic-tion-ar-y *n., pl.* -ies A reference book containing alphabetically arranged words together with their definitions and usages.

dic-tum *n., pl.* -ta *or* -tums An authoritative or positive utterance; a pronouncement; a saying that is popular.

did *v.* Past tense of do.

di-dac-tic *or* **didactical** *adj.* Being inclined to teach or moralize excessively. **didactically** *adv.,* **didacticism** *n.*

did-dle *v.* To cheat; to swindle; to waste valuable time.

did-n't *contr.* Did not.

di-do *n., pl.* -dos *or* -does *Informal* A mischievous caper; an antic.

die *v.* To expire; to stop living; to cease to exist; to fade away; to cease operation or functioning, as an engine. **to die hard** To resist defeat or death to the end. **to die off** To be removed one after another by death.

die cast-ing *n.* The process of giving an alloy or metal a desired shape; the act of cutting, stamping, or shaping with or as with a die.

diel-drin *n.* A highly toxic and persistent chemical which is used as an insecticide.

di-e-lec-tric *n., Elect.* A nonconductor of electricity.

di-er-e-sis *n., pl.* -ses The mark over a vowel indicating that it is to be pronounced in a separate syllable.

die-sel *n.* A diesel engine or a vehicle driven by a diesel engine.

die-sel en-gine *n.* An internal-combustion engine in which an air-fuel mixture is ignited by the heat generated from the high compression in the cylinder.

die-sink-er *n.* A person who engraves metal dies.

di-et *n.* A regulated selection of food and drink, especially one followed for medical or hygienic reasons; something that is taken or provided regularly; an assembly or legislature.

di-e-tet-ics *pl., n.* The study of diet or the regulations of a diet. **dietetical, dietetic** *adj.,* **-ally** *adv.*

di-eth-yl-stil-bes-trol *n.* A synthetic estrogen used especially to treat menstrual disorders.

dif-fer *v.* To have different opinions; to disagree.

dif-fer-ence *n.* The quality, state, or degree of being different or unlike; a

controversy or cause for a disagreement; in mathematics, the amount by which a number or quantity is less or greater than another.

dif-fer-ent *adj.* Not the same; separate; other; marked by a difference; unlike; differing from the ordinary. **differently** *adv.,* **differentness** *n.*

dif-fer-en-tia *n., pl.* -tiae A specific difference; something that distinguishes a species from others of the same genus.

dif-fer-en-tial *adj.* Relating to or showing a difference or differences. *n.* The amount or degree to which similar things differ.

dif-fer-en-tial cal-cu-lus *n.* In mathematics, the difference or variation of a function with respect to changes in independent variables.

dif-fer-en-tial gear *n., Mech.* A coupling consisting of a train of gears used to connect two or more shafts to allow different rates of wheel rotation, as on curves.

dif-fer-en-ti-ate *v.* To show, state, or distinguish the difference; to become or make different. **differentiation** *n.*

dif-fi-cult *adj.* Hard to do, deal with, or accomplish; hard to please.

dif-fi-cul-ty *n., pl.* -ties The quality or state of being difficult; something that requires great effort; conflicts or problems.

dif-fi-dent *adj.* Lacking confidence in oneself; timid. **diffidence** *n.,* **-ly** *adv.*

dif-frac-tion *n., Phys.* A modification of light rays, especially a beam of light as it passes an aperture or obstacle.

dif-fuse *v.* To pour out and spread freely in all directions; to scatter. -ion *n.*

dig *v.* To turn up, break up, or remove the earth with a shovel; to discover or learn by investigation or research. *Slang* To understand, like, appreciate or enjoy. *Informal* To work intensively.

di-gest *v.* To change ingested food into usable form; to mentally assimilate; to endure; to tolerate patiently; to decompose or soften with moisture or heat. **digestibility** *n.,* **digestible, digestive** *adj.*

di-ges-tion *n.* The chemical and muscular action of transforming food into an assimilable state.

dig-it *n.* A toe or finger; the Arabic numerals 0 through 9.

dig-i-tal *adj.* Pertaining to or like the fingers or digits; expressed in digits, especially for computer use; reading in digits, as a clock.

dig-i-tal com-put-er *n.* In computer science, a computer using data that is represented as digits to perform operations.

dig-i-tal-is *n.* The foxglove plant; a drug prepared from dried leaves of foxglove, used as a heart stimulant.

dig-ni-fied *adj.* Showing or possessing dignity; poised.

dig-ni-fy *v.* To give dignity or distinction to something.

dig-ni-tary n., pl. **-ies** A person of high rank, notability, and influence.

dig-ni-ty n., pl. **-ties** The quality or state of being excellent; the quality of being poised or formally reserved in appearance and demeanor; a high rank, office, or title.

di-graph n. A pair of letters, as the ea in seat or oa in boat, that represents a single sound. **digraphic** adj.

di-gress v. To turn away or aside from the main subject in a discourse; to wander. **digression** n., **digressive** adj., **digressively** adv.

dik-dik n. A very small African antelope.

dike n. An embankment made of earth, built to hold and control flood waters, also known as a levee.

di-lap-i-dat-ed adj. Being in a state of decay or disrepair. **dilapidation** n.

di-late v. To become or make enlarged; to expand. **-able** adj., **-ion**, **dilator** n.

di-la-to-ry adj. Tending to cause decay; characterized by delay; slow; tardy.

di-lem-ma n. A predicament requiring a choice between equally undesirable alternatives.

dil-et-tante n., pl. **-tantes** or **-tanti** One who has an amateurish and superficial interest in something.

dil-i-gent adj. Showing painstaking effort and application in whatever is undertaken; industrious. **-ce** n., **-ly** adv.

dill n. An aromatic herb with aromatic leaves and seeds used as seasoning.

dil-ly n., pl. **-lies** Slang Someone or something that is extraordinary.

dil-ly--dal-ly v. To waste time with indecision or hesitation.

di-lute v. To weaken, thin, or reduce the concentration of by adding a liquid.

dim adj. Dull; lacking sharp perception or clarity of understanding; obscured or darkened from faintness of light; pessimistic or negative. **dim** v., **dimly** adv., **dimness** n.

dim abbr. Dimension.

dime n. A United States coin worth ten cents or one tenth of a dollar.

di-men-sion n. A measurable extent, as length, thickness, or breadth. **dimensions** pl. The magnitude or scope of something. **-al** adj., **dimensionality** n.

di-min-ish v. To become or make smaller or less; to reduce in power, rank, or authority; to decrease; to taper. **diminishable** adj., **diminishment**, **diminution** n.

dim-in-ished adj. Reduced; lessened.

di-min-u-en-do adv. Gradually lessening in volume. **diminuendo** adj. & n.

di-min-u-tive adj. Very small; tiny.

dim-i-ty n., pl. **-ties** A sheer cotton fabric woven with cords, stripes, or checks.

dim-mer n. A rheostat used to reduce the intensity of an electric light.

dim-ple n. A slight depression in the surface of the skin, especially one made visible in the cheek by smiling; a slight surface depression. **dimple** v.

dim-wit n., Slang A simpleminded or stupid person. **dimwitted** adj.,

dimwittedly adv., **dimwittedness** n.

din n. A loud, confused, harsh noise.

dine v. To eat dinner.

din-er n. A dining car on a train; a restaurant usually shaped like a railroad car.

di-nette n. A small room or alcove which is used as a dining room.

ding--a--ling n., Slang A silly person.

din-ghy n., pl. **-ghies** A small rowboat; an inflatable rubber raft.

din-ky adj., Informal Insignificant or small.

din-ner n. The last meal of the day, taken usually between the hours of 5:00 and 7:00 P.M.; a banquet or formal meal.

din-ner-ware n. The tableware used in serving a meal.

di-no-saur n., Paleon.

A group of extinct reptiles from the Mesozoic period, some of which were the largest land animals known to exist.

dint n. Means; force; effort. v. To drive with force.

di-o-cese n. The territory under the jurisdiction of a bishop. **diocesan** adj. & n.

di-ode n. An electron tube which permits electrons to pass in only one direction, used as a rectifier.

di-o-ra-ma n. A miniature scene in three dimensions.

dip v. To let or put down into a liquid momentarily; to lift up and out by scooping or bailing; to be baptized by immersion; to make candles in wax or tallow; to sink or go down suddenly. n. A sauce made of liquid, into which something is to be dipped; a depression or hollow. Slang A silly person.

diph-the-ri-a n., Pathol. An acute contagious disease caused by bacillus and characterized by formation of a false membrane in the throat and other air passages by weakness and by fever.

diph-thong n., Phon. A blend of a single speech sound which begins with one vowel sound and moves to another in the same syllable, as oi in oil, oi in coil or oy in toy.

di-plo-ma n. A document issued by a college, school, or university testifying that a student has earned a degree or completed a course of study.

di-plo-ma-cy n., pl. **-cies** The art or practice of conducting international negotiations; skill and tact in dealing with people.

dip-lo-mat n. A person employed in diplomacy. **diplomatic** adj.

dip-per n. One that dips; a container for dipping; a long-handled cup for dipping water. Astron. The Big Dipper and the Little Dipper, two northern constellations.

dip-so-ma-ni-a n. An insatiable craving

for alcohol. **dipsomaniac** *n. & adj.*

dip-ter-ous *adj.* Pertaining to or of animals having a single pair of wings such as the fly, gnat, and mosquito.

dip-tych *n.* A pair of painted or carved panels which are hinged together.

dir *abbr.* Director.

dire *adj.* Dreadful or terrible in consequence. **direly, -fully** *adv.,* **-ness** *n.*

di-rect *v.* To control or regulate the affairs of; to command or order; to direct or tell someone the way; to cause something to move in a given or direct course; to indicate the destination of a letter; to supervise or instruct the performance of a job; to move or lie in a straight line; to do something immediate. *adj.* Without compromise; absolute; in the exact words of a person, as a direct quote.

di-rect cur-rent *n.* An electrical current which flows in only one direction.

di-rec-tion *n.* The act of directing; an order or command; the path or line along which something points, travels, or lies. **directional** *adj.*

di-rec-tive *n.* A regulation or order from someone with authority.

di-rect-ly *adv.* Immediately; at once; in a direct manner or line; doing without an agent, medium, or go-between.

di-rec-tor *n.* A person who manages or directs; one of a group of persons who supervises the affairs of an institute, corporation or business. **-ship** *n.*

di-rec-to-ry *n., pl.* **-ries** A book listing data, alphabetically or classified, containing the names and addresses of a specific group, persons, organizations, inhabitants, or businesses.

di-rect tax *n.* A tax which is charged directly to the taxpayer.

dirge *n.* A slow mournful song; a funeral hymn.

dir-i-gi-ble *n.* A lighter-than-air plane which may be steered by means of its own motive power.

dirk *n.* A dagger.

dirn-dl *n.* A lady's full-skirted dress with a gathered waistband.

dirt *n.* Soil or earth; obscene or profane language; scandalous or hateful gossip. *Min.* Broken ore or rock; washed-down earth, containing precious metal. **dirt-bike** A light-weight motorbike used on rough roads, surfaces, or trails. **dirt-cheap** Extremely cheap.

dirty *adj.* Not clean; grimy; indecent; obscene; mean; despicable; lacking in brightness or clarity; relating to excessive radioactive fallout. *v.* To become or make soiled. **dirtiness** *n.*

dirty tricks *pl., n., Informal* Unethical behavior, especially in politics.

dis-a-ble *v.* To make powerless or to incapacitate; to disqualify legally.

dis-a-buse *v.* To free from delusion, misunderstanding, or misconception.

dis-ad-van-tage *n.* A circumstance that is unfavorable; loss or damage; detriment. **disadvantage** *v.*

dis-af-fect *v.* To weaken or destroy the affection or loyalty of. **-ion** *n.,* **disaffectedly** *adv.,* **disaffected** *adj.*

dis-a-gree *v.* To vary in opinion; to differ; to argue; to quarrel; to be unfavorable or unacceptable.

dis-a-gree-able *adj.* Offensive or unpleasant. **disagreeably** *adv.*

dis-al-low *v.* To refuse to allow; to reject as invalid or untrue. **disallowance** *n.*

dis-ap-pear *v.* To vanish; to drop from sight. **disappearance** *n.*

dis-ap-point *v.* To fail to satisfy the desires, hopes, or expectations of. **disappointment** *n.*

dis-ap-pro-ba-tion *n.* Disapproval; condemnation.

dis-ap-prove *v.* To refuse to approve; to reject; to condemn. **disapproval** *n.*

dis-arm *v.* To make harmless; to deprive or take away the weapons or any means of attack or defense. **-ment** *n.*

dis-ar-range *v.* To disturb the order of something. **disarrangement** *n.*

dis-ar-ray *n.* A state of confusion or disorder; an upset or turmoil.

dis-as-sem-ble *v.* To take apart.

dis-as-so-ci-ate *v.* To break away from or to detach oneself from an association. **disassociation** *n.*

dis-as-ter *n.* An event that causes great ruin or distress; a sudden and crushing misfortune. **-ous** *adj.,* **-ously** *adv.*

dis-a-vow *v.* To disclaim or deny any responsibility for or knowledge of.

dis-band *v.* To disperse; to break up.

dis-bar *v.* In law, to be expelled officially from the legal profession. **-ment** *n.*

dis-be-lieve *v.* To refuse to believe in something. **disbelief, disbeliever** *n.*

dis-burse *v.* To pay out. **disbursement, disbursal, disburser** *n.*

disc *or* **disk** *n., Informal* A phonograph record.

disc *abbr.* Discount.

dis-card *v.* To remove a playing card from one's hand; to throw out. *n.* The act of discarding; something which is cast aside or rejected. **discarder** *n.*

dis-cern *v.* To detect visually; to detect with senses other than that of vision; to comprehend mentally; to perceive as separate and distinct. **discerner, discernment** *n.,* **discernible** *adj.*

dis-charge *v.* To relieve of a charge, duty, load, or burden; to release as from confinement, custody, care, or duty; to dismiss from employment; to send forth; to shoot or fire a weapon; to get rid of; to release from service or duty; to fulfill an obligation, duty, or debt. *n.* The act of discharging or the condition of being discharged.

dis-ci-ple *n.* One who accepts and assists in spreading the doctrines of another. **Disciple** One of Christ's followers.

dis-ci-pline *n.* Training which corrects, molds, or perfects the mental faculties or moral character; behavior which results from such training; obedience to authority or rules; punishment meant to correct poor behavior. *v.* To train or develop by teaching and by control; to bring order to; to penalize. **disciplinary** *adj.*

dis-claim *v.* To disavow any claim to or association with. **disclaimer** *n.*

dis-close *v.* To make known; to bring into view. **disclosure** *n.*

dis-co *n., pl.* **-cos** A discotheque.

dis-color *v.* To alter or change the color of. **discoloration** *n.*

dis-com-fit *v.* To defeat in battle; to make upset or uneasy. **discomfiture** *n.*

dis-com-fort *n.* Physical or mental uneasiness; pain; an inconvenience. *v.* To make uncomfortable.

dis-com-mode *v.* To inconvenience.

dis-com-pose *v.* To disrupt the composure or serenity of; to unsettle; to destroy the order of. **discomposure** *n.*

dis-con-cert *v.* To upset; to discompose; to perturb. **disconcertingly** *adv.*

dis-con-nect *v.* To sever or break the connection of or between. **-ion** *n.*

dis-con-nect-ed *adj.* Not connected.

dis-con-so-late *adj.* Without consolation; dejected; cheerless; sorrowful. **-ly** *adv.*

dis-con-tent *n.* Lack of contentment; dissatisfaction. *v.* To make unhappy. **discontent** *v.*, **-edly** *adv.*, **-ed** *adj.*

dis-con-tin-ue *v.* To come or bring to an end; to break the continuity of; to interrupt; to stop trying, taking, or using. **discontinuance, discontinuation** *n.*

dis-cord *n.* Lacking accord or harmony; a harsh combination of musical sounds. **discordant** *adj.*

dis-co-theque *n.* A nightclub where music is provided for dancing.

dis-count *v.* To sell or offer for sale at a price lower than usual; to leave out of account; to disregard; to give discounts; to underestimate the importance of something. *n.* A reduction from the full amount of a debt or from the standard price; the act or practice of discounting; a deduction taken or an allowance made. **discountable** *adj.*

dis-coun-te-nance *v.* To look upon with disfavor; to make uneasy.

dis-cour-age *v.* To deprive or be deprived of enthusiasm or courage; to hinder by disfavoring. **discouragement** *n.*, **discouragingly** *adv.*

dis-course *n.* A conversation; a formal and lengthy discussion of a subject. *v.* To write or converse extensively.

dis-cour-te-ous *adj.* Lacking consideration or courteous manners. **discourteously** *adv.*, **discourtesy** *n.*

dis-cov-er *v.* To make known or visible; to observe or learn of for the first time. **-able** *adj.*, **discoverer, -y** *n.*

dis-cred-it *v.* To mar the reputation of or disgrace someone or something; to injure the reputation of. *n.* Loss of credit or reputation; doubt; disbelief. **discreditable** *adj.*, **discreditably** *adv.*

dis-creet *adj.* Tactful; careful of appearances; modest. **-ly** *adv.*, **-ness** *n.*

dis-crep-an-cy *n., pl.* **-cies** A difference in facts; an instance of being discrepant. **discrepant** *adj.*

dis-crete *adj.* Separate; made up of distinct parts.

dis-cre-tion *n.* The quality or act of being discreet; the ability to make responsible choices; power to decide; the result of separating or distinguishing. **discretionary** *adj.*

dis-crim-i-nate *v.* To distinguish or differentiate between someone or something on the basis of race, sex, class, or religion; to act prejudicially. **discriminatingly** *adv.*, **-ion** *n.*, **-ive** *adj.*

dis-cur-sive *adj.* Covering a wide field of subjects in a quick manner; rambling from subject to subject. **discursively** *adv.*, **discursiveness** *n.*

dis-cus *n.* A heavy disk made of wood, rubber, or metal, which is hurled for distance in athletic competitions; a brightly-colored, disk-shaped fresh water fish of South America.

dis-cuss *v.* To investigate by argument or debate; to consider or examine something through discourse. **discussible** *adj.*, **discussion** *n.*

dis-cus-sant *n.* A participant in a discussion.

dis-dain *v.* To treat contemptuously; to look on with scorn. **disdainfully** *adv.*

dis-ease *n.* A condition of the living animal, plant body, or one of its parts which impairs normal functioning; a condition of ill health. **diseased** *adj.*

dis-em-bark *v.* To go or put ashore from a ship; unload.

dis-em-body *v.* To release or free the soul or physical existence.

dis-em-bow-el *v.* To remove the bowels or entrails; to eviscerate. **-ment** *n.*

dis-en-chant *v.* To free from false beliefs or enchantment. **-ingly** *adv.*, **-ing** *adj.*

dis-en-cum-ber *v.* To relieve of hardships; to free from encumbrance; unburden.

dis-en-fran-chise *v.* To disfranchise. **disenfranchisement** *n.*

dis-en-gage *v.* To free from something that holds or otherwise engages; to set free. **disengagement** *n.*

dis-en-tan-gle *v.* To relieve of entanglement, confusion, etc. **-ment** *n.*

dis-es-teem *v.* To regard with little esteem. *n.* Lack of esteem.

dis-fa-vor *n.* Disapproval; the state of being disliked. **disfavor** *v.*

dis-fig-ure *v.* To mar, deface, or deform the appearance of something or someone. **disfigurement** *n.*

dis-fran-chise *v.* To deprive of a legal right or privilege, especially the right to vote. **disfranchisement** *n.*

dis-gorge *v.* To discharge by the throat or mouth; to regurgitate; to give up on request or under pressure; to discharge violently or as a result of force; to discharge the contents of; to spew forth violently.

dis-grace *n.* The state of having lost grace, favor, respect, or honor; something that disgraces. *v.* To bring reproach or shame to; to humiliate by a superior showing; to cause to lose favor or standing. **disgracer,**

-fulness *n.*, **-ful** *adj.*, **disgracefully** *adv.*

dis-grun-tle *v.* To make dissatisfied or discontented.

dis-guise *v.* To alter the customary appearance or character of in order to prevent recognition; to conceal the actual existence or character of. *n.* Clothes and or make-up assumed to disguise one's identity or to copy that of another; an artificial manner; the act of disguising. **disguisedly** *adv.*, **disguiser** *n.*, **disguisable** *adj.*

dis-gust *v.* To affect with nausea, repugnance, or aversion; to cause one to become impatient or lose attention. *n.* A marked aversion to something distasteful; repugnance. **disgustedly, disgustfully, disgustingly** *adv.*, **disgusted, disgusting, disgustful** *adj.*

dish *n.* A concave vessel on which food is served; the amount a dish holds; the food served in a dish; a particularly prepared food; fashion; a directional microwave antenna having a concave reflector. *Slang* Something that is favored; an attractive woman. *v.* To make sarcastic, cutting remarks; to put food into a dish.

dis-ha-bille *n.* The state of being carelessly dressed; undress.

dis-har-mo-ny *n.* Lack of harmony or agreement; discord.

dish-cloth *n.* A cloth used for washing dishes; also called a dishrag.

dis-heart-en *v.* To cause to lose spirit or courage; to discourage, demoralize, or dispirit.

di-shev-el *v.* To mess up or disarrange; to throw into disorder or disarray.

dis-hon-est *adj.* Lack of honesty; arising from or showing fraud or falseness. **dishonesty** *n.*, **dishonestly** *adv.*

dis-hon-or *n.* The deprivation of honor; disgrace; the state of one who has lost honor; a cause of disgrace; failure to pay a financial obligation. *v.* To bring disgrace on something or someone; to fail to pay.

dish-rag *n.* A dishcloth.

dish-washer *n.* A person or a machine which washes dishes.

dis-il-lu-sion *v.* To deprive of illusion; to disenchant.

dis-in-cline *v.* To make or to be unwilling; to be or cause to be not interested.

dis-in-fect *v.* To cleanse and make free from infection, especially by destroying harmful microorganisms; to sterilize. **disinfection** *n.*

dis-in-gen-u-ous *adj.* Lacking frankness, sincerity, or simplicity; crafty; not straightforward.

dis-in-her-it *v.* To deliberately deprive of inheritance; to depose of previously held privileges.

dis-in-te-grate *v.* To break or reduce into separate elements, parts, or small particles; to destroy the unity or integrity of; to explode; to undergo a change in structure, as an atomic nucleus. **disintegration, disintegrator** *n.*

dis-inter *v.* To exhume or dig up something buried; to bring to light, disclose, uncover, or expose.

dis-in-ter-est-ed *adj.* The state of being unbiased, impartial, unselfish, or not interested; free from selfish motive or interest. **disinterest** *n.*, **-ly** *adv.*

dis-join *v.* To end the joining of; to become detached; to disconnect.

disk *or* **disc** *n.* A thin, flat, circular object; in computer science, a round, flat plate coated with a magnetic substance on which data for a computer is stored; a fairly flat, circular, metal object used to break up soil; the implement employing such tools.

disk op-er-at-ing sys-tem *n.* In computer science, the software which controls the disk drives and disk accessing; abbreviated as DOS.

disk pack *n.* In computer science, a computer storage device which has several magnetic disks to use and store as a unit.

dis-like *v.* To regard with aversion or disapproval. *n.* Distaste.

dis-lo-cate *v.* To put out of place or proper position. *Med.* To displace a bone from a socket or joint.

dis-lodge *v.* To remove or drive out from a dwelling or position; to force out of a settled position.

dis-loy-al *adj.* Not loyal; untrue to personal obligations or duty. **disloyally** *adv.*, **disloyalty** *n.*

dis-mal *adj.* Causing gloom or depression; depressing; lacking in interest or merit. **dismally** *adv.*, **dismalness** *n.*

dis-man-tle *v.* To strip of dress or covering or to strip of furniture and equipment; to take apart. **dismantlement** *n.*

dis-may *v.* To deprive or be deprived of courage or resolution through the pressure of sudden fear or anxiety. **dismay** *n.*, **dismayingly** *adv.*

dis-mem-ber *v.* To cut, pull off or disjoin the limbs, members, or parts of.

dis-miss *v.* To discharge or allow to leave; to remove from position or service; to bar from attention or serious consideration; in law, to disallow or reject any further judicial consideration on a claim or action. **dismissal** *n.*, **dismissible** *adj.*

dis-mount *v.* To get down from; to remove from a seat, setting, or support; to take apart; to disassemble.

dis-o-bey *v.* To refuse or fail to obey; to be disobedient. **disobedient** *adj.*, **disobediently** *adv.*

dis-o-blige *v.* To act contrary to the wishes of; to neglect or refuse to act in accordance with the wishes of; to offend; to inconvenience. **-ingly** *adv.*

dis-or-der *n.* Breach of peace or public order; lack of good order; an abnormal physical or mental condition; an ailment. *v.* To disturb the order of; to disturb the normal or regular functions of. **-ly** *adj.*, **disorderliness** *n.*

dis-or-gan-ize *v.* To destroy or break up the organization, unity, or structure of.

disorganization n.

dis-own v. To refuse to acknowledge or claim as one's own.

dis-pa-rate adj. Altogether dissimilar; unequal. **disparately** adv., **-ness** n.

dis-pas-sion-ate adj. Free from bias or passion. **dispassionately** adv.

dis-patch or **des-patch** v. To send off to a particular destination or on specific business; to dispose of quickly; to kill summarily. n. The act of dispatching; a message sent with speed; a message; a news story sent to a newspaper. **-er** n.

dis-pel v. To drive off or away.

dis-pense v. To give out; to distribute; to administer; to let go or exempt. **dispense with** To get rid of; to forgo.

dis-perse v. To break up or scatter in various directions; to spread or distribute from a common source; to distribute. **dispersible** adj., **-ion**, **-al** n.

di-spir-it v. To deprive of or be deprived of spirit; to discourage or be discouraged. **dispiritedly** adv.

dis-place v. To change the position of; to take the place of; to discharge from an office; to cause a physical displacement of. **displacement** n.

dis-play v. To put forth or spread; to put in view; to show off. n. The act of displaying; in computer science, a device which gives information in a visual form such as on a cathode-ray tube (computer screen or CRT).

dis-please v. To cause the disapproval or annoyance of; to cause displeasure. **displeasingly** adv., **displeasure** n.

dis-pose v. To put in place; to finally settle or come to terms. **dispose of** To get rid of; to attend to or settle; to transfer or part with, as by selling.

dis-pos-sess v. To deprive of possession or ownership of land, possessions, or property. **dispossession** n.

dis-pro-por-tion n. Lack of proportion, symmetry or proper relation. **disproportion** v., **disproportional**, **disproportionate** adj., **-ately** adv.

dis-prove v. Prove to be false or erroneous. **disproof** n., **disprovable** adj.

dis-pu-ta-tion n. The act of disputing; a debate.

dis-pute v. To debate or argue; to question the validity of; to strive against or to resist. n. A verbal controversy; a quarrel. **-able** adj., **disputably** adv., **disputant**, **disputer** n.

dis-qual-i-fy v. To deprive of the required properties or conditions; to deprive of a power or privilege; to make ineligible for a prize or further competition. **disqualification** n.

dis-quiet v. To take away the tranquillity of; to trouble. **-ing** adj., **-ingly** adv.

dis-qui-si-tion n. A formal inquiry into or discussion of a subject.

dis-re-gard v. To ignore; to neglect; to pay no attention to; to treat without proper attention. **disregardful** adj.

dis-re-pair n. The state of being in need of repair, usually due to neglect.

dis-re-pute n. A state of being held in low esteem; loss of a good reputation; disgrace. **disreputable** adj.

dis-re-spect n. Lack of respect or reverence. **disrespect** v. **disrespectful** adj., **disrespectfully** adv.

dis-robe v. To undress.

dis-rupt v. To throw into disorder or confusion; upset; to cause to break down. **disruption** n., **disruptive** adj.

dis-sat-is-fy v. To fail to satisfy; to disappoint. **dissatisfaction** n., **-ied** adj.

dis-sect v. To cut into pieces; to expose the parts of something, such as an animal, for examination; to analyze in detail. **dissector** n.

dis-sem-ble v. To conceal or hide the actual nature of; to put on a false appearance; to conceal facts. **-er** n.

dis-sem-i-nate v. To scatter or spread, as if by sowing, over a wide area. **dissemination**, **disseminator** n.

dis-sen-sion n. Difference of opinion; discord; strife.

dis-sent v. To differ in opinion or thought. n. Difference of opinion; refusal to go along with an established church.

dis-ser-ta-tion n. A formal written discourse or treaties, especially one submitted for a doctorate.

dis-serv-ice n. An ill turn; an ill service, injury, or harm.

dis-sev-er v. To sever; to divide; to separate. **disseverance**, **-ment** n.

dis-si-dent adj. Strong and open difference with an opinion or group. **dissident**, **dissidence** n.

dis-sim-i-lar adj. Different; not the same; unlike. **dissimilarity** n.

dis-si-mil-i-tude n. Lack of resemblance; unlikeness.

dis-sim-u-late v. To conceal under a false appearance; to dissemble.

dis-si-pate v. To disperse or drive away; to squander or waste; to separate into parts and scatter or vanish; to become dispersed; to lose irreversibly. **-ion** n.

dis-so-ci-ate v. To break from the association with another. **dissociation** n.

dis-so-lute adj. Loose in morals; lacking moral restraint. **-ly** adv., **-ness** n.

dis-so-lu-tion n. The act or process of changing from a solid to a fluid form; the separation of body and soul; death.

dis-solve v. To pass into solution, such as dissolving sugar in water; to overcome, as by emotion; to fade away; to become decomposed; to terminate.

dis-so-nance n., **Mus**. Lack of agreement; a conflict. **Mus**. A harsh or disagreeable combination of sounds; discord. **dissonant** adj., **dissonantly** adv.

dis-suade v. To alter the course of action; to turn from something by persuasion or advice. **dissuader**, **dissuasion** n., **dissuasive** adj.

dis-taff n. A staff rotation for holding the flax, tow, or wool in spinning; the female side of a family; women in general.

dis-tal n. Relatively remote from the

point of attachment or origin. **-ly** *adv.*

dis-tance *n.* Separation in time or space; the degree of separation between two points; the space that separates any two specified points in time; the quality or state of being distant; aloofness. *v.* To put space between; to keep at a distance.

dis-tant *adj.* Apart or separate by a specified amount of time or space; situated at a great distance; coming from, going to, or located at a distance; remotely related. **distantly** *adv.*, **distantness** *n.*

dis-taste *v.* To feel aversion to; to have an offensive taste; dislike. **-ful** *adj.*, **distastefully** *adv.*, **distastefulness** *n.*

dis-tem-per *n.* Bad humor or temper; a highly contagious viral disease of dogs, marked by fever and by respiratory and sometimes nervous symptoms. *v.* To throw out of order.

dis-tend *v.* To expand from internal pressure. **distensible** *adj.*, **distention, distension** *n.*

dis-till *v.* To extract by distillation; to give off in drops. **-er**, **distillery** *n.*

dis-til-late *n.* The condensed substance separated by distillation.

dis-til-la-tion *n.* The act or process of heating a liquid or other substance until it sends off a gas or vapor and then cooling the gas or vapor until it returns to a liquid or solid form, thus separating impurities.

dis-tinct *adj.* Distinguished from all others; clearly seen; unquestionable. **distinctly** *adv.*, **distinctness** *n.*

dis-tinc-tion *n.* The act of distinguishing; a difference; a special honor or recognition.

dis-tinc-tive *adj.* Serving to give style or distinction to. **distinctiveness** *n.*

dis-tin-guish *v.* To recognize as being different; to discriminate; to make something different or noticeable. **-able**, **-ed** *adj.*, **distinguishably** *adv.*

dis-tort *v.* To twist or bend out of shape; to twist the true meaning of; to give a misleading account of. **distortion** *n.*

dis-tract *v.* To draw or divert one's attention away from something; to cause one to feel conflicting emotions.

dis-trait *adj.* Absentminded.

dis-traught *adj.* Deeply agitated with doubt or anxiety; crazed.

dis-tress *v.* To cause suffering of mind or body. *n.* Pain or suffering; severe physical or mental strain; a very painful situation; a state of danger or desperate need. **distressingly** *adv.*

dis-trib-ute *v.* To divide among many; to deliver or give out; to classify. **distribution** *n.*, **distributive** *adj.*

dis-trib-u-tor *n.* A person that distributes, such as a wholesaler; a device which directs electrical current to the spark plugs of a gasoline engine.

dis-trict *n.* An administrative or political section of a territory; a distinctive area. **district** *v.*

dis-trict at-tor-ney *n.* The public prosecuting officer of a judicial district.

Dis-trict of Co-lum-bi-a *n.* The capital of the United States of America; the only part of the continental United States which is not a state, is not part of a state, and does not have a voting congressperson in the House of Representatives or an elected senator.

dis-trust *n.* Suspicion; doubt. *v.* To doubt; to suspect. **-ful** *adj.*, **-fully** *adv.*

dis-turb *v.* To destroy the tranquillity or composure of; to unsettle mentally or emotionally; to interrupt or interfere with; to bother. **disturbance**, **-er** *n.*

dis-u-nite *v.* To divide or separate.

dis-u-ni-ty *n.* Discord; unrest.

dis-use *n.* The state of not using; out of use.

ditch dig-ger *n.* One that digs ditches.

dith-er *n.* A state of nervousness or indecision; commotion.

dit-to *n.*, *pl.* **-tos** An exact copy; the same as stated before. **ditto mark** The pair of marks (" ") used to substitute the word *ditto*. *adv.* As before.

dit-ty *n.*, *pl.* **-ties** A short, simple song.

dit-ty bag *n.* A small bag used by sailors to hold small articles, such as thread, buttons, and other small personal effects.

di-u-ret-ic *adj.* Tending to cause an increase in the flow of urine. *n.* A drug given to increase the amount of urine produced.

di-ur-nal *adj.* Having a daily cycle or recurring every day; of, relating to, or occurring in the daytime; opening in the daytime and closing at night.

di-va *n.*, *pl.* **-vas** or **-ve** A prima donna; a female opera star.

di-van *n.* A long, backless and armless sofa or couch.

dive *v.* To plunge into water headfirst; to plunge downward at a sharp angle; to submerge; to rush headlong. *n.* The act or an instance of diving; a submerging of a submarine; a sharp decline. *Slang* A disreputable bar; in boxing, a faked knockout; in football, an offensive play in which the ball carrier plunges into the line for short yardage. **diver** *n.*

dive--bomb *v.* To bomb something from an airplane by making a steep dive toward the target and releasing the bomb. **dive-bomber** *n.*

div-er *n.* A person who dives; a person who stays underwater for prolonged periods by having air supplied either from the surface or from compressed air tanks.

di-verge *v.*

To move or extend in different directions from a common point; (diverging rays of light); to differ in opinion or manner.

divergence n., **divergent** adj.

di-vers adj. Various; several.

di-verse adj. Unlike in characteristics; having various forms or qualities. **diversely** adv., **diverseness** n.

di-ver-si-fy v. To give variety to something; to engage in varied operations; to distribute over a wide range of types or classes. **diversification** n.

di-ver-sion n. The act of diverting from a course, activity or use; something that diverts or amuses. **diversionary** adj.

di-ver-sion-ist n. A person characterized by political deviation.

di-ver-si-ty n., pl. -ties A difference; variety; unlikeness.

di-vert v. To turn from a set course; to give pleasure by distracting the attention from something that is burdensome or oppressive. **diversionary** adj., **diversion**, **diversity** n.

di-vest v. To undress or strip, especially of clothing or equipment; to deprive or dispossess of property, authority, or title; to take away from a person.

di-ves-ti-ture n. The act of divesting; the compulsory transfer of title or disposal of interests upon government order.

di-vide v. To separate into parts, areas, or groups; to separate into pieces or portions and give out in shares; to cause to be apart; in mathematics, to perform mathematical division on a number. n. An act of dividing; a dividing ridge between drainage areas.

div-i-dend n. An individual share of something distributed; a bonus; a number to be divided; a sum or fund to be divided and distributed.

di-vid-er n. A person who divides something. Something that serves as a partition.

di-vine adj. Of, relating to, preceding from, or pertaining to God. *Informal* Extremely pleasing. n. A clergyman or theologian. v. To foretell.

di-vin-ing rod n. A forked branch or stick that supposedly indicates the location of underground water or minerals by bending downward when held over a source.

di-vi-sion n. Separation; something which divides, separates, or marks off; the act, process, or instance of separating or keeping apart; the condition or an instance of being divided in opinion; in mathematics, the process of discovering how many times one quantity is contained in another. *Milit.* A self-sufficient tactical unit capable of independent action.

di-vi-sive adj. Tending to create dissension or disunity. **divisiveness** n.

di-vi-sor n In mathematics, the number by which a dividend is to be divided.

di-vorce n. The legal dissolution of a marriage; the complete separation of things. **divorce** v., **divorcee** n.

div-ot n. A square of turf or sod; a piece of turf torn up by a golf club while making a shot.

di-vulge v. To reveal or make known; to disclose; to reveal a secret.

Dix-ie n. The southern states of the continental U.S.

Dix-ie-crat n. A Democrat who supported a 1948 presidential ticket opposing the civil rights stand of the Democrats. **Dixiecratic** adj.

dix-ie-land n. Distinctly American jazz music, usually played by a small band and characterized by ensemble and solo improvisation.

diz-zy adj. Having a whirling sensation in the head with loss of proper balance; mentally confused; caused by or marked by giddiness; extremely rapid. **dizzily** adv., **dizzy** v.

DMZ abbr. Demilitarized zone.

DNA abbr. Deoxyribonucleic acid.

do v. To bring to pass; to bring about; to perform or execute; to put forth; to exert; to bring to an end. n. A festive get-together; a command to do something. *Mus.* The first tone of a scale. **do away with** To destroy; to kill. **do in** To tire completely; to kill. **do up** To adorn or dress lavishly; to wrap and tie.

DOA abbr. Dead on arrival.

Do-ber-man pin-scher n. A medium-sized, slender, smooth-coated dog.

do-cent n. A teacher at a college or university; a guide or lecturer in a museum.

doc-ile adj. Easily led, taught, or managed. **docility** n.

dock n. A landing slip or pier for ships or boats; a loading area for trucks or trains; an enclosure where the defendant sits or stands in a criminal trail. *Bot.* A weedy plant with small flower clusters. v. To haul or guide into a dock; to become docked. *Aeros.* To connect, as in two or more spacecrafts.

dock-age n. A charge for the use of a dock; docking facilities.

dock-et n. A brief written summary of a document; an agenda; an identifying statement about a document placed on its cover.

dock-yard n. A shipyard; a place where ships are repaired or built.

doc-tor n. A person trained and licensed to practice medicine, such as a physician, surgeon, dentist, or veterinarian; a person holding the highest degree offered by a university. v. To restore to good condition; to practice medicine; to administer medical treatment; to tamper with; to alter for a desired end. **doctoral** adj.

doc-tor-ate n. The degree, status, or title of a doctor.

doc-trine n. Something taught as a body of principles; a statement of fundamental government policy especially in international relations. -al adj.

doc-u-ment n. An official paper utilized as the basis, proof, or support of something. v. To furnish documentary evidence of; to prove with, support by, or provide by documents. -ation n.

doc·u·men·ta·ry *adj.* Relating to or based on documents; an artistic way of presenting facts. **documentary** *n.*

dod·der *v.* To tremble, shake, or totter from weakness or age. *n., Bot.* A parasitic, twining vine.

dodge *v.* To avoid by moving suddenly; to evade a responsibility by trickery or deceit; to shift suddenly. **dodge** *n.*

do·do *n., pl.* **-does** *or* **-dos** An extinct flightless bird, formerly present on the island of Mauritius. *Informal* One hopelessly behind the times. *Slang* A stupid person; an unimaginative person.

doe *n., pl.* **does** *or* **doe** A mature female deer; any of various mammals, as the hare or kangaroo.

does·n't *contr.* Does not.

dog *n.*

A usually domesticated carnivorous mammal, raised in a variety of breeds, probably descended from the common wolf; any of various animals, such as the dingo. *Informal* A mean, worthless person; a fellow; an undesirable piece of merchandise. *Slang* An unattractive woman or girl; a theatrical flop.

dog days *pl., n.* The hot, sultry part of summer between mid-July and September.

dog-fight *n.* An aerial combat between planes.

dog·ged *adj.* Stubbornly determined; obstinate. **doggedly** *adv.*, **-ness** *n.*

dog·gie bag *n.* A container used to carry home leftover food from a meal eaten at a restaurant.

dog·ma *n.* A rigidly held doctrine proclaimed to be true by a religious group; a principle or idea considered to be the absolute truth.

dog·mat·ic *adj.* Marked by an authoritative assertion of unproved or unprovable principles. **dogmatically** *adv.*

do--good·er *n., Informal* An earnest but usually impractical and often naive and ineffectual humanitarian or reformer.

dog paddle *n.* A beginner's swimming stroke in which the arms and legs move up and down. **dog-paddle** *v.*

do·jo *n.* A school of instruction in the Japanese martial arts.

dol·drums *pl., n.* A period of listlessness or despondency. *Naut.* The ocean region near the equator where there is very little wind.

dole *n.* The distribution of food, money, or clothing to the needy; a grant of government funds to the unemployed; something portioned out and distributed bit by bit. **dole** *adj.*

dole·ful *adj.* Filled with grief or sadness. **dolefully** *adv.*, **dolefulness** *n.*

doll *n.* A child's toy having a human form. *Slang* A woman; an attractive person. **dolled up** To dress up

elegantly, as for a special occasion.

dol·lar *n.* A coin, note, or token representing one dollar; the standard monetary unit of the U.S.

dol·lop *n.* A lump or blob of a semiliquid substance; an indefinite amount or form.

dol·ly *n., pl.* **-lies** A doll; a low, flat frame on wheels or rollers used to move heavy loads; a wheeled apparatus for moving a motion picture or television camera toward or away from the action.

dol·men *n.* A prehistoric monument made up of a huge stone set on upright stone.

do·lor·ous *adj.* Marked by grief or pain; sad; mournful. **-ly** *adv.*, **-ness** *n.*

dol·phin *n.*

Any of various small cetaceans with the snout in the shape of a beak and the neck vertebrae partially fused.

dolt *n.* A stupid person.

do·main *n.* A territory under one government; a field of activity or interest.

dome *n.* A roof resembling a hemisphere; something suggesting a dome.

do·mes·tic *adj.* Of or relating to the home, household or family life; interested in household affairs and home life; tame or domesticated; of or relating to policies of one's country; originated in a particular country. *n.* A household servant.

domestically *adv.*, **domesticity** *n.*

dom·i·cile *n.* A dwelling place, house, or home. **domicile** *v.*, **domiciliary** *adj.*

dom·i·nant *adj.* Having the most control or influence; most overwhelming; in genetics, producing a typical effect even when paired with an unlike gene for the same characteristic.

dominance *n.*, **dominantly** *adv.*

dom·i·nate *v.* To rule or control; to exert the supreme determining or guiding influence on; to occupy the most prominent position in or over.

domination, dominator *n.*

Dom·i·ni·ca Island *n.* Republic in the East Caribbean.

Do·min·i·can Republic *n.* Country occupying the east part of Hispaniola.

Dominion Day *n.* Canada Day.

dom·i·no *n., pl.* **-noes** *or* **-nos** A long, loose, hooded cloak usually worn with a half mask as a masquerade costume; a person wearing a domino; the mask itself; a small rectangular block of wood or plastic with the face marked with dots. *pl.* A game containing 28 of such pieces.

dom·i·no the·o·ry *n.* The theory that if a certain event occurs, a series of similar events will follow.

Don *n.* Sir; used as a courtesy title with a man's name in Spanish-speaking countries; a Spanish gentleman; a head, fellow, or tutor at an English university; a Mafia leader.

don *v.* To put something on; to dress.

done *adj.* Completely finished or through; doomed to failure, defeat, or death; cooked adequately.

do-nee *n.* A recipient of a gift.

done for *adj.* Mortally stricken; doomed; left with no opportunity for recovery; ruined.

don-key *n., pl.* **-keys** The domesticated ass. *Informal* A stubborn person.

do-nor *n.* One who gives, donates, or contributes.

Don Qui-xo-te *n.* The idealistic hero of Cervantes' *Don Quixote*; an impractical idealist.

don't *contr.* Do not.

doo-dle *v.* To scribble, design, or sketch aimlessly, especially when preoccupied. **doodle** *n.*

doom *n.* To pronounce judgment, particularly an official condemnation to a severe penalty or death; an unhappy destiny. *v.* To condemn; to make certain the destruction of.

dooms-day *n.* Judgment day; a dreaded day of judgment or reckoning; the end of the world.

door *n.* A barrier, normally swinging or sliding, by which an entry is closed and opened; a means of entrance or exit.

dope *n.* A preparation for giving a desired quality to a substance or surface, such as an antiknock added to gasoline. *Slang* A narcotic, especially one that is addictive; a stupid person; facts and details; all the details.

dor-mant *adj.* Asleep; a state of inactivity or rest. **dormancy** *n.*

dor-sal *adj., Anat.* Of, relating to, or situated on or near the back.

do-ry *n., pl.* **-ries** A small flat-bottomed boat with high, flaring sides and a sharp bow.

DOS *abbr.* Disk operating system.

dose *n.* The measured quantity of a therapeutic agent to be taken at one time or at stated intervals. *Med.* The prescribed amount of radiation to which a certain part of the body is exposed. **dosage** *n.*, **dose** *v.*

dos-si-er *n.* A complete file of documents or papers giving detailed information about a person or affair.

dot *n.* A small round spot; a mark made by or as if by a writing implement; a small round mark used in punctuation; a precise moment in time; a short click or buzz forming a letter or part of a letter in the Morse code.

dote *v.* To show excessive affection or fondness; to exhibit mental decline, especially as a result of senility. **-er** *n.*

dou-ble *adj.* Twice as much; composed of two like parts; designed for two. *Bot.* Having more than the usual number of petals. *n.* An actor who takes the place of another for scenes calling for special skill; in baseball, a two-base hit. *v.* In baseball, to make a double; to make or become twice as great; to fold in two; to turn and go back; to serve an additional purpose.

dou-ble--cross *v., Slang* To betray.

dou-ble--deck-er *n.* A vehicle, as a ship or other means of transportation, with two decks for passengers; a sandwich with three slices of bread and two layers of filling.

dou-ble dip *n.* A person holding a salaried position while receiving a pension from a previous job.

dou-ble-head-er *n.* Two games played consecutively on the same day or night.

dou-ble joint-ed *adj.* Having unusually flexible joints which allow connected parts to bend at abnormal angles.

doubt *v.* To be uncertain or mistrustful about something; to distrust. **-er** *n.*

dough *n.* A soft mixture of flour, liquids, and other ingredients which is baked to make bread, pastry, and other foods. *Slang* Money. **doughy** *adj.*

dough-nut *or* **donut** *n.* A small cake made of rich, light dough which is deep fried.

dough-ty *adj.* Marked by valor; brave.

dour *adj.* Stern and forbidding; morose and ill-tempered.

douse *v.* To plunge into liquid; to throw water on; to drench; to extinguish.

dove *n.*

Any of numerous pigeons; a gentle, innocent person. **dovish** *adj.*

dow-a-ger *n.* A widow holding a title or property from her dead husband; a dignified, elderly woman.

dow-dy *adj.* Not neat or tidy; old-fashioned. **dowdier, dowdiest** *adj.*

dow-el *n.* A round wooden pin which fits tightly into an adjacent hole to fasten together the two pieces.

dow-er *n.* The part of a deceased man's estate that is given to his widow by law. *v.* To provide with a dower.

down *adv.* Toward or in a lower physical condition; from a higher to a lower position; the direction that is opposite of up; a lower or worse condition or status; from a past time or past generations of people; partial payment at the time of purchase. *v.* To put something in writing; to bring, strike, put, or throw down; in football, any of a series of plays during which a team must advance at least ten yards in order to retain possession of the ball. *n.* A grassy highland used for grazing; soft, fluffy feathers of a young bird; a soft hairy growth, such as that on a peach.

down-er *n., Slang* A depressant or sedative drug; a barbiturate; something that is depressing.

Down's syn-drome *n.* Extreme mental deficiency; a condition in which a child is born with a broad, short skull, slanting eyes, and broad hands with short fingers; Mongolism.

down-ward *or* **down-wards** *adv.* From a higher to a lower place. **-ward** *adj.*

down-wind *adv. & adj.* In the direction toward which the wind blows.

dowse *v.* To search for with a divining rod to find underground water or minerals. **dowser** *n.*

dox-ol-o-gy *n., pl.* **-gies** A hymn or verse in praise of God.

doz-en *n.* Twelve of a kind; a set of twelve things. **dozen, dozenth** *adj.*

drab *adj.* Of a light, dull brown or olive brown color; commonplace or dull.

drach-ma *n., pl.* **-mas** *or* **-mae** A silver coin of ancient Greece.

draft *n.* A current of air; a sketch or plan of something to be made; a note for the transfer of money; the depth of water a ship draws with a certain load. *Milit.* A mandatory selection of men for service. *v.* To draw a tentative plan or sketch. *adj.* The drawing of a liquid from a keg or tap. **draftee** *n.*

drag *v.* To pull along or haul by force; to move with painful or undue slowness; to bring by force; to proceed slowly; to lag behind. *Slang* To puff on a pipe, cigarette, or cigar. *n.* Something which retards motion or action; a tool used under water to detect or collect objects; something which is boring or dull. *Slang* Someone or something that is bothersome; a street; a race.

drag-on *n.*

An mythical, giant, serpent-like, winged, fire-breathing monster.

drag-on-fly *n.*

A large insect which holds it's wings in a horizontal position, during during it's naiad stage has rectal gills.

drag queen *n., Slang* A male homosexual who dresses in female clothing, especially one who performs as a female publicly.

drain *v.* To draw off liquid gradually; to use up; to exhaust physically or emotionally; to flow off gradually. *n.* A means, such as a trench or channel, by which liquid matter is drained; something which causes depletion. **-er** *n.*

drake *n.* A male duck.

dram *n.* A small drink; a small portion; a measurement equaling approximately .06 ounces.

dra-ma *n.* A composition in prose or verse, especially one recounting a serious story; dramatic art of a particular period.

drank *v.* Past tense of drink.

drape *v.* To cover or adorn with something; to arrange or hang in loose folds. *n.* The manner in which cloth hangs or falls.

dras-tic *adj.* Acting extremely harsh or severe. **drastically** *adv.*

draught *n. & v.* A variation of draft.

draughts *pl., n.* The game of checkers, as referred to by the British.

draw *v.* To move or cause to move toward a direction or to a position as if by leading; to take out for use; to withdraw funds; to take in air; to sketch; to elicit a response; to attract; to formulate from evidence at hand; to displace water in floating; to provoke; to end something undecided or tied; to write in a set form.

draw-back *n.* An undesirable feature.

draw-bridge *n.* A bridge that can be raised or lowered to allow ships and boats to pass.

drawer *n.* One that draws pictures; a sliding box or receptacle in furniture. **drawers** *pl.* An article of clothing for the lower body.

draw-ing *n.* An act of drawing; the process of deciding something by choosing lots; the art of representing something or someone by means of lines; the amount drawn from an account.

drawl *v.* To speak slowly with prolonged vowels.

dray *n.* A low, heavy cart without sides, used for hauling.

dread *v.* To fear greatly; to anticipate with alarm, anxiety, or reluctance. *n.* A great fear.

dread-ful *adj.* Inspiring dread; very distasteful or shocking; awful. **dreadfully** *adv.*, **dreadfulness** *n.*

dream *n.* A series of thoughts, images, or emotions which occur during the rapid eye movement or REM state of sleep; an experience in waking life that has the characteristics of a dream; a daydream; something notable for its beauty or enjoyable quality; something that is strongly desired; something that fully satisfies a desire. **dreamful, dreamlike** *adj.*, **-fully** *adv.*, **-fulness** *n.*

drea-ry *adj.* Bleak and gloomy; dull. **drearily** *adv.*, **dreariness** *n.*

dredge *n.* An apparatus used to remove sand or mud from the bottom of a body of water; a boat or barge equipped with a dredge. *v.* To dig, gather, or deepen with a dredging machine; to use a dredge. **dredger** *n.*

dregs *pl., n.* The sediment of a liquid; the least desirable part.

drench *v.* To wet thoroughly; to throw water on. **drencher** *n.*

dress *n.* An outer garment for women and girls; covering or appearance appropriate to a particular time. *v.* To set straight; to put clothes on; to arrange in a straight line at proper intervals; to provide with clothing; to kill and prepare for market; to put on or wear formal or fancy clothes.

drew *v.* Past tense of draw.

drib-ble *v.* To drip; to slobber or drool; to bounce a ball repeatedly; to move in short bounces. **dribbler** *n.*

drift *v.* To be driven or carried along by or as if by currents of air or water; to move along the line of least resistance; to move about aimlessly; to be carried along with no guidance or control; to accumulate in piles, as sand; to deviate from a set course; in the western U.S., to drive livestock slowly to allow grazing.

drill *n.* A tool used in boring holes; the act of training soldiers in marching and the manual of arms; a physical or mental exercise to perfect a skill by regular practice; a marine snail which is destructive to oysters by boring through their shells and feeding on them. *v.* To make a hole with a drill; to train by repeated exercise.

drill-mas-ter *n.*, *Milit.* A non-commissioned officer who instructs in military drill.

drink *v.* To take liquid into the mouth and swallow; to take in or suck up; to receive into one's consciousness; to partake of alcoholic beverages. *n.* A liquid suitable for swallowing; alcoholic beverages; a sizable body of water. **drinkable** *adj.*, **drinker** *n.*

drip *v.* To fall in drops. *n.* Liquid or moisture which falls in drips; the sound made by falling drops. *Slang* A dull or unattractive person.

drip coffee *n.* Coffee made by allowing boiling water to drip slowly through ground coffee.

drip-dry *adj.* Made of a washable fabric which dries without wrinkling and needs no ironing. **drip-dry** *v.*

drive *v.* To propel, push, or press onward; to repulse by authority; to force into a particular act or state; to operate or be conveyed in a vehicle; to supply a moving force; to impress convincingly with force; in sports, to hit a ball hard in a game; to rush or advance violently. *n.* The act of driving; a trip taken in a vehicle; the means or apparatus by which motion is transmitted to a machine; an organized movement or campaign to accomplish something; initiative; the act of urging together animals. *Milit.* A full-scale military offensive.

drive-in *n.* A place of business which allows consumers to be accommodated while remaining in their vehicles.

driv-el *v.* To slobber; to talk nonsensically. **drivel** *n.*

driz-zle *n.* A fine, quiet, gentle rain. **drizzle** *v.*

droll *adj.* Whimsically comical. **-ery** *n.*

drom-e-dar-y *n.*, *pl.* **-ies** A one-humped camel, widely used in northern Africa and western Asia as a beast of burden.

drone *n.* A male bee, especially a honey bee, which has no sting, performs no work, and produces no honey; a person who depends on others for his survival; an unmanned boat or aircraft controlled by a remote control device. *v.* To make a low, continuous humming sound; to speak monotonously.

drool *v.* To let saliva dribble from the mouth. *Informal* To make an exaggerated expression of desire. **drool** *n.*

droop *v.* To hang or bend downward; to become depressed. **-iness** *n.*, **-y** *adj.*

drop *n.* A tiny, pear-shaped or rounded mass of liquid; a small quantity of a substance; the smallest unit of liquid measure; the act of falling; a swift decline; the vertical distance from a higher to a lower level; a delivery of something by parachute. *v.* To fall in drops; to descend from one area or level to another; to fall into a state of collapse or death; to pass into a given state or condition; to end or terminate an association or relationship with; to deposit at a specified place. **drop behind** To fall behind. **drop by** To pay a brief visit. **drop out** To quit school without graduating; to withdraw from society.

drop-sy *n.*, *Med.* A diseased condition in which large amounts of fluid collect in the body tissues and cavities.

dross *n.* An impurity which forms on the surface of molten metal; inferior, trivial, or worthless matter.

drought *or* **drouth** *n.* A prolonged period of dryness; a chronic shortage of something.

drove *n.* A herd being driven in a body; a crowd. *v.* Past tense of drive.

drown *v.* To kill or die by suffocating in a liquid; to cause not to be heard by making a loud noise; to drive out.

drowse *v.* To doze. **drowse** *n.*

drows-y *adj.* Sleepy; tending to induce sleep. **drowsiness** *n.*

drub *v.* To hit with a stick; to abuse with words; to defeat decisively.

drudge *n.* A person who does tiresome or menial tasks. **drudgery** *n.*

drug *n.* A substance used in the treatment of disease or illness; a narcotic. *v.* To take drugs for narcotic effect; to mix or dose with drugs.

drum *n.*

A musical percussion instrument consisting of a hollow frame with a cover stretched across one or both ends, played by beating with sticks or the hands; something with the shape of a drum; a cylindrical container; a metal container holding a capacity between 12 and 110 gallons; any of various percoid fishes that make a drumming noise. *v.* To beat a drum; to tap rhythmically or incessantly; to instill by repetition; to dismiss in disgrace. **drum up** To invent or devise; to go out and actively pursue new accounts or business.

drunk *adj.* Intoxicated with alcohol which impairs the physical and mental faculties of a person; overwhelmed by strong feeling or emotion. *n.* A drunkard.

drunk-ard *adj.* A person who is intoxicated by liquor.

drupe *n.* A fruit, as the peach, usually having one large pit or seed.

dry *adj.* Free from moisture or liquid; having little or no rain; devoid of running water; not liquid; thirsty; eaten without a garnish, such as jelly; humorous in a shrewd, impersonal way; not sweet, as in dry wines. *Informal* Opposed to the sale or consumption of alcoholic beverages. *v.* To remove the water from. -ly *adv.*

dry-ad *n.* A wood nymph.

dry--clean *v.* To clean cloth or fabrics with chemical solvents, as benzenes, rather than water.

dry goods *pl., n.* Textile fabrics as distinguished from foodstuffs and hardware.

du-al *adj.* Made up or composed of two parts; having a double purpose.

dub *v.* To confer knighthood upon; to nickname; to give a new sound track to; to add to a film, radio, or television production; to transpose a sound already recorded. **dub, dubber** *n.*

du-bi-ous *adj.* Causing doubt; unsettled in judgment; reluctant to agree; question as to quality or validity; verging on impropriety. **dubiously** *adv.*

du-cal *adj.* Pertaining to a duke or dukedom.

duch-ess *n.* The wife or widow of a duke; a female holding a ducal title in her own right.

duck *n.*

Any of various swimming birds with short necks and legs; the flesh of any of these birds used as food. *Slang* A person. *v.* To lower the head and body quickly; to evade; to plunge quickly under water.

duct *n.* A bodily tube or canal, especially one carrying a secretion; a tubular passage through which something flows.

duc-tile *adj.* Capable of being drawn into a fine strand or wire; easily influenced or persuaded.

dud *n., Informal* A bomb, shell, or explosive round which fails to detonate; something which turns out to be a failure. **duds** *pl.* Clothing; personal belongings.

dude *n., Informal* A city person vacationing on a ranch; a man who is a fancy dresser. *Slang* A fellow.

dudg-eon *n.* A sullen, displeased, or indignant mood.

due *adj.* Owed; payable; owed or owing as a natural or moral right; scheduled or expected to occur. *n.* Something that is deserved or owed. **dues** *pl.* A fee or charge for membership.

du-el *n.* A premeditated combat between two people, usually fought to resolve a point of honor; a struggle which resembles a duel. **duel** *v.,* **duelist** *n.*

du-et *n.* A musical composition for two performers or musical instruments.

duf-fel bag *n.* A large cloth bag for carrying personal belongings.

duke *n.* A noble ranking below a prince and above a marquis. **dukes** *pl., Slang* The fists. **dukedom** *n.*

dul-cet *adj.* Melodious; pleasing to the ear; having an agreeable, soothing quality.

dul-ci-mer *n.* A musical stringed instrument played with two small picks or by plucking.

dull *adj.* Stupid; lacking in intelligence or understanding; insensitive; having a blunt edge or point; not intensely felt; arousing no interest or curiosity; not bright; overcast or gloomy; unclear. *v.* To make or become dull; to blunt or to make blunt. **dullness** *n.,* **dully** *adv.*

du-ly *adv.* In a proper or due manner.

dumb *adj.* Unable to speak; temporarily speechless. *Informal* Stupid. **dumbly** *adv.,* **dumbness** *n.*

dumb-bell *n.* A short bar with two adjustable weighted disks attached to each end, used in pairs for calisthenic exercise.

dumb-waiter *n.* A small elevator, usually found in the kitchen of a home, which is used to convey goods, as food or dishes, from one floor to another.

dum-dum bullet *n.* A soft-nosed, small-arms bullet designed to expand on contact.

dum-found *or* **dumb-found** *v.* To confound with amazement.

dum-my *n., pl.* **-mies** One who is habitually silent; one who is stupid; the exposed hand in bridge; a bridge player whose hand is a dummy; an imitation or copy of something, used as a substitute; a person or agency secretly in the service of another.

dump *v.* To throw down or discard in a mass; to empty material out of a container or vehicle; in computer science to reproduce data stored in the working memory onto an external storage medium. *n.* A place where garbage or trash is dumped. *Milit.* A military storage facility. *Slang* A disreputable or messy place.

dump-ling *n.* A small mass of dough cooked in soup or stew; sweetened dough wrapped around fruit, baked, and served as desert.

dun *v.* To press a debtor for payment. *n.* A brownish gray to dull grayish brown color. **dun** *adj.*

dunce n. A slow-witted person.

dune n. A ridge or hill of sand blown or drifted by the wind.

dung n. The excrement of animals; manure.

dun-ga-ree n. A sturdy, coarse, cotton fabric, especially blue denim; pants or overalls made from this material.

dun-geon n. A dark, confining, underground prison chamber.

dunk v. To dip a piece of food into liquid before eating; to submerge someone in a playful fashion.

du-o n., pl. -os An instrument duet; two people in close association.

du-o-de-num n., pl. -dena or -denums The first portion of the small intestine, extending from the lower end of the stomach to the jejunum. duodenal adj.

dupe n. A person who is easily manipulated or deceived. v. To deceive or trick.

du-plex adj. Double. n. An apartment with rooms on two adjoining floors; having two parts.

du-pli-cate adj. Identical with another; existing in or consisting of two corresponding parts. n. Either of two things which are identical; an exact copy of an original. v. To make an exact copy of. duplication n.

du-ra-ble adj. Able to continue for a prolonged period of time without deterioration. durability n.

du-ra-tion n. The period of time during which something exists or lasts.

du-ress n. Constraint by fear or force; in law, coercion illegally applied; forced restraint.

dur-ing prep. Throughout the time of; within the time of.

dusk n. The earliest part of the evening, just before darkness.

dust n. Fine, dry particles of matter; the earth, as a place of burial; the surface of the ground; a scorned condition. v. To remove the dust from; to sprinkle or cover with a powdery material.

Dutch n. The people of the Netherlands; the language of the Netherlands. Dutch adj., Dutchman n.

Dutch elm disease n. A fungus which affects elm trees, eventually killing them.

Dutch treat n. A date during which each person pays his own way.

duty n., pl. -ties Something which a person must or ought to do; a moral obligation; a service, action, or task assigned to one, especially in the military; a government tax on imports.

DVM abbr. Doctor of Veterinary Medicine.

dwarf n., pl. -rfs or -rves A human being, plant, or animal of a much smaller than normal size. v. To stunt the natural growth of; to cause to seem small by comparison. dwarfish adj.

dwarf-ism n. A condition where one's growth is stunted.

dwell v. To live, as an inhabitant; to continue in a given place or condition; to focus one's attention. dweller n.

dwell-ing n. A house or building in which one lives.

DWI abbr. Driving while intoxicated.

dwin-dle v. To waste away; to become steadily less.

dy-ar-chy n. A type of government where the power is vested in two rulers.

dye v. To fix a color in or stain materials; to color with or become colored by a dye. n. A color imparted by a dye.

dye-wood n. A type of wood from which coloring material is taken for the purpose of dyeing things.

dying adj. Coming to the end of life.

dy-nam-ic adj. Marked by energy and productive activity or change; of or relating to energy, motion, or force. dynamically adv., dynamical adj.

dy-nam-ics n., Phys. The part of physics which deals with force, energy, and motion and the relationship between them.

dy-na-mism n. A kind of theory that explains the universe in terms of forces. dynamist n., dynamistic adj.

dy-na-mite n. An explosive composed of nitroglycerin or ammonium nitrate and an absorbent material, usually packaged in stick form. v. To blow up with or as if with dynamite.

dy-na-mo n. A person who is very energetic.

dy-na-mom-e-ter n. A type of device that is used for the purpose of measuring mechanical force.

dy-nap-o-lis n. A type of city that has been planned for orderly growth along a traffic artery.

dy-nas-ty n., pl. -ties A succession of rulers from the same family; a family or group which maintains great power, wealth, or position for many years. dynastic adj., dynastically adv.

dys-cra-sia n. A condition of the body that is abnormal.

dys-en-ter-ic adj. To be pertaining to dysentery.

dys-en-ter-y n. An infection of the lower intestinal tract which produces pain, fever, and severe diarrhea.

dys-func-tion n. An abnormal functioning. dysfunctional adj.

dys-gen-e-sis n. The defective development of the gonads of one's body such as in Turner's syndrome.

dys-gen-ic adj. To be biologically defective.

dys-lex-i-a n. An impairment in one's ability to read. dyslexic adj.

dys-men-or-rhea n. A menstruation of the woman that is painful, abnormal condition. dysmenorrheic adj.

dys-pep-sia n. Indigestion. dyspeptic adj., dyspeptically adv.

dys-pro-si-um n. A metallic element used in nuclear research, symbolized by Dy.

dys-tro-phy n. Atrophy of muscle tissue; any of various neuromuscular disorders, especially muscular dystrophy.

dz abbr. Dozen.

E, e The fifth letter of the English alphabet. *Mus.* The third tone in the natural scale of C.

each *adj.* Everyone of two or more considered separately. *adv.* To or for each; apiece.

each other *pron.* Each in reciprocal action or relation; one another.

ea-ger *adj.* Marked by enthusiastic interest or desire; having a great desire or wanting something. **-ly** *adv.,* **-ness** *n.*

ea-ger bea-ver *n.* A person who is overly or extremely zealous.

ea-gle *n.* A large, powerful bird of prey having a powerful bill, broad strong wings, and soaring flight; a U.S. gold coin worth ten dollars; a score of two under par on a hole in golf.

ea-gle eye *n.* The ability to see with exceptional keenness.

ea-gle ray *n.* A type of stingray which has broad pectoral fins.

ea-glet *n.* The young of an eagle.

eal-dor-man *n.* A person like a shire in Anglo-Saxon England; the chief officer in a district.

ear *n., Anat.*

The hearing organ in vertebrates, located on either side of the head; any of various organs capable of detecting vibratory motion; the ability to hear keenly; attention or heed; something that resembles the external ear. **all ears** Listen closely. **by ear** Without reference to written music.

ear-ache *n.* The pain which is associated with the ear.

ear-drop *n.* A type of earring which has a pendant attached to it.

ear-drum *n.* The tympanic membrane which is located inside the ear.

eared *adj.* Having ears.

eared seal *n.* Type of seal which has small well-developed external ears such as the fur seal and the sea lions.

ear-flap *n.* A covering for the ears which may be an extension of a cap.

ear-ful *n.* Gossip or news about someone.

ear-ing *n.* A line which is attached to a sail and is used for the purpose of attaching the sail to the gaff or yard.

earl *n.* A British title for a nobleman ranking above a viscount and is below a marquis. **earldom** *n.*

ear-less seal *n.* A type of seal which does not have external ears such as the hair seal.

earl mar-shal *n.* In England, an officer who is the royal attendant on ceremonial occasions.

ear-lobe *n.* The part of the ear which hangs below the pinna and is the location for earrings.

ear-lock *n.* A section of the hair which hangs in front of the ear.

ear-ly *adj.* Occurring near the beginning of a period of time; a development or a series; distant in past time; before the usual or expected time; occurring in the near future. *adv.* Near the beginning of time; far back in time. **earlier, earliest** *adj.*

Early American *n.* The style of architecture, furniture and fabric which has the characteristics of colonial America.

ear-ly bird *n.* An early riser; a person who arrives early.

ear-ly on *adv.* During on early stage.

ear-mark *n.* A mark which has been placed on the ear of an animal for identification.

ear-muff *n.* A pair of ear coverings which are attached with a band and worn over the head to cover the ears.

earn *v.* To receive payment in return for work done or services rendered; to gain as a result of one's efforts. **-er** *n.*

ear-nest *n.* A serious mental state; payment in advance to bind an agreement; a pledge. *adj.* Characterized by an intense and serious state of mind; having serious intent. **earnestly** *adv.,* **earnestness** *n.*

earn-ings *pl., n.* Something earned, such as a salary.

ear-phone *n.* A device that takes electrical energy and converts it into sound.

ear pick *n.* A tool or device which is used to remove the wax from the ear.

ear-plug *n.* A device which is inserted into the ear to prevent water or sound from entering.

ear-ring *n.* A piece or jewelry which is worn on the earlobe for decoration.

earth *n.* The third planet from the sun and the planet on which there is life; the outer layer of the world; ground; soil; dirt.

earth-born *adj.* Being born on this earth.

earth-en-ware *n.* The ceramic ware which is fired at a low heat.

earth-ling *n.* One who inhabits the earth.

earth-ly *adj.* Belonging to this earth.

earth-quake *n.* A trembling or violent shaking of the crust of the earth.

earth science *n.* A type of science which studies the earth or its parts.

earth-star *n.* A type of fungus whose outer layer splits into the shape of a star.

earth-ward *adv.* To be moving towards the earth.

earth-worm *n.* A type of annelid worm which lives in the soil.

ear-wig *n.* A type of insect that has a pair of cerci at the end of its body and antennae which are jointed.

ease *n.* A state of being comfortable; freedom from pain, discomfort, or care; freedom from labor or difficulty; an act of easing or a state of being eased. *v.* To free from pain or discomfort; to lessen the pressure or tension; to make less difficult; to move or pass with freedom. **at ease** Free from discomfort. *Milit.* Standing silently with the feet apart, as in a military formation. **easeful** *adj.*, **easefully** *adv.*

ea-sel *n.* A frame used by artists to support a canvas or picture.

east *n.* The direction opposite of west; the direction in which the sun rises.

East Berlin *n.* The capital of East Germany.

Easter *n.* A Christian festival which celebrates the resurrection of Christ.

Easter egg *n.* An egg that is dyed bright colors and associated with the celebration of Easter.

Easter lily *n.* A type of lily that blooms in the early spring.

easy *adj.* Capable of being accomplished with little difficulty; free from worry or pain; not hurried or strenuous; something readily obtainable.
easily *adv.*, **easiness** *n.*

easy going *adj.* Taking life easy; without worry, concern, or haste.

easy mark *n.* A person who is easily overcome.

eat *v.* To chew and swallow food; to erode; to consume with distress or agitation; to take a meal. **eat crow** To accept what one has been fighting against. **eat one's heart out** To grieve bitterly. **eat one's words** To retract what has been said. **eat out of one's hand** To accept the domination of another. **eater** *n.*

eat-ery *n.* A type of restaurant.

eat out *v.* To eat in a restaurant or not at home.

eaves *pl., n.* The overhanging edge of a roof.

eaves-drop *v.* To listen to what is said without the speakers knowing one is listening.

ebb *n.* The return of the tide towards the sea; a time of decline. *v.* To recede, as the tide does; to fall or flow back; to weaken.

eb-bet *n.* A type of green newt.

ebb tide *n.* The tide while at ebb; a period of decline.

eb-o-nite *n.* A type of hard rubber.

eb-o-ny *n., pl.* **-nies** The dark, hard, colored wood from the center of the ebony tree of Asia and Africa. *adj.* Resembling ebony; black.

e-bul-lient *adj.* Filled with enthusiasm. **ebullience** *n.*, **ebulliently** *adv.*

eb-ul-li-tion *n.* The process of boiling or bubbling; a sudden release of emotion.

ec-cen-tric *adj.* Differing from an established pattern or accepted norm; deviating from a perfect circle; not located at the geometrical center. *n.* An odd or erratic person; a disk or wheel with its axis not situated in the center. **eccentrically** *adv.*, **eccentricity** *n.*

ec-chy-mo-sis *n.* The escaping of blood into the surrounding tissues.

ec-cle-si-as-ti-cal *n.* A clergyman; a person officially serving a church. *adj.* Of or relating to a church.

ec-cle-si-ol-o-gy *n.* A study of the architecture of a church.

ec-crine *adj.* To be producing a fluid secretion which does not remove cytoplasm for the secreting cell.

ec-crine gland *n.* A type of sweat gland which produces an eccrine secretion.

ec-dy-sis *n.* The act of shedding the outer cuticular layer such as the insects.

ece-sis *n.* An establishment of animals in a new habitat.

ech-e-lon *n.* A formation, as of military aircraft or naval vessels, resembling a series of steps where each rank is positioned slightly to the right or left of the preceding one; a level of command or authority; a hierarchy.

echid-na *n.* A type of toothless spiny-coated nocturnal mammal found in Australia and feeds on ants.

echi-no-derm *n.* A member of the phylum Echinodermata having a radially symmetrical shape such as the starfish.

ech-o *n., pl.* **-oes** Repetition of a sound by reflecting sound waves from a surface; the sound produced by such a reflection; a repetition; the reflection of transmitted radar signals by an object. *v.* To repeat or be repeated by; to imitate.

ech-o cham-ber *n.* A room that has sound-reflecting walls and it is used for the production of hollow sounds.

ech-o-lo-ca-tion *n.* A method for locating objects with the use a sound waves.

ech-o sound-er *n.* A tool or device which is used to determine the depth of a body of water.

ec-lec-tic *adj.* Having components from diverse sources or styles. **eclectic** *n.*

e-clipse *n.* A total or partial blocking of one celestial body by another. *v.* To fall into obscurity or decline; to cause an eclipse of; to overshadow.

e-clip-tic *n., Astron.* The circle formed by the intersection of the plane of the earth's orbit and the celestial sphere.

ec-logue *n.* A short pastoral poem in the form of a dialogue.

ec-o-cide *n.* The deliberate destruction of the natural environment, caused by pollutants.

e-col-o-gy *n.* The branch of science concerned with the interrelationship of organisms and their environments; the relationship between living organisms and their environments. **ecologic** *adj.*, **ecologically** *adv.*, **ecologist** *n.*

ec-o-nom-ic *adj.* The science relating to the development, production, and management of material wealth; relating to the necessities of life.

ec-o-nom-i-cal *adj.* Not wasteful; frugal; operating with little waste. **-ly** *adv.*

ec-o-nom-ics *pl., n.* The science which treats production, distribution, and consumption of commodities. **-ist** *n.*

e-con-o-mize *v.* To manage thriftily; to use sparingly. **economizer** *n.*

e-con-o-my *n., pl.* **-mies** Careful management of money, materials, and resources; a reduction in expenses; a system or structure for the management of resources and production of goods and services.

eco-phys-i-ol-gy *n.* A study of the relationships of the environment and the physiology of organisms.

eco-spe-cies *n.* The subdivision of cenospecies.

eco-sphere *n.* The section of the universe which is inhabitable by living organisms.

ec-ru *n.* A light yellowish brown, as the color of unbleached linen.

ec-sta-sy *n., pl.* **-sies** The state of intense joy or delight. **ecstatic** *adj.*, **ecstatically** *adv.*

ec-to-derm *n.* An outer cellular membrane of a diploblastic animal.

ec-top-ic *adj.* To be occurring in an abnormal place or position.

ectopic pregnancy *n.* A pregnancy that takes place elsewhere in the body such as the fallopian tubes.

ec-to-therm *n.* An animal which is classified as cold-blooded.

Ec-ua-dor *n.* A country located in northwestern South America. **Ecuadorian** *adj. & n.*

ec-u-men-i-cal *adj.* Worldwide or general in extent, application, or influence; promoting unity among Christian churches or religions. **ecumenically** *adv.*, **ecumenism** *n.*

ec-ze-ma *n.* A noncontagious inflammatory skin condition, marked by itching and scaly patches. **-tous** *adj.*

edaph-ic *adj.* Pertaining to or relating to the soil. **edaphically** *adv.*

ed-dy *n., pl.* **-dies** A current, as of water, running against the direction of the main current, especially in a circular motion. **eddy** *v.*

eddy current *n.* A current of electricity which is induced by an alternating magnetic field.

Eddy, Mary Baker *n.* (1821-1910). American founder of Christian Science.

e-del-weiss *n.* An Alpine plant having woolly leaves and small flowers.

ede-ma *n.* An accumulation of serous fluid in the connective tissue that is abnormal. **edematous** *adj.*

E-den *n.* The garden which was the first home of Adam and Eve; a delightful area; a paradise. **Edenic** *adj.*

eden-tate *adj.* To be without teeth.

eden-tu-lous *adj.* To be without teeth.

edge *n.* The thin, sharp, cutting side of a blade; keenness; sharpness; the border where an object or area begins or ends; an advantage. *v.* To furnish with an edge or border; to sharpen; to move gradually. **on edge** Tense.

edged *adj.* To have a specified edge.

edge-less *adj.* To be without an edge.

edg-ing *n.* Something which can make or form an edge.

ed-i-ble *adj.* Safe or fit for consumption. **edibility, edible** *n.*

e-dict *n.* A public decree; an order or command officially proclaimed.

edif-i-ca-to-ry *adj.* To be suitable for edification.

ed-i-fice *n.* A massive building or structure.

ed-i-fy *v.* To benefit and enlighten morally or spiritually. **-ication, -er** *n.*

Edison, Thomas Alva *n.* (1847-1931). An American inventor.

ed-it *v.* To prepare and correct for publication; to compile for an edition; to delete or change. **editor** *n.*

e-di-tion *n.* The form in which a book is published; the total number of copies printed at one time; one similar to an original version.

ed-i-to-ri-al *n.* An article in a newspaper or magazine which expresses the opinion of a publisher or editor. *adj.* Of or relating to an editor or an editor's work; being or resembling an editorial. **editorially** *adv.*

ed-i-to-ri-al-ist *n.* A person who writes editorials for a paper or other publication.

editor in chief *n.* The editor who is in charge of an editorial staff.

ed-i-tress *n.* A woman who is an editor.

EDP *abbr.* Electronic data processing.

EDT *abbr.* Eastern Daylight Time.

ed-u-ca-ble *adj.* To be capable of being educated.

ed-u-cate *v.* To supply with training or schooling; to supervise the mental or moral growth of. **educator** *n.*

ed-u-cat-ed *adj.* To have an education.

ed-u-ca-tion *n.* The process of being educated. **-ally** *adv.*, **educational** *adj.*

ed-u-ca-tor *n.* Someone who educates.

e-duce *v.* To call forth or bring out; to develop from given facts.

edul-co-rate *v.* To make something pleasant.

eel *n., pl.* **eel** *or* **eels** A snake-like marine or freshwater fish without scales or pelvic fins. **eellike, eely** *adj.*

eel-grass *n.* A type of a marine plant that is under the water having narrow leaves.

eel-pout *n.* A type of marine fish which resembles blennies.

eel-worm *n.* A type of nematode worm.

ee-rie *or* **ee-ry** *adj.* Suggesting or inspiring the supernatural or strange spooky. **eerily** *adv.*, **eeriness** *n.*

ef-face *v.* To remove or rub out. **effacer, effacement** *n.*

ef-fect *n.* Something produced by a cause; the power to produce a desired result; the reaction something has on an object; a technique which produces an intended impression. **take effect** To become operative. **effecter** *n.*

ef-fec-tive *adj.* Producing an expected effect or proper result. **effectiveness** *n.*

ef-fec-tiv-i-ty *n.* The state of being effective.

ef-fec-tor *n.* An organ of the body that is active when it has been stimulated.

ef-fec-tu-al *adj.* To be able to produce an effect that is desired.

ef-fec-tu-al-ly *adv.* With a great effect.

ef-fem-i-nate *adj.* Having a more woman-like quality or trait than a man. effeminacy *n.*, effeminately *adv.*

ef-fen-di *n.* A man in the eastern Mediterranean area who has an education or property.

ef-fer-ent *adj., Physiol.* Carrying away or outward from a central organ or part. efferent *n.*, efferently *adv.*

ef-fer-vesce *v.* To foam with the escaping of a gas for something. -ntly *adv.*, effervescence *n.*, effervescent *adj.*

ef-fete *adj.* Exhausted of effectiveness or force; worn-out; decadent. effeteness *n.*, effetely *adv.*

ef-fi-ca-cious *adj.* Producing an intended effect. efficaciously *adv.*

ef-fi-cien-cy *n.* The degree of being efficient.

ef-fi-cient *adj.* Adequate in performance with a minimum of waste or effort; giving a high ratio of output.

ef-fi-gy *n., pl.* -gies A life-size sculpture or painting representing a crude image or dummy of a hated person.

ef-flo-resce *v.* To become covered with a powdery crust.

ef-flo-res-cence *n.* A time of flowering; a slow process of development; the highest point. efflorescent *adj.*

ef-flu-ence *n.* An act of flowing out; something that flows out or forth.

ef-flu-vi-um *n., pl.* -via *or* -viums An unpleasant vapor from something.

ef-flux *n.* The passing away of someone or something. effluxion *n.*

ef-fort *n.* Voluntary exertion of physical or mental energy; a difficult exertion; a normally earnest attempt or achievement; something done through exertion. *Phys.* A force applied against inertia. effortless *adj.*

ef-fort-ful *adj.* To be requiring effort.

ef-fron-ter-y *n., pl.* -ies Shameless boldness; impudence.

ef-ful-gent *adj.* Shining brilliantly; radiant. effulgence *n.*

ef-fuse *v.* To give off; to pour out.

ef-fu-sion *n.* An instance of pouring forth; an unrestrained outpouring of feeling. effusive *adj.*, effusively *adv.*

eg *abbr.* For example.

egal-i-tar-i-an *adj.* Being marked by egalitarianism. egalitarian *n.*

egest *v.* To defecate or rid the body of waste. egestive *adj.*, egestion *n.*

egg *n.* The hard-shelled reproductive cell of female animals, especially one produced by a chicken, used as food. *v.* To incite to action.

egg-beat-er *n.* A kitchen tool with rotating blades used to mix, blend, or beat food.

egg case *n.* A case which encloses an egg for the purpose of protecting it.

egg-cup *n.* A type of cup which is used to hold an egg so that it may be eaten in the shell.

egg-head *n., Informal* An intellectual; highbrow.

egg-head-ed *adj.* To have the characteristics of one who is an egghead.

egg-nog *n.* A drink of beaten eggs, sugar, and milk or cream, often mixed with alcohol.

egg-plant *n.* A widely cultivated perennial plant which yields an egg-shaped edible fruit.

egg-roll *n.* A thin egg-dough casing filled with minced vegetables and sometimes meat or seafood which is fried.

egg timer *n.* A sandglass which is used for the purpose of timing the cooking of an egg.

egg tooth *n.* The sharp prominence which is located on the tip of a bird's beak for the purpose of breaking through the egg at the time of its birth.

eg-lan-tine *n.* The sweetbrier; a type of rose.

e-go *n.* The self thinking, feeling, and acting distinct from the external world. *Physiol.* The conscious aspect that most directly controls behavior and is most in touch with reality.

e-go-cen-tric *adj.* Thinking, observing, and regarding oneself as the object of all experiences. egocentric, -ity *n.*

ego--de-fense *n.* A mechanism that is psychological and protects the self-image.

e-go-ma-ni-a *n.* Self obsession. egomaniac *n.*, egomaniacal *adj.*

ego trip *n. Slang* Something which satisfies the ego.

e-gre-gious *adj.* Outstandingly or remarkably bad; flagrant. egregiously *adv.*, egregiousness *n.*

e-gress *n.* The act of coming out; emergence; a means of departing; exit.

e-gret *n.*

Any of several species of white wading birds having long, drooping plumes.

E-gypt *n.* A country located in northeast Africa and southwest Asia.

Egyptian *adj. & n.*

ei-der *n.* A large sea duck found in northern regions, having soft down which is used for comforters, pillows, etc.

ei-der-down *n.* The down of the eider duck.

ei-det-ic *adj.* Involving vivid recall.

ei-do-lon *n.* An image that is unsubstantial.

eight *n.* The cardinal number which follows seven. eighth *adj.*

eight ball *n.* The black ball with the number eight in the game of pool. behind the eight ball *Slang* In a bad spot.

eigh-teen *n.* The number that follows seventeen. eighteenth *adj. & n.*

eight-fold *adj.* To be eight times as much or greater.

eight-pen-ny nail *n.* A type of nail which is under three inches and over two inches.

ein-korn n. The type of wheat that can be found in Europe and it has one grain.

Einstein, Albert n. (1879-1955). A German born American physicist.

Eisenhower, Dwight David n. (1890-1969). The 34th president of the United States, from 1953-1961.

ei-stedd-fod n. A festival of the Welsh people. **eisteddfodic** adj.

ei-ther pron. One or the other. conj. Used before the first of two or more alternatives linked by or. adj. One or the other of two. adv. Likewise; also.

e-jac-u-late v. To eject abruptly, as in semen; to utter suddenly and briefly; to exclaim. **-ion** n., **ejaculatory** adj.

e-ject v. To throw out; to expel. **ejection, ejector** n.

e-ject-ment n. An act for a recovery of possession of real property.

eke out v. To obtain with great effort; to make do.

EKG abbr. Electrocardiogram.

ekis-tics n. The science which dealing with the settlements of humans.

e-lab-o-rate adj. Planned or carried out with great detail; very complex; intricate. v. To work out or complete with great detail; to give more detail. **-ness, elaboration** n., **elaborately** adv.

e-land n. A large African antelope with a tan coat and spirally horns.

el-a-pid n. A member of the family of poisonous snakes that have grooved fangs.

e-lapse v. To slip or glide away; to pass away silently.

e-lapsed time n. The amount of time that has been taken to go through a course such as with a race.

elas-mo-branch n. A member of the class of fishes that have lamellate gills such members include the sharks, chimaeras, and rays.

elas-tase n. The enzyme found in the pancreatic juice which will digest elastin.

e-las-tic adj. Complying with changing circumstances; capable of easy adjustment. **elastically** adv., **elasticity** n.

elas-ti-cized adj. Being made with elastic.

elas-tic scat-ter-ing n. The scattering of particles due to a elastic collision.

elas-tin n. A type of protein which is similar to collagen.

elas-to-mer n. The elastic substances which resemble rubber.

e-late v. To make proud of. **elation** n.

el-a-ter n. The structure of a plant which aids in the distribution of spores.

elat-er-ite n. A mineral resin which is dark brown and occurs in flexible masses.

E layer n. The layer in the ionosphere above the earth that is able to reflect radio waves.

el-bow n. A sharp turn, as in a river or road, which resembles an elbow. Anat. The outer joint of the arm between the upper arm and forearm. v. To push or shove aside with the elbow.

el-bow grease n. An energy that is exerted with physical labor.

el-bow-room n. Ample room to move about; enough space for comfort.

eld-er adj. Older. n. One who is older than others; a person of great influence; an official of the church. Bot. A shrub bearing reddish fruit.

el-der-ber-ry n. An edible red or black berry which can be found in the honeysuckle family.

el-der-ly adj. Pertaining to later life; older. **elderliness** n.

el-dest adj. The oldest in age or seniority.

el-dest hand n. The one in a game of cards who receives the cards first in the deal.

elec abbr. Electricity; electric.

ele-cam-pane n. A type of European herb which has yellow flowers.

e-lect v. To choose or select by vote, as for an office; to make a choice. adj. Singled out on purpose; elected but not yet inaugurated. n. One chosen or set apart, especially for spiritual salvation.

e-lect-able adj. To be capable of being elected. **electability** n.

e-lect-ion n. The process of electing someone.

e-lec-tion-eer v. To help with the candidate's election. **electioneerer** n.

e-lec-tive adj. Pertaining to an election. **electiveness** n., **electively** adv.

e-lec-tor n. A person who is able to vote.

e-lec-tor-al adj. Pertaining to an elector.

e-lec-tor-ate n. A group of people who are able to vote in an election.

e-lec-tress n. A wife of the German elector.

e-lec-tric or **e-lec-tri-cal** adj. Relating to electricity; emotionally exciting. **electrically** adv.

e-lec-tri-cal storm n. A storm which contains lightening.

e-lec-tric chair n. The chair which is used to elkectrocute someone to death legally.

e-lec-tric eel n. A large which is shaped like an eel that able to give off an electrical shock.

e-lec-tri-cian n. A person whose job it is to install or maintain electric equipment.

e-lec-tric-i-ty n., Phys., Chem. A force that causes bodies to attract or repel each other, responsible for a natural phenomena as lightning; electric current as a power source; emotional excitement.

e-lec-tric or-gan n. A section of tissue which is capable of producing electricity such as with the electric eel.

e-lec-tric ray n. A type of ray which has a pair of electric organs and is found in warm waters.

e-lec-tri-fi-ca-tion n. The state of being electrified.

e-lec-tri-fy v. To charge something or someone with electricity.

e-lec-tro-car-di-o-gram n. The record produced by an electrocardiograph machine.

e-lec-tro-car-di-o-graph n. An electric instrument which detects and records the heartbeat.

e-lec-tro-cute v. To kill or execute by the use of electric current. electrocution n.

e-lec-trode n. A conductor by which an electric current enters or leaves.

e-lec-tro-de-pos-it n. The deposit which is formed at an electrode.

e-lec-tro-di-al-y-sis n. A dialysis which is accelerated with an electromotive force.

e-lec-tro-dy-nam-ics n., Phys. The study of the interactions of moving electric charges. electrodynamic adj.

e-lec-trol-y-sis n., Chem., Phys. A chemical decomposition by an electric current; destruction of tumors or hair roots by an electric current.

e-lec-tro-mag-net n. A magnet consisting of a soft iron core magnetized by an electric current passing through a wire which is coiled around the core.

e-lec-trom-e-ter n. An instrument for detecting or measuring electric potential or differences between two conductors.

e-lec-tro-mo-tive adj. Of, pertaining to, or tending to produce electric current.

e-lec-tron n., Elect. A subatomic particle with a negative electric charge found outside of an atoms nucleus.

e-lec-tro-stat-ic adj. Pertaining to static electric charges.

e-lec-tro-stat-ics pl. n., Phys. The physics of static electric charges.

e-lec-tro-type n. A duplicate metal plate made by electroplating a mold of the original plate which is used in printing. electrotype v.

e-lec-tro-va-lence n. The valence which is characterized by a transfer of electrons from one atom to another.

e-lec-tro-va-lent bond n. The bond which forms between ions of opposite charges.

e-lec-trum n. A type of pale yellow alloy of silver and gold.

el-e-doi-sin n. A protein that comes from the salivary glands of the octopus.

el-ee-mos-y-nar-y adj. Of, pertaining to, or contributed as charity.

el-e-gance n. Refinement in appearance, movement, or manners; an elegant quality. elegant adj.

ele-gi-ac adj. Consisting of two dactylic hexameter lines where the second of the two lacks the arses in the third and sixth feet. elegiacally adv.

el-e-gy n., pl. -gies A poem expressing sorrow and lamentation for one who is dead.

el-e-ment n. A constituent part. Chem. & Phys. A substance not separable into less complex substances by chemical means. elements pl. The conditions of the weather.

el-e-men-tal adj. Relating to an element.

elementally adv.

el-e-men-ta-ry adj. Fundamental, essential; referring to elementary school; introducing fundamental principles.

el-e-men-ta-ry school n. A school including the grades of first to sixth.

el-e-mi n. A fragrant oleoresins which is obtained from tropical trees and is used in inks and varnishes.

el-e-phant n.

A large mammal having a long, flexible trunk and curved tusks.

el-e-phant grass n. A cattail which is used for the purpose of making baskets.

el-e-phan-ti-a-sis n., Pathol. The enormous enlargement of affected parts along with hardening, caused by obstruction of lymphatics from parasitic worms.

el-e-phan-tine adj. To have a lot of strength or to be great in size.

el-e-phant seal n. A kind of seal that is almost extinct and has a long inflatable proboscis.

el-e-vate v. To lift up or raise; to promote to a higher rank.

el-e-vat-ed adj. To be above something such as the ground.

el-e-vat-ed rail-road n. A railroad which operated on an elevated track.

el-e-va-tion n. The height of something which is elevated or above the ground.

el-e-va-tor n. A platform or cage which raises cargo or person inside it to another level such as in a skyscraper or other building.

el-ev-en n. A cardinal number with a sum equal to ten plus one.

el-e-von n. A surface which is controlled by an airplane and operated as an elevator.

elf n., pl. elves An imaginary being with magical powers, often mischievous; a small, mischievous child. -in, -ish adj.

e-lic-it v. To bring or draw out; to evoke.

e-lide v. To omit, especially to slur over in pronunciation, as a vowel, consonant, or syllable. elision n.

e-li-gi-ble adj. Worthy of being chosen. eligibly adv., eligibility n.

e-lim-i-nate v. To get rid of, remove; to leave out, to omit; to excrete, as waste. -ion, -or n., -ive, eliminatory adj.

e-lite n. The most skilled members of a group; a small, powerful group; a type size yielding twelve characters to the inch. elite adj.

elit-ism n. A rule by the elite of a country or of a society.

e-lix-ir n., Phar. A sweetened aromatic liquid of alcohol and water, used as a vehicle for medicine; a medicine regarded as a cure-all; a sovereign remedy.

Elizabeth I n. (1533-1603). Queen of England and Ireland from 1558 until 1603. Elizabethan adj. & n.

elk n., pl. **elks** or **elk** The largest deer of Europe and Asia. **Elk** A member of a major benevolent and fraternal order.

ell n. An extension of a building at right angles to the main structure.

el-lag-ic acid n. A crystalline compound that is obtained from oak galls.

el-lipse n., Geom. A closed curve, somewhat oval in shape.

el-lip-sis n. An ommision of a few words which are understood in a sentence.

el-lip-tic or **el-lip-ti-cal** adj. Of, pertaining to, or shaped like an ellipse.

elm n. Any of various valuable timber and shade trees with arching branches.

elm bark beetle n. Type of beetle leading to the Dutch elm disease.

elm leaf beetle n. An orange-yellow beetle of the Old World.

el-o-cu-tion n. The art of effective public speaking. -ary adj., elocutionist n.

elo-dea n. A submerged aquatic monocotyledonous.

eloign v. To take someone or something to a place which is a great distance away.

elon-gate v. To stretch out in length.

elon-ga-tion n. The state of being elongated or stretched out in length.

e-lope v. To run away, especially in order to get married, usually without parental permission. elopement, eloper n.

el-o-quent adj. Having the power to speak fluently and persuasively; vividly expressive. eloquence n., -ly adv.

else adj. Different; other; more; additional. adv. In addition; besides.

else-where adv. To or in another place.

e-lu-ci-date v. To make clear, clarify; to explain. elucidator, elucidation n.

elu-cu-brate v. To work something out with an effort that is studious.

e-lude v. To evade or avoid; to escape understanding.

e-lu-sion n. An evasion of an order or of a problem that one may have.

e-lu-sive adj. Tending to evade something or someone. elusively adv.

e-lute v. To remove material from what has absorbed it with the use of a solvent. elution n.

e-lu-tri-ate v. To remove something by washing. elutriator n.

e-lu-vi-al adj. Related to eluviation.

e-lu-vi-a-tion n. Transportation of material that is in the soil by water.

E-ly-si-um n., Mythol. A place of exquisite happiness; a paradise. Elysian adj.

el-y-tron n. An anterior wing of a beetle which protect the functional wings.

em n., Print. A unit of measure for printed matter that is equal to the width of the letter M.

e-ma-ci-ate v. To become or cause to become extremely thin from the loss of appetite. emaciation n.

em-a-nate v. To come or give forth, as from a source. emanation n.

e-man-ci-pate v. To liberate; to set free from bondage. -ion, emancipator n.

e-mar-gin-ate adj. To have the margin notched. emargination n.

e-mas-cu-late v. To castrate; to deprive of masculine vigor. -ion, -or n.

em-balm v. To treat a corpse with preservatives in order to protect from decay. embalment, embalmer n.

em-bank v. To support, protect, or defend with a bank of earth or stone.

em-bar-go n., pl. -goes A prohibition or restraint on trade, as a government order forbidding the entry or departure of merchant vessels, for example the oil embargo of 1973. embargo v.

em-bark v. To board a ship; to set out on a venture. embarkation n.

em-bar-rass v. To cause to feel selfconscious; to confuse; to burden with financial difficulties. -ment n.

em-bas-sage n. The commission which has been entrusted to an ambassador.

em-bas-sy n., pl. -sies The headquarters of an ambassador.

em-bat-tle v. To prepare or to arrange for a battle. embattlement n.

em-bay v. To shelter.

em-bay-ment n. The formation of a bay.

em-bed v. To fix or enclose tightly in a surrounding mass. embedment n.

em-bel-lish v. To adorn or make beautiful with ornamentation; to decorate; to heighten the attractiveness by adding ornamental details. embellisher, embellishment n.

em-ber n. A small piece of glowing coal or wood, as in a dying fire. embers pl. The smoldering ashes or remains of a fire.

em-bez-zle v. To take money or other items fraudulently. embezzlement n.

em-bit-ter v. To make bitter; to create feelings of hostility. embitterment n.

em-blaze v. To set something ablaze.

em-bla-zon v. To decorate in bright colors. emblazonment n.

em-blem n. A symbol of something; a distinctive design. -atic, -atical adj.

em-bod-y v. To give a bodily form to; to personify. embodiment n.

em-bold-en v. To encourage; to make bold.

em-bo-lism n., Med. The blockage of a blood vessel, as by an air bubble or a detached clot.

em-bon-point n. Plumpness; stoutness.

em-boss v. To shape or decorate in relief; to represent in relief.

em-bou-chure n., Mus. The part of a wind instrument which is applied to the lips to produce a musical tone.

em-bow-er v. To enclose, cover, or shelter.

em-brace v. To clasp or hold in the arms; to hug; to surround; to take in mentally or visually. n. The act of embracing; a hug.

em-bra-sure n., Arch. A flared opening in a wall, as for a door or window.

em-bro-cate v. To moisten and rub an injured part of the body with a liquid medicine. **embrocation** n.

em-broi-der v. To decorate with ornamental needlework; to add fictitious details. **embroidery** n.

em-broil v. To involve in contention or violent actions; to throw into confusion. **embroilment** n.

em-bry-o n., pl. **-os** An organism in its early developmental stage, before it has a distinctive form; in the human species, the first eight weeks of development, especially before birth or germination; a rudimentary stage.

em-bry-ol-o-gy n. The science concerned with the origin, structure, and growth of embryos. **-ical** adj., **embryologist** n.

em-cee n., Informal A master of ceremonies. **emcee** v.

e-mend v. To correct or remove faults. **emendation, emender** n.

em-er-ald n. A bright-green, transparent variety of beryl, used as a gemstone.

e-merge v. To rise into view; to come into existence. **-ence** n., **emergent** adj.

e-mer-gen-cy n., pl. **-cies** A sudden and unexpected situation requiring prompt action.

e-mer-i-tus adj. Retired from active duty but retaining the honorary title held immediately before retirement.

Emerson, Ralph Waldo n. (1803-1882). An American poet and writer of essays.

em-er-y n. A grainy, mineral substance having impure corundum, used for polishing and grinding.

e-met-ic adj. A medicine used to induce vomiting. **emetic** n.

em-i-grate v. To move from one country or region to settle elsewhere. **emigrant, emigration** n.

e-mi-gre n. A refugee.

em-i-nent adj. High in esteem, rank, or office; conspicuous; outstanding. **eminent domain** n. The right of a government to take or control property for public use.

e-mir n. A Moslem prince.

em-is-sar-y n., pl. **-ies** A person sent out on a mission.

e-mit v. To send forth; to throw or give out. **emission** n.

e-mol-lient n. A substance for the soothing and softening of the skin.

e-mol-u-ment n. Profit; compensation, as a salary or perquisite.

e-mote v. To show emotion, as in acting.

e-mo-tion n. A strong surge of feeling; any of the feelings of fear, sorrow, joy, hate, or love; a particular feeling, as love or hate.

em-pa-thy n., Physiol. Identification with and understanding the feelings of another person. **empathetic, -ic** adj.

em-pen-nage n. The rear section or tail of an aircraft.

em-per-or n. The ruler of an empire.

em-pha-sis n., pl. **-ses** Significance or importance attached to anything.

em-phat-ic adj. Expressed or spoken with emphasis. **emphatically** adv.

em-pire n. The territories or nations governed by a single supreme authority.

em-pir-i-cal or **em-pir-ic** adj. Depending on or gained from observation or experiment rather than from theory and science. **empirically** adv.

em-place-ment n. A platform for guns or military equipment.

em-ploy v. To engage the service or use of; to devote time to an activity. **employable** adj., **employer, -ment** n.

em-ploy-ee or **em-ploy-e** n. A person who works for another in return for salary or wages.

em-po-ri-um n., pl. **-riums** or **-ria** A large store which carries general merchandise.

em-pow-er v. To authorize; to delegate; to license.

em-press n. A woman who rules an empire; an emperor's wife or widow.

emp-ty adj. Containing nothing; vacant; lacking substance. v. To empty. **emptily** adv., **emptiness** n.

em-py-re-an n. Pertaining to the highest part of heaven; the sky.

e-mu n. A swift-running Australian bird which is related to the ostrich.

em-u-late v. To strive to equal, especially by imitating. **-ion** n., **emulous** adj.

e-mul-sion n., Chem. A suspended mixture of small droplets, one within the other. Photog. A light-sensitive coating on photographic paper, film, or plates.

en-a-ble v. To supply with adequate power, knowledge, or opportunity; to give legal power to another.

en-act v. To make into law; to decree. **enactor, enactment** n.

en-nam-el n. A decorative or protective coating fused on a surface, as of pottery; a paint that dries to a hard, glossy surface; the hard outermost covering of a tooth. v. To apply, inlay, or decorate with enamel.

e-nam-el-ware n. A type of metalware which has been covered with a coating of enamel.

en-amine n. A type of amine that has a double bond linkage.

en-am-or v. To inflame with love; to charm.

en-an-tio-morph n. A pair of chemical compounds who have molecular structures that are alike.

ena-tion n. The outgrowth from a surface of an organ.

en bloc adv. As a unit.

enc or **encl** abbr. Enclosed; enclosure.

en-camp v. To form or stay in a camp.

en-cap-su-late v. To enclose or encase in a capsule. **encapsulation** n.

en-cap-su-lat-ed adj. To be surrounded with a membranous envelope.

en-case v. To close within a case.

en-case-ment n. The state of being encased.

en-caus-tic n. A type of paint which is made with melted beeswax.

en-ce-phal-ic adj. Pertaining to the brain.

en-ceph-a-li-tis n., Pathol. Inflammation

of the brain.

en-ceph-a-lo-my-eli-tis *n*. The inflammation of the spinal cord and the brain.

en-ceph-a-lop-a-thy *n*. The disease of the brain that alters structure.

en-chain *v*. To put or to hold in chains. enchainment *n*.

en-chant *v*. To put someone under a spell; to bewitch; to charm; to delight greatly.

en-chant-ment *n*. The state in which something or someone is enchanted.

en-chant-ress *n*. A female who does magic such as a sorceress.

en-chase *v*. To carve a relief into something.

en-chi-la-da *n*. A kind of rolled tortilla and is covered with chili-seasoned tomato sauce.

en-ci-pher *v*. To convert something such as a message in to a cipher.

en-cir-cle *v*. To form a circle around; to move around. encirclement *n*.

en-clasp *v*. To hold onto someone or something.

en-clave *n*. A country surrounded by a foreign country; a cultural group living within a larger group.

en-close *v*. To surround on all sides; to put in the same envelope or package with something else.

en-clo-sure *n*. The action of enclosing something; state of being enclosed.

en-code *v*. To conver or change a message into a code. encoder *n*.

en-co-mi-ast *n*. A person who praises. encomiastic *adj*.

en-co-mi-um *n*., *pl*. -miums *or* -mia High praise.

en-com-pass *v*. To surround; to form a circle; to enclose. encompassment *n*.

en-core *n*. An audience's demand for a repeat performance; a performance in response to an encore.

en-cor-ing *v*. To call for an encore.

en-coun-ter *n*. An unplanned or unexpected meeting or conflict. *v*. To come upon unexpectedly; to confront in a hostile situation.

en-coun-ter group *n*. A therapy group formed to increase people's sensitivity and to reveal their feelings so that they openly relate to others.

en-cour-age *v*. To inspire with courage or hope; to support. -ment *n*., -ingly *adv*.

en-crim-son *v*. To color or to make something the shade of crimson.

en-croach *v*. To intrude upon the rights or possessions of another. encroacher, encroachment *n*.

en-crust *v*. To cover with a crust; to crust. encrustation *n*.

en-cum-ber *v*. To hinder or burden with difficulties or obligations.

en-cum-brance *n*. An item which encumbers. encumbrancer *n*.

-en-cy *n*., *suffix* State.

en-cyc-li-cal *n*., *Rom. Cath. Ch.* A papal letter to the bishops of the world.

en-cy-clo-pe-di-a *n*. A comprehensive work with articles covering a broad range of subjects.

en-cy-clo-pe-dic *adj*. Pertaining to an encyclopedia.

en-cy-clo-pe-dist *n*. A person writes an encyclopedia.

en-cyst *v*. To become enclosed in a sac. encystment *n*.

en-cys-ta-tion *n*. A process of making or forming a cyst.

end *n*. A part lying at a boundary; the terminal point at which something concludes; the point in time at which something ceases; a goal; a fragment; a remainder; in football, either of the players in the outermost position on the line of scrimmage. *v*. To come or bring to a termination; to ruin or destroy; to die.

en-dam-age *v*. To cause damage to something or to someone.

end-amoe-ba *n*. A member of the genus that contains amoebas. -ic *adj*.

en-dan-ger *v*. To expose or put into danger or imperil. endangerment *n*.

en-dan-gered *adj*. Threatened with extinction.

en-darch *adj*. To be formed from the center outward. endarchy *n*.

end-ar-ter-ec-to-my *n*. The removal of the inner layer of an artery with surgery.

end-brain *n*. The anterior part of the forebrain.

end bulb *n*. The bulbous termination on a sensory nerve fiber.

en-dear *v*. To make beloved or dear.

en-dear-ment *n*. The state of being endeared.

en-deav-or *n*. An attempt to attain or do something. endeavor *v*.

en-dem-ic *adj*. Peculiar to a particular area or people.

en-der-mic *adj*. To act through the skin. endermically *adv*.

end-ex-ine *n*. A membranous inner layer of the exine.

end-ing *n*. Something which indicates an end.

en-dive *n*.

A herb with crisp succulent leaves, used in salads; a plant related to the endive.

end-less *adj*. To be without an end.

end line *n*. The line which marks the boundary of a playing field.

end-most *adj*. To be at the very end.

en-do-bi-ot-ic *adj*. To be living within the host's tissues.

en-do-car-di-tis *n*. An inflammation of the linings of the heart.

en-do-car-di-um *n*. The membrane lining of the cavities of the heart.

en-do-chon-dral *adj*. To be occurring in cartilage of the body.

en-do-crine *adj*. To be making secretions which are distributed in the body by the blood.

en-do-crine gland *n*. The gland which

makes and endocrine secretion.

en-do-cri-nol-o-gy *n.* The area of science or study of the endocrine glands and various secretions. **endocrinologist** *n.*

en-do-cy-to-sis *n.* The act of taking substances in to a cell with phagocytosis.

en-do-derm *n.* The inner germ layer in an embryo and becomes the epithelium of the digestive tract.

en-do-der-mis *n.* The most inner layer in the cortex of a plant.

en-do-en-zyme *n.* A kind of enzyme which functions inside the dell.

en-do-er-gic *adj.* To be absorbing energy.

en-do-eryth-ro-cyt-ic *adj.* To be occurring within the red cells of the blood.

en-dog-a-my *n.* The marriage that can only take place within a specific group due to customs. **endogamous** *adj.*

en-dog-e-nous *adj.*, *Biol.* Originating or growing from within.

en-do-me-tri-um *n.* The membrane that lines the woman's uterus.

en-do-mor-phic *adj.* To be pertaining to endomorphism.

en-do-nu-cle-ase *n.* An enzyme that will break down a chain of nucleotides.

en-do-par-a-site *n.* A kind of parasite that is able to live in the host's internal organs.

en-so-phyte *n.* A kind of plant which able to live within another plant.

en-do-plasm *n.* The fluid part of the cytoplasm. **endoplasmic** *adj.*

en-dor-phin *n.* Hormones with tranquilizing and pain-killing capabilities, secreted by the brain.

en-dorse *v.* To write one's signature on the back of a check, so as to obtain the cash indicated on the front, or on the back of a car title, so as to show transfer of ownership. **endorsee**, **endorsement** *n.*

en-do-scope *n.*, *Med.* An instrument used to examine a bodily canal or hollow organ. **endoscopic** *adj.*, **endoscopy** *n.*

en-do-skel-e-ton *n.* A skeleton which is on the inside of one's body.

en-do-sperm *n.* The tissue in seed plants which is nutritious.

end-os-te-al *adj.* To be pertaining to the endosteum. **endosteally** *adv.*

end-os-te-um *n.* A vascular connective tissue which lines the medullary cavities found in the bone.

en-do-sul-fan *n.* A kind of insecticide used for the control of crop insects.

en-do-the-ci-um *n.* The lining which is in a mature anther.

en-do-therm *n.* An animal that is warm-blooded.

en-do-tox-in *n.* A kind of poisonous substance which can be found in bacteria.

en-do-tra-che-al *adj.* To be placed within the trachea of the body.

en-dow *v.* To supply with a permanent income or incomeproducing property; to bestow upon. **endowment** *n.*

en-do-zo-ic *adj.* To be living in an animal.

end-pa-per *n.* A piece of paper placed on the front or the back cover of a book.

end point *n.* The point which marks the completion of a process.

end pro-duct *n.* A final product of a group of processes.

en-drin *n.* A type of insecticide.

end ta-ble *n.* A table that is about the height of the couch.

en-due *v.* To put on.

en-dur-able *adj.* Being able to endure. **endurably** *adv.*

en-dur-ance *n.* An ability to withstand stress or hardship.

en-dure *v.* To undergo; to sustain; to put up with; to tolerate; to bear.

en-duro *n.* A kind of long race that will stress endurance.

end-wise *or* **end-ways** *adv.* On end; lengthwise.

en-e-ma *n.* The injection of a liquid into the rectum for cleansing; the liquid injected.

en-e-my *n.*, *pl.* **-mies** One who seeks to inflict injury on another; a foe; a hostile force or power.

en-er-get-ic *adj.* Relating to energy. **energetically** *adv.*

en-er-get-ics *n.* An area of mechanics dealing with energy.

en-er-gize *v.* To bring or put forth energy.

en-er-gy *n.*, *pl.* **-gies** Capacity or tendency for working or acting; vigor; strength; vitality of expression. *Phys.* The capacity for doing work; usable heat or electric power.

en-er-vate *v.* To deprive of vitality or strength; to weaken. **enervation** *n.*

en-fant ter-ri-ble *n.* A person who has unconventional actions and causes embarrassment.

en-fee-ble *v.* To weaken; to make feeble. **enfeeblement** *n.*

en-fet-ter *v.* To tie up in fetters.

en-fi-lade *n.* An arrangement of things where they are parallel and opposite such as with rooms.

en-fleu-rage *n.* The process to extract perfumes for flowers.

en-fold *v.* To enclose; to wrap in layers; to embrace.

en-force *v.* To compel obedience; impose by force or firmness. **enforceable** *adj.*, **enforcement**, **enforcer** *n.*

en-fran-chise *v.* To grant with civil rights, as the right to vote; to give a franchise to. **enfranchisement** *n.*

eng *abbr.* Engineer.

Eng *abbr.* English.

en-gage *v.* To employ or hire; to secure or bind, as by a contract; to pledge oneself, especially to marry; to undertake conflict; to participate. *Mech.* To interlock.

en-gaged *adj.* To be involved in activity.

en-gage-ment *n.* The state of being engaged.

en-gag-ing *adj.* To draw the attention of others.

en-gen-der *v.* To give rise to; to exist; to cause.

en-glid *v.* To make something bright with light.

en-gine *n.* A machine which converts energy into mechanical motion; a mechanical instrument; a locomotive.

en-gined *adj.* To have an engine.

en-gi-neer *n.* A person who works in the field of engineering.

Eng-land *n.* Great Britian, also a part of the United Kingdom.

Eng-lish *adj.* Of, relating to, or characteristic of England, its people, language, and customs. *n.* The English language; the language of the United States and other countries that are or were formerly under English control. **Englishman, Englishwoman** *n.*

English Channel *n.* A section of the Atlantic Ocean which separates England from France.

en-gorge *v.* To swallow greedily. *Pathol.* To fill an artery with blood. **-ment** *n.*

en-graft *v., Bot.* To join or fasten, as if by grafting.

en-grave *v.* To carve or etch into a surface; to carve, cut, or etch into a stone, metal, or wood for printing; to print from plates made by such a process.

en-grav-ing *n.* The act or technique of one that engraves; the impression printed from an engraved plate.

en-gross *v.* To occupy the complete attention of; to copy or write in a large, clear hand. **engrossingly** *adv.*

en-gulf *v.* To enclose completely; to submerge; to swallow.

en-hance *v.* To make greater; to raise to a higher degree. **enhancement** *n.*

e-nig-ma *n.* One that baffles; anything puzzling; a riddle.

en-jamb-ment *or* **en-jambe-ment** *n.* Construction of a sentence from one line of a poem to the next, allowing related words to fall on different lines.

en-join *v.* To command to do something; to prohibit, especially by legal action.

en-joy *v.* To feel joy or find pleasure in; to have the use or possession of. **enjoyable** *adj.*, **-ably** *adv.*, **enjoyment** *n.*

en-large *v.* To make larger; to speak or write in greater detail. **enlargement, enlarger** *n.*

en-light-en *v.* To give a broadening or revealing knowledge; to give spiritual guidance or light to. **enlightenment** *n.*

en-list *v.* To secure the help or active aid of. *Milit.* To sign up for service with the armed forces. **enlistment** *n.*

en-liv-en *v.* To make livelier, cheerful or vigorous. **enlivener** *n.*

en masse *adv., Fr.* All together; grouped.

en-mesh *v.* To catch in a net; to entangle.

en-mi-ty *n., pl.* **-ties** Deep hatred; hostility.

en-no-ble *v.* To make noble or honorable in quality or nature; to confer the rank of nobility. **ennoblement** *n.*

en-nui *n.* Boredom; weariness.

e-nor-mi-ty *n., pl.* **-ties** Excessive wickedness; an outrageous offense or crime.

e-nor-mous *adj.* Very great in size or degree. **-ly** *adv.*, **enormousness** *n.*

e-nough *adj.* Adequate to satisfy demands or needs. *adv.* To a satisfactory degree.

en-quire *v.* Variation of inquire.

en-rage *v.* To put or throw into a rage.

en-rap-ture *v.* To enter into a state of rapture; to delight.

en-rich *v.* To make rich or richer; to make more productive.

en-roll *or* **en-rol** *v.* To enter or write a name on a roll, register, or record; to place one's name on a roll, register, or record. **enrollment** *n.*

en-sconce *v.* To settle securely; to shelter.

en-sem-ble *n.* A group of complementary parts that are in harmony; a coordinated outfit of clothing; a group of people performing together; music for two or more performers.

en-shrine *v.* To place in a shrine; to hold sacred. **enshrinement** *n.*

en-shroud *v.* To cover with a shroud.

en-sign *n.* An identifying flag or banner, as one displayed on a ship or aircraft. *Milit.* A commissioned officer of the lowest rank in the U.S. Navy or Coast Guard.

en-si-lage *n.* The process of storing and preserving green fodder in a silo; fodder that has been stored. **ensile** *v.*

en-slave *v.* To make a slave of; to put in bondage. **enslavement** *n.*

en-snare *v.* To catch; to trap.

en-sue *v.* To follow as a consequence.

en-sure *v.* To make certain of.

en-tail *v.* To have as a necessary accompaniment or result; to restrict the inheritance of property to a certain line of heirs. **entailment** *n.*

en-tan-gle *v.* To tangle; to complicate; to confuse. **entanglement** *n.*

en-tente *n., Fr.* A mutual agreement between governments for cooperative action; the parties to an entente.

en-ter *v.* To go or come into; to penetrate; to begin; to become a member of or participant in; in law, to make a record of.

en-ter-prise *n.* A large or risky undertaking; a business organization; boldness and energy in practical affairs.

en-ter-tain *v.* To harbor or give heed to; to accommodate; receive as a guest; to amuse. **entertainer, entertainment** *n.*

en-thrall *v.* To fascinate; to captivate. **enthrallment** *n.*

en-throne *v.* To place on a throne.

en-thu-si-asm *n.* Intense feeling for a cause; eagerness. **enthusiast** *n.*, **enthusiastic** *adj.*, **enthusiastically** *adv.*

en-tice *v.* To attract by arousing desire. **enticer, enticement** *n.*

en-tire *adj.* Having no part left out; whole; complete. **entirely** *adv.*

en-ti-tle *v.* To give a name to; to furnish with a right. **entitlement** *n.*

en-ti-ty *n., pl.* **-ties** The fact of real existence; something that exists alone.

en-tomb *v.* To place in a tomb. **-ment** *n.*

en-to-mol-o-gy *n.* Study of insects. **entomologist** *n.*, **entomologic, -ical** *adj.*

en-trails *pl.*, *n.* Internal organs of man or animals.

en-trance *n.* The act of entering; the means or place of entry; the first appearance of an actor in a play.

en-trance *v.* To fascinate; enchant. **entrancement** *n.*, **entrancingly** *adv.*

en-trap *v.* To catch in a trap. **-ment** *n.*

en-treat *v.* To make an earnest request of or for.

en-trench *v.* To dig a trench, as for defense; to fix or sit firmly. **-ment** *n.*

en-tre-pre-neur *n.*, *Fr.* A person who launches or manages a business venture. **entrepreneurial** *adj.*

en-trust *v.* To transfer to another for care or performance; to give as a trust or responsibility.

en-try *n.*, *pl.* **-tries** An opening or place for entering; an item entered in a book, list, or register.

en-twine *v.* To twine about or together.

e-nu-mer-ate *v.* To count off one by one. **enumeration, enumerator** *n.*

e-nun-ci-ate *v.* To pronounce with clarity; to announce; proclaim. **-ion** *n.*

en-ve-lope *n.* Something that covers or encloses; a paper case, especially for a letter, having a flap for sealing. *v.* To completely enclose.

en-ven-om *v.* To make poisonous; to embitter.

en-vi-a-ble *adj.* Highly desirable. **-ly** *adv.*

en-vi-ron-ment *n.* Surroundings; the combination of external conditions which affect the development and existence of an individual, group, or organism. **environmental** *adj.*, **-ally** *adv.*

en-vi-ron-men-tal-ist *n.* A person who seeks to preserve the natural environment.

en-vi-rons *pl.*, *n.* A surrounding region; a place; outskirts, especially of a city.

en-vis-age *v.* To have or form a mental image of; to visualize.

en-voy *n.* A messenger or agent; a diplomatic representative who is dispatched on a special mission.

en-vy *n.*, *pl.* **-vies** A feeling of discontent or resentment for someone else's possessions or advantages; any object of envy. *v.* To feel envy because of or toward. **envious** *adj.*

en-zyme *n.*, *Biochem.* Proteins produced by living organisms that function as biochemical catalysts. **enzymatic** *adj.*

Eo-cene *adj.* Pertaining to the epoch of Tertiary which is between the Oligocene and the Paleocene time periods.

eo-hip-pus *n.* A type of small primitive horse which had four toes and from the Lower Eocene time period.

e-o-li-an *adj.*, *Geol.* Caused by or transmitted by the wind.

eo-lith *n.* A kind of flint which is very crudely chipped.

Eo-lith-ic *adj.* To be pertaining to the early time period of the Stone Age.

e-on *n.* An indefinite period of time.

eo-sin *n.* A type of red dye that is obtained with the action of bromine on flourescein.

eo-sin-o-phil *n.* A type of leukocyte which has cytoplasmic inclusions.

eo-sin-o-phil-ia *n.* The abnormal increase of the number of eosinophils of the blood and may be caused by an allergic state or infection.

eo-sin-o-phil-ic *adj.* To be pertaining to eosinophilia.

EP *abbr.* Estimated position.

e-pact *n.* A period of time which has been added to harmonize the lunar with the solar calendar.

ep-ar-chy *n.* The diocese of the Eastern church.

ep-au-let *or* **ep-au-lette** *n.* A shoulder ornament, as on a military uniform.

ep-ei-rog-e-ny *n.* A deformation in the crust of the earth which causes the broader features of relief to form.

e-pen-the-sis *n.* An insertion of a sound into the body of a word.

e-pergne *n.* An ornamental centerpiece for holding flowers or fruit, used on a dinner table.

ep-ex-e-ge-sis *n.* The additional explanatory matter.

e-phah *n.* The ancient Hebrew unit of dry measure which is equal to a little over a bushel.

e-phe-bus *n.* A young person of Greece in the ancient times.

e-phe-dra *n.* A type of desert shrubs with leaves that are reduced to scales and its nodes.

e-phed-rine *n.*, *Chem.* A white, odorless alkaloid used to relieve nasal congestion.

e-phem-er-al *adj.* Lasting a very short time. **ephemerally** *adv.*

e-phem-er-al-i-ty *n.* The state of being ephemeral.

e-phem-er-is *n.* A statement of the positions of a celestial body at regular intervals.

eph-od *n.* A type of apron which was worn in the rites of the ancient Hebrew times.

eph-or *n.* A Spartan magistrates who had power over the king.

epi- *prefix* Attached to; upon.

ep-i-blast *n.* The layer which is the outside of the blastoderm.

e-pib-o-ly *n.* The act of one part growing about another part. **epibolic** *adj.*

ep-ic *n.* A long narrative poem celebrating the adventures and achievements of a hero. **epic** *adj.*

ep-i-ca-lyx *n.* A involucre which resembles the calyx.

ep-i-can-thic fold *n.* A fold of the upper eyelid skin over the inner angle of the eye.

ep-i-car-di-um *n.* The visceral part of the heart's pericardium.

ep-ic dra-ma *n.* A drama of the twentieth century that provokes critical thought.

ep-i-cene *adj.* To have the characteristics that are typical of the other sex.

ep-i-cen-ter *n.* The part of the earth's surface directly above the focus of an earthquake.

ep-i-chlo-ro-hy-drin *n.* A toxic liquid that has a chloroform odor.

ep-i-con-ti-nen-tal *adj.* To be located on a continent.

ep-ic thea-ter *n.* The theater where an epic drama may be seen.

ep-i-cure *n.* One having refined tastes, especially in food and wine.

ep-i-cur-ism *n.* The taste of an epicure.

ep-i-cy-cle *n.* The path or circle in which a plant will move.

ep-i-cy-clic train *n.* A type of train with gear wheels.

ep-i-dem-ic *adj.* Breaking out suddenly and affecting many individuals at the same time in a particular area, especially true of a contagious disease; anything that is temporarily widespread, as a fad. **epidemicity,** **epidemic** *n.* **epidemically** *adv.*

ep-i-den-drum *n.* A member of the genus that contains the tropical American orchids.

ep-i-der-mis *n., Anat.*

The outer, nonvascular layer of the skin. **epidermal** *adj.*

e-pi-der-moid *adj.* To resemble the epidermal cells.

e-pi-dia-scope *n.* Projector which is used for things which are opaque.

ep-i-did-y-mis *n.* The convoluted efferent tubes in the back of the testis.

ep-i-dote *n.* A mineral which occurs in grains and is sometimes used as a gem.

ep-i-du-ral *adj.* To be outside the dura mater.

ep-i-fau-na *n.* The benthic fauna which lives on the sea floor.

e-pi-gas-tric *adj.* Being over the stomach.

ep-i-ge-al *adj.* To be growing above the surface of the ground.

ep-i-ge-net-ic *adj.* To be formed after the laying of rock.

ep-i-glot-tis *n., Anat.* The leaf-shaped, elastic cartilage at the base of the tongue that covers the windpipe during the act of swallowing.

ep-i-gone *n.* A follower. **epigonism** *n.*

ep-i-gram *n.* A clever, brief, pointed remark or observation; a terse, witty poem or saying. **epigrammatic** *adj.*

ep-i-gram-ma-tize *v.* To make or create an epigram.

ep-i-graph *n.* An inscription on a tomb, monument, etc.; a motto or quotation placed at the beginning of a literary work.

e-pig-ra-phy *n.* The study and interpretation of inscriptions. **epigrapher** *n.*

e-pig-y-nous *adj.* Being adnate to the ovary surface and appearing to grow from the top.

ep-i-la-tion *n.* A removal of hair.

ep-i-lep-sy *n., Pathol.* A nervous disorder marked by attacks of unconsciousness with or without convulsions. **epileptic** *n. & adj.*

ep-i-lep-ti-form *adj.* To be resembling epilepsy.

ep-i-lep-to-gen-ic *adj.* Tending to be able to induce epilepsy.

ep-i-lep-toid *adj.* To be showing symptoms of epilepsy.

ep-i-logue *or* **ep-i-log** *n.* A short speech given by an actor to the audience at the end of a play; an appended chapter placed at the end of a novel or book, etc.

e-pi-my-si-um *n.* The connective tissue sheath of a muscle.

e-pi-nas-ty *n.* A movement where the leaf of a plant is bent down and outward.

ep-i-neph-rine *or* **ep-i-neph-rin** *n., Biochem.* A hormone secreted by the adrenal medulla of the adrenal glands that raises the blood pressure and quickens the pulse, used in synthesized form as a cardiovascular stimulant.

e-pi-neu-ri-um *n.* The connective sheath of a nerve trunk.

ep-i-phan-ic *adj.* To have the character of an epiphany.

e-piph-a-ny *n.* The Christian festival held on January 6th, celebrating the manifestation of Christ to the Gentiles as represented by the Magi; also known as the Twelfth Day.

ep-i-phe-nom-e-nal *adj.* To be pertaining to an epiphenumenon.

e-piph-y-se-al *adj.* To be pertaining to an epiphysis.

ep-i-phyte *n., Bot.* A plant that receives its nourishment from the air and rain while growing on another plant, as an orchid, moss, or lichen. **epiphytic** *adj.*

ep-i-scia *n.* A member of the genus of tropical American herbs having hairy foliage.

e-pis-co-pa-cy *n., pl.* **-cies** The government of a church by bishops; an episcopate.

e-pis-co-pal *adj.* Pertaining to or governed by bishops.

E-pis-co-pa-lian *n.* A member of the Protestant Episcopal Church.

e-pis-co-pate *n.* The term, rank, or position of a bishop; bishops as a group.

ep-i-scope *n.* The projector which is used for items that are opaque.

ep-i-sode *n.* A section of a poem, novel, etc., that is complete in itself; an occurrence; an incident. **episodic** *adj.*

ep-i-some *n.* The gene that can replicate autonomously in the bacterial cytoplasm.

ep-i-ster-num *n.* An anterior part of the sternum.

e-pis-tle *n.* A formal letter. **Epistle** One of the letters in the New Testament.

e-pis-tle side *n.* The right side of an altar as it is faced.

ep·i·taph *n.* An inscription, as on a tomb or gravestone, in memory of a deceased person. **epitaphic** *adj.*

e·pit·a·sis *n.* The portion of a play that develops the main action and leads it to a catastrophe.

ep·i·tha·la·mi·um *n.* A song in the honor of the groom and of the bride.

ep·i·the·li·o·ma *n.* A tumor either malignant or benign that is derived from epithelial tissue.

ep·i·the·li·um *n.*, *pl.* **-liums** *or* **-lia** *Biol.* The thin, membranous tissue consisting of one or more layers of cells, forming the covering of the outer bodily surface and most of the internal surfaces and organs.
epithelial, epithelioid *adj.*

ep·i·the·lize *v.* To convert to epithelium.

ep·i·thet *n.* A term, word, or phrase used to characterize a person or thing; an abusive phrase or word.

e·pit·o·me *n.* A concise summary, as of a book; an extreme or typical example.

e·pit·o·mize *v.* To be a perfect example.

e·pi·zo·ic *adj.* To be livings upon the body of an animal.

e·pi·zo·ot·ic *adj.* Pertaining to a disease which will effect a group of animals of the same kind. **epizootically** *adv.*

ep·och *n.* A point in time marking the beginning of a new era. **epochal** *adj.*

ep·ode *n.* Type of lyric poem.

ep·onym *n.* The one that something is named for. **eponymic** *adj.*

ep·o·pee *n.* A type of epic poem.

ep·ox·ide *n.* A kind of epoxy compound.

ep·ox·i·dize *v.* To change something into an epoxide.

ep·ox·y *n.*, *pl.* **-ies** *Chem.* A durable, corrosion-resistant resin used especially in surface glues and coatings.

ep·si·lon *n.* The fifth letter of the Greek alphabet.

Ep·som salts *pl.*, *n.* A hydrated magnesium sulfate, used as a purge or to reduce inflammation.

eq *abbr.* Equation.

eq·ua·ble *adj.* Not changing or varying; free from extremes; evenly proportioned; uniform; not easily upset.
equableness, equability *n.*, **equably** *adv.*

e·qual *adj.* Of the same measurement, quantity, or value as another; having the same privileges or rights.

e·qualed *v.* To be equal to another.

e·qual·i·ty *n.* The state of being equal.

e·qual·ize *v.* To become or make equal or uniform. **equalization, -er** *n.*

e·qual·ly *adv.* Doing something in an equal manner or method.

equal opportunity employer *n.* An employer who does not discriminate on the basis of age, race, sex, religion, etc.

e·qual sign *n.* The sign in math, ($=$), which denotes equality in an equation or etc.

e·qua·nim·i·ty *n.* Composure.

e·quate *v.* To consider or make equal.

e·qua·tion *n.* The act or process of being equal; a mathematical statement expressing the equality of two quantities, usually shown as ($=$).

e·qua·tion·al *adj.* To be involving an equation. **equationally** *adj.*

e·qua·tor *n.* The great imaginary circle around the earth; a line lying in a plane perpendicular to the earth's polar axis. **equatorial** *adj.*

e·qua·tor·i·al plane *n.* The plane in a cell which is perpendicular to a spindle of a cell and between the pole when is it dividing.

e·qua·tor·ward *adj.* To be moving toward the equator of the earth.

eq·uer·ry *n.*, *pl.* **-ries** The officer in charge of the horses of royalty; the personal attendant to a member of the British royal family.

e·ques·tri·an *adj.* Pertaining or relating to horsemanship. *n.* The person who rides or performs on a horse.

e·ques·tri·enne *n.* A woman who rides a horse.

e·qui·an·gu·lar *adj.*, *Geom.* Having all angles equal.

e·qui·ca·lor·ic *adj.* Being capable to yield equal amounts of energy that is required in the body.

e·qui·dis·tant *adj.* Having equal distances. **equidistance** *n.*, **-ly** *adj.*

e·qui·lat·er·al *adj.* Having all sides equal. **equilateral** *adj.*

e·qui·lat·er·al hy·per·bo·la *n.* A type of hyperbola that has the asymptotes and right angles.

e·quil·i·brate *v.* To keep something in equilibrium. **equilibrator** *n.*

e·qui·li·brist *n.* A person who can balance himself in positions which are unnatural. **equilibristic** *adj.*

e·qui·lib·ri·um *n.*, *pl.* **-ums** *Phys.* The state of balance between two opposing forces or influences; any state of compromise, adjustment, or balance.

e·qui·mol·al *adj.* To have an equal concentration of moles.

e·qui·mo·lar *adj.* Pertaining to an equal amount or number of moles.

e·quine *adj.* Pertaining to or like a horse.

e·qui·nox *n.* Either of the two times a year when the sun crosses the celestial equator and the days and nights are equal in time. **equinoctial** *adj.*

e·quip *v.* To furnish or fit with whatever is needed for any undertaking or purpose; to dress for a certain purpose or reason.

eq·ui·page *n.* A carriage that is equipped with horses and attendants.

e·quip·ment *n.* The state or act of being equipped; the material one is provided with for a special purpose.

e·qui·poise *n.* A state of balance.

e·qui·pol·lence *n.* The state of being equipollent.

e·qui·pol·lent *adj.* To have the same effect. **equipollently** *adv.*, **equipollent** *n.*

e·qui·pon·der·ant *adj.* To be balanced equally.

e·qui·pon·der·ate *v.* To make things equal in their weights.

e·qui·po·tent *adj.* To have equal effects

for development of something.

e-qui-prob-a-ble adj. To have the same degree of mathematical probability.

eq-ui-se-tum n. A type of perennial plant which can spread by creeping rhizomes such as the scouring rush.

eq-ui-ta-ble adj., pl. -ties Being impartial in treatment or judgment. **equitableness** n., **equitably** adv.

eq-ui-tant adj. To be overlapping one another at the base such as the iris.

eq-ui-ta-tion n. The art or act of horse riding.

eq-ui-ty n., pl. -ties Fairness or impartiality; the value of property beyond a mortgage or liability; in law, justice based on the concepts of fairness and ethics.

e-quiv-a-lent adj. Being equal or virtually equal, in effect or meaning. -ence, **equivalency, equivalent** n., -ly adv.

e-quiv-o-cal adj. Ambiguous; questionable. **equivocally** adv., -ness n.

e-quiv-o-cate v. To use intentionally evasive or vague language. **equivocation, equivocator** n.

e-qui-voque n. A double meaning.

-er n., suff. A thing or person that performs the action of the root verb; a person concerned with a trade or profession, as a banker, teacher, etc.; one who lives in or comes from a certain area, as a northerner, midwesterner, etc.; used to form the comparative usage degree of adverbs and adjectives.

e-ra n. An extended period of time that is reckoned from a specific date or point in the past and used as the basis of a chronology.

e-rad-i-cate v. To destroy utterly; to remove by the roots. **eradicator, -ion** n., **eradicable** adj.

e-rase v. To remove something written. Slang To kill. **erasable** adj., **eraser, erasure** n.

er-bi-um n., Chem. A soft, metallic, silvery, rare-earth element, symbolized by Er.

ere prep., Poet. Prior to; before.

e-rect adj. In a vertical position; standing up straight. v. To construct; build. Physiol. The state of erectile tissue, as through an influx of blood. **erectly** adv., -ness, -or, **erection** n.

ere-long adv., Archaic Before long.

er-e-mite n. A hermit.

erg n., Phys. A unit of work or energy.

er-go conj. & adv. Consequently; therefore.

er-gos-ter-ol n., Biochem. A steroid alcohol synthesized by yeast from sugars, converted under ultraviolet radiation to vitamin D.

er-got n. The disease of rye and other cereal plants; a drug used to contract involuntary muscles and to control hemorrhage.

er-got-ism n. The toxic condition that is produced by eating grain products or grasses that have been infected with ergot fungus.

E-rie n. One of America's five Great Lakes.

er-mine n.

A weasel whose fur changes from brown to white depending on the season.

e-rode v. To wear away gradually by constant friction; to corrode; to eat away.

e-rog-e-nous adj. Responsive to sexual stimulation.

e-ro-sion n. The state or process of being eroded. **erosional** adj.

e-ro-sive adj. Eroding or tending to erode. **erosiveness** n.

e-rot-ic adj. Pertaining to or promoting sexual desire. -ally adv., **eroticism** n.

err v. To make a mistake; to sin.

er-rand n. A short trip to carry a message or to perform a specified task, usually for someone else.

er-rant adj. Wandering or traveling about in search of adventure; straying from what is proper or customary.

er-rat-ic adj. Lacking a fixed course. Med. Irregular; inconsistent. -ally adv.

er-ro-ne-ous adj. To have or contain an error. **erroneously** adv., -ness n.

er-ror n. Something said, believed, or done incorrectly; a mistake; the state of being wrong or mistaken; in baseball, a misplay by a team member who is not batting.

er-satz adj. A substitute that is usually inferior; artificial.

erst-while adj., Archaic Former.

e-ruct v. To belch. **eructation** n.

er-u-dite adj. Scholarly.

er-u-di-tion n. Great learning.

e-rupt v. To burst forth violently and suddenly; to explode with steam, lava, etc., as a volcano or geyser; to break out in a skin rash or pimples.

-ery n., suff. A place of business; a business, or a place where something is performed or done: bakery; the collection of things; practice or act of something; the qualities or characteristics of something; slavery.

er-y-sip-e-las n. An acute, inflammatory, and very uncomfortable skin disease resulting from streptococcus.

e-ryth-ro-cyte n. A disk-shaped blood cell that contains hemoglobin and is responsible for the red color of blood.

es-ca-late v. To intensify, increase, or enlarge. **escalation** n.

es-ca-la-tor n. A moving stairway with steps attached to an endless belt.

es-cal-lop n. & v. Variation of scallop.

es-ca-pade n. Reckless or playful behavior; a prankish trick.

es-cape v. To break free from capture, confinement, restraint, etc.; to fade from the memory; to enjoy temporary freedom from unpleasant realities. **escape, escapee, escaper** n.

es-cape-ment n., Mech. A device used in timepieces to control the movement of the wheel and supply energy impulses to a pendulum or balance; a typewriter mechanism that controls the horizontal movement of the carriage.

escape velocity n., Phys. The minimum velocity that a rocket or anybody must attain to escape or overcome the gravitational field.

escape wheel n., Mech. The rotating notched wheel in an escapement.

es-cap-ism n. An escape from unpleasant realities through daydreams or other mental diversions. escapist n. & adj.

es-ca-role n. Endive leaves used for salads.

es-carp-ment n. A steep slope or drop; a long cliff formed by erosion.

-escense n., suff. To give off light in a certain way, as florescence.

-escent adj., suff. To give off light in a special way, as phosphorescent; beginning to be.

es-chew v. To shun or avoid. eschewal n.

es-cort n. A group or individual person accompanying another so as to give protection or guidance; a male who accompanies a female in public.

es-cri-toire n. A writing desk.

es-crow n. In law, a written deed, contract, or money placed in the custody of a third party until specified conditions are met.

es-cu-do n., pl. -dos The monetary unit of Portugal.

es-cutch-eon n. A shield-shaped surface with an emblem bearing a coat of arms; a protective plate, as for a keyhole.

-ese n. & adj., suff. An inhabitant or native of; in the language or style of.

Es-ki-mo n., pl. -mo or -mos One of a Mongoloid people living in the Arctic.

Eskimo dog n. A large dog of a sturdy, broad-chested breed used to draw sleds.

e-soph-a-gus n., pl. -gi Anat. The muscular, membranous tube through which food passes on the way from the mouth to the stomach. esophageal adj.

es-o-ter-ic adj. Confidential; kept secret; understood or meant for only a particular and often very small group.

ESP abbr. Extrasensory perception.

esp abbr. Especially.

es-pa-drille n. A shoe with a canvas upper and a flexible sole.

es-pal-ier n. A flat framework used to train shrubs to grow a particular way.

es-pe-cial adj. Having a very special place; apart or above others; exceptional. especially adv.

Es-pe-ran-to n. An artificial language with a vocabulary based on words in many European languages.

es-pi-o-nage n. The act or practice of spying to obtain secret intelligence.

es-pla-nade n. A flat, open stretch of land along a shoreline.

es-pou-sal n. Support or adoption, as of a cause; a wedding.

es-pouse v. To make something one's own; to take as a spouse; to marry; to give in marriage.

es-pres-so n., pl. -sos A strong coffee brewed by steam pressure from darkly-roasted beans.

es-prit n. Spirit; wit; mental liveliness.

es-prit de corps n., Fr. A group's spirit of enthusiasm and devotion to the common goals of the group.

es-py v. To catch a quick view or sight of.

Esq abbr. Esquire.

-esque adj., suff. Resembling.

es-quire n. The title of courtesy or respect; sometimes written as Esq. behind a man's last name.

-ess n., suff. Female.

es-say n. A short composition that deals with a single topic and expresses the author's viewpoint on a subject; an effort or attempt. essayer, essayist n., essay v.

es-sence n. The real nature in which something consists; the most important element; an immaterial spirit; being.

Es-sene n. A member of an ascetic Jewish sect of ancient Palestine.

es-sen-tial adj. Necessary; indispensable; containing, of, or being an essence. essential, essentiality, essentialness n., essentially adv.

est abbr. Established; estimate.

EST abbr. Eastern Standard Time.

-est adj. & adv., suff. Used to form the superlative degree of adverbs and adjectives.

es-tab-lish v. To make permanent, stable, or secure; to install; to create or find; to cause to be accepted or recognized; to prove.

es-tab-lish-ment n. The state of being established; a place of business or residence; those collectively who occupy positions of influence and status in a society.

es-tate n. A usually large or extensive piece of land containing a large house; in law, the nature, degree, and extent of ownership or use of property.

es-teem v. To regard with respect.

es-ter n., Chem. Any of a class of organic compounds formed by the reaction of an acid with an alcohol.

Esther n. In the Old Testament, the Jewish queen and wife of King Ahasuerus of Persia, who saved her people from massacre.

es-thet-ic adj. Variation of aesthetic.

es-ti-ma-ble adj. Worthy of respect or admiration. -ness n., estimably adv.

es-ti-mate v. To form or give an approximate opinion or calculation. n. A preliminary opinion or statement of the approximate cost for certain work.

es-ti-val adj. Pertaining to or of summer.

es-ti-vate v. To pass the summer in a state of dormancy.

Es-to-ni-a n. A former country located in western Europe, now a part of the U.S.S.R.

es-trange v. To arouse hated or indifference where there had been love and caring; to disassociate or remove oneself. **estrangement** *n.*

es-tro-gen *n.*, *Biochem.* Any of various steroid hormones that regulate female reproductive functions and secondary sex characteristics. **estrogenic** *adj.*

es-tu-ar-y *n.*, *pl.* **-ies** The wide mouth of a river where the current meets the sea and is influenced by tides.

ET *abbr.* Eastern Time; extra terrestrial.

et al *abbr.* And others.

etc *abbr.* And so forth.

etch *v.* To engrave or cut into the surface by the action of acid; to sketch or outline by scratching lines with a pointed instrument. **etcher** *n.*

etch-ing *n.* The process of engraving in which lines are scratched with a sharp instrument on a plate covered with wax or other coating after which the exposed parts are subjected to the corrosive action of an acid; a picture or impression made from an etched plate.

e-ter-nal *adj.* Existing without beginning or end; unending; meant to last indefinitely. **eternal, eternality, eternalness** *n.*, **eternally** *adv.*

e-ter-ni-ty *n.*, *pl.* **-ties** Existence without beginning or end; forever; the immeasurable extent of time; the endless time after a person dies.

eth-ane *n.*, *Chem.* An odorless, colorless, gaseous hydrocarbon from the methane series that is contained in crude petroleum and in illuminating gas.

eth-a-nol *n.*, *Chem.* The alcohol obtained after the distillation of certain fermented sugars or starches; the intoxicant in liquors, wines, and beers; alcohol.

e-ther *n.*, *Chem.* A highly flammable liquid compound with a characteristic odor, used as a solvent and an anesthetic; the clear upper regions of space.

e-the-re-al *adj.* Very airy and light; highly refined; delicate; heavenly.

eth-ic *n.*, *pl.* **-ics** The system of moral values; the principle of right or good conduct.

eth-i-cal *adj.* Relating to or of ethics; conforming to right principles of conduct as accepted by a specific profession, as medicine. **ethically** *adv.*

eth-nic *adj.* Relating to or of a national, cultural, or racial group. **ethnicity** *n.*

eth-nog-ra-phy *n.*, *pl.* **-phies** The branch of anthropology dealing with the classification and description of primitive human cultures.

eth-nol-o-gy *n.*, *pl.* **-gies** The branch of anthropology that is concerned with the study of ethnic and racial groups, their cultures, origins, and distribution.

eth-yl *n.*, *Chem.* An organic radical occurring in ether and alcohol; a univalent hydrocarbon radical; any gasoline that is treated with tetraethyl lead to reduce engine knock. **-ic** *adj.*

eth-yl-ene *n.*, *Chem.* A colorless, flammable gas refined from natural gas and petroleum and used as a fuel.

ethylene glycol *n.*, *Chem.* A colorless, syrupy alcohol used as an antifreeze, solvent, and lubricant.

ethyl ether *n.*, *Chem.* Ether.

e-ti-ol-o-gy *n.* The science and study of causes or origins. *Med.* The theory of the cause of a particular disease. **etiologic, etiological** *adj.*, **etiologically** *adv.*, **etiologist** *n.*

et-i-quette *n.* The prescribed rules, forms and practices, established for behavior in polite society or in official or professional life.

-ette *n.*, *suff.* Small; female.

et-y-mol-o-gy *n.*, *pl.* **-gies** The history of a word as shown by breaking it down into basic parts, tracing it back to the earliest known form, and indicating its changes in form and meaning; the branch of linguistics that deals with etymologies. **etymological** *adj.*, **-ist** *n.*

et-y-mon *n.*, *pl.* **-mons** or **-ma** The earlier form of a word in the same language or in the ancestral language.

eu-ca-lyp-tus *n.*, *pl.* **-tuses** or **-ti** A large, native Australian tree with very aromatic leaves that yield an oil used medicinally.

Eu-cha-rist *n.* The Christian sacrament of Communion in which bread and wine are consecrated and received in the remembrance of the passion and death of Christ. **Eucharistic** *adj.*

eu-chre *n.* A card game for two to four players played with 32 cards in which the winning side must take three of five tricks. *Informal* To trick or cheat.

eu-gen-ics *n.* The science of improving the physical and mental qualities of human beings through genetics. **eugenic** *adj.*, **eugenicist** *n.*

eu-lo-gize *v.* To write or deliver a eulogy for. **eulogist, eulogizer** *n.*

eu-lo-gy *n.*, *pl.* **-gies** A speech that honors a person or thing, usually delivered at a funeral; high praise. **eulogistic** *adj.*

eu-nuch *n.* A castrated man.

eu-phe-mism *n.* A substitution for a word or expression that is thought to be too strong, blunt, or painful for another person. **euphemistic** *adj.*, **euphemistically** *adv.*

eu-pho-ny *n.*, *pl.* **-nies** The agreeable sound of spoken words. **euphonious** *adj.*, **euphoniously** *adv.*

eu-pho-ri-a *n.* A very strong feeling of elation or well-being. **euphoric** *adj.*

eu-re-ka *interj.* An expression of triumph or achievement.

Eu-ro-pe-an *adj.* Derived from or related to Europe or its inhabitants; relating to a person of European descent.

eu-ro-pi-um *n.*, *Chem.* A soft, silvery-white, rare-earth element used in nuclear research, symbolized by Eu.

eu-sta-chian tube *n.*, *Anat.* The passage between the middle ear and the pharynx that equalizes the air pressure between the tympanic cavity and the atmosphere.

eu-tha-na-sia n. The act or practice of putting to death painlessly a person suffering from an incurable disease; also called mercy killing.

eu-then-ics n. The study of improving the physical and mental qualities of human beings by controlling the environmental factors. **euthenist** n.

e-vac-u-ate v. To leave a threatened area, town, building, etc.; to empty; to remove the contents. *Physiol.* To discharge or eject, as from the bowels. **evacuation, evacuator** n.

e-vac-u-ee n. A person who is evacuated from a hazardous place.

e-vade v. To baffle; to elude; to get away from by using cleverness or tricks.

e-val-u-ate v. To examine carefully; to determine the value of; to appraise. **evaluation, evaluator** n.

ev-a-nesce v. To disappear; to fade away.

ev-a-nes-cent adj. Vanishing or passing quickly; fleeting. **evanescence** n., **evanescently** adv.

e-van-gel-i-cal adj. Relating to the Christian gospel, especially the four Gospels of the New Testament; maintaining the doctrine that the Bible is the only rule of faith. **Evangelicalism** n., **evangelically** adv.

e-van-gel-ism n. The zealous preaching and spreading of the gospel.

e-van-gel-ist or **Evangelist** n. One of the four writers of the New Testament Gospels: Matthew, Mark, Luke, or John; a zealous Protestant preacher or missionary. **-ic** adj., **-ically** adv.

e-van-gel-ize v. To preach the gospel; to convert to Christianity. **-ation** n.

e-vap-o-rate v. To convert into vapor; to remove the liquid or moisture from fruit, milk, etc., so as to concentrate or dry it. **evaporative** adj., **evaporator** n.

evap-o-rat-ed milk n. A type of milk that is concentrated by evaporation.

evap-o-rite n. A type of sedimentary rock which originate by evaporation of sea water. **evaporitic** adj.

e-vasion n. The act or means of evading.

e-va-sive adj. Being intentionally vague; equivocal. **evasively** adv., **-ness** n.

eve n. The evening before a special day or holiday; the period immediately preceding some event; evening.

Eve n. The first woman created by God; the wife of Adam.

evec-tion n. The perturbation of the orbital motion of the moon that is caused due to the attraction of the sun.

e-ven adj. Having a flat, smooth, and level surface; having no irregularities; smooth; on the same line or plane; equally matched; not owing or having anything owed to one; exactly divisible by 2; opposed to odd. **to break even** *Informal* To end with neither profit or loss, as in business. **to get even** One's full measure of revenge. **evenly** adv., **evenness** n.

e-ven-fall n. The fall or the beginning of

the evening.

e-ven-hand-ed adj. Fair; impartial. **evenhandedly** adv., **evenhandedness** n.

eve-ning n. The time between sunset and bedtime.

evening dress n. Formal attire for evening.

evening primrose n. A biennial herb with conspicuous yellow flowers that open in the evening.

eve-nings adv. To be done or to occur in the evening repeatedly.

evening star n. The brightest planet visible in the western sky just after sunset, especially Venus.

e-ven-song n. An evening prayer.

e-vent n. A significant occurrence; something that takes place; the actual or possible set of circumstances; a real or contingent situation; the final outcome; one of the parts of a sports program. **eventless** adj.,

eventfully adv., **eventfulness** n.

e-vent-ful adj. To be rich in events.

e-ven-tide n. Evening.

e-ven-tu-al adj. Happening or expected to happen in due course of time.

e-ven-tu-al-i-ty n., pl. **-ties** A likely or possible occurrence; the conceivable outcome.

e-ven-tu-ate v. To result ultimately; to come out eventually.

ev-er adv. At any time; on any occasion; by any possible chance or conceivable way; at all times; throughout the entire course of time.

ev-er-bloom-ing adj. To be blooming more throughout the growing season.

Ev-er-est, Mount n. A mountain in the Himalayas, measuring 29,028 feet high.

ev-er-glade n. A tract of low, swampy land.

ev-er-green adj. A tree that has green foliage throughout the year.

ev-er-last-ing adj. Lasting or existing forever; eternal. n. One of several plants, chiefly of the aster family, whose flowers keep their form and color when dried. **everlastingly** adv., **everlastingness** n.

ev-er-more adv., *Poet.* For and at all time to come; always.

e-vert v. To turn inside out or outward.

ev-er-y adj. Without exceptions; the utmost; all possible. **every now and then** From time to time; occasionally. **every other** Each alternate. **every which way** *Informal* In every way or direction and with very little order.

ev-er-y-body pron. Every person.

ev-er-y-day adj. Happening every day; daily; suitable for ordinary days.

ev-er-y-one pron. Everybody; every person.

ev-er-y-place adv. Everywhere.

ev-er-y-thing pron. All things; whatever exists; whatever is needed, relevant, or important; the essential thing; the only thing that really matters.

ev-er-y-where adv. In, at, or to everyplace.

ev-er-y which way adv. To be in every

direction.

e-vict v. To put out or expel a tenant by legal process. **evictor, eviction** n.

e-vict-ee n. The person who is being evicted from a place of residence or business.

ev-i-dence n. Signs or facts on which a conclusion can be based. v. To indicate clearly. **in evidence** Clearly present; evident.

ev-i-dent adj. Easily understood or seen; obvious. **evidently** adv.

ev-i-den-tial adj. Pertaining to evidence.

e-vil adj. Morally bad or wrong; causing injury or any other undesirable result; marked by misfortune or distress; low in public esteem. **The Evil One** Satan.

e-vil-do-er n. A person who does evil to another. **evildoing** n.

e-vil-mind-ed adj. Obsessed with vicious or evil thoughts or intentions. **evil-mindedly** adv., **evil-mindedness** n.

e-vince v. To demonstrate or indicate clearly; to give an outward sign of having a quality or feeling.

e-vis-cer-ate v. To remove the vital part of something; to remove the entrails.

e-voke v. To call or summon forth; to draw forth or produce a reaction; to summon up the spirits by or as by incantations. **evocation** n., **evocative** adj., **evocatively** adv.

ev-o-lu-tion n. The gradual process of development or change. *Biol.* The theory that all forms of life originated by descent from earlier forms. **-ary** adj., **evolutionism, evolutionist** n.

e-volve v. To develop or change gradually. *Biol.* To be developed by evolutionary processes; to develop or work out. **evolvement** n.

ewe n.

A female sheep.

ew-er n.

A large, wide-mouthed pitcher or jug.

ex n. The letter x. *Slang* A former spouse.

ex- *pref.* Out of; former.

ex *abbr.* Example; exchange.

ex-ac-er-bate v. To make more severe or worse; to aggravate. **exacerbation** n.

ex-act adj. Perfectly complete and clear in every detail; accurate in every detail with something taken as a model; similar. v. To be extremely careful about accuracy and detail; to force unjustly for the payment of something; to insist upon as a strict right or obligation; to call for or require. **exaction, exactness** n., **exactly** adv.

ex-acting adj. Making severe demands; rigorous; involving constant attention, hard work, etc. **exactingly** adv., **exactingness** n.

ex-act-i-tude n. The quality of being exact.

ex-ag-ger-ate v. To look upon or to represent something as being greater than it really is; to make greater in intensity or size than would be normal or expected. **exaggerated, -ive** adj., **exaggeration, exaggerator** n.

ex-alt v. To raise in character, honor, rank, etc.; to praise or glorify; to increase the intensity of. **exalted** adj., **exaltedly** adv., **exalter, exaltation** n.

ex-am n., *Slang* An examination.

ex-am-i-na-tion n. A test of skill or knowledge; the act of examining or the state of being examined; medical testing and scrutiny. **-al** adj.

ex-am-ine v. To observe or inspect; to test by questions or exercises, as to fitness or qualification. **examinee, examiner** n.

ex-am-ple n. One that is representative as a sample; one worthy of imitation; an object or instance of punishment, reprimand, etc.; a previous instance or case that is identical with or similar to something that is under consideration; a problem or exercise in algebra, arithmetic, etc. **to set an example** To act in such a way as to arouse others to imitation.

ex-as-per-ate v. To make frustrated or angry; to irritate. **-ingly** adv., **-ion** n.

ex-ca-vate v. To dig a hole or cavity; to form or make a tunnel, hole, etc., by digging, scooping, or hollowing out; to remove or uncover by digging; to unearth. **excavation, excavator** n.

ex-ceed v. To surpass in quality or quantity; to go beyond the limit; to be superior. **exceeding** adj.

ex-ceed-ing-ly adv. Greater than; to an extraordinary degree or extreme.

ex-cel v. To surpass or to do better than others.

ex-cel-lence n. The state or quality of being superior or excellent; a superior trait or quality.

Ex-cel-len-cy n., pl. **-cies** An honorary title or form of address for high officials, as bishops or ambassadors.

ex-cel-lent adj. The best quality; exceptionally good. **excellently** adv.

ex-cel-si-or n. Long, firm wood shavings used in packing to protect delicate materials. adj. Upward; higher.

ex-cept prep. With the omission or exclusion of; aside from; not including; leaving out.

ex-cept-ing prep. With the exception that.

ex-cep-tion n. The act of or state of being excepted; something that is excluded from or does not conform to a general class, rule, or principle; criticism or objection.

ex-cep-tion-a-ble adj. Open to objection or exception. **exceptionability** n., **exceptionably** adv.

ex-cep-tion-al adj. Being an exception to the rule; unusual; well above average. **exceptionally** adv.

ex-cerpt n. A passage from a book, speech, etc. v. To select and cite.

ex·cess *n.* The amount or condition of going beyond what is necessary, usual, or proper; overindulgence, as in drink or food.

ex·ces·sive *adj.* Exceeding what is usual, necessary, or proper; extreme. **excessively** *adv.*, **excessiveness** *n.*

exch *abbr.* Exchange.

ex·change *v.* To give in return for something else; to trade; to return as unsatisfactory and get a replacement. *n.* The substitution of one thing for another; a place where brokers meet to buy, sell, or trade; the mutual receiving and giving of equal sums or money. **exchangeable** *adj.*

ex·cheq·uer *n.* The treasury of a nation or organization; financial resources; funds. *Slang* One's total financial resources.

Ex·cheq·uer *n.* The department of the British government that manages the public revenue.

ex·cise *n.* The indirect or internal tax on the production, consumption, or sale of a commodity, such as liquor or tobacco, that is produced, sold, and used or transported within a country.

ex·cise *v.* To remove surgically. **-ion** *n.*

ex·cit·a·ble *adj.* To be easily excited. **excitably** *adv.*, **excitability, -ness** *n.*

ex·cite *v.* To stir up strong feeling, action, or emotion; to stimulate the emotions of; to bring about; to induce. **excitation, -ment** *n.*, **-edly, -ingly** *adv.*

ex·claim *v.* To cry out abruptly; to utter suddenly, as from emotion.

ex·cla·ma·tion *n.* An abrupt or sudden forceful utterance. **exclamatory** *adj.*

exclamation point *n.* A punctuation mark (!) used after an interjection or exclamation.

ex·clude *v.* To keep out; to omit from consideration; to put out. **exclusion** *n.*

ex·clu·sive *adj.* Intended for the sole use and purpose of a single individual or group; intended for or possessed by a single source; having no duplicate; the only one; complete; undivided. **-ly** *adv.*, **exclusiveness, exclusivity** *n.*

ex·com·mu·ni·cate *v.* To deprive the right of church membership.

ex·co·ri·ate *v.* To tear the skin or wear off; to censure harshly. **excoriation** *n.*

ex·cre·ment *n.* Bodily waste, especially feces. **excremental** *adj.*

ex·cre·ta *pl., n.* Excretions from the body such as sweat, urine, etc.

ex·crete *v.* To throw off or eliminate waste matter by normal discharge from the body. **-ion** *n.*, **excretory** *adj.*

ex·cru·ci·at·ing *adj.* Intensely painful; agonizing. **excruciatingly** *adv.*

ex·cul·pate *v.* To free from wrong doing; to prove innocent of guilt. **exculpation** *n.*, **exculpatory** *adj.*

ex·cur·sion *n.* A short trip, usually made for pleasure; a trip available at a special reduced fare. *Phys.* The oscillating movement between two points; also, half of this total distance. **-ist** *n.*

ex·cur·sive *adj.* To go in one direction

and then another; rambling; digressive.

ex·cuse *v.* To ask forgiveness or pardon for oneself; to grant pardon or forgiveness; to overlook or accept; to apologize for; to justify; to allow one to leave; to release. *n.* A reason, justification, or explanation. **poor excuse** *Informal* An inferior example for something. **-able** *adj.*, **excusably** *adv.*

exec *abbr.* Executive; executor.

ex·e·cra·ble *adj.* Extremely bad; detestable; revolting. **-ness** *n.*, **-ly** *adv.*

ex·e·crate *v.* To detest; to feel or express detestation for; to abhor. **execration, execrator** *n.*

ex·e·cute *v.* To carry out; to put into effect; to validate, as by signing; to carry out what has been called for in a will; to put to death by the legal authority.

ex·e·cu·tion *n.* The act of executing a job or task; a putting to death as a result of a legal decision, as the death penalty.

ex·e·cu·tion·er *n.* A person who puts others to death; a person who carries out a legal execution.

ex·ec·u·tive *n.* A manager or administrator in an organization; the branch of the government responsible for activating or putting the laws of a country into effect and for carrying out plans or policies. **executively** *adv.*

executive Council *n.* The cabinet of a provincial government in Canada.

ex·ec·u·tor *n.* The person appointed to carry out the reading and execution of a will. **executorial** *adj.*

ex·e·ge·sis *n., pl.* **-ses** An interpretation or explanation of a text. **exegetic** *adj.*, **exegetically** *adv.*

ex·em·plar *n.* Something that serves as a worthy model or imitation; a typical example.

ex·em·pla·ry *adj.* Serving as a model; worthy of imitation; commendable.

ex·em·pli·fy *v.* To show by giving examples; to be an example of.

ex·empt *v.* To free or excuse from an obligation or duty to which others are subject. **exempt** *adj.*, **exemption** *n.*

ex·er·cise *n.* The act of performing drills; the act of training or developing oneself; something that is done to maintain or increase a skill, such as practice on the piano. **exercises** *pl.* A ceremony, etc., such as a graduation. **exercise** *v.*, **exerciser** *n.*

ex·ert *v.* To put into action, as influence or force; to put oneself through a strenuous effort. **exertion** *n.*

ex·hale *v.* To breathe out; the opposite of inhale; to breathe forth or give off, as air, vapor, or aroma.

ex·haust *v.* To make extremely tired; to drain oneself of resources, strength, etc. *n.* The escape or discharge of waste gases, working fluid, etc.; the waste gases, etc. that escape; the device through which waste gases are released or expelled. **exhaustible** *adj.*, **exhaustion** *n.*

ex-haus-tive *adj.* Tending to exhaust or that which exhausts. **exhaustively** *adv.*

ex-hib-it *v.* To display, as to put up for public view; to bring documents or evidence into a court of law. **exhibition, exhibitor** *n.*

ex-hi-bi-tion-ism *n.* The practice of deliberately drawing undue attention to oneself. **exhibitionist** *n.*

ex-hil-a-rate *v.* To elate, make cheerful, or refresh. **-ion** *n.*, **exhilarative** *adj.*

ex-hort *v.* To urge by earnest appeal or argument; to advise or recommend strongly. **exhortation** *n.*

ex-hume *v.* To dig up and remove from a grave; to disinter. **exhumation** *n.*

ex-i-gen-cy *n.*, *pl.* **-cies** The quality or state of being exigent. *usually pl.* A pressing need or necessity. **exigence** *n.*, **exigent** *adj.*

ex-ig-u-ous *adj.* Extremely small; scanty.

ex-ile *n.* The separation by necessity or choice from one's native country or home; banishment; one who has left or been driven from his or her country. *v.* To banish or expel from one's native country or home.

ex-ist *v.* To have actual being or reality; to live.

ex-is-tence *n.* The fact or state of existing, living or occurring; the manner of existing. **existent** *adj.*

ex-is-ten-tial *adj.* Based on experience; of or relating to existentialism.

ex-is-ten-tial-ism *n.* A philosophy that stresses the active role of the will rather than of reason in facing problems posed by a hostile universe.

ex-it *n.* A way or passage out; the act of going away or out; the departure from a stage, as in a play. **exit** *v.*

ex-o-bi-ol-o-gy *n.* The search for and study of extraterrestrial life. **-ist** *n.*

ex-o-dus *n.* A going forth; a departure of large numbers of people, as that of Moses and the Israelites as described in Exodus, the second book of the Old Testament.

ex officio *adj. & adv.*, *L.* By virtue of or because of office or position.

ex-og-e-nous *n.*, *Biol.* That which is derived from external causes.

ex-on-er-ate *v.* To free or clear one from accusation or blame; to relieve or free from responsibility. **exoneration** *n.*

ex-or-bi-tant *adj.* Beyond usual and proper limits, as in price or demand. **exorbitance** *n.*, **exorbitantly** *adv.*

ex-or-cise *v.* To cast out or expel an evil spirit by prayers or incantations; to free from an evil spirit. **exorciser** *n.*, **exorcism, exorcist** *n.*

ex-o-sphere *n.*, *Meteor.* The region of the earth's atmosphere starting about 400 miles up.

ex-o-ther-mic *adj.* Releasing rather than absorbing heat.

ex-ot-ic *adj.* Belonging by nature or origin to another part of the world; foreign; strangely different and fascinating. **exotically** *adv.*

exp *abbr.* Expenses; export; express.

ex-pand *v.* To increase the scope, range, volume, or size; to open up or spread out; to develop more fully in form or details. **expandable** *adj.*, **expander** *n.*

ex-panse *n.* A wide, open stretch.

ex-pan-sion *n.* The act of or state of being expanded; the amount of increase in range, size, or volume.

ex-pan-sive *adj.* Capable of expanding or inclined to expand; characterized by expansion; broad and extensive; open and generous; outgoing. **expansively** *adv.*, **expansiveness** *n.*

ex par-te *adj. & adv.* In law, giving only one side or point of view.

ex-pa-ti-ate *v.* To elaborate; to talk or write at length. **expatiation** *n.*

ex-pa-tri-ate *v.* To leave one's country and reside in another; to send into exile; to banish. **expatriate, expatriation** *n.*

ex-pect *v.* To look forward to something as probable or certain; to look for as proper, right, or necessary. *Slang* To presume or suppose.

ex-pec-tan-cy *n.*, *pl.* **-cies** The action or state of expecting; expectation; an object or amount of expectation.

ex-pec-tant *adj.* Expecting; pregnant.

ex-pec-ta-tion *n.* The state or act of expecting; something that is expected and looked forward to. **expectations** *pl.* Something expected in the future.

ex-pec-to-rant *adj.* Promoting the discharge by spitting of the mucus from the respiratory tract. *n.* Any medicine that is used to promote expectoration.

ex-pec-to-rate *v.* To spit. **expectoration** *n.*

ex-pe-di-en-cy *n.*, *pl.* **-cies** The state or quality of being expedient.

ex-pe-di-ent *adj.* Promoting narrow or selfish interests; pertaining to or prompted by interest rather than by what is right. **expediently** *adv.*

ex-pe-dite *v.* To speed up the progress or process of something; to do with quick efficiency. **expediter, expeditor** *n.*

ex-pe-di-tion *n.* A journey of some length for a definite purpose; the person or group and equipment that engage in such a journey; promptness.

ex-pe-di-tion-ar-y *adj.* Relating to or being an expedition; sent on military service abroad.

ex-pe-di-tious *adj.* Quick; speedy. **expeditiously** *adv.*, **expeditiousness** *n.*

ex-pel *v.* To drive or force out, as to dismiss from a school. **expellable** *adj.*, **expeller, expulsion** *n.*

ex-pend *v.* To consume; to pay out or use up.

ex-pend-a-ble *adj.* Available for spending. *Milit.* Equipment or supplies that can be sacrificed. **expendability** *n.*

ex-pen-di-ture *n.* An amount spent; the act or process of expending.

ex-pense *n.* The outlay or consumption of money; the amount of money required to buy or do something. **expenses** *pl.* The funds that have been allotted or spent to cover incidental costs; the charges incurred by an employee while at or pertaining to work. *Informal* The reimbursement for such charges incurred.

ex·pen·sive *adj.* Costing a lot of money; high-priced.

ex·pe·ri·ence *n.* The actual participation in something or the direct contact with; the knowledge or skill acquired from actual participation or training in an activity or event; one's total judgments or reactions based on one's past. **experience** *v.*

ex·pe·ri·enced *adj.* To be knowledgeable through actual practices, etc.

ex·per·i·ment *n.* The act or test performed to demonstrate or illustrate a truth; conducting of such operations. **experimental** *adj.*, **experimentally** *adv.*, **experimentation, experimenter** *n.*

ex·pert *n.* A person having great knowledge, experience, or skill in a certain field. *adj.* Skilled as the result of training or experience. **expertly** *adv.*, **expertness** *n.*

ex·per·tise *n.* A specialized knowledge, ability, or skill in a particular area.

ex·pi·ate *v.* To atone for; to make amends for. **expiation, -or** *n.*, **-ory** *adj.*

ex·pire *v.* To come to an end; to breathe out, as from the mouth; to exhale.

ex·plain *v.* To make understandable; to clarify; to give reasons for; to account for; to give an explanation for. **explainable, explanatory** *adj.*, **explainer, explanation** *n.*

ex·ple·tive *n.* An exclamation, often profane. *adj.* A word added merely to fill out a sentence.

ex·pli·ca·ble *adj.* Capable of explanation.

ex·pli·cate *v.* To clear up the meaning of. **-ion, explicator** *n.*, **explicative** *adj.*

ex·plic·it *adj.* Plainly expressed; specific; unreserved in expression; straightforward. **explicitly** *adv.*, **explicitness** *n.*

ex·plode *v.* To cause to burst or blow up violently with a loud noise; to increase rapidly without control; to show to be false.

ex·ploit *n.* A deed or act that is notable. *v.* To use to the best advantage of; to make use of in a selfish or unethical way. **exploitable, exploitative** *adj.*, **exploitation, exploiter** *n.*

ex·plore *v.* To examine and investigate in a systematic way; to travel through unfamiliar territory. **exploration, explorer** *n.*, **exploratory** *adj.*

ex·plo·sion *n.* A sudden, violent release of energy; the sudden, violent outbreak of personal feelings.

ex·plo·sive *adj.* Marked by or pertaining to an explosion. *n.* A chemical preparation that explodes. **explosively** *adv.*, **explosiveness** *n.*

ex·po·nent *n.* A person who represents or speaks for a cause or group; in mathematics, a number or symbol that indicates the number of times an expression is used as a factor. **exponential** *adj.*, **exponentially** *adv.*

ex·port *v.* To carry or send merchandise or raw materials to other countries for resale or trade. *n.* A commodity exported. **exportable** *adj.*, **-ation, -er** *n.*

ex·pose *v.* To lay open, as to criticism or ridicule; to lay bare and uncovered; to reveal the identity of someone; to deprive of the necessities of heat, shelter, and protection. *Photog.* To admit light to a sensitized film or plate.

ex·po·si·tion *n.* A statement of intent or meaning; a detailed presentation of subject matter; a commentary or interpretation; a large public exhibition. **expositor** *n.*, **expository** *adj.*

ex post facto *adj., L.* After the fact and retroactive.

ex·pos·tu·late *v.* To reason earnestly with someone about the inadvisability of his or her actions in an effort to correct or dissuade that person. **-ory** *adj.*, **expostulation, -or** *n.*

ex·po·sure *n.* The act or state of being exposed; an indication of which way something faces. *Photog.* The act of exposing a sensitive plate or film; the time required for the film or plate to be exposed.

ex·pound *v.* To give a detailed statement of something; to explain the meaning at length. **expounder** *n.*

ex·press *v.* To formulate in words; to verbalize; to state; to communicate through some medium other than words or signs; to squeeze or press out, as juice from fruit; to send goods, etc., by a fast or rapid means of delivery. *adj.* Explicit; precise.

ex·pres·sion *n.* Communication of opinion, thought, or feeling; the outward indication or manifestation of a condition, feeling, or quality; a particular phrase or word from a certain region of the country; a facial aspect or look that conveys a feeling; in mathematics, a symbol, sign, or set of that indicates something.

ex·pres·sion·ism *n.* An early 20th Century movement in the fine arts that emphasizes subjective expression of the artist's inner experiences rather than realistic representation. **expressionistic** *adj.*, **expressionist** *n.*

ex·pres·sive *adj.* Of or characterized by expression; serving to indicate or express; full of expression. **expressively** *adv.*, **expressiveness** *n.*

ex·press·way *n.* A multilane highway designed for rapid travel.

ex·pro·pri·ate *v.* To transfer or take property from the owner for public use; to deprive a person of property or ownership. **-ion, expropriator** *n.*

ex·pul·sion *n.* The act of expelling or the state of being expelled.

ex·punge *v.* To delete or remove; to erase. **expunger** *n.*

ex·pur·gate *v.* To remove obscene or objectionable material from a play, book, etc., before it is available to the public. **expurgation, expurgator** *n.*

ex·qui·site *adj.* Delicately or intricately beautiful in design or craftsmanship;

highly sensitive; keen or acute, as in pain or pleasure.

ex·quis·ite·ly *adv.*, **ex·quis·ite·ness** *n.*

ex·tant *adj.* Still in existence; not lost or destroyed; surviving.

ex·tem·po·ra·ne·ous *adj.* Acting or performing with little or no advance preparation; spoken with regard to content, but not memorized or read word for word. **extemporaneously** *adv.*

ex·tem·po·re *adj.* Extemporaneously.

ex·tem·po·rize *v.* To make, do, or perform with little or no advance preparation; to improvise to meet circumstances. **extemporization, -er** *n.*

ex·tend *v.* To stretch or open to full length; to make longer, broader, or wider; to continue; to prolong; to put forth or hold out, as the hand; to exert to full capacity; to offer something.

ex·tend·er *n.* A substance added to another to dilute, modify, or adulterate.

ex·ten·sion *n.* The act or state of being extended; an agreement with a creditor that allows a debtor further time to pay a debt. *Phys.* The property of matter by virtue of which it occupies space. **extensional** *adj.*

ex·ten·sive *adj.* Widespread; far-reaching; having a wide range; broad in scope. **extensively** *adv.*, **-ness** *n.*

ex·tent *n.* The degree, dimension, or limit to which anything is extended; the area over which something extends; the size.

ex·ten·u·ate *v.* To minimize the seriousness of something as a crime or fault. **extenuation** *n.*, **extenuating** *adj.*

ex·te·ri·or *adj.* Pertaining to or of the outside; the external layer.

ex·ter·mi·nate *v.* To annihilate; to destroy completely. **-ion, -or** *n.*

ex·tern *or* **externe** *n.* A person that is associated with but not officially residing in a hospital or an institution.

ex·ter·nal *adj.* For, of, or on the outside; acting from the outside; pertaining to foreign countries; outside; exterior. **externals** *pl.* Outward or superficial circumstances. **externally** *adv.*

ex·tinct *adj.* Inactive; no longer existing; extinguished. **extinction** *n.*

ex·tin·guish *v.* To put an end to; to put out; to make extinct.

extinguishable *adj.*, **extinguisher** *n.*

ex·tir·pate *v.* To pull up by the roots; to destroy wholly, completely. **-ion, extirpator** *n.*, **extirpative** *adj.*

ex·tol *also* **ex·toll** *v.* To praise highly.

extoller, extolment *n.*

ex·tort *v.* To obtain money from a person by threat, oppression, or abuse of authority. **-ion, extortionate** *adj.*

ex·tra *adj.* Over and above what is normal, required, or expected. *n.* An extra edition of a newspaper that covers news of special importance; a performer hired for a small part in a movie.

ex·tract *v.* To pull or draw out by force; to obtain in spite of resistance; to ob-

tain from a substance as by pressu or distillation; in mathematics, determine the root of a number. *n.* passage taken from a larger work; concentrated substance used in cool ing. **-able, extractible** *adj.*, **-or** *n.*

ex·trac·tion *n.* The process or act of e tracting; that which is extracted; one origin or ancestry.

ex·tra·cur·ric·u·lar *adj.* Pertaining to of activities not directly a part of th curriculum of a school or college; ou side the usual duties.

ex·tra·dite *v.* To obtain or surrender b extradition. **extraditable** *adj.*

ex·tra·di·tion *n.* The legal surrender an alleged criminal to the jurisdictio of another country, government, state for trial.

ex·tra·dos *n., pl.* **-dos** *or* **-doses** The e terior or upper curve of an arch.

ex·tra·ga·lac·tic *adj.* Coming fro beyond the galaxy; situated beyon the galaxy.

ex·tra·mar·i·tal *adj.* Adulterous.

ex·tra·mu·ral *adj.* Taking place outsid of an educational building or institu tion; involving teams from differe schools.

ex·tra·ne·ous *adj.* Coming from withou foreign; not vital or essential. **-ly** *adv.*

ex·tra·or·di·nar·y *adj.* Beyond what usual or common; remarkable.

ex·trap·o·late *v.* To infer the possibili beyond the strict evidence of a serie of events, facts, or observations; i mathematics, to infer the unknown ir formation by projecting or extendin known information. **extrapolation, extrapolator** *n.*, **extrapolative** *adj.*

ex·tra·sen·so·ry *adj.* Beyond the range c normal sensory perception.

extrasensory perception *n.* The ability t foresee something before it actuall happens; the ability to know some thing without any factual knowledge.

ex·tra·ter·res·tri·al *adj.* Occurring o originating outside the earth or its a mosphere. **extraterrestrial** *n.*

ex·tra·ter·ri·to·ri·al *adj.* Pertaining to o of extraterritoriality; situated outsid of the territorial limits.

ex·tra·ter·ri·to·ri·al·i·ty *n.* An exemptio from local legal jurisdiction, as tha extended to foreign diplomats.

ex·trav·a·gant *adj.* Overly lavish in ex penditure; wasteful; exceeding rea sonable limits; immoderate; unre strained. **extravagance** *n.*, **-ly** *adv.*

ex·trav·a·gan·za *n.* A lavish, spectacula showy entertainment.

ex·tra·ve·hic·u·lar *adj.* Occurring c done outside a vehicle, especially spacecraft in flight.

ex·treme *adj.* Greatly exceeding; goin far beyond the bounds of moderatio exceeding what is considered mode ate, usual, or reasonable; final; last; o the highest or utmost degree; one o the two ends of farthest limits of any thing; in mathematics, the first or la term of a proportion or series; a dras tic measure. **extremely** adv., **-ness** n.

ex-trem-ist n. A person who advocates or resorts to extreme measures or holds extreme views. **extremism** n.

ex-trem-i-ty n., pl. **-ties** The utmost or farthest point; the greatest degree of distress or peril; an extreme measure; an appendage or limb of the body; a hand or foot.

ex-tri-cate v. To free from hindrance, entanglement, or difficulties; to disengage. **extrication** n.

ex-trin-sic adj. Not inherent; outside the nature of something; from the outside; external. **extrinsically** adv.

ex-tro-vert or **extravert** n., Psychol. A person who is more interested in people and things outside himself than in his own private feelings and thoughts. **extroversion** n.

ex-trude v. To push or thrust out; to shape by forcing through dies under pressure; to project or protrude. **extrusion** n., **extrusive** adj.

ex-u-ber-ant adj. Full of high spirits, vitality, vigor, and joy; plentiful; abundant. **exuberance** n., **exuberantly** adv.

ex-ude v. To give off; to ooze or trickle forth, as sweat. **exudation, exudate** n.

ex-ult v. To be jubilant; to rejoice greatly. **exultant** adj., **exultation** n.

ex-ur-bi-a n. The often well-to-do residential area outside the suburbs of a large city. **exurbanite** n.

ey-as n. A type of bird which is unfledged.

eye n. An organ of sight consisting of the cornea, iris, pupil, retina, and lens; a look; gaze; the ability to judge, perceive, or discriminate. **eye of the storm** Meteor. The central area of a hurricane or cyclone. **eye of the wind** Naut. The direction from which the wind blows. **to catch one's eye** To get someone's attention. **see eye to eye** To be in complete agreement. **eye** v.

eye-ball n. The ball of the eye, enclosed by the socket and eyelids and connected at the rear to the optic nerve.

eye-bank n. A place where corneas removed from a recently-deceased person are stored for future use in restoring the sight of someone having a corneal defect.

eye-bolt n. A type of bolt which on its head is a loop.

eye-bright n. A type of herb that has opposite cut leaves.

eye-brow n. The short hairs covering the bony ridge over the eye.

eye-brow pen-cil n. A type of cosmetic pencil which is used to color the eyebrows.

eye--catch-er n. Something that is capable to attract the eye easily.

eye-cup n. A kind of cup which is oval and small and is used to cover the eye for the application of liquid into the eye.

eyed adj. To have an eye or many eyes.

eyed-ness n. A preference one has for the use of one eye over the other.

eye-ful n., pl. **-fuls** A satisfying or complete view. Slang A beautiful person.

eye-glass n. A corrective lens used to assist vision. **eyeglasses** pl. A pair of corrective lenses set in a frame.

eye-hole n. An opening to pass a hook, pin, rope, etc., through; a peephole.

eye-lash n. The stiff, curved hairs growing from the edge of the eyelids.

eye lens n. In an eyepiece, the lens which is located near the eye.

eye-let n. A small perforation or hole for a hook or cord to fit through in closing a fastening; the metal ring reinforcing an eyelet.

eye-lid n. Either of two folds of skin and muscle that open and close over an eye.

eye-lin-er n. Makeup used to highlight the outline of the eyes.

eye--open-er n. That which opens the eyes or enlightens, as a startling revelation. Slang A drink of liquor taken early in the morning.

eye-piece n. The lens or combination of lenses of an optical instrument closest to the eye.

eye-point n. The position where the eye is placed in the using of an optical instrument.

eye-pop-per n. A thing which will astonish. **eye-popping** adj.

eye-shade n. A type of visor which is used to shield the eyes from light which is strong.

eye-shot n. The range or area that one is able to see objects.

eye-sight n. The faculty or power of sight; the range of vision.

eye-sore n. Something ugly that offends the sight.

eye-spot n. The pigmented cells which cover a sensory termination; a spot of color.

eye-stalk n. A movable peduncle of the decapod crustacean that bears an eye at the tip.

eye-strain n. Fatigue or discomfort of the eyes, caused by excessive or improper use and marked by symptoms such as pain and headache.

eye-tooth n., pl. **teeth**

One of the canine teeth of the upper jaw.

eye-wash n. A medicinal wash for the eye. Slang Nonsense; bunk; meaningless or deceptive language.

eye-wink n. A glance or wink; an event or occurrence that happens in an instant.

eye-wit-ness n. A person who has seen something and can testify to it firsthand.

eyre n. An English court of medieval times.

Ezekiel n. A Hebrew prophet; a book in the Old Testament written by him.

Ezra n. Hebrew high priest; a book in the Old Testament written in part by him.

F, f The sixth letter of the English alphabet; in music, the fourth tone in the scale of C major; a failing grade.

F abbr. Fahrenheit, female.

fa-ble n. A brief, fictitious story embodying a moral and using persons, animals, or inanimate objects as characters; a falsehood; a lie. **fabulist, fabler** n., **fabled** adj.

fab-ric n. A cloth produced by knitting, weaving, or spinning fibers; a structure or framework, as the social fabric.

fab-ri-cate v. To make or manufacture; to build; to construct by combining or assembling parts; to make up in order to deceive; to invent, as a lie or story. **fabricating, fabricated** v., **fabrication, fabricator** n.

fab-u-lous adj. Past the limits of belief; incredible. *Slang* Very successful or pleasing. **fabulously** adv.

fa-cade n., Arch. The face or front of a building; an artificial or false appearance.

face n. The front surface of the head from ear to ear and from forehead to chin; external appearance, look, or aspect; the value written on the printed surface of a note or bond; the principal, front, finished, or working surface of anything; the most prominent or significant surface of an object. v. To confront with awareness. **face up to** To recognize the existence of something and confront it bravely. **faced, facing** v.

face brick n. A brick used for facing the exterior of a house or building.

face card n. In playing cards, a king, queen, or jack of a suit.

face--hard-en v. To harden the surface of metal or steel by chilling.

face--lift-ing or **face--lift** n. The plastic surgery for tightening facial tissues and improving the facial appearance. v. To modernize.

face--off n. The action of facing off in hockey, lacrosse, etc.

face--saver n. Something that preserves one's self-esteem or dignity. **-ing** adj.

fac-et n. One of the flat, polished surfaces cut upon a gemstone; the small, smooth surface on a bone or tooth; a phase, aspect, or side of a person or subject. **faceted** or **facetted** adj.

fa-ce-ti-ae n. Humorous or witty writings or remarks.

fa-ce-tious adj. Given to or marked by playful jocularity; humorous. **facetiously** adv., **facetiousness** n.

face value n. The apparent value of something; the value printed on the face of a bill or bond.

fa-cial adj. Near, of, or for the face; a massage or other cosmetic treatment for the face. **facially** adv.

fac-ile adj. Requiring little effort; easily achieved or performed; arrived at without due care, effort, or examination; superficial. **-ly** adv., **facileness** n.

fa-cil-i-tate v. To make easier or less difficult. **facilitating, facilitated** v.,

facilitation, facilitator n.

fa-cil-i-ty n., pl. **-ies** Ease in performance, moving, or doing something; something that makes an operation or action easier.

fac-ing n. The lining or covering sewn to a garment; any outer protective or decorative layer applied to a surface.

fac-sim-i-le n. An exact copy, as of a document; the method of transmitting drawings, messages, or such by an electronic method.

fact n. Something that actually occurred or exists; something that has real and demonstrable existence; actuality.

fac-tion n. A group or party within a government that is often self-seeking and usually in opposition to a larger group; conflict within a party; discord. **factional** adv., **factionalism** n.

fac-tious adj. Given to dissension; creating friction; divisive. **factiously** adv.

fac-ti-tious adj. Produced artificially; lacking authenticity or genuineness. **factitiously** adv., **factitiousness** n.

fac-tor n. One who transacts business for another person on a commission basis; one of the elements or causes that contribute to produce the result; in mathematics, one of two or more quantities that when multiplied together give or yield a given product; in biology, a gene. **factorship** n., **factorable** adj., **factorage** n.

fac-to-ry n., pl. **-ies** An establishment where goods are manufactured; a plant.

fac-to-tum n. An employee who performs all types of work.

fac-tu-al adj. Containing or consisting of facts, literal and exact. **factually** adv., **factualness, factuality** n.

fac-ture n. The process, manner or act of construction; making.

fac-ul-ty n., pl. **-ies** A natural ability or power; the inherent powers or capabilities of the body or mind; the complete teaching staff of a school or any other educational institution.

fad n. A temporary fashion adopted with wide enthusiasm. **faddish** adj., **faddishness, faddist** n.

fade v. To lose brightness, brilliance, or loudness gradually; to vanish slowly; to lose freshness, vigor, or youth; to disappear gradually. **faded, fading** v.

fa-er-ie n., variation of fairy

fag v. To exhaust by hard work. n. An English public school student required to perform menial tasks for an upperclassman. *Slang* A homosexual; a cigarette.

fag end n. The frayed end of a rope or cloth; a remnant; the last part.

fag-ot or **fag-got** n. A bundle of twigs, sticks, or branches that are used for fuel.

fag-ot-ing n. A method of ornamenting cloth by pulling out horizontal threads and tying the remaining vertical threads into hourglass shaped bunches.

Fahr-en-heit *adj.* Of or relating to the temperature scale in which the freezing point of water is 32 degrees and the boiling point of water is 212 degrees under normal atmospheric pressure.

fa-ience *n.* Earthenware that is decorated with a colorful opaque glaze.

fail *v.* To be totally ineffective, unsuccessful; to go bankrupt; to receive an academic grade below the acceptable standards; to issue such a grade; to omit or neglect. **failing, failed** *v.*

fail-ing *n.* A minor fault; a defect.

faille *n.* A ribbed material of cotton, silk, or rayon.

fail--safe *adj.* Of or relating to a system designed to prevent equipment failure or to compensate automatically for a mechanical failure; guaranteed not to fail.

fail-ure *n.* The fact or state of failing; a breaking down in health, action, strength, or efficiency; a situation in which a business becomes insolvent or bankrupt; in school, a failing grade.

faint *adj.* Having little strength or vigor; feeble; lacking brightness or clarity; dim. *n.* A sudden, temporary loss of consciousness; a swoon. **faintly** *adv.*, **faintness** *n.*

faint-hearted *adj.* Lacking courage or conviction; cowardly; timid. **faintheartedness** *n.*, **faintheartedly** *adv.*

fair *adj.* Visually light in coloring; pleasing to the eye; beautiful; impartial; free from blemish or imperfection; moderately large or good; not stormy; without precipitation. *n.* A periodic gathering for the buying and selling of goods and merchandise; a competitive exhibit of agricultural products, livestock, machinery, and other goods; a fund-raising event for a charity.

fair ball *n.* A ball that is situated, falls, or remains in the area bounded by the foul lines.

fair--haired *adj.* Having blonde or light colored hair; favored, favorite.

fair--mind-ed *adj.* Just and impartial.

fair--trade agree-ment *n.* A commercial agreement between a manufacturer and a seller under which a product cannot be sold at less than a minimum price set by the manufacturer.

fair-way *n.* The part of a golf course between the tees and putting greens; the usual course through a harbor or channel.

fair--weather *adj.* Friendly only during good times.

fair-y *n., pl.* **-ies** A tiny imaginary being, capable of working good or ill. *Slang* A male homosexual.

fair-y-land *n.* Any delightful, enchanting place; the land of the fairies.

fair-y tale *n.* An incredible or fictitious tale of fanciful creatures; a tale about fairies.

fait ac-com-pli *n.* An accomplished fact or deed that is irreversible.

faith *n.* A belief in the value, truth, or trustworthiness of someone or something; belief and trust in God, the Scriptures, or other religious writings; a system of religious beliefs.

faith-ful *adj.* True and trustworthy in the performance of duty, the fulfillment of promises or obligations, etc. **faithfully** *adv.*, **faithfulness** *n.*

faith-less *adj.* Not being true to one's obligations or duties; lacking a religious faith; unworthy of belief or trust. **faithlessly** *adv.*, **faithlessness** *n.*

fake *adj.* Having a false or misleading appearance; not genuine. *v.* To make a brief, deceptive movement in order to mislead one's opponent in certain sports. **fake, faker, fakery** *n.*

fa-kir *n.* A Moslem or Hindu religious mendicant, performing feats of endurance or magic.

fal-con *n.* A bird of prey noted for its powerful wings, keen vision, and swiftness of attack upon its prey. **falconer, falconry** *n.*

fall *v.* To drop down from a higher place or position due to the removal of support or loss of hold or attachment; to collapse; to become less in rank or importance; to drop when wounded or slain; to be overthrown by another government; to come as though descending, as night falls; to pass into a specified condition, as to fall asleep; to cut down or fell, as a tree; to surrender, as a city or fort. **to fall back on** To recede; to retreat. **to fall down on** To fail in. **to fall for** *Slang* To be deceived by. **to fall in** In the military, to meet and go along with. **to fall out** In the military, to leave ranks. **to fall short of** To fail to meet a standard or to reach a particular place. **to fall under** To be classified, as to be included. **the fall of man** The disobedience of Adam and Eve that began or resulted in original sin. *n.* A moral lapse or loss of innocence; autumn. **falling** *v.*

fal-la-cious *adj.* Containing or based on fundamental errors in reasoning; deceptive; misleading. **fallaciousness** *n.*, **fallaciously** *adv.*

fal-la-cy *n., pl.* **-ies** A deception; an error.

fall-back *n.* A place or position to which one can retreat.

fall guy *n., Slang* A person left to receive the blame or penalties; scapegoat.

fal-li-ble *adj.* Capable of making an error; liable to be deceived or misled; apt to be erroneous. **fallibility** *n.*, **fallibly** *adv.*

fall-ing--out *n.* A fight, disagreement, or quarrel.

fall-ing star *n.* A meteor, often visible as a result of being ignited by the atmospheric friction.

fall--off *n.* A decrease in something.

fal-lo-pi-an tube *n.* One of a pair of long, slender ducts serving as a passage for the ovum from the ovary to the uterus.

fall-out *n.* The descent of minute particles of radioactive material or debris after a nuclear explosion; an incidental result or side effect.

fal-low *n.* Ground that has been plowed but left unseeded during the growing season. **fallowness** *n.*

fal-low *adj.* Light yellowish-brown in color.

fal-low deer *n.* A European deer, about three feet high at the shoulders and spotted white in the summer.

false *adj.* Contrary to truth or fact; incorrect; deliberately untrue or deceptive; treacherous; unfaithful; not natural or real; artificial; in music, an incorrect pitch. *adv.* Faithless in manner. **falsely** *adv.*, **falseness**, **falsity** *n.*

false face *n.* A mask used for a disguise at Halloween.

false-hood *n.* The act of lying; an intentional untruth.

false ribs *pl.*, *n.* Ribs that are not united directly with the sternum. In man there are five on each side.

fal-set-to *n.* A high singing voice, usually male, that is artificially high.

fal-si-fy *v.* To give an untruthful account of; to misrepresent; to alter or tamper with in order to deceive; to forge. **falsifying**, **falsified** *v.*, **falsification**, **falsifier** *n.*

fal-ter *v.* To be uncertain or hesitant in action or voice; to waver; to move with unsteadiness. **falteringly** *adv.*, **faltering** *adj.*

fame *n.* Public esteem; a good reputation. **famed** *adj.*

fa-mil-iar *adj.* Being well-acquainted with; common; having good and complete knowledge of something; unconstrained or informal. *n.* A close friend or associate. **familiarly** *adv.*

fa-mil-i-ar-i-ty *n.*, *pl.* **-ties** An acquaintance with or the knowledge of something; an established friendship; an undue liberty or informality.

fa-mil-iar-ize *v.* To make oneself or someone familiar with something. **-ing**, **familiarized** *v.*, **familiarization** *n.*

fam-i-ly *n.*, *pl.* **-ies** Parents and their children; a group of people connected by blood or marriage and sharing common ancestry; the members of a household; a group or class of like things; in science, a taxonomic category higher than a genus and below an order. **family** *adj.*

family name *n.* A surname or last name.

family tree *n.* A genealogical diagram showing family descent; the ancestors and descendants of a family.

fam-ine *n.* A widespread scarcity of food; a drastic shortage of or scarcity of anything; severe hunger; starvation.

fam-ish *v.* To starve or cause to starve.

fa-mous *adj.* Well-known; renowned. *Slang* Excellent; admirable. **famously** *adv.*, **famousness** *n.*

fan *n.* A device for putting air into motion, especially a flat, lightweight, collapsible, wedge-like shape; a machine that rotates thin, rigid vanes. *Slang* an enthusiastic devotee or admirer of a sport, celebrity, diversion, etc. *v.* To move or stir up air with a fan; to direct air upon; to cool or refresh with or as with a fan; to spread like a fan; in baseball, to strike out. **fanned**, **fanning** *v.*

fa-nat-ic *n.* One who is moved by a frenzy of enthusiasm or zeal. **fanatical** *adj.*, **-ically** *adv.*, **fanaticism** *n.*

fan-ci-er *n.* A person having a special enthusiasm for or interest in something.

fan-ci-ful *adj.* Existing or produced only in the fancy; indulging in fancies; exhibiting invention or whimsy in design. **fancifully** *adv.*, **fancifulness** *n.*

fan-cy *n.*, *pl.* **-cies** Imagination of a fantastic or whimsical nature; a notion or idea not based on evidence or fact; a whim or caprice; judgment or taste in art, style, etc. *adj.* Adapted to please the fancy; highly decorated. *v.* To imagine; to visualize; to believe without proof or conviction; to suppose; to breed, as animals, for conventional points of beauty. **fanciness** *n.*

fan-cy-free *adj.* Unattached; not in love; carefree.

fan-cy-work *n.* Decorative or ornamental needle work.

fan-dan-go *n.* A Spanish or Spanish-American dance in triple time; the music for this dance.

fan-fare *n.* A short, loud trumpet flourish; a spectacular public display.

fang *n.*

A long, pointed tooth or tusk an animal uses to seize or tear at its prey; one of the hollow, grooved teeth with which a poisonous snake injects its venom. **fang** *v.*

fan-jet *n.* An aircraft with turbojet engines.

fan-ny *n.*, *pl.* **-ies** *Slang* The buttocks.

fan mail *n.* Mail received by a public figure from admirers.

fan-tail *n.* Any fan-shaped tail or end; a variety of domestic pigeons having fan-like tail feathers. **fantailed** *adj.*

fan-ta-sia *n.* A composition structured according to the composer's fancy and not observing any strict musical form.

fan-ta-size *v.* To create mental fantasies; to imagine or indulge in fantasies. **fantasizing**, **fantasized** *v.*

fan-tas-tic *adj.* Existing only in the fancy; unreal; wildly fanciful or exaggerated; impulsive or capricious; coming from the imagination or fancy. *Slang* Superb; wonderful. **fantastically** *adv.*

fan-ta-sy *n.*, *pl.* **-ies** A creative imagination; a creation of the fancy; an unreal or odd mental image; a whimsical or odd notion; a highly or ingeniously imaginative creation; in psychology, the sequence of pleasant mental images fulfilling a wish.

far *adv.* From, to, or at a considerable

distance; to or at a certain distance, degree, or point; very remote in time, quality, or degree. *adj. & adv.* Remote in space or time; extending widely or at great lengths; extensive or lengthy. **far and away** Decidedly. **far and wide** Everywhere. **far be it** from me Having no audacity or desire. **in so far as** To the extent that. **to go far** To accomplish a lot; to have success; to last a long time or to cover a great extent. **farther, further, farthest, furthest** *adj.*

far-ad *n.* A unit of capacitance equal to that of a capacitor having a charge of one coulomb on each plate and a potential difference of one volt between the plates.

far-away *adj.* Very distant; remote; absent-minded; dreamy.

farce *n.* A theatre comedy employing exaggerated or ludicrous situations; a ridiculous situation or action; a seasoned stuffing. **farcical** *adj.*

fare *v.* To be in a specific state; to turn out. *n.* A fee paid for hired transportation; food or a variety of foods.

Far East *n.* The countries of eastern Asia, including China, Japan, Korea, Manchuria, and the adjacent islands. **Far Eastern** *adj. & n.*

fare--thee--well *n.* The most extreme degree; perfection.

fare-well *n.* Good-by; a departure. *adj.* Closing; parting.

far--fetched *adj.* Neither natural nor obvious; highly improbable.

far--flung *adj.* Widely distributed over a great distance.

fa-ri-na *n.* A fine meal obtained chiefly from nuts, cereals, potatoes, or Indian corn, used as a breakfast food or in puddings.

far-i-na-ceous *adj.* Made from, rich in, or composed of starch; mealy.

farm *n.* Land that is cultivated for agricultural production; land used to breed and raise domestic animals; the area of water used for the breeding and raising of a particular type of aquatic animal, such as fish; the raising of livestock or crops as a business; in baseball, a minor league club used by a major league club for training its recruits. **farm out** To send work out to be done elsewhere. **farmer** *n.*

farm-house *n.* The homestead on a farm.

farm-land *n.* Land that is suitable for agricultural production.

farm-stead *n.* A farm, including its land and all of the buildings.

farm team *n.* A minor league baseball team.

farm-yard *n.* The area surrounded by farm buildings and enclosed for confining stock.

far--off *adj.* Distant; remote.

far--out *adj., Slang* Very unconventional.

far-ra-go *n., pl.* goes A confused mixture.

far--reach-ing *adj.* Having a wide range, effect, or influence.

far-row *n.* A litter of pigs.

far--see-ing *adj.* Having foresight; prudent; wise; having the ability to see distant objects clearly.

far--sight-ed *adj.* Able to see things at a distance more clearly than things nearby; having foresight; wise. **far-sightedly** *adv.,* **far-sightedness** *n.*

far-ther *adv.* To or at a more distant point. *adj.* More remote or distant.

far-ther-most *adj.* Most distant; farthest.

far-thest *adj.* To or at the greatest distance.

far-thing *n.* Something of little worth; a former British coin worth 1/4 of a penny.

far-thin-gale *n.* A hoop skirt of the 16th and 17th centuries, used to make a woman's skirt stick out.

fas-ci-nate *v.* To attract irresistibly, as by beauty or other qualities; to captivate; to hold motionless; to spellbind. **fascinating** *adj.,* **fascinatingly** *adv.,* **fascination, fascinator** *n.*

fas-cism *n.* A one-party system of government marked by a centralized dictatorship, stringent socioeconomic controls, and often belligerent nationalism. **fascisi** *n.,* **fascistic** *adj.*

fashion *n.* The mode or manner of dress, living, and style that prevails in society, especially in high society; good form or style; current style or custom; a piece of clothing made up in the current style. *v.* To make into a given shape or form; to make fitting. **fashionable, -ableness** *adj.,* **-ably** *adv.*

fast *adj.* Swift; rapid; performed quickly; constant; steadfast; firmly secured; sound or deep, as sleep; permitting or suitable for quick movement; requiring rapidity of motion or action; acting or moving quickly. *v.* To give up food, especially for a religious reason. *n.* A period prescribed for fasting.

fast-back *n.* A car with a downward slope from the roof to the rear.

fast-en *v.* To join something else; to connect; to securely fix something; to shut or close; to focus steadily. **fastener** *n.*

fast--food *adj.* Of or relating to a restaurant that specializes in foods prepared and served quickly.

fas-tid-i-ous *adj.* Exceedingly delicate or refined; hard to please in matters of taste. **fastidiously** *adv.,* **-ness** *n.*

fast--talk *v., Slang* To affect or influence someone with deceptive talk. **fast-talking** *v.,* **fast-talker** *n.*

fast--track *adj.* High-powered and aggressive.

fat *adj.* Having superfluous flesh or fat; obese; plump; containing much fat or oil; rich or fertile, as land; abundant; plentiful; profitable; thick; broad. **a fat chance** *Slang.* Very little or no chance at all. *n.* Any of a large class of yellowish to white, greasy liquid or solid substances that are widely distributed in animal and plant tissues, consisting of various fatty acids and glycerol, generally odorless, tasteless, and color-less; the richest or most desirable part. **fatness,**

fattiness n., fatty adj.

fat-al adj. Causing death; deadly; bringing ruin or disaster; destructive; decisively important; fateful; brought about by fate; destined; inevitable.

fa-tal-ism n. The belief that events or things are predetermined by fate and cannot be altered. fatalist n., fatalistical adj., fatalistically adv.

fa-tal-i-ty n., pl. -ies A death caused by a disaster or accident; the capability of causing death or disaster; the quality or state of being subject to or determined by fate.

fat-back n. The strip of unsmoked salt pork taken from the upper part of a pork side.

fat cat n., Slang A powerful and wealthy person; a rich person who contributes greatly to a political campaign.

fate n. The force or power held to predetermine events; fortune; inevitability; the final result or outcome; unfortunate destiny; doom. fated adj.

fate-ful adj. Determining destiny; governed by fate; bringing death or disaster. fatefully adv., fatefulness n.

fa-ther n. The male parent; any male forefather; ancestor; a male who establishes or founds something. Father A priest; one of the early Christian writers who formulated doctrines and codified observances. v. To beget; to act as a father toward. fatherhood, fatherliness n., fatherly adj.

fa-ther--in--law n. The father of one's spouse.

fa-ther-land n. The land where one was born; the native country of one's ancestors.

Father's Day n. A day set aside to honor all fathers, occurring on the third Sunday in June.

fath-om n. A unit of length that is equal to six feet or approximately 1.83 m, used mostly in measuring marine depths. v. To understand fully.

fath-om-less adj. Too deep to measure; too difficult to understand.

fa-tigue n. The state or condition of extreme tiredness or weariness from prolonged physical or mental exertion. fatigues Military clothes for heavy work and field duty. v. To become or make tired; to exhaust. fatiguing, fatigued v.

fat-ten v. To make or become fat; to increase the amount of something. fattening, fattened v.

fat-ty adj. Greasy; oily; having an excess of fat.

fatty acid n. Any of a class of organic acids derived from hydrocarbons, occurring in plant and animal fats.

fa-tu-i-ty n. Stupidity; foolishness.

fat-u-ous adj. Silly and foolish in a self-satisfied way. fatuously adv., -ness n.

fau-ces n. pl. The passage at the back of the mouth to the pharynx, formed by the membranous, muscular arches extending downward from each side of the soft palate. faucial adj.

fau-cet n. A fixture with an adjustable valve used to draw liquids from a pipe or cask.

faugh interj. An exclamation of contempt or disgust.

fault n. An impairment or defect; a weakness; a minor offense or mistake; a break in the earth's crust allowing adjoining surfaces to shift in a direction parallel to the crack; a bad serve, as in tennis. v. To criticize. at fault Open to blame; in the wrong. faultily, faultlessly adv., faultless, faulty adj.

fault-find-er n. One who finds fault; a petty critic. faultfinding n. & adj.

faun n. A woodland deity represented in Roman mythology as part goat and part man.

fau-na n., pl. faunas or faunae Animals living within a given area or environment. faunal adj.

Faust n. A German doctor of legend who sold his soul to the devil for youth, power, and worldly experience.

fau-vism n. An art movement noted for the use of very flamboyant colors and bold, often distorted forms.

faux pas n. A false step; a social blunder.

fa-vor n. A helpful or considerate act; the attitude of friendliness or approbation; the condition of being held in the regard; approval or support. favors Consent to sexual intimacy, especially as granted by a woman; a token of love or remembrance; a small gift given to each guest at a party. v. To benefit; to give advantage; to prefer or like one more than another; to support or approve; to look like or resemble; to treat with special care. favorer n., favoringly adv.

fa-vor-a-ble adj. Beneficial; antageous; building up hope or confidence; approving; promising. -ness n., -ably adv.

fa-vor-ite n. Anything regarded with special favor or preferred above all others; in sports, the contestant considered to be the most likely winner.

favorite son n. A person favored by his own state delegates for nomination at a national political convention.

fa-vor-it-ism n. Preferential treatment; a display of often unjust partiality.

fa-vour n. & v. British variety of favor.

fawn n. A young deer less than a year old; a light yellowish-brown color. v. To show cringing fondness; to display slavish affection. fawningly adv.

fay n. A fairy or elf.

faze v. To worry; to disconcert. fazed, fazing v.

FB abbr. Freight bill.

FBI abbr. Federal Bureau of Investigation.

fe-al-ty n., pl. -ies The obligation of allegiance owed to a feudal lord by his vassal or tenant; faithfulness; loyalty.

fear n. The agitated feeling caused by the anticipation or the realization of danger; an uneasy feeling that something may   happen contrary to one's hopes; a feeling of deep, reverential awe and dread. *v.* To be apprehensive; to suspect. **fearfulness** *n.*, **fearful** *adj.*, **fearfully** *adv.*

fear-less *adj.* Without fear; brave; courageous. **fearlessness** *n.*, **-ly** *adv.*

fear-some *adj.* Causing fear; timid. **fearsomely** *adv.*, **fearsomeness** *n.*

fea-si-ble *adj.* Capable of being put into effect or accomplished; practical. **feasibility** *n.*, **feasibly** *adv.*

feast *n.* A delicious meal; a banquet; a day or days of celebration set aside for a religious purpose or in honor of some person, event, or thing. *v.* To provide with pleasure. **feasting** *v.*, **feaster** *n.*

feat *n.* A notable act or achievement.

feath-er *n.* One of the light, hollow-shafted structures that form the covering of birds. **a feather in one's cap** An achievement one should be proud of; in rowing, to turn the oar blade following each stroke so that the blade is more or less horizontal as it is carried back to the position for reentering the water. **feathery** *adj.*

feather bed *n.* A mattress stuffed with feathers; a bed with a feather mattress.

feather-bedding *n.* The practice that requires an employer to hold back on production or to employ more workers than needed because of union rules or safety regulations.

feather-edge *n.* A very thin, fragile edge.

feather-stitch *n.* An embroidery stitch that resembles a feather, accomplished by taking one or more short stitches alternately on either side of a straight line.

feather-weight *n.* A boxer weighting between 118 and 127 pounds; any person or thing that is light in weight.

fea-ture *n.* The appearance or shape of the face; the main presentation at a movie theater; a special article in a magazine or newspaper that is given special prominence. **feature** *v.*

Feb *abbr.* February.

feb-ri-fuge *n.* A medicine used to reduce fever.

feb-rile *adj.* Feverish.

Feb-ru-ar-y *n.* The second month of the year, having 28 days or, in a leap year, 29 days.

fe-ces *pl. n.* Waste that is excreted from the bowels; excrement. **fecal** *adj.*

feck-less *adj.* Ineffective; weak; careless and irresponsible. **fecklessly** *adv.*

fe-cund *adj.* Fruitful; productive. **-ity** *n.*

fe-cun-date *v.* To make fertile. **-ing**, **fecundated** *v.*, **fecundation** *n.*

fed *v.* Past tense of feed.

fed *abbr.* Federal, federated.

fed-er-al *adj.* Of, relating to, or formed by an agreement between two or more states or groups in which each retains certain controlling powers while being united under a central authority; of or pertaining to the United States central government. **Federal** Pertaining to or of the central government of Canada; of or supporting the Union in the American Civil War. **federally** *adv.*

fed-er-al-ism *n.* The organization or system of a federal government; the advocacy or support of this system.

Federalist Party *n.* The political party of 1787-1830 which advocated the adoption of the U.S. Constitution and the formation of a strong national government.

fed-er-a-l-ize *v.* To join or unite in a federal union; to bring under the control of the federal government. **-ing**, **federalized** *v.*, **federalization** *n.*

fed-er-ate *v.* To unite in a federal union or alliance. **federating**, **federated** *v.*

fed-er-a-tion *n.* The joining together of two or more states or groups into a union or confederacy.

fe-do-ra *n.* A soft hat with a low crown creased lengthwise and a brim that can be turned up or down.

fed up *adj.* Extremely annoyed or disgusted.

fee *n.* A fixed charge, compensation, or payment for something; a charge for professional services; an inherited estate in land.

fee-ble *adj.* Very weak; lacking in strength; lacking force; ineffective. **feebleness** *n.*, **feebly** *adv.*

feeble minded *adj.* Mentally deficient; intellectually subnormal. **-ness** *n.*

feed *v.* To supply with food; to provide as food; to consume food; to keep supplied, as with fuel for a fire; to enter data into a computing machine; to draw support or encouragement. *n.* The mechanical part, as of a sewing machine, that keeps supplying material to be worked on. *Slang* A meal.

feed-back *n.* The return to the input of a portion of the output of a machine; the return of data for corrections or control.

feed lot *n.* A place where livestock are fattened for market.

feed-stock *n.* Raw materials required for an industrial process.

feel *v.* To examine, explore, or perceive through the sense of touch; to perceive as a physical sensation; to believe; to consider; to be aware of; to be emotionally affected by; to think; to suppose; to judge; to experience the full force or impact of; to produce a sensory impression of being soft, hard, hot or cold; to produce an indicated overall condition, impression, or reaction. **feeling** *v.*

feel-er *n.* Any action, hint, or proposal intended to draw out views and the intentions of another; one who or that which feels; an organ of touch.

feel-ing *n.* The sensation that is perceived by touch; a physical or emotional sensation; compassion; a generous, sympathetic attitude; the impression produced upon a person by an object, place, etc. **feelingly** *adv.*

feet *n.* The plural of foot.

feign *v.* To make a false show of; to

dream up a false story and tell it as the truth; to fabricate; to imitate so as to deceive. **feigned** *adj.*

feint *n.* A deceptive or misleading movement intended to draw defensive action away from the real target.

feld-spar *n.* Any of a large group of crystalline materials largely made up of silicates of aluminum. **feldspathic** *adj.*

fe-lic-i-tate *v.* To congratulate; to wish happiness. **felicitated**, **felicitating** *v.* **felicitation** *n.*

fe-lic-i-tous *adj.* Most appropriate; well chosen; pertinent or effective in manner or style. **felicitously** *adv.*

fe-lic-i-ty *n., pl.* **-ies** Happiness; bliss; an instance or source of happiness; an agreeably pertinent or effective style.

fe-line *adj.* Of or relating to cats, including wild and domestic cats; resembling a cat, as in stealth or agility. **felinity**, **feline** *n.*, **felinely** *adv.*

fell *v.* Past tense of fall; to strike or cause to fall down; to finish a seam with a flat, smooth strip made by joining edges, then folding under and stitching flat. *n.* Timber cut down during one season; an animal's hide; pelt. *adj.* Cruel and fierce; lethal.

fel-lah *n., pl.* **fellahin** *or* **fellaheen** An Arab peasant or laborer.

fel-low *n.* A boy or man; an associate, comrade; the counterpart; one of a pair. *Informal* A boyfriend.

fel-low-ship *n.* A friendly relationship; the condition or fact of having common interests, ideals, or experiences; the status of being a fellow at a college or university, also the financial grant made to a fellow.

fel-ly *n., pl.* **-ies**

The rim of a wooden wheel, into which spokes are inserted.

fel-on *n.* A person who has committed a felony; an inflammation in the terminal joint or at the cuticle of a finger or toe.

fel-o-ny *n., pl.* **-ies** A serious crime, such as rape, murder, or burglary, punishable by a severe sentence. **-ious** *adj.*, **feloniously** *adv.*, **feloniousness** *n.*

felt *v.* Past tense of feel. *n.* An unwoven fabric made from pressed animal fibers, as wool or fur; a piece of fabric or material made of felt.

fem *abbr.* Feminine.

fe-male *n.* The sex that produces ova or bears young; a plant with a pistil but no stamen, which is capable of being fertilized and producing fruit. *adj.* Of or relating to the sex that produces ova or bears young; suitable to this sex having a bore, slot, or hollow part designed to receive a projecting part, as a plug or prong.

fem-i-nine *adj.* Pertaining to or of the female sex; female; characterized by qualities generally attributed to women; lacking in manly qualities.

Gram. Applicable to females only or to persons or things classified as female. **femininely** *adv.*, **feminineness**, **femininity** *n.*

fem-i-nism *n.* The movement advocating the granting of the same social, political, and economic rights to women as the ones granted to men. **feminist** *n.*, **feministic** *adj.*

femme fa-tale *n., pl.* **femmes fatales** A seductive or charming woman.

fe-mur *n., pl.* **femurs** *or* **femora** The bone extending from the pelvis to the knee. **femoral** *adj.*

fen *n.* A low, marshy land; a bog.

fence *n.* A structure made from rails, stakes, or strung wire that functions as a boundary or barrier. *Slang* A seller and recipient of stolen goods; the location where such goods are sold. *v.* To close in, surround, or separate as if by a fence. **on the fence** Neutral or undecided. **fencer** *n.*

fenc-ing *n.* The sport of using a foil or saber; the practice of making quick, effective remarks or retorts, as in a debate; the material used to make fences; fences collectively.

fend *v.* To ward off or to keep off; to offer resistance. **fending**, **fended** *v.*

fend-er *n.* The protective device over the wheel of a car or other vehicle; a metal guard set in front of an open fireplace; the projection on the front of a locomotive or streetcar, designed to push obstructions from the tracks, also known as cow-catcher.

fen-es-tra-tion *n.* The design and position of doors and windows in a building.

fen-nel *n.* A tall herb from the parsley family which produces an edible stalk and aromatic seeds used as a flavoring.

fe-ral *adj.* Not tame nor domesticated; returned to a wild state; existing in a untamed state.

fer--de--lance *n.* A large, venomous snake of tropical America, with gray and brown markings.

fer-ment *n.* Any substance or agent producing fermentation, as yeast, mold, or enzyme; excitement; unrest; agitation. **fermentability**, **fermenter** *n.*, **fermentable** *adj.*

fer-men-ta-tion *n.* The decomposition of complex organic compounds into simpler substances; the conversion of glucose into ethyl alcohol through the action of zymase; great agitation; commotion.

fer-mi-um *n.* A metallic radioactive element, symbolized by Fm.

fern *n.* Any of a number of flowerless, seedless plants, having fronds with divided leaflets and reproducing by spores. **ferny** *adj.*

fe-ro-cious *adj.* Extremely savage, fierce, cruel, or bloodthirsty. *Slang* Very intense. **ferociously** *adv.*, **ferociousness**, **ferocity** *n.*

fer-ret *n.* A small, red-eyed polecat of

Europe, often domesticated and trained to hunt rodents or rabbits. *v.* To search out by careful investigation; to drive out of hiding.

ferreter *n.*, **ferrety** *adj.*

fer-ric *adj.* Pertaining to or containing iron.

fer-ric ox-ide *n.* A dark compound that occurs as hematite ore and rust.

Fer-ris wheel *n.* A large, power-driven wheel with suspended compartments in which passengers ride for amusement.

fer-ro-mag-net-ic *adj.* Relating to or being typical of substances, as iron and nickel, that are readily magnetized. **ferromagnetism** *n.*

fer-rous *adj.* Pertaining to or containing iron.

fer-rule *n.* A cap or ring used near or at the end of a stick, as a walking cane, to reinforce it or prevent splitting.

fer-ry *n.*, *pl.* **-ies** A boat or other craft used to transport people, vehicles, and other things across a body of water.

fer-ry-boat *n.* A boat used to transport passengers or goods.

fer-tile *adj.*, *Biol.* Having the ability to reproduce; rich in material required to maintain plant growth. **-ity, -ness** *n.*

fer-til-ize *v.* To make fertile; to cause to be productive or fruitful; to begin the biological reproduction by supplying with sperm or pollen; to make fertile by spreading or adding fertilizer. **fertilized, fertilizing** *v.*, **fertilizable** *adj.*, **fertilization** *n.*

fer-til-iz-er *n.* A material that fertilizes, such as nitrates or manure which enriches soil.

fer-ule *n.* A flat stick sometimes used to punish children. **ferule** *v.*

fer-vent *adj.* Passionate; ardent; very hot. **fervency, ferventness** *n.*, **fervently** *adv.*

fer-vid *adj.* Fervent to an extreme degree; impassioned; very hot; burning. **fervidly** *adv.*, **fervidness** *n.*

fer-vor *n.* Great emotional warmth or intensity.

fes-cue *n.* A type of tough grass, often used as pasturage.

fes-tal *adj.* Pertaining to or typical of a festival, holiday, or feast.

fes-ter *v.* To develop or generate pus; to be a constant source of irritation or resentment.

fes-ti-val *n.* A particular holiday or celebration; a regularly occurring occasion.

fes-tive *adj.* Relating to or suitable for a feast or other celebration. **festively** *adv.*, **festiveness** *n.*

fes-tiv-i-ty *n.*, *pl.* **-ies** A festival; gladness and rejoicing.

fes-toon *n.* A garland of flowers, leaves, colored paper, or ribbon hanging in loops between two points. *v.* To decorate, fashion into, or link together by festoons. **festoonery** *n.*

fet-a *n.* A white Greek cheese made of goat's or ewe's milk and preserved in brine.

fe-tal *adj.* Relating to or like a fetus.

fe-tal po-si-tion *n.* The bodily position of a fetus with the spine curved, the head bowed forward, and the arms and legs drawn in toward the chest.

fetch *v.* To go after and return with; to draw forth; to elicit; to bring as a price; to sell for; to strike a blow. **fetching, fetched** *v.*, **fetcher** *n.*

fetch-ing *adj.* Very attractive or pleasing to the eye.

fete *n.* A festival or feast; a very elaborate outdoor celebration. **fete** *v.*

fet-id *adj.* Having a foul odor; stinking. **fetidly** *adv.*, **fetidness** *n.*

fet-ish *n.* An object that is regarded as having magical powers; something that one is devoted to excessively or irrationally. *Psychiatry* A nonsexual object that arouses or gratifies sexual desires. **fetishistic** *adj.*, **fetishist** *n.*

fet-lock *n.* A tuft of hair that grows just above the hoof at the back of the leg of a horse.

fe-tol-o-gy *n.* The medical study of a fetus. **fetologist** *n.*

fet-ter *n.* A chain or other bond put around the ankles to restrain movement, preventing escape; anything that prevents free movement.

fet-tle *n.* State; the condition of something.

fe-tuc-ci-ne *n.* Narrow strips of pasta.

fe-tus *n.* The individual unborn organism carried within the womb from the time major features appear; especially in humans, the unborn young after the eighth week of development.

feud *n.* A bitter quarrel between two families, usually lasting over a long period of time. **feud** *v.*

feu-dal *adj.* Relating to or characteristic of feudalism. **-ize** *v.*, **feudally** *adv.*

feu-dal-ism *n.* The political, social, and economic organization produced by the feudal system. **feudalist** *n.*, **feudalistic** *adj.*

feu-da-to-ry *n.*, *pl.* **-ies** One holding a feudal fee. *adj.* Owing feudal homage or allegiance.

fe-ver *n.* Abnormally high body temperature and rapid pulse; a craze; a heightened emotion or activity. **feverish** *adj.* **feverishly** *adv.*, **-ishness** *n.*

fever blister *n.* A cold sore.

few *adj.* Small in number; not many. *n.* A select or limited group.

fey *adj.* Seemingly spellbound; having clairvoyance; acting as if under a spell.

fez *n.* A red felt, black-tasseled hat worn by Egyptian men.

fi-an-ce *n.* A man to whom a woman is engaged to be married.

fi-an-cee *n.* A woman to whom a man is engaged to be married.

fi-as-co *n.*, *pl.* **fiascoes** A complete or total failure.

fi-at *n.* A positive and authoritative order or decree.

fib *n.* A trivial lie. **fib** *v.*, **fibber** *n.*

fi-ber *n.* A fine, long, continuous piece of natural or synthetic material made from a filament of asbestos, spun glass, textile, or fabric; internal strength; character. **fibrous** adj.

fi-ber-board n. A tough, pliable building material made of plant fibers, as wood, compressed into rigid sheets.

fi-ber-glass n. A flexible, nonflammable material of spun glass used for textiles, insulation, and other purposes.

fi-ber op-tics pl., n. Light optics transmitted through very fine, flexible glass rods by internal reflection.

fi-ber-scope n. The flexible fiber optic instrument used to view otherwise inaccessible objects.

fib-ril-la-tion n., Pathol. The rapid and uncoordinated contraction of the muscle fibers of the heart.

fi-brin n., Biochem. An insoluble protein that promotes the clotting of blood.

fi-brin-o-gen n., Biochem. A complex blood plasma protein that is converted to fibrin during the process of blood clotting.

fi-broid adj. Made up or resembling fibrous tissue.

fib-u-la n. Anat.

The outer and smaller bone of the lower limb or hind leg, in humans located between the knee and ankle.

-fic adj., suffix Making; causing; rendering.

-fication n., suffix Making; production.

fi-chu n. A lightweight triangular scarf, worn about the neck and fastened loosely in front.

fick-le adj. Inconstant in purpose or feeling; changeable. **fickleness** n.

fic-tion n. Something that is created or imaginary; a literary work that is produced by the imagination and not based on fact. **fictional** adj.

fic-ti-tious adj. Nonexistent; imaginary; not genuine; false; not real. **fictitiously** adv., **fictitiousness** n.

fid-dle n. A violin. v. To play the violin; to fidget or make nervous or restless movements; to spend time in a careless way. Naut. A rack used at the table to prevent things from sliding off. **fit as a fiddle** To enjoy good or perfect health. **to play second fiddle** To be put into a position subordinate to that of another. **fiddling, fiddled** v., **fiddler** n.

fiddler catfish n. A freshwater, scaleless fish with long whisker-like feelers used for navigation; ranging in size from 8 to 14 inches in length and having a light taste and tender texture.

fiddler crab n. A small burrowing crab found mostly off the Atlantic coast of the United States, the male being much larger than the female.

fid-dle-sticks interj. Used to express mild disgust, annoyance; nonsense.

fi-del-i-ty n., pl. -ies Faithfulness or loyalty to obligations, vows, or duties. Elect. The degree to which a phonograph, tape recorder, or other electronic equipment receives and transmits input signals without distortion.

fidg-et v. To move nervously or restlessly. **fidgets** pl, n. The condition of being nervous or restless. **fidgeter, fidgetiness** n., **fidgety** adj.

fi-du-ci-ar-y adj. Relating to or pertaining to the holding of something in trust. n. An agent; a trustee.

fie interj. An expression of disgust or impatience in response to an unpleasant surprise.

fief n. A feudal estate in land.

field n. A piece of land with few or no trees; a cultivated piece of land devoted to the growing of crops; an area in which a natural resource such as oil is found; an airport; the complete extent of knowledge, research, or study in a given area; in sports, the bounded area in which an event is played; the members of a team actually engaged in active play; in business, the area away from the home office. Milit. A region of active operations or maneuvers. Physics A region of space that is marked by a physical property, as electromagnetic force, with a determinable value at each point in the region. **fielder** n.

field ar-til-lery n. Artillery that has been mounted for use in the fields.

field day n. A day full of pleasurable activities, usually out of doors. Slang The opportunity to express oneself with the greatest pleasure or success.

field e-vent n. An event at an athletic meet other than races, such as jumping and throwing.

field glass n., often **field glasses** A compact, portable binocular instrument for viewing distant objects.

field mag-net n. A magnet providing the magnetic field in a generator or electric motor.

field mar-shal n. An army official in Europe who ranks just below the commander-in-chief.

field mouse n. A small mouse inhabiting fields and meadows.

field of force n. A region where the force of a single agent, as an electric current, is operative.

fiend n. An evil spirit or demon; a person who is totally engrossed in something. Slang An addict. **fiendish** adj., **fiendishly** adv., **fiendishness** n.

fierce adj. Savage and violent in nature. Slang Very difficult or disagreeable. **fiercely** adv., **fierceness** n.

fier-y adj. Containing or composed of fire; brightly glowing; blazing; hot and inflamed; full of spirit or intense with emotion. **fieriness** n.

fi-es-ta n. A religious holiday or festival.

fife n. A small, shrill-toned instrument similar to a flute.

fif-teen n. The cardinal number equal to

14 + 1. **fifteen** *adj.*, **-th** *n.*, *adj. & adv.*

fifth *n.* The ordinal of five; one of five equal parts. *Mus.* The space between a tone and another tone five steps from it. **fifth** *adj. & adv.*

Fifth Amendment *n.* An amendment to the United States Constitution, ratified in 1791, guaranteeing due process of law and that no person shall be forced to testify against himself.

fifth column *n.* During wartime, the private civilians within defense lines who secretly assist the enemy. **-ist** *n.*

fifth wheel *n.* A superfluous thing or person.

fif-ty *n.* The cardinal number equal to 5 x 10. **fiftieth** *n.*, *adj. & adv.*, **fifty** *adj.*

fifty-fifty *adj.*, *Slang* Divided into two equal portions or parts.

fig *n.* A tree or shrub bearing a sweet, pear-shaped, edible fruit; the fruit of the fig tree.

fight *v.* To struggle against; to quarrel; to argue; to make one's way by struggling; to participate in wrestling or boxing until a final decision is reached. *n.* A physical battle; struggle; strife; conflict; combat. **fighting** *v.*

fight-er *n.* A person who fights. *Milit.* A fast, highly maneuverable airplane used in combat.

fig-ment *n.* An invention or fabrication.

fig-u-ra-tive *adj.* Based on, like, or containing a figure of speech; metaphorical; representing by means of a figure or symbol. **figuratively** *adv.*

fig-ure *n.* A symbol or character that represents a number; anything other than a letter; the visible form, silhouette, shape, or line of something; the human form or body; an individual, especially a prominent one; the impression or appearance a person makes; a design or pattern, as in a fabric; a figure of speech; a series of movements, as in a dance. **fig-ures** *pl.* In mathematics, calculations; an amount shown in numbers. *v.* To represent; to depict; to compute. **figured**, **figuring** *v.*

fig-ure eight *n.* A skating maneuver shaped like an 8; anything shaped like the number 8.

fig-ure-head *n.* A person with nominal leadership but no real power; a carved figure on a ship's prow.

fig-ure of speech *n.* An expression, as a metaphor or hyperbole, where words are used in a more forceful, dramatic, or illuminating way.

fig-u-rine *n.* A small sculptured or molded figure; a statuette.

Fi-ji *n.* A native of the Fiji Islands.

fil-a-ment *n.* A very thing, finely spun fiber, wire, or thread; the fine wire enclosed in an electric lamp bulb which is heated electrically to incandescence. **-ary**, **filamentous** *adj.*

fil-bert *n.* The edible nut of the hazel tree or the tree it grows on.

filch *v.* To steal. **filcher** *n.*

file *n.* A device for storing papers in proper order; a collection of papers so arranged; a line of persons, animals, or things placed one behind another; a hard, steel instrument with ridged cutting surfaces, used to smooth or polish. *v.* To march as soldiers; to make an application, as for a job. **filing**, **filed** *v.*

fi-let *n.* A filet of meat or fish; lace or net with a pattern of squares.

fi-let mi-gnon *n.* A small, tender cut of beef from the inside of the loin.

fil-i-al *adj.* Of or relating to a son or daughter; pertaining to the generation following the parents. **filially** *adv.*

fil-i-buster *n.* An attempt to prolong, prevent, or hinder legislative action by using delaying tactics such as long speeches. **filibuster** *v.*, **filibusterer** *n.*

fil-i-gree *n.* Delicate, lace-like ornamental work made of silver or gold intertwisted wire. **filigree** *v. & adj.*

fil-ing *n.*, *often* **fil-ings** Particles removed by a file.

Fil-i-pi-no *n.* A native or inhabitant of the Philippines. **Filipino** *adj.*

fill *v.* To put into or hold as much of something as can be contained; to supply fully, as with food; to put together or make up what is indicated in an order or prescription; to meet or satisfy a requirement or need; to occupy an office or position; to insert something, as to fill in a name or address. *Naut.* To trim the yards so the sails will catch the wind. *n.* A built-up piece of land or the material, as earth or gravel, used for it. **to fill in on** To give someone additional information of facts about something. **to fill out** To become or make fuller or more rounded. **filling** *v.*

fill-er *n.* Something that is added to increase weight or bulk or to take up space; a material used to fill cracks, pores, or holes in a surface before it is completed.

fil-let *or* **fi-let** *n.* A narrow ribbon or band for holding the hair; a strip of boneless fish or meat. *v.* To slice, bone, or make into fillets.

failing *n.* That which is used to fill something, especially the substance put into a prepared cavity in a tooth; the horizontal threads crossing the warp in weaving.

failing sta-tion *n.* A retail business where vehicles are serviced with gasoline, oil, water, and air for tires.

fil-lip *n.* A snap of the finger that has been pressed down by the thumb and then suddenly released; something that arouses or excites. **fillip** *v.*

Fill-more, Mil-lard *n.* The 13th president of the United States, from 1850-1853.

fil-ly *n.* A young female horse.

film *n.* A thin covering, layer, or membrane. *Photog.* A photosensitive strip or sheet of flexible cellulose material that is used to make photographic negatives or trans-

parencies; the film containing the pictures projected on a large screen; the motion picture itself. *v.* To cover with or as if with a film; to make a movie.

film-dom *n.* The movie industry or business.

film-strip *n.* A strip of film containing graphic matter for still projection on a screen.

fil-ter *n.* A device, as cloth, paper, charcoal, or any other porous substance, through which a liquid or gas can be passed to separate outsuspended matter. *Photog.* A colored screen that controls the kind and intensity of light waves in an exposure. *v.* To pass liquids through a filter; to strain.
filterer, filterability *n.*,
filterable, filtrable *adj.*

filth *n.* Anything that is dirty or foul; something that is considered offensive.

filth-y *adj.* Highly unpleasant; morally foul; obscene. **-ily** *adv.*, **filthiness** *n.*

fil-trate *v.* To pass or cause to pass through something. *n.* Anything which has passed through the filter.
filtrating, filtrated *v.*, **filtration** *n.*

fin *n.*

A thin membranous extension of the body of a fish or other aquatic animal, used for swimming and balancing. *Slang* A five dollar bill.

fi-na-gle *v.*, *Slang* To get something by trickery or deceit. **finagled** *v.*,
finagling *adj.*, **finagler** *n.*

fi-nal *adj.* Pertaining to or coming to the end; last or terminal. **-ity** *n.*, **-ly** *adv.*

finals *pl.*, *n.* Something decisively final, as the last of a series of athletic contests; the final academic examination.

fi-na-le *n.* The last part, as the final scene in a play or the last part of a musical composition.

fi-nal-ist *n.* A contestant taking part in the final round of a contest.

fi-nal-ize *v.* To put into final and complete form. **finalized, finalizing** *v.*,
finalization, finalizer *n.*

fi-nance *n.* The science of monetary affairs. **finances** Monetary resources; funds. *v.* To supply the capital or funds for something; to sell or provide on a credit basis.
financial *adj.*, **financially** *adv.*

fin-an-cier *n.* An expert who deals with large-scale financial affairs.

finch *n.* A small bird, as a grosbeak, canary, or goldfinch, having a short stout bill.

find *v.* To come upon unexpectedly; to achieve; to attain; to ascertain; to determine; to consider; to regard; to recover or regain something; to detect the true identity or nature of something or someone. **finding** *v.*

find-er *n.* A person who finds; the device on a camera that indicates what will be in the picture.

find-ing *n.* Something that is found or discovered. **findings** *pl.*, *n.* Conclusions or statistics that are the result of a study, examination, or investigation.

fine *adj.* Superior in skill or quality; very enjoyable and pleasant; light and delicate in workmanship, texture, or structure; made up or composed of very small parts. *Slang* To be in good health; very well. *n.* The sum of money required as the penalty for an offense.
fineness *n.* **fine** *v.* **finely** *adv.*

fi-ne *n.*, *Mus.* The end.

fine arts *pl.*, *n.* The arts of drawing, painting, sculpture, architecture, literature, music, and drama.

fin-er-y *n.*, *pl.* **-ies** Elaborate jewels and clothes.

fi-nesse *n.* A highly refined skill; the skillful handling of a situation.

fin-ger *n.* One of the digits of the hand, usually excluding the thumb; that part of a glove made to fit the finger; anything resembling the finger. *Mus.* The use of the fingers in playing an instrument.

fin-ger-board *n.* The strip of wood on the neck of a stringed instrument against which the strings are pressed by the fingers in order to play.

fin-ger bowl *n.* A small bowl which contains water for cleansing the fingers at the table after eating.

fin-ger-ing *n.*, *Mus.* The technique of using the fingers in order to play a musical instrument; the marking that indicates which fingers are to be used.

fin-ger-nail *n.* The transparent covering on the dorsal surface of the tip of each finger.

fin-ger-print *n.*

An inked impression of the pattern formed by the ridges of the skin on the tips of each finger and thumb. **fingerprint** *v.*

fin-ger-tip *n.* The extreme end of a finger.

fin-i-al *n.* The ornamental projection or terminating part, as on a lamp shade.

fin-ick-y *adj.* Hard to please; choosy.

fi-nis *n.* The end.

fin-ish *v.* To bring to an end; to conclude; to reach the end; to consume all. *Slang* To kill, defeat, or destroy. *n.* The last stage or conclusion of anything; the perfection or polish in manners, speech, or education; the surface quality or appearance of paint, textiles, or other materials. *adj.* Having glossy polish. **finishing** *v.*,
finisher *n.*, **finished** *adj.*

fi-nite *adj.* Having bounds or limits; of or relating to a number which can be determined, counted, or measured.
finitely *adv.*, **finiteness** *n.*

fink *n.*, *Slang* A person that breaks a strike; an unsavory person.

Finn *n.* A native or inhabitant of Finland

land.

fin-nan had-dle *n.* Smoked haddock.

fin-ny *adj.* Having or suggesting fins or fin-like extensions.

fir *n.* An evergreen tree with flat needles and erect cones.

fire *n.* The chemical reaction of burning, which releases heat and light. *v.* To have great enthusiasm; to ignite or cause to become ignited; to bake in a kiln; to discharge a firearm or explosive; to let a person go from a job; to dismiss. **fired, firing** *v.*

fire a-larm *n.* A safety device to signal the outbreak of a fire.

fire-arm *n.* A small weapon used for firing a missile; a pistol or rifle using an explosive charge.

fire-ball *n.* A very bright meteor; a hot, incandescent sphere of air and vaporized debris. *Slang* A remarkably energetic person or thing.

fire-box *n.* A box that contains a fire alarm; the compartment in which the fuel of a locomotive or furnace is burned.

fire-brand *n.* A piece of glowing or burning wood; one who stirs up or agitates conflict or trouble.

fire-break *n.* A strip of land that is cleared to prevent a fire from spreading.

fire-brick *n.* A highly heat-resistant brick, used to line furnaces and fireplaces.

fire-bug *n.* One who enjoys setting fire to buildings or homes; a pyromaniac.

fire-crack-er *n.* A small paper cylinder charged with an explosive that is set off to make noise.

fire-damp *n.* Gas, mainly methane, occurring naturally in coal mines and forming explosive mixtures with air.

fire en-gine *n.* A large motor vehicle equipped to carry firefighters and their equipment to a fire.

fire es-cape *n.* A structure, often metal, used as an emergency exit from a building.

fire ex-tin-guish-er *n.* A portable apparatus that contains fire extinguishing chemicals, which are ejected through a short nozzle and hose.

fire fight-er *n.* A person who fights fires as an occupation.

fire-fly *n.* A beetle that flies at night, having an abdominal organ that gives off a flashing light.

fire-house *n.* The building used to house fire fighting equipment and personnel.

fire irons *pl. n.* Equipment that includes tongs, shovel, and a poker used to tend a fire, usually in a fireplace.

fire-man *n., pl.* -**men** A person employed to prevent or extinguish fires; one who tends fires.

fire-place *n.* An open recess in which a fire is built, especially the base of a chimney that opens into a room.

fire-plug *n.* A hydrant for supplying water in the event of a fire.

fire-pow-er *n., Milit.* The capacity to deliver fire or missiles, as from a weapon, military unit, or ship.

fire-proof *adj.* Resistant to fires.

fire tow-er *n.* A forest fire lookout station.

fire-trap *n.* A building made from such construction or built in such a way that it would be hard to escape from if there were a fire.

fire wall *n.* A fireproof wall in a building used as a barrier to forestall or prevent a fire from spreading.

fire-works *pl. n.* Explosives used to generate colored lights, smoke, and noise for entertainment or celebrations.

fir-ing line *n.* In combat, the front line from which gunfire is delivered; the vulnerable front position of a pursuit or activity.

firm *adj.* Relatively solid, compact, or unyielding to pressure or touch; steadfast and constant; strong and sure. *n.* A partnership of two or more persons for conducting a business. *v.* To become or make firm or firmer.

firm-ly *adv.* Unwaveringly; resolutely. **firmness** *n.*

fir-ma-ment *n.* The expanse of the heavens; the sky.

firn *n.* Snow that is partially consolidated by thawing and freezing but has not converted to glacial ice.

first *adj.* Preceding all others in the order of numbering; taking place or acting prior to all others; earliest; ranking above all in importance or quality; foremost. *adv.* Above or before all others in time, order, rank, or importance; for the very first time. *n.* The ordinal number that matches the number 1 in a series, 1st; the transmission gear producing the lowest driving speed in an automotive vehicle. **firstly** *adv.*

first aid *n.* The emergency care given to a person before full treatment and medical care can be obtained.

First Amend-ment *n.* The amendment to the Constitution of the United States which forbids Congress to interfere with religion, free speech, free press, the right to assemble peaceably, or the right to petition the government, ratified in 1791.

first-born *adj.* First in order. *n.* The child who is born first.

first class *n.* The best quality or highest rank; a class of sealed mail that consists partly or wholly of written matter; the best or most luxurious accommodations on a plane, ship, etc.

first-de-gree burn *n.* A mild burn characterized by heat, pain, and redness of the skin surface but not exhibiting blistering or charring of tissues.

first-hand *adj.* Coming directly from the original source. **firsthand** *adv.*

first la-dy *or* **First La-dy** *n.* The wife of the President of the United States or the wife or hostess of the chief executive of a state, city, or other country.

first lieu-ten-ant *n.*, *Milit.* A commissioned officer ranking above a 2nd lieutenant and below a captain.

first per-son *n.* A category for verbs or pronouns indicating the speaker or writer of a sentence in which they are used.

first-rate *adj.* Of the finest rank, quality, or importance. **first-rate** *adv.*

firth *n.* A narrow inlet or arm of the sea.

fis-cal *adj.* Relating to or of the finances or treasury of a nation or a branch of government; financial. **fiscally** *adv.*

fish *n.*, *pl.* **fish** *or* **fishes**

A cold-blooded, vertebrated aquatic animal having fins, gills for breathing, and usually scales; the flesh of fish used as food. **like a fish out of water** Not at ease or comfortable. *v.* To try to catch fish; to seek or find one's way; to grope; to try and obtain something in an artful or indirect way. **fishing** *n.*

fish bowl *n.* A bowl usually made of glass, serving as a small aquarium for fish; a lack of privacy.

fish-er-man *n.*, *pl.* **-men** A person who fishes commercially or for sport and relaxation; a commercial fishing boat.

fish-er-y *n.*, *pl.* **-ies** The business of catching, processing, or selling fish; a fish nursery or hatchery.

fish sto-ry *n.* An extravagant, boastful story that is probably not true.

fish-tail *v.* To swing from side to side while moving forward, as the motion of the rear end of a vehicle.

fish-wife *n.*, *pl.* **-wives** A very coarse, abusive woman.

fish-y *adj.* Resembling fish, as in taste or odor; improbable; highly suspicious. **fishily** *adv.*, **fishiness** *n.*

fis-sile *adv.* Capable of being separated or split. *Physics* Fissionable. **-ity** *n.*

fis-sion *n.* The process or act of splitting into parts. *Physics* The exploding of the nucleus of an atom that leads to the formation of more stable atoms and the release of large quantities of energy. **fissionable** *adj.*

fis-sure *n.* A narrow opening, crack, or cleft in a rock. **fissure** *v.*

fist *n.* The hand closed tightly with the fingers bent into the palm. *Slang* The hand.

fist-fight *n.* A fight between two or more people without protection for the hands.

fist-ful *n.*, *pl.* **-fuls** A hand full.

fis-tu-la *n.*, *pl.* **-las** *or* **-lae** *Pathol.* A duct or other passage formed by the imperfect closing of a wound or abscess and leading either to the body surface or to another hollow organ. **-ous** *adj.*

fit *v.* To be the proper size and shape; to be in good physical condition; to possess the proper qualifications; to be competent; to provide a time or place for something; to belong. *adj.*

Adapted or adequate for a particular circumstance or purpose. *Med.* A convulsion; an impulsive and irregular exertion or action. **fitter**, **fitness** *n.*

fitch *n.* The polecat of the Old World or its fur.

fit-ful *adj.* Characterized by irregular actions; capricious; restless. **fitfully** *adv.*, **fitfulness** *n.*

fit-ing *adj.* Suitable or proper. *n.* The act of trying on clothes for alteration; a piece of equipment or an appliance used in an adjustment. **fittingly** *adv.*, **fittingness** *n.*

five *n.* The cardinal number equal to 4 + 1; any symbol of this number, as 5; anything with five units, parts, or members. **five** *adj. & pron.*

fix *v.* To make stationary, firm, or stable; to direct or hold steadily; to place or set definitely; to make rigid; to arrange or adjust; to prepare, as a meal. *n.* A position of embarrassment or difficulty. *Naut.* The position of a ship determined by observations, radio, or bearings. *Slang* The injection of a narcotic, such as heroin. **fixing, fixed** *v.*

fix-a-tion *n.* The act or state of being fixed; a strong, often unhealthy preoccupation. **fixate** *v.*

fix-ture *n.* Anything that is fixed or installed, as a part or appendage of a house; any article of personal property affixed to reality to become a part of and governed by the law of real property.

fizz *n.* A hissing or bubbling sound; effervescence; tiny gas bubbles. **fizz** *v.*

Fl *or* **FL** *abbr.* Florida.

flab *n.* Excessive, loose, and flaccid body tissue. **flabby** *adj.*, **flabbiness** *n.*

flab-ber-gast *v.* To astound; to amaze. **flabbergasting, flabbergasted** *v.*

flac-cid *adj.* Lacking resilience or firmness. **flaccidity** *n.*, **flaccidly** *adv.*

flac-on *n.* A small, stoppered decorative bottle.

flag *n.* A piece of cloth, usually oblong, bearing distinctive colors and designs to designate a nation, state, city, or organization. *Bot.* Any of various iris or cattail plants with long blade-shaped leaves. *v.* To mark with or adorn with flags for identification or ornamentation; to grow weak or tired.

Flag Day *n.* June 14, 1777, the day on which Congress proclaimed the Stars and Stripes the national standard of the United States.

flag-el-lant *n.* One who whips himself or has himself whipped by another for religious motives or for sexual excitement. **flagellation** *n.*

flag-on *n.* A vessel or container with a handle, spout, and hinged lid, used for holding wines or liquors.

fla-grant *adj.* Obvious; glaring; disgraceful; notorious; outrageous. **flagrance, flagrancy** *n.*, **flagrantly** *adv.*

flair *n.* An aptitude or talent for something; a dashing style.

flak *n.* Antiaircraft fire; abusive or excessive criticism.

flake *n.* A small, flat, thin piece which has split or peeled off from a surface. *Slang* Oddball; eccentric. **flake** *v.*, **flakily** *adv.*, **flakiness** *n.*, **flaky** *adj.*

flam-boy-ant *adj.* Extravagantly ornate; showy; florid; brilliant and rich in color. **flamboyance, flamboyancy** *n.*, **flamboyantly** *adv.*

flame *n.* A mass of burning vapor or gas rising from a fire, often having a bright color and forming a tongue-shaped area of light; something that resembles a flame in motion, intensity, or appearance; a bright, red-yellow color; violent and intense emotion or passion. *Slang* A sweetheart. **flaming, flamed, flame** *v.*

fla-men-co *n.* A fiery percussive dance of the Andalusian gypsies with strong and often improvised rhythms.

flame-out *n.* The combustion failure of a jet aircraft engine while in flight.

fla-min-go *n.* A large, long-necked, tropical wading bird, having very long legs, and pink or red plumage.

flam-ma-ble *adj.* Capable of catching fire and burning rapidly. **flammability, flammable** *n.*

flange *n.* A projecting rim or collar used to strengthen or guide a wheel or other object, keeping it on a fixed track. **flange** *v.*

flank *n.* The fleshy part between the ribs and the hip on either side of the body of an animal or human being; the lateral part of something. *Milit.* The right or left side of a military bastion or formation. *v.* To be stationed at the side of something. **flanker** *n.*

flan-nel *n.* A woven fabric made of wool or a wool, cotton, or synthetic blend. **flannels** *pl.*, *n.* Trousers made of flannel. **flannelly** *adj.*

flan-nel-ette *n.* Cotton flannel.

flap-per *n.* A young woman of the 1920's whose dress and behavior were considered unconventional; a young bird not yet able to fly.

flare *v.* To blaze up or burn with a bright light; to break out suddenly or violently, as with emotion or action; to open or spread outward. **flaring, flared** *v.*, **flare** *n.*

flash *v.* To burst forth repeatedly or suddenly into a brilliant fire or light; to occur or appear briefly or suddenly. *n.* A short and important news break or transmission. **flashed, flashing** *v.*

flash-back *n.* The interruption in the continuity of a story, motion picture, drama, or novel to give a scene that happened earlier.

flash card *n.* A card printed with numbers or words and displayed briefly as a learning drill.

flash flood *n.* A violent and sudden flood occurring after a heavy rain.

flash point *n.* The lowest temperature at which the vapor of a combustible liquid will ignite or burn.

flash-y *adj.* Showing brilliance for a moment; tastelessly showy; gaudy. **flashily** *adv.*, **flashiness** *n.*

flask *n.* A small container made of glass and used in laboratories.

flat *adj.* Extending horizontally with no curvature or tilt; stretched out level, prostrate or prone; lacking flavor or zest; deflated. *Mus.* Below the correct pitch. *n.* An apartment that is entirely on one floor of a building. **flat broke** Having little or no money. **to fall flat** Failing to achieve. **-ly** *adv.*, **-ness** *n.*

flat-bed *n.* A truck that has a shallow rear platform without sides.

flat-car *n.*

A railroad car having no roof or sides.

flat-foot *n.*, *pl.* **-feet** A condition in which the arch of the foot is flat. *Slang* A police officer. **flat-footed** *adj.*

flat--out *adv.* In a direct way; at top speed. *adj.* Out-and-out.

flat-ten *v.* To make flat; to knock down. **flattener** *n.*

flat-ter *v.* To praise extravagantly, especially without sincerity; to gratify the vanity of; to portray favorably; to show as more attractive. **flatterer** *n.*, **flattering** *adj.*, **flatteringly** *adv.*

flat-ter-y *n.* Excessive, often insincere compliments.

flat-top *n.* A United States aircraft carrier; a short haircut having a flat crown.

flat-u-lent *adj.* Marked by or affected with gases generated in the intestine or stomach; pretentious without real worth or substance. **flatulence** *n.*, **flatulently** *adv.*

flat-ware *n.* Tableware that is fairly flat and designed usually of a single piece, as plates; table utensils, as knives, forks, and spoons.

flaunt *v.* To display showily. **-ing** *v.*, **flaunter** *n.*, **flauntingly** *adv.*

flau-tist *n.* A flutist.

fla-vor *n.* A distinctive element in the taste of something; a distinctive, characteristic quality; a flavoring. *v.* To impart flavor to. **flavorful, flavorsome** *adj.*

fla-vor-ing *n.* A substance, as an extract or something else that is used to increase the flavor.

flaw *n.* A defect or blemish that is often hidden and that may cause failure under stress; a weakness in character; a fault in a legal paper that may nullify it. **flaw** *v.*

flaw-less *adj.* Without flaws or defects; perfect. **-ly** *adv.*, **flawlessness** *n.*

flax *n.* A plant with blue flowers, seeds that yield linseed oil, and slender stems from which a fine textile fiber is derived.

flax-en *adj.* Made of or pertaining to flax; pale yellow or golden as flax fiber.

flay *v.* To remove the skin of; to scold harshly.

flea *n.* A small, wingless, bloodsucking,

parasitic jumping insect; a parasite of warm-blooded animals.

flea-bit-ten *adj.* Bitten or covered by fleas. *Slang* Shabby.

flea mar-ket *n.* A place where antiques and used items goods are sold.

fleck *n.* A tiny spot or streak; a small flake or bit. *v.* To mark with flecks.

fledg-ling *or* **fledge-ling** *n.* A young bird with newly acquired feathers; a person who is inexperienced; a beginner.

flee *v.* To run away; to move swiftly away. fleeing *v.*, fleer *n.*

fleece *n.* A coat of wool covering a sheep; the soft wool covering a sheep. *v.* To shear the fleece from; to swindle; to cover with fleece. fleecer, fleeciness *n.*, fleecily *adv.*, fleecy *adj.*

fleet *n.* A number of warships operating together under the same command; a number of vehicles, as taxicabs or fishing boats, operated under one command. *adj.* Moving rapidly or nimbly. fleetly *adv.*, fleetness *n.*

flesh *n.* Soft tissue of the body of a human or animal, especially skeletal muscle; the meat of animals as distinguished from fish or fowl; the pulpy substance of a fruit or vegetable; the body as opposed to the mind or soul; mankind in general; one's family. *v.* To arouse the hunting instinct of dogs by feeding fresh meat.

flesh and blood *n.* Human nature together with its weaknesses; one biologically connected to another.

flesh-ly *adj.* Of or pertaining to the body; sensual; worldly. fleshliness *n.*

flesh-pot *n.* A place were physical gratification is received.

flesh-y *adj.* Of, resembling, or suggestive of flesh; firm and pulpy; juicy as fruit. fleshiness *n.*

fleur-de-lis *n., pl.* **fleurs-de-lis**

A heraldic emblem consisting of a three-petaled iris, at one time used as the armorial emblem of French sovereigns; the emblem of Quebec Province.

flew *v.* Past tense of fly.

flex *v.* To bend the arm repeatedly; to contract a muscle. flexing, flexed *v.*

flex-i-ble *adj.* Capable of being bent or flexed; pliable; responsive to change; easily yielding. flexibility *n.*, flexibly *adv.*

flex time *n.* A system which allows employees to set their own work schedules within a wide range of hours.

flick *n.* A light, quick snapping movement or the sound accompanying it. *v.* To strike or hit with a quick, light stroke; to cause to move with a quick movement. *Slang* A movie.

flick-er *v.* To burn or shine unsteadily, as a candle. *n.* A wavering or unsteady light; a North American woodpecker

having a brownish back and a spot breast. flickering *v.*

fli-er *or* **fly-er** *n.* One who or that wh flies, especially an aviator; a daring risky venture; a printed advertisem or handbill for mass distribution.

flight *n.* The act or manner of flying scheduled airline trip; a group t flies together; a swift or rapid pass or movement, as of time; a group stairs leading from one floor another; an instance of fleeing.

flight at-ten-dant *n.* A person employ to assist passengers on an aircraft.

flight bag *n.* A lightweight piece of l gage having flexible sides and outs pockets.

flight-y *adj.* Inclined to act in a fic fashion; marked by irresponsible b havior, impulse, or whim; easily cited, skittish. flightiness *n.*

flim-flam *n. Slang* A swindle; trick; ho flimflam *v.*

flim-sy *adj.* Lacking in physical streng or substance; unconvincing. flimsiness *n.*, flimsily *adv.*

flinch *v.* To wince or pull back, as fro pain; to draw away. flincher *n.*

fling *v.* To throw or toss violently; throw oneself completely into an tivity. *n.* An act of casting away; casual attempt; a period devoted self-indulgence; unrestraint.

flint *n.* A hard quartz that produces spark when struck by steel; an imp ment used by primitive man; an all which used in lighters to ignite t fuel. flinty *adj.*

flip *v.* To turn or throw suddenly with jerk; to strike or snap quickly a lightly. *Slang* To go crazy; to becor upset or angry; to react enthusias cally. flip *n.*, flipper *adj.*

flip-flop *n.* The sound or motion something flapping loosely; a bac ward somersault; a sudden reversal direction or point of view; electronic device or a circuit capab of assuming either of two stable state

flip-pant *adj.* Marked by or showi disrespect, impudence, or the lack seriousness. flippancy *n.*, -ly *adv.*

flip-per *n.* A broad flat limb, as of a se adapted for swimming; a paddle-li rubber shoe used by skin divers a other swimmers.

flip side *n.* The reverse or opposite side

flirt *v.* To make teasing romantic sexual overtures; to act so as to attra attention; to move abruptly; to dart. A person who flirts; a snappy, quic jerky movement. flirtation, flirtatiousness *n.*, flirtatious *adj.*

flit *v.* To move rapidly or abruptly.

flit-ter *v.* To flutter. flitter *n.*

float *n.* An act or instance of floatin something that floats on the surface or in a liquid; a device used to bu the baited end of a fishing line; floating platform anchored near shoreline, which is used by swimme or boats; a vehicle with a platfor used to carry an exhibit in a parade; a drink consisting of ice cream floating in a beverage. *v.* To be or cause to be suspended within or on the surface of a liquid; to be or cause to be suspended in or move through the air as if supported by water; to drift randomly from place to place; to move lightly and easily; to place a security on the market; to obtain money for the establishment or development of an enterprise by issuing and selling securities. -ing *v.*, -able *adj.*, -er *n.*

loat-ing rib *n.* One of the four lower ribs in the human being that are not attached to the other ribs.

lock *n.* A group of animals of all the same kind, especially birds, sheep, geese, etc., living, feeding or kept together; a group under the direction of a single person, especially the members of a church; a large number. *v.* To travel as if in a flock.

loe *n.* A large, flat mass of floating ice or a detached part of such a mass.

log *v.* To beat hard with a whip or stick.

lood *n.* The great deluge depicted in the Old Testament; an overflow of water onto land that is normally dry; an overwhelming quantity. *v.* To overwhelm with or as if with a flood; to fill abundantly or overwhelm; to supply the carburetor of an engine with an excessive amount of fuel; in football, to send more than one pass receiver into the same defensive area.

lood-gate *n.* A valve for controlling the flow or depth of a large body of water.

lood-light *n.* An electric lamp that gives off a broad and intensely bright beam of light. floodlight *v.*

loor *n.* The level base of a room; the lower inside surface of a structure; a ground surface; the right, as granted under parliamentary rules, to speak to a meeting or assembly; an area dividing a building into stories. *v.* To cover or furnish with a floor; to knock down; to overwhelm; to puzzle; to press the accelerator of a vehicle to the floorboard.

loor ex-er-cise *n.* A competitive gymnastics event with tumbling maneuvers performed on a mat.

loor show *n.* Entertainment consisting of singing, dancing; nightclub acts.

loor-walk-er *n.* A department store employee who supervises the sales force and gives assistance to customers.

loo-zy *n., pl.* -ies *Slang* A sleazy, loose woman; a prostitute.

lop *v.* To fall down clumsily; to move about in a clumsy way. *Slang* To completely fail; to go to bed. flop *n.*

lop house *n.* A cheap, rundown hotel.

lop-py *adj.* Flexible and loose. floppily *adv.*, floppiness *n.*

lop-py disk *n.* In computer science, a flexible plastic disk which is coated with magnetic material, used to record and store computer data.

flo-ra *n., pl.* -ras *or* -rae Plants growing in a specific region or season.

flo-ral *adj.* Of or pertaining to flowers.

flo-res-cence *n.* A state or process of blossoming. florescent *adj.*

flor-id *adj.* Flushed with a rosy color or redness; ornate. -ness *n.*, floridly *adv.*

Flor-i-da *n.* A state located on the southeastern coast of the United States.

flo-rist *n.* One who grows or sells flowers and also artificial ones which are made of silk or silk-like fibers.

floss *n.* A loosely-twisted embroidery thread; a soft, silky fiber, such as the tassel on corn; dental floss. *v.* To clean between the teeth with dental floss. flossed, flossing *v.*

flo-ta-tion *n.* The act or state of floating.

flo-til-la *n.* A fleet of small vessels; a group resembling a small fleet.

flot-sam *n.* Any goods remaining afloat after a ship has sunk.

flounce *n.* A gathered piece of material attached to the upper edge of another surface, as on a curtain. *v.* To move with exaggerated tosses of the body.

floun-der *v.* To struggle clumsily, as to gain footing; to act or speak in a confused way. *n.* Any of various edible marine flatfish. floundered, -ing *v.*

flour *n.* A soft, fine, powder-like substance obtained by grinding the meal of grain, especially wheat. *v.* To coat or sprinkle with flour. flourly *adj.*

flour-ish *v.* To thrive; to fare well; to prosper and succeed. *n.* A decorative touch or stroke, especially in handwriting; a dramatic act or gesture; a musical fanfare, as of trumpets. flourished, flourishing *v.*

flout *v.* To have or show open contempt for. floutingly *adv.*

flow *v.* To move freely, as a fluid; to circulate, as blood; to proceed or move steadily and easily; to rise; to derive; to be abundant in something; to hang in a loose, free way. flow *n.*

flow chart *n.* A chart or diagram showing the sequence and progress of a series of operations on a specific project.

flow-er *n.* A cluster of petals, bright in color, near or at the tip of a seed-bearing plant; blossoms; the condition of highest development; the peak; the best example or representative of something. *v.* To produce flowers; to bloom; to develop fully.

fl oz *abbr.* Fluid ounce.

flu *n., Informal* Influenza.

flub *v.* To bungle or botch; to make a mess of. flub *n.*

fluc-tu-ate *v.* To shift irregularly; to change; to undulate. fluctuation *n.*

flue *n.* A conduit or passage through which air, gas, steam, or smoke can pass.

flu-ent *adj.* Having an understanding of a language use; flowing smoothly and naturally; flowing or capable of flowing. fluency *n.*, fluently *adv.*

fluff *n.* A ball, tuft, or light cluster of

loosely gathered fibers of cotton or wool. *Slang* A mistake made by an actor or announcer in reading or announcing something. *v.* To make or become fluffy by patting with the hands. *Informal* To make an error in speaking or reading.

flu-id *n.* A substance, as water or gas, capable of flowing. *adj.* Changing readily, as a liquid.

fluidity, fluidness *n.,* **fluidly** *adv.*

fluke *n.* A flatfish, especially a flounder; a flattened, parasitic trematode worm; the triangular head of an anchor at the end of either of its arms; a barb or point on an arrow; an unexpected piece of good luck. **fluky** *adj.*

flung *v.* Past tense of fling.

flunk *v., Slang* To fail in, as an examination or course; to give a failing grade to. **flunking, flunked** *v.*

flun-ky *or* **flun-key** *n.* A liveried servant; a person who does menial work.

flu-o-res-cence *n., Chem., Phys.* Emission of electromagnetic radiation, especially of visible light, resulting from and occurring during the absorption of radiation from another source; the radiation emitted.

fluorescence *v.,* **fluorescent** *adj.*

fluorescent lamp *n.* A tubular electric lamp in which ultraviolet light is reradiated as visible light.

fluor-i-date *v.* To add a sodium compound to water in order to prevent tooth decay. **flouridating, flouridated** *v.,* **fluoridation** *n.*

flu-o-ride *n.* A compound of fluorine with another element or a radical.

flu-o-rine *n.* A pale yellow, corrosive, and extremely reactive gaseous element, symbolized by F.

fluor-o-scope *n.* A device for observing shadows projected upon a flourescent screen of an optically opaque object, as the human body, which may be viewed by transmission of x-rays through the object. **fluoroscope** *v.,* **fluoroscopic** *adj.,* **fluoroscopy** *n.*

flur-ry *n., pl.* **-ies** A sudden gust of wind; a brief, light fall of snow or rain, accompanied by small gusts; a sudden burst of activity or commotion.

flush *v.* To flow or rush out suddenly and abundantly; to become red in the face; to blush; to glow with a reddish color; to purify or wash out with a brief, rapid gush of water; to cause to flee from cover, as a game animal or bird. *n.* Glowing freshness or vigor; a hand in certain card games, as poker, in which all the cards are the same suit. *adj.* Having a heightened reddish color; abundant; affluent, prosperous; having surfaces that are even; arranged with adjacent sides close together; having margins aligned with no indentations; direct as a blow. *adv.* In an even position with another surface. **flushed, flushing** *v.*

flus-ter *v.* To make or become nervous or confused.

flute *n.* A high-pitched, tubular woo wind instrument equipped with fing holes and keys; a decorative groove the shaft of a column; a small groove pleat, as in cloth.

fluting *n.,* **fluted** *adj.*

flut-ist *n.* A fl:ute player.

flut-ter *v.* To flap or wave rapidly and i regularly; to fly as with a light, rapi beating of the wings; to beat errat cally, as one's heart; to move about i a restless way. **flutter** *n.* **fluttery** *adj.*

flux *n.* A flowing or discharge; a consta flow or movement; a state of consta fluctuation or change; a substance th promotes the fusing of metals an prevents oxide formation. *v.* To mak fluid; to melt; to apply a flux to.

fly *v.*

To move through the air on wings wing-like parts; to travel by air; float or cause to float in the air; to e cape; to flee; to pass by swiftly quickly; to hit a fly ball. *n.* A folde piece of cloth that covers the fastenin of a garment, especially trousers; a ball one has batted over the field; a of numerous winged insects, includi the housefly and the tsetse; a fishin lure that resembles an insect. **fly o the handle** To react explosively.

flyable *adj.*

fly--by--night *adj.* Unstable or ten porary; financially unsound.

fly-weight *n.* A boxer who belongs to t lightest weight class, weighing 11 pounds or less.

fly-wheel *n.* A rotating wheel hea enough to regulate the speed of machine shaft.

FM *abbr.* Field manual; frequenc modulation.

foal *n.* The young animal, as a hors especially one under a year old. *v.* give birth to a foal.

foam *n.* A mass of bubbles produced o the surface of a liquid by agitation froth; a firm, spongy material use especially for insulation an upholstery. *v.* To cause to form foa **foam at the mouth** To be very angry.

foaminess *n.,* **foamy** *adj.*

fob *n.* A chain or ribbon attached to pocket watch and worn dangling fro a pocket; an ornament or seal worn a fob. *v.* To dispose of by frau deceit, or trickery; to put off by e cuse.

focal length *n.* The distance to the foc from a lens surface or concave mirro

fo-cus *n., pl.* **cuses** *or* **ci** A point in an o tical system at which rays converge from which they appear to diverge; t clarity with which an optical syste delivers an image; adjustment f clarity; a center of activity or intere *v.* To produce a sharp, clear image to adjust a lens in order to produce a clean image; to direct; to come together at a point of focus.

fo·cal *adj.*, **focally** *adv.*

fod·der *n.* A coarse feed for livestock, made from chopped stalks of corn and hay.

foe *n.* An enemy in war; an opponent or adversary.

foe-tal *adj.* Variation of fetal.

foe-tus *n.* Variation of fetus.

fog *n.* A vapor mass of condensed water which lies close to the ground; a state of mental confusion or bewilderment. *v.* To obscure or cover with, as if with fog. -**gily** *adv.*, **fogginess** *n.*, -**gy** *adj.*

fog-horn *n.* A horn sounded in fog to give warning.

fo-gy or **fo-gey** *n.* A person with old-fashioned attitudes and ideas. -**ish** *adj.*

foi-ble *n.* A minor flaw, weakness, or failing.

foil *v.* To prevent from being successful; to thwart. *n.* A very thin, flexible sheet of metal; one that serves as a contrast; a fencing sword having a light, thin, flexible blade and a blunt point.

foiled, foiling *v.*

foist *v.* To pass off something as valuable or genuine.

fold *v.* To double or lay one part over another; to bring from an opened to a closed position; to put together and intertwine; to envelop or wrap; to blend in by gently turning one part over another. *Slang* To give in; to stop production; to fail in business. *n.* A line, layer, pleat or crease formed by folding; a folded edge; an enclosed area for domestic animals; a flock of sheep; a people united by common aims and beliefs; a church and its members. **folding, folded** *v.*

fol-de-rol *n.* Nonsense; a pretty but useless ornament.

fo-li-age *n.* The leaves of growing plants and trees; a cluster of flowers and branches.

fo-li-o *n.* A large sheet of paper folded once in the middle; a folder for loose papers; a book that consists of folios; a page number.

folk *n.*, *pl.* **folk** or **folks** An ethnic group of people forming a nation or tribe; people of a specified group. *Slang* A person's parents, family, or relatives.

fol-li-cle *n.* A small anatomical cavity or sac.

fol-low *v.* To proceed or come after; to pursue; to follow the course of; to obey; to come after in time or position; to ensue; to result; to attend to closely; to understand the meaning of. **following, followed** *v.*

fol-ly *n.*, *pl.* -**ies** Lack of good judgment; an instance of foolishness; an excessively costly and often unprofitable undertaking.

fo-ment *v.* To rouse; to incite; to treat therapeutically with moist heat. **foment, fomentation** *n.*

fond *adj.* Affectionate liking; cherished with great affection; deeply felt. **fondly** *adv.*, **fondness** *n.*

fon-dant *n.* A sweet, soft preparation of sugar used in candies and icings; a candy made chiefly of fondant.

fon-dle *v.* To stroke, handle, or caress affectionately and tenderly. **fondled, fondling** *v.*

font *n.* A receptacle in a church that holds baptismal or holy water; an assortment of printing type of the same size and face.

food *n.* A substance consisting essentially of carbohydrates and protein used to sustain life and growth in the body of an organism; nourishment, as in solid form; something that sustains or nourishes. **food for thought** Something to think about, something to ponder.

food-stuff *n.* A substance having food value.

fool *n.* One lacking good sense or judgment; one who can easily be tricked or made to look foolish. *v.* To dupe; to act in jest; to joke. *Slang* To amuse oneself. **fooling** *v.*

foot *n.*, *pl.* **feet**

The lower extremity of the vertebrate leg upon which one stands; a unit of measurement equal to 12 inches; a basic unit of verse meter that consists of a group of syllables; the end lower or opposite the head; the lowest part. *v.* To go on foot; to walk or run. *Slang* To pay the bill. **on foot** Walking rather than riding.

foot-ball *n.*

A game played by two teams on a long rectangular field having goals at either end whose object is to get the ball over a goal line or between goalposts by running, passing or kicking; the oval ball used in the game of football.

foot-bridge *n.* A bridge for pedestrians.

foot-fall *n.* A footstep; the sound of a footstep.

foot-hill *n.* A low hill at or near the foot of a mountain or a higher hill.

foot-hold *n.* A place providing support for the foot, as in climbing; a position usable as a base for advancement.

foot-ing *n.* Secure and stable position for placement of the feet; a foundation.

foot-less *adj.* Without feet.

foot-locker *n.* A small trunk for personal belongings, designed to be placed at the foot of a bed.

foot-loose *adj.* Free to move as one pleases; having no ties.

foot-note *n.* A note of reference, explanation, or comment usually below the text on a printed page; a commentary. **footnote** *v.*

foot-path *n.* A narrow path for people on foot.

foot-print *n.* The outline or impression of the foot on a surface.

foot-stool *n.* A low stool for resting the feet.

foot-wear *n.* Articles, as shoes or boots, worn on the feet.

foot-work *n.* The use of the feet, as in boxing.

fop *n.* A man unduly concerned with his clothes or appearance; a dandy. **foppery, foppishness** *n.,* **foppish** *adj.*

for *prep.* Used to indicate the extent of something; used to indicate the number or amount of; considering the usual characteristics of; on behalf of someone; to be in favor of. *conj.* Because; in as much as; with the purpose of.

for-age *n.* Food for cattle or other domestic animals; a search for supplies or food. *v.* To make a raid so as to find supplies; to plunder or rummage through, especially in search of provisions. **forager** *n.*

for-ay *n.* A raid to plunder. **foray** *v.*

for-bade *or* **for-bad** *v.* Past tense of forbid.

for-bear *v.* To refrain from; to cease from. **forbearance** *n.*

for-bid *v.* To command someone not to do something; to prohibit by law; to prevent.

forbidding *adj.* Very difficult; disagreeable.

force *n.* Energy or power; strength; the use of such power; intellectual influence; a group organized for a certain purpose. *Physics* Something that changes the state of rest or the body motion or influence. *v.* To compel to do something or to act; to obtain by coercion; to bring forth, as with effort; to move or drive against resistance; to break down by force; to press or impose, as one's will. **in force** In large numbers; in effect. **forceable.**

forceful *adj.,* **forcer** *n.,* **forcefully** *adv.*

force-meat *n.* Finely ground meat, fish, or poultry, used in stuffing or served separately.

for-ceps *n.* **forceps** *pl.*

An instrument resembling a pair of tongs used for manipulating, grasping or extracting, especially in surgery.

forc-i-ble *adj.* Accomplished or achieved by force; marked by force. **-y** *adv.*

ford *n.* A shallow place in a body of water that can be crossed without a boat. *v.* To wade across a body of water.

Ford, Gerald Rudolph *n.* The 38th president of the United States from, 1974-1977.

Ford, Henry *n.* (1863-1947). American automobile maker.

fore *adj. & adv.* Situated in, at, or toward the front; forward. *n.* The front of

something. *interj.* A cry used by a golfer to warn others that a ball is about to land in their direction.

fore--and--aft *adj.* Lying or going lengthwise on a ship; from stem to stern.

fore-arm *v.* To prepare in advance, as for a battle. *n.* The part of the arm between the elbow and the wrist.

fore-bear *or* **for-bear** *n.* An ancestor.

fore-bode *v.* To give an indication or warning in advance; to have a premonition of something evil. **foreboding** *n.,* **forbodingly** *adv.*

fore-cast *v.* To estimate or calculate in advance, especially to predict the weather. **forecast, forecaster** *n.*

fore-cas-tle *n.* The part of a ship's upper deck located forward of the foremast; living quarters for the crew at the bow of a merchant ship.

fore-close *v.* To recall a mortgage in default and take legal possession of the mortgaged property; to exclude; to shut out. **foreclosure** *n.*

fore-fa-ther *n.* An ancestor.

fore-fin-ger *n.* The finger next to the thumb.

fore-foot *n.* A front foot of an animal, insect, etc.

fore-front *n.* The foremost or very front of something; the vanguard.

fore-go *v.* To go before; to precede in time, place, etc. **foregoing** *v.*

fore-go-ing *adj.* Before; previous.

fore-gone *adj.* Already finished or gone.

fore-ground *n.* The part of a picture or landscape represented as nearest to the viewer.

fore-hand *n.* A stroke in tennis in which the palm of the hand holding the racket faces toward the direction of the stroke. **forehand** *adj. & adv.*

fore-head *n.* The part of the face that is above the eyebrows and extends to the hair.

for-eign *adj.* Situated outside one's native country; belonging to; located in or concerned with a country or region other than one's own; involved with other nations; occurring in a place or body in which it is not normally located.

for-eign-er *n.* A person from a different place or country; an alien.

fore-knowl-edge *n.* Prior knowledge of something; knowledge beforehand.

fore-lock *n.* A lock of hair growing from the front of the scalp and hanging over the forehead.

fore-man *n.* The person who oversees a group of people; the spokesperson for a jury. **forewoman** *n.*

fore-mast *n., Naut.* The forward mast of a sailing vessel; the mast nearest the bow of a ship.

fore-most *adj. & adv.* First in rank, position, time, or order.

fore-noon *n.* The period between sunrise and noon.

fo-ren-sic *adj.* Of, relating to, or used in courts of justice or formal debate.

forensically *adv.*

fo-ren-sic med-i-cine *n.* A science dealing with the application of medicine in legal problems.

fore-or-dain *v.* Appoint or dispose of in advance; predestine.

fore-part *n.* The first or earliest part of a period of time.

fore-run-ner *n.* One sent or going before to give notice of the approach of others; a harbinger.

fore-sail *n., Naut.* The sail carried on the foremast of a square-rigged vessel.

fore-see *v.* To know or see beforehand. **foreseeable** *adj.*, **foreseer** *n.*

fore-shad-ow *v.* To represent or warn of beforehand.

fore-shore *n.* The part of a shore uncovered at low tide.

fore-short-en *v.* To shorten parts of an object in order to give the illusion of depth.

fore-sight *n.* The act or capacity of foreseeing; the act of looking forward; concern for the future; prudence. **foresighted** *adj.*, **foresightedness** *n.*

fore-skin *n.* A fold of skin that covers the glans of the penis.

for-est *n.* A large tract of land covered with trees; something resembling a forest, as in quantity or density. *v.* To cover with trees. **forested** *adj.*, **forestland** *n.*

fore-stall *v.* To exclude, hinder, or prevent by prior measures.

for-est ran-ger *n.* An officer in charge of patrolling or protecting a public forest.

fore-taste *v.* To sample or indicate beforehand. **foretasting, foretasted** *v.*, **foretaste** *n.*

fore-tell *v.* To tell about in advance; to predict. **foretelling** *v.*, **foreteller** *n.*

fore-thought *n.* Prior thought or planning; a plan for the future.

fore-to-ken *v.* To warn beforehand.

for-ev-er *adv.* For eternity; without end.

fore-warn *v.* To warn in advance. **-ed** *v.*

fore-word *n.* An introductory statement preceding the text of a book.

for-feit *n.* Something taken away as punishment; a penalty; something that is placed in escrow and redeemed on payment of a fine; a forfeiture. *v.* To lose or give up the right to by some offense or error. **forfeiter** *n.*, **-able** *adj.*

for-fei-ture *n.* The act of forfeiting; something forfeited; a penalty.

for-gath-er *v.* To come together; to convene; to assemble. **-ing, forgathered** *v.*

forge *n.* A furnace where metals are heated and wrought; a smithy; a workshop that produces wrought iron. *v.* To form by heating and hammering; to give shape to; to imitate falsely; to advance slowly but steadily; to defraud; to counterfeit. **forging, forged** *v.*, **forger, forgery** *n.*

for-get *v.* To lose the memory of; to fail to become mindful or aware of at the right time. **forgetful, forgetable** *adj.*, **forgetfully** *adv.*, **forgetfulness** *n.*

for-give *v.* To pardon; to give up resentment of; to cease to feel resentment against. **forgiveness** *n.*, **forgivable** *adj.*

for-go *or* **fore-go** *v.* To give up or refrain from. **forgoer** *n.*

fork *n.* A tool consisting of a handle at one end of which are two or more prongs; the division of something into two or more parts that continue, as in a river or road.

forked *adj.* Shaped like or having a fork.

fork lift *n.* A self-propelled industrial vehicle with a pronged platform for hoisting and transporting heavy objects.

for-lorn *adj.* Abandoned or left in distress; hopeless; being in a poor condition. **forlornly** *adv.*, **forlornness** *n.*

form *n.* The shape or contour of something; a body of a living being; the basic nature or particular state of something; the way in which something exists; variety; manner, as established by custom or regulation; the style or manner determined by etiquette or custom; performance according to established criteria; fitness with regard to training or health; procedure of words, as in a ceremony; a document having blanks for insertion of information; style in musical or literary composition; the design or style of a work of art. *v.* To construct or conceive in the mind. *suffix* Having the form or shape of; cuneiform.

for-mal *adj.* Of or pertaining to the outward aspect of something; relating or concerned with the outward form of something; adhering to convention, rule, or etiquette; based on accepted conventions. **formally** *adv.*

for-mal-de-hyde *n.* A colorless, gaseous chemical used chiefly as a preservative and disinfectant in synthesizing other compounds.

for-mat *n.* A general style of a publication; the general form or layout of a publication. *v.* In computer science, to produce data in a specified form.

for-ma-tion *n.* The act or process of forming or the state of being formed; the manner in which something is formed; a given arrangement, as of troops, as a square or in a column.

for-ma-tive *adj.* Forming or having the power to form; of or pertaining to formation, growth, or development.

for-mer *adj.* Previous; preceding in place; being the first of two persons or things mentioned or referred to.

for-mer-ly *adv.* Previously.

form--fit-ting *adj.* Following closely to the contours of the body.

for-mi-da-ble *adj.* Extremely difficult; exciting fear by reason of size or strength. **formidably** *adv.*

form letter *n.* A standarized format of an impersonal letter sent to different people or to a large number of people.

for-mu-la *n.*, *pl.* **-las** *or* **-lae** A prescribed method of words or rules for use in a certain ceremony or procedure; a nutritious food for an infant in liquid form. *Math.* A combination or rule used to express an algebraic or symbolic form. *Chem.* A symbolic representation of the composition of a chemical compound. **formulaic** *adj.*

for-mu-late *v.* To state or express as a formula. **formulation, formulator** *n.* **formulating, formulated** *v.*

for-ni-ca-tion *n.* Voluntary sexual intercourse between two unmarried people. **fornicate** *v.,* **fornicator** *n.*

for-sake *v.* To abandon or renounce; to give up. **forsaking** *v.*

for-sooth *adv.* In truth; certainly.

for-swear *v.* To renounce emphatically or upon oath; to forsake; to swear falsely; to perjure oneself. **-ing** *v.*

for-syth-i-a *n.* An Asian shrub cultivated for its early-blooming, bright, yellow flowers.

fort *n.* A fortified structure or enclosure capable of defense against an enemy; a permanent army post.

forte *n.* An activity one does with excellence; a person's strong point; the part of a sword blade between the middle and the hilt.

forth *adv.* Out into plain sight, as from seclusion; forward in order, place, or time.

forth-com-ing *adj.* Ready or about to appear or occur; readily available.

forth-right *adj.* Straightforward; direct; frank. **-ly** *adv.,* **forthrightness** *n.*

forth-with *adv.* At once; promptly; immediately.

for-ti-fy *v.* To strengthen and secure with military fortifications; to provide physical strength or courage to; to strengthen; to enrich food, as by adding vitamins, minerals, etc. **fortification, fortifier** *n.,* **fortifying, fortified** *v.*

for-tis-si-mo *adv., Music.* Very loudly (used as a direction). **fortissimo** *adj.*

for-ti-tude *n.* Strength of mind in adversity, pain, or peril, allowing a person to withstand pain.

fort-night *n.* A period of two weeks. **fortnightly** *adj. & adv.*

FOR-TRAN *n.* In computer science, a programming language for problems that are expressed in algebraic terms.

for-tress *n.* A fort.

for-tu-i-tous *adj.* Occurring by chance; lucky; fortunate. **fortuitously** *adv.*

for-tu-nate *adj.* Brought about by good fortune; having good fortune.

for-tune *n.* A hypothetical force that unpredictably determines events and issues favorably and unfavorably; success that results from luck; possession of material goods; a very large amount of money.

fortune hunter *n.* A person who seeks wealth through marriage.

for-tune--tell-er *n.* A person who claims to predict the future. **-telling** *n. & adj.*

for-ty *n., pl.* **-ies** The cardinal number equal to four times ten.

fortieth *n., adj. & adv.,*

for-ty--nin-er *n.* A United States pioneer in the 1849 California gold rush.

forty winks *n., Slang* A short nap.

fo-rum *n., pl.* **-rums** *or* **-ra** A public marketplace in an ancient Rome city, where most legal and political business was transacted; a judicial assembly.

for-ward *adj.* At, near, or toward a place or time in advance; overstepping the usual bounds in an insolent or presumptuous way; extremely unconventional, as in political opinions; socially advanced. *n.* A player in football at the front line of offense or defense. *v.* To send forward or ahead; to help advance onward. **-ly** *adv.,* **-ness** *n.*

fos-sil *n.* The remains of an animal or plant of a past geologic age preserved in the rocks of the earth's surface; one that is outdated.

fossilization *n.,* **fossilize** *v.*

fos-ter *v.* To give parental care to; to nurture; to encourage. *adj.* Giving or receiving parental care.

foul *adj.* Revolting to the senses; spoiled or rotten; covered with offensive matter; morally offensive; vulgar or obscene; unfavorable; dishonorable; indicating the limiting lines of a playing area. *adj.* In a foul way. *v.* To physically contact or entangle; to become foul or dirty; to dishonor; to obstruct; to entangle; to make or hit a foul. **foul up** *Slang* To make a mistake. **foully** *adv.,* **foulness** *n.*

found *v.* To establish; to set up, often with funds to permit continuation and maintenance; to establish the basis or lay the foundation of; to melt metal and pour into a mold; to make by casting molten metal. **founder** *n.*

foun-da-tion *n.* The act of founding or establishing; the basis on which anything is founded; an institution supported by an endowment; a cosmetic base for make-up.

foun-dry *n., pl.* **ries** An establishment where metal is cast.

fount *n.* A fountain; an abundant source.

foun-tain *n.* A natural spring or jet of water coming from the earth; an artificially created spray of water; a basinlike structure from which such a stream comes; a point of origin or source.

fountain pen *n.* A pen having a reservoir of ink that automatically feeds the writing point.

four *n.* The cardinal number that equals 3 + 1; anything consisting of four units. **four** *adj. & pron.*

four-score *adj.* Being four times twenty; eighty.

four-teen *n.* The cardinal number that equals 13 + 1; anything consisting of fourteen units. **fourteen** *adj. & pron.,* **fourteenth** *n., adj. & adv.*

fourth *n.* The ordinal number matching the number four in a series; the fourth forward gear of a transmission in a motor vehicle. **fourth** *adj. & adv.*

Fourth of July *n.* American Independence Day celebrated as a national holiday.

four--wheel *adj.* An automotive transmission in which all four wheels are linked to the source of driving power.

fowl *n., pl.* fowl *or* fowls A bird used as food or hunted as game, as the duck, goose, etc.; the edible flesh of a fowl. *v.* To hunt or catch wild fowl. **-er** *n.*

fox *n.*

A wild mammal having a pointed snout, upright ears, and a long bushy tail; the fur of a fox; a sly or crafty person. *v.* To outwit; to trick.

fox-hole *n.* A shallow pit dug by a soldier as cover against enemy fire.

fox-hound *n.* A large dog breed developed for fox hunting.

fox terrier *n.* A small dog having a wiry or smooth white coat with dark markings.

fox--trot *n.* A ballroom dance in 4/4 or 2/4 time consisting of a variety of rhythmic steps.

fox-y *adj.* Like a fox; sly or crafty; sharp *Slang* Very pretty. **foxily** *adv.*

foy-er *n.* The public lobby of a hotel, theater, etc.; an entrance hall.

fpm *abbr.* Feet per minute.

fps *abbr.* Feet per second.

Fr *abbr.* Father (clergyman).

fra-cas *n.* A noisy quarrel or disturbance; fight or dispute.

frac-tion *n.* A small part; a disconnected part or fragment of anything; in mathematics, an indicated quantity less than a whole number that is expressed as a decimal. *Chem.* A component of a compound separated from a substance by distilling. **fractional** *adj.*

frac-ture *n.* The act of breaking; the state of being broken. *Med.* The breaking or cracking, as in a bone.

frag-ile *adj.* Easily damaged or broken; frail; tenuous; flimsy. **fragilely** *adv.*, **fragility** *n.*

frag-ment *n.* A part detached or broken; part unfinished or incomplete. *v.* To break into fragments. **-ation** *n.*

fra-grant *adj.* Having an agreeable, especially sweet odor. **fragrance** *n.*, **fragrantly** *adv.*

frail *adj.* Delicate; weak; easily damaged. **frailly** *adv.*, **frailness** *n.*

frame *v.* To put into a frame, as a picture; to build; to design; to adjust or adapt for a given purpose; to provide with a frame. *Slang* To incriminate so as to make a person appear guilty. *n.* Something made up of parts and joined together, such as a skeletal structure of a body; the pieces of wood or metal which surround a picture, photograph, or work of art; general structure; one exposure on a roll of film. **frame-up** *Slang* An act or actions which serve to frame someone or to make someone appear guilty when he is not. **-er** *n.*, **-ing, framed** *v.*

fran-chise *n.* A privilege or right granted to a person or group by a government; the constitutional right to vote; authorization to sell a manufacturer's products; the territory within which a privilege or immunity is authorized. **franchise** *v.*, **franchisee, franchiser** *n.*

Franco, Francisco *n.* (1892-1975). Spanish dictator.

Fran-co-A-mer-i-can *n.* An American of French descent. **Franco-American** *adj.*

fran-gi-ble *adj.* Breakable. **frangibility** *n.*

frank *adj.* Sincere and straightforward. *v.* To mark mail officially so that no charge is made for delivery. *n.* The right to send mail without charge; a signature or mark on mail indicating that mail can be sent without charge; mail sent without charge; to mail free. **frankly** *adv.*, **frankness** *n.*

Frank-fort *n.* The capital of Kentucky.

frank-furt-er *n.* A smoked sausage made of beef or beef and pork.

frank-in-cense *n.* An aromatic gum resin obtained from African and Asian trees used as incense and in medicine.

Frank-lin, Benjamin *n.* (1706-1790). American statesman, scientist and inventor.

Franklin stove *n.* A stove made of cast iron and shaped like a fireplace, which utilizes metal baffles to increase its energy efficiency.

fran-tic *adj.* Emotionally out of control with worry or fear. **-ally, -ly** *adv.*

fra-ter-nal *adj.* Pertaining to or relating to brothers; of, pertaining to, or befitting a fraternity. *Biol.* Of or relating to a twin or twins that developed from separately fertilized ova. **fraternalism** *n.*, **fraternally** *adv.*

frat-er-nize *v.* To associate with others in a friendly way; to mingle intimately with the enemy, often in violation of military law. **fraternizing, -ed** *v.*

frat-ri-cide *n.* The killing of one's brother or sister; one who has killed his brother or sister. **fratricidal** *adj.*

fraud *n.* A deliberate and willful deception perpetrated for unlawful gain; a trick or swindle; an impostor; a cheat.

fraud-u-lent *adj.* Marked by or practicing fraud. **fraudulence** *n.*, **-ly** *adv.*

fraught *adj.* Full of or accompanied by something specified.

fray *n.* A brawl, or fight; a heated argument or dispute. *v.* To wear out by rubbing; to irritate one's nerves.

fraz-zle *v., Slang* To wear out; to completely fatigue. **-ing, frazzled** *v.*

freak *n.* A seemingly capricious event; a whimsical quality or disposition. *Slang* A drug addict; a highly individualistic rebel; a person with an extreme physical abnormality; a fan or enthusiast. **freak out** To experience hallucinations or paranoia induced by a drug; to make or become highly excited.

freakish, freaky *adj.*, freakily *adv.*

freck-le *n.* One of the small, brownish, often sun induced spots on the skin usually due to precipitation of pigment increasing in number and intensity on exposure to the sun.

free *adj.* Not imprisoned; not under obligation; politically independent; possessing political liberties; not affected by a specified circumstance or condition; exempt; costing nothing; not being occupied or used; too familiar; forward; liberal, as with money. *adv.* In a free way; without charge. *v.* To set at liberty; to release or rid; to untangle. -ly *adv.*, -ness *n.*

free-dom *n.* The condition or state of being free; political independence; possession of political rights; boldness of expression; liberty; unrestricted access or use.

free lance *n.* One whose services are without long-term commitments to any one employer.

free--standing *adj.* Standing alone without any support.

free trade *n.* International exchange between nations or states which is unrestricted.

free-way *n.* A highway with more than two lanes.

free will *n.* The ability to choose freely; the belief that a human being's choices can be made freely, without external constraint. *adj.* Done willingly.

freeze *v.* To become ice or a similar solid through loss of heat; to preserve by cooling at an extremely low temperature; to become nonfunctional through the formation of ice or frost; to feel uncomfortably cold; to make or become rigid; to become suddenly motionless, rigid or inactive, as though through fear; to set prices at a certain level; to forbid further use of. *n.* An act of freezing or the state of being frozen; a cold snap. freezing *v.*

freeze--dry *v.* To preserve by drying in a frozen state under a high vacuum.

freeze-dried *adj.*

freez-er *n.* One that freezes or keeps cold; an insulated cabinet for freezing and storing perishable foods.

freight *n.* A service of transporting commodities by air, land or water; the price paid such transportation; a train that transports goods only. *v.* To carry as cargo.

freight-er *n.* A ship used for transporting cargo.

French *n.* The language of France; of or pertaining to the people of France. Frenchman, Frenchwoman *n.*

French Canadian *n.* A person from Canada whose first language is French.

French fries *pl.*, *n.* Thin strips of potatoes which have been fried crisp in deep fat.

French fry *v.* To fry in deep fat.

fren-zy *n.*, *pl.* -ies A state of extreme excitement or violent agitation; temporary insanity or delirium. -ied *adj.*

fre-quent *adj.* Happening or appearing often or time after time. *v.* To go to a place repeatedly. frequenter, frequentness *n.*, frequently *adv.*

fres-co *n.*, *pl.* -coes or -cos The art of painting on moist plaster with water-based paint; a picture so painted.

fresh *adj.* Newly-made, gathered, or obtained; not spoiled, musty, or stale; new; different; not soiled; pure and clean; having just arrived; refreshed; revived. *Slang* Impudent; disrespectful. freshly *adv.*, freshness *n.*

fresh-man *n.* A student in the first year of studies in a high school, university, or college; a beginner.

fret *v.* To be anxious or irritated; to wear away; to make by erosion; to ripple water. *n.* An ornamental design, composed of repeated symmetric figures; a ridge of metal fixed across the fingerboard of a stringed instrument, as a guitar.

Freud, Sigmund *n.* (1856-1939). Austrian psychoanalyst. Freudian *adj. & n.*

Fri *abbr.* Friday.

fri-a-ble *adj.* Easily crumbled or pulverized brittle. friability, -ness *n.*

fri-ar *n.* A member of a mendicant Roman Catholic order.

fric-as-see *n.* A dish of meat or poultry stewed in gravy. fricassee *v.*

fric-tion *n.* The rubbing of one surface or object against another; a conflict or clash. *Phys.* A force that retards the relative motion of two touching objects. frictional *adj.*

Fri-day *n.* The sixth day of the week.

friend *n.* Someone who is personally well known by oneself and for whom one holds warm regards; a supporter of a cause or group. Friend A member of the Society of Friends; a Quaker. friendless *adj.*, friendship *n.*

frieze *n.* A decorative horizontal band along the upper part of a wall in a room.

frig-ate *n.* A square-rigged warship of the 17th to mid 19th centuries; U.S. warship smaller than a cruiser but larger than a destroyer.

fright *n.* Sudden violent alarm or fear; a feeling of alarm. *Slang* Something very unsightly or ugly.

fright-en *v.* To fill with fear; to force by arousing fear. frightening *adj.*, frighteningly *adv.*

frig-id *adj.* Very cold; lacking warmth of feeling or emotional warmth; sexually unresponsive. frigidity, frigidness *n.*, frigidly *adv.*

frill *n.* A decorative ruffled or gathered border. *Slang* A superfluous item. frilly *adj.*

fringe *n.* An edging that consists of hanging threads, cords, or loops. fringe *v.*

frip-per-y *n.*, *pl.* -ies Showy and often cheap ornamentation; a pretentious display.

frisk *v.* To skip or leap about playfully;

to search someone for a concealed weapon by running the hands over the clothing quickly.

frit-ter v. To squander or waste little by little. n. A small fried cake made of plain batter, often containing fruits vegetables, or fish. **frittered, frittering** v.

friv-o-lous adj. Trivial; insignificant; lacking importance; not serious; silly. **frivolousness** n., **frivolously** adv.

frizz v. To form into small, tight curls. **frizziness** n., **frizzily** adv., **frizzy** adj.

fro adv. Away from; back, as running to and fro.

frock n. A smock or loose-fitting robe; a robe worn by monks.

frog n.

Any of various small, smooth-skinned, web-footed, largely aquatic, tailless, leaping amphibians; an ornamental braid or cord; an arrangement of intersecting railroad tracks designed to permit wheels to pass over the intersection without difficulty; a perforated holder for flower stems. *Slang* Hoarseness in the throat.

frol-ic n. Merriness; a playful, carefree occasion. v. To romp about playfully; to have fun. **frolicker** n., **-some** adj.

from prep. Starting at a particular time or place; used to indicate a specific point; used to indicate a source; used to indicate separation or removal; used to indicate differentiation, as knowing right from left.

frond n. A large leaf, as of a tropical fern, usually divided into smaller leaflets.

front n. The forward surface of an object or body; the area or position located before or ahead; a position of leadership; a field of activity for disguising objectionable or illegal activities; an apparently respectable person, group, or business used as a cover for illegal or secret activities. *Meteor.* The line of separation between air masses of different temperatures. **-al** adj., **-ally** adv.

front money n. Money paid in advance for a service or product that is promised.

fron-tier n. A part of an international border or the area adjacent to it; an unexplored area of knowledge or thought. **frontiersman** n.

fron-tis-piece n. An illustration that usually precedes the title page of a book or periodical.

frost n. A feathery covering of minute ice crystals on a cold surface; the act or process of freezing. v. To cover with frost; to apply frosting to a cake. **frostily** adv., **frostiness** n., **frosty** adj.

Frost, Robert Lee n. (1874-1963). American poet.

frost-bite n. The local destruction of bodily tissue due to exposure to freezing temperatures, often resulting in gangrene. **frostbite** v.

frost-ing n. Icing; a mixture of egg whites, sugar, butter, etc.; a lusterless or frosted surface on glass or metal.

froth n. A mass of bubbles on or in a liquid, resulting from agitation or fermentation; a salivary foam, as of an animal, resulting from disease or exhaustion; anything unsubstantial or trivial. v. To expel froth. **frothily** adv., **frothiness** n., **frothy** adj.

frou-frou n. A rustling sound, as of silk; a frilly dress or decoration.

for-ward adj. Obstinate. **forwardness** n.

frown v. To contract the brow as in displeasure or concentration; to look on with distaste or disapproval. **frown** n., **frowningly** adv., **frowned, frowning** v.

frow-zy or **frow-sy** adj. Appearing unkempt.

fro-zen adj. Covered with, changed into, surrounded by, or made into ice; extremely cold, as a climate; immobilized or made rigid, as by fear; coldly reserved; unfriendly; kept at a fixed level, as wages; not readily available for withdrawal, sale, or liquidation, as from a bank.

fru-gal adj. Economical; thrifty. **frugality, frugalness** n., **frugally** adv.

fruit n., pl. **fruit** or **fruits** The ripened, mature, seed-bearing part of a flowering plant, as a pod or berry; the edible, fleshy plant part of this kind, as an apple or plum; the fertile structure of a plant that does not bear seeds; the outcome or result. v. To produce or cause to produce fruit. **fruitage** n., **fruitful, fruitless** adj.

fru-i-tion n. Achievement or accomplishment of something worked for or desired; the state of bearing fruit.

frump-y adj. Unfashionable; dowdy. **frump, frumpiness** n.

frus-trate v. To keep from attaining a goal or fulfilling a desire; to thwart; to prevent the fruition of; to nullify. **frustration** n., **frustratingly** adv., **frustrating, frustrated** v.

fry v. To cook in hot fat or oil, especially over direct heat. n. A dish of any fried food; a social occasion at which foods are fried and eaten; a very young fish, especially a recently hatched one. **frying, fried** v.

fry-er n. Something which is intended for the purpose of frying, such as a young chicken.

fry-ing pan n. A type of metal pan that is used for the purpose of frying foods.

fub-sy adj. To be chubby and squat.

fuch-sia n. A chiefly tropical plant widely grown for its drooping, four-petaled flowers of purple, red, or white.

fuch-sine n. A type of dye that is made by the oxidation of a mixture of aniline and toluidines and it is a bright red.

fu-coid adj. To be pertaining to or to be like rockweeds.

fu-cose n. A type of aldose sugar.

fu-co-xan-thin n. A type of brown pigment that occurs in the ova of brown algea.

fu-cus *n.* A type of brown algea.

fud-dle *v.* To make someone or something confused.

fud-dy--dud-dy *n., pl.* -ies An old-fashioned person.

fudge *n.* A soft, cooked candy containing sugar, butter, and a flavoring, as chocolate. *v.* To falsify; to adjust, make, or fit together in a clumsy way; to evade.

Fue-gian *n.* A person who is a member of the group of American Indians of Tierra del Fuego.

fuel *n.* A combustible matter consumed to generate energy, especially a material such as wood, coal, or oil burned to generate heat. *v.* To take in or supply with fuel; to stimulate, as an argument. **fueler** *n.*

fuel cell *n.* A kind of cell which will change the chemical energy of a fuel to an electrical energy.

fug *v.* To hang around or loll indoors in an atmosphere that is stuffy.

fu-ga-cious *adj.* To be lasting a short time. **fagacity** *n.*

fu-gal *adj.* To be pertaining to the style of a musical fugue.

-fuge *n. comb. form* Something that drives away.

fu-gi-tive *adj.* Fleeing or having fled, as from arrest, pursuit, etc. *n.* One who flees or tries to escape.

fu-gle *v.* To act in the manner a fugleman does.

fu-gle-man *n.* A person who heads a group.

fugue *n., Mus.* A musical composition in which the theme is elaborately repeated by different voices or instruments; a psychological disturbance in which actions are not remembered after returning to a normal state.

fu-ji *n.* A type of spun silk fabric that was first made in Japan.

-ful *adj., suffix* Having the qualities of something; to be filled with or full of.

ful-crum *n., pl.* -crums *or* -cra The point on which a lever turns.

ful-fill *or* **ful-fil** *v.* To convert into actuality; to effect; to carry out; to satisfy. **fulfillment, fulfillment** *n.*

ful-gent *adj.* To be very or dazzling bright.

ful-gu-rant *adj.* To be flashing like lightening flashes.

ful-gu-rite *n.* A type of tubular crust that is formed by the fusion of rock by lightening.

ful-gu-rous *adj.* To be giving off flashes like that of lightening.

fu-lig-i-nous *adj.* To be murky or to have a color that is dark.

full *adj.* To have in something the maximum amount that the object is able to hold. **fullness** *n.*

full dress *n.* A style of dress that usually is found at a formal social gathering, very stylish.

full--fledged *adj.* To have full plumage.

full moon *n.* A phase of the moon where the whole side of the disk is able to be viewed.

full--size *adj.* To have the normal size of that of its kind.

ful-ly *adv.* To be done in a manner that is full.

ful-mar *n.* A type of artic seabird which is related to the petrels.

ful-mi-nate *v.* To condemn severely; to explode. **fulmination, fulminator** *n.*, **fulminated, fulminating** *v.*

ful-some *adj.* Offensively insincere. **fulsomely** *adv.*, **fulsomeness** *n.*

fum-ble *v.* To handle idly; to blunder; to mishandle a baseball or football. *n.* The act of fumbling; a fumbled ball. **fumbler** *n.*, **fumbling, fumbled** *v.*

fume *n., often* **fumes** An irritating smoke, gas, or vapor. *v.* To treat with or subject to fumes; to show or feel anger or distress.

fu-mi-gate *v.* To subject to fumes in order to exterminate vermin or insects. **-ion, fumigator** *n.*, **-ed, fumigating** *v.*

func-tion *n.* The characteristics or proper activity of a person or thing; specific occupation, duty, or role; an official ceremony; something depending upon or varying with another; in math, a quantity whose value is dependent on the value of another. *v.* To serve or perform a function as required or expected.

fund *n.* A source of supply; a sum of money or its equivalent reserved for a specific purpose. *v.* To convert into long-term arrangements for paying something off; to furnish or accumulate a fund for.

fun-da-men-tal *adj.* Basic or essential; of major significance; anything serving as the primary origin; most important. **fundamental** *n.*, **fundamentally** *adv.*

fu-ner-al *n.* The service performed in conjunction with the burial or cremation of a dead person.

fun-gus *n., pl.* -gi *or* -guses

Any of numerous spore-bearing plants which have no chlorophyll that include yeasts, molds, mildews, and mushrooms. **fungous, fungal** *adj.*

fu-nic-u-lar *n.* A cable railway along which cable cars are drawn up a mountain, especially one with ascending and descending cars that counterbalance one another.

funk *n.* Cowardly fright or panic; fear; a state of depression.

funk-y *adj., Slang* Having an earthy quality that is characteristic of the blues. **funkiness** *n.*

fun-nel *n.* A cone-shaped utensil having a tube for channeling a substance into a container. *v.* To pass or cause to pass through a funnel.

fur-be-low *n.* A ruffle or frill on clothing; a piece of showy decoration or ornamentation.

fur-bish *v.* To make bright, as by rubbing; to polish; to renovate.
furbishing, furbished *v.*

fu-ri-ous *adj.* Extremely angry; marked by rage or activity. **furiously** *adv.*

furl *v.* To roll up and secure to something, as a pole or mast; to curl or fold. **furl** *n.*

fur-long *n.* A distance equal to approximately 201 meters or 230 yards.

fur-lough *n.* Permission granted to be absent from duty, especially to members of the armed forces. **furlough** *v.*

fur-nace *n.* A large enclosure designed to produce intense heat.

fur-nish *v.* To outfit or equip, as with fittings or furniture.
furnisher *n.,* **furnishing** *v.*

fur-ni-ture *n.* Movable articles, such as chairs and tables, used in a home, office, etc.

fu-ror *n.* Violent anger; rage; great excitement; commotion; an uproar.

fur-row *n.* A long, narrow trench in the ground, made by a plow or other tool; a deep wrinkle in the skin, especially of the forehead. **furrow** *v.*

fur-tive *adj.* Done in secret; surreptitious; obtained underhandedly; stolen.

fu-ry *n., pl.* **-ies** Uncontrolled anger; turbulence; an angry or spiteful woman.

fuse *n.* An electrical safety device containing a wire or strip of fusible metal that melts and interrupts the circuit's flow when the current exceeds a particular amperage; a mechanical, electrical, or electronic device used to detonate explosives, such as bombs or grenades.

fu-see *or* **fu-zee** *n.* A large-headed friction match capable of burning in the wind; a colored signal flare used as a railroad signal.

fu-sil-lage *n.* The central section of an airplane, containing the wings and tail assembly.

fu-sil-lade *n.* A quickly repeated or simultaneous discharge of a number of firearms.

fu-sion *n.* The act or procedure of melting together by heat; a blend produced by fusion; a nuclear reaction in which nuclei of a light element combine to form more massive nuclei, with the release of huge amounts of energy.

fus-tian *n.* A sturdy, stout cotton cloth. *adj.* Pompous, pretentious language; bombastic.

fu-tile *adj.* Ineffectual; being of no avail; without useful result; serving no useful purpose.

fu-ture *n.* The time yet to come; a prospective condition regarding advancement or success; the future tense or a verb form in the future tense.

fuzz *n.* A mass of fine, loose particles, fibers, or hairs.

G, g The seventh letter of the English alphabet. *Mus.* The fifth tone in the scale of C major. *Slang* One thousand dollars; a grand. *Physiol* A unit of force equal to that due to the earth's gravity.

g *abbr.* Gravity; gram.

GA *abbr.* Georgia. The peach tree state.

gab *v., Slang* To talk or chat idly.

gab, gabber *n.*

gab-ar-dine *n.* A firm cotton, wool, or rayon material, having a diagonal raised weave, used for suits and coats.

gab-ble *v.* To speak rapidly or incoherently. **gabble** *n.*

gab-bro *n.* a granular igneous rock.
gabbroci, gabbroitic *adj.*

Gabriel *n.* A special messenger of God mentioned in the Bible.

ga-boon *n.* An African tree with reddish-brown wood and is used mainly in furniture.

gad *v.* To wander about restlessly with little or no purpose. **gadder** *n.*

gad-a-bout *n., Slang* A person who goes about seeking excitement and/or fun.

gad-fly *n.* A fly that bites or annoys cattle and horses; an irritating, critical, but often constructively provocative person; a person who is bothersome to others.

gadg-et *n., Slang* A small device or tool used in performing miscellaneous jobs, especially in the kitchen.

gad-o-lin-i-um *n.* A metallic element, silvery-white in color, of the lanthanide series, symbolized by Gd.

ga-droon *n.* The ornamental carving on a rounded molding.

gad-well *n.* A grayish brown duck.

Gae-a *n.* In Greek mythology, the mother and wife of Uranus, the goddess of earth.

gaff *n.* A sharp iron hook used for landing fish. *Naut.* A spar on the top edge of a fore-and-aft sail. *Slang* Abuse or harsh treatment. *v.* To land or hook with a gaff.

gaffe *n.* A social blunder; mistake; a faux pas.

gaf-fer *n.* An old man.

gag *n.* Something, as a wadded cloth, forced into or over the mouth to prevent someone from speaking or crying out; an obstacle to or any restraint of free speech, such as by censorship. *Slang* A practical joke or hoax. **to pull a gag** To perform a practical joke or trick on someone. *v.* To keep a person from speaking out by means of a gag; to choke on something. **gagger** *n.*

ga-ga *adj., Slang* Crazy; silly.

gage *n.* Something that is given as security for an action to be performed; a pledge; anything, as a glove, thrown down as a challenge to fight or a challenge for combat.

gag-gle *n.* A flock of geese; a group; a cluster.

gag rule *n.* A law or rule that prevents discussion or expression of an opinion.

gag-ster n. A person who plays practical jokes.

gai-e-ty n., pl. **-ies** The state of being happy; cheerfulness; showiness; finery; fun, festive activity.

gai-ly adv. A gay or cheerful manner; showily or brightly.

gain v. To earn or acquire possession of something; to succeed in winning a victory; to develop an increase of; to put on weight; to secure as a profit; to improve progress; to draw nearer to.

gain-er n. A fancy dive used in diving competition; one who gains.

gain-ful adj. Producing profits or advantage; lucrative.

gainfully adv., **gainfulness** n.

gain-say v. To deny; to contradict; dispute. **gainsayer** n.

gait n. A way or manner of moving on foot; one of the foot movements in which a horse steps or runs.

gai-ter n. A covering, as of leather or canvas, that covers the leg and extends from the knee to the instep; an old-fashioned shoe with a high top and elastic sides.

gal n., Slang A girl.

ga-la n. A festive; something that is suitable for a celebration. **gala** adj.

ga-lac-tic adj. Relating to the galaxy, or the Milky Way.

ga-lac-tose n. The sugar typically occurring in lactose.

ga-la-go n. A small nocturnal African primate with long ears, long tail and long hind limbs enabling them to leap at great lengths.

ga-lah n. A showy Australian cockatoo that is very distructive in wheat growing areas.

gal-an-tine n. A cold dish that consist of fish or meat that has been poached, stuffed, and covered with aspic.

gal-ax-y n., pl. **-ies** Astron. Any of the very large systems of stars, nebulae, or other celestial bodies that constitute the universe; a brilliant, distinguished group or assembly. **Galaxy** The Milky Way. **galactic** adj.

gal-ba-num n. A greenish or brown aromatic bitter gum resin used for medicinal purposes and in incense.

gale n., Meteor. A very powerful wind stronger than a stiff breeze; an outburst, as of hilarity.

ga-le-na n. A metallic, dull gray mineral that is the principal ore of lead.

gal-i-lee n. A porch at the entrance of an English church.

Gal-i-lee, Sea of n. The freshwater lake that is bordered by Syria, Israel, and Jordan.

gal-i-ma-ti-as n. A confused mixture of words.

gall n., Physiol. The bitter fluid secreted by the liver; bile; bitterness of feeling; animosity; impudence; something that irritates. v. To injure the skin by friction; to chafe. **-ing** adj., **gallingly** adv.

gal-lant adj. Dashing in appearance or

dress; majestic; stately; chivalrously attentive to women; courteous; having a fine appearance. **gallantly** adv.

gal-lant-ry n., pl. **-ries** Nobility and bravery; a gallant act.

gall-blad-der or **gall bladder** n.

The small sac under the right lobe of the liver that stores bile.

gal-le-on n. A large three-masted sailing ship.

gal-ler-y n., pl. **-ries** A long, narrow passageway, as a corridor, with a roofed promenade, especially an open-sided one extending along an inner or outer wall of a building; a group of spectators, as at a golf tournament; a building where statues, paintings, and other works of art are displayed; a room or building where articles are sold to the highest bidder; an underground passage in a mine. **galleried** adj., **gallery** v.

gal-ley n., pl. **-leys** A long medieval ship that was propelled by sails and oars; the long tray used by printers to hold set type; a printer's proof made from composed type, used to detect and correct errors.

gal-ley proof n. The proof take from type on a galley that permits corrections before the page is printed.

gal-ley slave n. A person who has been condemned to work at the oars on a galley; a person who is overworked; a drudge.

gal-ley--west adv. Into confusion or destruction.

gal-li-gas-kins n. Very loose fitting trousers of the 16th century.

gall-ing adj. Being very irritated; annoying; vexing.

gal-li-nule n. A wading bird with dark iridescent plumage, having a frontal shield on the head and unlobed feet.

gal-li-um n. A silvery metallic element used in semiconductor technology and as a component of various low-melting alloys, symbolized by Ga.

gal-li-vant v. To roam about in search of amusement or pleasure; to flirt; to run about.

gal-lon n. A liquid measurement used in the U.S., equal to 4 quarts; in Great Britain, a liquid measurement which equals 4 imperial quarts; a dry measurement that equals 1/8 bushel.

gal-loon n. A trimming of lace, or embroidery with metallic threads.

gal-lop n. A horse's gait that is faster than a canter and characterized by regular leaps during which all four feet are off the ground at once.

gal·low·glass *n.* A mercenary of an Irish chief.

gal·lows *n.* A wooden framework of two or more upright beams and a crossbeam, or any similar structure used for execution by hanging.

gall·stone *n., Pathol.* A small, hard concretion of cholesterol crystals that sometimes form in the gall bladder or bile passages.

ga·loot *n.* A strange or foolish person.

ga·lore *adj.* In great numbers; abundant; plentiful.

ga·losh *pl., n.* galoshes Waterproof overshoes, with a heavy sole, which are worn to keep the feet warm in bad weather.

ga·lump *v.* To bump or gallop along clumsily.

gal·van·ic *adj.* Produced by or pertaining to galvanism; stimulating or shocking.

gal·va·nism *n.* Electricity that is produced by chemical action. *Med.* A therapeutic application of continuous electric current from voltaic cells.

gal·va·nize *v.* To stimulate or shock muscular action by an electric current; to protect iron or steel with rust resistant zinc. *Slang* To infuse with energy. galvanization, galvanizer *n.*

gal·va·nom·e·ter *n., Electr.* An apparatus for detecting the presence of an electric current and for determining its strength and direction. -metric *adj.*

gal·va·no·scope *n.* An instrument used to detect the direction and presence of an electric current by the deflecting of a magnetic needle.

gal·yak *n.* A short-haired fur derived from the pelt of a stillborn lamb.

gam *n.* A school of whales.

gam·bit *n.* In chess, an opening in which a piece is sacrificed for a favorable position; a maneuver that is carefully planned.

gam·ble *v.* To take a chance on an uncertain outcome as a contest or a weekly lottery number. *n.* Any risky venture. gambler *n.*

gam·boge *n.* A gum resin that is orange to brown in color and is used as a yellow pigment.

gam·bol *v.* To frolic, skip, dance or leap about in play. *n.* Frolic; a playful leap or skip.

gam·brel roof *Archit.* A ridged roof with the slope broken on each side, the lower slope steeper than the upper.

game *n.* A contest governed by specific rules; a way of entertaining oneself; amusement; a calculated way to do something; animals, fish, or birds that are hunted for sport or food. gamer, gamest *adj.*, gamely *adv.*, gameness *n.*

game-cock *n.* A rooster bred and trained for cockfighting.

game fish *n.* A fish of a family that includes salmons, chars, and trouts.

game fowl *n.* A domestic fowl developed for the production of fighting cocks.

game-keep-er *n.* A person in charge of protecting and maintaining wildlife on a private preserve; a person who prevents illegal fishing or hunting.

gam-elan *n.* A string, flute, and percussion orchestra of southeast Asia, that resembles the xylophone.

game plan *n.* A game where chance rather that skill determines the outcome.

games-man-ship *n.* The art or skill of winning games by somewhat dubious means but without breaking the rules.

game-some *adj.* Frolicsome; sportive; playful.

gam-ete *n., Biol.* Either of two mature reproductive cells, an ovum or sperm, which produce a zygote when united. gametic *adj.*

gam-in *n.* A homeless child who wanders about the streets of a town or city.

gam-ma globulin *n., Biochem.* A globulin that is present in blood plasma and contains antibodies effective against certain infectious diseases.

gamma ray *n., Phys.* Electromagnetic radiation that has energy greater than several hundred thousand electron volts.

gam-mer *n.* An elderly woman.

gam-mon *n.* A cured ham; in the game of backgammon, a double victory in which a player removes all his pieces before the other player removes any.

gam-ut *n.* The whole range series or extent of anything.

gam-y *adj.* Having the strong flavor of game, especially when slightly tainted; scandalous. gaminess *n.*

gan-der *n.* A male goose. *Slang* A quick glance; a look or peek.

Gandhi, Mohandas Karamchand "Mahatma" *n.* Hindu leader of India, who was assassinated in 1948.

gan-dy dancer *n.* A seasonal laborer or one who works in a railroad section gang.

gang *n.* A group of persons who are organized and work together or socialize regularly; a group of adolescent hoodlums or criminals. gang up on To attack as a group.

gang hook *n.* Two or three fishhooks with shanks joined together.

gang-land *n.* The underworld; organized criminal elements of society.

gan-gling *adj.* Awkwardly tall and thin; lanky and loosely built.

gan-gli-on *n., pl.* -glia *or* -ons *Physiol.* A collection of nerve cells located outside the spinal cord or brain. ganglionic *adj.*

gang-plank *n.* A temporary board or ramp used to board or leave a ship.

gang-plow *n.* A plow that is so designed to turn two, three or more rows at a time.

gan-grene *n., Pathol.* The death and decay of tissue in the body caused by a failure in the circulation of the blood supply. gangrene *v.*, gangrenous *adj.*

gang-ster *n.* A member of a criminal

gang; a racketeer; a mobster.

gang-way *n.* A passageway through, into, or out of an obstructed area. *Naut.* A passage on a ship's deck offering entrance to passengers or freight; gangplank.

gan-net *n.* A large sea bird with white plumage and black wing tips, related to the pelican and heron.

gant-let *n.* Variation of gauntlet.

gan-try *n., pl.* **-ies** *Aeros.* A bridge-like framework support, especially a movable vertical structure with platforms, that is used in assembling or servicing rockets before they are launched.

gaol *n., Brit.* Jail. **gaol** *v.*

gap *n.* An opening or wide crack, as in a wall; a cleft; a deep notch or ravine in a mountain ridge, offering passage.

gape *v.* To open the mouth wide, as in yawning; to stare in amazement with the mouth wide open; to become widely separated or open. *n.* A yawn; the act of gaping. **gape, gaper** *n.*

gar *n.* A fish having a spearlike snout and elongated body covered with bony plates; a garfish.

ga-rage *n.* A building or structure in which motor vehicles are stored, repaired, or serviced.

garb *n.* Clothing; a particular way of dressing.

gar-bage *n.* Food wastes, consisting of unwanted or unusable pieces of meat, vegetables, and other food products; any unwanted or worthless material; trash.

gar-ble *v.* To mix up or confuse; to change or distort the meaning of with the intent to mislead or misrepresent. *n.* The act or process of garbling. **garble, garbler** *n.*

gra-boil *n.* A confused state.

gar-den *n.* A place for growing flowers, vegetables, or fruit; a piece of ground commonly used as a public resort. *v.* To work in or make into a garden. *adj.* Produced or referring to or in a garden. **gardener, gardening** *n.*

gar-de-nia *n.* A tropical shrub with glossy evergreen leaves and fragrant white flowers.

Garfield, James Abram *n.* (1831-1881). The 20th president of the United States, assassinated in 1881, after serving from March through September of 1881.

gar-gan-tu-an *adj.* Of enormous size; immense.

gar-gle *v.* To force air from the lungs through a liquid held in the back of the mouth and throat. *n.* A liquid preparation used to wash the mouth and throat. **gargle** *n.*

gar-goyle *n.* A waterspout made or carved to represent a grotesque animal or human figure, projecting from a gutter to throw rain away from the side of a building.

gar-ish *adj.* Too showy and bright; gaudy; dazzling. **garishly** *adv.*, **garishness** *n.*

gar-land *n.* A wreath, chain, or rope of flowers or leaves. *v.* To decorate with or form into a garland. *Naut.* A ring of rope attached to a spar to aid in hoisting or to prevent chafing.

gar-lic *n.* A plant related to the onion with a compound bulb which contains a strong odor and flavor, used as a seasoning.

gar-ment *n.* An article of clothing.

gar-ner *v.* To gather and store; to accumulate; to collect; to acquire.

gar-net *n.* A dark-red silicate mineral used as a gemstone and as an abrasive.

gar-nish *v.* To add something to, as to decorate or embellish; to add decorative or flavorful touches to food or drink. **garnish** *n.*

gar-nish-ee *v., Law* To attach a debt or property with notice that no return or disposal is to be made until a court judgment is issued; to take a debtor's wages by legal authority.

gar-nish-ment *n.* The act of garnishing; the legal proceeding that turns property belonging to a debtor over to his creditor.

gar-ni-ture *n.* Anything that is used to garnish or decorate.

gar-ret *n.* A room in an attic.

gar-ri-son *n.* The military force that is permanently placed in a fort or town; a military post.

gar-ron *n.* A small workhorse.

gar-rote *or* **gar-rotte** *n.* The former Spanish method of execution by strangulation with an iron collar tightened by a screw-like device; the instrument used; throttling or strangulation.

gar-ru-lous *adj.* Given to continual talkativeness; chatty; very talkative. **garrulity, garrulousness** *n.*

gar-ter *n.* An elastic band or strap that is worn around the leg or knee to hold a stocking in place; a band that holds up a sleeve.

garter snake *n.* A nonvenomous North American snake which is small, harmless and has brightly colored stripes.

garth *n.* A small yard.

gas *n., pl.* **gases** A form of matter capable of expanding to fill a container and taking on the shape of the container; a combustible mixture used as fuel; gasoline; a gas used to produce an irritating, poisonous, or asphyxiating atmosphere. **gas** *v.*, **gaseous, gassy** *adj.*

gas chamber *n.* An enclosure in which a condemned prisoner is put to death by the use of poisonous gas.

gas-e-ous *adj.* Pertaining to or of the nature of gas.

gas-con *n.* A boastful person.

gash *n.* A long, deep cut. **gash** *v.*

gas-ket *n., Mech.* A rubber seal, disk, or ring used between matched machine parts or around pipe joints to prevent the escape of fluid or gas.

gas-light *n.* A light produced by burning illuminating gas.

gas-log *n.* A imitation log used as fuel in

a fireplace.

gas mask *n.* A protective respirator which covers the face and contains a chemical air filter to protect against poisonous gases.

gas-o-hol *n.* A fuel blended from unleaded gasoline and ethanol.

gas-o-line *or* **gas-o-lene** *n.* A colorless, highly flammable mixture of liquid hydrocarbons made from crude petroleum and used as a fuel and a solvent.

gasp *v.* To inhale suddenly and sharply, as from fear or surprise; to make labored or violent attempts to breathe.

gas-tral *adj.* Relating to the stomach or digestive tract.

gas-tric *adj.* Of or pertaining to the stomach.

gas-tric juice *n.,* *Biochem.* The digestive fluid secreted by the stomach glands, containing several enzymes.

gas-tric ul-cer *n.,* *Pathol.* An ulcer formed on the stomach lining, often caused by excessive secretion of gastric juices.

gas-tri-tis *n.,* *Pathol.* Inflammation of the stomach lining. **gastritic** *adj.*

gas-tro-en-ter-ol-o-gy *n.* The medical study of the stomach and intestines. **gastroenterologist** *n.*

gas-tron-o-my *n.* The art of good eating. **gastronome** *n.,* **gastronomic,** **gastronomical** *adj.*

gas-tro-pod *n.* One of the large class of aquatic and terrestrial mollusks, including snails, slugs, limpets, having a single shell and a broad, muscular organ of locomotion. **-ous** *adj.,* **gastropodan** *adj. & n.*

gas-works *n.,* *pl.* **-works** An establishment where gas is manufactured.

gat *n.,* *Slang* A pistol; short for Gatling gun.

gate *n.* A movable opening in a wall or fence, commonly swinging on hinges, that closes or opens; a valve-like device for controlling the passage of gas or water through a conduit or dam; the total paid admission receipts or number in attendance at a public perform-ance.

gate--crash-er *n.* One who gains admittance without an invitation or without paying.

gate-leg ta-ble *n.* A table with legs that swing out to support drop leaves, the legs folding against the frame when the leaves are let down.

gate-way *n.* The opening in a fence, etc. for a gate.

gath-er *v.* To bring or come together into one place or group; to harvest or pick; to increase or gain; to accumulate slowly; to fold or pleat a cloth by pulling it along a thread. **gather, gathering** *n.*

Gat-ling gun *n.* An early machine gun.

gauche *adj.* Socially awkward; clumsy; boorish. **gauchely** *adv.,* **gaucheness** *n.*

gaud-y *adj.* Too highly decorated to be in good taste. **gaudiness** *n.*

gauge *or* **gage** *n.* A standard measurement, dimension, or capacity; an instrument used for measuring, testing, or registering; the distance between rails of a railroad; the diameter of the bore of a shotgun barrel. *v.* To determine the capacity, contents or volume of; to estimate; to evaluate. **gauger** *n.*

gaunt *adj.* Thin and bony; haggard; gloomy or desolate in appearance.

gaunt-let *or* **gant-let** *n.*

A challenge to fight; a glove to protect the hand; a former military punishment which forced an offender to run between two lines of men armed with clubs with which to strike him; criticism from all sides.

gauze *n.* A loosely-woven, transparent material used for surgical bandages; any thin, open-mesh material; a mist. **gauzy** *adj.,* **gauziness** *n.*

gave *v.* Past tense of give.

gav-el *n.* A mallet used by a presiding officer or by a person in charge to call for order or attention. **gavel** *v.*

ga-vi-al *n.* A large crocodile found in India, with long, slender jaws.

ga-votte *n.* A French dance resembling a quick-moving minuet.

gawk *v.* To gape; to stare stupidly.

gawk-y *adj.* Clumsy or awkward. **-iness** *n.*

gay *adj.* Merry; happy and carefree; brightly ornamental or colorful; homosexual. *n.* A homosexual. **-ness** *n.*

gaze *v.* To look steadily or intently at something in admiration or wonder; to stare.

ga-ze-bo *n.* A freestanding structure open on all sides.

ga-zelle *n.* A small, gracefully formed antelope of northern Arabia and Africa, having curved horns and large eyes.

ga-zette *n.* A newspaper; an official publication. *v.* To publish or announce in a gazette.

gaz-et-teer *n.* A dictionary consisting of geographical facts.

gaz-pa-cho *n.* A cold soup made from vegetables, spices , oils, etc.

gds *abbr.* Goods.

gear *n.,* *Mech.* A toothed wheel which interacts with another toothed part to transmit motion; an assembly of parts that work together for a special purpose; equipment. *v.* To regulate, match, or suit something. **gearing** *n.*

gear-shift *n.,* *Mech.* A mechanism used for engaging or disengaging the gears in a power transmission system.

gear-wheel *or* **gear wheel** *n.,* *Mech.* A cogwheel.

geck-o *n.,* *pl.* **-os** *or* **-oes** Any of various small lizards of warm regions having toes with adhesive pads enabling them to climb up or down vertical surfaces.

geese *n.* Plural of goose.

gee-zer *n., Slang* An old odd or eccentric man.

Ge-hen-na *n.* In the New Testament, hell; a place of torment.

ge-fil-te fish *n.* Chopped fish mixed with crumbs, seasoning, and eggs, then cooked in a broth and served chilled in oval-shaped cakes or balls.

Gei-ger coun-ter *n., Phys.* An instrument used to measure, detect, and record cosmic rays and nuclear radiation.

gei-sha *n., pl.* **-sha** *or* **-shas** A Japanese girl who furnishes entertainment and companionship for men.

gel *n., Chem.* A colloid that is in a more solid than liquid form. *v.* To change into or take on the form of a gel.

gel-a-tin *or* **gel-a-tine** *n.* An almost tasteless, odorless, dried protein, soluble in water and derived from boiled animal tissues, used in making foods, drugs, and photographic film; a jelly made from gelatin. **gelatinous** *adj.*

geld *v.* To castrate or spay, especially a horse.

geld-ing *n.* A gelded animal.

gel-id *adj.* Very cold; frigid. **gelidity** *n.*

gem *n.* A cut and polished precious or semiprecious stone; one that is highly treasured. *v.* To set or decorate with or as with gems.

gem-i-nate *v.* To become paired or arrange in pairs.

Gem-i-ni *n.* The third sign of the zodiac; a person born between May 21 and June 20.

gem-mule *n.* A small bud.

gem-ol-o-gy *or* **gem-mol-o-gy** *n.* The study of gems. **-ical** *adj.*, **gemologist** *n.*

Gem State *n.* Nickname of the state of Idaho.

gen *abbr.* Gender; general; generally.

gen-darme *n., pl.* **gendarmes** An armed policeman in France.

gen-der *n., Gram.* Any of two or more categories, as feminine, masculine, and neuter, into which words are divided and which determine agreement with or selection of modifiers or grammatical forms; the quality of being of the male or female sex.

gene *n., Biol.* A functional hereditary unit which occupies a fixed location on a chromosome and controls or acts in the transmission of hereditary characteristics.

ge-ne-al-o-gy *n., pl.* **-ies** A record, table, or account showing the descent of a family, group, or person from an ancestor; the study of ancestry. **genealogical** *adj.*, **genealogist** *n.*

gen-er-al *adj.* Pertaining to, including, or affecting the whole or every member of a group or class; common to or typical of most; not being limited to a special class; miscellaneous; not detailed or precise. *n., Milit.* An officer in the United States Army, Air Force, or Marine Corps ranking above a colonel. **generally** *adv.*

general admission *n.* A fee paid for an unreserved seating area.

gen-er-al as-sem-bly *n.* A legislative body. **General Assembly** The supreme deliberative body of the United Nations.

gen-er-al-i-ty *n., pl.* **-ies** The state or quality of being general; an inadequate, inexact or vague statement or idea.

gen-er-al-i-za-tion *n.* Something arrived at by generalizing, such as a broad, overall statement or conclusion.

gen-er-al-ize *v.* To draw a general conclusion from particular facts, experiences, or observations.

gen-er-al prac-ti-tion-er *n.* A doctor who treats a variety of medical problems rather than specializing in one.

gen-er-al-ship *n.* The office or rank of a general; leadership or management of any type.

gen-er-al staff *n., Milit.* A group of officers who assist the commander in planning and supervising military operations.

gen-er-al store *n.* A retail store selling a large variety of merchandise but not subdivided into departments.

gen-er-ate *v.* To cause to be; to produce; to bring into existence, especially by a chemical or physical process. **-ive** *adj.*

gen-er-a-tion *n.* A group of individuals born at about the same time; the average time interval between the birth of parents and that of their offspring. **generational** *adj.*

gen-er-a-tor *n., Mech.* A machine that changes mechanical energy into electrical energy.

ge-ner-ic *adj.* Relating to or indicating an entire class or group; general; pertaining to a genus or class of related things; of or relating to a class of product, or merchandise that does not bear a trademark or trade name. **generically** *adv.*

gen-er-ous *adj.* Sharing freely; abundant; overflowing. **-ity** *n.*, **generously** *adv.*

gen-e-sis *n., pl.* **-ses** The act or state of originating.

Genesis The first book of the Old Testament.

ge-net-ic *adj.* Of or pertaining to the origin or development of something; of or relating to genetics. **-ally** *adv.*

ge-net-ic code *n., Biochem.* The biochemical basis of heredity that specifies the amino acid sequence in the synthesis of proteins and on which heredity is based.

ge-ne-va *n.* An alcoholic liquor flavored with juniper berries.

Ge-ne-va Con-ven-tion *n.* The international agreement signed at Geneva in 1864 which governs the war-time treatment of prisoners of war and of the wounded, sick, and the dead.

gen-ial *adj.* Cheerful, kind, pleasant and good-humored in disposition or manner. **geniality** *n.*, **genially** *adv.*

ge-nie *n.* A supernatural creature, capable of taking on human form, who does one's bidding.

ge-nii *n.* In ancient mythology, a guardian spirit appointed to guide a person through life.

gen-i-tal *adj.* Of or pertaining to the reproductive organs or the process of reproduction. **genitalia** *n.*

gen-i-tals *pl.,n.* The external sexual organs. **genitalia** *n.*

gen-i-tive *adj., Gram.* Indicating origin, source, or possession. *n.* The genitive case. **genitival** *adj.*

gen-i-to-u-ri-nar-y *adj., Anat.* Of or pertaining to the genital and urinary organs or their functions.

gen-ius *n., pl.* **-ses** Exceptional intellectual ability or creative power; a strong, natural talent; a person who exerts powerful influence over another.

gen-o-cide *n.* The systematic extermination or destruction of a political, racial, or cultural group. **genocidal** *adj.*

gens *n., pl.* **gentes** In ancient Rome, a clan that included families of the same name that have descended through the male line.

gent *n., Slang* A gentleman.

gen-teel *adj.* Refined or well-bred; elegant; polite; stylish or fashionable. **genteelly** *adv.*, **genteelness** *n.*

gen-tian *n.* An annual or perennial plant with showy blue, red, yellow, or white flowers.

Gen-tile *n.* A person, especially a Christian, who is not a Jew; of or relating to non-Mormons.

gen-til-i-ty *n.* The quality of being genteel; the members of the upper class; well-born or well-bred persons collectively.

gen-tle *adj.* Not harsh, severe, rough, or loud; easily handled or managed; docile; not sudden or steep; from a good family of high social standing. *Meteor.* A soft, moderate breeze. *v.* To tame. **gently** *adv.*, **gentleness** *n.*

gen-tle-folk *or* **gen-tle-folks** *pl., n.* Persons from good family backgrounds.

gen-tle-man *n.* A man of noble birth and social position; a courteous or polite man; used as a form of address.

gen-tle-wom-an *n.* A woman of noble birth and social position; a woman attendant upon a lady of rank; a well-bred or polite woman.

gen-try *n.* People of good family or high social standing; the aristocracy; in England, the social class that is considered the upper ranks of the middle class.

ge-nu *n., pl.* **gennua** *Anat.* The knee.

gen-u-flect *v.* To bend down on one knee, as in worship. **genuflection** *n.*

gen-u-ine *adj.* Real; authentic; not counterfeit or spurious; not hypocritical; sincere. **genuinely** *adv.*, **-ness** *n.*

ge-nus *n., pl.* **nera** *Biol.* A group or category of plants and animals usually including several species.

geo- *combining form* Ground; earth; soil.

ge-o-cen-tric *adj.* Of or relating to the earth's center; formulated on the assumption that the earth is the center of the universe. **geocentrically** *adv.*, **geocentrical** *adj.*

ge-o-chem-is-try *n.* A branch of chemistry that deals with the chemical composition of the earth's crust. **geochemical** *adj.*, **geochemist** *n.*

ge-ode *n., Geol.* A hollow rock having a cavity lined with crystals. **geodic** *adj.*

ge-o-des-ic dome *n.* A vaulted or domed structure of lightweight straight elements that form interlocking polygons.

ge-o-des-ic line *n.* In mathematics, the shortest line that connects two points on a given surface.

ge-od-e-sy *n.* The geologic science dealing with the determination of the shape, area, and curvature of the earth. **geodesist** *n.*, **geodetic** *adj.*

geo-duck *n.* An edible clam of the Pacific coast.

ge-og-ra-phy *n., pl.* **-hies** The science that deals with the earth's natural climate, resources, and population. **geographer** *n.*, **geographic, geographical** *adj.*, **geographically** *adv.*

ge-ol-o-gy *n., pl.* **-ies** The science that deals with the history, origin, and structure of the earth. **geologic, geological** *adj.*, **geologically** *adv.*, **geologist** *n.*

ge-o-met-ric *adj.* According to or pertaining to the rules and principles of geometry; increasing in a geometric progression.

ge-o-met-ric pro-gres-sion *n.* A sequence of numbers, as 4, 8, 16, 32 where each term is the product of a constant factor and the term that precedes it.

ge-om-e-try *n., pl.* **ies** The branch of mathematics that deals with the measurement, properties, and relationships of lines, angles, points, surfaces and solids.

ge-o-phys-ics *pl., n.* The study of the earth as the product of complex physicochemical forces that act upon it internally from outer space, with reference to exploration of the less accessible regions.

ge-o-pol-i-tics *pl., n.* The study of the influence of economic and geographical factors on the politics and policies of a nation or region. **geopolitical** *adj.*

Geor-gia *n.* A state located in the southeastern part of the United States, known as the peach tree state.

ge-o-ther-mal *or* **ge-o-ther-mic** *adj.* Relating to the internal heat of the earth.

ge-ra-ni-um *n.* A plant having rounded leaves and clusters of pink, red, or white flowers; a plant of the genus Pelargonium, with divided leaves and purplish or pink flowers.

ger-bil *n.*

An animal of the rodent family found in the desert regions of Africa and

Asia Minor, having long hind legs and a long tail; a popular pet.

ger-i-at-rics *pl., n.* The medical study that deals with the structural changes, diseases, physiology, and hygiene of old age. **geriatric** *adj.*, **geriatrician** *n.*

germ *n.* A small cell or organic structure from which a new organism may develop; a micro-organism which causes disease. *Biol.* A reproductive cell.

Ger-man *n.* The language of Germany; an inhabitant or native of Germany.

ger-mane *adj.* Relevant to what is being considered or discussed.

Ger-man-ic *n.* Relating to the language or customs of the Dutch, German, English, Afrikaans, Flemish or Scandinavians. **Germanic** *adj.*

ger-ma-ni-um *n.* A grayish-white element widely used in electronics and optics, symbolized by Ge.

Ger-man meas-les *n., Pathol.* A contagious viral disease accompanied by sore throat, fever and a skin rash; a disease capable of causing defects in infants born to mothers infected during the first stages of pregnancy.

Ger-man shep-herd *n.* A large breed of dog, which is often trained to help the police and the blind.

germ cell *n.* An egg or sperm cell.

ger-mi-cide *n.* An agent used to destroy microorganisms or disease germs. **germicidal** *adj.*

ger-mi-nal *adj.* Of or relating to a germ or germ cell; of or in the earliest stage of development.

ger-mi-nate *v.* To begin to grow, develop, or sprout. **germination** *n.*

germ plasm *n., Biol.* The part of the protoplasm of a germ cell containing the chromosomes and genes.

ger-on-tol-o-gy *n.* The study of the processes and phenomena of aging. **-ical, -ic** *adj.*, **gerontologist** *n.*

ger-ry-man-der *v.* To divide a voting area so as to advance unfairly the interests of a political party; to adjust or adapt to one's advantage.

ger-und *n., Gram.* A verb form that is used as a noun.

ges-so *n.* Plaster of paris prepared with glue used in painting, etc.

gest *n.* A notable deed or feat.

ge-sta-po *n.* The secret police in Germany under the Nazi regime, known for its brutality.

ges-ta-tion *n.* The carrying of a developing offspring in the uterus; pregnancy. **gestate** *v.*, **gestational** *adj.*

ges-tic-u-late *v.* To make expressive or emphatic gestures, as in speaking.

ges-ture *n.* A bodily motion, especially with the hands in speaking, to emphasize some idea or emotion. *v.* To make gestures. **gesturer** *n.*

ge-sund-heit *interj. German* A phrase used to wish good health to a person who has just sneezed.

get *v.* To come into possession of, as by receiving, winning, earning or, buying.

to get ahead To attain success. to get back at To revenge oneself on. to get by To manage; to survive. get one's goat To make somebody angry.

get-a-way *n.* The act of or instance of escaping by a criminal; a start, as of a race.

get--to-geth-er *n.* A small informal family or social gathering.

get-up *n.* An outfit; a costume.

gew-gaw *n.* A little ornamental article of small value.

gey-ser *n.* A natural hot spring that intermittently ejects hot water and steam.

ghast-ly *adj.* Horrible; terrifying; very unpleasant or bad; ghost-like in appearance; deathly pale.

ghat *n.* A broad flight of steps that leads down to the edge of a river; a mountain pass, range, or chain.

gher-kin *n.* A very small, prickly cucumber pickled as a relish.

ghet-to *n.* A run-down section of a city in which a minority group lives because of poverty or social pressure.

ghost *n.* The spirit of a dead person which is believed to appear to or haunt living persons; a spirit; a ghostwriter; a false, faint secondary television image. **ghostly** *adj.*

ghost town *n.* A town that once flourished but is now deserted.

ghost-writer *n.* A person hired to write for another person and to give credit for the writing to that other person.

ghoul *n.* A person who robs graves; in Moslem legend, an evil spirit which plunders graves and feeds on corpses. **-ish** *adj.*, **ghoulishly** *adv.*, **-ishness** *n.*

GI *n., pl.* **GIs** *or* **GI's** An enlisted person in the United States armed forces. *adj.* In conformity with military regulations or customs. *v.* To clean or scrub in preparation for or as if for a military inspection.

GI *abbr.* Government issue, general issue.

gi-ant *n.* A legendary man-like being of supernatural size and strength; one of great power, importance, or size. **giantess** *n.*

gib-ber *v.* To talk or chatter incoherently or unintelligibly.

gib-ber-ish *n.* Meaningless speech.

gib-bet *n.* A gallows. *v.* To execute by hanging on a gibbet.

gib-bon *n.* A slender, long-armed Asian ape.

gib-bous *adj.* The moon or a planet which is seen with more than half but not all of the apparent disk illuminated. **-ly** *adv.*, **gibbousness** *n.*

gibe *v.* To ridicule or make taunting remarks. **gibe, giber** *n.*

gib-let *n., or* **giblets** The heart, liver, and gizzard of a fowl.

gid-dy *adj.* Affected by a reeling or whirling sensation; dizzy; frivolous and silly; flighty. **giddily** *adv.*, **giddiness** *n.*

gift *n.* Something that is given from one person to another; a natural aptitude;

a talent.

gift-ed adj. The state of having a special talent or ability.

gig n. A light, two-wheeled carriage drawn by one horse. *Naut.* A speedy, light rowboat; a spear with forks or prongs used for fishing. *Slang* A job, especially an engagement to play music. *Milit., Slang* A demerit; a punishment to military personnel.

gi-gan-tic adj. Of tremendous or extraordinary size; huge. **gigantically** adv.

gig-gle v. To laugh in high-pitched, repeated, short sounds. **giggle, giggler** n., **giggly** adj.

gig-o-lo n., A man who is supported by a woman not his wife; a man who is paid to be an escort or dancing partner.

Gi-la mon-ster n. A large, venomous lizard of the southwestern United States desert, having an orange and black body.

gild v. To coat with a thin layer of gold; to brighten or adorn. **gilded** adj., **gilding, gilder** n.

gill n., *Zool.* The organ, as of fishes and various other aquatic invertebrates, used for taking oxygen from water. n. A liquid measure that equals 1/4 pint.

gilt adj. Covered with or of the color of gold. n. A thin layer of gold or a gold-colored substance which is applied to a surface.

gilt-edge or **gilt-edged** adj. Of the highest value or the best quality.

gim-bal n. A three ringed device that keeps an object supported on it level, as the compass of a ship.

gim-crack n. A cheap and useless object of little or no value.

gim-let n. A small, sharp tool with a bar handle and a pointed, spiral tip which is used for boring holes.

gim-mal n. A series of interlocked rings.

gim-mick n. A tricky feature that is obscured or misrepresented; a tricky device, especially when used dishonestly or secretly; a gadget. **gimmickry** n., **gimmicky** adj.

gimp n., *Slang* A person who walks with a limp; a cripple. **gimp** v., **gimpy** adj.

gin n. An aromatic, clear, alcoholic liquor distilled from grain and flavored with juniper berries; a machine used to separate seeds from cotton fibers. v. To remove the seeds from cotton with a gin.

gin-ger n. A tropical Asian plant that has a pungent aromatic root, used in medicine and cooking.

gin-ger ale n. An effervescent soft drink flavored with ginger.

gin-ger-bread n. A dark, ginger and molasses flavored cake or cookie.

gin-ger-ly adv. Doing something very cautiously. **gingerliness** n.

gin-ger-snap n. A brittle, molasses and ginger cookie.

ging-ham n. A cotton fabric woven in solid colors and checks.

gin-gi-vi-tis n., *Pathol.* Inflammation of the gums.

gink-go n., pl. -goes or -koes A large Chinese shade tree cultivated in the United States, with edible fruits and nuts.

gin rum-my n. A variety of the card game rummy.

gin-seng n. A herb native to China and North America with an aromatic root believed to have medicinal properties.

Gip-sy n. & adj. Variation of gypsy.

gi-raffe n., pl. -fes or -fe

The tallest of all mammals, having an extremely long neck and very long legs, found in Africa.

gird v. To surround, encircle, or attach with or as if with a belt.

gird-er n. A strong, horizontal beam, as of steel or wood, which is the main support in a building.

gir-dle n. A cord or belt worn around the waist; a supporting undergarment worn by women to give support and to shape. **girdle** v.

girl n. A female child or infant; a young, unmarried woman; any woman of any age; one's sweetheart. **girlish** adj., **girlishly** adv., **girlishness** n.

girl Fri-day n. A woman employee responsible for a variety of tasks.

girl friend n. A female friend; a regular or frequent female companion of a boy or man.

Girl Scout n. A member of the Girl Scouts of the United States, an organization for girls between 7 and 17 years of age.

girth n. The circumference or distance around something; a strap that encircles an animal's body to secure something on its back, as a saddle.

gis-mo n., *Slang* A part or device whose name is unknown or forgotten; a gadget.

gist n. The central or main substance, as of an argument or question.

give v. To make a present of; to bestow; to accord or yield to another; to put into the possession of another; to convey to another; to donate or contribute; to apply; to devote; to yield as to pressure; to collapse; to furnish or provide; to deliver in exchange; to pay. **give away** To hand over the bride to the bridegroom at a wedding ceremony. **give out** To collapse; to be exhausted. **give up** To surrender; to submit oneself. **giver** n.

give--and--take n. To make a mutual exchange, as of conversation or opinions.

give-a-way n. Something that is given free as a premium; something that betrays, generally unintentionally.

giv-en adj. Bestowed; presented; specified or assumed.

giv-en name *n.* The name bestowed or given at birth or baptism.

giz-zard *n.* The second stomach in birds, where partly digested food is finely ground.

gla-brous *adj.*, *Biol.* Having no hair or down; having a smooth surface. **glabrousness** *n.*

gla-cial *adj.* Of or pertaining to, caused by, or marked by glaciers; extremely cold. **glacially** *adv.*

gla-cial e-poch *Geol.* A portion of geological time when ice sheets covered much of the earth's surface.

gla-cier *n.* A large mass of compacted snow that moves slowly until it either breaks off to form icebergs or melts when it reaches warmer climates.

glad *adj.* Displaying, experiencing, or affording joy and pleasure; a state of being happy; being willing to help; grateful. *n.* Short for gladiolus.

glad-den *v.* To make glad.

glade *n.* A clearing in a forest or woods.

glad-hand *n.* A warm welcome to people you meet.

glad-i-a-tor *n.* An ancient Roman slave, captive, or paid freeman who entertained the public by fighting to the death; one who engages in an intense struggle or controversy. **-ial** *adj.*

glad-i-o-lus *.,* *pl.* **-li** *or* **-luses** A plant with fleshy bulbs, sword-shaped leaves, and spikes of colorful flowers.

glad-some *adj.* Giving cheer; showing joy. **gladsomely** *adv.*, **gladsomeness** *n.*

glam-or-ize *or* **glam-our-ize** *v.* To make glamorous; to portray or treat in a romantic way.

glam-our *or* **glam-or** *n.* Alluring fascination or charm. **-ous**, **glamourous** *adj.*

glamour girl *n.* A woman considered to lead a glamorous life.

glance *v.* To take a brief or quick look at something; to obliquely strike a surface at an angle and be deflected; to give a light, brief touch; to brush against. **glancing** *adj.* **glanced** *v.*

gland *n.*, *Anat.* Any of various body organs which excrete or secrete substances. **glandular** *adj.*

glare *v.* To stare fiercely or angrily; to shine intensely; to dazzle. *n.* An uncomfortably harsh or bright light.

glar-ing *adj.* Shining with an extremely bright light; painfully obvious. **glaringly** *adv.* **glaringness** *n.*

glass *n.* A hard, amorphous, brittle, usually transparent material which hardens from the molten state, preceded by rapid cooling to prevent crystallization; any substance made of or resembling glass; a mirror, tumbler, windowpane, lens, or other material made of glass. **glasses** A pair of eyeglasses used as an aid to vision; glassware. **glass**, **glassy** *adj.*

glass blowing *n.* The art or process of shaping objects from molten glass by gently blowing air into them through a glass tube. **glass blower** *n.*

glass-ine *n.* A thin dense transparent paper highly resistant to air and grease.

glass-wool *n.* Glass fibers in a mass being used for thermal insulation and air filters.

glau-co-ma *n.*, *Pathol.* A disease of the eye characterized by abnormally high pressure within the eyeball and partial or complete loss of vision.

glau-cous *adj.* Yellowish green.

glaze *n.* A thin, smooth coating as on ceramics. *v.* To become covered with a thin glassy coating of ice; to coat or cover with a glaze; to fit with glass, as to glaze a window.

glazer *n.*, **glazing**, **glazed** *v.*

gla-zier *n.* A person who sets glass. **glaziery** *n.*

gleam *n.* A momentary ray or beam of light. *v.* To shine or emit light softly; to appear briefly. **gleamy** *adj.*

glean *v.* To collect or gather facts by patient effort; to collect part by part; to pick bits of a crop left by a reaper. **gleaner** *n.*, **gleanings** *pl.*, *n.*

glee *n.* Joy; merriment; an unaccompanied song for male voices. **gleeful** *adj.*, **gleefully** *adv.*

glee club *n.* A singing group that is organized to sing short pieces of choral music.

glen *n.* A small, secluded valley.

glen-gar-ry *n.* A woolen cap worn by the Scottish people.

glen plaid *n.* A twill pattern of checks.

glib *adj.* Spoken easily and fluently; superficial. **glibly** *adv.*, **glibness** *n.*

glide *v.* To pass or move smoothly with little or no effort; to fly without motor power. **glidingly** *adv.*, **gliding** *v.*

glid-er *n.* One that glides; a swing gliding in a metal frame. *Aeron.* An aircraft without an engine, constructed to soar on air currents.

glim-mer *n.* A faint suggestion; an indication; a dim unsteady light. *v.* To give off a faint or dim light. **glimmering** *v.*

glimpse *n.* A momentary look.

glis-sade *n.* A gliding ballet step; a controlled slide in either a sitting or standing position, used to descend a steep, snowy, or icy incline. **glissade** *v.*, **glissader** *n.*

glis-san-do *n.*, *pl.* **-di** A rapid passing from one tone to another by a continuous change of pitch.

glis-ten *v.* To shine softly as reflected by light. **glistening**, **glistened** *v.*

glitch *n.* A minor mishap or malfunction. *Elect.* A false signal caused by an unwanted surge of power.

glit-ter *n.* A brilliant sparkle; small bits of light-reflecting material used for decoration. *v.* To sparkle with brilliance. **glittery** *adj.*, **glittering**, **glittered** *v.*

gloam-ing *n.* Twilight; the dusk of early evening.

gloat *v.* To express, feel, or observe with great malicious pleasure or self-satisfaction. **gloater** *n.*, **gloating** *v.*

glob n. A drop of something; a rounded, large mass of something.

glob-al adj. Spherical; involving the whole world. -ize v., globally adv.

globe n. A spherical object; anything that is perfectly rounded; the earth; anything like a sphere, such as a fishbowl; a spherical representation of the earth, usually including geographical and political boundaries.

globe--trot-ter n. One who travels all over the world.

glob-u-lin n., Biochem. Any of a class of simple proteins found widely in blood, milk, tissue, muscle and plant seeds.

gloom n. Partial or total darkness; depression of the mind or spirits. gloomily adv., -iness n., gloomy adj.

glop n., Slang A messy mixture of food; something that is considered worthless.

glo-ri-fy v. To worship and give glory to; to give high praise. glorification n.

glo-ri-ous adj. Magnificent; resplendent; delightful; illustrious; full of glory. gloriously adv.

glory n., pl. -ies Distinguished praise or honor; exalted reputation; adoration and praise offered in worship; a wonderful asset; the height of one's triumph, achievement, or prosperity. v. To rejoice with jubilation.

gloss n. The sheen or luster of a polished surface; a deceptively or superficially attractive appearance; a note that explains or translates a difficult or hard to understand expression. v. To cover over by falsehood in an attempt to excuse or ignore.

glos-sa-ry n., pl. -ries A list of words and their meanings.

gloss-y adj. Having a bright sheen; lustrous; superficially attractive. n. A photo print on smooth, shiny paper. glossily adv., glossiness n.

glot-tis n., pl. -ises or -ides Anat. The opening or cleft between the vocal cords at the upper part of the larynx. glottal adj.

glove n. A covering for the hand with a separate section for each finger; an oversized protective covering for the hand, as that used in baseball, boxing, or hockey. gloved adj.

glow v. To give off heat and light, especially without a flame; to have a bright, warm, ruddy color. n. A warm feeling of emotion. glowing adj., glowingly adv.

glow-er v. To look sullenly or angrily at; to glare. glower n., gloweringly adv.

glow-worm n. A European beetle; the luminous larva or grub-like female of an insect which displays phosphorescent light; the firefly.

glox-in-i-a n. A tropical South American plant with large, bell-shaped flowers.

glu-ca-gon n. A protein that increases the content of sugar in the blood by increasing the rate of breakdown of glycogen in the liver.

glu-cose n., Chem. A substance less sweet than cane sugar, found as dextrose in plants and animals and obtained by hydrolysis; a yellowish to colorless syrupy mixture of dextrose, maltose, and dextrins with a small amount of water, used especially in confectionery and baking.

glue n. Any of various adhesives in the form of a gelatin, made from animal substances, as bones or skins, and used to stick and hold items together. glue v., gluey adj.

glum adj. Moody and silent. glumly adv., glumness n.

glut v. To feed or supply beyond capacity; to provide with a supply that exceeds demand. n. An overabundance.

glu-ten n. A mixture of plant proteins that is used as an adhesive and as a substitute for flour. glutenous adj.

glu-te-us n. The large muscles of the buttock.

glut-ton n. Someone who eats immoderately; one who has a large capacity for work or punishment. gluttonous adj., -ously adv., -y n.

glyc-er-ol n., Chem. A sweet, oily, syrupy liquid derived from fats and oils and used as a solvent, sweetener, antifreeze, and lubricant.

gly-co-side n., Chem. Any of a group of carbohydrates which, when decomposed, produce glucose or other sugar.

G--man n., pl. -men. An agent of the Federal Bureau of Investigation.

gnarl n. A hard, protruding knot on a tree. gnarled adj.

gnash v. To grind or strike the teeth together, as in a rage or pain.

gnat n. A small, winged insect, specially one that bites or stings.

gnaw v. To bite or eat away with persistence; to consume or wear away. gnawer n., gnawing, gnawed v.

gneiss n. A banded, coarse-grained rock with minerals arranged in layers.

gnome n. In folklore, a dwarf-like creature who lives underground and guards precious metals and treasures.

gno-mon n. An object that by the position of its shadow is an indicator of the hour of the day.

GNP abbr. Gross national product.

gnu n., pl. gnus or gnu South African antelope with an ox-like head, curved horns, a long tail, and a mane.

go v. To proceed or pass along; to leave; to move away from; to follow a certain course of action; to function; to function correctly; to be in operation; to be awarded or given; to have recourse; to resort to; to pass, as of time; to be abolished or given up; to pass to someone, as by a will. n. An attempt; a try. go back on To abandon. go for To try; to try to obtain. go places To be on the road to success. go under To suffer destruction or defeat. going v.

goad v. To drive cattle to move; to incite or rouse.

go--a-head n. Permission; a signal to

move ahead or proceed.

goal *n.* A purpose; the terminal point of a race or journey; in some games, the area, space, or object into which participants must direct play in order to score.

goal-ie *n.* A goalkeeper.

goal-keep-er *n.* The player responsible for defending the goal in hockey, soccer, and other games, preventing the ball or puck from passing over the goal for a score; a goal tender.

goal-post *n.* Two vertical poles with a crossbar which constitutes the goal line in some sports.

goat *n.* A horned, cud-chewing mammal related to the sheep; a lecherous man. *Slang* One who is a scapegoat. **-ish** *adj.*, **goatishly** *adv.*, **goatishness** *n.*

goat-ee *n.* A short, pointed beard on a man's chin.

goat-skin *n.* The skin of a goat, often used for leather.

gob *n.* A piece or lump of something. *Slang* A sailor.

gob-ble *v.* To eat and swallow food greedily; to take greedily; to grab.

gob-ble-dy-gook *n., Informal* Wordy and often unintelligible language.

gob-bler *n.* A male turkey.

go--be-tween *n.* A person who acts as an agent between two parties.

gob-let *n.* A drinking glass, typically with a base and stem.

gob-lin *n.* In folklore, an ugly, grotesque creature said to be mischievous and evil.

go-bo *n.* A dark strip to shield a television camera from light.

god *n.* Someone considered to be extremely important or valuable; an image, symbol, or statue of such a being.

God *n.* The Supreme Being; the ruler of life and the universe.

god-child *n.* A child for whom an adult serves as sponsor at baptism, circumcision, and other rites.

god-dess *n.* A female of exceptional charm, beauty, or grace.

god-father *n.* A man who sponsors a child at his or her baptism or other such ceremony.

god-for-sak-en *adj.* In a remote desolate place.

god-head *n.* Godhood; divinity. **Godhead** The essential and divine nature of God.

god-hood *n.* The state or quality of being a god; divinity.

god-less *adj.* Not recognizing a god. **godlessness** *n.*

god-ly *adj.* Filled with love for God.

god-mother *n.* A woman who sponsors a child at his or her baptism or other such ceremony.

god-par-ent *n.* A godfather or godmother.

god-send *n.* Something received unexpectedly that is needed or wanted.

god-son *n.* A male godchild.

God-speed *n.* Best wishes for someone's venture or journey.

go--get-ter *n.* An enterprising, aggressive person.

gog-gle *n., pl.* **-gles**

Spectacles or eyeglasses to protect the eyes against dust, wind, sparks, and other debris. *v.* To gaze or stare with bulging eyes.

go-ing *n.* The act of moving, leaving, or departing; the condition of roads or ground that affects walking, riding, and other movement; a condition influencing activity or progress. **goings on** Actions or behavior, used to express disapproval.

goi-ter *n., Pathol.* Any abnormal enlargement of the thyroid gland, visible as a swelling in the front of the neck. **goitrous** *adj.*

gold *n.* A soft, yellow, metallic element that is highly ductile and resistant to oxidation; used especially in coins and jewelry; a precious metal; a bright, vivid yellow; money; the element symbolized by Au.

gold-brick *n., Slang* A person who avoids work. **goldbricker** *n.*

gold dig-ger *n., Slang* A woman who seeks money and gifts from men.

gold-en *adj.* Made of or containing gold; bright yellow in color; rich; lustrous; marked by prosperity.

gold-en age *n.* Any period marked by peace, happiness, prosperity, or excellence.

gold-en an-ni-ver-sa-ry *n.* The 50th anniversary.

Gold-en Gate *n.* A large bridge in San Francisco, California, that connects the Pacific Ocean and San Francisco Bay.

gold-en-rod *n.* A North American plant with small yellow flowers; the state flower of Alabama, Kentucky, and Nebraska.

gold-en rule *n.* The principle of treating others as one wants to be treated.

Gold-en State *n.* Nickname of the state of California.

gold--fill-ed *adj.* Made of a hard base metal over which a thick covering of gold is laid.

gold-finch *n.* A small bird, the male of which has yellow plumage with black forehead, tail, and wings.

gold-fish *n.* A reddish or brass-colored freshwater fish, cultivated as an aquarium fish.

gold mine *n.* A mine which produces gold ore; any source of great riches or profit.

gold stand-ard *n.* The monetary system based on gold of a specified weight and fineness as the unit of value and exchange.

golf *n.* A game played outdoors with a hard ball and various clubs, on a grassy course with 9 or 18 holes.

golf v., **golfer** n.

Gol-go-tha n. The place near Jerusalem where Jesus was crucified; also known as Calvary.

Go-li-ath n. In the Bible, a giant Philistine killed by David with a stone from a sling shot.

gon-ad n., Anat. The male or female sex gland where the reproductive cells develop; an ovary or testis. **gonadal, gonadial, gonadic** adj.

gon-do-la n. A long, narrow, flat-bottomed boat propelled by a single oar and used on the canals of Venice.

gone adj. Past; bygone; dead; beyond hope; marked by faintness or weakness. **far gone** Exhausted; wearied; almost dead.

gon-er n., Slang One that is ruined, close to death, or beyond all hope of saving.

gon-fa-lon n. A banner hung from a crosspiece and cut so as to end in streamers.

gong n. A heavy metal disk which produces a deep resonant tone when struck.

gon-o-coc-cus n., pl. -**cocci** The bacterium which causes gonorrhea. **gonococcal, gonococcic** adj.

gon-or-rhe-a n., Pathol. A contagious venereal infection transmitted chiefly by sexual intercourse. **gonorrheal** adj.

goo n. Any sticky substance. **gooey** adj.

goo-ber n., Regional A peanut.

good adj. Having desirable or favorable qualities or characteristics; morally excellent; virtuous; well-behaved; tractable; proper; excellent in degree or quality; unspoiled; fresh; healthy; striking or attractive. **goods** Merchandise or wares; personal belongings; cloth; fabric. **for good** Forever; permanently. **better, best** adj.

Good Book n. The Bible.

good--by or **good--bye** interj. Used to express farewell. n. A farewell; a parting word; an expression of farewell. adj. Final.

good--for--noth-ing n. A person of little worth or usefulness.

Good Fri-day n. The Friday before Easter, a day observed by Christians as a commemoration of the crucifixion of Jesus.

good--heart-ed adj. Having a kind and generous disposition. -**heartedness** n.

good--hu-mored adj. Having a cheerful temper or mood; amiable. **good-humoredly** adv., -**humoredness** n.

good--look-ing adj. Handsome; having a pleasing appearance.

good--na-tured adj. Having an easygoing and pleasant disposition. **good-naturedly** adv., -**naturedness** n.

good-ness n. The state or quality of being good.

good-will n. A desire for the well-being of others; the pleasant feeling or relationship between a business and its customers.

good-y n., pl. -**ies** Something that is good

to eat; a prissy person.

goof n., Slang A stupid or dull-witted person; a mistake. v. To blunder; to make a mistake.

goof--off n. A person who shuns responsibility or work. v. To be doing something else when there is work to be done.

goof-y adj. Ridiculous; silly. **goofily** adv., **goofiness** n.

gook n., Slang A slimy, sludgy, or dirty substance.

goon n., Slang A thug or hoodlum hired to intimidate or injure someone; a person hired to break strikes; a stupid person.

goose n., pl. **geese**

A large water bird related to swans and ducks; a female goose. Informal A silly person.

goose-ber-ry n., pl. -**ies** The edible greenish berry of a spiny shrub used for pies, jams, and other foods.

goose bumps pl., n. A prickling sensation of the skin caused by fear or cold, also known as goose pimples and goose skin.

goose egg n. A score of zero in a contest or game.

goose-neck n. Any various devices curved like a goose's neck.

go-pher n. A burrowing North American rodent with large cheek pouches.

gore v. To stab or pierce. n. Blood that has been shed; a triangular or tapering piece of cloth as in a sail or skirt.

gorge n. A deep, narrow ravine; deep or violent disgust. v. To eat or devour something greedily. **gorger** n.

gor-geous adj. Beautiful; dazzling; extremely beautiful; magnificent. **gorgeously** adv., **gorgeousness** n.

Gor-gon-zo-la n. A pungent, strongly flavored Italian cheese.

go-ril-la n.

A large African jungle ape, having a massive, stocky body, long arms, and tusk-like canine teeth.

gorse n. A spiny plant bearing fragrant yellow flowers.

go-ry adj. Covered or stained with blood; resembling gore; marked by much bloodshed or violence.

gos-hawk n. A large, short-winged hawk formerly used in falconry.

gos-ling n. A young goose.

gos-pel or **Gos-pel** n. The teachings of Christ and the apostles; any information which is accepted as unquestionably true; any of the first four books of the New Testament.

gos-pel mus-ic n. American religious music based on simple folk melodies blended with rhythmic and melodic elements of spirituals and jazz.

gos-sa-mer *n.* The fine film or strands of a spider's web floating in the air; anything sheer, delicate, light, or flimsy.

gos-sip *n.* Idle, often malicious talk; a person who spreads sensational or intimate facts. *v.* To spread or engage in gossip. **gossiper** *n.*, **gossipy** *adj.*

got *v.* Past tense of get.

Goth *n.* A member of a Germanic people that invaded the Roman Empire early in the Christian era; a barbarian.

Goth-am *n.* A nickname for New York City.

Goth-ic *adj.* Of or pertaining to the Goths or to their language; of or relating to an architectural style popular from about 1200 to 1500, which was characterized by pointed arches and ribbed vaulting.

gouache *n.* A method of painting with opaque watercolors.

Gou-da cheese *n.* A mild, yellow Dutch cheese made from milk.

gouge *n.* A chisel with a scoop-shaped blade used for woodcarving; a groove or hole made with or as if with a gouge *v.* To make a hole or groove with a gouge; to cheat, as to charge exorbitant prices. **gouger** *n.*

gou-lash *n.* A stew made from beef or veal and vegetables seasoned chiefly with paprika.

gourd *n.* A vine fruit related to the pumpkin, squash, and cucumber and bearing inedible fruit with a hard rind; the dried, hollowed-out shell can be used as a drinking utensil.

gour-mand *n.* A person who takes excessive pleasure in eating.

gour-met *n.* Someone who appreciates and understands fine food and drink.

gout *n., Pathol.* A disease caused by a defect in metabolism and characterized by painful inflammation of the joints. **gouty** *adj.*

gov *abbr.* Government.

gov-ern *v.* To guide, rule, or control by right or authority; to control or guide the action of something; to restrain. **governable** *adj.*, **governance** *n.*

gov-ern-ess *n.* A woman employed in a private household to train and instruct children.

gov-ern-ment *n.* The authoritative administration of public policy and affairs of a nation, state or city; the system or policy by which a political unit is governed; any governed territory, district, or area. **governmental** *adj.*, **governmentally** *adv.*

gov-er-nor *n.* Someone who governs, as the elected chief executive of any state in the United States; an official appointed to exercise political authority over a territory. *Mech.* A device which will automatically controls the speed of a machine. **governorship** *n.*

govt *abbr.* Government.

gow-an *n.* A yellow or white field flower.

gown *n.* A woman's dress, especially for a formal affair; any long, loose-fitting garment; a robe worn by certain officials, scholars, and clergymen.

GP *abbr.* General practitioner.

GPO *abbr.* General Post Office.

gr *abbr.* Grade; gross; grain.

grab *v.* To snatch or take suddenly; to take possession of by force or by dishonest means. *Slang* To capture the attention of someone or something. **grab, grabber** *n.*, **grabby** *adj.*

grab bag *n.* A bag or container full of miscellaneous unidentified articles from which one may draw an object at random.

gra-ben *n., Geol.* An elongated depression in the earth, caused by the downward faulting of a portion of the earth's crust.

grace *n.* Seemingly effortless beauty, ease, and charm of movement, proportion, or form; a charming quality or characteristic; an extension of time that is granted after a set date, as for paying a debt. **graceful, graceless** *adj.*, **-fully** *adv.* **-fulness** *n.*

gra-cious *adj.* Marked by having or showing kindness and courtesy; full of compassion; merciful. **graciously** *adv.*, **graciousness** *n.*

grack-le *n.* Any of various New World blackbirds having long tails and iridescent blackish plumage.

grad *n., Slang* A graduate.

gra-date *v.* To shade into the next color or stage.

gra-da-tion *n.* A gradual and orderly arrangement or progression according to quality, size, rank, or other value; the act of grading. **gradational** *adj.*

grade *n.* A step or degree in a process or series; a group or category; a level of progress in school, usually constituting a year's work; a letter or number indicating a level of achievement in school work; the degree to which something slopes, as a road, track, or other surface. *Milit.* Rank or rating. **grade** *v.*

grad-er *n.* A machine used to level earth.

grade school *n.* Elementary school, which will usually teach from kindergarten to grade 6 or grade 8.

gra-di-ent *n.* A slope or degree of inclination. *Phys.* A rate of change in variable factors, as temperature or pressure.

gra-din *n.* One in a series of steps.

grad-u-al *adj.* Moving or changing slowly by degrees; not steep or abrupt. **gradually** *adv.*, **gradualness** *n.*

grad-u-ate *v.* To receive or be granted an academic diploma or degree upon completion of a course of study; to divide into categories, grades or steps. *n.* A person who holds an academic degree; a type container or beaker marked in units or degrees, used for measuring liquids.

grad-u-ate stu-dent A student who has received a college degree and is working toward an advanced or higher degree.

grad-u-a-tion *n.* The state of graduating; a commencement ceremony; issuing of diplomas or degrees.

graf-fi-to *n., pl.* **graf-fi-ti** An inscription or drawing made on a public wall, subway train, rock, or any other surface.

graft *v.* To insert a shoot from a plant into another living plant so that the two will grow together as a single plant. *Surg.* To transplant a piece of tissue or an organ. *n.* Living tissue or skin used to replace damaged or destroyed tissue or skin; the act of acquiring or getting personal profit or advantage by dishonest or unfair means through one's public position.

gra-ham *n.* Whole wheat flour.

gra-ham cracker *n.* A semi sweet cracker made of whole wheat flour.

grail *n.* The legendary cup used by Christ at the Last Supper; also called the Holy Grail.

grain *n.* A small, hard seed or kernel of cereal, wheat, or oats; the seeds or fruits of such plants as a group; a very small amount; a small, hard particle, as a grain of sand; the side of a piece of leather from which the hair has been removed; the characteristic markings or pattern of this side; texture; basic nature. **against the grain** Contrary to one's inclinations or temperament. **grainer** *n.*, **grainless** *adj.*

grain al-co-hol *n.* Ethanol.

grain el-e-va-tor *n.* A building used to store grain.

grain-y *adj.* Having a granular texture; resembling the grain of wood. **-iness** *n.*

gram *n.* A metric unit of mass and weight equal to 1/1000 kilogram and nearly equal to one cubic centimeter of water at its maximum density.

gram-mar *n.* The study and description of the classes of words, their relations to each other, and their arrangement into sentences; the inflectional and syntactic rules of a language. **grammarian** *n.*, **grammatical** *adj.*, **grammatically** *adv.*

gram-mar school *n.* An elementary school. *Brit.* A secondary or preparatory school.

gram mol-e-cule *n., Chem.* The quantity of a compound, expressed in grams, that is equal to the molecular weight of that compound.

gran-a-ry *n., pl.* **ries** A building for storing threshed grain; an area or region where grain grows in abundance.

grand *adj.* To be large in size, extent, or scope; magnificent; of high rank or great importance; lofty; admirable; main or principal; highly satisfactory; excellent. *Slang* A thousand dollars. **grandly** *adv.*, **grandness** *n.*

Grand Can-yon State *n.* Nickname for the state of Arizona.

grand-child *n.* The child of one's son or daughter.

grand-dad *n.* The father of one's mother or father.

grand-daugh-ter *n.* The daughter of one's son or daughter.

gran-deur *n.* The quality or condition of being grand; splendor; magnificence.

grand-fa-ther *n.* The father of one's father or mother; an ancestor.

grand-fa-ther clock *n.* A pendulum clock enclosed in a tall narrow cabinet.

gran-di-flo-ra *n.* A rose bush producing both single blooms and clusters of blooms on the same plant due to crossbreeding tea roses and floribunda.

gran-dil-o-quent *adj.* Speaking in or characterized by a pompous or bombastic style. **grandiloquence** *n.*

gran-di-ose *adj.* Impressive and grand; pretentiously pompous; bombastic. **grandiosely** *adv.*, **grandiosity** *n.*

grand jury *n.* A jury that listens to accusations against people who have committed a crime and passes judgment as to whether they are guilty or innocent.

grand mal *n., Pathol.* A form of epilepsy characterized by severe convulsions and loss of consciousness.

grand-moth-er *n.* The mother of one's father or mother; a female ancestor.

grand op-era *n.* A form of opera having a serious and complex plot with the complete text set to music.

grand-par-ent *n.* A parent of one's mother or father.

grand pi-ano *n.* A piano with the strings which are arranged horizontally in a curved, wooden case.

grand prix *n.* An international long-distance car race through the streets.

grand slam *n.* In bridge, the taking of all the tricks; in baseball, a home run hit with runners on first, second, and third bases.

grand-son *n.* A son of one's son or daughter.

grand-stand *n.* A raised stand of seats, usually roofed, for spectators at a racetrack or sports event.

gran-ite *n.* A hard, coarse-grained igneous rock composed chiefly of quartz, mica, and orthoclase, which is used for building material and in sculpture. **granitic** *adj.*

gran-ite-ware *n.* Ironware utensils coated with hard enamel.

gran-ny *or* **gran-nie** *n.* A grandmother; an old woman; a fussy person.

gra-no-la *n.* Rolled oats mixed with dried fruit and seeds and eaten as a snack.

grano-lith *n.* A artificial stone made of crushed granite and cement.

grant *v.* To allow; to consent to; to admit something as being the truth; in law, to transfer property by a deed. *n.* That which is granted. **grantee**, **granter**, **grantor** *n.*

Grant, Ulysses S. *n.* The 18th president of the United States, from 1869-1877.

gran-u-lar *adj.* The state of being composed or seeming to be composed or containing grains or granules.

granularity n.

gran-u-late v. To make or form into granules or crystals; to become or cause to become rough and grainy.

granulation n.

gran-ule n. A very small grain or particle forming a larger unit.

grape n. Any of numerous woody vines bearing clusters of smooth-skinned, juicy, edible berries, having a dark purplish blue, red, or green color, eaten raw or dried and used in making wine.

grape-fruit n. A tropical, large, round citrus fruit with a pale yellow rind and tart, juicy pulp; the tree bearing this fruit.

grape hyacinth n. Several small bulbous spring flowering herbs of the lily family.

grape-shot n. A shot consisting of a cluster of small iron balls, formerly used to charge a cannon.

grape sug-ar n. Dextrose.

grape-vine n. A climbing vine that produces grapes; a secret or informal means of transmitting information or rumor from person to person.

graph n. A diagram representing the relationship between sets of things.

graph-ic or graph-i-cal adj. Describing in full detail; of or pertaining to drawings or blueprints, as in architecture.

graph-ite n. A soft black form of carbon having a metallic luster and slippery texture, used in lead pencils, lubricants, paints, and coatings.

graphitic adj.

graph-ol-o-gy n. The study of handwriting for the purpose of analyzing a person's character or personality.

graphologist n.

graph paper n. Paper ruled with lines for drawing graphs.

grap-nel n. A small anchor with several flukes at the end.

grap-ple n. An instrument with iron claws used to fasten an enemy ship alongside for boarding. v. To struggle or contend with; to fasten, seize or drag as with a grapple. grappler n.

grasp v. To seize and grip firmly; to comprehend; to understand. n. The power to seize and hold.

graspable adj., grasper n.

grasp-ing adj. Urgently desiring material possessions; greedy.

graspingly adv., graspingness n.

grass n. Any of numerous plants having narrow leaves and jointed stems; the ground on which grass is growing. Slang Marijuana.

grassiness n., grassy adj.

grass court n. A tennis court made with a grass surface.

grass-hop-per n.

Any of several jumping insects that has long powerful hind legs. Slang Any

type of small, lightweight airplane which can be used for dusting crops and military observation.

grass-land n. Land in which grasses are the main vegetation, as a prairie.

grass roots pl., n. A society of common people, thought of as having practical and highly independent views or interests. grassroots adj.

grass wi-dow n. A woman who is separated or divorced from her husband.

grassy adj. Abounding or covered with grass.

grate v. To reduce, shred or pulverize by rubbing against a rough or sharp surface; to make or cause to make a harsh sound. n. A rasping noise.

grater n., grating adj., gratingly adv.

grate n. A framework or bars placed over a window or other opening; an iron frame to hold burning fuel in a fireplace or furnace.

grate-ful adj. The state of being thankful or appreciative for benefits or kindnesses; expressing gratitude.

gratefully adv., gratefulness n.

grat-i-cule n. The network of lines of latitude and longitude from which maps are drawn.

grat-i-fy v. To give pleasure or satisfaction to; to fulfill the desires of; to indulge. gratification n.

gra-tin n. A brown crust formed on food cooked with a topping of crumbs or grated cheese.

grat-ing n. A grate.

grat-is adv. & adj. Without requiring payment; free.

grat-i-tude n. The state of appreciation and gratefulness; thankfulness.

gra-tu-i-tous adj. Given or obtained without payment; unjustified; unwarranted. gratuitously adv., -ness n.

gra-tu-i-ty n., pl. -ies A gift, as money, given in return for a service rendered; a tip.

gra-va-men n., pl. -mens or -mina In law, the part of an accusation or charge weighing most heavily against the accused.

grave n. A burial place for a dead body, usually an excavation in the earth. adj. Very serious or important in nature; filled with danger; critical. v. To sculpt or carve; to engrave. Mus. Solemn and slow. gravely adv.,

graveness, graver n.

grav-el n. Loose rock fragments often with sand. Pathol. The deposit of sand-like crystals that form in the kidneys; also known as kidney stones.

grave-stone n. A stone that marks a grave; a tombstone.

grave-yard n. An area set aside as a burial place; a cemetery.

grave-yard shift n. Slang A work shift that usually begins at midnight.

gra-vim-e-ter n. An implement for determining specific gravity. gravimetry n.

grav-i-tate v. To be drawn as if by an irresistible force; to sink or settle to a lower level.

grav-i-ta-tion *n., Physics* The force or attraction any two bodies exert towards each other. **gravitational, gravitatively** *adj.*, **gravitationally** *adv.*

grav-i-ty *n., pl.* **-ies** The gravitational force manifested by the tendency of material bodies to fall toward the center of the earth; gravitation in general; weight; importance; seriousness.

gra-vy *n., pl.* **-ies** The juices exuded by cooking meat; a sauce made by seasoning and thickening these juices. *Slang* Money or profit which is easily acquired.

gray *or* **grey** *adj.* A neutral color between black and white; gloomy; dismal; having gray hair; characteristic of old age. **grayish** *adj.*, **grayness** *n.*

gray-beard *n., Slang* An old man.

gray-ling *n., pl.* **-ling** *or* **-lings** Any of several freshwater food and game fish with a small mouth and a large dorsal fin.

gray mat-ter *n.* The grayish-brown nerve tissue of the spinal cord and brain, consisting mainly of nerve cells and fibers; brains.

graze *v.* To feed upon growing grasses or herbage; to put livestock to feed on grass or pasturage; to brush against lightly in passing; to abrade or scrape slightly.

gra-zier *n.* One who grazes cattle.

grease *n.* Melted or soft animal fat; any thick fatty or oily substance, as a lubricant. *v.* To lubricate or coat with grease. **greasiness** *n.*, **greasy** *adj.*

grease monkey *n.* An auto or airplane mechanic.

grease paint *n.* Makeup used for theatre performances.

greasy *adj.* Soiled with grease; oily in appearance.

greasy spoon *n.* A small cheap restaurant.

great *adj.* Very large in size or volume; prolonged in duration or extent; more than ordinary; considerable; remarkable; impressive; eminent; renowned; very good or first-rate; a generation removed from a relative. **greatly** *adv.*, **greatness** *n.*

great--aunt *n.* An aunt of either of one's parents.

Great Bear *n.* The constellation Ursa Major.

Great Brit-ain *n.* The island which is located off the west coast of Europe, made up of England, Scotland and Wales; the United Kingdom.

great--grand-child *n.* A child of a grandchild.

great--grand-daugh-ter *n.* A daughter of a grandchild.

great--grand-fa-ther *n.* The father of a grandparent.

great--grand-mo-ther *n.* The mother of a grandparent.

great--grand-par-ent *n.* The father or mother of a grandparent.

great--grand-son *n.* The son of a grandchild.

great-heart-ed *adj.* Noble or generous in spirit; magnanimous. **-ly** *adv.*, **greatheartedness** *n.*

Great Lakes *n.* The group of five freshwater lakes of central North America located on either side of the boundary between the United States and Canada and including Lake Superior, Lake Michigan, Lake Huron, Lake Erie, and Lake Ontario.

great--neph-ew *n.* A grandnephew.

great--niece *n.* A grandniece.

Great Pyr-e-nees *n.* A breed of large heavy-coated white dogs.

Great Salt Lake *n.* A lake composed of salt water located in the state of Utah.

great seal *n.* The chief seal of a government.

great--un-cle *n.* An uncle of either of one's parents; granduncle.

greave *n.* An armor for the leg worn below the knee.

grebe *n.* Any of various swimming and diving birds having partially webbed feet, very short tails, and a pointed bill.

Greece *n.* A country of southeast Europe. **Grecian** *adj.* & *n.*

greed *n.* Selfish desire to acquire more than one needs or deserves.

greed-y *adj.* Excessively eager to acquire or gain something; having an excessive appetite for drink and food; gluttonous. **greedily** *adv.*, **greediness** *n.*

Greek *n.* An inhabitant or native of Greece; the modern or ancient language of Greece. *adj.* Pertaining to or of the Greek Church; of or pertaining to the culture of Greece.

green *adj.* Of the color between yellow and blue in the spectrum; not fully matured or developed; lacking in skill or experience. *n.* A grassy plot or lawn, especially an area of closely mowed grass at the end of a golf fairway. **greenish** *adj.*, **greenness** *n.*

green-back *n.* A U.S. legal-tender currency note.

green bean *n.* A string bean; a vegetable commonly grown in private gardens.

green-er-y *n., pl.* **-ies** Green foliage or plants.

green--eyed *adj.* Jealous.

green-gro-cer *n.* A person who sells fresh vegetables and fruits.

green-horn *n.* An inexperienced person; a beginner; a person who is easily fooled.

green-house *n.* An enclosed structure equipped with heat and moisture designed for the cultivation of plants.

green light *n.* The traffic light which signals permission to proceed.

green monkey *n.* A long-tailed monkey of West Africa that has greenish colored hair.

green pep-per *n.* The unripened fruit of various pepper plants.

green-room *n.* The room or lounge in a theatre used by performers when they are off-stage.

greens fee n. The fee paid for playing golf on a golf course.

green thumb n. A special skill for making plants thrive.

greet v. To address someone in a friendly way; to welcome; to meet or receive in a specified manner. **greeter** n.

greet-ing n. A word of salutation on meeting.

gre-gar-i-ous adj. Habitually associating with others as in groups, flocks, or herds; enjoying the company of others; sociable. **gregariously** adv., **gregariousness** n.

grem-lin n. A mischievous elf said to cause mechanical trouble in airplanes.

Gre-na-da n. An island in the West Indies.

gre-nade n. A small explosive device detonated by a fuse and thrown by hand or projected from a rifle.

gren-a-dier n. A member of a special European corps which was formerly armed with grenades.

gren-a-dine n. A syrup made from pomegranates or red currants and used as a flavoring in mixed drinks.

grew v. Past tense of grow.

grey n., & adj. Variation of gray.

grey-hound n. One of a breed of slender, swift-running dogs with long legs.

grib-ble n. A small marine crustacean which destroys submerged timber.

grid n. An arrangement of regularly spaced bars; the system of intersecting parallel lines that divide maps, charts, and aerial photographs, used as a reference for locating points.

grid-dle n. A flat pan used for cooking. **griddle cake** n. A pancake.

grid-i-ron n. A metal framework used for broiling meat, fish, and other foods; a football field.

grief n. Deep sadness or mental distress caused by a loss, remorse, or bereavement.

griev-ance n. A real or imagined wrong which is regarded as cause for complaint or resentment; a complaint of unfair treatment.

grievance committee n. A group formed by a labor union or employees jointly to discuss and try to eliminate problems.

grieve v. To cause or feel grief or sorrow.

griev-ous adj. Causing grief, sorrow, anguish, or pain; causing physical suffering. **grievously** adv.

grif-fin or **grif-fon** n. In Greek mythology, a fabulous beast with a lion's body, an eagle's head, and wings.

grig n. A lively small or young person.

grill n. A cooking utensil made from parallel metal bars; a gridiron; food cooked on a grill; a restaurant where grilled foods are a specialty. v. To broil on a grill.

gril-lage n. A framework of lumber or steel for support in marshy soil.

grille or **grill** n. A grating with open metalwork used as a decorative screen or room divider.

grilse n. A young mature salmon returning from the sea to spawn for the first time.

grim adj. Stern or forbidding in appearance or character; unyielding; relentless; grisly; gloomy; dismal. **grimly** adv., **grimness** n.

grim-ace n. A facial expression of pain, disgust, or disapproval. **grimace** v.

grime n. Dirt, especially soot clinging to or coating a surface. **griminess** n., **grimy** adj.

grin v. To smile broadly. **grin** n.

grind v. To reduce to fine particles; to sharpen, polish, or shape by friction; to press or rub together; to work or study hard. n. A person who works hard or who studies very hard. **grind-er** n. One that grinds.

grind-ers pl.,n. Slang The teeth.

grind-stone n. A flat, circular stone which revolves on an axle and is used for polishing, sharpening, or grinding.

grip n. A firm hold; a grasp; the ability to seize or maintain a hold; the mental or intellectual grasp; a suitcase. v. To grasp and keep a firm hold on; to capture the imagination or attention. **gripper** n., **grippingly** adv.

gripe v. To cause sharp pain or cramps in the bowels; to anger; to annoy; to complain.

grippe n. Influenza. **grippy** adj.

gris-ly adj. Ghastly; gruesome.

grist n. Grain that is to be ground; a batch of such grain.

gris-tle n. Cartilage of meat. **gristly** adj.

grist-mill n. A mill for grinding grain.

grit n. Small, rough granules, as of sand or stone; having great courage and fortitude. v. To clamp the teeth together. **gritty** adj.

grits pl., n. Coarsely ground hominy or coarse meal; eaten primarily in the southern states of the U.S.

griz-zle v. To become or cause to become gray.

grizzly bear n.

A large, grayish bear of western North America. **grizzlies** pl.,n., Slang Grizzly bears.

groan v. To utter a deep, prolonged sound of or as of disapproval or pain. **groan** n., **groaningly** adv.

groat n. A former British coin worth four-pence; any grain without its hull; a tiny sum.

gro-cer n. A storekeeper who deals in foodstuffs and various household supplies.

groceries pl., n. The merchandise sold in a grocery.

grocery n., pl. -ies A store in which foodstuffs and household staples are sold.

grog n. Any alcoholic liquor, especially

rum, mixed with water.

grog-gy adj. To be dazed, weak, or not fully conscious, such as from a blow or exhaustion; drunk. **groggily** adv., **grogginess** n.

gro-gram n. A loosely woven fabric of silk and mohair or silk and wood.

grog-shop n. A low-class barroom.

groin n., Anat. The crease or fold where the thigh meets the abdomen. Archit. The curved edge of a building formed by two intersecting vaults.

grom-met n. A reinforcing eyelet through which a rope, cord, or fastening may be passed. Naut. A ring of rope or metal used to secure the edge of a sail.

groom n. A male person hired to tend horses; a stableman; a bridegroom. v. To make neat in appearance; to prepare for a particular position, as for a political office.

grooms-man n., pl. -men The best man at a wedding; any one of a bridegroom's attendants.

groove n. A long, narrow channel or indentation; a fixed, settled habit or routine; a rut. **groove** v.

groovy adj., Slang A state or condition of being wonderful; delightful.

grope v. The act of feeling about with or as with the hands, as in the dark; to look for uncertainly or blindly. **grope** n., **gropingly** adv.

gros-beck n. Any of several colorful birds which are related to the finch, having a stout, short beak.

gros-grain n. A heavy, horizontally corded silk or rayon fabric, woven as a ribbon.

gross adj. Exclusive of deductions; of or relating to the total amount received; excessively large or fat; lacking refinement or delicacy; coarse; vulgar. n. The entire amount without deduction; an amount that equals 12 dozen or 144 items. **grossly** adv., **grossness** n.

gross na-tion-al pro-duct n. The total market value of all goods and services produced by a nation in a year.

gro-tesque adj. Distorted, incongruous or ludicrous in appearance or style; bizarre; outlandish. **grotesque**, **grotesqueness** n., **grotesquely** adv.

grot-to n., pl. -toes or -tos A cave or cave-like structure.

grouch n. An habitually irritable or complaining person. **grouch** v., **grouchily** adv., **grouchiness** n., -y adj.

ground n. The surface of the earth; soil, sand, and other natural material at or near the earth's surface; the connecting of an electric current to the earth through a conductor.

ground v. Past tense of grind.

ground ball n. A batted ball that bounds or rolls along the ground.

ground cov-er n. A low-growing plant which forms a dense, extensive growth and tends to prevent soil erosion.

ground crew n. The mechanics who maintain and service an airplane.

ground glass n. Glass that has been treated so that it is not fully transparent.

ground hog n. A woodchuck.

Ground-hog Day n. February 2nd, on which, if the ground hog sees his shadow, he goes underground again because there will be six more weeks of winter.

ground ivy n. A trailing mint with rounded leaves purple flowers.

ground-less adj. Without foundation or basis.

ground rent n. Rent paid by a lessee for the use of land.

ground rule n. A basic rule; the rule in sports that modifies play on a particular field, course, or court.

grounds n. The land that surrounds a building; the basis for an argument, action or belief; the sediment in the bottom of a liquid, such as coffee, or tea. v. To prevent an aircraft or pilot from flying. Naut. To run a boat aground.

ground sheet n. A waterproof cover to protect an area of ground, such as a baseball or football field.

ground wave n. A radio wave along the surface of the earth.

ground ze-ro n. The point on the ground vertically beneath or above the point of detonation of an atomic bomb.

group n. A collection or assemblage of people, objects, or things having something in common.

grou-per n. A large fish related to the sea bass.

group-ie n., Slang A female follower of a rock group, especially when it is on tour.

group ther-a-py n. Psychotherapy which involves sessions guided by a therapist and attended by several patients who discuss their problems.

grouse n., pl. grouse Any of a family of game birds characterized by mottled, brownish plumage and rounded bodies. v. To complain; to grumble.

grout n. A material used to fill cracks in masonry or spaces between tiles. **grout** v., **grouter** n.

grove n. A small group of trees, lacking undergrowth.

grov-el v. To lie or crawl face downward, as in fear; to act with abject humility. **groveler** n., **grovelingly** adv.

grow v. To increase in size, develop, and reach maturity; to expand; to increase; to come into existence. **to grow on** To become increasingly acceptable, necessary, or pleasing to. **grower** n., **growing** v.

growl v. To utter a deep, guttural, threatening sound, as that made by a hostile or agitated animal. **growl** n., **growling** v.

grown adj. Fully matured; cultivated in a specified way.

grown-up n. A mature adult.

growth n. The act or process of growing; a gradual increase in size or amount.

Pathol. An abnormal formation of bodily tissue, as a tumor.

growth factor *n.* A substance that enhances the growth of an organism.

grub *v.* To dig up by the roots; to lead a dreary existence; to drudge. *n.* The thick, worm-like larva of certain insects, as of the June beetle. *Slang* Food; to scrounge. **grubbing** *v.*

grub-by *adj.* Sloppy, unkempt. **grubbily** *adv.*, **grubbiness** *n.*

grub-stake *n.* Funds and supplies furnished a miner until he can fend for himself.

grudge *n.* A feeling of ill will, rancor, or deep resentment. *v.* To be displeased, resentful, or envious of the possessions or good fortune of another person. **grudger** *n.*, **grudgingly** *adv.*

gru-el *n.* A thin liquid made by boiling meal in water or milk.

gru-el-ing *or* **gru-el-ling** *adj.* Extremely tiring; exhausting. **gruelingly** *adv.*

grue-some *adj.* The state of causing horror or fright. **-ly** *adv.*, **gruesomeness** *n.*

gruff *adj.* Brusque and rough in manner; harsh in sound; hoarse. **gruffly** *adv.*, **gruffness** *n.*

grum-ble *v.* To complain in low, throaty sounds; to growl. **grumble, grumbler** *n.*, **grumbly** *adj.*

grump-y *adj.* Irritable and moody; ill tempered. **grumpily** *adv.*, **-iness** *n.*

grun-gy *adj. Slang* Dirty, run-down, or inferior in condition or appearance.

grunt *n.* The deep, guttural sound of a hog. **grunt** *v.*

grun-tle *v.* To put in a good mood.

G-string *n.* A very narrow loincloth with a waistband, worn by strip-teasers.

G-suit *n.* A flight garment designed to counteract the effects of high acceleration on a person by exerting pressure on the body parts.

GU *abbr.* Guam.

gua-ca-mo-le *n.* Mashed avocado seasoned with condiments.

gua-na-co *n.* A South American mammal with a fawn-colored coat, related to the camel but without a hump.

qua-neth-i-dine *n.* A drug used in treating severe high blood pressure.

gua-no *n.* The excrement of sea birds, used as a fertilizer.

guar *abbr.* Guaranteed.

guar-an-tee *n.* The promise or assurance of the durability or quality of a product; something held or given as a pledge or security. *v.* To assume responsibility for the default or debt of; to certify; to vouch for.

guar-an-tor *n.* One who gives a guarantee or guaranty.

guar-an-ty *n., pl.* **-ies** A pledge or promise to be responsible for the debt, duty, or contract of another person in case of default; something that guarantees.

guard *v.* To watch over or shield from danger or harm; to keep watch as to prevent escape, violence, or indiscretion. *n.* A defensive position, as in boxing or fencing; in football, one of two linemen on either side of the center; in basketball, one of the two players stationed near the middle of the court; a device or piece of equipment that protects against damage, loss, or harm. **guarding, guarded** *v.*

guard-house *n.* A military jail; a building used by soldiers on guard duty.

guard-i-an *n.* One who is legally assigned responsibility for the care of the person and property of an infant, minor or person unable to be do for himself because of physical or mental disability. **guardianship** *n.*

guard-rail *n.* The protective rail, as on a highway or any area that proposes a threat or danger.

guards-man *n.* A member of the U.S. National Guard.

guar gum *n.* A gum from ground guar seeds used as a thickening agent and as a sizing material.

gua-va *n.* A tree or shrub of the myrtle family bearing small, pear-shaped, edible, yellow-skinned fruit.

gub-ba *v., Slang* To tickle the neck area, especially of children and babies. *n.* The area that is tickled.

gu-ber-na-to-ri-al *adj.* Of or pertaining to a governor.

gudgeon *n.* A small European freshwater fish related to the carp.

gue-non *n.* A long tailed arboreal African monkey.

guern-sey *n., pl.* **-seys** A breed of brown and white dairy cattle.

guer-ril-la *n.* A member of an irregular military force that is capable of great speed and mobility, often operating behind enemy lines.

guess *v.* To make a judgment or form an opinion on uncertain or incomplete knowledge; to suppose; to believe.

guess-ti-mate *n. Slang* An estimate made without all the facts.

guest *n.* A person who is the recipient of hospitality from another; a customer who pays for lodging.

guff *n., Slang* Nonsense or empty talk.

guf-faw *n.* A loud burst of laughter.

guid-ance *n.* The act, process, or result of guiding.

guide *n.* One who leads or directs another, as in a course of action; a person employed to conduct others on trips through museums and sightseeing tours. **guidable** *adj.*, **guider** *n.*

guide-book *n.* A handbook containing directions and other information for tourists and visitors.

guid-ed mis-sile *n., Mil.* An unmanned missile that can be controlled by radio signals while in flight.

guide-line *n.* Any suggestion, statement, or outline of policy or procedure; a rope or cord to guide a person over a difficult point.

gui-don *n.* A small flag carried by a military unit as a unit market.

guild *n.* An association of persons of the same trade or occupation.

guil·lo·tine n. An instrument of capital punishment in France, used for beheading condemned prisoners.

guilt n. The condition or fact of having committed a crime or wrongdoing; the feeling of responsibility for having done something wrong.

guilt·less adj. A state or condition of being without guilt; innocent.

guilt·y adj. Deserving of blame for an offense that has been committed; convicted of some offense; pertaining to, involving or showing guilt. **guiltily** adv., **guiltiness** n.

guin·ea n. Formerly, a British gold coin worth one pound and five pence.

guin·ea fowl n. A widely domesticated bird of African origin with dark gray plumage speckled with white.

guin·ea hen n. The female guinea fowl.

guin·ea pig n. A small, domesticated rodent usually with a short white tail, widely used for biological experimentation.

gui·tar n. A musical instrument with six strings, played by plucking or strumming.

gulch n. A deep cleft or ravine.

gulf n. A large area of ocean or sea partially enclosed by land; a wide, impassable separation, as in social position or education.

gull n. A long-winged, web-footed sea bird, usually white and gray with a hooked upper mandible.

gull n. A gullible person; one who is easily tricked.

gul·let n., *Pathol.* The passage from the mouth to the stomach; esophagus; the throat; the pharynx.

gul·li·ble adj. Easily cheated or fooled. **gullibility** n., **gullibly** adv.

gul·ly n., pl. -ies A ditch or channel cut in the earth by running water.

gulp v. To swallow rapidly or in large amounts; to gasp or choke, as in nervousness; in computer science, small group of bytes that may be either data or instructions. **gulping, gulped** v.

gum n. A sticky, viscous substance exuded from various trees and plants, soluble in water and hardening on exposure to air; chewing gum; the firm connective fleshly tissue that surrounds the base of the teeth. v., *Slang* To bungle. **gummy** adj.

gum·bo n. A thick soup or stew containing okra and other vegetable, chicken, meat or seafood.

gum·boil n. A type of small boil or abscess on the gum.

gum·drop n. A small, round, firm piece of jelly-like, sugar-coated candy usually, colored and coated with sugar.

gum·my adj. Covered with or containing gum; sticky. **gumminess** n.

gump·tion n., *Slang* Boldness; initiative; enterprise; personal initiative; practical common sense.

gum·shoe n. A shoe made of rubber *Slang* A detective. **gumshoe** v.

gun n. A weapon made of metal from which a projectile is thrown by the force of an explosion; a portable firearm. v. To shoot; to open up the throttle of an engine in order to accelerate. **gun for** To try to ruin, catch, or acquire.

gun-fight n. A duel with pistols.

gung ho adj., *Slang* Extremely enthusiastic.

gun·man n., pl. -men One who is armed with a gun, especially an armed criminal.

gun·ner·y n. The science and art of constructing and operating guns; the use of guns in general.

gun·ny n., pl. -ies A type of coarse, heavy fabric made of jute or hemp and used for making sacks.

gun·pow·der n. An explosive powder used in blasting, fireworks, and guns.

gun·shot n. A shot fired from a gun.

gun--shy adj. Afraid of loud noises, as gunfire; wary.

gun·smith n. A person who makes or repairs guns.

gun·wale or **gun·nel** n. The upper edge of a ship's side.

gup·py n., pl. -ies

A small, tropical freshwater fish, popular in home aquariums.

gur·gle v. To flow in a broken, uneven current, making low, bubbling sounds. **gurgle** n., **gurglingly** adv.

gu·ru n. A spiritual teacher or guide of Hinduism.

gush v. To flow or rush forth in volume and with sudden force; to be overly sentimental or enthusiastic. **gush** n., **gushy** adj.

gush·er n. An oil well with a plentiful natural flow of oil; a person who gushes.

gus·set n. A piece of armor that covers the joints in a suit of armor giving additional strength.

gust n. A sudden, violent rush of wind or air; a sudden outburst, as of emotion. v. To blow in gusts. **gustily** adv., **gustiness** n., **gusty** adj.

gus·ta·to·ry adj. Associated with or pertaining to the sense of taste or the act of tasting.

gus·to n. Hearty enjoyment or enthusiasm.

gut n. The alimentary canal or part of it. v. To disembowel. **guts** Bowels; entrails; the prepared intestines of certain animals, used as strings for musical instruments and surgical sutures; fortitude; courage.

gut·less adj., *Slang* Lacking courage. Appealing or expressing strongly to physical passions.

guts·y n., *Slang* Courageous.

gut·ter n. A channel or ditch at the side of a street for carrying off surface water; a trough attached below or along the eaves of a house for carrying off rain water from the roof.

gut-ter-snipe *n.* A person of the lowest class; a street urchin.

gut-tur-al *adj.* Pertaining to the throat; having a harsh, muffled, or grating quality. **guttural** *n.*, **gutturally** *adv.*

guy *n., Slang* A man; a fellow.

guz-zle *v.* To drink greedily or to excess. **guzzler** *n.*, **guzzling, guzzled** *v.*

gym *n., Informal* A gymnasium. An assortment of outdoor play equipment such as a seesaw, rings and a swing.

gym-na-si-um *n., pl.* -ums *or* -sia A room or building equipped for indoor sports.

gym-nas-tic *adj.* Of or pertaining to athletic exercises.

gym-nas-tics *pl., n.* A sport or physical exercises, especially those performed with special apparatus in a gym. **gymnast** *n.*, **gymnastic** *adj.*

gym-no-sperm *n.* One of a class of plants whose seeds are not enclosed within an ovary.

gy-ne-coid *adj.* Having female characteristics; being typical of a woman.

gy-ne-col-o-gy *n.* The branch of medicine dealing with the female reproductive organs, female diseases, and female organs. **gynecology.** **gynecologic** *adj.*, **gynecologist** *n.*

gyp *v., Informal* To swindle, cheat, or defraud. *n.* A fraud. **gypper** *n.*

gyp-sum *n.* A mineral, hydrous calcium sulfate, used to make plaster of Paris, gypsum plaster, and plasterboard.

Gyp-sy *n., pl.* -ies A person who looks like or leads the life of a Gypsy. *v.* To wander or live like a Gypsy or the Gypsies.

Gyp-sy *n., pl.* -ies A member of a wandering, dark-haired, dark-skinned, Caucasian people originally from India and now living mainly in Europe and the U.S.

gyp-sy moth *n.* A moth whose larvae are destructive to foliage.

gy-rate *v.* To rotate or revolve around a fixed point or axis; to move or turn in a spiral motion. *adj.* Coiled or winding about. **gyrator** *n.*, **gyratory** *adj.*

gyr-fal-con *n.* A falcon with color phases ranging from black to white.

gy-ro *n.* A gyroscope or gyrocompass.

gy-ro-com-pass *n.* A type of compass which has a motor-driven gyroscope so mounted that its axis of rotation maintains a constant position with reference to the true or the geographic north.

gy-ro pi-lot *n., Aeron.* An automatic pilot.

gy-ro-scope *n.* A spinning wheel or disk whose spin axis maintains its angular orientation when not subjected to external torques. **gyroscopic** *adj.*

gy-ro-sta-bi-liz-er *n.* A gyroscopic instrument designed to reduce the rolling motion of ships.

Gy Sgt. *abbr.* Gunnery sergent.

gyve *n.* A shackle for the legs. *v.* To chain; to shackle.

H, h The eighth letter of the English alphabet.

ha *interj.* An exclamation denoting joy, wonder, sudden emotion or surprise.

ha-ba-ne-ra *n.* Cuban dance.

ha-be-as cor-pus *n.* In law, a writ commanding a person to appear before a judge or court for the purpose of releasing that person from unlawful detention or restraint.

hab-er-dash-er *n.* A person who deals in men's clothing and men's furnishings.

hab-er-dash-er-y *n., pl.* -ies The goods sold by a haberdasher.

ha-ber-geon *n.* A medieval jacket.

hab-ile *adj.* Having skill; able.

ha-bil-i-ment *n., pl.* -ments Clothing characteristic of an office, rank, or occasion.

hab-it *n.* Involuntary pattern of behavior acquired by frequent repetition; manner of conducting oneself; an addiction. *Biol.* The characteristic form of a plant or animal. Clothing that indicated membership or rank in a religious order, or activity.

hab-it-a-ble *adj.* Suitable for habitation. **habitability,** -ness *n.*, **habitably** *adv.*

hab-i-tat *n.* The region in which an animal or plant lives or grows; the place of residence of a person or group.

hab-i-ta-tion *n.* A place of residence; a house or other dwelling where man or animals dwell.

hab-it--form-ing *adj.* Producing physiological addiction.

ha-bit-u-al *adj.* Practicing by or acting according to habit; resorted to on a regular basis; regular. **habitually** *adv.*, **habitualness** *n.*

ha-chure *n.* Shading used to denote surfaces in relief on a map.

ha-ci-en-da *n.* A large estate or ranch in Spanish-speaking countries; the main building of a hacienda; a stock-raising ranch.

hack *v.* To cut with repeated irregular blows; to manage successfully. *n.* A tool used for hacking; a rough, dry cough; *Informal* a taxi driver.

hack-a-more *n.* A bridle with a loop placed over the nose with a slip noose passed over the lower jaw used in place of a bit.

hack-ber-ry *n.* Trees and shrubs of the elm family with small edible berries.

hack-le *n.* One of the long, slender, often narrow glossy feathers on the neck of a rooster; the hair on the back of the neck, especially of a dog, that rise in anger or fear.

hack-ney *n.* A horse of medium size for ordinary driving or riding; a carriage or coach available for hire. *v.* To make common or frequent use of.

hackney coach *n.* A carriage drawn by two horses with seating for six persons.

hack-neyed *adj.* Trite; commonplace.

hack-saw *n.* A finetoothed saw in a narrow frame used for cutting metal.

had *v.* Past participle and past tense of have.

had-dock *n.* A food fish that is usually smaller than the related cod and is found on both sides of the Atlantic.

Ha-des *n.* The underground abode of the dead in Greek mythology; hell.

had-n't *contraction* Had not.

haft *n.* A handle of a weapon or tool.

hag *n.* A malicious, ugly old woman; a witch. **haggish** *adj.*

hag-fish *n.* A fish that resembles the eel but has a round mouth surrounded by eight tentacles.

Hag-ga-dah *n.* Ancient Jewish lore forming especially the nonlegal part of the Talmud; the Jewish ritual for the Seder.

hag-gard A worn-out, exhausted, and gaunt look, as from hunger or fatigue; appearing wasted by suffering or want. **haggardly** *adv.*, **haggardness** *n.*

hag-gle *v.* To argue or bargain on price or terms. *n.* The process or act of haggling someone.
haggler *n.*, **haggling**, **haggled** *v.*

hag-i-og-ra-phy *n.*, *pl.* -phies Biography of the lives of saints or revered persons. **hagiographer** *n.*, **hagiographic**, **hagiographical** *adj.*

hai-ku *n.* An unrhymed Japanese verse form with three short lines.

hail *n.* Precipitation of small, hard lumps of ice and snow; a hailstone; an exclamation, greeting, acclamation; *v.* To pour down as hail; to call loudly in greeting or welcome; to shout with enthusiasm; to signal in order to draw the attention of.

hail-stone *n.* A type of hard pellet made of frozen snow & ice.

hair *n.* One of the pigmented filaments that grow from the skin of most mammals; a covering of such structures, as on the human head and on the skin; a slender margin. **hairy** *adj.*

hair follicle *n.* The tubular sheath that surrounds the lower part of the hair shaft providing the growing basal part of the hair with nourishment.

hair-less *adj.* Being bald; lacking hair. **hairlessness** *n.*

hair--raising *adj.* Causing fear or horror. **hairraiser** *n.*

hair-split-ting *n.* The process of making petty distinctions. **hairsplitter** *n.*

hair-spring *n.* A fine, coiled spring that regulates and controls the movement of the balance wheel in a clock or watch.

hair trig-ger *n.* A gun trigger set to react to the slightest pressure. **hair trigger** *adj.* Reacting immediately to the slightest provocation.

hake *n.* A marine food fish related to the cod.

ha-kim *n.* A Muslim physician, ruler or governor.

ha-la-tion *n.* A light that spreads beyond its proper boundaries in a developed photographic image.

hal-berd *n.* A medieval weapon used in the 15th and 16th centuries, having both an ax-like blade and a steel spike on the end of a long pole.

hal-cy-on *adj* Calm and tranquil; peaceful;

hale *adj.* Healthy and robust; free from defect. *v.* To compel to go. **haleness** *n.*

half *n.*, *pl.* **halves** One of two equal parts into which a thing is divisible; art of a thing approximately equal to the remainder; one of a pair. *adj.* Being one of two equal parts; being partial or incomplete. **half** *adv.*

half-and-half *n.* A mixture of whole milk and cream.

half-breed *n.* The offspring of an American Indian and a white man; offspring of parents having different races.

half-brother *n.* A brother who is related through only one parent.

half--caste *n.* A person having one European and one Asian parent.

half--dol-lar *n.* A coin which represents one half of a dollar.

half gainer *n.* A dive performed in a diving competition.

half heart-ed *adj.* Lacking in spirit or interest.

half-hitch *n.* A knot that is tied so it can be easily unfastened.

half hour *n.* Thirty minutes; time representing half of an hour.

half-nelson *n.* A wrestling hold in which one arm is placed under the opponents arm and one arm behind the opponents neck.

half pint *n.* A measurement equaling half of a pint; a nickname for a small person.

half-sister *n.* A sister that is related through one parent only.

half-sole *v.* To repair shoes by replacing the sole that is worn out.

half step *n.*, *Mus.* A semitone.

half time *n.* An intermission in the sport of football, basketball, etc.

half--track *n.* A vehicle propelled by continuous rear treads and front wheels.

half-truth *n.* A statement which is only partially true.

halfway house *n.* A house for formerly institutionalized individuals which is designed to help them adjust to private life.

half--wit *n.* A mentally disturbed person; a feeble-minded person. **--witted** *adj.*

hal-i-but *n.* Any of the edible flat fishes of the North Atlantic or Pacific waters.

hal-ite *n.* Large crystal or masses of salt; also known as rock salt.

hal-i-to-sis *n.* A condition or state of having bad breath.

hal-le-lu-jah *interj.* Used to express joy, praise, or jubilation. **hallelujah** *n.*

hall-mark *n.* An official mark placed on gold and silver products to attest to their purity; an indication of quality or superiority; a distinctive characteristic.

Hall of Fame *n.* A building which

houses memorials to famous individuals.

hal·low v. To sanctify; to make holy; to honor.

Hal·low·een n. October 31, the eve of All Saints' Day, celebrated particularly by children.

hal·lu·ci·na·tion n. An illusion of seeing something that is nonexistent; something one thinks is seen during a hallucination; a delusion. **hallucinate** v., **hallucinational**, **hallucinative**, adj. **hallucinatory** adj.

hal·lu·ci·no·gen n. A drug or other agent which causes hallucination. **hallucinogenic** adj.

hall·way n. A corridor; an entrance hall.

ha·lo n. A ring of colored light surrounding the head; an aura of glory. **halo** v.

hal·o·gen n. Any of the group of nonmetallic elements including fluorine, chlorine, bromine, iodine, and astatine. **halogenous** adj.

hal·o·ge·ton n. A annual herb of the goosefoot family found in western America.

halo·phile n. An organism that grows in a salty environment.

halt v. To bring to a stop.

hal·ter n. A rope or strap for leading or tying an animal; a noose for hanging a person; a woman's upper garment tied behind the neck and across the back.

hal·vah n. A flaky confection of sesame seeds in a base of syrup or honey.

halve v. To divide into two equal parts; to lessen by half. *Informal* Share equally.

hal·yard n. A rope for hoisting or lowering a sail, flag, or yard.

ham n. The meat of a hog's thigh; the back of the knee or thigh. **ham** v.

ham·burg·er n. A patty of ground beef on a bun.

hame n. The curved projections attached to the collar of a draft horse to fasten the traces to.

ham·let n. A small rural village or town.

ham·mer n.

A hand tool with a heavy head used to drive or strike forcefully, especially nails; the part of a gun which strikes the primer or firing pin; any of the padded wooden levers which strike the strings of a piano. v. To strike or pound forcibly and repeatedly. **hammerer** n.

ham·mer·head n. A large, predatory shark of warm seas, whose eyes are set in long, fleshy projections at the sides of the head.

ham·mer·lock n. A hold in wrestling in which the opponent's arm is twisted upward behind his back.

ham·mer·toe n. A toe that is bent downward and malformed.

ham·mock n. A hanging bed or couch of

fabric or heavy netting, suspended from supports at each end.

ham·per v. To interfere with movement or progress of. n. A large, usually covered, receptacle used to store dirty laundry.

ham·ster n. Any of various rodents with large cheek pouches and a short tail.

ham·string n. Either of two tendons located at the back of the human knee; the large tendon at the back of the hock of four-footed animals. v. To cripple by cutting the hamstring; to frustrate.

hand n. The part of the arm below the wrist, consisting of the palm, four fingers and a thumb; a unit of measure, four inches, used especially to state the height of a horse; a pointer on a dial, as of a clock, meter, or gauge; the cards dealt to or held by a player in one round of a game; a manual laborer, worker, or employee. v. To give, offer, or transmit with the hand; direct with the hands.

hand·bag n. A woman's purse held in the hand or with a shoulder strap.

hand·ball n. A court game in which the players bat a small rubber ball against the wall with their hands.

hand·bar·row n. A flat rectangular frame with handles at both ends for carrying loads.

hand·bill n. A small hand-distributed advertisement.

hand·book n. A small guide or reference book giving information or instructions.

hand·car n. A small open four-wheeled railroad car propelled by a small motor or by hand.

hand·craft·man n. A person skilled in handicrafts.

hand·cuff v. To put handcuffs on; to make ineffective. **handcuffs** pl., n. A pair of circular metal shackles chained together that can be fastened around the wrists.

hand·ful n. As much as the hand will hold.

hand·gun n. A gun that can be held and fired with one hand.

hand·i·cap n. A race or contest in which advantages or penalties are given to individual contestants to equalize the odds; any disadvantage that makes achievement unusually difficult; physical disability; an obstacle. v. To give a handicap to.

hand·i·cap·per n. A person who predicts the winners in a race.

hand·i·craft or **hand·craft** n. Skill and expertise in working with the hands; an occupation requiring manual dexterity; skilled work produced by the hands.

hand·ker·chief n. A type of small piece of cloth used for wiping the face or nose; a kerchief or scarf.

han·dle v. To touch, pick up, or hold with the hands; to represent; to trade or deal in. **handler** n.,

handleless *adj.*, **handleable** *adj.*

han-dle-bars *n.* A bent bar with a handle at each end used to steer a bicycle or similar vehicle.

hand-made *adj.* Made by hand or by a hand process.

hand-maid *or* **hand-maid-en** *n.* A female maid or personal servant.

hand--me--down *n.* Something, such as an article of clothing, used by a person after being outgrown or is carded by another. **hand-me-down** *adj.*

hand-out *n.* Free food, clothing, or cash given to the needy; a folder distributed free of charge; a flyer; a press release for publicity.

hand-pick *v.* To select with care.

hand-rail *n.* A narrow rail used for support.

hand-saw *n.* A saw operated with one hand.

hand-set *n.* A telephone receiver and transmitter combined in a single unit.

hand-shake *n.* The act of clasping hands by two people, as in greeting, agreement, or parting.

hand-some *adj.* Very good-looking or attractive; very generous, as with money. **handsomely** *adv.*, **handsomeness** *n.*

hand-spring *n.* An acrobatic feat in which the body flips entirely backward or forward, while the feet pass quickly in an arc over the head.

hand-stand *n.* The feat of supporting the body on the hands with the feet balanced in the air.

hand--to--mouth *adj.* Providing or having barely enough to exist.

hand truck *n.* A hand operated truck for moving heavy objects.

hand work *n.* Work which is done by hand.

hand-wo-ven *adj.* Produced by hand.

hand-writ-ing *n.* Writing performed with the hand, especially cursive; the type of writing of a person. **handwriting on the wall.** An omen of one's unpleasant fate.

hand-y *adj.* Easy to use or reach; helpful or useful. **handily** *adv.*, **handiness** *n.*

handy-man *n.* A person who does odd jobs.

hang *v.* To be attached to from above and unsupported from below; to fasten or be suspended so as to swing freely; to be put to death by hanging by the neck; to fasten or attach something as a picture to a wall. **hangout** *Slang* To spend one's time in a particular place.

han-gar *n.* A building for housing aircraft.

han-ger *n.* A device from which something may be hung or on which something hangs.

hang gli-der *n.* A device shaped like a kite from which a person hangs suspended in a harness while gliding through the air.

hang gliding *n.*, **hang glide** *v.*

hang-man *n., pl.* **-men** One hired to execute people by hanging.

hang-nail *n.* The small piece of skin that hangs loose from the side or root of a fingernail.

hang-over *n.* Something remaining from what has passed; the effects of excessive alcohol intake.

hang--up *n., Slang* A psychological or emotional problem; an obstacle.

hank *n.* A loop, coil, or piece of hair, thread, or yarn.

han-ker *v.* To have a yearning or craving for something. **hankerer, hankering** *n.*

han-som *n.* A two-wheeled covered carriage with the driver's seat elevated behind the cab.

Ha-nuk-kah *or* **Ha-nu-kah** *n.* An eight-day Jewish holiday remembering the rededication of the Temple in Jerusalem.

hao-le *n.* A person who is not of the Hawaiian race, especially a Caucasian.

hap-haz-ard *adj.* Occurring by accident; happening by chance or at random; hit-or-miss. **haphazardly** *adv.*, **haphazardness** *n.*

hap-less *adj.* Unfortunate; unlucky. **haplessly** *adv.*, **haplessness** *n.*

hap-pen *v.* To occur or come to pass; to take place; to discover by chance; to turn up or appear by chance.

hap-pen-ing *n.* A spontaneous event or performance; an important event.

happen-stance *n.* An event occurring by chance.

hap-py *adj.* Enjoying contentment and well-being; glad, joyous, satisfied or pleased. **happily** *adv.*, **happiness** *n.*

hap-py--go--luck-y *adj.* Carefree and unconcerned.

ha-ra--ki-ri *n.* A Japanese suicide ritual committed by ripping open the abdomen with a knife.

ha-rangue *n.* A long, extravagant, speech; a lecture. **haranguer** *n.*

ha-rass *v.* To disturb or annoy constantly; to torment persistently. **harassment, harasser** *n.*

har-bin-ger *n.* A person that initiates or pioneers a major change; something that foreshadows what is to come.

har-bor *n.* A place of refuge or shelter; a bay or cove; an anchorage for ships. *v.* To provide shelter; to entertain, as a feeling or thought. **harborage, harborer** *n.*

hard *adj.* Difficult to perform, endure, or comprehend; solid in texture or substance; resistant to cutting or penetration; containing salts which make lathering with soap difficult; high in alcoholic content. **hardness** *n.*

hard-back *adj.* Text bound between hard covers as opposed to paper ones.

hard--bit-ten *adj.* Tough or seasoned by hard experiences.

hard-board *n.* A composition board made by compressing wood chips at high temperatures.

hard--boiled *adj.* Boiled or cooked in the shell to a hard or solid state.

hard candy *n.* A confection made of sugar and corn syrup.

hard ci-der *n.* Apple juice that has become fermented.

hard co-py *n.* In computer science, the printed information or data from a computer.

hard--core *or* **hard-core** *adj.* Extremely graphic in presentation; obstinately resistant to change.

hard disk *n.* In computer science, magnetic storage consisting of a rigid disk of aluminum coated with a magnetic recording substance; contained within a removable cartridge or mounted in the hard disk of a microcomputer.

hard-en *v.* To make or become hard or harder; to make or become physically or mentally tough; to make or become callous or unsympathetic.

hard hat *n.* A protective head covering made of rigid material, worn by construction workers.

hard-head-ed *adj.* Having a stubborn character; obstinate. **hardheadedly** *adv.,* **hardheadedness** *n.*

hard-heart-ed *adj.* Heartless; unfeeling. **hardheartedly** *adv.,* **hardheartedness** *n.*

har-di-hood *n.* Resolute courage; audacious boldness; vitality; vigor.

har-di-ment *n.* A bold deed.

Hard-ing, Warren Gamaliel *n.* (1865-1923) The 29th President of the United States, from 1921-1923, died in office.

har-ding-grass *n.* A perennial grass of Australia and Africa used as a forage grass.

hard-ly *adj., Slang* Very little; almost certainly not. *adv.* Forcefully; painfully; barely.

hard--nosed *adj.* Stubborn; hard-headed; unyielding.

hard pal-ate *n.* The bony forward part of the palate that forms the roof of the mouth.

hard-pan *n.* A layer of very hard clay-like matter or subsoil which roots cannot penetrate.

hard rock *n.* Rock music featuring amplified sound and modulations, and feedback.

hard sauce *n.* A mixture of butter and powdered sugar with cream and flavoring.

hard sell *n.* Slang A sales method involving aggressive, high-pressure selling and closing techniques.

hard-ship *n.* A painful, difficult condition causing suffering.

hard-tack *n.* A hard, crackerlike biscuit made with flour and water.

hard-top *n.* A car with a permanent top designed to resemble a convertible.

hard-ware *n.* Manufactured machine parts, such as tools and utensils; the mechanical components of a computer installation.

hard-wood *n.* The wood of an angiospermous tree as opposed to that of a coniferous tree; a tree that yields hardwood.

har-dy *adj.* Bold and robust; able to survive very unfavorable conditions, as extreme cold; daring. **hardiness** *n.,* **hardily** *adv.*

hare *n.*

Various mammals related to the rabbits but having longer ears and legs.

hare-bell *n.* A small blue-flowered herb with leaves on the stem.

hare-brained *adj.* Foolish or silly.

hare-lip *n.* A congenital deformity in which the upper lip is split. **-ped** *adj.*

har-em *n.* The women living in a Muslim residence; the living quarters of a harem.

hark *v.* To listen closely.

har-le-quin *n.* A jester; a clown. *adj.* Patterned with vividly colored diamond shapes.

har-lot *n.* A prostitute.

harm *n.* Emotional or physical damage or injury. *v.* To cause harm to.

harmful *adj.,* **-fully** *adv.,* **-fulness** *n.*

har-ma-line *n.* A hallucinogenic alkaloid used in medicine as a stimulant of the central nervous system.

harm-less *adj.* Without harm; not harmful.

har-mon-ic *adj.* Relating to musical harmony; in harmony; concordant. **harmonically** *adv.*

har-mon-i-ca *n.* A small, rectangular musical instrument having a series of tuned metal reeds that vibrate with the player's breath.

har-mo-ni-ous *adj.* Pleasing to the ear; characterized by agreement and accord; having components agreeably combined. **harmoniously** *adv.*

har-mo-ny *n., pl.* **-ies** Complete agreement, as of feeling or opinion; an agreeable combination of component parts; pleasing sounds; a combination of musical tones into chords. **harmonize** *v.,* **harmonizer** *n.*

har-ness *n.* The working gear, other than a yoke, of a horse or other draft animal. **harnesser** *n.*

harness racing *n.* A racing sport in which horses are harnessed to a 2-wheeled sulky with a driver.

harp *n.* A musical instrument having a triangular upright frame with strings plucked with the fingers. *v.* To play a harp. **harp on** To write or talk about excessively. **harpist** *n.*

har-poon *n.* A barbed spear used in hunting whales and large fish.

harp-si-chord *n.* A piano-like instrument whose strings are plucked by using quills or leather points. **-ist** *n.*

har-py *n., pl.* **-pies** A vicious woman; a predatory person.

har-ri-dan *n.* A mean, hateful old woman.

har-ri-er *n.* A slender, narrow-winged hawk that preys on small animals; a hunting dog; a cross-country runner.

Har-ri-son, Benjamin *n.* (1833-1901). The 23rd president of the United States from 1889-1893.

Har-ri-son, William Henry *n.* (1773-1841) The 9th president of the United States, from March 4th - April 4th 1841; died in office.

har-row *n.* A tool with sharp teeth for breaking up and smoothing soil.

har-ry *v.* To harass.

harsh *adj.* Disagreeable; extremely severe. **harshly** *adv.*, **harshness** *n.*

hart *n.* A fully grown male deer after it has passed its fifth year.

harte-beest *n.* A large African antelope.

Hart-ford *n.* The capital of the state of Connecticut.

har-um—scar-um *adj.* Reckless; irresponsible.

har-vest *n.* The process or act of gathering a crop; the season or time for gathering crops. *v.* To reap; to obtain as if by gathering. **harvester** *n.*

harvest moon *n.* The full moon closest to the time of the September equinox.

harvest-time *n.* The time during which the annual crops are harvested.

ha-sen-pfef-fer *n.* A highly seasoned stew made from rabbit meat.

hash *n.* A fried or baked mixture of chopped meat and potatoes. *v.* To chop up into small pieces. *Slang* To make a mess of; to discuss at great length.

hash-ish *n.* The leaves and flowering tops of the hemp plant, which are chewed, drunk, or smoked for their intoxicating and narcotic effect.

hasp *n.* A clasp or hinged fastener that passes over a staple and is secured by a pin, bolt, or padlock.

has-sle *n., Slang* A type of quarrel or argument. **hassle** *v.*

has-sock *n.* A firm upholstered cushion used as a footstool.

haste *n.* Speed; swiftness of motion or action; excessive eagerness to act. **make haste** To hurry.

has-ten *v.* To act or move with haste or speed.

hast-y *adj.* Rapid; swift; made or done with excessive speed. **hastily** *adv.*, **hastiness** *n.*

hat *n.* A covering for the head with a crown and brim.

hat-band *n.* A strip of leather, cloth, etc. around the crown of a hat.

hat-box *n.* A container or box used for storing or carrying hats.

hatch *n.* A small opening or door, as in a ship's deck. *v.* To bring forth, as young from an egg; to devise; to contrive secretly. **hatchery** *n.*

hatch-back *n.* An automobile with a sloped roof in the back that opens upward.

hatch-et *n.* A small ax with a short handle.

hatch-way *n.* An opening covered by a hatch in a ship's deck.

hate *v.* To feel hostility or animosity toward; to dislike intensely. **hatefully** *adv.*, **hatefulness, hater** *n.*

ha-tred *n.* A deep-seated dislike or animosity.

hat-ter *n.* A person who makes, sells, or repairs hats.

hau-berk *n.* A tunic of chain worn as defensive armor.

haugh-ty *adj.* Arrogantly proud; disdainful. **haughtily** *adv.*, **haughtiness** *n.*

haul *v.* To pull or draw with force; to move or transport, as in a truck or cart. *n.* The distance over which someone travels or something is transported; an amount collected at one time.

haul-age *n.* The process or act of hauling; a charge for hauling.

haunch *n.* The hip; the buttock and upper thigh of a human or animal; the loin and leg of a four-footed animal.

haunt *v.* To appear to or visit as a ghost or spirit; to visit frequently; to linger in the mind. **haunting** *adj.*

haut-bois or **haut-boy** *n.* An oboe.

haute cou-ture *n.* Designers who create exclusive fashions for women.

hau-teur *n.* A disdainful arrogance.

Ha-van-a *n.* The capital of Cuba; a cigar made from Cuban tobacco.

have *v.* To hold or own, as a possession or as property. **have to** Need to; must. **have had it** Suffered or endured all that one can tolerate.

ha-ven *n.* A safe refuge.

hav-er-sack *n.* A bag for carrying supplies on a hike or march.

hav-oc *n.* Mass confusion; widespread destruction; devastation.

haw *n.* A hesitating sound made by a speaker who is groping for words. *v.* To hesitate in speaking; to falter in speaking.

Ha-wai-i or **Ha-wai-ian Is-lands** A state and island group of the United States, located in the central Pacific.

haw-finch *n.* A Eurasian finch with a large bill and a short thick neck.

hawk *n.*

Any of several predatory birds, with a short, hooked bill and strong claws for seizing small prey; one who advocates a war-like foreign policy; one having an aggressive attitude.

hawkish *adj.*, **-ishly** *adv.*, **-ishness** *n.*

haw-ser *n.* A heavy cable or rope for towing or securing a ship.

haw-thorn *n.* A thorny shrub or tree bearing white or pink flowers and red fruit.

hay *n.* Alfalfa or grass that has been cut and dried for animal food.

Hayes, Rutherford Birchard *n.* (1822-1893) The 19th president of the United States from 1877-1881.

hay fe-ver *n.* An acute allergy to certain airborne pollens, marked by severe irritation of the upper respiratory tract and the eyes.

hay-fork *n.* A hand held or mechanical tool used to move hay.

hay-loft *n.* A upper loft in a barn or stable used to store hay.

hay-mow *n.* A large mound of hay stored in a loft.

hay ride *n.* A pleasure ride on a wagon or truck partly filled with straw or hay.

hay-seed *n.* The seeds from hay; a person from the country.

hay-stack *n.* A pile of hay stored outdoors.

hay-wire *adj., Slang* Broken; emotionally out of control; crazy.

haz-ard *n.* A risk; chance; an accident; a anger or source of danger. *v.* To take a chance on; to venture. **hazardous** *adj.*

haze *n.* A fog-like suspension of dust, smoke, and vapor in the air; a confused or vague state of mind. *v.* To harass with disagreeable tasks. **-er** *n.*

ha-zel *n.* A small tree or shrub bearing edible brown nuts with smooth shells; a light brown or yellowish brown.

ha-zel-nut *n.* The edible nut of the hazel.

haz-y *adj.* Lacking clarity; vague; obscured or cloudy. **hazily** *adv.,* **haziness** *n.*

hdqrs. *abbr.* Headquarters.

H--Bomb *n.* Hydrogen bomb.

head *n.* The upper part of a human or animal body, containing the brain, the principal nerve centers, the eyes, ears, nose and mouth. **headed** *adj.*

head-ache *n.* A pain or ache in the head. *Slang* A bothersome problem. **-y** *adj.*

head-band *n.* A band of cloth worn around the head.

head-board *n.* A frame or panel that stands at the head of a bed.

head cold *n.* A common cold or viral infection that centers primarily in the nasal passages.

head-first *adv.* With the head in a forward position; headlong.

head-gear *n.* A protective covering worn on the head.

head-hunt-ing *n.* A tribal custom of decapitating slain enemies and preserving the heads as trophies.

head-ing *n.* A title or caption that acts as a front, beginning, or upper part of anything; the direction or course of a ship or aircraft.

head-land *n.* A high ridge or cliff projecting into the water.

head-light *n.* A light with special lens mounted on the front of an automobile; a miners light worn on the head.

head-line *n.* A title, caption, or summarizing words of a newspaper story or article printed in large type. *v.* To provide with a headline; to serve as the star performer. **headliner** *n.*

head-lock *n.* A wrestling hold in which the head of a wrestler is locked under the arm of his opponent.

head-long *adv.* Headfirst; not having deliberation. **headlonging** *adj.*

head-mas-ter *n.* A school principal of a private school.

head-mis-tress *n.* A female school principal of a private school.

head-phone *n.* A phone held over the ear by a band worn on the head.

head-piece *n.* A helmet, cap or other covering for the head; a headset.

head-quar-ters *pl., n.* The official location from which a leader directs a military unit.

head-rest *n.* A pad at the top of the back of an automobile seat to support the head.

head-set *n.* A pair of headphones.

head-stall *n.* The part of a bridle that goes over a horse's head.

head-stand *n.* The act of balancing the body's weight on the top of the head, with the aid of the arms.

head start *n.* An early or advance start; an advantage.

head-stone *n.* A memorial stone marker at the head of a grave, indicating a name, date of birth and date of death.

head-strong *adj.* Not easily restrained; obstinate.

heads up *n.* A warning given to look out for danger overhead.

head-wait-er *n.* The waiter in charge of a restaurant or dining room staff.

head-wat-er *n.* The source of a river or stream.

head-way *n.* Motion in a forward direction; progress toward a goal; clearance beneath an arch or ceiling.

head wind *n.* A head blowing in the direction opposite the course of a ship or aircraft.

head-y *adj.* Tending to intoxicate; affecting the senses; headstrong.
headily *adv.,* **headiness** *n.*

heal *v.* To restore to good health; to mend. **healable** *adj.,* **healer** *n.*

health *n.* The overall sound condition or function of a living organism at a particular time; freedom from disease or defect. **healthful** *adj.,*
healthfully *adv.,* **healthfulness** *n.*

health-y *adj.* In a state of or having good health; characteristic of a sound condition. **healthily** *adv.,* **healthiness** *n.*

heap *n.* A haphazard assortment of things; a large number or quantity. *v.* To throw or pile into a heap.

hear *v.* To perceive by the ear; to listen with careful attention; to be informed of; to listen to officially or formally, as in a court of law. **hearer** *n.*

hear-ing *n.* One of the five senses; the range by which sound can be heard; an opportunity to be heard; in law, a preliminary examination of an accused person.

hear-ing aid *n.* An electronic device used to amplify the hearing of partially deaf persons.

heark-en *v.* To listen carefully.

hear-say *n.* Information heard from another; common talk; rumor.

hearse *n.* A vehicle for conveying a dead body to the place of burial.

heart *n.*

The hollow, primary muscular organ of vertebrates which circulates blood throughout the body; the emotional center, such as in love, hate, consideration, or compassion; the most essential part of something.

heart-ache *n.* Emotional grief; sorrow.

heart at-tack *n.* An acute malfunction or interrupted heart function.

heart-beat *n.* A pulsation of the heart, consisting of one contraction and one relaxation.

heart-break *n.* Great sorrow; deep grief. **heartbreaking** *adj.*, **-ingly** *adv.*

heart-burn *n.* A sensation of burning in the stomach and esophagus, usually caused by excess acid in the stomach.

heart-en *v.* To give courage to.

heart-felt *adj.* Deeply felt; sincere.

hearth *n.* The floor of a fireplace, furnace; the stone that forms the front of a fireplace.

heart-land *n.* A strategically important central region, one regarded as vital to a nation's economy or defense.

heart-less *adj.* Having no sympathy; lacking compassion. **heartlessness** *n.*, **heartlessly** *adv.*

heart-rend-ing *adj.* Causing great distress, suffering emotional anguish.

heart-sick *adj.* Profoundly dejected. **heartsickness** *n.*

heart-throb *n.* One pulsation of the heart; tender emotion; a loved one.

heart--to--heart *adj.* Sincere; frank.

heart--warm-ing *adj.* A feeling of warm sympathy.

heart-wood *n.* The older, no longer active central wood of a tree.

heart-y *adj.* Marked by exuberant warmth; full of vigor; nourishing; substantial. **heartily** *adv.*, **heartiness** *n.*

heat *n.* A quality of being hot or warm; a degree of warmth; depth of feeling; a period of sexual ardor in female animals. *Slang* Pressure or stress.

heat ex-haus-tion *n.* A reaction to intense heat, a mild form of heat stroke.

heath *n.* An open tract of uncultivated wasteland covered with low-growing shrubs and plants.

hea-then *n.* A person or nation that does not recognize the God of Christianity, Judaism, or Islam; in the Old Testament, a Gentile; non-Jew. **heathen**, **heathenish** *adj.*, **heathendom**, **heathenism** *n.*

heath-er *n.* A shrub that grows in dense masses and has small evergreen leaves and small pinkish flowers. **heather**, **heathery** *adj.*

heat light-ning *n.* Flashes of electric light, without thunder, seen near the horizon.

heat pump *n.* A heating plant for heating and cooling a building by transferring heat to a reservoir outside the building.

heat stroke *n.* A state of collapse or exhaustion, accompanied by fever and marked by clammy skin, caused by excessive heat.

heat wave *n.* An extended period of unusually hot weather.

heave *v.* To raise or lift, especially forcibly; to hurl or throw. *Naut.* To push, pull, or haul, as by a rope. *Slang* To vomit. *n.* The act of throwing.

heaves *n.* A disease of horses affecting the lungs and marked by coughing and difficult breathing.

heav-en *n.* The sky; the region above and around the earth; the abode of God, the angels, and the blessed souls of the dead; a state or place of blissful happiness. **heavenliness** *n.*, **heavenly** *adj.*, **heavenward** *adv. & adj.*,

heav-y *adj.* Of great weight; very thick or dense; forceful; powerful; rough and violent, as stormy weather; of great significance; grave; painful, as bad news; oppressive. **heavily** *adv.*, **heaviness** *n.*

heavy--du-ty *adj.* Designed for hard use.

heavy--hand-ed *adj.* Clumsy; not tactful; oppressive. **heavy-handedly** *adv.*, **heavy-handedness** *n.*

heavy--heart-ed *adj.* Melancholy; depressed; sad. **heavyheartedly** *adv.*, **heavyheartedness** *n.*

heavy--set *adj.* Having a stocky build.

heavy--weight *n.* A person of above average weight; a competitor in the heaviest class; a boxer weighing more that 175 pounds.

heb-do-mad *n.* The period of seven days.

he-be-phre-nia *n.* A schizophrenic reaction causing silliness, hallucinations and regression.

He-bra-ic *or* **He-bra-i-cal** *adj.* Of or relating to the Hebrews or their language or culture. **Hebraist** *n.*

He-brew *n.* A member of a Semitic people claiming descent from Abraham, Isaac, and Jacob; the modern form of the language of the Hebrews. **Hebrew** *adj.*

heck-le *v.* To badger or annoy, as with questions, comments, or gibes. **-er** *n.*

hec-tic *adj.* Intensely active, rushed, or excited; marked by a persistent and fluctuating fever caused by a disease, such as tuberculosis; feverish; flushed.

hec-to-graph *n.* A machine for making copies of a drawing on a gelatin surface.

he'd *conj.* He had; he would.

hed-dle *n.* A set of parallel cords or wires that guide warp threads in a loom.

hedge *n.* A boundary or fence formed of shrubs or low-growing trees; a means to guard against financial loss; a deliberately ambiguous statement. **hedge** *v.*, **hedger** *n.*

hedge-hog *n.* A small nocturnal mammal with dense, erectile spines on the back, which are presented when the animal rolls itself into a ball in self-defense; a porcupine.

hedge-hop v. To fly an aircraft close to the ground, as in spraying crops.

hedge-row n. A dense row of bushes, shrubs, or trees forming a hedge.

he-don-ism n. The doctrine devoted to the pursuit of pleasure; the philosophy that pleasure is the principal good in life. hedonist n., hedonistic adj.

heed v. To pay attention; to take notice of something. n. Attention. -ful adj., heedfully adv., heedfulness n.

heel n. The rounded back part of the human foot under and behind the ankle; the part of a shoe supporting or covering the heel; a lower or bottom part; the crusty ends of a loaf of bread.

heft n., Slang Weight; bulk. v. To gauge or estimate the weight of by lifting; to lift up.

heft-y adj. Bulky; heavy; sizable.

he-gem-o-ny n. Dominance or leadership, as of one country over another.

he-gi-ra n. A journey or departure to flee an undesirable situation.

heif-er n. A young cow, particularly one that has not produced a calf.

height n. The quality of being high; the highest or most advanced point; the distance from the base of something; the apex; the distance above a specified level; altitude; the distance from head to foot.

height-en v. To increase or become high in quantity or degree; to raise or lift.

Heim-lich ma-neu-ver n. An emergency maneuver used to dislodge food from a choking person's throat; the closed fist is placed below the rib cage and pressed inward to force air from the lungs upward.

hei-nous adj. Extremely wicked; hateful or shockingly wicked. heinously adv., heinousness n.

heir n. A person who inherits another's property or title.

heir ap-par-ent n. An heir who is legally assured of his right to inherit if he survives his ancestor.

heir-ess n. A female heir, especially a large fortune.

heir-loom n. A family possession handed down from generation to generation; an article of personal property acquired by legal inheritance.

heist v., Slang To take from; to steal. n. A robbery.

hel-i-cal adj. Of or pertaining to the shape of a helix. helically adv.

hel-i-con n. A large, circular tuba that encircles the player's shoulder.

hel-i-cop-ter n.

An aircraft propelled by rotors which can take off vertically rather than needing an approach or a rolling start.

he-lio-graph n. An apparatus fo telegraphing using the sun's ray reflected from a mirror.

hel-i-port n. A designated area wher helicopters land and take off.

he-li-um n. An extremely light, nonflam mable, odorless, gaseous elemen symbolized by He.

hell or **Hell** n. The abode of the dea souls condemned to eternal punish ment; a place of evil, torment, destruction; great distress; anguish; cause of trouble or misery.

hellish adj., hellishly adv.

he'll contr. He will.

hel-le-bore n. A North American plai bearing white or greenish flowers ar yielding a toxic alkaloid used medicine.

Hel-le-nism n. Ancient Greek civ lization, character or culture; adoptio of Greek thought, style, or cultur customs. Hellenist n., Hellenistic ad

hell hole n. A place of extrem wretchedness or horror.

hel-lion n. A mischievous person.

hel-lo n. An expression of greeting.

helm n. A wheel or steering apparat for a ship; a position or any place control or command.

hel-met n. A protective covering for tl head made of metal, leather, or pla tic.

helms-man n. One who guides a ship.

hel-ot n. A serf; a slave. helotry n.

help v. To assist or aid. n. Assistanc relief; one that assists; one hired help. helper n., -ful adj., -fully adv.

help-ing n. A single serving of food.

help-less adj. Without help; powerles lacking strength.

help-mate n. A helper, partner or cor panion.

Hel-sin-ki n. The capital of Finland.

hel-ter--skel-ter adv. In a confused hurried manner; in an aimless wa adj. Rushed and confused. n. Gre confusion; a tumult.

helve n. A handle on a tool such as an or hatchet.

hem n. A finished edge of fabric folde under and stitched. interj. A sou made as in clearing the throat, us especially to attract attention or to l a pause in speech. v. To fold und and stitch down the edge of; to co fine and surround.

he--man n. Slang A man marked strength; a muscular man.

hem-an-gi-o-ma n. A benign tumor th occurs as a reddish elevated area the skin.

he-ma-tol-o-gy n. The branch of biolo cal science that deals with blood a blood-generating organs. -ist n.

he-ma-to-ma n. A tumor containi blood.

hemi-ple-gia n. The paralysis of one h of the body or part of it resulting fro injury to the motor center of t brain.

hem-i-sphere n. A half sphere that

divided by a plane passing through its center; either symmetrical half of an approximately spherical shape; the northern or southern half of the earth divided by the equator or the eastern or western half divided by a meridian. **hemispherical** *adj.*

hem-lock *n.* An evergreen tree of North America and eastern Asia, having flat needles and small cones; the wood of a hemlock; any of several poisonous herbaceous plants, having compound leaves and small whitish flowers; a poison obtained from the hemlock plant.

he-mo-dy-nam-ics *n.* The branch of physiology that deals with the circulation of the blood.

he-mo-glo-bin *n.* The respiratory pigment in the red blood cells of vertebrates containing iron and carrying oxygen to body tissues.

he-mo-ly-sin *n.* A substance which causes the dissolution of red blood cells.

he-mo-phil-i-a *n.*, *Pathol.* An inherited blood disease characterized by severe, protracted, sometimes spontaneous bleeding. **hemophiliac** *n.*

hem-or-rhage *n.* Bleeding, especially excessive bleeding. **hemorrhage** *v.*

hem-or-rhoid *n.*, *Pathol.* A painful mass of dilated veins in swollen anal tissue.

hem-or-rhoids *pl.*, *n.* A condition in which hemorrhoids occur.

he-mo-stat *n.* An agent that stops bleeding; a clamp-like instrument for preventing or reducing bleeding.

hemp *n.* An Asian herb; the female plant from which hashish and marijuana are produced; the tough fiber of the male plant from which coarse fabrics and rope are made. **hempen** *adj.*

hem-stitch *n.* An ornamental stitch, made by pulling out several threads and tying the remaining threads together in groups. **hemstitch** *v.*

hen *n.* A mature female bird, especially an adult female domestic fowl.

hence-forth / hence-for-ward *adv.* From this time on.

hench-man *n.* A loyal and faithful follower; one who supports a political figure chiefly for personal gain.

hen-e-quen *n.* A strong hard fiber obtained from the leaves of a tropical American agave used for binder twine.

hen-na *n.* An Asian and North African ornamental tree bearing fragrant white or reddish flowers; a brownish-red dye derived from henna leaves and used as a cosmetic dye; a strong reddish brown.

heno-the-ism *n.* The worship of one god although not denying the existence of other gods.

hen-peck *v.* To domineer over one's husband by persistent nagging.

Hen-ry, Patrick *n.* (1736-1799). An American Revolutionary leader.

hep-a-rin *n.*, *Biochem* A substance found especially in liver tissue having the power to slow or prevent blood clotting.

he-pat-ic *adj.* Of or like the liver.

he-pat-i-ca *n.* A small perennial herb having three-lobed leaves and white or lavender flowers.

hep-a-ti-tis *n.*, *Pathol.* Inflammation of the liver causing jaundice.

hep-ta-gon *n.* A polygon of seven angles and sides.

her-ald *n.* A person who announces important news; one that comes before as a sign of what is to follow.

he-ral-dic *adj.* An official whose duty is to grant royal proclamations. *v.* To announce.

her-ald-ry *n.*, *pl.* **-ries** The art or science of tracing genealogies and devising and granting coats of arms.

herb *n.* A soft-stemmed plant without woody tissue that usually withers and dies each year; an often pleasant-smelling plant. **herbal** *adj. & n.*

her-ba-ceous *adj.* Like, or consisting of herbs; green and leaf-like.

herb-age *n.* Grass or vegetation used especially for grazing; the succulent edible parts of plants.

herb-al-ist *n.* One who gathers, grows, and deals in herbs.

her-bar-i-um *n.*, *pl.* **-iums** *or* **-ia** A collection of dried plant specimens that are scientifically arranged for study; a place housing a herbarium.

her-bi-cide *n.* A chemical agent used to kill weeds. **herbicidal** *adj.*

her-bi-vore *n.* A type of herbivorous animal.

her-biv-o-rous *adj.* Feeding chiefly on plant life or vegetables. **-ly** *adv.*

her-cu-le-an *adj.* Of unusual size, force, or difficulty; having great strength.

Her-cu-les *n.* A mythical Greek hero famous for his great strength.

herd *n.* A number of cattle or other animals of the same kind, kept or staying together as a group; a large crowd of people. *v.* To bring together in a herd. **herder, herdsman** *n.*

here-af-ter *adv.* From now on; at some future time. *n.* Existence after death.

here-by *adv.* By means or by virtue of this.

he-red-i-tar-y *adj.* Passing or transmitted from an ancestor to a legal heir; having an inherited title or possession; transmitted or transmissible by genetic inheritance. **hereditarily** *adv.*

he-red-i-ty *n.* The genetic transmission of physical traits from parents to offspring.

here-in *adv.* In or into this place.

here-of *adv.* Relating to or in regard to this.

her-e-sy *n.*, *pl.* **-sies** A belief in conflict with orthodox religious beliefs; any belief contrary to set doctrine.

her-e-tic *n.* A person holding opinions different from orthodox beliefs, especially religious beliefs. **heretical** *adj.*

here-to *adv.* To this matter, proposition, or thing.

here-to-fore *adv.* Up to the present time; previously.

here-un-to *adv.* Hereto; to this.

here-up-on *adv.* Immediately following or resulting from this.

here-with *adv.* Together or along with this; hereby.

her-i-ta-ble *adj.* Something capable of being inherited.

her-i-tage *n.* Property that is inherited; something handed down from past generations; a legacy.

her-maph-ro-dite *n.* A person having both male and female reproductive organs. **hermaphroditic** *adj.*

her-met-ic *or* **her-met-i-cal** *adj.* Tightly sealed against air and liquids; made impervious to outside influences. **hermetically** *adv.*

her-mit *n.* A person who lives in seclusion, often for religious reasons.

her-mit-age *n.* The dwelling place or retreat of a hermit; a secluded hideaway.

hermit crab *n.* A chiefly marine decapod crustacean having soft abdomens and which occupy the empty shells of gastropods.

her-ni-a *n.* The protrusion of a bodily organ, as the intestine, through an abnormally weakened wall that usually surrounds it; a rupture. **hernial** *adj.*

he-ro *n., pl.* **-roes** A figure in mythology and legend renowned for exceptional courage and fortitude. **heroic** *adj.,* **heroically** *adv.*

he-ro-ic coup-let *n.* A verse consisting of two rhyming lines of iambic pentameter.

her-o-in *n.* A highly addictive narcotic derivative of morphine.

her-o-ine *n.* A woman of heroic character; the principal female character in a story or play.

her-o-ism *n.* Heroic behavior.

her-on *n.* A bird having a long slender bill, long legs, and a long neck.

her-pes *n., Pathol.* A viral infection, characterized by small blisters on the skin or mucous membranes. **herpetic** *adj.*

her-pe-tol-o-gy *n.* The scientific study and treatment of reptiles and amphibians. **-ic**, **herpetological** *adj.,* **herpetologically** *adv.,* **herpetologist** *n.*

Herr *n., pl.* **Herren** A courtesy title of address to the name or a professional title of a German, equivalent to Mister.

her-ring *n.* A valuable food fish of the North Atlantic, the young of which are prepared as sardines, the adults are pickled, salted, or smoked.

her-ring-bone *n.* A pattern utilizing rows of short slanted parallel lines with connected rows slanting in the opposite direction.

hertz *n.* A unit of frequency equaling one cycle per second.

he's *contr.* He has; he is.

hes-i-tant *adj.* Given to hesitating; lacking decisiveness. **hesitancy** *n.*

hes-i-tate *v.* To pause or to be slow before acting, speaking, or deciding; to be uncertain. **hesitatingly** *adv.,* **hesitation** *n.,* **hesitating** *v.*

hes-sian *n.* A German mercenary soldier.

het-er-o-dox *adj.* Not in accord with established beliefs or religious doctrine; holding unorthodox opinions or beliefs. **heterodoxy** *n.*

het-er-o-sex-u-al *adj.* Of or having sexual desire to the opposite sex; involving different sexes. **heterosexual**, **heterosexuality** *n.*

hew *v.* To make or shape with or as with an axe; to adhere strictly; to conform.

hex *n.* One held to bring bad luck; a jinx. *v.* To put under an evil spell; to be a witch.

hex-a-gon *n.*

A polygon having six sides and six angles. **-al** *adj.,* **-ally** *adv.*

hex-am-e-ter *n.* A line of verse containing six metrical feet.

hey-day *n.* A time of great power, prosperity or popularity; a peak.

HI *abbr.* Hawaii.

hi-a-tus *n.* A slight gap, break, or lapse in time from which something is missing; a break.

hi-a-tus *n.* A break between shooting of television shows; a break in continuity.

hi-ba-chi *n., pl.* **-chis** A deep, portable charcoal grill used for cooking food.

hi-ber-nac-u-lum *n.* A shelter occupied during the winter by a dormant animal.

hi-ber-nate *v.* To pass the winter in an inactive, dormant, sleep-like state. **hibernation**, **hibernator** *n.*

hi-bis-cus *n.* A chiefly tropical shrub or tree, bearing large colorful flowers.

hic-cup *or* **hic-cough** *n.* An involuntary contraction of the diaphragm that occurs on inhalation and spasmodically closes the glottis, producing a short sharp sound. **hiccup** *v.*

hick *n., Slang* A clumsy, unsophisticated country person. *adj.* Typical of hicks.

hick-o-ry *n., pl.* **-ries** A North American tree with a smooth or shaggy bark, hard edible nuts, and heavy, tough wood.

hi-dal-go *n., pl.* **-goes** A Spanish nobleman of lesser nobility.

hid-den *adj.* Out of sight; away from the public eye.

hide *v.* To put, or keep out of sight; to keep secret; to obscure from sight; to seek shelter. *n.* The skin of an animal.

hide-bound *adj.* Obstinately narrow-minded or inflexible.

hid-e-ous *adj.* Physically repulsive; extremely ugly. **-ly** *adv.,* **hideousness** *n.*

hi-er-ar-chy *n., pl.* **-chies** An authoritative body or group of things or persons arranged in successive order; a ranked series of persons or things. **hierachical, hierachic** *adj.,* **-ically** *adv.*

hi-er-o-glyph-ic *n.* A pictorial symbol representing an idea, object, or sound. **hieroglyphically** *adv.*

hi--fi *n.* High fidelity; electronic equipment, such as a phonograph, radio, or recording equipment capable of reproducing high-fidelity sound.

high *adj.* Extending upward; located at a distance above the ground; more than normal in degree or amount.

high and dry *adv.* In a helpless position; away from the current or tide.

high-ball *n.* A mixed drink often served in a tall glass.

high-born *adj.* Of noble birth or ancestry.

high-boy *n.* A tall chest of drawers often in two sections with the lower one mounted on four legs.

high-bred *adj.* Highborn; descending from superior breeding stock.

high-brow *n., Slang* One who claims to have superior knowledge or culture. **highbrow, highbrowed** *adj.*

high chair *n.* A child's chair also used as a feeding table.

higher education *n.* An education beyond the secondary level; college education.

high-er--up *n., Slang* A person having superior rank or status.

high-fa-lu-tin *adj.* Pretentious or extravagant in manner or speech.

high fash-ion *n.* The newest in fashion, style, or design.

high fi-del-i-ty *n., Elect.* The reproduction of sound with minimal distortion, as on records or tapes.

high--flown *adj.* Pretentious in language or style.

high fre-quen-cy *n.* A radio frequency in the band from three to thirty megacycles.

high-grade *n.* Having superior quality.

high--hand-ed *adj.* Overbearing and arbitrary. **-ly** *adv.*, **highhandedness** *n.*

high--hat *adj., Slang* Supercilious; patronizing; snobbish; fashionable.

high jump *n.* A jump for height in athletics.

high-land *n.* Land elevated as a plateau. **highlands** *pl.* A hilly or mountainous region.

high-light *n.* A significant event or detail of special importance. *v.* To give emphasis to; to provide with highlights.

high--mind-ed *adj.* Possessing noble principles or behavior. **-ness** *n.*

high-ness *n.* The state of being high. **Highness** A title used for royalty.

high noon *n.* The middle of the day; 12:00 noon.

high-pow-ered *n.* Having great energy.

high--pres-sure *adj., Informal* Using insistent persuasive methods or tactics. *v.* To try to persuade by using high-pressure techniques.

high--rise *n.* An extremely tall building.

high roller *n.* A person who spends freely and gambles for high stakes.

high-road *n.* A main road; a direct or guaranteed method or course.

high school *n.* A secondary school of grades nine through twelve or grades ten through twelve. **high schooler** *n.*

high seas *pl., n.* The open waters of an ocean or sea that are beyond the territorial jurisdiction of any one nation.

high--sound-ing *adj.* Pretentious or imposing in implication or sound.

high--spirited *adj.* Unbroken in spirit; proud.

high--stick-ing *n.* In hockey, an offense in which a player holds the stick above the shoulders of other players or himself.

high--strung *adj.* A state of being very nervous and excitable.

high tech *n.* An interior design that incorporates industrial materials or motifs; high technology.

high tech-nol-o-gy *n.* The technology that involves highly advanced or specialized systems or devices.

high--test *adj.* Relating to gasoline with a high octane number.

high tide *n.* The highest level reached by the incoming tide each day.

high-water *adj.* A high state of water in a river.

high-way *n.* A main or principal road or thoroughfare of some length which connects towns and cities and is open to the public.

high-way-man *n.* Formerly, a robber who waylaid travelers on highways.

highway robbery *n.* An excessive profit derived from a business transaction.

hi-jack *v., Slang* To seize illegally or steal while in transit; to coerce or compel someone; to commandeer a vehicle, especially an airplane in flight.

hike *v.* To walk for a lengthy amount of time usually through rugged terrain or woods; to pull up clothing with a sudden motion. **hike, hiker** *n.*

hi-lar-i-ous *adj.* Boisterously happy or cheerful. **hilariously** *adv.*, **hilarity** *n.*

hill *n.* A rounded, elevation of the earth's surface, smaller than a mountain; a pile or heap; a small pile or mound, as of soil. *v.* To surround or cover with hills, as potatoes. **hilliness** *n.*, **hilly** *adj.*

hill-bil-ly *n., pl.* **-lies** *Slang* A person living or coming from an isolated rural region, as from the mountains or a backwoods area, especially of the southern U.S.

hill-ock *n.* A small or low hill or mound. **hillocky** *adj.*

hill-side *n.* The side or slope of a hill.

hill-top *n.* The summit or top of a hill.

hilt *n.* The handle of a dagger or sword. **to the hilt** Fully; completely; thoroughly.

him *pron.* The objective case of the pronoun he.

Hi-ma-la-yas *n.* A mountain range in Asia.

hi-mat-i-on *n.* A rectangular cloth draped over the left shoulder and body and worn as a garment in Greece.

him-self *pron.* That identical male one; a form of the third person, singular masculine pronoun.

hind *adj.* Located at or toward the rear part; posterior.

hin-der *v.* To interfere with the progress or action of. **hinderer** *n.*

Hin-di *n.* The principal language of northern India. **Hindi** *adj.*

hind-most *adj.* Farthest to the rear or back.

hind-quar-ter *n.* The back or hind part of a side of meat. **hindquarters** *pl.* The rump.

hin-drance *n.* The act of hindering or state of being hindered.

hind-sight *n.* Comprehension or understanding of an event after it has happened.

Hin-du *n.* A native of India; a person whose religion is Hinduism.

Hin-du-ism *n.* The religion, philosophy, and cultural beliefs of the Hindus of India.

hinge *n.* A jointed device which allows a part, as a door or gate, to swing or turn on another frame. *v.* To attach by or to equip with a hinge or hinges.

hint *n.* An indirect indication or suggestion. *v.* To make something known by a hint.

hin-ter-land *n.* A region remote from cities; an inland area immediately adjacent to a coastal area.

hip *n.* The part of the human body that projects outward below the waist and thigh; the hip joint.

hip *n.* The bright, red seed case of a rose.

hip *adj., Slang* Said to be aware of or informed about current goings on.

hip-bone *n.* The large, flat bone which forms a lateral half of the pelvis.

hip joint *n.* The joint between the hipbone and the thighbone.

hip-pie *or* **hip-py** *n., pl.* -ies A young person who adopts unconventional dress and behavior along with the use of drugs to express withdrawal from middle class life and indifference to its values.

hip-po-drome *n.* An oval stadium for chariot races in ancient Greece.

hip-po-pot-a-mus *n.*

A large, aquatic mammal, native to Africa, having short legs, a massive, thick-skinned hairless body, and a broad wide-mouthed muzzle.

hire *v.* To obtain the service of another for pay. **hirer** *n.*

hir-sute *n.* Covered with hair.

his *adj.* The possessive case of the pronoun he.

His-pan-ic *adj.* Of or relating to the language, people, or culture of Spain or Latin America.

hiss *n.* A sound resembling a prolonged, sibilant sound, as that of *sss* *v.* To emit such a sound as an expression of disapproval. **hisser** *n.*

his-ta-mine *n., Biochem.* A white, crystalline substance that occurs in plant and animal tissue, found to reduce blood pressure and to have a contracting action on the uterus and believed to cause allergic reactions. **-ic** *adj.*

his-tol-o-gy *n., pl.* -ies The study of the minute structures of animal and plant tissues as seen through a microscope. **histological** *adj.*, **histologist** *n.*

his-to-ri-an *n.* A person who specializes in the writing or study of history.

his-tor-ic *adj.* Significant or famous in history; historical.

his-tor-i-cal *adj.* Relating to or taking place in history; serving as a source of knowledge of the past; historic. **historically** *adv.*, **historicalness** *adj.*

his-to-ry *n., pl.* -ries Past events, especially those involving human affairs; an account or record of past events that is written in chronological order, especially those concerning a particular nation, people, activity, or knowledge; the study of the past and its significance.

his-tri-on-ics *pl., n.* Theatrical arts; feigned emotional display.

hit *v.* To give a blow to; to strike with force; to come forcibly in contact with; to collide with; to inflict a blow on; to move or set in motion by striking; in baseball, to make a successful hit while at bat. **hitter** *n.*

hitch *v.* To fasten or tie temporarily, with a hook or knot. *Slang* To unite in marriage; to obtain a ride by hitchhiking. *n.* A delay or difficulty. *Milit.* A period of time in the armed forces.

hitch-hike *v.* To travel by signaling and obtaining rides from passing drivers.

hith-er *adv.* To this place. *adj.* Situated toward this side.

hith-er-to *adv.* Up to now.

hive *n.* A natural or man-made structure serving as a habitation for honeybees; a beehive.

hives *pl., n.* Any of various allergic conditions marked by itching welts.

hoar *adj.* Having white or gray hair; grayish or white, as with frost. **-iness** *n.*

hoard *n.* The accumulation of something stored away for safekeeping or future use. *v.* To amass and hide or store valuables, money. **hoarder** *n.*

hoar-frost *n.* The deposit of ice crystals that form on a cold surface exposed to moist air.

hoarse *adj.* Having a husky, gruff, or croaking voice. **-ly** *adv.*, **-ness** *n.*

hoars-en *v.* To become or make hoarse.

hoar-y *adj.* Ancient; aged; gray or white with age.

hoax *n.* A trick or deception. *v.* To deceive by a hoax. **hoaxer** *n.*

hob *n.* The projection at the side or interior of a fireplace used to keep things warm; an elf or hobgoblin.

hob-ble v. To limp or walk with a limp; to progress irregularly or clumsily; to fetter a horse or other animal. n. A hobbling gait or walk.

hob-by n., pl. -bies An activity or interest undertaken for pleasure during one's leisure time.

hob-by-horse n. A child's rocking horse; a long stick surmounted by a horse's head.

hob-gob-lin n. An imaginary cause of terror or dread.

hob-nail n. A short, broad-headed nail used to stud the soles of heavy shoes against wear or slipping.

hob-nob n. To associate in a friendly manner; to be on familiar terms.

ho-bo n., pl. **ho-boes** or **ho-bos** A vagrant who travels aimlessly about; a tramp.

hock n. The joint of the hind leg of a horse, ox, or other animal which corresponds to the ankle in man.

hock-ey n. A game played on ice between two teams of skaters whose object is to drive a puck into the opponent's goal using curved wooden sticks; a similar kind of hockey played on a field with a small ball instead of a puck.

ho-cus--po-cus n. Any deception or trickery, as misleading gestures; nonsense words or phrases used in conjuring or sleight of hand.

hod n. A V-shaped trough held over the shoulder to carry loads, as bricks or mortar.

hod carrier n. A laborer employed to carry supplies to bricklayers, plasterers, etc. on the job.

hodge-podge n. A jumbled mixture or collection.

Hodg-kin's dis-ease n., Pathol. A disease characterized by progressive enlargement of the lymph nodes, lymphoid tissue, and spleen, generally fatal.

hoe n. A tool with a long handle and flat blade used for weeding, cultivating, and loosening the soil. hoe v., hoer n.

hoe-cake n. A thin, flat cake made of cornmeal.

hoe-down n., Slang A lively country square dance; party.

hog n. A pig, especially one weighing more than 120 pounds and raised for the market; a greedy, selfish, or dirty person. v. To take something selfishly; to take more than one's share. hoggish adj., -gishly adv., -gishness n.

ho-gan n. A building made of legs and mud and used as a dwelling by the Indians.

hog-nose snake n. Any of several nonvenomous American snakes with flat heads and prominent snouts.

hogs-head n. A large barrel or cask that holds from 63 to 140 gallons.

hog--tie v. To tie together the four feet of an animal or the hands and feet of a person.

hog-wash n. Kitchen scraps fed to hogs; any nonsense; false or ridiculous talk or writing.

hoi pol-loi n. The common people; the masses.

hoist v. To haul or raise up. n. A machine used for raising large objects.

hold v. To take and keep as in one's hand; to grasp; to possess; to put or keep in a particular place, position, or relationship; to suppress; to keep under control. n. A cargo storage area inside a ship or aircraft.

hold-ing n. Property, as land, money, or stocks.

hold-ing pat-tern n. A usually circular course that is flown by an aircraft awaiting clearance to land at an airport.

hold-o-ver n. Something that remains from an earlier time.

hold-up n. A robbery at gun point; a delay.

hole n. A cavity or opening in a solid mass or body. hole v.

hol-i-day n. A day set aside by law to commemorate a special person or event; a day set aside for religious observance; a day free from work; any day of rest.

ho-li-ness n. The state of being holy.

hol-lan-daise sauce n. A creamy sauce made from butter, egg yolks, and lemon juice or vinegar.

hol-ler v. To shout loudly; to yell.

hol-low adj. Having a cavity or space within; concaved or sunken; lacking significance or substance; not genuine; empty; meaningless. hollowly adv., hollowness n.

hol-ly n., pl. -ies A tree or shrub that bears glossy spiny leaves and bright-red berries.

hol-ly-hock n. A tall, cultivated plant of the mallow family, widely cultivated for its tall spikes of large, variously colored flowers.

Hol-ly-wood n. A district of Los Angeles, Ca., the capital of the American motion-picture industry.

hol-mi-um n. A metallic element of the rare-earth group, symbolized by Ho.

hol-o-caust n. A widespread or total destruction, especially by fire.

hol-o-grah n. A handwritten document, as a letter or will, signed by the person who wrote it. holographic, holographical adj.

ho-lo-gram n. A three-dimensional picture made on a photographic plate without the use of a camera and viewed with coherent light from behind.

Hol-stein n. One of a breed of black-and-white dairy cattle.

hol-ster n. A leather case designed to hold a pistol or gun. holstered adj.

ho-ly adj. Regarded with or characterized by divine power; sacred.

Ho-ly Com-mu-nion n. The Eucharist.

Ho-ly Ghost n. The third person of the Trinity.

Ho-ly Land n. Palestine.

Ho-ly Spir-it n. The Holy Ghost.

hom-age n. Great respect or honor, especially when expressed publicly.

hom-burg *n.* A man's felt hat having a stiff brim and high crown creased lengthwise.

home *n.* The place where one resides; a place of origin; one's birthplace or residence during the formative years; a place one holds dear because of personal feelings or relationships; a place of security and comfort.

home-bod-y *n., pl.* **-ies** One who prefers to stay at home or whose main interest centers around the home.

home-com-ing *n.* A return to one's home; a yearly celebration during which alumni return to visit their old schools.

home eco-nom-ics *n.* The principles of home management.

home-ly *adj.* Having a simple, familiar, everyday character; having plain or ugly features; unattractive. **-iness** *n.*

ho-me-op-a-thy *n.* A system of treating a disease with minute doses of medicines that produce the symptoms of the disease being treated. **homeopath** *n.*, **homeopathic** *adj.*

ho-me-o-sta-sis *n., Biol.* A state of equilibrium that occurs between different but related functions or elements.

home plate *n.* In baseball, the rubber slab or plate at which a batter stands when batting and which must be touched by a base runner in order to score.

home run *n.* In baseball, a hit that allows the batter to circle all the bases and to score.

home-sick *adj.* Longing or yearning for home and family. **homesickness** *n.*

home-spun *adj.* Something made, woven, or spun at home; anything that is simple and plain.

home-stead *n.* A house and its land. *v.* To occupy land granted under the Homestead Act. **homesteader** *n.*

home-stretch *n.* The straight portion of a racecourse between the last turn and the finish line; the last or final stage of anything.

home-work *n.* Work done at home, especially school assignments.

home-y *or* **hom-y** *adj.* Suggesting the coziness, intimacy, and comforts of home. **homeyness** *or* **hominess** *n.*

hom-i-cide *n.* The killing of one person by another; a person killed by another.

hom-i-let-ic *n.* Pertaining to the nature of a sermon.

hom-i-ly *n., pl.* **-ies** A sermon, particularly one based on a Biblical text.

hom-ing pi-geon *n.* A pigeon trained to find its way home from great distances.

hom-i-ny *n.* Kernels of hulled and dried corn, often ground into a coarse white meal and boiled.

hominy grits *n.* Hominy in uniform particles served as a side dish in the South.

ho-mo-ge-ne-ous *adj.* Of the same or similar nature or kind. **homogeneity,**

homogeneousness *n.*, **-ly** *adv.*

ho-mog-e-nize *v.* To process milk by breaking up fat globules and dispersing them uniformly. **homogenization, homogenizer** *n.*

hom-o-graph *n.* A word that is identical to another in spelling, but different from it in origin and meaning.

hom-o-nym *n.* A word that has the same sound and often the same spelling as another but a different meaning and origin.

hom-o-phone *n.* One of two or more words that have the same sound but different spelling, origin, and meaning.

Ho-mo sa-pi-ens *n.* The scientific name for the human race.

ho-mo-sex-u-al *adj.* Having sexual attraction or desire for persons of the same sex. **homosexual, homosexuality** *n.*

hon-cho *n., pl.* **-chos** The main person in charge; the boss; the manager.

hone *n.* A fine-grained stone used to sharpen cutting tools, such as knives or razors. *v.* To perfect something; to sharpen.

hon-est *adj.* Not lying, cheating, or stealing; having or giving full worth or value. **honestly** *adv.*, **honesty** *n.*

hon-ey *n., pl.* **hon-eys** A sweet, sticky substance made by bees from the nectar gathered from flowers; sweetness. *Slang* Dear; darling. **honeyed** *or* **honied** *adj.*

hon-ey-bee *n.* Any of various bees living in colonies and producing honey.

hon-ey-comb *n.* A structure consisting of a series of hexagonal cells made by bees for the storage of honey, pollen, or their eggs.

hon-ey-dew *n.* A sweet fluid deposited on plant leaves by certain insects.

hon-ey-dew mel-on *n.* A smooth-skinned, white melon with a sweet, greenish pulp.

hon-ey-moon *n.* A trip taken by a newly-married couple. **honeymooner** *n.*

hon-ey-suck-le *n.* A shrub or vine bearing a tubular, highly fragrant flower.

honk *n.* The harsh, loud sound made by a goose; the sound made by an automobile horn. **honk** *v.*, **honker** *n.*

hon-ky--tonk *n., Slang* A cheap bar or nightclub.

Hon-o-lu-lu *n.* The capital of the state of Hawaii, located on the island of Oahu.

hon-or *n.* High regard or respect; personal integrity; reputation; privilege; used as a title for mayors and judges. *v.* To accept something as valid.

hon-or-a-ble *adj.* Worthy of honor.

honorable mention *n.* A distinction conferred on someone for exceptional merit but not deserving of top honors.

hon-or-ar-y *adj.* Relating to an office or title bestowed as an honor, without the customary powers, duties, or salaries.

honor guard *n.* A guard assigned to accompany a distinguished person or accompany a casket at a military funeral.

hon-or-if-ic *adj.* Giving or conveying

respect or honor.

Hon-shu n. The largest island of Japan.

hood n. A covering for the head and neck, often attached to a garment; the movable metal hinged cover of an automobile engine. **hooded** adj.

-hood suff. The quality or state of; sharing a given quality or state.

hood-lum n. A young, tough, wild, or destructive fellow.

hoo-doo n. Voodoo. Slang One who is thought to bring bad luck.

hood-wink v. To deceive; to blind-fold.

hoo-ey n., & interj., Slang Nonsense.

hoof n., pl. **hooves** The horny covering of the foot in various mammals, as horses, cattle, and oxen. Slang To dance; to walk. **on the hoof** Alive; not butchered. **hoofed** adj.

hook n. A curved or bent piece of metal used to catch, drag, suspend, or fasten something; in golf, a stroke that sends the ball curving to the left; in boxing, to strike with a short, swinging blow; in hockey, to check illegally with the hockey stick. Slang v. To cause to become dependent or addicted. Naut., Slang An anchor. **by hook or by crook** In one way or another. **hook, line, and sinker** Unreservedly; entirely. to **hookup with** To marry; to form an association.

hoo-kah n. A smoking pipe having a long, flexible tube that passes through a vessel of water which cools the smoke as it is drawn through.

hook-er n., Slang A prostitute.

hook-worm n. A parasitic intestinal worm with hooked mouth parts.

hook-y n., Slang Truant. to **play hooky** To be out of school without permission.

hoop n. A circular band of metal or wood used to hold staves of a cask or barrel together; in basketball, the basket.

hoop-la n., Slang Noise and excitement.

hoose-gow n., Slang A jail.

Hoo-sier n., Slang A native or resident of Indiana.

Hoo-sier State n. Nickname for the state of Indiana.

hoot n. The loud sound or cry of an owl. **hooter** n., **hoot** v.

hoot n., Slang A very insignificant amount. **not give a hoot** Not caring.

hoot-en-an-ny n., pl. **-ies** An informal gathering of folk singers for a public performance.

Hoo-ver, Herbert Clark n. (1874-1964). The 31st president of the United States, from 1929-1933.

hop n. A perennial herb with lobed leaves and green flowers that resemble pine cones; the dried flowers of the plant, yielding an oil used in brewing beer. Slang A dance; a quick trip on a plane. v. To move by making short leaps on one foot; to move with light springing motions.

hope v. To want or wish for something with a feeling of confident expecta-

tion. to **hope against hope** To continue hoping for something even when it may be in vain.

hopeful adj. & n., **hopefully** adv.

hope-ful adj. Manifesting or full of hope. n. A young person who shows signs of succeeding. **-ly** adv., **hopefulness** n.

hope-less adj. Totally without hope; despairing; having no grounds for hope. **hopelessly** adv., **hopelessness** n.

hop-ped--up adj., Slang Stimulated by narcotics; drugged.

hop-per n. One that hops; a jumping insect; a receptacle in which coal, sand, grain, or other materials are held ready for discharge through the bottom.

hop-scotch n. A child's game in which the player throws an object, as a stone, into areas drawn on the ground and then hops on one foot over the lines of a diagram so as to recover the object.

horde adj. A large crowd.

hore-hound n. A whitish, bitter, aromatic plant, whose leaves yield a bitter extract used as a flavoring in candy.

ho-ri-zon n. The line along which the earth and sky seem to meet; the bounds or limit of one's knowledge, experience or interest.

hor-i-zon-tal adj. Parallel to the horizon. **horizontal** n., **horizontally** adv.

hor-mone n., Physiol. An internal secretion carried by the bloodstream to other parts of the body where it has a specific effect.

horn n.

A hard, bone-like, permanent projection on the heads of certain hoofed animals, as cattle, sheep, or deer; the two antlers of a deer which are shed annually. Mus. Any of the various brass instruments, formerly made from animal horns. **horn in** To join in a conversation or other activities without being invited. **-y** adj.

horn-ed toad n. A lizard with a flat body, a short tail, and horn-like projections on the head.

hor-net n. Any of various wasps which are capable inflicting a severe sting.

horn-pout n. A freshwater catfish with a large head and barbels for navigation.

horn-swog-gle v. To deceive.

horn-stone n. A quartz mineral much like flint but more brittle.

horn-wort n. A rootless aquatic herb that has flowers with a single carpel.

ho-rol-o-gy n. The scientific method of measuring time.

hor-o-scope n. A chart or diagram of the relative positions of the planets and signs of the zodiac at a certain time, as that of a person's birth; used to predict the future.

hor-ri-ble adj. Shocking; inducing or

producing horror. *Informal* Excessive; inordinate. **horribly** *adv.*

hor-rid *adj.* Horrible. **horridly** *adv.*

hor-ri-fy *v.* To cause a feeling of horror; to dismay or shock.

hor-ror *n.* The painful, strong emotion caused by extreme dread, fear, or repugnance. *Informal* Something that is disagreeable or ugly.

hors d'oeuvre *n.* An appetizer served with cocktails before dinner.

horse *n.*

A large, strong, hoofed quadruped mammal with a long mane and tail, used for riding and for pulling heavy objects; a device that generally has four legs, used for holding or supporting something; in gymnastics, a wooden, leather-covered block of wood on four legs, used for vaulting and other exercises.

horse chest-nut *n.* Any of several Eurasian trees with palmate leaves, clusters of flowers, and chestnut-like fruit.

horse-fly *n.* A large fly, the female of which sucks the blood of various mammals, such as horses and cattle.

horse-hair *n.* The hair from a horse's tail or mane; a fabric made from such hair; haircloth.

horse-hide *n.* The hide of a horse; leather made from a horse's hide. *Informal* A baseball.

horse-laugh *n.* A loud, scornful laugh.

horse-man *n.* A person who rides horseback; one who breeds or raises horses. **horsemanship** *n.*

horse-play *n.* Rough, boisterous fun or play.

horse-pow-er *n.*, *Mech.* A unit of power that is equal to 746 watts and nearly equivalent to the gravitational unit that equals 550 foot-pounds per second.

horse-rad-ish *n.* A tall, coarse, white-flowered herb from the mustard family; the pungent root of this plant is used as a condiment.

horse sense *n.*, *Slang* Common sense.

horse-shoe *n.*

A protective U-shaped shoe for a horse, consisting of a narrow plate of iron shaped to fit the rim of a horse's hoof. **horseshoes** A game in which the object is to encircle a stake with tossed horseshoes.

horse-shoe crab *n.* Any closely related marine arthropod with a rounded body and a stiff pointed tail.

horse show *n.* An exhibition of horse skills such as riding, jumping, etc.

horse-whip *n.* A whip used to control horses. *v.* To whip or flog.

horst *n.* A block of the earth's crust separated by faults from an adjacent block.

hort *abbr.* Horticultural; horticulture.

hor-ti-cul-ture *n.* The art or science of raising and tending fruits, vegetables, flowers, or ornamental plants. **-al** *adj.*, **-ally** *adv.*, **horticulturist** *n.*

ho-san-na *interj.* Used to praise or glorify God.

hose *n.* A sock; a stocking; a flexible tube for carrying fluids or gases under pressure. *v.* To wash; to water; to squirt with a hose.

ho-sier-y *n.* Stockings and socks.

hosp *abbr.* Hospital.

hos-pice *n.* A lodging for travelers or the needy maintained by a religious order.

hos-pi-ta-ble *adj.* Treating guests with warmth and generosity; receptive.

hos-pi-tal *n.* An institution where the injured or sick receive medical, surgical, and emergency care.

hos-pi-tal-i-ty *n.* Hospitable treatment, disposition, or reception.

hos-pi-tal-ize *v.* To place or admit in a hospital as a patient for care or treatment. **hospitalization** *n.*

hospital ship *n.* A ship equipped as a hospital to assist the wounded, sick or shipwrecked in time of war.

host *n.* One who receives or entertains guests; one who provides a room or building for an event or function. *Biol.* A living organism, as a plant or an animal, on or in which a parasite lives.

hos-tage *n.* A person held as security that promises will be kept or terms met by a third party.

hos-tel *n.* A low-priced, supervised lodging for young travelers.

hos-tel-ry *n.* An inn or hotel.

host-ess *n.* A woman who entertains socially; a woman who greets patrons at a restaurant and escorts them to their tables.

hos-tile *adj.* Of or relating to an enemy; antagonistic. **hostilely** *adv.*

hos-til-i-ty *n.*, *pl.* **-ies** A very deep-seated opposition or hatred; war.

hot *adj.* Having heat that exceeds normal body temperature; sexually excited or receptive; electrically charged, as a hot wire. *Slang* Recently and or illegally obtained.

hot air *n.*, *Slang* Idle talk.

hot-bed *n.* A glass-covered bed of soil heated by fermenting manure and used for raising seedlings; an environment that is conducive to rapid growth or development.

hot cake *n.* A pancake.

hot dog *n.* A cooked frankfurter, served in a long roll. *Slang* A person who enjoys showing off.

hot-el *n.* A business that provides lodging, meals, entertainment, and other services for the public.

hot flash *n.* A sudden sensation of heat that is caused by the dilation of skin capillaries and usually associated with menopausal endocrine imbalance.

hot-foot v. To hasten.

hot-head-ed adj. Having a fiery temper. **hotheadedly** adv., **hotheadedness** n.

hot-house n. A heated greenhouse used to raise plants.

hot line n. A direct telephone line that is in constant operation and ready to facilitate immediate communication.

hot plate n. A portable electric appliance for heating or cooking food.

hot po-ta-to n. An issue or problem that involves unpleasant or dangerous consequences for anyone dealing with it.

hot rod n. An automobile modified or rebuilt for greater power and speed.

hot seat n., Slang An electric chair; a position of embarrassment, anxiety, or uneasiness.

hot spring n. A natural spring with water temperature above 98 degrees.

hound n. Any of several kinds of long-eared dogs with deep voices which follow their prey by scent; a person unusually devoted to something; a fan. v. To pursue or drive without letting up; to nag continuously.

hour n. A measure of time equal to 60 minutes; one 24th of a day; the time of day or night. **hours** pl. A specific or certain period of time.

hour-glass n.

A two-chambered glass instrument for measuring time with sand, water, or mercury trickling down from the top chamber to the bottom in order to measure the passage of an hour in time.

hour-ly adj. Something that happens or is done every hour. **hourly** adv.

house n. A building that serves as living quarters for one or more families; home; the shelter or refuge.

house-boat n. A boat equipped to serve as a dwelling or for cruising.

house-break v. To teach acceptable manners.

house-coat n. A woman's informal garment to be worn around the house.

house-keeper n. A woman employed to take care of the running of the house.

housemaid's knee n. The swelling of the knee due to an enlargement of the bursa in the front of the patella due to over use of the knee usually.

house moth-er n. A woman acting as a chaperon and sometimes a housekeeper in a residence for young people.

house of correction n. An institution where persons who have committed a minor offense are housed until they are reformed and released back into society.

house-warming n. A party to celebrate a family moving into a new house.

housing development n. A group of usually individual dwellings or apartment houses typically of similar design.

housing project n. A publicly supported housing development planned for low-income families.

hov-el n. A small dirty house.

hov-er v. To remain suspended over something.

how adv. In what manner or way; to what effect; in what condition or state; for what reason; with what meaning.

how-dy interj. A word used to express a greeting.

how-ev-er adj. In whatever way. conj. Nevertheless.

how-it-zer n. A short cannon that fires projectiles at a high trajectory.

howl v. To utter a loud, sustained, plaintive sound, as the wolf.

howl-er n. One that howls; a ridiculous or stupid blunder.

how-so-ev-er adv. To whatever degree or extent.

hp abbr. Horsepower.

hr abbr. Hour.

HS abbr. High School.

ht abbr. Height.

hua-ra-che n. A sandal with a low heel and an upper made of interwoven leather thongs.

hub n. The center of a wheel; the center of activity.

hub-cap n. The removable metal cap that covers the end of an axle, such as one used on the wheel of a motor vehicle.

huck-le-ber-ry n. A type of bush, related to the blueberry and bearing glossy, blackish, usually acidic berries.

HUD abbr. Department of Housing and Urban Development.

hud-dle n. A crowd together; in football, a brief meeting of teammates to prepare for the next play. v. To nestle or crowd together; to confer.

hue n. A gradation of color running from red through yellow, green, and blue to violet; a particular color; a shade.

huff n. A fit of resentment or of ill temper. v. To exhale or breathe heavily, as from extreme exertion. **huffily** adv., **huffiness** n., **huffy** adj.

hug v. To embrace; to hold fast; to keep, cling, or stay close to. **huggable** adj., **hugger** n.

huge adj. Of great quantity, size, or extent. **hugely** adv., **hugeness** n.

hu-la n. A Hawaiian dance characterized by beautiful rhythmic movement of the hips and gestures with the hands.

hulk n. A heavy, bulky ship; the body of an old ship no longer fit for service.

hulk-ing adj. Unwieldy or awkward.

hull n. The outer cover of a fruit or seed; the framework of a boat; the external covering of a rocket, spaceship, or guided missile.

hul-la-ba-loo n. A confused noise; a great uproar.

hum v. To make a continuous low-pitched sound; to be busily active; to sing with the lips closed. **hummer** n.

hu-man adj. Of, relating to, or typical of man; having or manifesting human form or attributes.

humanly *adv.*, **humanness** *n.*

hu-mane *adj.* To be marked by compassion, sympathy, or consideration for other people or animals.

humanely *adv.*, **humaneness** *n.*

hu-man-i-tar-i-an *n.* A person who is concerned for human welfare, especially through philanthropy.

humanitarian *adj.*, **humanitarianism** *n.*

hu-man-i-ty *n.*, *pl.* **-ies** The quality or state of being human; humankind.

hum-ble *adj.* Marked by meekness or modesty; unpretentious; lowly. *v.* To make humble. **-ness, -er** *n.*, **-y** *adv.*

hum-din-ger *n.*, *Slang* Someone or something that is marked as superior.

hum-drum *n.*, *Slang* Boring; dull.

hu-mer-us *n.*, *pl.* **meri** The long bone of the upper arm or forelimb extending from the shoulder to the elbow.

hu-mid *adj.* Containing or characterized by a large amount of moisture; damp.

hu-mid-i-fy *v.* To make humid or more moist. **humidifier** *n.*

hu-mid-i-ty *n.* A moderate amount of wetness in the air; dampness.

hu-mi-dor *n.* A container used to keep cigars in which the air is kept properly humidified by a special device.

hu-mil-i-ate *v.* To reduce one's dignity or pride to a lower position. **-ion** *n.*

hum-ming-bird *n.*

A very small bird with narrow wings, long primaries, a slender bill, and a very extensile tongue.

hum-mock *n.* A rounded knoll or hill of snow or dirt. **hummocky** *adj.*

hu-mor *n.* Something that is or has the ability to be comical or amusing. *Physiol.* Fluid contained in the body such as blood or lymph.

humorous *adj.*, **humorously** *adv.*

hu-mor-ist *n.* A person who has a sense of humor; one who uses humor to amuse others.

hump *n.* The rounded lump or protuberance, as on the back of a camel. **over the hump** To be past the difficult or most critical state.

hu-mus *n.* A complex material resulting from partial decomposition of plant or animal matter forming the organic portion of soil.

hunch *n.* A strong, intuitive feeling about a future event or result. *v.* To bend into a crooked position or posture.

hun-dred *n.*, *pl.* **-dreds** *or* **-dred** The cardinal number equal to 10 X 10.

hundredth *n.*, *adj. & adv.*

hun-ger *n.* A strong need or desire for food. **hungrily** *adv.*, **hungry** *adj.*

hunt *v.* To search or look for food; to pursue with the intent of capture; to look in an attempt to find.

hunter, huntress *n.*

hur-dle *n.* A portable barrier used to jump over in a race; an obstacle one must overcome. *v.* To leap over.

hur-dy-gur-dy *n.* A musical instrument where the sound is produced by turning a crank.

hurl *v.* To throw something with great force; in baseball, to pitch. **hurler** *n.*

hur-rah *interj.* Used to express approval, pleasure, or exultation. **hurrah** *n. & v.*

hur-ri-cane *n.* A tropical cyclone with winds exceeding 74 miles per hour, usually accompanied by rain, thunder, and lightning.

hur-ry *v.* To move or cause to move with haste. **hurriedly** *adv.*, **hurriedness** *n.*

hurt *v.* To experience or inflict with physical pain; to cause physical or emotional harm to; to damage.

hus-band *n.* A man who is married.

hush *v.* To make or become quiet; to calm; to keep secret; to suppress. *n.* A silence.

husk *n.* The dry or membranous outer cover of certain vegetables, fruits, and seeds, often considered worthless.

husk-y *adj.* Having a dry cough or grating sound; burly or robust.

huskily *adv.*, **huskiness** *n.*

husk-y *n.*, *pl.* **-ies** A heavy-coated working dog of the arctic region.

hus-sy *n.*, *pl* **-ies** A saucy or mischievous girl; a woman with doubtful morals; a disreputable woman.

hus-tings *n.*, *pl.* A platform used for making political speeches from.

hus-tle *v.* To urge or move hurriedly along; to work busily and quickly. *Slang* To make energetic efforts to solicit business or make money.

hustle, hustler *n.*

hy-a-cinth *n.* A bulbous plant that has a cluster of variously colored, highly fragrant, bell-shaped flowers.

hy-brid *n.* An offspring of two dissimilar plants or of two animals of different races, breeds, varieties, or species; something made up of mixed origin or make-up. **hybrid** *adj.*

hybrid computer *n.* A system which consists of a combination of analog and digital computer systems.

hy-drant *n.* A pipe with a valve and spout which supplies water from a main source.

hy-drate *n.* A chemical compound formed by the union of water with another substance in definite proportions. **hydrate** *v.*, **hydration** *n.*

hy-drau-lic *adj.* Operated, moved, or effected by the means of water; hardening or setting under water. **-ally** *adv.*

hy-drau-lics *pl.*, *n.* The scientific study that deals with practical applications of water or other liquids in motion and the laws that govern its action.

hy-dro-elec-tric *adj.* Relating to the production of electricity by the use of waterpower.

hy-dro-foil *n.* A motorboat built with metal plates and fins attached by struts for lifting the hull clear of the water as speed is attained.

hy-dro-gen *n.* A colorless, normally odorless, highly flammable gas that is the simplest and lightest of the elements, symbolized by H. **hydrogenous** *adj.*

hy-dro-gen bomb *n.* A bomb that is extremely destructive, with an explosive power obtained from the rapid release of atomic energy.

hy-dro-gen per-ox-ide *n.* A colorless, unstable, liquid compound that is used as an antiseptic solution and as a bleach.

hy-dro-pho-bi-a *n.* A fear of water; rabies. **hydrophobic** *adj.*

hy-dro-plane *v.* To skim over water with only the hull more or less touching the surface.

hy-dro-scope *n.* A mirror device which enables a person to see at a considerable distance below the surface of the water.

hy-gro-scope *n.* An instrument which shows the changes in humidity in the atmosphere.

hy-e-na *n.*

Any of several strong carnivorous mammals of Africa and Asia, with coarse hair and very powerful jaws.

hy-giene *n.* The science of the establishment and maintenance of good health and the prevention of disease. **hygienic** *adj.*, **-ically** *adv.*, **hygienist** *n.*

hy-men *n.* The thin membrane that partly closes the external vaginal orifice.

hymn *n.* A song of praise giving thanks to God; a song of joy. **hymn** *v.*

hym-nal *n.* A book that contains hymns compiled for worshipping.

hype *v.*, *Slang* To put on; to stimulate; to promote or publicize extravagantly.

hy-per *pref.* Excessive in anything that is performed or done physically.

hy-per-ac-tive *adj.* Abnormally active. **hyperactivity** *n.*

hy-er-cho-les-ter-emia *n.* A disease in which there is excessive cholesterol in the blood.

hy-per-chro-mic anemia *n.* An anemia which has an increase in hemoglobin and a reduction in the number of red blood cells.

hy-per-crit-i-cal *adj.* Being excessively critical.

hy-per-ga-my *n.* The act of marrying into an equal or higher social group.

hy-per-gly-ce-mia *n.* An excessive amount of sugar in the blood.

hy-per-li-pe-mia *n.* The presence of excessive fat in the blood.

hy-perm-ne-sia *n.* The ability of having complete memory or recall of the past.

hy-per-os-to-sis *n.* An excessive thickening of bone tissue.

hy-per-pha-gia *n.* An abnormal desire for the consumption of food associated with injury to the hypothalamus.

hy-per-pnea *n.* Abnormally rapid breathing. **hyperpneic** *adj.*

hy-per-ten-sion *n.* The condition of abnormally high blood pressure especially in the arteries. **-ive** *adj. & n.*

hy-per-ven-ti-la-tion *n.* An excessive rate of respiration leading to loss of carbon dioxide from the blood.

hy-per-vi-ta-min-osis *n.* An abnormal condition resulting from the excessive use of one or more vitamins.

hy-phen *n.* A punctuation mark (-) used to show connection between two or more words. **hyphen** *v.*

hy-phen-ate *v.* To separate or join with a hyphen. **hyphenation** *n.*

hyp-no-sis *n.*, *pl.* **hypnoses** A state that resembles sleep but is brought on or induced by another person whose suggestions are accepted by the subject.

hyp-not-ic *adj.* Inducing sleep. *n.* An agent, such as a drug, which induces sleep; a sedative; a person subject to hypnotic influence or under the influence of hypnotism. **-ally** *adv.*

hyp-no-tism *n.* The study or act of inducing hypnosis. **hypnotist** *n.*

hyp-no-tize *v.* To induce hypnosis; to be dazzled by; to be overcome by suggestion.

hy-po *n.*, *pl.* **hypos** *Slang* A hypodermic needle or syringe.

hy-po-chon-dri-a *n.* A mental depression accompanied by imaginary physical ailments. **hypochondriac** *n. & adj.*, **hypochondriacal** *adj.*

hy-po-der-mic sy-ringe *n.* A syringe and hypodermic needle used for injecting a substance into one's body.

hy-po-gly-ce-mia *n.* An unusual decrease of sugar in the blood.

hy-poth-e-sis *n.* An assumption made in order to draw out and test the logical consequences.

hy-po-thy-roid-ism *n.* A condition which lowers the metabolic rate of the thyroid gland causing loss of vigor.

hyp-ox-ia *n.* A condition which causes a deficiency of oxygen reaching the tissues of the body.

hyp-sog-ra-phy *n.* The branch of geography which deals with the measurement of the varying elevations of the earth's surface.

hy-rax *n.* A small ungulate mammal with thickset body, short legs and ears and a rudimentary tail.

hys-sop *n.* An aromatic herb from the mint family.

hys-ter-ec-to-my *n.*, *pl.* **-ies** Surgery on a female which partially or completely removes the uterus.

hys-ter-ia *n.* A psychological condition characterized by emotional excess and or unreasonable fear.

hys-ter-ic *n.* A person suffering from hysteria. *pl.*, *n.* A fit of uncontrollable laughter or crying; hysteria.

hys-ter-i-cal *adj.* Emotionally out of control. **hysterically** *adv.*

I, i The ninth letter of the English alphabet; the Roman numeral for one.

I *pron.* The person speaking or writing. *n.* The self; the ego.

I *or* **i** *abbr.* Island; isle.

IA *abbr.* Iowa.

i-amb *or* **i-am-bus** *n.* A metrical foot consisting of a short or unstressed syllable followed by an accented syllable. **iambic** *adj. & n.*

-i-at-ric *adj.* Pertaining to medicine or a physician.

i-at-ro-gen-ic *adj.* Induced inadvertently by a physician or his treatment. **iatrogenically** *adv.*

ib *or* **ibid** *abbr., L.* Ibidem, in the same place.

I band *n.* A band of the striated muscle fiber.

I-beam *n.* A steel girder or crossbeam with an I-shaped cross section.

i-bex *n.*

An Old World mountain goat with long curved horns.

ibid *abbr.* ibidem.

i-bi-dem *adv.* Used in footnotes to indicate a part of literary work that was just mentioned.

i-bis *n.* A long-billed wading bird related to the heron and stork.

IBM *abbr.* Intercontinental ballistic missile.

Ibo *n.* A person of the Negro people who live around the area of the lower Niger.

ICA *abbr.* International Cooperation Administration.

ice *n.* Solidly frozen water; a dessert of crushed ice which is flavored and sweetened. *Informal* Extreme coldness of manner. *v.* To change into ice; to cool or chill; to cover with icing. **icily** *adv.*, **iciness** *n.*, **icy** *adj.*

ice age *n.*, *Geol.* A time of widespread glaciation.

ice ax *n.* A pick and adz that has a spiked handle that is used for mountain climbing.

ice bag *n.* A small, flexible, waterproof bag designed to hold ice, used on parts of the body.

ice-berg *n.* A thick mass of floating ice separated from a glacier.

ice-blink *n.* A luminous appearance under a cloud or near the horizon, caused by the reflection of light on distant formations of ice.

ice-boat *n.* A vehicle with runners and usually a sail, used for sailing over ice; an icebreaker.

ice-boat-ing *n.* A sport of sailing in iceboats. **iceboater** *n.*

ice-bound *adj.* Obstructed or covered by ice so as to be inaccessible or immovable.

ice-box *n.* A structure designed for holding ice in which food and other perishables are stored.

ice-break-er *n.* A sturdy vessel for breaking a path through icebound waters; a pier or dock apron for deflecting floating ice from the base of a pier or bridge.

ice cap *n.* An extensive perennial covering of ice and snow that covers a large area of land.

ice--cold *adj.* To be very cold; freezing.

ice cream *n.* A smooth mixture of milk, cream, flavoring, sweeteners, and other ingredients, beaten and frozen.

ice--cream chair *n.* An armless chair small in size having a circular seat.

ice--cream cone *n.* A crisp and edible cone for the purpose of holding ice cream.

ice-fall *n.* A waterfall which is frozen.

ice field *n.* Pieces of glaciers that have joined and frozen together causing a sheet of ice so large that one cannot see its end.

ice floe *n.* A mass of sea ice that floats free upon the water.

ice fog *n.* A type of fog that is composed of many ice particles.

ice hock-ey *n.* A version of hockey which is played on ice.

ice-house *n.* A building for the purpose of storing ice.

Icel *abbr.* Icelandic.

Ice-land *n.* An island country in the North Atlantic near the Arctic Circle. **Icelander** *n.*, **Icelandic** *adj.*

Ice-land moss *n.* A kind of lichen of the arctic areas which can be used for food.

Ice-land pop-py *n.* A type of perennial poppy having small pastel flowers.

ice-man *n.* A man who is able to travel upon the ice with ease; one who delivers and sells ice.

ice milk *n.* A food similar to ice cream but made with skim milk.

ice nee-dle *n.* A slender ice particle which floats in the air in cold weather.

ice pack *n.* A large mass of floating, compacted ice; a folded bag filled with ice and applied to sore parts of the body.

ice pick *n.* A pointed tool used for breaking ice into small pieces.

ice plant *n.* An herb of the Old World that is related to the carpetweed.

ice point *n.* A temperature of zero degrees centigrade.

ice sheet *n.* A glacier.

ice show *n.* An entertaining show involving ice skaters.

ice skate *n.* A shoe or boot with a runner fixed to it for skating on ice. **ice-skate** *v.*, **ice skater** *n.*

ice storm *n.* a type of storm with frozen rain.

ice water *n.* Water cooled by ice.

ich-nol-o-gy *n.* The study of fossil footprints of animals. **ichnological** *adj.*

ich-thy-ol-o-gy *n.* The zoological study of

fishes. **ichthyologic,**
ich-thy-o-log-i-cal *adj.*, **ichthyologist** *n.*

i-ci-cle *n.* A hanging spike of ice formed by dripping water that freezes.

ic-ing *n.* A sweet preparation for coating cakes and cookies.

i-ci-ness *n.* The state of being very cold or icy.

ic-ing *n.* The sweet preparation for frosting cakes.

i-con *or* **i-kon** *n.* A sacred Christian pictorial representation of Jesus Christ, the Virgin Mary, or other sacred figures.

i-con-o-clasm *n.* The attitude or practice of an iconoclast. **iconoclastic** *adj.*

i-con-o-clast *n.* One who opposes the use of sacred images; one who attacks traditional or cherished beliefs. **iconoclasm** *n.*, **iconoclastic** *adj.*

ico-nog-ra-phy *n.* A pictorial material illustrating a subject; a published work dealing with iconography.

icon-o-scope *n.* A camera tube containing an electron gun and a mosaic screen which produces a charge proportional to the light intensity of the image on the screen.

i-cy *adj.* Covered with or consisting of ice; extremely cold; freezing; characterized by coldness.

id *n., Psychol.* The unconscious part of the psyche associated with instinctual needs and drives.

I'd *contr.* I had; I should; I would.

ID *abbr.* Idaho.

ID *abbr.* Identification.

I-da-ho *n.* A state located in the northwest part of the United States.

i-de-a *n.* Something existing in the mind; conception or thought; an opinion; a plan of action.

i-de-al *n.* A concept or imagined state of perfection; highly desirable; perfect; an ultimate objective; an honorable principle or motive. *adj.* Conforming to absolute excellence. **ideally** *adv.*, **idealness** *n.*

i-de-al-ism *n.* The practice or tendency of seeing things in ideal form; pursuit of an ideal; a philosophical system believing that reality consists of ideas or perceptions.

i-de-al-ist *n.* A person who practices or advocates idealism in writing.

i-de-al-is-tic *adj.* To be pertaining to idealism or idealists.

i-de-al-i-ty *n.* The state of being ideal.

i-de-al-ize *v.* To regard or represent as ideal. **idealization** *n.*

i-de-al-ly *adv.* In respect to an ideal; theoretically.

i-de-al point *n.* The point added to a space to eliminate special cases.

i-de-ate *v.* To make an idea of something.

i-de-ation *n.* The act of forming ideas.

i-de-ation-al *adj.* To be pertaining to ideation; referring to ideas of objects not immediately present to the senses.

i-dem *pron. & adj., L.* The same; used to indicate a previously mentioned reference.

i-dem-po-tent *adj.* To be pertaining to a mathematical quantity that is not zero.

i-den-tic *adj.* Constituting an expression which a government follows precisely the same course.

i-den-ti-cal *adj.* Being the same; exactly equal or much alike; designating a twin or twins developed from the same ovum. **identically** *adv.*, **-ness** *n.*

i-den-ti-fi-a-ble *adj.* Having the capability of being identified or recognized. **identifiably** *adv.*

i-den-ti-fi-ca-tion *n.* The act of identifying; the state of being identified; a means of identity.

i-den-ti-fi-er *n.* A person who identifies someone or something.

i-den-ti-fy *v.* To recognize the identity of; to establish as the same or similar; to equate; to associate oneself closely with an individual or group. **identifiable** *adj.*

i-den-ti-ty *n., pl.* **-ties** The condition or state of being a specific person or thing and recognizable as such; the condition or fact of being the same as something else; individuality.

i-den-ti-ty cri-sis *n.* A type of psychosocial confusion that arises when one is unable to attain psychological identification due to demands that conflict and other pressures.

i-den-ti-ty ele-ment *n.* The element which leaves an element of a set to which it belongs unchanged when it is combined with that element such as, $1 \times 3 = 3$, where 1 is the identity element.

id-e-o-gram *or* **id-e-o-graph** *n.* A pictorial symbol used in a writing system to represent an idea or thing, as Chinese characters; a graphic symbol, as $ or %.

id-e-og-ra-phy *n.* A representation of some ideas by the use of graphic symbols.

id-eo-log-i-cal *adj.* Concerned with ideas.

id-e-o-logue *n.* A person who adheres to a particular ideology.

i-de-ol-o-gy *n., pl.* **-gies** A body of ideas that influence a person, group, culture, or political party. **ideological** *adj.*

ides *pl., n.* In the ancient Roman calendar, the fifteenth day of March, May, July, and October or the thirteenth day of the other months.

-i-din *n., suffix* A chemical compound that is related in structure to another compound.

id-i-o *comb. form* Personal; distinct; separate.

id-i-o-blast *n.* A type of plant cell which differs from neighboring cells in a great manner. **idioblastic** *adj.*

id-i-o-cy *n., pl.* **-cies** A condition of an idiot.

id-i-o-graph-ic *adj.* Pertaining to the concrete or unique.

id-i-o-lect *n.* The speech patterns of an individual at a period of time in his life. **idiolectal** *adj.*

id-i-om *n.* A form of expression having a meaning that is not readily understood from the meaning of its component words; the dialect of people or a region; a kind of language or vocabulary.

id-i-o-mat-ic *adj.* Pertaining to an idiom; being peculiar to a group.

id-i-o-mor-phic *adj.* To have the right or proper shape. **idiomorphically** *adj.*

id-i-o-path-ic *adj.* To be peculiar to an individual. **idiopathically** *adv.*

id-i-o-syn-cra-sy *n.,* *pl.* **-sies** A peculiarity, of behavior. **idiosyncratic** *adj.,* **-ically** *adv.*

id-i-ot *n.* A mentally deficient person; an extremely foolish or stupid person.

idiotic *adj.* Showing of complete lack or thought or common sense by someone. **idiotically** *adv.,* **-alness** *n.*

id-i-ot sa-vant *n.* A person who mentally defective but exhibits exceptional skill.

i-dle *adj.* Doing nothing; inactive; moving lazily; slowly; running at a slow speed or out of gear; unemployed or inactive. **idleness,** **idler** *n.,* **idly** *adv.*

id-ler pul-ley *n.* A type of guiding pulley which is used for a chain or a belt.

id-ler wheel *n.* A kind of wheel or roller which is used to transfer motion to something.

id-lesse *n.* The state of being idle.

i-do-crase *n.* A type of mineral which is a complex silicate of calcium, iron, magnesium, and aluminum.

i-dol *n.* A symbol or representation of a god or deity that is worshiped; a person or thing adored.

i-dol-a-ter *n.* The worship of idols; blind adoration; devotion. **idolater** *n.*

i-dol-a-trous *adj.* Pertaining to idolatry; having a character of idolatry. **idolatrousness** *n.,* **idolatrously** *adv.*

i-dol-a-try *n.* An immoderate attachment to something.

i-dol-ize *v.* To admire with excessive admiration or devotion; to worship as an idol. **idolization,** **idolizer** *n.*

IDP *abbr.* Integrated data processing.

i-dyll *or* **i-dyl** *n.* A poem or prose piece about country life; a scene, event, or condition of rural simplicity; a romantic interlude. **-ic** *adj.,* **idyllically** *adv.*

i-dyll-ist *n.* A person who composes idylls.

IE *abbr.* Industrial engineer.

-ie *suff.* Little; dear.

IEA *abbr.* International Education Association.

IEEE *abbr.* Institute of Electrical and Electronic Engineers.

if *conj.* On the condition that; allowing that; supposing or granting that.

if-fy *adj., Slang* Marked by unknown qualifies or conditions.

IFO *abbr.* Identified flying object.

I for-ma-tion *n.* A kind of offensive football formation where the players form a line directly behind the quarterback.

ig-loo *n.* A dome-shaped Eskimo dwelling or hut often made of blocks of snow.

ig-ne-ous *adj., Geol.* Relating to fire; formed by solidification from a molten magma.

ig-nes-cent *adj.* To be capable of giving off sparks.

ig-nis fat-u-us *n.* A type of light which will appear over marshy ground in the night and it is often attributable to the combustion of gas from organic matter that is decomposed.

ig-nite *v.* To start or set a fire; to render luminous by heat. **igniter** *n.,* **ignitable, ignitible** *adj.,* **ignitability** *n.*

ig-ni-tion *n.* An act or action of igniting; a process or means for igniting the fuel mixture in an engine.

ig-ni-tron *n.* A type of mercury-containing rectifier tube.

ig-no-ble *adj.* Dishonorable in character or purpose; not of noble rank; mean, worthless; of a low family or birth right. **ignobly** *adv.,* **ignobleness** *n.*

ig-no-min-i-ous *adj.* Marked by or characterized by shame or disgrace; dishonorable. **ignominiously** *adv.*

ig-no-min-y *n.* A disgraceful conduct or action; dishonor; shame. **-iousness** *n.,* **ignominiously** *adv.,* **ignominious** *adj.*

ig-no-ra-mus *n.* A totally ignorant person.

ig-no-rance *n.* The state of being ignorant.

ig-no-rant *adj.* Lacking education or knowledge; not aware; lacking comprehension. **ignorantness** *n.*

ig-no-ra-tio elen-chi *n.* An act to disprove something which is not an issue.

ig-nore *v.* To pay no attention to; to reject; to disregard; refuse to consider, recognize or notice. **ignorable** *adj.*

Igo-rot *n.* Person who is a member of the group of people of Luzon, Philippines.

i-gua-na *n.*

A large, dark-colored tropical American lizard.

i-guan-odon *n.* A member of the genus of the gigantic herbivorous dinosaurs which are from the early Cretaceous of England.

IGY *abbr.* International Geophysical Year.

IHP *abbr.* Indicated horsepower.

ike-ba-na *n.* A Japanese art of arranging flowers that emphasizes balance and form.

IL *abbr.* Illinois.

ilang--ilang *n.* A type of tree from the custard-apple family which has a very fragrant greenish yellow flowers.

-ile *adj., suffix* Capable of.

il-e-i-tis *n.* Inflammation of the ileum.

il-e-um *n., pl.* **ilea** The lower part of the small intestine between the jejunum and the large intestine.

ile-us n. A functional obstruction of the bowel.

ilex n. A type of European evergreen oak which is located in the southern region.

il-i-ac adj. Pertaining to the ilium.

Il-i-ad n. An epic in the Homeric tradition; a series of disastrous events.

il-i-um n. The largest bone of the pelvis.

ilk n. Sort; kind.

ill adj. Not healthy; sick; destructive in effect; harmful; hostile; unfriendly; not favorable; not up to standards. adv. In an ill manner; with difficulty; scarcely. n. Evil; injury or harm; something causing suffering.

Ill abbr. Illinois.

I'll contr. I will; I shall.

ill-ad-vised adj. Done without careful thought or sufficient advice.

il-la-tion n. Action of inferring.

il-la-tive n. A phrase which introduces an inference. **illatively** adv.

il-laud-able adj. To be deserving no praise. **illaudably** adv.

ill-be-ing n. The state of being deficient in one's health or prosperity.

il-bod-ing adj. To be boding evil.

ill-bred adj. Ill-mannered; impolite; rude.

il-le-gal adj. Contrary to law or official rules. **illegality** n., **illegally** adv.

il-le-gal-ize v. To declare illegal. **illegalization** n.

il-leg-i-ble adj. Not readable; not legible. **illegibly** adv., **illegibility** n.

il-le-git-i-mate adj. Against the law; unlawful; born out of wedlock. **illegitimacy** n., **illegitimately** adv.

ill-fat-ed adj. Destined for misfortune; doomed; unlucky; that which causes or marks the beginning of misfortune.

ill-fa-vored adj. Unattractive; objectionable; offensive; unpleasant.

ill-got-ten adj. Obtained in an illegal or dishonest way.

ill-hu-mored adj. Irritable; cross.

il-lib-er-al adj. To be lacking or missing culture or refinement. **illiberalness**, **illiberality** n., **illiberally** adv.

il-lib-er-al-ism n. A lack of liberalism.

il-lic-it adj. Not permitted by custom or law; unlawful. **illicitly** adv.

il-lim-it-able adj. To be incapable of being bounded or limited in any way. **illimitably** adv., **illimitability** n.

Il-li-nois n. A state located in the central part of the northern United States. **Illinoisan** adj. & n.

il-liq-uid adj. Not being readily convertible into cash. **liquidity** n.

il-lite n. A clay mineral that has essentially the crystal structure of muscovite. **illitic** adj.

il-lit-er-ate adj. Unable to read and write; uneducated; having or showing a lack of knowledge of fundamentals on a particular subject. **illiteracy**, **illiterate** n., **illiterately** adv.

ill-man-nered adj. Lacking or showing a lack of good manners; rude; having bad manners.

ill-na-tured adj. Disagreeable or unpleasant disposition. **ill-naturedly** adv.

ill-ness n. Sickness; a state of being in poor health; the unhealthy condition of ones body or mind.

il-log-ic n. The state or quality of being illogical.

il-log-i-cal adj. Contrary to the principles of logic; not logical. -ity, **illogicalness** n., **illogically** adv.

ill-sort-ed adj. To be not matched well.

ill-tem-pered adj. Having or showing a cross temper or disposition.

ill-treat v. To treat someone or something improperly or cruelly.

il-lu-mi-nate v. To give light; to make clear; to provide with understanding; to decorate with pictures or designs; spiritually or intellectually enlightened. **illumination**, -or n.

il-lu-mi-na-tive adj. Pertaining to or producing illumination.

il-lu-mi-nism n. A claim to a personal enlightenment which is not accessible to mankind in general.

ill-us-age n. An unkind treatment toward someone or something.

ill-use v. To treat cruelly or unjustly. n. Unjust treatment.

il-lu-sion n. A misleading perception of reality; an overly optimistic idea or belief; misconception; the act of deceiving. **illusive**, **illusory** adj.

il-lu-sion-ary adj. To be factual; a matter-of-fact.

il-lu-sion-ism n. The action of using artistic techniques that creates an illusion of reality. **illusionistic**, **illusionist** adj.

il-lus-trate v. To explain or clarify, especially by the use of examples; to clarify by serving as an example; to provide a publication with explanatory features. **illustrator**, **illustrational** n.

il-lus-tra-tion n. The act of illustrating; an example or comparison used to illustrate.

il-lus-tra-tive adj. Serving, designed, or tending to illustrate. **-ly** adv.

il-lus-tri-ous adj. Greatly celebrated; renowned; brilliantly outstanding because of actins or achievements. **illustriousness** n., **illustriously** adv.

il-lu-vi-al adj. To be pertaining to or marked by illuviation.

il-lu-vi-ate v. To go through illuviation.

il-lu-vi-a-tion n. A gathering of dissolved soil materials in an area as the result of eluviation form another.

il-lu-vi-um n. The material that is leached from one soil horizon to another soil horizon.

ill will n. Unfriendly or hostile feelings; malice.

ill-wisher n. A person who wishes ill or harm to another.

il-men-ite n. A type of massive black mineral which is made of iron, oxygen, and titanium.

I'm contr. I am.

im-age n. A representation of the form and features of someone or something; an optically formed representation of an object made by a mirror or lens; a mental picture of something imaginary. *v.* To make a likeness of; to reflect; to depict vividly.

im-ag-ery *n., pl.* **-ies** Mental pictures; existing only in the imagination.

im-ag-in-a-ble *adj.* Capable of being imagined. **imaginably** *adv.,* **-ness** *n.*

im-ag-i-nar-y *adj.* Existing only in the imagination. **imaginarily** *adv.*

im-ag-i-nar-y num-ber *n.* A complex number where its imaginary part is not zero, 2 + 6i.

im-ag-i-nar-y part *n.* The portion of a complex number which has an imaginary unit as a factor such as the 2i in 7 + 2i.

im-ag-i-nar-y un-it *n.* A positive square root of negative one, -1.

im-ag-i-na-tion *n.* The power of forming mental images of unreal or absent objects; such power used creatively; resourcefulness.
imaginative *adj.,* **imaginatively** *adv.*

im-ag-ine *v.* To form a mental picture or idea of; to suppose; to guess.

im-ag-ism *n.* The movement in poetry in the 20th century where expression of ideas and emotions are through precise images.
imagistically *adj.,* **imagist** *n.*

i-ma-go *n., pl.* **-goes** *or* **-gines** An insect in its sexually mature adult stage; the idealized image of self or another person.

i-mam *n.* A prayer leader of Islam; rulers that claim descent from Muhammad.

imam-ate *n.* The country which is ruled over by an imam; office of an imam.

ima-ret *n.* A hospice of Turkey.

im-bal-ance *n.* A lack of functional balance; defective coordination.

im-be-cile *n.* A mentally deficient person who requires supervision in the daily routine of caring for himself.
imbecilic *adj.,* **imbecilely** *adv.*

im-be-cil-i-ty *n.* The state of being an imbecile.

im-bibe *v.* To drink; to take into the mind and retain; to absorb light, heat, gas, or moisture. **imbiber** *n.*

im-bi-bi-tion *n.* The action of imbibing. **imbibitional** *adj.*

im-bri-cate *adj.* With edges overlapping in a regular arrangement, as roof tiles or fish scales. **imbricately** *adv.*

im-bri-ca-tion *n.* A pattern which shows imbrication or overlapping.

im-bro-glio *n., pl.* **-glios** A complicated situation or disagreement; a confused heap; a tangle; an embarrassing or painful misunderstanding.

im-brue *v.* To drench something.

im-brute *v.* To degrade someone to the level of that of a brute.

im-bue *v.* To saturate, or penetrate as with a stain or dye.

imdtly *abbr.* Immediately.

IMF *abbr.* International Monetary Fund.

im-id-az-ole *n.* A type of white crystalline which is an antimetabolite that i related to histidine.

im-ide *n.* A type of compound whic contains the NH group and is derive from ammonia. **imidic** *adj.*

im-i-do *adj.* To be pertaining to th group NH which is united to a radica which is not an acid radical.

im-ine *n.* A kind of compound that ha an NH group and is derived fro ammonia with the replacement of tw hydrogen atoms by a hydrocarbon.

im-i-no *adj.* To be pertaining to the NH group which is united to a radica which is not an acid radical.

imip-ra-mine *n.* A kind of antidepres sant drug.

imit *abbr.* Imitative.

im-i-ta-ble *adj.* Capable or worthy of im itation.

im-i-tate *v.* To copy the actions or ap pearance of another; to adopt the styl of; to duplicate; to appear like.
imitator *n.*

im-i-ta-tion *n.* An act of imitating; some thing copied from an original.

im-i-ta-tive *adj.* To be marked by imita tion. **imitatively** *adv.*

im-mac-u-la-cy *n.* The state of some thing being immaculate.

im-mac-u-late *adj.* Free from sin, stair or fault; impeccably clean.
immaculately *adv.,* **immaculateness** *n.*

im-mane *adj.* To be large or monstrou in character.

im-ma-nence *n.* The quality of bein immanent.

im-ma-nent *adj.* Existing within restricted to the mind; subjective.
immanence, immanency *n.,* **-ly** *adv.*

im-ma-nent-ism *n.* A theory accordin to which God or other spirit is im manent in the world. **immanentist** *n.*

im-ma-te-ri-al *adj.* Lacking materia body or form; of no importance o relevance. **immaterially** *adv.,* **-ness** *n*

im-ma-te-ri-al-ism *n.* The theory whic believes that external bodies are in es sence mental. **immaterialist** *n.*

im-ma-te-ri-al-i-ty *n.* The state of bein immaterial.

im-ma-te-ri-al-ize *v.* To cause or t make something immaterial.

im-ma-ture *adj.* Not fully grown; un developed; suggesting a lack o maturity. **immaturely** *adv.,*
immaturity, immatureness *n.*

im-meas-ur-a-ble *adj.* Not capable c being measured. **immeasurably** *adv.,* **immeasurableness** *n.*

im-me-di-a-cy *n., pl.* **-ies** The quality c being immediate; directness; some thing of urgent importance.

im-me-di-ate *adj.* Acting or happenin without an intervening object, agen or cause; directly perceived; occurrin at once; close in time, location, o relation; being next in time.

im-me-di-ate con-stit-u-ent *n.* A mean ingful constituent that directly forms bigger linguistic construction.

im-me-di-ate-ly *adv.* In direct relationship or connection.

im-me-mo-ri-al *adj.* Beyond the limits of memory, tradition, or records. immemorially *adv.*

im-mense *adj.* Exceptionally large. immensely *adv.*, immenseness *n.*

im-men-si-ty *n.* The state of something being immense or very large in size.

im-merge *v.* To immerse someone or oneself into something such as water.

im-merse *v.* To put into a liquid; to baptize by submerging in water; to engross; to absorb. immersible *adj.*, immersion *n.*

im-mersed *adj.* To be growing completely underwater such as a plant.

im-mers-ible *adj.* Having the capability of being totally underwater without damaging any working parts.

im-mersion *n.* The act or state of being totally immersed.

im-me-thod-i-cal *adj.* Not being methodical. immethodically *adv.*

im-mi-grant *n.* One who leaves his country to settle in another and who takes up permanent residence in the new country.

im-mi-grate *v.* To leave one country and settle in another; to bring in as immigrants. -ion *n.*, immigrational *n.*

im-mi-nent *adj.* About to happen or take place. imminentness *n.*, imminence *n.*, imminently *adv.*

im-min-gle *v.* To intermingle or to blend into something such as a group.

im-mis-ci-ble *adj.* To be incapable of attaining homogeneity or mixing. immiscibly *adv.*, immiscibility *n.*

im-mit-i-ga-ble *adj.* To not be capable of being mitigated. immitigableness *n.*, immitigably *adv.*

im-mix *v.* To mix something intimately.

im-mo-bile *adj.* Not moving or incapable of motion. immobility *n.*

im-mo-bi-lize *v.* To render motionless, preventing movement. immobilization, immobilizer *n.*

im-mod-er-a-cy *n.* The lack of moderation.

im-mod-er-ate *adj.* Exceeding normal bounds. immoderately *adv.*, immoderateness, immoderation *n.*

im-mod-est *adj.* Lacking modesty; indecent; boastful. immodestly *adv.*, immodesty *n.*

im-mo-late *v.* To kill, as a sacrifice; to destroy completely. immolator *n.*

im-mor-al *adj.* Not moral; confliction with moral principles. immorally *adv.*

im-mor-al-ist *n.* One who practices immorality.

im-mo-ral-i-ty *n.*, *pl.* -ies Lack of morality; an immoral act or practice.

im-mor-tal *adj.* Exempt from death; lasting forever, as in fame. *n.* A person of lasting fame. -ity *n.*, immortally *adv.*

im-mor-tal-ize *v.* To make something immortal. -ation, immortalizer *n.*

im-mo-tile *adj.* To be lacking motility. immotility *n.*

im-mov-a-ble *adj.* Not capable of moving or being moved. immovably *adv.*, immovability, immovableness *n.*

immun *abbr.* Immunization.

im-mune *adj.* Not affected or responsive; resistant, or protected as to a disease.

im-mu-ni-ty *n.* The state at which something is immune.

im-mu-nize *v.* To make immune.-ation *n.*

im-mu-no-as-say *n.* An identification of a substance by the way it acts as an antigen. immunoassayable *adj.*

im-mu-no-chem-is-try *n.* The part of chemistry which deals with the chemical aspect of immunology. -ist *n.*, immunochemical *adj.*, -ically *adv.*

im-mu-no-dif-fu-sion *n.* A separation of antigens by the way they pass through a semipermeable membrane.

im-mu-no-gen-e-sis *n.* The production of immunity. immunogenicity *n.*, immunogenic *adj.*, -ically *adv.*

im-mu-no-ge-net-ics *n.* A branch of immunology concerned with heredity, disease, and the immune system and its components. immunogenetic *adj.*, immunogenetically *adv.*

im-mu-no-glob-u-lin *n.* A type of protein which is made up of heavy and light chains and is used as an antibody by the body.

immunol *abbr.* Immunology.

im-mu-nol-o-gy *n.* The study of immunity to diseases. immunologic, immunological *adj.*, -ically *adv.*

im-mu-no-pa-thol-o-gy *n.* The branch of medicine dealing with immunologic abnormalities. immunopathologist *n.*, immunopathological *adj.*

im-mu-no-re-ac-tive *adj.* To be reacting to an antigen. immunoreactivity *n.*

im-mu-no-sup-pres-sion *n.* The suppression of the body's natural immune responses. immunosuppressant *adj.*, immunosuppressive *adj.*

im-mu-no-sup-pres-sive *adj.* Acting to suppress a natural immune response to an antigen.

im-mu-no-ther-a-py *n.* The treatment of disease by the means of antigenic preparations or with antigens.

im-mure *v.* To confine by or as if by walls; to build into a wall. -ment *n.*

im-mu-ta-ble *adj.* Unchanging or unchangeable. immutability *n.*, -y *adv.*

imp *n.* A mischievous child.

im-pact *n.* A collision; the impetus or force produced by a collision; an initial, usually strong effect. *v.* To pack firmly together; to strike or affect forcefully. impactive *adj.*

im-pac-ted *adj.* Wedged together at the broken ends, as an impacted bone; wedged inside the gum in such a way that normal eruption is prevented, as an impacted tooth.

im-pac-tion *n.* Something wedged in a part of the body.

im-pac-tor *n.* The one which impacts; a kind of tool or instrument which is used for the purpose of collecting samples of suspended particles.

im-pair *v.* To diminish in strength, value,

quantity, or quality.

impairer, impairment *n.*

im-pa-la *n.* A large African antelope, the male of which has slender curved horns.

im-pale *v.* To pierce with a sharp stake or point; to kill by piercing in this fashion. **impalement** *n.*

im-pal-pa-ble *adj.* Not perceptible to touch; not easily distinguished. **impalpability** *n.*, **impalpably** *adv.*

im-pan-el *v.* To enroll on a panel.

im-par-a-dise *v.* To enrapture.

im-par-i-ty *n.* Disparity.

im-part *v.* To grant; to bestow; to convey; to make known; to communicate. **impartment, impartation** *n.*

im-par-tial *adj.* Not partial; unbiased. **impartiality** *n.*, **impartially** *adv.*

im-par-ti-ble *adj.* Being not subject to partition. **impartibly** *adv.*

im-pass-a-ble *adj.* Impossible to travel over or across. **-ness** *n.*, **-y** *adv.*

im-passe *n.* A road or passage having no exit; a difficult situation with no apparent way out; a deadlock.

im-pas-si-ble *adj.* To be inaccessible to an injury. **impassibility** *n.*, **-y** *adv.*

im-pas-sion *v.* To arouse the passions of someone by another person.

im-pas-sioned *adj.* To be filled with passion.

im-pas-sive *adj.* Unemotional; showing no emotion; expressionless. **-ly** *adv.*, **impassiveness, impassivity** *n.*

im-paste *v.* To make or form something into a crust or a paste.

im-pas-to *n.* A kind of raised decoration on ceramic ware. **impastoed** *adj.*

im-pa-tience *n.* The quality of being impatient.

im-pa-tiens *n.* A type of watery-juiced annual herb that has irregular saccate flowers.

im-pa-tient *adj.* Unwilling to wait or tolerate delay; expressing or caused by irritation at having to wait; restlessly eager; intolerant. **impatience** *n.*, **impatiently** *adv.*

im-pawn *v.* To put or place something in pawn.

im-peach *v.* To charge with misconduct in public office before a proper court of justice; to make an accusation against. **impeachable** *adj.*, **-ment** *n.*

im-pearl *v.* To form something into pearls.

im-pec-ca-ble *adj.* Having no flaws; perfect; not capable of sin. **impeccably** *adv.*, **impeccability** *n.*

im-pe-cu-ni-ous *adj.* Having no money. **impecuniousness, impecuniosity** *n.*, **impecuniously** *adv.*

im-ped-ance *n.* A measure of the total opposition to the flow of an electric current, especially in an alternating current circuit.

im-pede *v.* To obstruct or slow down the progress of.

im-ped-i-ment *n.* One that stands in the way; something that impedes, especially an organic speech defect.

im-ped-i-men-ta *pl.*, *n.* Things that impede or encumber, such as baggage.

im-pel *v.* To spur to action; to provoke to drive forward; to propel.

im-pel-ler *n.* One that impels something

im-pend *v.* To hover threateningly; to be about to happen.

im-pen-dent *adj.* To be near at hand.

im-pen-e-tra-bil-i-ty *n.* The inability of two parts of anything to occupy the same space at exactly the same time.

im-pen-e-tra-ble *adj.* Not capable of being penetrated; not capable of being seen through or understood; unfathomable. **impenetrableness** *n.*, **impenetrably** *adv.*

im-pen-i-tence *n.* The quality of being impenitent.

im-pen-i-tent *adj.* Not sorry; unrepentant. **impenitence** *n.*, **-ly** *adv.*

im-per-a-tive *adj.* Expressing a command or request; empowered to command or control; compulsory. **imperative** *n.*, **imperatively** *adv.*

im-pe-ra-tor *n.* The commander in chief of the ancient Romans. **-ial** *adj.*

im-per-cep-ti-ble *adj.* Not perceptible by the mind or senses; extremely small or slight. **-y** *adv.*, **imperceptibility** *n.*

im-per-cep-tive *adj.* Not being perceptive. **imperceptiveness** *n.*

im-per-cip-i-ence *n.* The state of being unperceptive.

im-per-cip-i-ent *adj.* Being not percipient.

imperf *abbr.* Imperforate.

im-per-fect *adj.* Not perfect; of or being a verb tense which shows an uncompleted or continuous action or condition. *n.* The imperfect tense. **imperfectly** *adv.*, **imperfectness** *n.*

im-per-fect fun-gus *n.* A type of fungus of which only the conidial stage is known.

im-per-fec-tion *n.* The quality or condition of being imperfect; a defect.

im-per-fec-tive *adj.* To be expressing action as being incomplete.

im-per-fo-rate *adj.* To have no opening lacking a normal opening.

im-pe-ri-al *adj.* Of or relating to an empire or emperor; designating a nation or government having dependent colonies; majestic; regal. *n.* A pointed beard on the lower lip or chin. **imperially** *adv.*

im-pe-ri-al-ism *n.* The national policy or practice of acquiring foreign territories or establishing dominance over other nations. **imperialist** *n.*, **imperialistic** *adj.*, **-ically** *adv.*

im-pe-ri-al moth *n.* A large New World moth with yellow wings and brownish or purplish markings.

im-per-il *v.* To put in peril; endanger.

im-pe-ri-ous *adj.* Commanding domineering; urgent. **imperiousness** *n.*, **imperiously** *adv.*

im-per-ish-a-ble *adj.* Not perishable permanently enduring. **imperishably** *adv.*, **imperishable** *n.*

im-pe-ri-um *n.* An absolute dominion

the right to employ the force of the state.

im-per-ma-nence n. The state of being impermanent.

im-per-ma-nen-cy n. The state of something being impermanent.

im-per-ma-nent adj. Not permanent; temporary. **impermanently** adv.

im-per-me-a-ble adj. Not permeable. **-ness, impermeability** n., **-y** adv.

im-per-mis-si-ble adj. Not permissible; not allowed. **-y** adv., **-ility** n.

im-per-son-al adj. Having no personal reference or connection; showing no emotion or personality. **impersonally** adv., **impersonality** n.

im-per-son-al-ize v. To make something impersonal. **impersonalization** n.

im-per-son-ate v. To assume the character or manner of. **impersonation, impersonator** n.

im-per-ti-nence n. The instance of impertinence.

im-per-ti-nent adj. Overly bold or disrespectful; not pertinent; irrelevant. **impertinently** adv.

im-per-turb-a-ble adj. Unshakably calm. **imperturbability** n., **imperturbably** adv.

im-per-vi-ous adj. Incapable of being penetrated or affected. **imperviously** adv., **imperviousness** n.

im-pe-tig-i-nous adj. To be pertaining to or related to impetigo.

im-pe-ti-go n. A contagious skin disease marked by pustules.

im-pe-trate v. To obtain something by a request. **impertration** n.

im-pet-u-os-i-ty n. An action which is impetuous.

im-pet-u-ous adj. Marked by sudden action or emotion; impulsive. **impetuosness** n., **impetuously** adv.

im-pe-tus n. A driving force; an incitement; a stimulus; momentum.

im-pi-e-ty n., pl. **-ies** The quality of being impious; irreverence.

im-pinge v. To strike or collide; to impact; to encroach. **impingement** n.

im-pi-ous adj. Not pious; irreverent; disrespectful. **impiously** adv.

imp-ish adj. Mischievous. **impishly** adv., **impishness** n.

im-pla-ca-ble adj. Not capable of being placated or appeased. **implacability** n., **implacably** adv.

im-plant v. To set in firmly; to fix in the mind; to insert surgically. **implant, implantation** n.

im-plau-si-ble adj. Difficult to believe; unlikely. **implausibility** n., **-y** adv.

im-plead v. To prosecute by law.

im-ple-ment n. A utensil or tool. v. To put into effect; to carry out; to furnish with implements. **implementation** n.

im-pli-cate v. To involve, especially in illegal activity; to imply.

im-pli-ca-tion n. The act of implicating or state of being implicated; the act of implying; an indirect expression; something implied. **implicatively** adv.

im-plic-it adj. Contained in the nature of someone or something but not readily apparent; understood but not directly expressed; complete; absolute.

im-plode v. To collapse or burst violently inward. **implosion** n.

im-plore v. To appeal urgently to. **implorer** n., **imploringly** adv.

im-plo-sion n. The action of bringing to a center. **implosive** adj.

im-ply v. To involve by logical necessity; to express indirectly; to suggest.

im-po-lite adj. Rude. **impoliteness** n., **impolitely** adv.

im-pol-i-tic adj. Not expedient; tactless. **impolitically** adv.

im-pon-der-a-ble adj. Incapable of being weighed or evaluated precisely. **imponderableness, imponderable** n.

im-pone v. To bet or to wager.

im-port v. To bring in goods from a foreign country for trade or sale; to mean; to signify; to be significant. n. Something imported; meaning; significance; importance. **importer** n., **importable** adj.

im-por-tance n. The quality of being important; significance.

im-por-tant adj. Likely to determine or influence events; significant; having fame or authority. **importantly** adv.

im-por-ta-tion n. the act or business of importing goods; something which is imported by a country.

im-port-ed cab-bage-worm n. A type of small white butterfly which is a pest of cruciferous plants such as cabbage.

im-port-ed fire ant n. A type of small South American ant which is destructive in the southeastern U.S.

im-por-tu-nate adj. Persistent in pressing demands or requests. **-ly** adv.

im-por-tune v. To press with repeated requests. **importunity, importuner** n.

im-pose v. To enact or apply as compulsory; to obtrude or force oneself or a burden on another; to take unfair advantage; to palm off. **imposer, imposition** n.

im-pos-ing adj. Awesome; impressive. **imposingly** adv.

im-po-si-tion n. The act of imposing upon someone or something; an excessive or uncalled for burden.

im-pos-si-ble adj. Not capable of existing or happening; unlikely to take place or be done; unacceptable; difficult to tolerate or deal with. **impossibility** n., **impossibly** adv.

im-post n. A tax or duty.

im-pos-tor or **im-pos-ter** n. One who assumes a false identity or title for the purpose of deception.

im-pos-tume n. A type of abscess.

im-pos-ture n. Deception by the assumption of a false identity.

im-po-tent adj. Without strength or vigor; having no power; ineffectual; incapable of sexual intercourse. **impotence, impotency** n., **-ly** adv.

im-pound v. To confine in or as if in a pound; to seize and keep in legal custody; to hold water, as in a reservoir.

im-pound-ment n. A type of a body of

water which is formed by impounding.

im-pov-er-ish v. To make poor; to deprive or be deprived of natural richness or fertility. **impoverishment** n.

im-pov-er-ish-ed adj. To be poor.

im-prac-ti-ca-ble adj. Incapable of being done or put into practice. **-ness**, **impracticability** n., **impracticably** adv.

im-prac-ti-cal adj. Unwise to put into effect; unable to deal with practical or financial matters efficiently. **impracticality** n.

im-pre-cate v. To utter curses or to invoke evil upon someone or something. **im-pre-ca-tion** n. An act of imprecating. **imprecatory** adj.

im-pre-cise adj. Not precise.

im-preg-na-ble adj. To be beyond question or criticism.

im-preg-nate v. To make pregnant; to fertilize, as an ovum; to fill throughout; to saturate. **impregnation, impregnator** n.

im-pre-sa n. A type of device that was used in the 16th and 17th century that had a motto.

im-pre-sa-ri-o n., pl. **-os** A theatrical manager or producer, especially the director of an opera company.

im-press v. To apply or produce with pressure; to stamp or mark with or as if with pressure; to fix firmly in the mind; to affect strongly and usually favorably. n. The act of impressing; a mark made by impressing; a stamp or seal for impressing. **impressible** adj., **impresser** n.

im-pres-sion n. A mark or design made on a surface by pressure; an effect or feeling retained in the mind as a result of experience; an indistinct notion or recollection; a satiric or humorous imitation; the copies of a publication printed at one time.

im-pres-sion-a-ble adj. Easily influenced. **impressionably** adv.

im-pres-sion-ism n. A style of late nineteenth century painting in which the immediate appearance of scenes is depicted with unmixed primary colors applied in small strokes to simulate reflected light.

im-pres-sion-ist n. A person who adheres to the theories of impressionism.

im-pres-sion-is-tic adj. Pertaining to impressionism.

im-pres-sive adj. Making a strong impression; striking. **impressively** adv., **impressiveness** n.

im-press-ment n. An act of seizing something for public use.

im-pres-sure n. A type of mark which is made by the application of pressure.

im-prest n. An advance of money.

im-pri-ma-tur n. Official permission to print or publish; authorization.

im-pri-mis adv. In the first place.

im-print v. To make or impress a mark or design on a surface; to make or stamp a mark on; to fix firmly in the mind. n. A mark or design made by

imprinting; a lasting influence or effect; a publisher's name, often with the date and place of publication, printed at the bottom of a title page.

im-print-ing n. A type of behavior pattern which is established early in the life of a member of a social species.

im-pris-on v. To put in prison. **-ment** n.

im-prob-a-ble adj. Not likely to occur or be true. **improbability** n., **-y** adv.

im-promp-tu adj. Devised or performed without prior planning or preparation.

im-prop-er adj. Unsuitable; indecorous; incorrect. **improperly** adv.

im-prop-er frac-tion n. A fraction having a numerator larger than or the same as the denominator.

im-prop-er in-te-gral n. A type of definite integral.

im-pro-pri-e-ty n., pl. **-ies** The quality or state of being improper; an improper act or remark.

im-prove v. To make or become better; to increase something's productivity or value. **improvable** adj.

im-prove-ment n. The act or process of improving or the condition of being improved; a change that improves.

im-prov-i-dent adj. Not providing for the future. **improvidence** n., **-ly** adv.

im-pro-vise v. To make up, compose, or perform without preparation; to make from available materials. **-ation**, **improviser, -ator** n., **improvisatory, improvisatorial** adj., **-atorially** adv.

im-pru-dent adj. Not prudent; unwise. **imprudence** n., **imprudently** adv.

im-pu-dent adj. Marked by rude boldness or disrespect. **-ce** n., **-ly** adv.

im-pu-dic-i-ty n. A lack of modesty.

im-pugn v. To attack as false; to cast doubt on. **impugner** n.

im-puis-sance n. A weakness.

im-puis-sant adj. Being weak.

im-pulse n. A driving force or the motion produced by it; a sudden spontaneous urge; a motivating force; a general tendency. Physiol. A transfer of energy from one neuron to another.

im-pulse buy-ing n. The buying of items and merchandise on an impulse.

im-pul-sion n. The state of being impelled.

im-pul-sive adj. Acting on impulse rather than thought; resulting from impulse; uncalculated. **impulsively** adv., **impulsiveness** n.

im-pu-ni-ty n. Exemption from punishment.

im-pure adj. Not pure; unclean; unchaste or obscene; mixed with another substance; adulterated; deriving from more than one source or style. **impurely** adv., **impureness, impurity** n.

im-pu-ta-tion n. An act of imputing. **imputative** adj.

im-pute v. To attribute something as a mistake, to another; to charge.

in abbr. Inch.

IN or **In** abbr. Indiana.

in-abil-i-ty n. A lack of sufficient power or capacity.

in ab·sen·tia *adv.* In the absence of.

in·ac·ces·si·ble *adj.* Not accessible.
inaccessibility *n.*, **inaccessibly** *adv.*

in·ac·cu·ra·cy *n.* The state of being inaccurate. **inaccurately** *adv.*

in·ac·tion *n.* The lack of activity or lack of action.

in·ac·ti·vate *v.* To make something or someone inactive.

in·ac·tive *adj.* Not active or inclined to be active; out of current use or service. **inactively** *adv.*, **inactivity**, **-ness** *n.*

in·ad·e·quate *adj.* Not adequate. **inadequacy** *n.*, **inadequately** *adv.*

in·ad·ver·tence *n.* The action of something being inadvertent.

in·ad·ver·tent *adj.* Unintentional; accidental; inattentive. **-ly** *adv.*

in·ad·vis·a·ble *adj.* Being not advisable. **inadvisability** *n.*

in·al·ien·a·ble *adj.* Not capable of being given up or transferred. **inalienably** *adv.*, **inalienability** *n.*

in·al·ter·a·ble *adj.* Being not alterable. **inalterability** *n.*

in·amo·ra·ta *n.* The woman with whom a person is in love with.

in--and--in *adv. or adj.* Being in repeated generations of the same related stock families.

in·ane *adj.* Without sense or substance. **inanely** *adv.*, **inanity** *n.*

in·an·i·mate *adj.* Not having the qualities of life; not animated. **inanimately** *adv.*, **inanimateness** *n.*

in·a·ni·tion *n.* Exhaustion, especially from malnourishment.

inan·i·ty *n.* The state of being inane.

in·ap·par·ent *adj.* Being not apparent. **inapparently** *adv.*

in·ap·pe·tence *n.* The loss of the appetite.

in·ap·pre·cia·ble *adj.* Too slight to be significant. **inappreciably** *adv.*

in·ap·pre·cia·tive *adj.* Being not appreciative. **inappreciatively** *adv.*

in·ap·proach·a·ble *adj.* Being not approachable.

in·ap·pro·pri·ate *adj.* Being not appropriate. **inappropriateness** *n.*

in·apt *adj.* Being not suitable or not apt. **inaptness** *n.*, **inaptly** *adv.*

in·ap·ti·tude *n.* The lack of aptitude.

in·ar·gu·a·ble *adj.* Being not arguable. **inarguably** *adv.*

in·ar·tic·u·late *adj.* Not uttering or forming intelligible words or syllables; unable to speak; speechless; unable to speak clearly or effectively; unexpressed. **inarticulately** *adv.*, **-ness** *n.*

in·as·much as *conj.* Because of the fact that; since.

in·at·ten·tion *n.* Not paying attention.

in·au·gu·ral *adj.* Of or for an inauguration.

in·au·gu·rate *v.* To put into office with a formal ceremony; to begin officially. **inauguration**, **inaugurator** *n.*

in--be·tween *adj.* Intermediate. *n.* An intermediate or intermediary.

in between *adv. & prep.* Between.

in·board *adj.* Within a ship's hull; close to or near the fuselage of an aircraft.

in·born *adj.* Possessed at birth; natural; hereditary.

in·bound *adj.* Incoming.

in·bounds *adj.* Pertaining to putting the ball into play by throwing or passing it onto a court such as with the game of basketball.

in·breathe *v.* To breath something such as a small particle in the air into the lungs.

in·bred *adj.* To be rooted into someone's nature possibly by hereity.

in·breed *v.* To produce by repeatedly breeding closely related individuals.

in·breed·ing *n.* The act of interbreeding of individuals which are closely related to preserve desirable characteristics of the stock or thing being breed.

in·built *adj.* To be built into something.

inc *or* **Inc** *abbr.* Income; increase;incorporated.

In·ca *n.*, *pl.* **-ca** *or* **-cas** An Indian people who ruled Peru before the Spanish conquest in the sixteenth century.

in·cal·cu·la·ble *adj.* Not calculable; indeterminate; unpredictable; very large. **incalculably** *adv.*

in·can·des·cent *adj.* Giving off visible light when heated; shining brightly; ardently emotional or intense. **incandescence** *n.*

incandescent lamp *n.*

A lamp in which a filament is heated to incandescence by an electric current.

in·can·ta·tion *n.* A recitation of magic charms or spells; a magic formula for chanting or reciting.

in·ca·pa·ble *adj.* Lacking the ability for doing or performing.

in·ca·pac·i·tate *v.* To render incapable; to disable; in law, to disqualify. **incapacitation** *n.*

in·ca·pac·i·ty *n.*, *pl.* **-ies** Inadequate ability or strength; a defect; in law, a disqualification.

in·car·cer·ate *v.* To place in jail. **incarceration** *n.*

in·car·nate *v.* To give actual form to.

in·car·na·tion *n.* The act of incarnating or state of being incarnated; the embodiment of God in the human form of Jesus; one regarded as personifying a given abstract quality or idea.

in·cen·di·ar·y *adj.* Causing or capable of causing fires; of or relating to arson; tending to inflame; inflammatory.

in·cense *v.* To make angry. *n.* A substance, as a gum or wood, burned to produce a pleasant smell; the smoke or odor produced.

in·cen·tive *n.* Something inciting one to action or effort; a stimulus.

in·cep·tion *n.* A beginning; an origin. **inceptive** *adj.*

in·cer·ti·tude *n.* Uncertainty; lack of confidence; instability.

in·ces·sant *adj.* Occurring without interruption; continuous. **incessantly** adv.

in-cest n. Sexual intercourse between persons so closely related that they are forbidden by law to marry. **incestuous** adj., **incestuously** adv.

inch n. A unit of measurement equal to 1/12th of a foot. v. To move slowly.

in-cho-ate adj. In an early stage; incipient. **inchoately** adv., **-ness** n.

in-ci-dence n. The extent or rate of occurrence.

in-ci-dent n. An event; an event that disrupts normal procedure or causes a crisis.

in-ci-den-tal adj. Occurring or likely to occur at the same time or as a result; minor; subordinate. n. A minor attendant occurrence or condition. **-ly** adv.

in-cin-er-ate v. To burn up. **-ion** n.

in-cin-er-a-tor n. One that incinerates; a furnace for burning waste.

in-cip-i-ent adj. Just beginning to appear or occur. **incipience** n., **-ly** adv.

in-cise v. To make or cut into with a sharp tool; to carve into a surface; to engrave.

in-ci-sion n. The act of incising; a cut or notch, especially a surgical cut.

in-ci-sive adj. Having or suggesting sharp intellect; penetrating; cogent and effective; telling. **incisively** adv., **incisiveness** n.

in-ci-sor n.

A cutting tooth at the front of the mouth.

in-cite v. To provoke to action. **incitement**, **inciter** n.

in-clem-ent adj. Stormy or rainy; unmerciful. **inclemency** n.

in-cli-na-tion n. An attitude; a disposition; a tendency to act or think in a certain way; a preference; a bow or tilt; a slope.

in-cline v. To deviate or cause to deviate from the horizontal or vertical; to slant; to dispose or be disposed; to bow or nod. n. An inclined surface.

in-cli-nom-e-ter n. An apparatus for indicating the direction of the earth's magnetic field in reference to the plane of the horizon.

in-clude v. To have as a part or member; to contain; to put into a group or total. **inclusion** n., **-ive** adj., **-ively** adv.

in-cog-ni-to adv. & adj. With one's identity hidden.

in-cog-ni-zant adj. Lacking awareness.

in-co-her-ent adj. Lacking order, connection, or harmony; unable to think or speak clearly or consecutively. **incoherence** n., **incoherently** adv.

in-com-bus-ti-ble adj. Incapable of burning. **incombustible** n.

in-come n. Money or its equivalent received in return for work or as profit from investments.

income tax n. A tax on income earned by an individual or business.

in-com-ing adj. Coming in or soon to come in.

in-com-men-su-rate adj. Not commensurate; disproportionate. **-ly** adv.

in-com-mode v. To inconvenience; to disturb.

in-com-mu-ni-ca-do adv. & adj. Without being able to communicate with others.

in-com-pa-ra-ble adj. Incapable of being compared; without rival. **-y** adv.

in-com-pat-i-ble adj. Not suited for combination or association; inconsistent. **incompatibility** n., **incompatibly** adv.

in-com-pe-tent adj. Not competent. **incompetence**, **incompetency** n.

in-com-plete adj. Not complete; lacking. **incompletely** adv., **incompleteness** n.

in-com-pre-hen-si-ble adj. Being unable to understand.

in-con-ceiv-a-ble adj. Impossible to understand.

in-con-clu-sive adj. Having no definite result.

in-con-dite adj. Being put together badly.

in-con-gru-ous adj. Not corresponding; disagreeing; made up of diverse or discordant elements; unsuited to the surrounding or setting. **incongruity** n., **incongruously** adv.

in-con-se-quen-tial adj. Without importance; petty. **inconsequentially** adv.

in-con-sid-er-a-ble adj. Unimportant; trivial. **inconsiderably** adv.

in-con-sid-er-ate adj. Not considerate; thoughtless. **inconsiderately** adv., **inconsiderateness** n.

in-con-sis-tent adj. Lacking firmness, harmony, or compatibility; incoherent in thought or actions.

in-con-sol-a-ble adj. Not capable of being consoled. **inconsolably** adv.

in-con-spic-u-ous adj. Not readily seen or noticed. **inconspicuously** adv., **inconspicuousness** n.

in-con-stant adj. Likely to change; unpredictable; faithless; fickle. **inconstancy** n., **inconstantly** adv.

in-con-sum-able adj. Unfit to be consumed.

in-con-ti-nent adj. Not restrained; uncontrolled; unable to contain or restrain something specified; incapable of controlling the excretory functions. **incontinence** n., **-ly** adv.

in-con-tro-vert-i-ble adj. Unquestionable; indisputable. **-y** adv.

in-con-ven-ience n. The quality or state of being inconvenient; something inconvenient. v. To cause inconvenience to; to bother.

in-con-ven-ient adj. Not convenient. **inconveniently** adv.

in-co-or-di-na-tion n. The lack of coordination of muscular functions resulting from loss of voluntary control.

in-cor-po-rate v. To combine into a unified whole; to unite; to form or cause to form a legal corporation; to give a physical form to; to embody.

incorporation, incorporator n.
in-cor-po-re-al adj. Without material
form or substance. Incorporeally adv.
in-cor-ri-gi-ble adj. Incapable of being
reformed or corrected. incorrigibility,
incorrigible n., incorrigibly adv.
in-cor-rupt-i-ble adj. Not capable of
being corrupted morally; not subject
to decay. incorruptibility n., -y adv.
in-crease v. To make or become greater
or larger; to have offspring; to
reproduce. n. The act of increasing;
the amount or rate of increasing.
increasingly adv.
in-cred-i-ble adj. Too unlikely to be
believed; unbelievable; extraordinary;
astonishing. incredibility n., -y adv.
in-cred-u-lous adj. Skeptical; disbeliev-
ing; expressive of disbelief.
incredulity n., incredulously adv.
in-cre-ment n. An increase; something
gained or added, especially one of a
series of regular additions. -al adj.
in-crim-i-nate v. To involve in or charge
with a wrongful act, as a crime.
incrimination n., incriminatory adj.
in-cu-bate v. To warm and hatch eggs, as
by bodily heat or artificial means; to
maintain a bacterial culture in
favorable conditions for growth.-ion n.
in-cu-ba-tor n. A cabinet in which a
desired temperature can be maintained, used for bacterial culture; an
enclosure for maintaining a premature
infant in a controlled environment; a
temperature controlled enclosure for
hatching eggs.
in-cu-bus n., pl. -buses or -bi An evil
spirit believed to seize or harm sleeping persons; a nightmare; a
nightmarish burden.
in-cul-cate v. To impress on the mind by
frequent repetition or instruction.
inculcation, inculcator n.
in-cul-pate v. To incriminate.
in-cum-bent adj. Lying or resting on
something else; imposed as an obligation; obligatory; currently in office. n.
A person who is currently in office.
incumbency n., incumbently adv.
in-cu-nab-u-lum n., pl. -la A book
printed before 1501.
in-cur v. To become liable or subject to,
especially because of one's own actions. incurrence n.
in-cur-able adj. Unable to be cured of a
disease.
in-cu-ri-ous adj. Lacking interest;
detached.
in-cur-sion n. A sudden hostile intrusion
into another's territory.
in-cur-vate v. To cause something to
curve inward.
in-cus n., pl. incudes An anvil-shaped
bone in the middle ear of mammals.
Ind abbr. Indiana.
in-debt-ed adj. Obligated to another, as
for money or a favor; beholden.
indebtedness n.
in-de-cent adj. Morally offensive or contrary to good taste. indecency n.,
indecently adv.

in-de-ci-pher-a-ble adj. Not capable of
being deciphered or interpreted.
in-de-ci-sion n. Inability to make up
one's mind; irresolution.
in-de-ci-sive adj. Without a clear-cut
result; marked by indecision.
indecisively adv., indecisiveness n.
in-dec-o-rous adj. Lacking good taste or
propriety. indecorously adv., -ness n.
in-deed adv. Most certainly; without
doubt; in reality; in fact. interj. Used
to express surprise, irony, or disbelief.
in-de-fat-i-ga-ble adj. Tireless. -y adv.
in-de-fen-si-ble adj. Incapable of being
justified; not able to protect against a
physical fight.
in-de-fin-a-ble adj. Not capable of being
defined. -ness n., indefinably adv.
in-def-i-nite adj. Not decided or
specified; vague; unclear; lacking fixed
limits. indefinitely adv., -ness n.
in-del-i-ble adj. Not able to be erased or
washed away; permanent. -y adv.
in-del-i-cate adj. Lacking sensitivity; tactless. indelicacy n., indelicately adv.
in-dem-ni-fy v. To secure against hurt,
loss, or damage; to make compensation for hurt, loss, or damage.
indemnification, indemnifier n.
in-dem-ni-ty n., pl. -ties Security against
hurt, loss, or damage; a legal exemption from liability for damages; compensation for hurt, loss, or damage.
in-dent v. To set in from the margin, as
the first line of a paragraph; to notch
the edge of; to serrate; to make a dent
or depression in; to impress; to stamp.
n. An indentation.
in-den-ta-tion n. The act of indenting or
the state of being indented; an angular
cut in an edge; a recess in a surface.
in-den-ture n. A legal deed or contract; a
contract obligating one party to work
for another for a specified period of
time. v. To bind into the service of
another.
in-de-pend-ence n. The quality or state of
being independent.
In-de-pend-ence Day n. July 4, a legal
holiday in the United States, com-
memorating the adoption of the Declaration of Independence in 1776.
in-de-pend-ent adj. Politically self-
governing; free from the control of
others; not committed to a political
party or faction; not relying on others,
especially for financial support;
providing or having enough income to
enable one to live without working. n.
One who is independent, especially a
candidate or voter not committed to a
political party. independently adv.
in--depth adj. Thorough; detailed.
in-de-scrib-a-ble adj. Surpassing description; incapable of being described.
indescribably adv.
in-de-struc-ti-ble adj. Unable to be
destroyed.
in-de-ter-mi-nate adj. Not determined;
not able to be determined; unclear or
vague. indeterminacy n., -ly adv.
in-dex n., pl. -dexes or -dices A list for

aiding reference, especially an alphabetical listing in a printed work which gives the pages on which various names, places, and subjects are mentioned; something serving to guide or point out, especially a printed character calling attention to a paragraph or section; something that measures or indicates; a pointer, as in an instrument; in mathematics, a small number just above and to the left of a radical sign indicating what root is to be extracted; any number or symbol indicating an operation to be performed on a expression; a number or scale indicating change in magnitude, as of prices, relative to the magnitude at some specified point usually taken as one hundred (100). *v.* To provide with or enter in an index; to indicate; to adjust through.

in-dex-a-tion *n.* The linkage of economic factors, as wages or prices, to a cost-of-living index so they rise and fall within the rate of inflation.

in-dex fin-ger *n.*

The finger next to the thumb.

in-dex of re-frac-tion *n.* The quotient of the speed of light in a vacuum divided by the speed of light in a medium under consideration.

In-di-a *n.* A country in southern Asia.

In-di-an *n.* A native or inhabitant of India; a member of any of various aboriginal peoples of the Americas.

Indian corn *n.* A tall American cereal grass bearing seeds on elongated ears.

Indian Ocean *n.* An ocean that extends from southern Asia to Antarctica and from eastern Africa to southeastern Australia.

In-di-an-a *n.* A state located in the central part of the northern United States. **Indianian** *n.* & *adj.*

In-di-an sum-mer *n.* A period of mild weather in late autumn.

in-di-cate *v.* To point out; to show; to serve as a sign or symptom; to signify; to suggest the advisability of; to call for. **indication, indicator** *n.*

in-dic-a-tive *adj.* Serving to indicate; of or being a verb mood used to express actions and conditions that are objective facts. *n.* The indicative mood; a verb in the indicative mood.

in-di-ca-tor *n.* A pressure gauge; a dial that registers pressures, etc.

in-dict *v.* To accuse of an offense; to charge; to make a formal accusation against by the findings of a grand jury. **indictable** *adj.*, **-er, -or, indictment** *n.*

in-dif-fer-ent *adj.* Having no marked feeling or preference; impartial; neither good nor bad. **indifference** *n.*, **indifferently** *adv.*

in-dig-e-nous *adj.* Living or occurring naturally in an area; native.

in-di-gent *adj.* Impoverished; needy. **indigence** *n.*

in-di-ges-tion *n.* Difficulty or discomfor in digesting food.

in-dig-nant *adj.* Marked by or filled with indignation. **indignantly** *adv.*

in-dig-na-tion *n.* Anger aroused by injustice, unworthiness, or unfairness.

in-dig-ni-ty *n.*, *pl.* **-ies** Humiliating treatment; something that offends one's pride.

in-di-go *n.*, *pl.* **-gos** or **-goes** A blue dye obtained from a plant or produced synthetically; a dark blue.

in-di-go bunt-ing *n.* A small North American bird, the male of which has deep-blue plumage.

in-di-go snake *n.* A non-venomous bluish-black snake found in the southern United States and northern Mexico.

in-di-rect *adj.* Not taking a direct course; not straight to the point. **indirection** *n.*, **indirectly** *adv.*

in-dis-creet *adj.* Lacking discretion. **indiscreetly** *adv.*, **indiscretion** *n.*

in-dis-pen-sa-ble *adj* Necessary; essential. **indispensability, indispensable** *n.*, **indispensably** *adv.*

in-dis-posed *adj.* Mildly ill. **-ition** *n.*

in-dis-tin-guish-able *adj.* Unable to determine in shape or structure; not clearly recognizable; lacking identity.

in-dite *v.* To write; to compose; to put down in writing. **inditer** *n.*

in-di-um *n.* A soft, silver-white, metallic element used for mirrors and transistor compounds, symbolized by In.

in-di-vid-u-al *adj.* Of, for, or relating to a single human being. **individually** *adv.*

in-di-vis-i-ble *adj.* Not able to be divided.

In-do-china *n.* The southeastern peninsula of Asia.

in-doc-tri-nate *v.* To instruct in a doctrine or belief; to train to accept a system of thought uncritically. **indoctrination** *n.*

In-do--Eu-ro-pe-an *n.* A family of languages comprising most of the languages of Europe and parts of southern Asia. **Indo-European** *adj.*

in-do-lent *adj.* Disinclined to exert oneself; lazy. **indolence** *n.*

in-dom-i-ta-ble *adj.* Incapable of being subdued or defeated. **indomitably** *adv.*

In-do-ne-sia *n.* A country of southeastern Asia. **Indonesian** *adj.* & *n.*

in-du-bi-ta-ble *adj.* Too evident to be doubted. **indubitably** *adv.*

in-duce *v.* To move by persuasion or influence; to cause to occur; to infer by inductive reasoning. **inducer** *n.*

in-duce-ment *n.* The act of inducing; something that induces.

in-duct *v.* To place formally in office; to admit as a new member; to summon into military service. **inductee** *n.*

in-duc-tance *n.* A circuit element, usually a conducting coil, in which electromagnetic induction generates electromotive force.

in-duc-tion n. The act of inducting or of being inducted; reasoning in which conclusions are drawn from particular instances or facts; the generation of electromotive force in a closed circuit by a magnetic field that changes with time; the production of an electric charge in an uncharged body by bringing a charged body close to it.

in-dulge v. To give in to the desires of, especially to excess; to yield to; to allow oneself a special pleasure. **-er** n.

in-dult n. A special dispensation granted in the Roman Catholic Church.

in-du-rate v. To make stubborn; to make hardy. **indurative** adj., **induration** n.

in-dus-tri-al adj. Of, relating to, or used in industry. **industrially** adv.

industrial arts n.,pl. A subject taught in schools that teaches manual skills and familiarity with tools and machines.

in-dus-tri-ous adj. Working steadily and hard; diligent.
industriously adv., **industriousness** n.

in-dus-try n., pl. **-tries** The commercial production and sale of goods and services; a branch of manufacture and trade; industrial management as distinguished from labor; diligence.

in-e-bri-ate v. To make drunk; to intoxicate. **inebriated**.
inebriant adj. & n., **inebriation** n.

in-ef-fa-ble adj. Beyond expression; indescribable. **ineffably** adv.

in-ef-fi-cient adj. Wasteful of time, energy, or materials. **inefficiency** n., **inefficiently** adv.

in-e-luc-ta-ble adj. Not capable of being avoided or overcome. **ineluctably** adv.

in-ept adj. Awkward or incompetent; not suitable. **ineptitude**, **ineptness** n., **ineptly** adv.

in-e-qual-i-ty n., pl. **-ies** The condition or an instance of being unequal; social or economic disparity; lack of regularity; in mathematics, an algebraic statement that a quantity is greater than or less than another quantity.

in-eq-ui-ty n., pl. **-ies** Injustice; unfairness.

in-ert adj. Not able to move or act; slow to move or act; sluggish; displaying no chemical activity.
inertly adv., **inertness** n.

in-er-tia n. The tendency of a body to remain at rest or to stay in motion unless acted upon by an external force; resistance to motion or change.
inertial adj., **inertially** adv.

in-ev-i-ta-ble adj. Not able to be avoided or prevented. **inevitability** n., **inevitably** adv.

in-ex-o-ra-ble adj. Not capable of being moved by entreaty; unyielding. **-y** adv.

in-ex-pe-ri-ence n. Lack of experience.

in-ex-pli-ca-ble adj. Not capable of being explained. **inexplicably** adv.

in ex-tre-mis adv. At the point of death.

in-ex-tri-ca-ble adj. Not capable of being untied or untangled; too complex to resolve. **inextricably** adv.

in-fal-li-ble adj. Not capable of making mistakes; not capable of failing; never wrong. **infallibility** n., **infallibly** adv.

in-fa-mous adj. Having a very bad reputation; shocking or disgraceful. **infamously** adv.

in-fa-my n., pl. **-ies** Evil notoriety or reputation; the state of being infamous; a disgraceful, publicly known act.

in-fan-cy n., pl. **-ies** The condition or time of being an infant; an early stage of existence; in law, minority.

in-fant n. A child in the first period of life; a very young child; in law, a minor.

in-fan-ti-cide n. The killing of an infant.

in-fan-tile adj. Of or relating to infants or infancy; immature; childish.

in-fan-tile pa-ra-ly-sis n. Poliomyelitis.

in-fan-try n., pl. **-ries** The branch of an army made up of soldiers who are trained to fight on foot. **-man** n.

in-farct n. An area of dead tissue caused by an insufficient supply of blood.
infarcted adj., **infarction** n.

in-fat-u-ate v. To arouse an extravagant or foolish love in.
infatuated adj., **infatuation** n.

in-fect v. To contaminate with disease-causing microorganisms; to transmit a disease to; to affect as if by contagion.

in-fec-tion n. Invasion of a bodily part by disease-causing microorganisms; the condition resulting from such an invasion; an infectious disease.

in-fe-lic-i-tous adj. Not happy; unfortunate; not apt, as in expression.
infelicity n., **infelicitously** adv.

in-fer v. To conclude by reasoning; to deduce; to have as a logical consequence; to lead to as a result or conclusion. **inferable** adj.

in-fer-ence n. A conclusion based on facts and premises.

in-fe-ri-or adj. Located under or below; low or lower in order, rank, or quality. **inferior**, **inferiority** n.

in-fer-nal adj. Of, like, or relating to hell; damnable; abominable. **-ly** adv.

in-fer-no n. A place or condition suggestive of hell.

in-fest v. To spread in or over so as to be harmful or offensive. **infestation** n.

in-fi-del n. One who has no religion; an unbeliever in a religion, especially Christianity.

in-field n. In baseball, the part of a playing field within the base lines.

in-fil-trate v. To pass or cause to pass into something through pores or small openings; to pass through or enter gradually or stealthily. **infiltration** n.

in-fi-nite adj. Without boundaries; limitless; immeasurably great or large; in mathematics, greater in value than any specified number, however large; having measure that is infinite.
infinite n., **infinitely** adv.

in-fin-i-tes-i-mal adj. Immeasurably small. **infinitesimally** adv.

in-fin-i-ty n., pl. **-ies** The quality or state

of being infinite; unbounded space, time, or amount; an indefinitely large number.

in-firm *adj.* Physically weak, especially from age; feeble; not sound or valid.

in-fir-ma-ry *n., pl.* -ries An institution for the care of the sick or disabled.

in-flame *v.* To set on fire; to arouse to strong or excessive feeling; to intensify; to produce, affect or be affected by inflammation.

in-flam-ma-ble *adj.* Tending to catch fire easily; easily excited.

in-flam-ma-tion *n.* Localized redness, swelling, heat, and pain in response to an injury or infection.

in-flate *v.* To fill and expand with a gas; to increase unsoundly; to puff up; to raise prices abnormally. inflatable *adj.*

in-fla-tion *n.* The act or process of inflating; a period during which there is an increase in the monetary supply, causing a continuous rise in the price of goods.

in-flect *v.* To turn; to veer; to vary the tone or pitch of the voice, especially in speaking; to change the form of a word to indicate number, tense, or person. inflective *adj.*, inflection *n.*

in-flex-i-ble *adj.* Not flexible; rigid; not subject to change; unalterable. inflexibility *n.*, inflexibly *adv.*

in-flict *v.* To cause to be suffered; to impose. inflicter, inflictor, -ion *n.*

in-flo-res-cence *n.*

A characteristic arrangement of flowers on a stalk. inflorescent *adj.*

in-flu-ence *n.* The power to produce effects, especially indirectly or through an intermediary; the condition of being affected; one exercising indirect power to sway or affect. *v.* To exert influence over; to modify. influential *adj.*

in-flu-en-za *n.* An acute, infectious viral disease marked by respiratory inflammation, fever, muscular pain, and often intestinal discomfort; the flu.

in-flux *n.* A stream of people or things coming in.

in-form-ant *n.* One who discloses or furnishes information which should remain secret.

in-for-ma-tive *adj.* Providing information; instructive.

in-frac-tion *n.* A violation of a rule.

in-fra-red *adj.* Of, being, or using electromagnetic radiation with wave lengths longer than those of visible light and shorter than those of microwaves.

in-fra-son-ic *adj.* Producing or using waves or vibrations with frequencies below that of audible sound.

in-fra-struc-ture *n.* An underlying base or foundation; the basic facilities needed for the functioning of a system.

in-fringe *v.* To break a law; to violate; to encroach; to trespass. infringement *n.*

in-fu-ri-ate *v.* To make very angry or furious; to enrage. infuriatingly *adv.*, infuriation *n.*

in-fuse *v.* To introduce, instill or inculcate, as principles; to obtain a liquid extract by soaking a substance in water. infusion *n.*

-ing *suff* Used in forming the present participle of verbs and adjectives resembling participles; activity or action; the result or a product of an action.

in-gen-ious *adj.* Showing great ingenuity; to have inventive ability; clever. ingeniously *adv.*, ingeniousness *n.*

in-ge-nu-i-ty *n., pl.* -ies Cleverness; inventive skill.

in-gen-u-ous *adj.* Frank and straightforward; lacking sophistication.

in-gest *v.* To take or put food into the body by swallowing. -ion *n.*, -ive *adj.*

in-gle-nook *n.* A recessed area or corner near or beside a fireplace.

in-glo-ri-ous *adj.* Not showing courage or honor; dishonorable. -ly *adv.*

in-got *n.* A mass of cast metal shaped in a bar or block.

in-grain *v.* To impress firmly on the mind or nature. *n.* Fiber or yarn that is dyed before being spun or woven.

in-grained *adj.* To be worked into the inmost texture; deep-seated.

in-grate *n.* A person who is ungrateful.

in-gra-ti-ate *v.* To gain favor or confidence of others by deliberate effort or manipulation. ingratiatingly *adv.*, ingratiation *n.*, ingratiatory *adj.*

in-grat-i-tude *n.* Lack of gratitude.

in-gre-di-ent *n.* An element that enters into the composition of a mixture; a part of anything.

in-gress *n.* A going in or entering of a building. ingression *n.*, ingressive *adj.*

in-grown *adj.* Growing into the flesh; growing abnormally within or into.

in-gui-nal *adj., Anat.* Of, pertaining to, or located in the groin.

in-hab-it *v.* To reside in; to occupy as a home. inhabitability, inhabiter, inhabitation *n.*, inhabitable *adj.*

in-hab-i-tant *n.* A person who resides permanently, as distinguished from a visitor.

in-ha-la-tion *n.* The act of inhaling.

in-ha-la-tor *n.* A device that enables a person to inhale air, anesthetics, medicated vapors, or other matter.

in-hale *v.* To breathe or draw into the lungs, as air or tobacco smoke; the opposite of exhale. inhalation *n.*

in-hal-er *n.* One that inhales; a respirator.

in-here *v.* To be an essential or permanent feature; to belong.

in-her-ent *adj.* Forming an essential element or quality of something. inherently *adv.*

in-her-it *v.* To receive something, as

property, money, or other valuables, by legal succession or will. *Biol.* To receive traits or qualities from one's ancestors or parents.
inheritable *adj.*, **inheritor** *n.*

in-her-i-tance *n.* The act of inheriting; that which is inherited or to be inherited by legal transmission to a heir.

in-her-i-tance tax *n.* A tax imposed on an inherited estate.

in-hib-it *v.* To restrain or hold back; to prevent full expression. **-able** *adj.*, **inhibitor, -er** *n.*, **-ive, inhibitory** *adj.*

in-hi-bi-tion *n.* The act of restraining, especially a self-imposed restriction on one's behavior; a mental or psychological restraint.

in--house *adj.* Of, relating to, or carried on within an organization.

in-hu-man *adj.* Lacking pity, emotional warmth, or kindness; monstrous; not being of the ordinary human type.

in-hu-mane *adj.* Lacking compassion or pity; cruel. **inhumanely** *adv.*

in-hu-man-i-ty *n., pl.* **-ties** The lack of compassion or pity; an inhumane or cruel act.

in-im-i-cal *adj.* Harmful opposition; hostile; malign. **inimically** *adv.*

in-im-i-ta-ble *adj.* Incapable of being matched; unique. **inimitably** *adv.*

in-iq-ui-ty *n., pl.* **-ies** The grievous violation of justice; wickedness; sinfulness. **iniquitous** *adj.*

in-i-tial *adj.* Of or pertaining to the beginning. *n.* The first letter of a name or word. *v.* To mark or sign with initials. **initially** *adv.*

in-i-ti-ate *v.* To begin or start; to admit someone to membership in an organization, fraternity, or group; to instruct in fundamentals. *adj.* Initiated. **initiator** *n.*, **initiatory** *adj.*

in-i-ti-a-tive *n.* The ability to originate or follow through with a plan of action; the action of taking the first or leading step. *Govt.* The power or right to propose legislative measures.

in-ject *v.* To force a drug or fluid into the body through a blood vessel or the skin with a hypodermic syringe; to throw in or introduce a comment abruptly. **injection** *n.*

in-junc-tion *n.* An authoritative command or order; in law, a court order requiring the party to do or to refrain from some specified action. **-ive** *adj.*

in-jure *v.* To cause physical harm, damage, or pain.

in-ju-ri-ous *adj.* Causing injury, damage or hurt; slanderous; abusive. **injuriously** *adv.*, **injuriousness** *n.*

in-ju-ry *n., pl.* **-ies** Damage or harm inflicted or suffered.

in-jus-tice *n.* The violation of another person's rights; an unjust act; a wrong.

ink *n.* Any of variously colored liquids or paste, used for writing, drawing, and printing. **inker** *n.*

ink-horn *n.* A small container to hold ink.

ink-ling *n.* A slight suggestion or hint; a vague idea or notion.

ink-stand *n.* A stand or device for holding writing tools and ink.

ink-well *n.* A small container or reservoir for holding ink.

ink-y *adj.* Resembling ink in color; dark; black; containing or pertaining to ink.

in-laid *adj.* Ornamented with wood, ivory, or other materials embedded flush with the surface.

in-land *adj.* Pertaining to or located in the interior of a country. **inlander** *n.*

in--law *n.* A relative by marriage.

in-lay *v.* To set or embed something, as gold or ivory, into the surface of a decorative design.

in-let *n.* A bay or stream that leads into land; a passage between nearby islands.

in-mate *n.* A person who dwells in a building with another; one confined in a prison, asylum, or hospital.

inn *n.* A place of lodging where a traveler may obtain meals and/or lodging.

in-nards *pl. n., Slang* The internal organs or parts of the body; the inner parts of a machine.

in-nate *adj.* Inborn and not acquired; having as an essential part; inherent.

in-ner *adj.* Situated or occurring farther inside; relating to or of the mind or spirit.

in-ner ear *n.* The part of the ear which includes the semicircular canals, vestibule, and cochlea.

in-ner-most *adj.* Most intimate; farthest within.

in-ner tube *n.* A flexible, inflatable rubber tube placed inside a tire.

in-ning *n.* In baseball, one of nine divisions of a regulation baseball game, in which each team has a turn at bat. **innings** *pl.* In the game of cricket, the time or period during which one side bats.

inn-keep-er *n.* The proprietor or manager of an inn.

in-no-cent *adj.* Free from sin, evil, or moral wrong; pure; legally free from blame or guilt; not maliciously intended; lacking in experience or knowledge; naive. **innocence** *n.*, **innocent** *n.*, **innocently** *adv.*

in-noc-u-ous *adj.* Having no harmful qualities or ill effect; harmless.

in-nom-i-nate bone *n., Anat.* One of the two large, irregular bones which form the sides of the pelvis.

in-no-vate *v.* To introduce or begin something new. **-ive** *adj.*, **innovator** *n.*

in-nu-en-do *n., pl.* **-dos** or **-does** An indirect or oblique comment, suggestion or hint.

in-nu-mer-a-ble *adj.* Too numerous or too much to be counted; countless.

in-oc-u-late *v.* To introduce a mild form of a disease or virus to a person or animal in order to produce immunity.

in-op-er-a-ble *adj.* Unworkable; incapable of being treated or improved by surgery.

in-op-er-a-tive *adj.* Not working; not functioning.

in-op-por-tune *adj.* Inappropriate; untimely; unsuitable. **-ly** *adv.*, **inopportuneness** *n.*

in-or-di-nate *adj.* Exceeding proper or normal limits; not regulated; unrestrained. **inordinately** *adv.*

in-or-gan-ic *adj.* Not having or involving living organisms, their remains, or products.

in-pa-tient *n.* A patient admitted to a hospital for medical treatment.

in-put *n.* The amount of energy delivered to a machine; in computer science, information that is put into a dataprocessing system. *Elect.* The voltage, current, or power that is delivered to a circuit.

in-quest *n.* A legal investigation into the cause of death.

in-quire *v.* To ask a question; to make an investigation. **inquirer** *n.*, **-ingly** *adv.*

in-quir-y *n.*, *pl.* **-ies** The act of seeking or inquiring; a request or question for information; a very close examination; an investigation or examination of facts or evidence.

in-qui-si-tion *n.* A former Roman Catholic tribunal established to seek out and punish heretics; an interrogation that violates individual rights; an investigation. **inquisitor** *n.*, **inquisitorial** *adj.*

in-quis-i-tive *adj.* Curious; probing; questioning. **-ly** *adv.*, **-ness** *n.*

in-sane *adj.* Afflicted with a serious mental disorder impairing a person's ability to function; the characteristic of a person who is not sane. **insanely** *adv.*, **insanity** *n.*

in-san-i-tar-y *adj.* Not sanitary; not hygienic and dangerous to one's health.

in-scribe *v.* To write, mark, or engrave on a surface; to enter a name in a register or on a formal list; to write a short note on a card. *Geom.* To enclose one figure in another so that the latter encloses the former. **inscriber** *n.*

in-scru-ta-ble *adj.* Difficult to interpret or understand; incomprehensible. **inscrutability**, **-ness** *n.*, **-y** *adv.*

in-sect *n.*, *Zool.* Any of a numerous cosmopolitan class of small to minute winged invertebrate animals with 3 pairs of legs, a segmented body, and usually 2 pairs of wings.

in-sec-ti-cide *n.* A substance for killing insects.

in-sec-tiv-o-rous *adj.* Feeding on insects.

in-se-cure *adj.* Troubled by anxiety and apprehension; threatened; not securely guarded; unsafe; liable to break, fail, or collapse. **insecurely** *adv.*, **insecurity** *n.*

in-sem-i-nate *v.* To introduce semen into the uterus of; to make pregnant; to sow seed. **insemination**, **-or** *n.*

in-sen-sate *adj.* Showing a lack of humane feeling; unconscious.

in-sen-si-ble *adj.* Deprived of consciousness; unconscious; incapable of perceiving or feeling; unmindful; unaware. **insensibility** *n.*, **-y** *adv.*

in-sen-ti-ent *adj.* Without sensation or consciousness. **insentience** *n.*

in-sep-a-ra-ble *adj.* Incapable of being separated or parted. **inseparability** *n.*, **inseparably** *adv.*

in-sert *v.* To put in place; to set. *n.* In printing, something inserted or to be inserted. **insertion** *n.*

in-set *v.* To set in; to implant; to insert.

in-shore *adj.* Near or moving toward the shore. **inshore** *adv.*

in-side *n.* The part, surface, or space that lies within. **insides** *n.* The internal parts or organs. **inside** *adj.*

in-sid-er *n.* One having special knowledge or access to confidential information.

in-sid-i-ous *adj.* Cunning or deceitful; treacherous; seductive; attractive but harmful. **insidiously** *adv.*, **-ness** *n.*

in-sight *n.* Perception into the true or hidden nature of things. **insightful** *adj.*, **insightfully** *adv.*

in-sig-ni-a *n.*, *pl.* **-nia** *or* **-nias** A badge or emblem used to mark membership, honor, or office.

in-sin-cere *adj.* Not sincere; hypocritical. **insincerely** *adv.*, **insincerity** *n.*

in-sin-u-ate *v.* To suggest something by giving a hint; to introduce by using ingenious and sly means. **insinuating** *adv.*, **insinuation** *n.*

in-sip-id *adj.* Lacking of flavor; tasteless; flat; dull; lacking interest. **insipidly** *adv.*, **insipidness** *n.*

in-sist *v.* To demand or assert in a firm way; to dwell on something repeatedly, as to emphasize. **-ence** *n.*, **insistent** *adj.*, **insistently** *adv.*

in-so-far *adv.* To such an extent.

in-sole *n.* The fixed inside sole of a shoe or boot; a removable strip of material put inside a shoe for protection or comfort.

in-sol-u-ble *adj.* Incapable of being dissolved; not soluble; not capable of being solved. **insolubility**, **insolubleness** *n.*, **insolubly** *adv.*

in-sol-vent *adj.* In law, unable to meet debts; bankrupt.

in-som-ni-a *n.* The chronic inability to sleep. **insomniac** *n.*

in-sou-ci-ant *adj.* Lighthearted and cheerful; unconcerned; not bothered.

in-spect *v.* To examine or look at very carefully for flaws; to examine or review officially. **inspection**, **inspector** *n.*

in-spi-ra-tion *n.* The stimulation within the mind of some idea, feeling, or impulse which leads to creative action; a divine or holy presence which inspires; the act of inhaling air. **inspirational** *adj.*, **inspirationally** *adv.*

in-spire *v.* To exert or guide by a divine influence; to arouse and create high emotion; to exalt; to inhale; breathe in. **inspirer** *n.*, **inspiringly** *adv.*

inst *abbr.* Instant; institute; institution.

in-sta-bil-i-ty *n.*, *pl.* **-ties** Lacking stability.

in-stall *or* **in-stal** *v.* To put in position for service; to place into an office or position; to settle. **installation, installer** *n.*

in-stall-ment *or* **in-stal-ment** *n.* One of several payments due in specified amounts at specified intervals.

in-stance *n.* An illustrative case or example; a step in proceedings. *v.* To illustrate.

in-stant *n.* A very short time; a moment; a certain or specific point in time. *adj.* Instantaneously; immediate; urgent.

in-stan-ta-ne-ous *adj.* Happening with no delay; instantly; completed in a moment. **instantaneously** *adv.*

in-stant-ly *adv.* Immediately; at once.

in-stead *adv.* In lieu of that just mentioned.

in-step *n.*, *Anat.* The arched upper part of the human foot.

in-sti-gate *v.* To urge forward; to stir up; to foment; to provoke. **instigation, instigator** *n.*

in-still *or* **in-stil** *v.* To introduce by gradual instruction or effort; to pour in slowly by drops. **instillation, instiller** *n.*

in-stinct *n.* The complex and normal tendency or response of a given species to act in ways essential to its existence, development, and survival. **instinctive, -ual** *adj.*, **-ively** *adv.*

in-sti-tute *v.* To establish or set up; to find; to initiate; to set in operation; to start. *n.* An organization set up to promote or further a cause; an institution for educating.

in-sti-tu-tion *n.* The principle custom that forms part of a society or civilization; an organization which performs a particular job or function, such as research, charity, or education; a place of confinement such as a prison or mental hospital. **-alize** *v.*, **institutional** *adj.*, **institutionally** *adv.*

in-struct *v.* To impart skill or knowledge; to teach; to give orders or direction. **instructive** *adj.*

in-struc-tion *n.* The act of teaching or instructing; important knowledge; a lesson; an order or direction.

in-struc-tor *n.* One who instructs; a teacher; a low-rank college teacher, not having tenure. **instructorship, instructress** *n.*

in-stru-ment *n.* A mechanical tool or implement; a device used to produce music; a person who is controlled by another; a dupe; in law, a formal legal document, deed, or contract.

in-stru-men-tal *adj.* Acting or serving as a means; pertaining to, composed for, or performed on a musical instrument. **instrumentally** *adv.*

in-stru-men-tal-ist *n.* A person who plays or performs with a musical instrument.

in-stru-men-tal-i-ty *n.*, *pl.* **-ies** Anything that serves to accomplish a purpose; means or agency.

in-stru-men-ta-tion *n.* The use of instruments or work performed with instruments. *Mus.* The arrangement of music for instruments.

in-sub-or-di-nate *adj.* Not obedient; not obeying orders. **insubordinately** *adv.*, **insubordination** *n.*

in-sub-stan-tial *adj.* Unreal; imaginary; not solid or firm; flimsy. **insubstantiality** *n.*

in-suf-fi-cient *adj.* Inadequate; not enough. **-ly** *adv.*, **insufficiency** *n.*

in-su-lar *adj.* Of or related to an island; typical or suggestive of life on an island; narrow-minded; limited in customs, opinions, and ideas. **insularity** *n.*

in-su-late *v.* To isolate; to wrap or surround with nonconducting material in order to prevent the passage of heat, electricity, or sound into or out of; to protect with wrapping or insulation. **insulation, insulator** *n.*

in-su-lin *n.*, *Biochem.* The hormone released by the pancreas, essential in regulating the metabolism of sugar; a preparation of this hormone removed from the pancreas of a pig or an ox, used in the treatment of diabetes.

in-sult *v.* To speak or to treat with insolence or contempt; to abuse verbally. *n.* An act or remark that offends someone. **insulter** *n.*, **insulting** *adj.*, **insultingly** *adv.*

in-su-per-a-ble *adj.* Insurmountable; not able to be overcome. **insuperability** *n.*, **insuperably** *adv.*

in-sur-ance *n.* Protection against risk, loss, or ruin; the coverage an insurer guarantees to pay in the event of death, loss, or medical bills; a contract guaranteeing such protection on future specified losses in return for annual payments; any safeguard against risk or harm. **insurability** *n.*, **insurable** *adj.*

in-sure *v.* To guarantee against loss of life, property, or other types of losses; to make certain; to ensure; to buy or issue insurance. **insurability** *n.*, **insurable** *adj.*

in-sured *n.* A person protected by an insurance policy.

in-sur-er *n.* The person or company which insures someone against loss or damage.

in-sur-mount-a-ble *adj.* Incapable of being overcome. **insurmountably** *adv.*

in-sur-rec-tion *n.* An open revolt against an established government. **-al** *adj.*, **insurrectionary** *adj.* & *n.*, **-ist** *n.*

in-sus-cep-ti-ble *adj.* Immune; incapable of being infected. **insusceptibility** *n.*

in-tact *adj.* Remaining whole and not damaged in any way. **intactness** *n.*

in-take *n.* The act of taking in or absorbing; the amount or quantity taken in or absorbed.

in-tan-gi-ble *adj.* Incapable of being touched; vague or indefinite to the mind. **intangibility, intangibleness** *n.*, **intangibly** *adv.*

in-te-ger *n.* Any of the numbers 1, 2, 3, etc., including all the positive whole numbers and all the negative numbers and zero; a whole entity.

in-te-gral *adj.* Being an essential and indispensable part of a whole; made up, from, or formed of parts that constitute a unity.

in-te-grate *v.* To make into a whole by joining parts together; to unify; to be open to people of all races or ethnic groups. **integration** *n.*, **-ive** *adj.*

in-teg-ri-ty *n.* Uprightness of character; honesty; the condition, quality, or state of being complete or undivided.

in-tel-lect *n.* The power of the mind to understand and to accept knowledge; the state of having a strong or brilliant mind; a person of notable intellect.

in-tel-lec-tu-al *adj.* Pertaining to, possessing, or showing intellect; inclined to rational or creative thought. *n.* A person who pursues and enjoys matters of the intellect and of refined taste. **intellectuality** *n.*, **-ly** *adv.*

in-tel-lec-tu-al-ize *v.* To examine objectively so as not to become emotionally involved. **intellectualization, intellectualizer** *n.*

in-tel-li-gence *n.* The capacity to perceive and comprehend meaning; information; news; the gathering of secret information, as by military or police authorities; information so collected.

in-tel-li-gent *adj.* Having or showing intelligence. **intelligently** *adv.*

in-tel-li-gen-tsia *n.* A group of intellectuals who form the social, artistic, political elite of a society.

in-tel-li-gi-ble *adj.* Having the capabilities of being understood; understanding. **intelligibleness** *n.*, **intelligibility** *n.*, **intelligibly** *adv.*

in-tem-per-ance *n.* The lack of moderation as in satisfying of the appetite or of one's passion for something.

in-tem-per-ate *adj.* To be not temperate. **intemperateness** *n.*

in-tend *v.* To have a plan or purpose in mind; to design for a particular use. **intended** *adj.*, **intender** *n.*

in-ten-dance *n.* The administrative department of some company or group.

in-ten-dant *n.* A type of administrative official such as a governor who is under the Spanish, French, or the Portugese monarchies.

in-tend-ed *adj.* To be planned for the future. **-ness** *n.*, **intendedly** *adv.*

in-tend-ing *adj.* Aspiring.

in-tend-ment *n.* The intention of something such as the law.

in-ten-er-ate *v.* To cause or to make something tender or softer than it was to begin with. **inteneration** *n.*

in-tense *adj.* Extreme in strength, effect, or degree; expressing strong emotion, concentration, or strain; profound. **intensely** *adv.*, **intenseness** *n.*

in-ten-si-fi-er *n.* The person who will intensify something.

in-ten-si-fy *v.* To become or make more intense or acute. **intensification** *n.*

in-ten-sion *n.* A connotation. **intensionally** *adv.*, **intensional** *adj.*

in-ten-si-ty *n.*, *pl.* **-ies** The quality of being intense or acute; a great effect, concentration, or force.

in-ten-sive *adj.* Forceful and concentrated; marked by a full and complete application of all resources. **intensively** *adv.*, **intensiveness** *n.*

intensive care *n.* The hospital care provided for a gravely ill patient in specially designed rooms with monitoring devices and life-support systems.

in-tent *n.* A purpose, goal, aim, or design. **intently** *adv.*, **intentness** *n.*

in-ten-tion *n.* A plan of action; purpose, either immediate or ultimate.

in-ten-tion-al *adj.* To be deliberately intended or done. **intentionality** *n.*, **intentionally** *adv.*

in-ter *v.* To place in a grave; bury. **interment** *n.*

inter- *pref.* Mutually; with each other; together; among or between.

in-ter-act *v.* To act on each other or with each other. **-ion** *n.*, **interactive** *adj.*

in-ter-ac-tant *n.* A person or thing that will interact with something else.

in-ter-ac-tion *n.* A reciprocal action or act. **interactional** *adj.*

in-ter alia *adv.* To be amoung other things.

in-ter ali-os *adv.* To be amoung other persons or people.

in-ter-atom-ic *adj.* To be acting between atoms.

in-ter-brain *n.* The diencephalon of the brain.

in-ter-breed *v.* To crossbreed; to breed together two different species.

in-ter-ca-la-ry *adj.* To be inserted in a calendar.

in-ter-ca-late *v.* To place or to insert between existing elements.

in-ter-cede *v.* To argue or plead on another's behalf. **interceder** *n.*

in-ter-cel-lu-lar *adj.* To be between cells. **intercellularly** *adv.*

in-ter-cept *v.* To interrupt the path or course of; to seize or stop. **intercept** *n.*

in-ter-cep-tion *n.* The state of being intercepted.

in-ter-cep-tor or **in-ter-cept-er** *n.* One who or that which intercepts; a fighter plane designed for the pursuit and interception of enemy aircraft.

in-ter-ces-sion *n.* An entreaty or prayer on behalf of others. **intercessor** *n.*, **intercessional, intercessory** *adj.*

in-ter-change *v.* To put each in the place of another; to give and receive in return. *n.* The intersection of a highway which allows traffic to enter or turn off without obstructing other traffic. -ably adv., interchanger n.

in-ter-change-able adj. To be capable of being interchanged with something. interchangeableness n.

in-ter-clav-i-cle n. The bone which is located between the clavicles and in front of the sternum of reptiles. interclavicular adj.

in-ter-col-le-gi-ate adj. Involving or pertaining to two or more colleges.

in-ter-co-lum-ni-a-tion n. A space between the columns of a series.

in-ter-com n., Informal A two-way communication system, as used in different areas of a home or business.

in-ter-com-mu-ni-cate v. To communicate with each other. -ion n., intercommunicative adj.

intercommunication system n. A type of communication system that has a loudspeaker and microphone at both ends allowing for two-way talking.

in-ter-con-nect v. To connect two or more things with one another. interconnection n.

in-ter-con-ti-nen-tal adj. Pertaining to or involving two or more continents.

in-ter-con-ver-sion n. A type of mutual conversion. intervertible adj., interconvertibility n.

in-ter-cool-er n. A type of device that is for cooling a fluid between successive heat-generating processes.

in-ter-cos-tal adj. To be located or situated between the ribs. intercostally adv., intercostal n.

in-ter-course n. Mutual exchange between persons or groups; communication; sexual intercourse.

in-ter-crop v. To raise or grow a crop in between another crop.

in-ter-cross n. A product of croosbreeding.

in-ter-cul-tur-al adj. To be pertaining or related to two or more cultures. interculturally adv.

in-ter-cur-rent adj. To be happening in the midst of a process.

in-ter-cut v. To insert something such as a contrasting camera shot.

in-ter-de-nom-i-na-tion-al adj. To be occurring between denominations which are different. -ism n.

in-ter-den-tal adj. To be intended for the use between the teeth.

in-ter-de-part-men-tal adj. To be involving or to be between departments. interdepartmentally adv.

in-ter-de-pend v. To rely or to depend on another person.

in-ter-de-pen-dence n. A mutual dependence. interdependency n.

in-ter-de-pen-dent adj. To be mutually dependent.

in-ter-dict v. To forbid or prohibit by official decree. interdiction, interdictor n., interdictory adj.

in-ter-dif-fuse v. To mix freely together to obtain a mixture which is homogeneous. interdiffusion n.

in-ter-dig-i-tate v. To be interlocked such as the fingers on one's hands can

when they are folded together.

in-ter-dis-ci-plin-ary adj. To be involving or containing two or more artistic, academic, or scientific disciplines.

in-ter-est n. Curiosity or concern about something; that which is to one's benefit; legal or financial right, claim, or share, as in a business; a charge for a loan of money, usually a percent of the amount borrowed.

in-ter-est-ed adj. Having or displaying curiosity; having a right to share in something. interestedly adv.

in-ter-est group n. The group of people who have a common identifying interest.

in-ter-est-ing adj. Stimulating interest, attention, or curiosity. interesting adv., interestingness n.

in-ter-face n. A surface forming a common boundary between adjacent areas; in computer science, the software or hardware connecting one device or system to another. interface v., interfacial adj.

in-ter-fas-cic-u-lar adj. To be located or situated between fascicles.

in-ter-fere v. To come between; to get in the way; to be an obstacle or obstruction. interferer n.

in-ter-fer-ence n. The process of interfering in something.

in-ter-Ter-o-gram n. A type of photographic record that is made by a device for recording optical interference phenomena. interferometry n.

in-ter-fer-tile adj. To be capable of interbreeding. interfertility n.

in-ter-file v. To place or to fit in with an existing file.

in-ter-fuse v. To make or to cause something to pass into another. -ion n.

in-ter-ga-lac-tic adj. To be occurring between galaxies.

in-ter-gen-er-a-tion-al adj. To be occurring between two or more generations.

in-ter-ge-ner-ic adj. To be existing between genera.

in-ter-gla-cial adj. To be occurring between glacial epochs.

in-ter-gov-ern-men-tal adj. To be happening between two or more governments.

in-ter-gra-da-tion n. A condition of a person or one that intergrades.

in-ter-grade v. To come together or to merge gradually one with another.

in-ter-group adj. To be occurring between tow or more social groups.

in-ter-growth n. The growing together of two things.

in-ter-hemi-spher-ic adj. To be happening or existing between hemispheres.

in-ter-im n. A time between events or periods. adj. Temporary.

in-ter-ion-ic adj. To be acting between two or more ions.

in-te-ri-or adj. Of, or contained in the inside; inner; away from the coast or border; inland; private; not exposed to view. interiority n.

in·te·ri·or dec·o·ra·tor *n.* A person who will supply furnishings for a home.

in·te·ri·or de·sign *n.* The practice of supervising and planning the design for a home in order to make it look better through the use of architectural interiors and the furnishings.

in·te·ri·or·ize *v.* To make something interior, such as a part of one's inner being. **interiorization** *n.*

interj *abbr.* Interjection.

in·ter·ject *v.* To go between other parts or elements; to add something between other things. **interjector** *n.*, **interjectory** *adj.*

in·ter·jec·tion *n.* A word used as an exclamation to express emotion, as *Oh!* or *Super!*.

in·ter·jec·tion·al *adj.* To be pertaining or to be constituting an interjection. **interjectionally** *adv.*

in·ter·lace *v.* To join things by weaving them together; to intertwine; to blend. **interlacement** *n.*

in·ter·lam·i·nate *v.* To place or to insert between laminae. **interlamination** *n.*

in·ter·lay·er *n.* The layer which is placed between other layers. **interlayering** *n.*

in·ter·leave *v.* To place in alternate layers.

in·ter·li·brary *adj.* To be taking place between two or more libraries.

in·ter·lin·e·ar *adj.* Situated or inserted between lines of a text.

in·ter·lin·ing *n.* A type of lining that is usually sewn between the outside fabric and the ordinary lining of a coat.

in·ter·link *v.* To put together or to link things together. **interlink** *n.*

in·ter·lo·cal *adj.* To be between localities.

in·ter·lock *v.* To join closely. **-er** *n.*

in·ter·lo·cu·tion *n.* The interchange on speech with others.

in·ter·loc·u·tor *n.* A person who takes part in a conversation.

in·ter·loc·u·to·ry *adj.* Having the nature of a dialogue; in law, pronounced while a suit is pending and temporarily in effect.

in·ter·lope *v.* To intrude or interfere in the rights of others. **interloper** *n.*

in·ter·lude *n.* A period of time that occurs in and divides some longer process; light entertainment between the acts of a show, play, or other more serious entertainment.

in·ter·lu·nar *adj.* To be pertaining to the intercal that is between the new and old moon, where the moon is invisible.

in·ter·mar·riage *n.* The marriage that takes place between the members of different groups.

in·ter·mar·ry *v.* To marry someone who is not a member of one's own religion, class, race, or ethnic group.

in·er·med·dle *v.* To interfere with things. **intermeddler** *n.*

in·ter·me·di·a·cy *n.* The action of intermediating.

in·ter·me·di·ar·y *n.*, *pl.* **-ies** A mediator. *adj.* Coming between; intermediate.

in·ter·me·di·ate *adj.* Situated or occurring in the middle or between. **intermediately** *adv.*, **-ness** *n.*

in·ter·me·di·a·tion *n.* The action or the act of coming in between two persons or two things.

in·ter·me·din *n.* A type of hormone which is secreted from the pituitary body and will induce the expansion of vertebrate chromatophores.

in·ter·ment *n.* The ceremony of interring.

in·ter·me·tal·lic *adj.* To be made of two or more metals.

in·ter·mi·na·ble *adj.* To seem to have no end. **interminableness** *n.*

in·ter·min·gle *v.* To blend or become mixed together.

in·ter·mis·sion *n.* A temporary interval of time between events or activities; the pause in the middle of a performance.

in·ter·mit *v.* To cause something to cease for a certain amount of time.

in·ter·mit·tent *adj.* Ceasing from time to time; coming at intervals.

in·ter·mit·tent cur·rent *n.* A type of electric current that will flow and stop at intervals but will not reverse.

in·ter·mix *v.* To mix two or more things together.

in·ter·mo·lec·u·lar *adj.* To be acting between two or more molecules. **intermolecularly** *adv.*

in·tern *or* **in·terne** *n.* A medical school graduate undergoing supervised practical training in a hospital. *v.* To confine, as in wartime. **internment, internship** *n.*

in·ter·nal *adj.* Of or pertaining to the inside; pertaining to the domestic affairs of a country; intended to be consumed by the body from the inside. **infernally** *adv.*, **internality** *n.*

in·ter·nal--com·bus·tion en·gine *n.* An engine in which fuel is burned inside the engine.

in·ter·nal·ize *v.* To incorporate within one's self. **internalization** *n.*

in·ter·nal med·i·cine *n.* The branch of medicine that studies and treats the nonsurgical diseases.

in·ter·nal res·pi·ra·tion *n.* The exchange of the gases, which are taken into the body through the lungs, between the cells and the blood on the body.

in·ter·na·tion·al *adj.* Pertaining to or involving two or more nations. **internationally** *adv.*, **internationality** *n.*

in·ter·na·tion·al·ism *n.* The policy of cooperation among nations where politics and economics are concerned. **internationalist** *n.*

in·ter·na·tion·al·ize *v.* To put or to place under an international control. **internationalization** *n.*

in·ter·ne·cine *adj.* Mutually destructive to both sides; involving struggle within a group.

in·tern·ee *n.* A person who is confined or

interned.

in-ter-nist *n.* A physician who is a specialist in internal medicine.

in-tern-ment *n.* The state of something being interned.

in-ter-node *n.* The interval that is between two nodes. internodal *adj.*

in-ter-nu-cle-ar *adj.* To be happening or occurring between biological nuclei.

in-ter-nun-ci-al *adj.* To link motor and sensory neurons.

in-ter-nun-cio *n.* The messenger who is between two parties.

in-ter-pen-e-trate *v.* To penetrate within or between something. -ion *n.*

in-ter-per-son-al *adj.* To be relating or to pertaining to relations between people.

in-ter-plan-e-tary *adj.* To be happening or operating between the planets.

in-ter-plant *v.* To plant or place a crop between other crops.

in-ter-play *n.* Action, movement, or influence between or among people.

in-ter-po-late *v.* To insert between other things or elements; to change something by introducing additions or insertions. -ion, interpolator *n.*

in-ter-pose *v.* To put between parts; to put in or inject a comment into a conversation or speech; to intervene. interposer, interposition *n.*

in-ter-pret *v.* To convey the meaning of something by explaining or restating; to present the meaning of something, as in a picture; to take words spoken or written in one language and put them into another language. interpretable *adj.*, interpretation *n.*

in-ter-pre-ta-tive *or* in-ter-pre-tive *adj.* Of or based on interpreting; to provide an interpretation. interpretatively *adv.*

in-ter-pret-er *n.* A person who will interpret things, such as languages, for others.

in-ter-pu-pil-lary *adj.* To be located or extending between the pupils of one's eyes.

in-ter-ra-cial *adj.* Between, among, or affecting different races.

in-ter-reg-num *n., pl.* -nums *or* -na An interval between two successive reigns; a break in continuity.

in-ter-re-late *v.* To have or to put into a mutual relationship. interrelation, interrelationship *n.*

in-ter-re-lat-ed *adj.* To have a mutual relation with someone or something. interrelatedly *adv.*, interrelatedness *n.*

in-ter-re-li-gious *adj.* To be existing between different religions.

in-ter-ro-gate *v.* To question formally. interrogation, interrogator *n.*

in-ter-rog-a-tive *adj.* Asking or having the nature of a question. *n.* A word used to ask a question. -ly *adv.*

in-ter-ro-ga-tor *n.* A person who will interrogate.

in-ter-ro-gee *n.* A person who is interrogated.

in-ter-rupt *v.* To break the continuity of

something; to intervene abruptly while someone else is speaking or performing. -er, -ion *n.*, interruptive *adj.*

in-ter-scho-las-tic *adj.* Conducted between or among schools.

in-ter se *adj. or adv.* To be between or amoung friends.

in-ter-sect *v.* To divide by cutting through or across; to form an intersection; to cross.

in-ter-sec-tion *n.* A place of crossing; a place where streets or roads cross; in mathematics, the point common to two or more geometric elements.

in-ter-ser-vice *adj.* To be relating to two or more of the armed services.

in-ter-ses-sion *n.* The period which is between two academic sessions that can be used for brief concentrated courses.

in-ter-sperse *v.* To scatter among other things. interspersion *n.*

in-ter-sta-di-al *n.* The subdivision that is within a glacial stage and marking a temporary retreat of the ice.

in-ter-state *adj.* Between, involving, or among two or more states.

in-ter-stel-lar *adj.* Among or between the stars.

in-ter-stice *n.* The small space between things.

in-ter-sti-tial *adj.* To be situating within a tissue or an organ.

in-ter-sub-jec-tive *adj.* To be happening or occurring between separate conscious minds. intersubjectively *adv.*

in-ter-till *v.* To cultivated the ground between the rows of a crop. -age *n.*

in-ter-trop-i-cal *adj.* To be located between the tropics.

in-ter-twine *v.* To unite by twisting together. intertwinement *n.*

in-ter-twist *v.* To intertwine things together. intertwist *n.*

in-ter-ur-ban *adj.* Between or among connecting urban areas.

in-ter-val *n.* The time coming between two points or objects; a period of time between events or moments. *Mus.* The difference in pitch between two tones.

in-ter-val-om-e-ter *n.* A type of device that operates a control such as one for the shutter of a camera.

in-ter-vene *v.* To interfere or take a decisive role so as to modify or settle something; to interfere with force in a conflict. intervention *n.*

in-ter-ve-nor *n.* A person who will intervene.

in-ter-ven-tion-ism *n.* The practice of intervening in something. -ist *n.*

in-ter-ver-te-bral *adj.* To be situated between the vertebrae, such as a disk. intervertebrally *adv.*

in-ter-ver-te-bral disk *n.* A elastic disk that is located between the vertebrae.

in-ter-view *n.* A conversation conducted by a reporter to elicit information from someone; a conversation led by an employer who is trying to decide whether to hire someone. interview *v.*, interviewer *n.*

in-ter-view-ee *n.* The person who is being interviewed.

in-ter-vi-vos *adv. or adj.* To be between living people.

in-ter-vo-cal-ic *adj.* To be preceded and followed immediately by a vowel.

in-ter-war *adj.* To be taking place between the wars.

in-ter-weave *v.* To weave things together; to intertwine. **interwoven** *adj.*

in-ter-zon-al *adj.* To be carried on between two or more zones.

in-tes-ta-cy *n.* The state of being intestate.

in-tes-tate *adj.* Having made no valid will; not disposed of by a will.

in-tes-ti-nal *adj.* To be pertaining to the intestines.

intestinal fortitude *n.* Stamina of a person.

in-tes-tine or **in-tes-tines** *n. Anat.*

The section of the alimentary canal from the stomach to the anus. **-inally** *adv.*

in-ti-ma *n.* The covering of an organ which is the innermost and is made up of a endothelial layer and is backed by connective tissue. **intimal** *adj.*

in-ti-mate *adj.* Characterized by close friendship or association. **-ly** *adv.*, **intimacy, intimateness** *n.*

in-tim-i-date *v.* To make timid or fearful; to frighten; to discourage or suppress by threats or by violence. **infimidation, intimidator** *n.*

in-tim-i-da-to-ry *adj.* Tending to intimidate others.

in-tine *n.* The layer that is innermost of a spore and it is a cellulose wall.

in-tit-ule *v.* To give or furnish with a title.

intnl *abbr.* International.

in-to *prep.* To the inside of; to a form or condition of; to a time in the midst of.

in-tol-er-a-ble *adj.* Not tolerable; unbearable. **intolerability, intolerableness** *n.*, **intolerably** *adv.*

in-tol-er-ant *adj.* Not able to endure; not tolerant of the rights or beliefs of others. **intolerance** *n.*, **-ly** *adv.*

in-to-nate *v.* To utter something.

in-to-na-tion *n.* The manner of speaking, especially the meaning and melody given to speech by changing levels of pitch. **intonational** *adj.*

in-tone *v.* To utter or recite in a monotone; to chant. **intoner** *n.*

in to-to *adv.* Totally.

in-tox-i-cate *v.* To make drunk; to elate or excite. **intoxicant, intoxication** *n.*

in-tox-i-cat-ed *adj.* To be affected by alcohol.

intra- *prefix* Within.

in-tra-ar-te-ri-al *adj.* To be located or situated within an artery.

in-tra-car-di-ac *adj.* To be occurring within one's heart.

in-tra-cel-lu-lar *adj.* To be occurring within a cell or cells.

in-tra-cra-ni-al *adj.* To be occurring within the skull. **intracarnially** *adv.*

in-trac-ta-ble *adj.* Hard to manage; difficult to cure or treat. **intractableness, intractability** *n.*

in-tra-cu-ta-ne-ous *adj.* To be occurring between the layers of one's skin. **intracutaneously** *adv.*

in-tra-der-mal *adj.* To be done within the layers of one's skin.

in-tra-der-mal test *n.* A type of which is used to test the immunity to an antigen by injecting it under a layer if the skin and then watching for a reaction.

in-tra-dos *n., pl.* **-dos** or **-doses** The interior curve of an arch or vault.

in-tra-ga-lac-tic *adj.* To be occurring within a single galaxy.

in-tra-mo-lec-u-lar *adj.* To be occurring or acting within a molecule. **intramolecularly** *adv.*

in-tra-mu-ral *adj.* Taking place within a school, college, or institution; the competition which is limited to a school community. **intramurally** *adv.*

in-tra-mus-cu-lar *adj.* Within a muscle. **intramuscularly** *adv.*

intrans *abbr.* Intransitive.

in-tran-si-gence *n.* The state of something being intransigent.

in-tran-si-gent *adj.* Refusing to moderate a position; uncompromising. **intransigency, intransigent** *n.*

in-tran-si-tive *adj.* To be not transitive. **intransitiveness** *n.*

in-trant *n.* A person who is entering or going into a learning institution.

in-tra-oc-u-lar *adj.* To be located within the eyeball.

in-tra-per-i-to-ne-al *adj.* To be going into the peritoneal cavity of the body. **intraperitoneally** *adv.*

in-tra-per-son-al *adj.* To be taking place between the members of a population.

in-tra-pop-u-la-tion *adj.* To be taking place between the members of a population.

in-tra-psy-chic *adj.* To be occurring in the mind. **intrapsychically** *adv.*

in-tra-spe-cif-ic *adj.* To be happening or occurring within members of one species. **intraspecifically** *adv.*

in-tra-state *adj.* To be occurring or happening within a state.

in-tra-u-ter-ine *adj.* To be occurring or happening within the uterus.

in-tra-u-ter-ine de-vice *n.* A metal or plastic loop, ring, or spiral which is inserted into the uterus and used for the purpose of contraception for the woman.

in-tra-vas-cu-lar *adj.* To be occurring within a vessel such as a blood vessel. **intravascularly** *adv.*

in-tra-ve-nous *adj.* To be ocurring within a vein. **intravenously** *adv.*

in-tra-zon-al *adj.* To be pertaining to a soil group which is found to be marked with relatively well-developed characteristics which are, in turn, determined by local factors instead by climate or vegetation.

in-trep-id adj. Courageous; unshaken by fear; bold. **intrepidly** adv., **intrepidity, intrepidness** n.

in-tra-ca-cy n. The state of something being intricate.

in-tri-cate adj. Having many perplexingly entangled parts or elements; complex; difficult to solve or understand. **intricately** adv.

in-tri-gant n. Something or someone that will intrigue.

in-trigue v. To arouse the curiosity or interest; to fascinate; to plot; to conspire; to engage in intrigues. n. A secret or illicit love affair; a secret plot or plan. **intriguer** n.

in-trigu-ing adj. To be engaging the interest of something or of someone to a marked degree.

in-trin-sic adj. Belonging to the true or fundamental nature of a thing; inherent. **intrinsically** adv.

in-trin-sic fac-tor n. A type of substance which is made by the gastrointestinal mucosa and is used for the purpose of the absorption of vitamin B12.

intro- prefix Into; in.

introd abbr. Introduction.

in-tro-duce v. To present a person face to face to another; to make acquainted; to bring into use or practice for the first time; to bring to the attention of. **-er** n., **introductory** adj.

in-tro-duc-tion n. A passage of a book that will introduce the story or the content of a book; something which introduces.

in-tro-gres-sion n. The introduction of a gene from one gene complex to another gene complex.

in-tro-it or **In-tro-it** n. A hymn or psalm sung at the beginning of a Roman Catholic Mass.

in-tro-ject v. To incorporate ideas in someone's personality unconsciously.

in-tro-mis-sion n. The process of intromitting.

in-tro-mit v. To put something in.

in-trorse adj. To be facing inward.

in-tro-spect v. To examine reflectively.

in-tro-ver-sion n. The state of being introverted. **introversive** adj.

in-tro-vert n., Psychol. A person who directs his interest to himself and not to friends or social activities. **introversion** n., **introverted** adj.

in-trude v. To thrust or push oneself in; to come in without being asked or wanted. **intruder** n.

in-tru-sion n. The act of intruding.

in-tru-sive adj. To be intruding where a person is not wanted or welcome. **intrusiveness** n., **intrusively** adv.

intsv abbr. Intensive.

in-tu-ba-tion n. The act of placing a tube into a hollow organ.

in-tu-it v. To understand through intuition. **intuitable** adj.

in-tu-i-tion n. The direct knowledge or awareness of something without conscious attention or reasoning; knowledge that is acquired in this way. **intuitive** adj., **intuitively** adv.

in-tu-ition-ism n. A type of doctrine that objects of one's perception are intuitively known to be real.

in-tu-mesce v. To enlarge.

in-tu-mes-cence n. The swelling or the bubbling that can be caused by the action of heat. **intumescent** adj.

in-tus-sus-cept v. To undergo an intussusception.

in-tus-sus-cep-tion n. The pulling or drawing in of something, such as with the intestines in one's body.

in-u-lin n. A type of white polysaccharide which can be found in the sap of the roots of composite plants.

in-unc-tion n. The action of placing ointment on a body part.

in-un-date v. To overwhelm with abundance or excess, as with work. **inundation** n., **inundatory** adj.

in-ure v. To become used to accepting something which is undesirable.

in-utile adj. To be unusable or useless.

in vac-uo adv. To be done in a vacuum.

in-vade v. To enter by force with the intent to conquer or to pillage; to penetrate and to overrun harmfully; to violate; to encroach upon. **invader** n.

in-vag-i-nate v. To sheathe something; to undergo an invagination.

in-va-lid n. A chronically sick, bedridden, or disabled person. **invalid** adj. & v., **invalidness** n.

in-val-id adj. Disabled by injury or disease; not valid; unsound. **invalidity** n., **invalidly** adv.

in-val-i-date v. To nullify; to make invalid. **invalidation, invalidator** n.

in-va-lid-ism n. A type of condition, which is chronic, of being an invalid.

in-val-u-able adj. Priceless; of great value; to be of great help or use. **invaluably** adv., **invaluableness** n.

in-vari-able adj. Constant and not changing. **invariably** adv.

in-vari-ance n. The state of being invariant.

in-va-sion n. The act of invading; an entrance made with the intent of overrunning or occupying.

in-va-sive adj. To be characterized by or with military aggression.

in-vec-tive adj. To be characterized by abuse or insult. **invectively** adv.

in-veigh v. To angrily protest something.

in-vei-gle v. To win over by flattery. **inveiglement, inveigler** n.

in-vent v. To devise or create by original effort or design. **inventor** n.

in-ven-tion n. The act or process of inventing; a new process, method, or device conceived from study and testing.

in-ven-tive adj. Skillful at invention or contrivance; ingenious. **inventively** adv., **inventiveness** n.

in-ven-to-ry n., pl. **-ies** A list of items with descriptions and quantities of each; the process of making such a list. **inventory** v.

in-ver-ness n. A type of loose belted coat that has a cape.

in-verse adj. Reversed in order or sequence; inverted. n. Something opposite. **inversely** adv.

in-ver-sion n. The act of inverting or the state of being inverted; that which is inverted.

in-ver-sive adj. To be marked or characterized by inversion.

in-vert v. To turn upside down; to reverse the position, condition, or order of something.

in-ver-tase n. A type of enzyme which is capable of inverting sucrose.

in-ver-te-brate adj. Lacking a backbone or spinal column. **invertebrate** n.

in-vert-ed com-ma n. A type of comma that is inverted to be upside down and placed at the top of a line.

in-vert-er n. Someone or something which will invert.

in-vert-ible adj. To be capable of being inverted.

in-vert su-gar n. A type of dextrose which can be obtained from starch.

in-vest v. To use money for the purchase of stocks or property in order to obtain profit or interest; to place in office formally; to install; to make an investment. **investor** n.

in-ves-ti-gate v. To search or inquire into; to examine carefully. **-ive** adj., **investigation, investigator** n.

in-ves-ti-ture n. The ceremony or act of investing or installing someone in a high office.

in-vest-ment n. The act of investing money or capital to gain interest or income; property acquired and kept for future benefit.

in-vet-er-a-cy n. The state of being persistent.

in-vet-er-ate adj. To be confirmed in a habit. **inveterately** adv.

in-vi-a-ble adj. To be unabe to survive. **inviability** n.

in-vid-i-ous adj. To be causing animosity or discontent.

in-vig-o-rate v. To give strength or vitality to. **invigoratingly** adv., **invigoration** n.

in-vin-ci-ble adj. Incapable of being defeated. **invincibility** n., **-y** adj.

in-vi-o-la-ble adj. Secure from profanation; safe from assault. **inviolability** n., **inviolably** adv.

in-vi-o-late adj. Not violated. **inviolately** adv., **inviolateness** n.

in-vis-cid adj. To have zero viscosity.

in-vis-i-ble adj. Not capable of being seen; not visible; not open to view; hidden. **invisibility** n., **invisibly** adv.

in-vi-ta-tion n. The act of inviting; the means or words that request someone's presence or participation.

in-vite v. To request the presence or participation of; to make a formal or polite request for; to provoke; to entice; to issue an invitation.

in-vit-ee n. The person who is being invited to something or somewhere.

in-vit-ing adj. Tempting; attractive. **invitingly** adv.

in vi-tro adv. To be done outside the body, such as fertilization.

in vi-vo adv. To be in the living body of an animal or in a plant.

in-vo-cate v. To invoke someone or something into doing something.

in-vo-ca-tion n. An appeal to a deity or other agent for inspiration, witness, or help; a prayer which is used at the opening of a ceremony or a service. **invocatory, invocational** adj.

in-voice n. An itemized list of merchandise shipped or services rendered, including prices, shipping instructions, and other costs; a bill. **invoice** v.

in-voke v. To call upon for aid, support, or inspiration; to conjure. **invoker** n.

in-vo-lu-cre n. The whorls of bracts which are situated below and close to a flower or a fruit. **involucred** adj.

in-vo-lu-crum n. A type of surrounding sheath.

in-vol-un-tar-y adj. Not done by choice or willingly. n. Physiol. Muscles which function without an individual's control. **involuntariness** n.

in-vo-lute v. To return to the former condition; to be cleared up.

in-vo-lu-tion n. The process where something returns itself to its fromer condition or state. **involutional** adj.

in-volve v. To include as a part; to make a participant of; to absorb; to engross. **involvement** n.

in-volved adj. To be complex in an extreme manner.

in-vul-ner-a-ble adj. To be immune to attack; impregnable; not able to be physically injured or wounded. **invulnerability** n., **invulnerably** adv.

in-ward adj. To be situated toward the inside, the center, or the interior; of or existing in the mind or thoughts. **inwardness** n., **inwardly** adv.

in-weave v. To interlace something.

in-wrought adj. To have the decoration worked in, such as with embroidery.

IOC abbr. International Olympic Committee.

i-o-date v. To treat something with iodine. **iodation** n.

i-od-ic adj. To be pertaining to or containing iodine.

i-od-ic ac-id n. An oxidizing solid that is formed by the oxidation of iodine.

i-o-dide n. A type of iodine compound that has a more electropositive element.

i-o-din-ate v. To cause a compound to combine with iodine.

i-o-dine n. A grayish-black, corrosive, poisonous element, symbolized by I; a solution made up of iodine, alcohol, and sodium iodide or potassium iodide which is used as an antiseptic.

io-dize v. To treat something with iodine or treat with an iodide.

io-do-form n. A type of yellow compound that has a penetrating persistent odor and is used as an antiseptic dressing.

io-do-phor *n.* A type of complex iodine and organic compound that will release iodine gradually and is used as a disinfectant.

io-dous *adj.* To be pertaining to or containing iodine.

io moth *n.* A type of yellow American moth that has a large ocellated spot on both of its hind wings.

i-on *n., Physics.* An atom or group of atoms which carries a positive or negative electric charge as a result of having lost or gained one or more electrons.

-ion *n., suffix* A process; a condition.

i-on-ize *v.* To convert completely or partially into ions. ionizer, ionization *n.*, ionizable *adj.*

io-ta *n.* The ninth letter that is in the Greek alphabet.

IOU *abbr.* I owe you.

Iowa *n.* A state which is located in the north central part of the United States.

ip-e-cac *n.* A type of South American creeping plant that has flowers which droop and is found in the tropical areas.

ipro-ni-a-zid *n.* A type of derivative of isoniazid that was formerly used for the purpose of treating tuberculosis.

ip-se dix-it *n.* A type of assertion which is made but not proven.

ip-si-lat-er-al *adj.* To be appearing on the same side of the body.

ip-so fac-to *adv.* By that very fact or act.

IQ *abbr.* Intelligence quotient.

Ir *abbr.* Irish.

i-ras-ci-ble *adj.* Easily provoked to anger; quick-tempered. irascibly *adv.*, irascibility, irascibleness *n.*

i-rate *adj.* To be raging; to be angry. irately *adv.*, irateness *n.*

IRBM *abbr.* Intermediate range ballistic missile.

Ire *abbr.* Ireland.

ire-nic *adj.* To be operating toward peace. irenically *adv.*

iri-da-ceous *adj.* To be pertaining to the iris family of flowers.

ir-i-des-cent *adj.* Displaying the colors of the rainbow in shifting hues and patterns. iridescence *n.*

irid-ic *adj.* To be pertaining to iridium or to the iris of the eye.

irid-i-um *n.* A type of silver-white brittle and very hard metallic element of the platinum group.

i-ris *n., pl.* irises *or* irides

The pigmented part of the eye which regulates the size of the pupil by contracting and expanding around it. *Bot.* A plant with narrow sword-shaped leaves and large, handsome flowers, as the gladiolus and crocus.

iris diaphragm *n.* Adjustable diaphragm made of thin opaque plates that is turned by a ring, so as to change the diameter of a central opening such as the aperture of a lens.

I-rish *adj.* Pertaining to Ireland and its people or their language.

I-rish cof-fee *n.* A type of coffee that contains Irish whiskey and whipped cream.

Irish confetti *n.* A brick, rock, or a fragment of either that is used as a missile.

I-rish Gaelic *n.* The Celtic language that has been used in Ireland since the end of the medieval period.

I-rish-ism *n.* A phrase or a word that is characteristic of the Irish.

Irish mail *n.* A child's toy with three or four wheels that is activated by a hand lever.

I-rish-man *n.* A person who is native to or an inhabitant of Ireland.

I-rish moss *n.* Red algar that has been dried and is used for thickening or emulsifying.

I-rish-ry *adj.* To be Irish in character or in quality.

I-rish set-ter *n.* A type of bird dog that has a chestnut-brown or reddish coat.

I-rish stew *n.* A type of stew that contains meat, (lamb) onions, and potatoes.

I-rish ter-ri-er *n.* A type of medium-sized terrior that was developed in Ireland and has a reddish wiry coat.

I-rish whis-key *n.* A type of whiskey, mainly of barley, that is made in Ireland.

I-rish wolf-hound *n.* A very large hound that resembles the Scottish deerhound but is much stronger and larger.

I-rish-wom-an *n.* A woman who was born in Ireland or is of Irish descent.

irk *v.* To annoy or to weary someone or something.

irk-some *adj.* Tending to irk someone or something. irksomeness *n.*

iron *n.* A type of heavy malleable ductile magnetic metallic element that is silver-white and will rust easily in moist air.

Iron Age *n.* The most recent of three early stages of human progress, following the Stone Age and the Bronze Age.

iron-bound *adj.* To be bound with iron; to be unyielding.

iron-clad *adj.* Covered with protective iron plates; strict; unbreakable.

iron curtain *n.* An impenetrable political and ideological barrier between the Soviet bloc and the rest of the world.

iron-er *n.* A person who irons things, such as clothing.

iron-fisted *adj.* To be ruthless and mean.

iron gray *n.* A type of color which is neutral and slightly greenish dark gray.

iron hand *n.* The rigorous control of someone or something.

ironhandedness n., **ironhanded** adj.

iron-heart-ed adj. To be hardhearted and cruel.

iron horse n. The engine of a train.

iron-ic adj. To be marked by or characterized by irony. **-al** adj., **-ally** adv.

iron-ing n. The process or action of pressing or smoothing with a heated iron. Clothes that have been ironed or are to be ironed.

iron lung n. A tank which encloses the entire body with the exception of the head and regulates the respiration of a patient by alternately increasing and decreasing air pressure.

iron-mas-ter n. The manufacturer of iron.

iron-stone n. A heavy, white, glazed pottery.

iron out v. To make harmonious or tolerable by modification of extremes.

iro-ny n., pl. -ies A literary device for conveying meaning by saying the direct opposite of what is really meant.

ir-ra-di-ate v. To subject to ultraviolet light, radiation, or similar rays. **irradiation**, **irradiator** n.

ir-ra-tion-al adj. Unable to reason; contrary to reason; absurd; in mathematics, a number which is not expressible as an integer or a quotient of integers. **irrationality** n., **-ly** adv.

ir-rec-on-cil-a-ble adj. Not able or willing to be reconciled. **irreconcilability** n., **irreconcilably** adv.

ir-re-deem-a-ble adj. Not capable of being recovered, bought back, or paid off; not convertible into coin.

ir-re-duc-i-ble adj. Not having the capabilities of reduction, as to a smaller amount. **irreducibility** n., **irreducibly** adv.

ir-re-fra-ga-ble adj. Cannot be refuted or disproved. **irrefragably** adv.

ir-re-fut-able adj. Cannot be disproved **irrefutability** n., **irrefutably** adv.

ir-reg-u-lar adj. Not according to the general rule or practice; not straight, uniform, or orderly; uneven. n. One who is irregular. **irregularity** n., **irregularly** adv.

ir-rel-e-vant adj. Not pertinent or related to the subject matter. **-ly** adv., **irrelevance**, **irrelevancy** n.

ir-re-li-gious adj. Lacking in religion; opposed to religion. **irreligiously** adv., **irreligiousness**, **irreligion** n.

ir-re-miss-ible adj. Unpardonable, as for sin. **irremissibility** n.

ir-re-mov-able adj. Not removable. **irremovably** adv.

ir-rep-a-ra-ble adj. Unable to be set right or repaired. **irreparability** n., **irreparably** adv.

ir-re-place-able adj. Unable to be replaced.

ir-re-press-ible adj. Impossible to hold back or restrain. **irrepressibility** n., **irrepressibly** adv.

ir-re-proach-able adj. Blameless; not meriting reproach. **-ness** n., **irreproachably** adv.

ir-re-sist-ible adj. Completely fascinating; impossible to resist.

ir-re-sol-u-ble adj. Admitting or having no explanation or solution.

ir-res-o-lute adj. Lacking resolution; indecisive; lacking firmness of purpose. **irresolutely** adv., **irresoluteness** n.

ir-re-spec-tive prep. Without regard to anything.

ir-re-spec-tive adj. Regardless of.

ir-re-spon-si-bil-i-ty n. The quality of being irresponsible.

ir-re-spon-si-ble adj. Lacking in responsibility; not accountable. **irresponsibility** n., **irresponsibly** adv.

ir-re-triev-a-ble adj. Unable to be retrieved or recovered.

ir-rev-er-ence n. A lack of reverence; a disrespectful action. **irreverent** adj., **irreverently** adv.

ir-re-vers-i-ble adj. Impossible to reverse. **irreversibility** n., **-y** adv.

ir-rev-o-ca-ble adj. Unable or incapable of being turned in the other direction; incapable of being repealed, annulled or undone. **irrevocability** n., **-y** adv.

ir-ri-gate v. To water the land or crops artificially, as by means of ditches or sprinklers; to refresh with water. Med. To wash out with a medicated fluid or water. **-ion**, **-or** n., **irrigational** adj.

ir-ri-ta-ble adj. Easily annoyed; ill-tempered. Pathol. To respond abnormally to stimuli. **irritability**, **irritableness** n., **irritably** adv.

ir-ri-tate v. To annoy or bother; to provoke; to be sore, chafed, or inflamed. **irritator**, **irritation** n., **irritant** adj. & n., **irritatingly** adv.

ir-rupt v. To burst or rush in; to invade. **irruption** n., **-ive** adj., **irruptively** adv.

IRS abbr. Internal Revenue Service.

is v. Third person, singular, present tense of the verb to be.

Is abbr. Island; islands.

is-al-lo-bar n. A line on a chart which connects the locations of equal change of atmospheric pressure.

is-ba n. The Russian log hut.

ISBN abbr. International Standard Book Number.

ISC abbr. International space Congress.

isch-emia n. The tissue anemia that is localized due to an obstruction of the inflow of arterial blood.

is-chi-um n. The posterior bone which comprises the pelvis of the body.

is-en-tro-pic adj. To be related to constant entropy.

-ish suffix Of or belonging to a nationality or ethnic group; characteristic of; the approximate age of; the approximate time of; somewhat.

Isis n. The nature goddess of the Egyptians.

is-land n. A piece of land smaller than a continent, completely surrounded by water.

is-land-er n. A person who makes his home on an island.

is-land uni-verse n. Any other galaxy besides the Milky Way.

isle *n.* A small island.

is-let *n.* A very small island.

ism *n.*, *Slang* A distinctive cause, doctrine, or theory.

-ism *suffix* Practice; process; a manner of behavior characteristic of person or thing; a system of principles.

is-n't *contr.* Is not.

iso-al-lox-a-zine *n.* A yellow solid which is the parent compound of flavins.

iso-bu-tyl-ene *n.* A type of gaseous butylene used for the purpose of making gasoline compounds.

iso-chro-nal *adj.* To have equal duration. isochronism *n.*

iso-cli-nal *adj.* To be having an equality of inclination.

iso-cy-clic *adj.* Being a ring that is composed of atoms only of one element.

iso-elec-tron-ic *adj.* To have the same number of electrons.

iso-gen-ic *adj.* To be characterized be having identical genes.

iso-gloss *n.* A boundary line that divides areas which differ in a particular linguistic feature. isoglossal *adj.*

iso-gon-ic *adj.* To be growing so that sizes of parts remain equvalent.

i-so-late *v.* To set apart from the others; to put by itself; to place or be placed in quarantine. isolation, isolator *n.*

i-so-la-tion-ism *n.* A national policy of avoiding political or economic alliances or relations with other countries. isolationist *n.*

i-so-mer *n.* A compound having the same kinds and numbers of atoms as another compound but differing in chemical or physical properties due to the linkage or arrangement of the atoms.

i-sos-ce-les tri-an-gle *n.*

A triangle which has two equal sides.

i-so-therm *n.* A line on a map linking points that have the same t e m p e r a t u r e . isothermal *adj.*

i-so-tope *n.* Any of two or more species of atoms of a chemical element which contain in their nuclei, the same number of protons but different numbers of neutrons. isotopic *adj.*, isotopically *adv.*

i-so-trop-ic *adj.* Having the same value in all directions. isotropy *n.*

Is-rae-li *adj.* Of or pertaining to the country of Israel or its inhabitants. Israeli, Israel *n.*

Is-ra-el-ite *n.* A Hebrew. Israelite *adj.*

is-sue *n.* The act of giving out; something that is given out or published; a matter of importance to solve. *Med.* A discharge as of pus or blood. *v.* To come forth; to flow out; to emerge; to distribute or give out, as supplies. issuable *adj.*, issuer *n.*

isth-mus *n.* A narrow strip of land which connects two larger pieces of land. isthmian *adj.*

it *pron.* Used as a substitute for a specific noun or name when referring to places, things, or animals of unspecified sex; used to refer to the general state of something.

I-tal-ian *adj.* Italian in character. *n.* A person living in Italy.

i-tal-ic *adj.* A style of printing type in which the letters slant to the right. Italics *pl.* Italic typeface.

i-tal-i-cize *v.* To print in italics. italicization *n.*

It-a-ly *n.* A country in southern Europe, bordered by the Mediterranean Ocean. Italian *adj. & n.*

itch *n.* A skin irritation which causes a desire to scratch; a contagious skin disease accompanied by a desire to scratch; a restless desire or craving. itch *v.*, itchiness *n.*, itchy *adj.*

-ite *suffix* A native or inhabitant of; an adherent of; a sympathizer or follower; a descendant of; a rock or mineral.

i-tem *n.* A separately-noted unit or article included in a category or series; a short article, as in a magazine or newspaper.

i-tem-ize *v.* To specify by item; to list. itemizer, itemization *n.*

it-er-ate *v.* To state or do again; to repeat. iteration *n.*

i-tin-er-ant *adj.* Traveling from place to place; wandering. itinerant *n.*

it'll *contr.* It will; it shall.

its *adj.* The possessive case of the pronoun it.

it's *contr.* It is; it has.

-ity *n.*, *suffix* Quality or state.

IUD *abbr* Interuterine device.

IV *abbr* Intervenous.

-ive *adj.*, *suffix* Tends toward an action.

I've *contr.* I have.

ivied *adj.* To be overgrown with ivy.

i-vo-ry *n.*, *pl.* -ies A hard, smooth, yellowish-white material which forms the tusks of elephants, walruses, and other animals; any substance similar to ivory. ivories The teeth; the keys on a piano. ivory *adj.*

i-vo-ry--billed wood-peck-er *n.* A type of large and almost extinct woodpecker living in the southeastern U.S.

i-vo-ry black *n.* A type of black pigment which can be made by calcining ivory.

i-vo-ry nut *n.* A nutlike seed in S. America's palm which can be used for carving.

i-vo-ry tow-er *n.* A condition or attitude of withdrawal from the world and reality. ivory tower *adj.*

i-vo-ry tow-ered *adj.* To be divorced from practical matters.

i-vy *n.*, *pl.* -ies A climbing plant having glossy evergreen leaves.

-ization *n.* *suffix* The process, action, or result of doing a specified thing.

-ize *suffix* To cause to become or resemble.

iz-zard *n.* The letter Z.

J, j *n.* The tenth letter of the English alphabet.

JA *abbr.* Joint account; judge advocate.

jab *v.* To poke or thrust sharply with short blows; a rapid punch.

jab-ber *v.* To speak quickly or without making sense.

Jab-ber-wock-y *n.* A poem characterized by meaningless speech and nonsense syllables; an imitation of this in speech or in writing; gibberish.

jab-ot *n.* A ruffle or decoration on the front of a blouse, dress, or shirt; a lace decoration that was formerly worn by men.

ja-bot-i-ca-ba *n.* A tropical tree that yields an edible fruit that resembles the grape grown in warm climates such as, Florida and California.

ja-cal *n.* A small hut found in the southwestern United States and Mexico, with wall made of rows and rows of thin vertical poles filled in with mud.

jac-a-mar *n.* A tropical, brilliantly colored, insectivorous bird of tropical America.

ja-ca-na *n.* A small aquatic bird having long, straight claws that are adapted for walking on floating objects such as aquatic plants.

jac-a-ran-da *n.* A tall tropical tree; or the fragrant wood of such a tree.

jack *n.* The playing card that ranks just below a queen and bears a representation of a knave; any of various tools or devices used for raising heavy objects; the male of certain animals; a man or boy; fellow; a small flag on a ship that indicates nationality. *Electr* A socket into which a plug is inserted to make an electric circuit.

jacks *n.* A game played with a set of six-pronged metal pieces and a small ball.

jack-al *n.* An African or Asian dog-like, carnivorous mammal; a person who works as a slave for another.

jack-a-napes *n.* An impudent person; an impudent child.

jack-ass *n.*

A male donkey or ass; a stupid person or one who acts in a stupid fashion.

jack-boot *n.* A heavy military boot which reaches above the knee.

jack-daw *n.* A glossy, black, crow-like bird.

jack-et *n.* A short coat worn by men and women; an outer protective cover for a book; the skin of a cooked potato. **jacketed, jacketless, jacketlike** *adj.*

Jack Frost *n.* A name given to frost or winter weather.

jack-hammer *n.* A tool operated by air pressure, used to break pavement and to drill rock.

jack--in--the--box *n.* A toy consisting of a small box from which a puppet springs up when the lid is unfastened.

jack--in--the--pul-pit *n.* A common herb which grows from a turnip-shaped bulb.

Jack Ketch *n.* An executioner.

jack-knife *n.* A large pocketknife; a dive executed by doubling the body forward with the knees unbent and the hands touching the ankles and then straightening before entering the water. *v.* To bend in the manner of a jackknife.

jack-leg *adj.* Deficient in skill or training; having questionable practices; below professional quality or standards.

jack-light *n.* A light used for hunting or fishing at night. *v.* To fish or hunt with a light. **jacklighter** *n.*

jack--of--all--trades *n.* A person who is able to do many types of work.

jack-o--lan-tern *n.* A lantern made from a hollowed out pumpkin which has been carved to resemble a face.

jack-pot *n.* Any post, prize, or pool in which the amount won is cumulative.

jack rab-bit *n.*

A large American hare with long back legs and long ears.

Jackson, Andrew *n.* (1767-1845) The seventh president of the United States from 1829-1837.

Ja-cob *n.* A Hebrew patriarch.

Ja-cob's ladder *n.* The ladder Jacob saw in his dreams, which extended from earth to heaven. *Naut.* A ladder with wooden or metal rungs and nonrigid sides. *Bot.* A plant with blue flowers and ladder-like leaflets.

jade *n.* A hard, translucent, green gemstone; an old, worn-out unmanageable horse; a mean old woman; hussy. *adj.* Worn-out; exhausted; worn-out. **jade** *v.*

jag *n.* A very sharp projection or point; a notch or indentation. *Slang* A binge or spree.

jag-ged *adj.* Having jags or sharp notches; serrated. **jaggedly** *adv.*, **jaggedness** *n.*

jag-uar *n.* A large, spotted, feline mammal of tropical America with a tawny coat and black spots.

jai alai *n.* A game similar to handball in which players catch and throw a ball with long, curved, wicker baskets strapped to their arms.

jail *n.* A place or building of confinement for incarceration.

jail-bird *n.*, *Slang* A prisoner or ex-prisoner.

jail-break *n.* A prison escape obtain by force.

jail de-liv-er-y *n.* The freeing of a

prisoner by force.

jail-er *n.* The officer in charge of a jail and its prisoners.

Jain-ism *n.* An ancient religion of India.

ja-lop-y *n., pl.* **-ies** *Slang* An old, run-down automobile.

ja-lou-sie *n.* A window, blind, or door having adjustable horizontal slats.

jam *v.* To force or wedge into a tight position; to apply the brakes of a car suddenly; to be locked in a position; to block; to crush. *Mus.* To be a participant in a jazz session. *Slang* To be in a difficult situation or to be crowded together, as of people, cars; a difficult situation. **jam** *v.*

jam *n.* A preserve of whole fruit boiled with sugar.

jamb *n.* The vertical sidepiece of a door.

jam-ba-lay-a *n.* A dish of rice that is cooked with vegetable, and various kinds of fish meat, but usually shrimp or ham.

jam-bo-ree *n.* A large, festive gathering.

jam session *n.* An informal gathering of a group of jazz musicians, usually for their own enjoyment.

Jan *abbr.* January.

Jane Doe *n.* A womans name that is used in hypotheses, especially in a legal proceeding when a womans name is unknown or unimportant.

jan-gle *v.* To make a harsh unmusical sound; to dispute something in a angrily way; to cause to become angry, tense or mad. *n.* A discordant sound; a dispute or quarrel. **jangle, jangler** *n.*

jan-i-tor *n.* A person who cleans and cares for a building, office, school, apartment etc. **janitorial** *adj.*

Jan-u-ar-y *n.* The first month of the year, having thirty-one days.

ja-pan *n.* A black varnish used for coating metal, wood and other objects. *v.* To varnish an object with japan.

Jap-a-nese *adj.* Pertaining to Japan, its people, or their language.

Ja-pan clo-ver *n.* A clover bush grown in the southern states of the United States and used as a forage crop.

Jap-a-nese bee-tle *n.* A green and brown beetle which is very damaging to plants.

Jap-a-nese mil-let *n.* A coarse grass that is grown for its forage and it's seeds used in bird feed.

Jap-a-nese per-sim-mon *n.* An edible fruit grown in the United States; the fruit itself, either red or orange in color.

Jap-a-nize *v.* To conform to Japanese ideas or usages. **Japanization** *n.*

Ja-pan wax *n.* A derivative from berries of Chinese and Japanese sumacs, used in the manufacturing of furniture and floor polishes.

jape *v.* To joke; to make fun of or mock by words or actions.

jape, japer, japery *n.*

Jap-o-nism *n.* To adapt to Japanese styles or methods; any mannerism or trait that is characteristic of the Japanese.

jar *n.* A deep, cylindrical vessel with a wide mouth; a harsh sound. *v.* To strike against or bump into; to affect one's feelings unpleasantly.

jar-di-niere *n.* A decorative pot or stand for flowers or plants; a garnish for meat made from cooked and diced vegetables.

jar-gon *n.* The technical or specialized vocabulary used among members of a particular profession; a type of speech containing pretentious or unfamiliar words; unintelligible writing or speech; gibberish. **jargonistic** *adj.*

jar-gon-ize *v.* To write or communicate jargon; a means of expressing oneself with jargon

jasmine *or* **jes-sa-mine** *n.* A shrub with fragrant yellow or white flowers.

jas-per *n.* An opaque red, brown, or yellow variety of quartz, having a high polish and often used for jewelry and vases.

ja-to *n.* A takeoff of an airplane which is assisted by an auxiliary rocket engine.

jaun-dice *n., Pathol.* A diseased condition of the liver due to the presence of bile pigments in the blood and characterized by yellowish staining of the eyes, skin, and body fluids.

jaun-diced *adj.* To be affected with jaundice.

jaunt *n.* A short journey for pleasure. *v.* To make a short journey, trip, or excursion. **jaunt** *v.*

jaun-ty *adj.* Having a buoyantly carefree and self-confident air or matter about oneself. **januntily** *adv.*, **jauntiness** *n.*

jaunt-ing car *n.* A light weight, open air cart that has two seats, set back to back or facing each other, with an area in front for the driver.

Ja-va *n., Slang* Coffee.

Jav-a-nese *n.* A native of Java or their language.

jave-lin *n.* A light spear thrown as a weapon; a long spear with a wooden shaft, used in competitions of distance throwing.

jave-lin throw *v.* To wound or strike with a javelin.

jaw *n., Anat.* Either of the two bony structures forming the framework of the mouth and holding the teeth. *Slang* To talk excessively.

jaw-bone *n.* One of the bones of the jaw, especially the lower jaw or mandible.

jaw-break-er *n.* A very hard piece of candy. *Slang* A word which is hard to pronounce.

Jaws of Life *n.* A trademark for a metal device having pincer-like arms used to provide access to persons trapped inside a crushed vehicle.

jay *n.* Any of various corvine birds of brilliant coloring, as the blue jay.

Jay-cee *n.* A young man belonging to an organization connected with a city's chamber of commerce.

jay-hawk-er *n.* The nickname for a person who is a native of Kansas.

jay-walk v., *Slang* To cross a street carelessly, violating traffic regulations and or signals. **jaywalker** n.

jazz n. A kind of music which has a strong rhythmic structure with frequent syncopation and often involving ensemble and solo improvisation. *Slang* Lying and exaggerated talk; idle and foolish talk; liveliness. *Jazz up* To make more interesting; to enliven. **jazzer** n., **jazzy** adj.

jazz band n. A musical band that plays jazz, and typically uses the saxophone, clarinet, piano, trombone, and drums.

jct abbr. Junction.

jeal-ous adj. Suspicious or fearful of being replaced by a rival; resentful or bitter in rivalry; demanding exclusive love. **jealously** adv., **jealousness**, **jealousy** n.

jean n. A strong, twilled cotton cloth. **jeans** Pants made of denim.

jeep n. A trademark for a small, military, and civilian vehicle with four-wheel drive.

jeer v. To speak or shout derisively. **jeer**, **jeerer** n., **jerringly** adv.

Jef-fer-son City n. The capital of the state of Missouri.

Je-ho-vah n. God, in the Christian translations of the Old Testament.

je-june adj. Lacking in substance or nourishment; immature.

je-ju-num n., pl. **-na** *Ant.* The part of the small intestine which extends from the duodenum to the ileum.

jel-ly n. pl. **-ies** Any food preparation made with pectin or gelatin and having a somewhat elastic consistency; a food made of boiled and sweetened fruit juice and used as a filler or spread. v. To make into jelly; to become or take the form of jelly; to become gelatinous; to assume or cause to assume definite form.

jel-ly-bean n. A small candy having a hard, colored coating over a gelatinous center.

jel-ly-fish n., pl. **fishes** Any of a number of freeswimming marine animals of jellylike substance, often having bell or umbrella-shaped bodies with trailing tentacles. *Slang* A person lacking determination; a spineless weakling.

jeop-ard-ize v. To put in jeopardy; to expose to loss or danger.

jeop-ard-y n. Exposure to loss or danger.

jer-bo-a n.

Any of a type of small, nocturnal rodent of Asia and Africa with long hind legs.

jer-e-mi-ad n. A lament or prolonged complaint.

Jer-emi-ah n. A Hebrew prophet of the seventh century B.C.

jerk v. To give a sharp twist or pull to. n. A sudden movement, as a tug or twist. *Physiol.* An involuntary contraction of a muscle resulting from a reflex action. *Slang* An annoying or foolish person. **-y**, **jerkily** adv., **jerkiness** n.

jer-kin n. A close-fitting jacket, usually sleeveless.

jerk-wa-ter adj. Of little importance.

jer-ry--build v. To build flimsily and cheaply. **jerry--builder** n.

jer-sey n., pl. **-seys** A soft ribbed fabric of wool, cotton, or other material; a knitted sweater, jacket, or shirt; fawn-colored, small dairy cattle which yield milk rich in butter fat.

Je-ru-sa-lem n. Capital of Israel.

jest n. An action or remark intended to provoke laughter; a joke; a playful mood. **jester** n.

Jes-u-it n. A member of the Society of Jesus, a religious order founded in 1534.

Je-sus n. The founder of Christianity, son of Mary and regarded in the Christian faith as Christ the son of God, the Messiah; also referred to as Jesus Christ or Jesus of Nazareth.

jet n.

A sudden spurt or gush of liquid or gas emitted through a narrow opening; a jet airplane; a hard, black mineral which takes a high polish and is used in jewelry; a deep glossy black.

jet lag n. Mental and physical fatigue resulting from rapid travel through several time zones.

jet set n. An international social group of wealthy individuals who travel from one fashionable place to another for pleasure. **jet setter** n.

jet stream n. A high-velocity wind near the troposphere, generally moving from west to east often at speeds exceeding 250 mph.; a high-speed stream of gas or other fluid expelled from a jet engine or rocket.

jet-ti-son v. To throw cargo overboard; to discard a useless or hampering item.

jet-ty n., pl. **-ies** A wall made of piling rocks, or other material which extends into a body of water to protect a harbor or influence the current; a pier.

Jew n. A descendant of the ancient Hebrew people; a person believing in Judaism.

jew-el n. A precious stone used for personal adornment; a person or thing of very rare excellence or value. v. To furnish with jewels. **jewelry** n.

jew-eler or **jew-el-ler** n. A person who makes or deals in jewelry.

Jew-ish adj. Of, relating to, or resembling the Jews, their customs, or their religion. **Jewishness** n.

Jew's harp n. A small musical instrument

held between the teeth when played, consisting of a U-shaped frame with a flexible metal piece attached which is plucked with the finger to produce twanging sounds.

Jez-e-bel *n.* The wife of Ahab, queen of Israel in the 9th century B.C., notorious for her evil actions.

jib *n., Naut.* A triangular sail set on a stay extending from the head of the foremast to the bowsprit. *v.* To swing or shift from one side of a vessel to the other.

jif-fy *or* **jiff** *n., pl.* **-ies, jiffs** A very short time.

jig *n.* Any of a variety of fast, lively dances; the music for such a dance. *Mech.* A device used to hold and guide a tool. **jig** *v.*

jig-ger *n.* A small measure holding 1 1/2 oz. used for measuring liquor. *Naut.* A small sail in the stern of a sailing craft. *Slang* Any small item which does not have a particular name.

jig-gle *v.* To move or jerk lightly up and down. *n.* A jerky, unsteady movement.

jig-saw *n.* A saw having a slim blade set vertically, used for cutting curved or irregular lines.

jigsaw puzzle *n.* A puzzle consisting of many irregularly shaped pieces which fit together and form a picture.

jilt *v.* To discard a lover. *n.* A woman or girl who discards a lover.

jim-my *n., pl.* **-ies** A short crowbar, often used by a burglar. *v.* To force open or break into with a jimmy.

jim-son-weed *n.* A tall, coarse, foul-smelling, poisonous annual weed with large, trumpet-shaped purplish or white flowers.

jin-gle *v.* To make a light clinking or ringing sound. *n.* A short, catchy song or poem, as one used for advertising.

jin-go-ism *n.* Extreme nationalism which is marked by a belligerent foreign policy. **jingoist** *n.,* **jingoistic** *adj.*

jinn *n., pl.* **jin-ni** In the Moslem legend, a spirit with supernatural powers.

jinx *n., Slang* A person or thing thought to bring bad luck; a period of bad luck.

jit-ney *n.* A vehicle carrying passengers for a small fee.

jit-ter *v., Slang* To be intensely nervous. **jittery** *adj.*

jit-ter-bug *n., Slang* A lively dance or one who performs this dance.

jit-ters *n.* Nervousness.

jive *n., Slang* Jazz or swing music and musicians.

job *n.* Anything that is done; work that is done for a set fee; the project worked on; a position of employment. **jobless** *adj.,* **joblessness** *n.*

job-ber *n.* One who buys goods in bulk from the manufacturer and sells them to retailers; a person who works by the job; a pieceworker.

job-name *n.* Computer Science. A code that is assigned to a specific job in-

struction in a computer program, for the operator's use.

jock *n., Slang* A male athlete in college; a person who participates in athletics.

jock-ey *n.* A person who rides a horse as a professional in a race; one who works with a specific object or device.

joc-u-lar *adj.* Marked by joking; playful. **jocularity** *n.,* **jocularly** *adv.*

joc-und *adj.* Cheerful; merry; suggestive of high spirits and lively mirthfulness. **jocundity** *n.,* **jocundly** *adv.*

jog *n.* A slight movement or a slight shake; the slow steady trot of a horse, especially when exercising or participating in a sport; a projecting or retreating part in a surface or line. *v.* To shift direction abruptly; to exercise by running at a slow but steady pace.

jog-gle *v.* To move or shake slightly.

john *n., Slang* Toilet; a prostitute's client.

John *n.* One of the twelve Apostles.

John Doe *n., Law* A person in a legal proceeding whose true name is unknown.

John Hancock *n.* One of the signer's of the Declaration of Independence. *Slang* A signature.

john-ny-cake *n.* A thin bread made with cornmeal.

john-ny---come---late-ly *n., pl.* **-ies** *Slang* A late or recent arrival.

Johnson, Lyndon Baines (1908-1973) The 36th president of the United States from 1963-1969.

John the Baptist *n.* The baptizer of Jesus Christ.

join *v.* To bring or put together so as to form a unit; to become a member of an organization; to participate.

join-er *n.* A person whose occupation is to build articles by joining pieces of wood; a cabinetmaker; a carpenter.

joint *n.*

The place where two or more things or parts are joined; a point where bones are connected. *Slang* A disreputable or shabby place of entertainment. *adj.* Marked by cooperation, as a joint effort.

join-ture *n., Law* A settlement of property arranged by a husband which is to be used for the support of his wife after his death.

joist *n.* Any of a number of small parallel beams set from wall to wall to support a floor.

joke *n.* Something said or done to cause laughter, such as a brief story with a punch line; something not taken seriously. *v.* To tell or play jokes. **jokingly** *adv.*

jok-er *n.* A person who jokes; a playing card, used in certain card games as a wild card; an unsuspected or unapparent fact which nullifies a seeming advantage.

jol·li·fi·ca·tion *n.* Merrymaking; festivity.

jol·ly *adj.* Full of good humor; merry. **jollity** *n.*, **jolly** *v.*

jolt *v.* To knock or shake about. *n.* A sudden bump or jar, as from a blow. **jolty** *adj.*

Jon·ah *n.* An 8th or 9th century B.C. Hebrew prophet who was swallowed by a whale and then cast on the shore alive three days later; a person who brings bad luck.

jon·quil *n.* A widely grown species of narcissus related to the daffodil, having fragrant white or yellow flowers and long narrow leaves.

Joseph *n.* The husband of Mary, the mother of Jesus.

Joseph of Arimathea *n.* A very wealthy disciple of Christ who provided the tomb for his burial.

josh *v.*, *Slang* To make good-humored fun of someone; to tease; to joke.

Jos·hu·a *n.* The successor to Moses.

joss *n.* A Chinese idol or image.

joss stick *n.* A stick of incense burnt by the Chinese.

jos·tle *v.* To make one's way through a crowd by pushing, elbowing, or shoving. **jostler** *n.*

jot *v.* To make a brief note of something. *n.* A tiny bit.

jounce *v.* To bounce; to bump; to shake. **jounce** *n.*, **jouncy** *adj.*

jour *abbr.* Journal; journalist.

jour·nal *n.* A diary or personal daily record of observations and experiences; in book-keeping, a book in which daily financial transactions are recorded. *Mech.* The part of an axle which rotates in or against a bearing.

jour·nal·ese *n.* The vocabulary and style of writing supposedly characteristic of most newspapers.

jour·nal·ism *n.* The occupation, collection, writing, editing, and publishing of newspapers and other periodicals. **journalist** *n.*, **journalistic** *adj.*, **journalistically** *adv.*

jour·ney *n.* A trip from one place to another over a long distance; the distance that is traveled. *v.* to make a trip; to travel a long distance.

jour·ney·man *n.*, *pl.* **-men** A worker who has served an apprenticeship in a skilled trade.

joust *n.* A formal combat between two knights on horseback as a part of a medieval tournament.

Jove *Interj.* A mild expression of surprise or emphasis.

jo·vi·al *adj.* Good-natured; good-humored; jolly. **joviality** *n.*

jowl *n.* The fleshy part of the lower jaw; the cheek. **jowly** *adj.*

joy *n.* A strong feeling of great happiness; delight; a state or source of contentment or satisfaction; anything which makes one delighted or happy. **joyfully** *adv.*, **joyfulness** *n.*, **joyless** *adj.*, **joylessly** *adv.*, **joylessness** *n.*

joy·ous *adj.* Joyful; causing or feeling joy. **joyously** *adv.*, **joyousness** *n.*

joy ride *Slang* A ride taken for pleasure only.

joy stick *Slang* The control stick of an airplane or video game.

JP *abbr.* Justice of the Peace.

JR *abbr.* Junior.

ju·bi·lant *adj.* Exultantly joyful or triumphant; expressing joy. **jubilance** *n.*, **jubilantly** *adv.*

ju·bi·la·tion *n.* Rejoicing; exultation.

ju·bi·lee *n.* A special anniversary of an event; any time of rejoicing.

Ju·dah *n.* In the Old Testament, a son of Jacob and Leah; the ancient kingdom in southern Palestine.

Ju·da·ic *or* **Judaical** *adj.* Of or pertaining to Jews. **Judaically** *adv.*

Ju·da·ism *n.* The religious practices or beliefs of the Jews; a religion based on the belief in one God.

Ju·das *n.* One of the twelve Apostles; the betrayer of Jesus; one who betrays another under the guise of friendship.

Ju·de·a *or* **Ju·dea·a** *n.* The southern part of ancient Palestine. **Judea, Judean** *adj.* & *n.*

judge *v.*, *Law* A public officer who passes judgment in a court. *v.* To decide authoritatively after deliberation.

judg·ment *or* **judge·ment** *n.* The ability to make a wise decision or to form an opinion; the act of judging. *Law* The sentence or determination of a court. **judgmental** *adj.*

ju·di·ca·ture *n.* The function or action of administration of justice; law, courts, or judges as a whole.

ju·di·cial *adj.* Pertaining to the administering of justice, to courts of law, or to judges; enforced or decreed by a court of law. **judicially** *adv.*

ju·di·ci·ar·y *adj.* Of or pertaining to judges, courts, or judgments. *n.* The department of the government which administers the law; a system of courts of law.

ju·di·cious *adj.* Having, showing, or exercising good sound judgment. **judiciously** *adv.*, **judiciousness** *n.*

Judith *n.* A Jewish heroine who rescued her countrymen by slaying the Assyrian general, Holofernes.

ju·do *n.* A system or form of self-defense, developed from jujitsu in Japan in 1882, which emphasizes principles of balance and leverage.

jug *n.* A small pitcher or similar vessel for holding liquids. *Slang* A jail.

jug·ger·naut *n.* Any destructive force or object.

jug·gle *v.* To keep several objects continuously moving from the hand into the air; to practice fraud or deception.

jug·u·lar *adj.*, *Anat.* Of or pertaining to the region of the throat or the jugular vein.

jug·u·lar vein *n.*, *Anat.* One of the large veins on either side of the neck.

juice *n.* The liquid part of a vegetable, fruit, or animal. *Slang* Electric current.

juic·er *n.* A device for extracting juice from fruit.

juic·y *adj.* Full of; abounding with juice; full of interest; richly rewarding, especially financially. **juiciness** *n.*

ju·jit·su *or* **ju·jut·su** *n.* A Japanese system of using holds, throws, and stunning blows to subdue an opponent.

juke box *n.* A large, automatic, coin-operated record player equipped with push buttons for the selection of records.

ju·lep *n.* A mint julep.

ju·li·enne *adj.* Cut into thin strips. *n.* A clear meat soup containing vegetables chopped or cut into thin strips.

July *n.* The seventh month of the year, having 31 days.

jum·ble *v.* To mix in a confused mass; to throw together without order; to confuse or mix something up in the mind.

jum·bo *n.* A very large person, animal, or thing. *adj.* Extremely large.

jump *v.* To spring from the ground, floor, or other surface into the air by using a muscular effort of the legs and feet; to move in astonishment; to leap over; to increase greatly, as prices. *Informal* To attack by surprise. *Computer Science* To move from one set of instructions in a program to another set further behind or ahead.

jump·er *n.* One who or that which jumps; a sleeveless dress, usually worn over a blouse. *Electr.* A short wire used to bypass or join parts of a circuit.

jump shot *n., Basketball* A shot made at the highest point of a jump.

jump·y *adj.* Nervous; jittery. **-iness** *n.*

jun·co *n.* Any of various small birds of North America, having mainly gray plumage.

junc·tion *n.* The place where lines or routes meet, as roads or railways; the process of joining or the act of joining.

junc·ture *n.* The point where two things join; a crisis; an emergency; a point in time.

June *n.* The sixth month of the year, having 30 days.

Ju·neau *n.* The capital of the state of Alaska.

June beetle *or* **June bug** *n.* A large, brightly colored beetle which flies in June and has larvae that live in the soil and often destroy crops.

jun·gle *n.* A densely covered land with tropical vegetation, usually inhabited by wild animals. **jungle** *adj.*

jun·ior *adj.* Younger in years or rank, used to distinguish the son from the father of the same first name; the younger of two. *n.* The third year of high school or college.

junior high school *n.* A school which includes the 7th, 8th, and 9th grades.

ju·ni·per *n.* An evergreen shrub or tree of Europe and America with dark blue berries, prickly foliage, and fragrant wood.

junk *n.* Discarded material, as glass, scrap iron, paper, or rags; a flat-bottomed Chinese ship with battened sails; rubbish; worthless matter. *Slang* Heroin, narcotics or dope.

jun·ket *n.* A party, banquet, or trip; a trip taken by a public official with all expenses paid for by public funds; a custard-like dessert of flavored milk set with rennet. **junket** *v.*, **junketeer** *n.*

junk·ie *or* **junk·y** *n.* Slang A drug addict that uses heroin.

Juno *n.* In Roman mythology, the queen of heaven.

Ju·no·esque *adj.* Stately and beautiful.

jun·ta *n.* A body of men or persons, as military officers, in power following a coup d'etat.

Ju·pi·ter *n., Astron.* The fifth planet from the sun; the largest planet in the solar system.

ju·rid·i·cal *or* **ju·rid·ic** *adj.* Of or pertaining to the law and to the administration of justice.

ju·ris·dic·tion *n.* The lawful right or power to interpret and apply the law; the territory within which power is exercised. **jurisdictional** *adj.*

ju·ror *n.* A person who serves on a jury.

ju·ry *n., pl.* **-ies** A group of legally qualified persons summoned to serve on a judicial tribunal to give a verdict according to evidence presented.

just *adj.* Fair and impartial in acting or judging; morally right; merited; deserved; based on sound reason. *adv.* To the exact point; precisely; exactly right. **justly** *adv.*, **justness** *n.*

jus·tice *n.* The principle of moral or ideal rightness; conformity to the law; the abstract principle by which right and wrong are defined; a judge.

justice of the peace *n.* A local magistrate having limited jurisdiction with authority to try minor cases, administer oaths, and perform marriages.

justified margin *n.* A typing or typesetting margin with all the characters at the ends of the lines vertically aligned.

jus·ti·fy *v.* To be just, right, or valid; to declare guiltless; to adjust or space lines to the proper length. **-iable** *adj.*, justifiably *adv.*, justification *n.*

jut *v.* To extend beyond the main portion; to project.

jute *n.* A tall, annual Asian herb of the linden family, yielding a strong, coarse fiber used to make sacking and rope.

ju·ve·nile *adj.* Young; youthful; not yet an adult. *n.* A young person; an actor who plays youthful roles; a child's book.

ju·ve·nile court *n.* A court which deals only with cases involving dependent, neglected, and delinquent children.

ju·ve·nile de·lin·quent *n.* A person who is guilty of violations of the law, but is too young to be punished as an adult criminal; a young person whose behavior is out of control.

jux·ta·pose *v.* To put side by side; to place together. **-ed** *adj.*, **-ition** *n.*

K, k The eleventh letter of the English alphabet. In Computer science, a unit of storage capacity equal to 1024 bytes.

Kaa-ba n. Building in the Great Mosque at Mecca that contains the sacred stone said to have been turned black in color, by the tears of the repentant pilgrims or by the sins of people who have rubbed or touched it.

ka-bob n. Cubed meat and mushrooms, onions, and tomatoes placed on a skewer usually marinated, and broiled over an open fire.

ka-bu-ki n. A traditional Japanese drama in which dances and songs are performed in a stylized fashion.

Kad-dish n. A Jewish prayer recited by mourners after the death of a relative and during other daily prayers in the synagogue.

kaf-fee klatsch n. An informal get-to-gether to drink coffee and talk.

kaf-ir n. A grain sorghum that is cultivated in dry areas, having a tough leafy stalk and is used for fodder

kai-nite n. A mineral that is used as a fertilizer and a source of magnesium and potassium.

ka-ka n. A New Zealand parrot, having an olive-brown color.

ka-ka-po n. A large parrot.

kale n. A green cabbage having crinkled leaves which do not form a tight head.

ka-lie-do-scope n. A tubular instrument rotated to make successive symmetrical designs by using mirrors reflecting the changing patterns made by pieces of loose colored glass at the end of a tube. **kaleidoscopic, -ical** adj., **kaleidoscopically** adv.

kale-yard school n. A school of writers form the 19th century who wrote about Scottish life in a very sentimental manner, using heavy dialect.

kal-mi-a n. An evergreen shrub of North America, having pink, white, or purple flowers.

kame n. A short ridge of gravel and sand that remains after glacial ice melts.

kam-ik n. Boot made of sealskin, knee-high in length and worn in the eastern arctic regions.

ka-mi-ka-ze n. A Japanese pilot in World War II trained to make a suicidal crash; an aircraft loaded with explosives used in a suicide attack.

kam-pong n. A group of dwellings or a local village in countries that speak Malay.

kan-ga-roo n., pl. **-roo, roos**

Any of various herbivorous marsupials, of Australia, with short forelegs, large hind limbs, capable of jumping, and a large tail.

kan-ga-roo court n. A self-appointed, il-

legal court, usually marked by incompetence or dishonesty. where the laws are deliberately totally disregarded or misinterpreted.

Kan-sas n. A state in the central United States. **Kansan** n.

ka-o-lin or **ka-o-line** n. A fine clay which remains white after firing, used in ceramics an in manufacturing high quality porcelain.

Ka-pell-meis-ter n. The director of a choir, band, or orchestra.

ka-pok n. A silky fiber manufactured from the fruit of the silk-cotton tree and used for stuffing cushions, life preservers, pillows, and sleeping bags and also used for insulation.

ka-put adj., Slang Destroyed or out of order; something with no possibility of success.

kar-a-kul n. Any of a breed of fat-tailed sheep of central Asia having a narrow body and coarse wiry, brown fur.

kar-at n. A unit of measure for the fineness of gold; a measure of weight for precious gems.

ka-ra-te n. A Japanese art of self-defense, in which a person uses his elbows, feet, and knees in a quick, damaging blow to his opponent.

kar-ma n. The over-all effect of one's behavior, held in Hinduism and Buddhism to determine one's destiny in a future existence. **karmic** adj.

ka-ross n. Animal skins sewn together into the shape of a square and worn by natives; a throw rug made from animal skins.

kar-y-o-lymph n. Biol. The transparent substance surrounding the nucleus of a cell.

Kash-mir goat n. A goat from India that is raised for is find delicate wool, from which cashmere items are made.

ka-ty-did n. Any of various green insects related to grasshoppers and crickets, having specialized organs on the wings of the male that make a shrill sound when rubbed together.

katz-en-jam-mer n. A feeling of uneasiness, worry, or nervousness that follows intoxication.

kay-ak n. A watertight Eskimo boat, having a circular hole in the top for the occupant, and made from a light wooden frame, covered with sealskin.

kay-o v. To knock out an opponent, in boxing. n. A knockout

ka-zoo n. A toy musical instrument with a paper membrane which vibrates when a player hums into the tube.

ke-a n. A New Zealand parrot.

kedge n. A small anchor. v. Pull a ship by the rope of an anchor.

keel n. The central main stem on a ship or aircraft which runs lengthwise along the center line from bow to stern, to which a frame is built upwards. v. To capsize. **keel over**. To fall over suddenly; turn upside down. **keelless** adj.

keel-age n. A fee for mooring a ship in

port.

keel-boat n. A boat used on rivers; shallow boat used for freight.

keel-haul v. To drag a person under the keel of a ship as a form of punishment.

keel-son n., *Naut*. A structural member fastened above and parallel to the keel to give additional strength.

keen adj. Having a sharp edge or point; acutely painful or harsh; intellectually acute; strong; intense. *Slang* Great. **keenly** adv., **keenness** n., **keener** n.

keep v. To have and hold; to not let go; to maintain, as business records; to know a secret and not divulge it; to protect and defend. **keeper** n., **keeping** n., **keepable** adj.

keep back v. To withhold things; to prevent one from coming forward.

keep-er n. One who keeps, guards, or maintains something; a person who respects or observes a requirement; a device for holding something in place, as a latch, or clasp.

keep-ing n. Charge or possession; conformity or harmony; maintenance or support; be consistent with.

keep off v. To fend or avert off. v. To stay back or remain at a distance.

keep-sake n. A memento or souvenir; a token or remembrance of friendship.

keep up v. To persist in, sustain, or continue. To remain equal or even to; to stay informed; to continue without interruption.

kef n. A tranquil and dreamy state; a narcotic.

keg n. A small barrel usually having the capacity of five to ten gallons; the unit of measure for nails which equals 100 pounds.

keg-ler n. A bowler.

Keller, Helen n. 1880-1968 American author and lecturer who was deaf, mute, and blind.

kelp n. Any of a large brown seaweeds.

kel-pie n. A sheep dog originally bred in Australia.

kemp n. A course hairlike fiber used in the making of carpet.

ken-nel n. A shelter for or a place where dogs or cats are bred, boarded, or trained. **kenneled, kenneling.** v.

Ken-ny meth-od n., *Med*. A treatment for poliomyelitis that involves both exercise and hot applications.

ke-no n. A game of chance resembling bingo; a lottery game.

Ken-tuck-y n. A state located in the east central United States. **-ian** adj. & n.

Ken-tuck-y cof-fee tree n. A tree that has thick, wood pods whose seeds were at one time used as a coffee bean substitute.

kep-i n. A French military cap having a flat, round top and a visor.

ker-a-tin n. A fibrous protein which forms the basic substance of nails, hair, horns, and hoofs. **keratinous** adj.

ker-a-to-plas-ty n., *Surg*. An operation that replaces damaged corneal tissue with healthy corneal tissue. **keratoplastic** adj.

ker-chief n. A piece of cloth usually worn around the neck or on the head; scarf. **kerchiefed, kerchieft** adj.

ker-mis n. An annual fair of the Netherlands.

ker-nel n. A grain or seed, as of corn, enclosed in a hard husk; the inner substance of a nut; the central, most important part. **kernelly** adj.

ker-o-sene or **ker-o-sine** n. An oil distilled from petroleum or coal and used for illumination.

ker-ri-a n. A shrub of Japan, having ridged, green stems and double or single flowers that are yellow in color.

ker-sey n. A coarse cloth made from wool and cotton used mainly for rugged garments and outer wear.

ker-sey-mere n. A twill weave cloth made from fine wool; also sassimere.

ke-ryg-ma n. The apostolic teaching of the life and teachings of Jesus as Christ.

kes-trel n. A small falcon, that hovers in the air with its head in the direction of the wind, having a gray and brown plumage, common in Europe inhabiting coasts, moors, and farms.

ketch n. A small sailing vessel with two masts one large mainmast toward the bow of the ship, and a smaller mizzenmast in the direction of the stern but before the rudder.

ketch-up n. A thick, smooth sauce made form tomatoes; also catsup.

ke-tene n. A gas which is colorless and poisonous, having a penetrating odor.

ke-to adj. Having or pertaining to a ketone.

ke-tol n. Organic compound having both a ketone and alcohol group.

ke-tone n. An organic compound; used as a solvent; acetone. **ketonic** adj., **ketosis** n.

ket-tle n. A pot or vessel, usually made of metal, used for stewing or boiling liquids.

ket-tle-drum n. A musical instrument with a parchment head which can be tuned by adjusting the tension.

ket-tle of fish n. A mess; an awkward situation; matter of consideration.

key n. An object used to open a lock; button or level pushed on a keyboard of a typewriter, piano, etc.; the crucial or main element. **keyed** adj.

Key, Francis Scott n. 1779-1843. American poet and lawyer.

key-board n. A bank of keys, as on a piano, typewriter, or computer terminal. v. To set by means of a keyed typesetting machine; to generate letters by means of a word processor.

key club n. A private club that offers entertainment and serves liquor; a nightclub.

key-hole n. Lock; area or hole in a lock where a key is inserted.

key-note n., *Mus*. The first and harmonically fundamental tone of a scale;

main principle or theme.

key-note ad-dress *n.* An opening speech that outlines issues for discussion.

key-punch *n.* A machine operated from a keyboard that uses punched holes in tapes or cards for data processing systems. **keypunch** *n.*, **keypuncher** *v.*

key ring *n.* A metal ring upon which keys are kept.

key-stone *n.* The wedge-shaped stone at the center of an arch that locks its parts together; an essential part; the part upon which the other parts depend.

key-stroke *n.* A stroke of a key, as of a typewriter.

key-way *n.* A slot cut in a wheel hub or shaft for the reception of a key.

key word *n.* A word having special significance in relation to other phrases, words, etc.

kg *abbr.* Kilogram.

khad-dar *n.* Cloth made from cotton.

khak-i *n.* A yellowish brown or olive-drab color; a sturdy twilled cotton cloth being khaki in color. **khakis** A uniform of khaki cloth. **khaki** *adj.*

khan *n.* An Asiatic title of respect; a medieval Turkish, Mongolian or Tartar ruler. **khanate** *n.*

khe-dive *n.* A ruler of Egypt from 1867 to 1914 governing as a viceroy of the sultan of Turkey.

kib-itz *v.* **Slang** To look on and offer meddlesome advice to others. **-er** *n.*

kick *v.* To strike something with a force by the foot. **kick in** To put in money. **kick out** To expel with force. **kicker** *n.*

kick-back *n.* A secret payment to a person who can influence a source of income; repercussion; a strong reaction.

kick-off *n.* The play that begins a game of soccer or football.

kick-stand *n.* The swiveling bar for holding a two-wheeled vehicle upright.

kid *n.* A young goat; leather made from the skin of a young goat. **Slang** A child; youngster *v.* To mock or tease playfully to deceive for fun; to fool. **kiddish** *adj.*, **kiddishness**, **kidder** *n.*

kid-nap *v.* To seize and hold a person; unlawfully, often for ransom. **-per** *n.*, **kidnaping**, **kidnapping** *v.*

kid-ney *n.*, *pl.* **-neys**

Either of two organs situated in the abdominal cavity of vertebrates whose function is to keep proper water balance in the body and to excrete wastes in the form of urine.

kidney bean *n.* A bean grown for its edible seeds.

kidvid *n.*, **Slang** Television programming for kids.

kiel-ba-sa *n.* A smoked Polish sausage.

kill *n.* To put to death; nullify; cancel; to slaughter for food; to deprive of life; to neutralize or destroy the active qualities. **killer** *n.*

kill-deer *n.*, *pl.* **-deer, -deers** A bird characterized by a plaintive, penetrating cry.

killer whale *n.* A black and white carnivorous whale, found in the colder waters of the seas.

kil-lick *n.* An anchor for a boat sometimes consisting of a stone secured by wood.

kil-li-fish *n.* A fish found in North America belonging to the family Cyprinodontidea.

kill-ing *n.* The act of a person who kills; a slaying. **killingly** *adv.*

kill-joy *n.* One who spoils the enjoyment of others.

kiln *n.* An oven or furnace for hardening or drying a substance, especially one for firing ceramics, pottery, etc.

ki-lo *n.* A kilogram.

kil-o-bit *n.* In computer science, one thousand binary digits.

kil-o-cal-o-rie *n.* One thousand gram calories.

ki-lo-cy-cle *n.* A unit equal to one thousand cycles, one thousand cycles per second.

kil-o-gram *n.* A measurement of weight in the meteoric system equal to slightly more than one third of a pound.

kil-o-li-ter *n.* Metric measurement equal to one thousand liters.

kil-o-me-ter *n.* Metric measurement equal to one thousand meters.

kil-o-ton *n.* One thousand tons; an explosive power equal to that of one thousand tons of TNT.

kil-o-volt *n.* One thousand volts.

kil-o-watt *n.* A unit of power equal to one thousand watts.

kil-o-watt-hour *n.* A unit of electric power consumption of one thousand watts throughout one hour.

kilt *n.* A knee-length wool skirt with deep pleats, usually of tartan, worn especially by men in the Scottish Highlands.

kil-ter *n.* Good condition; proper or working order.

ki-mo-no *n.* A loose, Japanese robe with a wide sash; a loose robe worn chiefly by women.

kin *n.* One's relatives by blood; relatives collectively.

kind *n.* A characteristic; a particular variety or sort.

kind *adj.* Of a friendly, or good-natured disposition; coming from a good-natured readiness to please others. **kindness** *n.*

kin-der-gar-ten *n.* A school or class for young children from the ages of four to six to further their social, mental and physical development.

kin-der-gart-ner *n.* A child who attends kindergarten.

kind-heart-ed *adj.* Having much generosity and kindness.

kin-dle *v.* To ignite; to catch fire; to stir up; to arouse or excited; to excite, as the feelings.

kind-less *adj.* Mean, cruel, unkind, unfriendly. **kindlessly** *adv.*

kin-dling *n.* Easily ignited material such as, sticks, wood chips, etc. used to start a fire.

kind-ly *adv.* A kind nature, disposition, or character; benevolent. **kindliness** *n.*

kind-ness *n.* An act of good will; state or quality of being kind; a kind act.

kin-dred *n.* A person's relatives by blood. *adj.* Having a like nature; similar. **kindredness** *n.*

kin-e-mat-ics *n.* The branch or aspects of dynamics that deals with motion considered apart from force and mass. **kinematic, kinematical** *adj.*, **-ly** *adv.*

kin-e-scope *n.* A cathode-ray tube in a television set which translates received electrical into a visible picture on a screen; a film of a television on broadcast.

ki-ne-sics *n.* To study the relationship between communication and nonverbal body language. **kinesic** *adj.*, **kinesically** *adv.*

ki-ne-si-ol-o-gy *n.* Science that investigates organic and anatomy process in reference to human motion.

kin-es-the-sia *n.* The sense of muscular movement or effort. **kinesthesis, kinesthetic** *adj.*

ki-net-ic *adj.* Of, or pertaining to, or produced by motion.

ki-net-ic art *n.* The type of modern abstract art that attempts to present or indicate a sense of motion.

ki-ne-to-scope *n.* The early form of the motion picture, where a series of pictures pass beneath a small opening for viewing, at a high rate of speed.

kin-folk *n.* Relatives; family.

king *n.* One who rules over a country; a male ruler; a playing card with a picture of a king; the main piece in the game of chess; a crowned checker in the game of checkers. **kingship** *n.*

king-bird *n.* A North American bird belonging to the genus Tyrannus.

king-bolt *n.* A vertical central vehicle to the front axle.

king crab *n.* A large crab-like crustacean common in the coastal waters of Japan, Alaska, and Siberia.

king-craft *n.* The art of ruling as a king; the profession and techniques used by a king.

king-dom *n.* The area or the country which is ruled by a king or queen. **kingdomless** *adj.*

king-fish *n.* A large fish used for food.

king-fish-er *n.* A bright colored bird having a long stout bill and short tails and feeds on fish and insects.

King James Bible *n.* An English translation of the Bible from Hebrew and Greek published in 1611 authorized by King James I of England.

king-let *n.* A very small bird; a king of little importance.

king-ly *adj.* Pertaining to or belonging to a king or kings; monarchical; splendid; befitting a king.

king-pin *n.* The foremost pin of a set arranged in order for playing bowling or tenpins; the most important or essential person.

king post *n.* A post located between the tie beam and the apex of a roof truss.

king-ship *n.* A monarchy; the state, or dignity of a king.

king--size *adj.* Very large; larger than the standard size.

king snake *n.* Large snake found in the southern United States which is non-poisonous.

king-wood *n.* Wood of Brazil with violet-colored stripes.

kink *n.* A tight twist or knot-like curl; a sharp painful muscle cramp; a mental quirk. *v.* To form or cause to form a kink.

kink-y *adj.* Tightly curled; sexually uninhibited. **kinkily** *adv.*, **kinkiness** *n.*

kin-ka-jou *n.* A tropical American mammal having large eyes, brown fur and a long prehensile tail.

ki-osk *n.* A small building used as a refreshment booth or newsstand.

kip *n.* The untanned skin of a calf, a lamb and or an adult of any small breed; a bundle of such hides.

kip-per *n.* A salted and smoked herring or salmon. *v.* To cure by salting, smoking, or drying.

kirk *n.* The Presbyterian Church of Scotland as opposed to the Episcopal Church of Scotland.

Kir-man *n.* An elaborate Persian rug having elaborate floral designs and soft colors.

kir-tle *n.* A woman's long skirt or petticoat; a mans tunic or coat.

kis-met *n.* Fate; appointed lot.

kiss *v.* To touch two lips together in greeting; between two people. **kissable** *adj.*

kit *n.* A collection of tools, supplies, or items for a special purpose.

kitch-en *n.* A room in a house or building used to prepare and cook food.

kitch-en-ette *n.* A small area that functions ar a kitchen.

kitch-en-ware *n.* Dishes, pots, pans, and other utensils that are used in a kitchen.

kite *n.* A light-weight framework of wood and paper designed to fly in a steady breeze at the end of a string; any of various predatory birds of the hawk family having a long, usually forked tail.

kith *or* **kin** *n.* Acquaintances or family.

kitsch *n.* Anything that is pretentious and in poor taste.

kit-ten *n.*

A young cat. **-ish** *adj.*, **-ishly** *adv.*

kit-ty *n.* A small collection or accumulation of objects or money; a young cat or kitten.

kit-ty--cor-nered *adj.* Diagonally; catty-cornered.

ki-va *n.* A Pueblo Indian chamber, used in ceremonies, often underground.

Ki-wa-ni-an *n.* A member of a major national and international service club organized to promote higher business standards and provides service to the community.

ki-wi *n.* A flightless bird, of New Zealand having vestigial wings and a long, slender bill; a vine, native to Asia, which yields a fuzzy-skinned, edible fruit; the fruit of this vine; a student who has not piloted a plane solo.

klatch or klatsch *n.* A social gathering devoted primarily to small talk and gossip.

klep-to-ma-nia *n.* Obsessive desire to steal or impulse to steal, especially without economic motive.

kleptomaniac *n.*

kloof *n.* A ravine; gorge; deep mountain cleft.

kludge *n.* A computer system that is made up of poorly matched components.

klutz *n., Slang* A stupid or clumsy person. **klutziness** *n.*, **klutzy** *adj.*

km *abbr.* Kilometer.

knack *n.* A natural talent; aptitude. **knacker** *n.*

knack-wurst or knock-wurst *n.* A thick or short, heavily seasoned sauage.

knap-sack *n.* A supply or equipment bag, as of canvas or nylon, worn strapped across the shoulders.

knave *n.* Tricky; or dishonest person; a rascal. **knavish** *adj.*, **knavishly** *adv.*

knead *v.* To work dough into a uniform mass; to shape by or as if by kneading. **kneader, kneadability** *n.*, **-able** *adj.*

knee *n.* The joint in the human body which connects the calf with the thigh.

knee action *n.* The front-wheel suspension of an autombile that permits independent vertical movement of each front wheel.

knee-cap *n.* Patella; bone covering the joint of the knee.

knee--deep *adj.* So deep that it reaches ones knees.

keen--high *adj.* Reaching of rising upward toward the keen.

kneel *v.* To go down upon one's knees. **kneeler** *n.*

knell *v.* To sound a bell, especially when rung for a funeral; to toll. *n.* An act or instance of knelling; a signal of disaster.

knick-ers *pl. n.* Short loose-fitting pants gathered at the knee.

knick-knack *n.* A trinket; trifling article.

knife *n.* An instrument used to cut an item. **knifed, knifing** *v.*

knife--edge *n.* A very sharp edge; the edge of a knife.

knife switch *n.* A switch used to close a circuit.

knight *n.* A medieval soldier serving a monarch; a chess piece bearing the shape of a horse's head.

knightly *adj.*

knight bachelor *n.* A knight of the lowest and most ancient order of the English knights.

knight-hood *n.* The character of a knight.

knight-ly *adj.* Dealing with a knight.

knish *n.* Baked or fried dough stuffed with meat, cheese, or potatoes.

knit *v.*

To form by intertwining thread or yarn, by interlocking loops of a single yarn by means of needles; to fasten securely; to draw together.

knit, knitter, knitting *n.*

knitting needle *n.* A long, slender, pointed rod for knitting.

knob *n.* A rounded protuberance; a lump; a rounded mountain; a rounded handle. **knobbed** *adj.*, **knobby** *adj.*

knock *v.* To hit or strike with a hard blow; to criticize; to collide; to make a noise, as that of a defective engine.

knock-down *adj.* Designed to be easily assembled for storage or shipment.

knock down *v.* To strike to the ground with or as with a sharp blow.

knockdown-drag-out *adj.* Extremely violent or bitter.

knock-er *n.* One who or that which knocks; as a metal ring for knocking on a door.

knock-knee *n.* A condition in which one or both knees turn inward and knock or rub together while walking.

knoll *n.* A small round hill; a mound.

knot *n.* A interwinding as of string or rope; a fastening made by tying together lengths of material, as string; a unifying bond, especially of marriage; a hard node on a tree from which a branch grows. *Naut.* A unit of speed, also called a nautical mile which equals approximately 1.15 statute miles per hour. **knot, knotted, knotting** *v.*, **knottiness** *n.*, **knotty** *adj.*

knot-hole *n.* A hole in lumber left by the falling out of a knot.

knout *n.* A whip or scourge for flogging criminals. **knout** *v.*

know *v.* To perceive directly as fact or truth; to believe to be true; to be certain of; to be familiar with or have experience of. **knowable** *adj.*, **knowledge, knower** *n.*

know-how *n.* Knowing how to do something.

know-ing *adj.* To be astute; to know secret knowledge. **knowingly** *adv.*

knowl-edge *n.* Having ability to know facts, information.

knowl-edge-a-ble *adj.* The state of being intelligent.

know--noth-ing *n.* An extremely stupid person.

knuck-le *n.* On the finger; the joint of the finger. **knuckly** *adj.*

knuck-le ball *n.* A pitch used in baseball that is a slow pitch.

knuck-le-bone *n.* The bone of the finger which forms the knuckle.

knuck-le-head *n.* A person who is not very smart; dumb.

knur *n.* A lump or knot of a tree.

knurl *n.* A ridge. **knurled, knurly** *adj.*

ko-a-la *n.*

An Australian marsupial which has large hairy ears, gray fur, and feeds on eucalyptus leaves.

Ko-di-ak- bear *n.* A large bear found in Alaska.

kohl *n.* Dark powder used as cosmetics to darken under the eyes.

kohl-ra-bi *n.*, *pl.* **-ies** A variety of cabbage having a thick stem and eaten as a vegetable.

ko-la *n.* The tree which produces the kola nut.

ko-la nut *n.* The brownish nut used as a tonic and stimulant.

ko-lin-sky *n.* A mink found in Asia.

kook *n.*, *Slang* A crazy or eccentric person. **kookiness** *n.*, **kooky** *adj.*

Ko-ran *n.* The sacred book of Islam, accepted as containing the revelations made to Mohammed by Allah through the angel Gabriel.

ko-sher *adj.* Conformant to eat according to Jewish dietary laws. *Slang* Appropriate; proper.

kow-tow *v.* To show servile deference.

kph *abbr.* Kilometers per hour.

K ra-tion *n.* Emergency food pack used during W.W. II.

kraal *n.* A village of southern African natives; and enclosure for animals in southern Africa.

Krem-lin *n.* The citadel of Moscow which houses the major Soviet government offices; the Soviet government.

kryp-ton *n.* A white, inert gaseous chemical used mainly in fluorescent lamps; symbolized by Kr.

KS *abbr.* Kansas.

ku-dos *n.* Acclaim or prestige resulting from notable achievement or high position; glory; recognition; renown.

ku-miss *n.* The fermented camel's milk drank by Asiatic nomads.

kum-quat *n.* A small, round or oblong yellowish-orange fruit having a sour, acid pulp and edible rind; the tree bearing this fruit.

kung fu *n.* A Japanese art of self-defense similar to karate.

kw *abbr.* Kilowatt.

kwash-i-or-kor *n.* Severe malnutrition, especially in children, caused by protein deficiency.

Ky *abbr.* Kentucky.

ky-pho-sis *n.* Abnormal curving of the spine.

L, l *n.* The twelfth letter of the English alphabet; the Roman numeral for fifty.

LA *abbr.* Louisiana.

la-bel *n.* Something that identifies or describes. **label** *v.* To attach a label to.

la-bi-al *adj.* Pertaining to or of the labia or lips.

la-bi-um *n.*, *pl.* **labia** Any of the four folds of the vulva.

la-bor *n.* Physical or manual work done for hire. *Med.* The physical pain and efforts involved in childbirth. *v.* To work; to progress with great effort.

lab-o-ra-to-ry *n.*, *pl.* **-ies** A place equipped for conducting scientific experiments, research, or testing; a place where drugs and chemicals are produced. *adj.* Suggestive or referring to work done or the functions performed in a laboratory.

la-bor camp *n.* A group of prisoners who have been forced into labor; a place for migrant farm workers.

Labor Day *n.* A legal holiday, the first Monday in September, which recognizes the contributions of working people.

la-bored *adj.* Bearing the marks of constraint and effort; produced with a great amount of labor; heavy.

la-bo-ri-ous *adj.* Toilsome; not easy; requiring much labor; diligent in service or work; industrious. **laboriously** *adv.*, **laborousness** *n.*

la-bor-ite *n.* A person who promotes the theories, interests, and practices of a labor organization; one that belongs to a political party that is devoted mainly to labor interests.

la-bret *n.* A decorative ornament worn by primitive tribes or people, usually made from a piece of wood, bone, etc. and placed through a pierced lip.

la-brum *n.* The upper part of the mouth or an crustacean or insect. *anat.* The cartilage ring around the bony portion of a joint.

lab-y-rinth *n.*

A system of winding, intricate passages; a maze; a strange or bewildering arrangement of circumstances. *anat.* The bony and fluid-filled structures of the inner ear; the inner ear. **labyrinthine** *adj.*

lab-y-rin-thine *adj.* Pertaining to a labyrinth; intricate. **labyrinthically** *adv.*

lac *n.* The resinous secretion left on certain trees by the lac insect and used in making paints and varnishes and the production of red color matter.

lac-co-lith *n.*, *Geol.* A body of igneous rock between beds of overlying strata that causes the formation of domes.

lace *n.* A delicate open-work fabric of silk, cotton, or linen made by hand or on a machine; a cord or string used to fasten two edges together. *v.* To fasten or tie together; to interlace or intertwine. **lacy** *adj.*

lac-er-ate *v.* To open with a jagged tear; to wound the flesh by tearing. *adj.* Having the appearance of being torn.

lac-er-a-tion *n.* The act of tearing; a jagged tear caused by lacerating.

lac-er-til-i-an *n.* Belonging to the family of lizards.

lace-wing *n.* Any insects with bright eyes and lacelike wings, whose larvae prey on plant lice.

lach-es *n., pl.* Inexcusable delay in completing a duty or claiming a legal right.

lach-ry-mal or **lac-ri-mal** *adj.* Relating to or producing tears; relating to the glands that produce tears. *anat.* The organ that produces and secrets tears.

lach-ry-ma-to-ry *adj.* A small vase found in ancient tombs that is said to have held tears from mourners.

lach-ry-mose *adj.* Tearful; crying; trying to provoke tears. **lachrymosely** *adv.*

lac-ing *n.* The act of connecting or fastening; a cord used to draw tight; a trim or braid; a sprinkling of liquor in food or drink.

lack *n.* The deficiency or complete absence of something. *v.* To have little of something or to be completely without; absent; to want something.

lack-a-dai-si-cal *adj.* Lacking life, interest, or spirit; melancholy; listless; lacking in zest. **lackadaisically** *adv.*, **lackadaisicalness** *n.*

lack-ey *n.* A male servant of very low status; a servile follower.

lack-lus-ter *adj.* Lacking sheen; dull; without luster; vitality, or brightness.

lac-quer *n.* A transparent varnish which is dis-solved in a volatile solution and dries to give surfaces a glossy finish.

lac-ri-ma-tor *n.* An eye irritant that causes tears.

la-crosse *n.* A game of American Indian origin played with a ball and long-handled rackets, by two teams of ten men each, to advance the ball into the opponents' goal.

lac-tal-bu-min *n.* A protein that belongs to the albumin class, found in milk and derived from the residue whey, used in the preparation of adhesives, varnishes and some foods.

lac-tate *v.* To secrete or to milk. **-ion** *n.*

lac-ta-tion *n.* The production of milk in mammals; the act of nursing. **lactational** *adj.*, **lactationally** *adv.*

lac-te-al *adj.* Of, resembling, or like milk. *n., Anat.* Any of the lymphatic vessels carrying chyle from the small intestine to the blood.

lac-tic acid *n.* A limpid, syrupy acid that is present in sour milk, molasses, some fruits, and wines.

lac-tif-er-ous *adj.* Producing milk or a milky liquid substances.

lac-tose *n., Biochem.* A white, odorless crystal-line sugar that is found in milk.

la-cu-na *n., pl.* **-nas, -nae** A space from which something is missing; a gap.

lad *n.* A boy or young male; a term that is applied to any male.

laddish *adj.*, **ladhood** *n.*

lad-der *n.* An implement made of metal, wood, or rope used for climbing up or down in order to reach another place or area; a series of accomplishments with reference to position or status. **ladderless, ladderlike, laddery** *adj.*

lad-der-back *adj.* Referring to the back of a chair with horizontal pieces connection two vertical post.

lade *v.* To load down, as with cargo or a burden; to dip or lift out.

lad-en *adj.* Heavily burdened; oppressed; weighed down; loaded. **laden** *v.*

lad-ing *n.* Cargo; freight.

la-dle *n.*

A cup-shaped vessel with a deep bowl and a long handle, used for dipping or conveying liquids. **ladle** *v.*

la-dy *n., pl.* **ladies** A woman showing refinement, cultivation, and often high social position; the woman at the head of a household; an address or term of reference for any woman. *adj.* Having the qualities of a lady; to be ladylike.

la-dy-bug or **la-dy-bird** *n.* Any of a family of brightly colored beetles, black with red spots which feed mainly on aphids and other insects.

lady--in--waiting *n., pl.* **ladies** A lady appointed to wait on a queen or princess.

la-dy-like *adj.* Having the characteristics of a lady; delicate; gentle.

la-dy-love *n.* A mistress or sweetheart; a lady who is loved.

lag *v.* To stray or fall behind; to move slowly; to weaken or decrease gradually. *n.* The process or act of retardation or falling behind; the amount or period of lagging.

lag-an *n.* Something sunk at sea, but attached to a bouy in order to recover it.

lag-gard *adj.* Slow; backward; lagging. *n.* A person who lags behind everyone else; a loiterer. **laggardly** *adv.*, **laggardness** *n.*

la-gniappe *n.* A small gift which is given to a purchaser by a storekeeper. *Informal* Anything given as an extra bonus.

la-goon *n.* A body of shallow water separated from the ocean by a coral reef or sandbars. **lagoonal** *adj.*

la-i-cism *n.* A governmental system which is free from ecclesiastical influence or jurisdiction.

la-i-cize *v.* To take away the jurisdiction of the clergy. **laicization** *n.*

laid Past tense of lay.

laid back *adj., Slang* Casual or relaxed in character.

lain *v.* Past tense of lie.

lair *n.* The den or bed of a wild animal. *v.* To lie in a lair; to place in a lair.

lais-sez--faire *n.* A policy stating that a government should exercise very little control in trade and industrial affairs; noninterference. **laissezfaire** *adj.*

la-i-ty n. Laymen, as distinguished from clergy.

lake n. A large inland body of either salt or fresh water.

La-maze meth-od n. A method of childbirth in which the mother is prepared psychologically and physically to give birth without the use of drugs.

lamb n. A young sheep; the meat of a lamb used as food; a gentle person. v. To give birth, as a ewe.

lam-baste or **lambast** v., *Slang* To thrash or beat; to give an abrasive verbal or written attack on something or someone.

lam-bent adj. Lightly and playfully brilliant; flickering gently; softly radiant; softly bright. lambency n., -ly adv.

lamb-skin n. The skin of a lamb that is dressed with the fleece or wool attached, the leather made from this lamb's skin.

lame adj. Disabled or crippled, especially in the legs or feet so as to impair free movement; weak; ineffective; unsatisfactory. lamely adv., lameness n.

la-me n. A brocaded fabric woven with gold or silver thread, sometimes mixed with other fiber.

lame duck n., *Slang* An officeholder who has been defeated but continues in office until the inauguration of his or her successor. *milit.* A damaged or disabled aircraft. lameduck adj.

la-ment v. To express sorrow; to mourn. n. An expression of regret or sorrow. lamentable adj., -ably adv., -ion n.

lam-i-na n., pl. -nae, -nas A thin scale or layer. *Bot.* The blade or flat part of a leaf.

lam-i-nate v. To form or press into thin sheets; to form layers by the action of pressure and heat. lamination n., laminated adj., laminator n.

lamp n. A device for generating heat or light.

lamp-black n. A black soot of very fine texture of pure carbon.

lamp-light-er n. A person who lights street lamps; a torch or device for lighting lamps.

lam-poon n. A satirical, but often humorous, attack in verse or prose, especially one that ridicules a group, person, or institution. lampoon v., lampoonery, lampooner n.

lamp-post n. A post used to support a lamp that lights a path or street.

lam-prey n. ,pl. preys An eel-like fish having a circular, suctorial mouth with rasping teeth and no jaw.

lam-ster n., *Slang* A person who is fleeing for the law.

lance n. A spear-like implement used as a weapon by mounted knights or soldiers. *lance* v.

lance cor-po-ral n., *Mil.* In the U.S. Marine Corps, an enlisted man who ranks above a private first class and below a corporal.

lance-let n. A small fishlike marine animal, having a transparent body that is pointed at both ends, and usually found beneath sand in shallow waters.

lan-cet arch n. An arch having a sharply pointed apex.

lan-cet win-dow n. A narrow window characterized by a pointed apex.

lance-wood n. Elastic wood that is used for fishing rods and archery bows.

lan-ci-nate v. Pierce or stab; to tear. lancination n.

land n. The solid, exposed surface of the earth as distinguished from the waters. v. To arrive at a destination; to catch a fish; to receive a new job. landless adj.

lan-dau n. A four-wheeled vehicle with a closed carriage and a back seat with a collapsible top.

land-er n. A space vehicle for landing on a celestial body.

land-fall n. The first sight of land when on a trim or journey by air or sea.

land-fill n. A system of trash and garbage disposal in which the waste is burned in low-lying land so as to build up the ground surface; a section built up by landfill.

land grant n. A grant of land made by a government, especially for railroads, roads, or agricultural colleges.

land-hold-er n. An owner, holder, or proprietor of land.

land-ing n. The act of coming, going, or placing ashore from any kind of vessel or craft; the act of descending and settling on the ground in an airplane.

land-ing field n. A cleared area used for take off and landing of aircraft.

land-ing gear n., *Aeron* The area under an aircraft that includes the wheels and their supporting frame.

land-ing strip n. The are on an airstrip where the planes actually touch the surface in takeoffs and landings; a secondary runway.

land-la-dy n. A woman who rents and/or owns buildings or other property; a female landlord.

land-locked adj. Almost or completely surrounded or enclosed by land.

land-lord n. A person who owns property and rents or leases to another; innkeeper.

land-lub-ber n. An inexperienced person on a ship.

land-mark n. A fixed object that serves as a boundary marker of a territory; a turning point.

land mass n. A large body of land.

land meas-ure n. A unit of measurement that is used in giving the area of land, such as an acre.

land of-fice n. An office in which sales of public lands are recorded and open for public inspection.

land-own-er n. A person who owns land.

land-scape n. A view or vista of natural scenery as seen from a single point. v. To change or improve the features of a section of ground by contouring the land and planting shrubs, trees, or flowers.

land-slide n. The shifting or sliding of a large portion of soil from a higher level to a lower level.

lands-man n. An inexperienced seaman. A person who lives on the land.

land-ward adj. Facing, lying, or in the direction of land.

lane n. A small or narrow path between walls, fences, or hedges; any well-definded or narrow channel or passage; a portion of the highway, which is indicated by pavement lines or markings.

lang-syne n. The time long ago; times past.

lan-guage n. The words, sounds, pronunciation and method of combining words used and understood by people.

lan-guid adj. Lacking in energy; drooping; weak; sluggish, listless. languidly adv., languidness n.

lan-guish v. To become weak, dull, or feeble; to be or live in a state of depression. languisher n., -ment n.

lan-guor n. Feebleness; physical exhaustion; listlessness; oppressive stillness. languorous adj., languorously adv.

lank adj. Slender; lean; tall and bony. lanky adv., lankness n.

lank-y adj. Awkwardly tall and thin. lankily adv., lankiness n.

lan-o-lin n. Wool grease obtained from sheep's wool and refined for use in ointments and cosmetics.

Lan-sing n. The capital of the state of Michigan.

lan-tern n. A portable light having transparent or translucent sides.

lan-tern jaw n. A thin, long and projecting lower jaw.

lan-yard n. A piece of rope or line used to secure objects on ships.

la-pel n.

The front part of a garment, especially that of a coat, that is turned back, usually a continuation of the collar.

lap-in n. Rabbit fur that is sheared and dyed.

lap-is laz-u-li n. A semiprecious stone that is azure blue in color.

lap-pet n. A flap or fold on a headdress or on a garment.

lapse n. A temporary deviation or fall to a less desirable state; a gradual falling or slipping; a failure or denial due to neglect; a trivial error. v. To deviate from moral integrity, or the established standard; to slip into ruin; to cease to exist; Law To pass from one person to another through negligence or ommission. lapser n.

lar-ce-ny n., pl. -ies The unlawful taking of another person's property; theft. larcenous adj.

lard n. The soft, white, solid or semisolid fat obtained after rendering the fatty tissue of the hog.

lar-der n. A place, such as a pantry or room, where food is stored.

large adj. Greater than usual or average in amount or size. at large To be free and not confined.

large--heart-ed adj. Sympathetic; generous. large-heartedness n.

large in-tes-tine n. The portion of the intestine that extends from the end of the small intestine to the anus.

large--scale adj. Larger than others of the same kind; extensive; of or relating to a scale drawing to show detail, as a model or map.

lar-gess or lar-gesse n. Liberal or excessive giving to an inferior; generosity; a donation, present, or gift that is given unselfishly.

lar-go adv., Mus. In a very slow, broad, and solemn manner. largo adj. & n.

lar-i-at n. A long, light rope with a running noose at one end to catch livestock.

lark n. A bird having a melodious ability to sing; a merry or carefree adventure. v. Frolic; to behave in an impishly manner.

lar-va n., pl. larvae The immature, wingless, often worm-like form of a newly hatched insect; the early form of an animal that differs greatly from the adult, such as the tadpole. larval adj.

lar-yn-gi-tis n. Inflammation of the larynx. adj. Characteristic or pertaining to the larynx.

lar-ynx n., pl. larynges or larynxes The upper portion of the trachea which contains the vocal cords. laryngeal adj.

la-sa-gna or la-sa-gne n. Traditional Italian dish of wide flat noodles baked with a sauce of tomatoes, meat, and cheese.

la-ser n. A device which utilizes the natural oscillations of molecules or atoms between energy levels for generating coherent electromagnetic radiation in the visible, ultraviolet, or infrared parts of the spectrum.

lash v. To strike or move violently or suddenly; to attack verbally; to whip. n. Eyelash. lasher n.

lass n. A young girl or woman; a sweetheart.

las-si-tude n. A condition of weariness or weakness; fatigue.

las-so n., pl. -sos, -soes A long rope or long leather thong with a running noose used to catch horses and cattle. lasso v.

last adj. Following all the rest; of or relating to the final stages, as of life; worst; lowest in rank. adv. After all others in sequence or chronology. v. To continue. n. A form in the shape of a foot used to hold a shoe while it is repaired or to shape a shoe as it is being made.

last-ly adv. In the last place; finally.

Last Rites n., Eccl. Sacraments of the Roman Catholic Church given to a person near death.

Last Sup-per n. The last meal eaten by

Jesus Christ and his disciples, before his crucifixion.

last word *n.* A final comment in an argument or discussion; a decisive work.

latch *n.* A device used to secure a gate or door, consisting of a bar that usually fits into a notch. *v.* To fasten by means of a latch. **latch onto** To grab onto.

latch-et *n.* A narrow leather strap or thong used to fasten a shoe or sandal onto the foot.

latch-key *n.* A key for opening an outside door.

latch-key child *n* A child whose parent or parents work during the day and who carries a key to the front door because he or she returns home from school to an empty house.

late *adj.* Coming, staying, happening after the proper or usual time; having recently died. **lateness** *n.*, **lately** *adv.*

lat-er-al *adj.* Relating to or of the side. *n.* In football, an underhand pass thrown sideways or away from the line of scrimmage. **laterally** *adv.*

la-tex *n.* The milky, white fluid that is produced by certain plants, such as the rubber tree; a water emulsion of synthetic rubber or plastic globules used in paints and adhesives.

lath *n.* A thin, narrow strip of wood nailed to joists, rafters, or studding and used as a supporting structure for plaster. *v.* To line or cover with lath.

lathe *n.* A machine for holding material while it is spun and shaped by a tool. **lathe** *v.*

lath-er *n.* A foam or suds formed by detergent, or soap and water. **latherer** *n.*, **lathery** *adj.*

lat-i-tude *n.* The angular distance of the earth's surface north or south of the equator, measured in degrees along a meridian; freedom to act and to choose.

Lat-in *n.* A member of the latin peoples; language of the Roman Empire.

lat-i-tude *n.* The angular distance north and south of the equator. **latitudinal** *adj.*, **latitudinally** *adv.*

la-trine *n.* A public toilet, as in a camp or in a barracks.

lat-ten *n.* A brasslike alloy formed in thin sheets.

lat-ter *adj.* Being the second of two persons or two things.

lat-tice *n.* A structure made of strips of wood, metal, or other materials, interlaced or crossed, framing regularly spaced openings. **lattice** *v.*

laud *v.* To praise; to extol. *n.* A hymn or song of praise. **-able** *adj.*, **-ably** *adv.*

laugh *v.* To express amusement, satisfaction, merriment, or pleasure with a smile and inarticulate sounds; to be merry. **laughable** *adj.*

laugh-ter *n.* The expression, sound, or act produced by laughing.

launch *v.* To push or move a vessel into the water for the first time; to set a rocket or missile into flight; to put into operation.

launcher *n.* The mechanical instrument that discharges a rocket or other projectile.

laun-der *v.* To wash clothes or other materials in soap and water. **laundrer, laundress** *n.*

laun-dry *n.*, *pl.* **-ies** An establishment where laundering is done professionally; clothes or other articles to be or that have been laundered.

lau-re-ate A person honored for his accomplishment. **laureate** *v.*

la-va *n.* Molten rock which erupts or flows from an active volcano; the rock formed after lava has cooled and hardened.

lav-a-to-ry *n.*, *pl.* **-ies** A room with permanently installed washing and toilet facilities.

lav-en-der *n.* An aromatic plant having spikes of pale violet flowers; light purple in color. **lavender** *adj.*

lav-ish *adj.* Generous and extravagant in giving or spending. **lavisher** *n.*, **lavishly** *adv.*, **lavishness** *n.*

law *n.* A rule of conduct or action, recognized by custom or decreed by formal enactment, considered binding on the members of a nation, community, or group; a system or body of such rules.

law--a-bid-ing *adj.* Abiding by the laws.

lawn *n.* A stretch of ground covered with grass that is mowed regularly near a house, park, or building.

law-ren-ci-um *n.* A short-lived radioactive element, symbolized by LR.

law-suit *n.* A case or proceeding brought before a court of law for settlement.

law-yer *n.* A person trained in the legal profession who acts for and advises clients or pleads in court.

lax *adj.* Lacking disciplinary control; lacking rigidity or firmness. **laxity, laxness** *n.*, **laxly** *adv.*

lax-a-tive *n.* A medicine taken to stimulate evacuation of the bowels.

lay *v.* To cause to lie; to place on a surface; past tense of lie.

lay-er *n.* A single thickness, coating, or covering that lies over or under another. **layered** *adj.*, **layer** *v.*

lay-ette *n.* The clothing, bedding, and equipment for a newborn child.

lay-man *n.* A person not belonging to a particular profession or specialty; one who is not a member of the clergy.

lay-off *n.* A temporary dismissal of employees.

lay-out *n.* A planned arrangement of something, such as a street, room, park, or building.

la-zy *adj.* Unwilling to work; moving slowly; sluggish. **lazily** *adv.*, **-iness** *n.*

la-zy-bones *n.* *Slang* A lazy person.

lb *abbr.* Pound

L--do-pa *n.* A drug used in treating Parkinson's disease.

lea *n.*, *Poetic.* A grassy field or meadow.

leach *v.* To cause a liquid to pass through a filter; to remove or wash out by filtering. **leachable** *adj.*

lead v. To go ahead so as to show the way; to control the affairs or action of. n. A soft, malleable, heavy, dull gray metallic element symbolized by Pb, used in solder, paints, and bullets; a graphite stick used as the writing material in pencils; in printing, the thin strip of type metal used to provide space between printed lines. **leadenness** n., **leading, leaden** adj.

lead poisoning n. Poisoning of a person's system by the absorption of lead or any of its salts.

leaf n., pl. **leaves**

A flat outgrowth from a plant structure or tree, usually green in color and functioning as the principal area of photosynthesis; a single page in a book. v. To turn the pages of a book. **leafless, leafy** adj.

leaf-let n. A part or a segment of a compound leaf; a small printed handbill or circular, often folded.

league n. An association of persons, organizations, or states for common action or interest; an association of athletic competition; an underwater measurement of distance that equals 3 miles or approximately 4.8 km.

leak n. An opening, as a flaw or small crack, permitting an escape or entrance of light or fluid. **leakage** n., **leakiness** n., **leaky** adj.

lean v. To rest or incline the weight of the body for support; to rest or incline anything against a large object or wall; to rely or depend on; to have a tendency or preference for; to tend towards a suggestion or action. adj. having little or no fat; thin. **leanly** adv., **leanness** n.

lean-ing n. An inclination; a predisposition.

lean--to n. A structure of branches, sloping to the ground from a raised support, usually an outside wall.

leap v. To rise or project oneself by a sudden thrust from the ground with a spring of the legs; to spring, to jump. **leap, leaper** n.

leap-frog n. A game in which two players leap over each other by placing one's hands on the back of another who is bending over and leaping over him in a straddling position.

leap year n. A year containing 366 days, occurring every 4th year, with the extra day added to make 29 days in February.

learn n. The process of acquiring knowledge, understanding, or mastery of a study or experience. **learner** n., **learnable** adj., **learn** v.

lease n. A contract for the temporary use or occupation of property or premises in exchange for payment of rent.

leash n. A strong cord or rope for restraining a dog or other animal.

least-wise adv., Slang At least; at any rate.

leath-er n. An animal skin or hide with the hair removed, prepared for use by tanning.

leath-er-neck n., Slang A United States Marine.

leave v. To go or depart from; to permit to remain behind or in a specified place or condition; to forsake; to abandon; to bequeath, as in a will. n. Official permission for absence from duty.

leav-en n. An agent of fermentation, as yeast, used to cause batters and doughs to rise; any pervasive influence that produces a significant change.

lech-er-y n. Unrestrained indulgence in sexual activity. **lecher** n., **lecherous** adj., **lecherously** adv.

lec-i-thin n. Any of a group of phosphorus containing compounds found in plant and animal tissues, commercially derived from egg yolks, corn, and soybeans, and used in the production of foods, cosmetics, pharmaceuticals, and plastics.

lec-tern n. A stand or tall desk, usually with a slanted top, on which a speaker or instructor may place books or papers.

lec-ture n. A speech on a specific subject, delivered to an audience for information or instruction. v. To give a speech or lecture; to criticize or reprimand.

led v., p.t. & p.p. Past tense of lead.

ledge n. A narrow, shelf-like projection forming a shelf, as on a wall or the side of a rocky formation.

ledg-er n. A book in which sums of money received and paid out are recorded.

lee n. The side of a ship sheltered from the wind.

Lee, Robert E. (Edward) n. (1807-1870) A commander and general of the American Confederacy during the American Civil War.

leech n. Any of various carnivorous or bloodsucking worms; a person who clings or preys on others.

leek n. A culinary herb of the lily family, related to the onion, with a slender, edible bulb.

leer n. A sly look or sideways glance expressing desire or malicious intent.

lee-way n., Naut. The lateral drift of a plane or ship away from the correct course.

left adj. Pertaining to or being on the side of the body that faces north when the subject is facing east.

leg n. A limb or appendage serving as a means of support and movement in animals and man; a part or division of a journey or trip. **leg** v.

leg-a-cy n., pl. -ies Personal property, money, and other valuables that are bequeathed by will; anything that is handed down from an ancestor, predecessor, or earlier era.

le-gal *adj.* Of, pertaining to, or concerned with the law or lawyers; something based on or authorized by law. **legality, legalization** *n.,* **legalize** *v.,* **legally** *adv.*

le-gal-ism *n.* A strict conformity to the law, especially when stressing the letter and forms of the law rather than the spirit of justice. **legalist** *n.,* **legalistic** *adj.*

le-ga-tion *n.* The official diplomatic mission in a foreign country, headed by a minister; the official residence or business premises of a diplomatic minister of lower rank than an ambassador.

le-ga-to *adv., Music* Smooth and flowing with successive notes connected. **legato** *adj. & n.*

leg-end *n.* An unverifiable story handed down from the past; a body of such stories, as those connected with a culture or people.

leg-en-dar-y *adj.* Presented as, based on, or of the nature of a legend.

leg-horn *n.* A hat made from finely plaited wheat straw.

leg-i-ble *adj.* Capable of being read or deciphered. **legibility** *n.,* **legibly** *adv.*

le-gion *n.* In ancient Rome, an army unit that comprised between 4,200 and 6,000 men; any of various honorary or military organizations, usually national in character.

leg-is-late *v.* To pass or make laws.

leg-is-la-tion *n.* The act or procedures of passing laws; lawmaking; an officially enacted law.

leg-is-la-tive *adj.* Of or pertaining to legislation or a legislature; having the power to legislate.

leg-is-la-ture *n.* A body of persons officially constituted and empowered to make and change laws.

leg-ume *n.* A plant of the pea or bean family, that bears pods which split when mature; the seeds or pod of a legume used as food. **leguminous** *adj.*

leg-work *n., Slang* A chore, task, or gathering of information accomplished by going about on foot.

lei *n., pl.* **leis**

A wreath of flowers worn around the neck; the customary greeting of welcome in the state of Hawaii.

lei-sure *n.* The time of freedom from work or duty. **leisurely** *adj. & adv.,* **leisured** *adj.*

LEM *abbr.* Lunar excursion module.

lem-on *n.* An oval citrus fruit grown on a tree, having juicy, acid pulp and a yellow rind that yields an essential oil used as a flavoring and as a perfuming agent. *Slang* Something, as an automobile, that proves to be defective or unsatisfactory.

lem-on-ade *n.* A drink made from water, lemon juice, and sugar.

lend *v.* To allow the temporary use or possession of something with the understanding that it is to be returned; to offer oneself as to a specific purpose.

length *n.* The linear extent of something from end to end, usually the longest dimension of a thing as distinguished from its thickness and width; the measurement of something to estimate distance. **lengthy** *adj.*

length-en *v.* To make or become longer.

length-wise *adv. & adj.* Of or in the direction or dimension of length; longitudinally.

le-ni-ent *adj.* Gentle, forgiving, and mild; merciful; undemanding; tolerant. **leniency, lenience** *n.*

len-i-tive *adj.* Having the ability to ease pain or discomfort. **lenitive** *n.*

lens *n.*

In optics, the curved piece of glass or other transparent substance that is used to refract light rays so that they converge or diverge to form an image; the transparent structure in the eye, situated behind the iris, which serves to focus an image on the retina.

lent *v.* Past tense of lend.

Lent *n., Eccl.* The period of forty days, excluding Sundays, of fasting and penitence observed by many Christians from Ash Wednesday until Easter. **Lenten** *adj.*

len-til *n.* A leguminous plant, having broad pods and containing edible seeds.

Leo *n.* The fifth sign of the zodiac; a person born between (July 23 - August 22.)

leop-ard *n.*

A large member of the cat family of Africa and Asia, having a tawny coat with dark brown or black spots grouped in rounded clusters, also called a panther. **leopardess** *n.*

le-o-tard *n.* A close-fitting garment worn by dancers and acrobats.

lep-er *n.* One who suffers from leprosy.

lep-re-chaun *n.* A mischief-making elf of Irish folklore, supposed to own hidden treasure.

lep-ro-sy *n., Pathol.* A chronic communicable disease characterized by nodular skin lesions and the progressive destruction of tissue. **leprous, leprotic** *adj.*

les-bi-an *n.* A homosexual woman.

lese maj-es-ty *or* **leze** *n.* An offense against a ruler or supreme power of state.

le-sion *n., Pathol.* An injury; a wound; any well-defined bodily area where the tissue has changed in a way that is characteristic of a disease.

less *adj.* Smaller; of smaller or lower importance or degree.. *prep.* With the subtraction of; minus.

-less *suffix.* Without; lacking.

les-see *n.* One who leases a property.

les-son *n.* An instance from which something is to be or has been learned; an assignment to be learned or studied as by a student.

les-sor *n.* One who grants a lease to another.

let *v.* To give permission; to allow. *n.* An invalid stroke in a game such as tennis, that must be repeated because of some interruption or hindrance of playing conditions.

let-down *n.* A decrease or slackening, as in energy or effort. *Slang* A disappointment.

le-thal *adj.* Pertaining to or being able to cause death. **lethally** *adv.*

leth-ar-gy *n., Pathol.* A state of excessive drowsiness or abnormally deep sleep; laziness. **lethargic** *adj.*, **lethargically** *adv.*

let's *contr.* Let us.

let-ter *n.* A standard character or sign used in writing or printing to represent an alphabetical unit or speech sound; a written or printed means of communication sent to another person.

let-ter-head *n.* Stationery printed with a name and address, usually of a company or business establishment.

let-ter--perfect *adj.* Absolutely correct; perfect.

let-tuce *n.* A plant having crisp, edible leaves that are used especially in salads.

leu-ke-mi-a *n., Pathol.* A generally fatal disease of the blood in which white blood cells multiply in uncontrolled numbers. **leukemic** *adj.*

le-vee *n.* An embankment along the shore of a body of water, especially a river, built to prevent over-flowing.

lev-el *n.* A relative position, rank, or height on a scale; a standard position from which other heights and depths are measured. *adj.* Balanced in height; even. *v.* To make or become flat or level. **leveler, -ness** *n.*, **levelly** *adv.*

lev-el--head-ed *adj.* Showing good judgment and common sense.

level-headedness *n.*

lever *n.* A handle that projects and is used to operate or adjust a mechanism.

lever-age *n.* The use of a lever; the mechanical advantage gained by using a lever; power to act effectively.

lev-i-tate *v.* To rise and float in the air in apparent defiance of gravity. **-ion** *n.*

Le-vit-i-cus *n.* The third book of the Old Testament.

lev-i-ty *n., pl.* **-ies** Lack of seriousness; frivolity; lightness.

lev-y *v.* To impose and collect by authority or force, as a fine or tax; to draft for military service; to prepare for, begin, or wage war. **levy** *n.*

lewd *adj.* Preoccupied with sex; lustful.

lewdly *adv.*, **lewdness** *n.*

lex-i-cog-ra-phy *n.* The practice or profession of compiling dictionaries. **lexicographer** *n.*, **-ic, -ical** *adj.*

lex-i-con *n.* A dictionary; a vocabulary or list of words that relate to a certain subject, occupation, or activity.

lexical *adj.*

li-a-bil-i-ty *n., pl.* **-ies** The condition or state of being liable; that which is owed to another.

li-a-ble *adj.* Legally or rightly responsible.

li-ai-son *n.* A communication, as between different parts of an armed force or departments of a government; a close connection or relationship; an illicit love affair.

li-ar *n.* A person who tells falsehoods.

lib *n., Slang* Liberation.

li-bel *n., Law* A written statement in published form that damages a person's character or reputation. **libel** *v.*, **libelous** *adj.*

lib-er-al *adj.* Characterized by generosity or lavishness in giving; abundant; ample; inclining toward opinions or policies that favor progress or reform, such as religion or politics. **liberalism, liberality** *n.*, **liberalize** *v.*, **liberally** *adv.*

liberal arts *pl. n.* Academic courses that include literature, philosophy, history, languages, etc., which provide general cultural information.

lib-er-ate *v.* To set free, as from bondage, oppression, or foreign control. **liberation** *n.*

lib-er-ty *n., pl.* **-ies** The state of being free from oppression, tyranny, confinement, or slavery; freedom; in Navy terms, the permission to be absent from one's ship or duty for less than 48 hours.

Lib-er-ty Bell *n.* The bell rung July 4, 1776, to celebrate the adoption of the Declaration of Independence and cracked in 1835; located in Philadelphia, Pennsylvania.

li-bi-do *n.* One's sexual desire or impulse; the psychic energy drive that is behind all human activities. **libidinal, libidinous** *adj.*

Libra *n.* The seventh sign of the Zodiac; a person born between (September 23 - October 22.)

li-brar-i-an *n.* A person in charge of a library; one who specializes in library work.

li-brar-y *n., pl.* **-ies** A collection of books, pamphlets, magazines, and reference books kept for reading, reference, or borrowing; a commercial establishment, usually in connection with a city or school, which rents books.

lice *n.* Plural of louse.

li-cense *n.* An official document that gives permission to engage in a specified activity or to perform a specified act. **licensee, licenser** *n.*

li-cen-ti-ate *n.* A person licensed to practice a specified profession.

li-cen-tious *adj.* Lacking in moral restraint; immoral. **licentiously** *adv.*, **licentiousness** *n.*

li-chen *n.* Any of various flowerless plants consisting of fungi, commonly growing in flat patches on trees and rocks. **lichened, lichenous** *adj.*

lic-it *adj.* Lawful. **licitly** *adv.*, **-ness** *n.*

lick *v.* To pass the tongue over or along the surface of. *Slang* To beat; to thrash.

lick-e-ty--split *adv.* Full speed; rapidly.

lic-o-rice *n.* A perennial herb of Europe, the dried root of which is used to flavor medicines and candy.

lid *n.* A hinged or removable cover for a container; an eyelid. **lidded, -less** *adj.*

lie *v.* To be in or take a horizontal recumbent position; to recline. *n.* A false or untrue statement.

liege *n.* A feudal lord or sovereign. *adj.* Loyal; faithful.

lien *n.* The legal right to claim, hold, or sell the property of another to satisfy a debt or obligation.

lieu *n.* Place; stead. **in lieu of** In place of.

lieu-ten-ant *n.* A commissioned officer in the U.S. Army, Air Force, or Marine Corps who ranks below a captain.

life *n., pl.* **lives** The form of existence that distinguishes living organisms from dead organisms or inanimate matter in the ability to carry on metabolism, respond to stimuli, reproduce, and grow.

life-guard *n.* An expert swimmer employed to protect people in and around water.

life pre-serv-er *n.* A buoyant device, as one in the shape of a ring or jacket, used to keep a person afloat in water.

lifer *n.* *Slang* A person sentenced to life in prison.

life-raft *n.* A raft made of wood or an inflatable material used by people who have been forced into the water.

life--sup-port sy-stem *n.* A system giving a person all or some of the items, such as oxygen, water, food, and control of temperature, necessary for a person's life and health while in a spacecraft or while exploring the surface of the moon; a system used to sustain life in a critical health situation.

life-time *n.* The period between one's birth and death.

life-work *n.* The main work of a person's lifetime.

life zone *n.* A biogeographic zone.

lift *v.* To raise from a lower to a higher position; to elevate; to take from; to steal. *n.* The act or process of lifting; force or power available for lifting; an elevation of spirits; a device or machine designed to pick up, raise, or carry something; an elevator. **lifter** *n.*

lift-off *n.* The vertical takeoff or the instant of take-off of an aircraft or spacecraft.

lig-a-ment *n.* A tough band of tissue joining bones or holding a body organ in place. **ligamentous** *adj.*

li-gate *v.* To tie with a ligature.

lig-a-ture *n.*

Something, as a cord, that is used to bind; a thread used in surgery; something that unites or connects; a printing character that combines two or more letters.

light *n.* Electromagnetic radiation that can be seen by the naked eye; brightness; a source of light; spiritual illumination; enlightenment; a source of fire, such as a match. *adj.* Having light; bright; of less force, quantity, intensity, weight, than normal; having less calories or alcoholic content; dizzy; giddy. **light** *v.*, **lightness** *n.*

light-er *n.* A device used to light a pipe, cigar or cigarette; a barge used to load and unload a cargo ship.

light-fast *adj.* Resistant to sunlight.

light-heart-ed *adj.* Free from anxiety or care; hopefull and optimistic.

light-ing *n.* An artificial supply of light.

light-ly *adv.* With little weight or force.

light-ning *n.* The flash of light produced by a high-tension natural electric discharge into the atmosphere. *adj.* Moving with or as if with the suddenness of lightning.

light-ning bug *n.* A firefly.

light-ning rod *n.* A grounded metal rod positioned high on a building to protect it from lightning.

light op-er-a *n.* An operetta.

lights *pl. n.* The lungs, especially of a slaughtered animal.

light-ship *n.* A ship, having a powerful light or horn, that is anchored in dangerous waters to warn other vessels.

light show *n.* A display of colored lights in kaleidoscopic patterns, often accompanied by film, slides, or music.

light-weight *n.* A person who weighs very little; a boxer or wrestler weighing between 127 and 135 pounds.

light--year *or* **light year** *n.* A measure equal to the distance light travels in one year, approximately 5.878 trillion miles.

lig-ne-ous *adj.* Of or resembling wood; woody.

lig-ni-fy *v.* To make or become woody or wood-like.

lig-nite *n.* A brownish-black soft coal, especially one in which the texture of the original wood is distinct.

lig-ro-in *n.* A volatile, flammable fraction of petroleum used as a solvent.

like--mind-ed *adj.* Of the same way of thinking.

lik-en *v.* To describe as being like; to compare.

like-ness *n.* Resemblance; a copy.

lik-ing *n.* A favorable regard to something.

li-lac *n.* A shrub widely grown for its large, fragrant purplish or white flower cluster; a pale purple. **lilac** *adj.*

Lil-li-pu-tian *n.* A very small person. *adj.* Tiny.

lilt *n.* A light song; a rhythmical way of speaking.

lil-y *n., pl.* **-ies**

Any of various plants bearing trumpet-shaped flowers; a plant similar or related to the lily, as the water lily.

lil-y--liv-ered *adj.* Timid; cowardly.

lily of the valley *n., pl.* **lilies** A widely cultivated plant which bears fragrant, bell-shaped white flowers on a short stem.

Li-ma *n.* The capital of Peru.

li-ma bean *n.* Any of several varieties of tropical American plants having flat pods with light green edible seeds.

limb *n.* A large bough of a tree; an animal's appendage used for movement or grasping; an arm or leg.

lim-ber *adj.* Bending easily; pliable; moving easily; agile. *v.* To make or become limber. **limberly** *adv.*, **-ness** *n.*

lim-bo or **Lim-bo** *n.* The abode of souls kept from entering Heaven; a place or condition of oblivion or neglect.

Lim-burg-er *n.* A soft white cheese having a strong odor and flavor.

lime *n.* A tropical citrus tree with evergreen leaves, fragrant white flowers, and edible green fruit; calcium oxide. **limy** *adj.*

lime-light *n.* A focus of public attention; the center of attention.

lim-er-ick *n.* A humorous verse of five lines.

lime-stone *n.* A form of sedimentary rock composed mainly of calcium carbonate which is used in building and in making lime and cement.

lim-it *n.* A boundary; a maximum or a minimum number or amount; a restriction on frequency or amount. *v.* To restrict; to establish bounds or boundaries. **limitation** *n.*

li-mo-nite *n.* A natural iron oxide used as an ore of iron.

lim-ou-sine *n.* A luxurious large vehicle; a small bus used to carry passengers to airports and hotels.

limp *v.* To walk lamely. *adj.* Lacking or having lost rigidity; not firm or strong. **limply** *adv.*, **limpness** *n.*

lim-pet *n.* Any of numerous marine gastropod mollusks having a conical shell and adhering to tidal rocks.

lim-pid *adj.* Transparently clear. **limpidity** *n.*, **limpidly** *adv.*

linch-pin *n.* A locking pin inserted through a shaft to keep a wheel from slipping off.

Lin-coln *n.* The capital of the state of Nebraska.

Lincoln, Abraham *n.* The 16th president of the United States from 1861-1865, who was assassinated.

Lind-berg, Charles A. *n.* (1902-1974) American aviator; the first man to make a nonstop flight across the Atlantic Ocean, linking the United States and France.

lin-den *n.* Any of various shade trees having heart-shaped leaves.

lin-e-age *n.* A direct line of descent from an ancestor.

lin-e-a-ment *n.* A contour, shape, or feature of the body and especially of the the face.

lin-e-ar *adj.* Of, pertaining to, or resembling a line; long and narrow.

lin-e-ar per-spec-tive *n.* A technique in painting and drawing in which parallel lines converge to give the illusion of distance and depth.

line-back-er *n.* In football, one of the defensive players positioned directly behind the line of scrimmage.

line drive *n.* In baseball, a ball hit with force whose path approximates a straight line parallel or nearly parallel to the ground.

line-man *n.* A person who works on telephone or electric power lines; a player on the forward line of a team, especially football.

lin-en *n.* Thread, yarn, or fabric made of flax; household articles, such as sheets and pillow cases, made of linen or a similar fabric. **linen** *adj.*

line of scrim-mage *n.* In football, an imaginary line that extends across the field from the position of the football on any given play.

lin-er *n.* A ship belonging to a ship line or an aircraft belonging to an airline; one that lines or serves as a lining.

line score *n.* In baseball, a statistical record of each inning of a game.

lines-man *n.* An official in a court game, as tennis or volleyball, who calls shots which fall out-of-bounds; an official in football who marks the downs.

line--up *n.* A line of persons formed for the purpose of inspection or identification; the members of a team who take part in a game; a group of television programs that are aired sequentially.

ling *n.* Any of various marine food fishes related to the cod.

lin-ger *v.* To be slow in parting or reluctant to leave; to be slow in acting; to procrastinate.

lingerer *n.*, **lingeringly** *adv.*

lin-ge-rie *n.* Women's undergarments.

lingo *n., pl.* **goes** Language that is unfamiliar; a specialized vocabulary.

lin-guist *n.* One who is fluent in more than one language; A person specializing in linguistics.

lin-i-ment *n.* A liquid or semiliquid medicine applied to the skin.

lin-ing *n.* A material which is used to cover an inside surface.

link *n.* One of the rings forming a chain; something in the form of a link; a tie or bond; a cuff link. *v.* To connect by or as if by a link or links.

link-age *n.* The act or process of linking; a system of connecting structures.

links *pl., n.* A golf course.

li-no-le-um *n.* A floor covering consisting of a surface of hardened linseed oil and a filler, as wood or powdered cork, on a canvas or burlap backing.

lin-seed *n.* The seed of flax, used in paints and varnishes.

lin-sey--wool-sey *n.* A coarse, sturdy fabric of wool and linen or cotton.

lin-tel *n.* A horizontal beam across the top of a door which supports the weight of the structure above it.

li-on *n.*

A large carnivorous mammal of the cat family, found in Africa and India, having a short, tawny coat and a long, heavy mane in the male; a person of great importance or prestige.

li-on--heart-ed *adj.* Very courageous.

li-on-ize *v.* To treat someone as a celebrity.

lip service *n.* An expression of acquiescence that is not acted upon.

liq-ue-fy *or* **liq-ui-fy** *v.* To make liquid. **liquefaction, liquefier** *n.*

li-queur *n.* A sweet alcoholic beverage; a cordial.

liq-ui-date *v.* To settle a debt by payment or other settlement; to close a business by settling accounts and dividing up assets; to get rid of, especially to kill. **liquidation** *n.*

lia-ui-da-tor *n.* A person who liquidates, usually appointed by law to liquidate assets.

liq-uid-ize *v.* To cause something to become liquid.

liq-uor *n.* A distilled alcoholic beverage; a liquid substance, as a watery solution of a drug.

Lis-bon *n.* The capital of Portugal.

lisle *n.* A fine, tightly twisted cotton thread.

lisp *n.* A speech defect or mannerism marked by lisping. *v.* To mispronounce the s and z sounds, usually as th. **lisper** *n.*

lis-some *adj.* Nimble. **lissomely** *adv.*, **lissomeness** *n.*

list *n.* A series of numbers or words; a tilt to one side. **list** *v.*

listen *v.* To monitor or tune in to conversation or a broadcast.

list-less *adj.* Lacking energy or enthusiasm. **listlessly** *adv.*, **-ness** *n.*

list price *n.* The basic price of an item.

lit *abbr.* Literary; literature.

lit-a-ny *n., pl.* **-ies** A prayer in which phrases recited by a leader are alternated with answers from a congregation.

li-tchi *or* **li-chee** *n.* A Chinese tree, bearing edible fruit; the fruit of the tree.

lit-er-al *adj.* Conforming to the exact meaning of a word; concerned primarily with facts; without embellishment or exaggeration. **literally** *adv.*, **literalistic** *adj.*

lit-er-al-ism *n.* Adherence to the explicit sense of a given test; literal portrayal; realism. **literalist** *n.*, **literalistic** *adj.*

lit-er-ar-y *adj.* Pertaining to literature; appropriate to or used in literature; of or relating to the knowledge of literature. **literarily** *adv.*

lit-er-ate *adj.* Having the ability to read and write; showing skill in using words. **literacy, literate** *n.*

lit-er-a-ti *pl., n.* The educated class.

lit-er-a-ture *n.* Printed material, as leaflets for a political campaign; written words of lasting excellence.

lithe *adj.* Bending easily; supple. **lithely** *adv.*, **litheness** *n.*

lith-i-um *n.* A silver-white, soft metallic element symbolized by Li.

li-thog-ra-phy *n.* A printing process in which a flat surface is treated so that the ink adheres only to the portions that are to be printed.

lithograph *n. & v.*, **lithographer** *n.*, **lithographic, lithographical** *adj.*

li-thol-o-gy *n.* The microscopic study and classification of rocks. **lithologist** *n.*

lit-i-gate *v.* To conduct a legal contest by judicial process. **litigant, litigation, litigator** *n.*

lit-mus *n.* A blue powder obtained from lichens which turns red in acid solutions and blue in alkaline solutions, used as an acid-base indicator.

lit-mus pa-per *n.* Unsized paper that is treated with litmus and used as an indicator.

lit-ter *n.* A covered and curtained couch, mounted on shafts and used to carry a single passenger; a stretcher used to carry a sick or injured person; material used as bedding for animals; the offspring at one birth of a multiparous animal; an accumulation of waste material. **litter** *v.*, **litterer** *n.*

lit-ter-bug *n.* One who litters a public area.

Little Dipper *n.* Ursa Minor.

Little Rock *n.* The capital of Arkansas.

lit-to-ral *adj.* Relating to or existing on a shore. *n.* A shore.

lit-ur-gy *n., pl.* **-ies** A prescribed rite or body of rites for public worship. **liturgical** *adj.*, **liturgically** *adv.*

live-li-hood *n.* A means of support or subsistence.

live-ly *adj.* Vigorous. **liveliness** *n.*

liv-er *n.* The large, very vascular, glandular organ of vertebrates which secretes bile.

liv-er-wurst *n.* A kind of sausage made primarily of liver.

liv-er-y *n., pl.* **-ies** A uniform worn by servants; the care and boarding of horses for pay; a concern offering horses and vehicles for rent. **-ied** *adj.*

liv-er-y-man *n.* A keeper or employee of a livery stable.

live-stock *n.* Farm animals raised for human use.

live wire *n., Slang* An energetic person.

liv-id *adj.* Discolored from a bruise; very angry.

liz-ard *n.*

One of various reptiles, usually with an elongated scaly body, four legs, and a tapering tail.

liz-ard fish *n.* A bottom-dwelling fish, having a lizard-like head and dwelling in warm waters of the seas.

lla-ma *n.* A South American ruminant, related to the camel family and raised for its soft wool.

load *n.* A mass or weight that is lifted or supported; anything, as cargo, put in a ship, aircraft, or vehicle for conveyance; something that is a heavy responsibility; a burden. **loader, loading** *n.* **load** *v.*

load-ed *adj.* Intended to trick or trap. *Slang* Drunk; rich.

loaf *n., pl.* **loaves** A food, especially bread, that is shaped into a mass. *v.* To spend time in idleness. **loafer** *n.*

loam *n.* Soil that consists chiefly of sand, clay, and decayed plant matter. **-y** *adj.*

loan *n.* Money lent with interest to be repaid; something borrowed for temporary use. *v.* To lend.

loan shark *n.* One who lends money to individuals at exorbitant rates of interest. **loan sharking** *n.*

loath *adj.* Averse.

loathe *v.* To dislike intensely.

loath-ing *n.* Intense dislike; abhorrence.

loath-some *adj.* Arousing disgust. **loathsomely** *adv.*, **loathsomeness** *n.*

lob *v.* To hit or throw in a high arc.

lob-by *n., pl.* **-ies** A foyer, as in a hotel or theatre; a group of private persons trying to influence legislators. **lobbyist** *n.* **lobby** *v.*

lobe *n.* A curved or rounded projection or division, as the fleshy lower part of the ear. **lobar, lobed** *adj.*

lob-lol-ly *n., pl.* **-ies** A mudhole; mire.

lo-bo *n.* The gray wolf, as referred to by those who reside in the western United States.

lo-bot-o-my *n., pl.* **-mies** Surgical severance of nerve fibers by incision into the brain.

lob-ster *n.*

Any of several large, edible marine crustaceans with five pairs of legs, the first pair being large and claw-like.

lob-ule *n.* A small lobe; a subdivision of a lobe. **lobular** *adj.*

lo-cal *adj.* Pertaining to, being in, or serving a particular area or place. **locally** *adv.*

lo-cale *n.* A locality where a particular event takes place; the setting or scene, as of a novel.

lo-cal-i-ty *n., pl* **-ties** A specific neighborhood, place, or district.

lo-cate *v.* To determine the place, position, or boundaries of; to look for and find; to establish or become established; to settle. **locator** *n.*

lo-ca-tion *n.* The act or process of locating; a place where something is or can be located; a site outside a motion picture or television studio where a movie is shot.

loch *n., Scot.* A lake.

lock *n.* A device used, as on a door, to secure or fasten; a part of a waterway closed off with gates to allow the raising or lowering of boats by changing the level of the water; a strand or curl of hair. **lock** *v.*

lock-et *n.* A small, ornamental case for a keepsake, often a picture, worn as a pendant on a necklace.

lock-jaw *n.* Tetanus; a form of tetanus in which a spasm of the jaw muscles locks the jaws closed.

lock-smith *n.* A person who makes or repairs locks.

lo-co *adj., Slang* Insane.

lo-co-mo-tion *n.* The act of moving; the power to move from place to place.

lo-co-mo-tive *n.* A self-propelled vehicle that is generally electric or diesel-powered and is used for moving railroad cars.

lo-co-weed *n.* Any of several plants found throughout the western and central United States which are poisonous to livestock.

lo-cust *n.* Any of numerous grasshoppers which often travel in swarms and damage vegetation; any of various hardwooded leguminous trees, such as carob, black locust, or honey locust.

lode-star *n.* A star; the North Star, used as a reference point.

lodge *n.* A house, such as a cabin, used as a temporary or seasonal dwelling or shelter; an inn; the den of an animal, such as a beaver; a local chapter of a fraternal organization; the meeting hall of such a chapter. **lodge** *v.*

lodg-er *n.* One who rents a room in another's house.

lodg-ment *or* **lodge-ment** *n.* An act of lodging; a place for lodging; an accumulation or deposit.

loft *n.* One of the upper, generally unpartitioned floors of an industrial or commercial building, such as a warehouse; an attic; a gallery in a church or hall.

lo-gan-ber-ry *n.* A prickly plant cultivated for its edible, acidic, red fruit.

loge *n.* A small compartment, especially a box in a theatre; a small partitioned area, as a separate forward section of a theatre mezzanine or balcony.

log-ger-head *n.* Any of various large marine turtles, especially the carnivorous turtle found in the warm waters of the western Atlantic. **at loggerheads** In a state of contention; at odds.

log-gi-a *n.* A roofed but open arcade along the front of a building; an open balcony in a theatre.

log-ic *n.* The science dealing with the principles of reasoning, especially of the method and validity of deductive reasoning; something that forces a decision apart from or in opposition to reason. **logician** *n.*

log-i-cal *adj.* Relating to; or in accordance with logic; something marked by consistency of reasoning. **-ly** *adv.*

lo-gis-tics *pl., n.* The methods of procuring, maintaining, and replacing material and personnel, as in a military operation. **logistic** *adj.*

lo-go-type *n.* Identifying symbol for a company or publication.

lo-gy *adj.* Something marked by sluggishness. **loginess** *n.*

loin *n.* The area of the body located between the ribs and pelvis; a cut of meat from an animal.

loin-cloth *n.* A cloth worn about the loins.

loins *n.* The thighs and groin; the reproductive organs.

loi-ter *v.* To stay for no apparent reason; to dawdle or delay. **loiterer** *n.*

loll *v.* To move or act in a lax, lazy or indolent manner; to hang loosely or laxly. **loller** *n.*

lol-li-pop *or* **lol-ly-pop** *n.* A piece of flavored hard candy on a stick.

lol-ly-gag *v., Slang* To fool around.

Lon-don *n.* The capital of England.

lone *adj.* Single; isolated; sole; unfrequented.

lone-iy *adj.* Being without companions; dejected from being alone. **-iness** *n.*

lon-er *n.* A person who avoids the company of others.

lone-some *adj.* Dejected because of the lack of companionship. **lonesomely** *adv.,* **lonesomeness** *n.*

long-bow *n.* A wooden bow that is approximately five to six feet in length.

lon-gev-i-ty *n.* Long life; long duration; seniority.

Longfellow, Henry Wadsworth *n.* (1807-1882) American poet.

long-hair *n.* A lover of the arts, especially classical music; a person with long hair.

long-hand *n.* Cursive handwriting.

long-horn *n.* One of the long-horned cattle of Spanish derivation, formerly common in the southwestern United States; a firm-textured cheddar cheese ranging from white to orange in color and from mild to sharp in flavor.

lon-gi-tude *n.* The angular distance that is east and west of the prime meridian at Greenwich, England.

lon-gi-tu-di-nal *adj.* Of or relating to the length; relating to longitude. **longitudinally** *adv.*

long-shore-man *n.* A dock hand who loads and unloads cargo.

look *v.* To examine with the eyes; to see; to glance, gaze, or stare at. *n.* The act of looking; the physical appearance of something or someone.

look-out *n.* A person positioned to keep watch or look for something or someone.

loom *v.* To come into view as a image; to seem to be threatening. *n.* A machine used for interweaving thread or yarn to produce cloth.

loop *n.* A circular length of line folded over and joined at the ends; a loop-shaped pattern, figure, or path. *v.* To form into a loop; to join, fasten, or encircle with a loop.

loop-hole *n.* A means of escape; a legal way to circumvent the intent of a law.

loose *adj.* Not tightly fastened; not confined or fitting; free.

loot *n.* Goods, usually of significant value, taken in time of war; goods that have been stolen. *v.* To plunder; to steal. **looter** *n.*

lop *v.* To remove branches from; to trim.

lope *v.* To run with a steady gait. **lope, lopper** *n.*

lop-sid-ed *adj.* Larger or heavier on one side than on the other; tilting to one side. **lopsidedly** *adv.,* **lopsidedness** *n.*

lo-qua-cious *adj.* Overly talkative. **loquaciously** *adv.,* **loquacity** *n.*

Lord *n.* God. A man having dominion and power over other people; the owner of a feudal estate.

lore *n.* Traditional fact; knowledge that has been gained through education or experience.

lor-gnette *n.* A pair of opera glasses with a handle.

lose *v.* To mislay; to fail to keep. **loser** *n.*

loss *n.* The suffering or damage used by losing; someone or something that is lost. **losses** *pl. n.* Killed, wounded, or captured soldiers; casualties.

loss ratio *n.* The ratio between insurance premiums and insurance losses in a given period of time.

lost *adj.* Unable to find one's way.

lot *n.* Fate; fortune; a parcel of land having boundaries; a plot.

lo-ta *n.* A small spherical water vessel of copper or brass used in India.

lo-tic *adj.* Living in or related to actively moving water.

lo-tion *n.* A liquid medicine for external use on the hands and body.

lot-ter-y *n., pl.* **-ies** A contest in which winners are selected by a random drawing.

lot-to *n.* A game of chance that resembles bingo.

lo-tus *n.* An aquatic plant having fragrant pinkish flowers and large leaves; any of several plants similar or related to the lotus.

lo-tus--eater *n.* One of a people represented in the Odyssey of Homer as eating the lotus fruit and living in the dreamy indolence it produced.

loud *adj.* Marked by intense sound and high volume. **loud, -ly** *adv.,* **-ness** *n.*

Louis XIV *n.* (1638-1715) King of France from 1643 to 1715.

Lou-i-si-an-a *n.* A state located in the

southern United States.

lounge v. To move or act in a lazy, relaxed manner. n. A room, as in a hotel or theatre, where people may wait; a couch. **lounger** n.

louse n., pl. **lice**

A small, wingless biting or sucking insect which lives as a parasites on various animals and also on human beings. *Slang* A mean, contemptible person.

lous-y adj. Lice-infested. *Slang* Mean; poor; inferior; abundantly supplied. **lousily** adv.

lout n. An awkward, stupid person. **loutish** adj.

lou-ver or **lou-vre** n. An opening in a wall fitted with movable, slanted slats which let air in, but keep precipitation out; one of the slats used in a louver.

love n. Intense affection for another arising out of kinship or personal ties; a strong feeling of attraction resulting from sexual desire; enthusiasm or fondness; a score of zero in tennis. **love** v., **lovable**, **loving** adj.

love-bird n. Any of various Old World parrots which show great affection for their mates.

love-ly adj. Beautiful. -iness, **lovely** n.

lov-er n. A person who loves another; a sexual partner.

love seat n. A small couch which seats two.

love-sick adj. Languishing with love; expressing a lover's yearning. -ness n.

loving cup n. A large, ornamental cup with two or more handles, often given as an award or trophy.

low adj. Not high; being below or under normal height, rank, or level; depressed. v. To moo, as a cow.

low-brow n. An uncultured person.

low-down n. The whole truth; all the facts adj. Despicable; mean; depressed.

low-er--case adj. Having as its typical form a, b, c, or u, v, w rather than A, B, C, or U, V, W.

low-er class n. The group in society that ranks below the middle class in social and economic status.

low-est com-mon de-nom-i-na-tor n. The least common multiple of the denominators of a set of fractions.

low-est com-mon mul-ti-ple n. Least common multiple.

low fre-quen-cy n. A radio-wave frequency between 30 and 300 kilohertz.

low-land n. Land that is low and level in relation to the surrounding countryside.

low-ly adj. Low in position or rank.

low profile n. A deliberately inconspicuous life style or posture.

low--rise adj. Having one or two stories and no elevator.

low--ten-sion adj. Having a low voltage;

built to be used at low voltage.

lox n. Smoked salmon; liquid oxygen.

loy-al adj. Faithful in allegiance to one's country and government; faithful to a person, cause, ideal, or custom. -ty n.

loy-al-ist n. One who is or remains loyal to political cause, party, government, or sovereign.

loz-enge n. Small medicated candy, normally having the shape of a lozenge.

lu-au n. A traditional Hawaiian feast.

lub-ber n. An awkward, clumsy or stupid person; an inexperienced sailor.

lu-bri-cant n. A material, as grease or oil, applied to moving parts to reduce friction.

lu-bri-cious or **lu-bri-cous** adj. Smooth, unstable; shifty. **lubricity** n.

lu-cid adj. Easily understood; mentally clear; rational; shining. **lucidity**, **lucidness** n., **lucidly** adv.

Lucifer n. The devil; Satan.

Lu-cite n., *Trademark* A transparent thermoplastic acrylic resin.

luck n. Good fortune; the force or power which controls odds and which brings good or bad fortune or success; fate. **lucky** adj., **luckily** adv., **luckiness** n.

lu-cra-tive adj. Producing profits, gain, or great wealth. **lucratively** adv.

lu-cre n. Money; profit.

lu-cu-brate v. To study or work laboriously.

lu-di-crous adj. Amusing or laughable through obvious absurdity; ridiculous; comical. **ludicrously** adv., -ness n.

luff v. To turn a sailing vessel toward the wind; the fullest part of a ship's bow.

lug n. An ear-like handle or projection used as a hold; a tab. v. To carry with difficulty; to tug or pull.

luge n. A small sled similar to a toboggan which is ridden in a supine position and used especially in competition.

lug-gage n. Something that is lugged, especially suitcases or a traveler's baggage.

lu-gu-bri-ous adj. Mournful; dejected; especially exaggeratedly or affectedly so. **lugubriously** adv., -ness n.

luke-warm adj. Mildly warm; tepid; unenthusiastic; soothing. **lukewarmly** adv., **lukewarmless** n.

lull v. To cause to rest or sleep; to cause to have a false sense of security. n. A temporary period of quiet or rest just before or after a confusion or storm.

lul-la-by n., pl. -bies A song to lull a child to sleep. v. To quiet with a lullaby.

lum-ba-go n. Painful rheumatic pain of the muscles and tendons of the lumbar region of the back.

lum-bar adj. Part of the back and sides between the lowest ribs and the pelvis.

lum-ber n. Timber, sawed or split into boards. v. To walk or move clumsily.

lum-ber-jack n. One who cuts and prepares timber for the sawmill.

lum-ber-yard n. A business place where lumber and other building materials

are sold.

lu-mi-nar-y *n., pl.* **-ies** A celestial body, as the sun; a notable person.

lu-mi-nes-cence *n.* An emission of light without heat, as in fluorescence.

lu-mi-nous *adj.* Emitting or reflecting light; bathed in steady light; illuminated; easily understood; clear. **luminously** *adv.,* **luminousness** *n.*

lum-mox *n.* A clumsy oaf; dull-witted person.

lump *n.* A projection; a protuberance; a swelling, as from a bruise or infection; amass or solid matter. *v.* To group things together. **lumpy** *adj.*

lum-pen *adj.* Lating to groups of people who have been uprooted from their normal routine or economic status.

lump-ish *adj.* Stupid or dull. **lumpishly** *adv.,* **lumpiness** *n.*

lump-y *adj.* Covered or full of lumps.

lu-na-cy *n., pl.* **-ies** Insanity.

lu-nar *adj.* Of, relating to, caused by the moon.

lu-nar e-clipse *n.* An eclipse where the moon passes partially or wholly through the umbra of the earth's shadow.

lu-na-tic *n.* A crazy person; mad; insane.

lunch *n.* A meal served between breakfast and supper.

lunch-eon *n.* A lunch; a meal taken at midday.

lunch-eon-ette *n.* A modest restaurant at which light meals are served.

lunch-room *n.* A room in a school, business, or establishments where individuals may eat lunch.

lung *n.*

One of the two spongy organs that constitute the basic respiratory organ of air-breathing vertebrates.

lunge *n.* A sudden forward movement; a thrust. **lunge** *v.*

lung-fish-es *n.* A bread of fish that used lungs as well as gills for breathing.

lu-pu-lin *n.* A yellow powder that is obtained from hops and used as a sedative.

lu-pus *n.* A bacterial disease of the skin caused by the tubercle bacillus and results in lesions of the skin and mucous membranes.

lurch *v.* To heave something to one side.

lure *n.* A decoy; something appealing; an artificial bait to catch fish. *v.* To attract or entice with the prospect of reward or pleasure.

lu-rid *adj.* Sensational; shining with a fiery glare. **luridly** *adv.,* **luridness** *n.*

lurk *v.* To lie in concealment, as in an ambush; to remain inconspicuous; to be unobserved. **lurker** *n.,* **-ingly** *adv.*

lus-cious *adj.* Very pleasant to smell or taste; appealing to the senses. **lusciously** *adv.,* **lusciousness** *n.*

lush *adj.* Producing luxuriant growth or vegetation. *Slang* An alcoholic. **lushly** *adv.,* **lushness** *n.*

lust *n.* Intense sexual desire; an intense longing; a craving; a passionate desire; to desire eagerly. **lustful** *adj.,* **lustfully** *adv.*

lus-ter *or* **lus-tre** *n.* A glow of reflected light; sheen; brilliance or radiance; brightness. **lustrous, lusterless** *adj.*

lus-ter-ware *n.* A glossy and often iridescent piece of pottery.

lust-ful *adj.* Having a strong desire for sexual satisfaction.

lus-tral *adj.* Pertaining to a rite of purification.

lus-trous *adj.* Characterized by sheen; bright; luminous. **-ly** *adv.,* **-ness** *n.*

lust-y *adj.* Vigorous; healthy; robust; lively. **lustily** *adv.,* **lustiness** *n.*

lute *n.* A medieval musical stringed instrument with a fretted finger board, a pear-shaped body, and usually a bent neck.

lu-te-ti-um *or* **lu-te-ci-um** *n.* A silvery rare-earth metallic element symbolized by Lu.

Luther, Martin (1483-1546) German religious leader.

lux-u-ri-ant *adj.* Growing or producing abundantly; lush; plentiful. **luxuriance** *n.,* **luxuriantly** *adv.*

lux-u-ri-ate *v.* To enjoy luxury or abundance; to grow abundantly.

lux-u-ry *n., pl.* **-ies** Something desirable but costly or hard to get; something which adds to one's comfort or pleasure but is not absolutely necessary; sumptuous surroundings or living.

ly-ce-um *n.* A hall where public programs are presented; an organization which sponsors such programs as lectures and concerts.

lye *n.* A powerful caustic solution yielded by leaching wood ashes; potassium hydroxide; sodium hydroxide.

ly-ing--in *n.* Confinement in childbirth.

lymph node *n.* A roundish body of lymphoid tissue; lymph gland.

lynch *v.* To execute without authority or the due process of law.

lynx *n.*

A wildcat. *adj.* Having acute eyesight.

lyre *n.* An ancient Greek stringed instrument related to the harp.

lyr-ic *adj.* Concerned with thoughts and feelings; romantic; appropriate for singing. *n.* A lyric poem. **lyrics** The words of a song. **lyrical** *adj.,* **lyrically** *adv.,* **lyricism** *n.*

ly-ser-gic acid di-eth-yl-am-ide *n.* An organic compound which induces psychotic symptoms similar to those of schizophrenia; LSD.

M, m The thirteenth letter of the English alphabet; the Roman numeral for 1,000.

mac n. An address for a man whose name is unknown.

ma-ca-bre adj. Suggesting death and decay; ghastly;gruesome. -ly adv.

mac-ad-am n. Pavement for roads consisting of layers of compacted, broken stone, usually cemented with asphalt and tar. v. The laying down of layers of small stones, held together with asphalt or tar. **macadamize** v.

mac-a-ro-ni n. Dried pasta made into short tubes and prepared as food.

mac-a-roon n. A small cookie made of sugar, egg whites, shredded coconut, and ground almonds.

ma-caw n. Any of various tropical American parrots with long tails, brilliant plumage, and harsh voices.

mace n. An aromatic spice made by grinding the cover of the nutmeg.

mac-e-doine n. A jellied salad, or mixture of diced vegetable or fruits.

mac-er-ate v. To make a solid substance soft by soaking in liquid; to cause to grow thin. **macerater** or **macerator**, **maceration** n.

ma-chet-e n. A large, heavy knife with a broad blade, used as a weapon.

mach-i-nate v. To plot; to devise or contrive, especially with an evil purpose. **machination**, **machinator** n.

ma-chine n. A device or system built to use energy to do work; a political organization. v. To produce precision tools; to prepare or finish something with a machine. **machinability** n., **machinable**, **machineable**, -like adj.

ma-chine lan-guage n., In Computer Science, the system of numbers or instructions for coding input data which can be then directly processed by a computer.

ma-chin-er-y n., pl. -ies A collection of machines as a whole; the mechanism or operating parts of a machine.

machine shop n. A work are where materials, especially metals, are cut and designed by machine tools.

machine tool n. A machine that is power-driven and used for chaping or cutting metals, wood, etc.

ma-chin-ist n. A Person who is skilled in the operation or repair of machines.

ma-chis-mo n. An exaggerated sense of masculinity.

mach-me-ter n. An indicator that measures airspeed relative to the speed of sound, and then indicates the speed that an airplane using such an indicator, can exceed without sustaining damage due to compressibility effects.

ma-cho adj., Slang Exhibiting machismo.

mack-er-el n. A fish with dark, wavy bars on the back and a silvery belly, found in the Atlantic Ocean.

mack-er-el sky n. The sky dotted with small, white in color, fleecy clouds.

Mack-i-naw n. A short coat of blanket-like material and thickness.

mack-in-tosh or **mac-in-tosh** n. A lightweight waterproof overgarment or cloak; a raincoat; any waterproof coat or outter covering.

mack-le n. To become blurred.

ma-cle n. The double crystal of a diamond.

mac-ra-me n. The craft or hobby of tying knots into a pattern.

mac-ro-bi-ot-ic adj. Relating to or being an extremely restricted diet to promote longevity, consisting mainly of whole grain, vegetables and fish.

mac-ro-cosm n. A large scale model of something that is smaller. -ic adj., **macrocosmically** adv.

mac-ro-cyte n. A red blood cell that is larger than normal. **macrocytic** adj., **macrocytosis** n.

mac-ro-graph n. A drawing or photograph that is at least life-size or larger.

ma-crog-ra-phy v. To investigate something by the use of the naked eye.

mac-cron n. A short mark (-) placed over a vowel to indicate the pronunciation as a long sound.

mac-ro-scop-ic or **mac-ro-scop-ic-al** adj. Large enough to be seen by the naked eye. **macroscopical**, -ally adv.

mac-u-la n. A discolored sport on the skin. **macular** adj.

mad adj. Angry; afflicted with a mental disorder; insane; mentally deranged; imprudent; affected with wild excitement; wild with fondness, desire, or eagerness. n. A time or period of anger, or bad temper. **madly** adv.

mad-am n., pl. **mes-dames** A title used to address a married woman; used without a name as a courtesy title when addressing a woman.

mad-cap adj. Impulsive, rash or reckless; harebrained.

mad-den v. To craze; to enrage; to make mad. v. To become mad. **maddening** adj., **maddeningly** adv.

mad-ding adj. Behaving senselessly; acting mad; inducing madness.

made v. Past tense of make. adj. Constructed not natural; invented or constructed.

mad-e-moi-selle n., pl. **mademoiselles** or **mesdemoiselles** An unmarried French girl or woman.

made--to--order adj. Custom-made; made per instructions.

made--up adj. Fabricated; invented; concocted; having only makeup on.

mad-house n., Slang A place of confusion and disorder; a hospital for mentally disturbed people.

Mad-i-son, James n. (1751-1836). The 4th U.S. president of the United States from (1809-1817).

mad-man n. A lunatic.

mad-ness n. The state of being mad; extreme excitement.

Ma-don-na n. Virgin Mary.

mad-ri-gal n., Music An unaccompanied song, usually for four to six voices, developed during the early Renaissance.

mael-strom n. Any irresistible or dangerous force.

maes-tro n., pl. -tros or -tri A person mastering any art, but especially a famous conductor of music.

Ma-fi-a n. A secret criminal organization in Sicily; an international criminal organization believed to exist in many countries, including the U.S.

mag-a-zine n. A publication with a paper cover containing articles, stories, illustrations and advertising; the part of a gun which holds ammunition ready for feeding into the chamber.

mag-da-len n. A prostitute that has been reformed; a house used for the purpose of reforming prostitutes.

ma-gen-ta n. A purplish red color.

mag-got n. The legless wormlike larva of any of various insects, as the housefly, often found in decaying matter. -y adj.

Ma-gi pl., n. Magus The three wise men of the East who traveled to Bethlehem to pay homage to the baby Jesus.

mag-ic n. The art which seemingly controls foresight of natural events and forces by means of supernatural agencies; any influence that proves strange or extraordinary. **magic, magical** adj., **magically** adv.

ma-gi-cian n. A person who is skilled in magic and performs magic.

mag-is-te-ri-al adj. Pertaining to the office or a magistrate; arrogant; pompous; authoritative. **magisterially** adv., **magisterialness** n.

mag-is-trate n. A civil officer with the power to enforce the law. **magistracy** n.

mag-ma n., pl. -mata or -mas Geol. The molten rock beneath the earth's surface from which igneous rocks are formed. **magmatic** adj.

Mag-na Car-ta n. The Great Charter of English liberties which the barons forced King John to sign on June 19, 1215; any document constituting a guarantee of rights and privileges.

mag-nan-i-mous adj. Generous in forgiving insults or injuries. **magnanimity, magnanimousness** n., -ly adv.

mag-nate n. A person notable or powerful, especially in business.

mag-ne-sia n., Chem. A light, white powder used in medicine as an antacid and laxative.

mag-ne-si-um n. A light, silvery metallic element which burns with a very hot, bright flame and is used in lightweight alloys, symbolized by Mg.

mag-net n.

A body having the property of attracting iron and other magnetic material. **magnetism** n.

mag-net-ic adj. Pertaining to magnetism or a magnet; capable of being attracted by a magnet; having the power or ability to attract. **magnetically** adv.

mag-net-ic field n. The area in the neighborhood of a magnet or of an electric current, marked by the existence of a detectable magnetic force in every part of the region.

mag-net-ite n. A black iron oxide in mineral form, which is an important iron ore.

mag-net-ize v. To have magnetic properties; to attract by personal charm or influence. -able adj., **magnetization, magnetizer** n.

mag-ne-to n. A small alternator which works by means of magnets that are permanently attached, inducing an electric current for the spark in some engines.

mag-ne-tom-e-ter n. An instrument used for measuring the direction and intensity of magnetic forces.

mag-ne-to-sphere n., Physics A region of the upper atmosphere extending from about 500 to several thousand km above the surface, forming a band of ionized particles trapped by the earth's magnetic field.

mag-ni-fi-ca-tion n. The act of magnifying; magnified reproduction.

mag-nif-i-cent adj. Having an extraordinarily imposing appearance; beautiful; outstanding; exceptionally pleasing. **magnificence** n., -ly adv.

mag-ni-fy v. To increase in size; to cause to seem more important or greater; to glorify or praise someone or something. **magnification magnifier** n.

mag-nil-o-quent adj. Speaking or spoken in a lofty and extravagant manner. **magniloquence** n., **magniloquently** adv.

mag-ni-tude n. Greatness or importance in size or extent. Astron. The relative brightness of a star expressed on a numerical scale, ranging from one for the brightest to six for those just visible.

mag-no-lia n. An ornamental flowering tree or shrub with large, fragrant flowers of white, pink, purple, or yellow.

Magnolia State n. Nickname of the state of Mississippi.

mag-num n. A wine bottle holding about two quarts or approximately 2/5 gallon.

mag-num o-pus n. A great work of art; literary or artistic masterpiece; the greatest single work of an artist, writer, or other creative person.

mag-pie n. Any of a variety of large, noisy bird found the world over having long tapering tails and black and white plumage.

ma-ha-ra-ja or **ma-ha-ra-jah** n. A king or prince who rules an Indian state.

ma-ha-ra-ni or **ma-ha-ra-nee** n. The wife of a maharajah.

ma-hat-ma n. In some Asian religions, a person venerated for great knowledge; a title of respect; wise person; saintly.

mahl-stick n. A stick used by painters to

steady their hand while painting.

ma-hog-a-ny *n.*, *pl.* **-ies** Any of various tropical trees having hard, reddish-brown wood, much used for cabinet work and furniture.

maid *n.* A young unmarried woman or girl; a female servant. **maiden** *n.*

maid-en-hair *n.* A delicate fern with dark stems and light-green, feathery fronds.

maid-en head *n.* Virginity.

maid-en name *n.* A woman's family name before marriage.

maid of hon-or *n.* An unmarried woman who is the main attendant of a bride at a wedding.

maid-ser-vant *n.* Female servant.

mail *n.* Letter, printed matter, or parcel handled by the postal system. *v.* To send something through the mail; to put in a mailbox for delivery. **-er** *n.*

mail-a-ble *adj.* Having the capabilities of being mailed. **mailability** *n.*

mail-bag *n.* A bag in which mail is carried and transported.

mail-box *n.* A box us to deposit mail awaiting for delivery and collection; a box at a private residence that receives mail.

mail-er *n.* A box or other container used to send mail in.

mail-lot *n.* The closefitting clothing worn by dancers, gymnasts, and acrobats.

mail-man *n.* A person who carries and deliverers mail; also postman.

mail or-der *n.* Goods which are ordered and sent by mail; the goods that are received.

maim *v.* To disable or to deprive of the use of a bodily part; to impair; to render defective. **maimer** *n.*

main *adj.* Being the most important part of something. *n.* A large conduit used to carry water, oil, or gas. **mainly** *adv.*

Maine *n.* A state located in the north-eastern corner of the United States.

main-land *n.* The land part of a country as distinguished from an island; the main or principle part or section of a country or continent. **mainlander** *n.*

main-line *v.*, *Slang* To inject a drug directly into a vein.

main-stream *n.* A main direction or line of thought; the main channel of a river. **mainstream** *adj. & v.*

main-tain *v.* To carry on or to keep in existence; to preserve in a desirable condition; to continue; to uphold; to defend. **-able** *adj.*, **maintenance** *n.*

maize *n.* Corn; a yellow color.

maj-es-ty *n.*, *pl.* **-ies** Stateliness; exalted dignity. **majestic, majestical** *adj.*, **majestically** *adv.*

ma-jor *adj.* Greater in importance, quantity, number, or rank; serious; size or extent. *n.* An officer in the U.S. Army, Air Force or Marines who ranks above a captain and below a lieutenant colonel; a subject or field of academic study. *Music* A major musical scale, interval, key, or mode. *n.* The subject in an academic study that is pursued by a student.

ma-jor-do-mo *n.* A butler who manages a large household.

ma-jor-ette *n.* A young woman or girl who marches and twirls a baton with a band.

ma-jor gen-er-al *n.* Military officer just below a lieutenant general, but above a brigadier general.

ma-jor-i-ty *n.*, *pl.* **-ies** The greater number of something; more than half; the age at which a person is considered to be an adult, usually 21 years old; a number of voters in agreement; a political party group with the most votes.

ma-jor-i-ty rule *n.* A majority vote that consists of at least one vote over half of the total.

ma-jor med-i-cal *n.* An insurance policy which pays partially or totally the medical bills that are incurred during an illness, usually after a certain deductible amount is paid.

make *v.* To cause something to happen; to create; to provide, as time; to produce; to earn; to manufacture a line of goods. *n.* A brand name, as a make of a car. **make a-way with** To carry off. **make hay** To take advantage of a given opportunity in the early stages. **make no bones** To perform unhesitating.

make--be-lieve *n.* A pretending to believe; fiction; pretense. *v.* To pretend. **make-believe** *adj.*

make do *v.* To carry on or manage with minimal materials.

make--read-y *n.* The procedure used to make a form ready for printing by the use of overlays and underlays in order to produce a distinct impression.

make-shift *n.* A temporary substitute. **makeshifty, makeshiftness** *n.*

make--up *n.* The manner in which something is formed together or assembled; con-structions; the qualities of physical or mental constitution; cosmetics such as face powder and lipstick. *v.* To invent a story.

make-weight *n.* Anything added to something to cover a deficiency.

mak-ing *n.* The act of one who or something that forms, or produces; the process of being constructed.

mal-a-chite *n.* A green basic copper carbonate, used as a common ore of copper and for decorating stoneware.

mal-ad-min-is-ter *v.* To conduct dishonestly. **maladministration** *n.*

mal-a-droit *adj.* Lacking skill; awkward; clumsy; not dexterous; tactless. **maladroitly** *adv.*, **maladroitness** *n.*

mal-a-dy *n.*, *pl.* **-ies** A chronic disease or sickness of the human body; a sickness; an ailment.

ma-laise *n.* The vague or unlocalized discomfort sometimes indicating the beginning of an illness.

mal-a-prop-ism *n.* A foolish misuse of a word. **malaprop, malapropian** *adj.*

mal-ap-ro-pos *adj.* Not appropriate. *adv.* Inappropriately. **malapropos** *adv.*

ma·lar·i·a n., *Pathol.* The infectious disease introduced into the blood by the bite of the infected female anopheles mosquito and characterized by cycles of fever, chills, and profuse sweating.

ma·lar·key n., *Slang* Foolish or insincere talk; nonsense; deceptive; nonsensical talk.

mal·con·tent adj. Unhappy with existing conditions or affairs; dissatisfied; discontented. malcontent n.

mal de mer n. Seasickness.

male adj. Of or belonging to the sex that has organs to produce spermatozoa and fertilizes the female; characteristic of this sex; masculine. *Bot.* A plant with stamens but no pistil. n. A male person or animal; man or boy. -ness n.

male al·to n. The unusually high adult male voice.

mal·e·dic·tion n. A curse against a person; execration. maledictory adj.

mal·e·fac·tor n. A person who commits a crime or an unlawful act; a criminal; an evildoer. malefaction n.

ma·lef·i·cent adj. Harmful; doing evil or wrong. maleficence n.

ma·lev·o·lent adj. Full of spite or ill will for another; malicious; sinister; rancorous. -ly adv., malevolence n.

mal·for·ma·tion n. Defective or abnormal structure or form. malformed adj.

mal·func·tion n. Failure to function correctly either partially or totally.

mal·ice n. The direct intention or desire to harm others. *Law* The willfully formed design to injure another without just reason or cause.

ma·lign v. To speak slander or evil of; defame traduce. adj. Of an evil disposition, nature, or character. tending to produce evil effect. maligner n., malignly adv.

ma·lig·nant adj., *Pathol.* Of or relating to tumors and abnormal or rapid growth, and tending to metastasize; opposed to benign; causing death or great harm. malignancy, malignity n., malignantly adv.

ma·lin·ger v. To pretend injury or sickness so as to avoid responsibility or work. malingerer n.

mall n. A walk or other shaded public promenade; a street with shops, restaurants, and businesses which is closed to vehicles.

mal·lard n., pl. mallard or -ards.

A wild duck having brownish plumage, the male of which has a green head and neck.

mal·le·a·ble adj. Able to be bent, shaped, or hammered without breaking; capable of being molded, altered, or influenced. malleability, malleableness n., malleably adv.

mal·let n. A hammer with a head made of wood or rubber and a short handle; a tool for striking an object without marring it, used mainly for driving another tool, such as a chisel.

mal·le·us n., pl. -lei *Anat.* The club-shaped bone of the middle ear or the largest of three small bones; also called the hammer.

mal·nour·ished adj. Undernourished; poorly nourished.

mal·nu·tri·tion n. Insufficient or faulty nutrition.

mal·oc·clu·sion n. Improper alignment of the teeth.

mal·o·dor n. An offensive stench; odor.

mal·o·dor·ous adj. Having a disagreeable or foul odor. malodorously adv., malodorousness n.

mal·po·si·tion n., *Pathol.* Wrong position as of a fetus in the uterus or a body organ.

mal·prac·tice n. Improper treatment or neglect of a patient by his doctor during surgery or treatment which results in damage or injury; failure to perform a professional duty in a proper, careful, or correct fashion, resulting in injury, loss, or other problems.

malt n. Grain, usually barley, used chiefly in brewing and distilling; an alcoholic beverage.

mal·tose n. A white, crystalline sugar found in malt.

mal·treat v. To treat badly, unkindly, or roughly. maltreatment n.

mal·ver·sa·tion n. Improper behavior in a position of trust.

ma·ma n. Mother.

mam·ba n. A venomous snake found in the tropics and in southern Africa.

mam·bo n. A dance resembling the rumba of Latin America.

mam·mal n. Any member of a class whose females secrete milk for nourishing their young, including man. mammalian adj. & n.

mam·ma·ry gland n. The milk-producing organ of the female mammal, consisting of small cavity clusters with ducts ending in a nipple.

mam·mog·ra·phy n. An X-ray examination of the breast for early detection of cancer.

mam·moth n. An extinct, early form of elephant whose tusks curved upwards and whose body was covered with long hair; anything of great or huge size.

man n., pl. men An adult or fully-grown male; the human race; any human being, regardless of sex. *Slang* Husband; an expression of pleasure or surprise.

man·a·cle n. A device for restraining the hands; handcuffs. manacle v.

man·age v. To direct or control the affairs or use of; to organize. -ability n., -able adj., manageably adv.

man·age·ment n. The act of directing, or managing for a purpose; administration.

man·ag·er n. One in charge of managing

an enterprise or business.
managerial adj., **managership** n.
man-a-tee n. An aquatic mammal of the coastal waters of Florida, West Indies, and the Gulf of Mexico.
man-date n. An authoritative order or command. Law A judicial order issued by a higher court to a lower one. **mandate** v.
man-da-to-ry adj. Required by, having the nature of, or relating to a mandate; obligatory. **mandatorily** adv.
man-di-ble n. The lower or under jaw bone. Biol. Either part of the beak of a bird. **mandibular** adj.
man-do-lin n. A musical instrument having a pear-shaped body and a fretted neck, usually with four strings.
man-drake n. A plant having purplish flowers and a branched root, yielding powerful extracts and sometimes resembling the human form.
man-drel or **man-dril** n. A spindle or shaft on which material is held for working on a lathe; a rod around which metal is cast or shaped.
man-drill n. A large, fierce West African baboon, identifiable by its blue and red ribbed facial features.

mane n.

The long hair growing on the neck or back of some animals, as the lion, and horse. **maned** adj.
man--eat-er n. An animal which feeds on human flesh, such as a shark or a tiger; a cannibal.
ma-nege n. The art of training, breaking and riding horses; the performance of a horse so trained; a school for teaching horsemanship.
ma-neu-ver n., Milit. A planned strategic regulated movement or shift, as of warships, or troops; any planned, skillful, or calculated move. **maneuver** v., **maneuverability** n., **maneuverable** adj.
man Fri-day n. A male person devoted to another as a servant, aide, or employee.
man-ful adj. Having a manly spirit; resolute, brave; bold.
manfully adv., **manfulness** n.
man-ga-nese n. A hard, brittle, gray-white metallic element which forms an important component of steel alloys, symbolized by Mn.
mange n. A contagious skin disease of dogs and other domestic animals caused by parasitic mites and marked by itching and hair loss. **mangy** adj.
man-ger n. A trough or box which holds livestock feed.
man-gle v. To disfigure or mutilate by bruising, battering, or crushing; to spoil; to damage or destroy. **-er** n.
man-go n., pl. **-goes** or **-gos** A tropical evergreen tree that produces a fruit having a slightly acid taste.
man-grove n. A tropical evergreen tree or shrub having aerial roots which

form dense thickets along tidal shores.
man-han-dle v. To handle very roughly; to move something by human force.
man-hole n. A circular covered, opening usually in a street, through which one may enter a sewer, drain, or conduit for repairs or cleaning.
man-hood n. The state of being an adult male; virility.
man--hour n. The amount of work that one person can complete in one hour, used to estimate wages and costs.
man-hunt n. An extensive organized hunt for a person, especially one who has committed a crime. **manhunter** n.
ma-ni-a n. An extraordinary enthusiasm or craving for something; intense excitement and physical overactivity, often a symptom of manic-depressive psychosis; a form of insanity that this characterized by great excitement.
-mania suffix. Unreasonable or intense desire or infatuation with.
ma-ni-ac n. A violently insane person.
maniac, **maniacal** adj.
man-ic--de-pres-sive adj. Of a mental disorder characterized by alternating periods of manic excitation and depression. **manic-depressive** n.
man-i-cot-ti n. Pasta shaped like a tube, filled with meat or ricotta cheese and served with hot tomato sauce.
man-i-cure n. The cosmetic care of the hands and fingernails
manicure v., **manicurist** n.
man-i-fest adj. Clearly apparent or visible to the eye; obvious. v. To display, reveal or show. n. A list of cargo or passengers. **manifestly** adv., **manifestative** adj., **manifester** n.
man-i-fes-ta-tion n. The act or state of being manifest; display; that which reveals or displays.
man-i-fest con-tent n. The images that take place within a dream.
man-i-fes-to n., pl. **-toes** or **-tos** A public or formal explanation of principles or intentions, usually of a political nature.
man-i-fold adj. Having many and varied parts, forms, or types; having an assortment of features. Mech. A pipe with several or many openings, as for the escaping of exhaust gas. v. To multiply. **manifoldly** adv., **-ness** n.
man-i-kin or **man-ni-kin** n. A little man; a dwarf; a mannequin; a scale model of the human body, used for demonstrating the anatomy or surgical procedures.
Ma-nil-a n. The capital of the Philippines.
Manila hemp n. The fiber of the banana plant, used for making paper, rope, and cord.
ma-nil-a pa-per n. Strong, light brown paper, originally made from Manila hemp but now made of various fibers.
ma-nip-u-late v. To handle or manage shrewdly and deviously for one's own profit. **manipulation**, **manipulator** n., **manipulative** adj.

man-kind n. The human race; men collectively, as opposed to women.

man-like adj. Resembling a man.

man-ly adj. Pertaining to or having qualities which are traditionally attributed to a man. -ly adv., -iness n.

man--made adj. Made by human beings and not developed by nature; manufactured by man.

man-na n. The food which was miraculously given to the Israelites in the wilderness on their flight from Egypt; anything of value that one receives unexpectedly.

manned adj. Operated by a human being.

man-ne-quin n. A life-sized model of a human figure, used to fit or display clothes; a person who models clothes.

man-ner n. The way in which something happens or is done; an action or style of speech; one's social conduct and etiquette. **mannered** adj.

man-ner-ism n. A person's distinctive behavioral trait or traits. -ist n., **manneristic, manneristical** adj.

man-ner-ly adj. Well-behaved; polite; showing good manners. -iness n.

man-nish adj. Resembling a man; masculine; unwomanly. **mannishly** adv., **mannishness** n.

man--of--war n., pl. **men--of--war** A warship.

ma-nom-e-ter n. An instrument used to measure pressure, as of gases or liquids. **manometric** adj.

man-or n. A landed estate; the house or hall of an estate. **manorial** adj.

man-pow-er n. The force of human physical power; the number of men whose strength and skill are readily available to a nation, army, project, or other venture.

man-que adj. Lacking fulfillment; frustrated.

man-sard n., Archit. A curved roof with the lower slope almost vertical and the upper almost horizontal.

manse n. The house of a clergyman.

man-sion n. A very large, dwelling or impressive house.

man--size or **man--sized** adj., Slang Quite large.

man-slaugh-ter n., Law The unlawful killing without malice of a person by another; homicide.

man-slay-er n. One who murders or kills human being.

man-ta n. A rough-textured cotton fabric; any of several very large fishes having large, very flat bodies with winglike fins.

man-teau n., pl. -teaus or -teaux A robe or cloak.

man-tel also **man-tle** n. A shelf over a fireplace; the ornamental brick or stone around a fireplace.

man-til-la n. A light scarf worn over the head and shoulders by women in Latin America and Spain.

man-tis n., pl. **mantises** or **mantes** A tropical insect with a long body, large eyes, and swiveling head, which stands with its forelegs folded as if in prayer. Also known as a praying mantis.

man-tle n. A loose-fitting coat which is usually sleeveless; something that covers or conceals; a device consisting of a sheath of threads, used in gas lamps to give off brilliant illumination when heated by a flame. **mantle** v.

man-u-al adj. Used or operated by the hands. n. A small reference book which gives instructions on how to operate or work something. -ly adv.

man-u-fac-ture v. To make a product; to invent or produce something; to produce artificially. **manufacturer** n.

ma-nure n. The fertilizer used to fertilize land, obtained from animal dung. v. To treat an area with fertilizing matter; apply manure. **manure** v.

man-u-script n. A typed or written material copy of an article, book, or document, which is being prepared for publication.

man-wise adv. According to the nature of men.

man-y adj. Amounting to a large or indefinite number or amount; considerable number.

man-y--sid-ed adj. Having many aspects or sides, talents or capabilities. **manysidedness** n.

map n. A plane surface representation of a region. v. To plan anything in detail. **mapmaker, mapper** n.

ma-ple n. A tall tree having lobed leaves and a fruit of two joined samaras; the wood of this tree, amber-yellow in color when finished and used for furniture and flooring.

ma-ple su-gar n. Sugar made from the sap of the maple tree.

ma-ple sy-rup n. The refined sap of the sugar maple.

mar v. To scratch or deface; to blemish; to ruin; to spoil.

Mar abbr. March.

mar-a-bou n. A stork of Africa, whose soft down is used for trimming women's garments.

ma-ra-ca n.

A percussion instrument made from gourds containing dried beans or pebbles.

mar-a-schi-no cherry n. A cherry preserved in a cordial distilled from the fermented juice of the small wild cherry and flavored with cracked cherry pits.

mar-a-thon n. A foot race of 26 miles, usually run on the streets of a city; any contest of endurance. **marathoner** n.

mar-ble n. A limestone which is partly crystallized and irregular in color. v. To contain sections of fat, as in meat. **marbles** A game played with balls of glass. Slang A person's common sense or sanity. **marble** *v.*, **marbly** *adj.*

march *n.* To walk with measured, regular steps in a solemn or dignified manner. *Mus.* A musical composition. *n.* The uniform and measured walk of soldiers, moving together. **marcher** *n.*

March *n.* The third month of the year, containing 31 days.

Mar-di Gras *n.* The Tuesday before Ash Wednesday, often celebrated with parades and costumed merrymaking.

mare *n.* The female of the horse and other equine animals.

ma-re *n.*, *pl. Astron.* Any of the dark areas or large depressions on the surface of the moon.

ma-re clau-sum *n.* The body of water that is controlled by one nation.

ma-re li-be-rum *n.* A body of water that is available to all nations for travel and navigation.

mare's-nest *n.* An accomplishment found to be worthless; a greatly confused state of affairs.

mar-ga-rine *n.* A butter substitute made from vegetable oils and milk.

mar-gin *n.* The edge or border around the body of written or printed text; the difference between the selling price and cost of an item.

mar-gi-na-li-a *pl.*, *n.* The notes in the margin of a book.

ma-ri-a-chi *n.* A Mexican band; the music performed by a musician playing in a mariachi.

Marie Antoinette *n.* (1755-1793). The queen of Louis XVI of France from 1774-1793.

mar-i-gold *n.* Any of a variety of plants having golden-yellow flowers.

mar-i-jua-na *or* **marihuana** *n.* Hemp; the dried flower tops and leaves of this plant, capable of producing disorienting or hallucinogenic effects when smoked in cigarettes or ingested.

ma-ri-na *n.* A docking area for boats, furnishing moorings and supplies for small boats.

mar-i-nade *n.* A brine made from vinegar or wine and oil with various herbs and spices for soaking meat, fowl, or fish before cooking.

mar-i-nate *v.* To soak in a marinade. **marination** *n.*

ma-rine *adj.* Of, pertaining to, existing in, or formed by the sea. *n.* A soldier trained for service on land and at sea. **Marine** *n.* A member of the Marine Corps.

ma-rine glue *n.* A water-insoluble glue used to coat areas on a ship's deck.

mar-i-ner *n.* A person whose job is to assist or navigate ships and seaman through an area.

mar-i-o-nette *n.* A small jointed animal or human figure of wood which is manipulated from above by attached strings or wires.

mar-i-tal *adj.* Pertaining to marriage; matrimonial. **maritally** *adv.*

mar-i-time *adj.* Located or situated on or near the sea; pertaining to the sea and its navigation and commerce.

mark *n.* A visible impression, trace, dent, or stain; an identifying seal, inscription, or label; a symbol to indicate ownership, degree of excellence, or distinction.

Mark *n.* The evangelist who wrote the second Gospel narratives in the New Testament; the second Gospel of the New Testament; Saint Mark.

mar-ket *n.* The trade and commerce in a certain service or commodity; a public place for purchasing and selling merchandise; the possible consumers of a particular product. *v.* To sell. **marketability** *n.*, **marketable** *adj.*

mar-ket-place *n.* A place, such as a public square, where ideas, opinions, and works are traded and tested.

marks-man *n.* A person skilled in firing a gun and hitting the mark. **-woman** *n.*

mark-up *n.* The amount of increase in price from the cost to the selling price. *v.* To raise the price.

mar-lin *n.* A large marine game fish of the Atlantic; the striped marlin found in the Pacific.

mar-line-spike *n.*, *Naut.* A pointed tool used in splicing ropes.

mar-ma-lade *n.* A preserve made from the pulp and rind of fruits.

ma-roon *v.* To put ashore and abandon on a desolate shore. *n.* A dull purplish red.

mar-que-try *n.* Inlaid work of wood or ivory used for decorating furniture.

mar-quis *n.* The title of a nobleman ranking below a duke.

mar-qui-sette *n.* A fabric of cotton, silk, nylon, or a combination of these, used in curtains, clothing, and mosquito nets.

mar-riage *n.* The state of being married; wedlock; the act of marrying or the ceremony entered into by a man and woman so as to live together as husband and wife. **marriageability** *n.*, **marriageable** *adj.*

mar-row *n.* The soft, vascular tissue which fills bone cavities; the main part or essence of anything.

mar-row-bone *n.* A bone that is rich in marrow.

mar-ry *v.* To take or join as husband or wife; to unite closely.

Mars *n.* The 4th planet from the sun.

marsh *n.* An area of low, wet land; a swamp. **marshy** *adj.*

mar-shal *n.* A military officer of high rank in foreign countries; the person in the U.S. in charge of a police or fire department. *v.* To bring troops together to prepare for a battle.

marsh-mal-low *n.* A soft, white confection made of sugar, corn syrup, starch, and gelatin and coated with powdered sugar.

mar-su-pi-al *n.* An animal, such as a kangaroo, koala, or opossum, which has no placenta, but which in the female has an abdominal pouch with teats to feed and carry the offspring.

mart *n.* A trading market; a center.

mar-ten *n.*

A weasel-like mammal of eastern North America with arboreal habits; the valuable brown fur of the marten.

mar-tial *adj.* Of, pertaining to, or concerned with war or the military life.

mar-tial arts *pl., n.* Oriental arts of self-defense, such as karate or judo, which are practiced as sports.

mar-tial law *n.* Temporary rule by military forces over the citizens in an area where civil law and order no longer exist.

mar-tin *n.* A bird of the swallow family with a tail that is less forked than that of the common swallow.

mar-ti-ni *n., pl.* -nis A cocktail of gin and dry vermouth, served with an olive or lemon peel.

mar-tyr *n.* A person who would rather die than renounce his religious principles; one making great sacrifices to advance a cause, belief, or principle. **martyr** *v.,* **martyrdom** *n.*

mar-vel *n.* Anything causing surprise, wonder, or astonishment. **marvel** *v.*

mar-vel-ous *or* **marvellous** *adj.* Causing astonishment and wonder; wondrous. *Informal* Excellent; very good, admirable. **marvelously** *adv.,* **-ness** *n.*

Marx-ism *n.* The body of socialist doctrines developed by Karl Marx.

Mary *n.* The mother of Jesus.

Mary-land *n.* A state located on the eastern coast of the United States.

mar-zi-pan *n.* A confection of grated almonds, sugar, and egg whites.

masc *abbr.* Masculine.

mas-car-a *n.* A cosmetic preparation used for coloring or darkening the eyelashes.

mas-cot *n.* A person, animal, or object thought to bring good luck.

mas-cu-line *adj.* Of or pertaining to the male sex; male; the masculine gender. **masculinity** *n.*

ma-ser *n., Physics* One of several devices which are similar to the laser but which operate with microwaves rather than light.

mash *n.* A soft, pulpy mass or mixture used to distill alcohol or spirits. *v.* To crush into a soft, pulpy mass. **-er** *n.*

mask *n.* A covering used to conceal the face in order to disguise or protect. *v.* To hide or conceal.

mas-o-chism *n.* A condition in which sexual gratification is marked by pleasure in being subjected to physical pain or abuse. **masochist** *n.,* **masochistic** *adj.*

ma-son *n.* A person working with brick or stone.

ma-son-ic *adj.* Pertaining to or like freemasonry or Freemasons.

masque *n.* An elaborately staged dramatic performance, popular during the 16th and 17th centuries in England; a masquerade.

mas-quer-ade *n.* A costume party in which the guests are masked and dressed in fancy costumes. *v.* To disguise oneself. **masquerader** *n.*

mass *n.* A body of matter that does not have definite shape but is relatively large in size; physical volume; the measure of a body's resistance to acceleration.

Mass *or* **mass** *n.* A celebration in the Roman Catholic and some Protestant churches; the service including this celebration.

Mass *or* **Ma** *abbr.* Massachusetts.

Mass-a-chu-setts *n.* A state located in the northeastern part of the United States.

mas-sa-cre *n.* The indiscriminate and savage killing of human beings in large numbers. **massacre** *v.*

mas-sage *n.* The manual or mechanical manipulation of the skin to improve circulation and to relax muscles.

mas-seur *n.* A man who gives massages.

mas-seuse *n.* A woman who gives massages.

mas-sive *adj.* Of great intensity, degree, and size. **massively** *adv.,* **-ness** *n.*

mast *n.* The upright pole or spar which supports the sails and running rigging of a sail boat.

mas-tec-to-my *n., pl.* -ies The surgical removal of breast.

mas-ter *n.* A person with control or authority over others; one who is exceptionally gifted or skilled in an art, science, or craft; the title given for respect or in address. *v.* To learn a skill, craft, or job; to overcome defeat.

mas-ter key *n.* A key which will open many different locks whose keys are not the same.

mas-ter-ly *adj.* Characteristic of a master. **masterliness** *n.*

mas-ter-mind *n.* A person who plans and directs at the highest levels of policy and strategy. *v.* To plan or direct an undertaking.

mas-ter of cer-e-mo-nies *n.* A person who hosts a formal event or program.

mas-ter-piece *n.* Something having notable excellence; an unusually brilliant achievement which is considered the greatest achievement of its creator.

mas-ter plan *n.* A plan providing complete instructions.

mast-head *n.* The top of a mast; the listing in a periodical giving the names of the editors, staff, and owners.

mas-ti-cate *v.* To chew. **mastication** *n.*

mas-to-don *n.* A large, extinct mammal which resembles an elephant.

mas-toid *n., Anat.* The nipple shaped portion at the rear of the temporal bone behind the ear.

mas-tur-ba-tion *n.* The act of stimulating the sexual organs by hand or other means without sexual intercourse.

mas·tur·bate v., **masturbator** n.

mat n. A flat piece of material made of fiber, rubber, rushes, or other material and used to cover floors; the border around a picture, which serves as a contrast between the picture and the frame.

mat·a·dor n. A bullfighter who kills the bull after completing various maneuvers with a cape.

match n. Anything that is similar or identical to another; a short, thin piece of wood or cardboard with a specially treated tip which ignites as a result of friction. v. To equal; to oppose successfully. **-able** adj., **-er** n.

match-maker n. A person who arranges a marriage.

mate n. A spouse; something matched, joined, or paired with another; in chess, a move which puts the opponent's king in jeopardy. Naval A petty officer. **mate** v.

ma·te·ri·al n. The substance from which anything is or may be composed or constructed of; anything that is used in creating, working up, or developing something.

ma·te·ri·al·ism n. The doctrine that physical matter is the only reality and that everything, including thought, feeling, will, and mind, is explainable in terms of matter; a preference for material objects as opposed to spiritual or intellectual pursuits. **-ist** n., **-istic** adj., **-istically** adv.

ma·te·ri·al·ize v. To give material or actual form to something; to assume material or visible appearance; to take form or shape.

materialization, materializer n.

ma·te·ri·el n. The equipment and supplies of a military force, including guns and ammunition.

ma·ter·nal adj. Relating to a mother or motherhood; inherited from one's mother.

ma·ter·ni·ty n. The state of being a mother; the qualities of a mother; the department in a hospital for the prenatal and postnatal care of babies and their mothers.

math n. Mathematics.

math·e·mat·ics n. The study of form, arrange-ment, quantity, and magnitude of numbers and operational symbols. **mathematical** adj., **mathematically** adv., **mathematician** n.

mat·i·nee n. An afternoon performance of a play, concert, movie, etc.

ma·tri·arch n. A woman ruler of a family, tribe, or clan. **matriarchal** adj., **matriarchy** n.

mat·ri·cide n. The killing of one's own mother; one who kills his mother.

ma·tric·u·late v. To enroll, or to be admitted into a college or university.

mat·ri·mo·ny n. The condition of being married; the act, sacrament, or ceremony of marriage. **matrimonial** adj., **matrimonially** adv.

ma·trix n., pl. **-rixes** or **-rices.** Something within which something else develops, originates, or takes shape; a mold or die.

ma·tron n. A married woman or widow of dignity and social position; the woman supervisor in a prison. **matronliness** n., **matronly** adj. & adv.

mat·ter n. Something that makes up the substance of anything; that which is material and physical, occupies space, and is perceived by the senses; something that is sent by mail; something that is written or printed.

mat·tock n. A tool having a blade on one side and a pick on the other or one with a blade on each side.

mat·tress n. A large cloth case filled with soft material and used on or as a bed.

mat·u·rate v. To ripen or mature.

ma·ture adj. Completely developed; at full growth; something, as a bond at a bank, that is due and payable.

mature v., **maturely** adv., **maturity** n.

mat·zo n., pl. **-zos** or **-zot** A large, flat piece of unleavened bread eaten during Passover.

maud·lin adj. Overly sentimental; tearfully and overwhelmingly emotional.

maul n. A heavy hammer or mallet used to drive wedges, piles, and other materials. v. To handle roughly; to abuse.

maun·der v. To wander or talk in an incoherent manner.

mau·so·le·um n., pl. **-leums** or **-lea** A large and stately tomb.

mauve n. A purplish rose shade; a moderately reddish to gray purple.

mav·er·ick n. An unbranded or orphaned calf or colt. Slang A person who is unorthodox in his ideas or attitudes.

maw n. The jaws, mouth, or gullet of a hungry or ferocious animal; the stomach.

mawk·ish adj. Disgustingly sentimental; sickening or insipid. **mawkishly** adv.

max abbr. Maximum.

max·i n. A floor-length garment, such as a skirt or coat.

max·il·la n., pl. **-lae** or **-las** The upper jaw or jawbone. **maxillary** adj.

max·im n. A brief statement of truth, general principle, or rule of conduct.

max·i·mize v. To increase as greatly as possible; to intensify to the maximum.

max·i·mum n., pl. **-mums** or **-ma** The greatest possible number, measure, degree, or quantity. **maximum** adj.

may v. To be permitted or allowed; used to express a wish, purpose, desire, contingency, or result.

May n. The fifth month of the year, having 31 days.

may-be adv. Perhaps; possibly.

May Day n. The first day of May, traditionally celebrated as a spring festival and in some countries as a holiday honoring the labor force.

may-flow·er n. A wide variety of plants which blossom in May.

Mayflower *n.* The ship on which the Pilgrims came to America in 1620.

may-hem *n., Law* The offense of injuring a person's body; any situation brought on by violence, confusion, noise, or disorder.

may-o *n., Slang* Mayonnaise.

may-on-naise *n.* A dressing for salads, made by beating raw egg yolk, oil, lemon juice, or vinegar and seasonings.

may-or *n.* The chief magistrate of a town, borough, municipality, or city. **mayoral** *adj.*, **mayoralty, mayorship** *n.*

may-pole *n.* A decorated pole hung with streamers around which May Day dancing takes place.

maze *n.* A complicated, intricate network of passages or pathways; a labyrinth; a state of uncertainty, bewilderment, or perplexity. **maze** *v.*

MBA *abbr.* Master of Business Administration.

MC *abbr.* Master of ceremonies.

McKinley, William *N.* (1843-1901). The 25th president of the United States, from 1897-1901, assassinated while in office.

MD *abbr.* Maryland *or* Md.

MD *abbr.* Doctor of Medicine.

mdse *abbr.* Merchandise.

me *pron.* The objective case of the pronoun I.

ME *abbr.* Maine.

mead *n.* An alcoholic beverage made from fermented honey and water with yeast and spices added.

mead-ow *n.* A tract of grassland used for grazing or growing hay.

mead-ow-lark *n.* A songbird of North America.

mea-ger *or* **mea-gre** *adj.* Thin; lean; deficient in quantity, richness, vigor, or fertility. **meagerly** *adv.*, **-ness** *n.*

meal *n.* The edible seeds of coarsely ground grain; any powdery material; the food served or eaten at one sitting at certain times during the day; the time or occasion of taking such food.

meal-tick-et *n., Slang* One who is a source of financial support for another; a ticket or card bought for a specified price and redeemable at a restaurant for food.

meal-y--mouthed *adj.* Unable to speak plainly and frankly; evasive.

mean *v.* To have in mind as a purpose or intent; to be of a specified importance or significance. *adj.* Poor or inferior in appearance or quality. *n.* The medium point. **means** The method or instrument by which some end is or may be accomplished; the available resources.

me-an-der *v.* To wander about without a certain course or a fixed direction.

mean-ing *n.* That which is meant or intended; the aim, end, or purpose; the significance; an interpretation. **meaningful, meaningfulness** *adj.*

mean-time *n.* The time or period between or during the intervening time.

mean-while *adv.* At the same time.

mea-sles *n.* A contagious viral disease usually occurring in children, characterized by the eruption of red spots.

mea-sly *adj., Slang* Very small; meager.

meas-ure *n.* The range, dimension, extent, or capacity of anything. *Mus.* The group of beats marked off by regularly recurring primary accents; the notes and rests between two successive bars on a musical staff. *v.* To determine the range, dimension, extent, volume, or capacity of anything. **measurable** *adj.* **-ably** *adv.*, **-er** *n.*

meas-ure-ment *n.* The process or act of measuring.

meat *n.* The flesh of an animal which is used as food; the core or essential part of something. **meatiness** *n.*, **-y** *adj.*

mech *abbr.* Mechanical; mechanics.

me-chan-ic *n.* A person skilled in the making, operation, or repair of machines or tools.

me-chan-i-cal *adj.* Involving or having to do with the construction, operation, or design of tools or machines; produced or operated by a machine. **-ly** *adv.*

me-chan-i-cal draw-ing *n.* A drawing done with the aid of squares, compasses, or other instruments.

me-chan-ics *pl., n.* The scientific study and analysis of the action of forces and motion on material bodies.

mech-a-nism *n.* The arrangement or parts of a machine; the technique or process by which something works.

mech-a-nize *v.* To make mechanical; to equip with tanks, trucks, mechanical and other equipment, as in the military. **mechanization** *n.*

med *abbr.* Medical.

med-al *n.*

A small piece of metal with a commemorative image or inscription which is presented as an award.

med-al-ist *n.* A person who designs, collects, or makes medals; one who has been awarded or received a medal.

me-dal-lion *n.* A large circular or oval medal which is used as a decorative element.

med-dle *v.* To interfere or participate in another person's business or affairs. **meddler** *n.*, **meddlesome** *adj.*

med-i-a *pl., n.* The instruments of news communication, as radio, television, and newspapers.

me-di-al *adj.* Pertaining to or situated in the middle; ordinary.

me-di-an *n.* Something that is halfway between two different parts. *adj.* Relating to or constituting the median of a set of numbers.

me-di-an strip *n.* The strip which divides highway traffic lanes which are going in opposite directions.

me-di-ate *v.* To help settle or reconcile opposing sides in a dispute.

mediation, mediator *n.*

med·ic *n.*, *Slang* A physician or intern; a medical student; in the armed forces, a corpsman or enlisted person trained to give first aid.

Med·i·caid *or* **medicaid** *n.* A governmental medical care or health insurance program providing medical aid for people who are unable to pay their own medical expenses.

med·i·cal *adj.* Relating to the study or practice of medicine. **medically** *adv.*

medical examiner *n.* A physician who is authorized by a governmental body to ascertain causes of death.

Med·i·care *or* **medicare** *n.* The program under the Social Security Administration which provides medical care for elderly people.

med·i·cate *v.* To treat an injury or illness with medicine. **medication** *n.*

med·i·cine *n.* Any agent or substance used in the treatment of disease or in the relief of pain; the science of diagnosing and treating disease; the profession of medicine.

med·i·cine ball *n.* A large, heavy ball used for physical exercise.

me·di·e·val *or* **mediaeval** *adj.* Like or characteristic of the Middle Ages. **medievalism, -ist** *n.*, **medievally** *adv.*

me·di·o·cre *adj.* Common; fair; undistinguished.

med·i·tate *v.* To be in continuous, contemplative thought; to think about doing something. **meditative** *adj.*, **meditation** *n.*

Med·i·ter·ra·ne·an *n.* A sea bounded by Africa, Asia, and Europe, which connects with the Atlantic Ocean through the Straits of Gibraltar. *adj.* Of or relating to the people or countries bounded by the Mediterranean.

me·di·um *n.*, *pl.* **-dia** *or* **-ums** Something which occupies a middle position between two extremes; the means of communicating information or ideas through publishing, radio, or television.

med·ley *n.* A mixture or confused mass of elements; a jumble. *Music* A musical composition made up of parts of different songs.

me·dul·la *n.*, *pl.* **-las** *or* **-lae** *Anat.* The center of certain vertebrate structures, such as bone marrow.

me·dul·la ob·lon·ga·ta The mass of nerve tissue found at the base of the brain, controlling bodily functions such as breathing and circulation.

meek *adj.* Showing patience and a gentle disposition; lacking spirit or backbone; submissive. **-ly** *adv.*, **-ness** *n.*

meet *v.* To come upon; to encounter; to come into conjunction or contact with someone or something; to cope or deal with; to handle; to fulfill an obligation or need.

meet·ing *n.* An assembly or gathering of persons; a coming together.

meg·a·bucks *n.*, *Slang* One million dollars; a lot of money.

meg·a·hertz *n.*, *pl.* **-hertz** *Physics.* One million cycles per second, used as a radio-frequency unit.

meg·a·lo·ma·ni·a *n.*, *Psychiatry* A mental disorder marked by fantasies of power, wealth, or omnipotence. **megalomaniac** *n.*, **-cal** *adj.*

meg·a·lop·o·lis *n.* A very large urban complex.

meg·a·phone *n.* A funnel-shaped device which is used to amplify or direct the voice.

meg·a·ton *n.* One million tons; the unit equal to the explosive power of one million tons of TNT.

meg·a·watt *n.* A unit of electrical power equal to one million watts.

mei·o·sis *n.*, *pl.* **-ses** *Biol.* The process by which undeveloped sex cells, sperm and ovum, mature by reduction division so that they contain only half of the full number of chromosomes.

mel·an·cho·li·a *n.*, *Psychiatry* A mental disorder of great depression of spirits and excessive brooding without apparent cause. **melancholiac** *adj.* & *n.*

mel·an·chol·ic *adj.* Depressed; sad.

mel·an·chol·y *adj.* Excessively gloomy or sad.

me·lange *n.*, *French* A medley or mixture.

mel·a·nin *n.*, *Biochem.* The brownish-black pigment which is contained in animal tissues, as the hair and skin.

mel·a·nism *n.* Anabnormally dark pigmentation of the skin.

mel·a·no·ma *n.*, *pl.* **-mas** *or* **-mata** A dark-colored tumor or malignant mole.

Mel·ba toast *n.* Very thinly sliced bread which is toasted until brown and crisp.

meld *v.* In pinochle and other card games, to declare or announce a combination of cards for inclusion in one's total score. *n.* The card or combination of cards declared for a score.

me·lee *n.* The confused and tumultuous mingling of a crowd.

mel·io·rate *v* To cause to improve or to improve. **-ion** *n.*, **-ive** *adj.* & *n.*

mel·lif·er·ous *adj.* Producing or bearing honey.

mel·lo *adj.* Sweet and soft; rich and full-flavored; rich and soft in quality, as in sounds or colors.

me·lo·di·ous *adj.* Characterized by a melody; tuneful; pleasant to hear.

mel·o·dra·ma *n.* A very dramatic presentation which is marked by suspense and romantic sentiment; sensational and highly emotional language or behavior. **melodramatic** *adj.*, **melodramatically** *adv.*

mel·o·dy *n.*, *pl.* **-ies** An agreeable succession of pleasing sounds. **melodic** *adj.*, **melodically** *adv.*

mel·on *n.*

The large fruit of any of various plants of the gourd family, as the watermelon.

melt v. To change from a solid to a liquid as a result of pressure or heat.

melt-down n. The melting of a nuclear-reactor core.

melt-ing pot n. A place where immigrants of different cultures or races are assimilated.

mem-ber n. A person who belongs to a society, party, club, or other organization. *Biol.* An organ or part of an animal or person's body, especially a limb.

mem-ber-ship n. The state or fact of being a member.

mem-brane n. A thin, pliable, sheet-like layer of tissue which covers body surfaces and separates or connects body parts. membranous adj.

me-men-to n., pl. -tos or -toes A keepsake.

mem-oir n. Personal records or reminiscences; an autobiography.

mem-o-ra-ble adj. Worth remembering or noting. memorably adv.

mem-o-ran-dum n., pl. -dums or -da A brief, informal note written as a reminder.

me-mo-ri-al n. Something that serves to keep in remembrance, as a person or event. adj. Perpetuating remembrance.

Memorial Day n. The holiday that recognizes members of the armed forces killed in wars, celebrated on the last Monday in May.

mem-o-rize v. To commit something to memory. memorization, memorizer n.

mem-o-ry n., pl. -ries The mental function or capacity of recalling or recognizing something that has been previously learned or experienced.

men pl. n. The plural of man.

men-ace n. Something or someone who threatens; an annoying person. menace v., menacingly adv.

me-nar-che n. The beginning or the first occurrence of menstruation.

mend v. To fix; to repair; to correct.

men-da-cious adj. Prone to lying; deceitful; untrue; false. mendaciously adv., mendacity n.

men-de-le-vi-um n. A short-lived radioactive element of the actinide series.

me-ni-al adj. Relating to a household servant or household chores requiring little responsibility or skill. -ly adv.

men-in-gi-tis n., Pathol. An inflammation of the membranes which enclose the brain and spinal cord.

me-ninx n., pl. meninges The membrane which encloses the spinal cord and brain. meningeal adj.

men-o-pause n., Physiol. The time of final menstruation, occurring normally between the ages of 45 and 50 menopausal adj.

men-ses pl., n. The blood and dead cell debris which are discharged from the uterus through the vagina by women who are not pregnant; menstruation, occurring at monthly intervals between puberty and menopause.

men-stru-ate v. To discharge the menses, approximately every 28 days. menstrual adj.

men-stru-a-tion n., Physiol. The process, act, or periodical flow of bloody fluid from the uterus, also called period.

-ment suffix The result or product of achievement; action; process.

men-tal adj. Relating to or of the mind. mentally adv.

men-tal de-fi-cien-cy n. Subnormal intellectual development, marked by deficiencies ranging from impaired learning ability to social incompetence.

men-tal-i-ty n., pl. -ies Mental faculties or powers; mental activity; habit of mind.

men-tal re-tar-da-tion n. A mental deficiency.

men-thol n., Chem. The white, waxy crystalline alcohol which is obtained from and has the odor of peppermint oil. mentholated adj.

men-tion v. To refer to incidentally, in passing, or briefly. mentionable adj., mentioner n.

men-tor n. A wise and trusted person.

men-u n. A list of food or dishes available at a restaurant; in Computer Science, a list of options displayed on the screen from which the operator may choose.

me-ow n. The cry of a cat. meow v.

me-phi-tis n. A sickening or foul smell; a stench emitted from the earth.

mer-can-tile adj. Of or relating to merchants, trading, or commerce.

mer-ce-nar-y n. A person who is concerned only with making money and obtaining material gain; a person paid to serve as a soldier in a foreign country. mercenary adj.

mer-cer-ize v. To treat cotton yarn or thread with sodium hydroxide so as to give strength and receptiveness to dyes.

mer-chan-dise n. Commodities or goods that are bought and sold. v. To buy and sell.

mer-chant n. A person who operates a retail business for profit.

mer-chant-man n. A ship used for commercial shipments.

mer-cu-ry n. A silvery, metallic, liquid element used in thermometers and barometers, symbolized by Hg.

mer-cy n., pl. -ies Compassionate and kind treatment. merciful, -iless adj., mercifully, mercilessly adv.

mere adj. Absolute; no more than what is stated. merest adj., merely adv.

merge v. To unite or bring together as one; in Computer Science, to combine two or more files into one, retaining the internal order of both.

mer-ger n. The act of combining two or more corporations into one.

me-ringue n. A mixture of stiffly beaten egg whites and sugar, used as a topping for cakes and pies or baked into crisp shells.

me-ri-no *n., pl.* **-nos** A Spanish breed of hardy, white, fine-wooled sheep; a soft, lightweight fabric originally made of merino wool. **merino** *adj.*

mer-it *n.* A characteristic act or trait which is worthy of praise. *v.* To earn; to be worthy of.

mer-i-toc-ra-cy *n., pl.* **-ies** A system which bases advancement on ability or achievement.

mer-i-to-ri-ous *adj.* Deserving honor, praise or reward. **meritoriously** *adv.*

mer-maid *n.* An imaginary sea creature having the upper body of a woman and the tail of a fish. **merman** *n.*

mer-ry *adj.* Delightful; gay; entertaining; festive; happy; joyous. **merrily** *adv.*, **merriness** *n.*

mer-ry--go--round *n.* A circular, revolving platform often with benches and animal figures, usually found in circuses and amusement parks.

me-sa *n.* A flat-topped hill or small plateau with steep sides.

mesh *n.* Open spaces in a thread, wire or cord net; something that entraps or snares; the fitting or coming together of gear teeth for transmitting power.

mes-mer-ize *v.* To hypnotize or put into a trance.

Mes-o-po-ta-mi-a *n.* The area between the Euphrates and Tigris rivers.

mes-quite *n.* A thorny, deep-rooted shrub or small tree which grows in the southwestern United States and in Mexico.

mess *n., pl.* **messes** A disorderly or confused heap; a jumble; a dish or portion of soft or liquid food; a meal eaten by a group of persons, usually in the military.

mes-sage *n.* Any information, command, or news transmitted from one person to another.

mes-sen-ger *n.* A person who carries a message or does an errand for another person or company.

Mes-si-ah *n.* The anticipated or expected king of the Jews; Jesus Christ.

mess-y *adj.* Untidy; upset; dirty; lacking neatness. **messily** *adv.*, **messiness** *n.*

met *v., p.t. & p.p.* Past tense of meet.

me-tab-o-lism *n.* The chemical and physical changes in living cells which involve the maintenance of life. **metabolic** *adj.*, **metabolize** *v.*

meta-car-pus *n.* The part of the forefoot or hand which connects the bones of the toes or fingers to the ankle or wrist.

met-a-gal-ax-y *n.* The universe; the entire system of galaxies.

metal *n.* One of a category of opaque, fusible, ductile, and typically lustrous elements. **metallic** *adj.*, **-lically** *adv.*

met-al-lur-gy *n.* The technology and science which studies methods of extracting metals from their ores and of preparing them for use. **metallurgical** *adj.*, **metallurgist** *n.*

met-a-mor-pho-sis *n.* The transformation and change in the structure and habits of an animal during normal growth, as the metamorphosis of a tadpole into a frog. **metamorphism** *n.*, **metamorphose** *v.*

met-a-phor *n.* A figure of speech in which the context demands that a word or phrase not be taken literally, as the sun is smiling; a comparison which doesn't use like or as.

me-tas-ta-sis *n.* A spread of cancer cells from the original tumor to one or more additional sites within the body. **metastasize** *v.*, **metastatic** *adj.*

met-a-tar-sus *n., pl.* **-si** The part of the human foot which forms the instep and contains five bones between the ankle and the toes; the hind foot of four-legged animals. **metatarsal** *adj.*

me-te-or *n.* A moving particle in the solar system which appears as a trail or streak in the sky as it comes into contact with the atmosphere of the earth.

me-te-or-ic *adj.* Of or relating to a meteor or meteors; resembling a meteor in speed, brilliance, or brevity.

me-te-or-ite *n.* A stony or metallic mass of a meteor which reaches the earth after partially burning in the atmosphere.

me-te-or-ol-o-gy *n.* The science concerned with the study of weather, weather conditions and weather forecasting. **meteorological,** **-ic** *adj.*, **-ically** *adv.*, **meteorologist** *n.*

me-ter *n.* The arrangement of words, syllables, or stanzas in verse or poetry; a measure equaling 39.37 inches.

meth-a-done *n.* A man-made narcotic used in the treatment of heroin addiction.

meth-ane *n.* A colorless, odorless flammable gas used as a fuel; a product of the decomposition of organic matter.

meth-a-nol *n.* A colorless, odorless flammable alcohol that is used as an antifreeze, as a fuel, and as a raw material in chemical synthesis.

me-thinks *v.* It seems to me.

meth-od *n.* A manner, a process, or the regular way of doing something; the orderly arrangement, development, or classification. **methodical,** **methodic** *adj.*, **methodically** *adv.*

Meth-od-ist *n.* A member of a Protestant denomination which was developed from a religious club formed by John and Charles Wesley in 1729. **Methodism** *n.*, **Methodist** *adj.*

Methuselah *n.* A Biblical ancestor of Noah who is said to have lived to the age of 969.

meth-yl *n.* An alkyl radical derived from methane which occurs in several organic compounds.

me-tic-u-lous *adj.* Very precise; careful; concerned with small details. **meticulously** *adv.*, **meticulousness** *n.*

me-tis *n.* A person of mixed blood, usually of French and Indian ancestry.

met-ric *adj.* Of or relating to the metric system. **metrical** *adj.*, **metrication** *n.*

met-ric sys-tem *n.* A decimal system of weights and measures based on the meter as a unit of length and the kilogram as a unit of mass, originated in France around 1790.

met-ri-fy *v.* To adopt or convert to the metric system. **metrification** *n.*

met-ro *n.* A subway system for transportation.

met-ro-nome *n.* An instrument designed to mark time by means of a series of clicks at exact intervals. **-ic** *adj.*

me-trop-o-lis *n.* A large or capital city of a state, region, or country.

mew *n.* A hideaway; a secret place.

Mexico *n.* A large country located in southwestern North America.

mez-za-nine *n.* A low story between two main stories of a building; the lowest balcony in a theatre.

MI *abbr.* Michigan.

MIA *abbr.* Missing in action.

mice *pl. n.* The plural of mouse.

Michelangelo *n.* Italian Renaissance painter and sculptor.

Mich-i-gan *n.* A state located in the mid-western part of the United States.

mi-crobe *n.* A germ, plant, or animal so small that is can be seen only with the aid of a microscope.

mi-cro-bi-ol-o-gy *n.* The scientific study of microorganisms. **microbiological** *adj.*, **microbiologist** *n.*

mi-cro-ceph-a-ly *n.* A condition of abnormal smallness of the head, usually associated with mental defects.

mi-cro-cir-cuit *n.* An electronic circuit composed of very small components.

mi-cro-com-put-er *n.* A computer which uses a microprocessor.

mi-cro-film *n.* A film used to photograph printed matter at a greatly reduced size.

micro-or-gan-ism *n.* An organism too small to see without the aid of a microscope.

mi-cro-phone *n.*

An instrument which converts acoustical waves into electrical signals and feeds them into a recorder, amplifier or broadcasting transmitter. **-ic** *adj.*

mi-cro-proc-es-sor *n.* In Computer Science, a semiconductor processing unit which is contained on an integrated circuit chip.

mi-cro-scope *n.*

An optical instrument consisting of a lens or combination of lenses, used to produce magnified images of very small objects.

mi-cro-scop-ic *adj.* Too small to be seen by the eye alone. **microscopical** *adv.*

mi-cro-sur-ger-y *n.* Surgery performed by means of a microscope and laser beam. **microsurgical** *adj.*

mi-cro-wave *n.* A very short electromagnetic wave.

microwave oven *n.* An oven which uses microwaves to heat and cook food.

mid *adj.* In the middle or center; central.

mid-air *n.* A point in the air just above the ground surface.

mid-day *n.* Noon; the middle of the day.

mid-den *n.* A refuse heap or dunghill.

mid-dle *adj.* Being equally distant from extremes or limits; the central. *n.* Anything which occupies a middle position; the waist.

middle age *n.* A period of life from about 40 to 60 years.

Middle Ages *pl. n.* The period of European history from about 500 to 1500.

Middle America *n.* The mid-western states of the U.S.; the class of American citizens with conservative values and attitudes, considered to have an average income and education. **Middle American** *adj.*

mid-dle class *n.* The social class of people between a high income and low income status.

mid-dle ear *n.* A small membrane-lined cavity between the tympanic membrane and the inner ear through which sound waves are carried.

mid-dle-man *n.* A person who serves as an agent between the producer and a product and the consumer.

mid-dle school *n.* A school which usually includes grades 6, 7, and 8.

mid-dle-weight *n.* A boxer weighing between 148 and 160 pounds.

midg-et *n.* A very small person.

mid-i *n. Slang* A dress, skirt, or coat which extends to the calf.

mid-night *n.* 12 o'clock p.m.; the middle of the night.

mid-point *n.* A point at or near the middle.

mid-riff *n.* The midsection of the human torso; the diaphragm.

mid-ship-man *n.* A person in training for a naval commission; a student at the U.S. Naval Academy.

midst *n.* The central or middle part or position; a person positioned among others in a group.

mid-sum-mer *n.* The middle of summer.

mid-term *n.* The middle of an academic term.

mid-way *n.* The section of a carnival or fair where shows and rides are located.

mid-week *n.* The middle of a calendar week.

mid-wife *n.* A woman who gives assistance in the birth of a baby. **-ry** *n.*

mid-win-ter *n.* The middle of the winter months.

mid-year *n.* The middle of a calendar year; academic examinations which are given in the middle of the academic year.

miff *n.* Ill humor; displeasure. **miff** *v.*

might *n.* Force, power, or physical

strength. *v.* To indicate a present condition contrary to fact; to ask permission politely.

might·y *adj.* Showing or having great power.

mi·graine *n.* A condition of severe, recurring headaches often accompanied by nausea.

mi·grant *n.* A person who moves from one place to another to find work in the fields.

mi·grate *v.* To move from one place to another or from one climate to another. migration *n.*,
migrational, migratory *adj.*

mike *n.*, *Slang* Microphone.

mil *n.* A unit of measure equal to 1/1000 of an inch, used in measuring wire.

milch *adj.* Giving milk.

mild *adj.* Gentle in manner, behavior, or disposition; not severe or extreme.
mildly *adv.*, mildness *n.*

mil·dew *n.* A fungal growth which is usually white in color.
mildew *v.*, mildewy *adj.*

mile *n.* A unit of measurement equaling 5,280 feet.

mile·age *n.* The distance traveled or measured in miles; an allowance given for traveling expenses at a set rate per mile; the average distance of miles a vehicle will travel on a gallon of gas.

mile·post *n.* A number posted along the side of a highway indicating the distance to a given place, also called a mile marker.

mile·stone *n.* A stone marker serving as a mile-post; an important point in development or progress.

mil·i·tant *adj.* Engaged in warfare or combat; aggressive.
militancy, militant *n.*

mil·i·ta·rize *v.* To train or equip for war.

mil·i·tar·y *adj.* Of or related to arms, war, or soldiers. *n.* A nation's armed forces. militarily *adv.*

mi·li·tia *n.* A military service or armed forces called upon in case of an emergency.

milk *n.* A whitish fluid produced by the mammary glands of all mature female mammals as a source of food for their young. *v.* To draw milk from the breast or udder. *Slang* To take advantage of every possibility in a given situation. milkiness *n.*, milky *adj.*

milk glass *n.* An opaque glassware used especially for ornamental and novelty objects.

milk of mag·ne·sia *n.* A milk-white liquid suspension of magnesium hydroxide, used as an antacid and laxative.

milk shake *n.* A refreshing drink made from milk flavoring and ice cream, which is thoroughly blended or shaken.

milk·sop *n.* A man who lacks manly qualities.

milk·weed *n.* Any of various plants which secrete latex and have pointed pods that open to release seeds and downy flowers.

Milk·y Way *n.* The broad, luminous galaxy in which the solar system is located.

mill *n.* A building housing machinery for grinding grain into meal or flour; any of various machines which grind, crush, or press; a unit of money which equals 1/1000 of a U.S. dollar. *v.* To grind.

mill·er *n.* A person who operates, works, or owns a grain mill; a moth whose wings are covered with a powdery substance.

mil·li·ner *n.* Someone who designs, sells, or makes women's hats.

mil·lion *n.* A very large number equal to 1,000 x 1,000. millionth *n.*, *adj.*

mil·lion·aire *n.* A person whose wealth is estimated at $1,000,000 or more.

mime *v.* To act a part or performance without using words. *n.* An actor who portrays a part, emotion, or situation using only gestures and body language. mimer *n.*

mim·e·o·graph *n.* A duplicating machine that makes duplicates of typed or drawn information from a stencil through which ink is pressed.

mim·ic *v.* To imitate another person's behavior or speech.

mince *v.* To cut or chop something into small pieces.

mince·meat *n.* A pie filling made from spiced raisins, apples, and meat that have been cut into small pieces.

mind *n.* The element of a human being which controls perception, thought, feeling, memory, and imagination. *v.* To obey; to take care of; to bring; to remember; to object to.

mine·less *adj.* Destitute of consciousness or mind.

mine *n.* A pit or underground excavation from which metals or coal can be uncovered and removed. miner *n.*

mine *pron.* The one that belongs to me.

mine·lay·er *n.* A navy ship used to lay underwater mines.

min·er·al *n.* A solid inorganic substance, such as silver, diamond, or quartz, which is taken from the earth.
mineral *adj.*, mineralize *v.*

min·e·stro·ne *n.* A very thick vegetable soup that may contain pasta and beans.

mine·sewwper *n.* A warship used to neutralize or remove mines by dragging the bottom.

min·gle *v.* To mix or come together.

min·i·a·ture *n.* A copy or model of something that has been greatly reduced in size.

mini·car *n.* A subcompact or very small car.

min·i·com·put·er *n.* In Computer Science, a computer designed on a very small scale.

mini·disk *n.* *Computer Science* The 5 1/4 inch floppy disk which is used for storing information.

min·i·mize *v.* To reduce something to a

minimum

min-i-mum *n.*, *pl.* **-ums** *or* **-uma** The least, smallest, or lowest amount, degree, number, or position.

mini-skirt *n.* A womens skirt that has a hem line several inches above the knee.

min-is-ter *n.* The pastor of a Protestant church; a high officer of state who is in charge of a governmental division.

mink *n.*, *pl.* **mink** *or* **minks**

A semiaquatic animal of the weasel family whose thick, lustrous fur is used for making fur coats.

Min-nes-o-ta *n.* A state located in the central part of the United States.

min-now *n.* A small, fresh-water fish used as bait.

mi-nor *adj.* Not of legal age; lesser in degree, size or importance.

mi-nor-i-ty *n.*, *pl.* **-ies** The smaller in number of two groups constituting a whole; a part of the population that differs, as in race, sex, or religion.

min-ster *n.* A large cathedral or church.

min-strel *n.* A medieval traveling musician or poet.

mint *n.* A place where coins are made by a government; any of a variety of aromatic plants used for flavoring; candy flavored by such a plant.

min-u-end *n.* A number of quantity from which another is to be subtracted.

min-u-et *n.* A slow, stately dance.

mi-nus *prep.*, *Math.* Reduced by subtraction. *n.* The minus sign (-); a negative number.

min-ute *n.* The unit of time which equals 60 seconds.

mi-nute *adj.* Extremely small in size.

mir-a-cle *n.* A supernatural event or happening regarded as an act of God.

mi-rage *n.* An optical illusion in which nonexistent bodies of water with reflections of objects are seen.

mire *n.* Soil or heavy mud.

mir-ror *n.* A surface of glass which reflects light, forming the image of an object.

mirth *n.* Merriment or joyousness expressed by laughter.

mis- *prefix* Wrong, bad, or ill.

mis-ad-ven-ture *n.* An unlucky mishap; a misfortune.

mis-an-thrope *n.* Someone who hates mankind.

mis-ap-pre-hend *v.* To understand something incorrectly; to misunderstand. **misapprehension** *n.*

mis-ap-pro-pri-ate *v.* To embezzle money; to use wrongly for one's own benefit. **misappropriation** *n.*

misc *abbr.* Miscellaneous.

mis-car-riage *n.* The premature birth of a fetus from the uterus.

mis-ce-ge-na-tion *n.* The marriage between two people of different races.

mis-cel-la-ne-ous *adj.* Consisting of a mixed variety of parts, elements, or characteristics.

mis-chance *n.* Bad luck or mishap.

mis-chief *n.* Behavior which causes harm, damage, or annoyance.

mis-chie-vous *adj.* Tending to behave in a playfully annoying way. **mischievously** *adv.*

mis-ci-ble *adj.*, *Chem.* Capable of being mixed. **miscibility** *n.*

mis-con-ceive *v.* To misunderstand the meaning. **-er; misconception** *n.*

mis-con-duct *n.* Improper conduct or behavior; bad management.

mis-count *v.* To count incorrectly; to miscalculate.

mis-cre-ant *n.* A person who is involved in criminal or evil acts; a heretic.

mis-cue *n.* An error; a mistake.

mis-deed *n.* A wrong or improper act; an evil deed.

mis-de-mean-or *n.*, *Law* A crime less serious than a felony.

mis-er *n.* A person who hoards money; a person who lives a meager life in order to hoard his money.

mis-er-a-ble *adj.* Very uncomfortable or unhappy; causing misery. **miserableness** *n.*, **miserably** *adv.*

mis-er-y *n.* A state of great unhappiness, distress, or pain.

mis-feed *n.* In computer science, the failure of paper or other media to pass through a printer or other device properly.

mis-fire *v.* To fail to explode, ignite, or fire. **misfire** *n.*

mis-fit *n.* A person who is not adjusted to his environment; anything which does not fit correctly.

mis-for-tune *n.* Bad luck or fortune.

mis-giv-ing *n.* A feeling of doubt.

mis-guide *v.* To guide incorrectly; to misdirect. **misguidance** *n.*, **-edly** *adv.*

mis-han-dle *v.* To handle clumsily; to manage inefficiently.

mis-hap *n.* An unfortunate accident; bad luck.

mish-mash *n.* A jumble or hodgepodge.

mis-in-ter-pret *v.* To understand or explain incorrectly. **misinterpretation** *n.*

mis-judge *v.* To make a mistake in judgment. **misjudgment** *n.*

mis-lay *v.* To lose; to put something in a place and not remember where.

mis-lead *v.* To lead in a wrong direction; to deliberately deceive. **misleader** *n.*, **misleading** *adj.*

mis-no-mer *n.* A wrong or inappropriate name.

mis-pro-nounce *v.* To pronounce a word incorrectly.

mi-sog-a-my *n.* Hatred of marriage.

mi-sog-y-ny *n.* Hatred of women.

mis-place *v.* To mislay; to put in a wrong place.

mis-read *v.* To read or interpret incorrectly.

mis-rep-re-sent v. To represent wrongly, misleadingly, or falsely. -ation n.

mis-rule n. Misruling; the condition of being misruled; disorder.

Miss n. The proper title for an unmarried woman or girl. v. To fail to hit, reach, or make contact with something; to omit; to feel the absence or loss of.

mis-sal n. A book containing prayers and services, used in the Roman Catholic Church throughout the year.

mis-shape v. To deform; to shape badly; to distort. **misshapen** adj.

mis-sile n. An object that is thrown or shot at a target. **missilery** n.

mis-sion n. An instance or the act of sending; an assignment or task to be carried out.

mis-sion-ar-y n., pl. -ies A person sent to do religious or charitable work, usually in a foreign country.

Miss-i-ssip-pi n. A state located in the south central part of the United States.

Miss-ou-ri n. A state located in the central part of the United States.

mis-spell v. To spell a word incorrectly. misspelling n.

mis-take n. A wrong statement, action, or decision. **mistaken**, mistakable adj., mistakably adv.

Mis-ter n. A courtesy title used before a man's name, abbreviated as Mr.

mis-tle-toe n. A parasitic plant with thick leaves, small yellowish flowers and white berries.

mis-treat v. To treat badly or wrongly. mistreatment n.

mis-tress n. A woman having authority, ownership, or a position of control; a woman having a sexual relationship with a man who is not her husband.

mis-tri-al n. A trial that is invalid because of an error during the procedure.

mis-trust v. To have doubt; to lack trust in something or someone. mistrust n. mistrustful adj., mistrustfully adv.

mis-un-der-stand v. To interpret incorrectly; to fail to understand.

mite n. A very small insect; a small amount of money.

mi-ter n.

A joint made by cutting two pieces at an angle and then fitting them together.

mit-i-gate v. To make or become less severe or painful.

mi-to-sis n., pl. mitoses A process of cell division in which chromatin divides into chromosomes.

mitt n. A women's glove that covers only the wrist and hand, leaving the fingers exposed; in baseball, a glove for a catcher or first baseman made in the style of a mitten.

mix v. To blend or combine into one; to come or bring together. **mixable** adj.

mixed num-ber n. A number representing the sum of an integer and a fraction, such as 5 1/2.

mix-ture n. The state of being mixed; the process or act of mixing; a combination of two or two substances.

mix-up n. An instance or state of confusion.

MN abbr. Minnesota.

MO abbr. Missouri.

mo abbr. Money order; mail order.

moan n. A very low, dull sound indicative of pain or grief.

moat n. A deep and wide trench surrounding a castle, usually filled with water.

mob n. A large, unruly crowd. v. To overcrowd.

mo-bi-lize v. To put into motion; to make ready. **mobilization** n.

moc-ca-sin n. A shoe or slipper made of a soft leather.

mo-cha n. An Arabian coffee of superior quality; a flavoring with coffee, often used with chocolate.

mock v. To treat with contempt or scorn; to imitate a mannerism or sound closely; to mimic. adv. An insincere manner. n. An imitation; a copy. mockingly adv.

mock-er-y n., pl. -ies Insulting or contemptuous action or speech; a subject of laughter or sport; a false appearance.

mock--he-ro-ic n. A satirical imitation of the heroic manner or style.

mock-ing-bird n.

A common bird that is remarkable for its exact imitations of the notes of other birds.

mock orange n. Any of several deciduous shrubs.

mock-up or **mock--up** n. A model of a structure used for study, testing, or demonstration.

mod n. A modern and unusual style of dress. adj. Modern.

mode n. A way or method of doing something; a particular manner or form; the value or score that occurs most frequently in a set of data; the current fashion or style, as in dress.

mod-el n. A small representation of an object; a pattern that something will be based on; a design or type; one serving as an example; one who poses for an artist or photographer. model v., modeler n.

mod-er-ate adj. Not excessive; tending toward the mean or average extent or quality; opposed to extreme political views. **moderate** v., **moderation** n.

mod-er-a-tor n. A person who moderates; a person who presides over a discussion or meeting but takes no sides.

mod-ern *adj.* Typical of the recent past or the present; advanced or up-to-date. **modern, -ity** *n.*, **modernly** *adv.*

mod-ern-ism *n.* A thought, action, or belief characteristic of modern times. **modernistic** *adj.*

mod-ern-ize *v.* To make or become modern. **modernization** *n.*

mod-est *adj.* Placing a moderate estimate on one's abilities or worth; retiring or reserved; limited in size or amount. **modesty** *n.*

mod-i-cum *n.* A small amount.

mod-i-fy *v.* To alter; to make different in character or form; to change to less extreme; to moderate. **modified, modifiable** *adj.*, **modification, -ier** *n.*

mod-ish *adj.* Fashionable. **-ly** *adv.*

mo-diste *n.* A person dealing in fashionable clothing for women.

mod-u-late *v.* To soften; to temper; to vary the intensity of. *Music* To change from one key to another; to vary the tone or intensity of. **modulation, modulator** *n.*, **modulative, -ory** *adj.*

mod-ule *n.* One of a series of standardized components which work together in a system. *Electr.* A self-contained subassembly of electronic components, as a computer stage; the self-contained area of a spacecraft for performing a particular task. **-ar** *adj.*

mod-us op-er-an-di *n.* A method of operating or proceeding.

mod-us vi-ven-di *n.* A compromise which avoids difficulties.

mo-gul *n.* A very great or important person; a small hill or bump of ice and snow on a ski slope.

mo-hair *n.* The fabric or yarn made from the silky hair of the Angora goat.

Mo-ham-med *n.* The Arab founder of Islam.

Mo-ham-med-an *adj.* Moslem. **Mohammedan, Mohammedanism** *n.*

Mohs scale *n.* A scale that classifies the hardness of minerals ranging from one for the softest, which is talc, to fifteen for the hardest, which is diamond.

moi-e-ty *n., pl.* **-ies** A half; any portion; part or share.

moil *v.* To work hard; to drudge. **moil** *n.*

moi-re *n.* Fabric, especially silk or rayon having a wavy pattern.

moist *adj.* Slightly wet; damp; saturated with moisture or liquid. **moistly** *adv.*, **moistness** *n.*

mois-ten *v.* To make or become moist or slightly wet. **moistener** *n.*

mois-ture *n.* Liquid diffused or condensed in a relatively small quantity; dampness. **moisturize** *v.*, **-izer** *n.*

Mo-ja-ve *or* **Mo-ha-ve** *n.* A desert region located in southern California.

mol *abbr.* Molecular; molecule.

mo-lar *n.* A grinding tooth which has a broad surface for grinding food, located in the back of the mouth.

mo-las-ses *n.* A thick, dark syrup produced when sugar is refined.

mold *n.* A superficial, often woolly growth produced on damp or decaying organic matter or on living organisms; a fungus that produces such a growth; crumbling, soft, friable earth suited to plant growth; distinctive nature or character; the frame on or around which an object is constructed; a cavity in which an object is shaped; general shape; form. **mold** *v.*, **moldable** *adj.*

mold-board *n.* The curved blade of a plow.

mold-er *v.* To crumble or decay gradually and turn to dust.

mole *n.*

A pigmented spot or mark on the human skin; a small, insectivorous mammal that lives mostly underground and has a narrow snout, small eyes, and silky fur; a large wall of stone or masonry used as a breakwater or pier.

mo-lec-u-lar *adj.* Of, relating to, or caused by molecules.

mo-lec-u-lar bi-ol-o-gy *n.* The branch of biology dealing with the structure and development of biological systems which are studied in terms of their molecular constituents. **molecular biologist** *n.*

mol-e-cule *n.* The simplest structural unit into which a substance can be divided and still retain its identity.

mole-hill *n.* A small ridge of earth thrown up by a mole.

mole-skin *n.* The dark gray pelt of the mole; a heavy, durable cotton fabric with a short, thick velvety nap on one side.

mo-lest *v.* To bother, annoy, or persecute; to accost sexually. **molestation, molester** *n.*

mol-li-fy *v.* To make less angry; to soften; to make less intense or severe. **mollification** *n.*

mol-lusk *or* **mol-lusc** *n.* Any of various largely marine invertebrates, including the edible shellfish.

mol-ly-cod-dle *v.* To spoil by pampering; to coddle.

Mol-o-tov cock-tail *n.* A homemade, flammable bomb consisting of a combustible liquid in a breakable bottle fitted with a rag that is ignited before the bomb is thrown.

molt *v.* To cast off or shed an external covering, as horns, feathers, or skin, which is periodically replaced by new growth. **molt** *n.*

mol-ten *adj.* Transformed to liquid form by heat.

mo-lyb-de-num *n.* A hard, gray metallic element used to harden steel alloys, symbolized by Mo.

mo-men-tar-i-ly *adv.* For just a moment; soon; from moment to moment.

mo-men-tar-y *adj.* Lasting just a moment; occurring presently or at every moment.

mo-men-tous *adj.* Of great importance or consequence; significant.
 momentously *adv.*, **momentousness** *n.*

mo-men-tum *n.*, *pl.* **-ta** *or* **-tums** A property of a moving body which determines the length of time required to bring it to rest when under the action of a constant force.

Mon *abbr.* Monday.

mon-arch *n.* A person who reigns over a kingdom or empire; a large orange and black butterfly.
 monarchic, monarchical *adj.*

mon-ar-chism *n.* The principles or system of a monarchic government.
 monarchist *n.*, **monarchistic** *adj.*

mon-ar-chy *n.*, *pl.* **-chies** Government by a monarch; sovereign control; a government or nation ruled by a monarch.

mon-as-ter-y *n.*, *pl.* **-ies** A house for persons under religious vows.
 monasterial *adj.*

mo-nas-tic *adj.* Of, relating to, or typical of monasteries, monks, or life in monasteries.

mo-nas-ti-cism *n.* The monastic lifestyle or system.

mon-au-ral *adj.* Of or relating to a system of transmitting or recording sound by techniques in which one or more sources are channeled into one carrier.

Mon-day *n.* The second day of the week.

Monet, Claude *n.* (1840-1926). French Impressionist painter.

mon-e-tar-y *adj.* Of or relating to money or how it is circulated. **-ily** *adv.*

mon-ey *n.* Anything which has or is assigned value and is used as a medium of exchange.

mon-ey-lend-er *n.* Someone whose business is lending money to others with interest.

mon-ger *n.* One who attempts to stir up or spread something that is undesirable; one who deals.

Mon-gol *n.* A native or inhabitant of Mongolia; a member of one of the chiefly pastoral Mongoloid peoples of Mongolia.

Mon-go-li-a *n.* A region of Asia that extends from Siberia to northern China; a country in Asia.

Mon-go-li-an *n.* A native or inhabitant of Mongolia; a member of the Mongoloid ethnic division. **Mongolian** *adj.*

Mon-gol-ism *n.* Down's syndrome.

Mon-gol-oid *adj.* Of, constituting, or characteristic of a people native to Asia, including peoples of northern and eastern Asia, Malaysians, Eskimos, and American Indians. **Mongoloid** Of, affected with, or pertaining to Down's syndrome. **Mongoloid** *n.*

mon-goose *n.*, *pl.* **-ses** A chiefly African or Asian mammal which has the ability to kill venomous snakes.

mon-grel *n.* An animal or plant, especially a dog, produced by interbreeding.

mo-ni-tion *n.* A caution or warning, as for an impending danger.

mon-i-tor *n.* A student assigned to assist a teacher; a receiver used to view the picture being picked up by a television camera; the image being generated by a computer. **monitorial** *adj.*

mon-i-to-ry *adj.* Giving a caution or conveying a warning.

monk *n.* A man who is a member of a religious order and lives in a monastery. **monkish** *adj.*,
 monkishly *adv.*, **monkishness** *n.*

mon-key *n.*, *pl.* **-keys**

A member of the older primates, excluding man, having a long-tail; a smaller species as distinguished from the larger apes. *v.* To play or fool around; to tamper with.

mon-key wrench *n.* A tool which has one adjustable jaw. *Slang* Something that hinders or stops a normally flowing system or procedure.

monk's cloth *n.* A sturdy cotton cloth having a coarse basket weave.

monks-hood *n.* A normally poisonous plant of the genus Aconitum, having variously colored hooded flowers.

mon-o-n. Mononucleosis.

mon-o-chro-mat-ic *adj.* Of, consisting of, or having one color.
 monochromatically *adv.*

mon-o-cle *n.* An eyeglass for one eye.

mon-o-cot-y-le-don *n.* Any of various plants having a single embryonic seed leaf appearing at germination.
 monocotyledonous *adj.*

mo-noc-u-lar *adj.* Of, relating to, or having one eye.

mo-nog-a-my *n.* Marriage or sexual relationship with only one person at a time. **-ist** *n.*, **monogamous** *adj.*

mon-o-gram *n.* A design consisting of one or more initials. **monogram** *v.*

mon-o-graph *n.* A scholarly pamphlet or book on a particular and usually limited subject. **monographic** *adj.*

mon-o-lin-gual *adj.* Knowing only one language.

mon-o-lith *n.* A single block of stone, as one used in architecture or sculpture. **monolithic** *adj.*

mon-o-logue *or* **mon-o-log** *n.* A speech by one person which precludes conversation; a series of jokes and stories delivered by a comedian. **-ist** *n.*

mon-o-ma-ni-a *n.* A pathological obsession or mental disorder in which a person is totally obsessed with a single idea. **-c** *n.*, **monomaniacal** *adj.*

mon-o-mi-al *n.* An algebraic expression consisting of only one term.

mon-o-nu-cle-ar *adj.* Having only one nucleus.

mon-o-nu-cle-o-sis *n.* An infectious disease marked by an abnormal increase of too many cells having one nucleus.

mon-o-nu-cle-o-tide *n.* A nucleotide containing one molecule each of a phosphoric acid, a pentose, and either a purine or pyrimidine base.

mon-o-phon-ic *adj.* Having only one part; a solo voice with accompaniment, as a piano.

mon-o-plane *n.* An aircraft with one wing or one set of wings.

mo-nop-o-ly *n., pl.* -ies Exclusive ownership or control, as of a service or commodity, by a single group, person, or company; a group, person, or company having a monopoly; exclusive possession; a service or commodity controlled by a single group. -ist, **monopolization** *n.,* -istic *adj.,* -ize *v.*

mon-o-rail *n.* A single rail serving as a track on which a wheeled vehicle can travel; a vehicle that travels on such a rail.

mon-o-so-di-um glu-ta-mate *n.* Sodium glut-amate used as a seasoning, abbreviated as MSG.

mon-o-syl-la-ble *n.* A word of one syllable. **monosyllabic** *adj.,* **monosyllabically** *adv.*

mon-o-the-ism *n.* The belief that there is just one God. **monotheist** *n.,* **monotheistic** *adj.*

mon-o-tone *n.* The utterance of sounds, syllables, or words in a single unvarying tone.

mo-not-o-nous *adj.* Spoken in a monotone; lacking in variety. **monotonously** *adv.,* **monotony** *n.*

mon-ox-ide *n.* An oxide that contains one oxygen atom per molecule.

Monroe, James N. (1758-1831). The 5th President of the United States.

Mon-si-gnor *n., pl.* -ors *or* -ori A title given to Roman Catholic priests who have received papal honors.

mon-soon *n.* A periodic wind, especially in the Indian Ocean and southern Asia; the season of the monsoon in India and parts of Asia.

mon-ster *n.* An animal or plant having an abnormal form or structure; an animal, plant, or object having a frightening or deformed shape; one unusually large for its kind. **monstrosity, monstrousness** *n.,* **monstrous** *adj.,* **monstrously** *adv.*

mon-tage *n.* A composite picture made by combining several separate pictures or parts of several pictures; a rapid succession of images in a motion picture, designed to illustrate an association of ideas.

Mon-tan-a *n.* A state located in the northwestern United States.

Mont-gom-er-y *n.* The capital of the state of Alabama.

month *n.* One of the twelve divisions of a calendar year.

month-ly *adj.* Occurring, done, or payable each month. *n.* A publication issued once a month. **monthly** *adv.*

Mont-pe-lier *n.* The capital of the state of Vermont.

mon-u-ment *n.* An object, such as a statue, built as a memorial to a person or an event; a burial vault; an area set aside for public use by a government because of its aesthetic, historical, or ecological significance.

mon-u-men-tal *adj.* Serving as or similar to a monument; massive; extremely important. **monumentally** *adv.*

mooch *v. Slang* To acquire by begging; to steal. **moocher** *n.*

mood *n.* A conscious yet temporary state of mind or emotion; the prevailing spirit; a verb form or set of verb forms inflected to show the understanding of the person speaking regarding the condition expressed.

mood-y *adj.* Subject to moods, especially depression; gloomy. **moodily** *adv.,* **moodiness** *n.*

moon *n.* The earth's only natural satellite; a natural satellite which revolves around a planet. *v.* To dream.

moon-beam *n.* A ray of moonlight.

moon-light *n.* The light of the moon. *v.* To hold a second job in addition to a regular one. **moonlighter** *n.*

moon-lit *adj.* Lit by the moon.

moon-rise *n.* The rising of the moon above the horizon; the time of the moon's rising.

moon-scape *n.* The surface of the moon as seen or as depicted.

moon-set *n.* The descent of the moon below the horizon; the time of the moon's setting.

moon-shine *n.* Moonlight; empty talk; nonsense; intoxicating liquor, especially illegally distilled corn whiskey.

moon-shin-er *n. Informal* A maker or seller of illicit whiskey; usually distributed in the night.

moon shot *n.* The launching of a spacecraft to the moon or its vicinity.

moon-stone *n.* A transparent or translucent feldspar of pearly or opaline luster used as a gem.

moon-struck *adj.* Mentally unbalanced; lunatic; romantically sentimental.

moon-ward *adv.* Toward the moon.

moor *v.* To make fast with cables, lines, or anchors. *n.* An expanse of open, rolling, infertile land. **moorage** *n.*

Moor *n.* Ancient North African people of whom Berber and Arab descent who invaded and conquered Spain in the eighth century. **Moorish** *adj.*

moor-ing *n.* A place where a ship or aircraft can be secured; a stabilizing device.

moose *n., pl.* **moose**

A very large North American deer having a large broad muzzle.

moot *v.* To bring up as for debate or discussion; to argue. *adj.* Open to debate; having no legal significance.

mope *v.* To be uncaring or dejected; to move in a leisurely manner. **moper** *n.*

mo-ped *n.* A motorbike that can be

pedaled.

mop-pet *n.* A child; a darling baby.

mop--up *n.* The process of completing a task.

mo-raine *n.* An accumulation of earth and stones carried and finally deposited by a glacier.

mor-al *adj.* Of or pertaining to conduct or character from the point of right and wrong; teaching a conception of right behavior. *n.* The lesson to be learned from a story, event, or teaching. **morals** Standards of right and wrong. **morally** *adv.*

mo-rale *n.* An individual's state of mind with respect to the tasks he or she is expected to perform; esprit de corps.

mor-al-ist *n.* Someone concerned with moral principles and questions; someone who practices morality. **moralism** *n.*, **-ic** *adj.*, **-ically** *adv.*

mo-ral-i-ty *n., pl.* **-ies** The quality of being morally right; moral behavior.

mor-al-ize *v.* To think, discuss, or judge in a moral sense. **-ation**, **moralizer** *n.*

mo-rass *n.* A marsh or bog; low-lying wet, soft ground; something which hinders or overwhelms.

mor-a-to-ri-um *n., pl.* **-iums** *or* **-ia** A temporary pause in activity; an authorization given legally to a debtor to suspend payments for a period of time.

mo-ray *n.* Any of various marine eels found usually in tropical waters.

mor-bid *adj.* Of, pertaining to, or affected by disease; suggesting an unhealthy mental state of being; gruesome. **morbidity**, **morbidness** *n.*, **morbidly** *adv.*

mor-da-cious *adj.* Violent in action; prone to biting. **mordacity** *n.*

mor-dant *adj.* Biting and caustic in thought, manner, or style. **mordancy** *n.*, **mordantly** *adv.*

more *adj.* Greater number, size, or degree; additional. *n.* An additional or greater number, degree, or amount. *adv.* To a greater extent or degree; in addition. *pron.* Additional things or persons.

mo-rel *n.* An edible mushroom having a sponge-like cap or hood.

more-o-ver *adv.* Furthermore; besides.

mo-res *n., pl.* The moral customs and traditional customs of a social group.

morgue *n.* A place in which dead bodies are kept until claimed or identified; the reference file at a newspaper or magazine office.

mor-i-bund *adj.* Approaching extinction; at the point of death. **moribundity** *n.*

Mor-mon *n.* A member of the Church of Jesus Christ of Latter-day Saints. **Mormonism** *n.*

morn *n.* Morning.

morn-ing *n.* The early part of the day; the time from midnight to noon.

morn-ing-glo-ry *n.* A usually twining, climbing plant with funnel-shaped flowers which are open in the morning, but closed later in the day.

morn-ing star *n.* A planet seen in the eastern part of the sky just before or at sunrise.

Mo-roc-co *n.* A country located in northwestern Africa.

mo-roc-co *n.* A soft, textured leather made of goatskin.

mo-ron *n.* An adult exhibiting an intelligence equal to that of a seven to twelve year old child; a very stupid person. **moronic** *adj.*, **-ically** *adv.*

mo-rose *adj.* Having a sullen disposition; marked by gloom. **-ly** *adv.*, **-ness** *n.*

mor-pheme *n.* A meaningful unit which cannot be divided into smaller meaningful parts. **morphemic** *adj.*, **morphemically** *adv.*

mor-phi-a *n.* Morphine.

mor-phine *n.* A highly addictive narcotic derived from opium which can be used as either a sedative or to dull pain.

mor-phol-o-gy *n.* The study of the form and structure of living organisms, considered separate from function; the study and description of word formation in a language. **morphological**, **morphologically** *adj.*, **morphologist** *n.*

mor-ris *n.* An old English folk dance.

mor-row *n.* The next day.

Morse code *n.* Either of two codes, developed by S. F. B. Morse, consisting of dots and dashes, long and short sounds, or long and short flashes of light.

mor-sel *n.* A small piece or quantity of food; a tasty dish.

mor-tal *adj.* Having caused or about to cause death; fatal; subject to death; very tedious or prolonged; unrelentingly hostile; of, relating to, or connected with death. *n.* A human being.

mor-tal-i-ty *n., pl.* **-ies** The state or condition of being mortal; the death rate; deaths.

mor-tar *n.* A strong vessel in which materials can be crushed or ground with a pestle; a muzzle-loading cannon for firing shells at short ranges and at high angles; a mixed building material, as cement with sand and water, which hardens and is used with masonry or plaster.

mor-tar-board *n.*

A square board with a handle, for holding mortar; an academic cap topped by a stiff, flat square.

mort-gage *n.* A temporary conveyance of property to a creditor as security for the repayment of a debt; a contract or deed defining the terms of a mortgage. *v.* To pledge or transfer by means of a mortgage. **mortgagee**, **mortgagor** *n.*

mor-ti-cian *n.* An undertaker.

mor-ti-fy *v.* To destroy the strength or functioning of; to subdue or deaden through pain or self-denial; to subject to severe humiliation; to become gangrenous **-ication** *n.*, **-ingly** *adv.*

mor-tise n. A usually hollowed out rectangular hole in a piece of wood which receives a tenon of another piece to form a joint.

mor-tu-ar-y n., pl. -ies A place in which dead bodies are temporarily held until burial or cremation.

mo-sa-ic n. A decorative inlaid design of small pieces, as of colored glass or tile, in cement. **mosaic** adj.

Mos-es n. Hebrew prophet and lawgiver; in the Old Testament, the person who lead the Israelites out of Egypt to the Promised Land; the person whom God presented the Ten Commandments to.

mo-sey v. Slang To move slowly; to shuffle along.

Mos-lem n. A believer of Islam.

mosque n. A Moslem house of worship.

mos-qui-to n., pl. -toes or -tos Any of various winged insects of which the females suck the blood of animals or humans.

mos-qui-to net n. A fine net or screen to keep out mosquitoes.

moss n. Delicate, small green plants which often form a dense, mat-like growth. **mossiness** n., **mossy** adj.

moss-back n. An old-fashioned person.

moss rose n. An old-fashioned garden rose which has a glandular, mossy calyx and flower stalk.

most adj. The majority of. n. The greatest amount. pron. The largest part or number. adv. In or to the highest degree.

most-ly adv. For the most part; principally.

mot n. A short, witty saying.

mote n. A particle, as of dust; a speck of dust.

mo-tel n. A temporary, roadside dwelling for motorists with rooms opening directly onto a parking area.

mo-tet n. A polyphonic vocal composition, based on a religious text and usually sung without accompaniment.

moth n. A usually nocturnal insect of the order Lepidoptera, having antennae that are often feathered, duller in color and with wings smaller than the butterflies.

moth-ball n. A ball, usually of camphor, used to repel moths from clothing during storage.

moth--eat-en adj. Partially eaten by moths; in a state of disrepair.

moth-er n. A female parent; one who holds a maternal relationship toward another; an old or elderly woman; a woman in a position of authority. adj. Of, relating to, or being a mother. v. To give birth to; to care for or protect like a mother. **motherhood**, **motherliness** n., **mothery** adj.

moth-er--in--law n. The mother of one's spouse.

moth-er-land n. The country or land of one's birth.

moth-er--of--pearl n. The pearly iridescent internal layer of a mollusk shell.

mo-tif n. An underlying main element or theme that recurs in a musical, artistic, or literary work.

mo-tile adj. Exhibiting or capable of movement.

mo-tion n. The act or process of changing position; a purposeful movement of the body or a bodily part; a formal proposal or suggestion that action be taken. **motion** v., **motionless** adj.

mo-tion pic-ture n. A sequence of filmed pictures that gives the illusion of continuous movement, when projected on a screen.

mo-tion sick-ness n. Dizziness; nausea brought on by motion as traveling by land or water.

mo-ti-vate v. Causing to act.

mo-tive n. Something, as a need or desire, which causes a person to act; a musical motif. adj. Causing or having the power to cause motion.

mot-ley adj. Composed of a variety of components.

mo-tor n. Any of various devices which develop energy or impart motion. adj. Imparting or producing motion; driven by or equipped with a motor; of, relating to or designed for motor vehicles; of, relating to, or involving muscular movement. v. To travel or transport by motor vehicle. **-ist** n.

mo-tor-bike n. A small motorcycle.

mo-tor-boat n. A boat propelled by an internal-combustion engine or an electric motor.

mo-tor-cade n. A procession of motor vehicles.

mo-tor-car n. An automobile.

mo-tor-cy-cle n. A two-wheeled automotive vehicle. **motorcyclist** n.

mo-tor home n. A motor vehicle built on a truck frame and equipped to provide a self-contained home during travel.

mo-tor-ize v. To equip with a motor; to supply with motor-propelled vehicles. **motorization** n.

mo-tor-man n. An operator of a locomotive engine, streetcar, or subway train.

mo-tor scoo-ter n. A small two-wheeled vehicle similar to a scooter but having a low-powered gasoline engine.

mo-tor ve-hi-cle n. A motor-powered vehicle which travels freely without the need for rails.

mot-tle v. To mark or be marked with spots or streaks of different colors or shades; to blotch. n. A blotch.

mot-to n., pl. -toes or -tos A sentence, phrase, or word expressing purpose, character, or conduct; an appropriate phrase inscribed on something.

moue n. A grimace, as of disapproval or disdain.

mound n. A small hill of earth, sand, gravel or debris; the slightly elevated ground in the middle of a baseball diamond on which the pitcher stands.

mount v. To rise or ascend; to get up on; climb upon; to increase in amount or extent; to organize and equip; to launch and carry out. n. A horse or other animal used for riding; a support to which something is fixed.

moun·tain *n.* A land mass that rises above its surroundings and is higher than a hill.

moun·tain ash *n.* Any of various deciduous trees bearing clusters of small white flowers and orange-red berries.

moun·tain·eer *n.* An inhabitant of a mountainous region; one who climbs mountains for sport. **mountaineer** *v.*

moun·tain goat *n.* A long-haired Rocky Mountain goat.

mountain laurel *n.* A low-growing evergreen shrub with poisonous leaves and clusters of pink or white flowers.

moun·tain lion *n.* A large wildcat; puma.

moun·tain·ous *adj.* Of or relating to a region with many mountains.

moun·tain·side *n.* The side of a mountain.

moun·tain-top *n.* The top of a mountain.

moun·te·bank *n.* A quack doctor; a false and boastful pretender; a charlatan.

Mount·ie *n.* or **Mounty** A member of the Canadian Mounted Police.

mount·ing *n.* A supporting frame or structure of an article.

mourn *v.* To express grief; to feel grief or sorrow; to follow the religious customs and rituals surrounding the death of a loved one.

mouse *n., pl.* **mice**

A small rodent that frequents human habitations; a timid person.

mousse *n.* A light frozen dessert.

mouth *n., pl.* **mouths** The bodily opening through which food is taken in.

mouth-off *v.* To speak disrespectfully.

mouth--to--mouth *adj.* Pertaining to a method of artificial resuscitation.

move *v.* To set in motion; to change one's place or location; to make a recommendation in a formal manner. **movable, moveable** *adj.,* **-ably** *adv.*

move·ment *n.* The act of moving; a part of a musical composition; an excretion of the bowels.

mov·er *n.* One that moves; a person employed to help in moving the contents of a home or business.

mov·ie *n.* A motion picture; motion picture industry.

mow *v.* To cut down, as with a machine. *n.* The part of the barn where hay or grain is stored. **mower** *n.*

Mozart, Wolfgang Amadeus *N.* (1756-1791). Austrian composer.

moz·za·rel·la *n.* A soft white cheese with a mild flavor.

MP *abbr.* Military Police.

mpg *abbr.* Miles per gallon.

mph *abbr.* Miles per hour.

Mr *abbr.* Mister.

Mrs *abbr.* Mistress.

Ms *abbr.* A form of address used for a woman when her marital status is irrelevant or unknown.

MS *abbr.* Mississippi.

MST *abbr.* Mountain Standard Time.

much *adj.* In great amount, quantity, degree, or extent. *adv.* To a great extent. *n.* Something impressive.

mu·ci·lage *n.* A sticky substance that is similar to plant gums.

muck *n.* Moist farmyard manure; moist, sticky soil or filth. *v.* To dirty with or as with muck. **mucky** *adj.*

muck-rake *v.* To search out and publicly expose real or apparent misconduct on the part of well-known persons.

mu·co·sa *n.* A mucous membrane.

mu·cous *adj.* Of, pertaining to, or secreting mucus.

mu·cous mem·brane *n.* A membrane secreting mucus which lines bodily channels that come into contact with air.

mu·cus *n.* The viscous liquid secreted by glands by the mucous membrane.

mud *n.* A mixture of water and earth. *Slang* A slanderous remark. **-dily** *adv.,* **muddiness** *n.,* **muddy** *adj. & v.*

mud·dle *v.* To make muddy; to mix up or confuse; to make a mess of; to think or act in a confused way. **-er** *n.*

mud·guard *n.* A piece of material applied to a wheel well to prevent mud from splashing onto a vehicle.

mud·sling·er *n.* One who makes malicious statements or charges against a political opponent. **mudslinging** *n.*

muff *n.* A warm, tubular covering for the hands; a bungling performance. *v.* To handle awkwardly; to act or do something stupidly or clumsily.

muf·fin *n.* A soft, cup-shaped bread that is cooked in a muffin pan and often served hot.

muf·fle *v.* To wrap up so as to conceal or protect; to deaden the sound of; to suppress.

muf·fler *n.* A scarf worn around the neck; a device which deadens noise, especially one forming part of the exhaust system of an automotive vehicle.

mug *n.* A large drinking cup; a person's face; a photograph of someone's face. *v.* To make funny faces; to assault viciously, usually with the intent to rob.

mug·gy *adj.* Warm, humid and sultry. **muggily** *adv.,* **mugginess** *n.*

mug·wump *n.* A defector from the Republican Party in 1884; anyone who acts independently, especially in politics.

muk·luk *n.* A boot made from the skin of seals or reindeer, worn by Eskimos; a slipper that resembles a mukluk.

mu·lat·to *n., pl.* **-tos** *or* **-toes** A person with one white parent and one black parent; a person of mixed black and white ancestry.

mul·ber·ry *n.* Any of several trees having an edible, berry-like fruit.

mulch *n.* A loose protective covering, as of sawdust or compost, or wood chips spread on the ground to prevent moisture evaporation, to protect roots from freezing, and to retard the growth of weeds. **mulch** *v.*

mulct *n.* A financial penalty or fine. *v.* To punish by fining; to obtain by fraud or theft.

mule *n.* A hybrid animal that is the offspring of a female horse and a male ass. *Slang* A stubborn person.

mulish *adj.*, **mulishly** *adv.*, **-ishness** *n.*

mule deer *n.* A long-eared deer of western North America, heavier built and larger than the white-tail deer.

mule--foot *adj.* Having a solid foot; not cleft.

mule-skin-ner *n.* A muleteer.

mu-le-teer *n.* A person who drives mules.

mu-ley *adj.* Naturally without horns.

mull *v.* To mix or grind thoroughly; to ponder; to think about.

mul-lah *n.* A Muslim leader and clergyman.

mul-lein *n.* A plant having yellow flowers and downy leaves.

mul-let *n.* An edible marine and freshwater fish.

mul-li-gan stew *n.* A stew made of various vegetables and meats.

multi- *prefix* Much, many, multiple; more than two.

mul-ti-dis-ci-plin-ary *adj.* Using or related to a combination of several disciplines for a common cause.

mul-ti-far-i-ous *adj.* Having much diversity. **multifariously** *adv.*

mul-ti-form *adj.* Having many appearances or forms. **multiformity** *n.*

mul-ti-lane *adj.* Having several lanes.

mul-ti-lat-er-al *adj.* Having many sides; involving or participated in by more than two parties or nations. **multilaterally** *adv.*

mul-ti-lin-gual *adj.* Expressed in several languages. **multilingualism** *n.*

mul-ti-mil-lion-aire *n.* A person whose fortune is worth many millions of dollars.

mul-ti-na-tion-al *adj.* Involving or relating to several countries.

mul-tip-a-rous *adj.* Producing more than one at a birth.

mul-ti-ple *adj.* Relating to or consisting of more than one individual, part, or element. *Math.* A number into which another number can be divided with no remainders.

mul-ti-ple--choice *adj.* Offering several answers from which the correct one is to be chosen.

mul-ti-ple scle-ro-sis *n.* A degenerative condition marked by patches of hardened tissue in the spinal cord or the brain.

mul-ti-plex *n.* A communications system in which two or more messages can be transmitted simultaneously on the same circuit. **multiplex** *v.*

mul-ti-pli-ca-tion *n.* The mathematical operation by which a number indicates how many times another number is to be added to itself.

mul-ti-plic-i-ty *n.*, *pl.* **-ies** A large number or variety.

mul-ti-pli-er *n.* A number that is or is to be multiplied by another number.

mul-ti-ply *v.* To increase in amount or number; to combine by multiplication.

mul-ti-sense *adj.* Having several meanings.

mul-ti-stage *adj.* Consisting of propulsion units which operate in turn.

mul-ti-tude *n.* A very large amount or number. **multitudinous** *adj.*

mul-ti-vi-ta-min *n.* A pill containing several vitamins that are essential to health.

mum *adj.* Silent, not speaking.

mum-ble *v.* To speak or utter in a low, confused manner. **mumbler** *n.*

mum-ble-ty--peg or **mum-ble--the--peg** *n.* A game in which players try to throw a knife from various positions so that the blade will stick into the ground.

mum-bo jum-bo *n.* A complicated or obscure ritual; a confusing and complicated language or activity.

mum-mer *n.* A performer who acts in a pantomime.

mum-mery *n.*, *pl.* **-ies** A hypocritical or ridiculous ceremony.

mum-mi-fy *v.* To dry and embalm as a mummy; to cause to shrivel and dry up. **mummification** *n.*

mum-my *n.*, *pl.* **-ies** A body embalmed or treated for burial in the manner of the ancient Egyptians.

mumps *pl. n.* An acute, contagious viral disease marked by fever and swelling of the salivary glands.

mun *abbr.* Municipal; municipality.

munch *v.* To chew noisily. **muncher** *v.*

mun-dane *adj.* Pertaining to or relating to the world; characterized by the ordinary and practical. **mundanely** *adv.*

Mu-nich *n.* A city located in southwest Germany.

mu-nic-i-pal *adj.* Relating to or typical of a municipality; having self-government in local affairs. **municipally** *adv.*, **municipality** *n.*

mu-nif-i-cent *adj.* Very liberal in giving; lavish. **munificence** *n.*, **-ly** *adv.*

mu-ni-tions *pl. n.* Guns and ammunition.

mu-ral *n.* A painting created on a wall.

mur-der *n.* The crime of unlawfully killing a person. *Slang* Something very dangerous, difficult, or uncomfortable. *v.* To kill a person unlawfully and with premeditated malice. **murderer** *n.*

mur-der-ous *adj.* Intending or having the purpose or capability of murder. **murderously** *adv.*

murk *n.* Darkness; gloom. **murkily** *adv.*, **murkiness** *n.*, **murky** *adj.*

mur-mur *n.* A low, indistinct, and often continuous sound; a gentle or soft utterance. **murmur** *v.*

mur-mur-ous *adj.* Characterized by murmurs. **murmurously** *adv.*

Mur-phy bed *n.* A bed which folds into a closet.

mur-rain *n.* A plague affecting plants or

domestic animals.

mur-rey *n.* Mulberry colored; purplish-black.

mus *abbr.* Museum; musical; musician.

mus-cae vo-li-tan-tes *n.* A condition of spots before the eyes due to cells and cell fragments in the vitreous humor and lens.

mus-cle *n.* Bodily tissue which consists of long cells that contract when stimulated. **muscle** *v.*

mus-cle--bound *adj.* Having muscles which are overdeveloped and lack the capacity to flex fully, usually caused by too much exercise.

mus-cu-lar *adj.* Relating to or consisting of muscle; brawny; having well-developed muscles. **muscularity** *n.*

mus-cu-lar dys-tro-phy *n.* A noncontagious hereditary disease characterized by gradual but irreversible muscular deterioration.

mus-cu-la-ture *n.* The muscles of an animal's body.

muse *n.* A state of deep thought.

Muse *n.* One of the nine Greek goddesses in mythology, who are the inspiration for creativity, as music and art.

mu-sette *n* A small bagpipe having a soft, sweet tone or sound; a small bag with a shoulder strap.

mush *n.* A thick porridge of cornmeal boiled in water or milk; soft matter. **mushiness** *n.*, **mushy** *adj.*

mush-room *n.*

A fungus having an umbrella-shaped cap on a stalk. *v.* To grow or multiply quickly.

mu-sic *n.* Organized tones in sequences and combinations which make up a continuous composition. **musical** *adj.*

mu-sic box *n.* A box enclosing an apparatus which produces music when activated.

mu-si-cian *n.* A composer or performer of music. **musicianly** *adj.*, **-ship** *n.*

mu-si-col-o-gy *n.* The scientific and historical study of music. **musicological** *adj.*, **musicologist** *n.*

musk *n.* A substance with a strong, powerful odor which is secreted by the male musk deer. **-iness** *n.*, **musky** *adj.*

mus-keg *n.* A bog formed by moss, leaves, and decayed matter resembling peat.

mus-ket *n.* A heavy, large-caliber shoulder gun with a long barrel.

musk-mel-on *n.* A sweet melon having a rough rind and juicy, edible flesh.

musk-rat *n.*

A rodent of North America with

brown fur.

Mus-lim *n.* A follower of Islam.

mus-lin *n.* A plain-woven, sheer, or coarse fabric.

muss *v.* To make messy or untidy. *Slang* A confused conflict. **mussily** *adv.*, **mussiness** *n.*, **mussy** *adj.*

mus-sel *n.* A freshwater bivalve mollusk.

must *v.* To be forced to; to have to; to be obligated to do something; to be necessary to do something. *n.* A requirement; absolute; something indispensable.

mus-tache *also* **mous-tache** *n.* The hair growing on the human upper lip especially on the male upper lip.

mus-tang *n.* A wild horse of the western plains.

mus-tard *n.* A condiment or medicinal preparation made from the seeds of the mustard plant.

mus-tard gas *n.* An irritating liquid chemical used as a war gas.

mus-ter *v.* To come or bring together; to convene; to bring or call forth. *n.* The act of examining or inspecting critically.

mustn't *contr.* Must not.

mus-ty *adj.* Moldy or stale in odor or taste. **mustily** *adv.*, **mustiness** *n.*

mu-ta-ble *adj.* Prone to or capable of change. **mutability**, **mutableness** *n.*

mu-tant *n.* An individual or organism which differs from the parental strain as a result of mutation. **mutant** *adj.*

mu-tate *v.* To undergo or cause to undergo mutation. **mutative** *adj.*

mu-ta-tion *n.* A change in form. *Biol.* A sudden change in the hereditary makeup of an organism in which there is a physical or chemical change in the genes.

mute *adj.* Unable to speak. *n.* A person who cannot speak. **-ly** *adv.*, **-ness** *n.*

mu-ti-late *v.* To deprive of an essential part, as a limb of the body; to maim or cripple; to make imperfect. **mutilation**, **mutilator** *n.*

mu-ti-ny *n.*, *pl.* **-ies** Open revolt against lawful authority. **mutineer** *n.*, **mutinous** *adj.*, **mutiny** *v.*

mutt *n.*, *Slang* A mongrel; a dog of mixed breed.

mut-ter *v.* To speak or utter in a low voice; to grumble; to complain.

mut-ton *n.* The flesh of a fully grown sheep, used for food. **muttony** *adj.*

mut-ton-chops *pl. n.* The whiskers on the side of the face which are narrow at the temple and broad and round by the lower jaw.

mu-tu-al *adj.* Having the same relationship; received and directed in equal amounts. **mutuality** *n.*

mu-tu-al fund *n.* An investment company which invests its shareholders' money in diversified ways.

muu-muu *n.* A dress which hangs loosely, originally given to the native women of Hawaii by missionaries.

muz-zle *n.* The projecting mouth of certain animals; the open end or mouth of an implement such as the barrel of a gun. **muzzler** *n.*

my *adj.* Relating to or of myself or one. *interj.* Used to express surprise, dismay, or pleasure.

my-ce-li-um *n., pl.* **-lia** A mass of interwoven filaments which form the main growing structure of a fungus.

my-col-o-gy *n.* A branch of botany; the scientific study of fungi. **mycological** *adj.*, **mycologist** *n.*

my-e-li-tis *n.* An inflammation of the spinal cord or bone marrow.

my-elo-ma *n.* A tumor of the bone marrow.

my-na *or* **my-nah** *n.* A dark brown, slightly crested bird of southeastern Asia.

myo-car-dio-graph *n.* A recording tool which traces the action of the heart muscles.

myo-car-di-um *n.* The muscular layer of the heart, located in the middle of the heart wall.

my-o-pia *n.* A visual defect in which visual images come to a focus in front of the retina of the eye rather than on the retina, causing fuzzy images. **myopic** *adj.*, **myopically** *adv.*

myr-i-ad *adj.* Having extremely large, indefinite aspects or elements.

myr-i-a-pod *n.* An arthropod, having a segmented body and many legs.

myr-mi-don *n.* A loyal follower.

myrrh *n.* An aromatic gum resin yielded from shrubs and trees, used in incense and perfumes.

myr-tle *n.* An evergreen shrub.

my-self *pron.* The one identical with me; used reflexively; my normal, healthy state or condition.

mys-te-ri-ous *adj.* Relating to or being a mystery; impossible or difficult to comprehend. **mysteriously** *adv.*, **mysteriousness** *n.*

mys-ter-y *n., pl.* **-ies** Something not understood; a problem or puzzle; an enigma; a Christian sacrament.

mys-tic *adj.* Relating to mystics, mysticism, or mysteries. *n.* A person practicing or believing in mysticism. **mystical** *adj.*, **mystically** *adv.*

mys-ti-cism *n.* The spiritual discipline of communion with God.

mys-ti-fy *v.* To perplex, to bewilder. **mystification** *n.*, **mystifyingly** *adv.*

mys-tique *n.* A body of beliefs connected with a group, person, idea, or thing.

myth *n.* A traditional story dealing with supernatural ancestors; a person or thing having only an unverifiable imaginary existence. **mythical**, **mythic** *adj.*, **mythically** *adv.*

my-thol-o-gy *n., pl.* **-ies** A body of myths dealing with gods and heroes. **mythological** *adj.*, **mythologist** *n.*

my word *interj.* An expression of astonishment.

nyx-e-de-ma *n.* A disease caused by decreased activity of the thyroid gland and marked by loss of mental and physical vigor.

N, n The fourteenth letter of the English alphabet.

nab *v., Slang* To seize; to arrest; to seize unexpectedly.

na-cho *n.* A tortilla, often small and triangular in shape, topped with cheese or chili sauce and baked.

nag *v.* To bother by scolding or constant complaining; to find fault with something constantly. *n.* A worthless horse. **nagger** *n.*, **nagging** *adj.*, **naggingly** *adv.*

nai-ad *n., Gr. Mythol.* A nymph presiding over and living in springs, brooks, and fountains.

nail *n.* A thin pointed piece of metal for hammering into wood and other materials to hold pieces together. *v.* To fasten with nails. **nailer** *n.*

nail-brush *n.* A small brush with firm bristles used to clean the hands and nails.

nail file *n.* A small instrument with a rough surface, used to shape the fingernails.

na-ive *adj.* Simple and trusting; not sophisticated; lacking careful judgment; ingenuous. **-ly** *adv.*, **-ness** *n.*

na-ked *adj.* Without clothes on the body; nude. **nakedly** *adv.*, **nakedness** *n.*

nam-by--pam-by *adj.* Weak; indecisive.

name *n.* A title or word by which something or someone is known or called. *v.* To give a name. **nameable** *adj.*

name--call-ing *n.* The use of offending names to induce condemnation or rejection.

name-less *adj.* Having no name; anonymous. **-ly** *adv.*, **namelessness** *n.*

name-plate *n.* A plaque or plate bearing ones name, company, or title; the title of a book or other publication that is displayed on the cover or first page.

name-sake *n.* A person named after someone with the same name.

na-nism *n.* Unusually small in size; dwarfism.

nan-ny *n.* A child's nurse; one who cares for small children.

nan-ny goat *n.* A female domestic goat.

nap *n.* A short rest or sleep, often during the day; to drowse; the surface of a piece of leather or fabric. **napless**, **napped** *adj.*, **napper** *n.*

na-palm *n.* A mixture of aluminum soaps used in jelling gasoline for use in bombs or by flame throwers.

nape *n.* The back of the neck.

nap-kin *n.* A cloth or soft paper, used at the dinner table for wiping the lips and fingers.

na-po-le-on *n.* A pastry of several flaky layers filled with custard cream.

nar-cis-sism *n.* The excessive admiration with oneself; self-love.

nar-cis-sus *n.* A widely grown type of bulbous plant which includes the jonquil, narcissus, and daffodil.

nar-co-lep-sy *n.* An illness where one has a frequent, sudden, uncontrollable need for deep, but quick sleep.

nar-co-sis *n.* A deep drug-induced state of stupor or unconsciousness.

nar-cot-ic *n.* A drug which dulls the senses, relieves pain, and induces a deep sleep; if abused, it can become habit-forming and cause convulsions or comas. **narcotically** *adv.*

nar-co-tize *v.* To bring someone under the influence of a narcotic. **-ation** *n.*

nark *n.* An informer.

nar-rate *v.* To tell a story or give a description in detail. **narration** *n.*, **narrator** *v.*

nar-row *adj.* Slender or small in width; of less than standard width. **narrowly** *adj.*, **narrowness** *n.*

narrow--mind-ed *adj.* Lacking sympathy or tolerance. **narrow-mindedly** *adv.*, **narrow-mindedness** *n.*

nar-whal *n.*

An aquatic mammal of the Arctic regions, closely related to the white whale, having a long, twisted, protruding tusk in the male.

na-sal *adj.* Of or pertaining to the nose.

nas-cent *adj.* Beginning to grow. **nascence, nascency** *n.*

na-stur-tium *n.* A five-petaled garden plant usually having red, yellow, or orange flowers.

nas-ty *adj.* Dirty, filthy, or indecent; unpleasant. **nastily** *adv.*, **nastiness** *n.*

na-tal *adj.* Pertaining to or associated with birth. **natality** *n.*

na-tion *n.* A group of people made up of one or more nationalities under one government. **national** *adj.*, **nationally** *adv.*

na-tion-al-ism *n.* Devotion to or concern for one's nation.

na-tion-al-i-ty *n.* The fact or condition of belonging to a nation.

na-tion-al-ize *v.* To place a nation's resources and industries under the control of the state.

na-tive *n.* A person born in a country or place.

na-tiv-i-ty *n.* Birth, circumstances, or conditions.

nat-ty *adj.* Tidy and trimly neat. **nattily** *adv.*, **nattiness** *n.*

nat-u-ral *adj.* Produced or existing by nature. *Mus.* A note that is not sharp or flat. **naturalness** *n.*, **naturally** *adv.*

nat-u-ral child-birth *n.* Childbirth with little stress or pain, requiring training for the mother and father and medical supervision, but without the use of drugs, anesthesia, or surgery.

nat-u-ral-sit *n.* A person who studies animals and plants.

nat-u-ral-ize *v.* To confer the privileges and rights of full citizenship; to adapt. **naturalization** *n.*

nat-u-ral law *n.* Conduct that is founded on the natural religion, ethics, or nature of man, and is considered morally binding.

na-ture *n.* The universe and its phenomena; one's own character or temperament. **natured** *adj.*

na-tur-op-a-thy *n.* A treatment for illness or disease using proper foods, exercise, and heat and avoids using drugs or surgery.

naught *n.* Nothing; the number 0; zero.

naugh-ty *adj.* Unruly; not proper; ill behaved. **naughtily** *adv.*, **-iness** *n.*

nau-se-a *n.* An upset stomach with a feeling that one needs to vomit. **nauseous** *adj.*, **nauseate** *v.*, **-tingly** *adv.*

nau-ti-cal *adj.* Pertaining to ships or seamanship. **nautically** *adv.*

na-val *adj.* Of or relating to ships; maritime.

na-vel *n.* A small mark or scar on the abdomen where the umbilical cord was attached.

nav-i-ga-ble *adj.* Sufficiently deep and wide enough to allow ships to pass. **navigableness** *n.*, **navigably** *adv.*

nav-i-gate *v.* To plan the course of a ship or aircraft; to steer a course. **navigation, -or** *n.*, **navigational** *adj.*

na-vy *n.* One of a nation's organizations for defense; a nation's fleet of ships; a very dark blue.

na-vy bean *n.* A dried bean, white in color.

Na-vy Cross *n.* A medal awarded to persons of the United States Navy for heroic actions in time of war.

na-vy-yard *n.* An area for the repairing, building, and outfitting of naval vessels; dockyard.

nay *adv.* Used to express a negation or refusal; no. *n.* Refusal; denial.

Na-zi *n.*, *pl.* nazis A member of the German fascist party which controlled Germany from 1933-1945 under Adolf Hitler. **Nazi** *adj.*, **nazification** *n.*

NBA *abbr.* National Basketball Association; National Boxing Association.

NC *abbr.* North Carolina.

ND *abbr.* North Dakota.

NE *abbr.* Nebraska.

Ne-an-der-thal *adj.* Suggesting a caveman in behavior or appearance; primitive or crude; *n.* Rough mannered person. **Neanderthal** *n.*

neap tide *n.* A tide in the minimum range which occurs during the first and third quarter of the moon.

near *adv.* At, to, or within a short time or distance. **nearness** *n.*

near-by *adj. & adv.* Close by; near at hand; adjacent.

near-sight-ed *adj.* Able to see clearly at short distances only. **-ly** *adv.*, **nearsightedness** *n.*

neat *adj.* Tidy and clean; free from disorder and dirt. **neatly** *adv.*, **-ness** *n.*

neat-en *v.* To make neat; to set in order.

Neb-ras-ka *n.* A state located in the central part of the United States.

neb-u-lous *adj.* Confused or vague; hazy; unclear; indistinct. **nebulously** *adv.*, **nebulousness** *n.*

nec-es-sar-y *adj.* Unavoidable; required; essential; needed; indispensable. **necessarily** *adv.*

ne-ces-si-tate *v.* To make necessary; to oblige. To force or compel.

ne-ces-si-ty *n.*, *pl.* -ies The condition of being necessary; the condition making a particular course of action necessary.

neck *n.* The part of the body which connects the head and trunk; a narrow part or projection, as of land, a stringed instrument, or bottle. *v.* To caress and kiss.

neck-er-chief *n.* A scarf or piece of cloth worn around the neck of a man or woman.

neck-lace *n.* A decoration of beads, or other precious stones.

neck-tie *n.*

A narrow strip of material worn around the neck and tied.

nec-rop-o-lis *n.* The examination of a corpse; an autopsy.

nec-tar *n.* A sweet fluid in various flowers, gathered by bees to help make honey; refreshing beverage. nectarous *adj.*

nee *n.* The term place before a married woman's maiden name, indicating her parentage.

need *n.* The lack of something desirable, useful, or necessary.

need-ful *adj.* Necessary. *n.* Something needed. needfully *adv.*, -ness *n.*

nee-dle *n.* A small slender, pointed steel implement which contains an eye through which thread is passed. *v.* To tease; to sew or pierce with a needle; to work with a needle. needlelike *adj.*

nee-dle-fish *n.* A fish having a long jaw and needle sharp teeth.

nee-dle-point *n.* Decorative stitching done on canvas in even stitches across counted threads. needlepoint *adj.*

need-less *adj.* Unnecessary; not needed or wanted. needlessly *adv.*, -ness *n.*

nee-dle-work *n.* Work that is excuted with a needle and thread; the profession or business of a person who works with a needle.

need-n't *contr.* Need not.

ne'er--do--well *n.* A worthless person; worthless.

ne-far-i-ous *adj.* Extremely wicked; despicable; villainous. nefariously *adv.*, nefariousness *n.*

neg *abbr.* Negative.

ne-gate *v.* To nullify; to deny. -or *n.*

ne-ga-tion *n.* A judgement; a negative statement, or doctrine; the act of denying; a denial. negational, negatory *adj.*, negationist *n.*

neg-a-tive *adj.* Expressing denial or disapproval; not positive. *n.* In photography, a negative photo. *Med.* No signs of a particular disease or problem. -ly *adj.*, negativeness *n.*

neglect *v.* To ignore; to pay no attention to; to fail to perform. neglectful *adj.*

neg-li-gee *n.* A woman's loose-fitting dressing gown.

neg-li-gent *adj.* To neglect what needs to be done.

ne-go-ti-ate *v.* To confer with another person to reach an agreement.

negotiation, negotiator *n.*

neigh-bor *n.* One who lives near another. neighboring *adj.*, neighbor *v.*

neigh-bor-hood *n.* A section or small region that possesses a specific quality; nearness; the number of people living within a particular locality.

neigh-bor-ly *adj.* Characteristic of congenial neighbors; friendly. neighborliness *n.*

nei-ther *adj.* Not one or the other. *pron.* Not the one or the other.

nel-son *n.* A wrestling hold using the application of leverage against an opponent's arm, head, and neck.

nem-e-sis *n.* An agent of punishment; invincible opponent.

neo *prefix* Recent; new.

neo-dym-i-um *n.* A metallic element of the rare-earth group, symbolized by Nd.

ne-on *n.* An inert gaseous element used in lighting fixtures, symbolized by Ne. *adj.* Relating or pertaining to neon. neon, neoned *adj.*

ne-o-na-tal *adj.* Pertaining to a newborn child. neonatally *adv.*

ne-o-nate *n.* A newborn child less than a month old.

ne-o-na-tol-o-gy *n.* The medical study of the first 60 days of a baby's life.

neo-phyte *n.* A novice; a beginner.

ne-o-plasm *n.* A tumor tissue serving no physiologic function; any new abnormal growth of body tissue. neoplastic *adj.*

ne-o-prene *n.* Synthetic, oil resistant rubber used in paints and putties.

ne-pen-the *n.* Anything that is capable of bringing forgetfulness of pain.

neph-ew *n.* The son of one's sister, brother, sister-in-law, or brother-in-law.

neph-o-gram *n.* An instrument used to photograph the clouds.

neph-o-scope *n.* An instrument used to determine the altitude of clouds and their velocity and direction of motion. nephoscope *adj.*

ne-phrit-ic *adj.* Relating to the kidneys; afflicted with an inflammation of the kidneys.

ne-phri-tis *n.* The inflammation of the kidneys. nephritic *adj.*

nep-o-tism *n.* The act of showing favoritism to relatives or friends in the work force based upon relationship rather than merit. nepotist *n.*, nepotic, nepotistic, nepotistical *adj.*

Nep-tune *n.* The planet 8th in order from the sun.

nep-tu-ni-um *n.* A radioactive metallic element.

ner-va-tion *n.* The arrangement of nerves.

nerve *n.* The bundles of fibers which convey sensation and originate motion through the body. *Slang* Impudent.

nerve cen-ter *n.* Group of nerve cells connected closely with each other and act together in performing functions.

nerve fi-ber *n.* Primary threadlike fibers known as dendrites of a nerve cell.

nerve-less *adj.* Lacking courage or strength; not nervous; calm. **nervelessly** *adv.*, **nervelessness** *n.*

nerv-ous *adj.* Affecting the nerves or the nervous system; agitated; worried. **nervously** *adv.*, **nervousness** *n.*

nerv-ous sys-tem *n.*, *Physiol.* The body system that coordinates, regulates, and controls the various internal functions and responses to stimuli.

nerv-y *adj.* Courageous or bold. **-iness** *n.*

nest *n.* A place, shelter, or home built by a bird to hold its eggs and young. *v.* To build a nest; to settle in a nest; to provide with a nest.

nest egg *n.* A supply of money accumulated or saved for future use; an artificial egg placed in a nest to induce a hen to lay eggs.

nes-tle *v.* To lie close to. **nestler** *n.*

net *n.* A meshed fabric made of cords, ropes, threads, or other material knotted or woven together; the profit, weight, or price which remains after all additions, subtractions, or adjustments have been made. **net** *v.*

neth-er *adj.* Situated below or beneath.

neth-er-most *adj.* Lowest; farthest down.

neth-er world *n.* Hell; the world of eternal punishment awaiting sinners after death.

net in-come *n.* A person's gross income after all expenses and taxes incurred in acquiring this income, have been deducted.

net pro-fit *n.* The remaining profit of a business after all operating expenses have been deducted from the total receipts.

net-ting *n.* The process of fishing with nets; process of manufacturing nets.

net-tle *n.* A plant having toothed leaves covered with stinging hairs.

net-tle-some *adj.* Annoying; irritated easily.

net-work *n.* A system of interlacing tracks, channels, or lines; an interconnected system.

neu-ral *adj.* Relating to a nerve or the nervous system. **neurally** *adv.*

neu-ral-gia *n.* Pain that occurs along the course of a nerve.

neu-ri-tis *n.* An inflammation of a nerve which causes pain, the loss of reflexes, and muscular decline. **neurotic** *adj.*

neu-rol-o-gist *n.* A physician who specializes in diagnosing and treating diseases of the nervous system.

neu-rol-o-gy *n.* The medical and scientific study of the nervous system and disorders. **-ical** *adj.*, **neurologist** *n.*

neu-ron *or* **neu-rone** *n.*, *Anat.*

A granular cell nerve which is the main functional unit of the nervous system.

neu-rop-a-thy *n.* A disease of the nervous system.

neu-ro-sis *n.* Any one of various func tional disorders of the mind or emo tions having no physical cause. **neurotic** *adj. n.*, **neurotically** *adv.*

neu-ro-sur-geon *n.* A surgeon that spe cializes in neurosurgery.

neu-ro-surgery *n.* Surgery of the brain.

neu-ter *adj.* Neither feminine nor mas culine. *n.* A castrated animal. **neuter** *v.*

neu-tral *adj.* Not supporting either sid of a debate, quarrel, or party; a colo which does not contain a decided hue *Chem.* Neither alkaline nor acid. **neutrality** *n.*, **neutrally** *adv.*

neu-tral-ism *n.* Maintaining a neutral at titude. **neutralist** *n.*, **neutralistic** *adj.*

neu-tral-ize *v.* To make or declar neutral.

neu-tron *n.* An uncharged particle in th nucleus of an atom present in a atomic nuclei except the hydroge nucleus.

Ne-va-da *n.* A state located in the west ern part of the United States.

nev-er *adv.* Not ever; absolutely not; a no time; in no degree.

nev-er-the-less *adv.* Nonetheles however; notwithstanding; in spite of.

new *adj.* Not used before; unaccu tomed; unfamiliar; recently inventec produced, made or discovered; ne habituated. **newness** *n.*, **newish** *adj.*

new born *n.* A recently borned baby. *ac* Just borned.

new-com-er *n.* A person new to an are; new arrival.

New Hamp-shire *n.* A state located i the northeastern part of the Unite States.

New Jer-sey *n.* A state located on th eastern coast of the United States.

New Mex-i-co *n.* A state located in th southwestern part of the Unite States.

new moon *n.* The period when the moo is directly line up between the eart and sun, therefore, its illuminated sic is not visible from the earth.

news *n.*, *pl.* Current information an happenings.

news-cast *n.* A television or radio nev broadcast.

news-let-ter *n.* A letterlike repo printed for periodic distribution subscribers.

news-pa-per *n.* A weekly or daily publ cation which contains recent nev and information.

news-print *n.* An inexpensive machin finished paper made from wood pu and used chiefly for newspapers ar some paperback books.

news-reel *n.* A brief motion pictu featuring news events.

news-stand *n.* A stand or place of bus ness where newspapers and pe odicals are sold.

New Test-a-ment *n.* The second part the Christian Bible containing th Gospels, Acts, Epistles, and the Boc of Revelation.

New York *n.* A state located on the eas

ern coast of the United States.

next *adj.* Immediately following or proceeding; nearest in space, time, rank, degree, or position.

next of kin *n.* Closest living relative or relatives.

next to *prep.* Adjacent to; immediately following.

NH *abbr.* New Hampshire.

nib *n.* The beak of a bird.

nib-ble *v.* To bite a little at a time; to take small bites. **nibble, nibbler** *n.*

nice *adj.* Pleasing; enjoyable; polite and courteous; refined; agreeable. **nicely** *adv.*, **niceness** *n.*

niche *n.* A recess or alcove in a wall; a position or place suitable for a person or thing.

nick *n.* A small chip or cut on a surface; **in the nick of time** the final critical moment. *v.* To make a notch in; to count by making nicks in.

nick-el *n.* A hard, silver, metallic element used in alloys and symbolized by Ni; a United States coin worth five cents.

nick-el-plat-ing *n.* The coating of metals with nickel.

nick-el-o-de-on *n.* A movie theatre which charged five cents for admission; a coin-operated juke box.

nick-er *v.* To snicker; laugh. *n.* A laugh.

nick-name *n.* The familiar form of a proper name, expressed in a shortened form. *v.* To give a nickname to; to call by an improper name. **nickname** *v.*

nic-o-tine *or* **nicotin** *n.* A poisonous alkaloid found in tobacco and used in insecticides and medicine.

niece *n.* A daughter of one's sister or brother or one's sister-in-law or brother-in-law.

nigh *adv.* Near in relationship, time, or space. *adj.* Not distant; being near.

night *n.* The time between dusk and dawn or the hours of darkness.

night-cap *n.* An alcoholic drink usually taken before retiring for the night; a cap worn to bed.

night clothes *n.* Clothes worn while sleeping.

night club *n.* An establishment that serves liquor and food and presents entertainment.

night crawl-er *n.* A large nocturnal earthworm, used as fish bait.

night dress *n.* Clothing worn to bed; nightgown.

night-fall *n.* Evening; the end of day.

night-gown *n.* A loose fitting gown used for sleeping.

night her-on *n.* A nocturnal heron found in the United States.

night-in-gale *n.*

A songbird with brownish plumage, noted for the sweet, nocturnal song of the male.

night latch *n.* A latch for a door that opens from the outside with a key and from the inside by a knob.

night let-ter *n.* A message sent at night for delivery the next morning.

night-long *adj.* Lasting all night.

night-ly *adj.* Happening at night; occurring every night.

night-mare *n.* A frightening and horrible dream that causes feelings of anxiety, oppression or helplessness.

night-shirt *n.* A long pullover sleeping shirt usually worn by men and boys while sleeping.

night stick *n.* A heavy stick carried by a policeman or security guard as protection.

nim-ble *adj.* Marked by a quick, light movement; quick-witted. **nimbleness** *n.*, **nimbly** *adv.*

nin-com-poop *n.* A silly or stupid person.

nine *n.* The cardinal number that is equal to 8 + 1. **nine** *adj., pron.*

ni-o-bi-um *n.* A gray, metallic element used in alloys, symbolized by Nb.

nip *v.* To pinch, bite, or grab something. *n.* A pinch, bite, or grab; a sharp, stinging feeling caused by cold temperatures. **nipper** *n.*

nip-ple *n.* The small projection of a mammary gland through which milk passes; an artificial teat usually made from a type of rubber which a bottle-fed baby nurses.

ni-tro-gen *n.* A nonmetallic gaseous element which is essential to life.

ni-tro-glyc-er-in *n.* A highly flammable, explosive liquid, used to make dynamite and, in medicine, to dilate blood vessels.

Nixon Richard M. *n.* Born in 1913, the 37th president of the United States from 1969-1974 resigned August 9, 1974 due to Watergate scandal.

NM *abbr.* New Mexico.

no *adv.* Used to express rejection, disagreement, or denial; not so; not at all.

no-bel-i-um *n.* A radioactive element.

Nobel prize *n.* An award given to people with achievements in literature, economics, medicine, and other fields, established by the last will and testament of Alfred Nobel.

no-bil-i-ty *n., pl.* **ies** The state or quality of being noble.

no-ble *adj.* Morally good; superior in character or nature. *n.* A person of rank or noble birth. **noblemen, nobleness** *n.*, **nobly** *adv.*

no-bod-y *pron.* Not anybody; no person.

noc-tur-nal *adj.* Pertaining to or occurring during the night. **nocturnally** *adv.*

nod *n.* A quick downward motion of the head as one falls off to sleep; a downward motion of the head indicating acceptance or approval.

node *n.* A swollen or thickened enlargement.

no-el *n.* A Christmas carol.

noise *n.* A sound which is disagreeable or loud; in computer science, unwanted data in an electronic signal.

noisy *adj.*, noisily *adv.*

no-mad *n.* A member of a group of people who wander from place to place. nomadic *adj.*, nomadism *n.*

no-men-cla-ture *n.* The set of names used to describe the elements of art, science, and other fields.

nom-i-nal *adj.* Of or relating to something that is in name or form only. nominally *adv.*

nom-i-nate *v.* To select a candidate for an elective office.

nomination, nominator *n.*

nom-i-nee *n.* A person nominated for a position or office.

non- *prefix* Not.

non-a-ge-nar-i-an *adj.* A person between the ages of 90 and 100 years.

non-cha-lant *adj.* Giving an effect of casual unconcern. nonchalance *n.*, nonchalantly *adv.*

non com-pos men-tis *adj.* Mentally unbalanced.

non-con-form-ist *n.* A person who does not feel compelled to follow or accept his community's traditions. nonconformity *n.*

none *pron.* Not any; not one.

non-sec-tar-i-an *adj.* Not associated with or restricted to one religion, faction, or sect.

non-sense *n.* Something that seems senseless or foolish. nonsensical *adj.*

non seq-ui-tur *n.* An inference that does not follow as the logical result of what has preceded it.

non-sex-ist *adj.* Not discriminating on the basis of gender.

noo-dle *n.* A flat strip of dried dough made with eggs and flour.

nook *n.* A corner, recess, or secluded place.

noon *n.* The middle of the day; 12:00 o'clock.

noose *n.* A loop of rope secured by a slipknot, allowing it to decrease in size as the rope is pulled.

nor *conj.* Not either; or not.

norm *n.* A rule, model, or pattern typical for a particular group.

nor-mal *adj.* Ordinary, average, usual; having average intelligence. normalcy, normality *n.*, normally *adv.*

north *n.* The direction to a person's left while facing east.

North Car-o-li-na *n.* A state located in the southeastern part of the United States.

North Da-ko-ta *n.* A state located in the north central part of the United States.

nose *n.* The facial feature containing the nostrils; the sense of smell.

nose-dive *n.* A sudden plunge as made by an aircraft.

nos-tal-gia *n.* A yearning to return to the past. nostalgic *adj.*

nos-tril *n.* The external openings of the nose.

nos-y *or* nos-ey *adj.* Snoopy; inquisitive; prying.

not *adv.* In no manner; used to express refusal or denial.

no-ta-ble *adj.* Remarkable, distinguished. notably *adv.*

no-ta-rize *v.* To acknowledge and certify as a notary public.

notary public *n.* A person who is legally authorized as a public officer to witness and certify documents.

no-ta-tion *n.* A process or system of figures or symbols used in specialized fields to represent quantities, numbers, or values. notational *adj.*

notch *n.* A v-shaped indentation or cut. notch *v.*

note *v.*

A record or message in short form. *Mus.* A tone or written character. note *v.*

not-ed *adj.* Famous; well-known.

noth-ing *n.* Not any thing; no part or portion.

no-tice *n.* An announcement; a notification. noticeable *adj.*, noticeably *adv.*

no-ti-fy *v.* To give notice of; to announce. notifier, notification *n.*

no-tion *n.* An opinion; a general concept; an idea.

notions *pl., n.* Small useful articles, as thread or buttons.

no-to-ri-ous *adj.* Having a widely known and usually bad reputation.

not-with-stand-ing *prep.* In spite of. *adv.* Nevertheless; anyway. *conj.* Although.

noun *n.* A word which names a person, place, or thing.

nour-ish *v.* To furnish with the nutriment and other substances needed for growth and life; to support. nourishing *adj.*, nourishment *n.*

nou-veau riche *n.* A person who has recently become rich.

no-va *n.*, *pl.* -vae *or* -vas A star which flares up and fades away after a few years or months.

nov-el *n.* An inventive narrative dealing with human experiences; a book. novelist *n.*

nov-el-ty *n.*, *pl.* -ies Something unusual or new.

No-vem-ber *n.* The 11th month of the calendar year, having 30 days.

nov-ice *n.* A person who is new and unfamiliar with an activity or business.

now *adv.* At the present time; immediately.

no-where *adv.* Not in or at any place.

nox-ious *adj.* Harmful; obnoxious; corrupt.

noz-zle *n.* A projecting spout or vent of something.

nu-ance *n.* A slight variation.

nub *n.* A knob; a small piece or lump.

nu-bile *adj.* Suitable or ready for marriage.

nu-cle-ar *adj.* Pertaining to and resembling a nucleus; relating to atomic energy.

nu-cle-us *n.*, *pl.* -clei *or* -cleuses A central element around which other elements are grouped.

nude *adj.* Unclothed; naked. -ity, -ist *n.*

nudge *v.* To poke or push gently.

nug-get *n.* A lump, as of precious metal.

nui-sance *n.* A source of annoyance.

null *adj.* Invalid; having no value or consequence. **nullification** *n.*

nul-li-fy *v.* To counteract.

numb *adj.* Lacking physical sensation. **numb** *v.*, **numbness** *n.*

num-ber *n.* A word or symbol which is used in counting or which indicates how many or which one in a series.

number-less *adj.* Too many to be counted.

nu-meral *n.* A symbol, figure, letter, word, or a group of these which represents a number.

nu-mer-a-tor *n.* The term in mathematics indicating how many parts are to be taken; the number in a fraction which appears above the line.

nu-mer-ous *adj.* Consisting or made up of many units.

nun *n.* A woman who has joined a religious group and has taken vows to give up worldly goods and never to marry.

nup-tial *adj.* Of or pertaining to a wedding.

nuptials *pl.*, *n.* A wedding.

nurse *n.* A person who is specially trained to care for disabled or sick persons. *v.* To feed a baby from a mother's breast.

nurs-er-y *n.*, *pl.* **-ies** A room reserved for the special use of infants or small children; a business or place where trees, shrubs, and flowers are raised.

nur-ture *n.* The upbringing, care, or training of a child. **nurturer** *n.*

nut *n.* A hard-shelled fruit or seed which contains an inner, often edible kernal.

nut-crack-er *n.* A hinged tool for cracking nuts.

nut-meg *n.* The hard seed of a tropical ever-green tree, which is grated and used as a spice.

nu-tri-ent *n.* A substance which nourishes. **nutrient** *adj.*

nu-tri-tion *n.* The process by which a living being takes in food and uses it to live and grow. **nutritive**, **-al** *adj.*, **nutritionally** *adv.*, **nutritionist** *n.*

nuts *adj.*, *Slang* Foolish, crazy; insane; eccentric.

nuz-zle *v.* To gently rub against something with the nose; to cuddle; to root up with the nose; to touch something with the nose.

NV *abbr.* Nevada.

NY *abbr.* New York.

NYC *abbr.* New York City.

ny-lon *n.* A strong, elastic material; yarn or fabric made from nylon. **nylons** Stockings made of nylon.

nymph *n.*, *Gr. & Rom. Mythol.* Nature goddess who lived in woods, rivers, and trees; various immature insects, especially the larva which undergoes incomplete metamorphosis. **-al** *adj.*

O, o The 15th letter of the English alphabet.

O *n.* A word used before a name when talking to that person; an interjection.

O' *abbr.* o'clock.

oaf *n.* A stupid or clumsy person. **oafish** *adj.*, **oafishly** *adv.*, **oafishness** *n.*

oak *n.* A large tree of durable wood bearing acorns. **oaken** *adj.*

oar *n.* A long pole, flat at one end, used in rowing a boat.

oar-lock *n.* A U-shaped device, on a pivot used to hold an oar during rowing.

oars-man *n.* A person who rows in a racing crew; a person who is skilled in the use of oars. **oarsmanship** *n.*

oa-sis *n.*, *pl.* **oases** A fertile section in the desert which contains water; anything that provides refuge.

oat *n.* A cultivated cereal grass whose grain or seed is used as food.

oat-cake *n.* A thin, brittle cake made of oatmeal.

oath *n.* A solemn promise in the name of God or on a Bible that a person will speak only the truth.

oat-meal *n.* A cooked cereal food made from rolled oats.

ob-bli-ga-to *adj.* Necessary to; indispensable.

ob-du-rate *adj.* Stubborn; hardhearted; not giving in; indifferent to human feelings; inflexible; unyielding. **obduracy**, **-ness** *n.*, **obdurately** *adv.*

o-be-di-ence *n.* The habit of obeying; compliance; submission. **obedient** *adj.*, **obediently** *adv.*

o-be-di-ent *adj.* Obeying or willing to do what one is told. **obedience** *n.*

ob-e-lisk *n.* A tall, four-sided stone pillar which slopes from a pointed top.

o-bese *adj.* Very fat; overweight. **obesity**, **obeseness** *n.*, **obesely** *adv.*

o-bey *v.* To carry out instructions; to be guided or controlled; to follow directions. **obeyer** *n.*

ob-fus-cate *v.* To obscure; to confuse, muddle, or bewilder. **obfuscation** *n.*, **obfuscatory** *adj.*

o-bi *n.* A sash that is tied over a kimono and worn by the Japanese female.

o-bit *n.* *Slang* An obituary; the record of the date of a persons death.

o-bit-u-ar-y *n.*, *pl.* **-ies** A published announcement that a person has died, often containing a short biography of the person's life. **obituary** *adj.*

ob-ject *v.* To voice disapproval; to protest. *n.* Something that is visible or can be touched. *Grammar* A word in a sentence which explains who or what is acted upon. **objectless** *adj.*

ob-ject ball *n.* In billiards the first ball struck by the cue ball.

ob-ject glass *n.* The lens or combination of lenses in a microscope or telescope, that first receives the rays from an object and forms the image through the eyepiece.

ob-jec-tion *n.* A feeling of opposition or disagreement, etc.; the reason for a disagreement.

ob-jec-tion-a-ble *adj.* Provoking disapproval or protest; offensive or reprehensible. **objectionability**, **objectionableness** *n.*, **-ably** *adv.*

ob-jec-tive *adj.* Pertaining to or dealing with material objects rather than mental concepts. *n.* Something that one works toward, a goal; a purpose. **objectivity**, **-ness** *n.*, **objectively** *adv.*

ob-la-tion *n.* A religious offering or the act of sacrifice; that which is offered.

ob-li-ga-tion *n.* A promise or feeling of duty; something one must do because one's conscience or the law demands it; a debt which must be repaid.

ob-lig-a-to-ry *adj.* Binding legally or morally; imperative, compulsory; recording an obligation. **obligatorily** *adv.*, **obligatoriness** *n.*

o-blige *v.* To constrain; to put in one's debt by a service or favor; to do a favor. **obliger** *n.*, **obligingly** *adv.*

ob-li-gee *n.* The person to whom another is obligated or bound by a legal agreement.

o-blig-ing *adj.* Disposed to do favors or perform special services; willing; kind. **obligingly** *adv.*, **obligingness** *n.*

ob-li-gor *adj., Law* A person who is legally bound to discharge an obligation.

o-blique *adj.*

Inclined; not level or straight up and down; slanting; indirect. **obliqueness**, **obliquity** *n.*, **obliquely** *adv.*

ob-liq-ui-ty *n.* Divergence from ones moral standards, an instance of mental deviation; a confusing statement.

o-blit-er-ate *v.* To blot out or eliminate completely; to wipe out; to erase; to destroy and sign of something. **obliteration**, **obliterator** *n.*, **-ive** *adj.*

o-bliv-i-on *n.* The condition of being utterly forgotten; the act of our condition of forgetting; an official pardon.

ob-liv-i-ous *adj.* Not aware or conscious of what is happening; unmindful; forgetfulness; unaware. **obliviously** *adv.*, **obliviousness** *n.*

ob-long *adj.* Rectangular; longer in one direction than the other; normally, the horizontal dimension; the greater in length. **oblong**, **oblongness** *n.*

ob-lo-quy *n.* Abusive language; a strongly condemnatory utterance.

ob-nox-ious *adj.* Very unpleasant; repugnant. **obnoxiousness** *n.*

o-boe *n.* A double-reed, tube-shaped woodwind instrument. **oboist** *n.*

ob-scene *adj.* Indecent; disgusting; objectionable; tending to incit lust. **obscenity**, **-ness** *n.*, **obscenely** *adv.*

ob-scure *adj.* Remote; not clear; not easily understood; unknown, or unnoticed to fame faint. *v.* To make dim or dark; to conceal by covering. **obscurely** *adv.*, **obscurity**, **-ness** *n.*

ob-serve *v.* To pay attention; to watch without actively participating; to notice; to discover; to detect; to mention; to keep, as a holiday; to celebrate something; to perceive. **observable**, **observant** *adj.*, **observably**, **observingly** *adv.*, **observer** *n.*

ob-ser-vant *adj.* Paying strict attention to something. **observantly** *adv.*

ob-ser-va-tion *n.* The act of observing something; that which is observed; a judgment or opinion. **-al** *adj.*, **observationally** *adv.*

ob-ser-va-to-ry *n., pl.* **-ies** A building or station furnished with instruments for studying the natural phenomenon; a high tower affording a panoramic view.

ob-sess *v.* To preoccupy the mind with an idea or emotion; to be abnormally preoccupied. **obsession** *n.*, **obsessive** *adj.*, **obsessively** *adv.*

ob-so-lete *adj.* No longer in use; out-of-date. *Biol.* Something that is imperfectly developed. **obsolescence** *n.*, **obsolescent** *adj.*

ob-sta-cle *n.* An obstruction; anything which opposes or stands in the way of progress.

ob-ste-tri-cian *n.* A physician who specializes in the care of a woman during pregnancy and childbirth.

ob-stet-rics *pl., n.* The branch of medicine which deals with pregnancy and childbirth.

ob-sti-na-cy *n.* The instance, state, or quality of being obstinate.

ob-sti-nate *adj.* Stubbornly set to an opinion or course of action; difficult to control or manage; hardheaded. **obstinacy** *n.*, **obstinately** *adv.*

ob-strep-er-ous *adj.* Noisy, unruly, or boisterous in resistance to advice or control. **obstreperousness**, **obstreperosity** *n.*, **obstreperously** *adv.*

ob-struct *v.* To block, close, hinder or impede; stand in the way of. **-or**, **obstruction** *n.*, **obstructive** *adj.*

ob-struc-tion-ism *n.* The deliberate interference the progress or business. **obstructionist** *n.*, **obstructionistic** *adj.*

ob-tain *v.* To acquire or gain possession of; to get, receive, procure. **acquire**. **obtainable** *adj.*, **-er**, **obtainment** *n.*

ob-trude *v.* To thrust forward without request or warrant; to call attention to oneself. **obtruder**, **obtrusion** *n.*

ob-tuse *adj.* Lacking acuteness of feeling; insensitive; not distinct or clear to the senses, as pain or sound. *Bot.* Rounded or blunt at the end, as a petal or leaf. **obtusely** *adv.*, **-ness** *n.*

ob-vert *v.* To turn in order to present a different view or surface.

ob-vi-ate *v.* To counter or prevent by effective measures; to overcome. **obviation**, **obviator** *n.*

ob-vi-ous *adj.* Easily seen, discovered, or understood; perfectly evident or plain. **obviously** *adv.*, **obviousness** *n.*

oc-a-ri-na *n.* Wind instrument with an oval body that has finger holds and mouthpiece

oc·ca·sion *n.* The time an event occurs; the event itself; a celebration; a significant or important event or time. *v.* To bring about; to cause incidentally; to produce.

oc·ca·sion·al *adj.* Appearing or occurring irregularly or now and then; intended, made, or suitable for a certain occasion; incidental. **-ly** *adv.*

oc·ci·den·tal *adj.* Western. **-ly** *adv.*

oc·cip·i·tal *adj.* Pertaining the the back part of the skull or head.

oc·cip·i·tal bone *n. Anat.* The bone which forms the back of the skull.

oc·cult *adj.* Concealed; not disclosed; beyond the bounds of natural knowledge. *n.* The action or influence of supernatural agencies or secret knowledge of them. **occultist** *n.*

oc·cult·ism *n.* Study or belief in the influence or action of supernatural powers. **occultist** *n.*

oc·cu·pan·cy *n.* The state or act of being occupied; the act of holding in possession; the time or term during which something is occupied.

oc·cu·pant *n.* A person who acquires title by occupancy.

oc·cu·pa·tion *n.* A job, profession, or vocation; a foreign military force which controls an area. *adj.* Relating to an occupation; pertaining to a trade. **occupationally** *adv.*

oc·cu·pa·tion·al ther·a·py *n. Med.* The treatment of mental, nervous, or physical disabilities by means of work designed to promote recovery or readjustment. **occupational therapist** *n.*

oc·cu·py *v.* To take and retain possession of; to live in; to employ or use. **occupier** *n.*, **occupiable** *adj.*

oc·cur *v.* To suggest; to have something come to mind; to happen; to exist so as to be seen. **-rence** *n.*, **occurrent** *adj.*

o·cean *n.* An immense body of salt water which covers 3/4 of the earth's surface; one of the oceans. **oceanic** *adj.*

ocean·ar·i·um *n.* A large contained marine aquarium used for the display of fish.

o·ce·an·ic *adj.* Pertaining to, occurring in the ocean.

ocean-front *n.* An area or building that faces the ocean.

ocean-going *adj.* Being capable or designed for ocean travel.

o·ce·an·og·ra·phy *n.* The science of oceanic phenomena dealing with underwater research. **oceanographer** *n.*, **oceanographic, oceanographical** *adj.*, **oceanographically** *adv.*

o·cean sunfish *n.* A large tropical fish having short bodies and very long fins.

oc·el·lat·ed *adj.* Having eyelike markings. **ocellation** *n.*

o·cel·lus *n.* The simple eye of an insect that is present inboth the larval and adult.

o·cel·lot *n.* A leopardlike cat, both nocturnal and arboreal.

och·loc·ra·cy *n.* Rule by the common people. **ochlocrat** *n.*, **ochlocratic** *adj.*

och·lo·pho·bia *n.* The morbid fear of mobs and crowds.

o'clock *adv.* Of, or according to the clock.

o·co·til·lo *n.* A desert shrub, characterized by thorny stems and bright red flowers.

Oct *abbr.* October.

oc·ta·chord *n.* A musical instrument with eight strings; a standard scale of eight notes.

oc·ta·gon *n.* A polygon with eight angles and eight sides. **octagonal** *adj.*, **octagonally** *adv.*

oc·ta·he·dron *n.* A solid having eight sides. **octahedral** *adj.*

oc·tam·er·ous *adj.* Divided into or consisting of eight parts.

oc·tane *n.* Any of several hydrocarbon compounds which occur in petroleum.

oc·tave *n., Music* A tone on the eighth degree above or below another tone.

Oc·to·ber *n.* The 10th month of the calendar year, having 31 days.

oc·to·de·cil·lion *n.* A cardinal number represented by a 1 and followed by 57 zeros.

oc·to·ge·nar·i·an *n.* A person between the ages of 80 and 90.

oc·to·pod *n.* Any cephalopod from the octopoda order, having eight arms. **octopodan** *adj.*, **octopoduous** *adj.*

oc·to·pus *n., pl.* **-es** or **-pi**

A cephalopod with a saclike body, eight tentacles containing double rows of suckers, large eyes, and a naked body and a small internal shell.

oc·to·syl·la·ble *n.* An eight syllable word, verse, or line.

oc·tu·ple *adj.* Having eight units or elements; eight time as great.

oc·u·lar *adj.* Of or relating to the eye; perceived or done by the eye. **-ly** *adv.*

oc·u·list *n.* A person who has been trained in the examination and treatment of the eye; ophthalmologist.

oc·u·lo·mo·tor *adj.* Pertaining or connected to the eyeball movement.

oc·u·lo·mo·tor nerve *n.* Either of the pair of the cranial nerves that supply most of the muscles that move the eyeball.

OD *n. Slang* An overdose of a drug; one who has taken an overdose. *v.* To overdose; to die from an overdose.

odd *adj.* Unusual; strange; singular; left over after dividing into parts; not even; different from the ordinary. **oddly** *adv.*, **oddness** *n.*

odd·ball *n.* One who displays an eccentric, curious, or nonconforming manner. *adj.* Unusual.

odd·i·ty *n.* A singular occurrence, person, or thing; the quality of being unusual.

odd·ment *n.* An article left over.

odds *pl, n.* An equalizing advantage given to a weaker opponent; a ratio between the probability against and the probability for something happening or being true.

odds and ends *n.* Miscellaneous things; remnants; scraps.

odds--on *n.* Having a better than even chance to reach a goal.

ode *n.* A lyric poem usually honoring a person or event, expressing a personal feeling.

o-di-ous *adj.* Arousing extreme dislike. **odiously** *adv.,* **odiousness** *n.*

o-dom-e-ter *n.* A device in a vehicle used to measure distance traveled.

o-dor *n.* A smell; a sensation which occurs when the sense of smell is stimulated. **odored, odorless** *adj.*

o-dor-ous *adj.* Emitting an odor; fragrant.

od-ys-sey *n.* A long voyage marked by many changes of fortune; a spiritual quest.

Oedipus complex *n.* An unconscious sexual feeling a child develops towards the parent of the opposite sex.

of *prep.* Proceeding; composed of; relating to; at a distance from.

off *adv.* From a position or place; no longer connected or on. *adj.* Canceled. *prep.* Away from. *interj.* Go away.

off-beat *n., Slang* Unconventional; out-of-step; questionable.

off-cast *n.* A person who is rejected.

off-color *adj.* Varying from decency; varying from the desired color.

of-fend *v.* To make angry; to arouse resentment; to break a law; to cause discomfort. **offender** *n.*

of-fense *n.* A violation of a duty, rule, or a propriety; the act of causing displeasure; the act of assaulting or attacking; in football and other sports, the team having possession of the ball.

of-fen-sive *adj.* Disagreeable or unpleasant; causing resentment; displeasure, or anger; insulting. **offensively** *adv.,* **offensiveness** *n.*

of-fer *v.* To present for acceptance or rejection; to present as an act of worship; to make available; to present in order to satisfy a requirement. **offerer, offeror** *n.*

of-fer-ing *n.* The act of one who offers; a contribution, as money, given to the support of a church.

off-hand *adv. or adj.* Without preparation or premeditation. **offhanded, offhandedness** *n.*

of-fice *n.* A place where business or professional duties are conducted; an important job, duty, or position.

of-fi-cer *n.* A person who holds a title, position of authority, or office; a policeman.

of-fi-cial *adj.* Something derived from proper authority. *n.* One who holds a position or office; a person who referees a game such as football, basketball, or soccer. **officialism** *n.,* **officially** *adv.*

of-fi-ci-ate *v.* To carry out the duties and functions of a position or office.

of-fi-cious *adj.* Offering one's services or advice in an unduly forward manner. **officiously** *adv.,* **officiousness** *n.*

off-spring *n., pl.* **-springs** The descendants of a person, plant, or animal.

of-ten *adv.* Frequently; many times.

oh *interj.* Used to express surprise, fear, or pain.

OH *abbr.* Ohio.

O-hi-o *n.* A state in the midwestern section of the United States.

ohm *n.* A unit of electrical resistance equal to the resistance of a conductor in which one volt produces a current of one ampere.

oil *n.* Any of various substances, usually thick, which can be burned or easily melted; a lubricant. *v.* To lubricate.

oil-cloth *n.* A cloth treated with oil which therefore becomes waterproof.

oil field *n.* An area rich in petroleum; an area which has been made ready for oil production.

oil slick *n.* A layer of oil floating on water.

oint-ment *n.* An oily substance used on the skin as an aid to healing or to soften the skin.

OK *abbr.* Oklahoma.

Ok-la-ho-ma *n.* A state in the south central part of the United States.

o-kra *n.* A tall tropical and semitropical plant with green pods that can be either fried or cooked in soups.

old *adj.* Having lived or existed for a long time; of a certain age. *n.* Former times.

old-en *adj.* Of or relating to times long past; ancient.

old--fash-ioned *adj.* Pertaining to or characteristic of former times or old customs; not modern or up-to-date.

Old Glo-ry *n.* The flag of the United States of America.

Old Tes-ta-ment *n.* The first of two parts of the Christian Bible, containing the history of the Hebrews, the laws of Moses, the writings of the prophets, the Holy Scriptures of Judaism, and other material.

Old World *n.* The eastern hemisphere, including Asia, Europe, and Africa.

ol-fac-tory *adj.* Pertaining to the sense of smell.

oli-gar-chy *pl., n.* **-ies** A government controlled by a small group for corrupt and selfish purposes; the group exercising such control.

ol-ive *n.*

A small oval fruit from an evergreen tree with leathery leaves and yellow flowers, valuable as a source of oil.

O-lym-pic Games *pl., n.* International athletic competition held every four years, based on an ancient Greek festival.

om-buds-man *pl. n.* **-men** A government

official appointed to report and receive grievances against the government.

om-e-let *or* **om-e-lette** *n.* A dish made from eggs and other items, such as bacon, cheese, and ham, and cooked until set.

o-men *n.* A phenomenon which is thought of as a sign of something to come, whether good or bad.

om-i-nous *adj.* Foreshadowed by an omen or by a presentiment of evil; threatening.

o-mis-sion *n.* The state or act of being omitted; anything neglected or left out.

o-mit *v.* To neglect; to leave out; to overlook.

om-ni-bus *n.* A public vehicle designed to carry a large number of people; a bus. *adj.* Covering a complete collection of objects or cases.

om-nip-o-tent *adj.* Having unlimited or infinite power or authority.

om-nis-cient *adj.* Knowing all things; having universal or complete knowledge.

om-niv-or-ous *adj.* Feeding on both vegetable and animal substances; absorbing everything. **omnivorously** *adv.*

on *prep.* Positioned upon; indicating proximity; indicating direction toward; with respect to. *adv.* In a position of covering; forward.

once *adv.* A single time; at any one time. *conj.* As soon as.

once-over *n.*, *Slang* A swift but comprehensive glance.

on-col-o-gy *n.* The study of tumors. **oncological, oncologic** *adj.*, **-ist** *n.*

one *adj.* Single; undivided. *n.* A single person; a unit; the first cardinal number (1).

one-self *pron.* One's own self.

one--sid-ed *adj.* Partial to one side; unjust. **one-sidedness** *n.*

on-ion *n.* An edible bulb plant having a pungent taste and odor.

on--line *adj. Computer Science* Controlled directly by a computer.

on-ly *adj.* Sole; for one purpose alone. *adv.* Without anyone or anything else. *conj.* Except; but.

on-o-mat-o-poe-ia *n.* The use of a word, as buzz or hiss, which vocally imitates the sound it denotes. **onomatopoeic, onomatopoetic** *adj.*

on-shore *adj.* Moving or coming near or onto the shore. **onshore** *adv.*

on-slaught *n.* A fierce attack.

on-to *prep.* To a position or place; aware of.

o-nus *n.* A burden; a responsibility or duty which is difficult or unpleasant; the blame.

on-ward *adv.* Moving forward in time or space. **onwards** *adj.*

on-yx *n.* A gemstone; a chalcedony in layers of different colors.

oo-dles *pl.*, *n.*, *Slang* A great or large quantity.

ooze *n.* A soft deposit of slimy mud on the bottom of a body of water; muddy or marshy ground; a bog. *v.* To flow or leak slowly; to disappear little by little.

o-pal *n.* A translucent mineral composed of silicon, often marked with an iridescent play of colors. **opaline** *adj.*

o-paque *adj.* Not transparent; dull; obscure. **opacity, opaqueness** *n.*

OPEC *abbr.* Organization of Petroleum Exporting Countries.

o-pen *adj.* Having no barrier; not covered, sealed, locked, or fastened. *n.* A contest for both amateurs and professionals. *v.* To begin or start. **openness** *n.*, **openly** *adv.*

open--and--shut *adj.* Easily settled; simple to decide.

op-era *n.* A drama having music as a dominant factor, an orchestral accompaniment, acting, and scenery.

op-er-ate *v.* To function, act, or work effectively; to perform an operation, as surgery. **operative** *adj.*

op-er-a-tion *n.* The process of operating; the system or method of operating; a series of acts to effect a certain purpose; a process; a procedure performed on the human body with surgical instruments to restore health; various mathematical or logical processes.

op-er-a-tor *n.* A person who operates a machine; the owner or person in charge of a business. *Slang* A shrewd person.

oph-thal-mol-o-gy *n.* A branch of medical science dealing with diseases of the eye, its structure, and functions.

o-pin-ion *n.* A judgment held with confidence; a conclusion held without positive knowledge.

o-pi-um *n.* A bitter, highly addictive drug; a narcotic.

o-pos-sum *n.*, *pl.* **-sum** *or* **-sums**

A nocturnal animal which hangs by its tail and carries its young in a pouch.

op-po-nent *n.* An adversary; one who opposes another.

op-por-tune *adj.* Occurring at the right or appropriate time. **opportunist** *n.*, **opportunely** *adv.*

op-por-tu-ni-ty *n.*, *pl.* **-ies** A favorable position; a chance for advancement.

op-pose *v.* To be in direct contention with; to resist; to be against. **opposable** *adj.*, **opposition** *n.*

op-po-site *adj.* Situated or placed on opposing sides. **oppositeness** *n.*

op-press *v.* To worry or trouble the mind; to weigh down; to burden as if to enslave. **oppression, oppressor** *n.*

op-pres-sive *adj.* Unreasonably severe or burdensome.

op-tic *adj.* Pertaining or referring to

sight or the eye.

op-ti-cal *adj.* Pertaining to sight; constructed or designed to assist vision.

op-ti-cian *n.* A person who makes eyeglasses and other optical articles.

op-ti-mism *n.* A doctrine which emphasizes that everything is for the best.

op-ti-mum *n., pl.* **-ma** The degree or condition producing the most favorable result. *adj.* Conducive to the best result.

op-tion *n.* The act of choosing or the power of choice; a choice. **-ally** *adv.*

op-tion-al *adj.* Left to one's decision; elective; not required.

op-tom-e-try *n.* The occupation or profession of examining the eyes and prescribing corrective lenses.

op-u-lence *n.* Wealth in abundance; affluence.

or *conj.* A word used to connect the second of two choices or possibilities, indicating uncertainty. *suffix* Indicating a person or thing which does something.

OR *abbr.* Oregon.

or-a-cle *n.* A seat of worship where ancient Romans and Greeks consulted the gods for answers; a person of unquestioned wisdom. **oracular** *adj.*

o-ral *adj.* Spoken or uttered through the mouth; taken or administered through the mouth. **orally** *adv.*

o-ral con-tra-cep-tive *n.* A pill containing hormones, taken monthly to prevent pregnancy.

or-ange *n.* A citrus fruit which is round and orange in color. *adj.* Yellowish red.

o-rang-u-tan *n., pl.* **-tans** A large, anthropoid ape, having brownish-red hair and very long arms.

o-rate *v.* To speak in an elevated manner.

orb *n.* A globe or sphere.

or-bit *n.* The path of a celestial body or a manmade object. *v.* To revolve or move in an orbit; to circle. **orbital** *adj.*

or-chard *n.* Land that is devoted to the growing of fruit trees.

or-ches-tra *n.* A group of musicians performing together on various instruments. **orchestral** *adj.*

or-ches-tra pit *n.* In theatres, the space reserved for musicians.

or-chid *n.* A plant found the world over having three petals in various colors.

or-dain *v.* To appoint as a minister, priest, or rabbi by a special ceremony; to decree.

or-deal *n.* A painful or severe test of character or endurance.

or-der *n.* A condition where there is a logical arrangement or disposition of things; sequence or succession; method; an instruction for a person to follow; a request for certain objects. *v.* To command; to demand.

or-der-ly *adj.* Neat, tidy.

or-di-nance *n.* A command, rule, or order; a law issued by a municipal body.

or-di-nar-y *adj.* Normal; having no

exceptional quality; common; average; plain.

ore *n.* A natural underground substance, as a mineral or rock, from which valuable matter is extracted.

o-reg-a-no *n.* A bushy perennial herb of the mint family, used as a seasoning for food.

Or-e-gon *n.* A state in the northwestern part of the United States.

or-gan *n.* A musical instrument of pipes, reeds, and keyboards which produces sound by means of compressed air; a part of an animal, human, or plant that performs a definite function, as the heart, a kidney, or a stamen.

or-gan-dy *or* **or-gan-die** *n., pl.* **-ies** A translucent, stiff fabric of cotton or silk.

or-gan-ic *adj.* Effecting or pertaining to the organs of an animal or plant; of or relating to the process of growing plants with natural fertilizers with no chemical additives. **organically** *adv.*

or-gan-i-za-tion *n.* The state of being organized or the act of organizing; a group of people united for a particular purpose. **organizational** *adj.*

or-gan-ize *v.* To assemble or arrange with an orderly manner; to arrange by planning. **organization** *n.*

or-gasm *n.* Physiol. Intensive emotional excitement; the culmination of a sexual act.

o-ri-ent *v.* To determine the bearings or right direction with respect to another source.

O-ri-ent *n.* The countries located east of Europe. **Oriental** *adj.*

or-i-fice *n.* An opening through which something may pass; a mouth.

or-i-gin *n.* The cause or beginning of something; the source; a beginning place.

o-rig-i-nal *adj.* Belonging to the first or beginning. *n.* A new idea produced by one's own imagination; the first of a kind. **originality** *n.*, **originally** *adv.*

or-i-ole *n.* A songbird having brightly colored yellow and black plumage in the males.

or-na-ment *n.* A decoration. *v.* To adorn or beautify. **ornamental** *adj.*, **ornamentally** *adv.*, **ornamentation** *n.*

or-nate *adj.* Excessively ornamental; elaborate; showy, as a style of writing.

or-phan *n.* A child whose parents are deceased. **orphan** *v.*, **orphanage** *n.*

or-ris *n.* Any of several species having a fragrant root and used in medicine, perfumes, and cosmetics.

or-tho-don-tics *n.* The branch of dentistry dealing with the correction and prevention of irregularities of the teeth.

or-tho-dox *adj.* Following established traditions and beliefs, especially in religion.

Or-tho-dox Ju-da-ism *n.* The branch of Jewish faith which accepts the Mosaic Laws as interpreted in the Talmud.

or-tho-pe-dics *or* **or-tho-pae-dics** *n.* The

branch of surgery or manipulative treatment concerned with the disorders of the bones, joints, and muscles. **orthopedist** *n.*

os-cil-late *v.* To swing back and forth with regular motion, as a pendulum. **oscillation, oscillator** *n.*, **-ory** *adj.*

os-mi-um *n.* A hard, but brittle metallic element symbolized as OS.

os-mo-sis *n.* The tendency of fluids separated by a semipermeable membrane to pass through it and become mixed and equal in strength. **osmotic** *adj.*

os-ten-ta-tion *n.* The act of displaying pretentiously in order to excite.

os-teo *n. comb. form* Bone; pertaining to the bones.

os-te-op-a-thy *n.* A medical practice based on the theory that diseases are due chiefly to abnormalities of the body, which can be restored by manipulation of the parts by therapeutic measures.

os-te-o-po-ro-sis *n.* A disorder causing gradual deterioration of bone tissue, usually occurring in older women.

os-tra-cize *v.* To exile or exclude from a group; to shut out.

oth-er *adj.* Additional; alternate; different from what is implied or specified. *pron.* A different person or thing.

oth-er-wise *adv.* Under different conditions of circumstances.

ot-ter *n., pl.* **-ter** *or* **-ters**

Web-footed aquatic mammals, related to the weasel.

ouch *n. interj.* An exclamation to express sudden pain.

ought *v.* Used to show or express a moral duty or obligation; to be advisable or correct.

ounce *n.* A unit of weight which equals 1/16 of a pound.

our *adj.* Of or relating to us ourselves. *pron.* The possessive case of the pronoun we. **ourselves** Our own selves.

oust *v.* To eject; to remove with force.

out *adv.* Away from the center or inside. *adj.* Away. *n.* A means of escape. *prep.* Through; forward from.

out-age *n.* A loss of electricity.

out-break *n.* A sudden outburst; an occurrence.

out-cast *n.* A person who is excluded; a homeless person.

out-come *n.* A consequence or result; the conclusion.

out-cry *n.* A cry of distress; noisy opposition.

out-dated *adj.* Old-fashioned and obsolete.

out-dis-tance *v.* To surpass in any career or competition.

out-do *v.* To excel in achievement; to surpass; to perform beyonds ones normal expectations. **outdoer** *n.*

out-door *adj.* Belonging, or performed outside of the house.

out-doors *adv.* The area that exists beyond the boundaries of a house.

out-er space *n.* The space existing beyond the earth's atmosphere.

out-face *v.* To defy; to confront; to stare down.

out-fit *n.* The equipment or tools required for a specialized purpose; the clothes a person is dressed in. *v.* To supply. **outfitter** *n.*

out-flank *v.* To out maneuver. **-er** *n.*

out-fox *v.* To get the better of a person or situation by craftiness.

out-land-ish *adj.* Extremely ridiculous, unusual, or strange; foreign; remote; bizarre. **outlandishly** *adv.*, **-ness** *n.*

out-last *v.* To exceed; to outlive; to last longer that something else in comparison.

out-law *n.* A person who habitually defies or breaks the law; a criminal. *v.* To ban; prohibit; to deprive of legal protection.

out-lay *n.* Disbursement; a laying out of money.

out-let *n.* An exit.

out-li-er *n.* A person who resides outside of his place of duty, or business.

out-line *n.* A rough draft showing the main features of something. **outline** *v.*

out-live *v.* To survive or live longer.

out-look *n.* A person's point of view; a mental view; the act of keeping watch over something; an area offering a view.

out-ly-ing *adj.* Being beyond the limit or boundary.

out-ma-neu-ver *v.* To gain advantage over by using more skillful actions.

out-match *v.* To outdo or surpass.

out-mode *v.* To make obsolete or unfashionable. **outmoded** *adj.*

out-num-ber *v.* To go over or exceed in number.

out--of--date *adj.* Obsolete. **-datness** *n.*

out-pa-tient *n.* A patient who visits a clinic or hospital for treatment but does not spend the night.

out-post *n.* Troops stationed at a distance away from the main group as a guard against attack; a frontier or outlying settlement.

out-put *n.* Production or yield during a given time.

out-rage *n.* An extremely violent act of violence or cruelty; the violent emotion such an act engenders. **outrageous** *adj.*, **outrage** *v.*

out-right *adj.* Free from reservations or complications; complete; entire.

out-side *n.* The area beyond the boundary lines or surface; extreme. *adv.* Outdoors.

out-spo-ken *adj.* Spoken without reserve; candid. **outspokenly** *adv.*

out-stand-ing *adj.* Excellent; prominent; unsettled, as a bill owed; projecting.

out-ward *adj.* Pertaining to the outside or exterior; superficial. **outwards** *adv.*

out-wit *v.* To trick, baffle, or outsmart with ingenuity.

o-val *adj.* Having the shape of an egg; an ellipse.

o-va-ry *n.*, *pl.* **-ies** One of the pair of female reproductive glands. **-ian** *adj.*

o-va-tion *n.* An enthusiastic display of approval for a person or a performance; applause.

ov-en *n.* An enclosed chamber used for baking, drying, or heating.

o-ver *prep.* Above; across; upon. *adv.* Covering completely; thoroughly; again; repetition. *adj.* Higher; upper. *prefix* Excessive, as overstuffed or overcrowded.

o-ver-act *v.* To act in an exaggerated way.

o-ver-all *adj.* Including or covering everything; from one side or end to another; generally. *n.* Pants with a bib and shoulder straps.

o-ver-arm *adj.* Thrown or executed with the arms raised above the shoulders.

o-ver-bear *v.* To crush or bear down by superior force or weight. **-ing** *adj.*

o-ver-board *adv.* Over the side of a boat or ship into the water.

o-ver-cast *adj.* Gloomy; obscured. *Meteor.* Clouds covering more than 9/10 of the sky.

o-ver-coat *n.* A coat worn over a suit for extra warmth.

o-ver-come *v.* To prevail; to conquer or defeat. **overcomer** *n.*

o-ver-con-fi-dence *n.* Extreme or excessive confidence.

o-ver-do *v.* To do anything excessively; to overcook.

o-ver-dose *n.* To take an excessive dose of medication, especially narcotics.

o-ver-draw *v.* To withdraw money over the limits of one's credit.

o-ver-drive *n.* A gearing device in a vehicle that turns a drive shaft at a greater speed than that of the engine, therefore decreasing power output.

o-ver-due *adj.* Past the time of return or payment.

o-ver-flow *v.* To flow beyond the limits of capacity; to overfill.

o-ver-hand *v.* To execute something with the hand above the level of the elbow or shoulder. **over-handed** *adv.*

o-ver-haul *v.* To make all needed repairs.

o-ver-head *n.* The operating expenses of a company, including utilities, rent, and upkeep. *adj.* Situated above the level of one's head.

o-ver-look *v.* To disregard or fail to notice something purposely; to ignore.

o-ver-night *adj.* Lasting the whole night; from dusk to dawn. **overnight** *adv.*

o-ver-pass *n.* A raised section of highway which crosses other lines of traffic. *v.* To cross, pass over, or go through something; to overlook.

o-ver-ride *v.* To disregard; to take precedence over; to declare null and void.

o-ver-rule *v.* To put aside by virtue of higher authority.

o-ver-run *v.* To spread out; to extend or run beyond.

o-ver-seas *adv.* Abroad, across the seas.

o-ver-see *v.* To supervise; to direct.

o-ver-sexed *adj.* Having an overactive interest in sex.

o-ver-shoe *n.* A galosh worn over a shoe for protection from snow or water.

o-ver-sight *n.* A mistake made inadvertently.

o-ver-size *or* **o-ver-sized** *adj.* Larger than the average size of something.

o-ver-step *v.* To go beyond a limit or restriction.

o-vert *adj.* Open to view.

o-ver--the--coun-ter *adj.* Not traded on an organized security exchange; of or relating to drugs or medicine which can be purchased without a prescription.

o-ver-throw *v.* To remove from power by force; to bring about destruction.

o-ver-time *n.* The time worked beyond or before the specified hours.

o-ver-whelm *v.* To overcome completely; to make helpless.

o-void *adj.* Having the shape of an egg.

ovu-late *n.* To discharge or produce eggs from an ovary.

o-vum *n.*, *pl.* **ova** The female reproductive cell.

owe *v.* To be in debt for a certain amount; to have a moral obligation.

owl *n.*

A predatory nocturnal bird, having large eyes, a short hooked bill, and long powerful claws. **owlish** *adj.*

own *adj.* Belonging to oneself. *v.* To possess; to confess; to admit. **owner** *n.*

ox *n.*, *pl.* **oxen** A bovine animal used domestically in much the same way as a horse; an adult castrated bull.

ox-ford *n.* A shoe which is laced and tied over the instep.

ox-ide *n.* A compound of oxygen and another element.

ox-y-gen *n.* A colorless, odorless, tasteless gaseous element essential to life, symbolized by O.

ox-y-gen-ate *v.* To combine or treat with oxygen.

ox-y-gen mask *n.* A device worn over the mouth and nose through which a person can receive oxygen as an aid to breathing.

ox-y-gen tent *n.* The protective cover that is placed over the upper body of a patient, and makes it possible for delivering and retaining pure oxygen to aid breathing.

oys-ter *n.* An edible marine mollusk.

oz *abbr.* Ounce; ounces.

o-zone *n.* A pale-blue gas formed of oxygen with an odor-like chlorine, formed by an electrical discharge in the air. *Slang* Fresh air.

P, p The 16th letter of the English alphabet.

PA *abbr.* Pennsylvania; power of attorney; per annum.

PABA *n.* The paraaminobenzoic acid.

pab-u-lom *n.* Type of food such as in absorbable solution.

Pac *abbr.* Pacific

pa-ca *n.* Type of large and brown rodent that is from Central And South America having white spots.

pace *n.* A person's step in walking or the length of a person's step; stride; the gait of a horse in which the legs on the same side are moved at the same time; rate of progress. **pace** *v.*, **pacer** *n.*

pace car *n.* The automobile that leads a field of competitors around the track, in order to warm up the engines then falls out and does not continue in the race.

pace lap *n.* The warm up lap before the start of a car race.

pace-mak-er *n.* The person who sets the pace for another in a race; a type of surgically implanted electronic instrument used to stabilize or stimulate the heartbeat. **-making** *n.*

pac-er *n.* One that sets a particular speed or pace.

pa-chi-si *n.* Another name for the game Parcheesi; ancient board game played with dice.

pach-y-derm *n.* A group of animals which contains the elephant, the rhinoceros, and hippo; animals having thick skins. **pachydermal** *adj.*

pach-y-san-dra *n.* A type of species of the evergreen trailing herbs of the box family and is grown for the purpose of ground cover in areas that are shaded.

Pa-cif-ic *n.* The largest ocean on the earth, extending from North & South America westward to Asia and Australia.

pa-cif-i-ca-tion *n.* The state of something being pacified or calmed. **pacificatory** *adj.*, **pacificator** *n.*

pac-i-fi-er *n.* A person or something that will pacify another; nipple shaped device for babies to suck on.

pac-i-fism *n.* The policy dealing with the establishment of universal peace between all nations; opposition to violence or war as a means of settling problems or disputes. **pacifist** *n.*

pac-i-fy *v.* To quiet or soothe anger or distress; to calm. **pacifiable** *adj.*

pack *n.* A bundle; a group or number of things tied or wrapped up; a full set of associated or like things, such as a pack of cards; a group of wolves or wild dogs that hunt together. *v.* To put things together in a trunk, box, or suitcase; to put away for storage. **to send packing** To force to leave with haste and without ceremony. **packability** *n.*, **packable** *adj.*

pack-age *n.* Something tied up, wrapped or bound together. **packager** *n.*

pack-age deal *n.* An agreement or offer that involves a number of related items, the items offered.

pack-age store *n.* A retail establishment that sells alcoholic beverages only in sealed containers.

pack animal *n.* An animal used to carry heavy packs.

pack-board *n.* A metal frame that is usually covered with canvas, used to carry goods and equipment over ones shoulder.

packed *adj.* To be filled to capacity.

pack-er *n.* A person who packs; one who works in an establishment that packs meat; a machine that automatically packs.

pack-et *n.* A type of parcel or package that is small in size and can be used to carry or hold small items.

pack-ing *n.* The action of a person who packs.

pack-ing house *n.* A place where food, such as meats, are made and packed in order to be sent to the market for sale.

pack-man *n.* A person who carries a pack and tries to sell his wares; a peddler.

pack rat *n.* A type of rodent located in North America that has a habit of hiding or hoarding the items that it finds; one who collects useless items.

pack-sack *n.* A flexible baglike case of material or leather designed with straps for carrying items of ones back.

pack-sad-dle *n.* a saddle that is used on pack animals for carrying objects.

pack-thread *n.* The twine or rope that is used for the purpose of binding packages together to make carrying easier for carrying. **packthreaded** *adj.*

pact *n.* An agreement between nations, groups, or people; a contract.

pad *n.* Anything stuffed with soft material and used to protect against blows; a cushion; a drawing or writing tablet of paper gummed together at one edge; the cushion-like part of the foot on some animals, as the dog. *Slang* A person's home. *v.* To stuff, line, or protect with soft material; to extend or lengthen something by inserting unnecessary matter; to travel by foot in a soft and nearly inaudible way.

pad-ding *n.* The material, as cotton, or synthetic fibers, which is used for the purpose of protecting something.

pad-dle *n.* A broad-bladed implement usually made from wood, used to steer and propel a small boat; a tool used for mixing, turning, or stirring; a small wooden, rounded racket used in table tennis. **paddle** *v.*, **paddler** *n.*

pad-dle-fish *n.* A type of fish that is located in the Mississippi River and has a snout which is shaped like a paddle.

pad-dle-wheel *n.* A wheel with boards for propelling vessels; a boat that is propelled by paddle wheels.

pad-dock *n.* The area that is located near the racetrack and is used for the purpose of mounting and tending to the horses that will or have already ran in a race.

pad-dy n. The land, usually in China, which is flooded with water and used for the purpose of growing rice.

pad-dy wag-on n., *Slang* A police vehicle for transporting suspects.

pad-lock n. A detachable lock, having a pivoted u-shaped hasp which can be inserted through a ring and then locked. **padlock** v.

pa-dre n. A title used in Spain and Italy for a priest.

pa-dro-ne n. The person who is the master of a vessel; the owner or operator of a business; an innkeeper.

pad-u-a-soy n. A corded, rich silk fabric.

pae-an n. A song of praise or joy.

pae-do-gen-e-sis n. The reproduction by immature animals.
    paedogenetic, padogenic *adj.*

pae-on n. A type of metrical foot that is made up of four syllables.

pa-gan n. A person who does not acknowledge God in any religion; a heathen; an idolater. **pagan** *adj.*

pa-gan-ism n. The belief in and the worship of a false god; heathenism.

pa-gan-ize v. To make someone a pagan or to become a pagan. **paganizer** n.

page n. The person who is hired to deliver messages or run errands; one side of the leaf of a book or letter. v. To call or to summon a person.

pag-eant n. An elaborate exhibition or spectacular parade for public celebration; anything having a showy appearance with out duration.

pag-eant-ry n. A type of exhibition that is showy; a spectacle.

pag-i-nate v. To number or to place numbers on a page showing the order in which they should be placed in order to read.

pa-go-da n. A sacred Buddhist tower built as a memorial or shrine.

paid v. Past tense of pay.

pail n. A cylindrical container usually having a handle; a bucket.

pail-ful *adj.* The total amount that a pail is able to hold.

pail-lasse n. A type of mattress that is filled with wood shavings and can be used under another mattress for support.

pail-lon n. A type of metallic foil which is used for the purpose of enamel work.

pain n. The unpleasant feeling resulting from injury or disease; any distress or suffering of the mind; sorrow. v. To cause or experience pain.
    painless *adj.*, **painlessness** n.

pain-ful *adj.* To be distressing or having or causing pain to something or to someone. **-ness** n., **painfully** *adv.*

pain-kill-er n. Medication that relieves pain. **painkilling** n.

pains-tak-ing *adj.* To be given to taking pains; done with carefulness and diligence. **painstakingly** *adv.*

paint n. A mixture of colors or pigments which are spread on a surface as protection or as a decorative coating; make-up for the face, as rouge. v. To apply paint to a surface; the practice of using paint to express oneself on canvas.

paint-brush n. A type of brush that is used for painting surfaces.

paint-ed bunt-ing n. A type of bird that is found in North America and is brightly colored.

paint-er n. The person who paints for a living or for self enjoyment. **-ly** *adj.*

paint-er's col-ic n. The lead poisoning which is marked by acute pain in the stomach area and a pulse which is slowed.

paint-ing n. The piece of art that is made by a painter and can be hung on one's wall for decoration.

pair n., pl. **pairs** or **pair** Two things which are similar and used together; something made of two parts which are used together; two persons or animals which live or work together.

pair--oar n. A type of boat where the rowers sit in front of one another and pull one oar in order to move the boat. **pair-oared** *adj.*

pais-ley *adj.* To have colors that are bright and patterned into a design which is typical of paisley.

pa-ja-mas pl. n. A loose fitting garment for sleeping, consisting of a jacket and pants.

pal n. A good friend.

pal-ace n. The royal residence of a sovereign, as of a king; a mansion.

pal-a-din n. One who is an eminent hero.

pa-laes-tra n. A type of school of ancient Greece that was used to teach athletics.

pal-at-a-ble *adj.* Pleasant to the taste; agreeable to one's feelings or mind.
    -y *adv.*, **palatability, palatableness** n.

pal-a-tal *adj.* To be pertaining or to be related to the palate. **palatally** *adv.*

pal-ate n. The muscular tissue at the roof of a person's mouth, opposite the tongue; sense of taste.

pa-la-tial *adj.* Pertaining to a palace.
    palatialness n.

pal-a-tine *adj.* To be related to the palate of one's mouth. n. A lord invested with royal privileges within his territory.

pa-lav-er n. A type of discussion; superfluous talk.

pale n. The pointed stake of a fence; a picket; an area that is enclosed within bounds. *adj.* Having a whitish or lighter than normal complexion; pallid; weak. **-ly** *adv.*, **paly, -ish** *adj.*

pa-le-eth-nol-o-gy n. A part or branch of ethnology which deals with the early human races known.

pale-face n. A person who has white skin; term first used 'y the American Indians.

pa-le-o-bot-a-ny n. A study of plants

which are discovered in their fossilized state or condition.

pa-le-o-bot-an-i-cal-ly *adv.*, **paleobotanist** *n.*

pa-le-og-ra-phy *n.* The study of ancient writings. **paleographically**, **paleographically** *adv.*, **paleographer** *n.*

pa-le-o-lith *n.* A stone implement that is from the Paleolithic time period.

pa-le-on-tol-o-gy *n.* The study and the science which deals with ancient life and they lived.

pa-le-o-zo-ol-o-gy *n.* The science or the study of the fossil animals.

pal-ette *n.* A thin oval board with a hole for the thumb, on which an artist lays and mixes colors.

pal-ette knife *n.* A type of knife which has a blade that is rounded at the end.

pal-frey *n.* A type of small horse that is used by a lady.

pal-imp-sest *n.* A piece of writing paper from which something as been erased and another writing has been written over, leaving the first faintly visible.

pal-in-drome *n.* A word, number, or sentence which reads the same backward or forward, such as toot or 1991.

pal-ing *n.* A type of fence which is made from pales or pickets.

pal-in-gen-e-sis *n.* The regeneration or the rebirth of someone or something. **palingenetically** *adv.*, **palingenetic** *adj.*

pal-i-node *n.* A poem that contains something from a previous piece; a recantation. **palinodist** *n.*

pal-i-sade *n.* A fence made of stakes for protection. **palisade** *v.*

pall *n.* A heavy cloth used to cover a bier or coffin; a very gloomy atmosphere. *v.* To have a wearying effect.

pal-la-di-um *n.* A silvery-white metallic element symbolized by Pd.

pall-bear-er *n.* A person who assists in carrying a coffin at a funeral.

pal-let *n.* A wooden platform on which material for freight shipments can be moved or stored; a bed made of straw.

pal-let-ize *v.* To load items on pallets for transportation and storing.

pal-li-al *adj.* To be relating to or pertaining to pallium.

pal-li-ate *v.* To conceal something with an excuse.

pal-lid *adj.* Deficient in color; lacking sparkle. **pallidly** *adv.*, **pallidness** *n.*

pal-lor *n.* Lacking color; paleness.

palm *n.* The inner area of the hand between the fingers and the wrist; any of a large group of tropical evergreen trees, having an unbranched trunk with a top or crown of fan-like leaves. *v.* To hide something small in or about the hand.

pal-mar *adj.* To be located or situated in the palm of one's hand.

palm-er-worm *n.* A type of caterpillar that is very destructive to vegetation.

pal-met-to *n.* A type of palm tree that has fan- shaped leaves. *Palmetto* The nickname for the state of South

Carolina.

palm-is-try *n.* The practice of fortune telling by the configurations of the palm of the hands.

pal-mit-ic acid *n.* A type of fatty acid that is used for the making of soap.

pal-mi-tin *n.* A type of colorless compound that is found in palm oil and can be used in the making of soap.

palm oil *n.* The vegetable fat that is obtained from the fruit of an oil palm and used for the making of candles and soap.

Palm Sun-day *n.* The Sunday before Easter; celebrated as Christ's triumphal entry into Jerusalem.

palm-y *adj.* To be prosperous.

pal-my-ra *n.* A type of palm that is used for the making of stiff brushes.

pal-o-mi-no *n.* A type of horse that has a coat which is golden in color and a mane that is flaxen.

pal-pa-ble *adj.* To be capable of being touched or felt by someone or something; easily detected; obvious; plain. **palpably** *adv.*, **palpability** *n.*

pal-pate *v.* To check something through the use of touch, such as a doctor would examine a patient.

pal-pe-bral *adj.* To be located near the eyelid of someone or something.

pal-pus *n.* A type of organ that is found on certain insects and is used for the purpose of sensing.

pal-sy *n., pl.* **-ies** Paralysis; the loss of ability to control one's movements.

pal-ter *v.* To haggle over something, such as the price of a good.

pal-try *adj.* To be worthless or inferior. **paltriness** *n.*

pa-lu-dal *adj.* To be related to or referring to a marsh.

pal-u-drine *n.* A type of drug which is used for the purpose of treating the disease malaria in people.

pam-pas *n.* The grassy plains that can be found in South America.

pam-per *v.* To treat with extreme care. **pamperer** *n.*

pam-pe-ro *n.* The strong and cold wind that blows in the pampas of South America and coming from the Andes mountain chain.

pam-phlet *n.* A brief publication which is not permanently bound.

pan *n.* A type of vessel that is usually made of metal and is used for the cooking of foods over heat.

pan-a-ce-a *n.* A remedy for all diseases, difficulties, cr ills; a cure-all. **panacean** *adj.*

pa-nache *n.* A type of showy plume that is worn on a cap.

pan-cake *n.* A thin, flat cake made from batter and fried on a griddle, served with butter, powdered sugar, syrup, and other toppings.

pan-cake ice *n.* Type of ice pieces that float on the water and are too small to interfere with navigation of the ships.

pan-chro-mat-ic *adj.* To be sensitive to

pan-cra-ti-um *n.* A type of gymnastic contest that was held in ancient Greece and contained a combination of wrestling and boxing.

pan-cre-as *n., Anat.* A large, irregularly shaped gland situated behind the stomach which releases digestive enzymes and produces insulin. **pancreatic** *adj.*

pan-cre-atec-to-my *n.* The surgical removal of any part or all of the pancreas.

pan-cre-at-ic-juice *n.* A type of alkaline fluid that contains digestive enzymes and is secreted by the pancreas into the duodenum of the small intestine.

pan-da *n.*

A large bear-like animal of China and Tibet with black and white fur and rings around the eyes; a racoon-like animal of the southeastern Himalayas with a ringed tail and reddish fur.

pan-da-nus *n.* A member belonging to the screwpine family.

pan-de-mo-ni-um *n.* A place marked with disorder and wild confusion; disorder; confusion.

pan-der or pan-der-er *n.* A go-between in sexual affairs; a pimp; one who profits from the base desires or passions of others. *v.* To act as a panderer for someone.

pan-dit *n.* A man who is respected highly.

pan-dow-dy *n.* A type of deep-dish pie that has been made with apples.

pan-e-gry-ic *n.* A type of writing about a person that praises them.

pan-el *n.* A flat, rectangular piece of material, often wood, which forms a part of a surface; a group of people selected to participate in a discussion group or to serve on a jury. **panelist** *n.,* **panel** *v.*

pan-el-ing *n.* A type of wood that has been made into panels and is used to cover walls for decoration.

pan-el truck *n.* A type of truck that is used for small deliveries and is enclosed.

pan-e-tel-la *n.* A type of cigar that has one end that is slender.

pang *n.* A sudden and sharp pain that does not last for very long.

pan-go-lin *n.* A type of scaled mammal that has a pointed tail and eats ants, found in Africa.

pan-han-dle *n.* A projecting strip of land that is not a peninsula, such as with Texas.

pan-ic *n.* A sudden unreasonable fear which overpowers. *v.* To cause or to experience panic. **panicky** *adj.*

pan-ic grass *n.* A type of grass that is grown and cut for forage.

pan-ic--strick-en *adj.* To be overcome by great and intense fear.

panne *n.* A type of light-weight velvet.

pan-nier *n.* One of a pair of large baskets which are carried on either side of an animal or over a person's back.

pan-ni-kin *n.* A small cup or pan.

pa-no-cha *n.* A type of sugar that has a course grade and can be found in Mexico.

pan-o-ply *n., pl.* -lies The complete equipment of a warrior, including his armor and weapons. **panoplied** *adj.*

pan-o-ram-a *n.* An unlimited or complete view in all directions of what is visible. **panoramically** *adv.*

pan-sy *n., pl.* -ies A garden plant with flowers bearing blossoms in a variety of colors.

pant *v.* To breathe in rapid or short gasps; to yearn. *n.* A short breath.

pan-ta-lets *n.* A type of underpants that are long and have a fringed bottom.

pan-tech-ni-con *n.* A type of storehouse that is used to store furniture.

pan-the-ism *n.* The belief that the laws and forces of nature are all manifestations of God. **pantheist** *n.,* **pantheistic** *adj.*

pan-the-on *n.* A type of building or temple that was built in order to honor all the gods. **pantheonic** *adj.*

pan-ther *n.* A black leopard in its unspotted form.

pan-ther-ess *n.* The female panther.

pan-to-mime *n.* Communication done solely by means of facial and body gestures. *v.* To express or act in pantomime.

pan-to-then-ic ac-id *n.* A type of vitamin belonging to the B complex that promotes growth of the cells.

pan-try *n., pl.* -ies A closet or room for the storage of food, dishes, and other kitchen items.

pants *pl, n.* Trousers; underpants.

pan-zer *n.* A type of German tank.

pap *n.* A soft food for invalids or babies.

pa-pa-cy *n., pl.* -ies The dignity or jurisdiction of a pope; a pope's term in office.

pa-pa-in *n.* A type of enzyme that is found in the juice of the unripe fruit of the papaya trees.

pa-paw *n.* A type of small tree that has drooping leaves and purple flowers and can be found in North America.

pa-pa-ya *n.* A type of tropical tree that will yield melonlike fruits.

pa-per *n.* A type of substance made of pulp from wood and rags, formed into sheets for printing, wrapping and writing. **paperer, paperiness** *n.*

pa-per-back *n.* A type of book which has its cover made out of paper.

pa-per birch *n.* A type of tree found in North America and having white bark that will peel into layers.

pa-per cut-ter *n.* A type of device which has been designed to cut many sheets of paper at one time.

pa-per-hang-er *n.* A person who hangs wallpaper to make money.

pa-per mul-ber-ry *n.* A type of tree of

China and of Japan that is used for making paper.

pa-per-weight n. A heavy object that is placed upon paper to keep then from blowing around.

pa-pier--ma-che n. A material consisting of wastepaper mixed with glue or paste which can be molded when wet and becomes hard when dry.

pap-il-lo-ma n. A type of benign tumor that will exist on the mucous membranes or the skin.

pa-poose n. A North American Indian child or baby.

pa-pri-ka n. A dark red seasoning powder made by grinding red peppers.

Pap test n. A test in which a smear of bodily secretion from the uterus is examined for the early detection of cancer.

pap-ule n. A type of elevation in the skin that does not contain pus, but it is inflammatory. **papular** adj.

pa-py-rus n. A type of reedlike plant that was used as paper in early Egypt to write upon.

pai-a-bi-o-sis n. The joining or fusion of two separate organisms, such as Siamese twins.

par-a-ble n. A short, fictitious story which illustrates a moral lesson.

par-a-chute n.

A folding umbrella shaped apparatus of light fabric used to make a safe landing after a free fall from an airplane. **parachute** v., **parachutist** n.

pa-rade n. An organized public procession; a march. **parade** v., **parader** n.

par-a-di-chlor-ben-zene n. Atype of white compound that is used as an insecticide.

par-a-dise n. A state or place of beauty, bliss or delight; heaven.
paradisiac, **paradisiacal** adj.

par-a-dox n. A statement which seems opposed to common sense or contradicts itself, but is perhaps true.
paradoxical adj., **paradoxically** adv.

par-aes-the-sia n. A sensation that is abnormal such as the prickling of the skin.

par-af-fin n. A white, waxy substance derived from petroleum and used to make lubricants, candles, and sealing materials. **paraffin** v.

par-a-gen-e-sis n. A type of formation of minerals where they are too close together and impact on one another's development. **paragenetic** adj.
paragenetically adv.

par-ago-ge n. An addition of a letter to the end of a word that is incorrect.

par-a-gon n. A pattern or model of excellence or perfection.

par-a-graph n. A section of a composition dealing with a single idea, containing one or more sentences with the first line usually indented.

paragraphic adj., **paragrapher** n.

par-a-keet n.

A small parrot with a long, wedge-shaped tail.

par-al-de-hyde n. A type of colorless liquid that can be used in medicine as a hypnotic.

par-al-lel adj. Moving in the same direction but separated by a distance, as railroad tracks. n. A parallel curve, line, or surface; a comparison; one of the imaginary lines which circle the earth paralleling the equator and mark the latitude. **parallelism** n.

par-al-lel bars n. One pair of bars that are horizontal and supported by uprights.

par-al-lel-o-gram n. A four-sided figure having parallel opposite sides which are equal.

pa-ral-o-gism n. A type of argument that is fallacious.

pa-ral-y-sis n., pl. -ses Complete or partial loss of the ability to feel any sensation or to move. **paralytic** adj. & n.

par-a-lyze v. To cause to be inoperative or powerless.

par-a-mat-ta n. A type of light twilled fabric that can be used for the making of dresses.

par-a-med-ic n. A person trained to give emergency medical treatment until a doctor is available.

par-am-ne-sia n. The illusion of remembering things that have not yet been experienced.

par-a-mount adj. To be superior to all others in one's rank, importance, and power. **paramountly** adv.

par-a-mour n. An unlawful lover.

pa-rang n. A type of knife that is large and heavy.

par-a-noi-a n. Mental insanity marked by systematic delusions of persecution or grandeur.

par-a-noid adj. To be marked by paranoia.

par-a-nor-mal adj. To be supernatural in character. **paranormally** adv.

par-a-pet n. A type of covering or wall that is used to protect the soldiers from the attacks of the enemy in front of them.

par-a-pher-na-lia n. Personal effects or belongings; the apparatus or articles used in some activities; equipment.

par-a-phrase v. To put something written or spoken into different words while retaining the same meaning.

par-a-phras-tic adj. To be making or forming a paraphrase.

par-a-ple-gi-a n. The paralysis of the lower trunk and of both legs.

par-a-site n., Biol. An organism which lives, grows, feeds, and takes shelter in or on another organism; a person depending entirely on another without providing something in return.

par-a-sit-i-cide n. A type of agent that is

used to destroy parasites.

par-a-si-tize *v.* To live upon another object as a parasite.

par-a-sol *n.* A small umbrella used as protection from the sun.

par-a-thi-on *n.* A type of insecticide that is very poisonous.

par-a-thy-roid gland *n.* The four glands which are located in or near the thyroid gland and are used for the control of calcium in the blood.

par-a-troops *pl., n.* Troops which are equipped and trained to parachute behind enemy lines. **paratrooper** *n.*

par-a-ty-phoid *n.* A type of very infectious bacterial disease that has symptoms which are like those of typhoid fever.

par-boil *v.* To precook something in boiling water.

par-cel *n.* A wrapped package; a bundle; a portion or plat of land. **parcel** *v.*

parch *v.* To become very dry from intense heat; to become dry from thirst or the lack of water.

parch-ment *n.* Goatskin or sheepskin prepared with a pumice stone and used as a material for writing or drawing.

par-don *v.* To forgive someone for an offense. In law, to allow a convicted person freedom from the penalties of an office or crime. **pardonable** *adj.*, **pardonably** *adv.*, **pardon** *n.*

pare *v.* To cut away or remove the outer surface gradually. **parer** *n.*

par-e-go-ric *n.* A medication used to relieve stomach pains.

par-ent *n.* A mother or father; a forefather; an ancestor; a source; a cause. **parenthood** *n.*, **parental** *adj.*

par-ent-age *n.* The origin or birth of someone.

par-en-ter-al *adj.* To be introduced into the body by means other than the digestive tract. **parenterally** *adv.*

pa-ren-the-sis *n., pl.* **-ses** One of a pair of curved lines () used to enclose a qualifying or explanatory remark.

pa-re-sis *n.* A type of paralysis that is incomplete and affecting only movement. **paretic** *adj.*

par-fleche *n.* The hide of an animal that has been dried upon a frame, such as the buffalo.

par-get *v.* To cover something with plaster.

pa-ri-ah *n.* A person who is thought of as an outcast.

pa-ri-e-tal *adj.* To be referring to the two bones of the skull which form the side and the top.

par-ing *n.* The action of cutting or of paring a piece of a vegetable off, such as with a potatoe.

par-ish *n.* In association with the Roman Catholic Church, the district under the charge of a priest; the members of a parish. **parishioner** *n.*

par-i-ty *n.* The number which is used to state the fact of having borne children.

park *n.* A tract of land used for recrea-

tion. *v.* To leave something temporarily in a parking garage or lot, as a car. **parker** *n.*

par-ka *n.* A type of cloth jacket with an attached hood.

park-ing lot *n.* A cleared area that is used for the storage and parking of cars, such as at a mall.

Par-kin-son's disease *n., Pathol.* A progressive disease marked by partial facial paralysis, muscular tremor, weakness, and impaired muscular control.

park-way *n.* A type of thoroughfare that is lined with trees.

par-lia-ment *n.* The assembly which constitutes the lawmaking body of various countries, as the United Kingdom.

par-lia-men-ta-ry *adj.* To be relating or pertaining to a parliament.

par-lor *n.* A room for entertaining visitors or guests; a business offering a personal service, as beauty parlor, ice cream parlor, or funeral parlor.

par-lor car *n.* A type of railroad car that requires an extra fare but containing individual cars.

par-lor-maid *n.* A person who is employed as a maid to take care of a parlor.

par-lous *adj.* To be dangerous; clever.

pa-ro-chi-al *adj.* Belonging to a local parish; having to do with a parish.

pa-ro-chi-al-ism *n.* A condition or state of being parochial.

pa-ro-chi-al school *n.* A type of school which is maintained by the parish.

par-o-dy *n., pl.* **-ies** A composition, song, or poem which mimics another in a ridiculous way.

pa-rol *n.* An oral statement.

pa-role *n.* The conditional release of a prisoner which occurs before his sentence expires. **parole** *v. & adj.*

pa-rot-id gland *n.* A type of salivary gland that is located in front of each ear.

pa-rot-i-di-tis *n.* The swelling and inflammation of the parotid glands.

par-ox-ysm *n.* A violent attack or outburst; a spasm.

par-quet *n.* A main floor of the theater which will extend back from the orchestra pit.

par-quet cir-cle *n.* Those seats which are located at the rear of the main floor in a theater.

parr *n.* A type of salmon when it is young and has not yet entered the salt waters.

par-ri-cide *n.* A person who murders his mother or father; the crime of murdering one's parents. **-al** *adj.*

par-rot *n.*

A brightly colored, semitropical bird with a strong, hooked bill. *v.* To imitate or repeat.

par-rot-fish *n.* A type of fish that is

tropical and having bright colors.

par-ry v. To avoid something; to turnaside. **parry** n.

parse v. To identify the parts of speech in a sentence and to indicate their relationship to each other.

par-si-mo-ny n. Extreme reluctance to use one's resources or to spend money. **-ious** adj., **-iously** adv.

pars-ley n. An herb with curly leaves which is used for seasoning and garnishing.

pars-nip n. A plant from the carrot family cultivated for its long, edible root.

par-son n. A pastor or clergyman.

parsonage n. The home provided by a church for its parson.

part n. A segment, portion, or division of a whole; a component for a machine; the role of a character, as in a play; the line which forms where the hair is parted by combing or brushing. v. To leave or go away from; to be separated into pieces; to give up control or possession.

par-take v. To have a share or part; to take; to take a part in something.

par-tial adj. Incomplete; inclined to favor one side more than the other. **partiality** n., **partially** adv.

par-tic-i-pate v. To join in or share; to take part. **participant, participation, participator** n., **participatory** adj.

par-ti-cle n. A very small piece of solid matter. Gram. A group of words, such as articles, prepositions, and conjunctions which convey very little meaning but help to connect, specify, or limit the meanings of other words.

par-tic-u-lar adj. Having to do with a specific person, group, thing, or category; noteworthy; precise. **particularly** adv.

part-ing n. A division; a separation; the place where a division or separation occurs. adj. Done, given, or said on departing.

par-ti-tion n. A separation or division. v. To divide.

part-ner n. One who shares something with another.

part-ner-ship n. Two or more persons who run a business together and share in the profits and losses.

par-tridge n., pl. **partridges**

A plump or stout-bodied game bird.

par-ty n., pl. **-ies** A group of persons who gather for pleasure or entertainment; a group of persons associated together for a common purpose; a group which unites to promote or maintain a policy, a cause, or other purposes, as a political group. In law, a person or group of people involved in a legal proceeding.

pass v. To proceed; to move; to transfer; to go away or come to an end; to get through a course, trial or test; to approve; to vote for; to give as an opinion or judgment; to hit or throw a ball to another player. n. A ticket or note that allows a person to come and go freely. **come to pass** To happen. **pass away** To die or cease to live. **pass over** To leave out, to ignore.

pas-sage n. The act of going, proceeding, or passing; the enactment by a legislature of a bill into law; a small portion or part of a whole book or speech; something, as a path or channel, through, over or along which something else may pass.

pas-sen-ger n. One who travels in a vehicle, car, plane, boat, or other conveyance.

pas-sion n. A powerful feeling; lust; sexual desire; an outburst of strong feeling; violence or anger. **Passion** The suffering of Christ which followed the Last Supper to the time of his death. **passionless, passionate** adj.

pas-sive adj. Not working, acting, or operating; inactive; acted upon, influenced, or affected by something external. Gram. Designating the form of a verb which indicates the subject is receiving the action. **passively** adv., **passivity, passiveness** n.

Pass-o-ver n. The Jewish holiday which commemorates the Exodus from Egypt.

pass-port n. An official permission issued to a person allowing him to travel out of this country and to return; a document of identification.

pass-word n. A secret word allowing a person to prove authorization to pass or enter.

past adj. Having to do with or existing at a former time. n. Before the present time; a person's history or background. adv. To go by. prep. After; beyond in time; beyond the power, reach, or influence.

paste n. A mixture usually made from water and flour, used to stick things together; dough used in making pastry; a brilliant glass used in imitating precious stones. **paste** v.

pas-tel n. A crayon made of ground pigments; a drawing made with crayons of this kind. adj. Pale and light in color or shade.

Pasteur, Louis n. (1822-1895.) A French scientist who discovered a treatment for rabies and for killing bacteria in milk.

pas-teur-i-za-tion n. The process of killing disease producing microorganisms by heating the liquid to a high temperature for a period of time.

pas-time n. Spending spare time in a pleasant way; a diversion.

pas-tor n. A Christian clergyman in charge of a church or congregation.

pas-tor-al adj. Referring to the duties of a pastor; pertaining to life in the country; rural or rustic. n. A poem dealing with country life.

past par·ti·ci·ple *n.* A participle used with reference to actions and conditions in the past.

pas·try *n.* Food made with dough or having a crust made of dough, as pies, tarts, or other desserts.

pas·ture *n.* An area for grazing of domestic animals. **pastured, pasturing** *v.,* **pasturage, pasturer** *n.*

pat *v.* To tap lightly with something flat. *n.* A soft, caressing stroke.

patch *n.* A piece of fabric used to repair a weakened or torn area in a garment; a piece of cloth with an insignia which represents an accomplishment. *v.* To repair or put together hastily. **patchy, patchable** *adj.,* **patcher** *n.*

pat·ent *n.* A governmental protection assuring an inventor the exclusive right of manufacturing, using, exploiting, and selling an invention. *adj.* Evident; obvious. **patentee, patency** *n.,* **patently** *adv.*

pa·ter·nal *adj.* Relating to or characteristic of a father; inherited from a father. **paternally** *adv.,* **paternalism** *n.*

path *n.* A track or course; a route; a course of action or life.

pa·thet·ic *adj.* Arousing pity, tenderness, or sympathy. **pathetically** *adv.*

pa·thol·o·gy *n.* The science that deals with facts about diseases, their nature and causes. **pathologic, pathological** *adj.,* **pathologist** *n.*

pa·thos *n.* A quality in a person that evokes sadness or pity.

pa·tience *n.* The quality, state, or fact of being patient; the ability to be patient.

pa·tient *adj.* Demonstrating uncomplaining endurance under distress. *n.* A person under medical care. **patiently** *adv.*

pa·ti·o *n.* An area attached to a house, used for enjoyment and entertainment.

pa·tri·arch *n.* The leader of a tribe or family who rules by paternal right; a very old and revered man. **patriarchal** *adj.,* **patriarchy** *n.*

pa·tri·ot *n.* A person who loves and defends his country. **patriotic** *adj.,* **patriotically** *adv.,* **patriotism** *n.*

pa·trol *n.* Walking around an area for the purpose of maintaining or observing security; a person or group carrying out this action. **patrol** *v.*

pa·tron *n.* A person who fosters, protects, or supports some person, enterprise, or thing; a regular customer.

pat·sy *n., pl.* **-ies** *Slang* A person who is taken advantage of.

pat·tern *n.* Anything designed or shaped to serve as a guide in making something else; a sample. *v.* To make according to a pattern.

pat·ty *n., pl.* **-ies** A small, flat piece of chopped meat.

pau·per *n.* A very poor person who depends on charity. **pauperism** *n.,* **pauperize** *v.*

pause *v.* To linger, hesitate, or stop for a time. **pause** *n.*

pave *v.* To surface with gravel, concrete, asphalt, or other material.

pave·ment *n.* A surface that has been paved.

pa·vil·ion *n.* A large, roofed structure used for shelter.

paw *n.* The foot of an animal. *v.* To handle clumsily or rudely.

pawn *n.* Something given as security for a loan; a hostage; a chessman of little value. **pawn** *v.*

pawn·broker *n.* A person who lends money on pledged personal property.

pay *v.* To give a person what is due for a debt, purchase, or work completed; to compensate; to suffer the consequences.

pay·ment *n.* The act of paying.

pay·roll *n.* The amount of money to be paid to a list of employees.

pea *n.* A round edible seed contained in a pod and grown on a vine.

peace *n.* A state of physical or mental tranquillity; calm; serenity; the absence of war; the state of harmony between people. **peaceable, peaceful** *adj.,* **peaceably, -fully** *adv.*

peach *n.* A round, sweet, juicy fruit having a thin, downy skin, a pulpy yellow flesh, and a hard, rough single seed.

pea·cock *n.*

A male bird with brilliant blue or green plumage and a long iridescent tail that fans out to approximately six feet.

peak *n.* A projecting edge or point; the summit of a mountain; the top. *v.* To bring to the maximum.

peal *n.* The ring of bells; the long, loud sound of thunder or laughter. *v.* To ring.

pea·nut *n.* A nut-like seed which ripens underground; the plant bearing this nut.

pear *n.* A juicy, edible fruit which grows on a tree.

pearl *n.* A smooth, rounded deposit formed around a grain of sand in the shell of various mollusks, especially the oyster; anything which is precious, rare, or fine. **pearly** *adj.*

peas·ant *n.* A farmhand or rustic workman; an uneducated person of the lowest class. *Slang* Uneducated or uncouth.

peat *n.* The black substance formed when plants begin to decay in wet ground, as bogs. **peaty** *adj.*

peat moss *n.* A moss which grows in very wet areas, used as plant food and mulch.

peb·ble *n.* A small, smooth stone. *v.* To treat, as to give a rough texture.

pe·can *n.* A large tree of the central and southern United States with an edible oval, thin-shelled nut.

peck *v.* To strike with the beak; to eat

without any appetite, taking only small bites. *n.* A measure which equals 1/4 of a bushel.

pec-tin *n.* A complex carbohydrate found in ripe fruits and used in making jelly. **pectic** *adj.*

pe-cu-liar *adj.* Odd; strange. **peculiarity** *n.,* **peculiarly** *adv.*

ped-al *n.* A lever usually operated by the foot. **pedal** *v.*

ped-dle *v.* To travel around in an attempt to sell merchandise.

ped-es-tal *n.* A support or base for a statue. **to put on a pedestal** To hold something in high respect.

pe-des-tri-an *n.* A person traveling by foot.

pe-di-at-rics *n.* The branch of medicine dealing with the care of children and infants. **pediatric** *adj.,* **pediatrician** *n.*

ped-i-cure *n.* The cosmetic care of the toenails and feet. **pedicurist** *n.*

ped-i-gree *n.* A line of ancestors, especially of an animal of pure breed.

ped-i-ment *n.* A broad, triangular architectural or decorative part above a door.

pe-dom-e-ter *n.* An instrument which indicates the number of miles one has walked.

pe-dun-cle *n., Biol.* A stalk-like support in some plants and animals.

peek *v.* To look shyly or quickly from a place of hiding; to glance. **peek** *n.*

peel *n.* The natural rind or skin of a fruit. *v.* To pull or strip the skin or bark off; to remove in thin layers. *Slang* To undress. **peeler** *n.*

peen *n.* The ball-shaped end of a hammer opposite the flat, striking surface.

peep *v.* To utter a very small and weak sound, as of a young bird.

peer *v.* To look searchingly; to come partially into one's view. *n.* An equal; a member of the British nobility, as a duke or earl.

pee-vish *adj.* Irritable in mood; cross. **peevishly** *adv.,* **peevishness** *n.*

peg *n.* A small pin, usually of wood or metal; a projecting pin on which something may be hung. *Slang* An artificial leg, often made of wood. **peg** *v.*

pei-gnoir *n.* A woman's loose fitting dressing gown.

pe-koe *n.* A superior black tea made from young or small leaves.

pel-i-can *n.* A large, web-footed bird with a large pouch under the lower bill for the temporary storage of fish.

pel-let *n.* A small round ball made from paper or wax; a small bullet or shot.

pelt *n.* The skin of an animal with the fur.

pel-vis *n., pl.* **-vises** *or* **-ves** The structure of the vertebrate skeleton which rests on the lower limbs, supporting the spinal column.

pen *n.* An instrument used for writing.

pe-nal *adj.* Of or pertaining to punishment or penalties.

pen-al-ty *n., pl.* **-ties.** The legal punishment for an offense or crime; something which is forfeited when a person fails to meet a commitment; in sports, a punishment or handicap imposed for breaking a rule.

pen-ance *n.* A voluntary act to show sorrow or repentance for sin.

pen-cil *n.* A writing or drawing implement made from graphite. *v.* To make, write, or draw with a pencil.

pen-dant *or* **pen-dent** *n.* An ornament which hangs from a necklace.

pend-ing *adj.* Not yet decided; imminent. *prep.* During; until.

pen-du-lous *adj.* Hanging downward so as to swing; wavering.

pen-du-lum *n.* A suspended object free to swing back and forth.

pen-e-trate *v.* To force a way through or into; to pierce; to enter; to pass through something. **penetrable, penetrating** *adj.,* **penetration** *n.*

pen-guin *n.* A web-footed, flightless, marine bird of the southern hemisphere.

pen-i-cil-lin *n.* A powerful antibiotic derived from mold and used to treat certain types of bacterial infections.

pen-in-su-la *n.* A piece of land projecting into water from a larger land mass. **peninsular** *adj.*

pe-nis *n., pl.* **-nises** *or* **-nes** The male sex organ; the male organ through which urine leaves the body.

pen-i-tent *adj.* Having a feeling of guilt or remorse for one's sins or misdeeds; sorry. **penitence** *n.,* **penitential** *adj.*

Penn-syl-va-nia *n.* A state located in the eastern part of the United States.

pen-ny *n., pl.* **-ies** A United States coin worth one cent ($.01).

pen-sion *n.* The amount of money a person receives regularly after retirement. **pensioner** *n.*

pen-sive *adj.* Involved in serious, quiet reflection; causing melancholy thought. **pensively** *adv.,* **-ness** *n.*

pen-ta-gon *n.*

Any object or building having five sides and five interior angles. **Pentagon** The five-sided office building in Arlington, Va. which houses the Defense Department.

Pen-te-cost *n.* The seventh Sunday after Easter, celebrated by Christians as commemoration of the descent of the Holy Ghost on the Apostles. **-al** *adj.*

pent-house *n.* An apartment built on the roof of a building.

pe-on *n.* A servant; a person engaged in menial work. **peonage** *n.*

pe-o-ny *n., pl.* **-nies** A plant with a large, fragrant red, white, or pink flower.

peo-ple *n., pl.* **people** Human beings; a body of persons living in the same country, under the same government, and speaking the same language; one's relatives or family. **people** *v.*

pep-per *n.* A strong, aromatic condiment. *v.* To pelt or sprinkle.

pep-tic *adj.* Pertaining to or aiding digestion.

per an-num *adv.* For, by, or in each year; annually.

per-cale *n.* A closely woven cotton fabric.

per--cap-i-ta *adj. & adv., Latin* Of each individual.

per-ceive *v.* To become aware of by the senses; to understand; to feel or observe. **perceivable** *adj.*, **-ably** *adv.*

per-cent-age *n.* The rate per hundred; a part or proportion in relation to a whole. *Slang* Profit; advantage.

per-cept *n.* A mental impression of something perceived; the immediate knowledge obtained from perceiving.

perch *n.* A place on which birds rest or alight; any place for standing or sitting; a small, edible freshwater fish having tender white meat.

per-cip-i-ent *adj.* Having the power of perception. **percipience, percipiency** *n.*

per-co-late *v.* To pass or cause to pass through a porous substance; to filter. **percolation, percolator** *n.*

per-cus-sion *n.* The sharp striking together of one body against another; the striking of a cap in a firearm. *Music.* An instrument which makes music when it is struck, as a drum or cymbal.

per-en-ni-al *adj.* Lasting from year to year; perpetual. *n.* A plant which lives through the winter and blooms again in the spring. **perennially** *adv.*

per-fect *adj.* Having no defect or fault; flawless; accurate; absolute. *v.* To make perfect. **-ly** *adv.*, **perfectness** *n.*

per-form *v.* To execute or carry out an action; to act or function in a certain way; to act; to give a performance or exhibition. **performable** *adj.*, **performer, performance** *n.*

per-fume *n.* A fragrant substance which emits a pleasant scent; one distilled from flowers. **perfume** *v.*

per-haps *adv.* Possibly; maybe; not sure.

per-i-gee *n.* The point of an orbit when a satellite of the earth is closest to the earth; the lowest part of an orbit.

per-il *n.* A source of danger; exposure to the chance of injury; danger. **perilous** *adj.*, **perilously** *adv.*

pe-ri-od *n.* An interval of time marked by certain conditions; an interval of time that is regarded as a phase in development; menstruation; the punctuation mark (.) which indicates the end of a sentence or an abbreviation.

pe-riph-er-y *n., pl.* **-ies** The outer part, boundary, or surface. **peripheral** *adj.*

per-ish *v.* To ruin or spoil; to suffer an untimely or violent death.

per-i-win-kle *n.* Any of several edible marine snails; a trailing evergreen plant with blue and sometimes white flowers.

per-jure *v.* To give false testimony while under oath. **perjury** *n.*

per-ma-nent *adj.* Continuing in the same state; lasting indefinitely; enduring. *n.* A hair wave which gives long lasting curls or body to the hair. **permanence, permanency** *n.*, **-ly** *adv.*

per-me-ate *v.* To spread through; to pervade; to pass through the pores. **permeation** *n.* **permeable** *adj.*

per-mis-sion *n.* The act of permitting something; consent.

per-mit *v.* To consent to; to allow. *n.* An official document giving permission for a specific activity.

per-ni-cious *adj.* Very harmful; malicious. **perniciously** *adv.*, **-ness** *n.*

per-ox-ide *n., Chem.* Oxide containing the highest proportion of oxygen for a given series; a chemical used with other ingredients to bleach the hair.

per-pen-dic-u-lar *adj.* Being at right angles to the plane of the horizon. *Math.* Meeting a plane or given line at right angles. **perpendicular, perpendicularity** *n.*, **-ly** *adv.*

per-pe-trate *v.* To perform; to commit; to be guilty. **petration, perpetrator** *n.*

per-pet-u-al *adj.* Lasting or continuing forever or an unlimited time. **perpetually** *adv.*

per-plex *v.* To confuse or be confused; to make complicated. **perplexing** *adj.*, **perplexingly, -edly** *adv.*, **perplexity** *n.*

per-se-cute *v.* To harass or annoy persistently; to oppress because of one's religion, beliefs, or race. **persecution, persecutor** *n.*, **persecutive** *adj.*

per-se-vere *v.* To persist in any purpose or idea; to strive in spite of difficulties or obstacles. **perseverance** *n.*, **perseveringly** *adv.*

per-sim-mon *n.* A tree having reddish orange, edible fruit.

per-sist *v.* To continue firmly despite obstacles; to endure. **persistence, persistency** *n.*, **-ent** *adj.*, **-ently** *adv.*

per-son *n.* A human being; an individual; the personality of a human being. *Law* Any human being, corporation, or other entity having legal rights and duties.

per-son-al *adj.* Belonging to a person or persons; of the body or person; relating to oneself; done by oneself.

per-son-i-fy *v.* To think of or represent as having human qualities or life; to be a symbol of. **personifier, -ication** *n.*

per-son-nel *n.* The body of people working for a business or service.

per-spec-tive *n.*

A painting or drawing technique in which objects seem to have depth and distance.

per-spi-ra-tion *n.* The salty fluid excreted from the body by the sweat glands.

per-spire *v.* To give off perspiration.

per-suade *v.* To cause to convince or believe by means of reasoning or argument. **persuader, persuasiveness** *n.*, **persuasive** *adj.*

per-tain *v.* To relate to; to refer to; to belong as a function, adjunct or quality; to be appropriate or fitting.

per-ti-na-cious *adj.* Adhering firmly to an opinion, belief, or purpose; stubbornly persistent. **pertinaciously** *adv.*, **pertinacity** *n.*

per-ti-nent *adj.* Relating to the matter being discussed.

per-turb *v.* To disturb, make anxious, or make uneasy; to cause confusion. **perturbation** *n.*

per-vade *v.* To spread through every part of something; to permeate. **pervasive** *adj.*

per-ver-sion *n.* The act of being led away from the accepted course; a deviant form of sexual behavior.

per-vert *v.* To lead away from the proper cause; to use in an improper way. *n.* A person practicing or characterized by sexual perversion. **perverted,** **pervertible** *adj.*

pes-si-mism *n.* The tendency to take a gloomy view of affairs or situations and to anticipate the worst. **pessimist** *n.*, **pessimistic** *adj.*, **pessimistically** *adv.*

pest *n.* A person or thing which is a nuisance; an annoying person or thing; a destructive insect, plant, or animal.

pes-ter *v.* To harass with persistent annoyance; to bother.

pes-ti-cide *n.* A chemical substance used to destroy rodents, insects, and pests. **pesticidal** *adj.*

pes-ti-lence *n.* A widespread and often fatal infectious disease, as bubonic plague or cholera.

pet *n.* An animal, bird, or fish one keeps for companionship; any favorite or treasured thing. *adj.* Treated or tamed as a pet. *v.* To stroke or caress gently. *Slang* To make love by fondling and caressing.

pet-al *n., Bot.* One of the leaf-like parts of a flower.

pe-tite *adj.* Small in size; little. **-ness** *n.*

pet-it four *n., pl.* **petits fours** *or* **petit fours** A small decorated cake.

pe-ti-tion *n.* A solemn request or prayer; a formal written request addressed to a group or person in authority.

pet-ri-fy *v.* To convert into a stony mass; to make fixed or immobilize, as in the face of danger or surprise. **petrification** *n.*, **petrifactive** *adj.*

pe-tro-le-um *n.* An oily, thick liquid which develops naturally below the ground surface, used in products such as gasoline, fuel oil, and kerosene.

pet-ti-coat *n.* A woman's skirt-like garment worn as an underskirt.

pet-ty *adj.* To have little importance or value; insignificant; trivial; having a low position or rank; minor; small-minded. **pettiness** *n.*

pet-ty cash *n.* Cash held on hand for minor bills or expenditures.

pe-tu-nia *n.* A widely grown tropical plant having a funnel-shaped flower in various colors.

pew *n.* A row of bench-like seats for seating people in church.

pew-ter *n.* An alloy of tin with copper, silver-gray in color and used for tableware and kitchen utensils.

pfen-nig *n., pl.* **-nigs** *or* **-nige** A small coin of Germany, equal to one hundredth of a Deutschemark.

phal-lus *n., pl.* **-li** *or* **-luses** A representation of the penis, often as a symbol of generative power. **phallic** *adj.*

phan-tasm *n.* The creation of an imaginary image; a fantasy; a phantom. **phantasmal, phantasmic** *adj.*

phan-tom *n.* Something which exists but has no physical reality; a ghost.

phar-ma-ceu-ti-cal *adj.* Pertaining or relating to a pharmacy or pharmacists.

phar-ma-cy *n., pl.* **-cies.** A place of business which specializes in preparing, identifying, and disbursing drugs; a drugstore.

phar-ynx *n., pl.* **-ynges** *or* **-ynxes.** The part of the throat located between the palate and the esophagus, serving as a passage for air and food. **pharyngeal** *adj.*

phase *n.* Any decisive stage in development or growth. *Astron.* One of the forms or appearances of a planet.

pheas-ant *n.* A long-tailed game bird noted for the beautiful plumage of the male.

phe-nom-e-non *n., pl.* **-na** *or* **-nons.** Something that can be observed or perceived; a rare occurrence. *Slang* An outstanding person with remarkable power, ability, or talent.

phi-lan-der *v.* To make love without feeling or serious intentions. **-er** *n.*

phi-lat-e-ly *n.* The collection and study of postage stamps and postmarked material. **philatelic** *adj.*, **philatelist** *n.*

phil-har-mon-ic *adj.* Pertaining to a symphony orchestra. **philharmonic** *n.*

phi-los-o-phy *n., pl.* **-ies** The logical study of the nature and source of human knowledge or human values; the set of values, opinions, and ideas of a group or individual.

pho-bi-a *n.* A compulsive fear of a specified situation or object.

phone *n., Slang* A telephone. *v.* To call or communicate by telephone.

phon-ic *adj.* Pertaining to sounds in speech; using the same symbol for each sound. **-ally** *adv.*, **phonetics** *n.*

pho-no-graph *n.* A machine which uses a needle to reproduce sound from a grooved disc or record.

pho-ny *adj. Informal* Counterfeit; fraudulent; not real or genuine.

phos-phate *n., Chem.* A salt or phosphoric acid which contains mostly phosphorus and oxygen.

phos-pho-rus *n.* A highly flammable, poisonous, nonmetallic element used in safety matches, symbolized by P.

pho-to *n. Slang* A photograph.

pho-to-cop-y *v.* To reproduce printed material using a photographic process.

photocopier, photocopy *n.*

pho-to-graph *n.* A picture or image recorded by a camera and then reproduced on a photosensitive surface. photography *n.*

pho-to-stat *n.* A trademark for a camera designed to reproduce documents and graphic material.

pho-to-syn-the-sis *n.*, *Biochem.* The chemical process by which plants use light to change carbon dioxide and water into carbohydrates, releasing oxygen as a by-product.

photosynthesize *v.*, photosynthetic *adj.*

phrase *n.*, *Gram.* A brief or concise expression which does not contain a predicate.

phre-nol-o-gy *n.* The study of or the theory that the conformation of the human skull indicates the degree of intelligence and character.

phys-i-cal *adj.* Relating to the human body apart from the mind or emotions; pertaining to material rather than imaginary subjects. *n.* A medical exam to determine a person's physical condition. physically *adv.*

phy-si-cian *n.* A person licensed to practice medicine.

phys-ics *n.* The scientific study which deals with energy, matter, motion, and related areas of science.

phys-i-ol-o-gy *n.*, *pl.* -ies The scientific study of living animals, plants, and their activities and functions; the vital functions and processes of an organism. physiological, physiologic *adj.*, physiologist *n.*

phys-i-o-ther-a-py *n.* The treatment of disease or physical defects by the use of heat and massage.

pi-an-o *n.* A musical instrument with a manual keyboard and felt-covered hammers which produce musical tones when struck upon steel wires.

pi-az-za *n.* A public square or an open area in an Italian town or city.

pi-ca *n.* A printer's type size of 12 points, equal to about 1/6 inch; a typewriter type size with 10 characters to an inch.

pic-co-lo *n.* A small flute with a brilliant sound pitched an octave above the flute.

pick *v.* To select or choose from a number or group; to remove the outer area of something with the fingers or a pointed instrument; to remove by tearing away little by little; to open a lock without using a key; to harass or tease someone or something; to pluck a musical instrument. *n.* A pointed metal tool sharpened at both ends, used to break up hard surfaces. *Music* A small flat piece of plastic or of bone, used to pluck or strum the strings of an instrument, as a guitar or banjo.

pick-et *n.* A pointed stake driven into the ground as support for a fence; a person positioned outside of a place of employment during a strike. *Mil.* A soldier posted to guard a camp.

pick-le *n.* A cucumber preserved in a solution of brine or vinegar. *Slang* A troublesome situation.

pick-pock-et *n.* A person who steals from another's purse or pocket.

pic-nic *n.* An outdoor social gathering where food is provided usually by the people attending. picnicker *n.*

pic-ture *n.* A visual representation on a surface, which is printed, drawn or photographed; the mental image or impression of an event or situation.

piece *n.* An element, unit, or part of a whole; a musical or literary work. *Slang* A firearm.

piecemeal *adv.* Gradually, bit by bit.

pier *n.* A structure extending into the water, used to secure, protect, and provide access to vessels.

pierce *v.* To penetrate or make a hole in something; to force into or through.

piercing *adj.*

Pierce, Franklin *n.* The 14th president of the United States, from 1853-1857.

pi-e-ty *n.*, *pl.* -ties. Devoutness toward God.

pig *n.*

A cloven-hoofed mammal with short legs, bristly hair, and a snout for rooting; the edible meat of a pig; pork. *Slang* A greedy or gross person.

pi-geon *n.* A bird with short legs, a sturdy body, and a small head.

pig-gy-back *adv.* Carried on the back and shoulders. piggyback *adj.*

pig-head-ed *adj.* Stubborn. -ly *adv.*

pig-ment *n.* A material used as coloring matter, suitable for making paint. *Biol.* Any substance such as melanin and chlorophyll which imparts color to vegetable tissue or animals.

pig-skin *n.* Something made from the skin of a pig. *Slang* A football.

pike *n.* A long pole with a sharp, pointed steel head; a large edible fresh-water fish with a long snout and a slender body. *Slang* A turnpike or a major highway.

pile *n.* A quantity of anything thrown in a heap; a massive or very large building or a group of buildings.

pil-fer *v.* To steal in little quantities; to steal items of little value. pilferage *n.*

pil-grim *n.* A person who travels to a sacred place; a wanderer. Pilgrims The English Puritans who founded the Plymouth colony in New England in the year 1620.

pill *n.* A small tablet containing medicine which is taken by mouth; someone or something which is disagreeable but must be dealt with. the pill *Slang* An oral contraceptive drug taken by women.

pil-lar *n.* A freestanding column which serves as a support.

pil-low *n.* A cloth case filled with feathers or other soft material, used to cushion the head during sleep.

pi-lot *n.* A person who is licensed to operate an aircraft; someone who is trained and licensed to guide ships in and out of port. *v.* To act or serve as a pilot.

pi-men-to *n.* A sweet pepper used as a stuffing for olives or as a relish.

pimp *n.* A person who arranges customers for prostitutes in exchange for a share of their money.

pim-ple *n.* A small eruption of the skin, having an inflamed base. **pimpled, pimply** *adj.*

pin *n.* A small, stiff piece of wire with a blunt head and a sharp point, used to fasten something, usually temporarily; one of the rounded wooden clubs serving as the target in bowling.

pin-a-fore *n.* A sleeveless apron-like garment.

pin-cer *n.* An implement having two handles and a pair of jaws working on a pivot, used to hold objects.

pinch *v.* To squeeze between a finger and thumb causing pain or discomfort; to be miserly. *n.* The small amount that can be held between the thumb and forefinger.

pine *n., Bot.* Any of various cone-bearing evergreen trees; the wood of such a tree.

pine-ap-ple *n.*

A tropical American plant with spiny, curved leaves bearing a large edible fruit. *Slang* A hand grenade.

pine-cone *n.*

The cone of a pinetree.

pink *n.* Any of various plants related to the carnation, having fragrant flowers; a light or pale hue of crimson; the highest or best possible degree.

pink-eye *n., Pathol.* An acute, contagious conjunctivitis of the eye.

pin-na-cle *n.* The highest peak; a sharp point; a pointed summit.

pi-noch-le *or* **pi-noc-le** *n.* A card game for two, three, or four people, played with a double deck of 48 cards.

pint *n.* A liquid or dry measurement equal to half of a quart or two cups.

pin-to *n., pl.* **-tos** *or* **-toes** A horse with spots; a spotted bean of the southwestern United States.

pin-wheel *n.* A toy with revolving paper or plastic fastened to a stick; a fireworks display featuring a revolving wheel of colored flames.

pin-worm *n.* A nematode parasite which infests the human intestines and rectum.

pi-o-neer *n.* One of the first settlers of a new region or country; the first developer or investigator in a new

field of enterprise, research, or other endeavor.

pi-ous *adj.* Reverently religious; devout. **piously** *adv.,* **piousness** *n.*

pipe *n.* A hollow cylinder for conveying fluids; a small bowl with a hollow stem for smoking tobacco. *Music* A tubular flute.

pipe-line *n.* A pipe used to transfer gas or oil over long distances; a means for conveying information.

pique *n.* A feeling of resentment or irritation.

pi-rate *n.* A robber of the high seas. *Slang* Someone who uses or reproduces someone else's work without authorization. **piracy** *n.,* **pirate** *v.,* **piratical** *adj.*

Pis-ces *n.* The 12th sign of the zodiac; one born between February 19-March 20.

pis-ta-chi-o *n.* A small tree of western Asia; the edible fruit from this tree.

pis-til *n.* The seed-producing female reproductive organ of a flower.

pis-tol *n.* A small hand-held firearm.

pis-ton *n., Mech.* A solid cylinder fitted into a larger cylinder, moving back and forth under liquid pressure.

pit *n.* An artificial or manmade hole in the ground; a slight indentation in the skin, as a scar from the chicken pox; an area for refueling or repair at a car race; the stone in the middle of some fruit, as peaches. *the pits* Anything at its worst.

pitch *n.* A thick, sticky, dark substance which is the residue of the distillation of petroleum or coal tar; the degree of slope of an incline; the property of a musical tone which makes it high or low. *v.* To cover with pitch; to throw; to throw out; to slope.

pitch--black *adj.* Extremely dark.

pitch-er *n.* The person who throws the ball to the batter; a container for holding and pouring liquids.

pitch-fork *n.* A large fork with a wide prong span, used as a garden or farm tool.

pith *n., Bot.* The sponge-like soft tissue at the center of the branch or stem of many plants.

pit-i-ful *adj.* Evoking or meriting pity. **pitifully** *adv.*

pit-y *n., pl.* **-ies.** A feeling of compassion or sorrow for another's misfortune.

piv-ot *n.* A thing or person upon which development, direction, or effect depends. *v.* To turn.

piz-za *n.* An Italian food consisting of a doughy crust covered with tomato sauce, cheese, and other toppings and then baked.

pkg *abbr.* Package.

place *n.* A region; an area; a building or location used for a special purpose; the position of something in a series or sequence. *v.* To put in a particular order or place.

place-ment *n.* The act of being placed; a business or service which finds positions of employment for applicants.

pla-cen-ta *n., pl.* **-tas** *or* **-tae** *Anat.* The vascular, membranous structure which supplies a fetus with nourishment before its birth.

plague *n.* Anything that is troublesome. *Pathol.* A highly contagious and often fatal epidemic disease, as the bubonic plague.

plaid *n.* A rectangular wool cloth or garment, usually worn by men and women, having a crisscross or checkered design.

plain *adj.* Level; flat; clear; open, as in view; not rich or luxurious; not highly gifted or cultivated.
plainly *adv.,* **plainness** *n.*

plain-tiff *n.* A person who brings suit.

plan *n.* A scheme or method for achieving something; a drawing to show proportion and relationship to parts. *v.* To have in mind as an intention or purpose.

plane *n.* A tool for smoothing or leveling a wood surface. *Geom.* A surface as a straight line that joins any two points on it. *Slang* Airplane. **plane** *v.*

plan-et *n., Astron.* A celestial body which is illuminated by light from the star around which it revolves. **-ary** *adj.*

plan-e-tar-i-um *n., pl.* **-iums** *or* **-ia** A device for exhibiting celestial bodies as they exist at any time and for any place on earth.

plank *n.* A broad piece of wood; one of the issues or principles of a political platform.

plant *n.* A living organism belonging to the vegetable kingdom, having cellulose cell walls. *v.* To place a living organism in the ground for growing; to place so as to deceive or to spy.

plaque *n.* A flat piece, made from metal, porcelain, ivory, or other materials, engraved for mounting; the bacteria deposit which builds up on the teeth.

plas-ma *n.* The clear fluid part of blood, used for transfusions.

plas-ter-board *n.* A building material of layered gypsum bonded to outer layers of paper.

plas-tic *adj.* Pliable; capable of being molded. *n.* A synthetically made material which is molded and then hardened into objects.
plasticity *n.,* **plasticize** *v.*

plastic surgery *n.* Surgery dealing with the restoration or repair of deformed or destroyed parts of the body or skin.

plate *n.* A flat flexible, thin piece of material, as metal; a shallow, flat vessel made from glass, crockery, plastic, or other material from which food is served or eaten; a piece of plastic, metal, or vulcanite fitted to the mouth to hold one or more artificial teeth. *Baseball* The place or object marking home base. *v.* To cover something, as jewelry, with a thin layer of gold, silver, or other metal.

pla-teau *n.* An extensive level expanse of elevated land; a period or stage of stability.

plat-form *n.* Any elevated or raised surface used by speakers, or by other performers or for display purposes; a formal declaration of principles or policy of a political party.

plat-i-num *n.* A silver-white, metallic element which is corrosive-resistant, used in jewelry; symbolized by Pt.

Pla-to *n.* Greek philosopher.

pla-toon *n.* A military unit subdivision commanded by a lieutenant.

plat-ter *n.* A large, oblong, shallow dish for serving food.

plau-si-ble *adj.* Seeming to be probable; appearing to be trustworthy or believable.

play *v.* To amuse or entertain oneself, as in recreation; to take part in a game; to perform in a dramatic role; to perform with a musical instrument; in fishing, to allow a hooked fish to tire itself out; to pretend to do something. *n.* A dramatic presentation.

playful *adj.* Lightly humorous; full of high spirits.

playground *n.* The area set aside for children's recreation.

play--off *n.* A sports contest to break a tie; a series of games to decide the winner or championship.

pla-za *n.* An open-air marketplace or square; a shopping mall.

plea *n.* An urgent request. In law, an allegation made by either party in a law suit.

plea bargaining *v.* Making a pretrial agreement to plead guilty to a lesser charge if a more serious one will be dropped.

plead *v.* To argue for or against something in court; to ask earnestly.

pleas-ant *adj.* Giving or promoting the feeling of pleasure; very agreeable.
pleasantly *adv.,* **pleasantness** *n.*

please *v.* To make happy; to give pleasure; to be the will or wish of; to prefer.

pleas-ur-a-ble *adj.* Pleasant; gratifying.

pleas-ure *n.* A feeling of satisfaction or enjoyment; one's preference or wish.

pleat *n.* A fold in a cloth made by doubling the cloth back and fastening it down.

plebe *n.* A freshman or first year student at the United States Naval Academy.

pledge *n.* A solemn promise; a deposit of something as security for a loan; a promise to join a fraternity; a person who is pledged to join a fraternity. *v.* To promise or vow.

plen-ti-ful *adj.* Having great abundance.
plentifully *adv.* **plentifulness** *n.*

plen-ty *n.* An ample amount; prosperity or abundance.

pleu-ra *n., pl.* **pleurae** *Anat.* The membranous sac which envelops the lungs and provides a lining for the thoracic cavity.

pli-a-ble *adj.* Flexible; easily controlled or persuaded. **pliability,**
pliableness *n.,* **pliably** *adv.*

pli-ers *pl. n.* A pincers-like implement used for holding, bending, or cutting.

plight *n.* A distressing circumstance, situation, or condition.

plod *n.* To walk in a heavy, slow way.

plot *n.* A small piece of ground usually used for a special purpose; the main story line in a piece of fiction; a plan; an intrigue; a conspiracy. *v.* To represent something by using a map or chart; to scheme secretly. **plotter** *n.*

plow *n.* An implement for breaking up or turning over the soil. *v.* To dig out. *Slang* To hit with force.

pluck *v.* To remove by pulling out or off; to pull and release the strings on a musical instrument. *Slang* To swindle. **plucker** *n.*

plug *n.* Anything used to stop or close a hole or drain. *Electr.* A two-pronged device attached to a cord and used in a jack or socket to make an electrical connection. *Slang* To advertise favorably; to give a recommendation or a piece of publicity for someone.

plum *n.* A small tree bearing an edible fruit with a smooth skin and a single hard seed; the fruit from such a tree.

plum-age *n.* The feathers of a bird.

plumb *n.* A lead weight tied to the end of a string, used to test the exact perpendicular line of something.

plumb-er *n.* A person who repairs or installs plumbing in a home or business.

plumb-ing *n.* The profession or trade of a plumber; the connecting of pipes and fixtures used to carry water and waste.

plume *n.* A feather used as an ornament.

plun-der *v.* To deprive of goods or property in a violent way. **plunderer** *n.*

plunge *v.* To thrust or cast something, as into water; to submerge; to descend sharply or steeply.

plunk *v.* To put down or place suddenly; to pluck or strum a banjo. **plunk, plunker** *n.*

plu-ral *adj.* Consisting of or containing more than one. **plural** *n.*

plus *prep.* Add the symbol (+) which indicates addition; increase; extra quantity.

Plu-to *n.* The planet which is ninth in order from the sun.

plu-to-ni-um *n.* A radioactive metallic element symbolized by Pu.

ply *v.* To mold, bend, or shape. *n.* A layer of thickness; the twisted strands of thread, yarn,, or rope.

ply-wood *n.* A structural material consisting of thin layers of wood which have been glued and pressed together.

PM *abbr.* Prime Minster.

PM *abbr.* Post meridiem.

pneu-mo-nia- *n.* An inflammation caused by bacteria, virus of the lungs, or irritation.

poach *v.* To cook in a liquid just at the boiling point; to trespass on another's property with the intent of taking fish or wild game. **poacher** *n.*

pock-et *n.* A small pouch within a garment, having an open top and used for carrying items. *v.* To put in or deposit in a pocket.

pod *n., Bot.*

A seed vessel, as of a bean or pea. *Aeron* A separate and detachable compartment in a spacecraft.

po-di-a-try *n.* Professional care and treatment of the feet.

po-di-um *n.,pl.* **-ia** *or* **-iums** A small raised platform for an orchestra conductor or a speaker.

po-em *n.* A composition in verse with language selected for its beauty and sound.

po-et *n.* A person who writes poetry.

po-et-ry *n.* The art of writing stories, poems, and thoughts into verse.

point *n.* The sharp or tapered end of something; a mark of punctuation, as a period (.); a geometric object which does not have property or dimensions other than location; a degree, condition, or stage; a particular or definite spot in time. *v.* To aim; to indicate direction by using the finger.

poin-set-ti-a *n.* A tropical plant having large scarlet leaves, used in Christmas decorations.

poise *v.* To bring into or hold one's balance. *n.* Equilibrium; self-confidence; the ability to stay calm in all social situations.

poi-son *n.* A substance which kills, injures, or destroys. **-er** *n.,* **-ous** *adj.*

poke *v.* To push or prod at something with a finger or other implement.

po-lar *adj.* Having to do with the poles of a magnet or sphere; relating to the geographical poles of the earth.

po-lar-ize *v.* To cause something to vibrate in an exact pattern; to break up into opposite groups. **-ation** *n.*

pole *n.* Either of the two ends of the axis of a sphere, as the earth; the two points called the North and South Poles, where the axis of the earth's rotation meets the surface; a long, slender rod.

pol-i-o-my-e-li-tis *n.* Inflammation of the spinal cord causing paralysis.

po-lice *n.* A division or department organized to maintain order; the members of such a department. *v.* To patrol; to enforce the law and maintain order.

po-liceman *n.* A member of the police force. **policewoman** *n.*

pol-i-cy *n., pl.* **-ies** Any plan or principle which guides decision making.

pol-ish *v.*

To make lustrous and smooth by rubbing; to become refined or elegant.

po-lite *adj.* Refined, mannerly, and courteous.

po-lit-i-cal *adj.* Concerned with or pertaining to government; involved in politics.

pol-i-ti-cian *n.* A person active in governmental affairs or politics.

pol-i-tics *n.* The activities and methods of a political party.

Polk, James K. *n.* The 11th president of the United States from 1845-1849.

poll *n.* The recording of votes in an election; a public survey taken on a given topic. poll *v.*

pol-len *n.* The yellow dust-like powder which contains the male reproductive cells of a flowering plant.

pol-lute *v.* To contaminate; to make unclear or impure; to dirty. pollution *n.*

po-lo *n.* A game played on horseback in which players try to drive a wooden ball through the opposing team's goal using long-handled mallets. poloist *n.*

po-lo-ni-um *n.* A radioactive metallic element symbolized by PO.

pol-ter-geist *n.* A mischievous ghost or spirit which makes much noise.

pol-y-es-ter *n.* A strong lightweight synthetic resin used in fibers.

pol-y-graph *n.* A machine designed to record different signals given off by the body, as respiration, blood pressure, or heartbeats; may be used to detect a person who may be lying.

poly-gon *n.*

A closed figure bounded by straight lines.

pol-y-he-dron *n.*, *pl.* -dra *or* -drons *Geom.* A solid bounded by polygons.

pom-pa-dour *n.* A hairstyle which is puffed over the forehead.

pomp-ous *adj.* A showing or appearance of dignity or importance.

pond *n.* A body of still water, smaller in size than a lake.

pon-der *v.* To weigh or think about very carefully; to meditate.

pon-der-ous *adj.* Massive; having great weight.

pon-tiff *n.* A pope.

po-ny *n.*, *pl.* -ies A small horse.

pool *n.* A small body of water; the collective stake in gambling games.

poor *adj.* Lacking possessions and money; not satisfactory; broke; needy; destitute.

pop *v.* To cause something to burst; to make a sharp, explosive sound. *Slang* Soda. popper *n.*

pop-corn *n.* A variety of corn which explodes when heated, forming white puffs.

pope *n.* The head of the Roman Catholic Church.

pop-lar *n.* A rapid growing tree having a light, soft wood.

pop-u-lar *adj.* Approved of; widely liked; suited to the means of the people.

pop-u-la-tion *n.* The total number of people in a given area, country, or city.

por-ce-lain *n.* A hard, translucent ceramic which has been fired and glazed.

porch *n.* A covered structure forming the entrance to a house.

por-cu-pine *n.*

A clumsy rodent covered with long sharp quills.

pore *v.* To ponder or meditate on something. *n.* A minute opening, as in the skin.

pork *n.* The edible flesh of swine. *Informal* Favors given by a government for political reasons and not public necessity.

por-no *n.*, *Slang* Pornography.

por-nog-ra-phy *n.* Pictures, films, or writing which deliberately arouse sexual excitement.

por-poise *n.*

An aquatic mammal with a blunt, rounded snout.

port *n.* A city or town with a harbor for loading and unloading cargo from ships; the left side of a ship; a dark-red, sweet, fortified wine.

port-a-ble *adj.* Capable of being moved easily.

por-ter *n.* A person hired to carry baggage.

port-fo-li-o *n.* A carrying case for holding papers, drawings, and other flat items.

port-hole *n.* A small opening in the side of a ship providing light and ventilation.

por-tion *n.* A section or part of a whole; a share. *v.* To allot; to assign.

por-tray *v.* To represent by drawing, writing, or acting.

pose *v.* To place or assume a position, as for a picture.

po-si-tion *n.* The manner in which something is placed; an attitude; a viewpoint; a job; employment. *v.* To place in proper order.

pos-i-tive *adj.* Containing, expressing, or characterized by affirmation; very confident; absolutely certain; not negative. positively *adv.*, positiveness *n.*

pos-se *n.* A deputized group or squad.

pos-ses-sion *n.* The fact or act of possessing property; the state of being possessed, as by an evil spirit.

pos-ses-sive *adj.* Having a strong desire to possess; not wanting to share. *n.* The noun or pronoun case which indicates ownership.

pos-si-ble *adj.* Capable of being true, happening, or being accomplished. possibility *n.*, possibly *adv.*

post *n.* An upright piece of wood or metal support; a position or employment. *v.* To put up information in a public place. *prefix.* After; in order; or time; behind.

post-age *n.* The charge or fee for mailing something.

pos-te-ri-or *adj.* Located in the back. *n.* The buttocks.

post-mor-tem *adj.* The examination of a body after death; an autopsy.

post-op-er-a-tive *adj.* Following surgery.

post-pone *v.* To put off; to defer to a later time. **postponable** *adj.*, **postponement, postponer** *n.*

post-script *n.* A short message added at the end of a letter.

pos-ture *n.* The carriage or position of the body.

pot *n.* A rounded, deep container used for cooking and other domestic purposes. *Slang* A large sum of money which is shared by all members of a group; marijuana. **pot** *v.*, **potful** *n.*

po-tas-si-um *n.* A silvery-white, highly reactive metallic element symbolized by K.

po-ta-to *n., pl.* **-toes** A thick, edible, underground tuber plant native to America.

po-tent *adj.* Having great strength or physical powers; having a great influence on the mind or morals; sexually competent.

po-ten-tial *adj.* Possible, but not yet actual; having the capacity to be developed. *Electr.* The potential energy of an electric charge that depends on its position in an electric field. **potentiality** *n.*, **potentially** *adv.*

pot-pour-ri *n.* A mixture of sweet-smelling dried flower petals and spices, kept in an airtight jar.

pot-ter-y *n., pl.* **-ies** Objects molded from clay and fired by intense heat.

pouch *n.* A small bag or other container for holding or carrying money, tobacco, and other small articles. *Zool.* The sac-like structure in which some animals carry their young.

poul-try *n.* Domestic fowl as ducks and hens, which are raised for eggs or meat.

pound *n., pl.* **pounds** or **pound** A measure of weight equal to sixteen ounces; a public enclosure where stray animals are fed and housed. *v.* To strike repeatedly or with force; to throb or beat violently or rapidly.

pov-er-ty *n.* The condition or state of being poor and needing money.

POW *abbr.* Prisoner of war.

pow-der *n.* A dry substance which has been finely ground or pulverized; dust; an explosive, such as gunpowder. *v.* To dust or cover.

pow-er-ful *adj.* Possessing energy or great force; having authority.

power of attorney *n.* A legal document in which one person gives another the authority to act for him.

prac-ti-cal *adj.* Serving an actual use or purpose; inclined to act instead of thinking or talking about something; useful.

pract-ice *n.* A custom or habit of doing something. *v.* To work at a profession; to apply; to put into effect; to exercise or rehearse.

prai-rie *n.* A wide area of level or rolling land with grass and weeds but no trees.

praise *v.* To express approval; to glorify.

prank *n.* A mischievous, playful action or trick. **prankster** *n.*

pra-seo-dym-i-um *n.* A metallic element of the rare-earth group, symbolized by Pr.

prawn *n.* An edible shrimp-like crustacean found in both salt and fresh water.

pray *v.* To address prayers to God; to ask or request.

prayer *n.* A devout request; the act of praying; a formal or set group of words used in praying.

praying mantis *n.* An insect which holds its front legs folded as, in prayer.

pre- *pref* Earlier or prior to something; in front.

preach *v.* To advocate; to proclaim; to deliver a sermon. **preacher,** **preachment** *n.*, **preachy** *adj.*

pre-am-ble *n.* An introduction to something, as a law, which states the purpose and reasons for the matter which follows.

pre-cau-tion *n.* A measure of caution or care taken in advance to guard against harm.

pre-cede *v.* To be or go before in time, position, or rank. **precedence** *n.*

prec-e-dent *n.* An instance which may serve as a rule or example in the future.

pre-cept *n.* A rule, order, or commandment meant to guide one's conduct.

pre-cinct *n.* An electoral district of a county, township, city, or town; an enclosure with definite boundaries.

pre-cious *adj.* Having great worth or value; beloved; cherished.

pre-cip-i-ta-tion *n.* Condensed water vapor which falls as snow, rain, sleet or hail. *Chem.* The act of causing crystals to separate and fall to the bottom of a liquid.

pre-cip-i-tous *adj.* Very steep; marked with very steep cliffs.

pre-cise *adj.* Exact; definite; strictly following rules; very strict.

pre-ci-sion *n.* Exactness; the quality of being precise; accuracy.

pre-clude *v.* To shut out; to make impossible; to prevent.

pre-co-cious *adj.* Showing and developing skills and abilities very early in life.

pre-con-ceive *v.* To form a notion or conception before knowing all the facts. **preconception** *n.*

pre-da-cious *adj.* Living by preying on other animals.

pred-a-tor *n.* A person who lives or gains by stealing from another person; an animal that survives by killing and eating other animals.

pre-des-ti-na-tion n. Destiny; fate; the act by which God has predestined all events.

pred-i-ca-ble adj. Capable of being predicated; to foretell.

pred-i-cate n. Gram. The word or words which say something about the subject of a clause or sentence; the part of a sentence which contains the verb. v. To establish.

pre-dict v. To tell beforehand; to foretell; to forecast.
predictability n., predictable adj., predictably adv., prediction n.

pre-dom-i-nant adj. Superior in strength, authority, number, or other qualities.

pree-mie n. Slang A baby born before the expected due date.

pre-empt v. To take or get hold of before someone else; to take the place of; to do something before someone else has a chance to do it. preemption n., preemptive adj.

pre-fab-ri-cate v. To construct in sections beforehand. prefabrication n.

pref-ace n. The introduction at the beginning of a book or speech.

pre-fect n. A high administrative official. prefecture n.

pre-fer v. To select as being the favorite; to promote; to present.

pref-er-ence n. A choice; a special liking for anything over another.
preferential adj.

pre-fix v. To put at the beginning; to put before.

preg-nant adj. Carrying an unborn fetus; significant. pregnancy n.

pre-his-tor-i-cal adj. Of or related to the period before recorded history.

pre-judge v. To judge before one knows all the facts. prejudgment n.

prej-u-dice n. A biased opinion based on emotion rather than reason; bias against a group, race, or creed.

pre-lim-i-nar-y adj. Leading up to the main action. preliminaries n.

prel-ude n. An introductory action. Music The movement at the beginning of a piece of music.

pre-ma-ture adj. Occurring or born before the natural or proper time. prematurely adv.

pre-med-i-tate v. To plan in advance or beforehand.

pre-mi-er adj. First in rank or importance. n. The chief executive of a government. premiership n.

pre-mi-um n. An object offered free as an inducement to buy; the fee or amount payable for insurance; an additional amount of money charged above the nominal value.

pre-na-tal adj. Existing prior to birth.

pre-oc-cu-py v. To engage the mind or attention completely.

prep Slang Preparatory school; preparation.

prep-a-ra-tion n. The process of preparing for something.

pre-par-a-to-ry adj. Serving as preparation.

pre-pare v. To make ready or qualified; to equip. preparedly adv.

pre-pay v. To pay for in advance.

pre-pon-der-ate v. To have superior importance, weight, force, influence, or other qualities. preponderance, preponderancy n., preponderantly adv.

prep-o-si-tion n., Gram. A word placed in front of a noun or pronoun to show a connection with or to something or someone.

pre-pos-ter-ous adj. Absurd; ridiculous; beyond all reason.

prep-pie n. Slang A student attending a prep school; a young adult who behaves and dresses very traditionally.

pre-rog-a-tive n. The unquestionable right belonging to a person.

pres-age n. An omen or indication of something to come; a premonition.

pre-school adj. Of or for children usually between the ages of two and five. preschooler n.

pre-scribe v. To impose as a guide; to recommend.

pre-scrip-tion n., Med. A physician's written order for medicine.

pres-ence n. The state of being present; the immediate area surrounding a person or thing; poise.

pres-ent adj. Now going on; not past or future. Gram. Denoting a tense or verb form which expresses a current state or action. v. To bring into the acquaintance of another; to introduce; to make a gift of. n. A gift. adv. Currently.

pres-en-ta-tion n. A formal introduction of one person to another; to present something as an exhibition, show, or product.

pre-serv-a-tive adj. Keeping something from decay or injury. preservation n., preservable adj.

pre-serve v. To keep or save from destruction or injury; to prepare fruits or vegetables to prevent spoilage or decay. preserves Fruit which has been preserved with sugar.

pre-shrunk adj. Material which has been washed during the manufacturing process to minimize shrinkage later.

pre-side v. To have a position of authority or control; to run or control a meeting.

pres-i-dent n. The chief executive officer of a government, corporation, or association. presidency n., -ial adj.

press v. To act upon or exert steady pressure or force; to squeeze out or extract by pressure; to smooth by heat and pressure; to iron clothes. n. A machine used to produce printed material. presser n.

pres-sure n. The act of or the state of being pressed; a constraining moral force; any burden, force, painful feeling, or influence; the depressing effect of something hard to bear.

pres-tige n. Importance based on past reputation and achievements.

pres-to adv., Music Very fast and quick;

at once.

pre-sume *v.* To take for granted; to take upon oneself without permission; to proceed over-confidently. **-able** *adj.*, **presumably** *adv.*, **presumer** *n.*

pre-sump-tion *n.* Arrogance; presumptuousness; something that can be logically assumed true until disproved.

pre-tend *v.* To make believe; to act in a false way. **pretender** *n.*

pre-tense *n.* A deceptive and false action or appearance; a false purpose.

pre-ten-tions *n.* Having or making claims to worth, excellence, etc.; showy.

pre-text *n.* A motive assumed in order to conceal the true purpose.

pret-ty *adj.* Pleasant; attractive; characterized by gracefulness; pleasing to look at. **sitting pretty** In a favorable position; good circumstances. **prettier**, **prettiest** *adj.*

pret-zel *v.* A hard, cooked dough usually twisted in a knot and sprinkled with salt.

pre-vail *v.* To succeed; to win control over something; to predominate. **prevailer** *n.*, **prevailingly** *adv.*

pre-vent *v.* To keep something from happening; to keep from doing something.

pre-ven-tive *or* **preventative** *adj.* Protecting or serving to ward off harm, disease, or other problems. **preventive** *n.*

pre-view *or* **prevue** *n.* An advance showing or viewing to invited guests.

pre-vi-ous *adj.* Existing or occurring earlier. **previously** *adv.*

price *n.* The set amount of money expected or given for the sale of something.

prick *n.* A small hole made by a sharp point. *v.* To pierce something lightly.

pride *n.* A sense of personal dignity; a feeling of pleasure because of something achieved, done, or owned.

priest *n.* A clergyman in the Catholic church who serves as mediator between God and His worshipers.

pri-ma-ry *adj.* First in origin, time, series, or sequence; basic; fundamental.

prime *adj.* First in importance, time, or rank. *n.* A period of full vigor, success, or beauty. *v.* To make ready by putting something on before the final coat, as to prime wood before painting.

prim-i-tive *adj.* Of or pertaining to the beginning or earliest time; resembling the style or manners of an earlier time.

primp *v.* To dress or arrange with superfluous attention to detail.

prince *n.* The son of a king; a king.

prin-cess *n.* The daughter of a king.

prin-ci-pal *adj.* Chief; most important. *n.* The headmaster or chief official of a school; a sum of money invested or owed which is separate from the interest.

prin-ci-ple *n.* The fundamental law or truth upon which others are based; a moral standard.

print *n.* An impression or mark made with ink; the design or picture which is transferred from an engraved plate or other impression. *v.* To stamp designs; to publish something in print, as a book or magazine.

printer *n.* A person whose occupation is printing.

print-out *n.* *Computer Science* The output of a computer, printed on paper.

pri-or *adj.* Previous in order or time.

pri-or-i-ty *n.* Something which takes precedence; something which must be done or taken care of first.

prism *n.*

A solid figure with triangular ends and rectangular sides, used to disperse light into a spectrum.

pris-on *n.* A place of confinement where people are kept while waiting for a trial or while serving time for breaking the law; jail. **prisoner** *n.*

pri-vate *adj.* Secluded or removed from the public view; secret; intimate; owned or controlled by a group or person rather than by the public or government. *n.* An enlisted person holding the lowest rank in military service.

priv-i-lege *n.* A special right or benefit granted to a person.

priv-i-leged *adj.* To have or enjoy a given privilege.

prize *n.* An award or something given to the winner of a contest; something exceptional or outstanding.

pro *n.* An argument in favor of or supporting something. *Slang* A professional or an expert in a given field.

prob-a-bil-i-ty *n.*, *pl.* **-ies** The state or quality of being probable; a mathematical statement or prediction of the odds of something happening or not happening.

prob-a-ble *adj.* Likely to become a reality, but not certain or proved.

pro-bate *n.* The act of legally proving that a will is genuine.

pro-ba-tion *n.* A period used to test the qualifications and character of a new employee; the early release of lawbreakers who must be under supervision and must report as requested to a probation officer.

probe *n.* An instrument used for investigating an unknown environment; a careful investigation or examination.

prob-lem *n.* A perplexing situation or question; a question presented for consideration, solution, or discussion. **problem**, **problematic** *adj.*

pro-ce-dure *n.* A certain pattern or way of doing something; the normal methods or forms to be followed.

pro-ceed *v.* To carry on or continue an action or process. *Law* To begin or institute legal action.

pro-ceeds *pl.*, *n.* The profits received from a fund-raising venture.

proc-ess *n.* The course, steps, or methods toward a desired result. *Law* Any judicial request or order. *Computer Science* The sequence of operations which gives a desired result. *v.* To compile, compute, or assemble; data.

pro-ces-sion *n.* A group which moves along in a formal manner; a parade.

pro-ces-sion-al *n.* A hymn sung during a procession; *adj.* the opening of a church service; of or relating to a procession.

pro-ces-sor *n. Computer Science* The central unit of a computer which processes data.

pro-claim *v.* To announce publicly.

proc-la-ma-tion *n.* An official public declaration or announcement.

pro-cras-ti-nate *v.* To put off, defer, or postpone to a later time. procrastination, procrastinator *n.*

proc-tor *n.* A person in a university or college whose job it is to see that order is maintained during exams. proctorial *adj.*

pro-cure *v.* To acquire; to accomplish.

prod *v.* To arouse mentally; to poke with a pointed instrument. *n.* A pointed implement used to prod or poke.

prod-i-gal *adj.* Wasteful expenditure of money, strength, or time; extravagance. *n.* One who is a spendthrift or is wasteful.

pro-duce *v.* To bear or bring forth by a natural process; to manufacture; to make; to present or bring into view.

prod-uct *n.* Something produced, manufactured, or obtained *Math.* The answer obtained by multiplying.

pro-duc-tion *n.* The process or act of producing; something produced, as a play.

pro-fane *adj.* Manifesting disrespect toward sacred things; vulgar.

pro-fess *v.* To admit or declare openly; to make an open vow.

pro-fess-sion-al *adj.* Having to do with a job or profession; referring to or engaging in an occupation, usually a sport for money rather than for fun.

pro-fes-sor *n.* A faculty member of the highest rank in a college or university; a highly skilled teacher.

pro-fi-cient *adj.* Highly skilled in a field of knowledge. proficiency *n.*, proficiently *adv.*

pro-file *n.* The outline of a person's face or figure as seen from the side; a short biographical sketch indicating the most striking characteristics.

prof-it *n.* The financial return after all expenses have been accounted for. *v.* To gain an advantage or a financial reward. profitable *adj.*

pro-found *adj.* Deeply held or felt; intellectually penetrating.

pro-fuse *adj.* Extravagant; giving forth lavishly; overflowing. profusely *adv.*, profuseness *n.*

prog-e-ny *n., pl.* -ies One's offspring, children, or descendants.

prog-no-sis *n., pl.* -noses A prediction of the outcome and course a disease may take.

pro-gram *n.* Any prearranged plan or course; a show or performance, as one given at a scheduled time. *Computer Science* A sequence of commands which tell a computer how to perform a task or sequence of tasks.

prog-ress *n.* Forward motion or advancement to a higher goal; an advance; steady improvement.

pro-hib-it *v.* To forbid legally; to prevent.

pro-ject *n.* A plan or course of action; a proposal; a large job. *v.* To give an estimation on something.

pro-jec-tile *n.* Anything hurled forward through the air.

pro-jec-tion *n.* The act or state of being projected; the state or part that sticks out.

pro-lif-er-ate *v.* To grow or produce with great speed, as cells in tissue formation.

pro-logue *n.* An introductory statement at the beginning of a poem, song, or play.

pro-long *v.* To extend or lengthen in time.

prom-e-nade *n.* An unhurried walk for exercise or amusement; a public place for such a walk, as the deck of a ship.

prom-i-nent *adj.* Jutting out; widely known; held in high esteem.

pro-mis-cu-ous *adj.* Lacking selectivity or discrimination, especially in sexual relationships.

prom-ise *n.* An assurance given that one will or will not do something; or that something shall or shall not happen; vow; the indication of what is to be expected; a pledge. *v.* To make a promise. promisable, promisable *adj.*, promiser *n.*

Prom-ised Land *n.* Heaven.

prom-is-ee *n., Law* A person to whom a promise is given.

prom-is-ing *adj.* Giving hopeful and favorable promises of future success. promisingly *adv.*

prom-i-sor *n., Law* A person who promises.

prom-is-so-ry note *n.* A written document or agreement that contains a promise to pay a debt to a particular person by a specified date or on demand.

prom-on-to-ry *n.* A projecting rock that extends into the sea.

pro-mote *v.* To raise to a higher rank or position; to work on behalf of; to forward; to contribute to the enlargement,m growth, or power of; to advance to a higher grade in school; to attempt to increase the sale of an item by advertising. promotion *n.*, promotional *adj.*

pro-mot-er *n.* A person who encourages; one who aids in promoting a financial undertaking; a person who starts or sets up a business venture.

pro-mo-tion *n.* Elevation in rank; state of being raised in status; advancement. promotional *adj.*

prompt *adj.* Arriving on time; punctual; immediate. *v.* To suggest or inspire; to incite or move to action; suggest to the mind; to assist a speaker who has forgotten his lines; inspire.
promptly *adv.*, **promptness** *n.*
prompt-book *n.* A copy of a play to be used by the director or the prompter.
prompt-er *n.* One who prompts.
promp-ti-tude *n.* Promptness.
prom-ul-gate *v.* To proclaim; to make known to the public.
promulgation, promulgator *n.*
prone *adj.* Lying flat; face down; sloping downward; inclined. *-ly adv.*, *-ness n.*
prong *n.* A pointed, projecting part, as the end of a sharp instrument or the end of an antler; the tine of a fork or related instrument.
prong-horn *n.* An antelope having hollow horns that fall off seasonally.
pro-nim-i-nal *adj.* Belonging to the nature of a pronoun. *-ly adv.*
pro-noun *n.*, *Gram.* A word which can be used in the place of a noun or noun phrase.
pro-nounce *v.* To deliver officially; to articulate the sounds, as words or letters. *-able adj.*, **pronunciation** *n.*
pro-nounced *adj.* Strongly defined; decided. **pronouncedly** *adv.*
pro-nounce-ment *n.* Act of pronouncing a word or letter; a decision.
pron-to *adv.* Quickly; promptly.
pro-nun-ci-a-tion *n.* The act of uttering. **pronunciational** *adj.*
proof *n.* The establishment of a fact by evidence; the act of showing that something is true; a trial impression from the negative of a photograph. *v.* To proofread; to mark and make corrections.
proof-read *v.* To read in order to detect and mark errors in a printer's proof.
proofreader *n.*
proof-read-er's marks *n.*, *pl.* The symbols that indicate changes that are to be made by the typesetter.
proof spir-it *n.* Alcoholic liquor that contains a standard amount of alcohol.
prop *n.* A support to keep something upright. An article or item used in the set of a movie or play. The propeller of an airplane. *v.* To sustain; to support.
prop-a-gate *v.* To reproduce or multiply by natural causes; to pass on qualities or traits. **propagation** *n.*
pro-pel *v.* To thrust or cause to move forward; to motivate.
prop-er *adj.* Appropriate; especially adapted or suited; conforming to social convention; correct.
prop-er ad-jec-tive *n.* An adjective whose form is obtained from that of a proper noun.
prop-er frac-tion *n.* A fraction with a larger denominator than numerator.
prop-er-ly *adv.* In a suitable manner; fitly; correctly.
prop-er noun *n.* A noun denoting a specific person, place, or thing and is capitalized.
prop-er-ty *n.*, *pl.* *-ies* Any object of value owned or lawfully acquired, as real estate; a piece of land; right of possession or ownership.
propertied, **propertyless** *adj.*
prop-er-ty man *n.* A man employed by a theater to take care of the stage properties.
proph-e-cy *n.*, *pl.* *-ies* A prediction made under divine influence; a foretelling of something to come.
proph-et *n.* One who delivers divine messages; one who foretells the future; a predictor.
prophetess, **prophethood** *n.*
pro-pi-ti-ate *v.* To win the goodwill of; to stop from being angry. **propitiation** *n.*
pro-po-nent *n.* One who supports or advocates a cause; a person who makes a proposal.
pro-por-tion *n.* The relation of one thing to another in size, degree, or amount. *v.* To adjust or arrange with balance and harmony. **proportional**,
proportionate *adj.*, **proportionally** *adv.*
pro-por-tion-a-ble *adj.* In proportion; a due comparative relation.
proportionably *adv.*
pro-pose *v.* To present or put forward for consideration or action; to suggest someone for an office, position, membership, or candidacy; to make an offer; to offer marriage. **proposal** *n.*
prop-o-si-tion *n.* A scheme or plan offered for consideration; a subject or idea to be proved or discussed; an assertion. *v.* To make a sexual suggestion. **propositional** *adj.*,
propositionally *adv.*
pro-pri-e-tor *n.* The person who owns property and has the exclusive title or legal right.
proprietorship, **proprietress** *n.*
pro-pri-e-ty *n.*, *pl.* *-ies* The quality or state of being proper in accordance with recognized principles or usage.
prop root *n.*, *Bot.* The root of plants, as corn, that grows into the soil and provides the main support of the stalk.
pro-pul-sis *n.* The outward protuberance of an organ.
pro-pul-sion *n.* The act or process of propelling. **propulsive** *adj.*
pro-rate *v.* To distribute or divide proportionately. **proration** *n.*
pro-scribe *v.* To banish; to outlaw; to prohibit. **proscriber** *n.*
prose *n.* Ordinary language, speech, or writing which is not poetry.
pros-e-cute *v.* To carry on. *Law* To bring suit against a person; to seek enforcement for legal process. **prosecution** *n.*, **prosecutable** *adj.*
pros-pect *n.* Something that has the possibility of future success; a possible customer. *v.* To explore.
prospective *adj.*, **prospectively** *adv.*
pros-per *v.* To be successful; to achieve success. **prosperous** *adj.*
pros-tate *n.* A small gland at the base of

the male bladder.

pros-ti-tute *n.* One who sells the body for the purpose of sexual intercourse. **prostitutor** *n.*

pros-trate *adj.* Lying with the face down to the ground. *v.* To overcome; to adopt a submissive posture. **prostrative** *adj.*, **prostrator** *n.*

prot-ac-tin-i-um *n.* A radioactive metallic element symbolized by Pa.

pro-tect *v.* To guard or shield from attack or injury; to shield. **protective** *adj.*, **protectively** *adv.*

pro-tein *n.*, *Biochem.* Any of a very large group of highly complex nitrogenous compounds occurring in living matter and composed of amino acids which are essential for tissue repair and growth. **proteinaceous**, **proteinic** **proteinous** *adj.*

pro-test *v.* To make a strong formal objection; to object to. *n.* The act of protesting. **protester** *n.*

Prot-es-tant *n.* A member of any of the Christian churches who believes Jesus is the son of God and died for man's sins. **Protestantism** *n.*

pro-to-col *n.* The code and rules of diplomatic and state etiquette.

pro-ton *n.*, *Physics* A unit of positive charge equal in magnitude to an electron.

pro-tract *v.* To extend in space; to protrude. **protraction**, **-ive** *adj.*

pro-trude *v.* To project; to thrust outward. **protrusion** *n.*

proud *adj.* Showing or having a feeling that one is better than the others; having a feeling of satisfaction; having proper self-respect or proper self-esteem.

prove *v.* To show with valid evidence that something is true. **provable** *adj.*, **provably** *adv.*

prov-erb *n.* An old saying which illustrates a truth. **Proverbs** *n.* The book contained in the Bible which has many sayings supposed to have come from Solomon and others.

pro-vide *v.* To supply or furnish with what is needed. **providable** *adj.*, **provider** *n.*

prov-i-dence *adj.* The supervision of God over his people

pro-vi-sion *n.* A supply of food or needed equipment.

pro-voke *v.* To cause to be angry; to annoy. **provocation** *n.*

prox-i-mate *adj.* Immediate; direct; closely adjacent.

prox-y *n.*, *pl.* -ies The authority, usually written, to act for another.

prude *n.* A person who is very modest, especially in matters related to sex. **prudery**, **prudishness** *n.*, **prudish** *adj.*

pru-dent *adj.* Cautious; discreet; managing very carefully.

prune *n.* The dried fruit of a plum. *v.* To cut off that which is not wanted or not necessary.

PS *abbr.* Postscript.

psalm *n.* A sacred hymn, taken from the Book of Psalms in the Old Testament.

psalm-book *n.* A type of book which has the psalms in it.

psalm-ist *n.* A person who writes psalms.

psal-ter-y *n.* A type of musical instrument that was used many years ago.

pseu-do *adj.* To be counterfeit or fake.

pseu-do-nym *n.* A name that is a fake. **pseudonymous** *adj.*

psi *n.* The twenty-third letter that is found in the Greek alphabet.

psil-o-cy-bin *n.* A type of an alkaloid of the fungus.

pso-ri-a-sis *n.*, *Pathol.* A non-contagious, chronic, inflammatory skin disease characterized by reddish patches and white scales.

PST *abbr.* Pacific Standard Time.

psych *v.*, *Slang* To prepare oneself emotionally or mentally; to outwit or outguess.

psy-chas-the-ni-a *n.* A type of emotional disorder that is caused by morbid fears. **psychasthenic** *adj.*

psych-e-del-ic *adj.* To be causing extraordinary alterations in the consciousness of a person.

psy-chi-a-trist *n.* A person who is a specialist in the field of psychiatry.

psy-chi-a-try *n.* The branch of medicine which deals with the diagnosis and treatment of mental disorders.

psy-chic *adj.* Cannot be explained by natural or physical laws. *n.* A person who communicates with the spirit world. **psychically** *adv.*, **psychical** *adj.*

psy-cho-a-nal-y-sis *n.* The way of studying and analyzing one's subconscious thoughts. **psychoanalytic** *adj.*

psy-cho-an-a-lyst *n.* The person who has been trained and is qualified to practice psychoanalysis on others.

psy-cho-bi-ol-o-gy *n.* The science of the study of the relationships between the body and the mind.

psy-cho-gen-e-sis *n.* The development of the mind.

psy-chol-o-gy *n.*, *pl.* -ies The science of emotions, behavior, and the mind. **psychological** *adj.*, **psychologist** *n.*

psy-cho-path *n.* A person suffering from a mental disorder characterized by aggressive antisocial behavior. **psychopathic** *adj.*

PT *abbr.* Pacific Time.

PTA *abbr.* Parent Teacher Association.

ptar-mi-gan *n.* A type of species of grouse that has feathered feet and can be located in the cold regions.

PT boat *n.* A type of small vessel of the navy.

pter-i-dol-o-gy *n.* The section or part of botany that is concerned with the study of ferns. **pteridologist** *n.*

pter-o-dac-tyl *n.* A type of flying reptile that is now extinct and is believed to have live thousands of years ago. **pterodactylous**, **pterodactyloid** *adj.*

pter-o-saur *n.* A type of flying reptile that is now extinct.

pto-maine *n.* A type of compound that can be poisonous and made by an animal.

pto-sis *n.* The drooping of a body organ. **ptotic** *adj.*

pty-a-lin *n.* A type of enzyme that is found in the saliva of man and is used to digest starch into maltose and dextrin.

pty-a-lism *n.* The excessive production of saliva in one's mouth.

pub *n.* A type of tavern.

pu-ber-ty *n.* The stage of development in which sexual reproduction can first occur; the process of the body which culminates in sexual maturity. **pubertal, puberal** *adj.*

pu-ber-u-lent *adj.* To be covered or to have down.

pu-bes-cence *n.* The arrival of the stage of puberty in a person.

pu-bis *n.* The part of the bone that forms the pelvis which is located in the front.

pub-lic *adj.* Pertaining to or affecting the people or community; for everyone's use; widely or well known. **-ness** *n.*

pub-lic--ad-dress sys-tem *n.* An amplifying system that amplifies sound through a series of loudspeakers and microphones.

pub-li-can *n.* A person who collects taxes in a town or city; any collector of public revenues.

pub-li-ca-tion *n.* The action of publishing something such as a book or magazine; the state of being published and printed.

pub-lic de-fend-er *n.* The attorney who defends someone without cost because they cannot afford to furnish an attorney for themselves.

pub-lic do-main *n.* The public property; the published work whose copyrights have expired; state of being available for the general public.

pub-lic en-e-my *n.* A person who is considered to be a threat or menace to the public; government regarded as an enemy.

pub-lic house *n.* A type of inn.

pub-li-cist *n.* A press or publicity agent; a person who is a specialist in public relations; a specialist on international law.

pub-lic-i-ty *n.* The state of being known to the public; common knowledge.

pub-li-cize *v.* To give publicity to; advertise.

pub-lic law *n.* A type of statute that has been adapted for the public as a whole by the nation.

pub-lic-ly *adv.* Public manner; without concealment.

pub-lic prop-er-ty *n.* The property which is owned by the public.

pub-lic sale *n.* A type of sale which is made after a public notice.

pub-lic serv-ant *n.* A person who works for the government.

pub-lic speak-ing *n.* An art of speaking effectively to the public.

pub-lish *v.* To print and distribute a book, magazine, or any printed matter to the public. **publishable** *adj.*

pub-lish-er *n.* A person who will publish the works of others as in books.

puc-coon *n.* A type of North American herb that has yellow flowers and can grow in the dry sandy soils.

puce *adj.* To be a reddish brown.

puck *n.* A hard rubber disk used in playing ice hockey.

puck-er *v.* To gather or group something into small wrinkles.

puck-ish *adj.* Elfish in character.

pud-dle *n.* A type of small pool of water. **puddler** *n.*

pu-den-cy *n.* The modesty of someone.

pudg-y *adj.* To be fat and short.

pueb-lo *n.* A type of village of grouped houses and can be found in New Mexico, used by the Pueblo Indians of North America.

pu-er-ile *adj.* To be childish in character and actions.

pu-er-per-al *adj.* To be related to childbirth.

puff *n.* A brief discharge of air or smoke. *v.* To breathe in short heavy breaths.

puff ad-der *n.* A type of large African viper that will puff up its body when it becomes agitated.

puff-ball *n.* A type of fungus that is rounded and will discharge its spores in a mass of smoke.

puff-er *n.* A person or something that puffs.

puff-er-y *n.* A type of praise which is very exaggerated.

puf-fin *n.* A type of sea bird that has a red bill and can be found in the North Atlantic regions.

pug *n.* A type of dog which looks like a small bulldog.

pug-na-cious *adj.* To be inclined to fight. **pugnaciousness** *n.*

pug-ree *n.* A type of turban that is worn to keep the rays of the sun off one's head.

pu-is-sance *n.* Might; strength.

puke *v.* To throw up or vomit food.

puk-ka *adj.* To be good.

pull *v.* To apply force; to cause motion toward or in the same direction of; to remove from a fixed place; to stretch.

pull-back *n.* The action or the process of pulling something back.

pul-let *n.* A young chicken.

pull-o-ver *n.* A type of clothing that is put on the body by pulling it over one's head.

pul-lu-late *v.* To send off or forth buds.

pul-mo-nar-y *adj.* To be referring to the lungs.

pul-mo-nar-y ar-ter-y *n.* The artery which is going from the heart to the lungs and is carrying unoxygenated blood.

pul-mo-nar-y vein *n.* A vein which comes from the lungs to the heart and is carrying the blood which has received oxygen in the lungs and it is ready to be pumped through the rest of the body.

pulp *n.* The soft juicy part of a fruit; a soft moist mass; an inexpensive type of paper. **pulpy** *adj.*, **pulpiness** *n.*

pul-pit *n.* The elevated platform lectern which is used in a church from which a service is conducted.

pulp-wood *n.* A type of soft wood which is found in the pine and spruce, and it is used for the purpose of making paper.

pul-sate *v.* To beat rhythmically.

pul-sa-tile *adj.* To be throbbing.

pul-sa-tion *n.* The action or the process of beating.

pul-sa-tor *n.* Something which will pulsate, such as the heart.

pulse *n., Physiol.* The rhythmical beating of the arteries caused by the action of the heart. **pulse** *v.*

pul-sim-e-ter *n.* A type of device that is used to measure the rate and the strength of one's pulse.

pul-ver-a-ble *adj.* To be capable of being changed or reduced to dust.

pul-ver-ize *v.* To be reduced to dust or to a fine powder by the process of crushing. **pulverizer** *n.*

pul-ver-u-lent *adj.* To be made up of fine powder.

pul-vil-lus *n.* A type of cushionlike mass that is found on the feet of certain insects.

pu-ma *n.* A type of large cat that is tawny in color and is located in North and South America.

pum-ice *n.* A type of porous stone that is from volcanoes and is used for the purpose of smoothing skin.

pump *n.* A mechanical device for moving a gas or liquid. *v.* To raise with a pump; to obtain information through persistent questioning. **pumplike, pumpable** *adj.*

pum-per-nick-el *n.* A type of coarse bread that is made from rye.

pump-kin *n.* A large, edible yellow-orange fruit having a thick rind and many seeds.

pump-kin-seed *n.* A type of sunfish that can be found in fresh water of eastern North America.

pu-na *n.* A type of plateau that is arid.

punch *n.* A tool used for perforating or piercing; a blow with the fist; a drink made of an alcoholic beverage and a fruit juice or other non-alcoholic beverage. *v.* To use a punch on something; to hit sharply with the hand or fist.

punch bowl *n.* A type of bowl that is large in size and used to serve punch.

pun-cheon *n.* A type of tool used to punch holes into something.

pun-chi-nel-lo *n.* A person who is grotesque.

punch-ing bag *n.* A type of leather bag that is stuffed and used to punch on for practice.

punc-tate *adj.* To be ending with a point; marked with dots, that are variously scattered over a surface.

punctation *n.*

punc-til-i-ous *adj.* To be formal in one's be-havior.

punc-tu-al *adj.* Prompt; arriving on time. **punctualness** *n.*

punc-tu-ate *v.* To mark words or written material with punctuation; to give or show emphasis.

punc-tu-a-tion *n.* The practice of punctuating a sentence with marks, in order to make the meaning clear. **puchtuative** *adj.*, **punctuator** *n.*

punc-tu-late *adj.* To be marked with dots or depressions. **punctulation** *n.*

punc-ture *v.* To prick or pierce with a pointed instrument. *n.* The act or effect of puncturing. **puncturable** *adj.*

pung *n.* A type of one-horse sleigh having an oblong box on runners.

pun-gent *adj.* Sharply affects smell or taste; poignant. **pungency** *n.*

pun-ish *v.* To subject a person to confinement or impose a penalty for a crime. **punishability** *n.*, **-able** *adj.*

pun-ish-ment *n.* A penalty which is imposed for breaking the law or a rule.

pu-ni-tive *adj.* Referring to or pertaining to punishment. **punitively** *adv.*, **punitiveness** *n.*

punk *n., Slang* A young, inexperienced boy. *adj.* Of or relating to a bizarre style of clothing; relating to punk rock bands.

pun-kah *n.* A type of fan that is hung from the ceiling and is operated by servants.

punk-ie *n.* A type of midge that sucks blood and can be found along the beach of the northeastern U.S.

pun-ster *n.* A person who likes to make puns.

punt *n.* A type of narrow, long, flat-bottomed boat; in football, a kick of the football dropped from the hands. *v.* To kick a football. **punter** *n.*

pun-ty *n.* A rod that is made of iron and is used for the making of glassworks.

pu-ny *adj.* To be weak and under-developed; insignificant or petty.

pup *n.*

A puppy, young dog, or the young of other animals.

pu-pa *n.* The stage in the development of an insect that is between the larva and the adult stage.

pu-pil *n.* A person who attends school and receives instruction by a teacher. *Anat.* The round contractile part of the eye through which the rays of light pass to the retina. **pupillary, pupilar** *adj.*

pu-pil-age *n.* The state of being a pupil.

pup-pet *n.* A small figure of an animal or person which is manipulated by hand or by strings. **puppetry** *n.*

pup-pet-eer *n.* A person who operates or handles puppets.

pup-py *n.* The young of a dog.

pup tent *n.* A type of tent that sleep only a few people.

pur-blind *adj.* To be lacking in insight. **purblindness** *n.*

pur-chas-a-ble *adj.* To be capable of being bought by someone.

pur-chase *v.* To receive by paying money as an exchange. **purchaser** *n.*

pure *adj.* Free from anything that damages, weakens, or contaminates; innocent; clean. **pureness** *n.*

pure-ly *adv.* To be done in a manner which is pure in character.

pur-fle *v.* To decorate something with the use of a flowered border.

pur-ga-tion *n.* An action of purging.

pur-ga-tive *n.* A type of medicine that is used to clean the bowels in preparation for surgery.

purge *v.* To make clean; to free from guilt or sin; to rid of anything undesirable, as unwanted persons. *Med.* To cause or induce emptying of the bowels. **purge** *n.*

pu-ri-fy *v.* To make clean or pure; to free from guilt. **purification, purifier** *n.*

pur-ism *n.* Observance of rigid purity in language. **purist** *n.,* **puristic** *adj.*

pu-ri-tan *n.* A person who practices great strictness of life and religious principles.

pu-ri-ty *n.* The quality of being pure; freedom from guilt or sin; freedom from foreign matter; freedom from anything that is improper.

purl *v.* To embroider. *n.* A stitch in knitting that is inverted.

pur-lieu *n.* The place or area where a person can roam about freely; a part of land that lies adjacent.

pur-lin *n.* A piece of timber that is laid horizontally on the main rafters of a roof, gives support to the common rafters.

pur-loin *v.* To take things that do not belong to someone; to steal.

pur-ple *n.* A color between red and violet. **purplish** *adj.*

pur-port *v.* To give the appearance of intending; to imply, usually with the intent to deceive. **purported** *adj.*

pur-pose *n.* A desired goal; an intention. **purposeful, -less** *adj.,* **purposely** *adv.*

pur-pu-ra *n.* A type of disease that causes purple spots to appear on the skin or membranes.

purr *n.* The low, murmuring sound characteristic of a cat. **purr** *v.*

purse *n.* A small pouch or bag for money; a handbag; a pocketbook; the sum of money offered as a prize.

purse--proud *adj.* To be proud of the wealth that one has obtained.

purs-lane *n.* A type of herb having tiny flowers and paddle-shaped leaves.

pur-sue *v.* To seek to achieve; to follow in an attempt to capture. **pursuer** *n.*

pur-suit *n.* The act of pursuing an occupation.

pu-ru-lent *adj.* To be like or resembling pus. **purulence** *n.*

pur-vey *v.* To supply provisions as a service. **purveyance, purveyor** *n.*

pus *n.* A yellowish secretion formed in infected tissue which contains bacteria.

push *v.* To move forward by exerting force; to force oneself through a crowd; to sell illegally. *Slang* To sell illegal drugs. **pushiness** *n.*

push-cart *n.* A type of light cart that can be pushed by the hands.

push-pin *n.* A type of pin with a large head and is used to hold papers up on a wall or corkboard.

pus-sy *adj.* To be containing or to be filled with pus.

pus-tu-late *v.* To cause blisters.

put *v.* To cause to be in a location; to bring into a specific relation or state; to bring forward for debate or consideration, as to put up for. **put down** To humiliate.

pu-ta-tive *adj.* Commonly supposed.

put on *v.* To don, such as one's clothes.

pu-tre-fy *v.* To cause to decay; to decay. **putrefaction** *n.,* **putrefactive** *adj.*

pu-tres-cent *adj.* To be growing rotten. **putrescence** *n.*

pu-trid *adj.* To be in a state of decay. **putridness** *n.,* **putridly** *adv.*

putsch *n.* A secret uprising.

putt *n.* In golf, a light stroke made on a putting green to get the ball into the hole.

put-ter *n.* A type of golf club that has a perpendicular face.

put-ting green *n.* The smooth grass that surrounds the hole.

put-ty-root *n.* A type of orchid that produces one large leaf.

puz-zle *v.* To bewilder; to confuse. *n.* A toy, board game, or word game which tests one's patience and skills.

puz-zle-ment *n.* The condition of being puzzled.

pyc-mon-e-ter *n.* A type of flask which is used for the determination of the density of a solid or of a liquid.

py-e-li-tis *n.* The inflammation of the kidney or of the pelvis.

py-e-log-ra-phy *n.* The taking of pictures of the kidneys or other organs of the body.

py-e-lo-ne-phri-tis *n.* The inflammation of the kidney.

py-gid-i-um *n.* The terminal end of an insect or of an other invertebrate.

pyg-my *n., pl.* **-ies** A very small person or animal; a dwarf.

pyk-nic *adj.* Rounded in body type and characteristically short.

py-lon *n.* A tower serving as a support for electrical power lines.

py-lo-rus *n.* The valve that is between the stomach and the duodenum for the purpose of passing food into the small intestine for further digestion.

py-o-der-ma *n.* The inflammation of the skin that is caused by a bacteria and is marked by pus.

py-o-gen-ic *adj.* To be making or producing pus.

py-or-rhe-a *n., Pathol.* The inflammation

of the gums and of the sockets of the teeth. **pyorrheal** adj.

py-ral-i-did n. A type of moth that has a slender body.

pyr-a-mid n.

A solid structure that has a square base and triangular sides which meet at a point on its top.

py-rar-gy-rite n. A type of an ore of silver.

pyre n. A pile of combustible material for burning a dead body.

py-rene n. A stone which is located inside fruit.

py-ret-ic adj. To be referring to or starting a fever.

py-rex-ia n. The abnormal rise of the body temperature; also know as fever.

pyr-he-li-om-e-ter n. A type of device that is used to measure the intensity of the energy that is put off by the sun. **pyrheliometric** adj.

py-ric adj. To be caused by or relating to burning.

pyr-i-form adj. To have the same shape or form as that of a pear.

py-ro-cel-lu-lose n. A cellulose nitrate that is used in smokeless powders.

py-ro-chem-i-cal adj. To be making a chemical change at a high temperature.

py-ro-gen n. A type of toxin that can cause a fever.

py-ro-gen-ic adj. To be producing a fever or heat.

py-ro-lu-site n. A type of black ore of manganese that is used in glassmaking.

py-rol-y-sis n. The chemical change that is brought on by the action of heat.

py-ro-ma-ni-a n. A compulsion to set fires.

py-rom-e-ter n. A type of device that can measure very high temperatures. **pyrometrically** adv., **pyrometrical** adj.

py-rope n. A type of deep-red garnet.

py-ro-pho-bi-a n. A fear of fire that is considered to be abnormal.

py-ro-phor-ic adj. To be highly flammable.

pyr-rhic n. A type of ancient Greecian dance of war fhat simulated the movements of battle.

Pyr-rhic vic-to-ry n. A victory acquired at too great of a cost.

pyr-rhu-lox-i-a n. A type of gray grosbeak that has a rose-colored breast and crest.

py-thon n. A large nonvenomous snake which crushes its prey.

py-tho-ness n. A woman who is believed to by possessed by a spirit. **pythonic** adj.

py-u-ri-a n., Pathol. The condition where there is pus in the urine.

pyx-ie n. A type of evergreen plant that is located in the eastern U.S.

pyx-is n. A small box, used by the Romans to hold jewelry.

Q, q The seventeenth letter of the English alphabet.

qat n. A small plant found in Africa, the fresh leaf is chewed for a stimulating effect.

qi-vi-ut n. Yarn spun from the fine, soft hair of the musk ox.

quack n. The harsh, croaking cry of a duck; someone who pretends to be a doctor. **quack** v., **quackery** n.

quad-ran-gle n., Math A plane figure with four sides and four angles.

quad-rant n.

A quarter section of a circle, subtending or enclosing a central angle of 90 degrees; an instrument which is used to measure altitudes.

qua-draph-o-ny n. The recording of sound using four transmission channels.

quad-rate adj. Being square or almost square.

qua-drat-ics n. A branch of algebra concerned with equations.

quad-ra-ture n. An arrangement of two celestial bodies with a separation of 90 degrees.

quad-ren-ni-um n. A period consisting of four years.

quad-ri-cen-ten-ni-al n. An anniversary celebrating 400 years.

quad-ri-ceps n. The muscle located in the front of the thigh.

qua-dri-ga n. A chariot pulled by a team of four horses.

quad-rille n. A square dance with five or six figures executed by four couples.

quad-ril-lion n. A thousand trillions; one followed by fifteen zeros. **-th** adj.

quad-ri-par-tite adj. Consisting of four persons or parts.

quad-ri-ple-gic n. A person who is paralyzed in both arms and both legs.

qua-dru-ma-na n. A group of primates distinguished by hand-shaped feet.

quad-ru-ped n. Any animal having four feet.

quad-ru-ple adj. Consisting of four parts; multiplied by four.

qua-dru-plet n. One of four infants born at the same time.

qua-dru-pli-cate n. Consisting of four identical parts.

quaff v. To drink with abundance.

quag-ga n. A wild ass of Africa related to the zebras.

quag-mire n. An area of soft muddy land that gives away underfoot; a marsh.

qua-hog n. A clam found in the Atlantic Ocean.

quail n., pl. A small game bird.

quaint adj. Pleasing in an old-fashioned, unusual way. **quaintly** adj., **-ness** n.

quake v. To shake or tremble violently.

quak-er n. The religious sect called the Society of Friends.

qual-i-fi-ca-tion n. An act of qualifying; the ability, skill, or quality which makes something suitable for a given position.

qual-i-fy v. To prove something able; restrict; limit; modify.

qual-i-ty n., pl., **ties** A distinguishing character which makes something such as it is; a high degree of excellence.

qualm n. A sudden feeling of sickness; sensation of uneasiness or doubt. **qualmishly** adj., **qualmishness** n.

quan-da-ry n. A state of perplexity.

quan-ti-ty n. Number; amount; bulk; weight; a portion; as a large amount.

quan-tum n., pl., **quanta** An amount or quantity.

quar-an-tine n. A period of enforced isolation for a specified period of time used to prevent the spread of a contagious disease. **quarantine** v.

quar-rel n. An unfriendly or angry disagreement; a cause for dispute.

quar-ri-er n. A person who works in a stone quarry.

quar-ry n., pl. **quar-ries** An animal hunted for food; an open pit or excavation from which limestone or other material is being extracted.

quart n. A unit of measurement equaling four cups.

quar-tan n. Something happening every four days.

quar-ter n. One of four equal parts into which anything may be divided; a place of lodging, as a barracks; a U.S. coin equal to 1/4 of a dollar.

quar-ter-back n., Football The offensive player who directs the plays for his team.

quar-ter-deck n. The part of a deck used for ceremonial and official use only.

quarter horse n. A horse capable of high speed and great endurance.

quarterly adj. Payable in three month intervals.

quar-ter-mas-ter n. The officer in charge of supplies for army troops; a navy OD officer who steers a ship and handles signaling equipment.

quar-tet n. A musical composition for four voices or instruments; any group or set of four.

quartz n. A hard, transparent crystallized mineral.

qua-sar n. One of the most distant and brightest bodies in the universe; a quasar producing intense visible radiation but not emitting radio signals.

quash v. To nullify or suppress by judicial action.

quay n. A landing place beside water for loading and unloading ships.

quea-sy adj. Nauseated; sick. **-iness** n.

que-bra-cho n. A tree of the sumac family which has hard wood found in South America.

queen n. The wife of a king; a woman sovereign or monarch; in chess, the most powerful piece on the board, which can move any number of squares in any direction; the fertile female in a colony of social insects.

queer adj. Strange; unusual; different from the normal. Slang Homosexual.

queerly adj., **queerness** n.

quell v. To put down with force; to quiet; to pacify.

quench v. To extinguish or put out; to cool metal by thrusting into water; to drink to satisfy a thirst. **quenchless, quenchable** adj., **quencher** n.

quer-cit-ron n. A large oak tree rich in tannin used in dyeing and tanning.

quer-u-lous adj. Complaining or fretting; expressing complaints.

que-ry n. An injury; a question. v. To question. **querier** n.

quest n. A search; pursuit; an expedition to find something.

ques-tion n. An expression of inquiry which requires an answer; a problem; an unresolved matter; the act of inquiring or asking.

ques-tion-able adj. Being in doubt; not certain or sure.

ques-tion mark n. A mark of punctuation, (?), used in writing to indicate a question.

ques-tion-naire n. A written series of questions to gather statistical information often used for a survey.

queue n., Computer Science A sequence of stored programs or data on hold for processing.

quib-ble v. To raise trivial objection. **quibble, quibbler** n.

quiche n. Unsweetened custard baked in a pastry shell, usually with vegetables or seafood.

quick adj. Moving swiftly; occurring in a short time; responding, thinking, or understanding something rapidly and easily. **quickly** adv., **quickness** n.

quick-en adj. To become faster; to increase the pace.

quick-sand n. A bog of very fine, wet sand of considerable depth, that engulfs and sucks down objects, people, or animals.

quick-temp-ered adj. Being easily angered or upset.

quick-wit-ted adj. Being quick to understand something.

quid n. A small portion of tobacco; a cow's cud.

qui-es-cent adj. Being in a state of quiet repose. **quiescently** adv.

qui-et adj. Silent; making very little sound; still; tranquil; calm. v. To become or make quiet. n. The state of being quiet. **quietly** adv., **quietness** n.

quill n.

A strong bird feather; a spine from a porcupine; a writing instrument made from a long stiff feather.

quilt n. A bed coverlet made of two layers of cloth with a soft substance between and held in place by lines of stitching.

quince *n.* A fruit that resembles a yellow apple used for making marmalade, jellys, etc.

quin-i-dine *n.* An alkaloid used in treating cardiac rhythm irregularities.

qui-nine *n., Chem.* A very bitter, colorless, crystalline powder used in the treatment of malaria.

quin-quen-ni-al *adj.* Happening or being done every five years.

quin-sy *n., Pathol.* A severe inflammation of the tonsils, which is accompanied by fever.

quin-tes-sence *n.* The most essential and purest form of anything.

quin-tet *n.* A musical composition written for five people; any group of five.

quin-til-lion *n.* A thousand quadrillions, one followed by eighteen zeros.

quin-tu-ple *adj.* Increased five times; multiplied by five; consisting of five parts.

quip *n.* A sarcastic remark. quipster *n.,* quipping *v.*

quire *n.* Twenty-five sheets of paper removed from a complete ream of paper; a set of all the sheets of paper necessary to form a book.

quirk *n.* A sudden, sharp bend or twist; a personal mannerism.

quis-ling *n.* A person who is a traitor, working against his own country from within.

quit *v.* To cease; to give up; to depart; to abandon; to resign or leave a job or position.

quite *adv.* To the fullest degree; really; actually; to a great extent.

quit-tance *n.* A document which releases someone from an obligation.

quiv-er *v.* To shake with a trembling motion. *n.* The arrows used in archery; the case in which arrows are kept.

quix-ot-ic *adj.* Extravagantly romantic.

quiz *v.* To question, as with an informal oral or written examination.

quiz, quizzer *n.*

quoin *n.* The external corner or angle of a building; the stone forming such a corner or angle; a cornerstone.

quoit *n.* A game in which a metal ring connected to a rope is thrown in an attempt to encircle a stake.

quon-dam *adj.* Former.

quo-rum *n.* The number of members needed in order to validate a meeting.

quo-ta *n.* An allotment or proportional share to each person.

quo-ta-tion *n.* The exact quoting of words as a passage; the stated current price.

quo-ta-tion mark *n.* The marks of punctuation (" ") showing a direct quote.

quote *v.* To repeat exactly what someone else has previously stated.

quo-tid-i-an *adj.* Occurring or recurring daily.

quo-tient *n., Math* The amount or number which results when one number is divided by another.

R, r The eighteenth letter of the English alphabet.

R *abbr.* Radius.

ra-ba-to *n.* A wide lace-edged collar of the early 17th century.

rab-bet *n.* A recess or groove along the edge of a piece of wood cut to fit another piece to form a joint. rabbeted *v.*

rab-bi *n.* An ordained leader of Jews; the leader and teacher of a Jewish congregation. rabbinic *adj.*

rab-bin-ate *n.* The dignity of a rabbi.

rab-bin-i-cal *adj.* To be referring or pertaining to the rabbis. rabbinically *adv.*

rab-bit *n.*

A burrowing mammal related to but smaller than the hare.

rab-bit ears *n.* Indoor television antenna, having two extensible rods, connected to a base forming a V shape.

rab-bit-eye *n.* A blueberry found in the southeastern part of the United States.

rab-bit punch *n.* A hit that is aimed at the back of one's head.

rab-bit-ry *n.* The location where rabbits are kept.

rab-ble *n.* A disorderly crowd. rabbling, rabbled *v.*

rab-ble-ment *n.* A rabble; a tumult.

rab-ble-rous-er *n.* A person who stirs masses of people to riot.

rab-id *adj.* Affected with rabies; mad; furious. rabidly *adv.,* rabidness *n.*

ra-bies *n.* An acute, infectious viral disease of the central nervous system, often fatal, which is transmitted by the bite of an infected animal.

rac-coon *n., pl.* -coons, -coon

A nocturnal mammal with a black, masklike face and a black-and-white ringed, bushy tail.

race *n.* The zoological division of the human population having common origin and other physical traits, such as hair form and pigmentation; a group of people having such common characteristics or appearances; people united by a common nationality.

race *n.* A contest which is judged by speed; any contest, such as a race for an elective office. raced, racer *n.*

race course *n.* The track on which a race takes place.

race horse *n.* A type of horse which is bred strictly for the use of racing.

ra-ceme *n.* A type of plant bearing flowers along its stalk. racemed *adj.*

rac-er *n.* A person who takes part in a race; one who runs in a race.

race-track *n.* The course which is used for the purpose of racing horses.

race-way *n.* The channel for water to pass through; a race track.

ra-chis *n.* A type of axial structure.

ra-cial *adj.* A characteristic of a race of people. **racially** *adv.*

rac-ing form *n.* The form that gives needed information which is relevant to horse races.

rac-ism *n.* A thought or belief that one race is better than another race. -ist *n.*

rack *n.* An open framework or stand for displaying or holding something; an instrument of torture used to stretch the body; a triangular frame used to arrange the balls on a pool table. *Mech.* A metal bar with teeth designed to move a cogged bar and produce a rotary or linear motion. *v.* to strain, as with great effort in thinking.

rack-et or **racquet** *n.* A light-weight bat-like object with netting stretched over an oval frame, used in striking a tennis ball or a shuttlecock.

rack-et-eer *n.* A person who engages in acts which are illegal.

rack-e-ty *adj.* To be noisy.

rack--rent *n.* A rent that is very high.

ra-clette *n.* A Swiss dish with cheese melted over a fire then scraped onto bread or potatoes.

rac-on-teur *n.* One who is skilled in the act of telling stories.

rac-y *adj.* Having a spirited or strongly marked quality; slightly improper or immodest. **racily** *adv.*, **raciness** *n.*

ra-dar *n.* A system which uses radio signals to detect the presence of an object or the speed the object is traveling.

ra-dar as-tron-o-my *n.* Astronomy that deals with investigations of the celestial bodies of the solar system by comparing characteristics of reflected radar wave with characteristics of ones transmitted from earth.

ra-dar-scope *n.* A screen or oscilloscope that serves as a visual indicator in a radar receiver.

ra-dar tel-e-scope *n.* A transmitter-receiver with an antenna for use in astronomy.

rad-dled *adj.* To be in a state of confusion; broken down; worn; lacking composure.

ra-di-al *adj.* Pertaining to or resembling a ray or radius; developing from a center axis.

ra-di-ance *n.* The quality of being shiny; the state of being radiant; relating or emitting to radiant heat.

ra-di-ant *adj.* Emitting rays of heat or light; beaming with kindness or love; projecting a strong quality. -ly *adv.*

ra-di-ant en-er-gy *n.* The energy traveling as a wave motion.

ra-di-ant heat *n.* Heat that is transmitted by radiation.

ra-di-ate *v.* To move out in rays, such as heat moving through the air. -ly *adv.*

ra-di-a-tion *n.* An act of radiating; the process or action of radiating; the process of emitting radiant energy in the form of particles or waves. **radiationless** *adj.*, **radiative** *adj.*

ra-di-a-tor *n.* Something which radiates; a system of pipes for heating or cooling external or internal substances.

rad-i-cal *adj.* Proceeding from a foundation or root; drastic; making extreme changes in views, conditions, or habits; carrying convictions or theories to their fullest application. **radically** *adv.*, **radicalness** *n.*

rad-i-cal-ism *n.* A following of views which are extreme in character.

rad-i-cand *n.* Term located within the radical sign.

rad-i-cate *v.* To take root.

rad-i-cle *n.* The lower part of a plant embryo or seedling.

radii *pl.* of Radius.

ra-di-o *n.* The technique of communicating by radio waves; the business of broadcasting programmed material to the public via radio waves. **radioing, radioed** *v.*

ra-di-o-ac-tive *adj.* Exhibiting radioactivity. **radioactively** *adv.*

ra-di-o-ac-tiv-i-ty *n.*, *Physics* A spontaneous emission of electro-magnetic radiation, as from a nuclear reaction.

ra-di-o-broad-cast *n.* A broadcasting or transmission of messages by a radio.

ra-di-o-chem-is-try *n.* The part of chemistry that deals with radioactive bodies. **radiochemical** *adj.*

ra-di-o-fre-quen-cy *n.* A frequency which is above 15,000 cycles per second that is used in radio transmission.

ra-di-o-gram *n.* A type of radiograph.

ra-di-o-graph *n.* A picture which is made by rays from a radioactive substance. **-ically** *adv.*, **radiographic** *adj.*

ra-di-o-lar-o-an *n.* A member of the group of minute marine protozoans and having an amoeboid body.

ra-di-o-lo-ca-tion *n.* The finding of the location of something with the use of radar.

ra-di-ol-o-gy *n.* A science which deals with rays for a radioactive substance and use for medical diagnosis. **radiologist** *n.*, **radiological, -ic** *adj.*

ra-dio-lu-cen-cy *n.* The state of being permeable to radiation.

ra-di-o-man *n.* A person who operates a radio.

ra-dio-pho-to *n.* A picture transmitted via radio.

ra-dio-sonde *n.* A miniature radio transmitter with instruments for broadcasting the humidity, pressure and temperature.

rad-ish *n.* The pungent, edible root of the radish plant.

ra-di-um *n* A radioactive metallic element symbolized by Ra.

ra-di-us *n.*, *pl.* -dii or -uses

A line from the center of a circle to its surface or circumference.

ra-dix *n.* The origin of something; as a root.

RADM *abbr.* Rear admiral.

ra-dome *n.* A plastic housing which protects the antenna assembly on an airplane.

ra-don *n.* A heavy, colorless, radioactive gaseous element symbolized by Rn.

rad-u-la *n.* The chitinous band a mollusk's mouth that is used to break up its food. **radular** *adj.*

raff *n.* The rabble of a group or town.

raf-fi-a *n.* A fiber from an African palm tree used for making baskets, hats, and other woven articles.

raf-fi-nose *n.* A slightly sweet sugar obtained commercially from cottonseed meal.

raff-ish *adj.* Something that is marked by crudeness or flashy vulgarity. **raffishly** *adv.*, **raffishness** *n.*

raf-fle *n.* A game of chance; a lottery in which one buys chances to win something.

raf-fle-sia *n.* A type of plant that has foul-smelling flowers and appears to be stemless.

raft *n.* A floating structure made from logs or planks and used for water transportation.

raft-er *n.* A timber of a roof which slopes; a person who maneuvers logs into position.

rafts-man *n.* A person who engages in rafting.

rag *n.* A cloth which is useless and sometimes used for cleaning purposes.

ra-ga *n.* Ancient melodic patterns in Indian music.

rag-a-muf-fin *n.* A child who is unkempt.

rag bag *n.* A miscellaneous grouping or collection; a bag for holding scrap pieces of material.

rag doll *n.* A child's doll that is usually made from scrap material and has a hand painted face.

rage *n.* Violent anger; intense feelings. **raging** *adj.*, **ragingly** *adv.*

rag-ged *adj.* To be torn or ripped; unkempt. **raggedness** *n.*, **raggedly** *adv.*

rag-ged rob-in *n.* A perennial herb having pink flowers with narrow-lobed petals.

rag-gle *n.* A small groove cut in masonry.

rag-i *n.* An East Indian cereal grass used as a staple food in the Orient.

rag-lan *n.* A loose fitting coat with extra wide sleeves.

rag-lan sleeve *n.* A sleeve with slanted seams from the underarm to the neck.

rag-man *n.* A person who collects objects which have been discarded by others.

ra-gout *n.* A highly seasoned meat and vegetable dish with a thick sauce.

rag pick-er *n.* A person who collects refuse for a livelihood.

rag-time *n.* A type of music with a ragtime rhythm.

rag-weed *n.* A type of plant whose pollen can cause hay fever.

rag-wort *n.* A type of herb which has yellow-rayed flowers.

raid *n.* A sudden invasion or seizure.

rail *n.* A horizontal bar of metal, wood, or other strong material supported at both ends or at intervals; the steel bars used to support a track on a railroad.

rail-bird *n.* A person who sits on or near a race track rail and watches a race or workout.

rail-head *n.* A section on a railroad where traffic may begin or start.

rail-ing *n.* A barrier of wood.

rail-ler-y *n.* A teasing that is good-humored.

rail-road *n.* A road having a line of rails providing a track for cars driven by a locomotive. **railroader** *n.*

rail-road-ing *n.* The operation of railroads.

rail-road worm *n.* A fruit fly's larva.

rail-split-ter *n.* A person who chops logs into fence rails.

rai-ments *n.* Garments.

rain *n.* The condensed water from atmospheric vapor, which falls to earth in the form of drops.

rain-bird *n.* A type of American cuckoos that has a series of rapid calls.

rain-bow *n.* An arc that contains bands of colors of the spectrum and is formed opposite the sun and reflects the sun's rays, usually visible after a light rain shower.

rain-bow trout *n.* A large stout-bodied fish of western North America.

rain check *n.* A coupon or stub for merchandise which is out of stock; the assurance of entrance or availability at a later date.

rain-coat *n.* A water-resistant or waterproof coat.

rain-fall *n.* The amount of measurable precipitation.

rain for-est *n.* A tropical woodland that has an annual rainfall of at least 100 inches.

rain gauge *n.* An instrument used to measure rain fall.

rain-mak-ing *n.* The act or process of producing or attempting to produce rain by the use of artificial means.

rain-proof *adj.* To be impervious to rain.

rain spout *n.* A pipe which drains rain from the roof.

rain-wear *n.* Waterproof clothing.

rain-y *adj.* To be wet from the rain. **raininess** *n.*, **rainily** *adv.*

raise *v.* To cause to move upward; to build; to make greater in size, price, or amount; to increase the status; to grow; as plants; to rear as children; to stir ones emotions; to obtain or collect as funds or money.

raised *adj.* To be elevated.

rai-sin *n.* A grape dried for eating.

ra-ja *n.* An Indian prince or chief.

rake *n.* A tool with a long handle at the end and a set of teeth at the other end used to gather leaves and other matter; a slope or incline, as the rake of an auditorium. **rake** *v.*, **raker** *n.*

rak-ish *adj.* Having a stylish appearance.

rakishness *n*.

ral-len-tan-do *adj*. In music, a gradual decrease in tempo.

ral-ly *v*. To call together for a purpose. *n*. A rapid recovery, as from depression, exhaustion, or any setback; in a meeting whose purpose is to rouse or create support; an automobile run over public roads at average speeds between checkpoints over a route unfamiliar to the participants.

ral-ly-ing *n*. The sport of driving automobiles in rallies.

ram *n*. A male sheep; an implement used to drive or crush by impact; to cram or force into place.

RAM *abbr*. Random access memory.

ram-ble *v*. To stroll or walk without a special destination in mind; to talk without sequence of ideas. ramble *n*., ramblingly *adv*.

ram-bler *n*. A climbing rose with small flowers in large clusters.

Ram-bouil-let *n*. A large sheep found in France.

ram-bunc-tious *adj*. Rough or boisterous. rambunctiousness *n*.

ram-bu-tan *n*. A bright red spiny fruit found on the soapberry tree.

ram-e-kin *n*. A dish made of cheese with bread crumbs or eggs baked in a mold; a baking dish.

ra-men-tum *n*. A type of scaly material that adheres to the leaves and the stems of certain ferns.

ra-met *n*. A member of a clone.

ra-mie *n*. A perennial plant with strong fibers used in the manufacture of clothing.

ram-i-form *adj*. To have the shape of a branch.

ram-i-fy *v*. To send forth branches.

ra-mose *adj*. To have branching.

ramp *n*. An incline which connects two different levels; movable staircase allows passengers to enter or leave an aircraft.

ram-page *n*. A course of destruction or violent behavior. *v*. To storm about in a rampage. rampageous *adj*., rampageousness *n*.

ram-pan-cy *n*. The state or quality of being rampant.

ram-pant *adj*. Exceeding or growing without control; wild in actions; standing on the hind legs and elevating both forelegs. rampantly *adv*.

ram-part *n*. An embankment raised as a fortification or barrier.

ram-pike *n*. A erect dead tree.

ram-pi-on *n*. A tuberous root bellflower with leaves which can be used in salads.

ram-rod *n*. A metal rod used to drive or plunge the charge into a muzzle-loading gun or pistol; the rod used for cleaning the barrels of a rifle or other firearm.

ram-shack-le *adj*. Likely to fall apart from poor construction or maintenance.

rams-horn *n*. A snail used in an aquarium as a scavenger.

ram-til *n*. A tropical herb grown for its oil seeds.

ram-u-lose *adj*. To have small branches.

ranch *n*. A large establishment for raising cattle, sheep, or other livestock; a large farm that specializes in a certain crop or animals. rancher *n*.

ranch house *n*. A one story house with a low-pitched roof.

ran-cho *n*. A small Mexican ranch.

ran-cid *adj*. Having a rank taste or smell. rancidness *n*.

ran-cor *n*. Bitter ill will. rancorous *adv*., rancorousness *n*.

ran-dom *adj*. Done or made in a way that has no specific pattern or purpose; to select from a group whose members all had an even chance of being chosen. randomly *adv*., -ness *n*.

ran-dom-iza-tion *n*. An arrangement to simulate a chance distribution.

R and R *abbr*. Rest and relaxation.

rang *v*. Past tense of ring.

range *n*. An area over which anything moves; an area of activity; a tract of land over which animals such as cattle and horses graze; an extended line or row especially of mountains; an open area for shooting at a target; large cooking stove with burners and oven. *v*. to arrange in a certain order; to extend or proceed in a particular direction.

range find-er *n*. Instrument that is used in gunnery to determine the distance of a target.

rang-er *n*. A person who is hired to tend the public forests.

rang-y *adj*. To be adapted for moving around. ranginess *n*.

ra-ni *n*. A Hindu queen.

ra-nid *n*. A large family of frogs.

rank *n*. A degree of official position or status. *v*. To place in order, class, or rank. *adj*. A strong and disagreeable odor, smell, or taste. -ly *adv*. -ness *n*.

rank and file *n*. The enlisted men of the armed forces.

rank-er *n*. A commissioned officer who was promoted from the ranks.

rank-ing *adj*. To be holding the highest rank.

ran-kle *v*. To cause anger or deep bitterness.

ran-sack *v*. To search or plunder through every part of something.

ran-som *n*. The price demanded or paid for the release of a kidnapped person; the payment for the release of a person or property detained. ransom *v*.

rant *v*. To talk in a wild, excited loud way. ranter *n*.

ran-u-la *n*. A type of cyst that can occur under the tongue due to a blockage in a duct.

rap *v*. To talk with people with similar interest and problems.

ra-pa-cious *adj*. Living on prey seized alive; taking by force; plundering. rapaciously *adv*., -ness, rapacity *n*.

rape *n*. The crime of forcible sexual intercourse; abusive treatment.

rape oil *n.* Type of oil that is from the rapeseed and is used in making rubber substitutes.

rap-id *adj.* Having great speed; completed quickly or in a short time.
rapidity, rapidness *n.*

rap-id--fire *adj.* Pertaining to firing shots in close succession to one another.

rap-id trans-it *n.* The train system that runs with a city and the area around it.

ra-pi-er *n.* A long, slender, straight sword with two edges.

rap-ine *n.* The forcible taking of another's property.

rap-pa-ree *n.* An Irish soldier or bandit.

rap-pee *n.* A snuff made from dark tobacco leaves.

rap-pel *n.* A descent from a cliff using a rope under one thigh, across the back and over the opposite shoulder.

rap-per *n.* A door knocker; a person who raps on a door.

rap-pi-ni *n.* An immature turnip plant used for its greens.

rap-port *n.* A harmonious relationship.

rap-proche-ment *n.* The establishment of cordial relations.

rap-scal-lion *n.* A rascal.

rapt *adj.* Deeply absorbed or carried away with something and not to noticing anything else; engrossed.
raptness *n.,* **raptly** *adv.*

rap-tor *n.* A bird of prey.

rap-to-ri-al *adj.* Having the ability to seize prey.

rap-ture *n.* An experience of being carried away by emotion.
rapturous *adj.,* **rapturously** *adv.*

rare *adj.* Scarce; infrequent; often held in high esteem or admiration because of infrequency. **rareness** *n.*

rare-bit *n.* A dish made of cheese poured over toast or crackers.

rar-e-fy *v.* To make thin or less dense.

rare-ly *adv.* Seldom; not often.

rar-ing *adj.* Being full of eagerness and enthusiasm.

rar-i-ty *n.* The quality of something being rare.

ras-bo-ra *n.* A breed of brightly colored fish often kept in tropical aquariums.

ras-cal *n.* A person full of mischief; a person who is not honest. **rascally** *adj.*

ras-cal-i-ty *n.* Behavior which is mischievous.

rash *adj.* Acting without consideration or caution. *n.* A skin irritation or eruption caused by an allergic reaction.

rash-er *n.* A thin slice of bacon; a portion of several slices of bacon.

ra-so-ri-al *adj.* Scratching the ground in search of food.

rasp *n.*

A file with course raised and pointed projections. *v.* To scrape or rub with a course file; to utter something in a rough, grating voice.
rasper *n.,* **raspy** *adj.* **raspingly** *adv.*

rasp-ber-ry *n.* A small edible fruit, red or black in color and having many small seeds. *Slang* Contemptuous sound made by expelling air with the tongue between the lips in order to make a vibration.

rasp-y *adj.* Grating; irritable.

ras-ter *n.* An area onto which an image is reproduced in a kinescope.

rat *n.*

A rodent similar to the mouse, but having a longer tail. *Slang* A despicable person who betrays his friends or his associates. **ratlike** *adj.*

rat-a-fia *n.* A liqueur flavored with kernels of fruit and almonds.

rat-a-tat *n.* A sharp tapping, or repeated knocking.

rat-bite fe-ver *n.* A kind of disease that can be transmitted through the bite of a rat and is characterized by muscle soreness and fever.

ratch-et *n.* A mechanism consisting of a pawl that allows a wheel or bar to move in one direction only.

ratch-et wheel *n.* A wheel with teeth that is held place with a engaging handle.

rate *n.* The measure of something to a fixed unit; the degree of price or value; a fixed ratio or amount. *v.* To appraise.

ra-tel *n.* An African nocturnal carnivorous mammal resembling a badger.

rate of ex-change *n.* The amount of one currency which equals the given amount of another.

rathe *adj.* To be before the normal time.

rath-er *adv.* Preferably; with more reason or justice; more accurate or precise.

raths-kel-ler *n.* A basement restaurant patterned after the German city hall and in which beer is sold.

rat-i-cide *n.* A material that is used to kill rats.

rat-i-fy *v.* To approve something in an official way. **ratification** *n.*

ra-ti-ne *n.* A nubby ply yarn made by twisting a thick and a thin yarn under pressure.

rat-ing *n.* A relative evaluation or estimate of something.

ra-tio *n.,* *pl.* **-tios** The relationship between two things in amount, size, degree, expressed as a proportion.

ra-ti-o-ci-na-tion *n.* A reasoned train of thought.

ra-tion *n.* A fixed portion or share. *v.* To provide or allot in rations.
rationing *n.* **rationed** *v.*

ra-tion-al *adj.* Having the faculty of reasoning; being of sound mind.
rationality *n.,* **rationally** *adv.,* **-ness** *n.*

ra-tio-nale *n.* An explanation of principles of opinion, belief or phenomena.

ra-tio-nal-ize v. To provide plausible but not truthful reasons for conduct. **rationalization** n., **rationalizer** n.

ra-toon v. To grow or sprout up from the root.

rat race n. A strenuous activity or rush.

rats-bane n. A material that is poisonous to rats.

rat snake n. A large harmless rat-eating snake.

rat-tail n. A horse's tail which has very little hair.

rat-tail file n. A slender round tapered file.

rat-tan n. An Asian palm whose strong stems are used to make wickerworks.

rat-teen n. A woolen fabric which is coarse in texture.

rat-ter n. A person who likes to catch rats.

rat-tle v. To make a series of rapid, sharp noises in quick succession; to talk rapidly; chatter. n. A baby's toy made to rattle when shaken.

rat-tle-brain n. A thoughtless person. **rattlebrained** adj.

rat-tler n., Slang A venomous snake which has a series of horny, modified joints which make a rattling sound when moved; a rattlesnake; one that rattle.

rat-tle-snake n. An American venomous snake with a tail that makes a sharp rattling sound when shaken.

rat-tle-snake plan-tain n. A variety of an orchid with mottled leaves.

rat-tle-snake root n. A plant formerly believed to be effective against their venom.

rat-tle-snake weed n. An woody herb with purple-veined leaves grown in the western United States related to the carrot.

rat-tle-trap n. Something that is rickety or rattly; an old car.

rat-trap n. An instrument or device that is used to catch rats.

rat-ty adj. Shabby; unkempt.

rau-cous adj. Loud and rowdy; having a rough hoarse sound; disorderly. **raucously** adv., **raucousness** n.

raun-chy adj. Being dirty, slovenly.

rau-wol-fi-a n. A type of shrub which is used as a source of the drug reserpine.

rav-age v. To bring on heavy destruction; devastate. **ravaged** v., **ravagement** n., **ravager** n.

rave v. To speak incoherently; to speak with enthusiasm. n. The act of raving.

rav-el v. To separate fibers or threads; to unravel.

rav-el-ment n. A confusion.

ra-ven n. A large bird, with shiny black feathers. adj. Of or relating to the glossy sheen or color of the raven.

rav-en-ing adj. To be hunting in order to devour something.

rav-en-ous adj. Being very hungry and eager for food.

rav-in n. Something seized as prey.

ra-vine n. A deep gorge with steep sides in the earth's surface, usually created by flowing water.

rav-ing adj. An incoherent, wild, or extravagant outburst.

rav-i-o-li n. A small piece of dough filled with meat or cheese served in a tomato sauce.

rav-ish v. To seize and carry off; to rape. **ravishment** n., **ravisher** n.

rav-ish-ing adj. Unusually striking.

raw adj. Uncooked; in natural condition; not processed. inexperienced; damp, sharp, or chilly. **rawly** adv., **-ness** n.

raw-boned adj. Having a coarse lean appearance.

raw-hide n. The untanned hide of cattle.

raw ma-te-ri-al n. Material that is existing in its natural form.

ray n. A thin line of radiation or light; a small trace or amount; one of several lines coming from a point.

ray-less adj. Having no rays; dark.

ray-on n. A synthetic cellulose yarn; any fabric made from such yarn.

raze v. To destroy or demolish.

ra-zor n. A sharp cutting instrument used especially for shaving.

ra-zor-back n. A wild hog of the southeastern United States; the mascot of the University of Arkansas.

ra-zor-bill n. A North Atlantic auk.

ra-zor clam n. A type of bivalve mollusks having a shell that is long and narrow.

razz v., Slang To heckle; to tease.

raz-zle--daz-zle n. A state of complete confusion.

re- prefix Again, anew or reverse action.

reach v. To stretch out; to be able to grasp. n. The act of stretching out. **reachable** adj., **reacher** n.

re-act v. To act in response to. Chem. To undergo a chemical change; to experience a chemical reaction; to move in a reverse direction; to cause to react.

re-ac-tant n. Substance which enters into and is altered the course of a chemical reaction.

re-ac-tion n. The mental or bodily response to an activity; the process or act or reacting; the action that is induced by vital resistance to another action; exhaustion caused by excessive exertion of stimulation; a emotional disorder forming a person's response to his life; the force that a body exerts when force from another body in the opposite direction; a chemical change; the state resulting from an interaction of chemical entities. **reactional** adj., **reactionally** adv.

re-ac-tion-ary adj. Marked by, or relating to political reaction. **-ism** n.

re-ac-tion en-gine n. A jet engine or one similar that develops thrust by expelling a jet of fluid.

re-ac-ti-vate v. To activate something again. **reactively** adv., **reactiveness**, **reactivity** n.

re-ac-tor n. A person, object, device, or

substance which reacts to something.

read *v.* To visually go over something, as a book, and to understand its meaning; to learn or be informed; to perceive something in a meaning which may or may not actually be there; to become acquainted with or look at the contents; to recognize the nature of by observing outward expression or signs.

read-able *adj.* Able to be read with ease. **readability**, **-ness** *n.*, **readably** *adv.*

read-er *n.* A person who has been instructed to read to others.

read-er-ship *n.* The state or quality of being a reader; the office of a reader; a particular group of readers.

readi-ly *adj.* Without hestitation; without a lot of difficulty.

read-ing *n.* An interpretation of something; the act of reading; a particular interpretation or version; the indication of a state of affairs.

read-ing desk *n.* A desk used to support a book and allows a person to read in a standing position.

read-out *n.* In computer science, the process of removing information from a computer and displaying it in an understandable form; the process of reading something; the radio transmission of pictures or information from a space vehicle either immediately upon acquisition or by tape recording playback. **readiness** *n.*

read-y *adj.* Prepared for use or action; quick or prompt; willing.

ready-made *n.* Something made beforehand for sale to the public; something that is lacking individuality or originality.

ready room *n.* An area where pilots are briefed before flying.

ready-to-wear *n.* Clothing manufacture to sell to the general public.

Rea-gan, Ronald Wilson *n.* The 40th president of the United States inaugurated in 1981.

re-a-gent *n* Any substance which causes a chemical reaction.

re-ag-gre-gate *v.* To reform into a whole. **reaggregate**, **reaggreagation** *n.*

re-al *adj.* Something which is existing, genuine, true, or authentic. *Law* Property which is regarded as permanent, fixed, or immovable; not illusory, artificial, or fraudulent. **realness** *n.*

real estate *n.* The property in land and buildings.

re-al-gar *n.* An orange-red mineral consisting of arsenic sulfide with a resinous luster.

re-alia *n.* Objects used to relate classroom teaching to the real life of people studied.

re-al-ism *n.* Concern or interest with actual facts and things as they really are. **realist** *n.*, **realistic** *adj.*, **-ically** *adv.*

re-al-i-ty *n.*, *pl.* The fact or state of being real or genuine; an actual situation or real event; something that is neither dependent nor derivative but exists necessarily.

re-al-ize *v.* To understand correctly; to make real; to make or cause to seem real. **realizable** *adj.*, **realization** *n.*, **realizer** *n.*

re-al-ly *adv.* Actually; truly; indeed; unquestionably. **realizable** *adj.*, **realizer** *n.*

realm *n.* A scope or field of any power or influence.

re-al-po-li-tik *n.* Politics that are based on material and practical factors and not on ethical or theoretical objectives.

Re-al-tor *n.* A real estate agent who belongs to the National Association of Realtors.

re-al-val-ued *adj.* Using only real numbers for values.

ream *n.* A quantity of paper containing 500 sheets; *v.* To widen the opening of something.

ream-er *n.* A rotating tool with cutting edges used to enlarge or shape a hole; a fruit juice extractor that has a ridged and pointed center that rises from a shallow bowl.

reap *v.* To harvest a crop with a sickle or other implement; to cut with a scythe, sickle, or other harvesting machine.

reap-er *n.* A machine used to reap grain.

reap-hook *n.* An implement that is held by the hand and has a hook-shaped blade used in reaping grain.

rear *n.* The back. *adj.* Of or at the rear. *v.* To raise up on the hind legs; to raise as an animal or child; to erect by building something. **rearer** *n.*

rear admiral *n.* A commissioned officer in the Navy who ranks above a captain.

rear echelon *n.* A military unit or headquarters located at a considerable distance from the front line.

rear-guard *n.* A military detachment detailed to protect the rear of a main body of men.

re-arm *v.* To supply with new or better weapons. **rearmament** *n.*

rear-most *adj.* Being farthest in the rear.

rear-view mir-ror *n.* A mirror on the side of an automobile which gives a view of the area behind the vehicle.

rea-son *n.* A statement given to confirm or justify a belief, promise, or excuse; the ability to decide things, to obtain ideas, to think clearly, and to make logical and rational choices and decisions. *v.* To discuss something logically. **reasoning** *v.*, **reasoner** *n.*

rea-son-a-ble *adj.* Moderate; rational; not excessive or extreme. **reasonableness** *n.*, **reasonably** *adv.*

rea-son-ing *n.* Conclusions drawn through the use of reason.

rea-son-less *adj.* Lacking the faculty of reason; not supported by reason. **reasonlessly** *adv.*

re-as-sur-ance *n.* The act of reassuring; reinsurance.

re-as-sure *v.* To restore confidence. **reassuringly** *adv.*

reave v. To carry away. **reaver** n.

re-bar-ba-tive adj. The act of being repellent. **rebarbatively** v.

re-bate n. A deduction allowed on items sold; a discount; money which is returned to the purchaser from the original payment. v. To return part of the payment. **rebater** n.

reb-be n. A Jewish spiritual leader.

re-bec n. An ancient musical instrument with a pear-shaped body and slender neck.

re-bel v. To refuse allegiance; to resist any authority; to react with violence; to take arms against a government.

re-bel-lion n. An organized uprising to change or overthrow an existing authority.

re-bel-lious adj. Engaged in rebellion; relating to a rebel or rebellion; characteristic of a rebellion. **rebelliously** adv., **rebelliousness** n.

rebel yell n. A high-pitched yell given by Confederate soldiers in the Civil War.

re-birth n. A revival or renaissance; reincarnation; spiritual regeneration.

re-bound v. To spring back; to recover from a setback or frustration; to gain possession of a rebound ball in basketball. n. Recoil.

re-bound-er n. A basketball player skilled at rebounding the ball.

re-bo-zo n. A long scarf worn by Mexican women.

re-broad-cast v. To repeat or broadcast again at a later time or date. **rebroadcast**, **rebroadcaster** n.

re-buff v. To refuse abruptly; to snub.

re-build v. To restore or make extensive changes to a building; to reconstruct; remodel.

re-buke v. To reprimand; to criticize sharply; to turn back. n. Strong disapproval. **rebuker** n.

re-bus n. A riddle using words or syllables whose names resemble the intended words or syllables in sound.

re-but v. To try and prove someone wrong by argument or evidence; to contradict by formal argument. **rebuttal** n., **rebutable** adj.

re-but-tal n. An argument that rebuts.

re-but-ter n. The reply of a defendant to the plaintiff's surrejoinder.

rec abbr. Recreation; receipt; record.

re-cal-ci-trant adj. Being difficult to handle or operate.

re-cal-cu-late v. To calculate again to discover an error or formulate new conclusions. **recalculation** n.

re-ca-les-cence n. An increase in temperature occurring while cooling metal.

re-call v. To order or summon to return to ask for something to be returned; so that defects can be fixed or repaired; to remember; to recollect. **recallability** n., **-able** adj., **recaller** n.

re-cant v. To formally admit that a previously held belief was wrong by making public confession; to withdraw; renounce. **recantation** n.

re-cap v. To restore an old tire; to review or summarize something. **-pable** adj.

re-cap-i-tal-iza-tion n. A revision of the capital structure of a corporation.

re-ca-pit-u-la-tion n. A concise summary; the third section of a sonata.

re-cap-ture v. To take possession of again.

re-cast v. To cast new people in a play; to cast once again.

re-cede v. To move back; as floodwater; to withdraw from an agreement; to grow less or smaller.

re-ceipt n. The written acknowledgment of something received. pl., **receipts** The amount of money received.

re-ceiv-ables n. The amount of money received.

re-ceive v. To take or get something; to greet customers or guests; to accept as true or correct; to assimilate through senses.

re-ceiv-er n. A person that receives something.

re-ceiv-ing blan-ket n. A small lightweight blanket to wrap an infant.

re-ceiv-ing line n. A group of people who individually welcome arriving guests.

re-cen-sion n. A revision of a text.

re-cent adj. Happening at a time just before the present; relating to a short time ago. **recently** adv. **recentness** n.

re-cep-ta-cle n. Anything which holds something; an electrical outlet designed to receive a plug.

re-cep-tion n. The act or manner of receiving something; a formal entertainment of guests, as a wedding reception.

re-cep-tion-ist n. An employee who greets callers and answers the telephone for a business.

re-cep-tive adj. Able to receive; open and responsive to ideas. **-ly** adv., **receptiveness**, **receptivity** n.

re-cep-tor n. A group of cells that receive stimuli.

re-cess n. A break in the normal routine of something; a depression or niche in a smooth surface.

re-ces-sion n. The act of receding; withdrawal; a period or time of reduced economic activity. **-ary** adj.

re-ces-sion-al n. A musical piece at the conclusion of a service.

re-ces-sive adj. Having a tendency to go backward. **recessively** adj., **-ness** n.

re-charge v. To restore the active materials in a battery; make a new attack. **recharger** n., **rechargeable** adj.

re-cheat n. A hunting call on a horn to assemble the hounds.

re-cid-i-vism n. A tendency to relapse into a previous mode of behavior. **recidivist** adj., **recidivistic** adj.

rec-i-pe n. The directions and a list of ingredients for preparing food.

re-cip-i-ent n. A person who receives.

re-cip-ro-cal adj. To return the same way.

re-cip-ro-cal pro-noun n. A pronoun to

denote mutual action between members in a plural subject.

re-cip-ro-cate v. To give and return mutually, one gift or favor for another. reciprocator n.

re-cip-ro-ca-tion n. A mutual exchange; an alternating motion. -ive adj.

rec-i-proc-i-ty n. Mutual exchange of privileges; the state of being reciprocal.

re-cit-al n. A performance given by an individual musician or dancer. recitalist n.

rec-i-ta-tion n. An instance of repeating aloud; a student's oral reply to questions.

re-cite v. To repeat something from memory; give an account of something in detail. reciter n.

reck-less adj. State of being careless and rash when doing something. recklessness n., recklessly adv.

reck-on v. To calculate; to compute; to estimate; to consider; to assume. reckon with Take into consideration.

reck-on-ing n. The act of calculation or counting.

re-claim v. To redeem; to reform; to recall; to change to a more desirable condition or state. reclaimable adj.

rec-la-ma-tion n. The state of being reclaimed.

re-cline v. To assume a prone position.

re-clos-able adj. Capable of being shut or closed again.

rec-luse n. A person who chooses to live in seclusion.

rec-og-ni-tion n. An acknowledgment which is formal; the action of recognizing something; special attention or notice.

re-cog-ni-zance n. An amount of money which will be forfeited for a nonperformance of an obligation.

rec-og-nize v. To experience or identify something or someone as having been known previously; to appreciative. recognizable adj., recognizably adv., recognizer, recognizability n.

re-coil v. To fall back or to rebound; to spring back under pressure. recoilless adj.

rec-ol-lect v. To remember or recall to the mind. recollection n., -ed adj.

rec-om-mend v. To suggest to another as desirable; advise. recommendation n., recommendable adj.

re-com-mit v. To refer back to; to entrust or consign again. -ment, -al n.

rec-om-pense v. To reward with something for a service.

re-com-pose v. To restore the composure of. recomposition n.

rec-on-cile v. To restore a friendship after an estrangement. -ably adv., reconcilement n., -able adj., -er n.

rec-on-dite adj. Being obscure. reconditely adv., reconditeness n.

re-con-di-tion n. To return to a good condition.

re-con-firm v. Confirm something again. reconfirmation n.

re-con-nais-sance n. An observation of territory such as that of the enemy.

re-con-noi-ter v. To survey a region. reconnoitering v.

re-con-sid-er v. To think about again with a view to changing a previous action or decision. reconsideration n.

re-con-sti-tute v. To restore to a former condition. reconstitution n.

re-con-struct v. To build something again. reconstructible, reconstructive adj., reconstructor n.

re-con-struc-tion n. Something which has been reconstructed or rebuilt.

re-con-ver-sion n. Returning back to the previous or original state.

re-con-vey v. To return back to a previous position or owner. -ance n.

re-cord v. To write down for future use or permanent reference; to preserve sound on a tape or disk for replay; a phonograph record. n. Information which is recorded and kept permanently.

re-cord chan-ger n. A device that automatically positions and plays each of a stack of records.

re-curd-er n. A person who records things such as official transactions.

re-cord-ing n. The act of making a transcription of sounds.

rec-ord play-er n. The machine which is used to play recordings.

re-count v. To tell the facts; narrate or describe in detail; to count again. n. A second count to check the results of the first count. recounter n.

re-coup v. To be reimbursed; to recover. recoupable adj., recoupment n.

re-course n. A turning to or an appeal for help; a source of help.

re-cov-er v. To regain something which was lost; to be restored to good health. Law To obtain a judgment for damages. recoverability, recoverable adj., recoverer n.

re-cov-er-y n. The power to regain something.

re-cov-er-y room n. A room in a hospital especially equipped to care for patients after surgery.

rec-re-ant adj. Cowardly; unfaithful.

re-cre-ate v. To create again, to form in the imagination. recreative, recreatable, recreative adj.

rec-re-a-tion n. Refreshment of body and mind; a pleasurable occupation or exercise. recreational adj.

rec-re-ation-ist n. A person seeking recreation out of doors.

re-crea-tion room n. A room used for relaxation and play; a public room in a hospital for social activities.

re-crim-i-nate v. The charging of another of the same account. recriminatory, -ive adj., -ion n.

re-cru-desce v. To break out; become raw again. recrudescence n.

re-cruit v. To enlist someone for military or naval purposes; to look for someone as for a service or employment. n. A newly enlisted person.

recruiter n., **recruitment** n.

rec-tal adj. Referring to the rectum of the body. **rectally** adv.

rec-tan-gle n.

A parallelogram with all right angles. **rectangular** adj., **rectangularity** n.

rec-ti-fi-er n. That which rectifies something. **rectifiable** adj.

rec-ti-fy v. To make correct. Chem. To purify by repeated distillations. Electr. To make an alternating current a direct current. **rectification** n.

rec-ti-lin-ear adj. Made up of or indicated by straight lines; bounded by straight lines. **rectilinearly** adv.

rec-ti-tude n. Rightness in principles and conduct; correctness.

rec-to n. The right-hand page of a book.

rec-tor n. A member of the clergy in charge of a parish; a priest in charge of a congregation, church, or parish; the principal or head of a school or of a college. **rectorate** n., **rectorial** adj., **rectorship** n.

rec-to-ry n. The rector's residence.

rec-trix n. The quill feathers of a bird's tail that are important in controlling flight.

rec-tum n., pl. -tums, -ta Anat. The lower terminal portion of the large intestine connecting the colon and anus.

re-cum-bent adj. Lying down or reclining. **recumbently** adv.

re-cu-per-ate v. To regain strength or to regain one's health; to recover from a financial loss. **recuperation** n., **recuperative** adj.

re-cur v. To happen, to return, or to appear again. **recurrence, recurrent** adj.

re-cur-rent adj. Happening time after time. **recurrently** adv.

re-cu-san-cy n. The refusal to accept established authority.

re-cy-cle v. To return to an earlier usable condition. **recyclable** adj.

red n. Having the color which resembles blood, as pigment or dye which colors red. Slang A communist; one who is in favor of the overthrow of an existing political of social order; a condition indicating a loss, as in the red.

re-dact v. To adapt for publication. **redactional** adj.

red-breast n. A bird with a reddish colored breast.

red-brick adj. A commonly used brick in construction.

red-bud n. An American tree with a pale pinkish-rose flower.

red cap n. A porter who carries luggage at railroad stations, airports, etc.

red carpet n. A greeting reserved for very important people.

red clover n. A clover with reddish purple flowers cultivated as forage and a cover crop.

red-coat n. A British soldier in America during the Revolutionary War.

red coral n. A hard stony skeleton of a delicate red or pink color used for jewelry and ornaments found in the Atlantic Ocean.

Red Cross n. An organization which helps people in need, collects and preserves human blood for use in emergencies, and responds with help in time of disaster.

rede v. To advise or counsel.

re-dec-o-rate v. To change in appearance; to refurbish. **redecorator, redecoration** n.

re-deem v. To buy back; to pay off; to turn something in, as coupons or rain checks and receive something in exchange. **redeemable** adj., **redeemer** n.

re-de-fine v. To examine with a view to change. **redefinition** n.

re-demp-tion n. The act of redeeming; rescue; ransom; that which redeems; salvation. **redemptional** adj.

re-demp-tion-er n. An immigrant to America who obtained passage by becoming a servant.

re-demp-tive adj. Relating to redemption.

re-de-ploy v. To move men and equipment from one location to another.

re-de-scribe v. To give a more updated version of something.

re-de-sign v. To change or revise the appearance or function of something.

re-de-vel-op-ment n. The renovation of a rundown area.

red-hand-ed v. To be caught in the act of committing a crime.

red-hot adj. Extremely hot. n. A small red candy flavored with cinnamon.

red-in-gote n. A fitted double-breasted coat with wide flat cuffs and collar worn by men in the 18th century.

red ink n. A business loss.

red-in-te-grate v. To restore to a former sound state.

re-di-rect v. To change the course of. **redirection** n.

re-dis-trib-ute v. To spread to different areas. **redistributive** adj. **redistribution** n.

red light n. A traffic signal; a warning device.

re-dou-ble v. To make something twice in size or amount.

re-doubt n. A small enclosed fortification.

re-doubt-a-ble adj. To be dreaded. **redoubtably** adv.

re-dound v. To have an effect on something.

red pencil v. To correct; to censor.

re-dress v. To put something right; to remedy. **redresser** n.

red ribbon n. The ribbon which designates second place winner in a contest.

red-root n. An herb of the bloodwort family of the eastern United States.

red-snap-per n. A saltwater fish which is red in color and can be found in the Gulf of Mexico and near Florida.

red squirrel n. A squirrel reddish in color but smaller than the grey squirrel.

red-start n. An American warbler which is brightly colored.

red tape n. Routines which are rigid and may cause a delay in a process.

red tide n. The presence of large numbers of dinoflagellates in seawater which is fatal to many forms of marine life.

re-duce v. To decrease; lessen in number, degree, or amount; to put into order; to lower in rank; to lose weight by dieting. **reducer** n., **reducible** adj.

re-duc-tion n. The state of being reduced. **reductional** adj.

re-dun-dant adj. Exceeding what is necessary; repetitive.
redundantly adv. **redundancy** n.

re-du-pli-cate v. To repeat something.
reduplication n., **reduplicative** adj., **reduplicatively** adv.

red-wood n. A tree found in California which is very tall and wide.

re-ech-o v. To reverberate again.

reed n. Tall grass with a slender stem, which grows in wet areas; a thin tongue of wood, metal, cane, or plastic; placed in the mouthpiece of an instrument to produce sounds by vibrating. **reediness** n., **reedy** adj.

reed-buck n. An African antelope.

re-ed-u-cate v. To train again through education; rehabilitate.
reeducation n., **reeducative** adj.

reedy adj. Having the tone quality of a reed instrument.

reef n. A chain of rocks, coral, or sand at or near the surface of the water.

reef-er n. A double-breasted jacket which is close-fitting.

reef knot n. A square knot used on a sail.

reek v. To emit vapor or smoke; to give off a strong offensive odor.

reel n. A device which revolves on an axis and is used for winding up or letting out fishing line, rope, or other string-like material; a lively and fast dance; a bobbin for sewing thread.

re-e-lect v. The act of electing someone again for an office.

reel-to-reel adj. Pertaining to magnetic tape which is threaded to a take-up reel, which moves from one reel to another.

re-em-pha-size v. To stress something or an idea again.

re-em-ploy v. To rehire someone who previously worked for you.

re-en-act v. To perform again; to repeat the actions of a previous event.

re-en-list v. To enlist or join a group or an armed force again. **reenlistment** n.

re-en-ter v. To enter a room or area again.

re-en-try n. The return of a space craft after a mission into outer space.

reeve n. A medieval English manor officer responsible for overseeing feudal obligations.

re-ex-am-ine v. Examine something or someone another time or again.
reexamination n.

ref n. The person who controls sports games.

re-fec-to-ry n. The place in colleges where the students dine.

re-fer v. To direct for treatment, information, or help; to classify within a general category or cause.

ref-e-ree n. A person who supervises a game, making sure all the rules are followed.

ref-er-ence n. The act of referring someone to someplace or to something.

ref-er-ence mark n. A mark, such as an asterisk, to direct the reader's attention to a footnote.

ref-er-en-dum n. A public vote on an item for final approval or for rejection.

ref-er-ent n. What is referred to, such as a person; the thing that a word or sign stand for. **referent** adj.

re-fill v. To fill something with an item again. **refillable** adj.

re-fine v. To purify by removing unwanted substances or material; to improve.
refined adj., **refinement** n.

re-fin-er-y n. A place or location which is used for the purpose of refining, such as sugar.

re-fin-ish v. The act of putting a new surface onto something, such as wood.

re-fit v. To repair something.

re-flect v. To throw back rays of light from a surface; to give an image, as from a mirror; to ponder or think carefully about something. **reflection**, **reflectiveness** n., **reflectively** adv.

re-flec-tom-e-ter n. A device for measuring radiant energy.

re-flec-tor n. Something which is able to reflect things, such as light.

re-flex v. Turning, casting, or bending backward. n. An involuntary reaction of the nervous system to a stimulus.

re-flex-ive adj. A relation that exists between an entity and itself.
reflexiveness, **reflexivity** n.

re-flex-ive pro-noun n. A pronoun referring to subject of the sentence or phrase in which it stands.

re-flex-ol-gy n. The science of behavior of simple and complex reflexes.

re-flo-res-cent adj. Blooming again.

re-flow v. To flow back again.

re-fo-cus v. To change the direction of.

re-for-est v. The act of replanting a forest or wooded area with trees.
reforestation n.

re-forge v. To make over.

re-form v. To reconstruct, make over, or change something for the better; improve; to abandon or give up evil ways. **reformer** n., **reformed** adj.

re-for-ma-to-ry n. A jail-like institution for young criminals.

Reform Judaism n. The branch of Judaism which has adopted a simpler and more liberal approach to religious rites and observances.

re-fract v. The deflecting something,

such as a ray of light. **refractive** *adj.*

re-frac-tion *n.* The state of being refracted or deflected. **refractivity, refractiveness** *n.*, **refractively** *adv.*

re-frac-to-ry *adj.* Unmanageable; obstinate; difficult to melt; resistant to heat. *n.* Something which does not change significantly when exposed to high temperatures. **refractorily** *adv.*, **refractoriness** *n.*

re-frac-to-ry per-i-od *n.* The period immediately following the response of a muscle before it recovers to make a second response.

re-frain *v.* To hold back; to keep oneself from following a passing impulse. *n.* A recurring phrase at the end of each stanza of a poem or song.

re-fresh *v.* To freshen something again; to restore strength. **refreshing** *adj.*, **refreshingly** *adv.*, **refresher** *n.*

re-fresh-er *n.* A course taken to review what has been previously learned.

re-fresh-ment *n.* Something which will refresh someone, such as a cold drink or snack.

re-frig-er-ant *n.* An agent which cools something.

re-frig-er-ate *v.* To chill or cool; to preserve food by chilling; to place in a refrigerator. **refrigeration** *n.*

re-frig-er-a-tor *n.* A box-like piece of equipment which chills food and other matter.

re-fu-el *v.* To put fuel into something again; take on additional fuel.

ref-uge *n.* Shelter or protection from harm; any place one may turn for relief or help.

ref-u-gee *n.* A person who flees to find safety. **refugeeism** *n.*

re-ful-gent *adj.* State of being radiant or putting off a bright light.

re-fund *v.* To return or pay back; to reimburse. **refundable** *adj.*, **refund** *n.*, **refundability** *n.*

re-fur-bish *v.* To make clean; to renovate. **refurbisher, -ment** *n.*

re-fus-al *n.* The denial of something which is demanded.

re-fuse *v.* To decline; to reject; to deny.

ref-use *n.* Rubbish; trash.

re-fute *v.* To overthrow or to disprove with the use of evidence. **refutable** *adj.*, **refutably** *adv.*, **refuter** *n.*

re-gain *v.* To recover; to reach again.

re-gal *adj.* Of or appropriate for royalty. **regally** *adv.*

re-gale *v.* To entertain or delight; to give pleasure.

re-ga-li-a *n.* Something which represents royalty such as a scepter.

re-gard *v.* To look upon closely; to consider; to have great affection for. *n.* Careful attention or thought; esteem or affection. **regards** Greetings of good wishes.

re-gard-ful *adj.* State of being mindful. **regardfulness** *n.*

re-gard-less *adj.* State of being careless or showing no regard towards something or someone. **regardlessness** *n.*,

regardfully *adv.*

re-gat-ta *n.* A boat race.

re-gen-cy *n.*, *pl.* **-ies** The jurisdiction or office of a regent.

re-gen-er-ate *v.* To reform spiritually or morally; to make or create anew; to refresh or restore. **regenerateness** *n.*, **regenerately** *adv.*, **regenerable** *adj.*

re-gent *n.* One who rules and acts as a ruler during the absence of a sovereign, or when the ruler is underage.

reg-i-cide *n.* A person who kills a king.

re-gime *n.* An administration.

reg-i-men *n.* Government control; therapy; a systematic plan to improve the health.

reg-i-ment *n.* A military unit of ground troops which is composed of several battalions. **-al** *adj.*, **regimentation** *n.*

reg-i-men-tals *n.* Military uniforms.

re-gion *n.* An administrative, political, social, or geographical area.

re-gion-al *adj.* Typical or pertaining to a geographic region; limited to a particular region.

re-gion-al-ize *v.* To divide into regions or districts.

regional library *n.* A public library serving several counties within the same state.

reg-is-ter *n.* Something which contains names or occurrences; a book of public records.

reg-is-tered *adj.* Recorded with the owner's name; recorded on the basis of pedigree of an animal.

reg-is-ter-ed mail *n.* Mail registered in the post office and guaranteed special care in delivery.

reg-is-ter-ed nurse *n.* A trained graduate nurse who is licensed by a state and who has passed qualifying examinations for registration.

reg-is-trar *n.* The person who keeps a register; and officer of an educational institution who is in charge of registration, keeping academic records, and evaluating their credentials.

reg-is-tra-tion *n.* An act of recording things or names.

reg-is-try *n.* The nationality of a ship in a register; an official record book.

reg-let *n.* A narrow strip of molding.

re-gress *v.* To return to a previous state or condition. **regressor, regression** *n.*

re-gres-sion *n.* The progressive decline of a disease; a shift toward a lower state; gradual loss of memory and acquired skills. **regressive** *adj.*, **-iveness** *n.*

re-gret *v.* To feel disappointed or distressed about; to be sorry for. *n.* A sense of loss or expression of grief; a feeling of sorrow. **regretfully** *adv.*, **-ful, regretable** *adj.*

re-group *v.* To reorganize after a setback in an activity.

reg-u-lar *adj.* Usual; normal; customary; conforming to set principles, procedures, or discipline; well-ordered; not varying. **regularity** *n.*, **regularly** *adv.*

reg-u-lar-ize *v.* To conform to laws, rules

and customs.

reg·u·late v. To adjust to a specification or requirement; to bring order or authority. **regulative,**
regulatory adj., **regulator** n.

reg·u·la·tion n. A rule that is set down in order to govern an area or people.

reg·u·lus n. A star in the constellation Leo.

re·gur·gi·tate v. To pour something forth. **regurgitation** n.

re·ha·bil·i·tate v. To restore; to a former state, by education and therapy. **rehabilitation** n., **rehabilitative** adj.

re·hash v. To rework or go over old material; to discuss again.

re·hears·al n. The act of practicing for a performance; a practice session. **rehearse** v.

re·hu·man·ize v. To restore to a full life; restore human rights and dignity.

re·hy·drate v. To return fluid lost due to dehydration.

reichs·mark n. A German coin.

reign n. The period in time when the monarch rules over an area.

reign of terror n. A period in history marked by violence committed by those in power which produced widespread terror.

re·im·burse v. To repay; to make restitution. **reimbursement** n.

rein n. One of a pair of narrow, leather straps attached to the bit of a bridle and used to control a horse.

re·in·car·na·tion n. The state of rebirth in new forms of life.

rein·deer n. A large deer found in northern regions, both sexes having antlers.

re·in·force v. To support; to strengthen with additional people or equipment. **reinforcement** n.

re·in·state v. To restore something to its former position or condition. **-ment** n.

re·in·te·grate v. To reunite with something.

re·in·vent v. To remake something that has already been invented.

re·in·vest v. To invest money in additional securities.

re·in·vig·o·rate v. To restore vigor.

re·is·sue v. To make available again.

re·it·er·ate v. To say or do something over and over again. **reiteration** n., **reiterative** adj., **reiteration** n.

re·ject v. To refuse; to discard as useless. **reject, rejection** n.

re·jec·tion n. The process in which the body rejects an organ transplant or tissue.

re·joice v. To fill with joy; to be filled with joy. **rejoicer** n. **rejoicingly** adv.

re·joic·ing v. An occasion or expression of joy.

re·join v. To respond or to answer someone.

re·join·der n. The answer to a reply made by someone to another.

re·ju·ve·nate v. To restore to youthful appearance or vigor. **rejuvenation** n.

re·ju·ve·nes·cence n. A renewal of youthfulness. **rejuvenescent** adj.

re·kin·dle v. To inflame something again. **rekindler** n.

re·lapse v. To fall back or revert to an earlier condition. **relapser** n.

re·late v. To tell the events of; to narrate; to bring into natural association. **relater** n., **relatable** adj.

re·lat·ed adj. To be in the same family; connected to each other by blood or by marriage.

re·la·tion n. The relationship between people by marriage or blood lines.

re·la·tion·ship n. A connection by blood or family; kinship; friendship; a natural association.

rel·a·tive adj. Relevant; connected; considered in comparison or relationship to other. n. A member of one's family. **relatively** adv., **relativeness** n.

relative humidity n. The ratio of the amount of water vapor actually present in the air to the amount possible at the same temperature.

rel·a·tiv·i·ty n. A condition or state of being relative.

re·lax v. To make loose or lax; to relieve something from effort or strain; to become less formal or less reserved. **relaxation** n., **relaxedly** adv.

re·lax·ation n. A period of recreational activity or pastime.

re·laxed adj. Being at rest or ease. **relaxedly** adv., **relaxedness** n.

re·lay n. A race in which a fresh team replaces another. v. To pass from one group to another.

re·lease v. To set free from confinement; to unfasten; to free; to relinquish a claim on something. n. A release from an obligation. **releaser** n.

rel·e·gate v. To banish someone or something. **relegation** n.

re·lent v. To soften in temper, attitude, or determination; to slacken. **relentless** adj., **relentlessness** adj.

rel·e·vant adj. Related to matters at hand. **relevantly** adv.

re·li·a·ble adj. Dependable; capable of being relied upon. **-ness** n. **-y** adv.

re·li·ance n. Confidence and trust; something which is relied upon.

re·li·ant adj. State of being confident or having reliance.

rel·ic n. Something which is very old; a keepsake; an object whose cultural environment has disappeared.

re·lic·tion n. The recession of water from land leaving it permanently uncovered.

re·lief n. Anything which decreases or lessens anxiety, pain, discomfort, or other unpleasant conditions or feelings.

re·lief map n. A map which outlines the contours of the land.

relief pitcher n. In baseball, a pitcher who relieves another pitcher due to ineffectiveness.

re·lieve v. To lessen or ease pain, anxiety, embarrassment, or other problems; to release or free from a duty by providing a replacement.

reliever *n.*, relievable *adj.*, reliever *n.*

re-lig-ion *n.* An organized system of beliefs, rites, and celebrations centered on a supernatural being power; belief pursued with devotion. religious *adj.*, religiousness *n.*

re-li-gi-ose *adj.* Being excessively religious.

re-lin-quish *v.* To release something or someone; withdraw from; to give up. relinquishment *n.*

rel-i-quary *n.* A shrine in which sacred relics are kept.

re-lish *n.* Pleasure; a spicy condiment taken with food to lend it flavor.

re-live *v.* To experience something again in the imagination or fantasy.

re-lo-cate *v.* To move to another area; establish in another place. -ion *n.*

re-luct *v.* To revolt; to feel opposition.

re-luc-tance *n.* An unwillingness; opposition by a magnetic substance to magnetic flux.

re-luc-tant *adj.* Unwilling; not yielding. reluctation *n.*

re-lume *v.* To light again.

re-ly *v.* To trust or depend; to have confidence in someone.

REM *abbr* Rapid eye movement.

re-main *v.* To continue without change; to stay after the departure of others.

re-main-der *n.* Something left over. *Math* The difference which remains after division or subtraction.

re-mains *pl.*, *n.* What is left after all other parts have been taken away; corpse.

re-make *v.* To revise an old movie, etc.

re-mand *v.* To order back; to send to another court or agency for further action; to return to custody pending trial.

re-man-u-fac-ture *v.* To make into a new product. remanufacturer *n.*

re-mark *n.* A brief expression or comment; to take notice; to observe; to comment.

re-mark-a-ble *adj.* Extraordinary. remarkably *adv.* remarkableness *n.*

re-match *n.* A second contest between the same contestants or teams.

re-me-di-a-ble *adj.* Being able to be remedied.

re-me-di-al *adj.* Concerned with the correction of study habits.

rem-e-dy *n.*, *pl.* -ies A therapy or medicine which relieves pain; something which corrects an error or fault. *v.* To cure or relieve a disease; to rectify.

re-mem-ber *v.* To bring back or recall to the mind; to retain in the mind carefully; to keep a person in one's thought; to recall a person to another as a means of greetings. -ability, rememberer *n.*, remembrable *adj.*

re-mem-brance *n.* Something which is remembered by someone.

re-mex *n.* A quill feather in the wing of a bird. remigial *adj.*

re-mil-i-ta-rize *v.* To equip again with military installations.

re-mind *v.* To cause or help to remember. reminder *n.*

rem-i-nisce *v.* To recall the past things which have happened.

rem-i-nis-cence *n.* The practice or process of recalling the past. reminiscent *adj.*

re-mint *v.* To make old coins into a new coins by melting down the old coins.

re-mise *v.* To release a claim to.

re-miss *adj.* Lax in performing one's duties; negligent. remissness *n.*

re-mis-sion *n.* A forgiveness; act of remitting; a temporary state of a disease when it doesn't progress; forgiveness.

re-mit *v.* To send money as payment for goods; to forgive, as a crime or sin; to slacken, make less violent, or less intense. remittance *n.*, remitter *n.*

re-mit-tance *n.* A sum of money sent to reduce a debt.

re-mit-tent *adj.* Marked by periods of abatement and increase of symptoms.

rem-nant *n.* A small piece or a scrap of something.

re-mod-el *v.* To reconstruct something making it like new; to alter the structure of a building or house.

re-mon-e-tize *v.* To restore to use as legal tender. remonetization *n.*

re-mon-strance *n.* Statement of reasons against an idea or something.

re-mon-strate *v.* Giving strong reasons against an act or an idea. remonstrative *adj.*, remonstration *n.*

rem-o-ra *n.* Any of several fishes that have anterior dorsal fin converted into a disk on the head thereby allowing them to cling to other fishes or ships.

re-morse *n.* Deep moral regret for past misdeeds. remorseful *adj.* remorsefully *adv.*, remorsefulness *n.*

re-mote *adj.* Distant in time; space or relation. remotely *adv.*, remoteness *n.*

re-mount *v.* To mount something again.

re-mov-a-ble *adj.* Being able to be removed. removableness *n.*

re-mov-al *n.* The change of a site or place; the act of removing from a post.

re-move *v.* To get rid of; to extract; to dismiss from office; to change one's business or residence. *n.* An act of moving. removable *adj.*, removal *n.*

re-moved *adj.* State of being separate from others.

re-mu-da *n.* A herd of horses from which they chose the horses to be used for the day.

re-mu-ner-ate *v.* Pay an equivalent for a service; to reward. remunerator *n.*, remuneration *n.*, remuneratively *adj.*

ren-ais-sance *n.* A revival or rebirth; the humanistic revival of classical art, literature, and learning in Europe which occurred during the 14th through the 16th centuries.

re-nal *adj.* Of or relating to the kidneys.

re-nas-cence *n.* A revival or rebirth.

re-na-ture *v.* To restore to an original condition.

ren-con-tre *n.* A hostile contest between

forces or individuals.

ren-coun-ter v. A casual meeting; a duel; a debate.

rend v. To remove from with violence; to split. **renderable** adj.

ren-der v. To give or make something available; to submit or give; to represent artistically; to liquefy or melt fat by means of heat.
rendering n., **renderable** adj.

ren-dez-vous n. A meeting place that has been prearranged; an appointment made between two or more people. v. To meet at a particular time and place.

ren-di-tion n. An interpretation or a translation.

ren-dzi-na n. A grayish brown intrazonal soil developed in grassy regions of high humidity; a rich limy soil.

ren-e-gade n. A person who rejects one allegiance for another; an outlaw; a traitor. **renegade** adj.

re-nege v. To fail to keep one's word. **reneger** n.

re-new v. To make new or nearly new by restoring; to resume. **-able** adj.

re-ni-tent adj. Resisting pressure; opposed.

ren-net n. An extract taken from a calf's stomach and used to curdle milk for making cheese.

ren-nin n. An enzyme that coagulates milk used in making cheese.

re-nom-i-nate v. To nominate for a succeeding term.

re-nounce v. To reject something or someone. **renouncement** n.

ren-o-vate v. To return or to restore to a good condition; to make new.
renovation n., **renovator** n.

re-nown n. The quality of being widely honored. **renowned** adj.

rent n. The payment made for the use of another's property. v. To obtain occupancy in exchange for payment.
rental n., **rentable** adj.

rent con-trol n. A government regulation of the amount charged for housing.

rent-er n. The leasee of a property.

rent strike n. The refusal of tenants to pay rent in protest of increase in price.

re-nun-ci-a-tion n. Renouncing. **-ive** adj.

re-o-pen v. To resume again, as a discussion or session.

re-or-der n. An order for more of the same kind as previously ordered.

re-or-gan-i-za-tion n. The process of reorganizing something.

rep. n., Slang Representative. v. Represent.

re-pack-age v. To wrap into a more efficient and attractive form.

re-pair v. To restore to good or usable condition; to renew; refresh. **-able** adj.

re-pair-man n. The person who makes repairs of things that are broken; a person who makes his living repairing things.

re-pand adj. Having a slightly wavy margin.

rep-a-ra-ble adj. Being able to be corrected.

rep-a-ra-tion n. The act of repairing something.

re-par-a-tive adj. Able to make amends.

rep-ar-tee n. A quick, witty response or reply; an interchange of clever retorts.

re-pass v. To pass thru again. **-age** n.

re-past n. Something taken as food; food which comprises a meal.

re-pa-tri-ate v. To go back to one's own country; to return to the country of one's origin. **repatriation** n.

re-pay v. To pay back money; to recompensate; to do something in return.
repayable adj., **repayment** n.

re-peal v. To withdraw officially; to rescind; to revoke. **repealable** adj., **repeal** n., **repealer** n.

re-peat v. To utter something again; to do an action again.

re-peat-ed adj. Recurring again and again.

re-peat-er n. Something or person which repeats.

re-pel v. To discourage; to force away; to create aversion.

re-pel-lent adj. Able to repel; tending to drive away or ward off.

re-pent v. To feel regret for something which has occurred; to change one's sinful way. **repentance** n., **repentant** adj., **repenter** n.

re-per-cus-sion n. An unforeseen effect produced by an action. **-ive** adj.

rep-er-toire n. The accomplishments or skills of a person.

rep-er-to-ry n. A collection of things.

rep-e-tend n. A repeated sound or refrain.

rep-e-ti-tion n. The act of doing something over and over again; the act of repeating.

re-pine v. To feel discontent; to complain.

re-place v. To return something to its previous place. **replaceable** adj., **replacement** n., **replacer** n.

re-plant v. To provide with new plants; to move plants to a new location.

re-play v. To play something again.

re-plen-ish v. To add to something to replace what has gone or been used.
replenisher, **replenishment** n.

re-plete adj. Having plenty; abounding; full. **repleteness** n.

re-ple-tion n. An act of eating too much food.

rep-li-ca n. A reproduction or copy of something. **replicate** v.

re-ply v. To give an answer to either verbally or in writing. **reply** n.

re-port n. A detailed account; usually in a formal way. v. To tell about; to make oneself available; to give details of.
reportable adj., **reporter** n.

re-port-age n. The process of reporting something.

re-port card n. The report of the students progress in school submitted to the parents for review.

re-port-ed-ly adv. To be according to a report.

re-pos-al *n.* An act or action of reposing.

re-pose *n.* The act of being at rest. *v.* To lie at rest. reposeful *adj.*

re-pos-it *v.* To put something back into place.

re-po-si-tion *n.* The state of something being repositioned.

re-pos-i-tor-y *n.* The location where things may be placed for preservation; a side altar in a Catholic church.

re-pos-sess *v.* To restore ownership of something.

re-pow-er *v.* To return power anew to something or someone.

rep-re-hend *v.* To show or express disapproval of. reprehension *n.*, -sible *adj.*

rep-re-hen-sive *adj.* To be conveying reproof.

rep-re-sent *v.* To stand for something; to serve as the official representative for.

rep-re-sen-ta-tion *n.* The act of representing. representational *adj.*

rep-re-sent-a-tive *n.* A person or thing serving as an example or type. *adj.* Of or relating to government by representation; typical. -ly *adv.*

re-press *v.* To restrain; hold back; to remove from the conscious mind. repressibility, repression, -iveness *n.*, repressive *adj.*, repressively *adv.*

re-pressed *adj.* To be marked by repression.

re-pres-sor *n.* Someone or something that will repress.

re-prieve *v.* To postpone punishment; to provide temporary relief; a temporary suspension of an execution. -able *adj.*, reprieve *n.*, reprieve, reprieving *v.*

rep-ri-mand *v.* To censure severely; rebuke. reprimand *n.*

re-print *n.* An additional printing of a book exactly as the previous one. reprint *v.*, reprinter *n.*

re-pri-sal *n.* Retaliation with intent to inflict injury in return for injury received; a sum of money paid in restitution.

re-prise *v.* To take back by force.

re-proach *v.* To blame; to rebuke. reproachful *adj.*

rep-ro-bate *adj.* The state of being morally depraved or evil. *v.* To condemn as unacceptable or evil.

re-pro-cess *v.* To treat in a special way in preparation for reuse.

re-pro-duce *v.* To produce an image or copy. *Biol.* To produce an offspring; to recreate or produce again. reproducer *n.*, reproducible *adj.*, reproduction *n.*, reproductive *adj.*

re-pro-gram *v.* To rewrite an existing program for a computer.

re-proof *n.* A censure.

re-prove *v.* To tell or express a disapproval of something.

rep-tile *n.*

A cold-blooded, egg-laying vertebrate, as a snake, lizard, or turtle.

reptilian *n.*, *adj.*

re-pub-lic *n.* A political unit or state where representatives are elected to exercise the power.

re-pub-li-can *adj.* Having the character of a republic; one of two political parties of the United States.

re-pub-li-can-ism *n.* The Republican principles.

Republican Party *n.* One of the two political parties in the United States.

re-pu-di-ate *v.* To cast away; to refuse to pay something.

re-pugn *v.* To offer resistance.

re-pug-nance *n.* The state or condition of being opposed.

re-pug-nant *adj.* Distasteful; repulsive; offensive.

re-pulse *v.* To repel or drive back; to repel or reject rudely; to disgust or be disgusted. repulsion *n.*

re-pul-sive *adj.* State of causing aversion. repulsively *adv.*, -ness *n.*

rep-u-ta-ble *adj.* Considered to be honorable; held in high esteem. reputably *adv.*, reputability *n.*

re-put-a-tion *n.* The commonly held evaluation of a person's character.

re-pute *v.* To account or to consider something. reputedly *adj.*

re-quest *v.* To ask for something.

re-qui-em *n.* The Roman Catholic mass for a deceased person.

re-quire *v.* To demand or insist upon. requirement *n.*

req-ui-site *adj.* Absolutely needed; necessary.

req-ui-si-tion *n.* A demand or a request; a demand by one government to another for release of prisoners.

re-quit-al *n.* The act of requiting something.

re-quite *v.* To reward; to repay someone. requiter *n.*

rere-dos *n.* An ornamental screen or partition wall behind an altar.

re-run *n.* A television show which is shown again.

re-sale *n.* The act of selling something again. resalable *adj.*

re-scind *v.* To repeal; to void. rescinder, recindment *n.*

res-cue *v.* To free from danger. *n.* An act of deliverance. rescuer *n.*

re-search *n.* A scientific or scholarly investigation; to carefully seek out.

re-sec-tion *n.* The surgical removal a section of an organ.

re-se-da *n.* An herb of the mignonette family with greyish-green leaves.

re-sem-ble *v.* To have similarity to something. resemblance *n.*

re-send *v.* To send back.

re-sent *v.* To feel angry about. -ful *adj.*, resentfully *adv.*, resentment *n.*

res-er-va-tion *n.* The act of keeping something back.

re-serve *v.* To save for a special reason; to set apart; to retain; to put off. *n.* Something that is saved for a future point in time; the portion of a country's fighting force kept inactive until called upon.

reserve clause *n.* A clause in an athlete's contract which gives the club the exclusive rights of the athlete's services until he is traded or released.

res-er-voir *n.* A body of water stored for the future; large reserve; a supply.

re-shape *v.* To give new form to.

re-side *v.* To dwell permanently; to exist as a quality or attribute. **residence** *n.*

res-i-den-cy *n.* A period of training in a medical field.

res-i-due *n.* Matter remaining after treatment or removal of a part; something which remains.

re-sign *v.* To give up; to submit to something as being unavoidable; to quit. **resignedly** *adv.,* **resignation** *n.*

res-ig-na-tion *n.* A formal notification stating the resignation of one's job, etc.

re-sil-ience *n.* The ability to recover from a shock without permanent after-effects.

res-in *n.* A plant substance from certain plants and trees used in varnishes and lacquers. **resinous** *adj.*

re-sist *v.* To work against or actively oppose; to withstand. **resistible** *adj.*

re-sist-er *n.* A person who is opposed to the policies of the government.

re-sis-tor *n.* An electrical device used in an electric circuit for protection or current control.

res-ju-di-ca-ta *n.* A matter decided on its merits by a court and not subject to litigation again between the same parties.

res-o-lute *adj.* Coming from or characterized by determination. **resolutely** *adv.,* **resolution** *n.*

re-solve *v.* To make a firm decision on something; to find a solution. **resolvable** *adj.,* **-er** *n.,* **resolution** *n.*

res-o-nance *n.* The increase of sound by the vibration of other bodies.

res-o-na-tor *n.* A device for increasing sounds of a musical instrument.

re-sort *v.* To go frequently or customarily. *n.* A place, or recreation, for rest, and for a vacation.

re-sound *v.* To be filled with echoing sounds; to reverberate; to ring or sound loudly. **resounding** *adj.,* **resoundingly** *adv.*

re-source *n.* A source of aid or support which can be drawn upon if needed. **resources** One's available capital or assets. **resourceful** *adj.,* **-ness** *n.*

re-spect *v.* To show consideration or esteem for; to relate to. *n.* Courtesy or considerate treatment. **-fully** *adv.,* **respectful** *adj.,* **respectability** *n.*

res-pi-ra-tion *n.* The process or act of inhaling and exhaling; the act of breathing; the process in which an animal or person takes in oxygen from the air and releases carbon dioxide. **respirator** *n.,* **-al, respiratory** *adj.*

re-spire *v.* To inhale and exhale air; take in oxygen.

res-pi-rom-e-ter *n.* An instrument for studying the extent and character of respiration.

res-pite *n.* A temporary postponement.

re-splen-dent *adj.* Having a shining appearance. **resplendently** *adj.*

re-spond *v.* To answer or reply; to act when prompted by something or someone.

re-sponse *n.* A reply; the act of replying. **responsive** *adj.*

re-spon-si-ble *adj.* Trustworthy; in charge; having authority; being answerable for one's actions or the actions of others. **responsibility, responsibleness** *n.,* **responsibly** *adv.*

re-spon-sum *n.* A formal opinion from a rabbinic authority to a submitted question or problem.

rest *n.* A cessation of all work, activity, or motion. *Mus.* An interval of silence equal in time to a note of same value. *v.* To stop work; to place or lay. **rester** *n.,* **restful** *adj.,* **restfully** *adv.*

res-tau-rant *n.* A place which serves meals to the public.

res-tau-ra-teur *n.* The owner of a restaurant.

rest home *n.* An establishment for the aged or the convalescent.

res-ti-tu-tion *n.* The act of restoring something to its rightful owner; compensation for injury, loss, or damage.

res-tive *adj.* Nervous or impatient because of a delay; resisting control. **restively** *adv.,* **restiveness** *n.*

re-store *v.* To bring back to a former condition or original state; to make restitution of. **restoration** *n.*

re-strain *v.* To hold back or be held back; to control, limit, or restrict. **restrainer, restraint** *n.*

restraining order *n.* A legal document issued to keep a situation unchanged.

re-strict *v.* To confine within limits. **restriction** *n.,* **restrictive** *adj.,* **restrictively** *adv.*

re-sult *v.* To happen or exist in a particular way. *n.* The consequence of an action, course, or operation.

re-sume *v.* To start again after an interruption. **resumption** *n.*

res-u-me *n.* A summary of one's personal history, background, work, and education.

re-su-pi-nate *adj.* To bend backward to an inverted position.

res-ur-rec-tion *n.* The act of Christ risen from the dead.

re-sus-ci-ate *v.* To return to life; to revive; give mouth-to-mouth breathing technique to help a person to start breathing again. **resuscitation** *n.,* **resuscitator** *n.*

re-tail *v.* The sale of goods or commodities to the public. *v.* To sell to the consumer. **retail** *adj.,* **retailer** *n.*

re-tain *v.* To hold in one's possession; to remember; to employ someone, as for his services.

re-tain-er *n.* A person or thing that retains; a fee paid for one's services.

re-tal-i-ate *v.* To seek revenge against someone. **retaliation** *n.*

re-tard v. To delay or slow the progress of. **retardant** n. & adj.

re-tar-da-tion n. A condition in which mental development is slow or delayed; a condition of mental slowness.

re-ten-tion n. The act or condition of being retained.

re-ten-tive adj. Having the capacity of retaining knowledge with ease. **retentively** adv., **retentiveness** n.

ret-i-cent adj. Being uncommunicative in speech; reserved. **reticently** adv.

re-tic-u-late v. To divide or construct as to form a network.

ret-i-na n., pl. **-nas, nae** The light sensitive membrane lining the inner eyeball connected by the optic nerve to the brain. **retinal** adj.

re-tire v. To depart for rest; to remove oneself from the daily routine of working. *Baseball* To put a batter out. **retirement** n., **retired** adj., **retiree** n.

re-tired adj. No longer working at one's profession.

re-tir-ing adj. Being shy or withdrawn.

re-tort n. A witty or cutting reply to another person.

re-touch v. To alter a negative to produce a more desirable picture.

re-trace v. To go back over.

re-tract v. To draw back or to take back something that has been said. **retractable** adj., **retraction** n.

re-tral adj. Toward the back.

re-tread v. To replace the tread of a worn tire. **retread** n.

re-treat n. The act of withdrawing from danger; a time of study; prayer; and meditation in a quiet; isolated location.

ret-ri-bu-tion n. An act of getting revenge against another person. **retributively** adv., **retributive** adj.

re-trieve v. To regain; to find something and carry it back. **retrievable** adj., **retrieval** n.

ret-ro-ac-tive adj. Taking effect on a date prior to enactment; extending to a prior time. **retroactively** adv.

ret-ro-grade adj. Moving backward; contrary to normal order.

ret-ro-gres-sion n. A reversal in development from a higher to a lower state.

ret-ro-pack n. A system of rockets on a spacecraft which produce thrust used to reduce speed.

ret-ro-re-flec-tor n. A device that reflects radiation.

ret-ro-rock-et n. A rocket on an airplane, or spacecraft which produces thrust in the opposite direction to the motion of the spacecraft for deceleration.

ret-ro-spect n. A review of things in the past. **-ively** adv., **retrospective** adj.

re-turn v. To come back to an earlier condition; to reciprocate. n. The act of sending, bringing, or coming back. **returns** n. A yield or profit from investments; a report on the results of an election. **returnable** adj., **returnee, returner** n.

re-un-ion n. A reuniting; the coming together of a group which has been separated for a period of time.

re-us-able adj. Capable of using something over and over again.

re-val-u-ate v. To increase the value of something.

re-val-ue v. To reappraise something as jewelry.

re-vamp v. Patch or reconstruct something again.

re-veal v. To disclose or make known; to expose or bring into view.

rev-eil-le n. The sounding of a bugle used to awaken soldiers in the morning.

rev-el v. To take great delight in. **-er** n.

rev-e-la-tion n. An act of or something revealed; a manifestation of divine truth. **Revelation** The last book in the New Testament.

re-venge v. To impose injury in return for injury received. **-ful** adj., **-er** n.

rev-e-nue n. Income returned by an investment.

revenue stamp n. A stamp which serves as evidence of payment of a tax.

re-verb n. An echo effect produced electronically in recorded music.

re-vere v. To honor and respect.

re-ver-sal n. An act of overthrowing a legal proceeding or judgment.

re-verse adj. Turned backward in position. n. The opposite of something; a change in fortune usually from better to worse; change or turn to the opposite direction; to transpose or exchange the positions of. *Law* To revoke a decision. **reverser** n.

re-vert v. To return to a former practice or belief. **reversion** n.

re-view v. To study or look over something again; to give a report on. n. A reexamination; a study which gives a critical estimate of something.

re-vile v. To use verbal abuse.

re-vise v. To look over something again with the intention of improving or correcting it. **reviser** n., **revision** n.

re-vi-tal-ize v. To give new life or energy to. **revitalization** n.

re-viv-al n. The act or condition of reviving; the return of a film or play which was formerly presented; a meeting whose purpose is religious reawakening.

re-vive v. To restore, refresh, or recall; to return to consciousness or life. **revivable** adj., **reviver** n.

re-voke v. To nullify or make void by recalling. **revocation** n.

re-volt n. To try to overthrow authority; to fill with disgust.

rev-o-lu-tion n. The act or state of orbital motion around a point; the abrupt overthrow of a government; a sudden change in a system.

re-volve v. To move around a central point; to spin; to rotate. **-able** adj.

re-volv-ing charge ac-count n. A charge account in which payment is made in monthly installments.

re-vue n. A musical show consisting of songs, dances, skits, and other similar entertainment.

re-ward n. Something given for a special service. v. To give a reward.

R.F.D. abbr. Rural free delivery.

rhab-do-man-cy n. The discovery of things that are concealed in the ground by the use of a divining rod.

rham-na-ceous adj. To be pertaining to or belonging to the buckthorn family of plants.

rhap-sod-ic adj. To have the characteristics of a rhapsody. -al adj.

rhap-so-dist n. A person who speaks in a rhapsodical way or manner.

rhap-so-dize v. To recite rhapsodies.

rhap-so-dy n., pl. -ies An excessive display of enthusiasm.

rhat-a-ny n. A type of South American shrub whose roots are used as an astringent.

rhea n. A large flightless South American bird smaller that resembles the African ostrich and has three toes.

rhe-ni-um n. A metallic element symbolized by Re.

rhe-ol-o-gy n. The study of the behavior of a liquid matter. rheological adj.

rhe-om-e-ter n. A type of device that is used for measuring the flow of liquids.

rhe-sus n. A light-brown monkey that is used for laboratory tests.

rhe-tor n. One who is an orator.

rhet-o-ric n. Effective expression in writing or speech; language which is not sincere.

rhe-tor-i-cal adj. To be involving rhetoric. rhetoricalness n.

rhe-tor-i-cal ques-tion n. A kind of question that is used for an effect and no answer is expected.

rhet-o-ri-cian n. A person who writes elaborate prose.

rheum n. A fluid that is discharged from the mucus glands of the body.

rheu-mat-ic fe-ver n. A severe infectious disease that is characterized by the swelling of the heart lining and the heart valves.

rheu-ma-tism n. A kind of inflammation that affects the joints and muscles of the body and can be very painful.

Rh fac-tor n. A substance found in the red blood cells of 85% of all humans; the presence of this factor is referred to as PH positive; the absence as PH negative.

rhi-nal adj. To be referring to the nose.

rhi-ni-tis n. An inflammation that occurs in the nose or the membranes of the nose.

rhi-noc-er-os n.

A very large mammal with one or two upright horns on the snout. rhinocerotic adj.

rhi-noc-er-os bee-tle n. A beetle, large in size, that has a projecting horn on the top of its head.

rhi-zan-thous adj. To be bearing very short stemmed flowers.

rhi-zo-bi-um n. A type of bacteria that is important in maintain the soil's fertility.

rhi-zo-ceph-a-lan n. A kind of crustacean that lives off a host and causes the host to lose its ability to reproduce.

rhi-zoid n. The hair-like structure that provides a root for ferns and mosses.

rhi-zome n. A subterranean plant stem thickened by deposits of reserve food material which produces shoots above and roots below.

rhi-zo-mor-phous adj. To be shaped like a root.

rhi-zo-pus n. A type of mold fungus.

Rh--neg-a-tive adj. Lacking the Rh factor in the blood system.

rho-da-mine n. A red dye.

Rhode Is-land n. A state located in the northeastern part of the United States.

Rhode Is-land bent n. A kind of European grass that is used as a lawn grass.

Rhode Is-land Red n. An American breed of domestic fowl with rich brownish red plumage.

Rhode Is-land White n. A domestic chicken that has white feathers and is like the Rhode Island Red.

rho-di-um n. A metallic element symbolized by Rh.

rho-do-chro-site n. A kind of mineral that is made of manganese carbonate and is pink in color.

rho-do-den-dron n. A variety of cultivated shrubs and trees with showy flowers and evergreen leaves.

rho-do-lite n. A type of garnet that is rose-red in color.

rho-do-ra n. A shrub found in Canada and New England having delicate pink flowers produced before the leaves in spring.

rhom-boid n. A parallelogram where the angles are oblique and adjacent sides are unequal. rhombic adj.

rhom-bus n. A four sided figure whose sides are equal in length.

rhon-chus n. A type of rale that occurs in the bronchial tubes of the airway.

rhu-barb n. A garden plant with large leaves and edible stalks used for pies.

rhyme or rime n. A word or verse whose terminal sound corresponds with another. rhyme v. rhymer n.

rhy-thm n. Music, speech, or movements which are characterized by equal or regularly alternating beats. -ical, rhythmic adj., rhythmically adv.

rhyth-mics n. The science of rhythms.

RI abbr. Rhode Island.

ri-al-to n. The theatre district.

ri-ant adj. To be smiling. riantly adv.

rib n. One of a series of curved bones enclosed in the chest of man and animals. Slang To tease. ribber n.

rib-ald adj. To be using indecent humor.

rib-band n. A narrow strip used in shipbuilding to hold frames in position during construction.

rib-bon *n.* A narrow band or strip of fabric, such as satin, used for trimming.

rib-bon fish *n.* A kind of marine fish that has a long and flat body.

ri-bo-fla-vin *n.* A B complex vitamin that is found in milk, leafy vegetables, and liver.

rib-wort *n.* A type of weed having a flower head and three-ribbed leaves.

rice *n.* A cereal grass grown extensively in warm climates.

rice-bird *n.* A type of small bird that can be found in rice field in the southern United States.

rice pa-per *n.* A paper made from rice paper tree pith.

rice pa-per tree *n.* The tree that is grown in China to make rice paper.

ric-er *n.* A kitchen utensil thru which soft foods are pressed in order to produce strings about the diameter of rice grain.

rich *adj.* Having great wealth; of great value; satisfying and pleasing in voice, color, tone, or other qualities; extremely productive; as soil or land.

rich-es *n.* One's wealth.

rich-ly *adv.* To be done in a rich manner or way.

Rich-ter scale *n.* An instrument which measures a seismic disturbance such as an earthquake with 1.5 being the smallest and 8.5 being a very devastating earthquake.

ri-cin *n.* A white powder that is poisonous and is used to cause the agglutination of the red corpuscles.

rick-ets *n.* A childhood disease which is caused by lack of inadequate sunlight or vitamin D resulting in severely deformed bones.

rick-ett-si-a *adj.* A microorganism that is passed from arthropods to humans.

rick-et-y *adj.* To be ready to fall apart or fall down. **ricketiness** *n.*

rick-rack *n.* A zigzag braid used in trimming.

rick-sha *n.* A small 2-wheeled vehicle that is pulled by one man and that originated in Japan.

ric-o-chet *n.* A glancing blow off a flat surface.

ri-cot-ta *n.* A white whey cheese of Italy resembling cottage cheese.

ric-tus *n.* An opening.

rid *v.* To make free from anything objectionable. **ridable** *adj.*

rid-dance *n.* The getting rid of something or someone that is unwanted.

rid-dle *v.* To perforate with numerous holes. *n.* A puzzling problem or question which requires a clever solution. **riddled, riddling** *v.*

ride *v.* To travel in a vehicle or on an animal; to sit on and drive, as a motorcycle. **ride for a fall** to flirt with danger. **ride high** To experience great success. **ride roughshod over** To treat with abuse.

rid-er *n.* One who rides as a passenger; a

clause, usually having little relevance, which is added to a document.

ridge *n.* A long, narrow crest; a horizontal line formed where two sloping surfaces meet. **ridge** *v.*

ridge-pole *n.* Timber located at the top of a roof which is horizontal.

rid-i-cule *n.* Actions or words intended to make a person or thing the object of mockery. **ridiculer** *n.*

ri-dic-u-lous *adj.* To be causing derision or ridicule; to be laughable. **ridiculousness** *n.*, **ridiculously** *adv.*

rid-ing *n.* An action of a person who rides.

rid-ing hab-it *n.* An outfit that is worn by women while they ride.

rid-ley *n.* A marine turtle found in the Atlantic Ocean off the coast of the United States.

ri-dot-to *n.* A place of entertainment in masquerade popular in the 18th century England.

rife *adj.* State of being abundant or abounding. **rifely** *adv.*

rif-fle *n.* Ripply water which is caused by a ridge.

rif-fler *n.* A small scraping tool.

riff-raff *n.* The rabble; low persons in society; a disreputable person.

ri-fle *n.* A firearm having a grooved bore designed to be fired from the shoulder.

ri-fle bird *n.* Type of Australian bird that has a velvety-black plumage.

ri-fle-man *n.* A person skilled in the shooting of a rifle.

ri-fling *n.* The act of putting or cutting spiral grooves in the barrel of a gun.

rift *n.* A fault; disagreement; a lack of harmony; a shallow place in a stream.

rig *v.* To outfit with necessary equipment. *n.* The arrangement of sails, masts, and other equipment on a ship; the apparatus used for drilling water or oil wells.

rig-a-doon *n.* A lively dance of the 17th and 18th century.

rig-a-to-ni *n.* A curved macaroni with fluted edges.

rig-ger *n.* A long pointed paintbrush; a ship with special rigs.

rig-ging *n.* The lines used aboard a ship in working sails and supporting masts and spars; ropes, etc. used to support and manipulate scenery in the theatre.

right *adj.* In accordance with or conformable to law, justice, or morality; proper and fitting; properly adjusted, disposed, or placed; orderly; sound in body or mind. *n.* The right side, hand, or direction; the direction opposite left. *adv.* Immediately; completely; according to justice, morality, or law.

right an-gle *n.*, *Geom.*

An angle of 90 degrees; an angle with two sides perpendicular to each other.

right a-way *adv.* Immediately, without

hesitation.

right-eous *adj.* Free from guilt; morally right; acting in accordance with moral or divine law. **righteousness** *n.*

right-ful *adj.* Having a legal claim.

right-hand-ed *adj.* Using the right hand more easily than the left; designed to be used with the right. **-ly** *adv.*, **righthandedness** *n.*, **righthanded** *adv.*

right-ly *adv.* To be done suitably.

right--of--way *n.* A tract of land used by a public utility company.

right tri-an-gle *n.* A type of triangle where one angle is 90 degrees.

right whale *n.* A kind of whale that is found in the polar seas and having a large head.

right wing *n.* One who is a member of a conservative political party.

right-winger *n.*, **right-wing** *adj.*

rig-id *adj.* Not bending; inflexible; severe; stern. **rigidity, rigidness** *n.*

ri-gid-i-fy *v.* To make something rigid. **rigidification** *n.*

rig-ma-role *n.* A meanless or complex procedure.

rig-or *n.* The condition of being rigid or stiff; stiffness of temper; harshness. **rigorous** *adj.*, **rigorously** *adv.*

rig-or-ism *n.* A strictness in practice.

rig-or mor-tis *n.* The rigidity of muscles occurring after death.

rile *v.* To make angry.

rill-et *n.* A small brook.

rim *n.* The outer edge or border of something; the outer part of a wheel joined to the hub on a car. **-less** *adj.*

rime *n.* An accumulation of granular ice on the windward sides of exposed objects formed from supercooled fog or clouds.

ri-mose *adj.* To be filled with fissures. **rimosity** *n.*, **rimosely** *adv.*

rim-rock *n.* A overlying strata of rock on a plateau that outcrops to form a vertical face.

rind *n.* A tough outer layer which may be taken off or pealed off.

rin-der-pest *n.* A kind of contagious disease that affects the ruminant animals.

ring *n.* A circular mark, line, or object; a small circular band worn on a finger; a group of persons acting together; especially in an illegal way. *v.* To make a clear resonant sound, as a bell when struck. *n.* The sound made by a bell.

ring-bone *n.* The callus growth that occurs on the pastern bones of a horse.

ring-dove *n.* A kind of very large European pigeon.

ring-er *n.* A person who sound bells by ringing; in the game of horseshoes, a shoe that encircles the peg.

ring fin-ger *n.* The third finger on the left hand usually where the wedding band is worn.

ring-lead-er *n.* The person who is the leader of a group, usually one that will violate the law.

ring-let *n.* A small curl of hair.

ring-mas-ter *n.* The person in charge of performances in the circus.

ring--necked pheas-ant *n.* A chicken-like bird that has a white ring around its neck and is found in the northern regions of the United States.

ring-side *n.* A section or area that is located right around the ring, such as in a boxing match.

ring-taw *n.* A game where marbles are placed in a circle with the object being for the shooter to knock the marbles out of the ring.

ring-toss *n.* A type of game where rings are tossed in an attempt to get them around a small upright pole some distance away.

ring-worm *n.*, *Pathol.* A contagious skin disease caused by fungi and marked by discolored, ring-shaped, scaly patches on the skin.

rink *n.* A smooth area covered with ice used for hockey or ice-skating; a smooth wooden surface for roller skating.

rinse *v.* To wash lightly with water. *n.* The act of rinsing; a hair coloring or conditioning solution. **-er** *n.*, **rinsed** *v.*

rins-ing *n.* The action or act of a person who rinses.

ri-ot *n.* A wild and turbulent public disturbance. *Slang* An irresistibly amusing person. **riotous** *adj.*, **rioter** *n.*

rip *v.* To tear apart violently; to move violently or quickly. *n.* A torn place **rip-off** *Slang* To steal.

ri-par-i-an *adj.* To be located on the bank by water, such as a lake.

rip cord *n.* A cord which, when pulled releases a parachute from its pack.

rip cur-rent *n.* A strong surface current flowing outward from shore which results from the return flow of waves.

ripe *adj.* Fully developed or aged; mature. **ripeness** *n.*

rip-en *v.* To age; to develop to maturity.

ri-poste *n.* A quick return thrust used in fencing; a verbal sally.

rip-per *n.* A machine used to break up rock, ore, etc.

rip-ping *adj.* To be pertaining to the tearing of something.

rip-ple *v.* To cause to form small wave on the surface of water; to wave gently. **rippler** *n.*

rip rap *n.* A foundation wall of stone thrown together in random fashion.

rip--roar-ing *adj.* To be noisy and loud.

rip saw *n.* A coarse-toothed saw used to cut wood in the direction of the grain.

rip tide *n.* Water made rough by the meeting of opposite tides and currents.

rise *v.* To move from a lower position to a higher one; to extend upward; to meet a challenge or demand. *n.* The act of going up or rising; an elevation in condition or rank.

ris-er *n.* A person who rises; the upright part of a stairway.

ris-i-bil-i-ty *n.* The ability to laugh.

ris-i-ble *adj.* Being inclined to or causing laughter.

ris-ing *adj.* To be growing in height; to

be more active.

risk *n.* A chance of suffering or encountering harm or loss; danger; a person who is a hazard to an insurer.

risk-y *adj.* To be hazardous or full of risk. **riskiness** *n.*

ri-sot-to *n.* Rice cooked in meat stock, seasoned with cheese.

rite *n.* A formal religious ceremony; any formal custom or practice.

rit-u-al *n.* A prescribed method for performing a religious ceremony. *adj.* Pertaining to or practiced as a rite. **ritual** *adj.*, **ritualism** *n.*, **ritually** *adv.*

ritzy *adj.* To be fashionable; having a high fashion.

ri-val *n.* One who strives to compete with another; one who equals or almost equals another.

ri-val-ry *n.* Competition.

rive *v.* To tear or to rip. **river** *n.*

riv-er *n.* A relatively large natural stream of water, usually fed by another body of water.

riv-er bed *n.* The channel thru which the river flows.

riv-er-ine *adj.* To be caused or formed by a river.

riv-er-weed *n.* A type of submerged fresh-water plant.

ri-vet *n.* A metal bolt that is used to secure two or more objects.

riv-u-let *n.* A small stream.

RN *abbr.* Registered Nurse.

RNA *abbr.* Ribonucleic acid.

roach *n.* A European freshwater fish; cockroach. *Slang* The butt of a marijuana cigarette.

roach back *n.* A back that is curved.

road *n.* A public highway used for vehicles, people, and animals; a path or course; a course toward the achievement of something.

road-a-bil-i-ty *n.* In reference to a car, its ability to ride over all types of roads.

road-bed *n.* The surface of which a road is constructed.

road block *n.* An obstruction in a road, which prevents passage.

road hog *n.* A type of driver that drives in the center of the road preventing others from passing.

road-house *n.* An inn outside city limits which serves liquor, meals, etc. and often has gambling.

road met-al *n.* The material, such as stones, that is used for repairing a road.

road racing *n.* A race over public roads instead of a race track.

road-run-ner *n.* A large bird of the cuckoo family that is a speedy runner found in the southwestern part of the United States.

road show *n.* A theatrical show given by a traveling troupe on tour.

road-side *n.* The side or the edge of a road.

road-stead *n.* The covered place for ships may anchor off the shore.

road-ster *n.* The early kind of car that has a single seat for two people and a rumble seat in the rear.

road test *n.* The test for a car to know how it will handle on the road in normal conditions.

road-way *n.* The land the road passes through.

roam *v.* To travel aimlessly or without a purpose. **roamer** *n.*

roan *n.* The color of a horse; a sheepskin tanned with sumac.

roar *v.* To utter a deep prolonged sound of excitement; to laugh loudly; a coisterous outcry. **roar, roarer** *n.*

roar-ing *n.* A loud sound or cry that is given off by something.

roast *v.* To cook meat by using dry heat in an oven. A cut of meat.

roast-er *n.* A person that roasts.

rob *v.* To take property unlawfully from another person. **robber** *n.*, **robbery** *n.*

rob-a-lo *n.* A type of marine fish that is found in the West Indian waters.

ro-band *n.* A piece of woven yarn used to fasten the sail to a spar.

rob-ber *n.* A person who steals for others.

rob-ber fly *n.* A large predatory fly.

rob-ber-y *n.* The act of larceny from a person by violence or threat.

robe *n.* A long loose garment usually worn over night clothes; a long flowing garment worn on ceremonial occasions.

rob-in *n.* A large North American bird with a black head and reddish breast.

Rob-in Hood *n.* A legendary outlaw know for his archery and for robbing the rich and giving to the poor.

Rob-in-son Cru-soe *n.* A shipwrecked sailor who lived for many years on a desert island in Defoe's book Robinson Crusoe.

ro-ble *n.* Type of white oak tree that is found mainly in California.

ro-bot *n.* A machine capable of performing human duties.

ro-bot bomb *n.* Type of missile with a bomb and is directed to its target with an automatic pilot.

ro-bot-ize *v.* To make something automatic. **robotization** *n.*

ro-bust *adj.* Full of strength and health; rich; vigorous. **robustly** *adv.*, **-ness** *n.*

ro-bus-tious *adj.* To be sturdy or strong. **robustiousness** *n.*

roc-am-bole *n.* One type of garlic that is cultivated.

roch-et *n.* A white linen vestment with close-fitting sleeves worn by bishops and prelates.

rock *n.* A hard naturally formed material. *Slang* One who is dependable.

rock-a-way *n.* A carriage having three or four wheels and a top that stands.

rock bass *n.* The striped bass.

rock-bottom *n.* The lowest part.

rock--bound *adj.* To be surrounded by rocks.

rock brake *n.* A kind of fern that will grow in places which are rocky.

rock candy *n.* Candy made from boiling sugar and water and crystallized on string.

rock dove *n.* A type of pigeon that has a fan-shaped tail and is bluish-grey in color.

rock-er *n.* A curved piece, usually of wood, on which a cradle or chair rocks.

rock-er arm *n.* A pivoted lever to push an engine valve down.

rock-et *n.*

A device propelled with the thrust from a gaseous combustion. *v.* To move rapidly.

rock-e-teer *n.* One who operates rockets.

rock-et plane *n.* An airplane propelled by rockets.

rock-et-ry *n.* The study of rockets.

rock-fish *n.* The striped bass.

rock gar-den *n.* Type of garden that is grown in or on rocks.

rock-ing horse *n.* Toy horse that is mounted on rockers and a child can rock back and forth on.

rock-ling *n.* A little codfish.

rock-oon *n.* A research rocket carried by a balloon to a high altitude and then fired.

rock--ribbed *adj.* Being firm and unyielding.

rock-rose *n.* Type of flowering shrub.

rock salt *n.* Salt that is artificially prepared in large crystals, sometimes used in the preparation of ice cream made at home.

rock tripe *n.* An edible lichen that can be found on the rocks in the arctic areas.

rock-weed *n.* Type of seaweed that can be found on rocks during the low tide.

rock wool *n.* A mineral wool made by blowing steam through molten rock and used for heat and sound insulation.

rock-y *adj.* Unsteady or unstable; full of rocks. **rockiness** *n.*

Rocky Mountain spotted fever *n.* A disease contracted from the bite of a wood tick characterized by fever, chills pains in muscles and joints.

rod *n.* A straight stick growing from a tree or bush; a pole with a line attached for fishing. **rodlike** *adj.*

rode *v.* Past tense of ride.

ro-dent *n.* A mammal, such as a rat, mouse, or beaver having large incisors used for gnawing.

ro-den-ti-cide *n.* A material that is used to destroy rodents.

ro-de-o *n.* A public show, contest, or demonstration of ranching skills, as riding and roping.

rod-man *n.* A surveyor's assistant.

rod-o-mon-tade *n.* Boasting that is vain.

roe *n.* The eggs of a female fish.

roent-gen-o-gram *n.* Type of photograph which is made with the used of x-rays.

roentgenographic *adj.*

ro-ent-gen-o-ther-a-py *n.* Kind of medic treatment using x-rays.

rogue *n.* A scoundrel or dishonest pe son; an innocently or playful person. **roguishness** *n.,* **roguishly** *adv.*

rogue el-e-phant *n.* The elephant th has been excluded form the herd.

roil *v.* To make one angry.

role *n.* The position or character that a actor or actress plays.

roll *v.* To move in any direction by turn ing over and over; to sway or roc from side to side, as a ship; to make deep prolonged sound as thunder. A list of names. *Slang* A large amou of money.

roll call *n.* The act of calling out th names on a list, in order to determin who is present.

roll-er *n.* A cylinder for crushin smoothing or rolling something; a of a number of various cylindric devices.

rol-lick *v.* To frolic about.

roll-ing mill *n.* A type of mill whe metal is rolled in to sheets.

roll-ing pin *n.* A long cylinder havi two handles and is rolled over doug in order to flatten it out.

roll up *v.* To collect item together.

ro-maine *n.* Type of lettuce that has na row leaves.

ro-mance *n.* A love affair, usually of th young, characterized by ideals devotion and purity; a fictitious sto filled with extravagant adventures. **romance** *v.,* **romancer** *n.*

Ro-man nu-mer-al *n.* The letter or lette of the Roman system of numberi still used in formal contexts, as: V = X = 10,   L = 50,   C = 100,   D = 50 M = 1000.

ro-man-tic *adj.* Very amorous; referrin to romance.

romp *v.* To run, play, or frolic in carefree way.

romp-er *n.* A person who romp around.

ron-dure *n.* A form that is gracefull curved.

rood *n.* A measurement of land whic equals 1/4 acre.

roof *n.* The top or covering of a hous or other building keeping the ele ments of weather out. **rooflike** *adj.*

roof gar-den *n.* The garden that can b found on top of a building.

roof-ing *n.* The supplies and materi that are used to cover a roof.

rook *n.* A kind of European crow.

rook-er-y *n.* The location which is use by the rooks for nesting.

rook-ie *n.* An untrained person; a novic or inexperienced person.

room *n.* A section or area of a buildin set off by partitions or walls. *v.* To oc cupy or live in a room.

room-er *n.* Person who rents a roo from someone and pays rent.

room-ful *n.* The amount that a room able to hold.

room-ing house n. A place or house where the rooms are rented out.

room-mate n. A person who will share or live in the same room with another.

room-y adj. To be spacious. **-ily** adv.

roost n. A place or perch on which birds sleep or rest; a piece of meat which has been or is to be roasted.

roost-er n. The male chicken.

root n.

The part of a plant which grows in the ground. Math A number which, when multiplied by itself, will produce a given quantity. v. To search or rummage for something; to turn up the earth with the snout, as a hog.
rootlike adj., **rootless** adj.

root-age n. The action of taking root into.

root beer n. A non-alcholic beverage that is flavored with extracts of herbs and roots.

root bor-er n. Type of insect that will tunnel into the roots of plants.

root cel-lar n. A place that is used to store vegetables.

root crop n. A crop that is grown for its enlarged roots.

root-ed-ness n. The state of having roots.

root-hold n. The anchorage of a plant in the soil by the growing and spreading of its roots.

root-less adj. Having no roots at all.

root-let n. A small root.

root out v. To discover something.

root rot n. A plant disease which is recognized by the decaying of it's roots.

root-y adj. To have a lot of roots.

rope n. A heavy cord of twisted fiber. **know the ropes**. To be familiar with all of the conditions at hand.

roop-walk n. A long building, or room where ropes are made.

rope yarn n. The strands of hemp that makes up a rope.

ro-que-laure n. A knee-length coat that was worn in the 18th and 19th centuries.

ror-qual n. Large whale.

ro-sa-ry n., pl. **-ies** A string of beads for counting prayers; a series of prayers.

rose n. A shrub or climbing vine having sharp prickly stems and variously colored fragrant flowers.

ro-se-ate adj. To be of a deep pink color. **roseately** adv.

rose-bay n. A flowering shrub.

rose-bud n. The state of the rose just before it blooms.

rose-col-ored adj. To be optimistic and bright.

rose fe-ver n. The allergy that is associated to rose pollen.

rose-fish n. Type of marine fish which is red in color and can be found in the North Atlantic.

ro-se-o-la n. A rash that is rose colored and appearing on the skin.

rose slug n. A larva of the sawfly that will feed on the leaves of roses.

ro-sette n. An ornament gathered to resemble a rose and made of silk or ribbon.

rose wa-ter n. A fragrant product made from rose petals, steeped in water, and used in cosmetics.

rose-wood n. A tropical tree found in South America that yields a fine wood for building objects.

Rosh Ha-sha-nah n. The Jewish New Year.

ros-i-ly adv. In a cheerful manner; with a rosy color.

ros-in-weed n. A sunflowerlike plant that is found in North America.

ros-ter n. A list of names.

ros-y adj. To be pink, like the color of roses. **rosiness** n.

rot v. To breakdown or decompose.

ro-ta-ry adj. Turning or designed to turn; of or relating to axial rotation.

ro-tate v. To turn on an axis; to alternate something in sequence. **-able** adj., **rotation, rotator** n., **rotatory** adj.

ROTC abbr. Reserve Officer's Training Corps.

rote n. Repetition of sounds.

ro-te-none n. Type of compound that is used as an insecticide.

ro-tis-ser-ie n. A rotation device with spits for roasting food.

ro-tor n. A rotating part of a mechanical device.

rot-ten adj. Decomposed; morally corrupt; very bad.

rot-ten-stone n. Type of soft stone that is used for polishing brass.

rot-ter n. A person who is really bad.

ro-tund adj. Plump; rounded.

ro-tun-da n. A building that is round having a domed roof.

rouge n. A cosmetic coloring for the cheeks.

rough adj. Having an uneven surface; violent or harsh. n. The part of a golf course with tall grass. v. To treat roughly. adv. In a very rude manner. **roughly** adv., **roughness** n.

rough-age n. Material that is coarse in texture.

rough--and--ready adj. Crude in method but effective in action.

rough blue-grass n. Type of grass having bluish-green stems.

rough-en v. To cause something to become rough.

rou-leau n. A trimming for hats that is rolled.

rou-lette n. A gambling game in which players bet on which slot a small ball will land in.

round adj. Curved; circular; spherical. v. To become round; to surround. adv. Throughout; prescribed duties, places, or actions. **roundness** n.

round-a-bout adj. To be going round something.

rouse v. To awaken or stir up.

rout v. To dig something up, such as a root.

route n. A course of travel. v. To send in a certain direction.

rou-tine n. Activities done regularly. adj. Ordinary.

rove v. To wander over a wide area. **rover** n., **roving** adj.

rove bee-tle n. A beetle that has slender body and is able to run quickly.

row n. A number of things positioned next to each other; a continuous line. v. To propel a boat with oars.

row-an tree n. Type of smooth-barked tree that has clusters of red berries.

row-dy n. A person who is disorderly. **rowdily** adv., **rowdiness** n.

roy-al adj. Relating to a king or queen.

roy-al blue n. A dark and deep shade of blue.

roy-al-ist n. A person who supports the king.

roy-al palm n. Type of palm tree that is located in California and Florida.

roy-al-ty n., pl. **-ies** Monarchs and or their families; a payment to someone for the use of his invention, copyright, or services.

R.S.V.P. abbr. Respondez s'il vous plait; please reply.

rub v. To move over a surface with friction and pressure; to cause to become worn or frayed.

rub-ber n. A resinous elastic material obtained from the coagulated and processed sap of tropical plants or produced synthetically. **rubbery** adj.

rub-ber ce-ment n. A type of adhesive that is liquid and made of rubber.

rub-ber-ize v. Coat or cover something with rubber.

rub-ber-neck v. To turn the head in order to see something.

rub-ber plant n. Type of plant that is found in East India and yields rubber.

rub-ber stamp n. A type of rubber plate which is coated with ink and used for the purpose of leaving prints on paper or other objects.

rub-bing n. The action or act of a person or thing that rubs.

rub-bish n. Worthless trash; nonsense.

rub-ble n. The pieces of broken material or stones.

rub-down n. A type of quick and brisk massage.

ru-be-fa-cient n. A type of substance which will turn the area of skin it is applied to red. **rubefaction** n.

ru-bel-la n. The German measles.

ru-bel-lite n. A red gem stone.

ru-be-o-la n. The German measles. **rubeoloid, rubeolar** adj.

ru-bi-cund adj. State of being of a red color or hue. **rubicundity** n.

ru-bid-i-um n., Symbol A silvery, highly reactive element symbolized by Rb.

ru-bi-ous adj. Being red in color.

ru-bric n. A heading, title, or initial letter of a manuscript which appears in red. **rubrically** adv., **rubrical** adj.

ru-bri-cate v. To color something red. **rubricator, rubrication** n.

ru-by n., pl. **-ies** A deep-red precious stone. **rubylike** adj.

ru-by glass n. Type of red glass.

ru-by spi-nal n. A gem stone, red in color.

ruche n. Piece of crimped fabric which is used to trim a woman's clothes.

ruck n. Trash.

ruck-sack n. A knapsack that is carried by hikers.

ruck-us n., Slang A noisy uproar, or commotion.

ruc-tion n. A quarrel.

rud-beck-i-a n. A type of North American herb with dark brown center disks.

rud-der n., Naut. A broad, flat, hinged device attached to the stern of a boat used for steering.

rud-dock n. The robin that is found in Europe.

rud-dy adj. Being red in color or hue.

ru-di-ment n. A first step, element, skill or principle. Biol. An undeveloped organ. **rudimentarines** n.

rue v. To repent.

rue a-nem-o-ne n. A type of woodland flower of North America having pinkish flowers.

rue-ful adj. To be causing sorrow or remorse. **ruefully** adv.

ru-fes-cent adj. To be red in color or tint. **rufescence** n.

ruff n. A stiff collar which has pleats in it.

ruffed grouse n. A bird, like the chicken and living in North America having fan-shaped tail and tufted feathers at the neck.

ruf-fi-an n. A lawless, rowdy person. **ruffianly** adj., **ruffianism** n.

ruf-fle n. A pleated strip or frill; a decorative band. v. To disturb or destroy the smoothness.

ru-fous adj. To be red in color or tint.

rug n. A heavy textile fabric used to cover a floor.

ru-ga n. A wrinkle or fold in something.

Rug-by n. A game similar to football in which the ball is propelled toward the opponents goal by carrying or kicking.

rug-ged adj. Strong; rough; having an uneven or rough surface. **ruggedness** n., **ruggedly** adv.

ru-gose adj. To be filled with folds and wrinkles. **rugous** adj., **rugosely** adv.

ru-in n. Total destruction. v. To destroy. **ruination** n., **ruinous** adj.

rule n. Controlling power; an authoritative direction or statement which regulates the method of doing something; a standard procedure. v. To have control over; to make a straight line using a ruler; to be in command.

rule out v. To omit something.

rul-er n. A straight edge used for measuring; a person who rules as sovereign.

rul-ing n. A type of decision which is handed down by a judge in a trial.

rum *n.* A type of liquor made from molasses and is distilled.

rum-ba *n.* A type of dance which has a complex rhythm.

rum-ble *v.* To make a heavy, continuous sound. *n.* A long deep rolling sound.

rum-ble seat *n.* A seat that is uncovered and located in the back of a vehicle, such as an early roadster.

rum-bly *adj.* To be characterized by a rumble.

ru-men *n.* The first stomach of ruminant animals, such as a cow or goat.

ru-mi-nant *n.* A cud-chewing animal; as a cow, deer, sheep, or giraffe; an animal which chews something which was swallowed. **ruminantly** *adv.*

ru-mi-nate *v.* To chew a cud; to ponder at length. **rumination** *n.*, **ruminative** *adj.*, **ruminator** *n.*

rum-mage *v.* To look or search thoroughly by digging or turning things over; to ransack.

rum-mage sale *n.* A sale of second-hand objects, conducted to make money.

rum-mer *n.* A type of drinking glass that is large in size.

rum-my *n.* A card game in which each player tries to get rid of his hand in sequences of three cards or more of the same suit.

ru-mor *n.* An uncertain truth which is circulated from one person to another; gossip. *v.* To speed by rumor.

ru-mor-mon-ger *n.* One who aids in the spreading of rumors.

rump *n.* The fleshy hind quarter of an animal; the human buttocks.

rum-ple *v.* To form into creases or folds; to wrinkle.

rum-pus *n.* A loud noise or disturbance.

rum-pus room *n.* A type of room which is used for parties.

run *v.* To hurry busily from place to place; to move quickly in such a way that both feet leave the ground for a portion of each step; to make a rapid journey; to be a candidate seeking an office; to drain or discharge. *Law* To be effective, concurrent with. *n.* A speed faster than a walk; a streak, as of luck; the continuous extent or length of something; an outdoor area used to exercise animals. In baseball, the method of scoring a point by running the bases and returning to home plate.

run-a-bout *n.* A type of boat which is open.

run-a-way *n.* A person who leaves home with out telling anyone where they are going and does not plan on coming back.

rund-let *n.* A type of barrel which is small in size.

rung *n.* A bar or board which forms a step of a ladder.

run-nel *n.* A small stream.

run-ner *n.* The person who runs in a race.

run-ner bean *n.* A kind of plant from the tropics that has edible seeds and red flowers.

run-ner-up *n.* A contestant who finishes second in a competition.

run-ning *adj.* State of moving fast or rapidly.

run-ning knot *n.* A type of knot that is able to slide up and down a rope.

run-ny *adj.* To be tending to run.

run-off *n.* That which runs off of something.

run-of-the-mill *adj.* Ordinary; not special; average.

runt *n.* The smallest animal in a litter. **runty** *adj.*, **runtiness** *n.*

run-through *n.* The rehearsal of a play.

run-way *n.* A path over which something runs; a platform which extends from a stage into the middle of an auditorium; a strip of paved ground for the landing and takeoff of airplanes.

rup-ture *n.* A state of being broken; the act of bursting. **rupturable** *adj.*

ru-ral *adj.* Pertaining to the country or country life. **ruralist** *n.*

ru-ral-ize *v.* The act of moving to or living in the country or the rural area. **ruralization** *n.*

ru-ral route *n.* A mail route which runs through the country.

ruse *n.* A type of trick.

rush *v.* To move quickly; to hurry; to be in a hurry. **rushy** *adj.*

rusk *n.* A piece of toasted and sweet bread.

rus-set *n.* A reddish or yellowish brown color.

rust *n.* Ferric oxide which forms a coating on iron material exposed to moisture and oxygen; deterioration through neglect. *v.* To form rust.

rus-tic *adj.* Characteristic of country life. *n.* A simple person. **rustically** *adv.*

rus-ti-cate *v.* Living and staying in the country or rural area. **rusticator** *n.*

rus-tic-i-ty *n.* The quality of being rustic.

rus-tle *v.* To move making soft sounds, such as those made by leaves of a tree.

rus-tler *n.* A person who steals cattle.

rust-proof *adj.* Being unable to rust.

rust-y *adj.* To be covered by rust. **rustiness** *n.*, **rustily** *adv.*

rut *n.* An indented track made by the wheels of vehicles.

ru-ta-ba-ga *n.* A vegetable of the mustard family which makes an underground white tuber.

ruth *n.* Grief; sorrowful for another.

ru-the-ni-um *n.* A metallic element symbolized by Ru. **ruthenious** *adj.*

ruth-ful *adj.* To be mournful. **-ness** *n.*

ruth-less *adj.* Merciless. **ruthlessly** *adv.*

ru-ti-lant *adj.* To have a glow that is reddish in color or tine.

rut-ty *adj.* A state of having many ruts.

Rx *n.* A prescription for medicine.

rye *n.* A cultivated cereal grass used to make flour and whiskey.

rye-grass *n.* A type of cultivated grasses.

rye whis-key *n.* Whiskey distilled from rye.

S, s The nineteenth letter of the English alphabet.

SA *abbr.* Salvation Army.

Saa-nen *n.* A member of the Swiss breed that is a white hornless goat.

sab-a-dil-la *n.* A type of mexican plant such as of the lily family whose seeds can be used for insecticides.

sab-bat *n.* The midnight assembly of the diabolists.

Sab-ba-tar-i-an *n.* A person who observes the Sabbath on Saturday.

Sab-bath *n.* The seventh day of the week; sundown on Friday to sundown on Saturday; a day set apart as the day of worship for Jews and some Christians; Sunday, the first day of the week, a day set apart as the day of worship by most Christians.

sab-bat-i-cal *adj.* To be relating to the sabbath.

Sa-bel-li-an *n.* The member of the early Italian people which includes the Sabines and Samnited.

sa-ber *n.* A lightweight sword.

sa-ber saw *n.* A type of light and portable electric saw.

sa-ber--toothed ti-ger *n.* A type of extinct cat which was characterized by the great development of the upper canines.

sa-bin *n.* The unit of acoustic absorption.

Sa-bine *n.* The member of the people of the Apennines of the ancient times.

sa-ble *n.* A carnivorous mammal having soft, black or dark fur.

sa-ble-fish *n.* A type of large spiny-finned fish which is grey or black and of the Pacific coast.

sa-bot *n.* The kind of wooden shoe which is worn by the people in various European countries.

sab-o-tage *n.* An act of malicious destruction, intended to obstruct production of war material by the opposing side.

sab-o-teur *n.* A person who commits sabotage.

sac *n., Biol.* A membranous pouch in an animal or plant, containing a liquid.

SAC *abbr.* Strategic Air Command.

sa-ca-huis-te *n.* A kind of bear grass that has long linear leaves and is used for forage.

sac-cade *n.* A type of small rapid jerky movements of the eye.

sac-cate *adj.* To have the form of a pouch.

sac-cha-rate *n.* A type of a compound of sugar usually with a bivalent metal.

sac-char-i-fy *v.* To break some compound into a simple sugar.

sac-cha-rim-e-ter *n.* A kind of device which is used for the purpose of measuring the amount of sugar in a solution.

sac-cha-rin *n.* A white, crystalline powder used as a noncaloric sugar substitute.

sac-cha-rine *adj.* Pertaining to or like sugar.

sac-cha-roi-dal *adj.* Being of fine granular texture.

sac-cha-rom-e-ter *n.* A type of hydrometer that has a special scale.

sac-cu-lar *adj.* To be resembling a sac.

sac-cu-late *adj.* To be formed of a series of saccular expansions.

sac-cule *n.* A chamber which is the smaller of the membranous labyrinth of the ear.

sac-er-do-tal *adj.* Pertaining to the priesthood or to priests.

sa-chem *n.* A kind of North American Indian chief.

sa-chet *n.* A small bag of a sweet smelling powder used to scent clothes.

sack *n.* A strong bag for holding articles *Slang* Dismissal from a position or job; sleeping bag or bed.

sack-but *n.* A kind of medieval trombone.

sack-cloth *n.* A type of garment which is made of sackcloth and is worn as a sign of mourning.

sack coat *n.* A type of man's jacket that has a straight and unfitted back.

sack-ing *n.* The material that sacks are constructed from.

sack out *v.* To go or to get into bed.

sack race *n.* Type of race where the contestants jump inside a sack to the finish line.

sacque *n.* A type of infant jacket that is short and fastens at the neck.

sa-cral *adj.* Pertaining to the sacrum.

sac-ra-ment *n., Eccl.* A formal Christian rite performed in a church, as a baptism. **Sacrament** The consecrated bread and wine of the Eucharist; the Lord's Supper.

sac-ra-men-tal *adj.* Pertaining to the character of the sacrament.

sac-ra-men-tal-ism *n.* The use of the sacramental acts or rites.

sa-crar-i-um *n.* A kind of ancient Roman shrine which holds sacred articles.

sa-cred *adj.* Dedicated to worship; holy. **sacredly** *adv.*, **sacredness** *n.*

sa-cred mush-room *n.* A type of New World hallucinogenic fungi.

sac-ri-fice *n.* The practice of offering something, as an animal's life, to a deity. *v.* To give up something of value for something else. **sacrificial** *adj.*

sac-ri-lege *n.* A technical violation of what is sacred because consecrated to God. **sacrilegiousness** *n.*

sac-ris-tan *n.* A type of person who is in charge of the sacristy equipment.

sa-cro-il-i-ac *adj.* Pertaining to the region of juncture of the sacrum and the ilium.

sac-ro-sanct *adj.* Being most holy or sacred. **sacrosanctity** *n.*

sa-crum *n.* The section or part of the vertebral column which is directly connected with the pelvis and in man is made up of five fused vertebrae.

sad *adj.* Marked by sorrow; unhappy causing sorrow; deplorable. **sadly** *adv.*, **sadness** *n.*

sad-den *v.* To become or to make sad.

sad-dle *n.*

A seat for a rider, as on the back of a horse or bicycle; a cut of meat which includes the backbone. *v.* To put a saddle on; to load down; to burden.

sad-dle-bag *n.* A cover pouch which is put across the back of the horse.

sad-dle blan-ket *n.* A type of folded blanket which is placed under the saddle to prevent galling the horse.

sad-dle-bow *n.* The pieces which form the front of the saddle.

sad-dle-cloth *n.* A type of cloth which is placed under the saddle.

sad-dle horn *n.* The prolongation of the pommel of a saddle.

sad-dle horse *n.* A type of horse which is used for riding.

sad-dle leath-er *n.* A type of leather which is made from the hide of cattle that is vegetable tanned and is used for making saddles.

sad-dler *n.* A person who makes or sells saddles.

sad-dle roof *n.* A type of roof having one ridge and two gables.

sad-dlery *n.* The things and items which are for sale in the shop of a saddler.

sad-dle seat *n.* A type of slightly concave chair as a Windsor chair.

sad-dle soap *n.* A type of mild soap used for the purpose of cleaning leather.

sad-dle sore *n.* An open sore which will develop on the back of a horse at the points of pressure from the saddle.

sad-iron *n.* A type of flatiron which is pointed at both ends.

sa-dism *n.*, *Psychol.* A condition in which sexual gratification comes from inflicting pain on others; cruelty. **sadist** *n.*, **sadistic** *adj.* **sadistically** *adv.*

sad sack *n.* A kind of person who is inept.

sa-fa-ri *n.*, *pl.* **-ris.** A trip or journey; a hunting expedition in Africa.

safe *adj.* Secure from danger, harm, or evil; unharmed; not likely to cause harm. *n.* A strong metal container used to protect and store important documents or money. **safely** *adv.*, **safeness** *n.*

safe--con-duct *n.* The protection which is given to a person that is passing through a military zone.

safe-crack-er *n.* A person who breaks into a safe for stealing the things inside.

safe--de-pos-it box *n.* A box which can be found in a bank and used for the purpose of protecting the valuables of the one who uses it.

safe-guard *n.* A kind of precautionary measure.

safe-keep-ing *n.* The process of keeping safety.

safe-light *n.* A kind of darkroom lamp which has a filter to screen out the rays which can be harmful to film.

safe-ty *n.* A condition of being safe from injury or hurt.

safe-ty belt *n.* A type of belt that is used to prevent a person from injury or falling.

safe-ty glass *n.* A type of material that is transparent and is used for windows that are easily or likely to be broken.

safe-ty pin *n.* A type of pin with a clasp that has a guard to cover its point.

safe-ty valve *n.* A type of valve that is used to release pressure.

saf-flow-er *n.* A type of Old World herb that has large red and orange flowers.

saf-fron *n.* A type of purple-flowered crocus which is used to flavor foods.

saf-ra-nine *n.* Any of the various mixtures of safranine salts which are used in dyeing.

saf-role *n.* A type of poisonous ether and is used for perfuming and flavoring.

sag *v.* To droop; to sink from pressure or weight; to lose strength. **sag** *n.*

sa-ga *n.* A long heroic story.

sa-ga-cious *adj.* Being of keen penetration and judgment.

sa-gac-i-ty *n.* The state of being sagacious.

sag-a-more *n.* The subordinate chief of the Algonquian Indians who are of the north Atlantic coast.

sage *n.* A person recognized for judgment and wisdom. **sage** *adj.*

sage-brush *n.* A type of North American undershrubs that have a bitter juice and odor.

sage cheese *n.* A type of cheese which is similar to a mild cheddar and is flavored with sage.

sag-ger *n.* A type of box which is made of fireclay.

sag-it-tal *adj.* Pertaining to the suture between the parietal bones of the skull.

Sag-it-ta-ri-us *n.* The ninth sign of the zodiac; a person born between (November 22 - December 21.)

sag-it-tate *adj.* To be shaped like an arrowhead.

sa-go *n.* A type of powdered starch that is made from the pith of a sago palm.

sa-go palm *n.* A type of plant which yields sago.

sa-gua-ro *n.* A type of arborescent cactus which grows in the southwestern U.S. and Mexico.

said *v.* Past tense of say.

sail *n.* A strong fabric used to catch the wind and cause a ship to move; a trip on a sailing vessel or boat. *v.* To travel on a sailing vessel.

sail-board *n.* A type of small flat sailboat made for two passengers.

sail-boat *n.* A type of boat which is propelled with a sail.

sail-cloth *n.* A type of canvas which is used for boat sails.

sail-er *n.* A boat which has specified sailing qualities.

sail-fish *n.* A type of pelagic fish that has a large dorsal fin.

sail-ing *n.* The skill of managing a ship.

sail-or *n.* The person that sails a boat or a ship.

sail-or's--choice *n.* A small grunt of the Western Atlantic Ocean.

sail-plane *n.* A type of glider.

sain-foin *n.* A type of herb that has pink flowers.

saint *n.* A person of great purity who has been officially recognized as such by the Roman Catholic Church; a person who has died and is in heaven. **sainted** *adj.* **sainthood** *n.*

Saint Ber-nard *n.* A type of Swiss alpine breed of working dog.

saint-dom *n.* The state of being a saint.

saint-ed *adj.* Pertaining or relating to a saint.

saint-hood *n.* The state of being a saint.

saint-ly *adj.* Resembling a saint.

Saint Pat-rick's Day *n.* A day which is observed by the Roman Catholic Church on March 17th in honor of St. Patrick and is celebrated in Ireland.

Saint Val-en-tine's Day *n.* A day where St. Valentine is honored on February 14th.

sake *n.* Motive or reason for doing something.

sa-ker *n.* A type of Old World falcon.

sal-able *adj.* Fit to be sold.

sa-la-cious *adj.* To be appealing to sexual desire. **saliciousness** *n.*

sal-ad *n.* A dish usually made of green vegetables, fruit, or meat tossed with dressing.

sal-ad days *n.* The time of youthful indiscretion.

sal-ad dress-ing *n.* A type of dressing used for the flavoring of a salad such as French, Ranch, Italian, etc.

sal-ad oil *n.* A type of vegetable oil which is used for salad dressings.

sal-a-man-der *n.* A lizard-like amphibian with porous, scaleless skin.

sa-la-mi *n.* A spiced sausage made of beef and pork.

sa-lar-i-at *n.* A body of salaried persons.

sa-la-ry *n., pl. -ies* A set compensation paid on a regular basis for services rendered. **salaried** *adj.*

sale *n.* An exchange of goods for a price; disposal of items at reduced prices. **salable** *adj.*

sa-lep *n.* The dried tubers of various Old World orchids.

sal-era-tus *n.* A kind of leavening agent.

sales *adj.* Pertaining to selling.

sales-clerk *n.* A person who sells in a store.

sales-man *n.* A person who sells in a store or a given area.

sales tax *n.* A tax which is placed on the sale of goods.

sal-i-cin *n.* A bitter white glucoside that is found in the bark of willows.

sa-lic-y-late *n.* The ester of salicylic acid.

sa-lience *n.* The state of being salient.

sa-li-ent *adj.* Projecting beyond a line; conspicuous.

sa-li-en-tian *n.* Any of the group of amphibians which consist of frogs, toads, and tree toads.

sa-lim-e-ter *n.* Type of hydrometer for indicating a percentage of salt in a solution.

sa-li-nize *v.* To impregnate with salt. **salinization** *n.*

sa-li-nom-e-ter *n.* A type of instrument used for the purpose of measuring salt in a solution.

sa-li-va *n.* Tasteless fluid secreted in the mouth which aids in digestion.

sal-i-vary *adj.* Pertaining to saliva or the glands of the body that secret saliva.

sal-i-vate *v.* To produce or make an abnormal flow of saliva.

Salk vac-cine *n.* A vaccine used to immunize against polio.

sal-let *n.* A type of 15th century helmet.

sal-low *n.* A type of Old World broad-leaved willow.

sal-ly *n., pl. -ies.* A sudden rush to launch an assault on something or someone.

Sal-ly Lunn *n.* A type of lightly sweetened yeast-leavened bread.

sal-ly port *n.* A passage in a fortified place.

sal-ma-gun-di *n.* A kind of salad plate made with eggs, meats, vegetables, and anchovies.

sal-mi *n.* A ragot of roasted game that is stewed in a rich sauce.

salm-on *n., pl. -on or -ons* A large game fish with pinkish flesh.

salm-on-ber-ry *n.* A type of red-flowered raspberry found on the Pacific coast.

sal-mo-nel-la *n.* A type of aerobic rod-shaped bacteria that causes food poisoning.

sal-mo-nel-lo-sis *n.* A disease that is caused by salmonellae.

sal-mo-nid *n.* A member of the family of elongated soft-finned fished.

salm-on pink *n.* A yellowish pink which is lighter and redder that salmon.

sa-lon *n.* A large drawing room; a business establishment pertaining to fashion.

sa-loon *n.* A place where alcoholic drinks are sold; a barroom.

sa-loop *n.* A hot drink which is made from sassafras and salep.

sal-pa *n.* A oceanic tunicate which is found to be abundant in warm seas.

sal-pin-gian *adj.* Pertaining to or relating to a salpinx.

sal-pin-gi-tis *n.* The swelling or inflammation of a fallopian tube or an eustachian tube.

sal-si-fy *n.* A type of European biennial herb that has an edible root.

sal soda *n.* A crystalline hydrated sodium carbonate.

salt *n.* A white crystalline solid, mainly sodium chloride, found in the earth and sea water, used as a preservative and a seasoning. *adj.* Containing salt.

sal-ta-rel-lo *n.* A type of Italian dance with a lively hop at the beginning of the measures.

sal-ta-tion *n.* The process of jumping or of leaping.

sal-ta-to-ri-al *adj.* To be adapted for leaping.

sal-ta-to-ry *adj.* Pertaining to dancing.

salt away *n.* To put or lay away safely such as money.

salt-box *n.* A type of dwelling with two stories that has a roof with a long rear slope.

salt-bush *n.* A type of shrubby plant that are able to thrive in alkaline soil.

salt-cel-lar *n.* A vessel used for holding salt at the table.

salt dome *n.* An anticline in sedimentary rock which has a mass of rock salt located within its core.

salt-ed *adj.* Being immune to a disease because one was infected earlier and recovered.

salt-er *n.* A person who makes or sells salt.

sal-tern *n.* A location where salt is made.

salt gland *n.* The gland of a marine bird which is able to excrete a concentrated salt solution.

salt grass *n.* A type of grass which is native to a habitat which is alkaline.

sal-tine *n.* A crisp cracker which is sprinkled with salt.

salt-ing *n.* An area which if flooded by tides.

salt lake *n.* A lake that has become salty.

salt marsh *n.* An area of flat land which is subject to the overflow by salt water.

salt—marsh cat-er-pil-lar *n.* A type of American moth whose larva has been found to be very destructive to crops.

salt out *v.* To separate from a solution by adding salt.

salt-pe-ter *n.* Potassium nitrate.

salt pork *n.* The fat pork that has been cured in brine or salt.

salt-shak-er *n.* A type of container with is used for the purpose of sprinkling salt onto foods through a perforated top.

salt-wa-ter *adj.* Pertaining to salt water.

salt-works *n.* The plant or place where salt is made.

salt-wort *n.* A plant of the goosefoot family which is used in making soda ash.

salty *adj.* To be containing salt.

sa-lu-bri-ous *adj.* To be promoting well-being or health.

sa-lu-ki *n.* A type of old northern African and Asiatic breed of hunting dogs.

sal-u-tar-y *adj.* Wholesome; healthful. **salutariness** *n.*

sal-u-ta-tion *n.* An expression; a greeting of good will, as used to open a letter. **salutational** *adj.*

sa-lu-ta-to-ri-an *n.* A student that usually has the second highest rank in the class.

sa-lu-ta-to-ry *adj.* Pertaining to a salutation.

sa-lute *v.* To show honor to a superior officer by raising the right hand to the forehead. *n.* An act of respect or greeting by saluting.

salv-able *adj.* Capable of being salvaged.

sal-vage *v.* The act of rescuing a ship, its cargo, or its crew; property which has been saved. *v.* To save from destruction; to rescue. **salvageable** *adj.*

sal-va-tion *n.* The means which effect salvation; the deliverance from the effects of sin.

sal-va-tion-ism *n.* The religious teachings which emphasizes the saving of the soul.

Sal-va-tion-ist *n.* An officer of the Salvation Army.

salve *n.* A medicated ointment used to soothe the pain of a burn or wound.

sal-ver *n.* A type of tray which is used for serving food and drinks.

sal-ver-form *adj.* Being tubular with a spreading limb.

sal-via *n.* Type of herbs of the mint family that have a two-lipped open calyx.

sal-vif-ic *adj.* To have the intent to save or to redeem.

sal-vo *n., pl.* **-vos** *or* **-voes** The discharge of a number of guns at the same time.

sal vo-la-ti-le *n.* A solution of ammonium carbonate in alcohol.

SAM *abbr.* Surface-To-Air Missile.

sa-ma-ra *n.* A dry indehiscent, one-seeded winged fruit.

Sa-mar-i-tan *n.* A person who is ready to help others in need.

sa-mar-i-um *n.* A metallic element symbolized by Sm.

sa-mar-skite *n.* A black orthorhombic mineral which is a complex oxide.

sam-ba *n.* A type of Brazilian dance.

sam-bar *n.* A kind of large Asiatic deer that has long course hair on its neck.

sam-bo *n.* A type of international wrestling with judo techniques.

Sam Brown belt *n.* A type of leather belt used for a dress uniform.

same *adj.* Identical; exactly alike; similar; not changing. *pron.* The very same one or thing. **sameness** *n.*

sa-mekh *n.* The 15th letter which is found in the Hebrew alphabet.

sam-i-sen *n.* A type of Japanese musical instrument having three strings.

sa-mite *n.* A type of medieval silk fabric made with gold or silver which is interwoven.

Sam-nite *n.* A person who belongs to the ancient people of central Italy.

sam-o-var *n.* A type of Russian urn used to boil water for the making of tea.

samp *n.* A coarse hominy.

sam-phire *n.* A common glasswort that is sometimes pickled.

sam-ple *n.* A portion which represents the whole. *v.* To try a little.

sam-pler *n.* A person who collects or examines samples.

sam-ple room *n.* The room where samples are displayed.

sam-pling *n.* A small section, part, or portion which is collected as a sample or analysis.

sam-shu *n.* A type of alcoholic liquor that is distilled in China from large millet or rice.

sam-u-rai *n.* The warrior aristocracy of Japan.

san-a-to-ri-um *n., pl.* **-ums** *or* **-ria** An institution for treating chronic diseases.

sanc-ti-fy *v.* To make holy. **-ication** *n.*

sanc-ti-mo-nious *adj.* To be possessing sanctity. **sanctimoniousness** *n.*

sanc-ti-mo-ny *n.* An hypocritical holiness.

sanc-tion *n.* Permission from a person of authority; a penalty to ensure compliance. *v.* To officially approve an action.

sanc-ti-ty *n.* The state of being holy.

sanc-tu-ar-y *n., pl.* **-ies.** A sacred, holy place, as the part of a church, where services are held; a safe place; a refuge.

sanc-tum *n.* A place which is sacred.

sand *n.* Fine grains of disintegrated rock found in deserts and on beaches. *v.* To smooth or polish with sandpaper.

san-dal *n.*

A shoe which is fastened to the foot by straps attached to the sole; a low shoe or slipper with an ankle strap.

san-dal-wood *n.* A fragrant Asian tree used in wood carving and cabinet making.

san-dal-wood oil *n.* The oil which is obtained from the sandalwood.

san-da-rac *n.* A resin that is aromatic and brittle obtained from the African sandarac tree.

san-da-rac tree *n.* A type of northern African tree of the pine family.

sand-bag *n.* A sand-filled bag, used to hold back water.

sand-bank *n.* A deposit of sand which can be large in size.

sand-bar *n.* A sand ridge which has been built by currents of the water.

sand-blast *n.* A stream of sand that is projected by steam used for cleaning.

sand--blind *adj.* To have very poor eyesight.

sand-box *n.* A receptacle that contains loose sand.

sand-bur *n.* A type of weed that has burry fruit and occurs in waste places.

sand--cast *v.* To make a casting by pouring the metal into a mold which is made of sand.

sand casting *n.* A casting which is made from a mold in sand.

sand crack *n.* A crack or fissure in the hoof of a horse which may cause lameness.

sand dol-lar *n.* A flat circular sea urchins that lives in shallow water on the sandy bottom.

sand-er *n.* A person who sands.

sand-er-ling *n.* A type of small sandpiper that has gray-and-white plumage.

sand flea *n.* A type of flea that may be found on the sand.

sand fly *n.* A type of small biting fly that has two wings.

sand-fly fev-er *n.* A disease of short duration and is characterized by headache, fever, and malaise and is transmitted through the bite of the sand fly.

sand-glass *n.* A type of instrument for measuring the passing of time with the running of sand through it.

sand grouse *n.* Type of bird that is closely related to the pigeons and can be found in southern Europe, Africa, and Asia.

sand-hill crane *n.* The crane that is bluish grey tinged and can be found in central and eastern North America.

sand-hog *n.* A person who works in a caisson.

sand jack *n.* The device which is for lowering a heavy weight by allowing the sand that supports it to run out.

sand lance *n.* A type of marine teleost fishes that are able to remain buried in the sand at ebb tide.

sand lily *n.* A type of western North America herb of the lily family.

sand-ling *n.* A young or small flounder.

sand myr-tle *n.* A low-branching evergreen shrub of the heath family.

sand-pa-per *n.* A type of paper that is covered on one side with sand used for the purpose of smoothing rough edges.

sand-pile *n.* A large pile of sand that children can play in.

sand-pip-er *n.* A small shorebird having a long soft-tipped bill.

sand rat *n.* A type of rodent that inhabits sandy areas.

sand-soap *n.* A type of soap that is gritty and can be used for all-purpose cleaning.

sand-stone *n.* A type of sedimentary rock.

sand-storm *n.* A storm in the desert that can drive clouds of sand in front of it.

sand trap *n.* A hazard on the golf course which is filled with sand.

sand-wich *n.* Two or more slices of bread between which a filling, such as cheese or meat, is placed.

sand-worm *n.* A type of polychaete worm that lives in sand.

sand-wort *n.* A type of low tufted herb that will usually grow in a sandy region.

sandy *adj.* To be containing or consisting of sand.

sane *adj.* Having a healthy, sound mind; showing good judgment. **sanely** *adv.*, **sanity** *n.*

san-ga-ree *n.* An iced drink of wine or beer, ale, or liquor which has been garnished with nutmeg.

sang-froid *n.* A self-possession or imperturbability.

san-gui-nar-ia *n.* The roots and rhizome of the blootroot which can be used as an emetic or as an expectorant.

san-gui-nary *adj.* To be attended by bloodshed. **sanguinarily** *adv.*

san-guine *adj.* To be relating to the blood. **sanguinely** *adv.*

san-guin-e-ous *adj.* Pertaining to bloodshed; consisting of blood.

san-guin-o-lent *adj.* To be tinged by blood or to contain blood.

san-gui-no-pu-ru-lent *adj.* To be containing pus and blood in the discharge.

san-i-cle *n.* A type of plant that sometimes are held to have healing powers.

sa-ni-ous *adj.* To be slightly blood tinged.

sanit *abbr.* Sanitation; sanitary.

san-i-tar-i-an *n.* One who is a specialist in sanitary science and the public health.

san-i-tari-ly *adv.* Doing something in a sanitary manner or way.

san-i-tar-y *adj.* Free from bacteria or filth which endanger health.

san-i-tar-y ware *n.* The ceramic plumbing fixtures such as sinks or toilet bowels.

san-i-tate *v.* To make something sanitary.

san-i-ta-tion *n.* The process of making something sanitary.

san-i-tize *v.* To make sanitary; to make clean or free of germs.

san-i-ty *n.* The state of being sane.

sank *v.* Past tense of sink.

san-nup *n.* An American Indian male who is married.

sans-cu-lotte *n.* One who is of a lower class and lacking culture or refinement.

san-se-vie-ria *n.* A member of the group of tropical herbs of the lily family that yield a strong fiber.

Santa Claus *n.* The symbol of Christmas, represented as a jolly, fat, white-bearded old man dressed in a red suit.

sap *n.* The liquid which flows or circulates through plants and trees. *v.* To weaken or wear away gradually. *Slang* A gullible person; fool.

sa-pi-ent *adj.* Wise.

sap-phire *n.* A clear, deep-blue gem, used in jewelry.

sar-casm *n.* An insulting or mocking statement or remark.

sarcastic, sarcastically *adj.*

sar-dine *n.* A small edible fish of the herring family, often canned in oil.

sar-don-ic *adj.* Scornful; mockingly cynical.

sa-ri *n.* A garment consisting of a long piece of lightweight material wrapped around the body and over the shoulder of Hindu women.

sar-sa-pa-ril-la *n.* The dried root of a tropical American plant, which is used as flavoring.

sash *n.* A band worn over the shoulder or around the waist.

sass *n.*, *Slang* Rudeness; a disrespectful manner of speech. *v.* To talk with disrespect.

sas-sa-fras *n.* The dried root of a North American tree, used as flavoring.

Sat *abbr.* Saturday.

Sa-tan *n.* The devil.

sat-el-lite *n.* A natural or man-made object which orbits a celestial body.

sat-in *n.* A smooth, shiny fabric made of silk, nylon, or rayon, having a glossy face and dull back.

sat-ire *n.* The use of mockery, sarcasm, or humor in a literary work to ridicule or attack human vice.

sat-is-fac-tion *n.* Anything which brings about a happy feeling; the fulfillment of a need, appetite, or desire; a source of gratification.

sat-is-fy *v.* To fulfill; to give assurance to.

sat-u-rate *v.* To make completely wet; to soak or load to capacity.

saturable *adj.*, **saturation** *n.*

Sat-ur-day *n.* The seventh day of the week.

Sat-urn *n.* The sixth planet from the sun.

sat-yr *n.*, *Gr. Myth.* A Greek woodland god having a human body and the legs, horns, and ears of a goat.

sauce *n.* A liquid or dressing served as an accompaniment to food. **saucing** *v.*

sau-cer *n.* A small shallow dish for holding a cup.

sau-er-kraut *n.* Shredded and salted cabbage cooked in its own juices until tender and sour.

sau-na *n.* A steam bath in which one is subjected to heat produced by water poured over heated rocks.

sau-sage *n.* Chopped meat, usually pork, which is highly seasoned, stuffed into a casing and cooked.

sav-age *adj.* Wild; not domesticated; uncivilized; brutal.

savagely *adv.*, **savagery** *n.*

save *v.* To rescue from danger, loss, or harm; to prevent loss or waste; to keep for another time in the future; to be delivered from sin. **saver** *n.*

sav-ior *n.* One who saves. Christ Savior.

sa-voir-faire *n.* Social skill; the ability to say and do the right thing.

sa-vor *n.* The taste or smell of something. *v.* To have a particular smell; to truly enjoy. **savory** *adj.*

saw *n.* A tool with a sharp metal blade edged with teeth-like points for cutting. *v.* Past tense of see; to cut with a saw.

sax-o-phone *n.*

A brass wind instrument having finger keys and a reed mouthpiece.
saxophonist *n.*

say *v.* To speak aloud; to express oneself in words; to indicate; to show. *n.* The chance to speak; the right to make a decision.

sb *abbr.* Substantive.

SB *abbr.* Simultaneous broadcast; southbound.

SBA *abbr.* Small Business Administration.

SBN *abbr.* Standard Book Number.

SC *abbr.* South Carolina.

scab *n.* The stiff, crusty covering which forms over a healing wound. *Slang* A person who continues to work while others are on strike.

scab-bard *n.* A type of sheath for a bayonet or a dagger.

scab-ble *v.* To dress something, such as stone, with a rough furrowed surface.

scab-by *adj.* To be diseased with scab.

sca-bies *n.* A contagious skin disease characterized by severe itching, caused by a mite under the skin.

sca-bi-o-sa- *n.* A type of herb of the teasel family.

sca-bi-ous *n.* A type of fleabanes.

sca-brous *adj.* To be rough to the touch. **scabrousness** *n.*

scad *n.* A type of caragid fish.

scaf-fold *n.* A temporary support of metal or wood erected for workers who are building or working in a large structure.

scaf-fold-ing *n.* The system of scaffolds.

scal-able *adj.* Able to be scaled.

sca-lar *adj.* To have an uninterrupted series of steps such as a staircase.

sca-la-re *n.* A type of cichlid fish found in South America.

sca-lari-form *adj.* To be like or resembling a ladder.

scal-a-wag *n., Slang* A rascal.

scald *v.* To burn with steam or a hot liquid; to heat a liquid to a temperature just under boiling.

scald-ing *adj.* To be able to cause the sensation of scalding.

scale *n.* A flat plate which covers certain animals, especially fish and reptiles; a device for weighing; a series of marks indicating the relationship between a map or model and the actual dimensions. *Music* A sequence of eight musical notes in accordance with a specified scheme of intervals.

scale armor *n.* A type of armor where it is covered by small metallic scales for protection.

scale--down *n.* A kind of reduction that is according to a fixed ratio.

scale leaf *n.* A type of scaly leaf that is small in size.

scale-like *adj.* To resemble a scale.

sca-lene *adj.* To have three sides that are not equal in their lengths.

scale-pan *n.* A kind of pan which is used for the purpose of weighing things.

scal-er *n.* Someone or something that scales an object.

scale--up *n.* The increase that is according to a ratio which is fixed.

scall *n.* A type of scabby disorder which can occur on the skin.

scal-liom *n.* A type of onion that will form a thick basal part but without a bulb.

scal-lop *n.* A marine shellfish with a fan-shaped, fluted bivalve shell; the fleshy edible muscle of the scallop.

scalp *n.* The skin which covers the top of the human head where hair normally grows. *v.* To tear or remove the scalp from. *Slang* To buy or sell something at a greatly inflated price. **scalper** *n.*

scal-pel *n.* A small, straight knife with a narrow, pointed blade, used in surgery.

scalp lock *n.* A tuft of the hair on the crown of an otherwise shaved head.

scamp *n.* A scheming or tricky person.

scamp-er *v.* To run playfully about.

scam-pi *n.* A type of large shrimp that is prepared with a garlic sauce.

scan *v.* To examine all parts closely; to look at quickly; to analyze the rhythm of a poem. *Electron.* To move a beam of radar in search of a target. **scan, scanner** *n.*

scan-dal *n.* Something which brings disgrace when exposed to the public; gossip.

scan-dal-ize *v.* To offend someone in a moral sense.

scan-dal-mon-ger *n.* One who circulates scandal.

scan-dal-ous *adj.* Being offensive to morality. **scandalously** *adv.*

scan-dent *adj.* To be characterized by a climbing means of growth.

Scan-di-an *adj.* To be pertaining or related to the languages of Scandinavia.

Scan-di-na-vian *n.* A person who is of Scandinavian descent.

scan-di-um *n.* A metallic element symbolized by Sc.

scan-ner *n.* The device for sensing recorded data.

scan-sion *n.* An analysis of verse to show the meter of the verse.

scant *adj.* Not plentiful or abundant; inadequate. **scantly** *adv.*, **scantness** *n.*

scanty *adj.* To be somewhat less than is normal. **scantiness** *n.*

scant-ling *n.* The dimensions of material used in building, as wood and brick.

scape *n.* The shaft of a column.

scape-goat *n.* A person bearing a blame for others.

scape-goat-ing *n.* The process of casting blame for failure on an innocent individual.

scape-grace *n.* A rascal.

scaph-oid *adj.* To be shaped like a boat.

sca-pose *adj.* To be consisting of a scape.

scap-u-la *n., pl.* -lae One pair of large, flat, triangular bones which form the back of the shoulder.

scap-u-lar *adj.* To be pertaining to or related to the scapula or the shoulder.

scar *n.* A permanent mark which remains on the skin after a sore or injury has healed. **scarless** *adj.*

scar-ab *n.* The scarabaeid beetle.

scar-a-bae-id *n.* A type of stout bodied beetle.

scarce *adj.* Not common or plentiful; rare. **scarceness** *n.*

scarce-ly *adv.* Being done by a slight

margin.

scar-ci-ty *n.* The state of being scarce.

scare *v.* To become scared or to frighten someone suddenly.

scare-crow *n.* A human figure usually placed in a garden for the purpose of scaring off animals and preventing them from eating what is being grown.

scared *adj.* The state of fear one may be thrown into by another who frightens them.

scaredy--cat *n.* A person who is very fearful.

scare up *v.* To get together with considerable difficulty.

scarf *n.* A wide piece of cloth worn around the head, neck, and shoulders for warmth.

scarf-skin *n.* The skin which forms the cuticle of the nail.

scar-i-fi-ca-tion *n.* The marks which can be made by scarifying.

scar-i-fy *v.* To make small cuts into the skin. **scarifier** *n.*

scar-i-ous *adj.* To be membranous in texture.

scar-la-ti-na *n.* A mild form of scarlet fever.

scar-let *n.* A bright or vivid red.

scarlet fever *n.* A communicable disease caused by streptococcus and characterized by a sore throat, vomiting, high fever, and a rash.

scarlet letter *n.* A scarlet A which is worn by a woman as a punitive mark representing the act of adultery.

scarlet runner *n.* A type of American high-climbing bean that is grown as an ornamental tool.

scarlet sage *n.* A type of garden salvia found in Brizil with intense scarlet flowers.

scarlet tanager *n.* A type of American tanager.

scar tissue *n.* A connective tissue that forms a scar and is made mostly of fibroblasts.

scary *adj.* To be able to be easily scared.

SCAT *abbr.* School and College Ability Test.

scathe *v.* To assail something with withering denunciation.

scath-ing *adj.* To be bitterly severe. **scathingly** *adv.*

scat-ter *v.* To spread around; to distribute in different directions.

scat-ter-ation *n.* The process of scattering things.

scat-ter-brain *n.* A heedless person.

scat-ter-good *n.* A person who is very wasteful.

scat-ter-ing *n.* The process of something being scattered.

scat-ter pin *n.* A type of pin which is worn for decoration on one's clothes.

scat-ter rug *n.* A type of rug small enough so that several can be used in one room.

scaup *n.* A type of diving duck.

scav-enge *v.* To salvage something from being discarded; to take away from an area.

scav-en-ger *n.* An animal, as a vulture, which feeds on decaying or dead animals or plant matter.

SCCA *abbr.* Sports Car Club of America.

sce-na *n.* A solo vocal that consists of a recitative.

sce-nar-i-o *n.* A synopsis of a dramatic plot.

sce-nar-ist *n.* A person who creates and writes a scenanrio.

scend *v.* To heave up under the influence of a natural force.

scene *n.* A view; the time and place where an event occurs; a public display of temper; a part of a play.

scene dock *n.* An area or space which is near the stage in a theater and is used for the storage of the scenery.

scen-ery *n.* A printed scenes or other accessories that are used with a play.

scene-shift-er *n.* The person who moves the scenes around in a theater.

sce-nic *adj.* Pertaining to the stage or setting in a play.

scent *n.* A smell; an odor. *v.* To smell; to give something a scent.

scent-ed *adj.* To have a smell or a scent.

scep-ter *n.* A rod or staff carried by a king as a sign of authority.

scep-tered *adj.* To be invested with a scepter.

sch *abbr.* School.

scha-den-freu-de *n.* The enjoyment that is obtained through the troubles of other's.

sched-ule *n.* A list or written chart which shows the times at which events will happen, including a plan given for work and specified deadlines.

schee-lite *n.* A type of mineral that consists of the tungstate of calcium and is a source of tungsten.

sche-ma *n.* A presentation which is diagrammatic.

sche-mat-ic *adj.* To be pertaining to a scheme. **schematically** *adv.*

sche-ma-tize *v.* To form a scheme. **schematization** *n.*

scheme *n.* A plan of action; an orderly combination of related parts; a secret plot.

schem-ing *adj.* To be given to be forming schemes.

schil-ler *n.* A type of bronzy iridescent luster.

schism *n.* A formal separation from a religious body.

schis-mat-ic *n.* The person who creates schism.

schis-ma-tize *v.* To take part in schism.

schist *n.* A type of metamorphic rock that has a closely foliated structure.

schis-tose *adj.* To be pertaining to schist.

schizo-carp *n.* A type of dry compound fruit that will split at its maturity.

schiz-ont *n.* A type of multinucleate sporozoan that will reproduce by schizogony.

schle-miel *n.* A bungler who is unlucky.

schnapps *n.* A type of distilled liquors.

schnau-zer *n.* A type of dog that has a long head, small ears, and a wiry coat.

schnit-zel *n.* A type of garnished and seasoned veal cutlet.

schnor-rer *n.* A person who wheedles other people into supplying his wants.

schol-ar *n.* A student with a strong interest in learning.

schol-ar-ly *adj.* To be suitable to learned persons.

schol-ar-ship *n.* A grant of money which is given to a student to enable them to go to school.

scho-las-tic *adj.* Pertaining to the schools. **scholastically** *adv.*

scho-li-ast *n.* The maker of scholia.

scho-li-um *n.* A comment which is marginal.

school *n.* A place for teaching and learning; a group of persons devoted to similar principles.

school age *n.* The time of one's life when one is able to attend school and required to do so by the law.

school-bag *n.* A bag which is used for the purpose of toting one's school books.

school board *n.* The board of people who are in charge of the public schools.

school-book *n.* A textbook which is used for the schoolwork done in schools.

school bus *n.* A vehicle that is used to take the children to and from work.

school-house *n.* The building that is used for teaching and school.

school-ing *n.* The instruction that is given in school.

school-room *n.* A classroom that is used for teaching.

school-time *n.* The time that is designated for the beginning of a session of school.

school-work *n.* The lessons which are done in school.

schoon-er *n.* A sailing vessel with two or more masts.

Schwann cell *n.* A type of cell of the neurilemma of the fiber of the nerve.

sci *abbr.* Scientific; science.

sci-ae-nid *n.* A type of carnivorous marine percoid fish such as the croakers.

sci-at-ic *adj.* Relating to being located near the hip area of the body.

sci-at-ic nerve *n.* The largest nerve of the body that runs down both legs.

sci-ence *n.* The study and theoretical explanation of natural phenomena in an orderly way; knowledge acquired through experience. **scientific** *adj.*, **scientifically** *adv.*, **scientist** *n.*

sci-en-tism *n.* The attitudes that are typical of the natural scientist.

sci-fi *adj.* Pertaining to science fiction.

scil *abbr.* Scilicet.

scil-la *n.* A type of Old World herbs of the lily family that have pink, blue, or white flowers.

scim-i-tar *n.* A type of saber that is made of a curved blade and is used by the Turks and the Arabs.

scin-til-late *v.* To give off or emit quick flashes. **sciltillator** *n.*

scir-rhus *n.* A type of malignant tumor that has a preponderance of fibrous tissue.

scis-sile *adj.* Being able to be cut smoothly.

scis-sion *n.* The process of splitting or cutting.

scis-sors *pl., n.* A cutting tool consisting of two blades joined and pivoted so that the edges are close to each other.

scis-sor-tail *n.* A type of flycatcher that lives in Mexico and the southern U.S. having a tail that is deeply forked.

scle-ra *n.* A dense fibrous white outer coat that will enclose the eyeball except the section which is covered by the cornea.

scler-ite *n.* A type of hard chitinous plate or piece.

scle-ro-der-ma *n.* A kind of disease of the skin and causes thickening of the subcutaneous tissues.

scle-rom-e-ter *n.* A device which is used for the purpose of determining the hardness of something.

scle-ro-pro-tein *n.* A type of protein that can be found in the skeletal and the connective tissues of the body.

scle-ro-sis *n., pl.* **-ses** A hardening of a part of the body, as an artery.

scle-rot-ic *adj.* Pertaining to the sclera.

scler-o-ti-za-tion *n.* The state of being sclerotized.

scler-o-tized *adj.* To be made hard by a substance other than chitin.

scoff *n.* The expression of derision or scorn. **scoffer** *n.*

scold *v.* To accuse or reprimand harshly.

scold-ing *n.* The action of the person who scolds another person.

sco-lex *n.* A head of the tapeworm in the stages of its life.

sco-li-o-sis *n.* The lateral curvature of the spine. **scoliotic** *adj.*

sconce *n.* A wall bracket for holding candles.

scone *n.* A type of quick bread made of oatmeal and is baked on a griddle.

scoop *n.* A small, shovel-like tool. *v.* To lift up or out. *Slang* An exclusive news report. **scoopful** *n.*

scoot *v.* To go suddenly and quickly.

scoot-er *n.* Type of child's foot-operated toy that is a board mounted between two wheels and having a steering handle.

scop *n.* A poet of the Old English.

scope *n.* The range or extent of one's actions; the space to function or operate in.

-scope *suff.* A device for seeing or discovering.

sco-pol-a-mine *n.* A kind of poisonous alkaloid that can be found in the roots of some plants belonging to the nightshade family.

scop-u-la *n.* A tuft of bushy hairs. **scopulate** *adj.*

scor-bu-tic *adj.* To be like or resembling scurvy. **scorbutically** *adv.*

scorch v. To burn slightly, changing the color and taste of something; to parch with heat.

scorched adj. To be discolored by scorching.

scorcher n., Slang A very hot day.

score n. A numerical record of total points won in a game or other contest; the result of an examination; a grouping of twenty items; a written musical composition which indicates the part to be performed by each person; a groove made with a pointed tool. v. To achieve or win; to arrange a musical score for.

score-board n. A board which is used to display the score of a game.

score-card n. A card which is used for the recording of the score in a game.

score-keep-er n. The person in the game who is in charge of keeping the score.

score-less adj. Having no points scored in a game; each team's score is 0.

sco-ria n. A refuse form the melting of metals. scoriaceous adj.

scorn n. Contempt; disdain. v. To treat with scorn.

scorn-ful adj. Being full of scorn. scornfulness n.

scor-pae-nid n. A member of the group or family of marine spiny-finned fishes.

Scor-pi-o n. The eighth sign of the zodiac; a person born between (October 23 - November 21.)

scor-pi-oid adj. To be curved at the end like the tail of the scorpion.

scor-pi-on n.

An arachnid having an upright tail tipped with a poisonous sting.

scor-pi-on fish n. A type of fish that has a venomous spine on the dorsal fin.

Scor-pi-us n. The southern constellation that is located partly in the Milky Way and next to Libra.

Scot n. A member of the Gaelic people of northern Ireland that settled in Scotland around the year 500 A.D.

Scot abbr. Scottish; Scotland.

scotch v. To stamp something out.

Scoth broth n. A type of soup that has been made from beef and vegetables and then thickened with barley.

Scotch-man n. A man who is of Scotch descent.

Scotch pine n. A type of pine that is found in Asia and northern Europe yielding very hard wood used for building purposes.

Scotch whisky n. A type of whisky that is distilled from malted barley.

sco-ter n. A type of sea duck of the northern coasts of Europe and North America.

scot--free adj. To be totally free from harm or penalty.

Scot-ic adj. Pertaining to the ancient Scots.

sco-to-ma n. A dark spot in the visual field.

Scot-ti-cism n. The characteristic feature of Scottish English.

Scottish Gaelic n. The Gaelic language of the country of Scotland.

Scottish terrier n. A type of old Scottish breed of the terrier having short legs, broad chest, wiry hair, and a large head.

scroun-drel n. A villain or a robber.

scour v. To clean by rubbing with an abrasive agent; to clean thoroughly.

scour-er n. Someone or something that scours.

scout v. To observe activities in order to obtain information. n. A person whose job is to obtain information; a member of the Boy Scouts or Girl Scouts.

scout-ing n. The action of a person who scouts.

scow n. A large barge with a flat bottom and square ends, used to transport freight, gravel, or other cargo.

scowl v. To make an angry look; to frown. scowl n.

SCPO abbr. Senior chief petty officer.

scrab-ble v. To scratch about frantically, as if searching for something. scrabble, scrabbler n.

scrag v. To kill or to execute by hanging.

scrag-gly adj. Messy; irregular.

scram v. To leave or to go away at once.

scram-ble v. To move with panic.

scrap n. A small section or piece. v. To throw away waste.

scrap-book n. A book that will have miscellaneous things in it.

scrape v. To rub a surface with a sharp object in order to clean. Slang An embarrassing situation.

scrap heap n. A large pile of metal which has been discarded.

scra-pie n. A kind of viral disease of sheep where they become itchy, excited, excessively thirsty, weak, and eventually a paralysis occurs.

scrap-pi-ness n. The state of being scrappy.

scratch v. To mark or make a slight cut on; to mark with the fingernails. n. The mark made by scratching; a harsh, unpleasant sound.

scratch hit n. A batted ball that is not hit hard enough but is still credited to the batter as a base hit.

scratch line n. The starting line of a race.

scratch pad n. A pad of paper that is used to jot down notes.

scratch paper n. The paper that is used just to take notes upon.

scratch test n. A type of test for allergic susceptibility that involves placing an extract of an allergy-producing substance in to a scratch on the skin.

scratchy adj. To be marked with scratched. scratchiness n.

scrawl n. To write or draw quickly and

often illegibly. **scrawl** n.

scraw-ny adj. Being very thin; skinny.
scrawniness n.

screak v. To make or produce a shrill noise.

scream v. To utter a long, sharp cry, as of fear or pain. n. A long piercing cry. Slang A very funny person.

scream-er n. A person who screams.

scream-ing-ly adv. To do something to an extreme degree.

scree n. A gathering of stones lying on a slope.

screech v. To make a shrill, harsh noise.

screech owl n. A type of owl that has a tuft of feathers on its head.

screed n. A piece of writing that is informal.

screen n. A movable object used to keep something from view, to divide, or to decorate; a flat reflecting surface on which a picture is projected. v. To keep from view.

screen-ing n. A metal mesh that may be used to cover a window.

screen pass n. A type of forward pass in the game of football to a receiver at or behind the line of scrimmage.

screen test n. A type of short film sequence testing the abilities of a prospective movie actor.

screen-writ-er n. A person who writes screen-plays.

screw n.

A metal piece that resembles a nail, having a spiral thread which is used for fastening things together; a propeller on a ship. v. To join by twisting. **screw up** To make a mess of.

screw-ball n. A type of pitch in baseball where the ball spins and breaks in the opposite direction to a curve.

screw bean n. A type of leguminous shrub of the southwestern U.S.

screw-driv-er n. A type of tool which is used for turning screws.

screw up v. To tighten.

screw-worm n. A type of two-winged fly whose larva is found to develop in the nostrils of mammals, even man.

screwy adj. To be very unusual.

scrib-ble v. To write without thought.

scribe n. A person whose profession is to copy documents and manuscripts.

scrib-er n. A sharp tool fro the purpose of making marks in material to be cut.

scrieve v. To move along smoothly.

scrim n. A type of durable cotton fabric used for clothing and curtains.

scrim-mage n. In football, a practice game. **scrimmage** v.

scrimp v. To make something too small or short.

scrim-shaw n. The art of carving designs on whale ivory or whalebone.

scrip n. A type of small wallet.

script n. The written text of the play.

scrip-tur-al adj. According to a sacred writing. **scripturally** adv.

scrip-ture n. A sacred writing. **Scriptures** The Bible.

script-writ-er n. A person who writes screenplays and other scripts.

scriv-en-er n. A public copyist or writer.

scrod n. A type of young fish such as the haddock or the cod.

scrof-u-la n. A tuberculosis of the lymph glands.

scrof-u-lous adj. To be affected with scrofula.

scroll n. A roll of parchment or similar material used in place of paper.

scroll saw n. A type of thin handsaw that is used for the purpose of cutting curves and designs.

scroll-work n. An ornamentation that is characterized by scrolls.

scrooge n. A type of person who is miserly.

scro-tum n., pl. -ta The external sac of skin which encloses the testes.
scrotal adj.

scrounge v. To collect by foraging.

scrub v. To clean something by rubbing. Slang To cancel.

scrub-ber n. One that is able to scrub.

scrub brush n. A type of brush which is used for the purpose of scrubbing.

scrub-land n. An area of land which has been covered with scrub.

scrub pine n. A type of tree which is not used for lumber due to its size.

scruff n. The region on the back of the neck.

scrump-tious adj., Slang Delightful.
scrumptiously adv.

scru-ple n. A principle which governs one's actions.

scru-pu-los-i-ty n. The state of being scrupulous.

scru-pu-lous adj. To have moral integrity. **scrupulously** adv.

scru-ta-ble adj. To be able to be deciphered.

scru-ta-tor n. An examiner.

scru-ti-neer n. The person who examines.

scru-ti-nize v. To look at or to examine something very carefully.

scru-ti-ny n. An inspection of something.

sct abbr. Scout.

sctd abbr. Scattered.

scu-ba n. An apparatus used by divers for underwater breathing; from the initials for self-contained underwater breathing apparatus.

scu-ba div-er n. A person who swims under the water with the use of scuba gear.

scud v. To move or to go quickly.

scuff v. To drag or scrape the feet while walking. n. A rough spot.

scuf-fle v. To struggle in a confused manner. **scuffle** n.

scuf-fle hoe n. A type of hoe which has both edges sharpened.

scull n. An oar mounted at the stern of a boat, which is moved back and forth to produce forward motion.

scul-lery n. A room used for storing and

cleaning dishes.

scul·lion *n.* A type of kitchen helper.

scul·pin *n.* A type of large-headed scaleless fish.

sculpt *v.* To carve; to make a sculpture.

sculp·tor *n.* A person who creates statues from clay, marble, or other material.

sculp·ture *n.* The art of processing a hard or soft material into another form, such as a statue.

scum *n.* A thin layer of waste matter floating on top of a liquid.

scum·ble *v.* To make something less brilliant by covering it with a thin coat of color.

scun·ner *v.* To be in a state of irritation.

scup·per·nong *n.* A type of white aromatic table wine that is made from scuppernongs.

scurf *n.* Flaky dry skin; dandruff.

scur·ril·i·ty *n.* The state of being scurrilous.

scur·ri·lous *adj.* To be vulgar and evil.

scur·ry *v.* To move quickly; to scamper.

scur·vy *n.* A type of disease that is caused by the lack of ascorbic acid and is characterized by bleeding gums and bleeding into the skin.

scut *n.* A type of tail which is short and erect.

scu·tage *n.* A kind of tax that is levied on a tenant of a knight's land in the place of serving for the military.

scutch·er *n.* A type of machine used for the purpose of scutching cotton.

scute *n.* A external horny plate.

scu·tel·late *adj.* To be resembling scutellum.

scu·tel·lum *n.* A small shield-shaped plant structure.

scut·tle *n.* A small opening with a movable lid in the hull of a ship. *v.* To deliberately sink a boat or other floating object by cutting or making holes in the bottom or sides.

scut·tle·butt *n.* A type of cask on a shipboard that contains fresh water that is to be used during that day.

scu·tum *n.* A type of horny and bony plate.

scy·pho·zo·an *n.* A type of coelenterates that makes of the group of jellyfish and lacking a true polyp.

scythe *n.* A tool with a long handle and curved, single-edged blade, used for cutting hay, grain and grass.

Scyth·i·an *n.* A member of the people that inhabitated Scythia and were nomads.

SD *abbr.* South Dakota.

sea *n.* The body of salt water which covers most of the earth; a large body of salt water.

sea-coast *n.* Land that borders the sea.

seal *n.*

A device having a raised emblem, displaying word or symbol, used to certify a signature or the authenticity of a document; a tight closure which secures; a large aquatic mammal with a sleek body and large flippers; the fur or pelt of a seal. *v.* To hunt seals.

sealer, sealant *n.*

sea level *n.* The level of the sea's surface, used as a standard reference point in measuring the height of land or the depth of the sea.

seam *n.* The line formed at the joint of two pieces of material.

sear *v.* To wither or dry up; to shrivel; to burn or scorch.

search *v.* To look over carefully; to find something; to probe. **searcher** *n.*

sea·son *n.* One of the four parts of the year; spring, summer, fall or autumn and winter; a time marked by particular activities or celebrations. *v.* To add flavorings or spices; to add interest or enjoyment.

seasonal *adj.*, **seasonally** *adj.*

seat *n.* A place or spot, as a chair, stool, or bench, on which to sit; the part of the body used for sitting; the buttocks.

se·cede *v.* To withdraw from an organization or group.

secession, secessionist *n.*

se·clude *v.* To isolate; to keep apart.

sec·ond *n.* A unit of time equal to 1/60 of a minute; a very short period of time; an object which does not meet first class standards. *Math* A unit of measure equal to 1/60 of a minute of angular measurement.

sec·on·dar·y *adj.* Not being first in importance; inferior; pertaining to a secondary school; high school.

se·cret *n.* Knowledge kept from others; a mystery. **secretly** *adv.* **secrecy** *n.*

sec·re·tary *n., pl.* **-ies** A person hired to write and keep records for an executive or an organization; the head of a government department. **-ial** *adj.*

se·crete *v.* To produce and give off; to release or discharge.

sec·tion *n.* A part or division of something; a separate part. *v.* To divide or separate into sections.

sec·tor *n.* An area or zone in which a military unit operates; the part of a circle bounded by two radii and the arc they cut. *Math v.* To divide.

sec·u·lar *adj.* Relating to something worldly; not sacred or religious.

se·cure *adj.* Safe and free from doubt or fear; sturdy or strong; not likely to fail. *v.* To tie down, fasten, lock, or otherwise protect from risk or harm; to ensure. **securely** *adv.*

se·cu·ri·ty *n., pl.* **-ies** The state of being safe and free from danger or risk; protection; an object given to assure the fulfillment of an obligation; in computer science, the prevention of unauthorized use of a device or program.

se·dan *n.* A closed, hardtop automobile with a front and back seat.

se·date *adj.* Serene and composed. *v.* To keep or be kept calm through the use of drugs. **sedative** *n.*

sed-i-ment n. Material which floats in or settles to the bottom of a liquid. **sedimentary** adj., **sedimentation** n.

se-duce v. To tempt and draw away from proper conduct; to entice someone to have sexual intercourse. **seducer, seduction** n., **seductive** adj.

see v. To have the power of sight; to understand; to experience; to imagine; to predict. **see red** To be extremely angry.

seed n. A fertilized plant ovule with an embryo, capable of producing an offspring. v. To plant seeds; to remove the seeds from.

seek v. To search for; to try to reach; to attempt. **seeker** n.

seem v. To appear to be; to have the look of. **seeming** adj. **seemingly** adv.

seep v. To leak or pass through slowly.

seer n. A person who predicts the future.

see-saw n. A board supported in the center which allows children to alternate being up and down.

seg-ment n. Any of the parts into which a thing is divided. v. To divide. **segmental** adj., **segmentation** n.

seg-re-gate v. To separate or isolate from others.

seg-re-ga-tion n. The act of separating people based on the color of their skin.

seine n. A fishing net with weights on one edge and floats on the other.

seize v. To grasp or take possession forcibly.

sel-dom adv. Not often.

se-lect v. To choose from a large group; to make a choice. **select, selection** adj., **selector, selectness** n.

se-le-ni-um n. An element symbolized by Se.

self n., pl. **-selves.** The complete and essential being of a person; personal interest, advantage or welfare.

self--de-fense n. To act of defending oneself or one's belongings.

sell v. To exchange a product or service for money; to offer for sale. **seller** n.

se-man-tics n. The study of word meanings and the relationships between symbols and signs.

sem-a-phore n. A system for signaling by using flags, lights or arms in various positions. **semaphore** v.

se-men n. The secretion of the male reproductive system, thick and whitish in color and containing sperm.

se-mes-ter n. One of two periods of time in which a school year is divided.

sem-i-an-nu-al adj. Occurring twice a year.

sem-i-co-lon n. A punctuation mark (;) having a degree of separation stronger than a comma but less than a period.

sem-i-nar n. A course of study for students engaged in advanced study of a particular subject.

sem-i-nar-y n., pl. **-ies** A school that prepares ministers, rabbis, or priests for their religious careers. **-ian** n.

sen-ate n. The upper house of a legisla-ture, as the United States Senate.

send v. To cause something to be conveyed from one place to another; to dispatch.

se-nile adj. Having a mental deterioration often associated with old age. **senility** n.

sen-ior adj. Being the older of two; of higher office or rank; referring to the last year of high school or college. n. One who is older or of higher rank.

sen-ior-i-ty n. Priority over others based on the length of time of service.

sen-sa-tion n. An awareness associated with a mental or bodily feeling; something that causes a condition of strong interest.

sense n. Sensation; feeling; the physical ability which allows a person to be aware of things around him; the five senses: taste, smell, touch, sight, and hearing; an ethical or moral attitude; the meaning of a word; v. To feel through the senses; to have a feeling about.

sen-si-bil-i-ty n., pl. **-ies** The ability to receive sensations.

sen-si-ble adj. Capable of being perceived through the senses; sensitive; having good judgment. **sensibly** adv.

sen-si-tive adj. Capable of intense feelings; affected by the emotions or circumstances of others; tender-hearted; of or relating to secret affairs of state. **-ly** adv., **sensitivity, sensitiveness** n.

sen-sor n. A device which responds to a signal.

sen-su-al adj. Preoccupied with the gratification of the senses. **sensualist, sensuality** n. **sensually** adv., **sensuous** adj.

sent v. Past tense of send.

sen-tence n. A series of words arranged to express a single complete thought; a prison term for a convicted person, determined by a judge or jury. v. To impose or set the terms of punishment.

sen-ti-ment n. Feelings of affection; an idea, opinion, thought, or attitude based on emotion rather than reason.

sen-ti-men-tal adj. Emotional; affected by sentiment.

sen-ti-nel n. One who guards.

se-pal n. One of the leaves which forms a calyx in a flower.

sep-a-rate v. To divide or keep apart by placing a barrier between; to go in different directions; to set apart from others. adj. Single; individual.

sep-a-ra-tion n. The process of separating or being separated; an interval which separates.

Sept abbr. September.

Sep-tem-ber n. The ninth month of the calendar year, having 30 days.

se-quel n. A new story which follows or comes after an earlier one and which uses the same characters.

se-quence n. A set arrangement; a number of connected events; the regular order; the order in which something is done. **sequential** *adj.*, **-tially** *adv.*

ser-e-nade *n.* Music performed as a romantic expression of love.

se-rene *adj.* Calm; peaceful. **serenity** *n.*

serf *n.* A slave owned by a lord during the Middle Ages.

serge *n.* A twilled, durable woolen cloth.

ser-geant *n.* A noncommissioned officer who ranks above a corporal but below a lieutenant.

se-ri-al *adj.* Arranged in a series with one part presented at a time.

se-ries *pl. n.* A number of related items which follow one another.

se-ri-ous *adj.* Sober; grave; not trivial; important. **seriously** *adv.* **-ness** *n.*

ser-mon *n.* A message or speech delivered by a clergyman during a religious service.

ser-pent *n.* A snake.

ser-rate *adj.* Having sharp teeth; having a notched edge. **serration** *n.*

se-rum *n., pl.* **-rums** *or* **-ra** The yellowish fluid part of the blood which remains after clotting; the fluid extracted from immunized animals and used for the prevention of disease.

ser-vant *n.* One employed to care for someone or his property.

serve *v.* To take care of; to wait on; to prepare and supply; to complete a term of duty; to act in a certain capacity; to start the play in some sports. *n.* The manner of serving or delivering a ball.

serv-ice *n.* Help given to others; a religious gathering; the military; a set of dishes or utensils. *v.* To repair; to furnish a service to something or someone.

ses-a-me *n.* A tropical plant and its edible seeds.

ses-sion *n.* A meeting or series of meetings; a meeting set for a specific purpose; the period during the day or year during which a meeting takes place.

set *v.* To put or place; to cause to do; to regulate; to adjust; to arrange; to place in a frame or mounting; to go below the horizon; to establish or fix. *n.* A group of things which belong together; a piece of equipment made up of many pieces; a young plant. *adj.* Established; ready.

set-tee *n.* A small couch or bench with arms and a back.

set-ting *n.* The act of placing or putting something somewhere; the scenery for a show or other production; the place where a novel, play, or other fictional work takes place; a jewelry mounting.

set-tle *v.* To arrange or put in order; to restore calm or tranquillity to; to come to an agreement on something; to resolve a problem or argument; to establish in a new home or business.

sev-en *n.* The cardinal number 7, after 6 and before 8. **seven** *adj. & pron.*, **seventh** *adj., adv. & n.*

sev-en-teen *n.* The cardinal number 17, after 16 and before 18.

seventeenth *adj., adv. & n.*

sev-en-ty *n., pl.* **-ies** The cardinal number 70, after 69 and before 71.

seventieth *adj., adv. & n.*

sev-er *v.* To cut off or separate. **severance** *n.*

sev-er-al *adj.* Being more than one or two, but not many; separate. **-ly** *adv.*

se-vere *adj.* Strict; stern; hard; not fancy; extremely painful; intense. **severely** *adv.*, **severity** *n.*

sew *v.* To fasten or fix; to make stitches with thread and needle.

sew-age *n.* The solid waste material carried away by a sewer.

sew-er *n.* A conduit or drain pipe used to carry away waste.

sex *n.* One of two divisions, male and female, into which most living things are grouped; sexual intercourse.

sex-tet *n.* A group of six people or things; music written for six performers.

sgt *abbr.* Sergeant.

sh *abbr.* Share.

shab-by *adj.* Worn-out; ragged. **shabbily** *adv.*, **shabbiness** *n.*

shack *n.* A small, poorly built building.

shack-le *n.* A metal band locked around the ankle or wrist of a prisoner; anything that restrains or holds. *v.* To restrain with shackles. **shackler** *n.*

shad *n., pl.* **shad** *or* **shads** An edible fish which swims upstream to spawn.

shad-ber-ry *n.* A fruit that is grown by the serviceberry.

shad-dock *n.* A type of pear-shaped citrus fruit that is related to the grapefruit.

shade *n.* A shadow that will gather with the coming of darkness; a comparative darkness due to the interception of the rays of the sun by an object.

shade--grown *adj.* To be grown in the shade.

shade tree *n.* A type of tree which is grown for the purpose of providing shade.

shad-ing *n.* A filling up with color within outlines to give the object a three-dimensional shape or look.

shad-ow *n.* An area from which light is blocked; a shaded area. *v.* To cast or throw a shadow on. **shadowy** *adj.*

shad-ow dance *n.* A type of dance that is shown by throwing shadows of the actors upon a screen.

shady *adj.* Being sheltered or protected form the rays of the sun.

shaft *n.* A long, narrow part of something; a beam or ray of light; a long, narrow underground passage; a tunnel; a narrow, vertical opening in a building for an elevator.

shaft-ing *n.* The materials that are used for shafting.

shag *n.* A long matted fiber or covering.

shag-gy *adj.* To be covered with long, matted, or coarse hair.

shak-able *adj.* Being capable of being shaken.

shake *v.* To move or to cause a back-

and-forth or up and down motion; to tremble; to clasp hands with another, as to welcome or say farewell; to upset or disturb. **shake** n., **shaky** adj.

shake-down n. Type of search which is very thorough.

shak-er n. Someone or something that shakes.

sha-ko n. A type of stiff military hat that has a plume and high crown.

shale n. A type of fissile rock which is made by the consolidation of mud or clay and has a finely stratified structure.

shale oil n. A type of dark oil which is obtained from oil shale by heating.

shall v., p.t. Past tense of should; used with the pronouns I or we to express future tense; with other nouns or pronouns to indicate promise, determination or a command.

shal-loon n. The twilled fabric of wool which is used for linings of coats.

shal-lop n. A type of small boat that can be propelled with oars or sails.

shal-lot n. A type of perennial herb that resembles an onion and is used for seasoning.

shal-low adj. Not deep; lacking intellectual depth.

sham n. A person who is not genuine but pretends to be; a cover for pillows. v. To pretend to have or feel something.

sham-ble v. To walk while dragging one's feet. **shambles** A scene or state of complete destruction.

sham-bling adj. To be characterized with or by slow awkward movements.

shame n. A painful feeling of embarrassment or disgrace brought on by doing something wrong; dishonor; disgrace; a disappointment.

shame-fac-ed adj. To be showing shame. **shamefacedness** n.

shame-ful adj. To be arousing the feeling of shame within someone.

shame-less adj. To be showing a lack of shame. **shamelessness** n.

sham-poo n. A soap used to cleanse the hair and scalp; a liquid preparation used to clean upholstery and rugs.

sham-rock n. A form of clover with three leaflets on a single stem; regarded as the national flower and emblem of Ireland.

shan-dy n. A type of drink which is made of beer and lemonade.

shan-dy-gaff n. A type of drink which is made of beer and ginger ale.

shang-hai v. To put someone onboard a ship with the help of a drug.

shank n. The portion of the leg between the ankle and the knee; a cut of meat from the leg of an animal, such as a lamb.

shan-ty-man n. A person who resides in a shanty.

shan-ty-town n. A type of town where the buildings are shanties.

shap-able adj. To be capable of being shaped.

shape n. The outline or configuration of something; the form of a human body; the condition of something; the finished form in which something may appear. v. To cause to take a particular form.

shape-less adj. To have no real or definite shape. **shapelessness** n.

shape-ly adj. To have a pleasant or pleasing shape to the form.

shard n. A fragment of a substance which is brittle.

share n. A part or portion given to or by one person; one of equal parts, as the capital stock in a corporation. -er n.

share-able adj. To be capable of being shared. **shareability** n.

share-hold-er n. A person who holds a share in a piece of property.

shark n.

A large marine fish which eats other fish and is dangerous to man; a greedy, crafty person.

shark-skin n. The skin or hide of the shark that can be made into goods of leather.

sharp adj. Having a thin edge or a fine point; capable of piercing or cutting; clever; quick-witted; intense; painful. Slang Nice looking. n. Music A note raised half a tone above a given tone. **sharpness** n., **sharply** adv.

sharp-en v. To make something sharp.

sharp-eyed adj. To have sight that is keen.

sharp-nosed adj. To be keen in smelling.

sharp-shinned hawk n. A type of hawk who eats birds and can be found in North America with a square-tipped tail.

sharp-tongued adj. To have bitter or harsh speech.

shat-ter v. To burst suddenly into pieces. **shatteringly** adv.

shave v. To remove a thin layer; to cut body hair, as the beard, by using a razor; to come close to.

shav-er n. The person who shaves.

shawl n. An oblong or square piece of fabric worn over the head or shoulders.

she pron. A female previously indicated by name.

shea but-ter n. A type of pale solid fat that is from the seeds of the shea tree and can be used in candles and soap.

shear v. To trim, cut, or remove the fleece or hair with a sharp instrument; to clip. **shearer** n.

sheared adj. To be finished by shearing.

shear-wa-ter n. A type of oceanic bird that are related to the albatrosses.

sheat-fish n. A type of large catfish.

sheath n. A cover or case for a blade, as a sword.

sheath-bill n. A white shore bird that has a horny sheath on the base of the upper mandible.

sheath knife n. A type of knife that has a

fixed blade and is designed to be carried in a sheath.

shea tree *n.* A type of tree of Africa that yields fatty nuts which yield shea butter.

sheave *n.* A wheel that is grooved.

she-been *n.* A type of drinking establishment that is operated illegally.

shed *v.* To pour out or cause to pour; to throw off without penetrating; to cast off or leave behind, especially by a natural process. *n.* A small building for shelter or storage.

shed-der *n.* Something that sheds something such as skin.

sheen *n.* Luster.

sheep *n., pl.* **sheep**

A cud-chewing thick-fleeced mammal, widely domesticated for meat and wool; a meek or timid person.

sheep-ber-ry *n.* A type of viburnum of North America that is shrubby having white flowers.

sheep dog *n.* A type of dog that is raised for the purpose of herding or watching over sheep.

sheep-fold *n.* A shelter for sheep.

sheep-herd-er *n.* A person who is in charge of a herd of sheep.

sheep-ish *adj.* To be like a sheep in meekness. **sheepishness** *n.*

sheep-shear-er *n.* A person who cuts sheep's wool off.

sheep-shear-ing *n.* The act of cutting the wool off of the sheep.

sheep-skin *n.* The leather that is prepared form the skin of the sheep.

sheep walk *n.* A range for the sheep.

sheer *adj.* Very thin; almost transparent; complete; absolute; very steep, almost perpendicular.

sheet *n.* A large piece of cloth for covering a bed; a single piece of paper; a continuous, thin piece of anything.

sheet an-chor *n.* A type of anchor that was carried in the waist of a ship.

sheet glass *n.* A type of glass which is produced into sheets.

sheet metal *n.* A type of metal that is in the form of a sheet.

shelf *n., pl.* **shelves** A flat piece of wood, metal, plastic, or other rigid material attached to a wall or within another structure, used to hold or store things; something which resembles a shelf, as a ledge of rocks.

shelf ice *n.* An ice sheet that starts on land and continues out to sea and out to where it rests on the floor of the ocean.

shell *n.* The hard outer covering of certain organisms; something light and hollow which resembles a shell; the framework of a building under construction; a case containing explosives which are fired from a gun.

shel-lac *n.* A clear varnish used to give a smooth, shiny finish to furniture and floors. *Slang* To defeat. **shellac** *v.*

shell bean *n.* A type of bean that is grown for its seeds which are edible.

shelled *adj.* To have a shell.

shel-ter *n.* Something which gives protection or cover. *v.* To give protection.

shel-ter-belt *n.* The barrier of tree that protects crops from storms and winds.

shel-ter tent *n.* A type of tent that is made of two interchangeable pieces of waterproof cotton duck.

shelve *v.* To put aside; to place on a shelf. **shelver** *n.*

shelv-ing *n.* The degree of sloping of something.

shep-herd *n.* A person who takes care of a flock of sheep; a person who takes care of others.

shep-herd-ess *n.* A girl who tends to sheep.

shep-herd's pie *n.* A type of pie that is made with meat and has a mashed potato crust.

sher-bet *n.* A sweet frozen dessert made with fruit juices, milk or water, egg white, and gelatin.

sher-iff *n.* A high ranking law-enforcement officer.

sher-ry *n.* A type of wine that is of Spanish origin and has a nutty taste.

SHF *abbr.* Superhigh frequency.

shield *n.* A piece of protective metal or wood held in front of the body; anything which serves to conceal or protect; a badge or emblem. **shield** *v.*, **shielder** *n.*

shield law *n.* The law that will protect journalist from being force to reveal confidential sources.

shiel-ing *n.* A type of hut which is used by shepherds in the mountains for shelter.

shift *n.* A group of people who work together; a woman's loose-fitting dress. *v.* To change direction or place; to change or move the gears in an automobile.

shift-less *adj.* To be lacking in ambition. **shiftlessness** *n.*

shill *n.* A person or thing that acts as a decoy.

shim-mer *v.* To shine with a faint sparkle. **shimmer** *n.*, **shimmery** *adj.*

shin *n.* The front part of the leg from the knee to the ankle. *v.* To climb a rope or pole by gripping and pulling with the hands and legs.

shin-bone *n.* The tibia in the lower leg.

shin-dig *n.* A party or social gathering.

shine *v.* To give off light; to direct light; to make bright or glossy; to polish shoes. *n.* Brightness.

shiner *n.* A black eye.

shin-gle *n.* A thin piece of material, as asbestos, used to cover a roof or side of a house. *v.* To apply shingles to.

shin-gles *pl., n., Pathol.* An acute, inflammatory viral infection, characterized by skin eruptions along a nerve path.

shin-ning *adj.* To be reflecting light.

shin-nery *n.* A growth of trees that is dense.

shin-splints *n.* The inflammation and injury to the muscles of the lower leg due to running on hard surfaces.

ship *n.* A large vessel for deep-water travel or transport. *v.* To send or transport.

ship-board *n.* A side of a ship.

ship-borne *adj.* To be designed to be carried or transported by a ship.

ship-build-er *n.* A person who builds ships. **shipbuilding** *n.*

ship-mas-ter *n.* The commander of a ship that is not a warship.

ship-ment *n.* The process of shipping goods from one port to another.

ship-worm *n.* A type of marine clam that will burrow into the wharf and wooden ships causing damage to them.

ship-wreck *n.* The loss of a ship; destruction; ruin. *v.* To wreck.

ship-wright *n.* The carpenter who is skilled in the repair and construction of ships.

ship-yard *n.* A place where ships are built or repaired.

shire *n.* The administrative division such as a county.

shire town *n.* The town in which is located a court of jurisdiction.

shirt *n.* A garment worn on the upper part of the body.

shirt-ing *n.* The fabric which can be used to make shirts.

shirt-mak-er *n.* A person who is capable of making shirts.

shirt-tail *n.* The section of the shirt which falls below the waist in the back.

shiv-er *v.* To tremble or shake with excitement or chill. **shivery** *adj.*

shoal *n.* Large group.

shoat *n.* A hog less than one year old.

shock *n.* A sudden blow or violent impact; an unexpected, sudden upset of mental or emotional balance; a serious weakening of the body caused by the loss of blood pressure or sudden injury. *v.* To strike with great surprise, disgust, or outrage; to give an electric shock.

shock absorber *n.* A device which is used for absorbing the energy of impulses to something.

shock-er *n.* Something that produces shock into something or someone.

shock-ing pink *n.* A shade of pink that is intense.

shock-proof *adj.* To be incapable of being shocked.

shod *adj.* To be equipped with a shoe.

shoe *n.* An outer cover for a foot; the part of a brake which presses against the drum or wheel to slow or stop the motion. *v.* To put on shoes.

shoe-bill *n.* A type of large wading bird that is located in the valley of the White Nile and is related to the herons and storks.

shoe-horn *n.* Type of curved piece material that is used to put on a shoe.

shoe-lace *n.* A string that is used to fasten a shoe to the foot.

shoe tree *n.* A device that is foot-shaped and placed into the shoe to help it maintain the shape of the shoe.

shone *v.* Past tense of shine.

shoo-fly *n.* A type of plant that is believed to repel flies.

shoot *v.* To kill or wound with a missile, as a bullet, fired from a weapon; to discharge or throw rapidly; to push forward or begin to grow by germinating. *Slang* To inject drugs directly into the veins. **shooter** *n.*

shoot-'em--up *n.* A type of show or movie where there is a large amount of bloodshed and shooting.

shoot-ing gal-lery *n.* A range that is usually covered and having targets to shoot at for practice.

shoot-ing star *n.* A meteor that appears in the sky as a temporary streak of light.

shoot--out *n.* A fight with handguns.

shop *n.* A small business or small retail store; a place where certain goods are produced. *v.* To visit a store in order to examine or buy things. **shopper** *n.*

shop-keep-er *n.* A person who runs a store.

shop-lift *v.* To take something from a store without paying for it.

shop-lift-er *n.* The person who takes things from a store without paying form them.

shop-ping cen-ter *n.* A group of stores that are gathered in one area for easier access.

shop-talk *n.* The subject matter that is peculiar to an occupation.

shore *n.* The land bordering a body of water.

shore din-ner *n.* A meal or dinner that consists of mainly seafoods.

shore-front *n.* The land which is located along a shore.

shore-line *n.* A line or location where a body of water and the shore meet.

short *adj.* Having little height or length; less than normal in distance, time, or other qualities; less than the needed amount. **shorts** Underpants or outerpants which end at the knee or above. **shortage** A lack in the amount needed. **short-change** To give less than the correct amount, as change for money. **short circuit** An electrical malfunction.

short-bread *n.* A type of cookie that is made from sugar, flour, and shortening.

short-cut *n.* A type of route that is more direct than the one that is usually taken.

short-en-ing *n* A fat, such as butter, used to make pastry rich and light.

short-fall *n.* The failure to accomplish a goal.

short-hand *n.* A type of writing where words and phrases are substituted by symbols and characters.

short-horn *n.* A breed of roan, red, or white beef cattle that originated in England.

short--horned grass-hop-per *n.* A type of grasshopper that has a short antennae.

short-leaf pine *n.* A type of pine that has short leaves and can be found in the southern U.S.

short--lived *adj.* Not lasting long.

short or-der *n.* An order, usually for food, which can be quickly prepared and served.

short-sight-ed *adj.* To be missing or lacking one's foresight.

shot *n.* The discharging of a gun, rocket, or other device; an attempt; a try an injection; a photograph. *Slang* Useless; ruined.

shot hole *n.* The hole which is drilled for dynamite to be exploded in.

should *v.* Past tense of shall, used to express obligation, duty, or expectation.

shoul-der *n.* The part of the body located between the neck and upper arm; the side of the road. *v.* To use the shoulder to push or carry something; to take upon oneself.

shoul-der bag *n.* A type of bag that can be carried on the woman's shoulder.

shoul-der patch *n.* A patch which is worn on the arm just below the shoulder.

should-n't *contr.* Should not.

shout *v.* To yell. *n.* A loud cry.

shout-ing dis-tance *n.* A distance that is short.

shove *v.* To push something or someone in a manner that may be rough.

shov-el *n.* A tool with a long handle and a scoop, used for picking up material or for digging. *v.* To move, dig, or scoop up with a shovel; to push or move large amounts rapidly.

shov-el-er *n.* Someone or something that will shovel things such as dirt and debris.

shov-el-head *n.* A type of fish that has a head which looks like a shovel.

shov-el-man *n.* A person who works with a shovel.

shov-el--nosed *adj.* To have a flat nose that may resemble a shovel.

show *v.* To put within sight; to point out; to explain; to put on display. *n.* A display; a movie, play or similar entertainment.

show bill *n.* A type of poster which may be used for advertising purposes.

show-er *n.* A short period of rain; a party with gifts given in honor of someone; a bath with water spraying down on the bather. *v.* To take a shower; to be extremely generous. **showery** *adj.*

shrank *v.* Past tense of shrink.

shrap-nel *n.*, *pl.* shrapnel A large shell containing metal fragments; fragments of metal that are exploded with great force.

shed *n.* A narrow strip or torn fragment; a small amount. *v.* To rip, tear, or cut into shreds.

shrew *n.* A small mouse-like mammal, having a narrow, pointed snout.

shriek *n.* A loud, sharp scream or noise. **shriek** *v.*

shrill *adj.* A high-pitched, sharp sound.

shrimp *n.*, *pl.* **shrimp** or **shrimps** A small, edible shellfish. *Slang* A small person.

shrine *n.* A place for sacred relics; a place considered sacred because of an event or person associated with it.

shrink *v.* To make or become less or smaller; to pull back from; to flinch. *Slang* A psychiatrist.

shroud *n.* A cloth in which a body is wrapped for burial. *v.* To cover.

shrub *n.* A woody plant which grows close to the ground and has several stems beginning at its base.

shrug *v.* To raise the shoulders briefly to indicate doubt or indifference.

shrunk *v.* Past tense of shrink.

shuck *n.* The outer husk that covers an ear of corn. **shuck** *v.*

shud-der *v.* To tremble uncontrollably, as from fear. **shudder** *n.*

shuf-fle *v.* To drag or slide the feet; to mix together in a haphazard fashion; to rearrange or change the order of cards. **shuffle** *n.*

shun *v.* To avoid deliberately.

shut *v.* To move a door, drawer, or other object to close an opening; to block an entrance; to lock up; to cease or halt operations.

shut-tle *n.* A device used to move thread in weaving; a vehicle, as a train or plane, which travels back and forth from one location to another.

shy *adj.* Bashful; timid; easily frightened. *v.* To move suddenly from fear. **shyly** *adv.*, **shyness** *n.*

si-al-a-gogue *n.* A kind of agent that will promote the flow of saliva.

si-al-ic *adj.* Pertaining to the light rock which is rich in alumina and silica.

Siamese twin *n.* One of a pair of twins that are united at some part of the body with the other twin.

sib-ling *n.* One of two or more children from the same parents.

sick *adj.* In poor health; ill; nauseated; morbid. **sickness** *n.*

sick bay *n.* A room on a ship that can be used as a hospital.

sick-en *v.* To become sick.

sick-en-er *n.* Something that disgusts or sickens.

sick-ish *adj.* To be somewhat sick.

sick-le

A tool with a curved blade attached to a handle, used for cutting grass or grain.

sick leave *n.* The absence from one's work that is permitted due to an illness.

sick-le cell *n.* An abnormal red blood cell which will take the shape of a crescent.

sick-le feath-er *n.* A long curved tail feather of the cock.

sick-ly *adj.* To be somewhat unwell.

sick pay *n.* The wages which are paid to an employee while they are on sick leave.

sick-room *n.* A room where a person who is sick remains.

side *n.* A surface between the front and back or top and bottom of an object; either surface of a flat object; the part to the left or right of a vertical axis; the right or left portion of the human body; the space beside someone or something; an opinion or point of view which is the opposite of another. *v.* To take a stand and support the opinion of a particular side. *adj.* Supplementary; peripheral.

side-arm *adj.* To be pertaining to a baseball pitching style where the arm is not raised above the shoulder.

side-band *n.* A band of frequencies that are produced by modulation.

side bearing *n.* A space which is provided at the side of a typeset letter to prevent it from touching another letter.

side-burns *n.* The short side-whiskers that are worn by the man on the side of his face. **sideburned** *adj.*

side-car *n.* A type of car that is attached to the side of a motorcycle for the use of a passenger.

side effect *n.* The secondary effect.

side--glance *n.* A look that is directed to the side.

side issue *n.* The issue that is apart form the main point.

side-light *n.* The light that is produced for the side.

side-lin-er *n.* The person that remains on the sidelines during a sport or activity.

side-long *adj.* To be inclining on the side.

si-de-re-al *adj.* To be pertaining to the stars.

sid-er-ite *n.* A type of ferrous carbonate that is an iron ore.

sid-er-it-ic *adj.* Pertaining to siderite.

side-sad-dle *n.* A type of saddle usually for women which allows the rider to place both legs on the same side of the horse.

side-split-ting *adj.* To be very funny.

side-step *v.* To step to the side. **sidestepper** *n.*

side-stroke *n.* A type of swimming stroke where the swimmer is one their side.

side-walk *n.* A type of paved walk that is used by pedestrians at the side of the street.

side-wall *n.* A wall which forms the side of something.

side-ward *adv.* To move toward the side.

side-wind-er *n.* A type of snake which moves by thrusting its body diagonally forward.

SIDS *abbr., n.* Sudden infant death syndrome; an unexpected death of a seemingly healthy baby, occurring during sleep sometime in the first four months of life.

siege *n.* The action of surrounding a town or port in order to capture it; a prolonged sickness.

si-er-ra *n.* A rugged chain of mountains or hills.

si-es-ta *n.* A rest or short nap.

sie-va bean *n.* A type of bean which is closely related to the lima bean.

sieve *n.* A meshed or perforated device which allows small particles to pass through but which holds back larger particles; a device for separating liquids from solids. **sieve** *v.*

sieve plate *n.* A wall which is perforated located at the end of one of the cells that make up a sieve tube.

sieve tube *n.* A type of tube that is made of thin-walled cells.

sift *v.* To separate coarse particles from small or fine ones by passing through a sieve. **sift through** To carefully examine. **sifter** *n.*

sig *abbr.* Signature; signal.

SIG *abbr.* Special interest group.

sigh *v.* To exhale a long, deep breath, usually when tired, sad, or relieved.

sight *n.* The ability to see with the eyes; the range or distance one can see; a view; a device mounted on a firearm used to guide the eye or aim.

sighted *adj.* To have sight.

sight gag *n.* A comic episode where the effect is created by a camera shot rather than by the words.

sight-less *adj.* To be lacking or missing the sight. **sightlessness** *n.*

sight-ly *adj.* To be pleasing to the sight. **sightliness** *n.*

sight-see *v.* To travel about and see sights that are of interest.

sig-il *n.* A word that is suppose to occult power in magic.

sig-ma *n.* The 18th letter in the Greek alphabet.

sig-moid *adj.* To be curved in two directions. **sigmoidally** *adv.*

sign *n.* A piece of paper, wood, metal, etc., with information written on it; a gesture that tells or means something. *v.* To write one's name on. **signer** *n.*

sig-nal *n.* A sign that gives a warning; the image or sound sent by television or radio.

sig-nal-ize *v.* To make signals to someone. **signalization** *n.*

sig-nal-man *n.* A person who works with signals or signals others.

sig-nal-ment *n.* The description of something or someone by characteristic marks.

sig-na-ture *n.* The name of a person, written by that person; a distinctive mark which indicates identity. *Music* A symbol indicating the time and key.

sign-board *n.* A type of board that is used for the purpose of being noticed.

sig-net *n.* A type of seal which is used to

give personal authority to a document or papers instead of using a signature.

sig-net ring n. A type of ring that is engraved with a signet.

sig-ni-fi-able adj. Being represented with a symbol or a sign of some sort.

sig-nif-i-cance n. The quality of being important; the meaning of something which is considered important.

sig-ni-fi-er n. Something that signifies.

sig-ni-fy v. To express or make known by a sign; to indicate. **signification** n., **significant** adj.

sign in v. To record the arrival of someone at a particular time by the signing of a list or the punching of the time clock.

sign language n. A means of communicating by using hand gestures; the language of deaf people.

sign manual n. The signature of a king which is on a royal grant and is placed at the top or beginning of the document.

sign off v. To tell or to announce the end of a program or of a broadcast.

sign on v. To tell or to announce the beginning of the broadcast for the day.

si-gnor n. An Italian man of the gentility.

si-gno-ra n. An Italian woman who is married and is usually of the gentility.

si-gno-ri-na n. An Italian woman who is not yet married.

si-gno-ri-no n. A Italian boy.

sign out v. To tell of one's departure by signing a list depicting when the person left.

sign-post n. A type of post that bears signs on it for the use of giving directions.

sike n. A type of stream which is small in size.

si-lage n. The fodder which is converted into feed for livestock.

sild n. A herring at a young age in its development but older than a brisling.

si-lence n. The state or quality of being silent; quiet. v. To make quiet.

si-lenc-er n. Someone or something which will cause silence.

si-lent adj. Making no sound; not speaking; mute; unable to speak; an unpronounced letter, as the "g" in gnat. **silently** adv., **silentness** n.

si-lents n. A kind of motion picture where is not a spoken dialogue.

si-lent treat-ment n. The act of ignoring another person completely.

sil-hou-ette n.

The outline of something, as a human profile, filled in with a solid color, as black; the outline of an object.

sil-i-con n. The second most common chemical element, found only in combination with another substance, symbolized as Si.

sil-i-cone rub-ber n. A type of rubber that is made from silicone elastomers and it is flexible over a wide range of different temperatures.

silk n. A soft, thread-like fiber spun by silkworms; thread or fabric made from silk. **silken**, **silky** adj.

silk-aline n. A type of cotton fabric that has a smooth finish like that of silk.

silk cot-ton n. A type of silky covering that can be found on the seeds of various silk-cotton trees.

silk--cot-ton tree n. A type of tropical tree that has large fruits with the seeds covered by silk cotton.

silk gland The gland that will produce the fluid which is excreted in filaments and then hardens into silk when it comes into contact with the air.

silk oak n. A type of timber tree of Australia that had mottled wood which is used for the purpose of making cabinets.

silk stock-ing n. A person who is dressed in a fashionable manner.

silk-worm n. A type of larva that spins a large amount of silk when it is making its cocoon.

sill n. The horizontal support that forms the bottom part of the frame of a window or door.

sil-ly adj. Foolish; lacking good sense, seriousness, or substance. **silliness** n.

si-lo n. A tall, cylindrical structure for storing food for farm animals; an underground shelter or storage for guided missiles.

silt n. A deposit of soil and sediment that may have been caused by a river.

silt-stone n. A type of which is composed of silt.

sil-u-roid n. A member of the suborder of the fishes which contains the catfish.

sil-va n. The trees of a country or region.

sil-ver n. A soft, white metallic element used in tableware, jewelry, and coins, symbolized by Ag. v. To coat with silver. adj. Of the color silver.

sil-ver age n. A period in history that is secondary to the gold age.

sil-ver bell n. A type of tree located in the southeastern U.S. and it is grown for its bell-shaped flowers.

sil-ver-bey-ry n. A type of shrub which is located in North America and is related to the buffalo berry.

sil-ver fir n. A fir that has leave that are silver colored on the underneath.

sil-ver-fish n. A small wingless insect which has been known to be injurious to clothing and paper.

sil-ver fox n. A color phase of the red fox which is genetic and the coat is white with black tips.

sil-ver hake n. A type of hake that is located on the northern New England coast and is used as an important food fish.

sil-ver lin-ing n. A hopeful prospect.

sil-ver map-le n. A type of maple of

North America that has leaves which are silvery white beneath.

sil-vern *adj.* To be made of silver.

sil-ver pa-per *n.* A metallic paper, such as tinfoil, that has a silver-like coating.

sil-ver perch *n.* A type of fish which is silvery in color and resembles the perch.

sil-ver-sides *n.* A type of fish that has a silver stripe down both sides of its body.

sil-ver-smith *n.* A person who makes goods and articles out of silver.

sil-very *adj.* To have a musical tone which is clear and soft.

sil-vics *n.* A study of the characteristics and ecology of forest trees.

sim-i-lar *adj.* Almost the same, but not identical.

sim-i-lar-i-ty *n.* The state of two things or people being like or similar.

sim-i-le *n.* A part of speech which is used for the purpose of comparing two things that are often unlike.

sim-mer *v.* To cook just below boiling; to be near the point of breaking, as with emotion.

sim-mer down *v.* To calm.

sim-nel *n.* A bread that is made of fine wheat flour.

si-mo-nize *v.* To polish something with wax.

si-moom *n.* A type of dry wind that is found to be from the deserts of Africa and Asia.

sim-ple *adj.* Easy to do or understand; not complicated; ordinary; not showy; lacking intelligence or education. **simpleness** *n.*, **simply** *adv.*

sim-ple closed curve *n.* A type of curve that does not intersect itself.

sim-ple frac-tion *n.* A type of fraction where the denominator and the numerator are of whole numbers.

sim-ple mo-tion *n.* A type of motion that is in a straight line.

sim-plic-i-ty *n.* The state of being easy to understand; naturalness; sincerity.

sim-pli-fy *v.* To make easy or simple. **simplification** *n.*

sim-u-late *v.* To have the appearance, effect, or form of. **simulation, simulator** *n.*

sim-u-lat-ed rank *n.* The statue of a civilian that is equal to a military rank.

si-mul-ta-ne-ous *adj.* Occurring at exactly the same time. **-ly** *adj.*

sin *n.* The breaking of a religious law or a law of God. *v.* To do something which is morally wrong. **sinless** *adj.*, **sinner** *n.*

since *adv.* At a time before the present. *prep.* During the time later than; continuously from the time when something occurs.

sin-cere *adj.* Honest; not deceitful; genuine; true. **sincerely** *adv.*

sin-cer-i-ty *n.* The state of being sincere.

sin-cip-i-tal *adj.* To be pertaining to the sinciput.

sin-ci-put *n.* A upper half or section of the skull.

sine *n.* A function in trigonometry.

si-ne qua non *n.* Something which is indispensable.

sin-ful *adj.* To be tainted with sin. **sinfulness** *n.*, **sinfully** *adv.*

sing *v.* To use the voice to make musical tones; to make a humming or whistling sound. **singer** *n.*

singe *v.* To slightly burn the surface of something; to remove feathers.

sin-gle *adj.* Of or referring to only one, separate; individual; unmarried. *n.* A separate, individual person or item; a dollar bill; in baseball, a hit that allows the batter to progress to first base. **singly** *adv.*

sin-gle--breast-ed *adj.* To have a center closing that has one row of buttons.

sin-gle cross *n.* The first-generation hybrid that is between two selected lines.

sin-gle file *n.* A type of line where the people are one right behind each other.

sin-gle--hand-ed *adj.* To be done by one person. **single-handedly** *adv.*

sin-gle--mind-ed *adj.* To have one overriding purpose.

sin-gle-ness *n.* The state of being single.

sin-gle-stick *n.* Fencing with a wooden stick that is held in one hand.

sin-gle tax *n.* A type of tax that is levied on a single item.

sin-gu-lar *adj.* Separate; one; extraordinary; denoting a single unit, thing or person.

sin-gu-lar-i-ty *n.* A unit that is separate; a state of being singular.

sin-gu-lar-ize *v.* To make something singular.

sin-is-ter *adj.* To be evil or causing evil. **sinisterness** *n.*, **sinisterly** *adv.*

sink *v.* To submerge beneath a surface; to go down slowly; to become less forceful or weaker. *n.* A basin for holding water, attached to a wall and connected to a drain. **sinkable** *adj.*

sink-age *n.* The degree of sinking.

sink-er *n.* A weight which is used for the purpose of sinking a fishing line into the water.

sink-hole *n.* A type of hollow depression where drainage is able to collect.

si-no-logue *n.* A person who is a specialist in sinology.

si-nol-o-gy *n.* A study of the Chinese and the culture, history, and language. **sinological** *adj.*, **sinologist** *n.*

sin-u-ate *adj.* To have a margin that has indentations. **sinuately** *adv.*

sin-u-os-i-ty *n.* The state of being sinuous.

sin-u-ous *adj.* To be marked with strong lithe movements. **sinuousness** *n.*

si-nus *n.*, *pl.* **sinuses** *Anat.* A body cavity; one of eight air spaces in the bones of the face which drain into the nasal cavity.

si-nus-itis *n.* The swelling and inflammation of the sinuses of the skull.

sip *v.* To drink in small amounts. **sip** *n.*

si-phon *also* **syphon** *n.* A tube through

which liquid from one container can be drawn into another by forced air pressure. **siphon** v.

si-pho-no-phore n. A type of free-swimming hyfrozoans that are transparent and have specialized zooids.

sip-pet n. A small piece of toast used for garnishing.

sir n. A respectful term used when addressing a man.

sir-dar n. The person who holds a responsible position in India.

sire n. A man who has rank and authority.

si-ren n. A whistle which makes a loud wailing noise, as a warning or signal; a seductive woman.

si-re-ni-an n. A type of aquatic herbivorous mammal including the manatee.

sir-loin n. The cut of meat that is from the hindquarter.

sis-kin n. A type of finch which is yellow and green and is located in Europe and Asia and is related to the goldfinch.

sis-ter n. A female having the same parents as another; a woman in membership with others, as in a church group or sorority. **sisterly** adj.

sis-ter-hood n. The state of being a sister.

sis-ter-ly adj. Related to being a sister.

sis-trum n. A type of percussion instrument that is used in Egypt in ancient times.

sit v. To rest the body with the weight on the buttocks; to cover eggs for hatching; to pose for a portrait.

si-tar n. A type of Indian lute that has a long neck and varying number of strings.

site n. A location of planned buildings.

sit-ting n. An act of one that sits.

sit-ting duck n. A defenseless target.

sit-u-a-tion n. A way in which something or someone is placed in with its surroundings. **situationally** adv., **situational** adj.

six n. The cardinal number 6, after five and before seven.

six-fold adj. To have six members.

six--pack n. The container for six bottles so that they can be bought together.

six-pen-ny nail n. A type of that is about two inches in length.

six-teen n. The cardinal number 16, after 15 and before 17.

six-ty n. The cardinal number 60, after 59 and before 61.

siz-a-ble adj. Large in size or dimensions. **sizableness** n.

size n. The measurement or dimensions of something; a sticky substance used to glaze walls, before applying wall paper.

sized adj. To have a size which is specified.

siz-zle v. To make a hissing sound, as of fat frying. **sizzle** n.

siz-zler n. The one that will sizzle.

skald n. Type of ancient Scandinavian poet. **skaldic** adj.

skat n. A kind of three-handed game of cards where each player bids for the privilege to attempt any of the several contracts.

skate n. A device with rollers which attaches to the shoe and allows one to glide over ice or roll over a wooden or cement surface; a shoe fitted with rollers. **ice skate, roller skate** v.

skate-board n.

A narrow piece of wood with wheels attached.

skat-er n. A person who is able to skate.

skat-ing n. The action or the art of gliding on skates.

ska-tole n. A kind of foul smelling substance which is found in the intestines.

ske-dad-dle v. To leave or to run away from something or someone.

skeet n. The sport of trapshooting where the targets are made of clay and thrown in a way which resemble the manner in which birds fly.

skee-ter n. A type of iceboat that has one sail.

skeg n. A stern of the keel of a boat or ship which is near the sternpost.

skeigh adj. To be spirited.

skein n. A piece of thread which is wound onto a reel.

skel-e-tal adj. Pertaining to or relating to the skeleton.

skel-e-ton n. The framework of bones that protects and supports the soft tissues and organs.

skel-e-ton-ize v. To reduce something to skeleton form.

skel-e-ton key n. A type of key that has been filed in order to be able to open many locks and can be used as a master key.

skep n. A type of hive that is doomed and has been made of twisted straw.

skep-sis n. A philosophic doubt as to the reality of something.

skep-tic n. A person who doubts or questions. **skepticism** n., **skeptical** adj., **skeptically** adv.

sker-ry n. An island which is rocky.

sketch n. A rough drawing or outline; a brief literary composition. **sketchy** adj.

sketch-book n. A kind of book which is used for the purpose of sketching things.

skew v. To turn or slant. n. A slant.

skew-bald adj. To be marked with spots of white or another color or colors.

skew curve n. A type of curve which is three-dinensional and does not lie in the same plane or single plane.

skew-er n. A piece of metal used as a pin for the purpose of fastening foods together in order to broil them on a grill.

skew lines n. Type of lines which are straight and do not intersect and are not located within the same plane.

skew-ness *n.* The lack of symmetry or of straightness of an object such as a line or curve.

ski *n., pl.* **skis** One of a pair of long, narrow pieces of wood worn on the feet for gliding over snow or water. *v.* To travel on skis. **skier** *n.*

skia-gram *n.* The figure which is formed by shading the outline of a shadow that is created by the figure.

ski-ag-ra-phy *n.* The art of making skiagrams.

ski boot *n.* A type of rigid boot which is attatched to the ski and is used to hold the ski on the foot.

skid *v.* To slide to the side of the road; to slide along without rotating. **skid** *n.*

skid-der *n.* A person who uses a skid or who skids.

skid-dy *adj.* Being likely to cause skidding.

skid road *n.* A type of road where logs are skidded along.

skiff *n.* A type of small and light sailing ship.

ski-ing *n.* The sport of jumping and moving on skis.

ski jump *n.* The jump which is made by someone who is wearing skis and usually jumps off of a large ramp.

ski lift *n.* A type of conveyor that is used to bring the skiers to the top of the hill that they will ski back down.

skill *n.* Ability gained through practice; expertise.

skilled *adj.* To have acquired a skill for something.

skil-let *n.* A type of pot that has feet and is used for the purpose of cooking foods on the hearth.

skill-ful *adj.* To be displaying a skill. **skillfully** *adv.*

skil-ling *n.* Type of old Scandinavian units of value, such as a coin.

skill-less *adj.* To have no skill for anything. **skilllessness** *n.*

skim *v.* To remove the top layer; to remove floating matter; to read over material quickly; to travel over lightly and quickly. **skimmer** *n.*

ski mask *n.* A type of face covering that is made of fabric and can be worn while one is skiing for the protection from the elements.

skim milk *n.* A type of milk where the cream has been taken out.

skim-ming *n.* The substance or that which is skimmed from a liquid.

skimp *v.* To economize; to hold back. **skimpy** *adj.*

skin *n.* The tough, outside covering of man and some animals; the outside layer of a vegetable or fruit; the fur or pelt of an animal. **skin** *v.*, **skinless** *adj.*

skin--deep *adj.* To be as deep as the skin.

skin diving *n.* A sport that involves swimming under the water without a breathing device.

skin-flint *n.* A type of person who would extort or save money any way that is possible.

skin game *n.* A kind of game that involves a trick or swindling of the person.

skin graft *n.* A section of the skin that is removed from one area and placed in an area where the skin has been removed or damaged.

skin grafting *n.* The process of placing or of making a skin graft.

skin-head *n.* A person whose hair is very short.

skink *v.* To serve something like a drink.

skink-er *n.* A person who serves liquor.

skin-ner *n.* A person who deals or sells skins.

skin-ny *adj.* To be lacking a sufficient amount of flesh on the body making the one looking thin.

skin-tight *adj.* To be closely fitted to one's body.

skip *v.* To move in light jumps or leaps; to go from one place to another, missing what is between. **skip** *n.*

skip-jack *n.* A type of fish that will jump above the surface of the water.

ski pole *n.* The poles that are used in the sport of skiing for the purpose of pushing the skier along the snow.

skirl *n.* The high shrill sound which is produced by a bagpipe.

skir-mish *n.* A small and minor fight.

skirr *v.* To look or to search about in.

skirt *n.* A piece of clothing that extends down from the waist. *v.* To extend along the boundary; to avoid the issue.

skirt-ing *n.* The fabric which is suitable for the making of skirts.

ski run *n.* The trail which is used for the sport of skiing.

skit *n.* A type of humorous story.

ski tow *n.* A conveyor that is used for the purpose of bringing the skiers back up to the top of the hill so that they can ski back down.

skit-tish *adj.* To be frightened easily.

skiv-er *n.* A type of thin leather that is made from sheepskin.

ski-wear *n.* The clothing that is used while one is skiing to keep warm.

skul-dug-gery *n.* A type of devious trick.

skulk *v.* To conceal something out of fear; to move in a furtive way or manner. *n.* A person who skulks around.

skull *n.* The bony part of the skeleton which protects the brain.

skull-cap *n.* A type of cap that is close fitting.

skull practice *n.* A type of meeting for a discussion or the exchanging of ideas.

skunk *n.*

A black mammal with white streaks down its back, which sprays an unpleasant smelling liquid when annoyed or frightened.

skunk cab-bage *n.* A type of herb that has a very foul odor and is found in the eastern part of North America.

sky *n., pl.* **skies** The upper atmosphere above the earth; the celestial regions.

sky blue *n.* A color which may range from light blue or pale blue.

sky-cap *n.* A person who has the job of handling the luggage at an airport.

sky-div-ing *n.* The sport of jumping out of airplane while it is flying in the air.

sky-ey *adj.* Pertaining to or resembling the sky.

sky--high *adv. or adj.* To be located high in the air; to do in a manner which is exorbitant.

sky-lark *n.* A type of lark which is large in size and is especially noted for its song.

sky-light *n.* The light of the sky.

sky-line *n.* The outline of a building or other very large object against the sky.

sky-phos *n.* A type of drinking vessel that was used in ancient Greece and had two handles.

sky-scrap-er *n.* A type of building which is very tall and therefore seems to scrape the sky.

sky-ward *adv.* To be moving toward the sky.

sky-way *n.* The route which is used by airplanes.

sky-write *v.* To write letters or words in to sky.

sky-writ-ing *n.* The writing which is formed in the sky with the use of smoke.

sl *abbr.* Slightly.

SL *abbr.* Sea level; south latitude.

slab *n.* A thick piece or slice.

slab--sid-ed *adj.* To have sides which are flat.

slack *adj.* Not taut or tense; sluggish; lacking in strength. *v.* To make slack. *n.* A part of something which hangs loose. **slacks** Long pants or trousers.

slack--baked *adj.* To be underdone.

slack-en *v.* To slow something down.

slack-er *n.* One who shirks an obligation.

slain *v.* Past tense of slay.

slake *v.* To die or diminish.

sla-lom *n.* A type of skiing where the skier zig-zags down the hill between upright obstacles such as flags.

slam *v.* To shut with force; to strike with a loud impact. *n.* A loud noise produced by an impact.

slam--bang *adj.* Being very loud or violent.

slam-mer *n., Slang* Jail or prison.

slan-der *n.* A false statement that deliberately does harm to another's reputation. **slanderous** *adj.*

slang *n.* Informal language that contains made-up words or common words used in a different or uncommon way.

slant *v.* To lie in an oblique position; to slope; to report on something giving only one side or viewpoint. *n.* An incline or slope.

slap *n.* A sharp blow with an open hand.

slap-hap-py *adj.* To be recklessly foolish.

slap shot *n.* The shot which is taken in ice hockey that is made with a swinging stroke.

slap-stick *n.* A type of comedy that stresses or contains horseplay.

slash *v.* To cut with a fast sweeping stroke; to reduce or limit greatly. *n.* A long cut.

slash-ing *n.* The process of slashing something. **slashingly** *adv.*

slash pine *n.* A type of southern pine which is a source of lumber and of turpentine.

slat *n.* A narrow strip of wood.

slate *n.* A fine grained rock that splits into thin layers, often used as a writing surface or roofing material. **slate** *v.*

slate black *n.* A color that is purplish black.

slat-er *n.* A person who slates.

slath-er *v.* To spread something in a thick manner onto something else.

slat-ing *n.* The work that is done by a slater.

slat-tern-ly *adj.* To be dirty because fo neglect.

slaty *adj.* To have the characteristic of slate.

slaugh-ter *v.* To kill livestock for food; to kill in great numbers. *Slang* To soundly defeat. **slaughterer** *n.*

slaugh-ter-house *n.* A place where one butchers or slaughters animals.

slaugh-ter-ous *adj.* Pertaining to slaughter.

Slav *n.* One who is able to speak a Slavic language for his native tongue.

slave *n.* A person held against his will and made to work for another.

slave ant *n.* A type of ant that is enslaved by the slave-making ant of the colony.

slave driver *n.* A person who is the supervisor of slaves.

slave-hold-er *n.* A person who is the owner of the slaves.

Slav-ic *adj.* To be pertaining to the Slavs or the language that they speak.

Slav-i-cist *n.* A person who is a specialist in the Slavic language.

slav-ish *adj.* Pertaining to the characteristic of a slave.

slay *v.* To kill or to destroy something in a violent manner.

sleave *v.* To separate something such as silk fibers in to filaments.

sleave silk *n.* A type of floss silk that is easily separated into filaments.

sled *n.* A vehicle with runners, used to travel on snow or ice.

sled dog *n.* A type of dog which has been trained to pull a sledge.

sledge *n.* A kind of vehicle that has low runners and is used for the purpose of transporting loads over the snow and is pulled by dogs.

sledge-ham-mer *n.* A type of hammer which is very heavy and must be wielded with both hands.

sleek *adj.* Smooth and shiny; neat and trim. **sleekly** *adv.*, **sleekness** *n.*

sleep *n.* A natural state of rest for the mind and body. *v.* To rest in sleep.

sleep-ing bag *n.* The bag which is lined and is used for sleeping.

sleep-ing car *n.* A car of a train that has accommodations allowing a person to sleep.

sleep-ing pill *n.* A type of drug which is taken to help the person to fall asleep.

sleep-less *adj.* Being not able to get to sleep. **sleeplessness** *n.*

sleep out *v.* To sleep away in a place that is not one's home.

sleep-walk-er *n.* A person who is able to walk while still asleep.

sleepy *adj.* Pertaining to sleep.

sleet *n.* Rain that is partially frozen; a combination of snow and rain. **sleet** *v.*, **sleety** *adj.*

sleeve *n.* The part of a garment which covers the arm; a case for something.

sleeve-let *n.* A kind of covering which is worn on the forearm in order to protect the clothing form dirt and wear.

sleigh *n.* A vehicle mounted on runners, usually pulled over ice and snow by horses.

sleigh bell *n.* A type of bell that is attached to a sleigh.

slen-der *adj.* Slim; inadequate in amount. **slenderly** *adv.*, **slenderness** *n.*

slept *v.* Past tense of sleep.

sleuth *n.* A detective.

slew *n.* A large amount of something.

slice *n.* A thin cut; a portion or share; in sports, a ball in flight that curves off to the right of its target. *v.* To cut into slices. **slicer** *n.*

slice bar *n.* A type of steel bar that has a flat blade used for chipping.

slick *adj.* Smooth and slippery; quick; smart; clever; attractive for the present time but without quality or depth. *n.* Water with a thin layer of oil floating on top.

slick-en-side *n.* A striated surface that is produced on a rock by moving along a fault.

slick-er *n.* A raincoat made of yellow oilcloth.

slide *v.* To move smoothly across a surface without losing contact. *n.* The act of sliding; a slanted smooth surface usually found on playgrounds; a transparent picture which can be projected on a screen; a small glass plate for examining specimens under a microscope.

slid-er *n.* Something that slides.

slide valve *n.* A kind of vlave which opens and closes something such as a passageway by sliding across it.

slide-way *n.* The way which something slides.

slid-ing seat *n.* The rower's seat which will slide aft and fore.

slight *adj.* Minor in degree; unimportant. *v.* To ignore. **slightly** *adv.*

slight-ing *adj.* To be characterized by disrespect. **slightingly** *adv.*

slim *adj.* Slender; meager; not much.

slime *n.* A wet, slippery substance.

slim-ming *adj.* To be giving the appearance or effect of slenderness.

slim-sy *adj.* Being frail.

sling *n.* A piece of material, as leather, or a strap which secures something; a piece of fabric worn around the neck used to support an injured hand or arm; a weapon made of a strap, used to throw a stone.

sling-shot *n.* A type of v-shaped device which has an elastic band and is used to propel objects such as rocks through the air.

slink-y *adj.* To be sinuous and sleek in moving.

slip *v.* To move in a smooth, quiet way; to fall or lose one's balance. *Slang* To become less active, alert, or strong. *n.* The action of slipping; the place between two piers used for docking a boat; a woman's undergarment; a small piece of paper; a portion of a plant used for grafting.

slip-case *n.* A type of container that has one end open in order to slide books into for protection.

slip-cov-er *n.* A type of cover which can be slipped on and off of something.

slip-knot *n.* A type of knot that will slip along the rope of which it is made.

slip-o-ver *n.* A type of garment that will slip on and off with ease.

slip-page *n.* The process of slipping.

slip-pery *adj.* To cause something to slip. **slipperiness** *n.*

slip–sheet *v.* To put in or to insert a slip sheet between other sheets.

slip sheet *n.* A type of paper that is put between newly printed sheets.

slip-sole *n.* A type of thin insole.

slip stitch *n.* A type of stitch which is used for concealing folded edges in sewing.

slip up *v.* Make a blunder or mistake.

slit *v.* To cut a slit into something. *n.* a narrow opening or cut into something.

slith-er *v.* To slide or slip in an indirect manner; to move like a snake. **-y** *adj.*

slit trench *n.* A trench which is narrow and is used as shelter in a battle from shell fragments.

sliv-er *n.* A thin, narrow piece of something that has been broken off.

slob *n.* One who is slovenly.

slob-ber *v.* To dribble from the mouth.

sloe gin *n.* A type of sweet liquer that is made of grain spirits and is flavored with sloes.

slog *v.* To plod along slowly and heavily.

slo-gan *n.* A phrase used to express the aims of a cause.

slo-gan-ize *v.* To use something as a slogan.

sloop *n.* A type of boat with one mast and is rigged fore-and-aft.

slop *n.* A tasteless liquid food.

slop chest *n.* The store which is on a merchant ship and supplies the crew with goods such as tobacco.

slope *v.* To slant upward or downward. *n.* An upward or downward incline, as a ski slope.

slop jar *n.* A type of pail that is large in

size and is used for the purpose holding and receiving the waste water from a washbowel.

slop-py *adj.* To be wet so that it spatters easily.

slosh *v.* To splash in a liquid, as water.

slot *n.* A narrow, thin groove or opening. *Slang* A place or scheduled time for an event.

slot-back *n.* The offensive halfback in the game of football that lines up behind and between the tackle and the offensive end.

sloth *n.* Laziness; a slow mammal found in South America.

sloth-ful *adj.* To be inclined to sloth. **slothfulness** *n.*

slot machine *n.* A type of machine that requires money to play and something will give money to the one playing.

slouch *n.* A drooping or sagging posture; a lazy person. *v.* To sit or walk with poor posture.

slouch hat *n.* A kind of hat that has a wide flexible brim.

slouchy *adj.* To be lacking good posture. **slouchiness** *n.*

slough *n.* The skin which is cast off from a snake as he sheds it.

Slo-vak *n.* A person who is a member of the Slavic people of eastern Czecholsolvakia.

slov-en *n.* A person who is habitually negligent of cleanliness.

slov-en-ly *adj.* To be untidy as in one's personal appearance.

slow *adj.* Moving at a low rate of speed; requiring more time than usual; not lively; sluggish; not interesting. *adv.* At less speed; in a slow manner. **slowly** *adv.*, **slowness** *n.*

slow--foot-ed *adj.* To be moving at a slow pace. **slow-footedness** *n.*

slow-poke *n.* A person who is slow.

slow--wit-ted *adj.* To be mentally slow.

sludge *n.* A mass which is slushy.

slue *v.* To cause something to skid.

slug *n.* A slow animal related to the snail; a bullet or a lump of metal. *v.* To strike forcefully with the fist or a heavy object.

slug-fest *n.* A type of fight which is marked by the exchange of blows which are heavy.

slug-gard *n.* A person who is habitually lazy. **sluggardly** *adj.*

slug-ger *n.* A person who strikes with heavy blows such as a fighter.

slug-gish *adj.* To be slow to respond to a treatment or to a stimulation. **sluggishness** *n.*, **sluggishly** *adv.*

sluice *n.* A man-made ditch used to move water; a sloping trough used for floating logs. *v.* To wash with flowing water.

sluice-way *n.* A channel which is artificial and water is let in by a sluice.

slum *n.* A crowded urban neighborhood marked by poverty. **slum** *v.*

slum-ber *v.* To sleep; to doze. **-er** *n.*

slum-ber-ous *adj.* Being able to induce slumber.

slum-ber par-ty *n.* A type of overnight gathering usually of girls at someone's house.

slum-my *adj.* To be pertaining to a slum.

slump *v.* To fall or sink suddenly.

slung *v.* Past tense of sling.

slur *v.* To slide over without careful consideration; to pronounce unclearly. *n.* An insult. *Music* Two or more notes connected with a curved line to indicate they are to be slurred.

slurp *v.* To make or produce a sucking noise while one is drinking.

slur-ry *n.* A type of waterfy mixture of matter which is insoluble.

slush *n.* Melting snow; snow which is partially melted. **slushy** *adj.*

slut *n.* A woman of bad character; a prostitute. **sluttish** *adj.*

SLV *abbr.* Satellite launch vehicle.

sly *adj.* Cunning; clever; sneaky; underhanded. **slyly** *adv.*, **slyness** *n.*

sly-boots *n.* A person who is sly.

sm *abbr.* Small.

SM *abbr.* Sergeant major.

SMA *abbr.* Sergeant major of the army.

smack *v.* To slap; to press and open the lips with a sharp noise. *n.* The act or noise of slapping something. *adv.* Directly.

smack-er *n.* A person who smacks.

smack-ing *adj.* To be lively.

SMaj *abbr.* Sergeant major.

small *adj.* Little in size, quantity, or extent; unimportant. *n.* The part that is less than the other. **smallness** *n.*

small ale *n.* A kind of weak ale that is brewed with little malt and is a cheap drink.

small arm *n.* A type of firearm which can be fired while it is held in the hands.

small change *n.* The coins of a low denomination.

small-clothes *n.* The close-fitting knee breeches which were worn in the 18th century.

small--fry *adj.* To be pertaining to a child.

small hours *n.* The hours which occur in the early morning.

small in-tes-tines *n.* The section of the intestines which is located between the colon and the stomach.

small-mouth bass *n.* Type of black bass which can be found in clear lakes and rivers.

small-pox *n.* An acute, contagious disease marked by high fever and sores on the skin.

small--scale *adj.* To be small in scope.

small--sword *n.* A type of light tapering sword that is used for thrusting in fencing.

small talk *n.* A casual conversation.

smalt-ite *n.* A type of white or grey mineral which is an arsenide of nickel and cobalt.

smal-to *n.* A type of colored glass that can be used for mosaic work.

smarmy *adj.* To be marked by a smug.

smart *adj.* Intelligent; clever.
smart-ly *adv.*, smartness *n.*
smart-en *v.* To make someone smarter.
smart-weed *n.* A polygonums that has a strong acid juice.
smash *v.* To break into small pieces; to move forward violently, as to shatter; to ruin. *n.* The act or sound of crashing. *adj.* Outstanding. smasher *n.*
smat-ter *v.* To speak with a superficial knowledge.
smaze *n.* The combination of smoke and haze that is similar to smog in its appearance only.
smear *v.* To spread or cover with a sticky, oily, or moist substance. *Slang* To discredit one's reputation.
smear-y *adj.* To be marked with smears.
smell *v.* To notice an odor by means of the olfactory sense organs. *n.* An odor; the ability to perceive an odor; the scent of something.
smel-ly *adj.* To have a smell or odor.
smelt *v.* To heat metals or their ores to a high temperature in order to obtain pure metallic constituents.
smelt-er *n.* Something or someone that smelts.
smew *n.* A merganser which is of northern Europe and of Asia where the male has a white-crest.
smid-gen *n.* A little or small amount.
smi-lax *n.* A type of twinning plant which has ovate bright green cladophylls.
smile *n.* A grin; a facial expression in which the corners of the mouth turn upward, indicating pleasure. smile *v.*
smirch *v.* To make something stained or dirty.
smirk *v.* To smile in a conceited way. smirk, smirker *n.*
smite *v.* To hit with great force using the hand. smiter *n.*
smith *n.* One who repairs or shapes metal.
smith-ery *n.* The art of a smith.
smith-son-ite *n.* A type of zinc which is white.
smithy *n.* The place where a smith works.
smock *n.* A loose-fitting garment worn as a protection for one's clothes while working. *v.* To gather fabric into very small pleats or gathers.
smock frock *n.* An outer garment which is loose fitting and is worn by workmen.
smog *n.* A mixture of smoke and fog.
smoke *n.* A cloud of vapor released into the air when something is burning. *v.* To preserve or flavor meat by exposing it to smoke.
smokeless, smoky *adj.*, smoker *n.*
smoke-house *n.* A place or building where meat and fish are cured by using smoke.
smoke jump-er *n.* A type of forest fighter who will parachute to the area of a fire that may have become hard to reach by land.
smoke out *v.* To force or drive out with the use of smoke.
smoke-stack *n.* The chimney which gases and smoke are able to be discharged.
smoke tree *n.* A type of shrubby tree belonging to the sumac family.
smok-ing jack-et *n.* A type of jacket which is worn by the man at home.
smolder *v.* To burn slowly without a flame and with little smoke.
smolt *n.* A young sea trout or salmon.
smooth *adj.* Not irregular; flat; without lumps, as in gravy; without obstructions or impediments. *adv.* Evenly. *v.* To make less difficult; to remove obstructions. -ness *n.*, smoothly *adv.*
smooth-en *v.* To make something smooth.
smoothy *n.* A type of person who has manners which are greatly polished.
smor-gas-bord *n.* A buffet meal with a variety of foods to choose from.
smother *n.* Failure to receive enough oxygen to survive. *v.* To conceal; to be overly protective. smothery *adj.*
SMSgt *abbr.* Senior master sergeant.
smudge *v.* To soil by smearing with dirt. *n.* A dirty mark or smear.
smug *adj.* Complacent with oneself; self-satisfied. smugly *adv.*, -ness *n.*
smug-gle *v.* To import or export goods illegally without paying duty fees.
smug-ly *adv.* To be done in a smug manner.
smut *n.* A type of matter or substance which will soil something.
smut-ty *adj.* To be tainted or soiled by smut. smuttiness *n.*
SMV *abbr.* Slow moving vehicle.
snack *n.* A small amount of food taken between meals. snack *v.*
snack bar *n.* An eating place for the public that serves snacks at a counter.
snaf-fle *n.* A jointed bit used with a bridle.
sna-fu *v.* To being someone into a confused state.
snag *n.* A stump or part of a tree that is partly hidden under the surface of water; a pull in a piece of fabric. *v.* To tear on a rough place. *Slang* To catch unexpectedly; to snatch.
snail *n.* A type of gastropod mollusk that can live in a spiral shell.
snail--paced *adj.* To be moving at a slow pace.
snake *n.* Any of a large variety of scaly reptiles, having a long tapering body. *Slang* An untrustworthy person.
snake-bite *n.* A bite of a snake on the skin.
snake charmer *n.* A person who exhibits his power to charm a snake.
snake-mouth *n.* A type of bog orchid that is located in eastern North America and Japan and it has pink flowers.
snake pit *n.* The place of complete disorder.
snake-skin *n.* The leather that has been prepared from the skin of a snake.
snake-weed *n.* A plant that is associated

with snakes and used in the treatment of snakebite.

snaky *adj.* To be entwined with snakes.

snap *v.* To break suddenly with a sharp, quick sound; to fly off under tension; to snatch something suddenly.

snap-back *n.* A type of football snap.

snap-bean *n.* A type of bean which is grown for its pods that are broken and cooked.

snap-drag-on *n.* A type of plant of the figowrt family and having white, yellow, or crimson flowers.

snap-per *n.* A type of carnivorous fish that are found in the warm seas.

snap-per-back *n.* In the game of football, a center.

snap-pish *adj.* To be given to curt irritable speech. **snappishness** *n.*

snap-shot *n.* A type of photograph which is made by an amateur with a small camera.

snare *n.* Anything that entangles or entraps; a trap with a noose, used to catch small animals.

snare drum *n.* A type of drum that has snares stretched across the lower end.

snarl *v.* To speak in an angry way; to cause confusion; to tangle or be tangled. *n.* A growl. **snarly** *adj.*

snatch *v.* To seize or grasp something suddenly. *n.* The act of taking something; a brief or small part.

snatch block *n.* A type of block which can be opened on one side in order to get the bight of a rope.

snaz-zy *adj.* To be flashily attractive.

SNCC *abbr.* Student Nonviolent Coordinating Committee.

sneak *v.* To act or move in a quiet, sly way. *n.* A person who acts in a secret, underhanded way.

sneak-ing *adj.* To be characteristic of a sneak. **sneakingly** *adv.*

sneak pre-view *n.* An advance showing of a motion picture.

sneak thief *n.* A type of thief that will steal whatever he can without using violence.

sneaky *adj.* To be marked by shiftiness.

sneer *v.* To express scorn by the look on one's face.

sneeze *v.* To expel air from the nose suddenly and without control. **sneeze** *n.*

sneeze-weed *n.* A type of plant such as the North American yellow-flowered herb.

sneeze-wort *n.* A type of strong-scented herb found in Eurasia.

sneezy *adj.* To be causing sneezing.

SNG *abbr.* Substitute natural gas.

snick *v.* To cut at something slightly.

snide *adj.* To be unworthy of esteem. **snideness** *n.,* **snidely** *adv.*

sniff *v.* To inhale through the nose in short breaths with a noise; to show scorn. **sniff** *n.*

sniff-er *n.* Someone or something that sniffs.

sniff-ish *adj.* Expressing a attitude.

snif-ter *n.* A type of drink of liquor that has been distilled.

snig-gle *v.* To try to catch an eel by putting the baited hook into the place where they hide.

snip *v.* To cut off in small pieces and with quick strokes. *n.* A small piece.

snipe *n., pl.* **snipe** *or* **snipes** A bird with a long bill which lives in marshy places. *v.* To shoot at people from a hidden position. **sniper** *n.*

snip-pet *n.* A small part or thing.

snips *n.* A type of hand shears that can be used for the purpose of cutting metal.

sniv-el *v.* To whine with snuffling.

snob *n.* A person who considers himself better than anyone else and who looks down on those he considers to be his inferiors.

snob-bery *n.* A snobbish conduct.

snob-bish *adj.* Being like a snob. **snobbishness** *n.,* **snobbishly** *adv.*

snood *n.* A type of band that can be worn in a woman's hair.

snook *n.* A type of fish that is large and can be used as food or for sport.

snook-er *n.* A type of pool which is played with six colored balls and fifteen red balls.

snoop *v., Slang* To prowl or spy. *n.* One who snoops.

snoopy *adj.* To be given to snooping.

snoot *n.* An expression of contempt.

snooze *v.* To sleep for a short amount of time.

snore *v.* To breath with a harsh noise while sleeping. **snore, snorer** *n.*

snor-kel *n.* A tube that extends above the water, used for breathing while swimming face down.

snort *n.* To force air through the nostrils with a loud, harsh noise. *Slang* To inhale a narcotic through the nose.

snort-er *n.* Someone or something that snorts.

snout *n.* A nose of an animal such as a swine.

snout beetle *n.* A type of beetle that has a head which has produced into a snout.

snow *n.* Vapor that forms crystals in cold air and falls to the ground in white flakes. *Slang* To charm or overwhelm.

snow-ball *n.* A mass of snow which is usually round in shape and pressed together.

snow-bank *n.* A slope of the snow.

snow-ber-ry *n.* A type of white-berried shrub that has pink flowers.

snow-bird *n.* A type of small bird that can be seen in the winter.

snow--blind *adj.* To be affected with snow blindness.

snow-bound *adj.* To be blocked in by a large amount of snow.

snow-brush *n.* A type of white-flowered shrub that can be found in North America.

snow-cap *n.* A cap of snow that appears on the tops of mountains.

snow-fall *n.* The fall of the snow.

snow-flake *n.* A small crystal of snow.

snow leopard *n.* A type of large cat that

can be found in central Asia having a long pelt and turns almost white in the winter.

snow line *n.* The margin of a perennial snowfield.

snow-man *n.* A figure which is made out of snow and usually resemble a man or woman.

snow-mo-bile *n.* A type of vehicle that is used for the purpose of traveling on the snow. **snowmobiling** *n.*

snow plant *n.* A type of California herb that is able to grow at high altitudes and will susally appear just before the snow melts.

snow-plow *n.* A machine which is used for the purpose of removing the snow from an area of which it is not desires, such as a street.

snow-shed *n.* A type of shelter which is used for the protection against snowslides.

snow-shoe *n.* A type of shoe which is used to travel on top of the snow.

snow-storm *n.* A storm that is made up of storm.

snow tire *n.* A type of tire that is used by a car when there is snow on the street in order to get better traction.

snowy *adj.* To be covered by snow. **snowily** *adv.*, **snowiness** *n.*

snub *v.* To treat with contempt or in an unfriendly way. **snub** *n.*

snub-ber *n.* Someone that snubs.

snub--nosed *adj.* To have a stubby nose.

snuff *v.* To draw air in through the nostrils. **snuff** *n.*

snuff-box *n.* A type of small box that can be used for holding snuff.

snuff-er *n.* A type of device used for cropping and holding the snuff of a candle.

snuf-fle *v.* To breathe through a nose that is obstructed producing a sniffing sound.

snug *adj.* Warm, pleasant, comfortable and safe.

snug-gle *v.* To curl up to someone in an affectionate manner.

so *adv.* To a degree or extent as a result; likewise; also; indeed. *conj.* In order that; therefore.

soak *v.* To pass through something with the use of pores. **soaker** *n.*

soak-age *n.* The amount of liquid that is gained through absorption.

soap *n.* A cleansing agent made of an alkali and a fat, and used for washing. *v.* To rub with soap.

soap-ber-ry *n.* A type of tropical woody plant.

soap-box *n.* A platform that is used by an informal orator.

soap bubble *n.* A type of hollow globe which is formed by blowing a small film of soapsuds.

soap-less *adj.* Containing no soap.

soap plant *n.* A type of plant which has a part that may be used in the place of soap.

soapy *adj.* To be covered or smeared with soap.

soar *v.* To glide or fly high without any noticeable movement; to rise higher than usual.

sob *v.* To weep with short, quick gasps.

so-ber *adj.* Not drunk or intoxicated serious; solemn; quiet. **soberly** *adv.*, **soberness** *n.*

soc-cer *n.* A game in which two teams o eleven men each try to kick a ball into the opposing team's goal.

so-cia-ble *adj.* Capable of friendly social relations; enjoying the company o others. **sociableness** *n.*, **sociably** *adv.*

so-cial *adj.* Having to do with people living in groups; enjoying friendly companionship with others. *n.* An in formal party or gathering.

so-cial-ism *n.* A system in which people as a whole, and not individuals, con trol and own all property.

so-ci-e-ty *n.*, *pl.* **-ies** People working together for a common purpose; com panionship.

so-ci-ol-o-gy *n.* The study of society and the development of human society. **sociologic, sociological** *adj.*

sock *n.* A short covering for the foot ankle, and lower part of the leg; a hard blow. *Slang* To hit with force.

sock-et *n.* A hollow opening into which something is fitted.

Soc-ra-tes *n.* Greek philosopher.

so-da *n.* Sodium carbonate; a flavored carbonated drink.

sod-den *adj.* Completely saturated; very wet; lacking in expression.

so-di-um *n.* A metallic element symbol ized by Na.

sod-om-y *n.* Anal sexual intercourse.

so-fa *n.* An upholstered couch with arms and a back.

soft *adj.* Not stiff or hard; not glaring or harsh; mild or pleasant; gentle in sound.

soft-ball *n.* A game played on a smaller diamond than baseball, with a larger softer ball.

soft-ware *n.* In computer science, data as routines, programs and languages which is essential to the operation of computers.

sog-gy *adj.* Saturated with a liquid or moisture.

sol-ace *n.* Comfort in a time of trouble grief, or misfortune. **solacer** *n.*

so-lar *adj.* Relating to or connected with the sun; utilizing the sun for power or light; measured by the earth's move ment around the sun.

so-lar-i-um *n.*, *pl.* **-ia** *or* **-ums** A glassed in room exposed to the sun's rays.

solar system *n.* The sun and the planets, asteroids, and comets that orbit it.

sol-der *n.* Any alloy, as lead or tin, which is melted and used to mend or join other pieces of metal. **soldered** *adj.*

soldier *n.* An enlisted person who serves in the military.

sole *n.* The bottom of a foot or shoe; single, the only one; a flat fish very popular as seafood.

sol-emn *adj.* Very serious; characterized

by dignity; sacred.

solemnity, solemnness n.

so-lic-it v. To try to obtain; to ask earnestly; to beg or entice a person persistently. **solicitation** n.

sol-id adj. Having a definite firm shape and volume; having no crevices; not hollow; having height, weight and length; without interruption; reliable, sound and upstanding. n. A solid substance. **solidification, solidness** n., **solidify** v.

sol-i-taire n. A single gemstone set by itself; a card game played by one person.

sol-i-tude n. The act of being alone or secluded; isolation.

so-lo n. A musical composition written for and performed by one single person or played by one instrument.

sol-stice n. Either of the two times in a twelve month period at which the sun reaches an extreme north or south position.

sol-u-ble adj. Capable of being dissolved; able to be solved or explained. **solubility** n., **solubly** adv.

solve v. To find the answer to. **-able** adj.

som-ber adj. Dark; gloomy; melancholy.

some adj. Being an indefinite number or quantity; unspecified. pron. An undetermined or indefinite quantity. adv. An approximate degree. **somebody** n. A person unknown. **someday** adv. At an unspecified future time. **somehow** adv. In a way.

som-er-sault n. The act or acrobatic stunt in which one rolls the body in a complete circle, with heels over head.

som-nam-bu-lism n. The act of walking during sleep. **somnambulant** adj.

son n. A male offspring.

so-na-ta n. An instrumental composition with movements contrasting in tempo and mood but related in key.

song n. A piece of poetry put to music; the act or sound of singing.

son-ic adj. Pertaining to sound or the speed of sound.

son-net n. A poem made up of fourteen lines.

soon adv. In a short time; in the near future; quickly.

soot n. The black powder generated by incomplete combustion of a fuel, such as coal or wood.

soothe v. To make comfortable; to calm.

sop v. To soak up a liquid; to absorb. n. Anything softened by a liquid; something given as a conciliatory offering.

soph-o-more n. A second year college or high school student.

so-pran-o n., pl. **-nos** or **-ni** The highest female singing voice.

sor-cery n. The use of supernatural powers.

sor-did adj. Filthy, very dirty; morally corrupt.

sore adj. Tender or painful to the touch, as an injured part of the body; severe or extreme. n. A place on the body which has been bruised, inflamed, or injured in some way. **sorely** adv.

sor-ghum n. A cane-like grass grown for its sweet juices and used as fodder for animals; the syrup prepared from the sweet juices.

so-ror-i-ty n., pl. **-ies** A social organization for women.

sor-rel n. Any of several herbs with sour-tasting leaves, used in salads.

sor-row n. Anguish; mental suffering; an expression of grief. **sorrowful** adj., **sorrowfully** adv.

sor-ry adj. Feeling or showing sympathy or regret; worthless.

sort n. A collection of things having common attributes or similar qualities. v. to arrange according to class, kind, or size.

sor-tie n., Mil. An attack on enemy forces; a combat mission flown by an aircraft.

SOS n. A call for help; the international distress signal; a call made when a rescue is needed, especially by a ship or plane.

souf-fle n. A fluffy dish made of egg yolks, whipped egg whites, and other ingredients, served as a main dish or sweetened as a dessert.

sought v. Past tense of seek.

soul n. The spirit in man that is believed to be separate from the body and is the source of a person's emotional, spiritual, and moral nature. Slang A spirit or attitude derived from Blacks and their culture.

sound n. A sensation received by the ears from air, water, noise, and other sources. v. To make a sound; to make noise. adj. Free from flaw, injury, disease, or damage. **soundless** adj., **soundly** adv.

soup n. A liquid food made by boiling meat and/or vegetables, in water.

sour adj. Sharp to the taste; acid; unpleasant; disagreeable. v. To become sour or spoiled. **sourly** adv.

source n. Any point of origin or beginning; the beginning or place of origin of a stream or river.

south n. The direction opposite of north. adv. To or towards the south. adj. From the south. **southerly** adj. & adv., **southern, southward** adj.

South Car-o-li-na n. A state located in the southeastern part of the United States.

South Da-ko-ta n. A state located in the central northwestern part of the United States.

south-paw n. A left-handed person.

South Pole n. The southernmost part of the earth.

south-west n. The direction between south and west. **southwestern** adj.

sou-ve-nir n. An item kept as a remembrance of something or someplace.

sov-er-eign n. A ruler with supreme power; a monarch. adj. Possessing supreme jurisdiction or authority.

So-vi-et n. The elected governmental

council of the former USSR. **soviet** *adj.* Having to do with the USSR.

sow *v.* To scatter or throw seeds on the ground for growth. **sow** *n.* A female pig.

space *n.* The unlimited area in all directions in which events occur and have relative direction; an interval of time; the area beyond the earth's atmosphere; a division between objects; an interval of time. **space** *v.* To divide objects by an empty area or to divide words by a blank or a series of blanks.

spade *n.* A tool with a flat blade used for digging, heavier than a shovel; one of the four suits in a deck of cards. **spade** *v.* To dig in the earth.

spa-ghet-ti *n.* Pasta made in long, thin pieces.

span *n.* The extent of space from the end of the thumb to the end of the little finger of a spread hand; the section between two limits or supports. **span** *v.* To extend across.

sp-an-iel *n.* A dog with large drooping ears and short legs.

spank *v.* To strike or slap the buttocks with an open hand as a means of punishment.

spare *v.* To refrain from injuring, harming or destroying; to refrain from using; to do without. **spare** *n.* Something extra, as a spare tire or a spare room.

spark *n.* A glowing or incandescent particle, as one released from a piece of burning wood or one produced by means of friction. **spark** *v.* To give off sparks.

spar-kle *v.* To emit or reflect light.

spar-row *n.* A small bird with grayish or brown plumage.

sparse *adj.* Scant; thinly distributed. **sparsely** *adv.* **sparsity** *n.*

spasm *n.* An involuntary muscle contraction.

spat-ter *v.* To scatter or splash a liquid.

spat-u-la *n.* A kitchen utensil with a flexible blade for mixing soft substances.

spawn *n.* The eggs of fish or other water animals, as oysters or frogs. **spawn** *v.* To lay eggs.

speak *v.* To utter words; to express a thought in words.

speak-er *n.* A person who speaks, usually before an audience; a device to project sound from a radio, stereo, or other audio device.

spear *n.* A weapon with a long shaft and a sharply pointed head; a stalk of asparagus. **spear** *v.* To strike, pierce, or stab with a spear.

spear-mint *n.* A mint plant yielding an aromatic oil used as a flavoring.

spe-cial-ist *n.* A person, such as a doctor, who devotes his practice to one particular field.

spe-cial-ize *v.* To focus one's efforts or interests in one field of activity or study.

spec-i-men *n.* A sample; a representative of a particular thing.

speck *n.* A small particle, mark, or spot. **speck** *v.* To cover or dot with specks.

spec-ta-cle *n.* A public display of something unusual. **spectacles** *pl.* Eyeglasses.

spec-trum *n.* *Physics* The band of colors produced when light is passed through a prism or other means, separating the light into different wave lengths.

spec-u-late *v.* To reflect and think deeply; to take a chance on a business venture in hopes of making a large profit.

speech *n.* The ability, manner, or act of speaking; a talk before the public.

speed *n.* Rate of action or movement; quickness; rapid motion. *Slang* A drug used strictly as a stimulant.

spell *v.* To say out loud or write in proper order the letters which make up a word; to relieve; to take a turn at performing a duty. **spell** *n.* The state of being controlled by magic; a short period of time; a time or period of illness; an attack.

spellbind To fascinate or hold as if by magic.

spend *v.* To give out; to use up; to pay; to exhaust.

sperm *n.* The male cell of reproduction; semen. **spermatic** *adj.*

sphere *n.* *Math* A round object with all points the same distance from a given point; globe, ball, or other rounded object. **spherical** *adj.* **spherically** *adv.*

sphinx *n. pl.* **sphinxes** *or* **sphinges** An ancient Egyptian figure having the head of a man, male sheep, or hawk and the body of a lion; a very mysterious person.

spice *n.* A pungently aromatic plant used as flavoring in food, as nutmeg, cinnamon, pepper, or curry. **spice** *v.* **spicy** *adj.*

spi-der *n.* An eight-legged, wingless arach-nid with a body divided into two parts, noted for spinning webs used as nests and as a means of capturing and holding prey.

spike *n.* A large, thick nail; a pointed metal piece on the sole of a shoe to prevent slipping, as on a sports shoe.

spill *v.* To allow or cause something to flow or run out of something. **spill** *Slang n.* A fall from a horse; to make known.

spin *v.* To draw out fibers and twist into thread; to produce cobweb or silk by extruding from the body a filament of a natural material that hardens when exposed to air, as is done by spiders and silkworms; to run something around and around; to twirl; to resolve; to tell a story. **spin** *Slang n.* A short drive or ride in an auto.

spin-ach *n.* A widely cultivated plant with dark green leaves which are used in salads or as a cooked vegetable.

spin-dle *n.* A rod with a slit in the top and a piece of wood at the other end, used to hold yarn or thread; a needle-like rod mounted on a base, used to hold papers.

spine *n.* The spinal column; the backbone; the back of a bound book, inscribed with the title.

spin-ster *n.* An unmarried woman; an old maid.

spir-it *n.* The vital essence of man, considered divine in origin; the part of a human being characterized by personality and self-consciousness; the mind; the Holy Ghost; the creative power of God; a supernatural being, as a ghost or angel.

spir-i-tual *adj.* Of, like, or pertaining to the nature of spirit; relating to spirit; sacred. **spiritual** *n.* A type of religious song originating among the African-Americans of the southern United States. **spirituality** *n.* **spiritualize** *v.*

spite *n.* Hatred or malicious bitterness; a grudge; ill will. **spiteful** *adj.* **spitefully** *adv.*

spit-toon *n.* A cuspidor or receptacle for spit.

spitz n. A small dog with a tail which curls over its back.

splash v. To spatter a liquid; to wet or soil with a liquid or semi-liquid; to make a splash. **splash** n. **splashy** adj.

splash-down n. The landing of a missile or spacecraft in the ocean.

spleen n. Anat. A highly vascular, flattened organ which filters and stores blood, located below the diaphragm; in ancient times, believed to be the site of melancholy, ill temper, or anger.

splen-did adj. Illustrious; magnificent; gorgeous; admirable; excellent; shining or brilliant.

splice v. To join together by wearing, overlapping, and binding the ends. **splice** n. Slang A marriage or wedding.

splint n. A device used to hold a fractured or injured limb in the proper position for healing. **splint** v.

splotch n. A discolored and irregularly shaped spot.

splutter v. To make a slight, short spitting sound. **splutter** n.

spoil v. To destroy the value, quality, or usefulness; to overindulge as to harm the character. **spoils** n. booty or loot from a robbery or a raid; rewards for political support. **spoilage** n. **spoiler** n.

spoke n. One of the rods that serve to connect and support the rim of a wheel. **spoke** v. Past tense of the verb speak.

spokes-man n. One who speaks on behalf of another or others.

sponge n. Any of a number of marine creatures with a soft, porous skeleton which soaks up liquid; a sterile dressing used during surgery. **sponge** v. To clean with a sponge.

spon-sor n. A person who is responsible for a debt or duty of another; a business that finances a television or radio program that in turn advertises its product.

spon-ta-ne-ous adj. Done from one's own impulse without apparent external cause; describing plants that grow without human cultivation, such as weeds. **spontaneity** n. **spontaneously** adv.

spoof n. A deception; nonsense.

spook n. Slang A ghost. **spook** v. To scare or frighten. **spooky** adj.

spool n. A small cylinder for holding thread, tape or wire. v. To wind an item on a spool; to wind itself on a spool.

spoon n. An eating, cooking, or measuring utensil; a shiny metallic fishing lure. **spoon** v. Slang To make love, as by kissing and caressing.

spoon-ful n. The total amount a spoon will hold.

spo-rad-ic adj. Occurring occasionally or at irregular intervals.

spore n. Bot. The reproductive single-celled structure produced by non-flowering plants; any cell capable of developing into a new organism, seed, or germ.

spo-ri-cidal adj. Tending to kill or destroy spores.

sport n. An interesting diversion; a particular game or physical activity with set rules; a person who leads a fast life. **sport** v. Slang To amuse and have a good time. **sport** adj. Relating or pertaining to sports. **sportful** adj. **sportfully** adv.

sport-ing adj. Of or relating to risk taking or gambling; displaying sportsmanship.

sports-man-ship n. Fair play; the ability to win or lose graciously.

sports-writer n. A person who writes and gives detail information about sport events.

spot n. A small area that differs in size, portion, or color. **spot** adj. Delivered or made immediately. Slang A dangerous or difficult situation. **spot** v. **spotted, spotless** adj. **spotlessly** adv. **spotlessness** n.

spot-light n. A powerful light thrown directly at one area. **spotlight** v. To cast a light to make something or someone conspicuous; to focus attention on.

spouse n. One's husband or wife; a marriage partner.

spout v. To pour out forcibly, as under pressure; to cause to shoot forth. Slang To orate pompously; to declaim.

sprain n. A wrenching or twisting of a muscle or joint.

sprawl v. To sit or lie in an ungraceful manner; to develop haphazardly. **-er** n.

spray n. A liquid dispersed in a fine mist or droplets. v. To disperse or send forth in a spray. **sprayer** n.

spread v. To unfold or open fully; to apply or distribute over an area; to force apart; to extend or expand. **spread** v.

spree n. An excessive indulgence in an activity; a binge.

spright-ly adj. Vivacious, lively.

sprin-kle v. To scatter in small particles or drops; to rain in small drops.

sprint n. A short, fast race.

sprock-et n. Mech. A tooth-like projection from the rim of a wheel.

spruce n. An evergreen tree with needle-like foliage, cones, and soft wood.

sprung v. Past tense of spring.

spry adj. Quick; brisk; energetic.

spud n. Slang A potato.

spur n. A sharp, projecting device worn on a rider's boot, used to nudge a horse. v. To urge on.

sput-nik n. An unmanned Soviet earth satellite.

sput-ter v. To throw off small particles in short bursts; to speak in a confused or agitated manner.

spu-tum n. pl. **-ta** Saliva or mucus that is expectorated.

spy n. pl. **spies** A secret agent who obtains information; one who watches other people secretly.

squab n. A chair cushion.

squab-ble v. To engage in a petty argument. n. A loud quarrel usually over an unimportant matter.

squad n. A small group organized to perform a specific job.

squad-ron n. A type of acyclic hydrocarbon that is widely distributed in nature.

squad car n. A type of police vehicle.

squad room n. A room in a barracks used to house soldiers.

squal-id adj. To be marked by degradation for poverty or neglect.

squall v. To cry out. n. A sudden violent wind occurring during a storm.

squa-lor n. The state of being squalid.

squa-ma-tion n. A state of something being scaly or having an arrangement of scales.

squa-mo-sal *adj.* Pertaining to the membrane bone of the skull.

squa-mous *adj.* To be consisting of scales. **squamously** *adv.*

squa-mous cell *n.* A type of cell which is derived for squamous epithelium.

squan-der *v.* To spend extravagantly or wastefully.

square *n.* A parallelogram with four equal sides; an implement having a T or L shape used to measure right angles. *Math.* To multiply a number by itself. *Slang* An unsophisticated person; a person who is not aware of the latest fads or trends.

square dance *n.* A type of dance that involves couples forming a hollow square. **square dancing** *n.*

square deal *n.* A fair trade.

square knot *n.* A kind of knot that is comprised of two reverse half-knots.

squar-er *n.* Someone who squares something.

square rig *n.* A type of sailing-ship rig where the main sails are extended on yards which are fastened to the masts on the center and horizontally.

square root *n.* A number which when multiplied by itself gives the given number.

square shoot-er *n.* A person who is honest.

square--toed *adj.* To have a toe that is shaped like a square.

squar-ish *adj.* To be slightly square in appearance.

squash *n.*

An edible fruit of the gourd family; a sport played in a walled court with a hard rubber ball and racket. *v.* To press or squeeze into a soft pulp.

squash bug *n.* A type of large black American bug that can be injurious to squash vines.

squat *v.* To sit on the heels; to crouch; to settle on a piece of land in order to obtain legal title. **squatter, squatness** *n.*

squaw *n.* An American Indian woman.

squaw-fish *n.* A type of cyprinid fish found in western North America.

squawk *v.* To protest about something in a loud manner.

squawk box *n.* A type of intercom speaker.

squaw-root *n.* A type of herb of Noeth America and is parasitic on hemlock and oak roots.

squeak *v.* To utter a sharp, penetrating sound. **squeak** *n.*, **squeaky** *adj.*

squeak-er *n.* Someone or something that squeaks.

squeal *v.* To produce or to make a shrill cry. **squealer** *n.*

squea-mish *adj.* Easily shocked or nauseated. **squeamishly** *adv.*

squea-mish-ness *n.* A state of being squeamish.

squee-gee *n.* A tool having a stout rubber blade across a wooden handle, used to wash windows. **squeegee** *v.*

squeeze *v.* To press together; to extract by using pressure. *n.* An instance of squeezing for pleasure; a hug.

squeeze bot-tle *n.* A kind of bottle which is flexible and will dispense its contents when one squeezes the bottle.

squeg *v.* To oscillate in a manner which is irregular.

squelch *n.* The process or act of suppressing. **squelchy** *adj.*

squib *n.* A firecracker that does not explode.

squid *n.* A type of 10-armed cephalopod that has a tapered body.

squig-gle *n.* The short wavy line or twist.

squil-la *n.* A type of stomatopod crustacean that will dig into the mud.

squinch *v.* To make something more compact.

squint *v.* To view something through partly closed eyes; to close the eyes in this manner. **squint** *n.*

squint--eyed *adj.* To have eyes that squint.

squire *n.* An old-fashioned title for a rural justice of the peace, lawyer, or judge; a man who escorts a woman; a young man who ranks just below a knight. **squire** *v.*

squire-ar-chy *n.* The gentry.

squirm *n.* To twist the body in a wiggling motion. **squirm** *v.*

squir-rel *n.*

A rodent with gray or brown fur, having a long bushy tail and dark eyes. **squirrel** *v.*

squir-rel cage *n.* A type of cage that is used for small animals and has a rotatable cylinder for exercising.

squir-rel-ly *adj.* To be odd.

squir-rel mon-key *n.* A kind of monkey of South America that has a long tail that is not used for grasping.

squirt *v.* To eject in a thin stream or jet; to wet with a squirt. *n.* The act of squirting.

squirt-ing cu-cum-ber *n.* A type of plant of the Mediterranean that belongs to the gourg family and will burst to eject its seeds when it is ripe.

squishy *adj.* To be soft and damp.

Sr. *abbr.* Senior.

SRB *abbr.* Solid rocket booster.

sta-bi-lize *v.* To make firm; to keep from changing. **stabilization, stabilizer** *n.*

sta-ble *n.* A building for lodging and feeding horses or other farm animals. *adj.* Standing firm and resisting change. **stable** *v.*

stac-ca-to *adj., Music* Marked by sharp emphasis. **staccato** *n.* & *adv.*

stack *n.* A large pile of straw or hay; any systematic heap or pile; a chimney. *v.* To fix cards so as to cheat.

sta-di-um *n., pl.* **-dia** A large structure

for holding athletic events or other large gatherings.

staff *n., pl.* **staffs** *or* **staves** A pole or rod used for a specific purpose; the people employed to assist in the day-to-day affairs of running a business, organization, or government. *Mil.* A group of people on an executive or advisory board. *Music* The horizontal lines on which notes are written. **staff** *v.*

stag *n.* The adult male of various animals; a man who attends a social gathering without a woman companion; a social event for men only. *adj.* For men only.

stag-ger *v.* To walk unsteadily; to totter. *adj.* Strongly affected by defeat, misfortune, or loss of strength.

stag-nant *adj.* Not flowing; standing still; foul from not moving; inactive.

stair *n.* A step or a series of steps.

stair-case *n.* A series or a flight of steps that connect one level to another.

stake *n.* A bet placed on a game of chance; a sharpened piece of wood for driving into the ground. **stake** *v.*

stale *adj.* Having lost freshness; deteriorated; lacking in interest; dull; inactive.

stale-mate *n.* A position in chess when a player cannot move without placing his king in check.

stalk *n.* The main axis of a plant. *v.* To approach in a stealthy manner.

stall *n.* An enclosure in a barn, used as a place to feed and confine animals; a sudden loss of power in an engine; a booth used to display and sell. *v.* To try to put off doing something; to delay.

stal-lion *n.* An uncastrated, fully grown male horse.

sta-men *n., pl.* **stamens** *Bot.* The pollen-producing organs of a flower.

stam-i-na *n.* Physical or moral endurance.

stam-mer *v.* To make involuntary halts or repetitions of a sound or syllable while speaking. **stammerer** *n.*

stamp *v.* To put the foot down with force; to imprint or impress with a die, mark, or design. *n.* The act of stamping; the impression or pattern made by a stamp; a postage stamp.

stam-pede *n.* A sudden rush of panic, as of a herd of horses or cattle. *v.* To cause a stampede.

stance *n.* The posture or position of a standing person or animal.

stand *v.* To be placed in or maintain an erect or upright position; to take an upright position; to remain unchanged; to maintain a conviction; to resist. *n.* The act of standing; a device on which something rests; a small booth for selling or displaying items.

stand-ard *n.* A model which stands for or is accepted as a basis for comparison. **standard** *adj.*

stand-ing *n.* A status, reputation, or achievement; a measure of esteem. *adj.* Unchanging; stationary; not

moving.

sta-ple *n.* A principle commodity grown in an area; a major element; a metal fastener designed to hold materials such as cloth or paper. **stapler** *n.*

star *n., Astron.* A self-luminous body that is a source of light; any of the celestial bodies that can be seen in the night sky; a symbol having five or six points and resembling a star.

star-board *n.* The right side of a ship or boat. **starboard** *adj. & adv.*

starch *n.* Nutrient carbohydrates that are found in foods such as rice and potatoes. *v.* To stiffen clothing by using starch. **starchiness** *n.,* **-y** *adj.*

stare *v.* To look with an intent, direct gaze. **stare, starer** *n.*

stark *adj.* Bare; total; complete; forbidding in appearance.
starkness *n.,* **starkly** *adv.*

star-ling *n.* A common black or brown bird.

star-tle *v.* To cause a sudden surprise; to shock. **startle** *n.*

starve *v.* To suffer or die from not having food; to suffer from the need of food, love, or other necessities.

state *n.* A situation, mode, or condition of something; a nation; the governing power or authority of; one of the subdivisions or areas of a federal government, as the United States. *v.* To make known verbally.

stat-ic *adj.* Not moving. *n.* A random noise heard on a radio. **statically** *adv.*

sta-tion *n.* The place where someone or something is directed to stand; a scheduled stopping place; the place from which radio and television programs are broadcast.

sta-tion-ar-y *adj.* Not movable; unchanging.

sta-tion-er-y *n.* Writing paper and envelopes.

sta-tis-tic *n.* An estimate using an average or mean on the basis of a sample taken; numerical data.

stat-ue *n.* A form sculpted from wood, clay, metal, or stone.

stave *n.* A narrow piece of wood used in forming part of a container, as a barrel. **stave** *v.*

stay *v.* To remain; to pause; to maintain a position; to halt or stop; to postpone or delay an execution. *n.* A short visit.

stead *n.* The position, place, or job of another.

stead-fast *adj.* Not changing or moving; firm in purpose; true. **steadfastly** *adv.,* **steadfastness** *n.*

stead-y *adj.* Firmly placed, fixed or set; not changing; constant; uninterrupted.

steal *v.* To take another person's property; to move in a sly way; to move secretly. *Baseball* To take a base without the ball being hit. *Slang* A real bargain.

steam *n.* Water in the form of vapor; the visible mist into which vapor is condensed by cooling. **steamy** *adj.*

steel *n.* A various mixture of iron, carbon, and other elements; a strong material that can be shaped when heated. **steely** adj.

stem n. The main stalk of a plant; the main part of a word to which prefixes and suffixes may be added. v. To stop or retard the progress or flow of something.

sten-cil n. A form cut into a sheet of material, as cardboard or plastic, so that when ink or paint is applied, the pattern will reproduce on paper or another material.

ste-nog-ra-phy n. The skill of writing in shorthand. **-er** n., **stenographic** adj.

step n. A single completed movement in walking, dancing, or running; the distance of such a step; the part of a ladder that one places the feet on in ascending or descending. Music A musical scale; a degree.

ste-re-o n. A record player with stereophonic sound. **stereo** adj.

ste-reo-phon-ic adj. Relating to or giving a three-dimensional effect of auditory perspective.

ster-e-o-type n. A conventional opinion or belief; a metal printing plate.

ster-ile adj. Free from microorganisms; sanitary; unable to reproduce.

ster-ling n. An alloy of 92.5% silver and another metal, as copper.

stern adj. Inflexible; harsh. n. The rear of a boat or ship. **sternly** adv. **-ness** n.

ster-num n., pl. **-nums** or **-na** A long, flat bone located in the chest wall, connecting the collarbones and the cartilage of the first seven pairs of ribs.

steth-o-scope n.

An instrument used to listen to the internal sounds of the body.

stew v. To cook slowly; to simmer; to boil. n. A dish of stewed meat and potatoes. Slang To worry.

stew-ard n. A manager of another's financial affairs; a person responsible for maintaining household affairs; a male attendant on an airplane or ship. **stewardess, stewardship** n.

stick n. A slender piece of wood; a club, rod, or walking stick. v. To put a hole in something; to pierce; to cling; to become jammed.

stiff adj. Not flexible; not easily bent; awkward. n., Slang A dead body.

sti-fle v. To suffocate; to cut off; to suppress; to keep back.

stig-ma n., pl. **-mata** or **-mas** A mark of disgrace. **stigmata** The part of a flower where pollen is deposited at pollination; wounds resembling the crucifixion scars of Jesus Christ. **stigmatic** adj.

still adj. Silent; calm; peaceful; until now or another time. **still** v., **stillness** n.

still-birth n. The birth of a dead fetus.

stilt n. One of a pair of long poles with foot supports, used for walking.

stim-u-lant n. An agent which arouses or accelerates physiological activity.

stim-u-late v. To excite to a heightened activity; to quicken. **stimulation** n.

stim-u-lus n., pl. **-li** Something that excites to action.

sting v. To prick with something sharp; to feel or cause to feel a smarting pain; to cause or feel sharp pain, either physical or mental. n. The act of stinging; the injury or pain caused by the stinger of a bee or wasp. **stinger** n.

stin-gy adj. Not giving freely; cheap.

stink v. To give off a foul odor that is highly offensive.

stip-u-late v. To settle something by agreement; to establish conditions of agreement. **stipulation** n.

stir v. To mix a substance by moving round and round; to agitate or provoke. **stirrer** n.

stir-rup n. A loop extending from a horse's saddle, used to support the rider's foot.

stitch n. In sewing, a single loop formed by a needle and thread; the section of loop of thread, as in sewing. v. To join with a stitch.

stock n. A supply of goods kept on hand; animals living on a farm; a share in ownership, as in a company or corporation; the raw material or the base used to make something. v. To provide with stock. adj. Regular, common, or typical.

stock-ade n. A barrier placed around a fort for protection.

stock-ing n. A knitted covering for the foot.

stock-y adj. Short and plump; built sturdily.

stole n. A long, narrow scarf that is usually worn around a woman's shoulders, as a mink stole. v. Past tense of steal.

stom-ach n., Anat. The organ into which food passes from the esophagus; one of the primary organs of digestion. v. To tolerate or stand; to put up with.

stone n. Rock; compacted earth or mineral matter; a gem or jewel; the seed or pit of certain fruits. Med. A hard rock that forms inside a body organ, as the kidney. **stoned** To be overcome by an excessive amount of alcohol or drugs.

stood v. Past tense of stand.

stool n. A seat without a backrest and arms; a small version of this on which to rest the feet; a bowel movement.

stoop v. To bend the body forward and downward from the waist. n. A porch attached to a house.

stop v. To cease; to halt; to refrain from moving, operating, or acting; to block or obstruct; to visit for a short time. v. A location where a bus, train, or other means of mass transportation may pick up or drop off passengers. **stoppage** n.

stor-age n. The act of storing or keeping; in Computer Science, the part of a computer in which all information is held; the memory.

store *n.* A business offering merchandise for sale; a supply to be used in the future. *v.* To supply; to accumulate.

stork *n.* A large, wading bird.

storm *n.* An atmospheric condition marked by strong winds with rain, sleet, hail, or snow. *v.* To charge or attack with a powerful force. **stormy** *adj.*

sto-ry *n., pl.* **-ies.** A narration of a fictional tale or account; a lie; a level in a building or house.

stout *adj.* Strong; sturdy; substantial; courageous. **stoutly** *adv.*

stove *n.* An apparatus in which oil, electricity, gas, or other fuels are consumed to provide the heat for cooking.

stow *v.* To pack or put away.

strad-dle *v.* To sit or stand with the legs on either side of something; to favor both sides of an issue. **straddler** *n.*

straight *adj.* Being without bends, angles, or curves; upright; erect; honest; undiluted; unmodified; heterosexual. *n.* In poker, a numerical sequence of five cards not of the same suit. **straightly** *adv.*, **straightness** *n.*

strain *v.* To stretch beyond a proper limit; to injure by putting forth too much effort; to pass through a sieve to separate small particles from larger ones.

strait *n.* A narrow passageway which connects two bodies of water.

strand *n.* Land that borders a body of water; one of the threads that are twisted together to form a rope. *v.* To leave in a difficult situation.

strange *adj.* Not previously known or experienced; odd; peculiar; inexperienced; alien. **strangely** *adv.*, **strangeness** *n.*

stran-ger *n.* A person unknown; a newcomer.

stran-gle *v.* To kill by choking. **-er** *n.*

strap *n.* A long, narrow strip of leather or other material used to secure objects. **strap** *v.*

strat-e-gy *n., pl.* **-ies** The skillful planning and managing of an activity. **strategic** *adj.*, **strategist** *n.*

stra-tum *n., pl.* **-ta** *or* **-tums** A horizontal layer, as of the earth's crust.

straw *n.* A stalk of dried, threshed grain; a slender, plastic or paper straw used to suck up a liquid. *adj.* Yellowish brown.

straw-ber-ry *n.*

A low plant with white flowers and red fruit; the fruit of this plant.

stray *v.* To roam or wander. *n.* A lost or wandering animal or person. **strayer** *n.*

streak *n.* A narrow line or stripe that is different from the surrounding area; a run of good or bad luck. *v.* To rush or move rapidly; to make a streak.

stream *n.* A small body of flowing water; a steady or continuous succession or procession. *v.* To flow in or like a stream.

street *n.* A public thoroughfare in a town or city with buildings on either or both sides.

strength *n.* The quality of being strong; power in general; degree of concentration or potency.

strengthen *v.* To grow strong or stronger.

stren-u-ous *adj.* Necessitating or characterized by vigorous effort or exertion. **strenuously** *adv.*

stress *n.* Special significance; an emphasis given to a specific syllable, word, action, or plan; strain or pressure. **stressful** *adj.*

stretch *v.* To extend fully; to extend forcibly beyond proper limits; to prolong. *n.* The state or act of stretching. **stretchable**, **stretchy** *adj.*

strew *v.* To scatter about.

strick-en *adj.* Suffering, as from an emotion, illness, or trouble.

strict *adj.* Holding to or observing rules exactly; imposing absolute standards. **strictly** *adv.* **strictness** *n.*

stride *v.* To walk with a long, sweeping step.

strike *v.* To hit with the hand; to ignite, as with a match; to afflict suddenly with a disease; to discover; to conclude or make; to stop working as a protest against something or in favor of rules or demands presented to an employer. **strike** *n.*

string *n.* A strip of thin twine, wire, or catgut used on stringed musical instruments; a series of related acts, items, or events; in Computer Science, data arranged in an ascending or descending sequence according to a command within the data.

strin-gent *adj.* Of or relating to strict requirements; marked by obstructions or scarcity. **stringency** *n.*, **-ly** *adv.*

strip *v.* To take off the outer covering; to divest or pull rank; to remove one's clothes; to rob. **strip**, **stripper** *n.*

stripe *n.* A streak, band, or strip of a different color or texture; a piece of material or cloth worn on the sleeve of a uniform to indicate rank, award, or service.

stroke *n.* The movement of striking; a sudden action with a powerful effect; a single movement made by the hand or as if by a brush or pen. *Path.* A sudden interruption of the blood supply to the brain. *v.* To pass the hand over gently.

stroll *v.* To walk in a slow, leisurely way.

strong *adj.* Exerting or possessing physical power; durable; difficult to break. **strongly** *adv.*

stron-ti-um *n.* A metallic element symbolized by Sr.

struc-ture *n.* A construction made up of a combination of related parts. **structure** *v.*, **structural** *adj.*

strug-gle *v.* To put forth effort against

opposition. **struggle,
struggler** n., **strugglingly** adv.

strych-nine n. An extremely poisonous alkaloid derived from certain plants, used to kill rodents and as a neural stimulant.

stub n. A short, projecting part; the short end of something after the main part has been removed or used. **stub** v.

stub-born adj. Inflexible; difficult to control, handle, or manage.

stuc-co n., pl. **-coes** or **-cos** Fine plaster used to coat exterior walls and to decorate interior walls.

stud n. An upright post, as in a building frame, to which sheets of wallboard or paneling are fastened; a small removable button used as an ornament; a male horse used for breeding. **stud** v.

stu-dent n. A person who studies at a school or college.

stu-di-o n. The place of work for an artist, photographer, or other creative person; a place for filming movies.

stud-y n., pl. **-ies** The process of applying the mind to acquire knowledge.

stum-ble v. To trip and nearly fall over something; to come upon unexpectedly. **stumble** n.

stump n. The part of a tree which remains after the top is cut down. v. To puzzle or be puzzled; to walk heavily; to campaign.

stun v. To render senseless by or as if by a blow.

stu-pen-dous adj. Astonishing or highly impressive. **stupendousness** n., **stupendously** adv.

stu-pid adj. Slow in apprehension or understanding. **stupidity** n.

stur-dy adj. Possessing robust strength and health. **sturdily** adv. **sturdiness** n.

stur-geon n. A large freshwater fish highly valued as a source of caviar.

stut-ter v. To speak with involuntary repetitions of sound. **stutter** n.

sty n., pl. **sties** An inflammation of the edge of an eyelid.

style n. A method, manner, or way of performing, speaking, or clothing; elegance, grace, or excellence in performance or appearance. **stylish** adj.

suave adj. Ingratiating; smoothly pleasant in manner.

sub- prefix. Beneath, under, or below.

sub abbr. Substitute.

sub-con-scious adj. Below the level of consciousness. **subconscious** n.

sub-due v. To bring under control by influence, training, persuasion or force.

sub-ject n. The word in a sentence that defines a person or thing; a person who is under the control of another's governing power. v. To subdue or gain control over. **subjection** n.

sub-jec-tive adj. Taking place within, relating to or preceding from an individual's emotions or mind. **subjectively** adv., **subjectivity** n.

sub-ma-rine adj. Operating or existing beneath the surface of the sea. n. A ship that travels underwater. **-er** n.

sub-merge v. To plunge under the surface of the water. **submergible** adj., **submergence** n.

sub-mit v. To give into or surrender to another's authority. **submission**, **submittal** n., **submissive** adj.

sub-or-di-nate adj. Being of lower class or rank; minor; inferior. **subordination** n., **subordinative** adj.

sub-poe-na n. A legal document requiring a person to appear in court for testimony.

sub-se-quent adj. Following in time, place, or order. **subsequently** adv., **subsequentness** n.

sub-side v. To move to a lower level or sink; to become less intense.

sub-sid-i-ar-y adj., pl., n. **-ies**. Providing assistance in a lesser capacity. **subsidiaries** pl., n.

sub-si-dy n., pl. **-dies**. Financial aid granted directly to a private commercial enterprise from the government.

sub-sist v. To have continued existence.

sub-soil n. The layer of earth that comes after the surface soil. **subsoiler** n.

sub-stance n. Matter or material of which anything consists.

sub-sti-tute n. Something or someone that takes the place of another.

sub-ten-ant n. A person who rents property from a tenant.

sub-ter-ra-ne-an adj. Located, situated, or operating underground.

sub-ti-tle n. An explanatory title, as in a document, book, etc.; a written translation that appears at the bottom of a foreign motion picture screen.

sub-tract v. To deduct or take away from.

sub-trop-i-cal adj. Pertaining to regions adjacent to the tropics.

sub-urb n. A residential community near a large city. **suburban** adj.

sub-way n. An underground electrically-powered train, usually used as a means of transportation.

suc-ceed v. To accomplish what is attempted; to come next or to follow.

suc-cess n. Achievement of something intended or desired; attaining wealth, fame, or prosperity.

suc-ces-sion n. The act or process of following in order; sequence; series; the order, sequence or act by which something changes hands.

suc-ces-sive adj. Following in order or sequence. **successively** adv., **-ness** n.

suc-cu-lent adj. Juicy; full of juice or sap. **succulence** n., **succulently** adv.

such adj. Of this or that kind or thing; a great degree or extent in quality. pron. Of a particular degree or kind; a person or thing of such.

suck v. To pull liquid in the mouth by means of a vacuum created by the lips and tongue. n. The action of sucking.

su-crose n. Sugar obtained from the sugar beet or sugar cane.

suc-tion n. The process or act of sucking.

sud-den adj. Happening very quickly without warning or notice; sharp;

abrupt; marked by haste.

suddenly adv., **suddenness** n.

suds pl., n. Bubbles or soapy water.

suede n. Leather with a soft, napped finish.

su-et n. The hard fat around the kidney and loins of sheep.

suf-fer v. To feel pain or distress; to sustain injury, loss, or damage. **sufferer** n.

suf-fi-cient adj. As much that is needed or desired. **sufficiency** n., **-ly** adv.

suf-fix n. A form affixed to the end of a word.

suf-fo-cate v. To kill by depriving something or someone of oxygen. **-ion** n.

sugar n. A sweet, water-soluble, crystalline carbohydrate. Slang A nickname for someone.

sug-gest v. To give an idea for action or consideration; to imply; hint or intimate.

sug-ges-tion n. The act of suggesting; a slight insinuation; hint.

su-i-cide n. The act of taking one's own life. **suicidal** adj.

suit n. A set of articles, as clothing, to be used or worn together; in cards, one of the four sets: spades, hearts, clubs, and diamonds that make up a deck. v. To meet the requirements of; to satisfy.

sul-fur also **sulphur** n. A light, yellow, nonmetallic element occurring naturally in both combined and free form, used in making matches, gunpowder and medicines.

sulk v. To be sullenly silent.

sul-len adj. Ill-humored, melancholy; gloomy; depressing.

sul-try adj. Hot and humid; muggy.

sum n. The result obtained by adding; the whole amount, quantity, or number; summary.

sum-ma-ry n., pl. **-ries.** Giving the sum or substance. adj. A statement covering the main points. **summarily** adv.

sum-mer n. The warmest of the four seasons, following spring and coming before autumn. **summery** adj.

sum-mit n. The top and highest point, degree, or level.

sum-mons n., pl. **-monses.** An order or command to perform a duty; a notice to appear at a certain place.

sun n. The star around which other planets of the solar system orbit; the energy, visible light, and heat, that is emitted by the sun; sunshine. **-ny** adj.

Sun-day n. The Christian holy day; the first day of the week.

sun-down n. The time of day the sun sets.

sunk-en adj. Submerged or deeply depressed in.

su-per adj. Exceeding a norm; in excessive intensity or degree; surpassing most others; superior in rank, status or position; excellent. n. Slang Superintendent of a building.

su-perb adj. Of first-rate quality.

su-per-fi-cial adj. Pertaining to a surface; concerned only with what is not necessarily real.

su-pe-ri-or adj. Of higher rank, grade, or dignity. n. A person who surpasses another in rank or excellence. **superiority** n., **superiorly** adv.

su-per-la-tive adj. Of the highest degree of excellence; pertaining to the degree of comparison of an adverb or adjective that shows extreme extent or level. **superlatively** adv.

su-per-nat-u-ral adj. An order of existence beyond the natural world; pertaining to a divine power. **supernaturally** adv.

su-per-sede v. To take the place of; to set aside.

su-per-son-ic adj., Aero. Characterized by a speed greater than that of sound.

su-per-sti-tion n. A belief founded, despite evidence that it is irrational; a belief, resulting from faith in magic or chance. **superstitious** adj., **-ly** adv.

su-per-vise v. To have charge in directing the work of other people. **supervision, supervisor** n., **-ory** adj.

sup-per n. The last or evening meal of the day.

sup-ple-ment n. A part that compensates for what is lacking. **supplementary, supplemental** adj.

sup-ply v., pl., n. **-plies.** To provide with what is needed; to make available. **supplier** n.

sup-port v. To bear or hold the weight of; to tolerate; to give assistance or approval. **supportable, supportive** adj., **supporter** n.

sup-pose v. To think or assume as true; to consider probable. **supposed** adj., **supposedly** adv.

sup-pos-i-to-ry n., pl. **-ries.** A medication, in solid form, that melts when inserted into the body cavity, as the rectum.

sup-press v. To put an end to something by force.

su-preme adj. Of the highest authority, rank, or power.

sur-charge n. An extra fee added to the cost of something; to overcharge.

sure adj. Firm and sturdy; being impossible to doubt; inevitable; not liable to fail. **surer, surest** adj., **surely** adv.

sur-face n. The exterior or outside boundary of something; outward appearance. **surface** v.

surge v. To increase suddenly. n. A large swell of water.

sur-geon n. A physician who practices surgery.

sur-ger-y n., pl. **-ies.** The branch of medicine in which physical deformity or disease is treated by an operative procedure.

sur-mise v. To guess; to conjecture.

sur-mount v. To overcome; to be at the top.

sur-name n. A person's family's last name.

sur-pass v. To go beyond the limits of; to be greater than. **surpassingly** adv.

sur-plus n. An amount beyond what is needed.

sur-prise v. To come upon unexpectedly or suddenly; to cause to feel amazed or astonished. **surprise, surpriser** n., **surprisingly** adv.

sur-ren-der v. To give up or yield possession or power. n. The act of surrendering.

sur-rey n., pl. -reys. A four-wheeled, horse-driven carriage.

sur-ro-gate n. A person who puts himself in the place of another. **surrogate** v.

sur-round v. To extend around all edges of something; to enclose or shut in.

sur-veil-lance n. Close observation kept over one, especially as a suspect.

sur-vey v., pl., n. -veys. To examine in detail; to determine area, boundaries, or position and elevation of a section of the earth's surface. **surveyor** n.

sur-vive v. To continue to exist; to outlast; to outlive. **surviving** adj., **survival, survivor** n.

su-shi n. A Japanese dish of thin slices of fresh, raw fish.

sus-pect v. To have doubt or distrust; to have a suspicion or inkling of someone or something. **suspect** n.

sus-pend v. To bar from a privilege for a certain time, as a means of punishment; to hang so as to allow free movement.

sus-pense n. The feeling of being insecure or undecided, resulting from uncertainty.

sus-pi-cion n. The instance of suspecting something wrong without proof. **suspicious** adj., **suspiciously** adv.

sus-tain v. To hold up and keep from falling; to suffer or undergo an injury.

su-ture n. The stitching together or joining the edges of an incision or cut.

swab n. A small stick with a wad of cotton on both ends, used to apply medication. Slang A sailor. **swab** v.

swad-dle v. To wrap closely, using a long strip of flannel or linen.

swag-ger v. To walk with a proud or conceited air.

swal-low v. To cause food to pass from the mouth to the stomach; to retract or take back, as words spoken. n. The act of swallowing.

swan n.

A mostly pure white bird having a long neck and heavy body, related to geese.

swap v. To trade something for something in return. **swap** n.

swarm n. A large number of insects, as bees; a large group of persons or things. **swarm** v., **swarmer** n.

swat v. To hit something with a sharp blow.

swatch n. A strip of cloth cut off a larger piece, used as a sample.

swath n. The area or width of grass cut by a machine. **swathe** v.

sway v. To move or swing from right to left or side by side; to exert influence or control.

sway-back n. Unnatural sagging of the back. **swaybacked** adj.

swear v. To make an affirmation under oath. **swearer** n.

sweat v. To excrete a salty moisture from the pores of the skin. Informal To work hard; to cause to sweat. Slang Being impatient; having anxiety.

sweat-er n. A knitted or crocheted garment with or without sleeves attached.

sweat gland n., Anat. One of the tubular glands that secrete sweat externally through pores.

sweep v. To touch very lightly; to remove or clear away with a brush, broom, etc.; to move with an even action.

sweet adj. Having a sugary, agreeable flavor; arousing pleasant emotions; a beloved or dear person.

swell v. To increase in size or bulk; to grow in volume. n. The process, effect, or act of swelling; a continuous wave that is long and billowing. Informal Fine; excellent; smart.

swel-ter v. To suffer from extreme heat.

swerve v. To turn aside from the regular course.

swift adj. Moving with great speed; accomplished or occurring quickly. **swiftly** adv., **swiftness** n.

swim v. To move oneself through water by moving parts of the body, as arms, head, and legs.

swin-dle v. To cheat out of property or money; to practice fraud. **swindle, swindler** n.

swine n., pl. **swine** A hoofed mammal with a snout, related to pigs and hogs; a low, despicable person. **swinish** adj.

swing v. To move freely back and forth; to hang or to be suspended. n. The act of a swing; a seat that hangs from chains or ropes. Music Jazz played by a larger band and developed by using simple harmonic patterns. **swinger** n.

swirl v. To move with a whirling, rotating motion. **swirl** n., **swirly** adj.

switch n. A small, thin, flexible stick, twig or rod. Electr. A device for opening or closing an electric circuit; to shift to another train track by using a switch; to exchange.

swiv-el n. A coupling device, ring, or pivot that allows attached parts to rotate or move freely. **swivel** v.

sword n. A weapon with a long, pointed cutting blade.

Syb-a-rite n. One who is a native to the ancient city of Sybaris.

syc-a-more n. A North American tree that is used widely for shade.

syce n. One who is an attendant as in India.

sy-cee n. The silver money which was once used in China.

sy-co-ni-um n. A type of fleshy fruit where the ovaries are borne in an enlarged receptacle.

sy-co-phan-cy n. The behavior of a sycophant.

sy-co-phant n. A self-seeking flatterer.

sy-co-phan-tic *adj.* Pertaining to a sycophant. **sycophantically** *adv.*

sy-co-sis *n.* An inflammatory disorder of the hair follicles.

sy-enite *n.* A type of igneous rock that is made of feldspar.

syl-la-bary *n.* A listing of syllables.

syl-lab-ic *adj.* Pertaining to or denoting syllables.

syl-la-bic-i-ty *n.* The state of being a syllable.

syl-la-ble *n., Phonet.* A word or part of one that consists of a single vocal impulse, usually consisting of one or more vowels or consonants.

syl-la-bub *n.* A type of dessert that is made by curdling milk with an acid such as wine.

syl-la-bus *n.* An outline of a course of study.

syl-lo-gism *n.* An argument with a major premise, a minor premise and a conclusion that is logically drawn from the premises. **syllogistic** *adj.*

syl-lo-gist *n.* A person who applies syllogistic reasoning.

sylph *n.* A slender woman who is very graceful. **sylphlike** *adj.*

sylph-id *n.* A diminutive sylph.

syl-van *adj.* To be living or located in the woods.

syl-va-nite *n.* A kind of mineral which will often occur in crystals.

syl-vat-ic *adj.* To be affecting wild animals.

syl-vite *n.* A mineral which is a natural potassium chloride and occurs in colorless cubes.

sym *abbr.* Symmetrical; symbol.

sym-bi-ont *n.* An organism that is living in symbiosis.

sym-bi-o-sis *n.* A living together in close union or two dissimilar organisms.

sym-bol *n.* Something that stands for or represents something else. **symbolic, symbolical** *adj.*, **symbolically** *adv.*

sym-bol-ism *n.* The practice of using symbols.

sym-bol-ist *n.* A person who is skilled in the interpretation of symbols.

sym-bol-iza-tion *n.* An instance of symbolizing.

sym-bol-ize *v.* To serve as a symbol of or for something.

sym-bol-o-gy *n.* The interpretation of a symbol or symbols.

sym-met-ri-cal *adj.* Involving symmetry. **symmetricalness** *n.*

sym-me-trize *v.* To make something symmetrical in form or size.

sym-me-try *n., pl.* **-tries.** Balance in form, size, and position of parts that are on two sides of an axis.

sym-pa-thet-ic *adj.* Having or showing kindness or sympathy for others. **sympathetically** *adv.*, **sympathize** *v.*

sympathetic nervous system *n.* Part of the body's nervous system which when stimulated will decrease muscle tone, constriction of the blood vessels, and depresses secretions.

sympathetic vibration *n.* The vibration which is produced in a body by another body.

sym-pa-thin *n.* The substance which is produced by the sympathetic nerve endings in the body.

sym-pa-thize *v.* To respond to someone or something with sympathy.

sym-pa-tho-lyt-ic *adj.* To be tending to oppose physiological results of the sympathetic nervous activity.

sy,-pa-tho-mi-met-ic *adj.* To be able to simulate the sympathetic nervous system in effect and action.

sym-pa-thy *n., pl.* **-thies.** Mutual understanding or affection during a time of sadness or loss.

sym-pa-thy strike *n.* A kind of strike where the strikers have no direct grievance against their own employer but in an attempt to give support to another group.

sym-pat-ric *adj.* To be happening or occurring in the same area.

sym-phon-ic poem *n.* An extended composition for a symphony orchestra in a freer form than a symphony.

sym-pho-ni-ous *adj.* To be agreeing such as in sound.

sym-pho-nist *n.* One who composes or writes symphonies.

sym-pho-ny *n., pl.* **-nies.** A large orchestra with wind, percussion and string sections. **symphonic** *adj.*

sym-phy-se-al *adj.* Pertaining to or related to a symphysis.

sym-phy-sis *n.* A joining or an articulation of bony surfaces by pads of fibrous cartilage and not having a synovial membrane at the joining.

sym-po-di-al *adj.* To be involving the formation of a main axis from a secondary axis. **sympodially** *adv.*

sym-po-si-arch *n.* The person who will preside over a symposium.

sym-po-si-ast *n.* The person or persons who add to or contribute to a symposium.

sym-po-sium *n.* A gathering or meeting where several specialist will give short speeches on a topic or on subjects which are related.

symp-tom *n.* A sign of change in a body's functions or appearance.

symp-tom-at-ic *adj.* To be having the characteristics of a particular disease but arising from something else.

symp-tom-atol-o-gy *n.* The part of medical science that deals with symptoms of a disease or diseases.

syn *abbr.* Synonymous; synonym.

syn-aes-the-sis *n.* The harmony of opposing impulses which are produced by a piece of art.

syn-a-gogue *n.* A place for Jewish worship and prayer.

syn-a-loe-pha *n.* A reduction to one syllable of two vowels of syllables which are adjacent.

synapse *n.* A point where a nervous impulse passes from one neuron to the next neuron.

syn-ar-thro-di-al *adj.* Pertaining to or

related to a synarthrosis.

syn-ar-thro-sis n. A joining of bones that is immovable and is united by fibrous connective tissues.

syn-car-pous adj. To have the carpels of gynoecium to unite in a compound ovary. **syncarpy** n.

syn-chro-mesh adj. To be designed for effecting synchronized gear shifting.

syn-chro-nism n. The state of being synchronous.

syn-chro-ni-za-tion n. A result of synchronizing.

syn-chro-nize v. To operate or take place at the same time.

syn-chro-nous adj. To be existing at precisely the same time.

syn-chro-ny n. A synchroistic treatment or occurrence.

syn-chro-scope n. A device for showing the two associated machines are working in synchronism with one another.

syn-cli-nal adj. To be inclined down from opposidte directions so they meet.

syn-cline n. A section of stratified rock where the beds dip towards each other.

syn-co-pate v. To produce by a synscope. **syncopator** n.

syn-co-pat-ed adj. To be exhibiting syncopation.

syn-co-pe n. The suspension, either complete or partial, of respiration or circulation caused by cerebral ischemia.

syn-cret-ic adj. To be brought about by syncretism.

syn-cre-tism n. A combination of different beliefs or of practices.

syn-cy-tium n. The multinucleate mass made of protoplasm which is formed from the fusion or the joining of cells.

syn-des-mo-sis n. The joining or an articulation where contiguous surfaces of the bones is rough and bound together by a ligament. **syndesmotic** adj.

syn-det-ic adj. To be marked by a conjunctive. **syndetically** adv.

syn-dic n. A type of municipal magistrate in other countries.

syn-di-cal-ism n. A type of revolutionary doctrine in which the workers are able to seize control of the governemtn and economy by direct means such as a strike.

syn-di-cate n. An organization set up to carry out business transactions; a company that sells materials for simultaneous publication at a number of different locations. **syndication** n.

syn-drome n. A set of concurrent symptoms that indicate or characterize a disorder or disease.

syn-ecol-o-gy n. A section or branch of ecology which deals with the development, structure, and distribution of ecological communities. **-ic** adj.

syn-eph-rine n. A type of crystalline sympathomimetic amine.

syn-ere-sis n. A separation of a liquid

from a gel due to constraction.

syn-er-gic adj. To be working together. **synergically** adv.

syn-er-gid n. A small cell lying near the micropyle of the embryo sac of the seed plant.

syn-er-gist n. One that will enhance the effects of an active agent.

syn-er-gis-tic adj. Pertaining or relating to synergism.

syn-er-gy n. An operation as of the muscles.

syn-es-the-sia n. A kind of concomitant sensation.

syn-ga-my n. A type of sexual reproduction through the uniting of the gametes.

syn-o-nym n. A word that means the same or nearly the same as another. **synonymous** adj., **synonymy** n.

syn-op-sis n., pl. **-ses**. A shortened statement or narrative.

syn-os-to-sis n. The joining or the union of bones which are separate to form a single bone.

sy-no-vi-al adj. Pertaining to or relating to synovia.

sy-no-vi-tis n. The inflammation or the swelling of a synovial membrane.

syn-the-sis n. A production of a substance by the joining of chemical elements.

syn-the-size v. To produce or to make with synthesis.

syn-thet-ic adj. To be involving synthesis. **synthetically** adv.

syph-i-lis n. An infectious venereal disease transmissible by direct contact and usually progressing in severity.

syph-i-lol-o-gist n.0 One who specializes in the treatment and the diagnosis of syphilis.

syph-i-lol-o-gy n. The branch of medicine that deals with the disease syphilis.

sy-ringe n. A medical instrument used to inject or draw fluids from the body. **syringe** v.

sy-rin-go-my-elia n. A progressively chronic disease of the spinal cord associated with muscle atrophy, spasticity and sensory disturbances.

syr-up n. A sticky, thick, sweet liquid, used as a topping for food.

sys-tal-tic adj. To be marked by regular dilatation and contraction.

sys-tem n. A method or way of doing something; the human body or related parts of the body that perform vital functions; an orderly arrangement. **systematic** adj., **systematically** adv.

sys-to-le n., Physiol. The regular rhythmic contraction of the heart that pumps blood through the aorta and pulmonary artery. **systolic** adj.

sy-zy-gial adj. To be pertaining to syzygy.

syz-y-gy n. A configuration of three celestial bodies in one gravitational system such as the moon, the sun, and earth when an eclipse is taking place.

T, t The twentieth letter of the English alphabet.

tab *n.* A strip, flap, or small loop that projects from something. *Slang* A bill or total.

tab-ard *n.* A type of sleeveless coat that is worn as a tunic by a knight over top the armor.

tab-by *n.* A type of domestic cat that has a coat which is mottled and striped.

tab-er-na-cle *n.* A portable shelter or structure used by the Jews during their journey out of Egypt; a place of worship.

ta-bes *n.* The wasting that comes with or is accompanying a chronic disease.

ta-bes for-sa-lis *n.* A type of syphilitic disorder that effects the nervous system and is marked with wasting, incorrdination, and pain.

ta-bla *n.* A type of drum which is usually used in pairs of different sizes in the Hindu music.

ta-ble *n.* An article of furniture having a flat top, supported by legs; a collection of related signs, values, or items. *v.* To put off or postpone.

tab-leau *n.* The depiction of a scene that can be presented on a stage by motionless and silent costumed people.

ta-ble-cloth *n.* A type of covering that is placed on the top of tables for protection or for decoration.

ta-ble-ful *n.* The amount that a table is able to accomodate.

ta-ble--hop *v.* To go from one table to another in order to talk with one's friends such as in a restaurant. **-er** *n.*

ta-ble-land *n.* A area of land which is flat and is elevated, such like a table.

ta-ble salt *n.* The salt that is suitable for use in cooking and at the table for the food.

ta-ble-spoon *n.* A unit of measure; a large spoon for serving food.
tablespoonful *n., pl.*, **tablespoonsful**

ta-ble sug-ar *n.* A type of white sugar which is granulated and use in foods.

tab-let *n.* A pad used for writing; a thin, flat piece of stone or wood which is fit for or has an inscription.

ta-ble talk *n.* The conversation which is informal and takes place at the dinner table.

ta-ble ten-nis *n.* A type of game that is like lawn tennis and is played on a table top with a plastic ball and wooden paddles.

ta-ble-top *n.* A top of a table.

ta-ble-ware *n.* The utensils such as forks, knives, and plates that are used on the table to eat with.

ta-ble wine *n.* A type of wine that is served with the food and does not have more that 14 percent alcohol.

tab-loid *n.* A small newspaper.

ta-boo *n.* A custom or rule against doing, using, or mentioning something. *adj.* Forbidden by social authority, convention, or custom.

ta-bor *n.* A type of small drum that has one head made of calf skin.

tab-o-ret *n.* A type of cylindrical seat that is with out a back or arms.

tab-u-lar *adj.* Pertaining to or arranged in a table or list. **tabularly** *adv.*

ta-bu-la ra-sa *n.* A person's mind in its hypothetical empty state before receiving an impression from the outside.

tab-u-late *v.* To put something in a tabular form. **tabulation** *n.*

tab-u-la-tor *n.* Something or someone that tabulates.

TAC *abbr.* Tactical Air Command.

ta-chom-e-ter *n.* An instrument for measuring velocity and speed.

tachy-car-dia *n.* A rapid heart beat.

tachy-lyte *n.* A type of black basalt which is glossy in appearance.

ta-chym-e-ter *n.* A device that is used to determine bearings or distances quickly.

tac-it *adj.* Understood; expressed or implied nonverbally; implicit.
tacitly *adv.*, **tacitness** *n.*

tac-i-turn *adj.* To be temperamentally disinclined to speak or to talk.

tack *n.* A small, short nail with a flat head; a sewing stitch used to hold something temporarily; the changing of a sailboat from one direction to another. *v.* To change the direction in which a sailboat is going. **tacker** *n.*

tack-board *n.* A type of board that can be made of cork and used for the purpose of tacking notices up.

tack claw *n.* A small tool used to remove tacks.

tacki-fy *v.* To cause or to make something tacky. **tackifier** *n.*

tacki-ly *adv.* To be done in a tacky manner.

tacki-ness *n.* The state of being tacky.

tack-le *n.* Equipment used for fishing or other sports or occupations; an apparatus of ropes and pulley blocks for pulling and hoisting heavy loads. In football, a position on a football team; the lineman between the guard and end. **tackled** *v.*, **tackler** *n.*

tack-y *adj.* Slightly sticky; shabby; lacking style or good taste; flashy.

ta-co *n., pl.* **-cos** A type of Mexican or Spanish food made of a tortilla folded over with a filling inside.

tac-o-nite *n.* A type of flint-like rock which can be considered a low-grade iron ore.

tact *n.* Having the ability to avoid what would disturb or offend someone.
tactful, tactless *adj.*, **tactfully,**
tactlessly *adv.*, **tactfulness** *n.*

tac-tic *n.* A way or method of working toward a goal; the art of using strategy to gain military objectives or other goals. **tactical** *adj.*, **tactician** *n.*

tac-tics *n.* The art of disposing of forces in combat or war.

tac-tile *adj.* To be pertaining to the sense of touch. **tactilely** *adv.*

tac-til-i-ty *n.* The responsiveness of someone or thing to stimulation of the sense of touch.

tact-less *adj.* To be marked by a lack of

tact. **tactlessness** n., **tactlessly** adv.
tad n. A small boy; an insignificant degree or amount.

tad-pole n.

The early stage in the growth of a frog or toad during which it breathes by external gills, has a long tail, and lives in the water; a polliwog.

tae-nia n. A type of Greek fillet of ancient times.
tae-nia-cide n. The agent which will kill or destroy tapeworms.
tae-ni-a-sis n. A type of disease that can be caused by tapeworms.
taf-fe-ta n. A stiff, smooth fabric of rayon, nylon, or silk.
taf-fe-tized adj. To be having a finish that is crisp in nature.
taff-rail n. The rail around the stern of a boat or ship.
taf-fy n. A type of candy which is boiled and is made of brown sugar and it is pulled until it becomes porous.
taf-ia n. A type of rum of West India that is made from distilled sugarcane juice.
Taft, William H. n. The 27th president of the United States from 1909-1913.
tag n. A piece of plastic, metal, paper, or other material that is attached to something in order to identify it; a children's game in which one child is "it" and tries to catch another child, who then becomes "it." **tagger** n.
tag-along n. The person that follows the lead of another person.
tag-board n. A type of cardboard that is used for that making of shipping tags.
tag end n. A random bit.
tag up v. To touch base in the game of baseball before one runs after a fly ball is caught.
Ta-hi-tian n. A person who is a native or living in Tahiti.
tah-sil-dar n. One who is a revenue officer in the country of India.
Tai n. A group of people of southeast Asia.
tai-ga n. The moist subarctic forest which will begin where the tundra ends and contains firs and spruces.
tail n. The posterior extremity, extending from the end or back of an animal. Tails The opposite side of a coin from heads; formal evening dress for men. v. To follow or keep close watch on someone.
tail-back n. The position in football that is the farthest back on the offensive side from the line of scrimmage.
tail-coat n. A type of coat that has tails.
tail end n. The end of something or one.
tail fin n. The fin that is located on the tail of a fish.
tail-gate n. The hinged gate at the back of a truck or automobile for loading and unloading. v. To follow very closely in a car.
taille n. A type of tax that was levied by

a French king on his subjects or the land that they held in their possession.
tail-light n. A red light that is at the rear of a car or other vehicle for the purposing of warning other cars behind it.
tai-lor n. One whose profession is making, mending, and altering clothing. v. To adapt for a specific purpose.
tai-lor-bird n. Type of warbler that will stitch leaves together in order to build their nests.
tai-lored adj. To be made by a tailor.
tail-or-ing n. The occupation of a tailor
tail-or's chalk n. A type of chalk that is used by tailors in order to make a temporary mark on the cloth they are using.
tail pipe n. A pipe that will discharge gases for the muffler.
tail-spin n. An emotional collapse.
tail-wa-ter n. The water which can be found below a dam.
taint v. To spoil, contaminate, or pollute. n. A blemish or stain.
tai-pan n. One who is a foreigner and living in China wielding an economic power.
take v. To seize or capture; to get possession of; to receive, swallow, absorb, or accept willingly; to attack and surmount; to move, convey, or conduct to a different place; to require; to choose or pick. n. The process of acquiring; the total receipts for admission at an event. Slang To cheat; to subtract.
take back v. To make or state a retraction of something such as a statement.
take down v. To lower the vanity of someone.
take in v. To receive as a lodger; to encompass something within the limits of something else.
take on v. To deal with something or someone.
talc n. A soft, fine-grained, smooth mineral used in making talcum powder.
tal-cum pow-der n. A type of powder that is made of talc and a antiseptic.
tale n. A story or recital of relating events that may or may not be true; a malicious or false story; gossip.
tale-bear-er n. A person who will spread gossip. **talebearing** adj. or n.
tal-ent n. The aptitude, disposition, or characteristic ability of a person.
talented, talentless adj.
tal-ent scout n. A person who discovers and recruits people with talent for a specialized activity or field.
ta-lent show n. A type of show which consists of a series of individual performances which are done by amateurs.
ta-ler n. A silver coin which was issued by German states in the 15th to the 19th centuries.
talk v. To communicate by words or speech; to engage in chatter or gossip. n. A speech or lecture, usually given to a group of people. Slang To boast; to brag. **talker, talkativeness** n.,

talkative adj., **talkatively** adv.

talk down v. To belittle someone by talking.

talk o·ver v. To consider something in a conversation between persons.

talky adj. To be containing or having too much talk in something.

tall adj. Of greater than average height; of a designated or specified height; imaginary, as a tall tale. **tallness** n., **tallish** adj.

tal·lage n. A fee that is paid a lord for his feudal tenant.

tall-boy n. A type of chest of drawers where the top section is smaller that the lower section.

tal·low n. Hard fat rendered from sheep or cattle, used to make candles, lubricants, and soap. **tallow** adj.

tal·ly n., pl. **-ies** A record or counting of money, amounts, or scores. v. To agree with; to reckon or figure a score; to count.

tal·ly·man n. The person who checks or has a record of accounting.

tal·on n. A long, curved claw found on birds or animals. **taloned** adj.

ta·lus n. The slope which is formed by the gathering or accumulation of rock debris.

ta·ma·le n. The meat that is seasoned chili and then is rolled into a corn meal dough and is steamed.

tam·a·rind n. A type of leguminous tree that has hard wood and red-striped yellow flowers.

tam·bour n. A type of frame that can be used used for the purpose of embroidering.

tam·bou·rine n.

A percussion instrument made of a small drum with jingling metal disks around the rim.

tame adj. Not wild or ferocious; domesticated or manageable. v. To make docile or calm. **tamely** adv., **tamer**, **tameness** n.

tame·less adj. Being unable to be tamed.

tam·per v. To change, meddle, or alter something; to use corrupt measures to scheme. **tamperproof** adj., **-er** n.

tan v. To cure a hide into leather by using chemicals. n. A brownish skin tone caused by exposure to the sun.

tan·a·ger n. A type of American passerine bird which can be found in the woodlands.

tan-bark n. A type of bark that is rich in tannin and is used in the tanning process.

tan·dem n. Any arrangement that involves two or more things, animals or persons arranged one behind the other.

tan·dem bi·cy·cle n. A type of bicycle that was built for two persons.

tang n. A sharp, distinct taste, smell, or quality; a slender shank that projects from a tool and connects to a handle.

tan·ge·lo n. The hybrid that is between a tangerine and a pomelo or grapefruit.

tan·gent n. A line that touches a curved line but does not intersect or cross it; a sudden change from one course to another. **tangency** n., **tangential** adj.

tan·ger·ine n. A small citrus fruit with an easily peeled orange skin, resembling an orange.

tan·gi·ble adj. Capable of being appreciated or felt by the sense of touch; capable of being realized. **tangibility, tangibleness** n., **tangibly** adv.

tan·gle v. To mix, twist, or unite in a confused manner making separation difficult. **tangle, tanglement** n.

tan·gled adj. To be in a state of disorder.

tan·gly adj. To be full of tangles.

tan·go n. A ballroom dance with long, gliding steps. **tango** v.

tan·gram n. A type of Chinese puzzle that is made by cutting a square of material into different shapes, such as five triangles, a rhomboid, and a square and they are able to be combined in different figures.

tank n. A large container for holding or storing a gas or liquid. **tankful** n.

tank·age n. The contents of a tank.

tank·ard n. A large drinking mug, usually with a hinged top.

tank·er n. A type of boat that is fitted with tanks for the carrying of liquid in bulk.

tank farm n. An area that has tanks and is used used for the purpose of storing oil.

tan·nage n. A process of tanning something.

tan·nery n. The place where tanning is done.

tan·ning n. The browning of the skin with an exposure to the sun.

tan oak n. A type of evergreen oak that will yield tanbark.

tan·tal·ic adj. To be pertaining to tantalum.

tan·ta·lite n. The mineral that is made of dark oxide of iron, tantalum, manganese, and columbium.

tan·ta·lize v. To tease or tempt by holding or keeping something just out of one's reach. **tantalizer** n., **tantalizingly** adv.

tan·ta·liz·ing adj. To have a quality that stimulates an interest.

tan·ta·lum n. A metallic element symbolized by Ta.

tan·ta·mount adj. To be equivalent in effect, significance, or value.

tan·ta·ra n. A blare of the horn or trumpet.

tan·trum n. A fit; an outburst or a rage of bad temper.

tan·yard n. The part of the tannery that is used to house the tanning vats.

tan·za·nite n. A type of mineral that is a blue variety of zoisite.

tap v. To strike repeatedly, usually while making a small noise; to strike or touch gently; to make secret contact with something. In medicine, to remove fluids from the body. **tapper** *n.*

tap dance *n.* A type of step dance that is tapped out by the means of shoes that have taps on them. **tap dancer** *n.*

tape *n.* A narrow strip of woven fabric; a string or ribbon stretched across the finish line of a race. **tape** *v.*

tape grass *n.* A type of submerged plant that has leaves which are long and ribbonlike.

tape mea-sure *n.* A strip of cloth or other material that is marked off in units of measure and is used to measure things.

ta-per *n.*

A very slender candle. *v.* To become gradually smaller or thinner at one end.

ta-per-er *n.* The person who bears or carries a taper in a religious procession.

tap-es-tried *adj.* To be decorated with tapestry.

tap-es-try *n.*, *pl.* -ies A thick fabric woven with designs and figures.

ta-pe-tum *n.* The layer of the nutritive cells that is found in the sporogenous tissue.

tape-worm *n.* A type of cestode worm that is parasitic and found in the intestine of animals or of man.

tap-i-o-ca *n.* A bead-like substance used for thickening and for puddings.

ta-pis *n.* The tapestry material that is used for table coverings and hangings.

tap-ping *n.* Process where something is tapped.

tap-pet hen *n.* A hen that is crested.

tap-root *n.* A root that will grow vertically downward and has other lateral roots.

taps *n., pl. Mil.* A bugle call that signals lights out, also sounded at memorial and funeral services.

tap-ster *n.* The person who is hired to dispense liquors in a barroom.

tar *n.* A black bituminous viscous liquid that is made or obtained by the destructive distillation of organic matter.

tar-an-tel-la *n.* A type of folk dance of Italy.

ta-ran-tu-la *n.* A type of spider which is hairy and slow and not really poisonous to man.

ta-rax-a-cum *n.* A dried root of the dandelion which can be used as a tonic and diuretic.

tar-dy *adj.* Late; not on time; delayed past the expected time. **tardily** *adv.*, **tardiness** *n.*

tare *n.* An element which is undesirable.

targe *n.* A type of light shield.

tar-get *n.* An object marked to shoot at; an aim or goal.

tar-get date *n.* A date which has been set for the completion of something.

tar-iff *n.* Duty or tax on merchandise coming into or going out of a country.

tar-la-tan *n.* A type of cotton fabric that is heavily sized for stiffness.

tarn *n.* A type of steep-banked mountain pool.

tar-nish *v.* To become discolored or dull; to lose luster; to spoil. **tarnish** *n.*, **tarnishable** *adj.*

tar-nished plant bug *n.* A type of bug that is destructive to plants because it will suck the sap for the leaves, buds, and fruits.

ta-ro *n.* A type of plant of the arum family and is grown in the tropics for its rootstocks which can be eaten.

tar-ok *n.* The card game that was popular in Europe and was played with a deck of 40, 52, or 56 cards.

tar-ot *n.* A set of 22 cards used for fortune-telling, each card showing a virtue, an elemental force, or a vice.

tar pa-per *n.* A type of paper which is heavy and is impregnated with tar and used in building.

tar-pau-lin *n.* A sheet of waterproof canvas used as a protective covering.

tar-ra-gon *n.* A type of European wormwood that is grown for its aromatic foliage.

tar-ry *v.* To linger, delay, or hesitate.

tar-sal *adj.* To be pertaining to the tarsus.

tar-si-er *n.* A type of nocturnal mammal of East India which is related to the lemurs.

tar-sus *n.* A bone of the foot or hand which makes up the ankle or the wrist.

tart *adj.* Sharp; sour; cutting, biting in tone or meaning. **tartly** *adv.*, **-ness** *n.*

tar-tan *n.* A plaid fabric pattern of Scottish origin. **tartan** *adj.*

tar-tar *n.* The reddish, acidic, crust-like deposit which forms as grape juice turns to wine; a hard deposit which forms on the teeth, composed of secretions, food, and calcium salts. **tartaric** *adj.*

TAS *abbr.* Telephone answering service.

task *n.* A bit of work, usually assigned by another; a job.

task-mas-ter *n.* A person who imposes labor upon another person.

task-mis-tress *n.* A woman who is a taskmaster.

tasse *n.* An overlapping plate in a suit of armor which will make a short skirt below the waist.

tas-sel *n.*

An ornamental decoration made from a bunch of string or thread.

taste *n.* The ability to sense or determine flavor in the mouth; a personal liking or disliking. *v.* To test or sense flavors in the mouth. **tasteful**, **tasteless** *adj.*, **taster** *n.*

taste bud *n.* An organ on the tongue that will mediate the sensation of taste.

taste-mak-er *n.* A person who will set a standard of what is fashionable.

tasty *adj.* To have a taste which is pleasing. **tastiness** *n.*

TAT *abbr.* Thematic apperception test.

ta-ta-mi *n.* The straw matting which is used as a covering for the floor in the Japanese home.

tat-ter *n.* A torn scrap of cloth. *v.* To become or make ragged.

tat-ter-de-ma-lion *n.* One who is dressed in clothing that is ragged.

tat-tered *adj.* To be torn into pieces or shreds.

tat-tered-sail *n.* The pattern of colored lines which form squares.

tat-ting *n.* A type of handmade lace.

tat-tle *v.* To reveal the secrets of another by gossiping. **tattler** *n.*

tat-tle-tale *n.* One who betrays secrets concerning others; a person, usually a child, who informs on others.

tat-too *n.* A permanent design or mark made on the skin by pricking and inserting an indelible dye. **tattooer** *n.*

tat-ty *adj.* To be frayed.

taught *v.* Past tense of teach.

taunt *v.* To mock or insult someone.

taupe *n.* A color which is a brownish gray.

tau-rine *adj.* To be pertaining to a bull.

Tau-rus *n.* The second sign of the zodiac; a person born between April 20 - May 20.

taut *adj.* Tight; emotionally strained. **tautly** *adv.*, **tautness** *n.*

tau-tog *n.* A type of fish that is found along the Atlantic coast of the U.S.

tau-tol-o-gy *n., pl.* -ies Redundancy; a statement which is an unnecessary repetition of the same idea.

tau-to-mer-ic *adj.* To be pertaining to tautomerism.

tav-ern *n.* An inn; an establishment or business licensed to sell alcoholic drinks.

tav-ern-er *n.* A person who runs a tavern.

taw *v.* To dress such as skins by a dry process.

taw-dry *adj.* To be gaudy in appearance. **tawdriness** *n.*

taw-pie *n.* A person who is foolish.

tax *n.* A payment imposed and collected from individuals or businesses by the government. *v.* To strain. **taxable** *adj.*, **taxation, taxer, taxpayer** *n.*

tax eva-sion *n.* The failure, which is deliberate, to pay taxes.

tax--ex-empt *adj.* Exempted from tax; bearing tax-free interest on federal or state income.

taxi *v.* To travel or to move at a slow speed.

taxi-cab *n.* A vehicle that is used to transport people for a fare.

taxi-der-my *n.* The art of stuffing and mounting animals for displaying.

taxi-me-ter *n.* The device which is used in a taxicab to record the money that is owed by the passenger.

taxi-stand *n.* The place where a taxi will park while the driver waits for a passenger.

tax-pay-er *n.* A person who pays a tax.

tax-pay-ing *adj.* Pertaining to the paying of taxes by someone.

tax shel-ter *n.* A credit or allowance that reduces taxes on current earnings for an individual investor or corporation.

tax stamp *n.* The stamp which is placed on something to show that the tax for it has been paid.

Taylor, Zachary *n.* The 12th president of the United States from 1849-1850, died in office.

TBA *abbr.* To be announced.

tbs *abbr.* Tablespoon.

tchr *abbr.* Teacher.

TDY *abbr.* Temporary duty.

tea *n.* A small tree or bush which grows where the climate is very hot and damp; a drink made by steeping the dried leaves of this shrub in boiling water.

tea bag *n.* A filter paper bag that holds tea.

tea-board *n.* A type of tray which is used used for the purpose of serving tea.

tea-bowel *n.* A type of teacup that does not have a handle.

teach *v.* To communicate skill or knowledge; to give instruction or insight. **teachability, teachableness, teaching** *n.*, **-able** *adj.*

teach-er *n.* A person who teaches; one who instructs.

teach-er-ship *n.* A position of teaching.

teach-er's pet *n.* A student in the class who gets the special attention of the teacher.

teach-ing aid *n.* The device which is used to help reinforce the classroom instructions.

tea-cup *n.* A type of cup that is used for hot beverages. **teacupful** *n.*

teak *n.* A type of tall tree of East India that can be used for shipbuilding.

teal blue *n.* A color which is a greenish blue.

team *n.* Two or more players on one side in a game; a group of people trained or organized to work together; two or more animals harnessed to the same implement. *v.* To join or work together.

tea mak-er *n.* A type of covered spoon which is used for making tea in a cup.

team-mate *n.* A person who is a team with others.

team-ster *n.* A person who drives a team of animals or a vehicle as an occupation.

tea party *n.* A gathering that takes place in the afternoon where tea is served.

tea-pot *n.* A container that tea is brewed in.

tea-poy *n.* A type of stand for a tea service.

tear *v.* To become divided into pieces; to separate; to rip into parts or pieces; to move fast; to rush. *n.* A rip or torn place.

tear *n.* A fluid secreted by the eye to

moisten and cleanse. *v.* To cry.

tear-down *n.* The process of taking something apart.

tear-ful *adj.* To be accompanied by tears. **tearfulness** *n.*

tear gas *n.* A type of gaseous substance that will blinds the eye with tears.

tear-jerk-er *n.* A story that is pathetic. **tear-jerking** *n.*

tea-room *n.* A type of room in a restaurant that is designed for the female clientele.

tea rose *n.* A type of rose that descend from the Chinese rose.

tear-stain *n.* The streak that is left by a tear. **tearstained** *adj.*

tear up *v.* To remove or to damage something.

teary *adj.* To be stained with tears.

tease *v.* To make fun of; to bother; to annoy; to tantalize. *n.* A person who teases. **teaser** *n.*, **teasingly** *adv.*

tea-sel *n.* A type of herb which is prickly and is used in the wool industry.

tea ser-vice *n.* The set of china which contains the items needed to serve tea, such as a tray, cups, and a teapot.

teat *n.* The protuberance that milk flows out of.

tea-time *n.* A time for serving the tea.

tec *abbr.* Technician.

tech *abbr.* Technical; technician.

tech-ne-tium *n.* A metallic element symbolized by Tc.

tech-ne-tron-ic *adj.* To be pertaining to a society that is shaped by the impact of technology.

tech-ni-cal *adj.* Expert; derived or relating to technique; relating to industry or mechanics. **technically** *adv.*

tech-ni-cal-i-ty *n.* The state of something being technical.

tech-ni-cian *n.* A person who is a specialist in the technical details of a subject.

tech-nique *n.* A technical procedure or method of doing something.

tech-no-crat *n.* A person who is a member of a technocracy.

tech-no-crat-ic *adj.* To be pertaining to a technocracy.

technol *abbr.* Technology.

tech-nol-o-gist *n.* A person who is a specialist in technology.

tech-nol-o-gy *n.*, *pl.* **-ies** The application of scientific knowledge to serve man in industry, commerce, medicine and other fields.

tec-ton-ic *adj.* To be pertaining to the deformation of the crust of the earth. **tectonically** *adv.*

tec-ton-ics *n.* The art of construction and building of things, such as a building.

ted *v.* To turn and scatter something, such as grass for drying purposes.

ted-der *n.* Someone or something that teds.

ted-dy bear *n.* A type of bear that is stuffed and used as a child's toy.

te-di-ous *adj.* Boring; taking a long time. **tediously** *adv.*

te-di-um *n.* The state of being tedious.

tee *n.*

A peg used to hold a golf ball on the first stroke toward a hole or goal post; a peg used to support a football during a field goal attempt. **tee** *v.*

teed off *adj.* To be very angry.

teem *v.* To abound; to be full of; to swarm or crowd.

teen-ag-er *n.* A young adult who is in their teen years of life, such as 13 to 19 years old.

teens *pl.*, *n.* The ages between 13 and 19; the years of one's life between 13 and 19.

tee-ter *v.* To about in an unsteady manner.

teeth *pl.*, *n.* The plural of tooth.

teethe *v.* To grow one's teeth.

teeth-er *n.* An object which can be used by a baby while they are cutting teeth.

teff *n.* A type of grass which is grown for its grain in Africa.

tel-e-cast *n.* A television broadcast.

tel-e-com-mu-ni-ca-tion *n.* The communication between two points which are a great distance away from each other.

tel-e-course *n.* A school course which can be taught over the television.

tel-e-film *n.* A movie or picture which has been made or produced for television.

tel-e-gram *n.* A message sent or received by telegraph. **telegram** *v.*

tel-e-graph *n.* A system for communicating; a transmission sent by wire or radio. *v.* To send messages by electricity over wire. **telegrapher**, **telegraphist** *n.*, **telegraphic** *adj.*

tel-e-graph plant *n.* A type of tick trefoil of East India whose leaflets move up and down.

tele-man *n.* The petty officer of the navy who will do coding, clerical, and communication work.

te-le-ost *n.* The group of fishes that have a bony skeleton. **teleostean** *adj.*

te-lep-a-thy *n.* Communication by means of mental processes rather than ordinary means. **-ic** *adj.*, **telepathist** *n.*

tel-e-phone *n.* A system or device for transmitting conversations by wire. **telephone** *v.*, **telephoner** *n.*

tel-e-phone booth *n.* The booth where a telephone can be located and one makes a call while standing up.

tel-e-phone di-rec-to-ry *n.* The book which lists numbers, names, and addresses of people who have a telephone.

tel-e-phone num-ber *n.* The number which has been given to a person and one is able to call this person with this number.

tel-e-phon-ic *adj.* To be able to convey sound. **telephonically** *adv.*

tel-e-pho-to *adj.* Relating to a camera lens which produces a large image of a distant object. **telephotograph** n.

tel-e-pho-to-graph-ic adj. To be pertaining to the process of telephotography.

tel-e-play n. A type of play which has been written for the television.

tel-e-scope n. An instrument which contains a lens system which makes distant objects appear larger and nearer. **telescopic** adj.

tel-e-sis n. The progress which is directed and planned in an intelligent manner.

tel-e-thon n. A long telecast used to raise money for a worthy cause.

tel-e-view v. To watch something by the means of a television receiver.

tel-e-vise v. To broadcast some show with the use of a television.

tel-e-vi-sion n. Reception and transmission of images on a screen with sound; the device that reproduces television sounds and images.

tel-e-vis-or n. The apparatus that will transmit or will receive for a television.

tel-ex n. Teletype communications by means of automatic exchanges.

te-lio-spore n. A type of chlamydospore that is thick-walled and in its final stage in the life cycle of the rust fungus.

tell v. To relate or describe; to command or order. **tellable, telling** adj.

tell-er n. A person who will relate or tell.

tell-tale n. The device for recording something.

tel-lu-ri-an adj. To be pertaining to the earth.

tel-lu-ri-um n. An element symbolized by Te; a semimetallic element.

tel-lu-rom-e-ter n. The device that will measure the distance with the used of microwaves.

tel-lu-rous adj. To be pertaining to tellurium.

telo-phase n. The phase in the process of cell division, mitosis, which occurs last.

tel-pher n. A type of car which is suspended an aerial cables.

tel-son n. The segment of an arthropod that is the terminal part.

tem-er-ar-i-ous adj. To be rash or daring. **temerariousness** n.

temp abbr. Temperature.

tem-per n. The state of one's feelings. v. To modify something, making it flexible or hard. **temperable** adj.

tem-per-a-ment n. Personality; a characteristic way of thinking, reacting, or behaving. **temperamental** adj.

tem-per-ance n. Moderation; restraint; moderation or abstinence from drinking alcoholic beverages.

tem-per-ate adj. Avoiding extremes; moderate. **temperately** adv., **-ness** n.

tem-per-ate zone n. A region that is between the arctic circle and the tropic of Cancer or between the antarctic circle and the tropic of Capricorn.

tem-per-a-ture n. A measure of heat or cold in relation to the body or environment; an elevation in body temperature above the normal 98.6 degrees Fahrenheit.

tem-pest n. A severe storm, usually with snow, hail, rain, or sleet.

tem-pes-tu-ous adj. To be pertaining to a tempest. **tempestuousness** n.

tem-plate n. A mold which is used to guide something, such as a saw.

tem-ple n. A place of worship; the flat area on either side of the forehead.

tem-po n., pl. **-pos** or **-pi** Mus. The rate of speed at which a musical composition is to be played.

tem-po-ral adj. To be pertaining to earthly life. **temporally** adv.

tem-po-ral bone n. A bone which is located on the side of the skull above the ear.

tem-po-ral-i-ty n. The state of being temporal.

tem-po-rar-y adj. Lasting for a limited amount of time; not permanent.

tempt n. To encourage or draw into a foolish or wrong course of action; to lure. **temptation, tempter** n.

tempt-ing adj. To have an appeal to something. **temptingly** adv.

tem-pu-ra n. The vegetables or seafood which is dipped in batter and then fried.

ten n. The cardinal number equal to 9 + 1; the number before eleven.

ten-a-ble adj. Being able to be held.

te-na-cious adj. Persistent; stubborn. **tenaciously** adv., **tenaciousness** n.

te-nac-i-ty n. The state of being tenacious.

te-nac-u-lum n. A type of sharp-pointed hook that is used in surgery for holding onto body parts such as arteries.

ten-ant n. A person who pays rent to occupy another's property. **tenantless, tenantable** adj.

ten-ant farm-er n. The farmer who will work the land that is owned by another person and pays rent with his crops.

tench n. A type of fish that is related to the dace and has an ability to survive outside the water.

Ten Commandments n. The ten rules of moral behavior which were given to Moses by God.

tend v. To be inclined or disposed; to be directed; to look after.

ten-dance n. The people in attendance.

ten-den-cy n., pl. **-ies** A disposition to act or behave in a particular way; a particular direction, mode, outcome, or direction.

ten-den-tious adj. To be marked by a tendency in favor to a point of view. **tendentiousness** n., **tendentiously** adv.

ten-der adj. Fragile; soft; not hard or tough; painful or sore when touched. n. Something offered as a formal bid or offer; compassionate; a supply ship. v. To make an offer to buy or purchase; to present, as a resignation. **tenderhearted, tenderly** adv., **-ness** n.

ten-der-foot *n.* A beginner who is inexperienced in something.

ten-der-ize *v.* To make something to become tender with applying a process that will break down the connective tissues. **tenderizer, tenderization** *n.*

ten-der-loin *n.* A cut of tender pork or beef.

ten-der--mind-ed *adj.* To be marked by dogmatism.

ten-der-om-e-ter *n.* A device that is used to determine the tenderness of vegetables and fruit samples.

ten-di-ni-tis *n.* The swelling and the inflammation of a tendon.

ten-di-nous *adj.* To be pertaining to or related to a tendon.

ten-don *n.* A band of tough, fibrous tissues that connect, a muscle and bone.

ten-dril *n.*

A thread-like part of a climbing plant which attaches itself to a support. **-ed** *or* **tendrilled** *adj.*

ten-e-brif-ic *adj.* To be causing darkness.

ten-e-brous *adj.* To be hard to understand.

te-net *n.* A belief or principle that is generally held to be true.

ten-fold *adj.* to have ten members.

Tenn *abbr.* Tennessee.

Ten-nes-see *n.* A state located in the central southeastern part of the United States.

ten-nis *n.* A sport played with a ball and racket by 2 or 4 people on a rectangular court.

ten-or *n.* An adult male singing voice, above a baritone.

te-no-syn-o-vi-tis *n.* The swelling and inflammation of a tendon sheath.

ten-pen-ny *adj.* To be costing ten pennies.

ten-pen-ny nail *n.* A type of nail which can measure three inches long.

ten-pin *n.* A bowling pin.

tense *adj.* Taut or stretched tightly; nervous; under strain. **tense** *v.*

ten-sile *adj.* To be pertaining to or containing tension.

tensile strength *n.* The greatest longitudinal stress that can be applied without tearing apart.

ten-sim-e-ter *n.* A type of device that can be used to measure differences of vapor pressure.

ten-si-om-e-ter *n.* A type of device that is used to measure tension; an instrument that determines the moisture level of soil.

ten-sion *n.* The condition of stretching or the state of being stretched. **tensional, tensionless** *adj.*

ten-si-ty *n.* The state of being tense.

ten-sive *adj.* To be causing tension.

ten-sor *n.* The muscle that will stretch a particular part of the body.

ten--strike *n.* A successful achievement.

tent *n.*

A portable shelter made by stretching material over a supporting framework. **tentless** *adj.*

ten-ta-cle *n.* A long, unjointed, flexible body part that projects from certain invertebrates, as the octopus. **tentacled** *adj.*

ten-tac-u-lar *adj.* Resembling or related to tentacles.

tent-age *n.* A group of tents.

ten-ta-tive *adj.* Experimental; subject to change; not definite. **tentatively** *adv.*

tent cat-er-pil-lar *n.* A type of caterpillar that is destructive and will make a large silken web on trees.

tent-ed *adj.* To be covered with a tent.

ten-ter *n.* A frame having clips or hooks along two side and is used for stretching and drying cloth.

ten-ter-hook *n.* A sharp hook or clip used to fasten cloth on a tenter.

tenth--rate *adj.* To be of the lowest quality.

tent-mak-er *n.* A person who makes tents.

tent stitch *n.* A slanted short stitch to the right used in embroidery to form a solid background of even lines.

te-nu-ity *n.* The lack of thickness of something.

ten-u-ous *adj.* To have little strength. **tenuousness** *n.*

ten-ure *n.* The right, state, or period of holding something, as an office or property. **tenured,** **tenurial** *adj.,* **tenurially** *adv.*

te-o-sin-te *n.* A type of annual fodder grass of Central America and Mexico.

te-pee *n.* A tent made of hides or bark used by the Indians of North America.

teph-ra *n.* A type of solid material that is ejected for the volcano when it erupts and it is carried in the air.

tep-id *adj.* Lukewarm. **tepidly** *adv.,* **tepidness** *n.*

te-qui-la *n.* A type of Mexican liquor.

terr *abbr.* Territory.

te-rai *n.* A type of wide-brimmed felt hat that is worn by the people in subtropical areas.

ter-a-to-log-i-cal *adj.* To be abnormal in structure or the growth.

ter-a-to-ma *n.* A type of tumor that is made up of a heterogeneous mixture of the tissues. **teratomatous** *adj.*

ter-bi-um *n.* A metallic element of the rare-earth group symbolized by Tb.

ter-cen-ten-a-ry *n., pl.* **-ries.** The time span of 300 years; a 300th anniversary.

ter-cet *n.* A group of three lines of verse.

ter-e-binth *n.* A type of European tree that belongs to the sumac family and will yield Chian turpentine.

ter-e-bin-thine *adj.* To be pertaining to or resembling turpentine.

te-rete *adj.* To be almost cylindrical but to be tapering at both ends.

ter-gi-ver-as-tion *n.* The evasion of a clear-cut statement.

ter-gum *n.* A plate of an arthropod that is a dorsal section.

ter-i-ya-ki *n.* A type of Japanese dish where the ingredients are soaked in soy sauce then grilled.

term *n.* A phrase or word; a limited time or duration; a phrase having a precise meaning. *Math* The quantity of two numbers either added together or subtracted.

term-er *n.* One who serves or hold an office for a certain amount of time or a term.

ter-mi-na-ble *adj.* Being capable of being terminated or destroyed.

ter-mi-nal *adj.* Of, forming, or located at the end; final. *n.* A station at the end of a bus line, railway, or airline; In Computer Science, the instrument through which data enters or leaves a computer.

ter-mi-nate *v.* To bring to a conclusion or end; to finish. **termination** *n.*

ter-mi-na-tive *adj.* Tending to terminate someone or something.

ter-mi-na-tor *n.* Someone or something that terminates.

ter-mi-nus *n.* Something that will mark the boundary of something.

ter-mi-tar-i-um *n.* The nest of the termite.

ter-mite *n.* The winged or wingless insect which lives in large colonies feeding on wood.

term-less *adj.* To have no end.

term pa-per *n.* A type of written assignment that is usually large in size and difficult.

tern *n.* A type of sea gulls that are smaller than other gulls and having forked tails.

ter-na-ry *adj.* To have three elements.

ter-nate *adj.* To be arranged in threes. **ternately** *adv.*

terp-si-cho-re-an *adj.* To be pertaining to or related to dancing.

terr *abbr.* Territory.

ter-race *n.* An open balcony or porch; a level piece of land that is higher than the surrounding area; a row of houses built on a sloping or raised site.

ter-ra cot-ta *n.* A hard, baked clay used in ceramic pottery.

ter-ra--cot-ta *n.* The solid ground or dirt.

ter-rain *n.* The surface of an area, as land.

ter-ra-pin *n.* An edible turtle of North America, living in both fresh and salt water.

terr-aque-ous *adj.* To be consisting of water and land.

ter-raz-zo *n.* A type of mosaic floor covering that is made by embedding pieces of granite into mortar.

ter-res-tri-al *adj.* Something earthly; not heavenly; growing or living on land.

ter-ri-ble *adj.* Causing fear or terror; intense; extreme; horrid; difficult. **terribly** *adv.*, **terribleness** *n.*

ter-ric-o-lous *adj.* To be living on the ground.

ter-ri-er *n.* A very active small dog, originally bred by hunters to dig for burrowing game, now kept as a family pet.

ter-rif-ic *adj.* Terrifying. *Informal* Excellent; causing amazement. **-ally** *adv.*

ter-ri-fy *v.* To fill with fear or terror; to frighten; to menace. **terrified, terrifying** *adj.*

ter-ri-to-ri-al-i-ty *n.* The behavior that can be associated with the defense of the territory.

ter-ri-to-ry *n., pl.* **-ies** An area, usually of great size, which is controlled by a particular government; a district or area assigned to one person or group. **territorial** *adj.*, **territorially** *adv.*

ter-ror *n.* Extreme fear; one who causes terror.

ter-ror-ism *n.* The state of being terrorized or the act of terrorizing; the use of intimidation to attain one's goals or to advance one's cause.

ter-ror-ize *v.* To scare or to fill someone with terror. **terrorization** *n.*

terse *adj.* Brief; using as few words as possible without loss of force or clearness. **tersely** *adj.*, **terseness** *n.*

ter-tian *adj.* To be recurring at 48-hour intervals.

ter-tia-ry col-or *n.* A type of color that can be obtained with the mixing of two secondary colors.

tes-la *n.* The unit of magnetic flux density.

TE-SOL *abbr.* Teachers of English to Speakers of Other Languages.

tes-sel-late *v.* Adorn something with mosaic.

tes-sel-lat-ed *adj.* To have an appearance that is checkered.

tes-sel-la-tion *n.* A state of something being tessellated.

tes-sera *n.* A table that was used by ancient Romans as a tally or a ticket.

tes-si-tu-ra *n.* The range of a voice part.

test *n.* An examination or evaluation of something or someone; an examination to determine one's knowledge, skill, intelligence or other qualities. **test** *v.*, **tester** *n.*

tes-ta *n.* An external covering or coating that is hard and belonging to a seed.

tes-ta-cean *n.* The order of rhizopods.

tes-ta-ceous *adj.* To have a shell covering.

tes-ta-cy *n.* The state of being testate.

tes-ta-ment *n.* A legal document which states how one's personal property is to be distributed upon his death. **Testament** *n.* One of the two sections of the Bible: the Old Testament and the New Testament. **testamentary** *adj.*

tes-tate *adj.* Having left a valid will.

tes-ta-tor *n.* One who leaves a will that will be in forced at the time of his death.

test ban *n.* A type of ban that is placed on the testing of nuclear weapons.

test case *n.* A type of case which may

serve as a precedent to other cases of this same nature.

test--drive *v.* To drive a car before one buys it.

test-ed *adj.* To be qualified through testing.

test--fire *v.* To perform a firing test.

test--fly *v.* To fly something in order to test it.

tes-ti-cle *n.* The male gland in which the sperm are made.

tes-ti-fi-er *n.* A person that will testify.

tes-ti-fy *v.* To give evidence while under oath; to serve as proof. **testifier** *n.*

tes-ti-mo-ni-al *n.* A formal statement; a gift, dinner, reception, or other sign of appreciation given to a person as a token of esteem. **testimonial** *adj.*

tes-ti-mo-ny *n., pl.* -ies A solemn affirmation made under oath; an outward expression of a religious experience.

test-ing *adj.* To be very difficult or requires much effort.

tes-tis *n., pl.* **testes** The sperm producing gland of the male.

tes-ton *n.* A type of silver coin of old Europe.

tes-tos-ter-one *n.* The male hormone which is made by the testis.

test pi-lot *n.* The pilot who will specialize in testing new airplanes.

test tube *n.*

A thin glass tube closed at one end, used in biology and chemistry.

test--tube ba-by *n.* A baby conceived outside of a mother's womb by fertilizing an egg removed from the mother and then returning the fertilized egg to the mother's womb.

tes-tu-do *n.* The covering of overlapping shields which was used by the Romans in ancient times in order to protect their forces.

tes-ty *adj.* To be able to be annoyed easily. **testiness** *n.*

tet-a-nal *adj.* Pertaining to or being derived for tetanus.

te-tan-ic *adj.* Pertaining to tetany.

tet-a-nize *v.* To cause or to induce tetanus in a muscle or other part of the body.

tet-a-nus *n., Pathol* An often fatal disease marked by muscular spasms, commonly known as lockjaw.

tetchy *adj.* To be peevishly sensitive.

teth-er *n.* A rope or chain which fastens an animal to something but allows limited freedom to wander within its range.

teth-er-ball *n.* A type of game where a ball is suspended with a rope from a pole that is upright and each player tries to wrap the ball around the pole by hitting it.

tet-ra *n.* A type of fish of South America which is brightly colored and is usually bred in an aquarium.

tet-ra-caine *n.* A type of local anesthetic.

tet-ra-chlo-ride *n.* A type of chloride that has four atoms of chlorine.

tet-ra-cy-cline *n.* A type of broad-spectrum antibiotic.

te-frad-y-mite *n.* A type of steel-gray mineral that has a metallic luster to it.

tet-ra-eth-yl *adj.* To be containing four ethyl groups within one molecule.

tet-ra-flu-o-ride *n.* A type of fluoride that contains four atoms of fluorine.

tet-ra-he-dral *adj.* To be pertaining or having the form of a tetrahedron.

tet-ra-hy-drate *n.* A type of compound which is hydrated with four molecules of water.

tet-ra-hy-me-na *n.* A member of the group of the genus of ciliate protozoans.

te-tram-e-ter *n.* A type of line of verse that has four dipodies.

tet-ra-meth-yl *adj.* To be having or containing four methyl groups in one molecule.

tet-ra-meth-yl-lead *n.* A type of volatile liquid that is poisonous and can be used as an antiknock agent.

tet-ra-ploid *adj.* To be a chromosome number that is four times the monoploid number. **tetraploidy** *n.*

tet-ra-pod *n.* A type of vertebrate that has two pairs of legs or limbs.

te-trarch *n.* One who is a governor of the fourth part of a province.

te-trar-chy *n.* A type of government by four ruling people.

tet-rode *n.* A type of vacuum tube that has four electrodes.

Tex-as *n.* A state located in the southwestern part of the United States.

text *n.* The actual wording of an author's work distinguished his from notes; the main part or body of a book. **textual** *adj.*, **textually** *adv.*

text-book *n.* A book used by students to prepare their lessons.

tex-tile *n.* A cloth made by weaving; yarn or fiber for making cloth. **textile** *adj.*

tex-ture *n.* The look, surface, or feel of something; the basic makeup. **textural** *adj.*, **texturally** *adv.*

thal-li-um *n.* A metallic element resembling lead, symbolized by Tl.

than *conj.* In comparison with or to something.

thank *v.* To express one's gratitude; to credit.

thank-ful *adj.* Feeling or showing gratitude; grateful. **thankfully** *adv.*, **thankfulness** *n.*, **thankless** *adj.*

thanks *pl., n.* An expression of one's gratitude.

Thanks-giv-ing Day *n.* A United States holiday, set apart as a legal holiday for public thanksgiving, celebrated on the fourth Thursday of November.

that *adj., pl.* **those** The person or thing present or being mentioned. *conj.* Used to introduce a clause stating what is said.

thatch *n.* Grass, straw, or similar material used to make a roof. *v.* To overlay or cover with or as if with thatch.

thaw *v.* To change from a frozen state to a liquid or soft state; to grow warmer; to melt. **thaw** *n.*

the *definite adj. or article* Used before nouns and noun phrases as a determiner, designating particular persons or things. *adv.* Used to modify words in the comparative degree; by so much; by that much.

the·a·tre *n.* A building adapted to present dramas, motion pictures, plays, or other performances; a performance.

the·at·ri·cal *adj.* Extravagant; designed for show, display, or effect.

theft *n.* The act or crime of stealing; larceny.

their *adj. & pron.* The possessive case of they; belonging to two or more things or beings previously named.

the·ism *n.* The belief in the existence of God. **theist** *n.*, **theistic** *adj.*

them *pron.* The objective case of they.

theme *n.* The topic or subject of something. *Mus.* A short melody of a musical composition. **thematic** *adj.*

them·selves *pron.* Them or they; a form of the third person plural pronoun.

then *adv.* At that time; soon or immediately. *adj.* Being or acting in or belonging to or at that time.

thence *adv.* From that place, event, fact, or origin.

thenceforth, thence-for-ward *adv.* From that time on.

the·oc·ra·cy *n., pl.* **-ies** Government by God or by clergymen who think of themselves as representatives of God. **theocratic** *adj.*, **theocratically** *adv.*

the·ol·o·gy *n., pl.* **-ies** The religious study of the nature of God, beliefs, practices, and ideas. **theologian** *n.*

the·o·rize *v.* To analyze theories. **theoretician, -ion, -er, theorist** *n.*

the·o·ry *n., pl.* **-ies** A general principle or explanation which covers the known facts; an offered opinion which may possibly, but not positively, be true.

ther·a·peu·tics *n.* The medical treatment of disease. **therapeutist** *n.*

ther·a·py *n., pl.* **-ies** The treatment of certain diseases; treatment intended to remedy an undesirable condition. **therapist** *n.*

there *adv.* In, at, or about that place; toward, into, or to. **thereabouts, thereafter, thereby, therefore, therefrom, therein** *adv.*

ther·mal *adj.* Having to do with or producing heat.

ther·mom·e·ter *n.* A glass tube containing mercury which rises and falls with temperature changes. **thermometric** *adj.*

ther·mom·e·try *n.* Measurement of temperature.

ther·mo·phile *n.* Organism that grows at a high temperature. **thermophilic** *also* **thermophile** *or* **thermophilous** *adj.*

ther·mo·plas·tic *adj.* Pliable and soft when heated or warm but hard when cooled. **thermoplastic** *n.*

ther·mo·stat *n.*

A device that automatically responds to temperature changes and activates equipment such as air conditioners and furnaces to adjust the temperature to correspond with the setting on the device. **thermostatic** *adj.*

the·sau·rus *n., pl.* **-ruses** *or* **-ri** A book which contains synonyms.

these *pron.* The plural of this.

the·sis *n., pl.* **-ses** A formal argument or idea; a paper written by a student that develops an idea or point of view.

they *pron.* The two or more beings just mentioned.

they'd *contr.* They had.

they'll *contr.* They will.

they're *contr.* They are.

they've *contr.* They have.

thick *adj.* Having a heavy or dense consistency; having a considerable extent or depth from one surface to its opposite. *Slang* Excessive. **thickly** *adv.*, **thickness, thicken** *n.*

thief *n., pl.* **thieves** A person who steals.

thieve *v.* To take by theft. **thievery** *n.*

thigh *n.* The part of the leg between the hip and the knee of man.

thim·ble *n.*

A small cap-like protection for the finger, worn while sewing.

thin *adj.* Having very little depth or extent from one side or surface to the other; not fat; slender. **thinly** *adv.*, **thinness** *n.*

thing *n.* Something not recognized or named; an idea, conception, or utterance; a material or real object.

things One's belongings.

think *v.* To exercise thought; to use the mind; to reason and work out in the mind; to visualize. **thinkable** *adj.*, **thinker** *n.*

third *n.* Next to the second in time or place; the last in a series of three.

Third World *n.* The underdeveloped or nonaligned nations of the world, especially in Asia and Africa.

thirst *n.* An uncomfortably dry feeling in the throat and mouth accompanied by an urgent desire for liquids. **-y** *adj.*

thir·teen *n.* The cardinal number equal to 12 + 1.

this *pron., pl.* **these** The person or thing that is near, present, or just mentioned; the one under discussion.

this·tle *n.* A prickly plant usually producing a purplish or yellowish flower.

thith·er *adv.* To that place; there; on the farthest side.

thong *n.* A narrow strip of leather used for binding.

tho-rax *n., pl.* **-raxes** *or* **-races** The section or part of the human body between the neck and abdomen, supported by the ribs and breastbone. **thoracic** *adj.*

tho-ri-um *n.* A radioactive metallic element symbolized by Th.

thorn *n.* A sharp, pointed, woody projection on a plant stem. **thorniness** *n.,* **thorny** *adj.*

thor-ough *adj.* Complete; intensive; accurate; very careful; absolute. **thoroughness** *n.,* **thoroughly** *adv.*

thor-ough-bred *adj.* Being of a pure breed of stock.

thor-ough-fare *n.* A public highway, road or street.

those *adj. & pron.* The plural of that.

though *adv.* Nevertheless; in spite of.

thought *n.* The process, act, or power of thinking; a possibility; an idea. **thoughtful, thoughtless** *adj.*

thou-sand *n.* The cardinal number equal to 10 x 100. **thousand** *adj. & pron.*

thrash *v.* To beat or strike with a whip; to move violently about; to defeat.

thread *n.* A thin cord of cotton or other fiber; the ridge going around a bolt, nut or screw. *v.* To pass a thread through, as to thread a needle. **thread-bare** *adj.* Shabby.

threads *pl., n. Slang* Clothes.

threat *n.* An expression or warning of intent to do harm; anything holding a possible source of danger. **threaten** *v.,* **threatener** *n.,* **threateningly** *adv.*

three *n.* The cardinal number equal to 2 + 1.

three-D *or* **3-D** *n.* A three-dimensional form.

thresh *v.* To separate seed from a harvested plant mechanically; to strike severely.

thresh-old *n.* A horizontal piece of wood or other material which forms a doorsill; a beginning point.

threw *v.* Past tense of throw.

thrice *adv.* Three times.

thrift *n.* The careful use of money and other resources. **thriftily** *adv.,* **thriftiness** *n.,* **thrifty** *adj.*

thrill *n.* A feeling of sudden intense excitement, fear, or joy. **thrilling** *adj.,* **thrillingly** *adv.*

thrive *v.* To prosper; to be healthy; to do well in a position.

throat *n.* The front section or part of the neck containing passages for food and air.

throb *v.* To beat, move, or vibrate in a pulsating way; to pulsate. **throb** *n.*

throm-bo-sis *n., pl.* **-ses** The development of a blood clot in a blood vessel or in the heart cavity.

throng *n.* A large group or crowd. *v.* To crowd around or into.

throt-tle *n.* The valve which controls the flow of fuel to an engine. *v.* To control the speed or fuel with a throttle.

through *prep.* From the beginning to the end; in one side and out the opposite side. *Slang* Completed; finished.

through-out *prep., adv.* In every place; everywhere; at all times.

throw *v.* To toss or fling through the air with a motion of the arm; to hurl with force. *Slang* To entertain, as to throw a party. **throw up** To vomit. **throw out** To discard something.

thru *prep., adv., & adj.* Through.

thrush *n.* A small songbird having a brownish upper body and spotted breast.

thrust *v.* To push; to shove with sudden or vigorous force. *n.* A sudden stab or push.

thru-way *or* **throughway** *n.* A major highway; an expressway.

thud *n.* A heavy, dull thumping sound.

thug *n.* A tough or violent gangster.

thumb *n.* The short first digit of the hand; the part of the glove that fits over the thumb. *v.* To browse through something quickly.

thump *n.* A blow with something blunt or heavy. **thump** *v.*

thun-der *n.* The loud explosive sound made as air is suddenly expanded by heat and then quickly contracted again.

thun-der-bolt *n.* A flash of lightning immediately followed by thunder.

thun-der-cloud *n.* A dark cloud carrying an electric charge and producing lightning and thunder.

thun-der-show-er *n.* A brief rainstorm with thunder and lightning.

Thurs. *or* **Thur.** *abbr.* Thursday.

Thurs-day *n.* The fifth day of the week.

thus *adv.* In this or that way; therefore.

thwack *v.* To strike hard, using something flat.

thwart *v.* To prevent from happening; to prevent from doing something. *n.* A seat positioned crosswise in a boat.

thy *adj.* Pertaining to oneself; your.

thyme *n.* An aromatic mint herb whose leaves are used in cooking.

thy-roid *adj. Anat.* Pertaining to the thyroid gland. *n.* The gland in the neck of man that produces hormones which regulate food use and body growth.

thy-rox-ine *n.* A hormone secreted by the thyroid gland.

ti-ar-a *n.* A bejeweled crown in the form of a half circle and worn by women at formal occasions.

tick *n.* One of a series of rhythmical tapping sounds made by a clock; a small bloodsucking parasite, many of which are carriers of disease.

tick-et *n.* A printed slip of paper or cardboard allowing its holder to enter a specified event or to enjoy a privilege; a list of candidates who represent a political party.

tick-le *v.* To stroke lightly so as to cause laughter; to amuse or delight. **tickle, tickler** *n.*

tidal wave *n.* An enormous rise of destructive ocean water caused by a storm or earthquake.

tid-bit *n.* A choice bit of food, news, or gossip.

tide *n.* The rise and fall of the surface level of the ocean which occurs twice a day due to the gravitational pull of the sun and moon on the earth.

tid-ings *pl., n.* News; information about events.

ti-dy *adj.* Well arranged; neat; orderly. *v.* To make orderly and neat. **tidily** *adv.*, **tidiness** *n.*

tie *v.* To secure or bind with a rope, line, cord or other similar material; to make secure or fasten with a rope; to make a bow or knot in; to match an opponent's score. *n.* A string, rope, cord or other material used to join parts or hold something in place. A necktie; a beam that gives structural support. **railroad tie** A device, as timber, laid crosswise to support train tracks.

tier *n.* A layer or row placed one above the other. **tiered** *adj.*

ti-ger *n.*

A large carnivorous cat having tawny fur with black stripes.

tiger-eye *n.* A yellow-brown gemstone.

tight *adj.* Set closely together; bound or securely firm; not loose; taut; difficult. *adv.* Firmly. *Slang* Intoxicated.

tight-en *v.* To become or make tighter.

tight-rope *n.* A tightly stretched horizontal rope high above the ground for the use of acrobats.

tights *pl., n.* A skintight stretchable garment, covering the lower half of the body.

tile *n.* A thin, hard, flat piece of plastic, asphalt, baked clay, or stone used to cover walls, floors, and roofs. *v.* To cover with tile.

till *prep. & conj.* Until; unless or before. *v.* To cultivate; to plow. *n.* A small cash register or drawer for holding money.

till-er *n.* A machine or person that tills land.

tilt *v.* To tip, as by raising one end. *n.* The state of tilting or being tilted.

tim-ber *n.* Wood prepared for building; a finished piece of wood or plank.

tim-ber line *n.* The height on a mountain beyond which trees cannot grow.

time *n.* A continuous period measured by clocks, watches, and calendars; the period or moment in which something happens or takes place. *adj.* Of or pertaining to time; pertaining to paying in installments. *Slang* A period of imprisonment.

time--shar-ing *n.* The joint ownership of property with each individual sharing the use of the property.

time tri-al *n.* A race or competition where each participant is timed individually over a set distance.

tim-id *adj.* Lacking self-confidence; shy.

tin *n.* A white, soft, malleable metallic element, symbolized by Sn; a container made of tin. *adj.* Made of tin.

tinc-ture *n.* A tinge of color; an alcohol solution of some medicinal substance. *v.* To tint.

tin-der *n.* A readily combustible substance or material used for kindling.

tin-der-box *n.* A portable metal box for holding tinder; a building which is a fire hazard; a situation which is about to explode with violence.

tine *n.* A narrow pointed spike or prong, as of a fork or antler.

tinge *v.* To impart a faint trace of color; to tint. *n.* A slight trace of added color.

tin-gle *v.* To feel a stinging or prickling sensation. **tingle** *n.*, **tingly** *adj.*

tink-er *n.* A person who mends domestic household utensils; one who does repair work of any kind. *v.* To work as a tinker; to attempt to fix, mend, or repair something in a bumbling, unprofessional manner.

tin-kle *v.* To produce a slight, sharp series of metallic ringing sounds.

tin-ny *adj.* Pertaining to or composed of tin.

tin-sel *n.* Thin strips of glittering material used for decorations.

tint *n.* A slight amount or trace of color. *v.* To color.

ti-ny *adj.* Minute; very small.

tip *v.* To slant from the horizontal or vertical. *n.* Extra money given as an acknowledgment of a service; a gratuity; a helpful hint.

tip-ple *v.* To drink an alcoholic beverage to excess.

tip-sy *adj.* Partially intoxicated. **-iness** *n.*

ti-rade *n.* A long, violent speech or outpouring, as of censure.

tire *v.* To become or make weary; to be fatigued; to become bored. *n.* The outer covering for a wheel, usually made of rubber, serving to absorb shock and to provide traction.

tire-less *adj.* Untiring. **tirelessly** *adv.*

tis-sue *n.*, *Biol.* Similar cells and their products developed by plants and animals; a soft, absorbent piece of paper, consisting of two layers.

tis-sue pa-per *n.* Thin, almost transparent paper used for wrapping or protecting delicate articles.

ti-ta-ni-um *n.* A metallic element symbolized by Ti.

tithe *n.* A tenth of one's income given voluntarily for the support of a church. **tithe** *v.*, **tither** *n.*

tit-il-late *v.* To excite or stimulate in a pleasurable way. **titillating, -ive** *adj.* **titillatingly** *adv.*, **titillation** *n.*

ti-tle *n.* An identifying name of a book, poem, play, or other creative work; a name or mark of distinction indicating a rank or an office. In law, the evidence giving legal right of possession or control of something. In sports, a championship. *v.* To give a title or name to.

TN *abbr.* Tennessee.

to *prep.* Toward, opposite or near; in contact with; as far as; used as a function word indicating an action, movement, or condition suggestive of movement; indicating correspondence, dissimilarity, similarity, or proportion; indicating the one for which something is done or exists. *adv.* In the state, direction, or condition.

toad *n.* A tail-less amphibian, resembling the frog but without teeth in the upper jaw and having a rougher, drier skin.

toad-stool *n.* A poisonous mushroom or inedible fungus, shaped like an umbrella.

toast *v.* To heat and brown over a fire or in a toaster. *n.* Sliced bread browned in a toaster. **toasty** *adj.*

toaster *n.* A device for toasting bread.

to-bac-co *n.* A tropical American plant widely cultivated for its leaves, which are prepared in various ways, as for chewing or smoking.

to-bog-gan *n.* A long sled-like vehicle without runners, having long thin boards curved upwards at the forward end. **tobogganist** *n.*, **toboggan** *v.*

to-day *adv.* On or during the present day. *n.* The present time, period, or day.

tod-dle *v.* To walk unsteadily with short steps.

tod-dler *n.* A small child learning to walk.

tod-dy *n.*, *pl.* **-ies** A drink made with hot water, sugar, spices, and liquor.

toe *n.* One of the extensions from the front part of a foot; the part of a stocking, boot or shoe that covers the toes.

tof-fee *n.* A chewy candy made of butter and brown sugar.

to-geth-er *adv.* In or into one group, mass, or body; regarded jointly; in time with what is happening or going on. **togetherness** *n.*

toil *v.* To labor very hard and continuously. *n.* A difficult task.

toi-let *n.* A porcelain apparatus with a flushing device, used as a means of disposing body wastes.

toi-lette *n.* The act of washing, dressing, or grooming oneself.

toi-let wa-ter *n.* A liquid with a scent stronger than cologne and weaker than perfume.

to-ken *n.* A keepsake; a symbol of authority or identity; a piece of imprinted metal used in place of money. *adj.* Done as a pledge or indication.

tol-er-ate *v.* To put up with; to recognize and respect the opinions and rights of others; to endure; to suffer. **toleration** *n.*, **tolerance**, **tolerant** *adj.*

toll *n.* A fixed charge for travel across a bridge or along a road. *v.* To sound a bell in repeated single, slow tones.

tom *n.* A male turkey or cat.

tom-a-hawk *n.* An ax used as a weapon or tool by North American Indians.

to-ma-to *n.*, *pl.* **-toes** A garden plant cultivated for its edible fruit; the fruit of such a plant.

tomb *n.* A vault for burying the dead; a grave.

tom-boy *n.* A girl whose behavior is characteristic of a boy. **tomboyish** *adj.*

tomb-stone *n.* A stone used to mark a grave.

tom-cat *n.* A male cat.

to-mor-row *n.* The day after the present day. *adv.* On the day following today.

ton *n.* A measurement of weight equal to 2,000 pounds. *Slang* A large amount.

tone *n.* A vocal or musical sound that has a distinct pitch, loudness, quality, and duration; the condition of the body and muscles when at rest.

tongs *pl.*, *n.* An implement with two long arms joined at one end, used for picking up or lifting.

tongue *n.*

The muscular organ attached to the floor of the mouth, used in tasting, chewing, and speaking; anything shaped like a tongue, as the material under the laces or buckles of a shoe.

ton-ic *n.* A medicine or other agent used to restore health. In music, the first note of a scale. *Slang* Flavored carbonated soda.

to-night *n.* This night; the night of this day; the night that is coming. *adv.* On or during the present or coming night.

ton-sil *n.*

One of a pair of tissue similar to lymph nodes, found on either side of the throat.

ton-sil-lec-to-my *n.* The surgical removal of tonsils.

too *adv.* Also; as well; more than is needed.

tool *n.* An implement used to perform a task; anything needed to do one's work. *v.* To make or shape with a tool.

tooth *n.*, *pl.* **teeth** One of the hard, white structures rooted in the jaw and used for chewing and biting; the small, notched, projecting part of any object, such as a gear, comb or saw. **toothed**, **toothless** *adj.*

top *n.* The highest part or surface of anything; a covering or lid; the above-ground part of a rooted plant; the highest degree; a toy having a symmetric body with a tapered end upon which it spins. **top** *v.*

to-paz *n.* A gemstone, usually yellow in color.

top-coat *n.* An outer coat.

top-ic *n.* The subject discussed in an essay, thesis, speech or other discourse; the theme.

top-most *adj.* Uppermost.

to-pog-ra-phy *n.*, *pl.* **-ies** A detailed

description of a region or place; a physical outline showing the features of a region or place.

top-ple v. To fall; to overturn.

top-sy--tur-vy adv. With the top side down; upside down. adj. In a confused state. n. Confusion.

To-rah n. The body of law and wisdom contained in Jewish Scripture and oral tradition; a parchment scroll that contains the first five books of the Old Testament.

torch n. A stick of resinous wood which is burned to give light; any portable device which produces hot flame. Slang To set fire to.

tor-ment n. Extreme mental anguish or physical pain; a source of trouble or pain. v. To cause terrible pain; to pester, harass, or annoy. **tormentingly** adv., **tormentor** n.

tor-na-do n., pl. -does or -dos A whirling, violent windstorm accompanied by a funnel-shaped cloud that travels a narrow path over land; a whirlwind.

tor-pe-do n., pl. -oes A large, self-propelled, underwater missile launched from a ship, containing an explosive charge.

tor-pid adj. Having lost the power of motion or feeling; dormant. **torpidity** n., **torpidly** adv.

tor-rent n. A swift, violent stream; a raging flood. **torrential** adj.

tor-rid adj. Parched and dried by the heat. **torridly** adv.

tor-sion n. The act or result of twisting; the stress produced when one end is held fast and the other turned. **torsional** adj.

tor-so n., pl. -sos or -si The trunk of the human body.

tort n., Law A wrongful act requiring compensation for damages.

tor-toise n. A turtle that lives on the land; a person or thing regarded as slow.

tor-tu-ous adj. Marked by repeated bends, turns, or twists; devious. **tortuousness** n.

tor-ture n. The infliction of intense pain as punishment; something causing anguish or pain. v. To subject or cause intense suffering; to wrench or twist out of shape. **-er** n., **torturously** adv.

toss v. To fling or throw about continuously; to throw up in the air. n. A throw.

tot n. A young child; a toddler.

to-tal n. The whole amount or sum; the entire quantity. adj. Absolute; complete. **total** v., **totally** adv.

to-tal-i-tar-i-an adj. Characteristic of a government controlled completely by one party; exercising complete political control. **totalitarian** n.

tote v. To carry something on one's arm or back.

to-tem n. An animal or plant regarded as having a close relationship to some family clan or group; a representation or symbol.

tot-ter v. To walk unsteadily; to shake or sway as if about to fall.

tou-can n.

A brightly colored tropical bird having a very large thin bill.

touch v. To allow a part of the body, as the hands, to feel or come into contact with; to hit or tap lightly; to eat or drink; to join; to come next to; to have an effect on; to move emotionally. n. An instance or act of touching; the feeling, fact, or act of touching or being touched; a trace; a tiny amount; a method, manner, or style of striking the keys of an instrument with a keyboard. **touchable** adj.

tough adj. Resilient and strong enough to withstand great strain without breaking or tearing; strong; hardy; very difficult; difficult to cut or chew. n. An unruly person; a thug. **toughly** adv., **toughness** n.

tou-pee n. A wig worn to cover a bald spot on one's head.

tour n. A trip with visits to points of interest; a journey; a period or length of service at a single place or job. **tourism, tourist** n.

tour-na-ment n. A contest involving a number of competitors for a title or championship.

tour-ni-quet n. A device used to temporarily stop the flow of blood through an artery.

tou-sle v. To mess up; to disarrange.

tout v. To solicit customers. Slang In horse racing, a person who obtains information on racehorses and sells it to bettors. **touter** n.

tow v. To drag or pull, as by a chain or rope. n. An act of being pulled; a rope or line for pulling or dragging; coarse broken flax, hemp, or jute fiber prepared for spinning.

to-ward or **to-wards** prep. In the direction of; just before; somewhat before; regarding; with respect to.

tow-el n. An absorbent piece of cloth used for drying or wiping. **towel** v.

tow-er n. A very tall building or structure; a skyscraper; a place of security or defense. **towering** adj.

town n. A collection of houses and other buildings larger than a village and smaller than a city.

town-ship n. A subdivision of a county having corporate powers of municipal government.

tox-e-mi-a n., Pathol. Blood poisoning; a condition in which the blood contains toxins.

tox-ic adj. Relating to a toxin; destructive, deadly, or harmful.

tox-in n. A poisonous substance produced by chemical changes in plant and animal tissue.

toy n. An object designed for the enjoyment of children; any object having little value or importance; a small trinket; a bauble; a dog of a very small breed. *v.* To amuse or entertain oneself.

trace *n.* A visible mark or sign of a thing, person, or event; something left by some past agent or event. *v.* To follow the course or track of; to copy by drawing over the lines visible through a sheet of transparent paper. **traceable** *adj.*, **traceably** *adv.*, **-er** *n.*

track *n.* A mark, as a footprint, left by the passage of anything; a regular course; a set of rails on which a train runs; a circular or oval course for racing. *v.* To follow the trail of footprints of. **trackable** *adj.*, **-er** *n.*

tract *n.* An extended area, as a stretch of land. *Anat.* An extensive region of the body, one comprising body organs and tissues that together perform a specialized function.

trac-tion *n.* The act of drawing, as a load over a surface; the state of being drawn or pulled; rolling friction that prevents a wheel from skidding over the surface on which it runs.

trac-tor *n.* A diesel or gasoline-powered vehicle used in farming to pull another piece of machinery.

trac-tor trail-er *n.* A large truck having a cab and no body, used to pull large trailers.

trade *n.* A business or occupation; skilled labor; a craft; an instance of selling or buying; a swap. **trade** *v.*, **tradeable** *adj.*, **trader** *n.*

trade-mark *n.* A brand name which is legally the possession of one company and cannot be used by another.

trade--off *n.* A compromise of possibilities when all cannot be attained at the same time; a surrender of one consideration in order to obtain another.

tra-di-tion *n.* The doctrines, knowledge, practices, and customs passed down from one generation to another. **traditional** *adj.*, **traditionally** *adv.*

tra-duce *v.* To betray. **-ment**, **-er** *n.*

traf-fic *n.* The passage or movement of vehicles; trade, buying and selling; the signals handled by a communications system. **trafficker** *n.*

trag-e-dy *n.*, *pl.* **-ies** An extremely sad or fatal event or course of events; a story, play, or other literary work which arouses terror or pity by a series of misfortunes or sad events.

trail *v.* To draw, drag, or stream along behind; to follow in the tracks of; to follow slowly behind or in the rear; to let hang so as to touch the ground. *n.* Something that hangs or follows along behind; a rough path through a wooded area.

trail-er *n.* One who trails; a large vehicle that transports objects and is pulled by another vehicle.

train *n.* The part of a long gown that trails behind the wearer; a long

moving line of vehicles or persons; a group of railroad cars. *v.* To instruct so as to make skillful or capable of doing something; to aim; to direct. **-able** *adj.*, **-er**, **training**, **trainee** *n.*

trait *n.* A quality or distinguishing feature, such as one's character.

trai-tor *n.* A person who betrays his country, a cause, or another's confidence.

tra-jec-to-ry *n.*, *pl.* **-ies** The curved line or path of a moving object.

tram-mel *n.* A long, large net used to catch birds or fish; something that impedes movement. **trammeler** *n.*

tramp *v.* To plod or walk with a heavy step. *n.* A homeless person or vagrant who travels about aimlessly.

tram-ple *v.* To tread heavily; to stomp; to inflict injury, pain, or loss by heartless or brutal treatment. **trample**, **trampler** *n.*

tram-po-line *n.* A canvas device on which an athlete or acrobat may perform. **trampolinist** *n.*

trance *n.* A stupor, daze, mental state, or condition, such as produced by drugs or hypnosis.

tran-quil *adj.* Very calm, quiet, and free from disturbance. **tranquillity** *n.*, **tranquilly** *adv.*, **tranquilize** *v.*

trans-act *v.* To perform, carry out, conduct, or manage business in some way. **transaction**, **transactor** *n.*

tran-scend *v.* To pass beyond; to exceed; to surpass. **-ent** *adj.*, **transcendence** *n.*

tran-scribe *v.* To make copies of something; to adopt or arrange.

tran-script *n.* A written copy.

trans-crip-tion *n.* The process or act of transcribing.

trans-fer *v.* To remove, shift, or carry from one position to another. **transferable** *adj.*, **transference**, **-er** *n.*

trans-fig-ure *v.* To change the outward appearance or form; to exalt; to glorify. **transfiguration** *n.*

trans-fix *v.* To pierce; to hold motionless, as with terror, awe or amazement. **transfixion** *n.*

trans-form *v.* To change or alter completely in nature, form or function. **transformable** *adj.*, **-ation**, **-er** *n.*

trans-fuse *v.* To transfer liquid by pouring from one place to another. *Med.* To pass blood from the blood vessels of one person into the vessels of another. **transfusion**, **transfuser** *n.*

trans-gress *v.* To go beyond the limit or boundaries; to sin against or violate. **transgression**, **transgressor** *n.*, **transgressive** *adj.*

tran-sient *adj.* Not staying or lasting very long; moving from one location to another. **transient** *n.*, **transiently** *adv.*

tran-sit *n.* Passage or travel from one point to another; an instrument for surveying that measures horizontal and vertical angles.

trans-late *v.* To change from one language to another while retaining the original meaning; to explain.

translation, translator n.

trans-lu-cent adj. Diffusing and admitting light but not allowing a clear view of the object.

trans-mis-sion n. The act or state of transmitting. Mech. The gears and associated parts of an engine which transmit power to the driving wheels of an automobile or other vehicle.

trans-mit v. To dispatch or convey from one thing, person, or place to another. transmissible, -table adj., -ter n.

trans-mute v. To change in nature, kind, or substance. transmutation n.

tran-som n. A small, hinged window over a doorway; the horizontal crossbar in a window.

trans-par-ent adj. Admitting light so that images and objects can be clearly viewed; easy to understand; obvious. transparency n., transparently adv.

tran-spire v. To give off waste products through plant or animal pores in the form of vapor; to happen; to take place. transpiration n.

trans-plant v. To remove a living plant from where it is growing and plant it in another place; to remove a body organ from one person and implant it in the body of another, as a kidney transplant; to remove skin from one area of the body and move it to another area of the body, as a skin graft. transplantable adj.

trans-port v. To carry or move from one place to another. n. A vessel or ship used to carry military supplies and troops; the process or act of transporting. transportable adj., transportation, transporter n.

trans-pose v. To reverse the place or order of. Mus. To perform or write music in a key different from the one it was originally written in.

trans-sex-u-al n. A person whose sex has been changed surgically.

trap n. A device for holding or catching animals; a device which hurls clay pigeons, disks, or balls into the air to be fired upon by sportsmen; anything which deliberately catches or stops people or things. v. To catch in a trap; to place in an embarrassing position. Slang The mouth.

tra-peze n. A short horizontal bar suspended by two ropes, used for acrobatic exercise or stunts.

trap-shoot-ing n. The hobby or sport of shooting at clay pigeons, disks, and other objects hurled into the air.

trau-ma n., pl. -mas or -mata A severe wound caused by a sudden physical injury; an emotional shock causing lasting and substantial damage to a person's psychological development.

tra-vail n. Strenuous mental or physical exertion; labor in childbirth. v. To undergo the sudden sharp pain of childbirth.

trav-el v. To journey or move from one place to another. n. The process or act of traveling. traveler n.

tra-verse v. To pass over, across, or through. n. A path or route across; something that lies across something else. traversable adj., traversal, traverser n.

trawl n. A strong fishing net which is dragged through water.

tray n. A flat container having a low rim, used for carrying, holding, or displaying something.

treach-er-ous adj. Disloyal; deceptive; unreliable. -ly adv., treachery n.

tread v. To walk along, on, or over; to trample. n. The act or manner of treading; the part of a wheel which comes into contact with the ground.

trea-son n. Violation of one's allegiance to a sovereign or country, as giving or selling state secrets to another country or attempting to overthrow the government. treasonable, -ous adj.

treas-ure n. Hidden riches; something regarded as valuable. v. To save and accumulate for future use; to value.

treasurer n. A person having charge and responsibilities for funds.

treas-ur-y n., pl. -ies A place where public or private funds are kept. Treasury The executive department of the United States Government in charge of collection, management, and expenditure of public revenue.

treat v. To behave or act toward; to regard in a given manner; to provide entertainment or food for another at one's own expense or cost. n. A pleasant surprise; something enjoyable which was unexpected. treatable adj., treater n.

treat-ment n. The manner or act of treating; medical care.

treb-le adj. Multiplied by three; having three. Mus. Performing or having the highest range, part, or voice. n. A high-pitched sound or voice. treble v.

tree n. A tall woody plant, usually having a single trunk of considerable height; a diagram resembling a tree, as one used to show family descent. Slang To get the advantage of something. tree v., treeless adj.

tre-foil n. Any of various plants having three leaflets with red, purple, yellow, or pink flowers.

trek v. To make a slow and arduous journey. trek, trekker n.

trel-lis n. A latticework frame used for supporting vines and other climbing plants.

trem-ble v. To shake involuntarily, as with fear or from cold; to express or feel anxiety. trembler n., trembly adj.

tre-men-dous adj. Extremely huge, large, or vast. Slang Wonderful.

trem-or n. A quick, shaking movement; any continued and involuntary trembling or quavering of the body.

trench n. A ditch; a long, narrow excavation in the ground. v. To cut deep furrows for protection. trencher n.

trend n. A general inclination, direction,

or course; a fad. v. To have or take a specified direction. **trendsetter** n.

tres-pass v. To infringe upon another's property. In law, to invade the rights, property, or privacy of another without consent or knowledge.

tres-tle n. A bar or beam supported by four legs, used as a support, as for a table.

tri-al n. In law, the examination and hearing of a case before a court of law in order to determine the case; an attempt or effort; an experimental treatment or action to determine a result. adj. Pertaining to or of a trial; performed or used during an experiment or test.

tri-an-gle n., Geom.

A plane figure bounded by three sides and having three angles. **-ar** adj., **triangularity** n.

tribe n. A group of people composed of several villages, districts, or other groups which share a common language, culture, and name.

trib-u-la-tion n. Great distress or suffering caused by oppression.

trib-un-al n. A decision-making body.

trib-ute n. An action of respect or gratitude to someone; money or other goods given by one country to another showing obedience and insuring against invasion.

tri-ceps n., Anat. The large muscle at the back of the upper arm.

trick n. An action meant to fool, as a scheme; a prank; a feat of magic. v. To deceive or cheat. **tricky** adj.

trick-er-y n. Deception.

trick-le v. To flow in droplets or a small stream. **trickle** n.

tri-cy-cle n. A small vehicle having three wheels, propelled by pedals.

tri-dent n. A long spear with three prongs, used as a weapon.

tried adj. Tested and proven reliable or useful.

tri-en-ni-al adj. Happening every third year; lasting for a time period of three years. **triennial** n., **triennially** adv.

tri-fle n. Something of little value or importance; a dessert made with cake, jelly, wine, and custard. v. To use or treat without proper concern.

trig-ger n. A lever pulled to fire a gun; a device used to release or start an action. v. To start.

trill n. A tremulous utterance of successive tones. v. To utter with a fluttering sound.

tril-lion n. The cardinal number equal to one thousand billion.

trim v. To clip or cut off small amounts in order to make neater; to decorate. adj. Neat. **trim** n.

tri-ni-tro-tol-u-ene n. A very powerful explosive, abbreviated as TNT.

trin-ket n. A small piece of jewelry.

tri-o n. A set or group of three.

trip n. Travel from one place to another; a journey; a loss of balance. v. To stumble. Slang A hallucinatory effect induced by drugs.

tripe n. The stomach lining of oxen or similar animals, used as food. Slang Nonsense.

trip-le adj. Having three parts. v. To multiply by three; in baseball, a three-base hit.

trip-let n. One of three born at the same time.

trip-li-cate n. A group of three identical things. **triplicate** v.

tri-pod n. A three-legged stand or frame.

trite adj. Used too often; common.

tri-umph v. To be victorious. n. A victory. **triumphant** adj., **-antly** adv.

triv-i-al adj. Insignificant; of little value or importance; ordinary.

Tro-jan n. A determined, courageous person.

troll v. To fish by pulling a baited line slowly behind a boat; to sing with a loud, full voice. n. The act of trolling for fish; dwarf or elf.

trol-ley n. A streetcar powered by electricity from overhead lines; a small container or basket used to convey material, as in an underground tunnel or mine.

trom-bone n. A brass musical instrument, larger and lower in pitch than a trumpet.

troop n. A group or assembly of people or animals; a group of Boy Scouts or Girl Scouts having an adult leader; a military unit. **trooper** n.

tro-phy n., pl. **-ies** A prize or object, such as a plaque, awarded to someone for his success, victory, or achievement.

trop-ic n. Either of two imaginary parallel lines which constitute the Torrid Zone. **Tropics** The very warm region of the earth's surface between the Tropic of Cancer and the Tropic of Capricorn. **tropical** adj.

tro-po-sphere n. The lowest atmosphere between the earth's surface and the stratosphere.

trot n. The gait of a horse or other four-footed animal, between a walk and a run, in which the hind leg and opposite front leg move at about the same time. **trot** v.

troth n. Good faith; the act of pledging one's fidelity. **troth** v.

trou-ble n. Danger; affliction; need; distress; an effort; physical pain, disease or malfunction. v. To bother; to worry; to be bothered; to be worried. **troubler** n., **troublingly** adv.

trough n. A long, narrow, shallow container, especially one that holds food or water for animals.

trounce v. To whip or beat; to defeat decisively.

troupe n. A group, especially of the performing arts. **troupe** v.

trou-sers pl., n. An outer garment that

covers the body from the waist down.

trous-seau *n., pl.* **-seaux** *or* **-seaus** The wardrobe, linens, and other similar articles of a bride.

trout *n.* A freshwater game or food fish.

trowel *n.* A flat-bladed garden tool with a pointed blade, used for digging. **trowel** *v.*, **troweler** *n.*

tru-ant *n.* A person who is absent from school without permission. **truancy** *n.*, **truant** *adj.*

truce *n.* An agreement to stop fighting; a cease fire.

truck *n.* An automotive vehicle used to carry heavy loads; any of various devices with wheels designed to move heavy loads; garden vegetables for sale. **trucker** *n.*

trudge *v.* To walk heavily; to plod.

true *adj.* In accordance with reality or fact; not false; real; loyal; faithful. *adv.* Truthfully. **truly** *adv.*

Truman, Harry S *n.* The 33rd president of the United States from 1945-1953.

trump *n.* In cards, a suit of any cards which outrank all other cards for a selected period of time.

trum-pet *n., Mus.*

A brass instrument having a flared bell, valves, and a mouthpiece. *v.* To proclaim something loudly.

trunk *n.*

The main part of a tree; the human body, excluding the head, arms and legs; a sturdy box for packing clothing, as for travel or storage; the long snout of an elephant. **trunks** Men's clothing worn for swimming or athletics.

truss *v.* To fasten or tie securely. *Med.* A support or device worn to keep a hernia in place.

trust *n.* Confidence or faith in a person or thing; care or charge. *Law* The confidence or arrangement by which property is managed and held for the good or benefit of another person. *v.* To have confidence or faith in; to believe; to expect; to entrust; to depend on.

truth *n., pl.* **truths** The facts corresponding with actual events or happenings; sincerity or honesty. **truthful** *adj.*, **truthfully** *adv.*, **truthfulness** *n.*

try *v.* To make an attempt; to make an effort; to strain; to hear or conduct a trial; to place on trial. **trying** *adj.*, **tryout** *n.*

tryst *n.* A meeting between lovers; a prearranged meeting.

tsp *abbr.* Teaspoon.

tsu-na-mi *n.* An extensive and destructive ocean wave caused by an underwater earthquake.

tub *n.* A round, low, flat-bottomed,

vessel with handles on the side, as one used for washing.

tu-ba *n.* A large, brass wind instrument having a low range.

tube *n.* A hollow cylinder, made of metal, rubber, glass or other material, used to pass or convey something through. **tube, tubal** *adj.*

tu-ber *n.*

The underground stem of certain plants, as the potato, with buds from which new plants arise.

tu-ber-cu-lo-sis *n.* A contagious lung disease of humans and animals caused by microorganisms; abbreviated as TB.

tuck *n.* A flattened fold of material, usually stitched in place. *v.* To sew or make a tuck in material; to put in a safe place; to make secure.

Tues. *abbr.* Tuesday.

Tues-day *n.* The third day of the week.

tuft *n.* A small cluster of feathers, threads, hair, or other material fastened or growing closely together.

tug *v.* To strain and pull vigorously. *n.* A hard pull; a strong force.

tu-i-tion *n.* Payment for instruction, as at a private school or college.

tu-lip *n.*

A bulb-bearing plant, having upright cup-like blossoms.

tum-ble *v.* To fall or cause to fall; to perform acrobatic rolls, somersaults, and similar maneuvers; to mix up; to turn over and over. **tumbler, tumble** *n.*

tum-ble-down *adj.* Ramshackle; in need of repair.

tum-brel *n.* A cart which can discharge its load by tilting.

tu-mor *n., Pathol.* A swelling on or in any part of the body; an abnormal growth which may be malignant or benign.

tu-mult *n.* The confusion and noise of a crowd; a riot; any violent commotion. **tumultuous** *adj.*

tu-na *n., pl.* **-na** *or* **-nas** Any of several large marine food fish.

tun-dra *n.* A treeless area in the arctic regions having a subsoil which is permanently frozen.

tune *n.* A melody which is simple and easy to remember; agreement; harmony. *v.* To adjust. **tunable** *adj.*, **tunably** *adv.*, **tuner** *n.*

tung-sten *n.* A metallic element also known as wolfram, symbolized by W.

tu-nic *n.* A loose garment extending to the knees, worn by ancient Romans and Greeks.

tun-nel *n.* An underground or underwater passageway. **tunnel** v.

tur-ban n. A Moslem headdress that consists of a long scarf wound around the head.

tur-bine n. A motor having one or more rotary units mounted on a shaft, which are turned by the force of gas or a liquid.

tur-bu-lent adj. Marked by a violent disturbance. **turbulence** n., **-ly** adv.

tu-reen n. A large dish, often having a cover, used to serve soup or stew.

turf n. A layer of earth with its dense growth of grass and matted roots. Slang Home territory or ground.

tur-key n. A large game bird of North America, having a bare head and extensible tail; the meat of this bird. Slang A failure.

tur-moil n. A state of confusion or commotion.

turn v. To move or cause to move around a center point; to revolve or rotate; to transform or change; to move so that the bottom side of something becomes the top and the top becomes the bottom; to strain or sprain; to translate; to go beyond or to pass; to become 40; to make sour; to spoil, as food; to change or reverse the position or direction of; to become or cause to become hostile. **turn to** To seek comfort or advice from; to open a book to a certain page. **turn down** To refuse or deny. **turn in** To go to bed. **turn off** To be or cause to be disgusted with something. **in turn** One after another. **turn over** To ponder; to think about; to give up or transfer to another. **turn up** To arrive; to appear; to find. **turner** n.

turn on v., Slang To cause a person to experience with intense stimulation, as by means of LSD or marijuana.

turn-buck-le n. A metal coupling, used to regulate the distance or tension between two metal rods or wires.

turn-down n., Slang A rejection or refusal.

tur-nip n. An edible root from the mustard family of plants.

turn-key n. The person in charge of the keys at a prison.

turn-off n. A road branching off from a main highway. Slang Something which causes one to lose interest.

turn-over n. The process or act of turning over; an upset; a change or reversal; the number of times merchandise is bought, sold, and restocked in a certain period of time; the number of people hired in a given period of time to replace those who have left; a piece of pastry made by putting a filling on one half of the dough and turning the other half over to enclose the filling.

tur-pen-tine n. The thick sap of certain pine trees; a clear liquid manufactured from this sap, used to thin paint.

tur-quoise n. A blue-green gemstone; a light bluish-green color.

tur-ret n. A small ornamental tower on building; a raised, usually rotatin section of a ship, tank, or plane whe the gunner sits. **turreted** adj.

tur-tle n.

A scaly-skinned animal having a soft body covered with a hard shell into which the head, legs, and tail can retracted.

tur-tle-neck n. A high collar that f closely around the neck.

tusk n. A long, curved tooth, as of a elephant or walrus.

tus-sle n. A hard fight or struggle with problem or person. **tussle** v.

tu-tor n. A person who teaches anoth person privately. v. To teach, coach, instruct privately.

tut-ti-frut-ti n. An ice cream flavor th contains different types of candi fruits.

tu-tu n. A very short ballet skirt.

tux-e-do n. A semiformal dress suit wo by men.

TV abbr. Television.

twain n. Two.

twang n. A sharp, ringing sound like th of a violin or other stringed instr ment. v. To cause or make a twang.

tweak v. To pinch and twist sharply.

tweed n. A coarse woolen fabric, wov in two or more colors. **tweeds** Clo ing made of tweed.

tweez-ers pl., n. A small, pincer-li implement used to grasp or plu small objects.

twelve n. The cardinal number equal 11 + 1. **twelve** adj. & pron.

twen-ty n. The cardinal number equal 19 + 1 or 2 X 10. **twenty** adj. & pron

twice adv. Double; two times.

twid-dle v. To turn or twirl in an aimle way.

twig n. A small branch which grows fro a larger branch on a tree.

twi-light n. The soft light of the sky b tween sunset and complete darkness

twill n. A weave that produces the par lel rib on the surface of a fabric.

twin n. One of two persons born at same time to the same mother; one two similar persons or things. a Having two similar or identical parts

twine v. To weave or twist together. n strong cord or thread made by twisti many threads together.

twinge n. A sudden, sharp pain; a br emotional or mental pang. **twinged**

twin-kle v. To gleam or shine with qu flashes; to sparkle. **twinkle** n.

twirl v. To rotate or cause to tu around and around. **twirl** n.

twist v. To wind two or more pieces thread, twine, or other materi together to make a single strand; curve; to bend; to distort or chan the meaning of; to injure and wren n. The act of twisting.

twist-er *n., Slang* A tornado; a cyclone; one that twists. In baseball, a ball batted or thrown in a twisting, spinning motion.

twit *v.* To tease about a mistake. *n.* A taunting reproach.

twitch *v.* To move or cause to move with a jerky movement. *n.* A sudden tug.

twit-ter *v.* To utter a series of chirping sounds; to chatter nervously.

two *n.* The cardinal number of 1 + 1; the second in a sequence.

two-bit *adj.* Insignificant. **two bits** Twenty-five cents. **two-faced** Double-dealing. **twofold** Being double as much or as many.

two--time *v., Slang* To be unfaithful to.

TX *abbr.* Texas.

ty-coon *n., Slang* A business person of wealth and power.

tyke *n.* A small child.

Tyler, John *n.* The 10th president of the United States from 1841-1845.

type *n.* A class or group of persons or things; letters, numbers, and other symbols typewritten on paper or another surface; in printing, the piece of plastic, metal, or wood having the character or characters that are printed; a model or example of. *v.* To identify according to some sort of classification; to typewrite. **typecast** To use repeatedly in the same kind of role.

type-face *n.* A style or design of printing type.

type-set-ter *n.* A person who arranges or sets type. **typesetting** *n.*

ty-phe.d *n., Path.* An acute, infectious disease caused by germs in drink or food, resulting in high fever and intestinal hemorrhaging. **typhoid** *adj.*

ty-phoon *n.* A tropical hurricane, especially one in the western part of the Pacific Ocean.

typ-i-cal *adj.* Exhibiting the characteristics of a certain class or group.

typ-i-fy *v.* To be characteristic or typical of; to show all the traits or qualities of. **typified, typifying** *adj.*

typ-ist *n.* The operator of a typewriter.

ty-po *n., Slang* An error in typewriting or in setting type; any printed error which was not the fault of the author.

ty-ran-no-sau-rus *n.*

A large, flesh-eating dinosaur which walked on its hind legs.

tyr-an-ny *n.* Harsh, absolute, and unfair rule by a king or other ruler; complete control.

tyr-an-nize *v.* To rule or control completely.

ty-rant *n.* An absolute, unjust, or cruel ruler; one who exercises power or control unfairly.

ty-ro *also* **ti-ro** *n.* A novice or a beginner.

U, u The twenty-first letter of the English alphabet.

UWA *abbr.* United Automobile Workers.

Uban-gi *n.* A woman of Africa that has lips which are distended with wooden disks.

ubi-qui-none *n.* The quinone which is able to function as an electron transfer agent in the Kreb's cycle.

ubiq-ui-tous *adj.* To be everywhere at the same point in time.

ubiq-ui-ty *n.* A presence in many places or locations at the same time.

U--boat *n.* A type of submarine which is used by the Germans.

UDC *abbr.* Universal decimal classification.

ud-der *n.* The milk-producing organ pouch of some female animals, having two or more teats.

UFO *n.* An unidentified flying object such as a space ship from another planet in the science fiction films.

UFT *abbr.* United Federation of Teachers.

UG *abbr.* Underground.

Uga-rit-ic *adj.* Pertaining to the ancient city of Ugarit.

ugh *interj.* Used to express disgust or horror.

ug-li-fy *v.* To make something or someone ugly.

ug-ly *adj.* Offensive; repulsive; unpleasant to look at. **uglily** *adv.* **ugliest, uglier** *adj.*, **ugliness** *n.*

ug-ly duck-ling *n.* Someone or something which at first appears unpromising but in the end it is found to have great potential.

UGPA *abbr.* Undergraduate gradepoint average.

Ugri-an *adj.* A person who is a member of the eastern division of the Finno-Ugric people.

Ugric *adj.* Pertaining to the languages of the Ugrian people.

ug-some *adj.* To be loathsome.

ugt *abbr.* Urgent.

uh *interj.* To express hesitation.

uh--huh *interj.* Used for the purpose of showing or indicating agreement.

uh-lan *n.* Part of a body of the Prussian light cavalry that was originally modeled on Tartar lancers.

Ui-ghur *n.* The person who is a member of the Turkic people who were powerful in Mongolia and eastern Turkestan.

uin-ta-ite *n.* A type of black asphalt which can be found especially in Utah.

Uit-land-er *n.* The British person who lived in the former republics of the Orange Free State and Transvaal.

UK *abbr.* United Kingdom.

ukase *n.* The proclamation by a russian government that has the force of law.

uki-yo-e *n.* A kind of Japanese art movement which flourished during the 17th to the 19th century.

Ukrai-ni-an *n.* An inhabitant of the Ukraine. **Ukrainian** *adj.*

u-ku-le-le n. A small, four-stringed musical instrument, orginally from Hawaii.

ula-ma n. Body of mullahs.

-u-lar adj., suffix To be relating to.

ul-cer n. A festering, inflamed sore on a mucous membrane or on the skin that results in the destruction of the tissue. ulcerous adj. ulceration n., ulcerate v.

ul-cero-gen-ic adj. To be tending to develop into an ulcer.

-ule n., suffix Small or little one.

-u-lent adj., suffix That abounds in.

ulex-ite n. A kind of mineral that occurs in loose fibers that is able to transmit light lengthwise with very little diminished intensity.

ul-lage n. That amount a container lacks of being full.

ul-na n., Anat. One of the two bones of the forearm.

-u-lose n., suffix Ketose sugar.

ulot-ri-chous adj. To have crisp or woolly hair.

-u-lous adj., suffix Being slightly.

ul-ster n. A type of long loose overcoat that is of Irish origin and is made of heavy material.

ult abbr. Ultimo; ultimate.

ul-te-ri-or adj. To be located or situated on the further side of something or someone.

ul-ti-ma n. A last syllable of a word.

ul-ti-ma ra-tio n. A final argument or the last resort to a problem or discussion.

ul-ti-mate adj. Final; ending; most extreme. ultimately adv., ultimateness n., ultimacy n.

ul-ti-ma-tum n., pl -tums, -ta A final demand, proposal, or choice.

ul-ti-mo adj. To be happening or occurring in the month which precedes the present.

ul-ti-mo-gen-i-ture n. The system of inheritance where the youngest boy succeeds to the estate.

ul-tra adj. To be going beyond others.

ultra- prefix. Beyond the scope, range, or limit of something.

ul-tra-ba-sic adj. To be extremely basic. ultrabasic n.

ul-tra-cen-trif-u-gal adj. Pertaining to being obtained by the means or methods of ultracentrifuge.

ul-tra-cen-tri-fuge n. A kind of high speed centrifuge that is able to sediment colloidal and other small particles.

ul-tra-con-ser-va-tive adj. To be extremely cautious.

ul-tra-fash-ion-able adj. Being up-to-date with fashions and customs.

ul-tra-fiche n. A type of microfiche whose microimages are of printed matter which has been reduced 90 times or more.

ul-tra-fil-tra-tion n. The act of filtrating small particles through a membrane and holding back the larger particles.

ul-tra-high adj. To be exceedingly high.

ul-tra-ism n. An example of radicalism. ultraist n. or adj.

ul-tra-lib-er-al adj. To be very liberal. ultraliberal n.

ul-tra-ma-rine adj. To be situated beyond the sea or the ocean.

ul-tra-mi-cro adj. To be referring or dealing with something which is smaller than micro.

ul-tra-mi-cro-scope n. A type of instrument used for the purpose of viewing objects which are too small to be viewed through a regular microscope.

ul-tra-mi-cro-scop-ic adj. Being too small in size to be viewed with a regular microscope. ultramicroscopically adv.

ul-tra-mi-cro-tome n. A type of microtome that is made or designed to cut very thin sections off of something for the purpose of examining it. ultramicrotomy n.

ul-tra-mil-i-tant adj. To be very militant. ultramilitant n.

ul-tra-min-ia-ture adj. Extremely small; below miniature. ultraminiaturization n.

ul-tra-mod-ern adj. Extremely advanced or modern in style or ideas.

ul-tra-mon-tane adj. Pertaining to the peoples beyond the mountains such as the Alps. ultramontanism n.

ul-tra-na-tion-al-ism n. An excessive devotion to national interests.

ul-tra-pure adj. To be of the utmost purity. ultrapurely adv.

ul-tra-se-cret adj. To be highly secret.

ul-tra-short adj. To be short in duration.

ul-tra-son-ic adj. Relating to sound frequencies inaudible to humans. ultrasonically adv.

ul-tra-son-ics n. The science of the ultrasonic happenings and phenomena.

ul-tra-so-phis-ti-cat-ed adj. To be very sophisticated.

ul-tra-sound n. The vibrations of the same physical nature as sound.

ul-tra-struc-ture n. The invisible physiochemical make-up of protoplasm. ultrastructurally adv.

ul-tra-vi-o-let adj. Producing radiation having wave-lengths just shorter than those of visible light and longer than those of X rays. ultraviolet n.

ul-tra-vi-o-let light n. The ultraviolet radiation.

ul-tra vi-res adv. Beyond the scope of legal authority.

ul-u-lant adj. To have a howling sound or noise. ululation n.

um-bel n. The racemose inflorescence which is found in the carrot family where the axis is very contracted so the pedicels appear to come from the same point.

um-bel-late adj. To be consisting of umbels.

um-bel-li-fer n. A member or plant of the carrot family.

um-bel-lif-er-ous adj. Pertaining to the carrot family.

um-ber n. A moderate brown darker in

color than ochre.

um-bil-i-cal *adj.* Pertaining to the navel.

um-bil-i-cal cord *n.*

The structure by which a fetus is attached to its mother, serving to supply food and dispose of waste.

um-bil-i-cate *adj.* To be depressed such as the navel is in appearance.

um-bi-li-cus *n.* A little depression occurring in the abdominal wall where the umbilical cord was attached to the embryo.

um-bles *n.* Entrails of an animal such as a deer which is used to be used as food.

um-bo *n.* The elevation of the tympanic membrane of the ear.

um-bra *n.* The conical shadow that excludes all light from the given source.

um-brage *n.* A reason for doubt.

um-bra-geous *adj.* To be filled with shadows. **umbrageousness** *n.*

um-brel-la *n.* A collapsible frame covered with plastic or cloth, held above the head as protection from sun or rain.

um-brel-la bird *n.* A type of tropical bird that is related to the flycatchers.

um-brel-la leaf *n.* A kind of North American herb belonging to the barberry family.

um-brel-la plant *n.* A type of African sedge which has whorls of slender leaves.

um-brel-la tree *n.* A type of American magnolia that has clusters of leaves.

Um-bri-an *n.* A person who is a member of ancient Italy and occupying Umbria.

Um-bun-du *n.* The Congo language of Angola.

umi-ak *n.* A kind of open Eskimo boat which was propelled with broad paddles.

ump *v.* To act or to behave as an umpire such as in the game of baseball.

um-pir-age *n.* An act of umpiring.

um-pire *n.* In sports, the person who rules on plays in a game. *v.* To act as an umpire.

ump-teen *adj.*, *Slang* An indefinitely large number. **umpteenth** *adj.*

UMT *abbr.* Universal Military Training.

UMW *abbr.* United Mine Workers.

UN *abbr.* United Nations.

un- *prefix* The reverse or opposite of an act; removal or release from.

un-abat-ed *adj.* To be not abated. **unabatedly** *adv.*

un-able *adj.* Not having the mental capabilities.

un-abridged *adj.* To be the most complete of a group or of a class.

un-ac-cept-able *adj.* To be not welcome. **unacceptably** *adv.*

un-ac-com-mo-dat-ed *adj.* To be not accommodated.

un-ac-com-pa-nied *adj.* Alone; without a companion. *Mus.* Solo.

un-ac-count-a-ble *adj.* Without an explanation; mysterious; not responsible. -**ably** *adv.*, **unaccountability** *n.*

un-ac-count-ed *adj.* Not being accounted for.

un-ac-cus-tomed *adj.* Not used to or in the habit of; not ordinary.

una cor-da *adv.* With the soft pedal pressed downward, such as with a piano.

un-adorned *adj.* Being without decorations.

un-adorn-ment *n.* The state of being unadorned.

un-adul-ter-at-ed *adj.* To be pure. **unadulteratedly** *adv.*

un-ad-vised *adj.* To do something or an action without consideration.

un-af-fect-ed *adj.* Not being effected in any way by something or someone.

un-af-fec-tion-ate *adj.* Without or lacking affection.

un-al-loyed *adj.* To be not alloyed; pure.

un-al-ter-able *adj.* Incapable of being changed. **unalterableness** *n.*

un-am-biv-a-lent *adj.* Being not ambivalent. **unambivalently** *adv.*

unan *abbr.* Unanimous.

un-an-chor *v.* To remove or to loosen for an anchor, such as a boat.

un-anes-the-tized *adj.* Not have been subjected to the anesthetic.

u-na-nim-i-ty *n.* The state of being unanimous.

u-nan-i-mous *adj.* Agreed to completely; based on the agreement of all. **unanimously** *adv.*

un-an-tic-i-pat-ed *adj.* To be not anticipated. **unanticipatedly** *adv.*

un-apol-o-get-ic *adj.* To be put forward without an apology.

un-ap-peas-able *adj.* Not to be appeased.

un-ap-proach-able *adj.* To be physically inaccessible.

un-apt *adj.* Not likely.

un-armed *adj.* Lacking means for protection.

un-ar-tic-u-lat-ed *adj.* To be not carefully reasoned before something is done.

una-ry *adj.* To consist of a single item.

un-ashamed *adj.* To be without guilt. **unashamedly** *adv.*

un-as-sail-able *adj.* Being not liable to attack. **unassailableness** *n.*

un-as-ser-tive *adj.* Not being assertive.

un-as-sist-ed *adj.* To be made without being assisted by another.

un-as-sum-ing *adj.* Modest and not showy. **unassumingness** *n.*

un-at-tached *adj.* Not engaged, going steady, or married.

un-at-trac-tive *adj.* Not being attractive or pretty; dull.

un-avail-ing *adj.* To be not availing. **unavailingness** *n.*

un-a-void-able *adj.* Inevitable; unstoppable. **unavoidably** *adv.*

un-a-ware *adj.* Not realizing. **unawareness** *n.*, **unawarely** *adv.*

un-backed *adj.* To be lacking aid or support from another.

un-bal-ance *v.* To put someone or something out of balance.

un-bal-anced *adj.* Not in balance.

un-bal-last-ed *adj.* Not steadied with ballast.

un-ban-dage *v.* To take off or to remove a bandage form a wound.

un-bar-bered *adj.* To have unkempt long hair.

un-barred *adj.* Not being secured or fixed with a bar.

un-be *v.* To cease to have being.

un-bear-a-ble *adj.* Not possible to endure; intolerable. **unbearably** *adv.*

un-beat-a-ble *adj.* To be possessing unsurpassible qualities.

un-beat-en *adj.* Being not pounded.

un-be-coming *adj.* Unattractive; not pleasing; not proper.
unbecomingness *n.*

un-be-known *or* **un-be-knownst** *adj.* Not known; without one's knowledge.

un-be-lief *n.* The skepticism in the matters such as one's religious faith.

un-be-liev-able *adj.* Incredible; hard to accept; not to be believed.
unbelievably *adv.*

un-be-liev-er *n.* A person who does not believe certain things as being true.

un-belt-ed *adj.* To not be belted or furnished with a belt.

un-bend *v.* To make something straight.
unbendable *adj.*

un-bend-ing *adj.* To not bend.

un-bi-ased *adj.* To be free from bias.

un-bib-li-cal *adj.* To be unsanctioned by the Bible.

un-bid-den *adj.* Being not bidden.

un-bind *v.* To take or remove a band from something or from someone.

un-blessed *adj.* To be not blessed.

un-blind-ed *adj.* Existing free for illusion.

un-blink-ing *adj.* Not showing any emotions such as crying.

un-block *v.* To free something from being blocked by something else.

un-bod-i-ed *adj.* To have no body.

un-bolt *v.* To unfasten with the withdrawal of a bolt such as with a lock on a door.

un-born *adj.* To be existing without birth.

un-bo-som *v.* To disclose or tell the thoughts of oneself to another.

un-bound *adj.* Being free or not fastened to anything or by anything.

un-box *v.* To remove something from a box.

un-brace *v.* To detach as if removing a brace or a band from something or someone.

un-braid *v.* To take apart grouped strands of hair or cloth.

un-branched *adj.* To have no or be without branched.

un-bred *adj.* Being not taught.

un-bri-dle *v.* To free from or to unfasten a bridle.

un-bro-ken *adj.* Being not violated or broken; being in one piece.

un-buck-le *v.* To loosen or to remove the buckle of something such as a belt.

un-budg-ing *adj.* Unable to to moved or changed.

un-build *v.* To take down such as a house.

un-bun-dle *v.* To price or place something separately.

un-bur-den *v.* To relieve from a burden; to free from fears or problems.

un-but-tered *adj.* Being without butter.

un-but-ton *v.* To open the hatches; to loosen to buttons of a jacket or of a coat in order to remove the object from the body.

un-but-toned *adj.* Not provided with buttons.

un-cage *v.* To set something or someone free from a cage or the object which holds them.

un-cal-cu-lat-ed *adj.* Not thought about or out before it occurs.

un-called for *adj.* Not necessary or needed; not requested.

un-can-did *adj.* Not honest.

un-can-ny *adj.* Strange, odd, or mysterious; exceptional.
uncannily *adv.*, **uncanniness** *n.*

un-cap *v.* To take off a covering or lid of something.

un-caused *adj.* Having no cause or reason.

un-ceas-ing *adj.* To never cease or end.
unceasingly *adv.*

un-cel-e-brat-ed *adj.* Not being famous or well-known.

un-cer-e-mo-ni-ous *adj.* To be informal, not ceremonious.

un-cer-tain *adj.* Doubtful; not sure; not known; hard to predict.
uncertainly *adv.*, **uncertainness** *n.*

un-cer-tain-ty *n.* The state of being uncertain or unsure.

un-changed *adj.* Having nothing new or different.

un-change-able *adj.* To be not changing.
unchangeableness *n.*

un-char-ac-ter-is-tic *adj.* Being not typical.

un-charged *adj.* Not being charged with something.

un-char-i-ta-ble *adj.* To be lacking in charity. **uncharitableness** *n.*

un-chart-ed *adj.* Not plotted such as on a map.

un-chas-ti-ty *n.* The state of being unchaste.

un-chiv-al-rous *adj.* Not being chival rous. **unchivalrously** *adv.*

un-choke *v.* To unblock an obstruction such as a piece of food in the throat.

un-church *v.* To expel someone from a church. **unchurched** *adj.*

un-cial *n.* A style of writing used in Greek and Latin manuscripts.

un-ci-form *adj.* To be hook-shaped.

un-ci-nar-ia *n.* A type of parasitic worm in the shape of a hook; hookworm.

un-ci-nate *adj.* To be bent at the end of the tip.

un-cir-cum-cised *adj.* Being spiritually

impure.

un-civ-il *adj.* Being not civil.

un-civ-i-lized *adj.* Without culture or refinement; without an established cultural and social way of living.

un-clamp *v.* To remove the clamp off of something.

un-clar-i-ty *n.* A lack of clarity.

un-clasp *v.* To remove the clasp of or to open the clasp of something.

un-clas-si-cal *adj.* Not being classical.

un-clas-si-fied *adj.* To not be subject to a security classification.

un-cle *n.* The brother of one's mother or father; the husband of an aunt.

un-clean *adj.* Immoral; dirty; not decent. **-ness**, **uncleanliness** *n.*, **uncleanly** *adv.*

un-clench *v.* To open something from a clenched position.

Un-cle Sam *n.* The American nation of people.

un-climb-a-ble *adj.* Unable to be climbed. **unclimbableness** *n.*

un-cloak *v.* To remove a cover from.

un-closed *adj.* Not being settled.

un-clothe *v.* To uncover or undress. **unclothed** *adj.*

un-cloud-ed *adj.* Not being covered by clouds. **uncloudedly** *adv.*

un-clut-ter *v.* To take clutter from an area; to make neat.

un-cock *v.* To take away the hammer from such as with a gun.

un-cof-fin *v.* To take out of a coffin.

un-coil *v.* To release from a coiled state; to unwind.

un-coined *adj.* Not being minted.

un-com-fort-a-ble *adj.* Disturbed; not at ease physically or mentally; causing discomfort. **uncomfortably** *adv.*

un-com-mer-cial *adj.* Not related to commerce.

un-com-mit-ted *adj.* Not being committed to something or to someone.

un-com-mon *adj.* Rare; odd; unusual. **uncommonly** *adv.*, **uncommonness** *n.*

un-com-mu-ni-ca-ble *adj.* Being unable to communicate something.

un-com-mu-ni-ca-tive *adj.* Not able to give information about something.

un-com-pas-sion-ate *adj.* Being unfeeling; not compassionate.

un-com-pet-i-tive *adj.* Being unable to compete in a competition or sport.

un-com-plain-ing *adj.* Not complaining. **uncomplainingly** *adv.*

un-com-pli-cat-ed *adj.* To be not complex or complicated; simple.

un-com-pli-men-ta-ry *adj.* Not being complimentary.

un-com-pre-hend-ing *adj.* To be lacking in understanding of something.

un-com-pro-mis-ing *adj.* Firm; unwilling to give in or to compromise. **uncompromisingly** *adv.*

un-con-cern *n.* Lack of interest; disinterest; indifference.

un-con-cerned *adj.* The state of not having any interest in something or someone. **-ness** *n.*, **unconcernedly** *adv.*

un-con-di-tion-al *adj.* Without conditions or limits. **unconditionally** *adv.*

un-con-di-tioned *adj.* Not subjected to conditioning.

un-con-form-a-ble *adj.* Not conforming to anything such as ideals.

un-con-for-mi-ty *n.* The lack of conformity.

un-con-ge-nial *adj.* Not being compatible to something or to someone.

un-con-ge-nial-i-ty *n.* The state of being uncongenial.

un-con-quer-a-ble *adj.* Being unable to be conquered by someone.

un-con-scio-na-ble *adj.* To be not guided by the conscience. **unconscionability**, **-ness** *n.*

un-con-scious *adj.* Not mentally aware; done without thought; not on purpose. **unconsciously** *adv.* **unconsciousness** *n.*

un-con-sid-er-ed *adj.* To be not worth considering.

un-con-sol-i-dat-ed *adj.* To be arranged loosely.

un-con-sti-tu-tion-al *adj.* Contrary to the constitution or the basic laws of a state or country.

un-con-straint *n.* To be free from constraint.

un-con-trol-la-ble *adj.* To exist free from the control of another.

un-con-ven-tion-al *adj.* Not in accordance with convention.

un-con-vinc-ing *adj.* To not be convincing. **unconvincingly** *adv.*

un-cool *adj.* To be lacking or without assurance.

un-cork *v.* To release from a container that has been sealed with a cork.

un-cor-set-ed *adj.* To not be wearing a corset.

un-cou-ple *v.* To release or disconnect from as railroad cars.

un-couth *adj.* Acting or speaking crudely, unrefined; clumsy or awkward. **uncouthness** *n.*, **-ly** *adv.*

un-cov-er *v.* To remove the cover from something; to disclose. **uncovered** *adj.*

un-cre-at-ed *adj.* To not exist because of creation.

un-crit-i-cal *adj.* To be lacking in discrimination.

un-cross *v.* To remove or to change something from a crossed position.

un-crown *v.* To remove the crown from someone such as a king.

un-crum-ple *v.* To return something to its original smooth condition.

un-crush-a-ble *adj.* Not being able to be crushed by something or by someone.

unc-tion *n.* An ointment which is used for the purpose of anointing an injury.

unc-tu-ous *adj.* To be smooth in texture; have organic matter and be easily workable.

un-curl *v.* To straighten something from a curled position.

un-cut *adj.* Not being cut into.

un-cyn-i-cal *adj.* Not being cynical.

un-daunt-a-ble *adj.* To be incapable of being daunted.

un-daunt-ed *adj.* Being courageously resolute. **undauntedly** *adv.*

un-de-bat-a-ble *adj.* Being not subject to

debate. **undebatably** *adv.*

un-de-cid-ed *adj.* Unsettled; having made no firm decision; open to change. **undecidedly** *adv.*

un-dec-y-le-nic a-cid *n.* Type of acid which is found in perspiration.

un-de-fend-ed *adj.* Being not defended or protected.

un-dem-o-crat-ic *adj.* To not be agreeing with the ideals of the democratic party.

un-de-mon-stra-tive *adj.* Being restrained in the expression of one's feelings or emotions. **-ness** *n.*

un-de-ni-able *adj.* Not open to doubt or denial; not possible to contradict. **undeniably** *adv.*

un-der *prep.* Below, in place or position; in a place lower than another; less in degree, number, or other quality; inferior in rank, quality, or character; during the reign or period; in accordance with. less than the required amount; insufficient.

un-der *prefix.* Location beneath or below; lower in importance or rank, degree or amount.

un-der-achiever *n.* A kind of student that fails to achieve his/her scholastic potential.

un-der-act *v.* To perform something in a feeble manner.

un-der-ac-tiv-i-ty *n.* A low level of activity which is thought of as not being normal.

un-der-age *adj.* Being less than legal age.

un-der-arm *n.* The armpit.

un-der-bel-ly *n.* The surface which is under a body when on one's stomach.

un-der-bid *v.* To bid for something at a level which is too low.

un-der-body *n.* The parts or sections of the body which are low.

un-der-bred *adj.* Being of an inferior breed.

un-der-brim *n.* The area on the underside of a hat's brim.

un-der-brush *n.* Small bushes, vines, and plants that grow under tall trees.

un-der-bud-get-ed *adj.* To be provided with a budget which is inadequate.

un-der-car-riage *n.* The landing gear of an airplane.

un-der-charge *v.* To charge too little for something that one buys.

un-der-class *n.* The class which is lower such as in high school.

un-der-class-man *n.* A person who is a member of the freshman class in high school.

un-der-clothes *pl., n.* Clothes worn next to the skin; underwear.

un-der-coat *n.* A jacket which can be worn under another jacket.

un-der-coat-ing *n.* A kind of waterproof coating which is applied to the underside of cars for the prevention of rusting and other types of wear.

un-der-cov-er *adj.* To be executed in a secret manner; engaged in spying for one's country, etc.

un-der-croft *n.* A type of room which is subterranean.

un-der-cur-rent *n.* The current that is located below the surface currents in the water.

un-der-cut *v.* To sell something at a price which is lower than the competitor's price to get the business of the one being offered the price.

un-der-de-vel-oped *adj.* Not fully mature or grown; lacking modern communications and industry.

un-der-de-vel-op-ment *n.* The state of being underdeveloped.

un-der-do *v.* To do something less thoroughly than one is able to do it.

un-der-done *adj.* To be not completely cooked.

un-der-dress *n.* A piece of clothing which is made to be worn under the dress of a woman when the dress is sheer.

un-der-ed-u-cat-ed *adj.* Being educated poorly.

un-der-em-ployed *adj.* To have less than adequate employment.

un-der-es-ti-mate *v.* To place or to put a value or price on something which is too low. **underestimation** *n.*

un-der-feed *v.* To feed someone or something too little food.

un-der-foot *adj.* Underneath or below the feet; being so close to one's feet as to be in the way.

un-der-fur *n.* A thick and soft fur that is lying under the long and course hair of a mammal.

un-der-gar-ment *n.* A kind of garment that is made to be worn under another piece of garment, such as underwear.

un-der-gird *v.* To make the foundation of something.

un-der-glaze *adj.* Suitable for applying before glaze is applied to something.

un-der-go *v.* To have the experience of; to be subjected to.

un-der-grad-u-ate *n.* A college or university student studying for a bachelor's degree.

un-der-ground *adj.* A channel or space which is subterranean. *n.* A group which functions outside of the law.

un-der-ground-er *n.* The member of the underground.

un-der-growth *n.* A type of growth which is found growing on the floor of the forest.

un-der-hand *adj.* Done deceitfully and secretly; sneaky. **underhanded** *adj.*, **underhandedly** *adv.*

un-der-hung *adj.* To have an underhung jaw; protruding or projecting beyond the upper jaw.

un-der-in-sured *adj.* Being not sufficiently insured.

un-der-laid *adj.* To be placed beneath something.

un-der-lay *v.* To cover the bottom of something.

un-der-let *v.* To be below the real value.

un-der-lie *v.* To be at the basis of something.

un-der-line v. To draw a line directly under something. **underline** n.

un-der-ling n. The person who is under the orders of another person.

un-der-lip n. The lower lip of a person's mouth.

un-der-ly-ing adj. To be lying below something.

un-der-manned adj. Being inadequately staffed.

un-der-mine v. To weaken; to make less strong.

un-der-most adj. The lowest in position.

un-der-neath adv. Beneath or below; on the under side; lower. prep. Under; below.

un-der-nour-ished adj. To be supplied with less than the minimum amount of the needed food. **undernourishment** n.

un-der-nu-tri-tion n. The lacking or deficient bodily nutrition which is due to inadequate food intake.

un-der-paid adj. To receive less than enough or adequate pay.

un-der-pants n. The pants which are worn under another garment.

un-der-part n. An auxiliary part or section.

un-der-pass n. A road or walk that goes under another.

un-der-pin v. To strengthen the foundation of something.

un-der-pin-ning n. The material which is used for the support of a structure.

un-der-play v. To act with restraint.

un-der-plot n. A kind of dramatic plot in a play that is subordinate to the main action or plot.

un-der-powered adj. To be driven by an engine that is not sufficiently powered.

un-der-priv-i-leged adj. Deprived of economic and social advantages.

un-der-pro-duc-tion n. A type of production which is unable to satisfy the demand.

un-der-pro-duc-tive adj. Being unable to produce something adequately.

un-der-proof adj. To be containing less alcohol than the proof spirit.

un-der-rate v. To rate or value below the true worth.

un-der-re-port v. To report something as being less than it actually is.

un-der-ripe adj. To be insufficiently ripe.

un-der-run v. To pass something along under in order to look at it or examine it.

un-der-sat-u-rat-ed adj. To be less than normally saturated or wet with a liquid.

un-der-score v. To emphasize.

un-der-sea adj. Being carried under the sea or under the surface of the sea.

un-der-sec-re-tar-i-at n. The staff which is under the secretary.

un-der-sell v. To sell for less than a competitor.

un-der-shirt n. A shirt worn under another.

un-der-side n. The side or part on the bottom.

un-der-stand v. To comprehend; to realize; to know the feelings and thoughts of. **understanding** v.

un-der-stand-able adj. Able to sympathize or comprehend. -y adv.

un-der-state v. To make too little of the actual situation. **understatement** n.

un-der-stood adj. Agreed upon by all.

un-der-stud-y v. To learn another person's part or role in order to be able to replace him if necessary.

un-der-take v. To set about to do a task; to pledge oneself to a certain job; to attempt. **undertaking** v.

un-der-tak-er n. A person who prepares the dead for burial.

un-der-tone n. A low, quiet voice; a pale or subdued color visible through other colors.

un-der-tow n. The underwater current which runs in the opposite direction of the surface current.

un-der-wa-ter adj. Occurring, happening or used beneath the surface of the water. **underwater** adv.

un-der-write v. To sign or write at the end of something; to finance; to assume a risk by means of insurance. To assume responsibility for; to undertake to pay a written pledge of money.

un-de-sir-a-ble adj. Offensive; not wanted. **undesirably** adv.

un-do v. To cancel; to reverse; to loosen or unfasten; to open a package. **undoer** n., **undoing** v.

un-done adj. Not finished; unfastened; ruined.

un-du-late v. To move from side to side with a flowing motion; to have a wavy shape. **undulation** n.

un-dy-ing adj. Without end.

un-earth v. To dig up from the earth; to find or discover.

un-earth-ly adj. Strange; not from this world.

un-easy adj. Feeling or causing distress or discomfort; embarrassed; awkward; uncertain. **uneasily** adv., **uneasiness** n.

un-em-ployed adj. Without a job; without work. **unemployment** n.

un-en-thu-si-as-tic adj. Not being excited about something.

un-e-qual adj. Not even; not fair; not of the same size or time; lacking sufficient ability. **unequaled** adj.

un-equiv-o-cal adj. Being clear; having no doubts.

UNES-CO abbr. United Nations Educational Scientific, and Cultural Organization.

un-es-sen-tial adj. Not being important.

un-e-ven adj. Not equal; varying in consistency or form; not balanced.

un-e-vent-ful adj. Lacking in significance; calm. **uneventfully** adv.

un-ex-pect-ed adj. Surprising; happening without warning. **unexpectedly** adv.

un-fail-ing adj. Constant, unchanging. **unfailingly** adv.

un-fair adj. Not honest; marked by a lack of justice. **unfairly** adv., **-ness** n.

un-faith-ful adj. Breaking a promise or

agreement; without loyalty; guilty of adultery. **-ness** n., **unfaithfully** adv.

un-fa-mil-iar adj. Not knowing; strange; foreign. **unfamiliarity** n.

un-fath-om-able adj. Being unable to comprehend.

un-fa-vor-able adj. Not desired; harmful; unpleasant. **unfavorably** adv., **unfavorableness** n.

un-feel-ing adj. Without sympathy; hardhearted; without sensation. **unfeelingly** adv.

un-fin-ished adj. At loose ends; not completed.

un-fit adj. Not suitable; not qualified; in poor body or mental health. **unfitly** adv., **unfitness** n.

un-fold v. To open up the folds of and lay flat; to reveal gradually. **unfoldment** n.

un-fore-seen adj. Not anticipated or expected.

un-for-get-ta-ble adj. Impossible or hard to forget; memorable. **-y** adv.

un-for-tu-nate adj. Causing or having bad luck, damage, or harm. n. A person who has no luck. **-ly** adv.

un-found-ed adj. Not founded or based on fact; groundless; lacking a factual basis.

un-friend-ly adj. Showing a lack of kindness; not friendly; not favorable. **unfriendliness** n.

un-frock v. To remove from a position of honor; to relieve from the duties of an office, post, etc.

un-furl v. To unroll or unfold; to open up or out.

un-fur-nished adj. Without furniture.

un-god-ly adj. Wicked; evil; lacking reverence for God. **ungodliness** n.

un-grate-ful adj. Not thankful; showing no appreciation. **ungratefully** adv.

un-guent n. A healing or soothing salve; ointment.

ungulate n. A group of hoofed mammals, many having horns.

un-happy adj. Sad; without laughter or joy; not satisfied or pleased. **unhappily** adv., **unhappiness** n.

un-healthy adj. Sickly; not enjoying good healthy.

un-heard adj. Not heard; not listened to.

un-heard--of adj. Not known or done before; without precedent.

un-ho-ly adj. Wicked.

un-hook v. To release or undo from a hook.

un-hur-ried adj. At a leisurely pace. **unhurriedly** adv.

UNI-CEF abbr. United Nations Children's Fund.

u-ni-corn n.

A mythical animal resembling a horse, with a horn in the center of its forehead.

u-ni-cy-cle n. A one wheeled vehicle with pedals. **unicyclist** n.

un-i-den-ti-fied fly-ing ob-ject n. A flying object that cannot be explained or identified, abbreviated as UFO.

uni-fac-to-ri-al adj. Controlled by a single gene.

u-ni-form n. Identical clothing worn by the members of a group to distinguish them from the general population. adj. Having the same manner or degree or form. **uniformly** adv.

u-ni-fy v. To come together as one; to unite. **unifier** n.

uni-lat-er-al adj. Affecting only one side of a subject.

uni-lin-ear adj. Developing in a series of stages from primitive to advanced.

un-in-hab-it-ed adj. Not lived in; empty.

un-in-ter-est-ed adj. Having no interest or concern in; not interested.

un-ion n. The act of joining together of two or more groups or things; a group of countries or states joined under one government; a marriage; an organized body of employees who work together to upgrade their working conditions and wages. **Union** The United States, especially the federal government during the Civil War.

union card n. A card which certifies membership in good standing in a union.

unip-a-rous adj. Having produced one egg or offspring at a time.

u-nique adj. Unlike any other; sole. **uniqueness** n., **uniquely** adv.

u-ni-sex adj. Adaptable and appropriate for both sexes. **unisexually** adv., **unisexual** adj., **unisexuality** n.

u-ni-son n. In music, the exact sameness of pitch, as of a tone; harmonious agreement.

u-nit n. Any one of several parts regarded as a whole; an exact quantity that is used as a standard of measurement; a special section or part of a machine.

uni-tar-i-an n. A member of a denomination that believes the deity exists in one person.

u-nite v. To join or come together for a common purpose.

United Nations n. An international organization formed in 1945.

United States of America n. A country bordering the Atlantic and Pacific Oceans, Mexico, and Canada.

unit rule n. A ruling which allows a delegation to a Democratic national convention to cast its entire vote as a unit by majority vote.

u-ni-ty n., pl. **-ies** The fact or state of being one; accord; agreement; harmony.

u-ni-valve n. A mollusk having a one-piece shell, such as a snail.

u-ni-ver-sal adj. Having to do with the world or the universe in its entirety. **universally** adv., **universalness** n.

u-ni-verse n. The world, stars, planets,

space, and all that is contained.

u-ni-ver-si-ty *n., pl.* **-ies** An educational institution offering undergraduate and graduate degrees in a variety of academic areas.

un-just *adj.* Not fair; lacking justice or fairness. **unjustly** *adv.*

un-kempt *adj.* Poorly groomed; messy; untidy.

un-kind *adj.* Harsh; lacking in sympathy, concern, or understanding. **unkindly** *adj.* **unkindness** *n.*

un-known *adj.* Strange; unidentified; not known; not familiar or famous.

un-lead-ed *adj.* Containing no lead.

un-like *prep.* Dissimilar; not alike; not equal in strength or quantity; not usual for.

un-lim-it-ed *adj.* Having no boundaries or limitations.

un-load *v.* To take or remove the load; to unburden; to dispose or get rid of by selling in volume.

un-lock *v.* To open, release, or unfasten a lock; open with a key.

un-loose *v.* To loosen or undo; to release.

un-luck-y *adj.* Unfortunate; having bad luck; disappointing or unsuitable. **unluckily** *adv.*

un-manned *adj.* Designed to operate or be operated without a crew of people.

un-mask *v.* To reveal the truth of one's identity; to expose.

un-men-tion-a-ble *adj.* Improper or unsuitable.

un-mis-tak-a-ble *adj.* Very clear and evident; understood; obvious. **unmistakably** *adv.*

un-mor-al *adj.* Having no moral knowledge.

un-nat-u-ral *adj.* Abnormal or unusual; strange; artificial. **unnaturally** *adv.*

un-nec-es-sar-y *adj.* Not needed; not appropriate. **unnecessarily** *adv.*

un-nerve *v.* To frighten; to upset. **unnervingly** *adv.*

un-num-bered *adj.* Countless; not identified by number.

un-oc-cu-pied *adj.* Empty; not occupied.

un-pack *v.* To remove articles out of trunks, suitcases, boxes, or other storage places.

un-pleas-ant *adj.* Not agreeable; not pleasant. **unpleasantly** *adv.*, **-ness** *n.*

un-pop-u-lar *adj.* Not approved or liked. **unpopularity** *n.*

un-pre-dict-a-ble *adj.* Not capable or being foretold; not reliable. **-ably** *adj.*

un-pre-pared *adj.* Not equipped or ready.

un-pro-fes-sion-al *adj.* Contrary to the standards of a profession; having no professional status.

un-prof-it-a-ble *adj.* Showing or giving no profit; serving no purpose.

un-qual-i-fied *adj.* Lacking the proper qualifications; unreserved.

un-ques-tion-a-ble *adj.* Being indisputable.

un-rav-el *v.* To separate threads; to solve; to clarify; to come apart.

un-re-al *adj.* Having no substance or reality.

un-rea-son-a-ble *adj.* Not according to reason; exceeding all reasonable limits. **unreasonableness** *n.*

un-re-lent-ing *adj.* Not weakening in vigor or determination.

un-re-li-a-ble *adj.* Unable to be trusted; not dependable.

un-re-served *adj.* Done or given without reserve; unlimited. **unreservedly** *adv.*, **unreservedness** *n.*

un-re-strained *adj.* Not held back, forced, or affected.

un-ripe *adj.* Immature, not ready to harvest. **unripeness** *n.*

un-ruf-fled *adj.* Serene and calm in the face of setbacks.

un-ru-ly *adj.* Disorderly; difficult to subdue or control.

un-sat-is-fac-to-ry *adj.* Unacceptable; not pleasing.

un-sa-vory *adj.* Disagreeable; morally offensive.

un-screw *v.* To loosen or unfasten by removing screws from.

un-scru-pu-lous *adj.* Without morals, guiding principles, or rules. **unscrupulously** *adv.*, **-ness** *n.*

un-seat *v.* To cause to lose one's seat; to force out of office.

un-seg-re-gat-ed *adj.* Being free from racial segregation.

un-self-ish *adj.* Willing to share; thinking of another's well-being before one's own. **unselfishly** *adv.*, **unselfishness** *n.*

un-set-tle *v.* To cause to be upset or excited; to disturb. **unsettled** *adj.*

un-sheathe *v.* To draw a sword from a sheath or other case.

un-sight-ly *adj.* Not pleasant to look at; ugly.

un-skilled *adj.* Having no skills or training in a given kind of work.

un-skill-ful *adj.* Lacking in proficiency. **unskillfully** *adv.*, **unskillfulness** *n.*

un-sound *adj.* Having defects; not solidly made; unhealthy in body or mind. **unsoundly** *adv.*, **unsoundness** *n.*

un-speak-a-ble *adj.* Of or relating to something which cannot be expressed or described. **unspeakably** *adv.*

un-sta-ble *adj.* Not steady or firmly fixed; having the tendency to fluctuate or change.

un-stead-y *adj.* Not secure; unstable; variable. **unsteadily** *adv.*, **-iness** *n.*

un-sub-stan-tial *adj.* Lacking strength, weight, or solidity; unreal.

un-suit-a-ble *adj.* Unfitting; not suitable; not appropriate for a specific circumstance. **unsuitably** *adv.*, **-ness** *n.*

un-swerv-ing *adj.* Being loyal and steady.

un-tan-gle *v.* To free from snarls or entanglements.

un-thank-ful *adj.* Ungrateful.

un-think-a-ble *adj.* Unimaginable.

un-ti-dy *adj.* Messy; showing a lack of tidiness; not organized or neat. **untidily** *adv.*, **untidiness** *n.*

un-tie *v.* To unfasten or loosen; to free from a restraint or bond.

un-til *prep.* Up to the time of. *conj.* To the time when; to the degree or place.

un-time-ly *adj.* Premature; before the expected time.

un-told *adj.* Not revealed; not told; inexpressible; cannot be described or revealed.

un-touch-a-ble *adj.* Cannot be touched; incapable of being obtained or reached.

un-true *adj.* Not true; contrary to the truth; not faithful; disloyal.

un-truth *n.* Something which is not true; the state of being false. **-ful** *adj.*, **untruthfully** *adv.*, **untruthfulness** *n.*

un-used *adj.* Not put to use; never having been used.

un-u-su-al *adj.* Not usual; uncommon. **unusually** *adv.*, **unusualness** *n.*

un-ut-ter-a-ble *adj.* Incapable of being described or expressed; unpronounceable. **unutterably** *adv.*

un-veil *v.* To remove a veil from; to uncover; to reveal.

un-war-y *adj.* Not cautious or careful; careless.

un-wa-ver-ing *adj.* Steady.

un-whole-some *adj.* Unhealthy; morally corrupt or harmful.

un-will-ing *adj.* Reluctant; not willing. **unwillingly** *adv.*, **unwillingness** *n.*

un-wind *v.* To undo or reverse the winding of; to untangle.

un-wise *adj.* Lacking good judgment or common sense. **unwisely** *adv.*

un-wor-thy *adj.* Not deserving; not becoming or befitting; lacking merit or worth; shameful. **unworthiness** *n.*

up *adv.* From a lower position to a higher one; on, in, or to a higher level, position, or place; to a greater degree or amount; in or into a specific action or an excited state, as they stirred up trouble; to be even with in time, degree, or space, as up to date; under consideration, as up for discussion; in a safe, protected place, as vegetable are put up in jars; totally, completely, as the building was burned up; in baseball, at bat or, as up to bat. **up** front To be honest.

up-beat *n.*, *Mus.* The relatively unaccented beat preceding the down beat. *adj.* Optimistic; happy.

up-bring-ing *n.* The process of teaching and rearing a child.

up-com-ing *adj.* About to take place or appear.

up-date *v.* To revise or bring up-to-date; to modernize. **update** *n.*

up-draft *n.* An upward current of air.

up-grade *v.* To increase the grade, rank, or standard of. *n.* An upward slope.

up-hill *adv.* Up an incline. *adj.* Hard to accomplish; going up a hill or incline.

up-hold *v.* To support.

up-hol-ster *v.* To cover furniture with fabric covering, cushions, and padding. **upholsterer**, **upholstery** *n.*

up-keep *n.* The cost and work needed to keep something in good condition.

up-land *n.* A piece of land which is elevated or higher than the land around it.

up-lift *v.* To raise or lift up; to improve the social, economic, and moral level of a group or of a society.

up-on *prep.* On.

up-per *adj.* Higher in status, position or location. *n.* The part of a shoe to which the sole is attached. *Slang* A drug used as a stimulant. **upper case** *n.* The large or capital case of letters.

up-per--class *adj.* Economically or socially superior.

up-per-class-man *n.* A junior or senior at a high school or college.

up-right *adj.* Having a vertical direction or position; honest. *n.* Something standing vertically, such as a beam in a building.

up-ris-ing *n.* A revolt; a rebellion; an insurrection.

up-roar *n.* A confused, loud noise; a commotion.

up-root *v.* To detach completely by pulling up the roots. **uprooter** *n.*

up-set *v.* To capsize; to turn over; to throw into confusion or disorder; to overcome; to beat unexpectedly. *adj.* Capsized; overturned; distressed; troubled. **upsetter** *n.*

up-stage *adj. & adv.* Toward or at the back part of a stage. *Slang* To steal the show or scene from.

up-stairs *adv.* Up one or more flights of stairs. *adj.* Situated on the upper floor.

up-stand-ing *adj.* Straightforward; honest; upright.

up-start *n.* One who has risen quickly to power or wealth, especially one who is conceited.

up-stream *adv.* Toward the origin of a stream; against the current.

up-tight *adv.* Nervous, tense, or anxious. **uptightness** *n.*

up--to--date *adj.* Most current or recent; appropriate to the present time.

up-town *adv.* Toward or in the upper part of town. **uptown** *adv.*

up-ward *or* **up-wards** *adv.* From a lower position to or toward a higher one. *adj.* Directed toward a higher position. **upwardly** *adv.*

u-ra-ni-um *n.* A hard, heavy, shiny metallic element that is radioactive, used especially in research and in nuclear weapons and fuels, symbolized by U.

ura-nog-ra-phy *n.* The science concerned with the description of the heavens and the celestial bodies.

ura-nom-e-try *n.* A chart of celestial bodies.

U-ra-nus *n.* The seventh planet of the solar system in distance from the sun.

ur-ban *adj.* Pertaining to a city or having characteristics of a city; living or being in a city. **urbanite** *n.*, **urbanize** *v.*

ur-ban-ol-o-gy *n.* The study dealing with the problems of a city such as education, politics, planning, etc.

urge *v.* To encourage, push, or drive; to recommend persistently and strongly.

n. An influence, impulse, or force.

ur-gent *adj.* Requiring immediate attention. **urgency** *n.*, **urgently** *adv.*

urine *n.* In man and other mammals, the yellowish fluid waste produced by the kidneys.

Ur-sa Ma-jor *n.* The constellation of seven stars forming the Big Dipper.

Ur-sa Mi-nor *n.* The constellation of seven stars forming the Little Dipper.

Us *pl., pron.* The objective case of we; used as an indirect object, direct object, or object of a preposition.

US *abbr.* United States.

USA *abbr.* United States of America.

us-a-ble *or* **use-a-ble** *adj.* Fit or capable of being used. **usability** *n.*, **usably** *adv.*

us-age *n.* The way or act of using something; the way words are used.

use *v.* To put into action; to employ for a special purpose; to employ on a regular basis; to exploit for one's own advantage. *n.* The state or fact of being used; the act or way of using something; the reason or purpose for which something is used; the function of something; the occupation or utilization of property. **used** *adj.*, **useful** *adj.*, **useless** *adj.*

ush-er *n.* A person who directs people to the correct seats in a theatre. *v.* To show or escort someone to a place; to go before as a representative or sign of something that comes later.

USSR *abbr.* Union of Soviet Socialist Republics.

u-su-al *adj.* Ordinary or common; regular; customary. **usually** *adv.*, **usualness** *n.*

u-surp *v.* To take over by force without authority. **usurpation, usurper** *n.*

usu-ry *n.* An exorbitant rate of interest charged to a borrower.

U-tah *n.* A state located in the western part of the United States.

u-ten-sil *n.* A tool, implement, or container, especially one for the kitchen.

uter-ine *adj.* Relating to birth by the same mother but by a different father.

u-ter-us *n.* An organ of female mammals within which young develop and grow before birth. **uterine** *adj.*

u-til-i-ty *n., pl.* -ies The state or quality of being useful; a company which offers a public service, as water, heat, or electricity.

u-til-ize *v.* To make or put to use.

ut-most *adj.* Of the greatest amount or degree; most distant. **utmost** *n.*

u-to-pi-a *n.* A condition or place of perfection or complete harmony and peace.

ut-ter *v.* To say or express verbally; to speak. *adv.* Absolute; complete. **utterly** *adv.*, **utterance** *n.*

ut-ter-most *n.* To do or preform to our highest ability.

u-vu-la *n.* The fleshy projection which hangs above the back of the tongue. **uvular** *adj.*, **uvularly** *adv.*

ux-or-i-cide *adj.* Murderer of ones wife by her husband.

V, v The twenty-second letter of the English alphabet; the Roman numeral for 5.

va-cant *adj.* Empty; not occupied; without expression or thought.

va-cate *v.* To leave; to cease to occupy.

va-ca-tion *n.* A period of time away from work for pleasure, relaxation, or rest.

vac-ci-nate *v.* To inject with a vaccine so as to produce immunity to an infectious disease, as measles or smallpox.

vac-ci-na-tion *n.* The inoculation with a vaccine.

vac-cine *n.* A solution of weakened or killed microorganisms, as bacteria or viruses, injected into the body to produce immunity to a disease.

vac-u-um *n., pl.* -ums, -ua A space which is absolutely empty; a void; a vacuum cleaner.

vag-a-bond *n.* A homeless person who wanders from place to place; a tramp.

va-gar-y *n., pl.* -ies An eccentric or capricious action or idea. **vagarious** *adj.*

va-gi-na *n., pl.* -nas, -nae *Anat.* The canal or passage extending from the uterus to the external opening of the female reproductive system.

vag-i-ni-tis *n.* An inflammation of the vagina.

va-grant *n.* A person who wanders from place to place. *adj.* Roaming from one area to another without a job.

vague *adj.* Not clearly expressed; not sharp or definite. **vaguely** *adv.*

vain *adj.* Conceited; lacking worth or substance; having too much pride in oneself. **in vain** Irreverently. **-ly** *adv.*

val-ance *n.* A decorative drapery across the top of a window.

vale *n.* A valley.

val-e-dic-to-ri-an *n.* The student ranking highest in a graduating class, who delivers a speech at the commencement.

val-en-tine *n.* A card or gift sent to one's sweet-heart on Valentine's Day, February 14th.

val-et *n.* A man who takes care of another man's clothes and other personal needs; a hotel employee who attends to personal services for guests.

val-iant *adj.* Brave; exhibiting valor. **valiance, valor** *n.*

val-id *adj.* Founded on facts or truth. *Law* Binding; having legal force. **validity, validate** *n.*

val-ley *n., pl.* -leys Low land between ranges of hills or mountains.

val-or *n.* Bravery. **valorous** *adj.*, **valorously** *adv.*

val-u-a-ble *adj.* Of great value or importance; having a high monetary value.

val-ue *n.* The quality or worth of something that makes it valuable; material worth; a principle regarded as worthwhile or desirable. *Math* A calculated numerical quantity. *v.* To estimate the value or worth of; to regard very highly; to rate according to importance, worth, or usefulness.

valve *n.* The movable mechanism which

opens and closes to control the flow of a substance through a pipe or other passageway. *Anat.* A membranous structure in a vein or artery that prevents or slows the backward movement of fluid.

va-moose *v. Slang* To leave in a hurry.

vam-pire *n.* In folklore, a dead person believed to rise from the grave at night to suck the blood of sleeping persons; a person who preys on others.

vam-pire bat *n.*

A tropical bat that feeds on the blood of living mammals.

van *n.* A large closed wagon or truck.

va-na-di-um *n.* A metallic element symbolized by V.

Van Buren, Martin *n.* 1782-1862 The 8th president of the United States from 1837-1841.

van-dal-ism *n.* The malicious defacement or destruction of private or public property.

vane *n.* A metal device that turns in the direction the wind is blowing; a thin rigid blade of an electric fan, propeller, or windmill.

va-nil-la *n.* A flavoring extract used in cooking and baking; prepared from the vanilla bean.

van-ish *v.* To disappear suddenly; to drop out of sight; to go out of existence.

van-i-ty *n., pl.,* **-ies** Conceit; extreme pride in one's ability, possessions, or appearance.

van-tage *n.* A superior position; an advantage.

va-por *n.* Moisture or smoke suspended in air, as mist or fog. **vaporish, vaporous** *adj.,* **vaporize** *v.*

var-i-able *adj.* Changeable; tending to vary; inconstant. *n.* A quantity or thing which can vary. **-ness** *n.,* **-y** *adv.*

var-i-ance *n.* The state or act of varying; difference; conflict.

var-i-a-tion *n.* The result or process of varying; the degree or extent of varying. *Mus.* A different form or version of a given theme, with modifications in rhythm, key, or melody.

var-i-e-gat-ed *adj.* Having marks of different colors. **variegate** *v.*

va-ri-e-ty *n., pl.,* **-ies** The state or character of being varied or various; a number of different kinds; an assortment.

var-i-ous *adj.* Of different kinds.

var-mint *n., Slang* A troublesome animal; an obnoxious person.

var-nish *n.* A solution paint used to coat or cover a surface with a hard, transparent, shiny film. *v.* To put varnish on.

var-si-ty *n., pl.,* **-ies** The best team representing a college, university, or school.

var-y *v.* To change; to make or become different; to be different; to make of different kinds.

vas-cu-lar *adj., Biol.* Having to do with vessels circulating fluids, as blood.

va-sec-to-my *n., pl.* **-ies** Method of male sterilization involving the surgical excision of a part of the tube which conveys semen.

vast *adj.* Very large or great in size. **vastly** *adv.,* **vastness** *n.*

vault *n.* An arched structure that forms a ceiling or roof; a room for storage and safekeeping, as in a bank, usually made of steel; a burial chamber. *v.* To supply or construct with a vault; to jump or leap with the aid of a pole.

vb *abbr.* Verb; verbal.

veg-e-ta-ble *n.* A plant, as the tomato, green beans, lettuce, raised for the edible part. *adj.* Resembling a vegetable in activity; passive.

veg-e-tar-i-an *n.* A person whose diet is limited to vegetables. *adj.* Consuming only plant products. **vegetarianism** *n.*

veg-e-ta-tion *n.* Plants or plant life which grow from the soil.

ve-hi-cle *n.* A motorized device for transporting goods, equipment, or passengers; any means by which something is transferred, expressed, or applied.

veil *n.* A piece of transparent cloth worn on the head or face for concealment or protection; anything that conceals from view. *v.* To cover or conceal, as with a veil.

vein *n., Anat.*

A vessel which transports blood back to the heart after passing through the body; one of the branching support tubes of an insect's wing; a long wavy, ir regularly colored streak, as in marble, or wood. **vein** *v.*

ve-lour *n.* A soft velvet-like woven cloth having a short, thick nap.

vel-vet *n.* A fabric made of rayon, cotton, or silk, having a smooth, dense pile. **velvety** *adj.*

vend-er *or* **vend-or** *n.* A person who sells, as a peddler.

ven-det-ta *n.* A fight or feud between blood-related persons, involving revenge killings.

ven-er-a-ble *adj.* Meriting or worthy of respect by reason of dignity, position, or age.

ve-ne-re-al dis-ease *n.* A contagious disease, as syphilis, or gonorrhea, which is typically acquired through sexual intercourse.

ve-ne-tian blind *n.* A window blind having thin, horizontal slats which can be adjusted to desired angles so as to vary the amount of light admitted.

ven-i-son *n.* The edible flesh of a deer.

ven-om *n.* A poisonous substance secreted by some animals, as scorpions or snakes, usually transmitted to their prey or an enemy through a bite or sting. **venomous** *adj.*

ve-nous *adj.* Of or relating to veins. *Physiol.* Returning blood to the heart after passing through the capillaries, supplying oxygen for the tissues, and becoming charged with carbon dioxide. **venously** *adv.*

vent *n.* A means of escape or passage from a restricted area; an opening which allows the escape of vapor, heat, gas, or liquid.

ven-ti-late *v.* To expose to a flow of fresh air for refreshing, curing, or purifying purposes; to cause fresh air to circulate through an area; to expose to public discussion or examination. **ventilation, ventilator** *n.*

ven-ture *n.* A course of action involving risk, chance, or danger, especially a business investment. *v.* To take a risk.

ven-ue *n.* The place where a crime or other cause of legal action occurs; the locale of a gathering or public event.

Ve-nus *n.* The planet second in order from the sun.

verb *n.* The part of speech which expresses action, existence, or occurrence.

ver-bal *adj.* Expressed in speech; expressed orally; not written; relating to or derived from a verb. *n.* An adjective, noun, or other word which is based on a verb and retains some characteristics of a verb. **verbally** *adv.*, **verbalize** *v.*

ver-ba-tim *adv.* Word for word.

ver-be-na *n.* An American garden plant having variously colored flower clusters.

verge *n.* The extreme edge or rim; margin; the point beyond which something begins. *v.* To border on.

ver-min *n.*, *pl.* **vermins** A destructive, annoying animal which is harmful to one's health.

Ver-mont *n.* A state located in the north-eastern part of the United States.

ver-sa-tile *adj.* Having the capabilities of doing many different things; having many functions or uses. **versatility** *n.*

verse *n.* Writing that has a rhyme; poetry; a subdivision of a chapter of the Bible. *v.* To make verse; to tell or celebrate in verse; to familiarize by close association or study.

ver-sion *n.* An account or description told from a particular point of view; a translation from another language, especially a translation of the Bible; a form or particular point of view; a condition in which an organ, such as the uterus, is turned; manual turning of a fetus in the uterus to aid delivery.

ver-so *n.*, *pl.* **-sos** The left-hand page.

ver-sus *prep.* Against; in contrast to; as an alternative of.

ver-te-bra *n.*, *pl.* **-brae, -bras** One of the bony or cartilaginous segments making up the spinal column. **-al** *adj.*

ver-tex *n.*, *pl.* **-es, -tices** The highest or topmost point; the pointed top of a triangle, opposite the base; the point at which two lines meet to form an angle.

ver-ti-cal *adj.* In a straight up-and-down direction; being perpendicular to the plane of the horizon or to a primary axis; upright. **vertically** *adv.*

ver-y *adv.* To a high or great degree; truly; absolutely; exactly; actually; in actual fact.

ves-per *n.* An evening prayer service; a bell to call people to such a service.

ves-sel *n.* A hollow or concave utensil, as a bottle, kettle, container, or jar; a hollow craft designed for navigation on water, one larger than a rowboat. *Anat.* A tube or duct for circulating a bodily fluid.

vest *n.* A sleeveless garment open or fastening in front, worn over a shirt.

ves-tige *n.* A trace or visible sign of something that no longer exists. **vestigial** *adj.*, **vestigially** *adj.*

ves-try *n.*, *pl.* **vestries** A room in a church used for meetings and classes.

vet *n.*, *Slang* A veterinarian; a veteran.

vet-er-an *n.* A person with a long record or experience in a certain field; one who has served in the military.

vet-er-i-nar-i-an *n.* One who is trained and authorized to give medical treatment to animals.

vet-er-i-nar-y *adj.* Pertaining to or being the science and art of prevention and treatment of animals.

ve-to *n.*, *pl.* **vetoes** The power of a government executive, as the President or a governor, to reject a bill passed by the legislature. *v.* To reject a bill passed by the legislature.

vex *v.* To bother; or annoy. **vexation** *n.*

vi-a *prep.* By way of; by means of.

vi-a-duct *n.* A bridge, resting on a series of arches, carrying a road or railroad.

vi-al *n.* A small, closed container used especially for liquids.

vi-brate *v.* To move or make move back and forth or up and down. **vibration** *n.*

vi-car-i-ous *adj.* Undergoing or serving in the place of someone or something else; experienced through sympathetic or imaginative participation in the experience of another.

vice *n.* An immoral habit or practice; evil conduct. *prefix* One who takes the place of another.

vi-ce ver-sa *adv.* With the order or meaning of something reversed.

vi-chy-ssoise *n.* A soup made from potatoes, chicken stock, and cream, flavored with leeks or onions and usually served cold.

vi-cin-i-ty *n.*, *pl.* **-ies** The surrounding area or district; the state of being near in relationship or space.

vi-cious *adj.* Dangerously aggressive; having the quality of immorality. **viciously** *adv.*, **viciousness** *n.*

vic-tim *n.* A person who is harmed or killed by another; a living creature which is slain and offered as sacrifice;

one harmed by circumstance or condition. **victimize** v.

vic-tor n. A person who conquers; the winner.

vic-to-ri-ous adj. Being the winner in a contest. **victoriously** adv.

vic-to-ry n., pl. -ies A defeat of those on the opposite side.

vid-e-o adj. Being, related to, or used in the reception or transmission of television.

vid-e-o disc n. A disc containing recorded images and sounds which may be played on a television set.

vid-e-o game n. A computerized game displaying on a display screen, controlled by a player or players.

vid-e-o ter-mi-nal n. *Computer Science* A computer device having a cathode-ray tube for displaying data on a screen.

vie v. To strive for superiority.

view n. The act of examining or seeing; a judgment or opinion; the range or extent of one's sight; something that is kept in sight. v. To watch or look at attentively; to consider.

vig-il n. A watch with prayers kept on the night before a religious feast; a period of surveillance.

vig-or n. Energy or physical strength; intensity of effect or action.
vigorous adj.

vile adj. Morally disgusting, miserable, and unpleasant. **vilely** adv., **vileness** n.

vil-la n. A luxurious home in the country; a country estate.

vil-lage n. An incorporated settlement, usually smaller than a town. **villager** n.

vil-lain n. An evil or wicked person; a criminal; an uncouth person.
villainous adj., **villainy** n.

vin-ai-grette n. A small ornamental bottle with a perforated top, used for holding an aromatic preparation such as smelling salts.

vin-di-cate v. To clear of suspicion; to set free; to provide a defense or justification for. **vindication** n.

vin-dic-tive adj. Showing or possessing a desire for revenge; spiteful.

vine n. A plant whose stem needs support as it climbs or clings to a surface.

vin-e-gar n. A tart, sour liquid derived from cider or wine and used in flavoring and preserving food. **vinegary** adj.

vin-tage n. The grapes or wine produced from a particular district in one season.

vi-nyl n. A variety of shiny plastics, similar to leather, often used for clothing and for covering furniture.

vi-o-la n. A stringed instrument, slightly larger and deeper in tone than a violin.

vi-o-late v. To break the law or a rule; to disrupt or disturb a person's privacy.

vi-o-lence n. Physical force or activity used to cause harm, damage, or abuse.

vi-o-let n. A small, low-growing plant with blue, purple, or white flowers; a purplish-blue color.

vi-o-lin n.

A small stringed instrument, played with a bow.

VIP abbr. Very important person.

vi-per n. A poisonous snake; an evil or treacherous person.

vir-gin n. A person who has never had sexual intercourse. adj. In an unchanged or natural state.

Vir-gin-ia n. A state located in the eastern part of the United States.

Virgo n. The sixth sign of the zodiac; a person born between August 23rd and September 22nd.

vir-ile adj. Having the qualities and nature of a man; capable of sexual performance in the male. **virility** n.

vir-tu n. The love or knowledge of fine objects of art.

vir-tue n. Morality, goodness or uprightness; a special type of goodness.
virtuous adj., **virtuously** adv.

vi-rus n. Any of a variety of microscopic organisms which cause diseases.

vi-sa n. An official authorization giving permission on a passport to enter a specific country.

vis-cid adj. Sticky; having an adhesive quality.

vise or **vice** n. A tool in carpentry and metalwork having two jaws to hold things in position.

vis-i-bil-i-ty n., pl. -ies The degree or state of being visible; the distance that one is able to see clearly.

vis-i-ble adj. Apparent; exposed to view.

vi-sion n. The power of sight; the ability to see; an image created in the imagination; a supernatural appearance.

vis-it v. To journey to or come to see a person or place. n. A professional or social call. *Slang* To chat.
visitor, **visitation** n.

vi-sor n. A brim on the front of a hat which protects the eyes from glare, the sun, wind, and rain.

vi-su-al adj. Visible; relating to seeing or sight.

vi-tal adj. Essential to life; very important. **vitally** adv.

vi-tal signs pl., n., *Med.* The pulse rate, body temperature, blood pressure, and respiratory rate of a person.

vi-ta-min n. Any of various substances which are found in foods and are essential to good health.

vit-re-ous adj. Related to or similar to glass.

vit-ri-fy v. To convert into glass or a substance similar to glass, by heat and fusion.

vi-va-cious adj. Filled with vitality or animation; lively. **vivaciously** adv.

viv-id adj. Bright; brilliant; intense; having clear, lively, bright colors.

viv-i-fy v. To give life to. **vivifiction** n.

vo-cab-u-lar-y n., pl. -ies A list or group of words and phrases, usually in alphabetical order; all the words that a person uses or understands.

vo-cal *adj.* Of or related to the voice; uttered by the voice; to speak freely and loudly. *n.* A vocal sound. **vocally** *adv.*

vocal cords *pl., n.* The lower of two folds or bands in the throat which produce sound when made tighter or loosened when air is breathed out while speaking or singing.

vo-ca-tion *n.* A career, occupation, or profession.

vo-cif-er-ate *v.* To utter or cry out loudly; to shout. **vociferation** *n.* **vociferous** *adj.*, **vociferously** *adv.*

vod-ka *n.* A colorless liquor of neutral spirits distilled from fermented rye or wheat mash.

vogue *n.* The leading style or fashion; popularity. **vogue** *adj.*

voice *n.* The sounds produced by speaking; the ability or power to produce musical tones. *v.* To express; to utter; to give voice.

void *adj.* Containing nothing; empty; not inhabited; useless; vain; without legal force or effect; null. *n.* Empty space; the quality or state of being lonely. *v.* To make void; to discharge; to emit.

voile *n.* A fine, soft, sheer fabric used for making light clothing and curtains.

volt-age *n.* The amount of electrical power, given in terms of the number of volts.

vol-ume *n.* The capacity or amount of space or room; a book; a quantity; the loudness of a sound.

vol-un-tar-y *adj.* Done cooperatively or willingly; from one's own choice.

vol-un-teer *n.* One who offers himself for a service of his own free will. *adj.* Consisting of volunteers. *v.* To offer voluntarily.

vo-lup-tuous *adj.* Full of pleasure; delighting the senses; sensuous; luxury. **voluptuousness** *n.*

vo-ra-cious *adj.* Having a large appetite; insatiable. **voraciously** *adv.*

vote *n.* The expression of one's choice by voice, by raising one's hand, or by secret ballot. *v.* To express one's views. **voteless** *adj.*, **voter** *n.*

vo-tive *adj.* Performed in fulfillment of a vow or in devotion.

vouch *v.* To verify or support as true; to guarantee. **voucher** *n.*

vow *n.* A solemn pledge or promise, especially one made to God; a marriage vow. *v.* To make a vow.

vow-el *n.* A sound of speech made by voicing the flow of breath within the mouth; a letter representing a vowel, as a, e, i, o, u, and sometimes y.

voy-age *n.* A long trip or journey.

vul-gar *adj.* Showing poor manners; crude; improper; immoral or indecent.

vul-ner-a-ble *adj.* Open to physical injury or attack. **vulnerability** *n.*, **-ably** *adv.*

vul-ture *n.* A large bird of the hawk family, living on dead animals; a greedy person; one who feeds on the mistakes or bad luck of others.

W, w The twenty-third letter of the English alphabet.

WA *abbr.* Washington.

WAC *abbr.* Women's Army Corps.

wacky *adj.* Amusingly or absurdly irrational. **wackily** *adj.*, **wackiness** *n.*

wad *n.* A small crumpled mass or bundle; a soft plug used to hold shot or gunpowder charge in place. *Slang* A large roll of money. **wad** *v.*

wad-dle *v.* To walk with short steps and swing from side to side. **waddle, waddler** *n.*

wade *v.* To walk through a substance as mud or water which hampers one's steps.

wad-able *adj.* Having the capability of being wadded.

wad-ding *n.* Materials for wadding or wads; A sheet of loose fibers that is used for stuffing.

wad-dle *v.* To walk with short swinging steps; to move in a clumsily manner.

wade *v.* To move in a medium that offers resistance; to move with difficulty; to set to work with determination.

wad-er *n.* A person that wades; a name for high top waterproof boots.

wading bird *n.* A log-legged bird such as the sandpiper or snipe.

wading pool *n.* A portable shallow pool that is filled with water and used by children.

wae-sucks *interj.* A Scottish phrase used to express pity.

wa-fer *n.* A small, thin, crisp cracker, cookie, or candy; a thin piece of material of something such as, silicon that is used as a base for an electronic component.

waf-fle *n.* Pancake batter cooked in a waffle iron.

waft *v.* To drift or move gently, as by the motion of water or air; a flag used to indicate the wind direction. **waft** *n.*

waft-age *n.* The state or act of being wafted.

waf-ture *n.* A wavelike motion.

wag *v.* To move quickly from side to side or up and down. *n.* A playful, witty person. **waggish** *adj.*, **wagger** *n.*

wage *n.* A payment of money for labor or services. *v.* To conduct or engage in something. **wageless** *adj.*

wage earner *n.* A person who works for a salary or wages.

wage level *n.* The approximate position of wages at any given time.

wa-ger *v.* To make a bet. *n.* Something that is risked on an event. **wager** *n.*

wag-on *n.* A four-wheeled vehicle used to transport goods; a station wagon; a child's four-wheeled cart with a long handle; a delivery vehicle.

wag-on-er *n.* A person who drives a wagon.

wagon master *n.* The person in charge of one or more wagons while transporting freight or other items.

wag-tail *n.* An Old World bird having a slender body and long tail.

wa-hi-ne *n.* A Polnesian girl or woman.

waif *n.* An abandoned, homeless, or lost child; a piece of property found without the owner; a stray animal.

wail *v.* A loud, mournful cry or weep. *n.* To make such a sound.

waist *n.* The narrow part of the body between the thorax and hips; the middle part or section of something which is narrower than the rest. **waisted** *adj.*

waist-band *n.* The band on clothing that encircles the waist.

wait *v.* To stay in one place in expectation of; to await; to put off until a later time or date; to be ready or prepared; to available and ready. *n.* A time of waiting.

wait-er *n.* A man who serves food at a restaurant.

wait-ress *n.* A woman who serves food at a restaurant.

waive *v.* To forfeit of one's own free will; to postpone or dispense with; to voluntarily relinquish; to put off take immediate action.

waiv-er *n.* The act of intentionally abandoning a privilege or right.

wake *v.* To come to consciousness, as from sleep. *n.* A vigil for a dead body; the surface turbulence caused by a vessel moving through water.

walk *v.* To move on foot over a surface; to pass over, go on, or go through by walking; in baseball, to advance to first base after four balls have been pitched. **walker** *n.*

walk-out *n.* A labor strike against a company.

walk-ie-talk-ie *n.* A battery-operated radio transmitting and receiving set.

walk--in *n.* A walk-in freezer or refrigerator; a person who walks in without an appointment.

walking delegate *n.* Labor union personal who has been appointed to visit with their members and their companies to enforce the union agreements and rules.

walking stick *n.* A stick usually made of wood, used to aid a person in walking.

walk--on *n.* A small nonspeaking part in a playr.

walk-out *n.* To leave a job, organization, or meeting as an expression of anger or disapproval.

walk-way *n.* A passage that is used for walking.

wall *n.* A vertical structure to separate or enclose an area. *v.* To provide or close up, as with a wall.

wal-la-by *n.* A small or medium-sized kangaroo.

wal-lah *n.* A person who performs a specific service or duty.

wal-let *n.* A flat folding case for carrying paper money.

wall-flow-er *n.* A person who shys away from a group; one who is unpopular and stays away from other people.

wal-lop *n.* A powerful blow; an impact. *v.* To move with disorganized haste.

wall-pa-per *n.* Decorative paper for walls, usually having a colorful pattern.

Wall Street *n.* The street in New York City where the New York Stock Exchange is located.

wal-nut *n.* An edible nut with a hard, light-brown shell; the tree on which this nut grows.

wal-rus *n.*

A large marine mammal of the seal family, having flippers, tusks, and a tough hide.

waltz *n.* A ballroom dance in 3/4 time; music for a waltz. *v.* To dance a waltz; to advance successfully and easily.

wam-pum *n.* Polished shells, once used as currency by North American Indians. *Slang* Money.

wand *n.* A slender rod used by a magician.

wan-der *v.* To travel about aimlessly; to roam; to stray. **wanderer** *n.*

wane *v.* To decrease in size or extent; to decrease gradually. *n.* A gradual deterioration.

wan-gle *v.* To resort to devious methods in order to obtain something wanted. **wangler** *n.*

want *v.* To wish for or desire; to need; to lack; to fail to possess a required amount; to hunt in order to apprehend. *n.* The state of lacking a required or usual amount. **wanting** *adj.*

war *n.* An armed conflict among states or nations; a state of discord; the science of military techniques or procedures.

ward *n.* A section in a hospital for certain patients requiring similar treatment; a person under protection or surveillance. *v.* To keep watch over someone or something.

ware *n.* Manufactured items of the same general kind; items or goods for sale.

ware-house *n.* A large building used to store merchandise. **warehouse** *v.*

warm *adj.* Moderate heat; neither hot or cold; comfortably established; marked by a strong feeling; having pleasant feelings.

warn *v.* To give notice or inform beforehand; to call to one's attention; to alert.

warp *v.* To become bent out of shape; to deviate from a proper course. *n.* The condition of being twisted or bent; threads running down the length of a fabric.

war-rant *n.* A written authorization giving the holder legal power to search, seize, or arrest. *v.* To provide a reason; to give proof. **warrantable** *adj.*, **warrantor** *n.*

war-ri-or *n.* One who fights in a war or battle.

war-y *adj.* Marked by caution; alert to danger.

wash *v.* To cleanse by the use of water; to remove dirt; to move or deposit as if by the force of water. *n.* A process or instance of washing; a group of soiled clothes or linens.

Wash *abbr.* Washington.

wash--and--wear *adj.* Requiring little or no ironing after washing.

wash-board *n.* A corrugated board on which clothes are rubbed in the process of washing; an uneven surface as a washboard.

washed--out *adj.*, *Slang* Tired.

wash-er *n.* A small disk usually made of rubber or metal having a hole in the center, used with nuts and bolts; a washing machine.

wash-ing *n.* Clothes and other articles that are washed or to be washed; cleaning.

Wash-ing-ton *n.* A state located in the northwestern part of the United States.

Washington, George *n.* (1732-1799) The first president of the United States from 1789-1797.

was-n't *contr.* Was not.

wasp *n.* Any of various insects, having a slim body with a constricted abdomen, the female capable of inflicting a painful sting.

waste *v.* To be thrown away; to be available but not used completely. *n.* A barren region; the instance of wasting; useless material produced as a by-product. *Slang* To destroy or murder. **wasteful** *adj.*, **waster** *n.*

watch *v.* To view carefully; to guard; to keep informed. *n.* The act of staying awake to guard or protect; a small timepiece worn on the wrist, designed to keep the correct time of day.

watch-dog *n.* A dog trained to guard someone or his property.

watch-ful *adj.* Carefully observant or attentive. **watchfully** *adv.*

watch-man *n.* A person hired to keep watch; a guard.

wa-ter *n.* The clear liquid making up oceans, lakes, and streams; the body fluids as tears or urine. *v.* To pour or spray on water on something or someone; to give water to drink; to weaken or dilute with water.

wa-ter moc-ca-sin *n.* A venomous snake from the lowlands and swampy areas of the southern United States.

wa-ter po-lo *n.* A water game between two teams, the object of which is to get a ball into the opponent's goal.

wa-ter pow-er *n.* The power or energy produced by swift-moving water.

wa-ter-proof *adj.* Capable of preventing water from penetrating. *v.* To make or treat in order to make waterproof. *n.* A material or fabric which is waterproof.

wa-ter--re-pel-lant *adj.* A material or product treated to resist water, but not completely waterproof.

wa-ter-shed *n.* The raised area between two regions that divides two sections drained by different river sources.

wa-ter--ski *v.* To travel over water on a pair of short, broad skis while being

pulled by a motorboat.

wa-ter-spout *n.* A tube or pipe through which water is discharged; a funnel-shaped column of spray and mist whirling over an ocean or lake.

wa-ter ta-ble *n.* The upper limit of the portion of the ground completely saturated with water.

wa-ter-tight *adj.* Closed or sealed so tightly that no water can enter, leaving no chance for evasion.

wa-ter-way *n.* A navigable body of water; a channel for water.

wa-ter-y *adj.* Containing water; diluted; lacking effectiveness. **wateriness** *n.*

watt *n.* A unit of electrical power represented by current of one ampere, produced by the electromotive force of one volt.

wave *v.* To move back and forth or up and down; to motion with the hand. *n.* A swell or moving ridge of water; a curve or curl, as in the hair.

wa-ver *v.* To sway unsteadily; to move back and forth; to weaken in force. **waver** *n.*, **waveringly** *adv.*

wax *n.* A natural yellowish substance made by bees, solid when cold and easily melted or softened when heated. **waxy** *adj.*

way *n.* A manner of doing something; a tendency or characteristic; a habit or customary manner of acting or living; a direction; freedom to do as one chooses.

way-far-er *n.* A person who travels on foot.

way-lay *v.* To attack by ambush.

way-ward *adj.* Unruly; unpredictable.

we *pl.*, *pron.* Used to refer to the person speaking and one or more other people.

weak *adj.* Having little energy or strength; easily broken; having inadequate skills; not reasonable or convincing. **weakness** *n.*, **weakly** *adv.*

wealth *n.* An abundance of valuable possessions or property; all goods and resources having monetary value.

wealth-y *adj.* Having much wealth or money; abundant; rich.

wean *v.* To accustom an infant or small child to food other than a mother's milk or bottle.

weap-on *n.* A device used in fighting a war; a device which can be used to harm another person.

wear *v.* To have on or put something on the body; to display. *n.* The act of wearing out or using up; the act of wearing, as clothing. **wearable** *adj.*

wea-ri-some *adj.* Tedious, boring or tiresome.

wea-ry *adj.* Exhausted; tired; feeling fatigued. *v.* To make or become tired; to become fatigued. **wearily** *adv.*, **weariness** *n.*

wea-sel *n.* A mammal with a long tail and short legs; a sly, sneaky person.

weath-er *n.* The condition of the air or atmosphere in terms of humidity, temperature, and similar features. *v.*

To become worn by the actions of weather; to survive.

weath-er-man *n.* A man who reports or forecasts the weather.

weather vane *n.*

A device that turns, indicating the direction of the wind.

weave *v.* To make a basket, cloth, or other item by interlacing threads or other strands of material. **weaver** *n.*

web *n.*

A cobweb; a piece of interlacing material which forms a woven structure; something constructed as an entanglement; a thin membrane that joins the toes of certain water birds.

wed *v.* To take as a spouse; to marry.

we'd *contr.* We had; we should.

Wed *abbr.* Wednesday.

wed-ding *n.* A marriage ceremony; an act of joining together in close association.

wedge *n.* A tapered, triangular piece of wood or metal used to split logs, to add leverage, and to hold something open or ajar. *v.* To force or make something fit tightly.

wed-lock *n.* Marriage; the state of being married.

Wednes-day *n.* The fourth day of the week.

weed *n.* An unwanted plant which interferes with the growth of grass, vegetables, or flowers.

week *n.* A period of seven days, beginning with Sunday and ending with Saturday; the time or days normally spent at school or work.

week-day *n.* Any day of the week except Saturday or Sunday.

week-end *n.* The end of the week from the period of Friday evening through Sunday evening.

week-ly *adv.* Every week; once a week. *adj.* Taking place or done every week of or relating to a week.

weep *v.* To shed tears; to express sorrow, joy, or emotion; by shedding tears; to cry. **weeper** *n.*

wee-vil *n.* A small beetle having a downward-curving snout, which damages plants.

weigh *v.* To determine the heaviness of an object by using a scale; to consider carefully in one's mind; to be of a particular weight; to oppress or burden.

weight *n.* The amount that something weighs; heaviness; a heavy object used to hold or pull something down; an overpowering force; the quality of a garment for a particular season. *v.* To make heavy.

weight-less *adj.* Lacking the pull of gravity; having little weight.

weight-y *adj.* Burdensome; important.

weird *adj.* Having an extraordinary or strange character. **weirdly** *adv.*

weird-o *n., Slang* A person who is very strange.

wel-come *v.* To extend warm hospitality; to accept gladly. *adj.* Received warmly. *n.* A greeting upon one's arrival.

weld *v.* To unite metallic parts by applying heat and sometimes pressure, allowing the metals to bond together. *n.* A joint formed by welding.

wel-fare *n.* The state of doing well; governmental aid to help the disabled or disadvantaged.

well *n.* A hole in the ground which contains a supply of water; a shaft in the ground through which gas and oil are obtained. *adj.* Being in good health; in an agreeable state.

we'll *contr.* We will; we shall.

well--be-ing *n.* The state of being healthy, happy, or prosperous.

well--done *adj.* Completely cooked; done properly.

well--groomed *adj.* Clean, neat, and properly cared for.

well--known *adj.* Widely known.

well--man-nered *adj.* Polite; having good manners.

well--mean-ing *adj.* Having good intentions.

well--to--do *adj.* Having more than enough wealth.

welsh *v., Slang* To cheat by avoiding a payment to someone; to neglect an obligation. **welsher** *n.*

welt *n.* A strip between the sole and upper part of a shoe; a slight swelling on the body, usually caused by a blow to the area. *v.* To hit severely.

wel-ter-weight *n.* A boxer weighing between 136 and 147 pounds.

went *v.* Past tense of go.

wept *v.* Past tense of weep.

were *v.* Second person singular past plural of be.

we're *contr.* We are.

were-n't *contr.* Were not.

west *n.* The direction of the setting sun; the direction to the left of a person standing north. *adj.* At, of, or from the west. *adv.* To or toward the west. **western** *adj.*

West Vir-gin-ia *n.* A state located in the eastern part of the United States.

whack *v.* To strike with a hard blow, to slap. *n.* An attempt.

whale *n.*

A very large mammal resembling a fish which lives in salt water. *Slang* An outstanding or impressive example.

wharf *n.* A pier or platform built at the edge of water so that ships can load and unload.

what *pron.* Which one; which things; which type or kind. *adv.* In which way. *adj.* Which particular one.

what-ev-er *pron.* Everything or anything. *adj.* No matter what. *Slang* Which thing or things.

what's *contr.* What is.

wheat *n.* A grain ground into flour, used to make breads and similar foods.

wheel *n.* A circular disk which turns on an axle; an apparatus having the same principles of a wheel; something which resembles the motion or shape of a wheel. *v.* To move on or as if by wheels; to turn around a central axis; to rotate, pivot, or turn around.

wheel-bar-row *n.* A vehicle having one wheel, used to transport small loads.

wheel-chair *n.* A mobile chair for disabled persons.

wheel-er *n.* Anything that has wheels.

wheeze *v.* To breathe with a hoarse whistling sound. *n.* A high whistling sound.

whelk *v.* Any of various large water snails, sometimes edible.

when *adv.* At what time; at which time. *pron.* What or which time. *conj.* While; at the time that; although.

whence *adv.* From what source or place; from which.

when-ev-er *adv.* At any time; when. *conj.* At whatever time.

where *adv.* At or in what direction or place; in what direction or place.

where-a-bouts *adv.* Near, at, or in a particular location.

where-as *conj.* It being true or the fact; on the contrary.

where-by *conj.* Through or by which.

wher-ev-er *adv.* In any situation or place.

whet *v.* To make sharp; to stimulate.

wheth-er *conj.* Indicating a choice; alternative possibilities; either.

whet-stone *n.* A stone used to sharpen scissors, knives, and other implements.

whew *n., interj.* Used to express relief; or tiredness.

whey *n.* The clear, water-like part of milk that separates from the curd.

which *pron.* What one or ones; the one previously; whatever one or ones; whichever. *adj.* What one; any one of.

which-ev-er *pron.* Any; no matter which or what.

whiff *n.* A slight puff; a light current of air; a slight breath or odor.

while *n.* A length or period of time. *conj.* During the time that; even though; at the same time; although.

whim *n.* A sudden desire or impulse.

whim-per *v.* To make a weak, soft crying sound. **whimper** *n.*

whim-si-cal *adj.* Impulsive; erratic; light and spontaneous. **whimsically** *adv.*

whine *v.* To make a squealing, plaintive sound; to complain in an irritating, childish fashion.

whin-ny *v.* To neigh in a soft gentle way.

whip *v.* To spank repeatedly with a rod or stick; to punish by whipping; to move in a motion similar to whipping or beating. *n.* A flexible stick or rod used to herd or beat animals; a dessert made by whipping ingredients; the utensil used to do so. *Slang* To overcome. **whipper** *n.*

whip-lash *n.* An injury to the spine or neck caused by a sudden jerking motion of the head.

whip-poor-will *n.* A brownish nocturnal bird of North America.

whir *v.* To move with a low purring sound.

whirl *v.* To rotate or move in circles; to twirl; to move, drive, or go very fast. *n.* A rapid whirling motion. **whirler** *n.*

whirl-pool *n.* A circular current of water.

whirl-wind *n.* A violently whirling mass of air; a tornado.

whirl-y-bird *n., Slang* A helicopter.

whisk *v.* To move with a sweeping motion; to move quickly or lightly. *n.* A sweeping movement; a utensil used in cooking; to stir.

whisk-er *n.*

The hair that grows on a man's face; the long hair near the mouth of dogs, cats, and other animals. **whiskers** A man's beard.

whis-key *n.* An alcoholic beverage distilled from rye, barley, or corn.

whis-per *v.* To speak in a very low tone; to tell in secret. *n.* A low rustling sound; the act of whispering.

whis-tle *v.* To make a clear shrill sound by blowing air through the teeth, through puckered lips, or through a special instrument. *n.* A device used to make a whistling sound. **whistler** *n.*

white *n.* The color opposite of black; the part of something that is white or light in color, as an egg or the eyeball; a member of the Caucasian group of people. *adj.* Having a light color; pale; pure; blameless, without sin.

white-cap *n.* A wave having a top of white foam.

white--col-lar *adj.* Relating to an employee whose job does not require manual labor.

White House *n.* The official residence of the President of the United States, located in Washington, D.C.

white-wash *n.* A mixture made of lime and other ingredients and used for whitening fences and exterior walls. *v.* To cover up a problem; to pronounce someone as being innocent without really investigating.

whith-er *adv.* To what state, place, or circumstance; wherever.

whit-tle *v.* To cut or carve off small shavings from wood with a knife; to remove or reduce gradually. **-er** *n.*

whiz *v.* To make a whirring or buzzing sound, a projectile passing at a high rate of speed through the air. *Slang* A person having notable expertise, as with a computer.

who *pron.* Which or what certain individual, person, or group; referring to a person previously mentioned.

who'd *contr.* Who would; who had.

who-ev-er *pron.* Whatever person; all or any persons.

whole *adj.* Complete; having nothing missing; not divided or in pieces; a complete system or unity; everything considered. *Math* Not a fraction.

whole-heart-ed *adj.* Sincere; totally committed; holding nothing back.

whole-sale *n.* The sale of goods in large amounts to a retailer. *adj.* Relating to or having to do with such a sale. *v.* To sell wholesale. **wholesaler** *n.*

whole-some *adj.* Contributing to good mental or physical health. **wholesomely** *adv.*, **wholesomeness** *n.*

whole wheat *adj.* Made from the wheat kernel with nothing removed.

who'll *contr.* Who shall; who will.

whol-ly *adv.* Totally; exclusively.

whom *pron.* The form of who used as the direct object of a verb or the object of the preposition.

whom-ev-er *pron.* The form of whoever used as the object of a preposition or the direct object of a verb.

whoop-ing cough *n.* An infectious disease of the throat and breathing passages in which the patient has spasms of coughing often followed by gasps for breath.

whoop-ing crane *n.* A large bird of North America, nearly extinct, having long legs and a high, shrill cry.

whoosh *v.* To make a rushing or gushing sound, as a rush of air.

whop-per *n.* Something of extraordinary size. *Slang* A lie.

whore *n.* A prostitute.

who's *contr.* Who is; who has.

whose *pron.* Belonging to or having to do with one's belongings. *adj.* Relating to *which* or *whom.*

why *adv.* For what reason or purpose. *conj.* The cause, purpose, or reason for which. *interj.* Expressing surprise or disagreement.

WI *abbr.* Wisconsin.

wick *n.* The soft strand of fibers which extends from a candle or lamp and draws up the fuel for burning.

wick-er *n.* A thin, pliable twig used to make furniture and baskets.

wick-et *n.* A wire hoop in the game of croquet; a small door, window, or opening used as a box office.

wide *adj.* Broad; covering a large area; completely extended or open. *adv.* Over a large area; full extent.

wide-spread *adj.* Fully spread out; over a broad area.

wid-ow *n.* A woman whose husband is no longer living.

wid-ow-er *n.* A man whose wife is no longer living.

width *n.* The distance or extent of something from side to side.

wield *v.* To use or handle something skillfully; to employ power effectively.

wie-ner *n.* A frankfurter; a hot dog.

wife *n.* A married female.

wig *n.* Artificial or human hair woven together to cover baldness or a bald spot on the head.

wig-gle *v.* To squirm; to move with rapid side-to-side motions. **wiggler** *n.*

wig-wam *n.* An Indian dwelling place.

wild *adj.* Living in a natural, untamed state; not occupied by man; not civilized; strange and unusual. *adv.* Out of control. *n.* A wilderness region not cultivated or settled by man.

wild-cat *n.* A medium-sized wild, feline animal; one with a quick temper. *v.* To drill for oil or gas in an area where such products are not usually found. *adj.* Not approved or legal.

wil-der-ness *n.* An unsettled area; a region left in its uncultivated or natural state.

wild-life *n.* Animals and plants living in their natural environments.

will *n.* The mental ability to decide or choose for oneself; strong desire or determination; a legal document stating how one's property is to be distributed after death. *v.* To bring about by an act of a will; to decide as by decree; to give or bequeath something in a will.

wil-low *n.* A large tree, usually having narrow leaves and slender flexible twigs.

Wilson, Woodrow *n.* (1856-1924) The 28th president of the United States from 1913-1921.

wilt *v.* To cause or to become limp; to lose force; to deprive of courage or energy.

win *v.* To defeat others; to gain victory in a contest; to receive. *n.* Victory; the act of winning. **winner** *n.*

winch *n.* An apparatus with one or more drums on which a cable or rope is wound, used to lift heavy loads. **wincher** *n.*

wind *n.* A natural movement of air. *v.* To become short of breath. **windy** *adj.*

wind *v.* To wrap around and around something; to turn, to crank. *n.* A turning or twisting.

wind-bag *n.*, *Slang* A person who talks excessively without saying anything of importance.

wind-fall *n.* A sudden or unexpected stroke of good luck.

wind in-stru-ment *n.* A musical instrument which produces sound when a person forces his breath into it.

wind-mill *n.* A machine operated or powered by the wind.

win-dow *n.* An opening built into a wall for light and air; a pane of glass.

win-dow--shop *v.* To look at merchandise in store windows without going inside to buy. **window-shopper** *n.*

wind-pipe *n.* The passage in the neck used for breathing; the trachea.

wine *n.* A drink containing 10-15% alcohol by volume, made by fermenting grapes.

wing n. One of the movable appendages that allow a bird or insect to fly; one of the airfoils on either side of an aircraft, allowing it to glide or travel through the air. v. To move as if on wings; to fly.

wing-spread n. The extreme measurement from the tips or outer edges of the wings of an aircraft, bird, or other insect.

wink v. To shut one eye as a signal or message; to blink rapidly. n. The act of winking; a short period of rest; a nap.

win-ning adj. Defeating others; captivating. n. Victory.

win-some adj. Very pleasant; charming.

win-ter n. The coldest season, coming between autumn and spring. adj. Relating to or typically of winter.

win-ter-green n. A small plant having aromatic evergreen leaves which yield an oil, used as flavoring or medicine.

wipe v. To clean by rubbing; to take off by rubbing. n. The act or instance of wiping.

wire n. A small metal rod used to conduct electricity; thin strands of metal twisted together to form a cable; the telephone or telegraph system; the finish line of a race. v. To equip with wiring. Slang To convey a message by telegram or telegraph; something completed at the last possible time.

Wis-con-sin n. A state located in the north central part of the United States.

wis-dom n. The ability to understand what is right, true, or enduring; good judgment; knowledge.

wise adj. Having superior intelligence; having great learning; having a capacity for sound judgment marked by deep understanding. wisely adv.

wise-crack n., Slang A witty remark or joke usually showing a lack of respect.

wish v. To desire or long for something; to command or request. n. A longing or desire.

wish-bone n. The bone of a bird, which, according to the superstition, when broken brings good luck to the person who has the longer end.

wish-ful adj. Having or expressing a wish; hopeful. wishfully adv.

wish-y-wash-y adj., Slang Not purposeful; indecisive.

wisp n. A tuft or small bundle of hay, straw, or hair; a thin piece. wispy adj.

wit n. The ability to use words in a clever way; a sense of humor.

witch n. A person believed to have magical powers; a mean, ugly, old woman.

with prep. In the company of; near or alongside; having, wearing or bearing; in the judgment or opinion of; containing; in the possession or care of; supporting; among; occurring at the same time. v. To take away or back; to retreat.

with-draw v. To take away; to take back; to remove; to retreat.

with-draw-al n. The process of withdrawing; a retreat; the act of removing money from an account; the process of discontinuing or no longer using a drug which is addictive.

whither v. To dry up or wilt from a lack of moisture; to lose freshness or vigor.

with-hold v. To hold back or keep.

withholding tax n. The tax on income held back by an employer in payment of one's income tax.

with-in adv. Inside the inner part; inside the limits; inside the limits of time, distance, or degree. n. An inside area.

with-out adv. On the outside; not in possession of. prep. Something or someone lacking.

with-stand v. To endure.

wit-ness n. A person who has seen, experienced, or heard something; something serving as proof or evidence. v. To see or hear something; to give proof or evidence of; to give testimony.

wit-ty adj. Amusing or cleverly humorous.

wiz-ard n. A very clever person; a person thought to have magical powers. Slang One with amazing skill.

wob-ble v. To move unsteadily from side to side, as a rocking motion.

woe n. Great sorrow or grief; misfortune.

wok n. A convex metal cooker for stir-frying food.

woke v. Past tense of wake.

wolf n. A carnivorous animal found in northern areas; a fierce person. v. To eat quickly and with greed. wolfish adj., wolfishly adv.

woman n. The mature adult human female; a person who has feminine qualities.

womanhood n. The state of being a woman.

womb n. The uterus; the place where development occurs.

won v. Past tense of win.

won-der n. A feeling of amazement or admiration. v. To feel admiration; to feel uncertainty. wonderful adj.

won-der-ment n. A feeling or state of amazement.

won-drous adj. Wonderful; marvelous.

won't contr. Will not.

won-ton n. A noodle dumpling filled with minced pork and served in soup.

wood n. The hard substance which makes up the main part of trees. adj. Made of wood. woods n. A growth of trees smaller than a forest.

wood-chuck n.

A rodent having short legs and a heavyset body, which lives in a burrow.

wood-en adj. Made of wood; resembling wood; stiff; lifeless; lacking flexibility.

wood-peck-er n. A bird which uses its bill for drilling holes in trees looking for insects to eat.

wood-wind *n.* A group of musical instruments which produce sounds when air is blown through the mouthpiece, as the clarinet, flute, and oboe.

wool *n.* The soft, thick hair of sheep and other such mammals; a fabric made from such hair.

word *n.* A meaningful sound which stands for an idea; a comment; a brief talk; an order or command. *v.* To express orally. **wording** *n.*

word proc-ess-ing *n.* A system which produces typewritten documents with automated type and editing equipment.

work *n.* The action or labor required to accomplish something; employment; a job; a project or assignment; something requiring physical or mental effort. *v.* To engage in mental or physical exertion; to labor to have a job; to arrange.

work-book *n.* A book containing exercises and problems designed to be written in; usually advancing in difficulty from kindergarten through grade 6; ranging in subjects as math, reading, spelling, science.

work-er *n.* A person who works for wages; an employee; a bee or other insect which performs special work in the colony in which it lives.

work-ing *adj.* Adequate to permit work to be done; assumed to permit further work.

work-man-ship *n.* The skill or art of a craftsman; the quality given to something in the process of making it.

work-out *n.* A period of strenuous exercise.

world *n.* The planet Earth; the universe; the human race; a field of human interest or effort.

worldly *adj.* Interested in pleasure rather than religious or spiritual matters.

worm *n.*

A small, thin animal having a long, flexible, rounded or flattened body. *Slang* A crude person.

worn *adj.* Made weak or thin from use; exhausted.

wor-ry *v.* To be concerned or troubled; to tug at repeatedly; to annoy; to irritate. *n.* Distress or mental anxiety.

wor-ship *n.* Reverence for a sacred object; high esteem or devotion for a person. *v.* To revere; attend a religious service. **worshiper** *n.*

worst *adj.* Bad; most inferior; most disagreeable *adv.* In the worst degree.

worth *n.* The quality or value of something; personal merit; the quantity that can be purchased for a certain amount of money.

wor-thy *adj.* Valuable or useful; deserving admiration or honor.

would-n't *contr.* Would not.

wound *n.* A laceration of the skin. *v.* To injure by tearing, cutting, or piercing the skin.

wow *interj.* An expression of amazement, surprise, or excitement.

wran-gle *v.* To quarrel noisily. **-er** *n.*

wrap *v.* To fold in order to protect something; to encase or enclose. *n.* A coat, shawl, or other outer protection. *Slang* To finish doing something, to finish producing or making something.

wrath *n.* Violent anger or fury.

wreak *v.* To inflict punishment upon another person.

wreath *n.* A decorative ring-like form of intertwined flowers, bows, and other articles.

wreck *v.* To ruin or damage by accident or deliberately; to spoil. *n.* Destruction; the remains of something wrecked or ruined; someone in poor condition.

wren *n.* A small brown songbird having a slender beak, short tail, and rounded wings.

wrench *n.* A tool used to grip, turn, or twist an object as a bolt or nut. *v.* To turn or twist violently; to give emotional pain.

wrest *v.* To twist or pull away in a violent way. *n.* A forcible twist.

wres-tle *v.* To struggle with an opponent in order to pin him down. *n.* The instance of wrestling. **wrestler** *n.*

wretch *n.* An extremely unhappy person; a miserable person. **wretched** *adj.*

wrig-gle *v.* To squirm; to move by turning and twisting.

wring *v.* To squeeze and twist by hand or machine; to press together.

wrin-kle *n.* A small crease on the skin or on fabric. *v.* To have or make wrinkles.

wrist *n.*, *Anat.* The joint of the body between the hand and forearm; the part of a sleeve which encircles the wrist.

wrist-watch *n.* A timepiece worn on the wrist.

writ *n.*, *Law* A written court document directed to a public official or individual ordering a specific action.

write *v.* To form symbols or letters; to form words on a surface; to communicate by writing; to earn a living by writing books.

writhe *v.* To twist, as in pain; to suffer greatly with pain.

writ-ing *n.* A book or other written work; handwriting; the process of forming letters into words; the occupation of a writer.

wrong *adj.* Incorrect; against moral standards; not suitable; immoral; unsuitable; inappropriate. *n.* An act which is wicked or immoral. *v.* To do wrong; to injure or hurt. **wrongly** *adv.*

wrote *v.* Past tense of write.

wrought *adj.* Fashioned; formed; beaten or hammered into shape.

wrung *v.* Past tense of *wring.*

WV *abbr.* West Virginia.

WY *abbr.* Wyoming.

Wy-o-ming *n.* A state located in the western part of the United States.

X, x The twenty-fourth letter of the English alphabet.

Xan-a-du *n.* A place having idyllic beauty.

xan-thate *n.* Ester or slat of a xanthic acid.

xan-thic *adj.* The color yellow or all colors that tend toward the color yellow when relating to flowers.

xan-thin *n.* A carotenoid pigment that is soluble in alcohol.

xan-thine *n.* A crystalline nitrogen compound, closely related to uric acid, found in blood, urine and certain plant and animal tissues.

xan-tho-chroid *adj.* Pertaining to the light-complexioned caucasoid race.

xan-tho-ma *n.* A skin condition of the eyelids marked by small, yellow, raised nodules or plates.

X chro-mo-some *n.* The sex female chromosome, associated with female characteristics; occurs paired in the female and single in the male chromosome pair.

xe-bec *n.* A small vessel with three-masts having both lateen and square sails.

xe-nic *adj.* Relating to, or employing a culture medium that contains one or more unidentified organisms.

xe-non *n.* The colorless, odorless gaseous element found in small quantities in the air, symbolized by Xe.

xe-no-phile *n.* One attracted to foreign people, styles, manners, etc.

xen-o-phobe *n.* A person who dislikes, fears, and mistrusts foreigners or anything strange. **xenophobia** *n.*

xe-rarch *adj.* Originating or developing in a dry place.

xe-ric *adj.* Relating to or requiring only a small amount of moisture. **xe-ri-cal-ly** *adv.*

xe-roph-i-lous *adj.* Tolerant or characteristic of xeric environments. **xerophily** *n.*

xe-roph-thal-mi-a *n.* A itching soreness of the eyes that is caused by an insufficient amount of vitamin A. **xerophthalmic** *adj.*

xe-ro-phyte *n.* A plant that can live in a surrounding of extreme heat and drought. **xerophytic** *adj.*, **xerophytically** *adv.*, **xerophytism** *n.*

XL *abbr.* Extra large.

X-mas *abbr.*, *n.* Christmas.

X--ra-di-a-tion *n.* Treatment with X-rays.

X ray *n.* Energy that is radiated with a short wavelength and high penetrating power; a black and white negative image or picture of the interior of the body.

x--sec-tion *n.* Cross section of something. **x-sectional** *adj.*

xy-lo-phone *n.* A musical instrument consisting of mounted wooden bars which produce a ringing musical sound when struck with two small wooden hammers. **xylophonist** *n.*

xy-lose *n.* A crystalline aldose sugar.

xy-lot-o-mous *adj.* Capable of cutting or boring wood. **xylotomic** *adj.*

Y, y The twenty-fifth letter of the English alphabet.

yacht *n.* A small sailing vessel powdered by wind or motor, used for pleasure cruises. **yacht** *v.*

yacht-ing *n.* The sport of sailing in a yacht.

yachts-man *n.* A person who sails a yacht. **yachtsmanship, -ship** *n.*

yak *n.* A long-haired ox of Tibet and the mountains of central Asia.

yam *n.* An edible root; a variety of the sweet potato.

Yan-kee *n.* A native of the northern United States. **Yankee** *adj.*

yap *v.* To bark in a high pitched, sharp way. *Slang* To talk in a relentess, loud, or stupid manner.

yard *n.* A unit of measure that equals 36 inches or 3 feet; the ground around or near a house or building.

yard goods *n.* Fabric that is sold by the yard.

yard-man *n.* A person employed as a worker in a railroad yard.

yard-mas-ter *n.* A person in charge of a railroad yard.

yard-stick *n.* A graduated measuring stick that equals 1 yard or 36 inches; standard of measurement.

yarn *n.* Twisted fibers, as of wool, used in knitting or weaving. *Slang* An involved tale or story.

yawn *v.* To inhale a deep breath with the mouth open wide. **yawn, yawner** *n.*

yawn-ing *adj.* Expressing tiredness by a yawn.

Y-Chro-mo-some *n.* The sex chromosome associated with male characteristics.

ye *pron.* You, used especially in religious contexts, as hymns.

yea *adv.* Yes; indeed; truly.

yeah *adv.*, *Slang* Yes.

year *n.* A period of time starting on January lst and continuing through December 31st, consisting of 365 days or 366 days in a leap year.

year-book *n.* A book printed each year giving facts about the year; a book printed each year for a high school, college, etc.

year-ling *n.* An animal that is one year old.

year-ly *adj.* Pertaining to something that happens, appears, or comes once a year, every year.

yearn *v.* To feel a strong craving; deep desire; a wistful feeling. **-er, -ing** *n.*

year--round *adj.* Lasting or continuing for an entire year.

yeast *n.* Fungi or plant cells used to make baked goods rise or fruit juices ferment.

yell *v.* To cry out loudly. *n.* A loud cry; a cheer to show support for an athletic team.

yel-low *n.* The bright color of a lemon; the yolk of an egg. *v.* To make or become yellow. *adj.* Of the color yellow. *Slang* Cowardly.

yel-low fev-er *n.* An acute infectious

disease of the tropics, spread by the bite of a mosquito.

yel-low-jack-et *n.* A small wasp, having bright yellow markings, and usually makes its nest below ground level.

yelp *n.* A quick, sharp, shrill cry, as from pain.

yen *n.* An intense craving or longing.

yeo-man *n.* The owner of a small farm; a petty officer who acts as a clerk.

yes *adv.* To express agreement.

yes-ter-day *n.* The day before today; a former or recent time. *adv.* On the day before the present day.

yet *adv.* Up to now; at this time; even now; more so. *conj.* Nevertheless; but.

yield *v.* To bear or bring forward; to give up the possession of something; to give way to. *n.* An amount that is produced.

yield-ing *adj.* Ready to yield, comply, or submit; unresisting. **yieldingly** *adv.*

yo-del *v.* To sing in a way so that the voice changes from normal to a high shrill sound and then back again.

yo-ga *n.* A system of exercises which helps the mind and the body in order to achieve tranquillity and spiritual insight.

yo-del *n.* A very unsophisticated country person; a bumpkin.

yolk *n.* The yellow nutritive part of an egg.

Yom Kip-pur *n.* The Jewish holiday observed with fasting and prayer for the forgiveness of sins.

you *pron.* The person or persons addressed.

you all *pron.*, *Slang* **y'all** A southern variation used for two or more people in direct address.

you'd *contr.* You had; you would.

you'll *contr.* You will; you shall.

young *adj.* Of or relating to the early stage of life; not old. *n.* The offspring of an animal. **youngster** *n.*

your *adj.* Belonging to you or yourself or the person spoken to.

you're *contr.* You are.

your-self *pron.* A form of you for emphasis when the object of a verb and the subject is the same.

youth *n.* The appearance or state of being young; the time of life when one is not considered an adult; a young person.

youth-ful *adj.* Being of a young age or early stage in life. **-ly** *adv.*, **-ness** *n.*

you've *contr.* You have.

yowl *v.* To make a loud, long cry or howl. **yowl** *n.*

yo--yo *n.* A grooved spool toy with a string wrapped around the spool so it can be spun or moved up and down.

yt-ter-bi-um *n.* A metallic element of the rare-earth group symbolized by Yb.

yt-tri-um *n.* A metallic element symbolized by Y.

yuc-ca *n.* A tropical plant having large, white flowers and long, pointed leaves.

yule *n.* Christmas.

yule-tide *n.* The Christmas season.

Z, z The twenty-sixth letter of the English alphabet.

za-ny *n.*, *pl* **-nies** A clown; a person who acts silly or foolish. *adj.* Typical of being clownish. **-iness** *n.*, **-nily** *adv.*

zap *v.*, *Slang* To destroy; to do away with.

zeal *n.* Great interest or eagerness.

zeal-ot *n.* A fanatical person; a fanatic.

zeal-ous *adj.* Full of interest; eager; passionate. **zealously** *adv.*, **zealousness** *n.*

ze-bra *n.* An African mammal of the horse family having black or brown stripes on a white body.

zeph-yr *n.* A gentle breeze.

ze-ro *n.*, *pl.* **-ros, -roes** The number or symbol "0"; nothing; the point from which degrees or measurements on a scale begin; the lowest point. *v.* To aim, point at, or close in on. *adj.* Pertaining to zero; nonexisting.

zest *n.* Enthusiasm; a keen quality. **zestful** *adj.*, **zestfully**, *adv.*, **zesty** *adj.*

zig-zag *n.* A pattern with sharp turns in alternating directions. *adv.* To move in a zigzag course or path. **zigzag** *v.*

zilch *n.*, *Slang* Nothing; zero.

zinc *n.* A bluish-white crystalline metallic element, used as a protective coating for steel and iron, symbolized by Zn.

zip *n.* To act or move with vigor or speed. *v.* To move with energy, speed, or facility; to open or close with a zipper. *Slang* Energy; zero; nothing.

zip code *n.* The system to speed the delivery of mail by assigning a five digit number, plus four to each postal delivery location in the United States.

zip-per *n.* A fastener consisting of two rows of plastic or metal teeth that are interlocked by means of sliding a tab.

zir-co-ni-um *n.* A metallic element symbolized by Zr.

zit *n.*, *Slang* A pimple.

zom-bie *n.* A person who resembles the walking dead; a person who has a strange appearance or behavior.

zone *n.* An area or region set apart from its surroundings by some characteristic.

zonk *v.*, *Slang* To stun; to render senseless with alcohol or drugs.

zoo *n.*, *pl.* **zoos** A public display or collection of living animals.

zo-ol-o-gy *n.* The science that deals with animals, animal life, and the animal kingdom. **zoologist** *n.*

zoom *v.* To move with a continuous, loud, buzzing sound; to move upward sharply; to move toward a subject with great speed.

zuc-chi-ni *n.*, *pl.* **-ni** A summer squash that is long and narrow and has a dark-green, smooth rind.

zwie-back *n.* A sweetened bread which is baked, sliced, and toasted to make it crisp.

zy-mol-o-gy *n.* The branch of science dealing with ferments and fermentation. **zymologic** *adj.*

zy-mo-scope *n.* An instrument that measures yeast's fermenting power.

Commonly Used Abbreviations

A

A. A. Alcoholics anonymous, Associate in Accounting.
A.A.A. American Automobile Association, Amateur Athletic Association.
abbr. or abbrev. abbreviated, abbreviation.
acad. Academy, academic.
acct. Account.
A.D. In the year of our Lord.
A.D.A. American Dental Association, American Dairy Association.
adj. Adjective, adjourned, adjustment.
admr. Administrator.
adv. Adverb, advertising, advise, advocate.
A.I.D.S. Acquired Immune Deficiency Syndrome.
A.M.A. American Medical Association.
anat. Anatomy, anatomical.
APO Army Post Office.
approx. approximately.
ASCAP American Society of Composers, Authors and Publishers.
A.T.M. Automatic Teller Machine.
avg. Average.
A.W.O.L. Absent without leave.

B

B.A. Bachelor of Arts.
B.E. Bachelor of Education, Board of Education, Bank of England.
biol. Biology, biologist.
bkpr. Bookkeeper.
bkry. Bakery.
bldg. Building.
blvd. Boulevard.
B.S. Bachelor of Surgery, Bachelor of Science.
bsmt. Basement.
bu. Bushel, bureau.
bx. Box.

C

CAA Civil Aeronautics Board.
cal. Calendar, caliber, calorie.
car. Carat.
Card. Cardinal.
cash. Cashier
c.c. Cash credit, carbon copy.
C.C. Chamber of Comerce, Country Club, Circuit Court, County court.
cent. Century, central.
chem. Chemist, Chemistry.
C.I.A. Central Intelligence Agency.
C.O. Commanding Officer, conscientious objector.
C.O.D. Cash on Delivery.
colloq. Colloquialism, colloquial.
comb. Combined, combination.
Cong. Congress.
coop. Cooperative, cooperation.
C.P.A. Certified Public Accountant.
C.P.O. Chief Petty Officer.
C.R.T. Cathode Ray Tube.
C.S.T. Central Standard Time.
cu. Cubic
C.Z. Canal Zone.

D

D.A. District attorney.
D.A.R. Daughters of the American Revolution.
D.A.V. Disabled American Veteran.
dba. Doing business as.
dbl. Double.
D.C. District of Columbia, district court.
D.D.S. Doctor of Dental Surgery.
Dec. December.
deg. Degree.
Dem. Democratic, Democrat.
dept. Department.
diam. Diameter.
dir. Director, direction.
dist. District, distance.
D.O.A. Dead on Arrival.
doz. Dozen
D.S.T. Daylight Savings Time.

E

ea. Each.
E.D.T. Eastern Daylight Time.
elem. Element, elementary.
E.O.M. End of Month.
E.R.A. Earned run average.
E.S.T. Eastern Standard Time.
etc. And so forth.
exch. Exchange.

F

F.B.I. Federal Bureau of Investigation.
F.C.C. Federal Communication Commission.
F.I.C.A. Federal Insurance Contributions Act.
Fri. Friday.
fut. Future.

G

gal. Gallon.
gen. General, gender.
G.I. A member of the U.S. Armed Forces, especially an enlisted man, general issue.
G.P.O. Government Printing Office, General Post Office.
gr. wt. Gross weight.

H

hdkf. Handkerchief.
hf. Half.
hist. History, historical.
hosp. Hospital.
hr. Hour.
ht. Height.

I

I.D. Identification, Intelligence Deptment.
inc. Incorporated, increase, income.
Ind. Indian.

Commonly Used Abbreviations

J

Jan. January.
J.C.C. Junior Chamber of Commerce.
Jr. Junior.
Jun. June.

K

km. Kingdom, kilometer.
kt. Karat, knot.
kw. Kilowatt.

L

lab. Laboratory.
liq. Liquor, liquid.
lon. Longitude.
LSD Lysergic acid diethylamide.
Lt. Gen. Lieutenant General.

M

mag. Magazine, magnitude.
manuf. Manufacturing, manufacturer.
Mar. March.
meas. Measure.
med. Medical, medium.
mfg. Manufacturing.
Mid. Midshipmen.
mkt. Market.

N

NASA National Aeronautics and Space
  Administration.
neg. Negative.
nos. Numbers.
n.s.f. Not sufficient funds.
nt. wt. Net weight.

O

Oct. October.
o.d. On demand, over dose, over-drive.
opp. Opposite, opposed.
oz. Ounce.

P

payt. Payment.
pd. Paid.
pg. Page.
PGA Professional Golfers Association.
prem. Premium.
Pres. President.
priv. Private.
pron. Pronoun, pronunciation.
pub. Publisher, publication.

Q

qt. Quart, quality.
quar. Quarter, quarterly.

R

rd. Road, round, rendered.
recd. Received.
ref. Reference, referee, reformed,
  refund.

R.F.D. Ruarl free delivery.
R.N. Registered Nurse.
r.p.m. Revolutions per minute.
R.S.V.P. Reply, in you please.

S

Sat. Saturday, saturn.
sec. Secondary, section, sector,
  second.
secy. Secretary.
S.P.C.A. Society for the Prevention of
  Cruelty to Animals.
Sr. Senior.
std. Standard.
Sun. Sunday.
syst. System.

T

tbsp. Tablespoon.
TD Touchdown.
Thurs. Thursday.
tn. Ton.
tsp. Teaspoon.
Tues. Tuesday.

U

UAW United Automobile Workers.
U.P.I. United Press International.
U.S.A. United States of America.

V

V.A. Veterans Administration.

W

Wed. Wednesday.
wkly. Weekly.

X

Xmas Christmas.

Y

yr. Year.

Z

zod. Zodiac.

PRESIDENTS OF THE UNITED STATES

	Name and Party	State of Birth	Term	Born	Died
.	George Washington (F)	VA	1789-1797	1732	1799
2.	John Adams (F)	MA	1797-1801	1735	1826
.	Thomas Jefferson (D-R)	VA	1801-1809	1743	1826
.	James Madison (D-R)	VA	1809-1817	1751	1836
.	James Monroe (D-R)	VA	1817-1825	1758	1831
.	John Q. Adams (D-R)	MA	1825-1829	1767	1848
.	Andrew Jackson (D)	SC	1829-1837	1767	1845
.	Martin Van Buren (D)	NY	1837-1841	1782	1862
.	William H. Harrison (W)	VA	1841-1841	1773	1841*
0.	John Tyler (D-W)	VA	1841-1845	1790	1862
1.	James K. Polk (D)	NC	1845-1849	1795	1849
2.	Zachary Taylor (W)	VA	1849-1850	1784	1850*
3.	Millard Fillmore (W)	NY	1850-1853	1800	1874
4.	Franklin Pierce (D)	NH	1853-1857	1804	1869
5.	James Buchanan (D)	PA	1857-1861	1791	1868
6.	Abraham Lincoln (R)	KY	1861-1865	1809	1865+
7.	Andrew Johnson (R)	NC	1865-1869	1808	1875
8.	Ulysses S. Grant (R)	OH	1869-1877	1822	1885
9.	Rutherford B. Hayes (R)	OH	1877-1881	1822	1893
0.	James A. Garfield (R)	OH	1881-1881	1831	1881+
1.	Chester A. Arthur (R)	VT	1881-1885	1829	1886
2.	Grover Cleveland (D)	NJ	1885-1889	1837	1908
3.	Benjamin Harrison (R)	OH	1889-1893	1833	1901
4.	Grover Cleveland (D)	NJ	1893-1897	1837	1908
5.	William McKinley (R)	OH	1897-1901	1843	1901+
6.	Theodore Roosevelt (R)	NY	1901-1909	1858	1919
7.	William H. Taft (R)	OH	1909-1913	1857	1930
8.	Woodrow Wilson (D)	VA	1913-1921	1856	1924
9.	Warren G. Harding (R)	OH	1921-1923	1865	1923*
0.	Calvin Coolidge (R)	VT	1923-1929	1872	1933
1.	Herbert C. Hoover (R)	IA	1929-1933	1874	1964
2.	Franklin D. Roosevelt (D)	NY	1933-1945	1882	1945*
3.	Harry S. Truman (D)	MO	1945-1953	1884	1972
4.	Dwight D. Eisenhower (R)	TX	1953-1961	1890	1969
5.	John F. Kennedy (D)	MA	1961-1963	1917	1963+
6.	Lyndon B. Johnson (D)	TX	1963-1969	1908	1973
7.	Richard M. Nixon (R)	CA	1969-1974	1913	1994
8.	Gerald R. Ford (R)	NE	1974-1977	1913	
9.	James E. Carter, Jr. (D)	GA	1977-1981	1924	
0.	Ronald W. Reagan (R)	IL	1981-1989	1911	
1.	George Bush (R)	MA	1989-1993	1924	
2.	William (Bill) J. Clinton (D)	AR	1993-2001	1946	
3.	George W. Bush (R)	TX	2001-	1946	

(F) Federalist; (D)Democratic; (R)Republican; (W) Whip; (r) resigned
* died in office; + assassinated while in office

VICE-PRESIDENTS OF THE UNITED STATES

Name and Party	State of Birth	Term	Born	Died
John Adams (F)	MA	1789-1797	1735	1826
Thomas Jefferson(D-R)	VA	1797-1801	1743	1826
Aaron Burr (R)	NJ	1801-1805	1756	1836
George Clinton(R)	NY	1805-1812	1739	1812
Elbridge Gerry (R)	MA	1813-1814	1744	1814
Daniel D. Tompkins	NY	1817-1825	1774	1825
John C. Calhoun	SC	1825-1832	1782	1850
Martin Van Buren (D)	NY	1833-1837	1782	1862
Richard M. Johnson	KY	1837-1841	1780	1850
John Tyler (W)	VA	1841-1841	1790	1862
George M. Dallas (D)	PA	1845-1849	1792	1864
Millard Fillmore (W)	NY	1849-1850	1800	1874
William R. King (D)	NC	1853-1853	1786	1853
John C. Breckinridge (D)	KY	1857-1861	1821	1875
Hannibal Mamlin (R)	ME	1861-1865	1809	1891
Andrew Johnson (R)	NC	1865-1865	1808	1875
Schuyler Colfax (R)	NY	1869-1873	1823	1885
Henry Wilson (R)	NH	1873-1875	1812	1875
William A. Wheeler (R)	NY	1877-1881	1819	1887
Chester A. Arthur (R)	VT	1881-1881	1829	1886
Thomas A. Hendricks (D)	OH	1885-1885	1819	1885
Levi P. Morton (R)	VT	1889-1893	1824	1920
Adlai E. Stevenson (D)	KY	1893-1897	1835	1914
Garret A. Hobart (R)	NJ	1897-1899	1844	1899
Theodore Roosevelt (R)	NY	1901-1901	1858	1919
Charles W. Fairbanks (R)	OH	1905-1909	1852	1918
James S. Sherman (R)	NY	1909-1912	1855	1912
Thomas R. Marshal (D)	IN	1913-1921	1854	1925
Calvin Coolidge (R)	VT	1921-1923	1872	1933
Charles G. Dawes (R)	OH	1925-1929	1865	1951
Charles Curtis (R)	KS	1929-1933	1860	1936
John N. Garner (D)	TX	1933-1941	1868	1967
Henry A. Wallace (D)	IA	1941-1945	1888	1965
Harry S. Truman	MO	1945-1945	1884	1972
Alben W. Barkley (D)	KY	1949-1953	1877	1956
Richard M. Nixon (R)	CA	1953-1961	1913	1994
Lyndon B. Johnson (D)	TX	1961-1963	1908	1973
Hubert H. Humphrey (D)	SD	1965-1969	1911	1978
Spiro T. Agnew (R)	MD	1969-1973(r)	1918	1996
Gerald R. Ford (R)	NE	1973-1974	1913	
Nelson A. Rockefeller (R)	ME	1974-1977	1908	1979
Walter F. Mondale (D)	MN	1977-1981	1928	
George Bush (R)	MA	1981-1989	1924	
J. Danforth (Dan) Quayle (R)	IN	1989-1993	1947	
Albert Gore Jr. (D)	DC	1993-2001	1948	
Richard (Dick) Cheney (R)	NE	2001-	1941	

(F) Federalist; (D)Democratic; (R)Republican; (W) Whip; (r) resigned

STATE	ABBREVIATION	CAPITAL CITY
Alabama	AL.	Montgomery
Alaska	AK.	Juneau
Arizona	AZ.	Phoenix
Arkansas	AR.	Little Rock
California	CA.	Sacramento
Colorado	CO.	Denver
Connecticut	CT.	Harford
Delaware	DE.	Dover
Florida	FL.	Tallahassee
Georgia	GA.	Atlanta
Hawaii	HI.	Honolulu
Idaho	ID.	Boise
Illinois	IL.	Springfield
Indiana	IN.	Indianapolis
Iowa	IA.	Des Monies
Kansas	KS.	Topeka
Kentucky	KY.	Frankfort
Louisiana	LA.	Baton Rouge
Maine	ME.	Augusta
Maryland	MD.	Annapolis
Massachusetts	MA.	Boston
Michigan	MI.	Lansing
Minnesota	MN.	St. Paul
Mississippi	MS.	Jackson
Missouri	MO.	Jefferson City
Montana	MT.	Helena
Nebraska	NB.	Lincoln
Nevada	NV.	Carson City
New Hampshire	NH.	Concord
New Jersey	NJ.	Trenton
New Mexico	NM.	Santa Fe
New York	NY.	Albany
North Carolina	NC.	Raleigh
North Dakota	ND.	Bismark
Ohio	OH.	Columbus
Oklahoma	OK.	Oklahoma City
Oregon	OR.	Salem
Pennsylvania	PA.	Harrisburg
Rhode Island	RI.	Providence
South Carolina	SC.	Columbia
South Dakota	SD.	Pierre
Tennessee	TN.	Nashville
Texas	TX.	Austin
Utah	UT.	Salt Lake City
Vermont	VT.	Montpelier
Virginia	VA.	Richmond
Washington	WA.	Olympia
West Virginia	WV.	Charleston
Wisconsin	WI.	Madison
Wyoming	WY.	Cheyenne

STATE	NICKNAME	FLOWER
Alabama	Cotton State	Camellia
Alaska	Great Land	Forget-Me-Not
Arizona	Grand Canyon State	Saguaro Cactus
Arkansas	Land of Opportunity	Apple Blossom
California	Golden State	Golden Poppy
Colorado	Centennial State	Mountain Columbine
Connecticut	Constitution State	Mountain Laurel
Delaware	First State	Peach Blossom
Florida	Sunshine State	Orange Blossom
Georgia	Peach State	Cherokee Rose
Hawaii	Aloha State	Hibiscus
Idaho	Gem State	Syringa
Illinois	Prairie State	Native Violet
Indiana	Hoosier State	Peony
Iowa	Hawkeye State	Wild Rose
Kansas	Sunflower State	Sunflower
Kentucky	Blue Grass State	Goldenrod
Louisiana	Pelican State	Magnolia
Maine	Pine Tree State	Pine Cone and Tassel
Maryland	Free State	Black-eyed Susan
Massachusetts	Bay State	Mayflower
Michigan	Wolvering State	Apple Blossom
Minnesota	Gopher State	Lady's-slipper
Mississippi	Boyou State	Magnolia
Missouri	Show Me State	Hawthorn
Montana	Treasure State	Bitterroot
Nebraska	Cornhuskers State	Goldenrod
Nevada	Silver or Sagebrush	Sagebrush
New Hampshire	Granite State	Purple Lilac
New Jersey	Garden State	Purple Violet
New Mexico	Land of Enchantment	Yucca Flower
New York	Empire State	Rose
North Carolina	Tarheel State	Flowering Dogwood
North Dakota	Sioux State	Wild Prairie Rose
Ohio	Buckeye State	Scarlet Carnation
Oklahoma	Sooner State	Mistletoe
Oregon	Beaver State	Oregon Grape
Pennsylvania	Keystone State	Mountain Laurel
Rhode Island	Little Rhody State	Violet
South Carolina	Palmetto State	Carolina Jessamine
South Dakota	Coyote State	American Pasqueflower
Tennessee	Volunteer State	Iris
Texas	Lone Star State	Bluebonnet
Utah	Beehive State	Sego Lilly
Vermont	Green Mountain State	Red Clover
Virginia	Old Dominion	Flowering Dogwood
Washington	Evergeen State	Coast Rhododendron
West Virginia	Mountain State	Rhododendron
Wisconsin	Badger State	Wood Violet
Wyoming	Equality State	Indian Paintbrush

MOUNTAINS	LOCATION	HEIGHT IN FEET
McKinley	Alaska	20,320
St. Elias	Alaska-Canada	18,008
Foraker	Alaska	17,400
Bona	Alaska	16,550
Blackburn	Alaska	16,390
Kennedy	Alaska	16,286
Sanford	Alaska	16,237
South Buttress	Alaska	15,885
Vancouver	Alaska-Canada	15,700
Churchill	Alaska	15,638
Fairweather	Alaska-Canada	15,300
Hubbard	Alaska-Canada	15,015
Bear	Alaska	14,831
East Butress	Alaska	14,730
Hunter	Alaska	14,573
Alverstone	Alaska-Canada	14,565
Browne Tower	Alaska	14,530
Whitney	California	14,494
Elbert	Colorado	14,433
Massive	Colorado	14,421
Harvard	Colorado	14,420
Rainer	Washington	14,410
Williamson	California	14,375
Blanca Peak	Colorado	14,345
La Plata	Colorado	14,336
Uncompahgre	Colorado	14,309
Crestone	Colorado	14,294
Lincoln	Colorado	14,286
Grays Peak	Colorado	14,270
Antero	Colorado	14,269
Torreys	Colorado	14,267
Castle	Colorado	14,265
Quandary	Colorado	14,265
Evans	Colorado	14,264
Longs Peak	Colorado	14,256
Wilson	Colorado	14,246
White	California	14,246
North Palisade	California	14,242
Savano	Colorado	14,229
Belford	Colorado	14,197
Princeton	Colorado	14,197
Crestone Needle	Colorado	14,197
Yale	Colorado	14,196
Boss	Colorado	14,172
Kit Carson	Colorado	14,165
Wrangell	Alaska	14,163
Shasta	California	14,162
Sill	California	14,162
El Diente	Colorado	14,159
Maroon	Colorado	14,156

RIVERS	LENGTH IN MILES	FLOWS INTO
Alabama	729	Mobile River
Albany	610	James Bay
Arkansas	1,459	Mississippi River, AR.
Brazos	923	Gulf of Mexico
Canadian	906	Arkansas River, OK.
Cimarron	600	Arkansan River, OK.
Colorado (AZ.)	1,450	Gulf of Mexico
Colorado (TX.)	862	Matagorda Bay
Cumberland	720	Ohio River
Fraser	850	Strait of Georgia
Gila	649	Colorado River, AZ.
Green (UT.-WY.)	730	Colorado River, UT.
Illinois	420	Mississippi River
James (ND.-SD.)	710	Missouri River, SD.
Koyukuk	470	Yukon River
Kuskokwim	724	Kuskokwim River
Liard	693	Machenzie River
Little Missouri	560	Missouri River
Mississippi	2,348	Mouth of Southwest Pass
Mississippi, Upper	1,171	Mouth of Missouri River
Missouri	2,315	Mississippi River
Missouri-Red Rock	2,540	Mississippi River
Mobile-Alabama-Coosa	774	Mobile Bay
Neosho	460	Arkansas River, OK
Niobrara	431	Missouri River, NB.
North Canadian	800	Canadian River, OK.
North Platte	618	Platte River, NB.
Ohio	1,310	Mississippi River, IL.-KY.
Ohio-Allegheny	1,306	Mississippi River
Osage	500	Missouri River, MO.
Ouachita	605	Red River, LA.
Pearl	411	Gulf of Mexico, MS.-LA.
Pecos	926	Rio Grande, TX.
Pee Dee-Yadkin	435	Winyah Bay, SC.
Pend Oreille	490	Columbia River
Porcupine	569	Yukon River, AK.
Red (OK.-TX.-LA.)	1,290	Mississippi River
Republican	445	Kansas River, KS.
Rio Grande	1,760	Gulf of Mexico
St. Francis	425	Mississippi River, AR.
Salmon	420	Snake River, ID.
Somkey Hill	540	Kansas River, KS.
Snake	1,038	Columbia River, WA.
South Platte	424	Platte River, NB.
Susquehanna	444	Chesapeake Bay, MD.
Tanana	659	Yukon River, AK.
Tennessee	652	Ohio River, KY.
Wabash	529	Ohio River, IL.-IN.
Wisconsin	430	Mississippi River
Yellowstone	692	Missouri River, ND.